Handbook of Cultural Developmental Science

Handbook of Cultural Developmental Science

Edited by

Marc H. Bornstein

Psychology Press
Taylor & Francis Group
New York   London

Psychology Press
Taylor & Francis Group
711 Third Avenue,
New York, NY 10017

Psychology Press
Taylor & Francis Group
27 Church Road
Hove, East Sussex BN3 2FA

© 2010 by Taylor and Francis Group, LLC
Psychology Press is an imprint of Taylor & Francis Group, an Informa business

Transferred to digital print 2012

First issued in paperback 2012

International Standard Book Number: 978-0-8058-6330-7 (Hardback) 978-0-415-64819-6 (Paperback)

For permission to photocopy or use material electronically from this work, please access www.copyright.com (http://www.copyright.com/) or contact the Copyright Clearance Center, Inc. (CCC), 222 Rosewood Drive, Danvers, MA 01923, 978-750-8400. CCC is a not-for-profit organization that provides licenses and registration for a variety of users. For organizations that have been granted a photocopy license by the CCC, a separate system of payment has been arranged.

Trademark Notice: Product or corporate names may be trademarks or registered trademarks, and are used only for identification and explanation without intent to infringe.

Library of Congress Cataloging-in-Publication Data

Handbook of Cultural Developmental Science / edited by Marc H. Bornstein.
    p. cm.
Includes bibliographical references and index.
ISBN-13: 978-0-8058-6330-7
ISBN-10: 0-8058-6330-3
1. Ethnopsychology. 2. Developmental psychology. I. Bornstein, Marc H. II. Title.

GN502.H357 2009
155.8'2--dc22
    2009003461

Visit the Taylor & Francis Web site at
http://www.taylorandfrancis.com

and the Psychology Press Web site at
http://www.psypress.com

We do not inherit the earth from our parents;
we borrow it from our children.

For
Jon and Lea
citizens of the world

Contents

Preface	ix
Part I Domains of Development Across Cultures	**1**
1 Culture JACQUELINE J. GOODNOW	3
2 Methodology FONS J. R. VAN DE VIJVER, JAN HOFER, and ATHANASIOS CHASIOTIS	21
3 Survival and Health CAROL M. WORTHMAN	39
4 Motor Skill KAREN E. ADOLPH, LANA B. KARASIK, and CATHERINE S. TAMIS-LEMONDA	61
5 Perception JANET F. WERKER, DAPHNE M. MAURER, and KATHERINE A. YOSHIDA	89
6 Cognition MICHAEL COLE and XAVIER E. CAGIGAS	127
7 Language ELENA LIEVEN and SABINE STOLL	143
8 Literacy DANIEL A. WAGNER	161
9 Emotions and Temperament JEROME KAGAN	175
10 Self and Personality ROSS A. THOMPSON and ELITA AMINI VIRMANI	195
11 Gender DEBORAH L. BEST	209
12 Peers KENNETH H. RUBIN, CHARISSA CHEAH, and MELISSA M. MENZER	223
13 Socialization MARY GAUVAIN and ROSS D. PARKE	239
14 Parenting MARC H. BORNSTEIN and JENNIFER E. LANSFORD	259
15 Religion GEORGE W. HOLDEN and BRIGITTE VITTRUP	279

| Part II | Development in Different Places on Earth | 297 |

16 The United States of America 299
CATHERINE S. TAMIS-LEMONDA and KAREN E. MCFADDEN

17 Central and South America 323
RODOLFO DE CASTRO RIBAS, JR.

18 European Union 341
MARTIN PINQUART and RAINER K. SILBEREISEN

19 North Africa and the Middle East 359
RAMADAN A. AHMED

20 Afrique Noire 383
A. BAME NSAMENANG and JOSEPH L. LO-OH

21 Russia 409
DAVID A. NELSON, CRAIG H. HART, EMILY K. KEISTER, and KARINA PIASSETSKAIA

22 China 429
XINYIN CHEN and LI WANG

23 East and Southeast Asia: Japan, South Korea, Vietnam, and Indonesia 445
DAVID W. SHWALB, BARBARA J. SHWALB, JUN NAKAZAWA, JUNG-HWAN HYUN, HAO VAN LE, and MONTY P. SATIADARMA

24 India 465
T. S. SARASWATHI and RANJANA DUTTA

25 Australia and New Zealand 485
ANN V. SANSON and JANIS E. PATERSON

26 The HOME Environment 505
ROBERT H. BRADLEY

27 Immigration and Acculturation 531
MARC H. BORNSTEIN and LINDA R. COTE

Contributors 553
Author Index 569
Subject Index 601

Preface

Among the Greeks of the Classical period, Xenophon and Aristotle expressed special fascination with the Lycurgan system of Spartan childrearing, called the *agogé*. Xenophon, an Athenian of the fourth century BC, specifically contrasted Spartan with other Greek childrearing practices in the *Constitution of the Lacedaemonians* of 380. Likewise, Aristotle's lost essay on *Education* reputedly compared child development and childrearing in Sparta with family practices in other Greek cultures. These histories documented how the Spartans intentionally set about developing tough and austere, disciplined and obedient, self-denying and competitive children who confidently met and endured the harsh existence of the Peloponnese.

Human beings do not grow up, and adults do not parent, in isolation, but always in physical and social contexts. Children, parents, and cultures are, therefore, intimately bundled because children must learn and adapt to their culture to survive and thrive; a major goal of parenting is to successfully embed the next generation into the existing culture; and culture comprises the ways in which a collection of people process and make sense of their experiences and so shapes a wide array of family functions, including cognitions and practices related to childrearing and child development. As children experience widely varying conditions in growing up, culture dramatically influences their socialization and enculturation. Culture plays an overarching role in organizing and directing the ecology of childhood and parenthood. Cultural prescriptions and proscriptions help to determine, to a great extent, the goals parents have for children, parents' cognitions, the practices of parents, and ultimately the experiences children have. Thus, culture exerts significant and differential influences over child physical, mental, emotional, and social development. It has been observed that perhaps the most significant single factor in determining the overall course of a person's life is the culture into which the person was born. Culture is a principal reason why individuals, who are at once commonly but uniquely endowed, are who they are and are often so different from one another. The *Handbook of Cultural Developmental Science* is centrally concerned with human development, parenting, and culture.

Studies of culture, caregiving, and children are requisite to tell the full scope of childhood. Currently, however, three main limitations constrain our understanding of child development and parenting; all three are cultural: a narrow participant database in the research enterprise, a biased sampling of world cultures in authoring the theoretical and empirical literature, and a corresponding bias in the audience of that literature. Most contemporary research into child development and parenting is of Western (north European or North American) origin, and less than 10% of the literature in developmental science emanates from regions of the world that account for more than 90% of the world's population. Therefore, much less is currently known scientifically than is commonly acknowledged about children, parenting, and families generally or the majority of cultural settings of human development specifically. Moreover, the societies typically included in cultural developmental research have limited many sources of variation; families often adhere to the same basic organization, and parents play the same basic roles and share many of the same basic goals for their children. This restriction of range is overly limiting in terms of understanding idiosyncrasies of child development and childrearing as well as the generalizations and universals about childhood and parenting that are possible. Science can only benefit from an enlarged representation of the world's children, parents, and cultures.

In response to this state of affairs, cultural context is gaining greater recognition in mainstream behavioral and social science study. Developmental studies in culture promise deeper insights into how children and parents in a variety of contexts come to think, feel, and act the way they do. For example, such lessons illuminate how broad or circumscribed are the presumed universals of child development and childcare, how children's experiences in different settings affect the course of their development, how different settings affect parenting, and the extent to which children's experiences reflect the acquisition of culture.

The *Handbook of Cultural Developmental Science* focuses on documenting child and caregiver characteristics associated with cultural variation and on charting relations between cultural variation on the one hand and, on the other, developmental variation in physical, mental, emotional, and social development in children, parents, and cultures.

Many daunting theoretical, methodological, and practical questions arise when undertaking cultural developmental study. As researchers who engage in cultural developmental investigations recognize, the sheer logistics of this kind of work are formidable. Cultural developmentalists are not in a position to manipulate relevant independent variables experimentally; such manipulations are normally impractical, impossible, or ethically unacceptable. To meet multiple challenges, cultural developmentalists often turn to "natural experiments," essentially fortuitous occurrences of particular customs human beings have adopted or of particular environments in which human beings have adapted.

Notwithstanding these formidable complications, the reasons to pursue cultural developmental study are many and compelling. One is description. People are perennially curious about development in cultures not their own. For this reason, social commentary as a matter of course includes reports of child life, just as the Athenians expressed interest in the Spartan *agogé*. Insofar as cultural developmental descriptions of biopsychological constructs, structures, functions, and processes attempt to encompass the widest spectrum of human variation, they are also the most comprehensive in science. They are vital to delimiting the full range of human experience; in this sense they are also critical to establishing realistic and valid developmental norms. Furthermore, our awareness of alternative modes of development sharpens our perceptions and enhances our understanding of the nature of child development and childrearing in our own culture. Thus, one major motive of cultural developmental research has been to augment our basic understanding of human development and human caregiving across cultures. Description itself is also prerequisite to other formal rationales, significantly explanation.

A second reason for culturally informed developmental study is explanation. This motive for submitting human development and caregiving in different cultures to psychological scrutiny derives from the extraordinary and unique power that cultural developmental comparisons furnish science. Cultural developmental study helps to explain the origins and ontogenetic course of the widest possible variety of constructs, structures, functions, or processes. Only the comparative view can expose variables that regulate development and care but may be invisible from a single-culture perspective. This type of analysis helps distinguish those constructs, structures, functions, and processes that emerge and evolve in a culture-dependent fashion from those that transcend or are independent of culture; it holds out the possibility of exposing how forces that vary globally (e.g., family structure, urbanization, nationality, religion, economics, and the like) differentially mold key features of human behavior. Culture-specific patterns of child development and childrearing are adapted to each specific society's setting and needs. All societies require certain behaviors of their member citizens (for example, care of infants, socialization of children, interpersonal communication, exchange of social control and responsibility across generations), and most if not all societies differentiate among members (for example, by promoting sexual, developmental, or socioeconomic class distinctions). Even behaviors that are logical candidates for a strong genetic or biological interpretation (because they display regularity and submit to normative analysis in one place) may be subject to experiential or environmental variation and show variability (if studied in other places). In brief, cultural developmental inquiry provides natural tests of special circumstances that might surround development and is critical to exploring and distinguishing cultural uniformity and cultural diversity of biopsychological constructs, structures, functions, and processes.

A third motive driving cultural developmental study is interpretation. At the end of the day, the major goal of much of scientific inquiry is to lay bare meaning. Understanding the meaning of biopsychological constructs, structures, functions, and processes depends critically on examining them in the contexts of culture and development. For example, a given construct, structure, function, or process can have the same or a different meaning in different cultures. Conversely, different constructs, structures, functions, and processes can have similar or different meanings depending on culture. Culture is a prime context for determining relations between construct, structure, function, or process and meaning. Development in culture is a prime circumstance for examining how meaning is shaped. Furthermore, the study of cultural developmental meaning furnishes a check against the uncritical adoption of an ethnocentric worldview and the (often untoward) implications of such a view. Many of the reasons that motivate cultural developmental study are frankly descriptive or explanatory, but others concern meaning. At base, all of these motives culminate in better understanding adaptation in human beings.

The *Handbook of Cultural Developmental Science* was developed to address these goals. It consists of two main parts. Chapters in Part I cover *Domains of Development Across Cultures*. Authorities in each major subdiscipline of childhood, caregiving, and culture look at a topic of interest from a perspective informed by culture and development. Part I begins with considerations of *Culture* by Jacqueline J. Goodnow and *Methodology* by Fons J. R. van de Vijver, Jan Hofer, and Athanasios Chasiotis. Then, substantive chapters address *Survival and Health* by Carol M. Worthman; *Motor Skill* by Karen E. Adolph, Lana B. Karasik, and Catherine S. Tamis-LeMonda; *Perception* by Janet F. Werker, Daphne M. Maurer, and Katherine A. Yoshida; *Cognition* by Michael Cole and Xavier E. Cagigas; *Language* by Elena Lieven and Sabine Stoll; *Literacy* by Daniel A. Wagner; *Emotions and Temperament* by Jerome Kagan; *Self and Personality* by Ross A. Thompson and Elita Amini Virmani; *Gender* by Deborah L. Best; *Peers* by Kenneth H. Rubin, Charissa Cheah, and Melissa M. Menzer; *Socialization* by Mary Gauvain and Ross D. Parke; *Parenting* by Marc H. Bornstein and Jennifer E. Lansford; and *Religion* by George W. Holden and Brigitte Vittrup.

Chapters in Part II cover *Development in Different Places on Earth*. Authorities focus on major regions of the world to look at childhood, caregiving, and culture from the perspective of place. Substantive chapters include: *The United States of America* by Catherine S. Tamis-LeMonda and Karen E. McFadden; *Central and South America* by Rodolfo de Castro Ribas Jr.; the *European Union* by Martin Pinquart and Rainer K. Silbereisen; *North Africa and the Middle East* by Ramadan A. Ahmed; *Afrique Noire* by A. Bame Nsamenang and Joseph L. Lo-oh; *Russia* by David A. Nelson, Craig H. Hart, Emily K. Keister, and Karina Piassetskaia; *China* by Xinyin Chen and Li Wang; *East and Southeast Asia* by David W. Shwalb, Barbara J. Shwalb, Jun Nakazawa, Jung-Hwan Hyun, Hao Van Le, and Monty P. Satiadarma; *India* by T. S. Saraswathi and Ranjana Dutta, and *Australia and New Zealand* by Ann V. Sanson and Janis E. Paterson. In addition, the *HOME Environment* is addressed by Robert H. Bradley and *Immigration and Acculturation* by Marc H. Bornstein and Linda R. Cote.

The *Handbook of Cultural Developmental Science* is designed to constitute the first step that theoreticians, researchers, and students alike should take when entering the field of cultural developmental study.

Acknowledgments

I thank Eve Malakoff-Klein, Christian Muñoz, Debra Riegert, Lee Transue, and Richard Tressider.

Marc H. Bornstein
Bethesda, Maryland

Part I
Domains of Development Across Cultures

1
Culture

JACQUELINE J. GOODNOW

Introduction

This chapter reviews four ways of specifying cultural contexts, linking each to accounts of development and asking what new questions they open about the nature and course of development. This opening section briefly considers some background questions: What gives rise to interest in ways of specifying cultural contexts? What prompts the choice of four particular ways of doing so?

Sources of Interest in Ways of Specifying Cultural Contexts

As Bornstein (1980) points out in a review of the history of cultural developmental psychology, people who come from "other" places and are seen as "different" have always attracted interest, both among members of the general public and among social scientists. Long-standing also is curiosity about what might happen if circumstances were changed. To cite one of Bornstein's (1980) early examples, King James I wondered what form speech and language might take if infants were brought up in the company of only a deaf-mute nurse.

Over time, however, changes have occurred in the extent to which we are aware of differences. Changes have also occurred in the aims, the methods, and the settings chosen once interest turns to closer analyses or comparisons. Changes in awareness are the most widespread, occurring both within and outside the social sciences. More visible now to all of us are changes in population flow from one country to another and in population patterns within countries. Canada, for example, is seen by many as having become more "French," California as more "Hispanic," and Australia as more "multicultural" or at least less "Anglo." Coupled with that awareness has often been a sense of changing social needs. New immigrant groups or new commitments to changing other parts of the world, for example, bring the need to think about new services, ranging from health and education to legal or political structures, with questions raised about their possible design, reception, or impact. Interest in those questions is one of the reasons for developmental psychology being increasingly referred to as "developmental science." However, interest in those questions is not restricted to any one discipline or even to the social sciences in general.

For changes in aims and methods, focus for the moment on developmental psychology (see also van de Vijver, Hofer, and Chasiotis, Chapter 2, this volume). A first move was a shift away from interest only in "testing for generality," from asking whether what we are accustomed to seeing is perhaps "universal." As a check on universality, almost any other country could be chosen. Convenience could be the deciding factor, together with some preference for places where there appeared to be a difference in the way children were reared or schooled. That way of proceeding, however, tends to lock us into seeing "nature" and "nurture" as opposed opposites. It also tells us little about how any particular similarity or difference comes about.

A second change moved the field beyond choices based on nationality or country of origin. Turning to other nationalities or countries of origin has benefits. It is likely, for example, to make us more aware of the ways in which people may vary, and it can make us reflect on both what they do and what we ourselves do. How, for instance, do people make judgments and decisions about developmental status or schooling when they have no record of chronological age? What prompts our own addiction to knowing how old individuals are? Turning to other nationalities or countries of origin also highlights for us the extent to which some ways of thinking or acting are shared by members of a large social group, have a history, and are felt to be part of who one is—features that may transcend national boundaries.

Nationality, however, still takes us only part of the way toward understanding how any developmental effects come about—how settings give rise to similarities or differences and how contexts shape or construct the ways in which we see ourselves and the world around us. To move more directly toward that kind of understanding, we need to choose settings that allow us to focus on some particular links between features of contexts and aspects of development. What happens, we ask, when literacy has a pictorial or syllabary base rather than an alphabetic one; when children learn about the making of clothes or about biology by procedures that are strictly detailed or by methods that allow some experimentation and some encounters with error; or when most of the activities of children are in the company of adults rather than within groups that are strongly age-graded?

At this point, we may not need comparisons across nationalities. We may be able to focus on groups within a country. In either case, any move toward closer description of a context or toward choosing two or more contexts for comparative purposes comes to be guided by a view of development as related to some particular aspects of contexts, such as the demands they make, the tools they provide, and the forms of participation they allow or encourage. However, those specific qualities or features may still take several forms. Which ways of specifying contexts should we consider?

Ways of Specifying Cultural Contexts

Of the four ways of specifying social-cultural contexts selected for review in this chapter, three focus on ways of describing content. The first emphasizes the nature of ideologies, values, and norms—ways of viewing the world that are often summarized by the term "cultural models." The second emphasizes what people do—the practices, activities, or routines that mark a social group. The third emphasizes what is available to people in the form of paths, routes, or opportunities. The fourth cuts across these descriptions. Regardless of whether the focus is on values, practices, or paths, this kind of account emphasizes the extent to which a context is marked by homogeneity or heterogeneity—by uniformity or by competition and "contest" among diverse ways of thinking or acting.

These approaches do not exclude one another. Some analyses may combine them (see Bornstein, 2002). Other ways of grouping approaches (see Cooper & Denner, 1998; Goodnow, 1995) and of bringing out points of relevance to developmental topics and methods (see Goodnow, 1990b, 2002, 2006b; Rogoff, 2002) are also possible. This particular grouping into four approaches, however, helps meet several challenges.

One challenge comes from the varied descriptions now available for the nature of contexts. Currently at hand, for example, is a range of definitions of "culture," usually offered by people other than psychologists and often expressed in unfamiliar terms. We need to bring out how those descriptions often hang together, cutting across disciplines. We also need to find ways of cutting across descriptions of family, neighborhood, and cultural contexts. At the least, it is effortful to use different dimensions to describe each of these. It is also restricting to see each only as a surround for the others—for example, a neighborhood only as a surround for families or culture only as a surround for all other groups or settings.

A further challenge comes when we seek to link accounts of cultural contexts to accounts of development. One of the difficulties prompted by turning to "other" places is that analyses of cultural contexts may easily be seen as on the margins of what most developmental scientists see as important, to be exotica with no direct relevance to core developmental issues. To break down that marginalization, we need ways to bring out the parallels that often exist between descriptions of contexts and descriptions of development. We need also to explore the ways in which analyses of cultural contexts prompt new questions about development, alerting us to aspects we might easily miss or take so much for granted that no need is seen for closer attention or exploration. The four chosen ways of specifying cultural contexts help us move toward meeting those needs.

For each of the four accounts, a summary outline of the main proposals is given and then specific points of relevance to analyses of development are discussed. Each account draws on the fields of anthropology, psychology, and sociology, although these are not the only relevant fields. Analyses of cultural contexts and development, it has been pointed out, can benefit from attention to history (e.g., Cole, 2001), law (e.g., Shweder, Markus, Minow, and Kessel, 1998), and studies of literature and language (e.g., Cazden, 1993; Goodnow, 1997). Anthropology and sociology, however, are still the main sources for both descriptions of contexts and observations on the shape and the course of development.

Considered first are approaches that emphasize multiplicity and contest. That choice stems partly from this approach cutting across all other descriptions. It stems also from issues of novelty. This way of viewing context is perhaps the least familiar to developmental psychologists. However, it also offers the sharpest contrast to the assumptions we often hold about the significance of differences among groups or generations and about our own ways of thinking and acting.

Specification 1: Multiplicity and Context

Proposals about multiplicity usually start by noting that it is tempting to regard societies as monolithic. This region or country, for example, is "Islamic," and that one is "Christian;" this one is "modern," and that one "traditional." The reality is less one-eyed. In any society, for instance, there is usually more than one political position, one form of medicine or schooling, one way of arranging work, one source of news or entertainment, and one view of what children are like and how adults should behave toward them. The number of viewpoints or positions, however, is less important than the balance among them. One form, for example, may predominate. In Gramsci's (1971) terms, one form may be "hegemonic," and another may be "counter-hegemonic." In Salzman's (1981) terms, one may be "dominant," and another may be "recessive." For the description of any society, however, the general argument is that we would do well to assume heterogeneity and then to peg our description in terms of the forms that heterogeneity takes.

Interest in heterogeneity is not new among anthropologists. It appears, for example, in Whiting and Edwards' (1988) description of how societies differ. It is also central to Romney's analyses of differences among individuals (they may hold consensus values or be more on the margins) and of the way an individual's being "modal" influences the judgments of others (e.g., Romney, Weller, and Batchelder, 1986). Holding opinions that are "modal," for example, makes an individual more likely to be seen by others as trustworthy—in a sense, to be seen as a "solid citizen."

More marked in later anthropological analyses, however, is an accompanying emphasis on "contest." In one description, analyses have changed from regarding cultures as "integrated, stable sets of meanings" to recognizing the presence of "conflict, ambiguity, and change" (Strauss, 1992, p. 1). Contest may be open, in the sense that one group or one set of interests seeks to discount, devalue, suppress, or take over another. Even when there is official tolerance, however, the reality is one of spread, resistance, and perhaps negotiation rather than side-by-side acceptance.

Accounts of cultural contexts in terms of multiplicity and contest are now to be found in many content areas. They appear, for example, in analyses of changes in film productions. Whenever the independents begin to reach more than some minimal share of the market, the large studios begin to pick up their themes and styles, in much the same way that formal medicine takes over some aspects of "alternative" therapies (Gledhill, 1988). They appear also in analyses of neighborhoods. In Shaw and McKay's (1942/1969) classic analysis of acts against the law by juveniles, for example, neighborhoods vary in their "mix" of ethnic groups and of groups with interests that fall within or outside the law. Mixtures often reduce the likelihood of groups pulling together. Pulling together may still occur, however, when there is a common enemy, for example, when regulatory agencies threaten the independence of all groups or business interests seek to take over an area. The starting point, however, is always the assumption of competing interests (from within and "outside"), with each seeking to maximize their areas of control or at least to resist spread and takeover efforts.

To add another part of the "contest" argument, social groups are seen as drawing boundary lines, especially between those regarded as "us" and "them" (e.g., Kristeva, 1991). Groups also take evaluative stances toward each other. They approve of some and disapprove of others. They view some as "advanced" and others as more "primitive" or "unsophisticated." They see some as presenting no danger, whereas others should be kept at a distance or approached with caution. In the social identity or group membership terms more often used by social psychologists, people consistently see themselves ("us") in more positive terms than they see those categorized as "them." In a further example of concern with boundary lines, we often reject attempts at "passing" and regard some group memberships as incompatible with others (e.g., Tajfel, 1981; Turner, 1987).

By and large, developmental scientists have not made much use of this way of viewing cultural contexts. There is a long-standing recognition that people within national or ethnic groups may vary from one another in their values (e.g., in the extent to which they value individualist rather than collective orientations) (Triandis, 2001). Heterogeneity is also recognized as likely to become more marked when socioeconomic changes occur unevenly, for example, when subgroups move unevenly into modernization (Assadi et al., 2007). The dynamic interplay among segments of a society, however, has been given relatively little attention. One notable exception is Wertsch's (2002) analysis of discrepancies that can arise between official narratives and what one's own experience points to as really being the case, which are discrepancies that can result in an "internal immigration"—a private holding—of one's own views. That type of analysis clearly warrants expansion.

From among other ways in which developmental analyses may benefit, three possibilities are singled out, with examples for each from existing research.

Proposals about *homogeneity* provide the first line of benefit. They lead one to ask about the effects of children receiving the same message from several sources (e.g., the message that school is irrelevant; Watson-Gegeo, 1992). They also provide a conceptual home for observations about the effects of like-minded others when a competing message tempts one "off track." African American students, for example, are more likely to persist with school achievement when their schools and neighborhoods contain a sizeable number of others who also do so (Steinberg, Darling, and Fletcher, 1995). Proposals about homogeneity also prompt us to ask about the effects on children of parents being perceived as "modal." Teachers who perceive parents as holding modal values, for example, judge their children as well-adjusted (Deal, Halvorson, and Wampler, 1989). Children, however, might make more varied judgments, finding it a relief, embarrassing, or awkward when parents display modal or marginal ways of thinking or acting.

A second line of benefit comes from proposals about *contest*. One of the questions such proposals prompt is: How do parents prepare their children for competing messages? Goodnow (1997, p. 352) pointed to two strategies: "cocooning" and "pre-arming." Cocooning consists of keeping children within an enclave of like-minded people. Children progress, for example, from one Catholic, Christian, or Islamic school to another, from one set of family-related friends to another, or from one neighborhood to another with the same restricted range of people. Pre-arming consists of actively equipping children with strategies for dealing with negative encounters that cannot be avoided, such as being teased, called names, excluded, regarded as strange, or challenged to give reasons for the beliefs one holds or for the way one speaks or dresses (wearing the hijab, for example, is officially tolerated in Australian classrooms but regularly challenged by peers on the playground). Padilla-Walker and Thompson (2005) have taken the analysis further by splitting cocooning into two forms (controlled and reasoned cocooning) and by adding two further strategies: compromise and deference (allowing the child to make the decisions).

For any particular group then, we may ask about the specific strategies that are used. Hughes and Chen (1999), for example, describe African American parents as pre-arming their children for negative encounters by making them aware and proud of their group's own history or by teaching them specific ways of responding to negative encounters of various kinds. Correlated with the use of particular strategies were the child's age and the parent's own encounters with discrimination. For a nonminority group, Padilla-Walker and Thompson (2005) have found links between cocooning and some particular qualities among parents, such as religiosity, the importance for parents of the value in question, and the sense that the outside world is threatening. Clearly open now for further exploration are questions about the circumstances that influence—for parents or for children—the use and effectiveness of various strategies.

Worth particular note in the course of such exploration is a study of the effects and effectiveness of a strong form of cocooning. This study draws from an autobiographical account of growing up within a strongly orthodox Jewish group, a group that allowed as little contact as possible with people who held alternative values and that marked its difference in ways ranging from religious practices to styles of dress (Lawrence, Benedikt, and Valsiner, 1992). The study records the many ways in which contact with others was discouraged or forbidden. It also records how cocooning broke down. The mother of this family tolerated the daughter's reading (an apparently safe "at home" activity). The books from the public library, however, presented a different world. That exposure prompted an eventual break from the group, leading to both a sense of relief and a sense of being "homeless," of belonging fully neither to the group from which the daughter came nor to the world into which she had moved. The account fits well with the general proposal that social shifts can result in a "homeless mind" (Berger, Berger, and Kellner, 1973), which is at ease in neither the old world nor the new world. Of benefit now would be further accounts that flesh out, for individuals, the developmental impact of such contextual shifts.

The third and last line of benefit picks up proposals about social identity and group memberships. A particular example is the issue of *parents' and children's perceptions of boundary lines and possible memberships*. Proposals about multiplicity and contest prompt questions about the extent to which children and parents see it as possible to "navigate the borders" between groups (Phelan, Davidson, and Yu, 1992), to "bridge multiple worlds" (Cooper, 1999, p. 25), and perhaps even to "pass" as a member of a group for which one lacks the usual credentials.

We now begin to wonder how people feel when boundary lines are not observed. B. Thorne (personal communication, July 20, 2003), for example, has noted the way teachers may happily lump together as "Asian" children from countries ranging from India to Japan. Noted also are occasions when children fudge their self-descriptions. A girl whose parents come from Egypt, for example, describes herself as "African" when she wishes to join a particular sports group. When do children feel that these category errors are significant enough to warrant correction or indignation? When do parents feel that a child is "no longer one of us" or has ceased—in the words of an immigrant Italian in Australia—to be a "true Italian"? What ways of thinking or acting must be kept, even in remnant form, to be perceived as "still one of us" or to feel "able to go home again"?

From a different tack, but still with questions about identity and boundary lines in mind, we begin to see more easily the value of exploring links between well-being and perceptions of the group to which one belongs. A study by Chandler, Lalonde, Sokol, and Hallett (2003) provides an example. Within a group of adolescents in various "bands" among Canadian First Nation groups, the rates of suicide and self-harm were lowest in "bands" that had both a positive view of their historical past (e.g., they sought to keep the language alive) and a proactive approach to their future (e.g., they were fighting for native title or other rights or preparing to do so). Instead of a sense of incompatibility between past, present, and future, for these adolescents, there was now a sense of accomplishing continuity both for themselves and for the groups to which they belong. How that sense of continuing personal and social identity is achieved or can be promoted is clearly an aspect of development that warrants further attention, particularly at times when conventional accounts of history and of expected futures provide little support for a sense of positive identity and often undercut its development.

Specification 2: Ideologies, Values, and Norms

Analyses of cultural contexts often turn to ways of thinking to what have been termed "cultural models" (e.g., D'Andrade and Strauss, 1992; Goodnow, 2006a; Goodnow and Collins, 1990; Holland and Quinn, 1987). The adjective "cultural" refers to these ways of thinking as being shared by all or most members of a group. The term "models" refers to the presence of categories, distinctions, or assumptions that reach across a variety of experiences, situations, or judgments.

Some analyses of cultural models focus on ways of thinking that have little obvious affective content, for example, distinctions among colors or types of snow. However, here we will focus on those to which feelings are more clearly attached, such as those that attract the sense of a "significant error," "deviance," or "developmental delay" when a distinction is not made or not correctly made. That focus draws attention to the fact that some ways of thinking matter more than others. It highlights also the need to bring together analyses of cognitive and social development, raising questions about "the socialization of cognition" (Goodnow, 1990a) and about the nature of socialization in all content areas.

As examples of particular concern with ways of thinking that matter, proposals from D'Andrade (1981), Bourdieu (1979), and Fiske (1991) are given. D'Andrade (1981) took cognitive psychology to task for its assumption that all skills were equally important; the essential feature, in those analyses, was the nature of the logic required. In reality, he pointed out, all cultures specify some skills as essential (not to acquire them rules one out as a competent member of the group). Others are regarded as options or, further down the scale, as "trivial pursuits." Errors related to essential skills or essential ways of thinking are "significant." Other errors may be more readily ignored or even found amusing.

Bourdieu (1979) adds a close analysis of what we regard as displaying "distinction" or "good taste." We regard some intellectual productions, for example, as displaying "elegant solutions," "original," or "well-presented," whereas others are "pedestrian," "repetitive," or "lacking in style." We expect students to learn that the style to aim for—if they wish to do more than pass—is one that blends "a knowledge of the literature" with "a novel approach" or "a new idea." The vagueness of the formal ways in which we teach these aspects of style, Bourdieu

(1979) argued, provides one of the ways in which most approaches to teaching reproduce class inequality.

Fiske (1991) offers a step away from academic types of skill, turning instead to an understanding of relationships. All cultures, he argues, draw distinctions among four types of relationships. These he labels as communal, hierarchical, exchange, and market-pricing. Communal relationships are marked by a caring concern for another's welfare, as if that person was part of ourselves. Hierarchical relationships are marked by differences in power and authority—differences seen as needing to be respected and sustained. Exchange relationships are marked by the making of equal returns for any benefit received, and market-pricing relationships are marked by money as the form of return, with the amount guided by what is common in the local economy.

Constant across cultures, Fiske (1991) proposed, is also the sense that some social category errors are more significant than others, with confusions between communal and market-pricing relationships regarded as the most serious. People might, for example, regard as acceptable the selling of people who, in hierarchical fashion, are regarded as "slaves" but see it as a serious social error to sell people to whom one should have communal ties, such as a parent or a sibling. Some category errors may even come to be regarded as "taboo," "counterfactual," or "heretical" (e.g., Fiske and Tetlock, 1997; Tetlock, McGraw, and Kristel, 2004). If we are to understand ways of thinking, it is proposed, we especially need to understand those that are outside the range of what are seen as reasonable or legitimate to consider, let alone translate into action.

How can developmental scientists make more use of these proposals? A starting point would be a heightened awareness of *gaps in the ideologies or values we consider*. In a society that has, in many ways, become increasingly secular, we are often slow to recognize the developmental importance of religion or spirituality. That position is now changing (see Holden and Vittrup, Chapter 15, in this volume). An example is a study by Hudley, Haight, and Miller (2003) documenting the importance of church affiliation for the development of a sense of identity and as a means of socialization.

In contrast, we know more about the ways in which schools actively promote some ways of thinking and speaking, whereas others are "devalued" or vigorously "dismantled." "Dismantling," for instance, is a major part of analyses of what happens within classrooms when children bring to school ways of speaking and storytelling that do not match what teachers value (e.g., Heath, 1983; Michaels, 1991). Within schools, teachers also promote "the voice of science," or accounts that remove personal histories and feelings from the description of events, emphasizing instead expert sources of information and physical or quantitative features (Wertsch, 1991).

Those studies have emphasized what teachers do. In a less common approach, Cazden (1993) drew attention to minority students' accounts of such encounters. Those accounts, from adult students, show how the individuals feel when they need to change their style to attract attention and approval from their teachers, for example, to say that they have read about something rather than that they are speaking from their own personal experience.

A further example of developmental relevance and one that goes outside of school settings is the notion that some ways of thinking have *a taboo, heretical, or counterfactual status*. How do they acquire this status? In one major analysis of acts against the law, for example, most actions are regarded as based on estimates of the probabilities of benefit or risk. Some possible actions, however, are regarded as "not an option." This perception, in Wikström and Sampson's (in press) analysis, is the essence of "morality." It is acquired, they suggest, early in childhood, perhaps on a different basis from the ways in which probability estimates of options and possible consequences are formed and revised in the course of experience.

Acts against the law are not the only content area to bring out the sense that some ways of proceeding are "not an option." Parents, for example, are prepared to consider as possible a number of ways in which household tasks may be carried out, shifted over to others, or rewarded. Some ways of proceeding, however, are designated as "not on," and children seem quick to learn where this line is drawn (Goodnow, 1996c). At this point, we have much to learn about how a sense of "not an option" or "not on" is acquired, but this is clearly an aspect of what we call moral development that warrants closer attention.

Moral development, however, is not the only content area that may benefit from culturally oriented analyses of values. Studies of development in all areas, these analyses imply, may benefit from our asking about when delays or errors are felt to be especially important or especially indicative of developmental status and about the kinds of actions or ideas that are felt to be outside the realm of what is reasonable or decent to consider or question. We might then also explore the extent to which forms of socialization vary with perceived importance or any implication of "heresy" and give rise to various degrees of resistance to change.

Specification 3: Practices, Activities, and Routines

This type of approach to cultural contexts shifts the emphasis from ways of thinking to ways of acting, or to what people do. Particular attention is given to acts that are repeated in everyday fashion and come to be regarded as "right" or "natural."

Analyses of these actions often appear under the label "cultural practices," within both sociology (e.g., West and Zimmerman, 1987) and anthropology (e.g., Bourdieu, 1997, 1990). The adjective "cultural" again refers to these ways of acting being followed by all or most of the members of a social group. (It can also refer to their being the routes by which larger frames, such as prevailing structures or ideologies, become part of daily lived experience; see Chaiklin and Lave, 1996; Miller and Goodnow, 1995; Thorne, 2005.)

The term "practices" refers to the repeated, everyday quality of these actions and to the accompanying expectation that this is how people should act. The actions described as practices range from ways of storytelling (e.g., Miller, 1994) to ways of organizing classrooms (e.g., Gutiérrez, 2002), dividing work (e.g., Goodnow, 1996c), or dividing sleeping areas among family members (e.g., Shweder, Arnett Jensen, and Goldstein, 1995). In each case, however, several qualities apply. One is that these ways of acting are seldom reflected on or questioned. A second is that in the course of learning a practice, people also learn the values associated with it. A third is that the undoing of actions may be the necessary first step in the undoing of ideas. The undoing of gender schemas offers a prime example. Change may need to start by altering the several ways in which we "do gender" (West and Zimmerman, 1987), such as by replacing terms such as "he" or "everyman" with terms such as such as "they" or "people." Developmentally, it is proposed, actions come first. Ideas or schemas follow.

The actions often described as "activities" also take varied forms. In one list, for example, they cover "bedtime, playing video games, homework, watching TV, cooking dinner, soccer practice, visiting grandma, babysitting for money, algebra class" (Weisner, 2002, p. 275). The emphasis, as that list suggests, is now more on routines in families and schools than on what is common to members of a larger social group. In activity analyses, there is also more attention to the places in which activities occur, the people who are present, and, in some analyses, the "psychology" of those present, for example, their views of what is possible or should occur (e.g., Super and Harkness, 1997; Weisner, 1984). The conceptual base comes less from sources such as Bourdieu (1977, 1990) and more from Russian activity theory (e.g., Vygotsky, 1978). (Cole, 1995, offers a more thorough account of these bases.) For both practices and activities, however, the focus remains on what people routinely do.

Common to both lines of analysis is also the particular attention paid to the presence of others and what they contribute. In Clark's (1996) analysis of "joint activities" that range from conversation to soccer and chess, for example, people may be present as team players, fans, observers, judges, or score keepers. In other analyses, people may provide the needed tools or resources (e.g., Cole and Hatano, 2007; Gauvain, 2001), pass on their expertise (e.g., Rogoff, 2003), offer motivational support (e.g., Takahashi, Tokoro, and Hatano, 2006), be the audiences kept in mind (e.g., Oura and Hatano, 2001; Wertsch, 1991), or provide the "community of practitioners" that a learner may join once a certain level of competence has been reached (Lave and Wenger, 1988). No analysis of any individual's action, however, can proceed without attention to the way others structure a task before any action occurs or are present in the course of an action taking place.

Again, aspects of development that an approach alerts us to and that we might well explore more fully, gaining in the process new views and new questions about both the course and the bases of development, are emphasized.

The first has to do with the question: *How does innovation come about?* Especially if we start from proposals about cultural practices, the emphasis may readily fall on the reproduction of skills or ways of acting that already exist. Each new generation then repeats what is already in place, with the older generation expressing concern about departures from established ways. Most analyses of culture, however, point out that we need to account for "production" as well as "reproduction," for the emergence of new ways as well as for continuity in old ways. How can new ways come about?

One proposal is that changes are more likely to occur in activities where others express less concern with replication. In these areas of "acceptable ignorance" or "negotiable disagreement" (Goodnow, 1996a, p. 345), the invention of new ways may be tolerated or even admired. Adults may also foster departures from routines and technical accuracy either from the start or as learning progresses. This is the kind of base argued for by Hatano and his colleagues. When, from the start, routines are relaxed rather than strict (the raising of inexpensive goldfish at home is one example), children may develop "adaptive expertise" rather than only "routine expertise" (Hatano and Inagaki, 1986). When people begin learning to play the piano, the focus is likely to fall on technical correctness and on the teacher as the main audience. Those who are more expert, however, may perceive audiences as expecting a mixture of technical skill and individual interpretation. Unless they achieve that expected mix, in fact, they may never be regarded as truly "expert" (Oura and Hatano, 2001).

Broader than both of those proposals is the argument that participation in itself brings about change. As participation proceeds, individuals begin—in collaboration with others—to move toward new ways of proceeding. An analysis of participation in the practice of selling Girl Scout cookies provides an example (Rogoff, Baker-Sennett, Lacasa, and Goldsmith, 1995). Over time, the individuals who took part in this task changed in their understanding of the task and in the ways they proceeded. Over time also, some of those new ways were adopted by others and became standard practice.

In effect, analyses of practices and activities provide a productive springboard for exploring both continuity and innovation. In addition, both offer *ways of clarifying the concept of participation*. Effective participation must call for learning the "collaborative rules" (Goodnow, 1996b) that apply. To take part in conversations, for example, in classrooms or in households, we need to learn how to join in and to exit in acceptable ways and how to establish "common ground" (Clark, 1996). We need also to learn what each person should contribute and what can be left out or delegated to others (Goodnow, 1996c). The developmental aspects to these forms of competence are far from being well understood.

An understanding of nonparticipation is also needed. Blumenfeld and her colleagues, for example, have drawn attention to the need to break a context such as "school" into components and to ask which of these invites nonparticipation. Students who display low overall engagement in school activities, Blumenfeld et al. (2005) report, fall into three subgroups: the truly disaffected (except for "fun" excursions, school is irrelevant), the strugglers (interested in some subjects but finding many activities too demanding), and the socially troubled (a group that often likes schoolwork but is turned off school by difficulties with other children).

From a different angle, Rogoff (2003) pointed out that "nonparticipation" may be in the eyes of the observer. In many societies, the early stages of learning may seem distant from the overt trial-and-error that we expect; they may appear, in our eyes, to be "only observation." That kind of activity, Rogoff (2003) argues, is better thought of as "intent participation"—observation accompanied by the expectation that overt action will occur later and by a mental rehearsal of how one will participate. That kind of analysis alerts us to the need to explore, in any society, the content areas and the circumstances under which this particular style of participation is expected or adopted.

The last point of relevance to be singled out has to do with *negative aspects to contributions from others*. Most developmental accounts of what others provide are benign. The emphasis is on the ways in which others help development or encourage effective participation. We know less about occasions of refused help or of help that is felt to be intrusive and interfering. Sociologists such as Foucault (1980) point out that others are not always helpful, especially when they are the experts in an area. They may regard knowledge and expertise as forms of power, to be controlled in monopoly fashion or passed on only to a restricted group. Developmental analyses pay little attention to the occurrence and impact of actions by others that may be perceived as less than helpful. One example of what can be explored, however, is a study of perceptions of unsolicited help or unasked-for advice (Smith and Goodnow, 1999). The focus in that study was on perceptions among adults varying in age. Exploring those perceptions during early childhood and adolescence, however, would be a useful addition to our current understanding of how others may contribute to the shape of development.

Specification 4: Paths, Routes, and Opportunities
These ways of specifying cultural contexts can be described more briefly than has been the case for the earlier approaches. The general emphasis on progressions and movement—on journeys—fits easily with many accounts of development and will seem familiar.

Less likely to be familiar is the presence of three ways of referring to paths, each highlighting different developmental questions. To start with, the paths of interest may be physical. An example comes from an analysis of neighborhoods. Features of the natural or built environment may allow only some ways to go from point A to point B, with that restriction bringing an unavoidable exposure to groups or activities in the area (Wikström and Sampson, 2006).

Less concretely, the term "paths" may refer to the stages or steps that individuals are expected to follow as they move through school, paid work, or relationships. Questions are then raised about expected timetables, the acceptable excuses for being "off-time," the extent to which sequences have to be followed in lock-step fashion, the skills needed for each step, and the impact of having to make several transitions at one time (e.g., Neugarten, 1979).

In a third phrasing (paths as opportunity structures), the emphasis is on available progressions, for example, on the possibility of employment after involvement in acts against the law (e.g., Braithwaite, 1989) or continuing in high school while pregnant (e.g., Furstenberg, 1976). Highlighted are questions about the extent to which doors are open or closed, the presence of guides or gatekeepers, the information people have about possible routes and how to access them, and, again, the presence of flexibility, this time in the form of alternative structures or recovery routes.

What do analyses of paths especially offer for the study of development? The familiarity of path concepts to developmental scientists will help keep this section relatively short, with a restriction to two points of relevance.

The first of these has to do with *the way one step is related to later steps*. Developmentalists have a well-established interest in this issue. Regularly offered, for example, are reminders that life is "not a rocket launch" (Shonkoff and Phillips, 2000), that there are "straight and devious paths to adulthood" (Robins and Rutter, 1994), and that what needs to be watched for is the occurrence not only of persistence but also of declines or desistance (e.g., Nagin and Tremblay, 1997). Age changes in antisocial acts or acts against the law have provided an especially strong spur to such analyses (Lawrence, 2007, provides one review; a report from the Developmental Crime Prevention Consortium, 1999, provides another). Here are not only patterns of continuity but also, especially among adolescents and young adults, patterns of increases and then desistance.

Present also, in a less obvious fashion, are questions about sudden accelerations. One might expect, for example, that involvement in crime will follow a step-by-step move into greater involvement. The progression, Loeber and LeBlanc (1990) reported, is often more complex. To start with, there are likely to be two ladders: one into crimes against property and the other into crimes against people. In the main, there is little crossover between ladders. For some adolescents, however, sudden leaps across ladders occur, with the first act of the new kind taken at the top of its ladder, at the deep end (e.g., a serious first act against people after a time of involvement only in crimes against property). Those leaps, Loeber and LeBlanc (1990) suggested, often stem from new contexts, such as from new exposures or from memberships in new groups. The bases to change may be different in other content areas. However, the occurrence and the sources of sudden accelerations and "leaps across" are, like occasions of desistance, clearly worth watching for in any analysis of sequential steps, with the possibility kept in mind that the change has been prompted more by changes in contexts than by changes only within the individual.

The other highlighted aspect has to do with *ways of introducing change*. Progressions through and beyond high school provide some examples. That progression may come to a halt if early pregnancy "forecloses" the possibility of completing school (Furstenberg, 1976). Keeping the route open is then the action that makes it possible to continue schooling and that opens work opportunities.

A further way to introduce change alters the individual rather than the availability of a route. The proportion of minority students in California, for example, drops toward the upper ends of schooling. Two changes, however, can counter that decline. In one, students come to know what various steps involve. In effect, they come to know the opportunity structures and the demands that are part of these. In the other, they are helped to see various steps as part of a possible future self. Both ways of introducing change are needed (Cooper, Dominguez, and Rosas, 2005).

School progressions, however, are not the only area where developmental analyses may benefit from closer attention to issues of path access and path availability (Goodnow, 2005). Movement out of involvement in crime, for example, has been proposed as calling for two steps: blocking access to one activity and opening access to another (Braithwaite, 1989). Less dramatically, the bases to some youths "managing to make it" in situations of disadvantage may lie less in their parents' knowledge of child development and more in parental knowledge of what is available in their communities, for example, their knowledge of possible moves from one school to another or of supports that can be drawn upon (Furstenberg, Cook, Eccles, Elder, and Sameroff, 1999). That bringing together of family and community contexts is clearly a departure from conventional analyses of parenting skill and a departure that could profitably be kept in mind in all analyses of families and development.

Conclusion

Four ways of specifying cultural contexts have been covered in this chapter—ways that bring together a variety of descriptions and that open up new questions about the nature, the course, and the bases of development.

This final section touches on some aspects to the specification of cultural contexts that are highly relevant to analyses of development but have received short shrift in this account. The first has to do with the interrelation of biological and cultural influences, and the second deals with interconnections among cultural contexts—family, neighborhood, and cultural contexts—that are often seen as separate from one another.

Analyses of *biological–cultural influences* take a variety of forms, with the discussion often focused on their relative power, or on how much can be accounted for by what is biologically given or culturally driven (see Bugental and Goodnow, 1997). Cultural analyses, however, contain at least two other possibilities that are developmentally interesting.

One of these comes from the analysis of relationships that was noted earlier (Fiske, 1991). Biologically based relationships, Fiske proposes, are distinctions that occur in all cultures. All cultures, for example, distinguish between relationships that are communal (we function as a group with concerns for our unity and for each other's feelings and welfare) and relationships that are hierarchical or authority based in type. Contributed by cultural contexts are the particular relationships, even within families, that are expected to be of one kind or another. The specific placement of people in various categories is, then, the essence of what is to be learned in the course of development.

A different kind of contribution comes from Cole and Hatano (2007). To interests in what is biologically given, they add an interest in what is culturally given, for example, in the tools or resources that are readily at hand, easily accessed, or quickly provided early in life or in the early phases of learning a new skill. (These resources may range from physical tools to language.) The combination of the two "givens," they propose, may provide a more effective account of rapid acquisition than either "given" can provide when considered alone. In effect, the issue is no longer one of relative importance but the extent to which the two influences support each other and combine to move development in a particular direction.

The other final point has to do with *interconnections among contexts*. Contexts are often set apart from one another, with distinctions drawn between "micro" and "macro" or "proximal" and "distal." Among developmental scientists, the best-known form of such distinctions is Bronfenbrenner's (1979) set of contexts, which is graphically presented as a set of concentric circles. The individual is at the center, surrounded in layers by the family, the neighborhood, and the "macrosystems" of ideology and institutional structure. Each of these layers is described as interconnected with others in bidirectional fashion—a proposal that concepts of "spillover" helped make concrete (e.g., Crouter, 1984, 2006).

Bronfenbrenner's proposals certainly made developmentalists far more aware than they were earlier of the need to consider influences beyond those within the family. Nonetheless, reservations arose, often prompted by analyses of contexts other than family contexts and often focused on the questions about interconnections. Some of the reservations have to do with the overall separation of contexts. As long as contexts are treated as "surrounds" for each other or as if they are "separate containers" (Thorne, 2005, p. 63), the analysis of interconnections, it is argued, will be limited.

Separateness is also at the heart of concerns with the implication that the effects of contexts outside the family are always funneled through parents. Room for children to come into direct contact with features of their environment and for neighborhood contexts to have direct effects on children is needed. In a similar fashion, room is needed for the state to intervene directly in the lives of children, bypassing parents (the physical removal of children by the state is one example; Goodnow, 1995).

Prompted also by analyses of cultural contexts is the recognition of similarities among contexts. Family, neighborhood, and cultural contexts, for example, are usually seen as different from one another. In addition, the descriptions offered for each of these contexts often focus on different dimensions or qualities, making the descriptions difficult to map on to one another (Goodnow, 2006b). This way of adding to the kind of account that Bronfenbrenner (1979) offered has come up occasionally in earlier sections of this chapter. Neighborhoods, for example, may be usefully described in the same multiplicity and contest terms that have been, in the main, proposed for societies or cultures. Shaw and McKay (1942/1969), in fact, noted that the features they observed in the dynamics of neighborhoods are the same as those highlighted in accounts of physical ecology—accounts that describe regions as mixed in the types of plants that are present, as going through phases in which various types are dominant, and as constantly in danger of being overrun by other species.

To take another example of similar dimensions being used to specify contexts often seen as separate and as different from one another, analyses of "family routines" have a great deal in common with analyses of "cultural practices." Family routines refer to shared, taken-for-granted ways of greeting one another, preparing food, or celebrating special occasions (e.g., Fiese, 2006; Weisner, 2002). Like cultural practices, these routines involve questions about what can be moved from one possible contributor to another, for example, from one family member to another or from "the family" to "the state" (Goodnow, 2006b). Like cultural practices, family routines also promote a sense of belonging and identity and of being at ease with others. A break in those routines or encounters with the family routines of others may give rise to the same sense that analysts have noted as stemming from encounters with the practices of other societies—the sense of not being at home and of being a stranger (e.g., Schütz, 1967).

Are there then no differences among these several contexts? The differences, contextual analyses suggest, lie less in one context being more "distal" than another and more in features such as the extent to which ways of thinking and acting are shared by a large number of people, have a history that goes beyond family history, are seen as part of a social identity, are embedded in institutional structures (are embedded, for example, in school procedures and regulations or in law), and are perceived as open to change by various kinds of action.

In summary, analyses of cultural contexts offer several benefits. They can help guide our sense of how to bring about change and how to select contexts that will be like or unlike one another in their developmental effects. More broadly, they can expand the ways in which we think about contexts or settings of all kinds, open up new questions and ways of exploring the nature and bases of development, and, of major importance, diminish the sense that attention to cultural contexts is something remote from core developmental concerns.

Acknowledgments

I owe a great deal to some particular experiences and groups of people. The experiences of most relevance are times of being an "alien" in other countries, prompting an awareness of the need to reflect not only on those cultures but also on my own, the one I thought I understood. The list of scholars to whom my debt is large would be long. With difficulty, I single out three groups with a staying power that promoted consideration of each others' views. One came together as a subcommittee for the Social Sciences Research Council. It stayed together to produce an edited book on cultural practices (Goodnow, Miller, and Kessel, 1995) and two chapters on cultural psychology (Shweder, Goodnow, Hatano, LeVine, Markus, and Miller, 1998, 2006). The second, which was created to consider developmental approaches to crime prevention, stayed together to produce a large governmental report on that issue (Developmental Crime Prevention Consortium, 1999) and several chapter contributions to a later book (France and Homel, 2007). The third came together in Seoul and then contributed chapters to a book that again maintained the exchange of ideas (Rubin and Chung, 2006). To the members of these several groups, and others, I wish to express my appreciation of the special challenges and insights they provided.

References

Assadi, S. M., Zokaei, N., Kavaiani, H., Mohammadi, M. R., Ghaeli, P., Gohari, M. R., and van de Vijver, F. J. R. (2007). Effects of sociocultural context and parenting style on scholastic achievement among Iranian adolescents. *Social Development, 16*, 169–180.

Berger, P., Berger, K., and Kellner, H. (1973). *The homeless mind: Modernization and consciousness.* New York: Random House.

Blumenfeld, P., Modell, J., Bartko, T., Secada, W., Fredricks, J., Friedel, J., and Paris, A. (2005). School engagement of inner-city students during middle childhood. In C. R. Cooper, C. García Coll, T. Bartko, H. Davis, and C. Chatman (Eds.), *Developmental pathways through middle childhood* (pp. 145–170). Mahwah, NJ: Erlbaum.

Bornstein, M. H. (1980). Cross-cultural developmental psychology. In M. H. Bornstein (Ed.), *Comparative methods in psychology* (pp. 231–280). Hillsdale, NJ: Erlbaum.

Bornstein, M. H. (2002). Toward a multiculture, multi-age, multimethod science. *Human Development, 45*, 257–263.

Bourdieu, P. (1977). *Outline of a theory of practice.* Cambridge, England: Cambridge University Press.

Bourdieu, P. (1979). *Distinction: A social critique of the judgment of taste.* London: Routledge and Kegan Paul.

Bourdieu, P. (1990). *The logic of practice.* Palo Alto, CA: Stanford University Press.

Braithwaite, J. (1989). *Crime, shame, and reintegration.* Cambridge, England: Cambridge University Press.

Bronfenbrenner, U. (1979). *The ecology of human development.* Cambridge, MA: Harvard University Press.

Bugental, D., and Goodnow, J. J. (1997). Socialization processes: Biological, cognitive, and social-cultural perspectives. In W. Damon (Ed.), *Handbook of child psychology* (Vol. 4, pp. 389–462). New York: Wiley.

Cazden, C. (1993). Vygotsky, Hymes, and Bakhtin: From word to utterance and voice. In E. A. Forman, N. Minick, and C. A. Stone (Eds.), *Contexts for learning* (pp. 197–212). New York: Oxford University Press.

Chaiklin, S., and Lave, J. (Eds.). (1996). *Understanding practice: Perspectives on activity and context.* New York: Cambridge University Press.

Chandler, M. J., Lalonde, C. E., Sokol, B. W., and Hallett, D. (2003). Personal persistence, identity development, and suicide: A study of native and non-native North American adolescents. *Monographs of the Society for Research in Child Development, 68*, 2, Serial No. 273.

Clark, H. H. (1996). *Using language.* Cambridge, England: Cambridge University Press.

Cole, M. (1995). The supra-individual envelope of development: Activity and practice, situation and context. In J. J. Goodnow, P. J. Miller, and F. Kessel (Eds.), *Cultural practices as contexts for development* (pp. 105–119). San Francisco: Jossey-Bass.

Cole, M. (2001). Remembering history in sociocultural research. *Human Development, 44*, 166–169.

Cole, M., and Hatano, G. (2007). Cultural-historical activity theory: Integrating phylogeny, cultural history, and ontogenesis in cultural psychology. In D. Cohen and S. Kitayama (Eds.), *Handbook of cultural psychology.* New York: Guilford Press.

Cooper, C. R. (1999). Multiple selves, multiple worlds: Cultural perspectives on individuality and connectedness in adolescent development. In A. Masten (Ed.), *Minnesota Symposium on Child Development: Cultural processes in development* (pp. 25–57). Hillsdale, NJ: Erlbaum.

Cooper, C. R., and Denner, J. (1998). Theories linking culture and psychology: Universal and community-specific processes. *Annual Review of Psychology, 49*, 559–584.

Cooper, C. R., Dominquez, W., and Rosas, S. (2005). Soledad's dream: Diversity, children's worlds, and pathways to college in democracies. In C. R. Cooper, C. García Coll, T. Bartko, H. Davis, and C. Chatman (Eds.), *Developmental pathways through middle childhood* (pp. 235–260). Mahwah, NJ: Erlbaum.

Crouter, A. C. (1984). Spillover from family to work: The neglected side of the work-family interface. *Human Relations, 37*, 425–442.

Crouter, A. C. (2006). Mothers and fathers at work: Implications for families and children. In A. Clarke-Stewart and J. Dunn (Eds.), *Families count: Effects on child and adolescent development* (pp. 135–154). New York: Cambridge University Press.

D'Andrade, R. G. (1981). The cultural part of cognition. *Cognitive Science, 5*, 179–195.

D'Andrade, R. G., and Strauss, C. (Eds.). (1992). *Human motives and cultural models.* Cambridge, England: Cambridge University Press.

Deal, J. E., Halvorson, C. F., and Wampler, K. S. (1989). Parental agreement on child-rearing orientations: Relations to parental, marital, family and child characteristics. *Child Development, 60*, 1025–1034.

Developmental Crime Prevention Consortium. (1999). *Pathways to prevention: Developmental and early intervention approaches to crime.* Canberra, Australia: Attorney-General's Department.

Fiese, B. H. (2006). *Family routines and rituals.* Princeton, NJ: Yale University Press.

Fiske, A. P. (1991). *Structures of social life: The four elementary forms of social relations.* New York: Free Press.

Fiske, A. P., and Tetlock, P. E. (1997). Taboo trade-offs: Reactions to transactions that transgress spheres of justice. *Political Psychology, 18,* 255–297.

Foucault, M. (1980). *Power-knowledge: Selected interviews and other writing.* Brighton, England: Harvester.

France, A., and Homel, R. (Eds.). (2007). *Pathways and crime prevention: Theory, policy and practice.* Sheffield, England: Willan.

Furstenberg, F. F. Jr. (1976). *Unplanned parenthood: The social consequences of teenage child-rearing.* New York: Free Press.

Furstenberg, F. F. Jr., Cook, T. D., Eccles, J., Elder, G. H. Jr., and Sameroff, A. (1999). *Managing to make it: Urban families and adolescent success.* Chicago: University of Chicago Press.

Gauvain, M. (2001). Cultural tools, social interaction and the development of thinking. *Human Development, 44,* 126–143.

Gledhill, C. (1988). Pleasurable negotiations. In D. Pribham (Ed.), *Female spectators: Looking at film and television.* London: Verso.

Goodnow, J. J. (1990a). The socialization of cognition: Acquiring cognitive values. In J. Stigler, R. Shweder, and G. Herdt (Eds.), *Culture and human development* (pp. 259–286). Chicago: University of Chicago Press.

Goodnow, J. J. (1990b). Using sociology to extend psychological accounts of cognitive development. *Human Development, 33,* 81–107.

Goodnow, J. J. (1995). Differentiating among social contexts: By spatial features, forms of interaction, and social contracts. In P. Moen, G. H. Elder Jr., and K. Lüscher (Eds.), *Examining lives in context: Perspectives on the ecology of human development* (pp. 269–302). Washington, DC: American Psychological Association.

Goodnow, J. J. (1996a). Acceptable ignorance, negotiable disagreement: Alternative views of learning. In D. Olson and N. Torrance (Eds.), *Handbook of psychology in education: New models of teaching, learning, and schooling* (pp. 345–368). Oxford, England: Blackwell.

Goodnow, J. J. (1996b). Collaborative rules: From shares of the work to rights to the story. In P. Baltes and U. Staudinger (Eds.), *Interactive minds* (pp. 163–193). Cambridge, England: Cambridge University Press.

Goodnow, J. J. (1996c). From household practices to parents' ideas about work and interpersonal relationships. In S. Harkness and C. Super (Eds.), *Parents' cultural belief systems* (pp. 313–344). New York: Guilford.

Goodnow, J. J. (1997). Parenting and the "transmission" and "internalization" of values: From social-cultural perspectives to within-family analyses. In J. E. Grusec and L. Kuczynski (Eds.), *Handbook of parenting and the transmission of values* (pp. 333–361). New York: Wiley.

Goodnow, J. J. (2002). Adding culture to studies of human development: Changes in procedure and theory. *Human Development, 45,* 237–245.

Goodnow, J. J. (2005). Contexts, diversity, pathways: Advances and next steps. In C. R. Cooper, C. García Coll, T. Bartko, H. Davis, and C. Chatman (Eds.), *Developmental pathways through middle childhood* (pp. 295–312). Mahwah, NJ: Erlbaum.

Goodnow, J. J. (2006a). Cultural perspectives and parents' views of parenting and development: Research directions. In K. H. Rubin and O. B. Chung (Eds.), *Parenting beliefs, behaviors, and parent-child relations* (pp. 35–60). New York: Psychology Press.

Goodnow J. J. (2006b). Research and policy: Second looks at views of development, families, and communities, and at translations into practice. In A. Clarke-Stewart and J. Dunn (Eds.), *Families count: Effects on child and adolescent development* (pp. 337–360). New York: Cambridge University Press.

Goodnow, J. J., and Collins, W. A. (1990). *Development according to parents: The nature, sources, and consequences of parents' ideas.* London: Erlbaum.

Goodnow, J. J., Miller, P. J., and Kessel, F. (Eds.). (1995). *Cultural practices as contexts for development.* San Francisco: Jossey-Bass.

Gramsci, A. (1971). *Selections from the prison notebooks.* London: Lawrence and Wishart.

Gutiérrez, K. D. (2002). Studying cultural practices in urban learning communities. *Human Development, 45,* 313–321.

Hatano, G., and Inagaki, K. (1986). Two courses of expertise. In H. Stevenson, H. Azuma, and K. Haluta (Eds.), *Child development and education in Japan* (pp. 262–272). San Francisco: Jossey-Bass.

Heath, S. B. (1983). *Ways with words: Language, life and work in communities and classrooms*. New York: Cambridge University Press.
Holland, D., and Quinn, N. (1987). *Cultural models in language and thought*. New York: Cambridge University Press.
Hudley, E. V. P., Haight, W., and Miller, P. J. (2003). *"Raise up a child": Human development in an African American family*. Chicago: Lyceum.
Hughes. D., and Chen, L. (1999). The nature of parents' race-related communications to children: A developmental perspective. In L. Balter and C. S. Tamis-LeMonda (Eds.), *Child psychology: A handbook of contemporary issues* (pp. 467–490). Philadelphia: Psychology Press.
Kristeva, J. (1991). *Strangers to ourselves*. New York: Columbia University Press.
Lave, H., and Wenger, E. (1988). *Situated learning: Legitimate peripheral participation*. New York: Cambridge University Press.
Lawrence, J. A. (2007). Taking a developmental pathways approach to understanding and preventing antisocial behaviour. In A. France and R. Homel (Eds.), *Pathways and crime prevention: Theory, policy and practice*. Sheffield, England: Willan.
Lawrence, J. A., Benedikt, R., and Valsiner, J. (1992). Homeless in the mind: A case history of personal life in and out of a closed orthodox group. *Journal of Social Distress and the Homeless, 1*, 157–176.
Loeber, R., and LeBlanc, M. (1990). Toward a developmental criminology. *Crime and Justice—A Review of Research, 12*, 375–473.
Michaels, S. (1991). The dismantling of narrative. In A. McCabe and C. Peterson (Eds.), *Developing narrative structure*. Hillsdale, NJ: Erlbaum.
Miller, P. J. (1994). Narrative practices: Their role in socialization and self-construction. In U. Neisser and R. Fivush (Eds.), *The remembering of self: Construction and accuracy in the self-narrative* (pp. 158–179). New York: Cambridge University Press.
Miller, P. J., and Goodnow, J. J. (1995). Cultural practices: Toward an integration of culture and development. In J. J. Goodnow, P. J. Miller, and F. Kessel (Eds.), *Cultural practices as contexts for development* (pp. 5–16). San Francisco: Jossey-Bass.
Nagin, D., and Tremblay, R. E. (1999). Trajectories of boys' physical aggression, opposition, and hyperactivity on the path to physically violent and non-violent juvenile delinquency. *Child Development, 70*, 1181–1196.
Neugarten, B. (1979). Time, age, and the life cycle. *American Journal of Psychiatry, 136*, 887–894.
Oura, Y., and Hatano, G. (2001). The constitution of general and specific mental models of other people. *Human Development, 44*, 144–159.
Padilla-Walker, L. M., and Thompson, R. A. (2005). Combating conflicting messages of values: A closer look at parental strategies. *Social Development, 14*, 305–323.
Phelan, P., Davidson, A. L., and Yu, H. C. (1992). Students' multiple worlds: Navigating the borders of family, peer, and school cultures. In P. Phelan and L. Davidson (Eds.), *Cultural diversity: Implications for education* (pp. 52–88). New York: Teachers College Press.
Robins, L., and Rutter, M. (Eds.). (1994). *Straight and devious paths from childhood to adulthood*. Chichester, England: Wiley.
Rogoff, B. (Ed.). (2002). How can we study cultural aspects of human development? *Human Development, 45*, 209–321 (Whole Issue No. 2).
Rogoff, B. (2003). *The cultural nature of human development*. New York: Oxford University Press.
Rogoff, B., Baker-Sennett, J., Lacasa, P., and Goldsmith, D. (1995). Development through participation in sociocultural activity. In J. J. Goodnow, P. J. Miller, and F. Kessel (Eds.), *Cultural practices as contexts for development* (pp. 45–66). San Francisco: Jossey-Bass.
Romney, K. A., Weller, S. C., and Batchelder, W. H. (1986). Culture as consensus: A theory of culture and informant accuracy. *American Anthropologist, 88*, 313–332.
Rubin, K. H., and Chung, O. B. (Eds.). (2006). *Parenting beliefs, behaviors, and parent-child relations*. New York: Psychology Press.
Salzman, P. C. (1981). Culture as enhabilmentis. In L. Holy and M. Stuchlik (Eds.), *The structure of folk models* (pp. 233–256). London: Academic Press.
Schütz, A. (1967). *The phenomenology of the social world*. London: Heinemann.
Shaw, C. R., and McKay, H. D. (1942; revised edition 1969). *Juvenile delinquency and urban areas*. Chicago: University of Chicago Press.
Shonkoff, J. P., and Phillips, D. A. (2000). *From neurons to neighborhoods: The science of early childhood development*. Washington, DC: National Academy Press.

Shweder, R. A., Arnett Jensen, L., and Goldstein, W. M. (1995). Who sleeps by whom revisited: A method for extracting the moral goods implicit in practice. In J. J. Goodnow, P. J. Miller, and F. Kessel (Eds.), *Cultural practices as contexts for development* (pp. 21–40). San Francisco: Jossey-Bass.

Shweder, R. A., Goodnow, J. J., Hatano, G., LeVine, R. A., Markus, H., & Miller, P. J. (1998). The cultural psychology of development: One mind, many mentalities. In W. Damon (Ed.), *Handbook of child psychology* (5th ed., Vol. 1, pp. 865–938). New York: Wiley.

Shweder, R. A., Goodnow, J. J., Hatano, G., LeVine, R. A., Markus, H., & Miller, P. J. (2006). The cultural psychology of development: One mind, many mentalities. In W. Damon (Ed.), *Handbook of child psychology* (6th ed., Vol. 1, pp. 716–792). New York: Wiley.

Shweder, R. A., Markus, H. R., Minow, M. L., and Kessel, F. (1998). The free exercise of culture: Ethnic customs, assimilation, and American law. *Items: Newsletter of Social Science Research Council, 51,* 61–67.

Smith, J., and Goodnow, J. J. (1999). Unsolicited support, unasked-for advice: Age differences in interpretation and affective response. *Psychology and Aging, 14,* 108–121.

Steinberg, L., Darling, N. E., and Fletcher, A. C. (1995). Authoritative parenting and adolescent adjustment: An ecological journey. In P. Moen, G. H. Elder Jr., and K. Lüscher (Eds.), *Examining lives in context: Perspectives on the ecology of human development* (pp. 423–466). Washington, DC: American Psychological Association.

Strauss, C. (1992). Models and motives. In R. G. D'Andrade and C. Strauss (Eds.), *Human motives and cultural models* (pp. 1–20). Cambridge, England: Cambridge University Press.

Super, C., and Harkness, S. (1986). The developmental niche: A conceptualisation at the interface of child and culture. *International Journal of Behavioral Development, 9,* 545–569.

Tajfel, H. (1981). *Human groups and social categories.* Cambridge, England: Cambridge University Press.

Takahashi, K., Tokoro, M., and Hatano, G. (2006, July). *Senior shutterbugs: Successful aging through participation in social activities.* Paper presented at the meeting of the International Society for the Study of Behavioral Development, Melbourne, Australia.

Tetlock, P. E., McGraw, A. P., and Kristel, O. V. (2004). Proscribed forms of social cognition: Taboo trade-offs, blocked exchanges, and heretical counterfactuals. In N. Haslam (Ed.), *Relational models theory: A contemporary overview* (pp. 247–262). Mahwah, NJ: Erlbaum.

Thorne, B. (2005). Unpacking school lunchtime: Structure, practice, and the negotiation of differences. In C. R. Cooper, C. García Coll, T. Bartko, H. Davis, and C. Chatman (Eds.), *Developmental pathways through middle childhood* (pp. 235–260). Mahwah, NJ: Erlbaum.

Triandis, H. C. (2001). Individualism-collectivism and personality. *Journal of Personality, 69,* 907–924.

Turner, J. C. (1987). *Rediscovering the social group: A self-categorisation theory.* Oxford, England: Blackwell.

Vygotsky, L. S. (1978). *Mind in society.* Cambridge, MA: Harvard University Press.

Watson-Gegeo, K. A. (1992). Thick explanation in the ethnographic study of child socialization: A longitudinal study of the problem of schooling for Kwar'ae (Solomon Island) children. In W. A. Corsaro and P. J. Miller (Eds.), *Interpretive approaches to children's socialization* (pp. 53–66). San Francisco: Jossey-Bass.

Weisner, T. S. (1984). A cross-cultural perspective: Ecocultural niches of middle childhood. In W. A. Collins (Ed.), *The elementary school years: Understanding development during middle childhood* (pp. 335–369). Washington, DC: National Academy Press.

Weisner, T. S. (2002). Ecocultural understanding of children's developmental pathways. *Human Development, 45,* 275–281.

Wertsch, J. V. (1991). *Voices of the mind.* Cambridge, England: Cambridge University Press.

Wertsch, J. V. (2002). *Voices of collective remembering.* New York: Cambridge University Press.

West, C., and Zimmerman, D. (1987). Doing gender. *Gender and Society, 1,* 125–151.

Whiting, B. B., and Edwards, C. P. (1988). *Children of different worlds: The formation of social behavior.* Cambridge, MA: Harvard University Press.

Wikström, P.-O. H., and Sampson, P. J. (Eds.) (2006). *The explanation of crime: Context, mechanisms, and development.* Cambridge: Cambridge University Press.

2
Methodology

FONS J. R. VAN DE VIJVER, JAN HOFER, and ATHANASIOS CHASIOTIS

Introduction

There is a growing interest in the study of cultural factors in developmental science. It is easy to see why. Understanding development requires the delineation of both universal and culture-specific variations in processes and outcomes. Cross-cultural studies have clearly shown that we cannot assume that findings arrived at in Western societies have universal validity. Universality and culture specificity are testable claims rather than assumptions; moreover, we know from existing cross-cultural studies that methodological aspects require much attention because we can take less for granted in cross-cultural studies than in monocultural studies. For example, instruments that have shown good reliability and validity in Western cultures may lose these properties in a non-Western context. Cross-cultural developmental studies have yielded various interesting results. We present two examples.

Research indicates that the adverse academic effects of authoritarian parenting found in Western countries may not be universal. Chao (1994; Bornstein and Lansford, Chapter 14, this volume; Steinberg, Lamborn, Dornbusch, and Darling, 1992) administered questionnaires of parental control and authoritative–authoritarian parenting style and Chinese child-rearing items involving the concept of "training" (hard work, self-discipline, and obedience) to Chinese American and European American mothers of preschool-aged children. The Chinese American mothers were found to score significantly higher on authoritarian parenting style and training ideologies. In a second study by the same author, parenting styles and school performance of European American adolescents and first- and second-generation Chinese Americans were compared. A positive association between authoritative parenting and school performance was found for the European Americans and, to a lesser extent, for second-generation Chinese Americans, but not for first-generation Chinese Americans (Chao, 2001). Baumrind's (1967) distinction among authoritarian, authoritative, and permissive parenting may need conceptual elaboration if it is to be used in non-Western contexts.

A second example comes from a study on short-term memory span in Libyan children (Shebani, Van de Vijver, and Poortinga, 2005). Baddeley (1997) formulated the phonological loop hypothesis, which holds that memory traces decay rapidly unless refreshed by rehearsal. The hypothesis predicts that people have a longer memory span for shorter stimuli. In Arabic, each digit can be pronounced in two ways that differ in length (short form and long form). Libyan boys and girls of two grades were presented either the short or long form of digits in recall and pronunciation tasks. Rehearsal speed (a measure of refreshment rate) was positively related with memory span, and children showed a longer memory span for shorter stimuli, thereby confirming the validity of the phonological loop model. The Arabic language provides a context to test Baddeley's model that cannot be achieved in other languages.

The goal of this chapter is to provide an overview and illustration of the major methodological aspects of cross-cultural studies in developmental science. The chapter comprises four parts. The first part describes bias and equivalence of measurements. In the second part, the theoretical background on bias and equivalence is further elaborated, and then methodological implications of conceptual issues of defining of culture, sampling of cultures, and descriptions of developmental contexts are addressed. The third part describes methodological and statistical tools that hold important promise for enhancing the quality of cross-cultural developmental studies. Multilevel models, integrative research designs combining qualitative and quantitative data, and natural experiments are presented as examples. Conclusions are drawn in the final part; it is argued that to advance our level of knowledge, cross-cultural developmental studies should attempt to integrate conceptual models and advanced methodological and statistical tools and move beyond the dichotomy of qualitative and quantitative approaches.

Key Issues in the Methodology of Cross-Cultural Developmental Studies

Bias and Equivalence

Cross-cultural developmental studies require data from different groups. Once we have collected data from different contexts, we can compare data from various groups and examine cultural differences or similarities across groups. Are such comparisons valid? More than 30 years ago, Triandis (1976) noted that research may become increasingly complex when we depart from the neat designs of experimental psychology with their tight control of ambient variables. The questions of to what extent measurements are equally appropriate for each of the groups under investigation and whether observations and test scores can be interpreted in the same way across populations are particularly relevant in cross-cultural psychology (Van de Vijver and Tanzer, 2004).

Widely used psychological theories and constructs have been developed predominantly in Western contexts. Cross-cultural research is indispensable to evaluate the generalizability of these theories or constructs. In other cultures, other constructs may be important that have never been instantiated in standard Western instruments because they are only locally relevant or have been overlooked in the West (Winter, 1996; Zhang and Bond, 1998). In hindsight, various historical examples of generalizations about differences in traits and abilities of cultural groups can be seen as based on psychometrically poor measures (Van de Vijver and Tanzer, 2004). It is crucial in cross-cultural research to address the equivalence of measurements and test bias because cross-cultural measurements may be distorted by various factors (Van de Vijver and Leung, 1997). For example, test–retest studies of cognitive instruments have shown that persons with little previous test experience often show considerable score gains at retesting and that retesting increases the predictive validity of an instrument in such a population (e.g., Nkaya, Huteau, and Bonnet, 1994). Retest score gains that differ across cultures indicate that the scores at the first occasion were not fully comparable across these cultures; the score gains may be due to memory effects, a better understanding of the test instructions, or the lower novelty of the testing situation so that participants feel more comfortable (Van de Vijver, Daal, and Van Zonneveld, 1986). Without retest data, the nature and size of the cross-cultural differences could be easily misinterpreted. An evaluation of cross-cultural findings without any concern for the comparability of the findings is risky (Dana, 2000). The computation of cross-cultural differences in *t* tests or analyses of variance without examining the comparability of the findings can easily lead to incorrect conclusions. We explain later how comparability can be evaluated.

Three hierarchically linked levels of equivalence are commonly distinguished in the literature: construct (structural and functional) equivalence, measurement unit equivalence, and scalar (full score) equivalence (Van de Vijver and Leung, 1997; see also Poortinga, 1989). The term *bias* is generally used to describe "nuisance" factors that negatively affect the equivalence of measurements across different (cultural) groups. Concepts of equivalence and bias do not refer to intrinsic properties of an instrument but rather to characteristics of a given comparison of test scores between cultural groups. Van de Vijver and Leung (1997) described three major types of bias—construct bias, method bias, and item bias—depending on whether the comparability is challenged by the construct, the administration method or samples to measure the construct, or specific items.

Equivalence of Construct Construct equivalence is present when the same construct is measured across cultural groups (regardless of whether measurement procedures are identical in each cultural group). Nomological networks of the instruments in cultures at hand can be examined to demonstrate equivalence of constructs. Functional equivalence of constructs is observed when similar patterns of convergent and discriminant relations with theoretically relevant variables are found across groups. In contrast, construct inequivalence or bias is present when respondents from different cultural groups do not ascribe the same meaning to the construct as a whole or if there is only partial overlap in the construct's definition across cultures.

Cross-cultural studies of achievement motivation provide a good example of construct bias. In Western studies, the need for achievement is typically defined as an individualistic desire to do things well and to overcome obstacles (McClelland, 1985). McClelland and colleagues were criticized for neglecting contextual and cultural determinants of achievement motivation. In line with such arguments, a number of studies point to a qualitative difference in achievement motivation in non-Western societies that is characterized by a pronounced social-oriented element (e.g., Doi, 1982; Kagan and Knight, 1981). In particular, scholars studying Chinese culture emphasized that pushing oneself ahead of others and actively striving toward self-enhancement are not universally valued (Bond, 1986; Yu, 1996). Rather, the concept of a social-oriented achievement motive reflects a need to meet expectations of significant persons and groups (e.g., family and peers). Winter (1996) argued that a kind of mastery motive (a general desire for agency and control) is probably an evolved innate aspect of our biological heritage; still, cultural specificities in childrearing practices, socialization patterns, dominant religious belief systems, values, and social rules to sanction individuals' behavior (Keller and Greenfield, 2000) will involve distinct experiences of rewards and punishments. These differences in cultural practices will eventually lead to the development of differences in terms of concerns for achievement, releasing stimuli, domains of action, and evaluation standards (Phalet and Lens, 1995). Consequently, a monocultural approach based on a Western conception of achievement does not cover all relevant aspects of the construct in non-Western cultures.

Another example may be taken from cross-cultural research on theory of mind. A basic assumption of mainstream developmental science is that everyday knowledge of human psychology is the same everywhere. This universality claim for mentalistic understanding and its development ("theory of mind") (Premack and Woodruff, 1978) has important implications for cultural and interpersonal understanding. If the conviction that other humans are mental beings whose ways of behavior are based on certain states of mind (needs, beliefs, or emotions) holds true, we also tend to view mind as rational and able to control emotions, intentions, and thereby actions. However, there are also reasons to assume culture-specific conceptualizations of mind. There might be cultures that explain actions by referring less to inner mental states and more to contextual factors or even to spirits outside the body (Lillard, 1998). In a review discussing cultural variations in theory of mind, Lillard (1998) claimed that the European American model of folk psychology is not universal.

A way to answer the question of universality of the concept of folk psychology is to consider its development. Chasiotis, Kiessling, Hofer, and Campos (2006) investigated the relation of theory of mind (measured here as false-belief understanding) and inhibitory control (the ability to suppress a reaction and activate another). The latter is assumed to be an important prerequisite of the former (compare Chasiotis, Kiessling, Winter, and Hofer, 2006). Three samples of preschoolers from Europe (Germany), Africa (Cameroon), and Latin America (Costa Rica) were involved. After controlling for age, gender, siblings, language understanding, and mother's education, culture did not have a moderating effect; each culture showed the same relation between conflict inhibition and false-belief understanding. Furthermore, delay inhibition was not a significant predictor of false-belief understanding in any culture. These results are in line with studies involving American or Asian samples (Carlson and Moses, 2001; Sabbagh, Xu, Carlson, Moses, and Lee, 2006), indicating the possible universality of the relation between delay inhibition and false-belief understanding. Cameroonian children scored significantly lower in theory of mind than the other two cultures; they also showed lower scores in conflict inhibition and higher scores in delay inhibition. The differences in mean scores make the culture-invariant relation between conflict inhibition and false-belief understanding even more interesting because the mean differences are observed against a backdrop of culture-invariant relations between the concepts. These findings suggest that the interdependent parenting goals of obedience and compliance might be related to better delay inhibitory performance and lower false-belief understanding in children (Chasiotis, Bender, Kiessling, and Hofer, in press).

Equivalence of Measurement Unit The second level of equivalence is called measurement unit equivalence. It is present when measures have the same unit of measurement across cultures but have different origins. A difference in origin might emerge when sources of method bias shift mean scores in at least one of the cultures. Depending on its source, it is useful to differentiate three types of method bias, namely administration bias, sample bias, and instrument bias.

Administration bias is caused by sources associated with the particular form of test administration. For example, differences in physical and technical environmental administration conditions, such as noisy versus quiet test locations or the presence of unfamiliar measurement devices (e.g., tape recorder or video camera), and differences in social environmental conditions, such as individual versus group administration and amount of space between participants, may cause substantial cross-cultural differences in target variables (e.g., test performance) and various nontarget variables (e.g., willingness to self-disclose). Further examples of administration bias are ambiguous instructions for study participants and/or guidelines for administrators, communication problems between respondents and administrators (e.g., language problems and violation of cultural communication norms), or the obtrusiveness of the mere presence of a person from a different culture (Super, 1983).

Sample bias occurs when cultural samples are not comparable with respect to relevant background characteristics other than the target construct. As a consequence, observed cross-cultural differences may reflect the target construct but may also be attributed to the influence of "nuisance variables" (e.g., level of education and volunteer bias). For example, in research on theory of mind, mothers' educational level and/or socioeconomic status are predictors of the children's understanding of false-belief tasks (Cole and Mitchell, 2000). Thus, it is essential to carefully balance cultural samples early in the recruitment process.

Finally, instrument bias reflects instrument characteristics causing cross-cultural differences that are unrelated to the target construct. The most important bias that leads to differences in origins of an instrument is group differences in familiarity with test material (e.g., items and response procedures) and response styles (e.g., acquiescence, extremity ratings, and social desirability). Different familiarity with measurements is a recurrent problem in cross-cultural studies, especially if the study involves "remote" cultural samples. Deregowski and Serpell (1971) found differences in performance between Scottish and Zambian children in sorting photographs but not in sorting miniature models. To reduce group differences in familiarity with stimulus material and testing, Hofer and colleagues (Hofer and Chasiotis, 2004; Hofer, Chasiotis, Friedlmeier, Busch, and Campos, 2005) adapted test instructions for picture-story tests because people from non-Western cultures were more likely to produce mere descriptions of picture cards rather than to create fantasy stories. By giving participants from all cultural groups a detailed and vivid introduction to the picture-story test, such group differences were minimized. Probably the most studied sources of instrumental bias have been cultural differences in response styles (e.g., Marín, Gamba, and Marín, 1992; Van Hemert, Van de Vijver, Poortinga, and Georgas, 2002). Participants with a higher age, lower education, and lower socioeconomic status are more likely to show acquiescence and social desirability (Grimm and Church, 1999; Van de Vijver and Leung, 2001).

Full Score Equivalence   The third level of equivalence, namely scalar or full score equivalence, is present when the measurement has the same measurement unit and origin across cultures. This level of equivalence is needed for direct cross-cultural comparisons of means, such as in *t* tests and analyses of variance. A source of bias that may obstruct reaching this level of equivalence (in addition to the presence of construct bias or method bias) is called item bias or differential item functioning (Holland and Wainer, 1993). Item bias is based on characteristics of single items (e.g., nonequivalent content or wording). An item is taken to be biased when people with the same underlying psychological construct (e.g., achievement motivation) from different cultural groups respond diversely to a given item (e.g., test item or picture card). The problem of item bias has often been studied for educational and cognitive tests, has been less studied for self-report measurements such as personality scales, and has been largely neglected for other types of measurements such as projective measurements (Hofer et al., 2005; Van de Vijver, 2000).

Item bias is often caused by a poor translation or adaptation of items. Although translations are linguistically correct, the item may still not be suitable for use across cultures due to culture-bound connotations or linguistic idiosyncrasies (Van de Vijver and Tanzer, 2004). In some cases, items that are useful in one culture do not make sense or are inappropriate in another culture. For example, "I make all my own clothes and shoes" and "I have attended school at some time during my life" (taken from the Personality Research Form; Jackson, 1984) may be useful items to assess a careful and purposeful pattern of responding among Western participants. However, one can easily imagine cultural contexts where such items lose their intended meaning. Comparing the stimulus material used for the assessment of implicit motives among German and Zambian adolescents, Hofer and Chasiotis (2004) found that picture cards clearly differed in their strength to trigger motive imagery across cultural samples. One of the cards depicted a white-collar employee in an office with a family picture at his desk. Stories by German participants were scored much higher for need for affiliation, whereas stories written by Zambian respondents were scored higher for achievement motive.

How Can We Identify and Remedy Various Sources of Bias?

Numerous strategies are described in the literature to identify and remedy the three types of bias. Two main approaches have been proposed to detect biased items: the judgmental approach and the statistical approach. In judgmental procedures, inappropriate items are identified by cultural experts. Few studies have applied this approach. The majority of studies examine item bias by employing different statistical methods depending on the measurement level of items, number of (cultural) groups, or sample size (for an overview, see Van de Vijver and Leung, 1997; Van de Vijver and Tanzer, 2004). Despite the many statistical techniques available and the numerous studies conducted, our knowledge about factors that induce item bias is limited. It is often difficult to find convergence between judgmental and statistical approaches (e.g., Engelhard, Hansche, and Rutledge, 1990). No specific item features have been found to increase or decrease item bias. Therefore, it is recommended to combine both judgmental and statistical strategies in research. Cultural experts may initially scrutinize wording and content of items, and statistical procedures are used for bias examination in a second step.

To minimize or measure the influence of method bias, various steps can be taken in the design and implementation of a cross-cultural study, such as an intensive training of test administrators; detailed instructions and manuals for administration, scoring, and interpretation; and balancing samples with respect to important participant and context variables. Furthermore, test–retest designs and an examination of response styles may obviate the risk of method bias.

Both design- and analysis-oriented ways of addressing construct bias have been proposed. A combination of the two kinds of procedures is recommended. Various statistical techniques are available to identify construct bias that usually amount to a comparison of data structures across cultural groups, such as the comparison of factor structures (see Van de Vijver and Leung, 1997). One could avoid bias in cross-cultural research by developing culture-specific, indigenous measurements. This procedure might be particularly applicable when there are serious doubts about the expected equivalence or the universal nature of the construct under investigation (Church, 2001). For example, indigenous research on personality in China has provided evidence for the existence of an additional dimension beyond the Five-Factor Model, labeled *Interpersonal Relatedness* (Cheung, 2006). If the research focus is more on universal features and on developing instruments that are applicable across cultures, cultural decentering may be an adequate procedure to avoid construct bias. This procedure involves a simultaneous development of the instrument in several cultures accompanied by a gradual adaptation of the measure, such as elimination of culture-specific words and concepts (e.g., Tanzer, Gittler, and Ellis, 1995). An alternative is the convergence approach, which involves independent measurement development in different cultures and a subsequent employment of all measures in all cultural samples under investigation (see Campbell, 1986).

In conclusion, meaningful comparisons between cross-cultural groups can only be made if sources of bias are addressed and successfully ruled out. Neglecting issues of equivalence in cross-cultural research leads to interpretation problems because alternative explanations, such as differences in construct definition or response styles, cannot be ruled out. Thus, an integrated examination of construct, method, and item bias is highly desirable to enhance our understanding of cultural differences and universals.

How Do We Approach Culture?

There are two different traditions in defining culture in cross-cultural psychology (Goodnow, Chapter 1, this volume; Lonner and Adamopoulos, 1997; Rohner, 1984; Segall, 1984). The first views culture as a *molar* Gestalt consisting of interrelated parts. Psychological phenomena are inextricably linked to their cultural context. Culture and psyche are said to make up each other; an essential feature of culture is shared meaning, which is created in the process of interactions and communications among a culture's members. Negotiation between cultural members leads to shared meaning and intersubjectivity. This view is commonly found in cultural psychology (Greenfield, 1997; Miller, 1997). The emphasis on the interrelations of cultural elements is often based on the view that culture as a concept has a limited dimensionality. The best known example is the popular dimension of individualism–collectivism (e.g., Triandis, 1995). The dimension refers to how the relation to the individual and the group is viewed in a culture (Greenfield,

2000). Individualistic societies prioritize individuals and emphasize their independence and uniqueness, whereas collectivistic societies prioritize the group (particularly in-groups, such as the family) by emphasizing the relatedness of individuals. This difference has numerous ramifications for psychological functioning and the way in which a society is organized. For example, socialization practices can be seen as functional adaptations that prepare children for a more individualistic or more collectivistic lifestyle. There is evidence that mother–child interactions vary as a function of individualism–collectivism (Keller, Yovsi, et al., 2004). Mothers in collectivistic societies tend to emphasize relatedness more, whereas mothers in more individualistic societies put more emphasis on autonomy. This difference in emphasis starts when children are very young.

The second view on culture is more *molecular*. Culture is seen as a set of antecedent variables that are linked with psychological functioning in feedback loops (Poortinga and Van de Vijver, 1987). Studies in this tradition typically attempt to identify specific cultural factors that can account for psychological outcomes. A well-known example is the study by Segall, Campbell, and Herskovits (1966) on illusion susceptibility. They argue in their "carpentered world hypothesis" that living in a Western society where geometric shapes, such as trade lines, rectangles, straight lines, and square corners, abound affects susceptibility to some visual illusions, such as the Müller–Lyer illusion. Westerners are more susceptible to these illusions than non-Westerners. Westerners are inclined to apply perceptual habits (interpreting three-dimensional cues to two-dimensional pictures) that are functionally adaptive in daily life but that are maladaptive in the perception of illusion figures.

The literature has long been dominated by the view that molar and molecular conceptions of cultures are incompatible. The two views were even associated with different methodologies. The molar tradition was more associated with ethnographic and qualitative means of data collection and analysis ("cultural psychology"), and the molecular tradition was more associated with the comparative, quantitative tradition ("cross-cultural psychology"). Increasingly, investigators acknowledge that both approaches have their merits and shortcomings and should be seen as complementary (instead of incompatible). A study of the relation between parenting style and children's autonomy could be carried it out in a single country to see whether culture-specific aspects of the concepts and relations can be identified; alternatively, the relation could also be studied in a comparative perspective. The methodology that can be employed will largely depend on the availability and desirability to use standardized instruments. The use of such instruments is not recommended in a monocultural study that attempts to unravel culture-specific features, whereas their use is much more likely and desirable in a cross-cultural study. There is a growing rapprochement between the approaches and appreciation of the complementary nature of molar and molecular models and methods.

Description of Context   Comparisons are only possible with a common point of reference. One commonly used point of reference in developmental studies of behavior is defined by universal developmental tasks (Keller, 2007). Because enculturation is co-constructed through participation in cultural practices during everyday activities (Rogoff, 2003), behavioral expressions of these tasks are embedded in their cultural context. Keller and her collaborators (Keller, 2007) have documented systematic differences in cultural models of parenting defined by broader cultural models of the self. Two contrasting prototypes can be identified: a model of interdependence, which is more adaptive in subsistence-based, less affluent families with low education and early reproduction, and a model of independence, which is more adaptive in "Western," more affluent urban areas where parents have a higher education and reproduce late. Moreover, variations of these two cultural dimensions of independence and interdependence can be postulated (Kagitcibasi, 2005) and empirically verified (e.g., Keller, Yovsi, et al., 2004). An autonomous-related sociocultural orientation has been found to prevail in urban middle-class families in traditionally interdependent societies, such as in Costa Rica, China, and India (Kagitcibasi, 2005; Keller, 2007).

Because of these variations in sociocultural orientation, the cultural context of investigation can vary starting from the participation procedure (e.g., who decides about participation), the assessment situation (e.g., what do the participants expect from the research), or defined communication styles (e.g., politeness norms of visiting families and required unobtrusiveness of the researcher). Most important, for the urban Western context, common scenarios of mother–child interactions, like a free-play situation between mother and child, might not be equally familiar or accepted in rural or tribal contexts such as India or Cameroon (cf. Keller, 2007). Interview studies can also be problematic because of different cultural conventions pertinent to interview situation, such as who is allowed to provide what kind of information. Such problems can only be treated with a culturally informed methodology, preferably by combining qualitative and quantitative approaches.

Sampling of Cultures There are essentially three ways in which cultures are sampled in developmental studies. The first and most common is *convenience sampling*. Cultures are selected because of availability, easy access, networks of researchers from the countries involved, or some other reason not related to substantive research questions. Such comparisons were common and relevant in the first generation of cross-cultural studies. Those studies helped to set up an empirical database mapping cross-cultural similarities and differences; however, both the quality and quantity of comparative studies have increased so much in the last decades that convenience sampling is now often seen as problematic. First, it is often difficult to link cultural factors to observed differences in psychological variables without a theory to sample cultures. Second, decades of cross-cultural research have shown that convenience sampling leads to biased sampling. Meta-analyses of cross-cultural studies indicate that a few geographical areas dominate the cross-cultural literature; examples are North America, East Asia, and Western Europe. Areas with very different cultures, such as Africa and South America, are much less represented in the literature (Öngel and Smith, 1994; Smith, Harb, Lonner, and Van de Vijver, 2001).

In *systematic (or theory-guided) sampling*, cultures are selected on theoretical grounds. Berry (1976) was interested in field dependence (independence), which is the tendency to be more (or less) influenced in the perception of an object by its background. It was hypothesized that agricultural societies that are more focused on collectivism and conformity encourage their members to be less autonomous and hence can be expected to show a higher level of field dependence. Two types of cultural groups (Canadian hunters–gatherers and African agriculturists) were selected to evaluate this hypothesis. The main strength of systematic sampling is its theoretical basis. Cross-cultural differences that are based on systematic sampling are easier to interpret than differences found in studies using convenience sampling; systematic sampling makes it easier to rule out more alternative interpretations of the cross-cultural differences observed. The systematic sampling of cultures can also show some methodological weaknesses, in particular when only a few cultures are considered. Campbell (1986) has repeatedly argued that two-culture studies are often difficult to interpret because of the many rival explanations that can be put forward; studies involving more than two cultures are less prone to rival alternative explanations. The argument also pertains to studies using systematic sampling strategies. Berry's (1976) work involved a comparison of Canadian hunters–gatherers and African agriculturists. When the study was replicated in Central Africa with culturally similar groups, the findings only partially supported the original hypothesis (Berry et al., 1986).

Finally, in *random sampling*, a probability sample of cultures is drawn. This sampling frame is used for mapping cross-cultural differences and evaluating the universality of the structure of a construct (structural equivalence) or the accuracy of a pan-cultural theory. Because of practical constraints, it is almost impossible to obtain a truly random sample; however, samples of large-scale studies may approximate a probability sample. Recent examples of large-scale studies can be found in personality (McCrae et al., 2005), social psychology (Schwartz, 1992), organizational psychology (House et al., 2004; Smith, Peterson, and Schwartz, 2002), and survey research (Inglehart, 1997). Large-scale studies in the developmental area always involve comparisons of school performance and educational achievement. A good example is the Programme for International Student Assessment (PISA), which was initiated by the Organisation for Economic Co-operation and Development (OECD; 2003). Another example is the Trends in International Mathematics and Science Study 2003 (TIMSS), which was organized by the International Association for the Evaluation of Educational Achievement (Mullis, Martin, and Foy, 2005). Both projects involve more than 40 countries and aim at providing policymakers with international benchmarks for identifying the strengths and weaknesses of various educational systems. Despite the impressive size of these studies, the cultural variability of the participating countries is limited, with an overrepresentation of affluent countries and an underrepresentation of developing countries. As a consequence, these studies of educational achievement do not provide a truly universal picture but may well provide a random sample of affluent countries.

Culture and Data Analysis   There are various ways to approach culture in comparative designs. The distinction between molar and molecular approaches to culture can be used to describe the decisions to be made. In data analyses using a molar approach, there is a tendency to treat culture (or cultural syndromes such as individualism–collectivism) as a nominal variable and to contrast cultures, thereby examining the range of influence of culture in psychological functioning. These studies often have an implicit focus on finding cross-cultural differences. Studies using a molecular approach typically do not start from cultural syndromes but from more specific cultural factors, such as socialization practices and schooling quality.

Culture plays a slightly different role in the analyses of both approaches. A molar approach takes culture as a starting point and addresses psychological consequences of culture (e.g., Which developmental milestones are affected by a culture's level of individualism?). A molecular approach attempts to decompose culture by unpackaging it (Whiting, 1976). Observing a cross-cultural difference in some psychological process is the beginning rather than the endpoint of a study. Cross-cultural studies are more successful if they can explain more observed cross-cultural differences in psychological function. In statistical terms, the explanatory variables are used as covariates in an analysis of covariance or as independent variables in a hierarchical regression analysis. The analysis addresses the question of to what extent observed cross-cultural differences can be "explained away" by the explanatory variables (Poortinga and Van de Vijver, 1987; Van de Vijver and Leung, 1997). In an analysis of variance with culture as the independent variable and psychological scores as dependent variables, the significance and effect size of culture indicate how much cross-cultural variation there is to be explained; after correction for covariates, the same analysis of variance, now using the residual scores as dependent variables, indicates how much cross-cultural variation is still left. The more cross-cultural variation that is left, the less successful our explanatory variables have been.

Thus, the seemingly paradoxical consequence of analyses of this kind is that we want to get rid of culture as an explanatory variable in cross-cultural research and identify contextual variables that are held responsible for sample differences across cultures. As an example, Chasiotis, Hofer, and Campos (2006) first regressed implicit parenting motivation on the variable "younger siblings." In the next step, the unstandardized residual of implicit parenting motivation of that regression analysis was re-entered in an analysis of variance with culture as predictor. The analysis of variance with the residual of implicit parenting motivation as the dependent variable and culture as the predictor showed a remarkable decrease in effect size of culture from .050 to .041, which means that 18% of the impact of culture on implicit parenting motivation was caused by the existence of younger siblings. The psychologically rather crude measure of "number of siblings" reduced the effect from a medium (.050) to a small (.019) size, meaning that 62% of the original effect size of culture on implicit parenting motivation could be traced back to sibling effects.

Promising Avenues

In this section, we describe three methodological developments that hold potential for further integrating cultural factors in developmental studies: multilevel designs and multilevel models, integrative approaches, and natural experiments.

Multilevel Designs and Multilevel Models   Recent developments in statistics have made it possible to address variation in nested structures. For example, children are nested in families, which are nested in cultures. Multilevel studies consider variation at two or more levels concurrently, such as individual and cultural levels. Two kinds of multilevel approaches have been developed (Hox, 2002; Muthén, 1994; Raudenbush and Bryk, 2002). The first addresses the structural equivalence of concepts at different levels of aggregation. McCrae et al. (2005) were interested in the question of whether the five-factorial structure of personality that is found at the individual level would also be observed at country level. After aggregating their individual-level data ($N = 12{,}156$) at country level ($N = 51$), the authors found the same structure as commonly observed at individual level. This support for the structural equivalence of personality at the two levels implies that individual and country differences in personality scale scores have the same meaning. Similarity of meaning is not a foregone conclusion. It could well be that method bias (e.g., response style differences or incomparable samples) induces a change of meaning after aggregation. Shen and Pedulla (2000; see also Stanat and Luedtke, 2008) analyzed data from TIMSS 2003. The authors examined the relation between self-reported mathematics ability and actual mathematics performance. The relation was studied both at individual level per country and at country level. At the individual level, the findings revealed a positive relation (the values of the correlation ranged from $r = .12$ to $r = .47$ across the participating countries). However, the country-level correlation was negative, $r = -.57$. The authors attributed the reversal of the correlation to cross-cultural differences in self-evaluations of ability. Scale scores at the country level reflect not only self-evaluations of ability, but also the tendency of cultural groups to be self-critical or modest. There is evidence to the effect that persons from East Asian cultures do not display the self-presentation styles of Westerners and show a modesty bias (Fahr, Dobbins, and Cheng, 1991; Shikanai, 1978; Takata, 1987).

The second type of multilevel model addresses the interplay of levels. These models address the question of to what extent a phenomenon at a certain level (e.g., the reading achievement of a child) is associated with variables at different levels (e.g., intelligence and socioeconomic status at individual level, school quality at school level, and educational expenditure at country level). Most examples come from the educational domain. Van Langen, Bosker, and Dekkers (2006; see also Stanat and Luedtke, 2008) examined performance gaps between boys and girls in the 42 countries participating in the PISA project. Data were analyzed at individual, school, and country level. Student achievements in mathematics, science, and reading were predicted on the basis of individual-level characteristics (e.g., gender and socioeconomic status), school characteristics (e.g., mean socioeconomic status, gender composition, and public versus private school types), and country characteristics (e.g., mean socioeconomic status, female economic activity rate, and gender empowerment index). The analysis of reading test scores revealed a significant interaction between gender and economic activity rates of women; mathematics and science achievement did not show this expected interaction. The reading performance gap in favor of girls tends to be larger in countries with higher female economic activity rates.

Integrative Approaches The second important methodological avenue for developmental studies is the use of integrative approaches that combine input from different methods, cultures, and/or ages (Bornstein, 2002). An example is the cross-cultural study that uses "method triangulation" (Keller, 2007, p. 57); interviews and verbal material of observed interactions are used as qualitative methods, and a quantitative methodology is used in the analysis of questionnaires and videotaped or in situ spot observations of behavior. The goal of the inductive and recursive qualitative codings, namely to gather instances for further examination, is more pragmatic, and the quantitative methodology allows the analytical testing of hypotheses generated by qualitative means. The qualitative methodology can also be used to substantiate and differentiate quantitative results (Georgas, Berry, Van de Vijver, Kagitcibasi, and Poortinga, 2006; Keller, Hentschel, et al., 2004). As another example, Bornstein et al. (2004) asked mothers of 20-month-olds in Argentina, Belgium, France, Israel, Italy, the Republic of Korea, and the United States to fill out comparable vocabulary checklists for their children. In each language, children's vocabularies contained relatively more nouns than other word classes, such as verbs and adjectives. Furthermore, the authors provide a brief description of the main features of the languages. This (qualitative) description is used to provide the linguistic context against which the universally high prevalence of nouns can be interpreted.

Another integrative approach can be found in psychometrically sound cross-cultural applications of implicit measures on life satisfaction (Hofer, Chasiotis, and Campos, 2006), generativity (Hofer, Busch, Chasiotis, Kärtner, and Campos, 2008), and parenthood (Chasiotis, Hofer, et al., 2006). As an example of a multimethod integrative design, Hofer et al. (2006) replicated earlier findings in monocultural studies with German (Brunstein, Schultheiss, and Grässmann, 1998) and Zambian adolescents (Hofer and Chasiotis, 2003) in a cross-cultural study among Germans, Costa Ricans, and Cameroonians using bias-free implicit and explicit measures of relatedness as predictors of life satisfaction. As an explicit measure, the Benevolence Scale of the Schwartz Value Survey was used; and as an implicit measure, a bias-free Thematic Apperception Test–type picture-story test measuring the need for affiliation-intimacy was administered. Results revealed that an alignment of implicit motives and self-attributed values was associated with an enhanced life satisfaction across cultures. Chasiotis, Hofer, et al. (2006) assessed explicit and implicit motivation for parenthood combined with a cross-cultural developmental perspective. They assumed that childhood context is important for the emergence of caregiving motivation. A model was tested across cultures in which being exposed to interactive experiences with younger siblings in childhood elicits nurturant implicit motivations that, in turn, lead to more conscious feelings of love toward children in adulthood, which are linked to parenthood. The path model describing this developmental pathway was valid in male and female participants and in all cultures under examination. This study supported the view that childhood context variables such as birth order might exert similar influences on psychological, somatic, and reproductive trajectories across different cultures (see also Chasiotis, Keller, and Scheffer, 2003).

Natural Experiments The last promising area involves the use of *natural experiments* (Scheier, 1959). The large-scale natural experiment of the division of Germany provided an opportunity to compare the influence of four decades of different sociopolitical structures in the former East and West Germany, which were culturally largely similar before the country was split at the end of World War II (Noack, Hofer, Kracke, and Klein-Allermann, 1995). Chasiotis, Scheffer, Restemeier, and Keller (1998) compared two similar urban areas in East (Halle) and West Germany (Osnabrück). Mother–daughter dyads from West and East Germany were analyzed to test the assumption that the onset of puberty is a context-sensitive marker of a reproductive strategy by comparing female parental and filial childhood context and somatic development in both regions. The effect of two different conditions of childhood context continuity on daughter's age at menarche was tested with the maternal age at menarche controlled. Linear regression models showed that mother's age at menarche only predicted the daughter's age at menarche if the childhood contexts of the mother's and daughter's generations were similar, which was only the case in the West German sample. In East Germany, the mother's age at menarche had no significant effect, and the variance of daughter's age at menarche was explained by filial childhood context variables alone. The comparison of the two samples of mother–daughter dyads in Eastern and Western Germany demonstrated the context sensitivity of somatic development and also showed that this context sensitivity is in line with the evolutionary theory of socialization: What seems to be inherited is not the timing of puberty per se, but the sensitivity for the prepubertal childhood context.

Another example concerns schooling. The relevance of schooling in cognitive development has been discussed for a long time. The Russian cultural–historical school argued that the skill to read and write has a formative influence on abstract thinking (Tulviste, 1991). The problem with testing this position is that reading and writing are acquired in the school context; therefore, schooling and the skills to read and write are confounded in nearly all populations. The confounding does not exist among the Vai in Liberia, where indigenous script is taught by adults to children in an informal setting. The Vai culture provides a natural experiment to avoid this confounding. Scribner and Cole (1981) compared the cognitive test performance of Vai illiterate adults without schooling, literate adults without schooling, and literate adults who were formally schooled. Literates in Vai outperformed illiterates only on tasks that required skills that are also used in dealing with specific Vai script features. High levels of specificity in differences between schooled and unschooled literates of an indigenous script were replicated among the Cree in Canada by Berry and Bennett (1991). Schooling affords children with tangible gains in development that typically focus on their efficient problem-solving strategies and not on their overall level of cognitive functioning (Case, Demetriou, Platsidou, and Kazi, 2001; Cole and Cagigas, Chapter 6, this volume; Schliemann, Carraher, and Ceci, 1997).

Studies of the relation between schooling and cognitive development that are conducted among children suffer from confounding chronological and educational age. The strong correlation of both kinds of ages in countries with compulsory schooling makes it impossible to estimate their relative contribution to cognitive development. The educational system among the Kharwar in India provides a natural experiment to overcome this confounding (Brouwers, Mishra, and Van de Vijver, 2006). The sample comprised 201 schooled and unschooled children from 6 to 9 years of age. The test battery contained various cognitive tests that used either a formal (school-related) or local stimulus content. Confirmatory factor analyses supported similar hierarchical factor structures, with general intelligence in the apex, for both unschooled and schooled children. The per annum score increments of chronological age were approximately twice as large as those of educational age. The study pointed to the important role of everyday experiences in the development of basic features of cognitive functioning.

These examples show how natural experiments can provide important insights by unconfounding variables that co-occur in most cultures. However, such experiments also have limitations. The most salient is the impossibility to manipulate the natural conditions. For example, the finding by Brouwers et al. (2006) that chronological age has more influence on cognitive test scores than educational age has to be interpreted against the backdrop of an overall low quality of schooling among the Kharwar. It was impossible to contrast good and bad schools in the area because of a lack of quality differentiation among the schools.

Conclusion

Developmental science assumes a multidisciplinary vantage point to understand ontogenetic development. Factoring culture into the equation is essential for a comprehensive understanding of this development. A few models integrate individual- and culture-level perspectives on development, such as Bronfenbrenner's (1977) ecological model, Super and Harkness's (1986) ecological niche model, and Cole's (1999) cultural context model. These models provide important first steps; yet, their heuristic value is limited. For example, studies of the ecological niche are often aimed at merely demonstrating the existence of cross-level relations (Van de Vijver and Poortinga, 2002). Recent methodological and statistical advances, such as multilevel models and analyses of bias and equivalence, enable a more fine-grained analysis of interactions at different levels. It is important to use these tools at a larger scale; yet, the use of more sophisticated research designs and statistical techniques alone is unlikely to generate new insights. In our view, it is important to integrate theory, design, and analysis as much as possible so as to enhance study quality. Theoretical sophistication and methodological sophistication are sometimes seen as incompatible; relatively few studies combine both types of sophistication. Cross-cultural studies deepen our understanding of the cultural factor in development. This goal is more likely to be achieved if we combine a theoretical framework that captures the interaction of individual and cultural factors, such as the three models mentioned earlier, with a sophisticated design and a data analysis that can model the interactions studied. Furthermore, it is important to include relevant contextual data in our studies, either quantitative (as part of the statistical analyses) or qualitative (as a description of the cultural context of the study). Numerous methodological and statistical procedures described in the current chapter, such as analyses of bias and equivalence, multimethod approaches, multilevel models, and natural experiments, are useful tools to increase the quality of our studies and the validity of our findings. If we are successful in integrating theoretical and methodological innovation, developmental cross-cultural studies have a bright future. It is easy to recognize that cultural factors are important in understanding developmental processes and outcomes. However, to be successful, we need to move beyond this recognition; we need to generate knowledge that is relevant for developmental science in general. The current chapter is intended to show how sophisticated methodological tools in cross-cultural developmental studies can contribute to generate new knowledge and advance development science.

References

Baddeley, A. (1997). *Human memory: Theory and practice* (revised). Mahwah, NJ: Erlbaum.

Baumrind, D. (1967). Child care practices anteceding three patterns of preschool behavior. *Genetic Psychology Monographs, 75*, 43–88.

Berry, J. W. (1976). *Human ecology and cognitive style. Comparative studies in cultural and psychological adaptation*. Beverly Hills, CA: Sage.

Berry, J. W., and Bennett, J. A. (1991). *Cree syllabic literacy: Cultural context and psychological consequences*. (Cross-Cultural Psychology Monographs No. 1). Tilburg, The Netherlands: Tilburg University Press.

Berry, J. W., Van de Koppel, J. M. H., Sénéchal, C., Annis, R. C., Bahuchet, S., Cavalli-Sforza, L. L., et al. (1986). *On the edge of the forest: Cultural adaptation and cognitive development in Central Africa*. Lisse, The Netherlands: Swets and Zeitlinger.

Bond, M. H. (1986). The social psychology of Chinese people. In M. H. Bond (Ed.), *The psychology of Chinese people* (pp. 213–264). Hong Kong: Oxford University Press.

Bornstein, M. H. (2002). Toward a multiculture, multiage, multimethod science. *Human Development, 45*, 257–263.

Bornstein, M. H., Cote, L. R., Maital, S., Painter, K., Park, S. Y., Pascual, L., et al. (2004). Cross-linguistic analysis of vocabulary in young children: Spanish, Dutch, French, Hebrew, Italian, Korean, and American English. *Child Development, 75*, 1115–1139.

Bronfenbrenner, U. (1977). Toward an experimental ecology of human development. *American Psychologist, 32*, 513–531.

Brouwers, S. A., Mishra, R. C., and Van de Vijver, F. J. R. (2006). Schooling and everyday cognitive development among Kharwar children in India: A natural experiment. *International Journal of Behavioral Development, 30*, 559–567.

Brunstein, J. C., Schultheiss, O. C., and Grässmann, R. (1998). Personal goals and emotional well-being: The moderating role of motive dispositions. *Journal of Personality and Social Psychology, 75,* 494–508.

Campbell, D. T. (1986). Science's social system of validity-enhancing collective believe change and the problem of the social sciences. In D. W. Fiske and R. A. Shweder (Eds.), *Metatheory in social science* (pp. 108–135). Chicago: University of Chicago Press.

Carlson, S. M., and Moses, L. J. (2001). Individual differences in inhibitory control and children's theory of mind. *Child Development, 72,* 1032–1053.

Case, R., Demetriou, A., Platsidou, M., and Kazi, S. (2001). Integrating concepts and tests of intelligence from the differential and developmental traditions. *Intelligence, 29,* 307–336.

Chao, R. K. (1994). Beyond parental control and authoritarian parenting style: Understanding Chinese parenting through the cultural notion of training. *Child Development, 65,* 1111–1119.

Chao, R. K. (2001). Extending research on the consequences of parenting style for Chinese Americans and European Americans. *Child Development, 72,* 1832–1843.

Chasiotis, A., Bender, M., Kiessling, F., and Hofer, J. (in press). The emergence of the independent self: Autobiographical memory as a mediator of false belief understanding and motive orientation in Cameroonian and German preschoolers. *Journal of Cross-Cultural Psychology.*

Chasiotis, A., Hofer, J., and Campos, D. (2006). When does liking children lead to parenthood? Younger siblings, implicit prosocial power motivation, and explicit love for children predict parenthood across cultures. *Journal of Cultural and Evolutionary Psychology, 4,* 95–123.

Chasiotis, A., Keller, H., and Scheffer, D. (2003). Birth order, age at menarche, and intergenerational context continuity: A comparison of female somatic development in West and East Germany. *North American Journal of Psychology, 5,* 153–170.

Chasiotis, A., Kiessling, F., Hofer, J., and Campos, D. (2006). Theory of mind and inhibitory control in three cultures: Conflict inhibition predicts false belief understanding in Germany, Costa Rica, and Cameroon. *International Journal of Behavioral Development, 30,* 192–204.

Chasiotis, A., Kiessling, F., Winter, V., and Hofer, J. (2006). Sensory motor inhibition as a prerequisite for theory of mind: A comparison of clinical and normal preschoolers differing in sensory motor abilities. *International Journal of Behavioral Development, 30,* 178–190.

Chasiotis, A., Scheffer, D., Restemeier, R. and Keller, H. (1998). Intergenerational context discontinuity affects the onset of puberty: A comparison of parent-child dyads in West and East Germany. *Human Nature, 9,* 321–339.

Cheung, F. (2006). A combined emic–etic approach to cross-cultural personality test development: The case of the CPAI. In Q. Jing, H. Zhang, and K. Zhang (Eds.), *Psychological science around the world* (Vol. 2, pp. 91–103). London: Psychology Press.

Church, T. A. (2001). Personality measurement in cross-cultural perspective. *Journal of Personality, 69,* 979–1005.

Cole, K., and Mitchell, P. (2000). Siblings in the development of executive control and a theory of mind. *British Journal of Developmental Psychology, 18,* 279–295.

Cole, M. (1999). Culture in development. In M. H. Bornstein and M. E. Lamb (Eds.), *Developmental psychology: An advanced textbook* (pp. 73–123). Hillsdale, NJ: Erlbaum.

Dana, R. H. (2000). Culture and methodology in personality assessment. In I. Cuellar and F. Paniagua (Eds.), *Handbook of multicultural mental health: Assessment and treatment of diverse groups* (pp. 97–120). San Diego, CA: Academic Press.

Deregowski, J. B., and Serpell, R. (1971). Performance on a sorting task: A cross-cultural experiment. *International Journal of Psychology, 6,* 273–281.

Doi, K. (1982). A two dimensional theory of achievement motivation: Affiliative and non-affiliative. *Japanese Journal of Psychology, 52,* 344–350.

Engelhard, G., Hansche, L., and Rutledge, K. E. (1990). Accuracy of bias review judges in identifying differential item functioning on teacher certification tests. *Applied Measurement in Education, 3,* 347–360.

Fahr, J.-L., Dobbins, G., and Cheng, B. D. (1991) Cultural relativity in action: A comparison of self-ratings made by Chinese and US workers. *Personnel Psychology, 44,* 129–147.

Georgas, J., Berry, J. W., Van de Vijver, F. J. R., Kagitcibasi, C., and Poortinga, Y. H. (Eds.). (2006). *Families across cultures. A 30-nation psychological study.* Cambridge, United Kingdom: Cambridge University Press.

Greenfield, P. M. (1997). Culture as process: Empirical methods for cultural psychology. In J. W. Berry, Y. H. Poortinga, and J. Pandey (Eds.), *Handbook of cross-cultural psychology. Vol. 1: Theory and method* (2nd ed., pp. 301–346). Needham Heights, MA: Allyn and Bacon.

Greenfield, P. M. (2000). Three approaches to the psychology of culture: Where do they come from? Where can they go? *Asian Journal of Social Psychology, 3,* 223–240.

Grimm, S. D., and Church, T. A. (1999). A cross-cultural investigation of response biases in personality measures. *Journal of Research in Personality, 33,* 415–441.

Hofer, J., Busch, H., Chasiotis, A., Kärtner, J., and Campos, D. (2008). Concern for generativity and its relation to implicit power motivation, generative goals, and satisfaction with life: A cross-cultural investigation. *Journal of Personality, 76,* 1–30.

Hofer, J., and Chasiotis, A. (2003). Congruence of life goals and implicit motives as predictors of life satisfaction: Cross-cultural implications of a study of Zambian male adolescents. *Motivation and Emotion, 27,* 251–272.

Hofer, J., and Chasiotis, A. (2004). Methodological considerations of applying a TAT-type picture-story-test in cross-cultural research: A comparison of German and Zambian adolescents. *Journal of Cross-Cultural Psychology, 35,* 224–241.

Hofer, J., Chasiotis, A., and Campos, D. (2006). Congruence between social values and implicit motives: Effects on life satisfaction across three cultures. *European Journal of Personality, 20,* 305–324.

Hofer, J., Chasiotis, A., Friedlmeier, W., Busch, H., and Campos, D. (2005). The measurement of implicit motives in three cultures: Power and affiliation in Cameroon, Costa Rica, and Germany. *Journal of Cross-Cultural Psychology, 36,* 689–716.

Holland, P. W., and Wainer, H. (1993). *Differential item functioning.* Hillsdale, NJ: Lawrence Erlbaum.

House, R. J., Hanges, P. J., Javidan, M., Dorfman, P. W., Gupta, V., and GLOBE associates. (2004). *Leadership, culture and organizations: The GLOBE study of 62 nations.* Thousand Oaks, CA: Sage.

Hox, J. J. (2002). *Multilevel analysis: Techniques and applications.* Mahwah, NJ: Lawrence Erlbaum Associates.

Inglehart, R. (1997). *Modernization and postmodernization. Cultural, economic, and political change in 43 countries.* Princeton, NJ: Princeton University Press.

Jackson, D. N. (1984). *Manual for the Personality Research Form.* Port Huron, MI: Research Psychologists Press.

Kagan, S., and Knight, G. P. (1981). Social motives among Anglo American and Mexican American children: Experimental and projective measures. *Journal of Research in Personality, 15,* 93–106.

Kagitcibasi, C. (2005). Autonomy and relatedness in cultural context: Implications for self and family. *Journal of Cross-Cultural Psychology, 36,* 403–422.

Keller, H. (2007). *Cultures of infancy.* Mahwah, NJ: Erlbaum.

Keller, H., and Greenfield, P. M. (2000). History and future development in cross-cultural psychology. *Journal of Cross-Cultural Psychology, 31,* 52–62.

Keller, H., Hentschel, E., Yovsi, R. D., Abels, M., Lamm, B., and Haas, V. (2004). The psycho-linguistic embodiment of parental ethnotheories: A new avenue to understand cultural differences in parenting. *Culture and Psychology, 10,* 293–330.

Keller, H., Yovsi, R., Borke, J., Kärtner, J., Jensen, H., and Papaligoura, Z. (2004). Developmental consequences of early parenting experiences: Self-recognition and self-regulation in three cultural communities. *Child Development, 75,* 1745–1760.

Lillard, A. (1998). Ethnopsychologies: Cultural variations in theories of mind. *Psychological Bulletin, 123,* 3–32.

Lonner, W. J., and Adamopoulos, J. (1997). Culture as antecedent to behavior. In J. W. Berry, Y. H. Poortinga, and J. Pandey (Eds.), *Handbook of cross-cultural psychology. Vol. 1: Theory and method* (2nd ed., pp. 43–83). Needham Heights, MA: Allyn and Bacon.

Marín, G., Gamba, R. J., and Marín, B. V. (1992). Extreme response style and acquiescence among Hispanics: The role of acculturation and education. *Journal of Cross-Cultural Psychology, 23,* 498–509.

McClelland, D. C. (1985). *Human motivation.* New York: Cambridge University Press.

McCrae, R. R., Terracciano, A., and 79 Members of the Personality Profiles of Cultures Project. (2005). Personality profiles of cultures: Aggregate personality traits. *Journal of Personality and Social Psychology, 89,* 407–425.

Miller, J. G. (1997). Theoretical issues in cultural psychology. In J. W. Berry, Y. H. Poortinga, and J. Pandey (Eds.), *Handbook of cross-cultural psychology. Vol. 1: Theory and method* (2nd ed., pp. 85–128). Needham Heights, MA: Allyn and Bacon.

Mullis, I. V. S., Martin, M. O., and Foy, P. (2005). *IEA's TIMSS 2003 International report on achievement in the mathematics cognitive domains. Findings from a developmental project.* Chestnut Hill, MA: Boston College.

Muthén, B. O. (1994). Multilevel covariance structure analysis. *Sociological Methods and Research, 22,* 376–398.

Nkaya, H. N., Huteau, M., and Bonnet, J. (1994). Retest effect on cognitive performance on the Raven-38 Matrices in France and in the Congo. *Perceptual and Motor Skills, 78,* 503–510.

Noack, P., Hofer, M., Kracke, B., and Klein-Allermann, E. (1995). Adolescents and their parents facing social change: Families in East and West Germany after unification. In P. Noack, M. Hofer, and J. Youniss (Eds.), *Psychosocial responses to social change* (pp. 129–148). Berlin: Walter de Gruyter.

Öngel, U., and Smith, P. B. (1994). Who are we and where are we going? JCCP approaches its 100th issue. *Journal of Cross-Cultural Psychology, 25,* 25–53.

Organisation for Economic Co-operation and Development. (2003). *The PISA 2003 assessment framework—Mathematics, reading, science and problem solving knowledge and skills.* Paris: Organisation for Economic Co-operation and Development.

Phalet, K., and Lens, W. (1995). Achievement motivation and group loyalty among Turkish and Belgian youngsters. In M. L. Maehr and P. R. Pintrich (Eds.), *Advances in motivation and achievement: Vol. 9. Culture, motivation, and achievement* (pp. 31–72). Greenwich, CT: JAI Press.

Poortinga, Y. H. (1989). Equivalence of cross-cultural data: An overview of basic issues. *International Journal of Psychology, 24,* 737–756.

Poortinga, Y. H., and Van de Vijver, F. J. R. (1987). Explaining cross-cultural differences: Bias analysis and beyond. *Journal of Cross-Cultural Psychology, 18,* 259–282.

Premack, D., and Woodruff, G. (1978). Does the chimpanzee have a theory of mind? *Behavioral Brain Sciences, 1,* 515–526.

Raudenbush, S. W., and Bryk, A. S. (2002). *Hierarchical linear models: Applications and data analysis methods* (2nd ed.). Thousand Oaks, CA: Sage.

Rogoff, B. (2003). *The cultural nature of human development.* New York: Oxford University Press.

Rohner, R. P. (1984). Toward a conception of culture for cross-cultural psychology. *Journal of Cross-Cultural Psychology, 15,* 111–138.

Sabbagh, M. A., Xu, F., Carlson, S. M., Moses, L. J., and Lee, K. (2006). The development of executive functioning and theory of mind. A comparison of Chinese and U.S. preschoolers. *Psychological Science, 17,* 74–81.

Scheier, I. H. (1959). The method of natural variation in applied educational research. *Journal of Educational Research, 52,* 167–170.

Schliemann, A., Carraher, D., and Ceci, S. J. (1997). Everyday cognition. In J. W. Berry, P. R. Dasen, and T. S. Saraswathi (Eds.), *Handbook of cross-cultural psychology: Vol. 2. Basic processes and human development* (2nd ed., pp. 177–216). Needham Heights, MA: Allyn and Bacon.

Schwartz, S. H. (1992). Universals in the content and structure of values: Theoretical advances and empirical tests in 20 countries. In M. Zanna (Ed.), *Advances in experimental social psychology* (Vol. 25, pp. 1–65). Orlando, FL: Academic Press.

Scribner, S., and Cole, M. (1981). *The psychology of literacy.* Cambridge, MA: Harvard University Press.

Segall, M. H. (1984). More than we need to know about culture, but are afraid to ask. *Journal of Cross-Cultural Psychology, 15,* 153–162.

Segall, M. H., Campbell, D. T., and Herskovits, M. J. (1966). *The influence of culture on visual perception.* Indianapolis, IN: Bobbs-Merrill.

Shebani, M. F. A., Van de Vijver, F. J. R., and Poortinga, Y. H. (2005). A cross-cultural test of the phonological loop hypothesis. *Memory and Cognition, 33,* 196–202.

Shen, C., and Pedulla, J. J. (2000). The relationship between students' achievement and their self-perception of competence and rigour of mathematics and science: a cross-national analysis. *Assessment in Education, 7,* 237–253.

Shikanai, K. (1978). Effects of self-esteem on attributions of success-failure. *Japanese Journal of Experimental Social Psychology, 18,* 47–55.

Smith, P. B., Harb, C., Lonner, W., and Van de Vijver, F. J. R. (2001). JCCP between 1993 and 2000: Looking back and looking ahead. *Journal of Cross-Cultural Psychology, 32,* 9–17.

Smith, P. B., Peterson, M. F., and Schwartz, S. H. (2002). Cultural values, sources of guidance and their relevance to managerial behaviour: A 47 nation study. *Journal of Cross-Cultural Psychology, 33,* 188–208.

Stanat, P., and Luedtke, O. (2008). Multilevel issues in international large-scale assessment studies on student performance. In F. J. R. van de Vijver, D. A. van Hemert, and Y. H. Poortinga (Eds.), *Individuals and cultures in multilevel analysis.* Mahwah, NJ: Erlbaum.

Steinberg, L., Lamborn, S. D., Dornbusch, S. M., and Darling, N. (1992). Impact of parenting practices on adolescent achievement: Authoritative parenting, school involvement, and encouragement to succeed. *Child Development, 63,* 1266–1281.

Super, C. M. (1983). Cultural variation in the meaning and uses of children's "intelligence". In J. B. Deregowski, S. Dziurawiec, and R. C. Annis (Eds.), *Expiscations in cross-cultural psychology* (pp. 199–212). Lisse, The Netherlands: Swets and Zeitlinger.

Super, C. M., and Harkness, S. (1986). The developmental niche: A conceptualization at the interface of child and culture. *International Journal of Behavioral Development, 9,* 545–569.

Takata, T. (1987). Self-depreciative tendencies in self evaluation through social comparison. *Japanese Journal of Experimental Social Psychology, 27,* 27–36.

Tanzer, N. K., Gittler, G., and Ellis, B. B. (1995). Cross-cultural validation of item complexity in a LLTM-calibrated spatial ability test. *European Journal of Psychological Assessment, 11,* 170–183.

Triandis, H. C. (1976). Methodological problems of comparative research. *International Journal of Psychology, 11,* 155–159.

Triandis, H. C. (1995). *Individualism and collectivism.* Boulder, CO: Westview Press.

Tulviste, P. (1991). *The cultural-historical development of verbal thinking.* Commack, NY: Nova Science.

Van de Vijver, F. J. R. (2000). The nature of bias. In R. H. Dana (Ed.), *Handbook of cross-cultural and multicultural personality assessment* (pp. 87–106). Mahwah, NJ: Erlbaum.

Van de Vijver, F. J. R., Daal, M., and Van Zonneveld, R. (1986). The trainability of abstract reasoning: A cross-cultural comparison. *International Journal of Psychology, 21,* 589–615.

Van de Vijver, F. J. R., and Leung, K. (1997). *Methods and data analysis for cross-cultural research.* Newbury Park, CA: Sage.

Van de Vijver, F. J. R., and Leung, K. (2001). Personality in cultural context: Methodological issues. *Journal of Personality, 69,* 1007–1031.

Van de Vijver, F. J. R., and Poortinga, Y. H. (2002). On the study of culture in developmental science. *Human Development, 45,* 246–256.

Van de Vijver, F. J. R., and Tanzer, N. K. (2004). Bias and equivalence in cross-cultural assessment: An overview. *European Review of Applied Psychology, 54,* 119–135.

Van Hemert, D. A., Van de Vijver, F. J. R., Poortinga, Y. H., and Georgas, J. (2002). Structural and functional equivalence of the Eysenck Personality Questionnaire within and between countries. *Personality and Individual Differences, 33,* 1229–1249.

Van Langen, A., Bosker, R., and Dekkers, H. (2006). Exploring cross-national differences in gender gaps in education. *Educational Research and Evaluation, 12,* 155–177.

Whiting, B. (1976). The problem of the packaged variable. In K. Riegel and J. Meacham (Eds.), *The developing individual in a changing world* (Vol. 1, pp. 303–309). The Hague, The Netherlands: Mouton.

Winter, D. G. (1996). *Personality: Analysis and interpretation of lives.* New York: McGraw-Hill.

Yu, A. (1996). Ultimate life concerns, self, and Chinese achievement motivation. In M. H. Bond (Ed.), *The handbook of Chinese psychology* (pp. 227–246). Hong Kong: Oxford University Press.

Zhang, J., and Bond, M. H. (1998). Personality and filial piety among college students in two Chinese societies: The added value of indigenous constructs. *Journal of Cross-Cultural Psychology, 29,* 402–417.

3
Survival and Health

CAROL M. WORTHMAN

Introduction

This may be the best moment to be a child in the history of humankind—if one goes by the global statistics for survival. Dramatic declines in infant and child mortality have fueled remarkable increases in life expectancy in the last half of the twentieth century. These advances have been hailed as triumphs of public health and international development policy. Between 1975 and 1995 alone, mortality for children ages 1 to 5 years decreased by 80% in Asia and North Africa, 78% in South/Central America, and 39% in sub-Saharan Africa; for all children under age 5 years, the corresponding declines were 60%, 63%, and 32% (Pelletier and Frongillo, 2003).

The more sobering news is that many young lives are still needlessly lost. Furthermore, disparities in child health actually are increasing within and among countries around the globe. In addition, there is more to well-being than mere survival, and expectations for child health have expanded to encompass reduced morbidity, healthy development, and the roots of adult function and well-being.

Fundamental improvements in the health status of children, which commenced in Western industrialized countries and swept the globe during the previous century, have had several effects on developmental science. First, such improvements abated the historically urgent concern with child survival among privileged, healthy postindustrial populations where most human development research is conducted. Second, unequal advances led to widening and persistent population disparities in child health and development that carry forward into adulthood and even into the next generation. Third, as with other branches of science and medicine, developmental science assumed a universalizing stance that overlooked the possible role of culture in confounding the generalizability of its findings.

This chapter aims to advance ongoing efforts by developmental science to engage with culture and cultural diversity; to integrate biology, cognition, and behavior; and to expand the scope of study and practice to an inclusive, comprehensive perspective that will better represent and serve the interests of the young. Its purpose, therefore, is to review current trends and insights regarding the status of child health from a comparative global perspective by considering evidence, ideas, and models of the roles of culture in differential child health.

Indices of Child Health

Child survival and health are particularly sensitive indicators of the overall welfare of a population. Indeed, they are widely recognized among policy, economic development, and health agencies and actors worldwide and, as such, carry weight for documenting needs, setting priorities, allocating resources, and evaluating progress at the international, national, and even regional levels (de Onis and Blössner, 2003; Milman, Frongillo, de Onis, and Hwang, 2005; United Nations Children's Fund [UNICEF], 2006; World Bank, 1993). Specifically, the key indicators of child welfare are early mortality and physical growth.

Identification of early mortality and child growth as key indicators has emerged from extensive evidence compiled by epidemiologists and human biologists over the last 60 years (Eveleth and Tanner, 1990; Frongillo, de Onis, and Hanson, 1997; Semba and Bloem, 2001). This work has established unequivocal links connecting poor conditions at the household and community level (e.g., poverty, marginal living conditions, lack of clean water and sanitation, inadequate or unsafe food), as well as inadequate infrastructure and programs at the regional and state level (e.g., sanitation, clean water, health care, economic opportunity, gender and structural inequality), with poor survival and growth among infants and children. In turn, growth and mortality indices of poor early health predict long-term health risk and reduced life expectancy (Crimmins and Finch, 2006).

Adequacy of response to emergent understandings of disparities in child health has varied. Indeed, one of the paradoxes of apparent global progress in child health and survival is the concurrent exacerbation of inequities in life chances for the young, within and between countries. Current status and trends in indices of child health, as well as progress on health disparities, are reviewed in the following sections.

Early Mortality

The premier challenge of infancy and early childhood is survival. Extensive demographic and epidemiological data collected by international agencies such as the World Health Organization (WHO; WHO, 2005), UNICEF (UNICEF, 2007), and World Bank (World Bank, 2004) clearly document the magnitude of this challenge. As shown in Figure 3.1, children under age 5 suffer far greater mortality rates than any other age group until late in life (age 60 and greater). Several major sources of mortality contribute to the survival challenge (Figure 3.2), primarily communicable diseases (e.g., infection, parasitic and infectious diseases) and insults from maternal conditions, perinatal conditions, and nutritional deficiencies. Birth and the postpartum transition are periods of greatest risk; 36% of deaths in children less than age 5 years in 2001 occurred among neonates within 1 month after birth, and 90% occurred before the age of 1 year

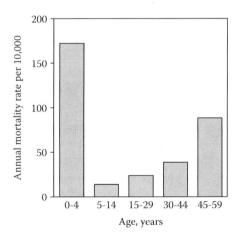

Figure 3.1 Crude annual mortality rates in 2001 for age groups under 60 years. (Rates calculated from data in Mathers, C. D., Lopez, A. D., and Murray, C. J. L., The burden of disease and mortality by condition: Data, methods, and results for 2001, in A. D. Lopez, C. D. Mathers, M. Ezzati, D. T. Jamison, and C. J. L. Murray (Eds.), *Global burden of disease and risk factors*, World Bank/Oxford University Press, New York, 2006, Table 3B9, pp. 174–179.)

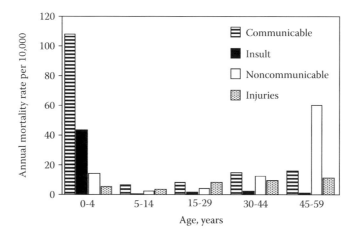

Figure 3.2 Crude annual mortality rates by cause for age groups under 60 years. Communicable diseases include infection and parasitic and infectious disease. Insults comprise maternal conditions, perinatal conditions, and nutritional deficiencies. Noncommunicable diseases include diabetes, cancer, cardiovascular disease, and other organic and mental disorders. Injury involves intentional and unintentional physical harm. (Rates calculated from data in Mathers, C. D., Lopez, A. D., and Murray, C. J. L., The burden of disease and mortality by condition: Data, methods, and results for 2001, in A. D. Lopez, C. D. Mathers, M. Ezzati, D. T. Jamison, and C. J. L. Murray (Eds.), *Global burden of disease and risk factors*, World Bank/Oxford University Press, New York, 2006, Table 3C9, pp. 174–179.)

(Black, Morris, and Bryce, 2003). Infections, preterm birth, and asphyxia account for most (86%) neonatal mortality worldwide, but the relative risk varies with infant mortality rates; the proportion of deaths in children under age 5 years (under-5 mortality) that occurs among neonates increases (24% to 56% of under-5 mortality) as national under-5 mortality rates decrease (Lawn, Wilczynska-Ketende, and Cousens, 2006). In affluent and poor countries, poverty is consistently associated with neonatal mortality, largely because of its influence on birth weight, access to care, and maternal health (Lawn, Cousens, and Zupan, 2005).

After the neonatal period, infections and parasitic and infectious diseases pose the greatest mortality risks (Figure 3.2). In particular, upper respiratory tract infections, diarrhea, and malaria account for nearly half (44%) of under-5 mortality (Brye, Boschi-Pinto, Shibuya, and Black, 2005). Behind these morbidities stands a powerful cofactor, malnutrition, which increases vulnerability to infection. Mildly to moderately malnourished young children ages 6 to 60 months are twice as likely to die during follow-up than their well-nourished peers, whereas severely malnourished children are nearly seven-fold more likely to die (Schroeder and Brown, 1994). Reciprocally, infections themselves promote malnutrition by reducing child appetite, eroding gut integrity and nutrient absorption, and claiming energy costs for the host's response to illness (Campbell, Elia, and Lunn, 2003; Dantzer, 2001). The global impact of malnutrition is substantial and insidious; formal country-specific estimates attribute 42% to 57% of child mortality in children ages 6 to 60 months to potentiation by malnutrition, with the majority related not to frank deprivation but to mild-to-moderate malnutrition (Pelletier, Frongillo, Schroeder, and Habicht, 1994).

Once a child survives the first 5 years, the risk for mortality decreases dramatically as the immune system becomes more robust (McDade, 2005). Communicable diseases and infections remain the primary sources of mortality through childhood and adolescence, although injuries (accidental and intentional) increase during adolescence and into the 20s. Injury-related mortality peaks during late adolescence and young adulthood (ages 15 to 24 years). This pattern is pronounced among males, robust across societies, and persistent through time (Heuveline and Slap, 2002).

Health Burden Among Children

Mortality profiles convey a picture of early vulnerability, but estimated burden of disease delineates a yet more compelling view by quantifying the actual human costs of early health challenges. During the 1990s, the Global Burden of Disease Study attempted to calculate burden as costs from the sources of morbidity and mortality in terms of their impact on well-being, or disability-adjusted life-years (DALYs) (Murray and Lopez, 1996). In this approach, early mortality is assigned a high cost in years of life lost, as are chronic conditions that impair well-being. Such an approach, therefore, weights the impact of early health risk, estimating that 28% of the total worldwide burden of disease is borne by young children (Figure 3.3). The burden is intensified by being narrowly concentrated in the first 5 years of life, rather than the 10- or 15-year age period over which the burden occurs in older groups.

Only much later in life (after age 60 years) do mortality rates exceed those in early childhood. A breakdown of the components of disease burden by source (Figure 3.4) reveals the toll levied

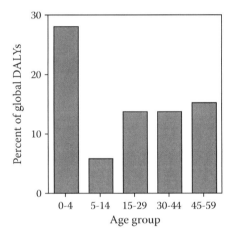

Figure 3.3 Percentage of total worldwide disability-adjusted life-years (DALYs) borne by age groups under 60 years. (Proportions calculated from data in Mathers, C. D., Lopez, A. D., and Murray, C. J. L., The burden of disease and mortality by condition: Data, methods, and results for 2001, in A. D. Lopez, C. D. Mathers, M. Ezzati, D. T. Jamison, and C. J. L. Murray (Eds.), *Global burden of disease and risk factors*, World Bank/Oxford University Press, New York, 2006, Table 3C9, pp. 228-233.)

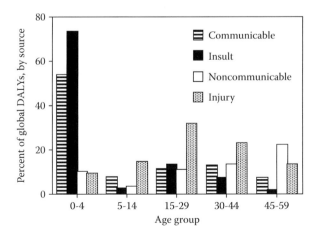

Figure 3.4 Distribution of the burden of disease by source across age groups under 60 years. Burden is gauged in terms of disability-adjusted life-years (DALYs). (Based on data in Mathers, C. D., Lopez, A. D., and Murray, C. J. L., The burden of disease and mortality by condition: Data, methods, and results for 2001, in A. D. Lopez, C. D. Mathers, M. Ezzati, D. T. Jamison, and C. J. L. Murray (Eds.), *Global burden of disease and risk factors*, World Bank/Oxford University Press, New York, 2006, Table 3C9, pp. 228-233.)

by communicable diseases and insults upon children under age 5 years, largely as a result of the substantial mortality from these causes. The high burden stems from two sources. An early death represents the loss of an entire lifetime's potential and thus poses a maximum burden from disease. Similarly, effects of illness or early insults (marginal malnutrition, low birth weight and other gestational conditions, or poor delivery care) on realization of developmental potential can impair lifetime cognitive capacity and resilience and also reduce health and life expectancy by increasing long-term risk for communicable and chronic diseases. For instance, a prospective study in the Philippines has linked number of infections in the first 6 months and growth in the first year to reduced immunocompetence (immunoglobulin E production and thymic function, respectively) in mid-adolescence at ages 14 to 15 years (McDade, 2005). Furthermore, a burgeoning literature documents the importance of gestational conditions for development and adult health, including links between low birth weight and later risk for depression in adolescent females (Costello, Worthman, Erkanli, and Angold, 2007) or cardiovascular disease in adult males (Barker, Eriksson, Forsén, and Osmond, 2002). The potentiating effects of early insult on later functional impairment and risk for ill health represent particularly insidious and persistent costs not only to individual quality of life, but also to human capital and the social burden of ill health.

By contrast, mid-childhood to mid-adolescence (ages 5 to 14 years) stands out as a period with the lightest burden of disease. Note that algorithms for estimation of burden in this period appear to place a low value on the impact of malnutrition (a component of insult) related to the understanding that most of the enduring effects from malnutrition, such as mortality or long-term health risk, are incurred early in life. Hence, evidence for both mortality and health burden describes a profile of early risk followed by a protected or buffered period of relative good health.

Temporal Trends: The Global Effort for Child Survival

The heavy burden of disease borne by the very young has focused attention on improving child survival (Black et al., 2003). Worldwide efforts have achieved dramatic reductions in early mortality over the last 50 years, during which time the global under-5 mortality rate was halved, from 159 to 70 per 1,000 live births (Figure 3.5). Vaccination campaigns, oral rehydration therapy

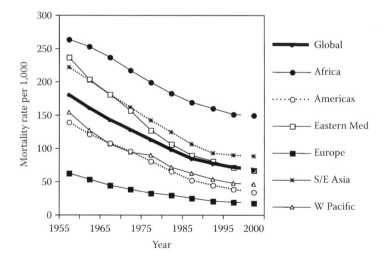

Figure 3.5 Changes in mortality rates per 1,000 live births among children under 5 years old. Trajectories are shown for global and regional figures. Numbers for 1999 are extrapolated estimates. (Data from Ahmad, O. B., Lopez, A. D., and Inoue, M., *Bulletin of the World Health Organization*, 78, 1175–1191, 2000.)

for diarrhea, widening health care access, and clean water and sanitation programs all have contributed to this effort. Nonetheless, several points of concern are apparent from the trends for 1955 to 1999 plotted in Figure 3.5 (Ahmad, Lopez, and Inoue, 2000). First, pre-existing mortality differences among world regions have not been reduced, much less eliminated, demonstrating that earlier visions for health equity remain unfulfilled (Stolnitz, 1965). Second, absolute and proportionate improvements during this period are distributed unequally among regions, such that rates of decline have been most dramatic in the eastern Mediterranean and most persistent in South and East Asia. By contrast, proportionate decreases have been greatest among developing countries of the Americas (76% reduction) and least in Africa (43% reduction). The low rate of change in developed nations relates to their low initial mortality and belies a 71% decrease in mortality rate in these privileged settings. Third, rates of decrease in mortality have decelerated markedly since the late 1980s. Such deceleration might reflect basement effects limiting survivorship, but the deceleration has been most pronounced and sustained in the two regions of highest mortality, namely Africa and South and East Asia. Mortality differentials have been related in part to the distribution of poverty; the poorest populations experience greater mortality than the richest populations (bottom versus top quintile), and more than three-fourths of this excess mortality is related to communicable disease (Heuveline, Guillot, and Gwatkin, 2002).

The diminishing returns on mortality reduction and the persistence and even exacerbation of inequities in early mortality risk have drawn increasing concern and renewed attention to factors with established relationships to early mortality trends (Ahmad et al., 2000). Such factors include fertility behavior (timing and spacing of births); nutrition (status markers, breastfeeding patterns, infant feeding); environmental risk (sanitation, clean water); health services use (by mother, for children); and socioeconomic status (poverty, social inequity). Indeed, comparative analyses of data from 56 countries collected between 1986 and 1998 show that maternal factors, child nutrition, environmental quality, and health care account for three-quarters of the variance in postneonatal mortality (Rutstein, 2000). Factors of increasing importance in specific regions include drug resistance of pathogens and parasites and prevalence of human immunodeficiency virus (HIV). These infectious risks apparently contribute to an actual reversal of mortality decline in regions of sub-Saharan Africa.

All of these mortality risk factors comprise behaviors and conditions strongly shaped by culture, including practices, goals/values, gender relations, and structures of status and power. Therefore, attention to underlying cultural conditions and change is needed to disentangle and explain the diversity of trends in child health. This theme is discussed after a review of global patterns and trends for the other major index of population welfare, namely child growth and nutritional status.

Survival Is Not Enough: Child Nutrition and Physical Development

Child growth and nutrition comprise the second set of sensitive indicators for the quality of conditions affecting human welfare (Frongillo et al., 1997). Child survival advocates sensibly emphasize that because death precludes further child development, averting mortality comes first; ensuring a future for all children remains an imperative (Lawn et al., 2005; WHO, 2005). Yet others press the need for measures to promote healthy development as essential for realizing the potential in each child's future. Reports by the International Child Development Steering Group document the magnitude of lost human potential (Grantham-McGregor, Cheung, Cueto, Glewwe, Richter, and Strupp, 2007), highlight the primary causes of loss (Walker et al., 2007), and identify effective strategies for promoting healthy development (Engle et al., 2007). The reports link global child health to meeting developmental needs and, as such, represent a timely and salutary expansion of the vision for child health.

Before considering this expanded vision, classic morphometric indices of child growth and nutrition, global patterns and trends, and the relations of poor early nutrition with manifold aspects of child welfare in terms of development and human potential are discussed.

Growth, Weight, and the Use of Growth Standards Measures of height and weight are widely used to monitor child welfare for several reasons. Some are empirical. Growth acts as a mirror for society by closely reflecting both quality and inequality of environments (Lindgren et al., 1998). Poor growth and underweight reflect acute and cumulative effects of environments that are inadequate for nutrition and energy load; pathogen, parasite, and toxin exposures; and psychosocial stress (Ulijaszek, Johnston, and Preece, 1998). Hence, these anthropometric indices predict impaired future health and longevity. Other reasons are practical; the measures are rapid, noninvasive, simple, inexpensive, and portable. Height reflects cumulative skeletal growth from gestation onward. Rates of growth respond to nutritional state (growth takes energy and nutrients), and although growth acceleration (catch-up) does occur after an interval of restricted growth, even temporary decelerations during periods of very rapid growth such as infancy are difficult to make up entirely (Martorell, Khan, and Schroeder, 1994). Infections and illness also exact a toll on growth by impairing energy and nutrient availability (Bhutta, 2006). Thus, even minor insults exert cumulative effects on height that reflect the recurrence of stress or challenge to the child (Checkley et al., 2004). Weight, like height, is related to body size but also reflects body composition and tissue mass. Unlike height, weight can decrease as body mass is expended to meet energetic needs. Thus, weight represents both acute and previous nutrition and disease states. Among children whose growth has been stunted by mild to moderate malnutrition, body mass and proportions commonly are conserved, and weight for height may scarcely differ from that of chronically healthy, well-nourished peers.

Growth standards are invaluable for assessing and comparing the nutritional status of children throughout the early years, but the choice of reference values is hotly debated (Butte, Garza, and de Onis, 2007; Roberfroid, Lerude, Perez-Cueto, and Kolsteren, 2006). The height and weight of children are moving targets that change over time, and rates of growth vary with age and stage of physical development. Therefore, anthropometric measures must be expressed in terms of height or weight for child age to derive comparable measures of status. But this approach requires norms (medians and distributions) of size for age, for which well-nourished healthy Western populations have been the source (most commonly, the United States National Center for Health Statistics [NCHS]). The logic behind the approach holds that, in principle, all child populations have the same distributions of growth potential reflected in optimal growth patterns that would be realized under nurturing, healthy conditions. Therefore, the same standards should apply for all populations. Although current thinking agrees with this logic for young children (WHO Multicentre Growth Reference Study Group, 2006), the presumption of cross-population universality of growth potential and the definition of optimal growth in school-age children and adolescents remain contested (Butte et al., 2007). The difficulties are further complicated by variation in the timing and pace of puberty and its association with environmental quality (Worthman, 1999a). Hence, WHO international growth standards apply to children through age 5 years (WHO, 2006b), and NCHS reference values for comparative purposes apply only to children through age 10 years.

With relative, standardized measures in hand, the status of an individual child is established vis-à-vis the reference and can be aggregated with children of other ages in the same sample for comparison with other groups. Weight-for-age or height-for-age less than two standard deviations below the reference median is classified as moderately malnourished, and weight-for-age or height-for-age three or more standard deviations below the median is considered severely malnourished (WHO, 1995). The next section discusses the use of anthropometric surveys for tracking differences and change in nutrition and health status across populations and through time.

Temporal Trends and Taking Stock

As late as 1980 and despite three decades of intensifying efforts toward global development and health promotion, roughly 40% of children in developing countries still manifested moderate to severe malnutrition (Pelletier and Frongillo, 2003). As Figures 3.6 and 3.7 show, global rates of moderate-to-severe malnutrition have declined according to both indices. But height and weight tell rather different stories about improvement and inequality. As with mortality rates, regional differences in the prevalence of stunting (height-for-age less than two standard deviations below median) are substantial (de Onis and Blössner, 2003; de Onis, Frongillo, and Blössner, 2000), being highest in Asia and lowest in the South America/Caribbean region. These differences were maintained as prevalence decreased throughout the last 25 years, during which the Africa region experienced little change. Consequently, height status of African children declined from being better than in developing countries overall to being the worst of any region.

Both globally and in developing countries, child nutrition has improved steadily over the last two decades and more; wasting (weight-for-age less than two standard deviations below median) declined by approximately 80% in the developing Americas and by nearly half in Asia, the region where the largest segment of human population resides. Despite this progress, current projections show that the Millennium Development goal set by international accord as a 50% reduction in under-5 undernutrition between 1990 and 2015 will not be achieved (de Onis, Blössner, Borghi, Frongillo, and Morris, 2004). Instead, only a 31% improvement is expected, largely as a result of deteriorating conditions in sub-Saharan Africa.

Juxtaposition of the temporal trends for both indicators (mortality and nutrition) suggests how gains have been achieved and reveals limitations that underlie both failures to meet

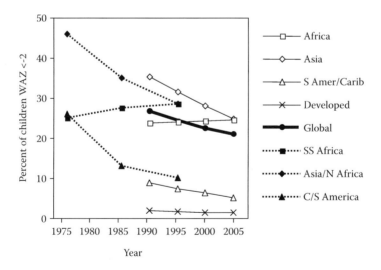

Figure 3.6 Trends in prevalence of child malnutrition as indexed by proportion of underweight children who are less than two standard deviations below weight-for-age (WAZ) reference values. Curves are drawn from two sets of analyses that cover overlapping time frames, 1975 to 1995 (dotted lines, solid symbol) (Pelletier and Frongillo, 2003) and 1990 to 2005, where 2005 was extrapolated (solid lines, open symbol) (de Onis, Blössner, Borghi, Morris, and Frongillo, 2004). Note the differences in definition of world region for the two time series. The similarity in trajectories yet absence of perfect overlap by each series is attributable to slightly different approaches to analysis and differences in definitions of region.

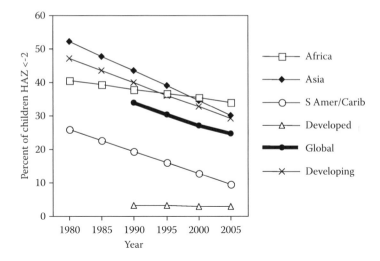

Figure 3.7 Trends in prevalence of child malnutrition based on proportion of small-statured children whose height is under two standard deviations below height-for-age (HAZ) reference values. (Data from de Onis, M., and Blössner, M., *International Journal of Epidemiology, 32*, 518–526, 2003; and de Onis, M., Frongillo, E. A., and Blössner, M., *Bulletin of the World Health Organization, 78*, 1222–1233, 2000.)

expectations and widening global health inequalities. The greatest gains in mortality reduction were attained earlier and more rapidly than for malnutrition. Sharp mortality reductions could be realized by acute interventions such as immunization and oral rehydration therapy. As mortality reductions slowed, the importance of continued improvements in nutrition for consolidation and, arguably, future progress of mortality gains became apparent (Pelletier and Frongillo, 2003). Concurrently, the understanding of child welfare as a litmus test for society reasserted itself to suggest that a reconceptualization of goals and indices of human welfare is needed. This reorientation is motivated by recognition that the fabric not just of societies, but also of the international order is imbricated with human welfare (Ahmad et al., 2000; Claeson and Waldman, 2000). Related to a refigured vision of child health within the social fabric is a reconsideration of an adequate indicator for child welfare, a theme that is taken up in the following section.

Toward Expanded Goals for Child Health: Realizing Developmental Potential

Child mortality and disease burden represent "the tip of the iceberg" of lost human potential (Grantham-McGregor et al., 2007, p. 60). In many respects, the markers of child nutritional status derive significance from their representation of embodied capital or the extent to which a child's potential is being supported and actuated under the conditions in which he or she is growing up. Embodied capital, in turn, fuels the future of societies as well as that of the children themselves. The number of children under age 5 years who fail to reach their psychosocial potential is estimated at 200 million (Grantham-McGregor et al., 2007).

In this inclusive view of child welfare, child psychosocial development comprises cognitive, socioemotional, and sensory-motor dimensions, all of which are affected by child health and nutrition. Child health and nutrition are, in turn, embedded in the material and social conditions of rearing. The estimation of 200 million children failing to meet potential is based on the performance of children with growth retardation (height-for-age less than two standard deviations below median) and absolute poverty (adjusted income under $1/day). Growth retardation and poverty were selected as indicators of poor child development because of their strong relations to deficient rearing conditions. Assessment of the impact of these indicators on school and cognitive performance reveals remarkably powerful effects. WHO and UNICEF data for 79 countries showed that attainment rates for the final grade of primary school drop by nearly 8% for every 10% increase in national prevalence of stunting. Data for 64 countries further indicate that for every 10% increase in poverty, school attainment rates drop by more than 6%. The prevalence of the risk factors is dauntingly high; nearly one-third of children in developing nations are stunted (Figure 3.7), and 37% live in absolute poverty (Gordon, Nancy, Pantazis, Pemberton, and Townsend, 2003).*

Poor early child health signals developmental risk that predicts diminished outcomes across the life course (Law, 2005). It also forms a link in the chain of intergenerational transmission for economic and health disparities. Environmental risks signaled by deficits in physical growth also impair cognitive and socioemotional development along with motor and other aspects of physical development. Even small differences in child growth have been linked to differences in school performance (reviewed in Grantham-McGregor et al., 2007).

For the purposes of this discussion, child development is taken to comprise physical development and health interacting dynamically with psychosocial development and well-being. This expanded view of both child health as including psychosocial development and child development as including physical development and health integrates the two worlds of human development and public health. It also raises the bar for defining what constitutes "developmental potential."

Culture and Child Health

Thus far, this chapter has surveyed the global record of progress and disparity in child health, the intimate ties between child health and culturally mediated conditions, and the emergence of an expanded developmental framework for child health. To meet the challenges of this expanded view, the following sections discuss concepts and models that have integrated culture to yield novel, practical insights into established and emergent health issues.

The Developmental Niche

The developmental niche, or the cultural organization of the environment in which the child grows up, is a powerful concept that links culture and human development (Super and Harkness, 2002). The niche is composed of the culturally constituted conditions (settings, experiences, resources, and challenges) under which development occurs (Valsiner, 1997). Cultural determinants of developmental niche include beliefs (e.g., parental beliefs about child development, health and illness, appropriate parenting, family relationships, proper behavior) and values (e.g., relative value of daughters versus sons, or relationships versus self, or religious versus pragmatic goals) that, in turn, inform social "goods" and priorities. Culture also includes practices, from those that define large-scale social structure, political economy, and living conditions to personal and domestic ones in daily life (e.g., cooking, hygiene, childcare) (Goodnow, Miller, and Kessel, 1995). From rituals to routines, practices both shape the settings in which children grow up and place children in specific settings. Most importantly, culture encompasses models of how the world is and works, along with context- and goal-contingent scripts for appropriate thought, action, and feeling (Shore, 1996). Thus, for example, parents hold models of family function, child development, and gender that are mapped to multiple scripts, as for mealtimes and child feeding, authority and minding, or task allocation and performance expectations.

---

* The criterion used for this estimate is severe deprivation of two of more basic human needs (e.g., food, safe water, shelter, sanitation). Poverty is difficult to both define and assess. Income/net resources take many forms, and consumption power can determine the leverage of available resources (Deaton, 2001). Then, relative rather than absolute deprivation accounts for some outcomes (Wilkinson, 1996).

Enacting cultural models and scripts through practices also exerts cumulative macrosocietal effects on social structure, political and material economy, degrees of inequity, and other circumstances that inform the range of possibilities and challenges afforded children and their families. Such effects also shape the characteristics of parents who themselves have grown up in the culture. These moderating factors influence the developmental niche of any specific child as well as the range of niches children experience in a particular society. Social marginalization or poverty impairs parental ability to enact cultural models and scripts for their children's welfare by, for instance, reducing their capacity to access prenatal and pediatric care, realize culturally appropriate hygienic practices, or regulate daily schedules and provide desirable opportunities to children (Grantham-McGregor et al., 2007).

The impact of moderating factors on the developmental niche and hence on child health can be both subtle and powerful. Consider this example regarding effects of household water storage and sanitation on child growth in an informal housing settlement (*pueblos jovenes*) near Lima, Peru (Checkley et al., 2004). Small water containers are stored uncovered inside the home and thus exposed to fecal contamination; large containers are kept outside, covered, and therefore less exposed. By age 24 months, children in households with small water containers had 28% more diarrheal episodes and were 0.8 cm shorter than were those in homes with medium or large storage containers. Moreover, a small water container plus lack of sewage and water connections in the home accounted for 40% of the average 2.5-cm height deficit in this population relative to the WHO/NCHS reference values for 24-month-olds. Hence, small within-community differences in household practices and access to infrastructure strongly contributed to child stunting.

The Developmental Niche and Child Health: Models and Exemplars

Therefore, as modeled in Figure 3.8, the developmental niche is the locus of action for determinants of child development and health. Pathways to differential well-being within and between cultures must operate through the niche. Culture shapes the developmental niche through models and scripts that orchestrate parental ethnotheories, practices, settings, and routines that make up the daily life of the child (Figure 3.8, top and middle). But the child also enters as an actor whose characteristics (biology/genetics, function, temperament, and abilities) and behaviors dynamically shape the niche and its effects on health and development (Figure 3.8, middle,

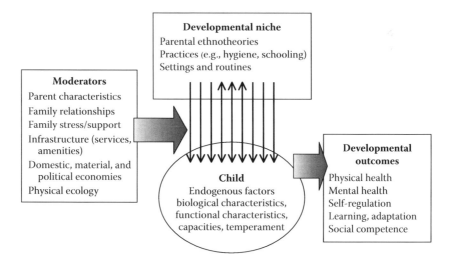

Figure 3.8 Components of and influences on the developmental niche and its relation to child outcomes.

bottom, and right). For instance, in many societies, child gender systematically colors the developmental niche by eliciting distinctive, elaborated cultural models and scripts for parenting and socialization that can lead to quite different survival and health prospects for boys and girls (Worthman, 1996). Additionally, child abilities and temperament interact with expectations for emotion regulation, appropriate demeanor, and task performance to modify parental affections, quality of care, and provision of opportunities. For instance, Masai babies whose mothers rated them difficult were more likely to survive during a subsequent drought, presumably because they claimed more care (deVries, 1984). By contrast, destitute mothers in *favelas* of northeast Brazil may respond to infant symptoms of severe malnutrition by withdrawing care, although these mothers, too, saw demanding children as fighters ready for life's hardships (Scheper-Hughes, 1992).

Cultural and social expectations also determine what caregivers monitor about the child and how they respond to what they see. Amele mothers of coastal New Guinea, for example, regard infant development in nonlinear terms including reversible behavioral-motor states to which infant feeding must be adjusted; an infant who was crawling and therefore fed stage-appropriate semisolids one day may be feverish, limp, and listless and therefore restricted to breast milk appropriate to their state the next day (Worthman, Jenkins, Stallings, and Lai, 1994). Similarly, Peruvian mothers encourage eating more when their infants show poor appetite during bouts of diarrhea but become more passive when infants eagerly accept food during recuperation (Bentley, Stallings, Fukumoto, and Elder, 1991).

An inclusive conception relating culture to child health ultimately must encompass all levels of a society and even the world order, from the political, economic, and social organizational, down to the domestic and personal. Nevertheless, such comprehensive accounts often lack specificity about *how* differential child health is produced and *what* those differences mean in terms of capacities, experiences, or welfare. Focus on the developmental niche draws culture out of the social ether and pulls it down to the ground by translating culture into the proximal dynamics of child development. Linking the global to the local, or macrostructural to microprocessual levels of analysis, remains more challenging. The moderators included in the developmental niche model (Figure 3.8, left) introduce these factors as constraints on dynamics operating in the niche. Hence, the distribution of sewage disposal and clean water, and access to schools, food, and medicines that condition the developmental niche of any child are shaped by values, availability and allocation of resources, and sociopolitical realities within and among nations.

The apparent and immediate needs of children and families prompt public health and policy to emphasize determinants of child welfare at the maternal, household, or community level (Engle et al., 2007). Yet the urgency of obvious need can deflect attention from larger determinants of inequity, poverty, and other challenges (Farmer, 2003). Hence, research and policy regarding child health, in particular, and social epidemiology, in general, continually struggle to formulate models of equivalent specificity and power at all levels of analysis. Nevertheless, frameworks that address all levels tend to be descriptive rather than predictive (Krieger, 2004; Mosley and Chen, 1984), whereas those with greater analytic purchase tend to offer more narrow specificity that makes a subset of relevant levels operational (Super and Harkness, 2002; Worthman, 1999b).

In view of these complexities, the following sections illustrate the insights generated by integrative, culturally informed analysis of human development and health in two domains, namely child feeding and transgenerational effects.

Child Feeding Humans are unique among mammals for systematic food sharing and provisioning of the young beyond weaning and into the adult period. This arrangement seems effective; infant mortality is much lower in humans than in other primates (Lancaster, 2000), and the infant feeding practices implemented by recent and contemporary preindustrial societies meet current global recommendations (Sellen, 2001). The downside of such unusual levels of nurturance and juvenile dependency surfaces where the cultural configurations and social arrangements for provisioning are inadequate or disrupted. Although global rates of acute and chronic hunger have declined, food insecurity remains common (Coates, Frongillo, Rogers, Webb, Wilde, and Houser, 2006) and increasingly is seen as related to perturbations in production, distribution, and consumption systems rooted in social, political, and economic disparities and crises (Baro and Deubel, 2006). Social macrostructure, inequalities, and instabilities shape food availability and household livelihood security (Frankenberger, 2003). These, in turn, affect child well-being. For example, dietary diversity is associated with child nutritional status (Arimond and Ruel, 2004), but diversity is reduced by poverty and market dependency.

The relation between feeding and survival is strongest in infancy; therefore, infant feeding practices have been intensively studied and targeted in interventions to improve child survival and growth (Labbok, Clark, and Goldman, 2004). Effects of early feeding ramify throughout life. Breastfed infants have less frequent infectious illness and higher survival (Jones, Steketee, Black, Bhutta, Morris, and Bellagio Child Survival Study Group, 2003) and, as adults, have lower risk of type 2 diabetes (Owen, Martin, Whincup, Smith, and Cook, 2006) and premenopausal breast cancer (Martin, Middleton, Gunnell, Owen, and Smith, 2005). Extensive evidence indicates that optimal infant feeding is defined by convergent ecological, maternal, cultural, and economic factors (McDade and Worthman, 1998). As such, infant feeding vividly illustrates both the roles of culture in child health and the feasibility of deriving a grounded model of those roles as a basis for intervention and policy. Exclusive breastfeeding provides ideal nutrition and developmental support as well as protection against pathogens causing early mortality (Labbok et al., 2004). Nevertheless, after 6 months, breast milk no longer meets infant needs. Supplementation becomes necessary but increases risk from pathogens and nutritional insufficiency. Infant needs and risks and caregiver intent and capacity for optimal feeding are influenced by household and community conditions. Hence, pathogen burden affecting mortality risk for the infant and maternal nutrition and workload affecting maternal health burden represent potentially opposing pressures—to delay or accelerate supplementation, respectively.

Figure 3.9 tracks how prevailing sociocultural factors determine the timing, pattern, quality, and quantity of infant feeding by influencing on-the-ground pressures on caregivers—usually mothers—around specific feeding behaviors comprising continuing exclusive breastfeeding,

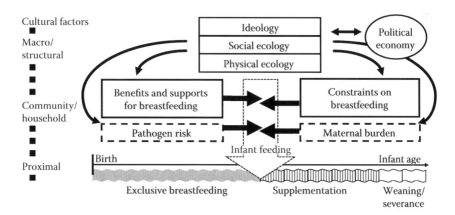

Figure 3.9 Biocultural determinants of infant feeding. Relation of the model to the impact of culture at three levels of analysis is indicated on the left side. (Modified from McDade, T. W., and Worthman, C. M., *Journal of Developmental and Behavioral Pediatrics, 19*, 286–299, 1998.)

supplementing, or weaning. Benefits and supports for breastfeeding, such as cultural views of maternal roles or infant development, weigh against constraints on breastfeeding, such as maternal workload and marital demands. For example, breastfeeding and supplementation patterns have been associated with mother–child transmission of HIV (Hartmann, Berlin, and Howett, 2006), but workload, illness, or partner pressure may erode maternal ability to maintain an exclusive breast- or bottle-feeding regimen to minimize transmission risk. Local forces are, in turn, shaped by macro-level factors (ideology, physical and social ecology, and political economy) related to conditions of life, prevailing values and knowledge, and access to resources and social capital. Poverty and social marginalization demonstrably affect infant feeding (Scheper-Hughes, 1992; Stallings, Worthman, Panter-Brick, and Coates, 1996), but the influence of macro–micro linkages often operate circuitously. For instance, household technologies of food storage and processing affect the nutritional value and safety of complementary foods fed to infants (Mensah and Tomkins, 2003).

Intergenerational Effects Explanations for parent effects on child health and survival have long focused on socioeconomic conditions of childrearing, particularly on income, parental education, and residence. An important insight gained by this work is the importance of women's education for reducing child mortality independent of the effects of paternal education, residence, or occupation (LeVine, LeVine, and Schnell, 2001; UNICEF, 2007). The effects of women's education extend to the community level; in India, for instance, the proportion of educated women at the district level predicts child immunization rates for the district (Parashar, 2005). Hence, child welfare reflects not only culturally determined gender norms, but also social stratification and living conditions that affect both parents' own developmental histories and consequent capacities and their priorities and resources for parenting as adults.

Recent epidemiological work has revealed another direct route for transmission of intergenerational effects, namely during gestation. Evidence that fetal conditions, indexed by low birth weight, have early and enduring effects on the child's health has directed attention to gestational environment and maternal welfare. Formative observations identified relationships of low birth weight with risk for cardiovascular disease and metabolic dysfunction in adulthood (Barker, 1991). The resultant thrifty phenotype hypothesis proposed that poor fetal nutrition induces alterations in regulatory mechanisms that facilitate coping with challenging postnatal conditions including poor nutrition and high activity but predispose to chronic disease within a "mismatching" postnatal environment of overnutrition and low activity (Hales and Barker, 1992).

Subsequent research has established relationships and mediating mechanisms between maternal conditions (diet, nutrition, stress, and activity levels) and child function as well as health from infancy onward (Gluckman and Hanson, 2004; Kajantie, Osmond, Barker, Forsén, Phillips, and Eriksson, 2005). Many factors influence fetal nutrition beyond maternal nutrition, including maternal behaviors (smoking or physical activity), maternal conditions (hyperglycemia or hypertension), maternal stress (low social support or distress), composition of maternal diet (high protein or low micronutrient intake), or vagaries of placentation (Harding, 2001; Perkins, Pivarnik, Paneth, and Stein, 2007). Context plays significant roles not only in producing gestational conditions that affect fetal development, but also in determining the postnatal health consequences of fetal outcomes (Leon, 2004; Worthman and Kuzara, 2005). For example, persons exposed during gestation to the 1944 to 1945 famine in Holland exhibit increased obesity, reduced glucose tolerance, higher blood pressure and risk for hypertension, and likelihood of mortality in middle age (Kyle and Pichard, 2006; Stein, Zybert, van der Pal-de Bruin, and Lumey, 2006). Conversely, undernourished offspring of Guatemalan mothers supplemented in pregnancy grew faster as children and had greater glucose tolerance as young adults compared with unsupplemented controls (Conlisk, Barnhart, Martorell, Grajeda, and Stein, 2004; Stein et al., 2004). Such effects can carry forward across generations; gestational and postnatal conditions that alter physiological regulation and increase sensitivity to stressors potentiate subsequent stress in pregnancy with consequent transmission of the phenotypes of vulnerability to the next generation (Drake and Walker, 2004). Via the uterine pathway, the treatment of girls and women may translate into well-being of their offspring—daughters *and* sons.

Fetal programming and environmental mismatch may underlie the emerging worldwide epidemics of obesity and secondary, or acquired, type 2 diabetes that became apparent by the 1990s (Zimmet, Alberti, and Shaw, 2001). Initially, the trends to increasing prevalence of non-communicable diseases were seen as afflictions of affluence (Armelagos, Brown, and Turner, 2005). But the global epidemic also afflicts developing and transitional economies, including their less affluent sectors, and coincident over- and undernutrition within households or communities is increasing (Monteiro, Moura, Conde, and Popkin, 2004). The trends first manifested in adults now are appearing in children and adolescents. Onset of type 2 diabetes historically has occurred later in life, but high prevalence in adults has been associated with its novel appearance among the young; child-onset type 2 diabetes was seen earliest in countries having the world's highest adult rates of the disorder (Pinas-Hamel and Zeitler, 2005). Ironically, diseases of affluence began disproportionately to burden the disadvantaged just as improved life circumstances were achieved (Leon and Walt, 2001). Thus, adolescents from disadvantaged minorities in the United States, Canada, and New Zealand have disproportionately high rates of secondary diabetes (Pinas-Hamel and Zeitler, 2005).

Other likely complementary explanations for these epidemiological trends also command supporting evidence (Davey Smith, Sterne, Tynelius, and Rasmussen, 2004; Dowse and Zimmet, 1993; Neel, 1962; Sniderman, Bhopal, Prabhakaran, Sarrafzadegan, and Tchernof, 2007; Spiegel, Knutson, Leproult, Tasali, and Van Cauter, 2005). During this period of very rapidly shifting epidemiological and scientific landscapes, final conclusions must await events. Nevertheless, the consensus is that changes in diet, activity, and daily experiences and stressors play a role in the emergence of chronic diseases and that such diseases have a developmental course that begins early on and is affected by conditions throughout life.

Behind these causal conditions is cultural change, on local and global levels. Therefore, now more than ever, culture has assumed a major place in our understanding of human development and health. From this point, this chapter turns to a final consideration of cultural factors in the epidemiology of early life.

Cultural Factors and Global Trends in Child Health

If child survival and growth are sensitive indicators of environmental quality, then advances in child health must draw on culture change. Global interventions that leveraged improvements in child survival, health, and nutrition also have involved culture change regarding social values, ideas, practices, and structures of power and authority. For instance, global achievement of high rates of child vaccination has relied on parental acceptance (Streefland, Chowdhury, and Ramos-Jimenez, 1999), political and media support (Gangarosa et al., 1998), and shared understandings of risk (Hacking, 1990), alongside reallocation of resources as well as organizational and logistical capacities required to implement and maintain immunization programs. Beliefs and values remain important even when material, technical, and logistical constraints are relaxed; in the United States where vaccination rates had slumped, completion of childhood immunization was attributable to "positive immunization-related beliefs and attitudes" among mothers (Gore et al., 1999).

Indeed, an analysis to explain differential reductions in growth stunting using the WHO Global Database on Child Growth found that both starting conditions and change in multiple domains were necessary to account for just two-thirds of national differences in stunting reduction among children under 4 years old (Milman et al., 2005). These factors comprised initial and change in immunization rate, initial and change in safe water rate, initial female literacy rate, initial government consumption, initial income distribution, and initial proportion of the economy devoted to agriculture. Accordingly, biomedicine and public health have begun to engage seriously with the role of culture in health, including critical analysis of the cultural context of customary medical, public health, and policy practices themselves.

Movements such as social medicine and ethnopediatrics have emerged to inform pediatric research, practice, and even popular childcare manuals on such disparate topics as feeding (McDade and Worthman, 1998), sleep (Jenni and O'Connor, 2005), and parenting in general (Small, 1998). "Pediatricians need to recognize the cultural environment in which children live and be knowledgeable about how cultural beliefs and values of both families and physicians interact with the needs and biological characteristics of individual children" (Jenni 2005, p. 204). Important as it is, individual-level action is demonstrably insufficient to secure child welfare. Rather, household, community, national, and international conditions influence the developmental niche and shape the welfare of any given child. Concurrently, social epidemiology has been launched to unravel the roles of psychosocial factors such as social capital, inequality, and perceived status or insecurity in paving the pathways to differential well-being based on a multilevel framework stretching from the molecular to the macrostructural (Adler, 2002; Krieger, 2004).

Conclusion

Views of child health and its relation to the social order are undergoing a paradigm shift related to forces of globalization and widespread culture change with corresponding struggles for local and global welfare (Worthman and Kohrt, 2005). The shift is precipitated by diminishing gains and even reversals in advancing child survival and health that are rooted in the limitations of current policies and their informing paradigms. Concerted public practice and research around the world during the last half century have taught us that not only psychosocial factors, but also physical development and health of the young are closely tied to the fabric of society. We are still learning how to bring these lessons most effectively to bear for securing the physical and psychobehavioral health of young people. The social sciences currently are grappling with this problem by engaging sources of human diversity (Part 2 of this book), characterizing the roles of culture and context (Part 1 of this book), and formulating multilevel models that span the individual to societal to global.

This discussion commenced by characterizing the exceptional burden of mortality and ill health borne by children, particularly during the early years. The burden remains substantial despite dramatic improvements in child survival from the latter part of the twentieth century to the present. Child health indicators also improved during this period, although not as rapidly as did survival. More worrisome are persistent or even widening disparities in child health within and among countries. Public and scientific constituencies agree that child survival and health denote the welfare and functioning of the population as a whole. This insight has had two consequences. First, indices of child health (particularly survival, growth, and weight) not only guide national and international policy with regard to public health, but also act as a litmus test for the performance of governments, agencies, and societies as a whole. Second, these indices have propelled an engagement with the sociocultural factors that drive child health.

If the survival and development of the young rely on the package of care and ambient conditions from conception onward, then improvements in child health must entail improvements in these conditions. Early efforts in this direction focused on proximal levels, particularly the mother and child, household, and local community. The concept of a developmental niche permits integration of cultural factors into the analysis of the determinants that form the particular envelope of care and experiences a child encounters. The model has been expanded to include both sociostructural and biological levels and has proven to be an effective tool for guiding new work to discover key factors and dynamics in child health and development (Richter, 2004; Weisner, 1998). Flexible integrative models are required for an effective and comprehensive global approach to child health because the nature and importance of these factors and dynamics vary within and across societies. A model for a basic element of care, child feeding, was discussed to show the feasibility for integration of structural down to biological levels of analysis in a biocultural model for determinants of infant feeding and its health consequences.

The shock waves from upheavals in thought and practice regarding human welfare and child health in particular will continue to reverberate for some time. Developmental and health sciences are transforming themselves in the process. The current move to define child health in terms of physical as well as psychosocial development and well-being orients social goals and policies around a realization of child developmental potential. The value of this integrated approach to child health is compellingly illustrated by the recognition of fetal programming and environmental mismatch as potentially powerful forces in shaping health across the life span and into the next generation. Social conditions that cause physical and mental hardship have been found to translate into adjusted functional capacities of offspring that, if confronted with a mismatching postnatal environment during current conditions of culture change and globalization, can lead to impaired development and health.

The cutting edge of current evidence for integrative cultural-contextual analysis has carved deep into outmoded distinctions between mind and body, individual and society, personal and political, and qualitative and quantitative analysis. Attention to child health and the use of developmental analysis have helped both to unravel these distinctions and to build new science and practice toward promotion of human equity, realized potential, and well-being.

References

Adler, N. E. (2002). Socioeconomic disparities in health: pathways and policies. Inequality in education, income, and occupation exacerbates the gaps between the health "haves" and "have-nots." *Health Affairs, 21,* 6–76.

Ahmad, O. B., Lopez, A. D., and Inoue, M. (2000). The decline in child mortality: A reappraisal. *Bulletin of the World Health Organization, 78,* 1175–1191.

Arimond, M., and Ruel, M. T. (2004). Dietary diversity is associated with child nutritional status: Evidence from 11 demographic and health surveys. *Journal of Nutrition, 134,* 2579–2585.

Armelagos, G. J., Brown, P. J., and Turner, B. (2005). Evolutionary, historical and political economic perspectives on health and disease. *Social Science and Medicine, 61,* 755–765.

Barker, D. J. (1991). The intrauterine environment and adult cardiovascular disease. *Ciba Foundation Symposium, 156,* 3–10; discussion 10–16.

Barker, D. J. P., Eriksson, J. G., Forsén, T., and Osmond, C. (2002). Fetal origins of adult disease: Strength of effects and biological basis. *International Journal of Epidemiology, 31,* 1235–1239.

Baro, M., and Deubel, T. F. (2006). Persistent hunger: Perspectives on vulnerability, famine, and food security in sub-Saharan Africa. *Annual Review of Anthropology, 35,* 521–538.

Bentley, M. E., Stallings, R. Y., Fukumoto, M., and Elder, J. A. (1991). Maternal feeding behavior and child acceptance of food during diarrhea, convalescence, and health in the central Sierra of Peru. *American Journal of Public Health, 81,* 43–47.

Bhutta, Z. A. (2006). Effect of infections and environmental factors on growth and nutritional status in developing countries. *Journal of Pediatric Gastroenterology and Nutrition, 43*(Suppl. 3), S13–S21.

Black, R. E., Morris, S. S., and Bryce, J. (2003). Where and why are 10 million children dying every year? *Lancet, 361,* 2226–2234.

Brye, J., Boschi-Pinto, C., Shibuya, K., and Black, R. E. (2005). WHO estimates of the causes of death in children. *Lancet, 365,* 1147–1152.

Butte, N., Garza, C., and de Onis, M. (2007). Evaluation of the feasibility of international growth standards for school-aged children and adolescents. *Journal of Nutrition, 137,* 153–157.

Campbell, D. I., Elia, M., and Lunn, P. G. (2003). Growth faltering in rural Gambian infants is associated with impaired small intestinal barrier function, leading to endotoxemia and systemic inflammation. *Journal of Nutrition, 133*, 1332–1338.

Checkley, W., Gilman, R. H., Black, R. E., Epstein, L. D., Cabrera, L., Sterling, C. R., et al. (2004). Effect of water and sanitation on childhood health in a poor Peruvian peri-urban community. *Lancet, 363*, 112–118.

Claeson, M., and Waldman, R. J. (2000). The evolution of child health programmes in developing countries: From targeting diseases to targeting people. *Bulletin of the World Health Organization, 78*, 1234–1245.

Coates, J., Frongillo, E. A., Rogers, B. L., Webb, P., Wilde, P. E., and Houser, R. (2006). Commonalities in the experience of household food insecurity across cultures: What are measures missing? *Journal of Nutrition, 136*, 1438–1448.

Conlisk, A. J., Barnhart, H. X., Martorell, R., Grajeda, R., and Stein, A. D. (2004). Maternal and child nutritional supplementation are inversely associated with fasting plasma glucose concentration in young Guatemalan adults. *Journal of Nutrition, 134*, 890–897.

Costello, E. J., Worthman, C. M., Erkanli, A., and Angold, A. (2007). Prediction from low birth weight to female adolescent depression: A test of competing hypotheses. *Archives of General Psychiatry, 64*, 338–344.

Crimmins, E. M., and Finch, C. E. (2006). Infection, inflammation, height, and longevity. *Proceedings of the National Academy of Sciences, 103*, 498–503.

Dantzer, R. (2001). Cytokine-induced sickness behavior: Where do we stand? *Brain, Behavior, and Immunity, 15*, 7–24.

Davey Smith, G., Sterne, J. A. C., Tynelius, P., and Rasmussen, F. (2004). Birth characteristics of offspring and parental diabetes: Evidence for the fetal insulin hypothesis. *Journal of Epidemiology and Community Health, 58*, 126–128.

Deaton, A. (2001). Counting the world's poor: Problems and possible solutions. *World Bank Research Observer, 16*, 125–147.

de Onis, M., and Blössner, M. (2003). The World Health Organization Global Database on Child Growth and Malnutrition: Methodology and applications. *International Journal of Epidemiology, 32*, 518–526.

de Onis, M., Blössner, M., Borghi, E., Frongillo, E. A., and Morris, R. (2004). Estimates of global prevalence of childhood underweight in 1990 and 2015. *JAMA, 291*, 2600–2606.

de Onis, M., Blössner, M., Borghi, E., Morris, R., and Frongillo, E. A. (2004). Methodology for estimating regional and global trends of child malnutrition. *International Journal of Epidemiology, 33*, 1–11.

de Onis, M., Frongillo, E. A., and Blössner, M. (2000). Is malnutrition declining? An analysis of changes in levels of child malnutrition since 1980. *Bulletin of the World Health Organization, 78*, 1222–1233.

deVries, M. W. (1984). Temperament and infant mortality among the Masai of East Africa. *American Journal of Psychiatry, 141*, 1189–1194.

Dowse, G., and Zimmet, P. (1993). The thrifty genotype in non-insulin-dependent diabetes. The hypothesis survives. *British Medical Journal, 306*, 532–533.

Drake, A. J., and Walker, B. R. (2004). The intergenerational effects of fetal programming: Non-genomic mechanisms for the inheritance of low birth weight and cardiovascular risk. *Journal of Epidemiology, 180*, 1–16.

Engle, P. L., Black, M. M., Behrman, J. R., Cabral de Mello, M., Gertler, P. J., Kapiriri, L., et al. (2007). Strategies to avoid the loss of developmental potential in more than 200 million children in the developing world. *Lancet, 369*, 229–242.

Eveleth, P., and Tanner, J. (1990). *Worldwide variation in human growth* (2nd ed.). New York: Cambridge University Press.

Farmer, P. (2003). *Pathologies of power*. Berkeley, CA: University of California Press.

Frankenberger, T. (2003). *Managing risks, improving lives: Program guidelines for conditions of chronic vulnerability* (2nd ed.). Tucson, AZ: Tango International.

Frongillo, E. A., de Onis, M., and Hanson, K. M. P. (1997). Socioeconomic and demographic factors are associated with worldwide patterns of stunting and wasting of children. *Journal of Nutrition, 127*, 2302–2309.

Gangarosa, E. J., Galazka, A. M., Wolfe, C. R., Phillips, L. M., Gangarosa, R. E., Miller, E., et al. (1998). Impact of anti-vaccine movements on pertussis control: The untold story. *The Lancet, 351*, 356–361.

Gluckman, P. D., and Hanson, M. A. (2004). The developmental origins of the metabolic syndrome. *Trends in Endocrinology and Metabolism, 15*, 183–187.

Goodnow, J. J., Miller, P. J., and Kessel, F. (Eds.). (1995). *Cultural practices as contexts for development*. San Francisco: Jossey-Bass Inc, Publishers.

Gordon, D., Nancy, S., Pantazis, C., Pemberton, S., and Townsend, P. (2003). *Child poverty in the developing world*. Bristol, United Kingdom: Policy Press.

Gore, P., Madhavan, S., Curry, D., McClung, G., Castiglia, M., Rosenbluth, S. A., et al. (1999). Predictors of childhood immunization completion in a rural population. *Social Science and Medicine, 48,* 1011–1027.

Grantham-McGregor, S., Cheung, Y. B., Cueto, S., Glewwe, P., Richter, L., and Strupp, B. (2007). Developmental potential in the first 5 years for children in developing countries. *The Lancet, 369*(9555), 60–70.

Hacking, I. (1990). *The taming of chance.* New York: Cambridge University Press.

Hales, C. N., and Barker, D. J. P. (1992). Type 2 (non-insulin-dependent) diabetes mellitus: The thrifty phenotype hypothesis. *Diabetologia, 35,* 595–601.

Harding, J. E. (2001). The nutritional basis of the fetal origins of adult disease. *International Journal of Epidemiology, 30,* 15–23.

Hartmann, S. U., Berlin, C. M., and Howett, M. K. (2006). Alternative modified infant-feeding practices to prevent postnatal transmission of human immunodeficiency virus type 1 through breast milk: Past, present, and future. *Journal of Human Lactation, 22,* 75–88; quiz 89–93.

Heuveline, P., Guillot, M., and Gwatkin, D. R. (2002). The uneven tides of the health transition. *Social Science and Medicine, 55,* 313–322.

Heuveline, P., and Slap, G. B. (2002). Adolescent and young adult mortality by cause: Age, gender, and country, 1955 to 1994. *Journal of Adolescent Health, 30,* 29–34.

Jenni, O. G., and O'Connor, B. B. (2005). Children's sleep: An interplay between culture and biology. *Pediatrics, 115,* 204–215.

Jones, G., Steketee, R. W., Black, R. E., Bhutta, Z. A., Morris, S. S., and Bellagio Child Survival Study Group. (2003). How many child deaths can we prevent this year? *Lancet, 362,* 65–71.

Kajantie, E., Osmond, C., Barker, D. J. P., Forsén, T., Phillips, D. I. W., and Eriksson, J. G. (2005). Size at birth as a predictor of mortality in adulthood: A follow-up of 350,000 person-years. *International Journal of Epidemiology, 34,* 655–663.

Krieger, N. (Ed.). (2004). *Embodying inequality: Epidemiologic perspectives.* Amityville, NY: Baywood Publishing.

Kyle, U. G., and Pichard, C. (2006). The Dutch Famine of 1944-1945: A pathophysiological model of long-term consequences of wasting disease. *Current Opinion in Clinical Nutrition and Metabolic Care, 9,* 388–394.

Labbok, M. H., Clark, D., and Goldman, A. S. (2004). Breastfeeding: Maintaining an irreplaceable immunological resource. *Nature Reviews Immunology, 4,* 565–572.

Lancaster, J. B. (2000). Human reproduction, the evolution of the brain, and fat storage. *American Journal of Physical Anthropology, 30*(Suppl.), 205.

Law, C. (2005). Early growth and chronic disease: A public health overview. *Maternal and Child Nutrition, 1,* 169–176.

Lawn, J. E., Cousens, S. N., and Zupan, J. (2005). 4 million neonatal deaths: When? Where? Why? *Lancet, 365,* 891–900.

Lawn, J. E., Wilczynska-Ketende, K., and Cousens, S. N. (2006). Estimating the causes of 4 million neonatal deaths in the year 2000. *International Journal of Epidemiology, 35,* 706–718.

Leon, D. A. (2004). Biological theories, evidence, and epidemiology. *International Journal of Epidemiology, 33,* 1167–1171.

Leon, D. A., and Walt, G. (2001). *Poverty, inequality and health: An international perspective.* Oxford, United Kingdom: Oxford University Press.

LeVine, R. A., LeVine, S. E., and Schnell, B. (2001). "Improve the women": Mass schooling, female literacy, and worldwide social change. *Harvard Educational Review, 71,* 1–50.

Lindgren, G., Goodman, A. H., Hermanussen, M., Floud, R., Steegman, J., Carlin, L., et al. (1998). Changing human growth patterns. In S. Ulijaszek, F. E. Johnston, and M. A. Preece (Eds.), *The Cambridge encyclopedia of human growth and development* (pp. 381–411). Cambridge, United Kingdom: Cambridge University Press.

Martin, R. M., Middleton, N., Gunnell, D., Owen, C. G., and Smith, G. D. (2005). Breast-feeding and cancer: The Boyd Orr cohort and a systematic review with meta-analysis. *Journal of the National Cancer Institute, 97,* 1446–1457.

Martorell, R., Khan, L. K., and Schroeder, D. G. (1994). Reversibility of stunting: Epidemiological findings in children from developing countries. *European Journal of Clinical Nutrition, 48* (Suppl. 1), S45–S57.

Mathers, C. D., Lopez, A. D., and Murray, C. J. L. (2006). The burden of disease and mortality by condition: Data, methods, and results for 2001. In A. D. Lopez, C. D. Mathers, M. Ezzati, D. T. Jamison, and C. J. L. Murray (Eds.), *Global burden of disease and risk factors.* New York: World Bank/Oxford University Press.

McDade, T. W. (2005). The ecologies of human immune function. *Annual Review of Anthropology, 34,* 495–521.
McDade, T. W., and Worthman, C. M. (1998). The weanling's dilemma reconsidered: A biocultural analysis of breastfeeding ecology. *Journal of Developmental and Behavioral Pediatrics, 19,* 286–299.
Mensah, P., and Tomkins, A. (2003). Household-level technologies to improve the availability and preparation of adequate and safe complementary foods. *Food and Nutrition Bulletin, 24,* 104–125.
Milman, A., Frongillo, E. A., de Onis, M., and Hwang, J. Y. (2005). Differential improvement among countries in child stunting is associated with long-term development and specific interventions. *Journal of Nutrition, 135,* 1415–1422.
Monteiro, C. A., Moura, E. C., Conde, W. L., and Popkin, B. M. (2004). Socioeconomic status and obesity in adult populations of developing countries: A review. *Bulletin of the World Health Organization, 82,* 940–946.
Mosley, W. H., and Chen, L. C. (1984). An analytical framework for the study of child survival in developing countries. *Population and Development Review, 10*(Suppl.), 25–45.
Murray, C. J. L., and Lopez, A. D. (1996). *The global burden of disease.* Cambridge, MA: Harvard University Press/WHO.
Neel, J. (1962). Diabetes mellitus: A thrifty genotype rendered detrimental by "progress"? *American Journal of Human Genetics, 14,* 353–362.
Owen, C. G., Martin, R. M., Whincup, P. H., Smith, G. D., and Cook, D. G. (2006). Does breastfeeding influence risk of type 2 diabetes in later life? A quantitative analysis of published evidence. *American Journal of Clinical Nutrition, 84,* 1043–1054.
Parashar, S. (2005). Moving beyond the mother-child dyad: Women's education, child immunization, and the importance of context in rural India. *Social Science and Medicine, 61,* 989–1000.
Pelletier, D. L., and Frongillo, E. A. (2003). Changes in child survival are strongly associated with changes in malnutrition in developing countries. *Journal of Nutrition, 133,* 107–119.
Pelletier, D. L., Frongillo, E. A., Schroeder, D. G., and Habicht, J.-P. (1994). A methodology for estimating the contribution of malnutrition to child mortality in developing countries. *Journal of Nutrition, 124,* 2106S–2122S.
Perkins, C. C. D., Pivarnik, J. M., Paneth, N., and Stein, A. D. (2007). Physical activity and fetal growth during pregnancy. *Obstetrics and Gynecology, 109,* 81–87.
Pinas-Hamel, O., and Zeitler, P. (2005). The global spread of type 2 diabetes mellitus in children and adolescents. *Journal of Pediatrics, 146,* 693–700.
Richter, L. (2004). *The importance of caregiver-child interactions for the survival and healthy development of young children: A review.* Geneva, Switzerland: World Health Organization.
Roberfroid, D., Lerude, M.-P., Perez-Cueto, A., and Kolsteren, P. (2006). Is the 2000 CDC growth reference appropriate for developing countries? *Public Health Nutrition, 9,* 266–268.
Rutstein, S. O. (2000). Factors associated with trends in infant and child mortality in developing countries during the 1990s. *Bulletin of the World Health Organization, 78,* 1256–1270.
Scheper-Hughes, N. (1992). *Death without weeping: The violence of everyday life in Brazil.* Berkeley, CA: University of California Press.
Schroeder, D., and Brown, K. (1994). Nutritional status as a predictor of child survival: Summarizing the association and quantifying its global impact. *Bulletin of the World Health Organization, 72,* 569–579.
Sellen, D. W. (2001). Comparison of infant feeding patterns reported for nonindustrial populations with current recommendations. *Journal of Nutrition, 131,* 2707–2715.
Semba, R. D., and Bloem, M. W. (Eds.). (2001). *Nutrition and health in developing countries.* Totawa, NJ: Humana Press.
Shore, B. (1996). *Culture in mind: Cognition, culture, and the problem of meaning.* New York: Oxford University Press.
Small, M. F. (1998). *Our babies, ourselves: How biology and culture shape the way we parent.* New York: Anchor.
Sniderman, A. D., Bhopal, R., Prabhakaran, D., Sarrafzadegan, N., and Tchernof, A. (2007). Why might South Asians be so susceptible to central obesity and its atherogenic consequences? The adipose tissue overflow hypothesis. *International Journal of Epidemiology, 36,* 220–225.
Spiegel, K., Knutson, K., Leproult, R., Tasali, E., and Van Cauter, E. (2005). Sleep loss: A novel risk factor for insulin resistance and type 2 diabetes. *Journal of Applied Physiology, 99,* 2008–2019.
Stallings, J. F., Worthman, C. M., Panter-Brick, C., and Coates, R. J. (1996). Prolactin response to suckling and maintenance of postpartum amenorrhea among intensively breastfeeding Nepali women. *Endocrine Research, 22,* 1–28.

Stein, A. D., Barnhart, H. X., Wang, M., Hoshen, M. B., Ologoudou, K., Ramakrishnan, U., et al. (2004). Comparison of linear growth patterns in the first three years of life across two generations in Guatemala. *Pediatrics, 113*, 270–275.

Stein, A. D., Zybert, P. A., van der Pal-de Bruin, K., and Lumey, L. H. (2006). Exposure to famine during gestation, size at birth, and blood pressure at age 59 y: Evidence from the Dutch Famine. *European Journal of Epidemiology, 21*, 759–765.

Stolnitz, G. J. (1965). Recent mortality trends in Latin America, Asia and Africa: Review and reinterpretation. *Population Studies, 19*, 117–138.

Streefland, P., Chowdhury, A. M., and Ramos-Jimenez, P. (1999). Patterns of vaccination acceptance. *Social Science and Medicine, 49*, 1705–1716.

Super, C. M., and Harkness, S. (2002). Culture structures the environment for development. *Human Development, 45*, 270–274.

Ulijaszek, S., Johnston, F. E., and Preece, M. A. (Eds.). (1998). *The Cambridge Encyclopedia of Human Growth and Development*. Cambridge, U.K.: Cambridge University Press.

United Nations Children's Fund. (2006). *The state of the world's children report 2006. Excluded and invisible.* New York: United Nations Children's Fund.

United Nations Children's Fund. (2007). *The state of the world's children 2007. Women and children: The double dividend of gender equality.* New York: United Nations Children's Fund.

Valsinger, J. (1997). *Culture and the development of children's action: A theory of human development* (2nd ed.). New York: Wiley.

Walker, S. P., Wachs, T. D., Meeks Gardner, J., Lozoff, B., Wasserman, G. A., Pollitt, E., et al. (2007). Child development: Risk factors for adverse outcomes in developing countries. *The Lancet, 369*, 145–157.

Weisner, T. S. (1998). Human development, child well-being, and the cultural project of development. *New Directions for Child Development, 81*, 69–85.

Wilkinson, R. G. (1996). *Unhealthy societies: The afflictions of inequality*. London: Routledge.

World Bank. (1993). *World development report 1993: Investing in health*. New York: Oxford University Press.

World Bank. (2004). *World development indicators 2004*. Washington, DC: World Bank.

World Health Organization. (1995). *Physical status: The use and interpretation of anthropometry*. Geneva, Switzerland: World Health Organization.

World Health Organization. (1996). *World health report: Fighting disease, fostering development*. Geneva, Switzerland: World Health Organization.

World Health Organization. (1998). *Obesity. Preventing and managing the global epidemic* (No. WHO/NUT/NCD/981). Geneva, Switzerland: World Health Organization.

World Health Organization. (2005). *World health report 2005: Make every mother and child count*. Geneva, Switzerland: World Health Organization.

World Health Organization. (2006a). *Preventing child maltreatment: A guide to taking action and generating evidence*. Geneva, Switzerland: World Health Organization.

World Health Organization. (2006b). *WHO child growth standards*. Geneva, Switzerland: World Health Organization.

World Health Organization Multicentre Growth Reference Study Group. (2006). Assessment of differences in linear growth among populations in the WHO Multicentre Growth Reference Study. *Acta Paediatrica Supplement, 450*, 56–65.

Worthman, C. M. (1996). Biosocial determinants of sex ratios: Survivorship, selection, and socialization in the early environment. In C. J. K. Henry and S. J. Ulijaszek (Eds.), *Long-term consequences of early environment* (pp. 44–68). Cambridge, United Kingdom: Cambridge University Press.

Worthman, C. M. (1999a). Evolutionary perspectives on the onset of puberty. In W. R. Trevathan, E. O. Smith, and J. J. McKenna (Eds.), *Evolutionary medicine*. New York: Oxford University Press.

Worthman, C. M. (1999b). The epidemiology of human development. In C. Panter-Brick and C. M. Worthman (Eds.), *Hormones, health, and behavior: A socio-ecological and lifespan perspective* (pp. 47–104). Cambridge, United Kingdom: Cambridge University Press.

Worthman, C. M., Jenkins, C. L., Stallings, J. F., and Lai, D. (1994). Attenuation of nursing-related ovarian suppression and high fertility in well-nourished, intensively breast-feeding Amele women of lowland Papua New Guinea. *Journal of Biosocial Science, 25*, 425–443.

Worthman, C. M., and Kohrt, B. (2005). Receding horizons of health: Biocultural approaches to public health paradoxes. *Social Science and Medicine, 30*, 698–714.

Worthman, C. M., and Kuzara, J. L. (2005). Life history and the early origins of health differentials. *American Journal of Human Biology, 17*, 95–12.

Zimmet, P., Alberti, K. G. M. M., and Shaw, J. (2001). Global and societal implications of the diabetes epidemic. *Nature, 414*, 782–787.

4
Motor Skill

KAREN E. ADOLPH, LANA B. KARASIK, and CATHERINE S. TAMIS-LEMONDA

Introduction

Frequently, science writers and journalists for parenting magazines and television specials ask us for expert advice about infant motor development. At what age should children master a particular motor skill? What can parents do to promote skill acquisition? What patterns of development should give parents cause to worry? One aim of this chapter is to show how cross-cultural research provides new insights into such questions about normative development. Cross-cultural research illustrates the range in the human condition and the plasticity of developmental processes in ways that laboratory studies with human children cannot. A second aim is to address assumptions inherent in these types of questions—whether there is such a thing as a sequence of motor skills that children attain at particular ages and whether childrearing practices and other contextual factors can alter the course of motor development. More generally, this chapter describes what cross-cultural research tells us about motor development. With a few notable exceptions (Bril, 1986b; Dennis, 1960; Hopkins, 1976), cross-cultural and laboratory research programs on motor development have been undertaken by different investigators, fueled by different questions, and informed by different research traditions. Thus, these two distinct literatures have arisen with little overlap or connection.

The chapter begins with a brief history of developmental norms and the use of normative data for understanding cultural differences. The next section outlines central issues in cross-cultural research on motor development, setting the stage for bringing research out of the laboratory and into the field. The following sections provide evidence that childrearing practices and contextual factors have a powerful influence on motor development. We show that the timing of motor milestones, the shape of the developmental trajectory, the forms of children's movements, and some of the skills that children acquire depend on cultural context.

Although fascinating group comparisons could be drawn from populations living around the globe, most cross-cultural studies of motor development involve comparisons between American or Western European children and African or Asian children. Figure 4.1 shows the locations of 106 studies, representative of the literature. Researchers have gathered little data about the effects of extreme climates and physical conditions on motor development, and little is known about the acquisition of motor skills that seem rarified in our culture (e.g., using dangerous implements, climbing, swimming, and pounding) but are commonplace in others.

The Science of Comparing Children

The science of *describing* motor development began more than 100 years ago with parent diaries (e.g., Preyer, 1890) and questionnaires (e.g., Trettien, 1900). Inspired by Darwin's natural

62 • Handbook of Cultural Developmental Science

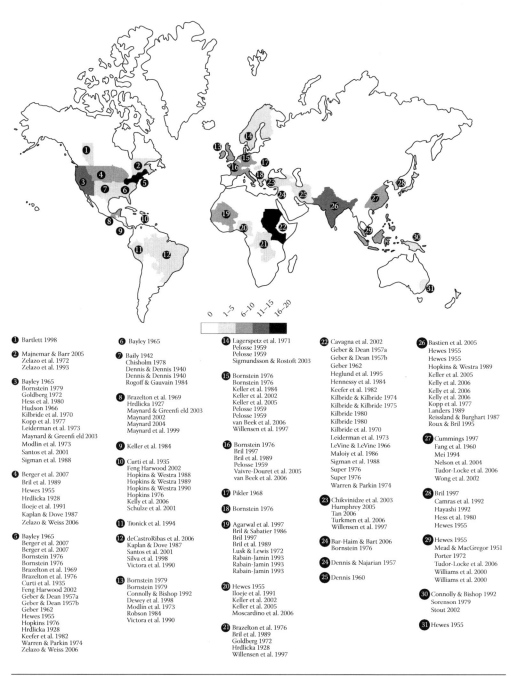

Figure 4.1. World map showing location of cross-cultural research on motor development. Darker regions denote a higher concentration of studies; unshaded regions denote geographical areas that are not represented in the literature. Combining adjacent regions results in a higher concentration of studies (e.g., Western Europe includes three regions that are represented separately), and separating adjacent regions results in a lower concentration of studies (e.g., Georgia, Israel, Lebanon, and Turkey are represented as one Middle Eastern region). Studies that described specific locations within countries (cities, states, and counties) allowed us to make subdivisions within countries for greater detail (e.g., United States, China). Studies that involved multiple sites are listed multiple times under the respective regions in the legend. Most studies focused on infants and children; however, a few instances of cross-cultural research with adults were included (e.g., Turkish adult crawlers). All studies on motor development conducted outside the United States that turned up in the literature search were included. Laboratory training studies conducted outside the United States were included. Normative studies were not included unless they involved geographical comparisons within the United States or children living outside the United States.

science descriptions, researchers focused on both the remarkable intraindividual and interindividual variability among children in motor behaviors. Trettien (1900), for example, reported a dozen forms of locomotion prior to walking in middle-class American children, including "bear crawling" on hands and feet, hitching in a sitting position, log-rolling, and cruising.

The Popularization of Developmental Norms

Inspired by the publication of Binet's intelligence scales, the science of comparing children's motor development also began more than 100 years ago. In standardizing the course of motor development, researchers focused on the typical child (who is, of course, no child), rather than on within-individual variability and individual differences. The idea of age-appropriate activities as an index of intrinsic biological functioning is the received legacy of early work on motor skill acquisition. Ages and stages so thoroughly pervade our conception of motor development that every pediatrician's office and developmental textbook sports a requisite table of developmental norms (Figure 4.2).

No one did more to popularize the use of developmental norms than Gesell (Thelen and Adolph, 1992), who reported a list of motor accomplishments for each month of life and provided a minutely detailed sequence of stages for each skill. Each accomplishment was vividly illustrated with photographs and line drawings traced from film records, with an infant centered on a white page, divorced from the surrounding physical and social context. Gesell's (1928) scales of motor development completed the reification of infants' motor development, transforming descriptive data (what is displayed) to prescriptive data (what is desirable). The scales depicted infants as progressing lock step through a series of requisite motor milestones. Despite the small size and homogeneous composition of Gesell's original sample (51 infants from middle-class families of Northern European extraction living in New Haven, Connecticut) and the fact that the items on his scales were derived from the mother–child interactions of this select

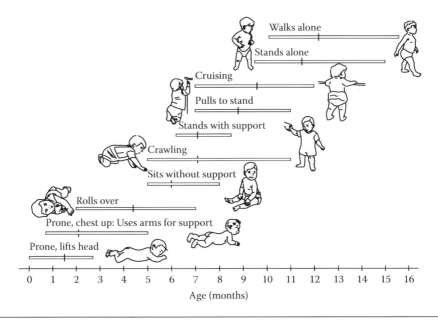

Figure 4.2. Typical normative depiction of infant motor milestones. The illustrations reflect an age-related sequence of several postural and locomotor skills acquired over the first 2 years of life. Vertical lines represent average ages of attainment; bars represent the normative range. Data drawn from Bayley (1969) and Frankenburg et al. (1992). (Adapted from Santrock, J. *Life-Span Development,* 10th ed., McGraw-Hill, New York, 2006. With permission.)

group, the tasks that comprised Gesell's scales of development provided the inspiration for the Bayley (1935, 1969, 1993, 2006) and Denver (Frankenburg and Dodds, 1967; Frankenburg et al., 1992) developmental scales, which continue to guide expectations for children's motor development.

After the appearance of the Gesell and Bayley scales, age-related stages of motor development became established as scientific fact, and the "normal" sequence of skills was limited largely to those behaviors first identified as important by Gesell. Like stages proposed for cognitive, social, and personality development, stages in motor development imply a universal sequence of skills, meaning that all children display all the skills in the sequence; skills in the sequence cannot be skipped; and earlier appearing skills cannot occur concurrently or after later appearing skills. Moreover, the developmental timing of skills was a central feature of these normative templates—group averages came to guide assumptions about the ages when children ought to acquire each skill in the sequence.

Cross-Cultural Comparisons

Gesell's work inspired social anthropologists (Mead and Macgregor, 1951) to document motor development with series of photographs ordered by children's age and to compare milestone ages and developmental quotients of children growing up in exotic locales relative to Western age norms (e.g., Curti, Marshall, and Steggerda, 1935). Indeed, among social anthropologists, psychologists, and clinicians, cross-cultural comparisons of age norms and the standardization of popular developmental scales continue to be the most prevalent form of cross-cultural research on motor development (e.g., Brazelton, Robey, and Collier, 1969; Santos, Gabbard, and Goncalves, 2001).

An influential series of articles by Geber and colleagues (Gerber 1958, 1962; Geber and Dean, 1957a, 1957b) concentrated researchers' attention on normative comparisons with children in Africa. On Geber's account, motor skills of infants in Uganda were remarkably advanced relative to Gesell's norms; Ugandan newborns maintained excellent head control and fully extended their limbs, but American newborns' heads lolled, and limbs were flexed. Ugandan infants sat independently at 4 months, stood upright at 7 months, walked well at 10 months, and ran at 14 months. In contrast, as illustrated in Figure 4.2, on the Bayley and Denver scales, American infants sit at 6 months, stand at 11 months, walk at 11.7 to 12.5 months, and run at 18 months. Dozens of studies replicated the findings of accelerated onset dates in African infants (e.g., Iloeje, Obiekwe, and Kaine, 1991; Kilbride, Robbins, and Kilbride, 1970; Leiderman, Babu, Kagia, Kraemer, and Leiderman, 1973; see Werner, 1972, for review), and similar patterns of accelerated onset dates for sitting, standing, and walking were found in infants of African descent from Jamaica (Hopkins and Westra, 1989, 1990) and other locations, including the United States (Bayley, 1965; Capute, Shapiro, Palmer, Ross, and Wachtel, 1985).

Given the racial implications of so-called African infant precocity, these findings were highly controversial. Methodological flaws shared by many studies led some researchers to doubt whether there was, in fact, a phenomenon to be explained (Warren, 1972). Geber's claims about the newborns were especially contentious because these data were potentially the strongest evidence for explanations based on genetic differences. Although supported by photographs showing newborns' remarkable head control and so on, the data were qualitative. Later studies using Brazelton's (1973) Neonatal Assessment Scales (normed with American newborns) showed mixed results. Zambian newborns initially lagged behind Western norms (Brazelton, Koslowski, and Tronick, 1976); Ugandan and European newborns showed no important group differences (Warren and Parkin, 1974); but Kenyan newborns displayed such qualitative differences in muscle tone that new items had to be added to the Brazelton scale to describe their behavior adequately (Keefer, Tronick, Dixon, and Brazelton, 1982).

Always lurking at the edges of the controversy surrounding African infant precocity was the nature versus nurture debate. Differences in motor development between African and European American/Western European infants were accompanied by possible genetic differences (skin pigmentation and lineage standing in for genetic assays) and striking differences in childrearing practices and other contextual factors. However, several lines of evidence support the view that cultural differences play a causal role in findings of accelerated development: Only the skills that were encouraged by the cultural context showed acceleration (e.g., Kilbride, 1980; Super, 1976); the precocity lasted only as long as the special physical and social stimulation (Geber and Dean, 1957a); and the African advantage was lost when children were reared in a more modern, Western way (e.g., Hopkins and Westra, 1988, 1990).

Central Issues in Motor Development

The case of the African infants raises three important issues in a cross-cultural approach to motor development. First, cross-cultural comparisons can serve as natural—albeit typically confounded—experiments about the effects of context on motor development. At issue is the extent to which the natural experiments provided by cultural differences are informative about motor development. The repeated finding of acceleration in African infants living in poverty with poor nutrition, sanitation, and medical care compared with more privileged Western infants begs for increased understanding about the complex factors that influence motor development. Second, cross-cultural research raises the question of universals in motor development: What, if anything, is common across cultures with different childrearing practices and physical and social contexts? Third, what are the most informative dependent measures in cross-cultural comparisons? In the case of the African infants, researchers focused on the timing of various milestones, but age at onset is only one of many possible outcome measures.

Natural Experiments

For many researchers, the natural experiment is the quintessence of cross-cultural research (Brazelton et al., 1969; Harkness, 1992; Kilbride, 1980; Super, 1976). Optimally, the comparison would involve groups that differ only on some critical factor that can be treated as the independent variable. Most frequently, however, the variable of interest does not occur in isolation but is accompanied by a host of other factors that confound clear interpretation. Typically, confounds in cross-cultural research are forgiven because the critical factor involves conditions that are not easily amenable to experimental manipulation for ethical or practical reasons. An irony in research on motor development is that laboratory researchers—beginning with the early pioneers in the 1930s—actually conducted controlled experiments with human infants showing that social and physical enrichment accelerates the timing of motor milestones and that deprivation delays onset dates (described in the following sections). Nonetheless, the natural experiments of cross-cultural and intracultural comparisons, especially in studies of deprivation, call researchers' attention to the immense cascade of interacting factors that may influence motor development, including climate, housing, terrain, man-made artifacts, parents' expectations and naïve theories, and particular childrearing practices.

A particularly nice example of a natural experiment is the question of handedness. Right handedness is nearly universal in cultures that emphasize writing and manual control of tools. Some cultures enforce right handedness with verbal admonitions or by tying down children's left hand (Bailey, 1942). Would children show a stronger preference for their right hand if they were reared in a culture with no formal schooling, no writing implements, limited use of manual tools, and no social pressures toward handedness? Children in Papua New Guinea had exactly this background and were compared with children growing up in England (Connolly and Bishop, 1992). Despite lack of social pressures to use their right hand,

Papuan children showed stronger right hand preferences for using novel tools such as pencils and scissors.

Universals

Historically, researchers have assumed universals in motor development. The notion of universal stages requires that infants cannot skip a stage and stages cannot occur concurrently or in different orders. The instructions for administration of the Bayley scale (Bayley, 2006) highlight the pervasive assumption of an invariant motor sequence. Children's scores on the Bayley scale are determined by failures on three consecutive skills in the sequence, despite the possibility that infants might succeed on a later appearing skill or fail on an earlier appearing skill.

However, invariant sequence is a misconception of motor development. After the first flush of studies instigated by Geber's reports, researchers found surprising deviations in the presumed sequence. Many African infants did not crawl, and infants who did crawl did so at later ages (e.g., Kilbride, 1980; Super, 1976). In Jamaica, for example, 29% of infants skipped crawling, and the remaining infants began crawling at the same age as they began walking—10.1 months and 10.0 months for crawling and walking, respectively (Hopkins and Westra, 1989, 1990). The surprise is that crawling—a skill featured on the Gesell and Bayley scales as a major milestone en route to walking—could be entirely missing from the repertoire of healthy infants or misplaced in the normative sequence. Indeed, up to 17% of British infants skipped crawling (10% hitched in a sitting position, and 7% simply stood up and walk), providing further evidence that crawling is not an obligatory milestone (Robson, 1984). One hundred years ago, 40% of American infants skipped crawling (Trettien, 1900). Instead, they hitched, crabbed on their backs, or log-rolled, perhaps to avoid catching their knees and feet at the edge of their long gowns. Moreover, modern American infants display skills such as rolling, sitting, crawling, cruising, walking, and stair ascent and descent in a staggering variety of orders, rather than in the invariant sequence suggested by ordering average onset ages in normative data (Berger, Theuring, and Adolph, 2007).

Deviations from a presumably invariant sequence are surprising because developmental norms, like all empirical data, reflect both the proclivities of the researcher and the propensities of the sample that contributed the data. Other skills arguably could have been included on the scales, and some of researchers' top picks could have been excluded. Cruising, for example, when infants walk sideways holding onto furniture for support, was not added to the Bayley scale until 1993. Crawling on hands and knees is not included on the 1992 Denver Developmental Screening Test. None of the major scales include crawling on the belly, crawling on hands and feet, and hitching on the buttocks, although both earlier researchers (e.g., Gesell, 1946; Trettien, 1900) and later researchers (e.g., Adolph, Vereijken, and Denny, 1998; Freedland and Bertenthal, 1994) observed these behaviors.

Part of the surprise surrounding the absence of crawling in substantial proportions of infants is also a result of the long-standing prejudice of laboratory researchers to assume biologically based, culture-free universals in development (Super and Harkness, 1986). Gesell's images of a lonely child isolated on the otherwise blank page reflect psychologists' search for the culture-free child. Images of children dressed in exotic costumes surrounded by other people in exotic clothing fit into a very different sort of framework; in the social anthropology research tradition, the appropriate object of study is not the solitary child, but the socially supported child in a particular cultural context. According to this alternative view, a single exception—Mead's (1928) demonstration that adolescence in Bali is not traumatic or the fact that some African infants do not crawl—can disprove assumed universals in development (Harkness, 1992). Moreover, universals do not need to be culture free. Despite dramatic differences in childrearing, climate, and so on, healthy children in every culture acquire basic motor functions such as reaching, sitting, and walking. Equifinality—different means to common outcomes—must reflect, at least in part, the fact that every culture places a premium on manual, postural, and locomotor skills that are foundational to human survival.

Dependent Measures

A final issue concerns the question of what develops and how—that is, what are the appropriate dependent measures in cross-cultural research on motor development? As strikingly illustrated by the case of African infant precocity, one measure that changes is the timing of motor milestones. However, it is only a historical accident that cross-cultural research on motor development is dominated by normative comparisons of onset ages. The same is not true in laboratory research. After Gesell's itemized stages and Bayley's refined developmental scales, there seemed little else to do in terms of normative descriptions. Instead, inspired by Shirley's (1931) and McGraw's (1935) pioneering microgenetic studies, laboratory research on motor development has always emphasized the processes of change, using detailed longitudinal designs with heroically dense observation schedules to chart developmental trajectories and a multitude of motion recording devices to describe the changing form of movements in real time (for reviews, see Adolph and Berger, 2005, 2006; Bertenthal and Clifton, 1998).

Onset Ages

Researchers have long debated the effects of experience on the timing of motor milestones, but parents in many cultures believe that childrearing practices can affect onset ages, just as they believe that parenting affects when children become toilet trained and use tools such as eating utensils. In modern, Western society, formal training to stimulate motor development often takes place outside the home (e.g., in swim and gym classes). In other cultures, formal training to promote motor skills (e.g., massage) is integral to daily childrearing routines.

Informal handling practices—how infants are held, carried, bathed, dressed, fed, placed for sleep, and so on—affect the timing of motor milestones by providing varying amounts of stimulation and opportunities for spontaneous movement. American parents hold a newborn like a fragile carton of eggs, with the head always supported against gravity. As illustrated in Figure 4.3A, Americans bathe newborns by dabbing them with a damp cloth as they lie supine on a dry blanket and gently pat them dry (Shelov and Hannemann, 1998). In Mali, caregivers lift a young infant by gripping the baby under an armpit with one hand, as shown in Figure 4.3B (Bril and Sabatier, 1986). They bathe infants propped in a sitting position in a bowl of water, scrub them vigorously with rough sponges, and shake them dry (Bril, 1988). In general, cultural factors that augment practice and enrich or intensify stimulation can accelerate developmental timing; contextual factors that restrict practice and reduce stimulation can delay onset ages.

Augmented Practice Accelerates Onset Ages

In many cultures in Africa, the Caribbean, and India, formal massage and stretching accompany infants' daily baths. Infants' limbs are passively limbered and extended, their skin is rubbed and plied with special oils, and their bodies are suspended, shaken, and tossed (Figure 4.4A–F). The mother or grandmother brings the infant's foot to the forehead, crosses the infant's arms behind the baby's back (Bril and Sabatier, 1986; Rabain-Jamin and Wornham, 1993), and crosses all four limbs over each other until the baby is folded into a little ball (Reissland and Burghart, 1987). Massage includes pulling the limbs, fingers, feet, and penis (Rabain-Jamin and Wornham, 1993); cosmetic molding of the head and face (Hopkins, 1976); and thumping the back, buttocks, and joints until they "crack" (Hopkins and Westra, 1988). The mother tosses the infant into the air and shakes and swings the infant while holding the baby under the arms, around the head, or upside down by the ankles (Bril and Sabatier, 1986; Rabain-Jamin and Wornham, 1993). The bathing routine typically ends with swaddling to calm infants. The order of massage,

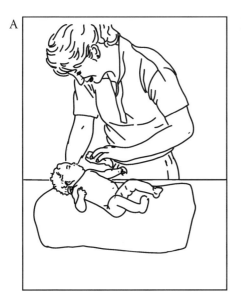 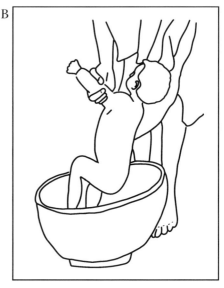

Figure 4.3. Typical manner of bathing a young infant in (A) middle-class Western societies and (B) the Bambara society in Mali. ([A] adapted from Shelov, S. P., and Hannemann, R. E., *Caring for your baby and young child,* Bantam, New York, 1998. With permission from Random House, Inc.; [B] adapted from Bril, B., *Bain et gymnastique neonatale: Enfants Bambara du Mali* [Motion Picture], Centre d'Etude des Processus Cognitifs et du Langage Ecole des Hautes Etudes en Sciences Socieles, France, 1988. With permission from B. Bril.)

stretching, and suspension events can be highly ritualized (Reissland and Burghart, 1987), but mothers adjust the vigor and frequency of their ministrations as infants acquire more postural control (Bril and Sabatier, 1986).

Among African and Caribbean cultures, childcare routines include formal exercises to stimulate development of particular skills. To facilitate sitting, mothers hold newborns on their laps and support them around the waist (Kilbride and Kilbride, 1975; Kilbride, 1980). When infants are 3 months of age, mothers sit them on the floor, supported by a hole in the ground (Figure 4.4G), a mound of sand, or a basin with cloth wrapped around the hips, or are propped with a cushion (Ainsworth, 1967; Konner, 1977; Super, 1976). To facilitate walking (Figure 4.4H–I), mothers stand children in their laps and bounce them vigorously in a routine the Kenyan Kipsigis call "kitwalse," meaning "to make jump" (Super, 1976). The child responds with stepping movements, sometimes "walking" up the adult's body (Hopkins, 1976). When children can support their own weight, mothers prop them against stools (Bril, 1986b), hold their hands, and encourage them to take steps (Hopkins, 1976). Novice walkers are lured with bits of food (Konner, 1977). Jamaican children who had not begun walking by 1 year are taken to the beach and buried up to the knees in sand, where the sight of the incoming waves soon develops the urge to walk (Hopkins and Westra, 1988). In Bali, parents set up a bamboo rail for children to hold as they practice taking independent walking steps (Mead and Macgregor, 1951).

In addition to formal training, informal handling also facilitates the development of reaching, sitting, crawling, and walking by holding or placing children in positions that give them opportunities to practice manual, prone, and upright skills. French infants, for example, spend 50% to 60% of their day lying down (Bril, 1997). In contrast, infants in Uganda, Botswana, and Mali spend 40% to 90% of their day in sitting or standing positions (Ainsworth, 1967; Bril and Sabatier, 1986; Konner, 1977; Super, 1976).

Figure 4.4. Formal routines practiced in Africa, India, and the Caribbean that are used to facilitate infants' motor development: (A–C) massage and cosmetic molding of infants' head and face; (D–F) suspension and shaking by ankles, arms, and head; (G) practice of sitting position; and (H–I) practice of upright stepping movements. (Images for Figure 4.4A–F and 4.4H–I redrawn from Hopkins, B., and Westra, T., *Genetic, Social and General Psychology Monographs, 114,* 379–408, 1988. With permission of the Helen Dwight Reid Educational Foundation. Published by Heldref Publications, 1319 Eighteenth St., NW, Washington, DC 20036-1802. Copyright © 1988.)

Riding in a sling on the hip or back of an active adult provides vestibular, visual, and proprioceptive stimulation. A typical woman in Mali bends down 1.5 times per minute to prepare food or tend to the fire (Bril, 1986b). Carrying also facilitates the development of muscle strength and coordination because infants must continually adjust their posture to the movements of the caregiver (Bril and Sabatier, 1986). Being carried in a sling can confer additional advantages for manual exploration. !Kung mothers of Botswana, for example, wear decorative objects and beads around their necks. Infants grasp onto these beads to stabilize their mouth on the breast while feeding, and they swipe, grasp, and manipulate the beads and dangling objects throughout the day, like American infants would play with a mobile or crib toy (Konner, 1972).

Does all the rubbing, stretching, shaking, and carrying make a difference? Natural experiments provided by cross-cultural and intracultural comparisons demonstrate the powerful effects of childrearing practices. The !Kung, for example, show acceleration in prehension skills, presumably as a consequence of continual access to manipulanda and the demands of grasping a support to breastfeed on demand (Konner, 1977). The evidence is especially strong for facilitation provided by formal training, which shows a dose–response relation with onset age, and facilitative effects are limited to the skills that receive special practice (Hopkins and Westra, 1988, 1990; Rabain-Jamin and Wornham, 1993; Super, 1976).

One way to control for extraneous factors in a natural, cross-cultural experiment is to hold constant the geographical region while comparing effects of different cultures. For example, East African groups vary in whether they promote crawling. Teso mothers of Uganda teach infants to crawl, and infants' average age at the onset of crawling is 5.5 months. Kipsigis mothers of Kenya do not give infants opportunities to crawl, and their onset age is delayed (Super, 1976). The correlation between the percentage of mothers who teach infants to crawl and the average age of crawling onset is .77 and increases to .97 if opportunities to practice crawling are factored in (Super, 1976).

Immigration provides a second method to control for extraneous factors in a natural and, in this case, intracultural experiment. Some immigrants continue to practice the childrearing routines of their home culture, but others assimilate into the new culture by adopting new childrearing routines. Some Jamaican mothers, for instance, continue to practice massage and formal exercise of sitting and walking after immigrating to England, but others do not (Hopkins, 1976). Infants who receive formal training exhibit better head control at 1 month of age, and they sit and walk at earlier ages compared with infants whose mothers do not exercise these skills. The trained Jamaican infants also are accelerated compared with English infants (Hopkins and Westra, 1988, 1990); frequency of formal exercise predicted the ages at which infants sat and walked. Finally, facilitative effects are limited to sitting and upright skills (no group differences in crawling onset age), indicating that precocity is specific to the skills that are practiced.

Actual experiments with random assignment to training and control groups confirm the facilitative effects of exercise and handling. Like the formal training routines in African and Caribbean cultures, experiments showed that a few minutes of stimulation per day distributed over a few weeks is sufficient to accelerate the timing of motor skills. Four weeks of vestibular stimulation (20 biweekly spins in an office chair) resulted in higher scores for infants on the Denver Developmental Screening Test compared with infants who were not spun (Clark, Kreutzberg, and Chee, 1977). Eight weeks of passive exercise (20 minutes of daily leg pumping) resulted in higher scores on the Gesell scale compared with controls who did not receive exercise (Porter, 1972). Three weeks of training in crawling (moving infants' limbs in a crawling position for 30 to 45 minutes per day) resulted in higher scores on the Bayley scale and more advanced crawling skills compared with infants who were handled but not trained in crawling (Lagerspetz, Nygard, and Strandvik, 1971). Eight weeks of training in upright stepping (12 minutes per day) resulted in more stepping movements, retention of the stepping pattern for longer periods, and earlier onset of walking compared with infants who were passively exercised or did not receive exercise (Zelazo, Zelazo, and Kolb, 1972b). The experimenter's own son, Philip, was exercised beyond the 8-week cut-off, and he began walking at 7.5 months (Zelazo, Zelazo, and Kolb, 1972a). Experimental evidence also indicates that training effects are specific to the skills receiving practice, rather than generalized precocity as the result of training (Zelazo, Zelazo, Cohen, and Zelazo, 1993).

Indeed, with the appropriate environmental supports and social encouragements, children can be trained to perform an amazing array of activities. In McGraw's (McGraw, 1935) classic co-twin study, the trained twin learned to swim underwater at 9.5 months, dive headfirst into a pool at 13.8 months, roller skate at 12.3 months, and climb 70-degree inclines at 21.4 months. Similarly, 4 months of training facilitated swimming behaviors in 12- to 16-month-old infants compared with untrained controls (Zelazo and Weiss, 2006).

Restricted Practice Delays Onset Ages

Since the 1930s, researchers have reported dramatic delays in the motor development of orphan children reared under impoverished conditions (e.g., Skodak and Skeels, 1949; Spitz, 1945). Dennis and Najarian (1957), for example, described neonates in a Lebanese orphanage swaddled tightly in their cribs, deprived of visual stimulation as a result of heavy drapes between cribs, fed with a bottle propped on a pillow, and handled by caregivers only for brief diaper changes; older infants had nowhere to locomote and little access to toys. Between 3 and 12 months of age, the average developmental score for the orphans was 63 on the Cattell Scale; the average American infant scored 101. Under similar rearing conditions in an Iranian orphanage, only 15% of the orphans could walk by 3 years of age (Dennis, 1960).

In a shocking series of reports, Dennis (1935, 1941) deliberately replicated the orphanage conditions with two infant girls under controlled conditions. By withholding stimulation and practice of particular skills (e.g., grasping, sitting, and standing) until after the expected onset date, he showed that initially healthy infants' development could be delayed by 2 to 10 months beyond the normal range. The girls reached and grasped a dangling ring at 8.0 months, sat unsupported at 9.8 and 10.7 months, stood without balancing at 12.0 months, raised to sitting at 12.7 and 13.9 months, and walked at 17 and 26 months.

Like the orphanages and Dennis's deprivation experiment, cultural practices that severely limit spontaneous movement can delay the onset of motor milestones. The widespread use of sandbags in Northern China provides a dramatic example (Mei, 1994). For the first 12 to 24 months of life, infants spend more than 16 hours per day lying supine inside a small sleeping bag filled with fine sand (parents use sandbags instead of diapers to preserve their scarce supply of water). Only infants' arm movements are unrestricted. Consequently, sandbag-reared infants show significant delays in sitting and walking compared with infants from the same region whose movements were unrestricted because their parents use diapers instead of sandbags.

Even mild restriction of infants' spontaneous movements can delay the onset of motor milestones. Japanese infants show delays for rolling and crawling if they are dressed in heavy, restrictive clothing or if their bed coverings include heavy winter blankets (Hayashi, 1992). Similarly, infants growing up in Denver, Colorado, are adversely affected by restrictions that accompany cold weather. Crawling was delayed by 3 weeks for infants who were born in the summer and came of crawling age in the winter compared with infants who were born in the winter and came of crawling age in the summer (Bensen, 1993). In addition to restrictive clothing that weighs down their limbs, fewer daylight hours during the winter months, lower average outdoor temperatures, and less access to outdoors may curtail children's spontaneous motor activity and thereby delay the onset of motor milestones.

In some cultures, caregivers deliberately restrict children's movements to ensure their safety (Ishak, Tamis-LeMonda, and Adolph, 2007). For example, caregivers in some societies discourage independent mobility for fear that young children will encounter dangers. The Gusii of Kenya have a cryptically worded proverb, "Lameness is up," meaning that when children get big enough to walk by themselves (somewhere between 1 and 2 years of age), they will be confronted with physical dangers and may be injured so badly as to become lame (LeVine and LeVine, 1966). The fears are realistic because Gusii who are learning to walk sometimes stumble into the fire and are burned. The Ache, a foraging society of Eastern Paraguay, travel for extended trips through uncleared, dangerous forests. For fear that children will "get into trouble" in the forest, mothers rarely put their infants down or let them venture more than a meter away (Kaplan and Dove, 1987). Locomotor development is severely delayed in the Ache; they begin walking between 23 and 25 months. Scores on the Denver Developmental Screening Test lag 2.3 months behind Western norms at 1 year of age and 17 months behind Western norms at 3 to 4 years of age (Kaplan and Dove, 1987). By age 5, however, Ache children begin to spend time away from their mothers, and by 8 to 10 years of age, they surpass American children by climbing 7.6-meter high trees, chopping branches with machetes, and using sharp knives.

In American households, parents impose safety restrictions on mobility by initially limiting children's access to stairs and later teaching infants to use stairs safely (Berger et al., 2007). Parents use safety gates on indoor stairs and carry their infants into homes with outside stairs. Childrearing practices interact with home characteristics. Infants with stairs in their home ascend stairs at a younger age than children without stairs in their home. Because stairs are alluring but potentially dangerous, home-stair parents are more likely to teach their infants to descend stairs. Because safety is paramount, the teaching involves explicit hands-on instruction; 76% of parents physically move infants' limbs from riser to riser, and 85% use verbal instructions. In contrast, no parent moves infants' legs back and forth to teach them to walk or tells them to move the right foot and then the left.

In some cultures, caregivers deliberately restrict practice because of cultural taboos associated with the particular skill. For example, some groups in Africa and the Caribbean consider crawling "hazardous and nonhuman," and discourage infants from crawling (Hopkins and Westra, 1988, 1989). Consequently, crawling is delayed or missing from infants' repertoires. Balinese mothers view crawling on hands and knees to be animal-like (Mead and Macgregor, 1951). Thus, if infants move around on their bellies or crawl a step or two, someone picks them up. Moreover, during the ages when most Western infants begin crawling, Balinese infants are rarely placed on the ground.

Although parents in Western cultures value crawling, caregivers deliberately restrict infants' exposure to the prone position for health-related reasons. Restricted practice was an unforeseen consequence of an institutionalized health initiative. For most of the twentieth century, Western pediatricians recommended that parents put infants to sleep on their stomachs to prevent aspiration of regurgitated milk. In 1992, the American Academy of Pediatrics, responding to research findings linking the prone sleep position with sudden infant death syndrome (SIDS), issued a recommendation that parents should not put infants to sleep on their bellies (Kattwinkel, Brooks, and Myerberg, 1992). In 1994, the Academy launched a "Back to Sleep" campaign to educate the public that belly-sleeping is not safe. Between 1992 and 2004, prone sleeping decreased from 70% to 13% in American infants (Kattwinkel, Hauck, Keenan, Malloy, and Moon, 2005). However, parents also are less likely to place infants on their bellies while awake because they mistakenly link waking prone time with SIDS (Mildred, Beard, Dallwitz, and Unwin, 1995; Salls, Silverman, and Gatty, 2002), and infants tend to fuss in the unfamiliar prone position. In addition, back-sleepers have less incidental exposure to the prone position as they fall asleep and wake up. At 4 months of age, 75% of back-sleepers spend less than 20 minutes per day awake on their bellies, and at 6 months of age, 50% spend less than 20 minutes (Majnemer and Barr, 2005).

Restricted time in a prone position in back-sleepers is linked with later onset ages for crawling and related skills that require use of the upper trunk and arms (Pin, Eldridge, and Galea, 2007). Back-sleepers are more likely to skip belly crawling and to display hitching compared with belly-sleepers (Davis, Moon, Sachs, and Ottolini, 1998). They roll, tripod sit, belly and hands-knees crawl, and pull to stand at later ages (Davis et al., 1998; Dewey, Fleming, Golding, and Team, 1998; Jantz, Blosser, and Fruechting, 1997); 22% of 6-month-olds show gross motor scores below the cut-off used by clinicians to identify motor delay (Majnemer and Barr, 2005).

Simply depriving children of adult postural support and handling also leads to delays. In the belief that children develop best when left alone, orphans reared in the National Methodological Institute for Infant Care and Education in Budapest were dressed in loose, unrestrictive clothing, given space in their cribs and pens in which to move, and provided with age-appropriate toys. However, the institute withheld "teaching" in any form (Pikler, 1968). Infants were always placed on their backs, and caregivers never helped them to roll, sit up, stand, or locomote by handling, placing, encouraging, or any other means. Infants acquired all of these skills but at later ages than expected on Gesell's norms.

Expectations About Onset Ages

Cultural differences in the timing of motor milestones are often accompanied by culture-specific expectations about when children should acquire various milestones. As Hess (1980, p. 260) put it, parents conceptualize infants' motor skill acquisition in terms of a "developmental timetable of expectations against which children's progress is gauged—a private version of Gesell's norms about what is possible and desirable."

The "private" normative timetables of mothers from cultures that use daily formal exercise routines, however, have accelerated expectations for the items receiving special practice (Bril, Zack, and Nkounkou-Hombessa, 1989; Rabain-Jamin and Wornham, 1993). For example, mothers from Jamaica who practiced formal sitting and walking exercises with their 1-month-olds expected their infants to achieve sitting and walking at earlier ages compared with English and Jamaican mothers who did not use formal exercise (Hopkins and Westra, 1989, 1990). Mothers in the exercise group had accelerated expectations only for the skills receiving specific practice, not for crawling. When expected and actual onset dates were compared, the mothers in the exercise group were also more accurate in their expectations for sitting and walking compared with mothers in the no-exercise groups, but they showed no advantage for accuracy regarding the unexercised skill of crawling.

In what direction does the causal arrow point in the link between expected and actual age of attainment? Mothers' expectations could arise as a reflection of the actual ages of attainment in the particular culture. Reciprocally, expectations could feed into childrearing practices and thereby affect the ages at which children in the culture acquire the skills, in a sort of self-fulfilling prophecy (Hopkins and Westra, 1990). The data are consistent with both explanations and likely reflect the bidirectional nature of the child in context.

Mothers hear about the ages of attainment from their own mothers, midwives, pediatricians, and parenting books (Hopkins and Westra, 1989), and they observe the ages at which children in the culture acquire various skills, particularly skills that are important to the culture. Mothers in cultures that use formal exercise routines may be especially attuned to the timing of the trained milestones. Sitting, for example, is critical to Ugandan mothers because it reflects social manners (Kilbride and Kilbride, 1975) and is required for a special naming ceremony (Ainsworth, 1967). Walking is important to Ugandan and Malian mothers because it is linked with the age of weaning and toilet training (Ainsworth, 1967; Bril et al., 1989). German mothers watching videotapes of Cameroonian mothers performing formal exercise routines with their infants remarked only about the unusually rough handling, not infants' level of motor skill (Keller, Yovsi, and Voelker, 2002). In contrast, Cameroonian mothers watching videotapes of German mothers playing with their infants as the infants lay supine in a crib made frequent remarks about the lack of motor handling. They were shocked that the German mothers did not train their infants in sitting and walking skills and worried that the infants would be delayed.

Of course, mothers in cultures that practice formal training may do so precisely because their expectations about onset ages are linked with their naïve theories about motor development and the importance that their culture places on the timing of particular skills. These mothers make special efforts so that their expectations are realized. Jamaican mothers use formal exercise routines because they believe that the routines will help their infants to sit and to walk and will make them grow strong and healthy (Hopkins, 1976; Hopkins and Westra, 1988). They are attuned to their own infant's developmental progress, viewing the exercise and massage routines as an opportunity to assess their infant's health.

Surprising Exceptions

Historically, swaddling—tightly wrapping infants' bodies and extended limbs with cloth bands, blankets, or sheets—is the most common form of culture-imposed restriction on infants' movements (for review, see van Sleuwen et al., 2007). Various forms of swaddling have been used in Asia, the Middle East, North and South America, and Northern Europe (Lipton, Steinscheider, and Richmond, 1965). Swaddling has many virtues. It protects infants against cold and sharp climate transitions (Tronick, Thomas, and Daltabuit, 1994) and against unsafe home environments (Masataka, 1996). It promotes continuous sleep (Lipton et al., 1965), reduces arousal and crying (Giacoman, 1971), and soothes pain (Campos, 1989). When bound against a cradleboard, as practiced by many Native American tribes, infants can be carted from place to place, hung by hooks to maintain proximity to caregivers as they work, and swung to and fro to reduce fussing (Chisholm, 1978; Dennis and Dennis, 1940). On the face of it, swaddling also has the obvious, seemingly negative, effect of limiting infants' movements and postures.

However, swaddling poses a puzzle for understanding the effects of restricted practice on motor onset ages. As reviewed, restrictions that impede spontaneous movement or limit access to various postures are related to delays in motor onset dates. Yet surprisingly, researchers have found no evidence that swaddling against a cradleboard delays motor development; Hopi (Dennis, 1940) and Navaho infants (Chisholm, 1978) reared on cradleboards began walking at the same ages as infants who were not reared on cradleboards. One explanation is that muscle strength was preserved by isometric exercise as infants pressed their limbs against the bindings (Hudson, 1966). An alternative explanation is that deleterious effects of restricted movements on walking were mitigated by increasing time spent unswaddled over the first year. From birth to 3 months, for example, Navaho infants spend 15 to 18 hours per day on the cradleboard; by 9 to 12 months, swaddling time has decreased to 6 to 9 hours per day; and, at every age, 80% to 85% of the time on the cradleboard is spent asleep (Chisholm, 1978). Thus, skills such as sitting and crawling that typically appear in the first 6 to 8 months of life may have been adversely affected but were not reported because the investigators focused on walking. A third possibility is that swaddling as used in the Navaho way simply has no adverse effects on motor development. Perhaps infants have adequate amounts of practice during time off the cradleboard to achieve milestones on the same schedule as unswaddled infants.

Some African mothers proved an exception to the specificity of parents' expectations. Mothers from Mali and Congo showed accelerated expectations for crawling compared with French mothers, despite the fact that the African mothers professed not to value prone skills and did not train crawling (Bril et al., 1989). Nonetheless, accelerated expectations in the African mothers were not generalized beyond the motor domain; African and French mothers showed no differences in expectations for cognitive and language skills.

Developmental Trajectories

The prevailing focus on onset ages in cross-cultural research is unfortunate because it draws attention away from outcome measures that can inform understanding about motor development. In particular, features of a developmental trajectory—the shape and rate of developmental change—provide a record of the resultant processes and clues about the underlying mechanisms. The final endpoint speaks to the plasticity and potential of human motor development.

Shape of the Trajectory

Culturally determined childrearing practices and other accoutrements of culture can affect the trajectory of motor skill acquisition in several ways. The best-studied example, upright stepping, concerns the *qualitative shape* of the developmental function. American infants display upright stepping movements as neonates, but by 2 months of age, stepping disappears. Infants stand rooted to the ground. Steps reappear toward the end of the first year as infants begin walking with parents' support and then independently. Thus, stepping shows a distinctive U-shaped function (McGraw, 1935).

Practice, however, can change the shape of the function by decreasing the dip between 2 and 8 months of age or by maintaining stepping movements intact throughout infants' first year (Zelazo, 1983). Practice effects on the shape of the developmental trajectory were observed in African mothers who exercised their children as part of their formal childcare routines (Super, 1976). Similarly, under controlled conditions, daily practice with Zelazo's (1983) own twin daughters resulted in a linear, rather than U-shaped, function over the first year of life. A few minutes of daily practice with upright stepping caused stepping to increase from birth to walking onset, rather than to disappear for several months, and both girls walked before 9 months of age. Despite African mothers' belief that formal training should begin at particular ages (Bril et al., 1989), Zelazo (1983) found no critical period for practice to be initiated. Practice reinstated stepping even in 10- to 16-week-old infants who had previously stopped stepping. These findings provided new insights into developmental mechanisms by showing that upright stepping movements are only masked in the typical U-shaped function, not suppressed by neural growth.

A second way that culture could influence the trajectory of motor development is by altering the *slope* of a developmental function. For Western infants, the developmental trajectories for crawling and walking, as in most motor learning tasks, show a negatively accelerated performance curve; initial improvements are rapid and dramatic, and later improvements are more gradual and subtle. For walking, improvements are most rapid over the first 3 to 6 months after onset; thereafter, the rate of change slows until the function reaches asymptote after 5 to 7 years of walking (Adolph, Vereijken, and Shrout, 2003; Bril and Ledebt, 1998). The initial phase where the slope of the function is steepest may reflect children's identification of the relevant parameters that control forward progression and balance. The subsequent period where the slope begins to flatten may reflect a process of honing and fine-tuning the values of the parameters to maximize the biomechanical efficiency of walking (Bril and Ledebt, 1998). Possibly, exercise or deprivation, either before or after onset, could accelerate or hinder the rate of the initial improvements and affect the point in the trajectory where the rate of improvements slows. Focus on the slope of the developmental function reveals whether the identification or tuning periods are most open to intervention.

A third way that culture could affect developmental trajectories concerns *periods of intermittent expression* in the initial appearance of new skills. Most American children acquire new motor skills in an intermittent manner (Adolph, Robinson, Young, and Gill-Alvarez, 2008). Skills such as reaching, sitting, crawling, and walking do not suddenly appear, as if turning on a faucet. Instead, skills sputter into children's repertoires early in the developmental trajectory and only stabilize after weeks or months of experience. A child might walk on Monday but not walk again until Thursday, and then not again until the following week, and so on. The African exercises to encourage sitting and upright skills might affect initial appearance by compressing the period of intermittent expression, especially as mothers are likely to adjust their handling practices as they observe children's initial successes. By affecting the variability and abruptness of initial expression, the data could speak to the issue of continuity and discontinuity in motor development.

Endpoint of Development

Another way that culture could affect developmental trajectories concerns the *endpoint* of development. The final level of skill performance could be higher or lower because of the amount and type of practice encouraged by the culture and differences in the climate and environment. For example, cross-cultural research shows that the dynamics of walking and running can be developed to extraordinary degrees in an entire society, like training a culture of Olympians with an endpoint far exceeding that of typical Western pedestrians. In some societies in South America and Asia, whole families, including children, take walking trips on foot of 56 to 64 km, often while carrying loads and in the heat or extreme cold (Devine, 1985). Most notorious is the endurance running of the Tarahumaran Indians in northern Mexico. They run kickball races of 150 to 300 km—more than the distance of six modern marathons—in 24 to 48 hours (Devine, 1985). They run down deer until the creatures fall from exhaustion (about 2 days of constant running).

Women in Western Kenya have developed new gait patterns to carry prodigious loads—up to 70% of their body weight—on their heads in an upright posture or supported by a strap across their foreheads (Figure 4.5). In a feat unmatched by brawny, young, army recruits, the African women can carry head-supported loads of up to 20% of their body weight without increased energetic costs (Heglund, Willems, Penta, and Cavagna, 1995; Maloiy, Heglund, Prager, Cavagna, and Taylor, 1986). Subtle adaptations of their walking gait conserve mechanical energy so that the mechanical work of walking does not increase.

Figure 4.5. Carrying head loads in (A) an upright position and (B) supported by a strap across the forehead. ([A] adapted from Maloiy, G. M. O., Heglund, N. C., Prager, L. M., Cavagna, G. A., and Taylor, C. R., *Nature, 319,* 668–669, 1986. Reprinted by permission from Macmillan Publishers Ltd.; [B] adapted from Bastien, G. J., Schepens, B., Willems, P. A., and Heglund, N.C., *Science, 308,* 1755, 2005. Reprinted with permission from American Association for the Advancement of Science.)

Advanced walking abilities in the African women result from years of practice. Training in load carriage begins in childhood. In Ghana, by 8 years of age, young girls called "kayayoos" begin transporting loads on their heads for fees (Agarwal et al., 1997). In Bali, where women also carry heavy head loads, little girls practice carrying objects on their head when playing (Mead and Macgregor, 1951). The Balinese pay close attention to balance. It is forbidden to place things on the head that may fall.

Endpoints can also stop short of what is expected. Many infants across cultures "bear crawl" on their hands and feet before they learn to walk (e.g., Adolph et al., 1998; Hrdlicka, 1928). Scientists discovered a family living on an isolated farm in Turkey where 5 of 19 living, adult children crawled on their hands and feet *instead* of walking (J. Harrison, personal communication, November 28, 2005; Humphrey, Skoyles, and Keynes, 2005; Tan, 2006; Turkmen et al., 2006). The gait of the adult crawlers was like that of healthy infants in several respects (compare panels A and B in Figure 4.6). They bore weight on their palms and sometimes crawled while carrying objects in their hands or mouths. They displayed both diagonal (near-trot) and ipsilateral gaits (limbs on the same side of body move together). They crawled up and down stairs.

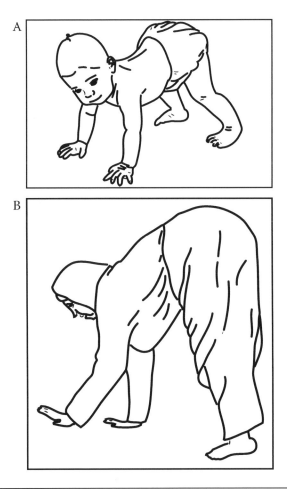

Figure 4.6. Crawling on hands and feet in (A) healthy infant and (B) Turkish adult crawler. ([B] adapted from Humphrey, N., Skoyles, J., and Keynes, R., Human hand-walkers: Five siblings who never stood up. *LSE Research Online*, 2005. Retrieved December 21, 2007, from http://eprints.lse.ac.uk/archive/00000463. With permission from N. Humphrey.)

The male "ran on all fours" quickly and effortlessly as Hrdlicka (1928) described in infants. The females were slower and less graceful, hampered by their long dresses, head scarves, and heavier body builds.

Both the scientific articles and sensational news reports that followed stressed the remarkable fact that the Turkish siblings crawled on hands and feet (J. Harrison, personal communication, November 28, 2005; Humphrey et al., 2005; Tan, 2006; Turkmen et al., 2006). Perhaps more remarkable is the fact that a group of people who could have walked did not. Several factors contributed to their needlessly arrested development. All of the Turkish crawlers had a genetic disorder and were missing part of their cerebellums. However, children who are missing the entire cerebellum can learn to walk, and indeed, one sibling with the disorder was bipedal. In contrast to healthy infants in most cultures, the children's parents never encouraged them to walk or provided supports to walk, believing that the children's affliction was their fate. The primary models for locomotion on this isolated farm were the other siblings. All 19 siblings bear crawled, and walking onset was delayed until the preschool years for the children who eventually walked. Happily, notoriety changed the course of development for the Turkish crawlers. A television documentary team provided the siblings with support rails, mechanical walkers, and a physiotherapist who encouraged them to walk. The five adult crawlers, for the first time in their lives, stood up and began learning to walk.

Form of Movements

Everyone has heard the clichés that Italians gesture flamboyantly when they talk, Native Americans walk softly, New Yorkers move at a frenetic pace, and Asian women sit and walk demurely. In fact, group membership is reflected in the form of most everyday movements. Even within Western cultures, the way people walk can indicate their sex, sexual orientation, race, profession, and favorite music.

Implicit Effects on Movement Form

Culture can exert effects on the form of people's movements through the assimilation and absorption of unspoken norms and group tendencies. Frame-by-frame film analyses show that Italians' communicative gestures involve wide, symmetrical sweeping motions of the arms, whereas Jewish gestures are asymmetrical and jerky (Boas, 1936). Navaho gestures involve smooth, circular motions, whereas European Americans use angular, staccato movements (Bailey, 1942). Even gestures that accompany behaviors as subtle as eye contact differ among cultures, with Americans leaning forward and looking straight at the listener's face and Japanese looking downward or at other parts of the face.

The frenetic tempo of a large, urban city and the relaxed mien of a small town are implicitly reflected in the form of occupants' movements. Comparisons between large, urban cities and smaller, rural settings in the United States, Europe, and the Middle East show that the speed of everyday activity is related to population density (Bornstein, 1979; Bornstein and Bornstein, 1976; Lowin, Hottes, Sandler, and Bornstein, 1971; Pelosse, 1959). Literally, the "pace of life" is culture specific: People walk at a faster pace and conduct transactions more rapidly in areas of higher population density.

Explicit Shaping of Movement Forms

Many motor actions, including everyday activities such as sitting and walking, are explicitly shaped by cultural practices. Etiquette (avoiding genital exposure as in Figure 4.7, position no. 34), religion (appropriate postures for prayer, position no. 29), labor (weaving, paddling a canoe, and so on), and other cultural factors lead to explicit instruction in the form of sitting (Hewes, 1955). In Uganda, proper sitting entails different positions for children, women, and men in

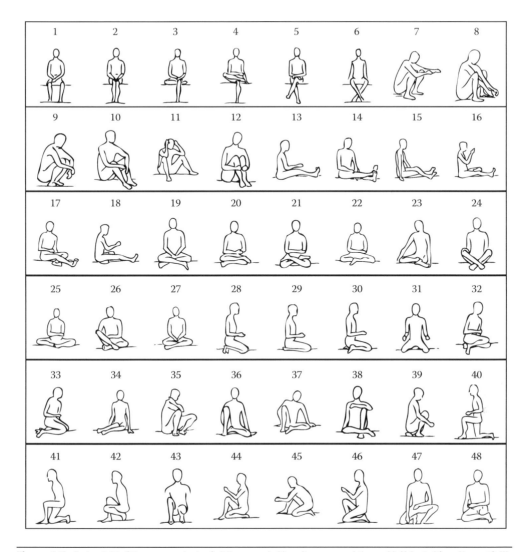

Figure 4.7. Forty-eight of the many variants of sitting recorded in cultures around the world. (Adapted from Hewes, G. W., *American Anthropologist*, 57, 231–244, 1955.)

social settings such as ceremonies, speeches, while eating, and in the presence of important people (Kilbride and Kilbride, 1975). For many people, certain postures (e.g., the yoga positions no. 20 to 23 and the deep squat positions no. 7 to 9) are not possible without years of practice.

Foot binding in China is an astounding example of explicit cultural practices designed to shape the form of movement (Figure 4.8). For more than 1,000 years, most of the mothers in China—billions of women—deformed their daughters' feet to give them the walking gait of a "tender young willow shoot in a spring breeze" (Chew, 2005). "Lotus flower" feet, 3 inches in length and half an inch wide in the front, were achieved through 7 to 10 years of terrible pain and a lifetime of maintenance; infections were a constant feature, necrosis was frequent, and 10% of girls died (Fang and Yu, 1960; Mackie, 1996). Training typically began between 5 and 8 years of age when girls were mature walkers and old enough to understand their duty and the bones of their feet were still malleable. In wealthy families, training began as young as 2 years of age (Fang and Yu, 1960). The mother broke the four small toes of each foot, bent them under

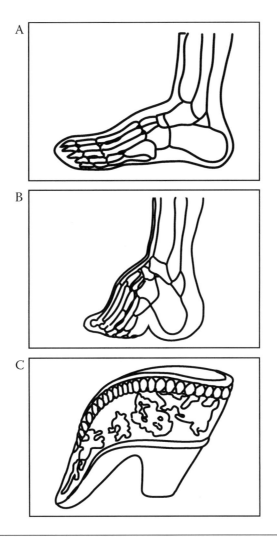

Figure 4.8. Footbinding in China. (A) Normal unbound foot. (B) Foreshortened foot as a consequence of years of binding. (C) Tiny, embroidered shoe with raised heel to accommodate the bound foot.

the foot, and held them in place with long rolls of bandages. By tightening the bindings, the ball of the foot was forced toward the heel to mold a bowed, pointed appendage meant to resemble a deer hoof because of the deep cleft (Blake, 1994; Ebrey, 1999; Fang and Yu, 1960; Mackie, 1996). Mothers forced their girls to walk and hop about on their broken feet to train the bones, and the girls wore bandages and tiny, embroidered shoes day and night (Ping, 2000). As the flesh deteriorated and sloughed off, the feet became smaller and more slender (Ping, 2000).

The pain of putting body weight on their feet and the new balance requirements of foreshortened feet forced girls to relearn how to walk (Chew, 2005). Now walking evoked the illusion of a floating lily because foot-bound women ambulated in short, tottering, mincing steps (Fang and Yu, 1960). The calves of the legs became atrophied as a result of a redistribution of body weight, whereas the thighs and buttocks became enlarged from constant tension (Dworkin, 1974; Ebrey, 1999; Fang and Yu, 1960). These characteristics were considered part of the allure for men, transferring the woman's strength from her feet to her groin. Feet were rarely made so small that women could not stand and walk because this would interfere with their worth (Blake, 1994). Reports differ as to the extent of impairment on endurance, speed, and balance over the course of women's lifetime, although researchers agree that women had difficulty standing from a sit, walking up and down stairs, and walking over sloping ground (Cummings, Ling, and Stone, 1997; Ebrey, 1999; Fang and Yu, 1960). China eradicated foot binding in a generation in the early twentieth century by organizing parents to agree not to bind their daughters' feet and not to allow their sons to marry foot-bound women (Gamble, 1943; Mackie, 1996).

Specialized Movement Patterns

Every society encourages a large set of special motor skills that are specific to the food, tools, toys, games, sports, leisure activities, and forms of labor in the culture. Chopsticks, skis, bicycles, and other cultural objects extend body parts and augment physical capabilities. Enculturation into the world of the Tarahumaran Indians, the video game world of American teens, or any other society dictates the motor patterns that children acquire. Children's bodies and brains change to support these new motor skills (Green and Bavelier, 2003).

Fine Motor

Eating utensils illustrate specialized fine motor skills because childrearing practices and the implements used for self-feeding differ culturally. Western children learn to self-feed using a spoon, but culture plays a role in mothers' expectations and in the actual age of attainment. Most American mothers (63%) expect children to eat with a spoon by 12 months, and indeed, 84% of children have tried to feed themselves with a spoon by 12 months (Schulze, Harwood, and Schoelmerich, 2001). In contrast, only 14% of Puerto Rican mothers expect children to use a spoon by 12 months, and only 52% of their 12-month-olds have tried to use a spoon. In everyday practice, 82% of American mothers compared with 4% of Puerto Rican mothers allow their 12-month-olds to self-feed.

Using chopsticks requires more fine motor control than a spoon because the fingers must work in coordination to clamp the food and increased visual guidance is required to steer the food to the mouth. Several grips are possible—pliers, scissors, tripod, and so on—and are differentially effective depending on the size and type of food to be transported (Ho and Wu, 2006). Chopsticks are the primary eating utensil in China, Japan, Korea, Vietnam, and Thailand. Parents view chopstick use as a major accomplishment and as a form of assessment and comparison with others: "Of course! My child is very clever; he could manipulate chopsticks one year ago. He is better than his cousins" (Wong, Chan, Wong, and Wong, 2002, p. 160). On average, Chinese children can eat most of a meal with chopsticks by 4.6 years of age.

Gross Motor

Pounding and weaving are excellent examples of specialized gross motor skills because the whole body is involved in the action and because both skills are central to the business of their respective cultures. In Mali, women pound millet, corn, and rice for 1 to 2 hours per day by repeatedly lifting and slamming a pestle down onto the grains in the mortar (Bril, 1986a). The torso raises and lowers with the arms; the legs are stationary and stable. Pounding can be done alone or in synchrony with a partner who times her lift to correspond with the other's slam. At 3 years of age, girls begin learning to pound using smaller child-sized implements. By 5 to 6 years, girls' basic coordination pattern resembles that of adults, but they are less stable and move their feet. Adult women do not teach children with verbal instructions, but they help children to discover the appropriate coordination by adapting their movements when pounding in synchrony and by tacitly modeling the most energy efficient body pattern.

Weaving is a critical technological skill for Zinacantec women in Mexico (Maynard, Greenfield, and Childs, 1999). All members of the group wear woven clothing, and skilled weaving is an asset in finding a husband. Using the ancient Mayan loom technique, women tie one end of the frame threads to a stationary post and strap the other end of the loom around their back. Weaving requires tremendous postural control and coordination. The weaver must rise up and down and lean forward and backward in a kneeling position, while simultaneously lifting the vertical threads, beating them tight, and passing the horizontal threads through them. The hips must remain level so that the loom does not tilt to the side allowing the spacer bar to fall. The foundations for weaving are set from early childhood (Maynard et al., 1999). Girls kneel with their legs under them (and watch their mothers do the same) while cooking, playing, and resting. They practice balance by carrying heavy head loads. They begin playing with a toy loom between 3 and 4 years of age and transition to a real loom with tiny bits of cloth between 5 and 9 years. Mothers provide some instruction about how to lean and kneel and support early training by doing some parts of the movements for the girls. As the girls master each component, they begin to coordinate the body and hand activities. Design elements come last and become increasingly unique to the individual weaver.

Conclusion

Normally, motor development is not the first thing to come to mind when people think of cross-cultural research on children's development. Instead, we conjure images of alternative social groups, strange linguistic conventions, variations in aspects of children's thinking, and culturally determined emotional displays. Motor development, however, provides a fascinating arena for cross-cultural research. What images are more vivid and powerful than children suspended by their ankles, buried in sandbags, and walking on their mothers' laps; young girls carrying huge head loads, tottering on 3-inch bound feet, and kneeling for hours to weave; boys running the distance of six marathons as part of a kickball game; and a family of adults who still crawl on their hands and feet? Indeed, cross-cultural research on motor development has proven rich and informative for understanding the development of perceptual-motor control and for illuminating some of the general issues that challenge developmental scientists.

Although most quantitative data concern onset dates of children's motor milestones, cross-cultural research speaks in important ways to issues concerning the shape and endpoint of developmental trajectories, the formal structure of motor actions, and the special motor skills that characterize a culture throughout the lifespan. Since the 1930s, training experiments have been a staple of laboratory studies of motor development. Cross-cultural research informs laboratory investigations about significant factors to study, just as laboratory studies test claims that originate in natural cross-cultural experiments.

For historical reasons, cross-cultural studies have been overly concentrated on infancy and on comparisons between American and Western European children versus African and Indian children (see Figure 4.1). A unique aspect of motor development is that important changes occur throughout the lifespan as new motor skills are acquired and old ones are lost, and many of these changes are specific to people's culture. Societies from Russia, Australia, and much of Asia and South America are grossly underrepresented in the literature. Studies of societies from unusual climates and environmental conditions and societies with variations in body build would be especially informative in evaluating contextual forces that affect motor development.

An important point that is often overlooked in cross-cultural research concerns what is common across dramatic disparities in physical and social context. One commonality is the set of basic motor functions—manual, postural, and locomotor skills—that are universally useful and adaptive and that are present in every society studied. A second commonality across studies and cultures is the prevalence of inter- and intraindividual variability. Wide age ranges (as illustrated in Figure 4.2) hold true for onset ages in every culture. Qualitative differences are also typical. Infants find unique and idiosyncratic solutions for the problem of moving, and their solutions may differ from one observation to the next. The sturdiest truism in the literature is that variability is endemic in motor development (Adolph and Berger, 2006).

Cross-cultural research has important implications for applied issues of education and rehabilitation. Clinicians rely on research with typically developing children to identify and treat abnormal motor development. Cross-cultural research shows a range of variation in the timing, sequence, form, and endpoint of motor skills that can be useful for understanding abnormal development and for planning interventions (Cintas, 1988). To the extent that childrearing practices influence motor development, therapists and families of children with disabilities can benefit from knowledge of childrearing methods in other cultures.

Finally, cross-cultural research challenges our assumptions about motor development (Goldberg, 1972). For most Western readers, studies of children from around the world prompt us to question whether young infants are inherently fragile and their natural position is horizontal, whether infant reflexes must disappear and development must consist of an obligatory sequence of motor milestones, and what it might mean for a society of healthy children to walk at 24 months of age. Perhaps most important, cross-cultural research raises awareness of possibilities formerly not envisaged and provides a new set of questions to ask.

Acknowledgements

This research was supported by National Institute of Child Health and Human Development Grant HD42697 to Karen E. Adolph and Catherine S. Tamis-LeMonda and by Grant HD33486 to Karen E. Adolph. We thank Michael Smith and Julia Leibowich for their assistance with figures and Marc H. Bornstein for his useful suggestions.

References

Adolph, K. E., and Berger, S. E. (2005). Physical and motor development. In M. H. Bornstein and M. E. Lamb (Eds.), *Developmental science: An advanced textbook* (5th ed., pp. 223–281). Mahwah, NJ: Lawrence Erlbaum Associates.

Adolph, K. E., and Berger, S. E. (2006). Motor development. In D. Kuhn and R. S. Siegler (Eds.), *Handbook of child psychology: Volume 2. Cognition, perception, and language* (6th ed., pp. 161–213). New York: John Wiley and Sons.

Adolph, K. E., Robinson, S. R. R., Young, J. W., & Gill-Alvarez, F. (2008). What is the shape of developmental change? *Psychological Review, 115*, 527–543.

Adolph, K. E., Vereijken, B., and Denny, M. A. (1998). Learning to crawl. *Child Development, 69*, 1299–1312.

Adolph, K. E., Vereijken, B., and Shrout, P. E. (2003). What changes in infant walking and why. *Child Development, 74*, 474–497.

Agarwal, S., Attah, M., Apt, N., Grieco, M., Kwakye, E. A., and Turner, J. (1997). Bearing the weight: The kayayoo, Ghana's working girl child. *International Social Work, 40*, 245–263.

Ainsworth, M. D. S. (1967). *Infancy in Uganda: Infant care and the growth of love*. Baltimore: Johns Hopkins Press.

Bailey, F. (1942). Navaho motor habits. *American Anthropologist, 44*, 210–234.

Bayley, N. (1935). The development of motor abilities during the first three years. *Monographs of the Society for Research in Child Development, 1*, 1–26.

Bayley, N. (1965). Comparisons of mental and motor test scores for ages 1-15 months by sex, birth, order, race, geographical location, and education of parents. *Child Development, 36*, 379–411.

Bayley, N. (1969). *Bayley Scales of Infant Development*. New York: The Psychological Corporation.

Bayley, N. (1993). *Bayley Scales of Infant Development* (2nd ed.). New York: The Psychological Corporation.

Bayley, N. (2006). *Bayley Scales of Infant and Toddler Development* (3rd ed.). San Antonio, TX: The Psychological Corporation.

Bensen, J. B. (1993). Season of birth and onset of locomotion: Theoretical and methodological implications. *Infant Behavior and Development, 16*, 69–81.

Berger, S. E., Theuring, C. F., and Adolph, K. E. (2007). How and when infants learn to climb stairs. *Infant Behavior and Development, 30*, 36–49.
Bertenthal, B. I., and Clifton, R. K. (1998). Perception and action. In D. Kuhn and R. S. Siegler (Eds.), *Handbook of child psychology. Volume 2: Cognition, perception, and language* (5th ed., pp. 51–102). New York: John Wiley and Sons.
Blake, C. F. (1994). Foot-binding in neo-Confucian China and the appropriation of female labor. *Signs, 19*, 676–712.
Boas, F. (1936). The effects of American environment on immigrants and their descendants. *Science, 84*, 522–525.
Bornstein, M. H. (1979). The pace of life: Revisited. *International Journal of Psychology, 14*, 83–90.
Bornstein, M. H., and Bornstein, H. G. (1976). The pace of life. *Nature, 259*, 557–558.
Brazelton, T. B. (1973). *Neonatal Behavioral Assessment Scale*. London: SIMP/Heinemann.
Brazelton, T. B., Koslowski, B., and Tronick, E. (1976). Neonatal behavior among urban Zambians and Americans. *Journal of American Academy of Child Psychiatry, 15*, 97–107.
Brazelton, T. B., Robey, J., and Collier, G. (1969). Infant development in the Zinacanteco Indians of Southern Mexico. *Pediatrics, 44*, 274–290.
Bril, B. (1986a). The acquisition of an everyday technical motor skill: The pounding of cereals in Mali (Africa). In M. G. Wade and H. T. A. Whiting (Eds.), *Themes in motor development* (pp. 315–326). Dordrecht, The Netherlands: Martinus Nijhoff.
Bril, B. (1986b). Motor development and cultural attitudes. In J. Wade and H. T. A. Whiting (Eds.), *Themes in motor development* (pp. 297–313). Dordrecht, The Netherlands: Martinus Nijhoff.
Bril, B. (Writer). (1988). Bain et gymnastique neonatale: Enfants Bambara du Mali [Motion Picture]. France: Centre d'Etude des Processus Cognitifs et du Langage Ecole des Hautes Etudes en Sciences Socieles.
Bril, B. (1997). Culture et premieres acquisitions motrices: Enfants d'Europe, d'Asie, d'Afrique. *Journal de Pediatrie et de Puericulture, 10*, 305–314.
Bril, B., and Ledebt, A. (1998). Head coordination as a means to assist sensory integration in learning to walk. *Neuroscience and Biobehavioral Reviews, 22*, 555–563.
Bril, B., and Sabatier, C. (1986). The cultural context of motor development: Postural manipulations in the daily life of Bambara babies (Mali). *International Journal of Behavioral Development, 9*, 439–453.
Bril, B., Zack, M., and Nkounkou-Hombessa, E. (1989). Ethnotheories of development and education: A view from different cultures. *European Journal of Psychology of Education, 4*, 307–318.
Campos, R. G. (1989). Soothing pain-elicited distress in infants with swaddling and pacifiers. *Child Development, 60*, 781–792.
Capute, A. J., Shapiro, B. K., Palmer, F. B., Ross, A., and Wachtel, R. C. (1985). Normal gross motor development: The influences of race, sex and socio-economic status. *Developmental Medicine and Child Neurology, 27*, 635–643.
Chew, S. (2005). "Double binds around my feet": The enormity of the everyday in women's writing and writing about women. *Journal of Gender Studies, 14*, 137–146.
Chisholm, J. S. (1978). Swaddling, cradleboards, and the development of children. *Early Human Development, 2*, 255–275.
Cintas, H. (1988). Cross-cultural variation in infant motor development. *Physical and Occupational Therapy in Pediatrics, 8*, 1–20.
Clark, D., Kreutzberg, J., and Chee, F. (1977). Vestibular stimulation influence on motor development in infants. *Science, 196*, 1228–1229.
Connolly, K. J., and Bishop, D. V. M. (1992). The measurement of handedness: A cross-cultural comparison of samples from England and Papua New Guinea. *Neuropsychology, 30*, 13–26.
Cummings, S. R., Ling, X., and Stone, K. (1997). Consequences of foot binding among older women in Beijing, China. *American Journal of Public Health, 87*, 1677–1679.
Curti, M. W., Marshall, F. B., and Steggerda, M. (1935). The Gesell schedules applied to one-, two- and three-year-old Negro children of Jamaica, B. W. I. *Journal of Comparative Psychology, 20*, 125–156.
Davis, B. E., Moon, R. Y., Sachs, H. C., and Ottolini, M. C. (1998). Effects of sleep position on infant motor development. *Pediatrics, 102*, 1135–1140.
Dennis, W. (1935). The effect of restricted practice upon the reaching, sitting, and standing of two infants. *Journal of Genetic Psychology, 47*, 17–32.
Dennis, W. (1940). The effect of cradling practices upon the onset of walking in Hopi children. *Journal of Genetic Psychology, 56*, 77–86.
Dennis, W. (1941). Infant development under conditions of restricted practice and of minimum social stimulation. *Genetic Psychology Monographs, 23*, 143–189.

Dennis, W. (1960). Causes of retardation among institutional children: Iran. *Journal of Genetic Psychology, 96*, 47–59.

Dennis, W., and Dennis, M. G. (1940). Cradles and cradling practices of the Pueblo Indians. *American Anthropologist, 42*, 107–115.

Dennis, W., and Najarian, P. (1957). Infant development under environmental handicap. *Psychological Monographs, 71*, 1–13.

Devine, J. (1985). The versatility of human locomotion. *American Anthropologist, 87*, 550–570.

Dewey, C., Fleming, P., Golding, J., and Team, A. S. (1998). Does the supine sleeping position have any adverse effects on the child? II. Development in the first 18 months. *Pediatrics, 101*, e5.

Dworkin, A. (1974). Gynocide: Chinese footbinding. In A. Dworkin (Ed.), *Woman hating.* New York: Dutton.

Ebrey, P. (1999). Gender and sinology: Shifting western interpretations of footbinding, 1300-1890. *Late Imperial China, 20*, 1–34.

Fang, H. S. Y., and Yu, F. Y. K. (1960). Foot binding in Chinese women. *Canadian Journal of Surgery, 293*, 195–202.

Frankenburg, W. K., and Dodds, J. B. (1967). The Denver Developmental Screening Test. *Journal of Pediatrics, 71*, 181–191.

Frankenburg, W. K., Dodds, J., Archer, P., Bresnick, B., Maschka, P., Edelman, N., et al. (1992). *Denver II screening manual.* Denver, CO: Denver Developmental Materials, Inc.

Freedland, R. L., and Bertenthal, B. I. (1994). Developmental changes in interlimb coordination: Transition to hands-and-knees crawling. *Psychological Science, 5*, 26–32.

Gamble, S. D. (1943). The disappearance of foot-binding in Tinghsien. *The American Journal of Sociology, 49*, 181–183.

Geber, M. (1958). The psycho-motor development of African children in the first year, and the influence of maternal behavior. *Journal of Social Psychology, 47*, 185–195.

Geber, M. (1962). Longitudinal study and psycho-motor development among Baganda children. In G. Nielson (Ed.), *Proceedings of the XIV International Congress of Applied Psychology* (Vol. 3, pp. 50–60). Oxford, United Kingdom: Munksgaard.

Geber, M., and Dean, R. (1957a). Gesell tests on African children. *Pediatrics, 20*, 1055–1065.

Geber, M., and Dean, R. (1957b). The state of development of newborn African children. *Lancet*, 1216–1219.

Gesell, A. (1928). *Infancy and human growth.* Oxford, United Kingdom: Macmillan.

Gesell, A. (1946). The ontogenesis of infant behavior. In L. Carmichael (Ed.), *Manual of child psychology* (pp. 295–331). New York: John Wiley.

Giacoman, S. L. (1971). Hunger and motor restraint on arousal and visual attention in the infant. *Child Development, 42*, 605–614.

Goldberg, S. (1972). Infant care and growth in urban Zambia. *Human Development, 15*, 77–89.

Green, C. S., and Bavelier, D. (2003). Action video game modifies visual selective attention. *Nature, 423*, 534–537.

Harkness, S. (1992). Cross-cultural research in child development: A sample of the state of the art. *Developmental Psychology, 28*, 622–625.

Hayashi, K. (1992). The influence of clothes and bedclothes on infants' gross motor development. *Developmental Medicine and Child Neurology, 34*, 557–558.

Heglund, N. C., Willems, P. A., Penta, M., and Cavagna, G. A. (1995). Energy-saving gait mechanics with head-supported loads. *Nature, 375*, 52–54.

Hess, R. D., Kashiwagi, K., Azuma, H., Price, G., and Dickson, W. P. (1980). Maternal expectations for mastery of developmental tasks in Japan and the United States. *International Journal of Psychology, 15*, 259–271.

Hewes, G. W. (1955). World distribution of certain postural habits. *American Anthropologist, 57*, 231–234.

Ho, C. P., and Wu, S. P. (2006). Mode of grasp, materials, and grooved chopstick tip on gripping performance and evaluation. *Perceptual and Motor Skills, 102*, 93–103.

Hopkins, B. (1976). Culturally determined patterns of handling the human infant. *Journal of Human Movement Studies, 2*, 1–27.

Hopkins, B., and Westra, T. (1988). Maternal handling and motor development: An intracultural study. *Genetic, Social and General Psychology Monographs, 114*, 379–408.

Hopkins, B., and Westra, T. (1989). Maternal expectations of their infants' development: Some cultural differences. *Developmental Medicine and Child Neurology, 31*, 384–390.

Hopkins, B., and Westra, T. (1990). Motor development, maternal expectations, and the role of handling. *Infant Behavior and Development, 13*, 117–122.

Hrdlicka, A. (1928). Children running on all fours. *American Journal of Physical Anthropology, XI*, 149–185.

Hudson, C. (1966). Isometric advantages of the cradle board: A hypothesis. *American Anthropologist, 68*, 470–474.

Humphrey, N., Skoyles, J. R., and Keynes, R. (2005). Human hand-walkers: Five siblings who never stood up. Discussion Paper. Centre for Philosophy of Natural and Social Science, London, United Kingdom.

Iloeje, S. O., Obiekwe, V. U., and Kaine, W. N. (1991). Gross motor development of Nigerian children. *Annals of Tropical Paediatrics, 11*, 33–39.

Ishak, S., Tamis-LeMonda, C. S., and Adolph, K. (2007). Ensuring safety and providing challenge: Mothers' and fathers' expectations and choices about infant locomotion. *Parenting: Science and Practice, 7*, 57–68.

Jantz, J., Blosser, C. D., and Fruechting, L. A. (1997). A motor milestone change noted with a change in sleep position. *Archives of Pediatrics and Adolescent Medicine, 151*, 565–568.

Kaplan, H., and Dove, H. (1987). Infant development among the Ache of Eastern Paraguay. *Developmental Psychology, 23*, 190–198.

Kattwinkel, J., Brooks, J., and Myerberg, D. (1992). Positioning and SIDS. *Pediatrics, 89*, 1120–1126.

Kattwinkel, J., Hauck, F. R., Keenan, M. E., Malloy, M., and Moon, R. Y. (2005). The changing concept of sudden infant death syndrome: Diagnostic coding shifts, controversies regarding the sleeping environment, and new variables to consider in reducing risk. *Pediatrics, 116*, 1245–1255.

Keefer, C. H., Tronick, E., Dixon, S., and Brazelton, T. B. (1982). Specific differences in motor performance between Gusii and American newborns and a modification of the Neonatal Behavioral Assessment Scale. *Child Development, 53*, 754–759.

Keller, H., Yovsi, R. D., and Voelker, S. (2002). The role of motor stimulation in parental ethnotheories. *Journal of Cross-Cultural Psychology, 33*, 398–414.

Kilbride, J., and Kilbride, P. (1975). Sitting and smiling behavior of Baganda infants: The influence of culturally constituted experience. *Journal of Cross-Cultural Psychology, 6*, 88–107.

Kilbride, J., Robbins, M., and Kilbride, P. (1970). The comparative motor development of Baganda, American white, and American black infants. *American Anthropologist, 72*, 1422–1428.

Kilbride, P. (1980). Sensorimotor behavior of Baganda and Samia infants. *Journal of Cross-Cultural Psychology, 11*, 131–152.

Konner, M. J. (1972). Aspects of the developmental ethology of a foraging people. In N. Jones (Ed.), *Ethological studies of child behavior*. Oxford, United Kingdom: Cambridge University Press.

Konner, M. J. (1977). Infancy among the Kalahari Desert San. In P. H. Leiderman, S. R. Tulkin, and A. Rosenfield (Eds.), *Culture and infancy: Variations in the human experience* (pp. 287–328). New York: Academic Press.

Lagerspetz, K., Nygard, M., and Strandvik, C. (1971). The effects of training in crawling on the motor and mental development of infants. *Scandinavian Journal of Psychology, 12*, 192–197.

Leiderman, P., Babu, B., Kagia, J., Kraemer, H., and Leiderman, G. (1973). African infant precocity and some social influences during the first year. *Nature, 242*, 247–249.

LeVine, R. A., and LeVine, B. B. (1966). *Nyansongo: A Gusii community in Kenya* (Vol. II). New York: John Wiley and Sons, Inc.

Lipton, E. L., Steinscheider, A., and Richmond, J. B. (1965). Swaddling, a child care practice: Historical, cultural, and experimental observations. *Pediatrics, 35*, 521–567.

Lowin, A., Hottes, J. H., Sandler, B. E., and Bornstein, H. G. (1971). The pace of life and sensitivity to time in urban and rural settings: A preliminary study. *Journal of Social Psychology, 83*, 247–253.

Mackie, G. (1996). Ending footbinding and infibulation: A convention account. *American Sociological Review, 61*, 999–1017.

Majnemer, A., and Barr, R. G. (2005). Influence of supine sleep positioning on early motor milestone acquisition. *Developmental Medicine and Child Neurology, 47*, 370–376.

Maloiy, G. M. O., Heglund, N. C., Prager, L. M., Cavagna, G. A., and Taylor, C. R. (1986). Energetic costs of carrying loads: Have African women discovered an economic way? *Nature, 319*, 668–669.

Masataka, N. (1996). On the function of swaddling as traditional infant-care practiced by Native Americans. *Japanese Journal of Psychology, 67*, 285–291.

Maynard, A. E., Greenfield, P. M., and Childs, C. P. (1999). Culture, history, biology, and body: Native and non-native acquisition of technological skill. *Ethos, 27*, 379–402.

McGraw, M. B. (1935). *Growth: A study of Johnny and Jimmy*. New York: Appleton-Century Co.

Mead, M. (1928). *Coming of age in Samoa*. Oxford, United Kingdom: Morrow.

Mead, M., and Macgregor, F. C. (1951). *Growth and culture: A photographic study of Balinese childhood.* Oxford, United Kingdom: Putnam.

Mei, J. (1994). The Northern Chinese custom of rearing babies in sandbags: Implications for motor and intellectual development. In J. H. A. van Rossum and J. I. Laszlo (Eds.), *Motor development: Aspects of normal and delayed development.* Amsterdam: VU Uitgeverij.

Mildred, J., Beard, K., Dallwitz, A., and Unwin, J. (1995). Play position is influenced by knowledge of SIDS sleep position recommendations. *Journal of Pediatric Child Health, 31,* 499–502.

Pelosse, J. L. (1959). Cadence spontanee de la marche en milieu urbain. *Biotypologie, 20,* 72–77.

Pikler, E. (1968). Some contributions to the study of the gross motor development of children. *Journal of Genetic Psychology, 113,* 27–39.

Pin, T., Eldridge, B., and Galea, M. P. (2007). A review of the effects of sleep position, play position, and equipment use on motor development in infants. *Developmental Medicine and Child Neurology, 49,* 858–867.

Ping, W. (2000). *Aching for beauty: Footbinding in China.* Minneapolis, MN: University of Minnesota Press.

Porter, L. S. (1972). The impact of physical-physiological activity on infants' growth and development. *Nursing Research, 21,* 210–219.

Preyer, W. (1890). *The mind of the child. Part I, the senses and the will, observations concerning the mental development of the human being in the first years of life.* New York: D. Appleton and Co.

Rabain-Jamin, J., and Wornham, W. L. (1993). Practice and representations of child care and motor development among West Africans in Paris. *Early Development and Parenting, 2,* 107–119.

Reissland, N., and Burghart, R. (1987). The role of massage in South Asia: Child health and development. *Social Science and Medicine, 25,* 231–239.

Robson, P. (1984). Prewalking locomotor movements and their use in predicting standing and walking. *Child: Care, Health, and Development, 10,* 317–330.

Salls, J. S., Silverman, L. N., and Gatty, C. M. (2002). The relationship of infant sleep and play positioning to motor milestone achievement. *The American Journal of Occupational Therapy, 56,* 577–580.

Santos, D., Gabbard, C., and Goncalves, V. (2001). Motor development during the first year: A comparative study. *Journal of Genetic Psychology, 162,* 143–153.

Schulze, P. A., Harwood, R. L., and Schoelmerich, A. (2001). Feeding practices and expectations among middle-class Anglo and Puerto Rican mothers of 12-month-old infants. *Journal of Cross-Cultural Psychology, 32,* 397–406.

Shelov, S. P., and Hannemann, R. E. (1998). *Caring for your baby and young child.* New York: Bantam.

Shirley, M. M. (1931). *The first two years: A study of twenty-five babies.* Westport, CT: Greenwood Press.

Skodak, M., and Skeels, H. M. (1949). A final follow-up study of one hundred adopted children. *Journal of Genetic Psychology, 75,* 85–125.

Spitz, R. A. (1945). Hospitalism—An inquiry into the genesis of psychiatric conditions in early childhood. *Psychoanalytic Study of the Child, 1,* 53–74.

Super, C. M. (1976). Environmental effects on motor development: The case of "African infant precocity." *Developmental Medicine and Child Neurology, 18,* 561–567.

Super, C. M., and Harkness, S. (1986). The developmental niche: A conceptualization at the interface of child and culture. *International Journal of Behavioral Development, 9,* 545–569.

Tan, U. (2006). A new syndrome with quadrupedal gait, primitive speech, and severe mental retardation as a live model for human evolution. *International Journal of Neuroscience, 116,* 361–369.

Thelen, E., and Adolph, K. E. (1992). Arnold L. Gesell: The paradox of nature and nurture. *Developmental Psychology, 28,* 368–380.

Trettien, A. W. (1900). Creeping and walking. *The American Journal of Psychology, 12,* 1–57.

Tronick, E., Thomas, R., and Daltabuit, M. (1994). The Quechua manta pouch: A caretaking practice for buffering the Peruvian infant against multiple stressors of high altitude. *Child Development, 65,* 1005–1013.

Turkmen, S., Demirhan, O., Hoffmann, K., Diers, A., Zimmer, C., Sperling, K., et al. (2006). Cerebellar hypoplasia and quadrupedal locomotion in humans as a recessive trait mapping to chromosome 17p. *Journal of Medical Genetics, 43,* 461–464.

van Sleuwen, B. E., Engelberts, A. C., Boere-Boonekamp, M. M., Kuis, W., Schulpen, T. W. J., and L'Hoir, M. P. (2007). Swaddling: A systematic review. *Pediatrics, 120,* 1097–1106.

Warren, N. (1972). African infant precocity. *Psychological Bulletin, 78,* 353–367.

Warren, N., and Parkin, M. (1974). A neurological and behavioral comparison of African and European newborns in Uganda. *Child Development, 45,* 966–971.

Werner, E. E. (1972). Infants around the world: Cross-cultural studies of psychomotor development from birth to two years. *Journal of Cross-Cultural Psychology, 3,* 111–134.

Wong, S., Chan, K., Wong, V., and Wong, W. (2002). Use of chopsticks in Chinese children. *Child: Care, Health, and Development, 28,* 157–161.
Zelazo, N. A., Zelazo, P. R., Cohen, K. M., and Zelazo, P. D. (1993). Specificity of practice effects on elementary neuromotor patterns. *Developmental Psychology, 29,* 686–691.
Zelazo, P. R. (1983). The development of walking: New findings on old assumptions. *Journal of Motor Behavior, 2,* 99–137.
Zelazo, P. R., and Weiss, M. J. (2006). Infant swimming behaviors: Cognitive control and the influence of experience. *Journal of Cognition and Development, 7,* 1–25.
Zelazo, P. R., Zelazo, N. A., and Kolb, S. (1972a). Newborn walking. *Science, 177,* 1058–1059.
Zelazo, P. R., Zelazo, N. A., and Kolb, S. (1972b). "Walking" in the newborn. *Science, 176,* 314–315.

5
Perception

JANET F. WERKER, DAPHNE M. MAURER, and KATHERINE A. YOSHIDA

Introduction

Perception refers to the way we take in information from the world through our senses. It is through the perceptual systems that children learn about the properties of the world around them, including those that specifically define their culture. Perceptual development thus provides a unique lens for understanding cross-cultural psychology.

How perceptual information is acquired has been a topic of philosophical debate for millennia. According to empiricist views, the child is born as a blank slate, a tabula rasa that experience—as it comes in through the sensory systems—must write upon (Locke, 1689/1959). Others argue that it would be logically impossible to make sense of the sights, sounds, and other sensory data without some initial organization to direct information uptake and to link it ultimately to meaning (Kant, 1724–1804). Developmental psychologists who ascribe to this rationalist view disagree as to the initial organization. Some argue that only primitives, such as figure/ground distinction and the ability to detect relations, form categories, and so on, are given at birth and that subsequent knowledge is constructed through interaction with the world (e.g., Piaget, 1953). Others argue that more specified knowledge needs to be provided by evolution to guide perception (e.g. Spelke, 2000) and that the "core knowledge" extends across domains including objects, faces, language, causality, number, and so on. A Gibsonian view (Gibson, 1979) avoids the debate about the specificity of the initial representation and instead argues that information in the world has inherent organization that can be perceived directly and stresses that perceptual development primarily involves increasing attention to and differentiation of those aspects of the organized world that are most relevant to the child's successful adaptation to their world (Gibson, 1969).

Humans require social groups for survival. Children growing up in different cultures are exposed to different languages; different facial types; different forms of music, dance, and art; different types of information; different religions; and so forth. Indeed, the very concept of culture is grounded in the differences, rather than the similarities, among groups of people. Hence, experience and learning are essential for recognizing and responding appropriately to members of one's social group (Gauvain and Parke, Chapter 13, this volume). Work on perceptual development reveals substantial organization from birth that prepares the child for learning about whatever culture he or she might be born into and almost astonishingly rapid perceptual attunement to key components of the culture within the first year of life. In this chapter, we describe some of the perceptual biases infants have at birth that prepare them for learning about the native culture and then review evidence illustrating how perception is shaped by experience

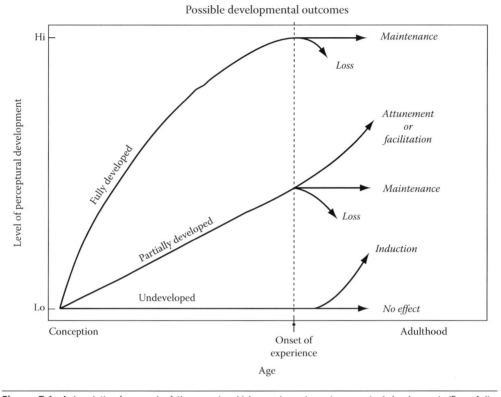

Figure 5.1. A descriptive framework of the ways in which experience impacts perceptual development. (From Aslin, R. N., and Pisoni, D. B., Some developmental processes in speech perception, in G. H. Yeni-Komshian, J. Kavanagh, and C. A. Ferguson [Eds.], *Child phonology: Perception* [Vol. 2, pp. 67–96], Academic Press, New York, 1980. Copyright © Elsevier. With permission.)

with the native culture. Through this review, we hope to illustrate how perceptual tuning allows culture to guide cognitive and social development, thus facilitating transmission and maintenance of cultural norms. Although we focus on some of the key changes that occur in infancy, we illustrate as well ways in which perception continues to reflect and guide social interaction beyond the early years.

As initially outlined by Gottlieb (1981) and elaborated specifically for speech perception by Aslin (1981), there are several theoretically possible roles for how experience can shape perception (see Figure 5.1). A perceptual ability can be "undeveloped" prior to experience, with experience required to bring about its appearance. This is referred to as *Induction*. A perceptual ability can be "partially" developed prior to the onset of experience, with experience functioning to maintain or improve that sensitivity that is already there and with lack of experience leading to a decline. This role of experience is referred to as *Attunement*. In addition, a perceptual ability can be fully present prior to the onset of experience, with experience serving only to maintain the ability and with lack of experience leading to its loss. Finally, an ability can be fully present regardless of experience.

In the review that follows, we illustrate how cultural experience functions in accord with an *Attunement* model, enhancing sensitivity to distinctions required and diminishing sensitivity to environmental cues that are not needed to function in the native culture. We review many aspects of perceptual development but focus on speech perception and face processing. Both of these are likely candidates for deep grounding in evolution because the ability to identify individuals and to learn the basic building blocks for communication is essential to survival. Moreover, languages and facial characteristics are among the most salient dimensions that distinguish one cultural group from another. Thus it is not surprising to find partial development of sensitivity even prior to the onset of specific experience. However, given the importance of differences in language and facial characteristics as identifying elements of distinct cultures, it is also not surprising to discover that experience plays an important role in reorganizing perceptual sensitivities. Hence, we will use these two domains—speech and face perception—as illustrations of the ways in which humans are prepared at birth for perceptual learning and how perceptual development reflects and guides acculturation. But, of course, cross-cultural perception involves much more than learning about the faces and language(s) of the native culture. To give a flavor of the many, many ways in which perceptual development provides a foundation for cultural transmission, music and color perception will be touched upon as well, as examples of the more general principles established in the review of speech and face perception.

Language Processing

Language communication involves processing speech at many different levels simultaneously. To recover the message in spoken language, listeners must parse the input into clauses, phrases, and words and must map individual words to representations in their lexicon. Those lexical representations include not just the meaning of the word, but also its grammatical class (e.g., noun, verb, and so on) and both phonological and morphological (e.g., stem of the word or stem plus past tense) form. As mature language users, we perform these tasks with remarkable efficiency, with the speed of word processing being many times faster than could be predicted by any sequential word recognition algorithm, suggesting that the multiple levels of language are not only processed in parallel, *but in a deeply facilitative, multilevel fashion.*

There are fundamental properties of the world's languages that are universal. Each language includes a semantic component in which certain aspects of the world (e.g., color, gender, names of objects, description of motion, and so on) are encoded in its lexicon. Each language employs syntactic classes to encode different types of relations, and each language has a form (usually sound, but also sign) to convey meaning. However, languages differ profoundly in the precise realization of these universals. For example, although all languages likely distinguish between content words that carry meaning (nouns, verbs, adjectives, and so forth) and function words that are primarily relational and hence carry mostly syntactic structure (for example, determiners such as the and an, and prepositions such as with and through), the precise types of content versus function words vary from language to language. English, for example, uses prepositions, whereas other languages use postpositions. Word order also differs between languages; for example, English is primarily an SVO (subject-verb-object) order language. Sentences such as "I like cookies" are more common than the secondary but also accepted OSV (object-subject-verb) order ("Cookies, I like"). Some languages, such as Japanese, Turkish, and Korean are primarily SOV ("I cookies like"). The third most common word order is VSO (verb-subject-object; "Like I cookies"). There are correlations, albeit imperfect, between basic word order and many other properties of a language, including phrase level order (e.g., do modifiers come before or after nouns) and morphology (see Mehler and Nespor, 2004; Peters, 1997).

Languages also differ in their surface level acoustic and phonological properties. All languages are made up of an inventory of segments (consonants and vowels). Although linguists disagree on the precise number, the world's languages use a finite number of consonants and vowels. All languages use segments as the smallest unit to combine and recombine to form syllables and words. They differ in the consonants and vowels they contain and in the precise specification of each particular consonant and vowel even when that consonant or vowel is used in both languages. Some languages, such as Mandarin or Thai and unlike English, additionally distinguish meaning based on tone differences, whereas others, such as Hausa or isiZulu, distinguish meaning based on different clicks. Languages differ as well in syllable form (Polish allows complex consonant clusters, whereas Japanese does not), in rhythm, and in intonation. Despite the differences between language families in rhythm, the rhythmical properties of any human language can be distinguished from nonlinguistic rhythms.

Infants from different communities are born into different language environments, and learning the native language is perhaps the most central component to acquiring cultural fluency. Learning a language entails breaking into its multilayered form to ultimately translate form into meaning. The development of speech perception is thus the story of how infants use the level of form (sound and sign) to acquire meaning and structure.

Beginnings

Infants begin life with a number of perceptual biases that prepare them for learning language. At birth, they show a preference for speech over matched complex nonspeech and will increase their frequency of high-amplitude sucks during test minutes in which such sucks lead to the presentation of speech sounds (Vouloumanos and Werker, 2007a). When presented with forward versus backward speech, optical imaging studies reveal greater activation of left hemisphere language areas in response to the forward speech but symmetric activation of both left and right hemisphere in response to the backward speech (Peña et al., 2003). Studies using functional magnetic resonance imaging (fMRI) with infants of 2 months also reveal the involvement of different neural systems in response to forward versus backward speech (Dehaene-Lambertz, Dehaene, and Hertz-Pannier, 2002). Although the preference for speech could potentially result from prenatal listening experience, the research fails to find support for such an experience-based explanation; newborn infants show a preference for speech over complex nonspeech but do not show a preference for speech filtered to match that heard in utero over complex nonspeech (Vouloumanos and Werker, 2007b). Moreover, the preference for linguistic over nonlinguistic information is not confined to oral speech; young hearing infants also show a preference for hand shapes and movements that correspond to possible signs over similarly complex shapes and movements that are more like nonlinguistic gestures (Krentz and Corina, 2008). Hence human language attracts close infant attention from the very beginning of life, positioning the infants to learn the characteristics of the native language.

Another perceptual capacity at birth that prepares neonates for language acquisition is categorical discrimination of content versus function words. After being habituated to a set of words from one category (e.g., content words) excised from a mother's speech, neonates show greater recovery to a new set of words from the other grammatical category (e.g., function words) than they do to a new set of words from the same grammatical category (Shi, Werker, and Morgan, 1999). At birth, this sensitivity is universal; neonates who were exposed to only a Chinese language throughout gestation showed the same categorical perception of English words. This shows that, at birth, neonates have biases in perception that will allow infants to ultimately assign word forms to their grammatical classes, which is a necessary step in language acquisition. By 6 months of age, infants selectively listen to content over function words (Shi and Werker, 2001), revealing a bias to listen more carefully to those words that carry meaning. At 6 months, the preference still appears to be universal; infants prefer content over function words even in a language they have not previously heard (Shi and Werker, 2003). By 8 to 11 months, however, the influence of language experience is apparent; infants begin to show a preference for noun phrases that contain a real versus a nonsense function word (e.g., *the breek* versus *kuh breek*) (Shi, Werker, and Cutler, 2006), and highly frequent function words facilitate learning of content words (Shi, Cutler, Werker, and Cruickshank, 2006). Of interest, the exact age of tuning varies somewhat depending on the frequency and consistency of the function words used in the language, with a slightly earlier age of segmentation reported in both German (Höhle and Weissenborn, 2003) and Quebec French (Shi, Lepage, Gauthier, and Marquis, 2006), where a small inventory of function words are very common, than in English (Shi, Lepage, et al., 2006). By 18 months of age, in languages like Spanish where all nouns have grammatical gender and their gender is marked by the determiner that precedes the noun (e.g., "la" versus "el" in Spanish), children begin to use grammatical gender in function words to constrain their choices in word recognition (Lew-Williams and Fernald, 2007).

Some of the biases infants show at birth result from listening experience in the womb. Neonates (up to 4 days old) prefer listening to their mother's voice (DeCasper and Fifer, 1980), a preference that could be instantaneously triggered by "expected" postnatal experience but that more likely reflects prenatal learning because it is only seen in response to the mother's—not the father's—voice. Further support for the role of prenatal listening experience is the evidence that in utero, term fetuses (average age, 38 weeks) show a differential response to their mother's voice (heart rate acceleration) than to a stranger's voice (heart rate deceleration) (Kisilevsky et al., 2003). Prenatal learning is evident as well for stories and songs read or played to the fetus in the last weeks of pregnancy and recognized after birth (DeCasper and Spence, 1986).

Evidence of prenatal listening influencing cultural perception is revealed in the preference neonates show at birth for the native language, although some influence from a few days of postnatal experience cannot be ruled out. In the first illustration, monolingual Spanish or English newborns were examined with a high-amplitude contingent sucking procedure in which their sucking controlled how long each language type played (Moon, Cooper, and Fifer, 1993). During the final 6 minutes of an 18-minute session, infants sucked more to hear the native language than the other language, which is evidence for a culture-specific newborn preference. More recently, monolingual English newborns have been compared to bilingual English–Tagalog newborns on their preference for low-pass filtered samples of English versus Tagalog (Byers-Heinlein, Burns, and Werker, manuscript under revision). Low-pass filtering at 400 Hz is similar to the filtering characteristics of the human uterus and preserves intonation and timing while removing most of the information that allows word recognition. English newborns showed a preference for English, producing more high-amplitude sucks to hear English than Tagalog, whereas the bilingual-exposed infants sucked at the equivalent high level to hear both languages.

Phonetic Perception

The most basic unit of sound in spoken language is the segment, the individual consonants and vowels that comprise syllables, words, and sentences. As noted earlier, the languages of the world differ in their phoneme inventories. For example, standard North American English uses 12 vowels to contrast meaning, whereas Spanish has only 5. English and Spanish share the vowel /e/ (as in late), but its precise acoustic/phonetic form is somewhat different in each. English-learning infants need not only to learn the specification of the vowels, but also to be able to discriminate all 12 vowels from one another, whereas a Spanish infant does not need to discriminate all 12 vowels, and indeed, will be a more proficient user of Spanish if he or she attends to only the 5 vowel differences that are used.

There is considerable evidence indicating that infants begin life with a broad-based sensitivity to phonetic distinctions that are employed across the worlds' languages, including many that are not used in the native language (Lasky, Syrdal-Lasky, and Klein, 1975; Streeter, 1976; Trehub, 1976; Werker, Gilbert, Humphrey, and Tees, 1981). It is important here to note that it is not just the case that neonates and young infants discriminate *any* acoustic difference. Rather, they show enhanced sensitivity to acoustic/phonetic differences that correspond roughly to a category boundary that is used in an adult language (Eimas, Siqueland, Jusczyk, and Vigorito, 1971; see also Bertoncini, Bijeljac-Babic, Blumstein, and Mehler, 1987; Werker and Lalonde, 1988).

Moreover, there is some evidence that specific neural circuits are privileged from birth for these types of discriminations (Dehaene-Lambertz and Gliga, 2004).

During the first year of life, infants become poorer at discriminating phonetic differences that are not used in the native language (Best, McRoberts, LaFleur, and Silver-Isenstadt, 1995; Pegg and Werker, 1997; Tsao, Liu, Kuhl, and Tseng, 2000; Tsushima et al., 1994; Werker and Lalonde, 1988; Werker and Tees, 1984a) and better at discriminating phonetic differences that are used (Burns, Yoshida, Hill, and Werker, 2007; Kuhl et al., 2006; Narayan, 2006; Narayan, Werker, and Beddor, in press). Throughout this chapter, we refer to this pattern of reduced discrimination of nonnative distinctions and improved discrimination of native distinctions as perceptual attunement (see Aslin and Pisoni, 1980).

Attunement in phonetic perception occurs between 6 and 10 months for consonants (e.g., Werker and Tees, 1984b) and is evident by 6 months for vowels (Kuhl, Williams, Lacerda, Stevens, and Lindblom, 1992; Polka and Werker, 1994). Moreover, it is seen in both behavioral studies (e.g., conditioned head turn, visual habituation) and event-related potential studies (Cheour et al., 1998; Rivera-Gaxiola, Silva-Pereyra, and Kuhl, 2005). Interestingly, it has been suggested that to modify perceptual attunement, at least after it has begun, the exposure must be "live"—that is, exposure of 5 hours over the course of 2 weeks via a noninteractive prerecorded auditory stream or even a noninteractive audiovisual stream may not be sufficient to maintain the nonnative contrasts at 9 months, whereas the same duration of live, contingent interaction is effective (Kuhl, Tsao, and Liu, 2003; Kuhl, 2007). Although the claim that live interaction is necessary is currently being challenged by results from a number of different learning tasks (see Yoshida, Pons, Cady, and Werker, under review), the suggestion that social interaction may be particularly effective in inducing perceptual change, particularly once attunement is well underway, links perceptual development to the acquisition of culture even more strongly.

Infants raised in bilingual environments appear to hold on to the distinctions used in both of their languages. In the single study on consonant perception, English infants showed discrimination of only their native ba-pa contrast at 10 to 12 months of age, whereas bilingual French–English infants discriminated across both the French and the English boundary (Burns et al., 2007). However, the path to maintenance of both contrasts is not always the same in infants growing up bilingual. In a study comparing Spanish, Catalan, and Spanish–Catalan bilingual infants, Bosch and Sebastián-Gallés (2003) reported a temporary decline at 8 months in the bilingual infants' discrimination of a vowel distinction that is used in Catalan, but not Spanish. Importantly, by 10 months, the bilingual Spanish–Catalan infants were again able to discriminate the Catalan-only distinction.

Tones In some languages, tone also serves as a phonetic feature to distinguish one possible word from another. For example, in Mandarin, the syllable "ma" carries four different meanings depending on its pitch. A high level tone /ma_1/ means "mother"; high rising /ma_2/ means "hemp", low falling to rising /ma_3/ means "horse", and high falling /ma_4/ means "scold." Perceptual attunement in the first year of life has recently been reported to extend to the perception of tone contrasts. Monolingual English infants were compared to Chinese (Mandarin and Cantonese) infants on their ability to discriminate two lexical tone contrasts. The two tone contrasts selected were distinctions that occur in Chinese but that were recorded from a Thai speaker. They were ba-rising versus ba-falling (two contour tones) and ba-rising versus ba-low (a contour versus a level tone distinction). At 6 months, both English- and Chinese-learning infants performed equally well, whereas at 9 months, only the Chinese-learning infants discriminated the lexical tone distinctions. To test whether the effect of listening experience was specific to language, the infants were also tested on their ability to discriminate identical pitch differences carried by a violin sound rather than by the syllable "ba." When listening to the violin sounds, the English and Chinese infants performed equally at both 6 and 9 months of age and comparably to how the young English- and both young and older Chinese-learning infants performed on the tone distinctions (Mattock and Burnham, 2006).

The research on phonetic perception provides strong and consistent support for cultural attunement. Across a wide variety of types of speech sounds and across a number of studies using different testing techniques, there is evidence that listening experience functions to maintain and improve discrimination of native phonetic contrasts.

Sign Perhaps most surprising is the evidence for perceptual attunement in the perception of sign language. To investigate this question, a group of researchers created three different 11-step hand-shape continua, with the endpoints of each continuum being nonsense signs (like nonsense syllables such as "ba" and "da") that correspond to morphological, but not meaningful, words in American Sign Language (ASL). Adult native signers showed categorical discrimination, with enhanced discrimination at a single point in the continuum, whereas nonsigning adults showed relatively equal (and high) discrimination at many points along the continuum (Baker, Idsardi, Golinkoff, and Petitto, 2005). When tested at 4 months of age on the hand-shape continuum that yielded the most robust results with adults, hearing infants who had not been exposed to a sign language showed categorical discrimination at the same location along the continuum as did the signing adults. At 14 months, however, the infants, like the nonsigning adults, showed equal (and high) discrimination at all steps along the continuum (Baker, Golinkoff, and Petitto, 2006) unless they had been raised by a parent who uses sign (in this case, ASL) as a primary language (Baker, Werker, and Golinkoff, manuscript in preparation).

Auditory–Visual Tuning to the phonetic properties of the native language is also seen in auditory–visual speech perception. Infants seem to either begin life with, or very rapidly learn, the correspondence between speech sounds heard and the mouth movements that produce them. By 4 months (Kuhl and Meltzoff, 1982) and even 2 months (Patterson and Werker, 2003), infants can match the speech sound heard with a visual display of talking faces. When shown two side-by-side talking faces, one articulating "ah" and the other "ee," infants will look preferentially to the side matching whichever of the two vowel sounds is centrally presented auditorily. Moreover, for both adults and infants (Rosenblum, Schmuckler, and Johnson, 1997; Burnham and Dodd, 2004; Kushnerenko, Teinonen, Volein, and Csibra, 2008; but see Desjardins and Werker, 2004 for limitations), the speech sound heard is influenced by the visible articulation seen. The classic illustration comes from McGurk and MacDonald (1976) wherein adults reported "hearing" a /da/ when they were presented auditorily with a /ba/ and visually with someone articulating a /ga/. There are cross-linguistic influences on the McGurk effect, such that only those articulations used in the native language influence the percept heard (Massaro, Cohen, and Smeele, 1995; Werker, Frost, and McGurk, 1992). In cultures where it is less appropriate to look directly at speakers' faces while they are speaking, McGurk effects are much less pronounced (Sekiyama and Tohkura, 1993). Although infants have not been tested for auditory–visual speech with nonnative languages, they have been tested with nonhuman vocalizations and show a similar perceptual attunement as that described earlier for phonemes. When tested in a two-choice matching task in which two vocalizing monkeys are shown, adult monkeys will look preferentially to the monkey face articulating the matching sound ("coo" or "grunt threat" sound; Ghazanfar and Logothetis, 2003). At 4 and 6 months, human infants also look toward the monkey producing the call that matches the auditory stimulus being played. By 8 and 10 months of age, however, human infants perform randomly on the same test (Lewkowicz and Ghazanfar, 2006).

Caveats Two caveats are important for understanding the pattern of attunement described earlier. First, the change in perceptual sensitivity involves a reorganization into language-relevant phonetic categories rather than a "loss" of sensory/acoustic level discrimination ability. When tested in very sensitive psychoacoustic tasks, adults can often perform better than chance on nonnative distinctions (e.g., Pisoni and Tash, 1974; Werker and Logan, 1985), and training regimens can lead to marked improvements (e.g., Logan, Lively, and Pisoni, 1991; McCandliss, Fiez, Protopapas, Conway, and McClelland, 2002). The remaining sensitivity, however, may not be identical to that which was present prior to perceptual attunement. For example, although the majority of event-related potential (ERP) studies with adults and older infants fail to reveal evidence of brain-based discrimination of nonnative distinctions (e.g., Cheour et al., 1998; Dehaene-Lambertz, 1997; Näätänen et al., 1997; Sharma and Dorman, 2000), a few recent studies do reveal auditory ERPs to nonnative contrasts. Importantly, however, even when ERP responses are seen to nonnative contrasts, they are longer in latency, different in polarity, and/or are recorded from different electrode sites than are the ERP responses of adults for whom the distinction is native (Rivera-Gaxiola, Csibra, Johnson, and Karmiloff-Smith, 2000; Rivera-Gaxiola et al., 2005).

The second caveat is that lack of listening experience does not always lead to a decline in perception. The most striking example comes from work by Best and colleagues on phonetic distinctions involving click sounds from languages such as isiZulu and Hausa (Best and McRoberts, 2003). English-learning infants and even English-speaking adults continue to discriminate many of the click contrasts even though they have most likely never heard them spoken (Best, McRoberts, and Sithole, 1988). It is argued that these distinctions remain discriminable, at least in part, because the click sounds are so unlike any of the speech sounds used in nonclick languages (such as English) that the clicks are not assimilated to linguistic categories. Hence the clicks are not subject to the influence of native-language category attunement and remain discriminable based on the same acoustic information that was available at 6 to 8 months (Best et al., 1988; for a more recent interpretation, see Best and McRoberts, 2003).

Perhaps the strongest support for attunement involving linguistic rather than acoustic processing comes from a recent study on word learning in English and Dutch infants age 18 months. Both Dutch and English use the vocalic difference /a/-/E/ as in "bag" versus "beg" to distinguish meaning in the language. Dutch and English infants of 18 months not only discriminate, but also use this difference to learn to associate two different words ("tam" and "tem") to two different objects. Vowel length differences are also used in both Dutch and English. However, it is only in Dutch that a vowel length difference alone signals a difference in meaning between two words. Vowel length is particularly interesting because it remains discriminable across the life span to English speakers. At 18 months, although both English (Kajikawa, Fais, Mugitani, Werker, and Amano, 2006) and Dutch infants can discriminate vowel length differences in a nonsense syllable discrimination task, only Dutch infants can use a vowel length difference to learn to associate two different words ("tam" and "ta:m") to two different objects (Dietrich, Swingley, and Werker, 2007). These findings reinforce the notion that attunement in the case of phonetic perception occurs at a linguistic rather than acoustic mode of processing.

Second Language Perception How permanent are the changes described in the previous section? Can attunement to the properties of the native language be overcome by exposure to another language? There are many situations in which humans must learn a language after infancy, either as an additional language to their first language or, in the case of adoption, relocation, and so forth, as a substitute language for their first. Hence, it is of not only theoretical, but also practical importance to consider how permanent the perceptual attunement of phonetic perception is. The vast literature on phonetic discrimination in second language acquisition reveals important effects of age (Flege, Yeni-Komshian, and Liu, 1999), similarity to the first language (Bosch, Costa, and Sebastián-Gallés, 2000), and acoustic salience (Flege, Bohn, and Jang, 1997) (acoustic salience is defined by the total amount of physical difference between the stimuli, the duration of those differences [longer differences are more perceptible], and the relative place in the spectrum [differences in the first and second formants are more salient than differences only in higher formants]). If the languages are quite distinct, high levels of discrimination in the second language may ultimately be acquired, but if the phonetic inventories are very similar, even if the second language is acquired in childhood, there may be a continuing advantage of one language over another, even into the adult years (Navarra, Sebastián-Gallés, and Soto-Faraco, 2005; Sebastián-Gallés, Echeverria, and Bosch, 2005), perhaps as a result of interference. Moreover, even in cases where adults can discriminate a nonnative or second language phonetic distinction to which they were exposed from childhood, they may not be able to use it as fluidly in a word recognition task (Pallier, Colomé and Sebastián-Gallés, 2001). Similarly, when native levels of discrimination of phonetic contrasts in the second language are evident, different brain systems may be involved (see Best and Avery, 1999, for a dichotic listening study of click discrimination in speakers of nonclick languages; see Minagawa-Kawai, Mori, Naoi, and Kojima, 2007 for an optical imaging study of native Korean/Japanese second language learners' discrimination of Korean).

Discrimination of phones in a new language in cases where the first language has been lost yields a different picture. Adults who learned Korean as their first language and were adopted into French homes between the ages of 3 and 8 *with no further exposure to Korean* are equally poor at discriminating Korean-specific phonetic distinctions as are French adults, even after being re-exposed to Korean as adults (Ventureyra, Pallier, and Yoo, 2004). However, exposure of just a few hours a week to Korean starting in childhood is sufficient to maintain native-like Korean discrimination in a primarily English environment (Oh, Jun, Knightly, and Au, 2003). Similarly, a study of native Italian speakers of English revealed that although the early learners of English were, as a group, not as proficient as English native speakers, the bilinguals who used their primary language less did not differ from the English natives (Flege and MacKay, 2004). This interference account is strengthened by comparing simultaneous bilinguals, who have been exposed to two languages from birth, to early sequential bilinguals, who learned their second language from a young age (Sebastián-Gallés et al., 2005). Simultaneous Spanish–Catalan bilinguals do not appear to attain the same level of proficiency in discriminating a Catalan-specific contrast as do the sequential Catalan–Spanish bilinguals who learned Spanish early (before 6 years of age), but nonetheless after they first learned Catalan.

Rhythmical Perception

The languages of the world fall into different rhythmical classes, initially characterized as "machine-gun rhythm" versus "Morse-code rhythm" (Lloyd James, 1940) but later relabeled "syllable-timed" and "stress-timed" rhythms, respectively (Pike, 1945). Stress-timed languages allow for more vowel reduction and more complex syllable structures, resulting in a greater variety of syllable types, than do syllable-timed languages, and a third category, mora-timed languages, has the least variable types of syllables (Bertinetto, 1981; Dasher and Bolinger, 1982). Two different groups have quantified and operationalized rhythmical classifications. Ramus and colleagues (Ramus, 2002; Ramus, Nespor, and Mehler, 1999) describe languages in terms of two primary variables: % vowel and + (standard deviation) of the consonant (+ C). Measurement of acoustic samples of various languages revealed that syllable-timed languages have a higher % vowel and lower + C than do stress-timed languages, and mora-timed languages have the lowest of all. Grabe, Low, and colleagues (Grabe and Low, 2002; Low, Grabe, and Nolan, 2000) operationalize the rhythmical differences between languages using the normalized pair-wise variability index (nPVI), which is a measure of the magnitude of durational contrast (i.e., the change in duration between successive items) for vocalic intervals, and sometimes using the raw pair-wise variability index (rPVI) for consonant intervals. These two related but distinct operationalizations yield nearly identical classifications of languages on the basis of rhythm (Ramus, 2002).

Infants can distinguish languages based on their rhythm. First shown with French newborns discriminating the native syllable-timed French from stress-timed Russian (Mehler et al., 1988), this finding has now been replicated across many different languages and with infants up to 5 months of age (Bahrick and Pickens, 1988; Nazzi, Bertoncini, and Mehler, 1998; see Nazzi and Ramus, 2003, for a review). When much of the consonantal and vowel information is removed with low-pass filtering, and/or when the individual syllables are replaced with a single repeated syllable such as "la," young infants continue to succeed (Dehaene-Lambertz and Houston, 1998; Mehler et al., 1998; Ramus, 2002). Removing the intonational information and leaving only the syllable-to-syllable timing is sufficient, providing robust evidence that languages are discriminated on the basis of rhythmical information.

Data from monolingual and bilingual infants of age 4 months learning Spanish and/or Catalan (both syllable-timed languages) suggest that within-rhythmical class discrimination is also possible when infants have familiarity with one of the languages. Monolingual-learning Spanish and Catalan infants both discriminate their native language from English and also from the other language (Spanish or Catalan; Bosch and Sebastián-Gallés, 1997). Bilingual-learning infants, hearing both Catalan and Spanish, are also able to discriminate their dominant language (defined as the language that their mother spoke) from English (Bosch and Sebastián-Gallés, 1997) as well as from their secondary language (Bosch and Sebastián-Gallés, 2001).

One of the most exciting recent findings is that very young infants can discriminate languages not just by listening, but actually by watching silent videos of bilingual speakers producing speech (Weikum et al., 2007). When shown silent talking heads, adults are able to discriminate the speech of their native language from that of an unfamiliar language, even when the two languages are as similar as Spanish and Catalan (Soto-Faraco et al., 2007). Critically, however, the adults must be speakers of one or both of the languages to discriminate successfully. A detailed analysis of error patterns suggests that subtle rhythmical cues (as evident in the timing of mouth openings and closings), rather than mouth-shape (visemic) cues, allow adults with knowledge of one of the languages to be successful.

As in so many other domains, the perceptual attunement seems to occur within the first year of life. To test visual language discrimination, infants were shown silent video displays of three bilingual French–English adults reciting sentences from *The Little Prince* in either English or French until they habituated (i.e., their looking time declined to 50% or less of what it had been in the first block of three trials). Following habituation, infants were shown either new sentences from the same language (control group) or new sentences from the opposite language (experimental group). A greater recovery in looking time in the experimental versus control condition is taken as evidence of discrimination. English-learning infants of 4 and 6 months of age showed a recovery in looking time to a change in language being spoken but not to a change to new sentences from within the same language. At 8 months of age, discrimination of the language change was no longer seen in the infants who were growing up in monolingual English homes, but it was still seen in infants growing up with both English and French (Weikum et al., 2007). This reveals how adaptive perceptual learning can be, in this case by providing bilingual-learning infants with continued sensitivity to one source of information that will allow them to keep their two native languages distinct.

Within the first year of life, infants become attuned to many other phonological properties of the native language, including the native language stress pattern (Jusczyk, Cutler, and

Redanz, 1993), phonotactics (sequence of consonants and vowels; Jusczyk et al., 1993), and prosody (Mattys, Jusczyk, Luce, and Morgan, 1999) (for a review, see Gerken and Aslin, 2005). This emerging sophistication of the acoustic and visual attributes of the native language not only prepares infants for learning the native language, but also, as will be reviewed later in the chapter, directly influences their preferences and choices for social partners.

Effects of Linguistic Rhythm on Other Aspects of Perception

Sensitivity to the rhythmic information in the native language may provide important information for identifying members of one's own cultural group, even when speech is "seen" and not heard.

Tone Sequences Rhythm in language seems to lead to cultural differences in perception of basic tone sequences (Iversen, Patel, and Ohgushi, 2006). When hearing a repeating sequence of tones of variable duration (short-short-long), English adults and infants perceive a break after the long tone (Trainor and Adams, 2000), whereas with similar stimuli (short-long), Japanese adults as a group have a slight tendency to segment after the short tone (Iversen et al., 2006). These differences are attributed to the rhythm of the language spoken, wherein English but not Japanese contains many phrases that have short-long durational differences in clitic groups (e.g., "the book"), perhaps biasing speakers of such languages to segment tones after long durations. If linguistic rhythm influences something as basic as simple tone perception, could it influence more culturally relevant and communicative auditory domains?

Music There has been a long-standing intuition that linguistic rhythm is reflected in the instrumental music of a culture (Abraham, 1974; Wenk, 1987). Using the nPVI measure described earlier to measure linguistic rhythm (e.g., Low et al., 2000), Patel and Daniele (2003) compared classical English-composed instrumental music (as an example of a stress-timed culture) to that of classical French-composed music (from a syllable-timed language) and found the predicted higher nPVI in the English music, paralleling the rhythmical differences in language. This initial work has been extended to a number of other cultures, including the United States, Austria, Germany, Scandinavia (stress-timed), and Italy and Spain (syllable-timed), with the results confirming higher durational contrastiveness in the music of stress-timed languages (Huron and Ollen, 2003).* The same pattern of results has been found in a comparison of English and Japanese (mora-timed) popular music refrains (Sadakata, Desain, Honing, Patel, and Iversen, 2004).

There are additional cultural differences in rhythm beyond those linked to language noted earlier. In North American music, simple meters predominate (e.g., simple or compound duple), whereas in Bulgarian and Macedonian, music tends to use more complex meter (Clayton, 2000). Exposure to complex rhythms seems to be required for ease of processing, at least among adults. In one study, North American, Bulgarian, and Macedonian adults were tested on their ability to detect differences that violated the metrical structure and differences that preserved the metrical structure of musical pieces (Hannon and Trehub, 2005a). The North Americans rated structure-violating differences to be more extreme than structure-preserving differences in music with simple meter only; the Bulgarians and Macedonians rated structure-violating differences to be more extreme in both simple and complex meter music.

This cultural difference in musical processing seems to be another example of perceptual attunement within the first year of life; North American infants of 6 months of age behave

---

* The findings were not replicated with Austrian and German music (the analysis yielded results indicative of syllable-timed roots; the lower than expected nPVI values are argued to be swayed by the historic musical influence from Italian music (Patel and Daniele, 2003).

like the Bulgarian and Macedonian adults, discriminating structure-violating from structure-preserving differences in both simple and complex meter music (Hannon and Trehub, 2005a). However, by 11 to 12 month of age, North American infants resemble North American adults and are able to detect structure-violating differences only in simple meter music (Hannon and Trehub, 2005b). Re-exposure within the infancy period rescues the ability to process complex rhythm. When North American infants age 11 months were exposed to Macedonian, Bulgarian, and Bosnian music for 20 minutes per day for 2 weeks before testing, these infants behaved like the Bulgarian and Macedonian infants, discriminating structure-violating and structure-preserving differences in the complex meters (Hannon and Trehub, 2005b). Of interest, unlike the report for phonetic discriminations, a noninteractive tape was adequate.

Pitch Perception

One particularly interesting aspect of sound is pitch. Pitch, with its primary acoustic correlate fundamental frequency, carries the melody in music. But pitch is also used in speech—it is one of the cues distinguishing individual voices and distinguishing between registers, such as the higher pitch of infant-directed speech. Structurally, pitch is one of the signals for boundaries between clauses, phrases, and sentences in spoken language and is one of the stress cues signaling, for example, new versus old information. As noted earlier, in tone languages, pitch also serves as a phonetic feature to distinguish one possible word from another.

Culture has a profound effect on tone perception. Numerous studies have shown that in adult speakers of tone languages, unlike speakers of nontone languages, specialized language areas in the left hemisphere are recruited to produce and perceive linguistic tone (see Xu et al., 2006). In addition, there is some specificity in that some perisylvian areas are activated more by tone as used in the native language than by tone as used in a different but nonnative tone language (Gandour et al., 2000). In speakers of nontone languages, the typical pattern of neural response is one of bilateral activation, similar to that seen in both speakers of tone languages and nontone languages in response to pitch differences that are presented outside of a linguistic context.

Behavioral studies similarly reveal specialized linguistic processing for tone only among speakers of tone languages. For example, Burnham and Mattock (2007) compared speakers of tone languages (Thai and Mandarin) to speakers of a nontone language (English) on their discrimination of pitch changes both within a linguistic context (carried on speech syllables) and outside of a linguistic context (filtered speech and violin sounds). The speakers of tone languages showed equally good discrimination of all the pitch changes, whereas the English speakers showed as rapid and as accurate discrimination of the pitch differences when nonlinguistic stimuli were used but slower and less accurate discrimination of the lexical pitch differences.

Music Perception

One of the most intriguing aspects of pitch perception is the phenomenon of perfect pitch, or absolute pitch (AP). We all have some degree of implicit pitch perception. We carry tunes more or less well, and when asked to sing a common song, there is a high degree of consistency across and within individuals across time in the note that we use to begin the song (Levitin, 1999). AP requires more explicit knowledge. It is commonly defined as the ability to label a particular note when played, for example, on the piano or to produce (sing) a particular pitch when given the name of the note (Levitin and Rogers, 2005). Individual differences in AP are seen not only in behavior, but also in brain organization (e.g., Keenan et al., 2001). Reports place the incidence of AP at only 1 to 5 people out of every 10,000 (e.g., Brown, Sachs, Cammuso, and Folstein, 2002; Ward and Burns, 1982). This is in sharp contrast to the much more common phenomenon of relative pitch (RP) perception. RP is shown by the ability to identify intervals in music (e.g., an octave), to detect a violation in a melodic contour, and to recognize a melody across a transposition in scale.

Cultural differences early in life have been shown to have an enormous influence on AP perception. The cultural influences are of two types. The first is musical training. There is a robust correlation between early musical training and the incidence of AP perception (Brown et al., 2002; Crozier, 1997; Levitin and Zatorre, 2003; Trainor, Desjardins, and Rockel, 1999). There seems to be a cut-off at age 9, after which experience no longer induces AP perception (see Chin, 2003), with particular advantages if the musical training begins before age 4 (Baharloo, Johnston, Service, Gitschier, and Freimer, 1998). The second type of cultural influence is language. Adult speakers of tone languages show greater precision than do speakers of nontone languages in implicit pitch processing tasks such as repeating a word on the same note or beginning a song on the same note (Deutsch, Henthorn, and Dolson, 2004). Moreover, speakers of tone languages are also more likely to show AP than are speakers of nontone languages (Deutsch et al., 2004). Early musical training and language experience interact such that the proportion of early trained musicians with AP is significantly greater among speakers of tone than of nontone languages (Deutsch, Henthorn, Marvin, and Xu, 2006). (Although this body of work has classically been understood to reveal an effect of experience on AP, a recent study indicates that there actually may be genetic differences that influence neural processing of pitch between population groups that have tone language and those that do not; see Dediu and Ladd, 2007.)

Based on findings such as these, Deutsch (2002) has hypothesized that infants are born with AP perception, perhaps in preparation for acquiring tone in language, and that the lack of AP perception among the majority of the citizens of the world reflects a kind of deprivation of expected experience). At present, however, this claim is difficult to evaluate because the definition of AP requires explicit labeling or singing on demand—two tasks that are beyond the skill level of young infants. Nevertheless, there is an active debate about the origins of AP perception. Word segmentation studies indicate that at 8 months of age, infants growing up in a nontone language show a processing bias for AP sequences over RP, even though adults from nontone language environments show an advantage for RP (Saffran and Griepentrog, 2001). This led Saffran and Griepentrog to conclude that the advantage for RP pitch emerges only after 8 months of age and does so only in listeners growing up in nontone languages. On the other hand, melody recognition studies indicate that infants use RP to process melodic sequences (Plantinga and Trainor, 2005) and treat the same melody presented in a new key as unchanged (Trainor and Trehub, 1992). Irrespective of whether infants are born with AP and lose it without appropriate experience or whether listening experience is required to induce AP perception, there is unequivocal evidence of a critical window early in life during which cultural experience impacts pitch perception.

Face Processing

Faces are highly similar around the world; they all have a similar oval outer shape and similar inner features, most prominently two eyes above a nose, which is in turn above a mouth. Yet just as languages differ in specific features, details of faces can differ among cultural groups, with the most striking differences being in skin color; however, other differences can be found in the prominence of the cheekbones, the bushiness of the eyebrows, the diversity of hair color (little for Asian faces; much for Caucasian faces), and so forth. A quick and dirty (although increasingly less accurate) way to distinguish members of one's own culture from members of other cultures is by facial appearance. Using facial appearance to distinguish the cultural in from out group is facilitated by a process of perceptual attunement for face processing akin to that described earlier for language. This attunement involves developing expertise in face processing that is not used for nonface objects and that generalizes only partially to faces of other ethnic groups/races to which the individual is rarely exposed. The expertise includes becoming adept at recognizing facial identity, despite variations in point of view, direction of eye gaze, facial expression, hairdo, and aging.

Recognizing facial identity is critical if individuals are to use culturally differentiated behaviors toward kin, same-sex strangers, opposite-sex strangers, elders, and so forth. At the same time, humans must be adept at recognizing facial expressions and other changeable aspects of the face, such as direction of gaze and sound being spoken, that transmit socially relevant information such as threat and acceptance. These cues are important modulators of social interactions and attention and, as noted earlier, can contribute to the decoding of language. All of these skills develop postnatally and become attuned to faces of the infant's own race and ethnic group, unless the infant is exposed to faces from multiple groups.

Learning to Recognize Facial Identity

Just as infants show an initial preference for speech over nonspeech (Vouloumanos and Werker, 2007a), infants' learning about faces is built on an initial bias to look toward stimuli with facelike structure (Morton and Johnson, 1991). The face bias may be based on a more general attraction to bounded stimuli with more or larger visible elements in the top, which is enhanced if eyes are present with direct gaze (e.g., Cassia, Turati, and Simion, 2004; Farroni, Menon, and Johnson, 2006; Johnson, 2005; Mondloch et al., 1999; Simion, Turati, Valenza, and Leo, 2006). This initial bias—combined with parents' interest—guarantees that babies spend more waking time looking at faces than at any other visual stimulus and hence that they begin to learn the characteristics of faces in their environment. By 3 days of age, infants recognize the face of their mother from visual cues alone (Bushnell, 2001; Bushnell, Sai, and Mullin, 1989; Pascalis and de Schonen, 1994), even if they have seen the mother for as little as 5.5 hours during those 3 days (Bushnell, 2001). Thus, cultural distinctiveness in the structure of the face (e.g., skin color) can begin to influence babies' face processing from birth. Perhaps because of newborns' poor acuity and contrast sensitivity, the external contour of the face is initially more salient than its internal features, but with age (and associated improvements in acuity and contrast sensitivity), the internal features become more salient (Hainline, 1978; Haith, Bergman, and Moore, 1977; Maurer and Salapatek, 1976; Turati, Macchi Cassia, Simion, and Leo, 2006).

Despite these initial advances and abundant exposure to faces, children do not reach adult levels of expertise in recognizing facial identity until adolescence (Bruce et al., 2000; Carey, Diamond, and Woods, 1980; Mondloch, Geldart, Maurer, and Le Grand, 2003; Mondloch, Le Grand, and Maurer, 2002). Some of the prerequisite skills do develop much earlier. By age 4 to 6 years, children process faces holistically. Like adults, they integrate the parts into a whole or Gestalt-like representation, thereby reducing the accessibility of information about individual features (reviewed in Maurer, Le Grand, and Mondloch, 2002). A classic measure of holistic processing is the *composite face effect*. When adults are asked to recognize the top half of a face (as belonging to a celebrity or being the same as the top half of the face that preceded it), they have difficulty if the top half has been combined with the bottom half of a different face (Hole, 1994; Young, Hellawell, and Hay, 1987). Presumably, holistic processing binds the two halves together, creating a novel face in which it is difficult to selectively attend to the top. Performance improves if the top and bottom halves are misaligned, presumably because misalignment disrupts holistic processing. Similarly, adults recognize that a feature belongs to a particular individual (e.g., Larry's nose) more easily if it is presented in the context of the rest of the face (within Larry's face) than if it is presented in isolation, a phenomenon called the *whole/part advantage* (Tanaka and Farah, 1993). By 4 to 6 years of age (the youngest age tested), children show both the composite face effect and the whole/part advantage, with the magnitude of both effects similar to those in adults (Carey and Diamond, 1994; De Heering, Houthuys, and Rossion, 2007; Mondloch, Pathman, Maurer, Le Grand, and de Schonen, 2007; Pellicano and Rhodes, 2003;

Tanaka, Kay, Grinnell, Stansfield, and Szechter, 1998). Although all of these studies were conducted in the West, both Asian and Caucasian Western adults show the composite face effect and the whole/part advantage, and hence, there is no reason to suspect that the developmental trajectory varies cross-culturally, although it may be biased toward faces from a familiar ethnic group (see below).

By age 4 to 6 years, children are also quite good at recognizing faces that differ only in the shape of the external contour or the shape of the internal features, although they rely more than adults on the external contour until around age 10 and are more easily fooled by paraphernalia (e.g., John wearing Bill's hat; Campbell, Walker, and Baron-Cohen, 1995; Carey and Diamond, 1977; Freire and Lee, 2001; Mondloch et al., 2002; Mondloch, Leis, and Maurer, 2006). By age 6 to 10 years, children are as good as adults in aspects of face processing that rely on featural processing. This includes the relative expertise in identifying emotional expressions across different identities, lip reading, and decoding direction of eye gaze across different identities and head orientations (Mondloch, Geldart, et al., 2003). All of these studies have been conducted with white participants growing up in the West, and hair cues *do* usually reliably differentiate among individual white faces. It is not known whether the developmental pattern is different when hair cues are less reliable, as among Asian faces.

Although individuals can be identified from featural cues, these cues change when the person is seen from a new point of view, expresses a different emotion, or is seen after many years of aging. Under these conditions, the viewer needs to rely on the spacing among facial features that comes from the bone structure of the face, a configural cue that has been called "sensitivity to second-order relations." Adults are exquisitely sensitive to metric differences among individuals in the spacing of facial features, with the limit of their sensitivity for own-race faces corresponding to the limits on visual acuity (Ge, Luo, Nishimura, and Lee, 2003; Haig, 1984). By 5 months of age, infants discriminate between a schematic face with typical spacing of features and one with unnaturally large spacing between the eyes and the eyes and mouth (Bhatt, Bertin, Hayden, and Reed, 2005), but children do not reach adult accuracy in discriminating among individual faces based on natural variations in the spacing of features until adolescence (Mondloch et al., 2002; Mondloch, Dobson, Parson, and Maurer, 2004; Mondloch, Le Grand, and Maurer, 2003). Likely as a result, up to at least age 10, children are not as good as adults at recognizing a face previously seen from a different point of view (e.g., turned to the side versus en face; Mondloch, Geldart, et al., 2003). Thus, it is likely that the slow development of sensitivity to second-order relations underlies the slow development of adult-like expertise in recognizing facial identity. Because experience affects the development of sensitivity to second-order relations, the recognition of facial identity may be biased throughout development toward faces from a familiar ethnic group (see section titled *Perceptual Attunement: Other Races.*).

Roles of Experience

Experience modifies the development of face processing and, not surprisingly, leads to cross-cultural differences in the processing of faces from familiar versus unfamiliar ethnic groups. Evidence comes from children treated for congenital cataract that previously blocked all patterned visual input to the retina. After years of delayed visual input, such children are normal on tests of lipreading, recognizing facial expression, decoding direction of eye gaze, and identifying faces on the basis of the shape of the external contour or the internal features—all tasks that can be solved based on featural processing (Geldart, Mondloch, Maurer, de Schonen, and Brent, 2002; Le Grand, Mondloch, Maurer, and Brent, 2001). Despite early removal of the cataract and fitting with compensatory contact lenses, in some cases by 2 to 3 months of age, and despite years of visual input following treatment, children treated for bilateral congenital cataract do not develop holistic face processing. Unlike normal controls, they do not show a composite face effect and are significantly *better* than controls in seeing that the top halves of two aligned faces are the same despite different bottom halves (Le Grand, Mondloch, Maurer, and Brent, 2004). They also are abnormally poor at detecting differences between faces in the spacing of features and the related skill of recognizing the identity of a face despite a change in its point of view (e.g., from en face to profile) (Geldart et al., 2002; Le Grand et al., 2001; Le Grand, Mondloch, Maurer, and Brent, 2003). Thus, early visual experience is necessary for the later development of two types of configural face processing: holistic processing and sensitivity to second-order relations.

Indirect evidence for a role of continuing experience comes from the face inversion effect; adults' accuracy plummets and their reaction times increase when they are asked to recognize upside down faces, with much larger changes than seen for upside down objects (e.g., Diamond and Carey, 1986; Yin, 1969). The inversion cost is much larger for identifying faces based on second-order relations (spacing differences) or despite a change in point of view than for featural processing (Freire, Lee, and Symons, 2000; Leder and Bruce, 1998; Malcolm, Leung, and Barton, 2005; Mondloch et al., 2002; Mondloch, Geldart, et al., 2003). Inversion also disrupts holistic processing, as indexed by the whole/part advantage or the composite face effect (Tanaka and Farah, 1993; Young et al., 1987). Combined, the data suggest that holistic processing and sensitivity to second-order relations are tuned by experience with upright faces. Converging evidence comes from the finding that adults are more sensitive to spacing differences in human faces than in monkey faces, even when the physical differences are identical (Mondloch, Maurer, and Aloha, 2006). In the following section, we show that by adulthood both of these skills are stronger for faces from a familiar ethnic group than for those from an unfamiliar ethnic group.

Perceptual Attunement: Other Races

At birth, babies do not look longer at faces from their own race/ethnic group than at faces from other groups (Kelly et al., 2005). By 3 months, they have developed a looking preference correlated with the relative frequency of own group and other group faces in their environment. Thus, when tested with Middle Eastern, Chinese, African, and Caucasian faces, white babies growing up in predominantly white areas of Sheffield, England had a looking preference for the Caucasian faces (Kelly et al., 2005), and Han Chinese babies growing up in China with no exposure to foreigners had a looking preference for the Chinese faces (Kelly, Liu, et al., 2007). When 3-month-old infants were tested with Caucasian and Ethiopian faces, white Israeli babies growing up in a predominantly white environment looked longer at the Caucasian faces, black Ethiopian babies growing up in a predominantly black environment in Ethiopia looked longer at the Ethiopian faces, and black Ethiopian babies growing up in an integrated environment showed no looking preference (Bar-Haim, Ziv, Lamy, and Hodes, 2006). Thus, by 3 months, infants growing up in a culturally segregated environment have developed a preference to look at faces of individuals of that culture, that is, their own race or ethnic group.

There is conflicting evidence on whether by 3 months, biased exposure to faces of the own race/ethnic group has also begun to tune discrimination and memory. When tested for discrimination following habituation to a single face, white French babies discriminated between Caucasian faces but not between Asian faces (Sangrigoli and de Schonen, 2004). However, when white English babies were tested with Caucasian, Chinese, Middle Eastern, and African faces, 3-month-olds discriminated among individual faces in all ethnic categories, and it was only between 6 and 9 months that the white babies started to fail the discrimination test for other race faces (Kelly, Quinn, et al., 2007). Moreover, in the original study of white French babies, familiarization with as few as three Asian faces was sufficient to induce discrimination among Asian faces equivalent to the discrimination shown for Caucasian faces. Converging evidence of environmental tuning of face processing comes from studies with male and female faces. At 3 to

4 months, infants being reared primarily by mothers are able to discriminate among individual female faces, but not among individual male faces, and look longer at unfamiliar female than unfamiliar male faces based on the internal features in the upright face (Quinn, Yahr, Kuhn, Slater, and Pascalis, 2002). Infants being reared primarily by fathers look longer at unfamiliar male faces than at unfamiliar female faces (Quinn et al., 2002). Together, these results suggest that during early infancy, face processing begins to be tuned to the characteristics of faces in the infant's individual environment, much as speech processing attunes to the properties of the ambient language. The tuning is first expressed as a preference for faces from the familiar race/ethnic groups, a preference that biases attention away from faces from the unfamiliar category (Kelly, Quinn, et al., 2007) and that, by 9 months of age, leads to a difference in discriminability. Paradoxically during this age period, infants are adept at processing monkey faces to which they never are exposed. Thus, 6-month-olds readily discriminate between individual human faces *and* between individual monkey faces, unlike 9-month-olds who fail the discrimination test for monkey faces unless exposed to named pictures of six monkeys in the intervening months (Pascalis, de Haan, and Nelson, 2002; Pascalis et al., 2005). Although this resembles some aspects of the attunement to same-race faces (more selectivity at 9 than at 6 months), other aspects do not match, namely the early manifestations of an own-race preference/face processing advantage at 3 months when there is apparently no advantage for human over monkey faces.

The Other-Race Effect in Adulthood

Adults are better at recognizing that they have seen an unfamiliar face before if the face is from their own race or ethnic group rather than from an unfamiliar race or ethnic group, the classic *other-race* effect that matches adults' experiences that "they all look alike to me" (see Meissner and Brigham, 2001, for a meta-analysis of 91 experiments). The difficulty does not arise from less variability in the structure of individual faces for some groups than others (i.e., Japanese faces are not less variable than Caucasian faces; Goldstein, 1979), and in most studies, a crossover has been observed that rules out a simple explanation based on the faces of some races/ethnic groups being physically less distinct (e.g., Caucasian faces that are easier than Japanese faces for Caucasians to remember are harder for Japanese to remember). The most common measure of the other-race effect is an old/new memory test in which a person learns faces during the first phase of the task and then later must recognize which faces were seen before among novel foils. For faces from their own group, adults are more likely to correctly recognize the old faces (i.e., more hits) and less likely to incorrectly identify a novel face as having been seen before (i.e., fewer false alarms). The other-race effect also is evident in matching tasks (reviewed in Meissner and Brigham, 2001), sequential same/different judgments (Walker and Tanaka, 2003), judgments of facial similarity (Ng and Lindsay, 1994), and change blindness (Humphreys, Hodsoll, and Campbell, 2005), suggesting that it originates in differential perceptual sensitivity. For example, East Indian and Western Caucasian observers take longer to see that one of four Indian or Caucasian faces in a scene has changed if it is from the less familiar ethnic group/race, but there is no such effect for seeing changes in one of the four bodies or in objects in the scene (Humphreys et al., 2005).

Although the other-race effect has been shown for a large number of cultural groups (Africans, European and African Americans, Japanese, Koreans, Chinese, and East Indians), the size varies across groups, perhaps as a result of different amounts of exposure to faces from other race/ethnic groups, different general processing styles, and/or the differences in prejudice or in power that affect the attention paid to faces from other ethnic groups (e.g., stronger effects in European Americans than Africans; Meissner and Brigham, 2001; Slone, Brigham, and Meissner, 2000; Valentine and Endo, 1992, but see Bothwell, Brigham, and Malpass, 1989). The perceptual other-race effect guarantees that adults are good at individuating members of their own culture, where it is most likely to matter to their economic and social interactions. They are not so good at recognizing "foreigners" with whom they interact less frequently and for whom "foreignness" may be a more salient characteristic than individual identity. Indeed, race is an especially salient characteristic for adults.

Adults generally process the race of a face faster than other characteristics, such as sex, age, or identity (Ito and Urland, 2003; Levin, 2000; Maclin and Malpass, 2003; Montepare and Opeyo, 2002). The rapid identification of the race/ethnic group of faces from an unfamiliar category may lead to processing of features that distinguish the racial category (Levin, 2000) and prevent their being processed automatically at the subordinate level of individual identity where information is extracted that distinguishes among individuals (Walker and Tanaka, 2003), as is routine for own-race faces and nonface categories for which an adult has expertise (Tanaka, Curran, and Sheinberg, 2005). A similar effect can be induced by defining faces as from an out-group; adults are less accurate at recognizing the identity of faces of *their own race* when the faces are arbitrarily defined as part of an out-group (different university or different personality) compared to faces from the in-group (same university or same personality group), perhaps because the out-group label promotes more superficial processing at the category level (Bernstein, Young, and Hugenberg, 2007). Indirect evidence for deeper processing of own-race faces comes from an fMRI study of European American adults showing that a 30-millisecond presentation was sufficient to activate the fusiform face area (FFA) bilaterally for white faces but not for black faces (Cunningham et al., 2004) and from a study of African American and European American adults showing greater overall activation of the FFA when adults attempted to remember own-race rather than other-race faces (Golby, Gabrieli, Chiao, and Eberhardt, 2001). The negative effect of superficial processing on other-race faces can be mitigated by instruction. In a study of European Americans, the other-race deficit for black faces in a typical old/new recognition paradigm was eliminated by preceding the experiment with a description of the typical effect and instructions to try to avoid it by carefully individuating the other-race faces (Hugenberg, Miller, and Claypool, 2007). Not surprisingly, there is no other-race effect for identifying a stimulus as a face or a scrambled image; Japanese and white British adults are equally good at classifying faces as intact or scrambled, whether the faces are of Japanese or white British adults (Valentine and Endo, 1992).

Emotional reactions to race when shown faces from an unfamiliar group may in part mediate the other-race memory effect. White Western adults show stronger activation in a brain area associated with emotional processing, especially of fear—the (right) amygdala—for black than for white faces, even when the face has a neutral expression and is presented for a mere 30 milliseconds before being masked, which is too short a time to be consciously perceived (Cunningham et al., 2004). Indirect evidence for the role of emotional reactions comes from a study in which the mood of white Western adults was manipulated by videos. When the video induced positive emotions either before they viewed the faces to be remembered or before they began the old/new memory task, the other-race effect diminished because the happy subjects were more accurate at recognizing black faces that were seen before than subjects who saw a neutral or fear-eliciting video (Johnson and Fredrickson, 2006). Positive emotions may facilitate the recognition of facial identity because they are known to widen the scope of attention toward more global processing that may facilitate the processing of configural cues and/or because they may offset negative emotional reactions that block processing below the superficial level of race. When faces have an angry expression rather than the typical neutral expression, the other-race memory effect disappears or even reverses; whites are better at recognizing black angry faces than white angry faces or black neutral faces, consistent with evidence that angry expressions attract and hold attention (Ackerman et al., 2006) and that emotional reactions (in this case of threat) moderate the other-race memory effect. Thus, angry faces may hold attention long enough for additional processing to occur at the individual level, perhaps because it is adaptive to remember the identity of threatening members of an out-group (Ackerman et al., 2006). Like the studies on the amygdala, such studies have not been reported for Asians or Asian faces, and the effects might be different when interracial social relationships are less charged or when there has been less previous contact with individuals from the less familiar race/ethnic group.

Consistent with the results from visual deprivation, adults process faces from their own race and ethnic group more holistically than faces from a less familiar race/ethnic group, as measured by both the whole/part advantage and the composite face effect (Michel, Caldara, and Rossion, in press; Michel, Rossion, Han, Chung, and Caldara, 2006; Tanaka, Kiefer, and Bukach, 2004). The difference is stronger in Western white adults, who showed no evidence of holistic processing for Asian faces in any of three studies, than for Asian adults, who showed evidence of holistic processing for both Asian and Caucasian faces, even in the one study that tested Asian adults who had had little contact with white faces (Michel et al., 2006). Holistic processing—as indexed by the composite face effect—activates areas in the middle fusiform gyrus near the classic fusiform face area, especially in the right hemisphere, and to a lesser extent, in the inferior occipital gyrus near the occipital face area (Schiltz and Rossion, 2006). As would be predicted from these findings, a Caucasian adult whose corpus callosum had been severed as treatment for epilepsy showed better memory for Caucasian than Japanese faces when they were presented to the right hemisphere but not when they were presented to the left hemisphere (Turk, Handy, and Gazzaniga, 2005).

There is indirect evidence that memory for second-order relations is better for faces from a familiar race/ethnic group than an unfamiliar group, just as sensitivity to second-order relations is better in other cases where there is a difference in the amount of experience (better for human than monkey faces; for upright than inverted faces; or after normal visual experience than after visual deprivation from congenital cataract). When faces are blurred to remove the high spatial frequencies that define facial features, adults can still recognize faces learned earlier during an experiment, presumably based on their second-order relations (Collishaw and Hole, 2000; Hayward, Rhodes, and Schwaninger, 2008). However, their accuracy is higher if the face is from their own race/ethnic group (Caucasian or Asian) than if it is from an unfamiliar group (Hayward et al., 2008). Adults are much poorer at recognizing the faces if, for the test, their features are cut into pieces and rearranged into a scrambled pattern, as would be expected from the elimination of information about second-order relations and the interference with holistic processing. However, adults' recognition of scrambled features is nevertheless above chance *and* better for own race/ethnic group than other race/ethnic group (Hayward et al., 2008). That finding indicates that adults are better at processing and remembering *both* the features and their spacing in faces from their own race/ethnic group, although the recognition of *isolated facial features* is not consistently better for faces from the same rather than different race or ethnic group (Michel et al., in press; Tanaka et al., 2004). Converging evidence for an own-race advantage for the processing of both features and second-order relations comes from a discrimination study in which Caucasian adults living in Australia and Chinese adults living in Hong Kong were better at recognizing which face they had just seen if it was from their own race/ethnic group, whether the foil differed in the spacing of the eyes and mouth or in the features (nose shape and lightness of the lips and eyebrows; Rhodes, Hayward, and Winkler, 2006).

Experience and the Other-Race Effect

Although it is obvious that the other-race effect in face processing results from lack of experience with faces from another race/ethnic group, what is less clear is how much exposure is necessary to ameliorate or eliminate the effect, whether there is less plasticity in adults than children, and what type of exposure is necessary. Many studies of the other-race effect with adults have evaluated the *contact hypothesis,* namely that the other-race effect is larger in adults with less contact with the unfamiliar race or ethnic group. A meta-analysis of 29 samples showed a small but significant correlation between self-reported contact and accuracy in discriminating other-race faces. (Limited variance may have contributed to the low value; Meissner and Brigham, 2001; see Michel et al., 2006, for similar evidence for holistic processing, at least by white Westerners.) There are also differences between groups that would be predicted by the contact hypothesis. White American students attending a university with only white students were best at recognizing white faces and equally poor at recognizing black and Japanese faces, whereas white American students attending an integrated university were best at recognizing white faces but better at recognizing black faces than Japanese faces (Chance, Goldstein, and McBride, 1975). Black students at the integrated university were best at recognizing black faces and better at recognizing white faces than Japanese faces. Similarly, black American adults are better than black Nigerian adults at recognizing white faces, with accuracy for both groups correlated positively with some measures of interracial experience (Carroo, 1986; but see Ng and Lindsay, 1994, for contradictory data for Asians tested in Singapore versus Ontario). Similarly, training of Western white adults on the discrimination of Asian faces improves recognition memory for a novel set of Asian faces, with no evidence of loss over 5 months (Elliott, Willis, and Goldstein, 1973; Goldstein and Chance, 1985). Western white adults with minimum previous contact with Asians can rapidly learn to identify the faces of four Asian "friends" as accurately as they recognize the faces of four new Caucasian friends; after just 1 hour of training, they appear to process the familiarized Asian faces holistically, as they do the familiarized Caucasian faces but not familiarized dogs (McKone, Brewer, MacPherson, Rhodes, and Hayward, 2007). Training with white faces does not induce any general improvements in the recognition of facial identity, as would be expected if performance had already been optimized by real-world experience.

The results for the contact hypothesis and for training suggest that there is considerable plasticity even in the adult brain that allows improvement in the processing of faces from an unfamiliar race or ethnic group. Such plasticity is consistent with recent evidence that faces are represented in an n-dimensional face space centered on a norm that is constantly being updated based on experience (reviewed in Rhodes et al., 2005). The strongest evidence comes from studies using adaptation. After adaptation to distorted faces (e.g., all expanded or all contracted), there is a shift in what looks most normal in the direction of the distortion, such that an average face appears distorted in the opposite direction (Maclin and Webster, 2001; Rhodes, Jeffery, Watson, Clifford, and Nakayama, 2003; Watson and Clifford, 2003; Webster and Maclin, 1999). Similarly, adaptation to anti-Dan (a face different from an average face in the opposite direction from Dan) causes an average face to begin to look like Dan and hence the neutral norm to shift in the direction of the adapting face (Jeffrey, Rhodes, and Busey, 2006; Leopold, O'Toole, Vetter, and Blanz, 2001; Rhodes and Jeffrey, 2006). Such adaptation generalizes across changes in position, size, and, to some extent, point of view (Jeffrey et al., 2006; Leopold and Bondar, 2005; Leopold, Bondar, and Giese, 2006). These laboratory effects suggest that adults constantly recalibrate their face space based on the collection of faces they see (Rhodes et al., 2006; Webster, Kaping, Mizokami, and Duhamel, 2004), updating the norm to which faces are compared and likely refining the dimensions to those most useful for discriminating among the represented faces. Consequently, the other race effect can diminish if the diet of faces begins to include those of the other race. Indirect evidence comes from a study with a face continuum created by morphing between Japanese and Caucasian faces in small steps. The neutral or boundary point was shifted in the direction of own race/ethnicity for both Caucasians and Japanese, except for Asians who had been in the United States for a year. Their boundary was closer to that of Caucasians, and its location was correlated with the length of their stay in the United States and amount of contact with Caucasians (Webster et al., 2004).

However, it is not clear whether the other-race effect can be eliminated completely in adulthood. For example, Asian students living in the West show holistic processing for both Asian and Caucasian faces, as indexed by the whole/part advantage (Michel et al., 2006; Tanaka et al., 2004), but nevertheless still show a strong other-race effect on tests of recognition memory for unfamiliar faces (Michel et al., 2006). Similarly, adults brought up in Korea but residing in France for an average of 4.5 years are nevertheless better at recognizing an unfamiliar face to which they were just exposed 1 second previously if the face is Asian rather than Caucasian (Sangrigoli, Pallier, Argenti, Ventureyra, and de Schonen, 2005).

There may be greater plasticity during childhood. There is evidence for the other-race memory effect from 3 years of age and possibly as early as 9 months (Kelly, Quinn, et al., 2007). For example, 3-year-olds are better at recognizing which of two faces was presented during the preceding second if the faces are from their own race/ethnic group than from an unfamiliar race/ethnic group (Sangrigoli and De Schonen, 2004). By kindergarten, children show an advantage in recognition memory for own-race faces that is as large as in adults (Pezdek, Blandon-Gitlin, and Moore, 2003). Despite the early emergence of a robust other-race effect, changes in the faces to which children are exposed can eliminate or actually reverse it (Sangrigoli et al., 2005; see also Feinman and Entwistle, 1976). Korean children adopted into French Caucasian homes when 3 to 9 years old later show a complete *reversal* of the other-race effect, such that, like native French Caucasian adults and unlike Koreans who moved to France as adults, they are better at recognizing an unfamiliar face to which they were exposed 1 second previously if it is Caucasian rather than Asian. That contrast suggests that the child's brain is sufficiently plastic for later biased experience to overwrite completely the effects of earlier experience biased in a different direction. As with speech, a critical feature in this example may be the large degree of bias in the later experience, such that the adopted Korean child encountered many Caucasian faces and very few Asian faces.

In summary, culture affects perception by leading to better expert processing of faces from one's own culture than those from other groups. This serves to facilitate social interactions within a culture and to provide perceptual support for a prejudice against members of a culture with a different appearance who normally will be processed at the level of race or ethnic group rather than as individuals. However, the perceptual bias can be reduced by contact, by positive emotions or the perception of threat, and by even short-term training.

Facial Expressions

Adults from widely different cultures agree at rates far exceeding chance on what emotion a face is expressing. For example, Ekman and colleagues (Ekman and Friesen, 1971; Ekman et al., 1987) and Izard (1971) found that adults from a variety of cultures agreed at high rates on which basic emotion (sadness, fear, surprise, happiness, disgust, or anger) was being posed in photographs of Western white adults, although accuracy was lower overall for preliterate groups (reviewed in Elfenbein and Ambady, 2002). In one meta-analysis, the average accuracy in recognizing the correct emotion on the photographed faces of adults from another race/ethnic group was found to be 58% and varied from a high of 79% for happiness to a low of 43% for contempt (meta-analysis in Elfenbein and Ambady, 2002). Such data indicate that there are universal signals in a static face that convey emotion in similar ways cross-culturally. These same emotions can also be signaled in the voice, although the accuracy of cross-cultural recognition is lower for voices than faces (Elfenbein and Ambady, 2003a). The basic set of emotions that are recognized cross-culturally result from the contraction of particular facial muscles and can signal to others that there is an environmental change that may require action (e.g., escape from the source of fear or threat, approach to the source of happiness) (Ekman, 1993). Infants discriminate among emotional expressions from an early age and by the end of the first year have begun to alter their behavior in response to emotions in ways that suggest they understand their meaning (e.g., avoiding a cliff or toy if the mom looks fearful, approaching a toy if mom looks happy) (Klinnert, Emde, Butterfield, and Campos, 1986; Rosen, Adamson, and Bakeman, 1992; Sorce, Emde, Campos, and Klinnert, 1985). Thus, the ubiquitous sensitivity to basic emotional expressions allows parents to use facial expressions to convey cultural expectations to children from an early age. It also allows parent, teachers, and elders to reinforce cultural norms through nonverbal feedback to adolescents in group settings (e.g., which individuals are unsuitable friends or marriage partners, what language is [literally] "frowned upon"), a role it continues to play in adulthood (e.g., shaming).

Nevertheless, the cross-cultural agreement in recognizing facial expressions is not perfect, and overall accuracy is greater for those from the same race/ethnic group as the person posing the expression than those from another group, an own-group advantage analogous to the own-race advantage in recognizing the identity of faces. On average, adults are 9% more accurate in recognizing emotional expressions on faces from their own ethnic/racial group, although the size of the effect varies from a high of 13% to 15% for disgust and fear to a low of 7% for anger and happiness (Elfenbein and Ambady, 2002), and the advantage is present for recognizing emotional voices as well as faces. The differences remain in studies with well-controlled stimuli and a balanced crossover design (e.g., Americans and Africans rating American and African faces). The own-group advantage for recognizing facial expression no doubt arises in part from sensitivity to culturally specific rules for the display of emotion (Ekman, 1993; Matsumoto, Takeuchi, Andayani, Kouznetsove, and Krupp, 1998); for example, in East Asian cultures, the control of emotions is emphasized more than in individualistic Western cultures. The resulting prediction is that cues to how a person is feeling will be more subtle for East Asians than Western adults. Consistent with this prediction, Japanese adults judge the happiness or sadness of a composite face from the subtle cues around the eyes, whereas American adults judge the emotion from the more blatant cues in the mouth region (Yuki, Madduz, and Masuda, 2007). Like the other-race effect for facial identity, the own-group advantage for recognizing facial expressions also appears to be related to contact; the greater the physical distance is between two groups, the larger the own-group advantage, even among white Western adults living in English-speaking countries (e.g., England, Scotland, Ireland, New Zealand, Australia; Elfenbein and Ambady, 2002, 2003a). It also appears to be somewhat malleable. University students studying in a foreign country are more accurate in judging the expressions on faces of natives of the country than their compatriots at home are, although they are still less accurate than native viewers are (Elfenbein and Ambady, 2003b). There have been no studies of the development of the own-group advantage for facial expressions. Like the own-race memory advantage for facial identity, the own-group advantage for recognizing basic facial expressions assures that adults are more sensitive to nonverbal cues arising from members of their own culture than cues from foreigners. Although this is adaptive within the cultural group, it can lead to awkward situations abroad when the out-group member misinterprets emotional expressions and reacts in an inappropriate way.

Perceptual Attunement

The reviews of language, music, and face processing provide strong evidence in support of perceptual attunement across the first year of life (see Scott, Pascalis, and Nelson, 2007, for a more general review). In all three domains, infants begin life with perceptual biases that differentially direct their attention and influence their information processing. They prefer speech over nonspeech at birth, preferentially attend to faces and face-like stimuli, and seem to favor some auditory stream segmentation strategies over others. The preferences infants show allow them to be relatively equal in their facility at processing those elements of speech, faces, and music that are common across cultures. During the first weeks and months of life, infants rapidly attune to the characteristics of their native language, native faces, and native music, improving in their ability to discriminate features that are regularly seen and heard in the native language, faces, and music and becoming less sensitive to those features that are not experienced in the native culture.

The examples we have reviewed here each address how the developing child becomes gradually attuned to one of these domains at a time. But of course, perceptual attunement to the language, music, and faces of a culture work together to drive social development and acculturation. A recently published study by Kinzler, Dupoux, and Spelke (2007) provides an excellent illustration of how infants and young children integrate perceptual knowledge of the native language with an ability to discriminate individual faces in making choices for social partners. At 5 to 6 months, after being shown side-by-side images of two female speakers, one speaking backward and the other speaking forward, infants show a preference for looking at a still image of the person who was speaking forward, revealing an early preference for social partners who speak "naturally." This preference is restricted to potential social partners; when forward versus backward speech was paired with two different geometric forms, infants of 5 to 6 months showed no subsequent preference for one form over the other. However, when the original experiment was repeated, but this time one of two bilingual speakers spoke the native language (English) and the other spoke Spanish (with person and side counterbalanced across infants), English-learning infants showed a preference for the still image of the person who was speaking English. This remarkably early preference for an individual face that has been associated with the native language requires that the infant recognize the still face after first seeing it moving and that their preference for the face be driven by its association with, what has become to the infant, the native language.

The study by Kinzler et al. (2007) showed that the preference for "native" faces is expressed in several other social domains over the next months and years as well. At 10 months, English- and French-learning infants were shown films of two bilingual speakers talking in either English or French. In the final part of the film, each speaker offered the child one of two toys. Infants in Boston chose the toy that had originally been offered, on film, by the person they saw speaking English, whereas infants in Paris chose the toy that had originally been offered by the person they saw speaking French. At 5 years, these earlier preferences were expressed in full-fledged friendship choices. When shown photographs of unfamiliar children while either English or French was played, 5-year-old children later stated a friendship preference for the picture of the child who they thought spoke their native language. When shown pictures paired with either accented or unaccented native speech, 5-year-old children indicated a friendship preference for the photograph associated with accent-free native speech (Kinzler et al., 2007). Taken together, these findings show that knowledge of the native language directs children's preferences and thus deeply influences their acquisition of culture.

Cultural Influences on Other Aspects of Perception

The influence of culture extends far beyond speech, music, and face perception. There are reported cultural influences on visual-spatial processing (Levinson, 1997), visual scene processing (Nisbett, 2003), visual illusions such as the rod and frame task (Kitayama, Duff, Kawamura, and Larsen, 2003), processing of time and space (Boroditsky, 2001), mathematical processing (e.g., Tang et al., 2006), and virtually every aspect of perception and cognition one could test. In many of these cases, the influence is argued to be from living in a specific type of world (e.g., see Segall, Campbell, and Herskovits, 1963, for one of the first articulations of the "carpentered world hypothesis"), and in many others, the influence is understood to come from language.

As an example of a change brought about by language, Hespos and Spelke (2004) showed that English-learning 5-month-old infants perceive the difference between tight- and loose-fitting events, where objects either fit together snugly or roomily. This conceptual distinction is made in Korean but not English. Here experience with linguistic terms that make this distinction seems to be critical for maintaining it. Only Korean adults, not English adults, treat tight-fitting and loose-fitting events as separate categories.

The evidence for cultural differences in processing is undeniable. What distinguishes the interpretations offered by different researchers, however, and hence remains highly controversial is whether the influence extends into the fundamental act of perception, as would be predicted by a strong Whorfian hypothesis (Whorf, 1956) or whether culture exerts its influence at a level of abstraction above that of perception, with perception and its neural correlates fundamentally unchanged (see Li and Gleitman, 2002, for example of a counter-explanation for the Levinson, 1997, results). Because it is beyond the scope of this chapter to give any semblance of fair coverage to that enormous literature, we provide a more in-depth examination of cultural influences of perception on one visual domain, color perception.

Color perception is perhaps one of the most widely studied and, in many ways, controversial areas of perceptual development (for comprehensive reviews, see Bornstein, 2006; Bornstein, Artreberry, and Mash, 2005). In many ways, research on color perception introduced and presaged the explosion of research reviewed earlier on the relation between perceptual attunement and acculturation. Highlights of classic research that has withstood the test of time and of current areas of controversy are provided here.

By 4 months of age, infants discriminate primary color categories (red, yellow, green, and blue) from each other and from secondary categories (such as orange, purple, and pink) (Bornstein, Kessen, and Weiskopf, 1976; Franklin and Davies, 2004). Infants are not born with this impressive range of discrimination; a developmental trajectory is found whereby 1-month-olds appear to already discriminate *red* from *green*, but neither from *yellow*; *green-yellow* discrimination comes in at 2 months of age, and finally, *red-yellow* discrimination appears at 3 months (Adams and Courage, 1995). This evidence suggests an early organization of the color space, one present before the many facets of culture-specific experience come into play. By 4 months, Western babies, like Western adults, are more sensitive to changes between the primary color categories than to changes of the same physical magnitude within a color category (Bornstein et al., 1976).

Given the evidence that hue categories are discriminated in infancy, the difficulty and confusion experienced by children in learning labels for the categories is puzzling (Bornstein, 1985). One reason may be that labels in the language do not always correspond to initial categories; for example, infants discriminate the color category *green* from *blue*, which is not distinguished in all languages. Category boundaries significantly sharpen in early childhood and remain stable through the lifespan (Raskin, Maital, and Bornstein, 1983), perhaps as a result of cementing linguistic influence in childhood. Cultural experience could perhaps influence the development of new color categories, but if and how culture affects color perception after infancy are matters of great debate. Indeed, it is possible that although the color category repertoire may differ between cultures, perception may remain fundamentally unchanged.

Potential cultural differences in adult color perception rest on methods testing the categorical nature of initial/universal versus culture-specific categories. But just how categorical is color perception? The terms *turquoise*, *navy*, and *azure*, which are all variants on the primary colors, along with the myriad of paint chips at home hardware stores attest to the fact that adults are acutely sensitive to and often able to label even slight variations within (or between) primary colors. Moreover, experimental evidence shows that both adults and infants are able to discriminate many more hue variations than they are able to readily label (Bornstein, 1987;

Franklin, Pilling, and Davies, 2005). Although hue discrimination is nonetheless better across than within categories for which adults have labels, this within-category sensitivity suggests that color perception is not as strongly categorical as are some types of perception, such as speech perception. This broad sensitivity could ultimately leave an opening for reorganization of initial categories.

In answering the questions of whether and how much culture-specific color terms influence color perception and cognition, initial investigations were supportive of universal patterns of perception, irrespective of linguistic labels (Rosch Heider, 1972). In this work, the Dugum Dani, a stone-age culture located in New Guinea, were compared to Americans. The Dani have only two color terms (roughly corresponding to dark and light), yet the results suggested that they used and remembered colors based on the Western primary color categories rather than just two as would be predicted by a strong linguistic relativity model (Rosch Heider and Olivier, 1972). However, some recent research has failed to replicate the initial Rosch Heider findings in another group with limited color terms. Specifically, Roberson and her colleagues studied Bernimo speakers (a small hunter-gatherer tribe of Papua New Guinea). The Bernimo language has only five color terms, and these terms divide the color space differently than would be predicted by the primary colors of red, green, blue, and yellow. Among the Bernimo, those colors that fall within the same linguistic category are perceived as more similar than colors that are from two different Bernimo linguistic categories (but importantly, still within one of the categories expected to be universal from the infant and Rosch Heider findings). Moreover, the Bernimo discriminate more easily between two colors that cross a Bernimo boundary than two colors that cross a more "universal" color boundary (Roberson, Davies, and Davidoff, 2000). These results support a stronger influence of language on color perception than the original Rosch Heider work.

The compelling evidence for both universal and cultural-specific influences on color perception requires an approach the goes beyond a simple back and forth debate. One such synthetic approach was first suggested by Jameson and D'Andrade (1997) and more recently developed by Kay, Reiger, and colleagues. Although acknowledging that there exist striking differences across cultures in the number and type of labeled color categories (Berlin and Kay, 1969), the core feature of this approach is that there is a universal organization to the color space but that it is less regularly shaped than the categories originally described by Rosch Heider. Specifically, it is suggested that although any color can potentially be focal for a particular cultural group, hue interacts with brightness to yield some colors that are more salient and hence more universally "focal" than others. These focal colors yield irregularly shaped natural categories that constrain how color terms are applied and used in languages with different numbers of color terms (Kay and Reiger, 2006). Indeed, mathematical modeling beginning with the initial irregular color space and crossing it with the number of color terms in a language successfully predicts the precise shades (using the Munsell set of color chips) that will be treated as members of a single linguistic color category in a language (Reiger, Kay, and Khetarpal, 2007).

A helpful distinction can be made between perceptually based categories that are initially present (and may or not develop further with experience) and conceptually based categories that will arise with experience and with the learning of color labels (Bornstein, 1987). The color space of these two levels may be divided differently and be tapped by different tasks, so if there is change in "perception," the question still remains at what level this change occurs. Two lines of work suggest that there are effects on only the higher cognitive language labeling level. For example, when articulatory suppression is imposed, hence blocking access to color terms, cultural differences in color perception are reduced (Roberson and Davidoff, 2000). Similarly, when color labels are made more accessible by presenting stimuli to the right visual hemisphere (thus activating the left cerebral hemisphere where much of language is localized), there is a stronger effect of language labels on color perception (Gilbert, Regier, Kay, and Ivry, 2006). However, although the linguistic effect is stronger for processing in the right visual field, a weaker but still significant effect is also found for stimuli processed in the left visual field. This weakened left visual field effect could be either a result of delayed transfer of information from the linguistically affected left cerebral hemisphere across the corpus callosum or a result of lingering categorical effects for primary colors first observed in infancy (Drivonikou et al., 2007). Thus, it appears that, at least at higher cognitive levels, color perception may remain more open to changes in cultural experience.

A remaining challenge is how best to account for the cross-cultural differences in color terms and in at least some aspects of color perception, despite the equally strong evidence for universal primary colors as revealed both by the initial infant biases described earlier and well-documented physiologically based constraints on coding. In what way could different higher order sets of color categories develop in individuals from different language and cultural groups? One possibility is that the documented sensitivities to subtle differences in hue that go far beyond either the primary colors or even the labeled categories of the language with the richest color vocabulary could be exploited in perceptual learning to create new categories (Ribar, Oakes, and Spalding, 2004; Werker and Curtin, 2005; Younger and Johnson, 2006). This could function as an opening whereby experience could change perception later in life, with linguistic labels potentially functioning as "invitations" to form categories (Waxman and Markow, 1995). Like speech sound categories in infancy, experience with the culturally nonmeaningful distinction between, for example, *green* and *blue* could result in decreasing attention to the contrast and creation of the category *grue*. In fact, categorical perception of color can be induced for arbitrary categories and in a relatively short amount of time even in adulthood (Özgen and Davies, 2002). In the Özgen and Davies study, individuals were trained over 3 days on a within-category distinction dividing either the blue or the green category. Feedback was given on same-different judgments on pairs of stimuli, where the category focal point now became the induced boundary. This perceptual training resulted in categorical perception of the trained boundaries (Özgen and Davies, 2002). Although within-category discrimination can also be demonstrated for speech sounds, both in infants (McMurray and Aslin, 2005) and in adults (McMurray and Aslin, 2004; Pisoni and Tash, 1974) and simple statistical learning manipulations can change category structure (Maye, Werker, and Gerken, 2002), it may be easier to bring about lasting change in color than in phonetic perception.

Conclusion

Human beings begin life with perceptual capacities that prepare them to acquire the knowledge necessary to live in any of the world's cultures. Specific experience interacts with developing sensitivities to attune perception to optimally match the requirements of the native culture. Culture as a form of experience can penetrate some perceptual systems so deeply as to lead to permanent deficits in the ability to process information from a nonnative culture. This is seen, for example, in the apparent critical periods in the other-race effect in individual recognition and in discrimination of many phones. In other cases, culture may affect only the outputs from perception, as might be the case in color naming and color memory. In either case, once culture has affected perception, perception in turn helps assure cultural cohesiveness. We prefer faces, speech, and songs from our native culture. We name and better remember colors, shapes, and even spatial layouts that carry import in our native culture. As such, whether it changes the actual functioning of the sensory systems or impacts at the level of language and thought, it can be seen that culture shapes perception and perception, in turn, shapes culture.

Acknowledgments

This chapter was prepared with assistance from Social Sciences and Humanities Research Council of Canada (SSHRC) and Natural Sciences and Engineering Research Council of Canada (NSERC) grants to J. Werker, a NSERC grant to D. Maurer, and SSHRC and Michael Smith Foundation for Health Research (MSFHR) fellowships to K. Yoshida.

References

Abraham, G. (1974). *The tradition of western music*. Berkeley, CA: University of California Press.

Ackerman, J. M., Shapiro, J. R., Neuberg, S. L., Kenrick, D. T., Becker, D. V., Griskevicius, V., et al. (2006). They all look the same to me (unless they're angry): From out-group homogeneity to out-group heterogeneity. *Psychological Science, 17*, 836–840.

Adams, R. J., and Courage, M. L. (1995). Development of chromatic discrimination in early infancy. *Behavioral Brain Research, 67*, 99–101.

Aslin, R. N. (1981). Experiential influences and sensitive periods in perceptual development: A unified model. In R. N. Aslin, J. R. Alberts, and M. R. Peterson (Eds.), *Development of perception: Psychobiological perspectives. Volume 2: The visual system*. New York: Academic Press.

Aslin, R. N., and Pisoni, D. B. (1980). Some developmental processes in speech perception. In G. H. Yeni-Komshian, J. Kavanagh, and C. A. Ferguson (Eds.), *Child phonology: Perception* (Vol. 2, pp. 67–96). New York: Academic Press.

Baharloo, S., Johnston, P. A., Service, S. K., Gitschier, J., and Freimer, N. B. (1998). Absolute pitch: An approach for identification of genetic and nongenetic components. *American Journal of Human Genetics, 62*, 224–231.

Bahrick, L. E., and Pickens, J. N. (1988). Classification of bimodal English and Spanish language passages by infants. *Infant Behavior and Development, 11*, 277–296.

Baker, S. A., Golinkoff, R. M., and Petitto, L. A. (2006). New insights into old puzzles from infants' categorical discrimination of soundless phonetic units. *Language Learning and Development, 2*, 147–162.

Baker, S. A., Idsardi, W. J., Golinkoff, R. M., and Petitto, L. (2005). The perception of handshapes in American Sign Language. *Memory and Cognition, 33*, 897–904.

Baker, S. A., Werker, J. F., and Golinkoff, R. M. (manuscript in preparation). Understanding the role of experience in perception of American Sign Language.

Bar-Haim, Y., Ziv, T., Lamy, D., and Hodes, R. (2006). Nature and nurture in own-race face processing. *Psychological Science, 17*, 159–163.

Berlin, B., and Kay, P. (1969). *Basic color terms: Their universality and evolution*. Berkeley, CA: University of California Press.

Bernstein, M., Young, S., and Hugenberg, K. (2007). The cross-category effect. Mere social categorization is sufficient to elicit an own-group bias in face recognition. *Psychological Science, 18*, 706–712.

Bertinetto, P. M. (1981). *Strutture prosodiche dell' italiano. Accento, quantità, sillaba, giuntura, fondamenti metrici*. Firenze, Italy: Accademia della Crusca.

Bertoncini, J., Bijeljac-Babic, R., Blumstein, S. E., and Mehler, J. (1987). Discrimination in neonates of very short CVs. *The Journal of the Acoustical Society of America, 82*, 31–37.

Best, C. T., and Avery, R. A. (1999). Left hemisphere advantage for click consonants is determined by linguistic significance. *Psychological Science, 10*, 65–69.

Best, C. T., and McRoberts, G. W. (2003). Infant perception of non-native consonant contrasts that adults assimilate in different ways. *Language and Speech, 46*, 183–216.

Best, C. T., McRoberts, G. W., LaFleur, R., and Silver-Isenstadt, J. (1995). Divergent developmental patterns for infants' perception of two nonnative consonant contrasts. *Infant Behavior and Development, 18*, 339–350.

Best, C. T., McRoberts, G. W., and Sithole, N. M. (1988). Examination of perceptual reorganization for non-native speech contrasts: Zulu click discrimination by English-speaking adults and infants. *Journal of Experimental Psychology: Human Perception and Performance, 14*, 345–360.

Bhatt, R. S., Bertin, E., Hayden, A., and Reed, A. (2005). Face processing in infancy: Developmental changes in the use of different kinds of relational information. *Child Development, 76*, 169–181.

Bornstein, M. H. (1985). On the development of color naming in young children: Data and theory. *Brain and Language, 26*, 72–93.

Bornstein, M. H. (1987). Perceptual categories in vision and in audition. In S. Harnad (Ed.), *Categorical perception* (pp. 287–300). New York: Cambridge University Press.

Bornstein, M. H. (2006). Hue categorization and color naming: Cognition to language to culture. In R. M. MacLaury, G. V. Paramel, and D. Dedrick (Eds.), *Anthropology of colour: Interdisciplinary multilevel modelling*. Amsterdam: John Benjamins.

Bornstein, M. H., Artreberry, M. E., and Mash, C. (2005). Perceptual development. In M. H. Bornstein and M. E. Lamb (Eds.), *Developmental science: An advanced textbook*. Mahwah, NJ: Lawrence Erlbaum Associates.

Bornstein, M. H., Kessen, W., and Weiskopf, S. (1976). The categories of hue in infancy. *Science, 191*, 201–202.

Boroditsky, L. (2001). Does language shape thought. Mandarin and English speakers' conceptions of time. *Cognitive Psychology, 43*, 1–22.

Bosch, L., Costa, A., and Sebastián-Gallés, N. (2000). First and second language vowel perception in early bilinguals. *European Journal of Cognitive Psychology, 12*, 189–222.

Bosch, L., and Sebastián-Gallés, N. (1997). Native-language recognition abilities in 4-month-old infants from monolingual and bilingual environments. *Cognition, 65*, 33–69.

Bosch, L., and Sebastián-Gallés, N. (2001). Evidence of early language discrimination abilities in infants from bilingual environments. *Infancy, 2*, 29–49.

Bosch, L., and Sebastián-Gallés, N. (2003). Simultaneous bilingualism and the perception of a language specific vowel contrast in the first year of life. *Language and Speech, 46*, 217–244.

Bothwell, R., Brigham, J., and Malpass, R. (1989). Cross-racial identification. *Personality and Social Psychology Bulletin, 15*, 19–25.

Brown, W. A., Sachs, H., Cammuso, K., and Folstein, S. E. (2002). Early music training and absolute pitch. *Music Perception, 19*, 595–597.

Bruce, V., Campbell, R. N., Doherty-Sneddon, G., Import, A., Langton, S., McAuley, S., et al. (2000). Testing face processing skills in children. *British Journal of Developmental Psychology, 18*, 319–333.

Burnham, D., and Dodd, B. (2004) Auditory-visual speech integration by pre-linguistic infants: Perception of an emergent consonant in the McGurk effect. *Developmental Psychobiology, 44*, 209–220.

Burnham, D., and Mattock, K. (2007) The perception of tones and phones. In O.-S. Bohn and M. J. Munro (Eds.), *Language experience in second language speech learning. In honor of James Emil Flege* (pp. 259–280). Amsterdam: John Benjamins.

Burns, T. C., Yoshida, K. A., Hill, K., and Werker, J. F. (2007). Bilingual and monolingual infant phonetic development. *Applied Psycholinguistics, 28*, 455–474.

Bushnell, I. W. R. (2001). Mother's face recognition in newborn infants: Learning and memory. *Infant and Child Development, 10*, 67–74.

Bushnell, I. W. R., Sai, F., and Mullin, J. T. (1989). Neonatal recognition of the mother's face. *British Journal of Developmental Psychology, 7*, 3–15.

Byers-Heinlein, K., Burns, T. C., and Werker, J. F. (under revision). The roots of bilingualism in newborns.

Campbell, R., Walker, J., and Baron-Cohen, S. (1995). The development of inner and outer face features in familiar face identification. *Journal of Experimental Child Psychology, 59*, 196–210.

Carey, S., and Diamond, R. (1977). From piecemeal to configurational representation of faces. *Science, 195*, 312–314.

Carey, S., and Diamond, R. (1994). Are faces perceived as configurations more by adults than by children? *Visual Cognition, 1*, 253–274.

Carey, S., Diamond, R., and Woods, B. (1980). Development of face recognition: A maturational component? *Developmental Psychology, 16*, 257–269.

Carroo, A. (1986). Other race recognition: A comparison of black American and African subjects. *Perceptual and Motor Skills, 62*, 135–138.

Cassia, V. M., Turati, C., and Simion, F. (2004). Can a nonspecific bias toward top-heavy patterns explain newborns' face preference? *Psychological Science, 15*, 379–383.

Chance, J., Goldstein, A., and McBride, L. (1975). Differential experience and recognition memory for faces. *Journal of Social Psychology, 97*, 243–253.

Cheour, M., Ceponiene, R., Lehtokoski, A., Luuk, A., Allik, J., Alho, K., et al. (1998). Development of language-specific phoneme representations in the infant brain. *Nature Neuroscience, 1*, 351–353.

Chin, C. (2003). The development of absolute pitch: A theory concerning the roles of music training at an early developmental age and individual cognitive style. *Psychology of Music, 31*, 155–171.

Clayton, D. F. (2000). The genomic action potential. *Neurobiology of Learning and Memory, 74*, 185–216.

Collishaw, S. M., and Hole, G. J. (2000). Featural and configural processes in the recognition of faces of different familiarity. *Perception, 29*, 893–909.

Crozier, J. B. (1997). Absolute pitch: Practice makes perfect, the earlier the better. *Psychology of Music, 25*, 110–119.

Cunningham, W., Johnson, M., Raye, C., Gatenby, J., Gore, J., and Banaji, M. (2004). Separable neural components in the processing of black and white faces. *Psychological Science, 15*, 806–813.

Dasher, R., and Bolinger, D. (1982). On pre-accentual lengthening. *Journal of the International Phonetic Association, 12*, 58–69.

DeCasper, A. J., and Fifer, W. P. (1980). Of human bonding: Newborns prefer their mothers' voices. *Science, 280*, 1174–1176.

DeCasper, A. J., and Spence, M. J. (1986). Prenatal maternal speech influences newborns' perception of speech sounds. *Infant Behavior and Development, 9*, 133–150.

Dediu, D., and Ladd, R. (2007). Linguistic tone is related to the population frequency of the adaptive haplogroups of two brain-size genes, ASPM and microcephalin. *Proceedings of the National Academy of Sciences, 104*, 10944–10949.

Dehaene-Lambertz, G. (1997). Electrophysiological correlates of categorical phoneme perception in adults. *NeuroReport, 8*, 919–924..

Dehaene-Lambertz, G., Dehaene, S., and Hertz-Pannier, L. (2002) Functional neuroimaging of speech perception in infants. *Science, 298*, 2013–2015.

Dehaene-Lambertz, G., and Gliga, T. (2004). Common neural basis for phoneme processing in infants and adults. *Journal of Cognitive Neuroscience, 16*, 1375–1387.

Dehaene-Lambertz, G., and Houston, D. (1998). Language discrimination response latencies in two-month-old infants. *Language and Speech, 41*, 21–43.

de Heering, A., Houthuys, S., and Rossion, B. (2007). Holistic face processing is mature at 4 years of age: Evidence from the composite face effect. *Journal of Experimental Child Psychology, 96*, 57–70.

Desjardins, R., and Werker, J. F. (2004). Is the integration of heard and seen speech mandatory for infants? *Developmental Psychobiology, 45*, 187–203.

Deutsch, D. (2002). The puzzle of absolute pitch. *Current Directions in Psychological Science, 11*, 200–204.

Deutsch, D., Henthorn, T., and Dolson, M. (2004). Speech patterns heard early in life influence later perception of the tritone paradox. *Music Perception, 21*, 357–372.

Deutsch, D., Henthorn, T., Marvin, E., and Xu, H.-S. (2006). Absolute pitch among American and Chinese conservatory students: Prevalence differences, and evidence for a speech-related critical period. *Journal of the Acoustical Society of America, 119*, 719–722.

Diamond, R., and Carey, S. (1986). Why faces are and are not special: An effect of expertise. *Journal of Experimental Psychology: General, 115*, 107–117.

Dietrich, C., Swingley, D., and Werker, J. F. (2007). Native language governs interpretation of salient speech sound differences at 18 months. *Proceedings of the National Academy of Sciences, 104*, 16027–16031.

Drivonikou, G. V., Kay, P., Regier, T., Ivry, R.B., Gilbert, A. L., Franklin, A., et al. (2007). Further evidence that Whorfian effects are stronger in the right visual field than the left. *Proceedings of the National Academy of Sciences, 104*, 1097–1102.

Eimas, P. D., Siqueland, E. R., Jusczyk, P., and Vigorito, J. (1971). Speech perception in infants. *Science, 171*, 303–306.

Ekman, P. (1993). Facial expression and emotion. *American Psychologist, 48*, 384–392.

Ekman, P., and Friesen, W. V. (1971). Constants across cultures in the face and emotion. *Journal of Personality and Social Psychology, 17*, 124–129.

Ekman, P., Friesen, W. V., O'Sullivan, M., Chan, A., Diacoyanni-Tarlatzis, I., Heider, K., et al. (1987). Universals and cultural differences in the judgments of facial expressions of emotion. *Journal of Personality and Social Psychology, 53*, 712–717.

Elfenbein, H., and Ambady, N. (2002). On the universality and cultural specificity of emotion recognition: A meta-analysis. *Psychological Bulletin, 128*, 203–235.

Elfenbein, H., and Ambady, N. (2003a). Cultural similarity's consequences. A distance perspective on cross-cultural differences in emotion recognition. *Journal of Cross-Cultural Psychology, 34*, 92–110.

Elfenbein, H., and Ambady, N. (2003b). When familiarity breeds accuracy: Cultural exposure and facial emotion recognition. *Journal of Personality and Social Psychology, 85*, 276–290.

Elliott, E., Wills, E., and Goldstein, A. (1973). The effects of discrimination training on the recognition of white and oriental faces. *Bulletin of the Psychonomic Society, 2*, 71–73.

Farroni, T., Menon, E., and Johnson, M. H. (2006). Factors influencing newborns' preference for faces with eye contact. *Journal of Experimental Child Psychology, 95*, 298–308.

Feinman, S., and Entwistle, D. (1976). Children's ability to recognize other children's faces. *Child Development, 47*, 506–510.

Flege, J., Bohn, O.-S., and Jang, S. (1997). The effect of experience on nonnative subjects' production and perception of English vowels. *Journal of Phonetics, 25,* 437–470.
Flege, J. E., and MacKay, I. R. A. (2004). Constraints on the perception of vowels in a second language. *Studies in Second Language Acquisition, 26,* 1–34.
Flege, J. E., Yeni-Komshian, G. H., and Liu, S. (1999). Age constraints on second-language acquisition. *Journal of Memory and Language, 41,* 78–104.
Franklin, A., and Davies, I. R. L. (2004). New evidence for infant colour categories. *British Journal of Developmental Psychology, 22,* 349–377.
Franklin, A., Pilling, M., and Davies, I. R. L. (2005). The nature of infant colour categorisation: Evidence from eye-movements on a target detection task. *Journal of Experimental Child Psychology, 91,* 227–248.
Freire, A., and Lee, K. (2001). Face recognition in 4- to 7-year-olds: Processing of configural, featural, and paraphernalia information. *Journal of Experimental Child Psychology, 80,* 347–371.
Freire, A., Lee, K., and Symons, L. A. (2000) The face-inversion effect as a deficit in the encoding of configural information: Direct evidence. *Perception, 29,* 159–170.
Gandour, J., Wong, D., Hsieh, L., Weinzapfel, B., Van Lancker, D., and Hutchins, G. (2000). A crosslinguistic PET study of tone perception. *Journal of Cognitive Neuroscience, 12,* 207–222.
Ge, L., Luo, J., Nishimura, M., and Lee, K. (2003). The lasting impression of Chairman Mao: Hyperfidelity of familiar-face memory. *Perception, 32,* 601–614.
Geldart, S., Mondloch, C. J., Maurer, D., de Schonen, S., and Brent, H. P. (2002). The effect of early visual deprivation on the development of face processing. *Developmental Science, 5,* 490–501.
Gerken, L. A., and Aslin, R. N. (2005). Thirty years of research on infant speech perception: The legacy of Peter W. Jusczyk. *Language Learning and Development, 1,* 5–21.
Ghazanfar, A. A., and Logothetis, N. K. (2003). Facial expressions linked to monkey calls. *Nature, 423,* 937–938.
Gibson, E. J. (1969). *Principles of perceptual learning and development.* New York: Appleton-Century-Crofts.
Gibson, J. J. (1979). *The ecological approach to visual perception.* Boston: Houghton-Mifflin.
Gilbert, A., Regier, T., Kay, P., and Ivry, R. (2006). Whorf hypothesis is supported in the right visual field but not the left. *Proceedings of the National Academy of Sciences 103,* 489–494.
Golby, A., Gabrieli, J., Chiao, J., and Eberhardt, J. (2001). Differential fusiform responses to same- and other-race faces. *Nature Neuroscience, 4,* 845–850.
Goldstein, A. (1979). Race-related variation of facial features: Anthropometric data I. *Bulletin of the Psychonomic Society, 13,* 187–190.
Goldstein, A., and Chance, J. (1985). Effects of training on Japanese face recognition: Reduction of the other-race effect. *Bulletin of the Psychonomic Society, 23,* 211–214.
Gottlieb, G. (1981). Roles of early experience in species-specific perceptual development. In R. N. Aslin, J. R. Alberts, and M. R. Peterson (Eds.), *Development of perception* (Vol. 1). New York: Academic Press.
Grabe, E., and Low, E. L. (2002). *Durational variability in speech and the rhythm class* (pp. 515–546). Berlin: Mouton de Gruyter.
Haig, N. (1984). The effect of feature displacement on face recognition. *Perception, 13,* 505–512.
Hainline, L. (1978). Developmental changes in visual scanning of face and nonface patterns by infants. *Journal of Experimental Child Psychology, 25,* 90–115.
Haith, M. M., Bergman, T., and Moore, M. J. (1977). Eye contact and face scanning in early infancy. *Science, 198,* 853–855.
Hannon, E. E., and Trehub, S. E. (2005a). Metrical categories in infancy and adulthood. *Psychological Science, 16,* 48–55.
Hannon, E. E., and Trehub, S. E. (2005b). Tuning in to musical rhythms: Infants learn more readily than adults. *Proceedings of the National Academy of Sciences, 102,* 12639–12643.
Hayward, W. G., Rhodes, G., and Schwaninger, A. (2008). An own-race advantage for components as well as configurations in face recognition. *Cognition, 106,* 1017–1027.
Hespos, S. J., and Spelke, E. S. (2004). Conceptual precursors to language. *Nature, 430,* 453–456.
Höhle, B., and Weissenborn, J. (2003) German-learning infants' ability to detect unstressed closed-class elements in continuous speech. *Developmental Science, 6,* 122–127.
Hole, G. (1994). Configurational factors in the perception of unfamiliar faces. *Perception, 23,* 65–74.
Hugenberg, K., Miller, J., and Claypool, H. (2007). Categorization and individuation in the cross-race recognition deficit: Toward a solution to an insidious problem. *Journal of Experimental Social Psychology, 43,* 334–340.
Humphreys, G., Hodsoll, J., and Campbell, C. (2005). Attending but not seeing: The "other race" effect in face and person perception studied through change blindness. *Visual Cognition, 12,* 249–262.

Huron, D., and Ollen, J. (2003). Agogic contrast in French and English themes: Further support for Patel and Daniele (2003). *Music Perception, 21*, 267–272.

Ito, T., and Urland, G. (2003). Race and gender on the brain: Electrocortical measures of attention to the race and gender of multiply categorizable individuals. *Journal of Personality and Social Psychology, 85*, 616–626.

Iversen, J. R., Patel, A. D., and Ohgushi, K. (2006). Nonlinguistic rhythm perception depends on culture and reflects the rhythms of speech: Evidence from English and Japanese. *Journal of the Acoustical Society of America, 120*, 3167.

Izard, C. E. (1971). *The face of emotion*. New York: Appleton-Century-Crofts.

Jameson, K., and D'Andrade, R. G. (1997). It's not really red, green, yellow, blue: An inquiry into perceptual color space. In C. L. Hardin and L. Maffi (Eds.), *Color categories in thought and language* (pp. 295–319). Cambridge, United Kingdom: Cambridge University Press.

Jeffery, L., Rhodes, G., and Busey, T. (2006). View-specific coding of face shape. *Psychological Science, 17*, 501–505.

Johnson, M. H. (2005). Subcortical face processing. *Nature Reviews Neuroscience, 6*, 766–774.

Johnson, K., and Fredrickson, B. (2006). "We all look the same to me." Positive emotions eliminate the own-race bias in face recognition. *Psychological Science, 16*, 875–880.

Jusczyk, P., Cutler, A., and Redanz, N. (1993). Infants' preference for the predominant stress patterns of English words. *Child Development, 64*, 675–687.

Kajikawa, S., Fais, L., Mugitani, R., Werker, J. F., and Amano, S. (2006). Cross-language sensitivity to phonotactic patterns in infants. *Journal of the Acoustical Society of America, 120*, 2278–2284.

Kay, P., and Regier, T. (2006). Language, thought, and color: Recent developments. *Trends in Cognitive Sciences, 10*, 51–54.

Keenan, J. P., Halpern, A. R., Thangaraj, V., Chen, C., Edelman, R. R., and Schlaug, G. (2001). Absolute pitch and planum temporale. *NeuroImage, 14*, 1402–1408.

Kelly, D., Liu, S., Ge, L., Quinn, P., Slater, A., Lee, K., et al. (2007). Cross-race preferences for same-race faces extend beyond the African versus Caucasian contrast in 3-month-old infants. *Infancy, 11*, 87–95.

Kelly, D., Quinn, P., Slater, A., Lee, K., Ge, L., and Pascalis, O. (2007). The other-race effect develops during infancy: Evidence of perceptual narrowing. *Psychological Science, 18*, 1084–1089.

Kelly, D. J., Quinn, P. C., Slater, A. M., Lee, K., Gibson, A., Smith, M., et al. (2005). Three-month-olds, but not newborns, prefer own-race faces. *Developmental Science, 8*, F31–F36.

Kinzler, K. D., Dupoux, E., and Spelke, E. S. (2007). The native language of social cognition. *Proceedings of the National Academy of Sciences, 104*, 12577–12580.

Kisilevsky, B. S., Hains, S. M. J., Lee, K., Xie, X., Huang, H., Ye, H.-H., et al. (2003). Effects of experience on fetal voice recognition. *Psychological Science, 14*, 220–224.

Kitayama, S., Duffy, S., Kawamura, T., and Larsen, J. T. (2003). Perceiving an object and its context in two cultures: A cultural look at New Look. *Psychological Science, 14*, 201–206.

Klinnert, M. D., Emde, R. N., Butterfield, P., and Campos, J. (1986). Social referencing: The infant's use of emotional signals from a friendly adult with mother present. *Developmental Psychology, 22*, 427–432.

Krentz, U. and Corina, D. (2008). Infant perception of American Sign Language and non-linguistic biological motion: The language instinct is not speech specific. *Developmental Science, 11(1), 1–9*.

Kuhl, P. K. (2007). Is speech learning 'gated' by the social brain? *Developmental Science, 10*, 110–120.

Kuhl, P. K., and Meltzoff, A. N. (1982). The bimodal perception of speech in infancy. *Science, 218*, 1138–1141.

Kuhl, P. K., Stevens, E., Hayashi, A., Degushi, T., Kiritani, S., and Iverson, P. (2006). Infants show a facilitation effect for native language phonetic perception between 6 and 12 months. *Developmental Science, 9*, F13–F21.

Kuhl, P. K., Tsao, F.-M., and Liu, H.-M. (2003). Foreign-language experience in infancy: Effects of short-term exposure and social interaction on phonetic learning. *Proceedings of the National Academy of Sciences, 100*, 9096–9101.

Kuhl, P. K., Williams, K. A., Lacerda, F., Stevens, K. N., and Lindblom, B. (1992). Linguistic experience alters phonetic perception in infants by 6 months of age. *Science, 255*, 606–608.

Kushnerenko, E., Teinonen, T., Volein, A., and Csibra, G. (2008). Electrophysiological evidence of illusory audiovisual speech integration in human infants. *Proceedings of the National Academy of Sciences, 105*, 11442–11445.

Lasky, R. E., Syrdal-Lasky, A., and Klein, R. E. (1975). VOT discrimination by four to six and a half month old infants from Spanish environments. *Journal of Experimental Child Psychology, 20*, 215–225.

Leder, H., and Bruce, V. (1998). Local and relational aspects of face distinctiveness. *The Quarterly Journal of Experimental Psychology A: Human Experimental Psychology, 51A,* 449–473.

Le Grand, R., Mondloch, C. J., Maurer, D., and Brent, H. P. (2001). Early visual experience and face processing. *Nature, 410,* 890. Erratum: 2001, *412,* 786.

Le Grand, R., Mondloch, C. J., Maurer, D., and Brent, H. P. (2003). Expert face processing requires visual input to the right hemisphere during infancy. *Nature Neuroscience, 6,* 1108–1112. Erratum: 2003, *8,* 1329.

Le Grand, R., Mondloch, C. J., Maurer, D., and Brent, H. P. (2004). Impairment in holistic face processing following early visual deprivation. *Psychological Science, 15,* 762–768.

Leopold, D. A., and Bondar, I. (2005). Adaptation to complex visual patterns in humans and monkeys. In C. Clifford and G. Rhodes (Eds.), *Fitting the mind to the world: Adaptation and after-effects in high-level vision.* London: Oxford University Press.

Leopold, D. A., Bondar, I. V., and Giese, M. A. (2006). Norm-based face encoding by single neurons in the monkey inferotemporal cortex. *Nature, 442,* 572–575.

Leopold, D. A., O'Toole, A. J., Vetter, T., and Blantz, V. (2001). Prototype-referenced shape encoding revealed by high-level aftereffects. *Nature Neuroscience, 4,* 89–94.

Levin, D. T. (2000). Race as a visual feature: Using visual search and perceptual discrimination tasks to understand face categories and the cross-race recognition deficit. *Journal of Experimental Psychology: General, 129,* 559–574.

Levinson, S. (1997). Language and cognition: The cognitive consequences of spatial description in Guugu Yimithirr. *Journal of Linguistic Anthropology, 7,* 98–131.

Levitin, D. J. (1999). Absolute pitch: Self-reference and human memory. *International Journal of Computing Anticipatory System, 4,* 255–266.

Levitin, D. J., and Rogers, S. E. (2005). Absolute pitch: Perception, coding, and controversies. *Trends in Cognitive Sciences, 9,* 26–33.

Levitin, D. J., and Zatorre, R. J. (2003). On the nature of early music training and absolute pitch: A reply to Brown, Sachs, Cammuso, and Folstein. *Music Perception, 21,* 105–110.

Lewkowicz, D. J., and Ghazanfar, A. A. (2006) The decline of cross-species intersensory perception in human infants. *Proceedings of the National Academy of Sciences, 103,* 6771–6774.

Lew-Williams, C., and Fernald, A. (2007). Young children learning Spanish make rapid use of grammatical gender in spoken word recognition. *Psychological Science, 18,* 193–198.

Li, P., and Gleitman, L. (2002). Turning the tables: Language and spatial reasoning. *Cognition, 83,* 265–294.

Lloyd James, A. (1940). *Speech signals in telephony.* London: Pitman & Sons.

Locke, J. (1689; reprinted in 1959). *An essay concerning human understanding.* New York: Dover.

Logan, J. S., Lively, S. E., and Pisoni, D. B. (1991). Training Japanese listeners to identify English /r/ and /l/: A first report. *Journal of the Acoustical Society of America, 89,* 874–886.

Low, E.-L., Grabe, E., and Nolan, F. (2000). Quantitative characterizations of speech rhythm: Syllable-timing in Singapore English. *Language and Speech, 43,* 377–401.

Maclin, O., and Malpass, R. (2003). The ambiguous-race face illusion. *Perception, 32,* 249–252.

Maclin, O. H., and Webster, M. A. (2001). The influence of adaptation on the perception of distortions in natural images. *Journal of Electronic Imaging, 10,* 100–109.

Malcolm, G., Leung, C., and Barton, J. J. S. (2005). Regional variations in the inversion effect for faces: Differential effects for feature shape, spatial relations, and external contour. *Perception, 33,* 1221–1231.

Massaro, D. W., Cohen, M. M., and Smeele, P. M. T. (1995). Cross-linguistic comparisons in the integration of visual and auditory speech. *Memory and Cognition, 23,* 113–131.

Matsumoto, D., Takeuchi, S., Andayani, S., Kouznetsove, N., and Krupp, D. (1998). The contribution of individualism vs collectivism to cross-national differences in display rules. *Asian Journal of Social Psychology, 1,* 147–165.

Mattock, K., and Burnham, D. (2006). Chinese and English infants' tone perception: Evidence for perceptual reorganization. *Infancy, 10,* 241–265.

Mattys, S. L., Jusczyk, P. W., Luce, P. A., and Morgan, J. L. (1999) Phonotactic and prosodic effects on word segmentation in infants. *Cognitive Psychology, 38,* 465–494.

Maurer, D., Le Grand, R., and Mondloch, C. J. (2002). The many faces of configural processing. *Trends in Cognitive Science, 6,* 255–260.

Maurer, D., and Salapatek, P. (1976). Developmental changes in the scanning of faces by young infants. *Child Development, 47,* 523–527.

Maye, J., Werker, J. F., and Gerken, L. A. (2002). Infant sensitivity to distributional information can affect phonetic discrimination. *Cognition, 82,* B101–B111.

McCandliss, B. D., Fiez, J. A., Protopapas, A., Conway, M., and McClelland, J. L. (2002). Success and failure in teaching the [r]–[l] contrast to Japanese adults: Tests of a Hebbian model of plasticity and stabilization in spoken language perception. *Cognitive, Affective, and Behavioral Neuroscience, 2*, 89–108.

McGurk, H., and MacDonald, J. (1976). Hearing lips and seeing voices. *Nature, 264*, 746–748.

McKone, E., Brewer, J., MacPherson, S., Rhodes, G., and Hayward, W. (2007). Familiar other-race faces show normal holistic processing and are robust to perceptual stress. *Perception, 36*, 224–248.

McMurray, B., and Aslin, R. N. (2004). Anticipatory eye movements reveal infants' auditory and visual categories. *Infancy, 6*, 203–229.

McMurray, B., and Aslin, R. N. (2005). Infants are sensitive to within-category variation in speech perception. *Cognition, 95*, B15–B26.

Mehler, J., Jusczyk, P., Lambertz, G., Halsted, N., Bertoncini, J., and Amiel-Tison, C. (1988). A precursor of language acquisition in young infants. *Cognition, 29*, 143–178.

Mehler, J., and Nespor, M. (2004). Linguistic rhythm and the development of language. In A. Belletti and L. Rizzi (Eds.), *Structures and beyond: The cartography of syntactic structures* (pp. 213–221). Oxford, United Kingdom: Oxford University Press.

Meissner, C., and Brigham, J. (2001). Thirty years of investigating the own-race bias in memory for faces. *Psychology, Public Policy, and Law, 7*, 3–35.

Michel, C., Caldara, R., and Rossion, B. (in press). Same-race faces are perceived more holistically than other-race faces. *Visual Cognition*.

Michel, C., Rossion, B., Han, J., Chung, C.-S., and Caldara, R. (2006). Holistic processing is finely tuned for faces of our own race. *Psychological Science, 17*, 608–615.

Minagawa-Kawai, Y., Mori, K., Naoi, N., and Kojima, S. (2007). Neural attunement processes in infants during the acquisition of a language-specific phonemic contrast. *Journal of Neuroscience, 27*, 315–321.

Mondloch, C. J., Geldart, S., Maurer, D., and Le Grand, R. (2003). Developmental changes in face processing skills. *Journal of Experimental Child Psychology, 86*, 67–84.

Mondloch, C. J., Le Grand, R., and Maurer, D. (2002). Configural face processing develops more slowly than featural face processing. *Perception, 31*, 553–566.

Mondloch, C. J., Le Grand, R., and Maurer, D. (2003). Early visual experience is necessary for the development of some—but not all—aspects of face processing. In O. Pascalis and A. Slater (Eds.), *The development of face processing in infancy and early childhood* (pp. 99–117). New York: Nova.

Mondloch, C. J., Leis, A., and Maurer, D. (2006). Recognizing the face of Johnny, Suzy, and me: Insensitivity to the spacing among features at four years of age. *Child Development, 77*, 234–243.

Mondloch, C. J., Lewis, T. L., Budreau, D. R., Maurer, D., Dannemiller, J. L., Stephens, B. R., et al. (1999). Face perception during early infancy. *Psychological Science, 10*, 419–422.

Mondloch, C., Maurer, D., and Ahola, S. (2006). Becoming a face expert. *Psychological Science, 17*, 930–934.

Mondloch, C., Pathman, T., Maurer, D., Le Grand, R., and de Schonen, S. (2007). The composite face effect in six-year-old children: Evidence of adultlike holistic face processing. *Visual Cogntion, 15*, 564–577.

Montepare, J., and Opeyo, A. (2002). The relative salience of physiognomic cues in differentiating faces: A methodological tool. *Journal of Nonverbal Behavior, 26*, 43–59.

Moon, C., Cooper, R. P., and Fifer, W. P. (1993). Two-day-olds prefer their native language. *Infant Behavior and Development, 16*, 495–500.

Morton, J., and Johnson, M. H. (1991). CONSPEC and CONLERN: A two-process theory of infant face recognition. *Psychological Review, 98*, 164–181.

Näätänen, R., Lehtokoski, A., Lennes, M., Cheour, M., Huotilainen, M., Iivonen, A., et al. (1997). Language-specific phoneme representations revealed by electric and magnetic brain responses. *Nature, 385*, 432–434.

Narayan, C. (2006). Acoustic-perceptual salience and developmental speech perception. Unpublished doctoral dissertation, University of Michigan, Ann Arbor, MI.

Narayan, C., Werker, J. F., and Beddor, P. (in press). Acoustic salience effects speech perception in infancy: Evidence from nasal place discrimination. *Developmental Science*.

Navarra, J., Sebastián-Gallés, N., and Soto-Faraco, S. (2005). Studying cross-linguistic phoneme perception: Evidence from an implicit task. *Journal of Experimental Psychology: Human Perception and Performance, 31*, 912–918.

Nazzi, T., Bertoncini, J. and Mehler, J. (1998). Language discrimination by newborns: Toward an understanding of the role of rhythm. *Journal of Experimental Psychology: Human Perception and Performance, 24*, 756–766.

Nazzi, T., and Ramus, F. (2003). Perception and acquisition of linguistic rhythm by infants. *Speech Communication, 41*, 233–243.

Ng, W.-J., and Lindsay, R. C. L. (1994). Cross-race facial recognition: Failure of the contact hypothesis. *Journal of Cross-Cultural Psychology, 25*, 217–232.

Nisbett, R. E. (2003). *The geography of thought: How Asians and Westerners think differently…and why*. New York: The Free Press.

Oh, J. S., Jun, S.-A., Knightly, L. M., and Au, T. K.-F. (2003). Holding on to childhood language memory. *Cognition, 86*, B53–B64.

Özgen, E., and Davies, I. R. L. (2002). Acquisition of categorical color perception: A perceptual learning approach to the linguistic relativity hypothesis. *Journal of Experimental Psychology: General, 131*, 477–493.

Pallier, C., Colomé, A., and Sebastián-Gallés, N. (2001). The influence of native-language phonology on lexical access: Exemplar-based versus abstract lexical entries. *Psychological Science, 12*, 445–448.

Pascalis, O., de Haan, M., and Nelson, C.A. (2002). Is face processing species-specific during the first year of life? *Science, 296*, 1321–1323.

Pascalis, O., and de Schonen, S. (1994). Recognition memory in 3- to 4-day-old human neonates. *Neuroreport, 5*, 1721–1724.

Pascalis, O., Scott, L. S., Kelly, D. J., Shannon, R. W., Nicholson, E., Colemen, M., et al. (2005). Plasticity of face processing in infancy. *Proceedings of the National Academy of Sciences, 102*, 5297–5300.

Patel, A. D., and Daniele, J. R. (2003). An empirical comparison of rhythm in language and music. *Cognition, 87*, B35–B45.

Patterson, M. L., and Werker, J. F. (2003). Two-month-old infants match phonetic information in lips and voice. *Developmental Science, 6*, 191–196.

Pegg, J. E., and Werker, J. F. (1997). Adult and infant perception of two English phones. *Journal of the Acoustical Society of America, 102*, 3742–3753.

Pellicano, E., and Rhodes, G. (2003). Holistic processing of faces in preschool children and adults. *Psychological Science, 14*, 618–622.

Peña, M., Maki, A., Kovacic, D., Dehaene-Lambertz, G., Bouquet, F., Koizumi, H., et al. (2003). Sounds and silence: An optical topography study of language recognition at birth. *Proceedings of the National Academy of Sciences, 10*, 11702–11705.

Peters, A. M. (1997). Language typology, prosody and the acquisition of grammatical morphemes. In D. I. Slobin (Ed.), *The crosslinguistic study of language acquisition* (Vol. 5, pp. 136–197). Hillsdale NJ: Lawrence Erlbaum Associates.

Pezdek, K, Blandon-Gitlin, I., and Moore, C. (2003). Children's face recognition memory: More evidence for the cross-race effect. *Journal of Applied Psychology, 88*, 760–763.

Piaget, J. (1953). *Origins of intelligence in the child*. London: Routledge and Kegan Paul

Pike, K. (1945). *The intonation of American English*. Ann Arbor: University of Michigan Press.

Pisoni, D. B., and Tash, J. (1974). Reaction times to comparisons within and across phonetic categories. *Perception and Psychophysics, 15*, 285–290.

Plantinga, J., and Trainor, L. J. (2005). Memory for melody: Infants use a relative pitch code. *Cognition, 98*, 1–11.

Polka, L., and Werker, J. F. (1994). Developmental changes in perception of non-native vowel contrasts. *Journal of Experimental Psychology: Human Perception and Performance, 20*, 421–435.

Quinn, P., Yahr, J., Kuhn, A., Slater, A., and Pascalis, O. (2002). Representation of the gender of human faces by infants: A preference for female. *Perception, 31*, 1109–1121.

Ramus, F. (2002). Language discrimination by newborns: Teasing apart phonotactic, rhythmic, and intonational cues. *Annual Review of Language Acquisition, 2*, 85–115.

Ramus, F., Nespor, M., and Mehler, J. (1999). Correlates of linguistic rhythm in the speech signal. *Cognition, 72*, 1–28.

Raskin, L., Maital, S., and Bornstein, M. H. (1983). Perceptual categorization of color: A life-span study. *Psychological Research, 45*, 135–145.

Regier, T., Kay, P., and Khetarpal, N. (2007). Color naming reflects optimal partitions of color space. *Proceedings of the National Academy of Sciences, 104*, 1436–1441.

Rhodes, G., Hayward, W., and Winkler, C. (2006). Expert face coding: Configural and component coding of own-race and other-race faces. *Psychonomic Bulletin and Review, 13*, 499–505.

Rhodes, G., and Jeffery, L. (2006). Adaptive norm-based coding of facial identity. *Vision Research, 46*, 2977–2987.

Rhodes, G., Jeffery, L., Watson, T. L., Clifford, C. W. G., and Nakayama, K. (2003). Fitting the mind to the world: Face adaptation and attractiveness aftereffects. *Psychological Science, 14*, 558–566.

Rhodes, G., Robbins, R., Jaquet, E., McKone, E., Jeffery, L., and Clifford, C. (2005). Adaptation and face perception: How aftereffects implicate norm based coding of faces. In C. W. G. Clifford and G. Rhodes (Eds.), *Fitting the mind to the world: Aftereffect in high-level vision* (pp. 213–240). Oxford, United Kingdom: Oxford University Press.

Ribar, R. J., Oakes, L. M., and Spalding, T. L. (2004). Infants can rapidly form new categorical representations. *Psychonomic Bulletin and Review, 11*, 536–541.

Rivera-Gaxiola, M., Csibra, G., Johnson, M. H., and Karmiloff-Smith, A. (2000). Electrophysiological correlates of cross-linguistic speech perception in adults. *Behavioural Brain Research, 111*, 11–23.

Rivera-Gaxiola, M., Silva-Pereyra, J., and Kuhl, P. K. (2005). Brain potentials to native and non-native speech contrasts in 7- and 11-month-old American infants. *Developmental Science, 8*, 162–172.

Roberson, D., and Davidoff, J. (2000) The categorical perception of colours and facial expressions: The effect of verbal interference. *Memory and Cognition, 28*, 977–986.

Roberson, D., Davies, I., and Davidoff, J. (2000) Color categories are not universal: Replications and new evidence from a Stone-age culture. *Journal of Experimental Psychology: General, 129*, 369–398.

Rosch Heider, E. (1972). Universals in color naming and memory. *Journal of Experimental Psychology, 93*, 10–20.

Rosch Heider, E., and Olivier, D. C. (1972). The structure of the color space in naming and memory for two languages. *Cognitive Psychology, 3*, 337–354.

Rosen, W., Adamson, L., and Bakeman, R. (1992). An experimental investigation of infant social referencing: Mother's messages and gender differences. *Developmental Psychology, 28*, 1172–1178.

Rosenblum, L. D., Schmuckler, M. A., and Johnson, J. A. (1997). The McGurk effect in infants. *Perception and Psychophysics, 59*, 347–357.

Sadakata, M., Desain, P., Honing, H., Patel, A. D., and Iverson, J. R. (2004). A cross-cultural study of the rhythm in English and Japanese popular music. Proceedings of the International Symposium on Musical Acoustics, Nara, Japan.

Saffran, J. R., and Griepentrog, G. J. (2001). Absolute pitch in infant auditory learning: Evidence for developmental reorganization. *Developmental Psychology, 37*, 74–85.

Sangrigoli, S., and de Schonen, S. (2004). Recognition of own-race and other-race faces by three-month-old infants. *Journal of Experimental Psychology and Psychiatry, 45*, 1219–1227.

Sangrigoli, S., Pallier, C., Argenti, A. M., Ventureyra, V. A. G., and de Schonen, S. (2005). Reversibility of the other-race effect in face recognition during childhood. *Psychological Science, 16*, 440–444.

Schiltz, C., and Rossion, B. (2006). Faces are represented holistically in the human occipito-temporal cortex. *NeuroImage, 32*, 1385–1394.

Scott, L. S., Pascalis, O., and Nelson, C. A. (2007). A domain-general theory of the development of perceptual discrimination. *Current Directions in Psychological Science, 16*, 197–201.

Sebastián-Gallés, N., Echeverria, S., and Bosch, L. (2005). The influence of initial exposure on lexical representation: Comparing early and simultaneous bilinguals. *Journal of Memory and Language, 52*, 240–255.

Segall, M. H., Campbell, D. T., and Herskovits, M. J. (1963). Cultural differences in the perception of geometric illusions. *Science, 139*, 769–771.

Sekiyama, K., and Tohkura, Y. (1993). Inter-language differences in the influence of visual cues in speech perception. *Journal of Phonetics, 21*, 427–444.

Sharma, A., and Dorman, M. (2000). Neurophysiologic correlates of cross-language phonetic perception. *Journal of the Acoustical Society of America, 107*, 2697–2703.

Shi, R., Cutler, A., Werker, J., and Cruickshank, M. (2006). Frequency and form as determinants of functor sensitivity in English-acquiring infants. *Journal of the Acoustical Society of America, 119*, EL61–EL67.

Shi, R., Lepage, M., Gauthier, B., and Marquis, A. (2006). Frequency factor in the segmentation of function words in French-learning infants. *Journal of the Acoustical Society of America, 119*, 3420.

Shi, R., and Werker, J. (2001). Six-month-old infants' preference for lexical words. *Psychological Science, 12*, 70–75.

Shi, R., and Werker, J. (2003). Basis of preference for lexical words in six-month-old infants. *Developmental Science, 6*, 484–488.

Shi, R., Werker, J., and Cutler, A. (2006). Recognition and representation of function words in English-learning infants. *Infancy, 10*, 187–198.

Shi, R., Werker, J., and Morgan, J. (1999). Newborn infants' sensitivity to perceptual cues to lexical and grammatical words. *Cognition, 72*, B11–B21.

Simion, F., Turati, C., Valenza, E., and Leo, I. (2006). The emergence of cognitive specialization in infancy: The case of face preference. In M. Johnson and Y. Munakata (Eds.), *Attention and performance XXI: Process of change in brain and cognitive development* (pp. 189–208). Oxford, United Kingdom: Oxford University Press.

Slone, A., Brigham, J., and Meissner, C. (2000). Social and cognitive factors affecting the own-race bias in whites. *Basic and Applied Social Psychology, 22*, 71–84.

Sorce, J., Emde, R., Campos, J., and Klinnert, M. (1985). Maternal emotional signaling: Its effect on the visual cliff behavior of 1-year-olds. *Developmental Psychology, 21*, 195–200.

Soto-Faraco, S., Navarra, J., Weikum, W. M., Vouloumanos, A., Sebastián-Gallés, N., and Werker, J. F. (2007). Discriminating languages by speech reading. *Perception and Psychophysics, 69*, 218–237.

Spelke, E. S. (2000). Core knowledge. *American Psychologist, 55*, 1233–1243.

Streeter, L. A. (1976). Language perception of two-month old infants shows effects of both innate mechanisms and experience. *Nature, 250*, 39–41.

Tanaka, J. W., Curran, T., and Sheinberg, D. L. (2005). The training and transfer of real-world perceptual expertise. *Psychological Science, 16*, 145–151.

Tanaka, J. W., and Farah, M .J. (1993). Parts and wholes in face recognition. *Quarterly Journal of Experimental Psychology, Human Experimental Psychology, 46*, 225–245.

Tanaka, J. W., Kay, J. B., Grinnell, E., Stansfield, B., and Szechter, T. (1998). Face recognition in young children: When the whole is greater than the sum of its parts. *Visual Cognition, 5*, 479–496.

Tanaka, J. W., Kiefer, M., and Bukach, C. M. (2004). A holistic account of the own-race effect in face recognition: Evidence from a cross-cultural study. *Cognition, 93*, B1–B9.

Tang, Y., Zhang, W., Chen, K., Feng, S., Ji, Y., Shen, J., et al. (2006). Arithmetic processing in the brain shaped by cultures. *Proceeding of the National Academy of Sciences, 28*, 10775–10780.

Trainor, L. J., and Adams, B. (2000). Infants' and adults' use of duration and intensity cues in the segmentation of auditory patterns. *Perception and Psychophysics, 62*, 333–340.

Trainor, L. J., Desjardins, R. N., and Rockel, C. (1999). A comparison of contour and interval processing in musicians and non-musicians using event-related potentials. *Australian Journal of Psychology: Special Issue on Music as a Brain and Behavioural System, 51*, 147–153.

Trainor, L. J., and Trehub, S. E. (1992). A comparison of infants' and adults' sensitivity to Western musical structure. *Journal of Experimental Psychology: Human Perception and Performance, 18*, 394–402.

Trehub, S. E. (1976). The discrimination of foreign speech contrasts by infants and adults. *Child Development, 47*, 466–472.

Tsao, F., Liu, H., Kuhl, P. K., and Tseng, C. (2000, July). Perceptual discrimination of a Mandarin fricative-affricate contrast by English-learning and Mandarin-learning infants. Poster presented at the meeting of the International Society on Infant Studies, Brighton, United Kingdom.

Tsushima, T., Takizawa, O., Sasaki, M., Shiraki, S., Nishi, K., Kohno, M., et al. (1994). Discrimination of English /r-l/ and /w-y/ by Japanese infants at 6-12 months: Language-specific developmental changes in speech perception abilities. *The Emergence of Human Cognition and Language, 3*, 57–61.

Turati, C., Macchi Cassia, V., Simion, F., and Leo, I. (2006). Newborns' face recognition: Role of inner and outer facial features. *Child Development, 77*, 297–311.

Turk, D., Handy, T., and Gazzaniga, M. (2005). Can perceptual expertise account for the own-race bias in face recognition? A split-brain study. *Cognitive Neuropsychology, 22*, 877–883.

Valentine, T., and Endo, M. (1992). Towards an exemplar model of face processing: The effects of race and distinctiveness. *The Quarterly Journal of Experimental Psychology, 44A*, 671–703.

Ventureyra, V., Pallier, C., and Yoo, H. (2004). The loss of first language phonetic perception in adopted Koreans. *Journal of Neurolinguistics, 17*, 79–91.

Vouloumanos, A., and Werker, J. F. (2007a) Listening to language at birth: Evidence for a bias for speech in neonates. *Developmental Science, 10*, 159–164.

Vouloumanos, A., and Werker, J. F. (2007b). Why voice melody alone cannot explain neonates' preference for speech. *Developmental Science, 10*, 170–172.

Walker, P., and Tanaka, J. (2003). An encoding advantage for own-race versus other-race faces. *Perception, 32*, 1117–1125.

Ward, W. D., and Burns, E. M. (1982). Absolute pitch. In D. Deutsch (Ed.), *The psychology of music* (pp. 431–451). New York: Academic Press.

Watson, T. L., and Clifford, W. G. (2003). Pulling faces: An investigation of the face-distortion aftereffect. *Perception, 32*, 1109–1116.

Waxman, S. R., and Markow, D. B. (1995). Words as invitations to form categories: Evidence from 12-month-old infants. *Cognitive Psychology, 29*, 257–302.

Webster, M. A., Kaping, D., Mizokami, Y., and Duhamel, P. (2004). Adaptation to natural facial categories. *Nature, 428*, 557–561

Webster, M. A., and Maclin, O. H. (1999). Figural aftereffects in the perception of faces. *Psychonomic Bulletin and Review, 6*, 647–653.

Weikum, W., Vouloumanos, A., Navarro, J., Soto-Faraco, S., Sebastián-Gallés, N., and Werker, J. F. (2007). Visual language discrimination in infancy. *Science, 316*, 1159.

Wenk, B. J. (1987). Just in time: On speech rhythms in music. *Linguistics, 25*, 969–981.

Werker, J. F., and Curtin, S. (2005). PRIMIR: A developmental model of speech processing. *Language Learning and Development, 1*, 197–234.

Werker, J. F., Frost, P. E., and McGurk, H. (1992). La langue et les lèvres: Cross-language influences on bimodal speech perception. *Canadian Journal of Psychology, 46*, 551–568.

Werker, J. F., Gilbert, J. H. V., Humphrey, K., and Tees, R. C. (1981). Developmental aspects of cross-language speech perception. *Child Development, 52*, 349–353.

Werker, J. F., and Lalonde, C. E. (1988). Cross-language speech perception: Initial capabilities and developmental change. *Developmental Psychology, 24*, 672–683.

Werker, J. F., and Logan, J. S. (1985). Cross-language evidence for three factors in speech perception. *Perception and Psychophysics, 37*, 35–44.

Werker, J. F., and Tees, R. C. (1984a). Cross-language speech perception: Evidence for perceptual reorganization during the first year of life. *Infant Behavior and Development, 7*, 49–63.

Werker, J. F., and Tees, R. C. (1984b). Phonemic and phonetic factors in adult cross-language speech perception. *Journal of the Acoustical Society of America, 75*, 1866–1878.

Whorf, B. (1956). *Language, thought, and reality: Selected writings of Benjamin Lee Whorf*. J. B. Carroll (Ed.). Cambridge, MA: MIT Press.

Xu, Y., Gandour, J., Talavage, T., Wong, D., Dzemidzic, M., Tong, Y., et al. (2006). Activation of the left planum temporale in pitch processing is shaped by language experience. *Human Brain Mapping, 27*, 173–183.

Yin, R. K. (1969). Looking at upside down faces. *Journal of Experimental Psychology, 81*, 141–145.

Yoshida, K. A., Pons, F., and Werker, J. F. (under review). Attention aids infants' phonetic learning.

Young, A. W., Hellawell, D., and Hay, D. C. (1987). Configurational information in face perception. *Perception, 16*, 747–759.

Younger, B. A., and Johnson, K. E. (2006). Infants' developing appreciation of similarities between model objects and their real world referents. *Child Development, 77*, 1518–1520.

Yuki, M., Madduz, W., and Masuda, T. (2007). Are the windows to the soul the same in the East and West? Cultural differences in using the eyes and mouth as cues to recognize emotions in Japan and the United States. *Journal of Experimental Social Psychology, 43*, 303–311.

6
Cognition

MICHAEL COLE and XAVIER E. CAGIGAS

Introduction

To understand the role of culture in cognitive development, it is helpful to consider the processes involved in terms of three levels of social grouping: human beings as a mammalian species, societies (thought of as the population of a particular geographical and political region that exhibits common cultural features), and cultural practices (thought of as recurrent ways of accomplishing valued social activities in concert with some group of one's proximally circumscribed social unit). These levels are not independent of each other. It is helpful to think of each "smaller" unit of cultural analysis as embedded within the more inclusive levels both spatially (in terms of the number of people involved) and temporally (in terms of time span over which the given cultural feature or formation has existed). Just as geopolitically defined populations can be thought of as branches of a tree of human life extending back to *Australopithecus*, so the different cultural practices within a society represent variations in the ways that people organize their everyday lives within the set of possibilities to be found in highly similar ecological circumstances. Consequently, specifying the linkages among specific cultural practices within more inclusive sociocultural formations and the linkages of those sociocultural formations within historically formed modes of life is a major ongoing challenge to the study of culture and cognitive development.

Our presentation is organized as follows. We begin by providing working definitions of the core concepts of culture, cognition, and development—the phenomena that must be related to understand the role of culture in cognition. We then consider cognition at each of the levels of social grouping associated with culture: cultural universals as they relate to human beings as a biological species, the level of large populations and social groups, and the level of cultural practices within social groups. We end by considering the crucial issue of arriving at a more systematic understanding the generality of cultural patterns across populations, their sources, and their consequences for cognition.

Culture, Cognition, and Development: Some Definitional Considerations

In its most general sense, the term "culture" as applied to human beings refers to the socially inherited body of past human behavioral patterns and accomplishments that serves as the resource for the current life of a social group (D'Andrade, 1996). Although scholars usually agree on the notion that culture constitutes the social inheritance of a population, anthropologists have historically emphasized culture either as "something out there" (the "man made part of the environment"; Herskovitz, 1948) or as "something inside the head" (as "what one needs to know to participate acceptably as a member in a society's affairs"; Goodenough, 1994, p. 265).

At present, many anthropologists and psychologists seek to transcend this dichotomy between "ideal" versus "material." For example, Geertz (1973, p. 45) wrote that his view of culture begins with the assumption that "human thought is basically both social and public—that its natural habitat is the house yard, the market place, and the town square. Thinking consists not of 'happenings in the head' (though happenings there and elsewhere are necessary for it to occur) but of trafficking in…significant symbols—words for the most part but also gestures, drawings, musical sounds, mechanical devices like clocks."

Our own proposal for transcending the ideal–material dichotomy with respect to culture and development is to think of the cultural medium in which human beings live as an environment transformed by the artifacts created by prior generations, extending back to the beginning of the species. As we are using the term, an artifact is an aspect of the material world that has been modified over the history of its incorporation into goal-directed human action (Cole, 1996). By virtue of the changes wrought in the process of their creation and use, artifacts are *simultaneously ideal (conceptual) and material.* They are ideal in that their material form has been shaped by their historical participation in the (successful, adaptive) social interactions of which they were previously a part and which they mediate in the present. They are material in that they are embodied in physical artifacts, whether in the morphology of a spoken, written, or signed word, or in a solid object such as a pencil. D'Andrade (1986, p. 22) made this point when he wrote: "Material culture—tables and chairs, buildings and cities—is the reification of human ideas in a solid medium." The basic function of these artifacts is to coordinate human beings with the physical world and each other; in the aggregate, culture is then seen as the species-specific *medium* of human development that organizes and configures the human nervous system for interaction with the world.

This conception of artifacts extends to what Wartofsky (1973) refers to as secondary artifacts, representations of primary artifacts and their modes of use. Secondary artifacts play a central role in preserving and transmitting the kinds of social inheritance referred to as recipes, beliefs, norms, conventions, and the like. This extension brings the mental entities psychologists refer to as schemas or scripts into contact with the notion of artifact. The term schema is ordinarily used by psychologists to refer to a mental structure that represents some aspect of the world. When thinking about culture and cognition, Bartlett's (1932) notion of schemas as conventions is useful because it emphasizes that schemas are simultaneously aspects of material practices and mental structures/functions. Scripts are an especially important kind of schema for purposes of thinking about the role of culture in cognitive development because they represent the everyday, culturally organized activities that people engage in. A script is an event schema that specifies the appropriate people who participate in an event, the social roles they play, the objects they use, and the sequence of actions and causal relations that they apply.

Both Bruner (1990) and Nelson (1981) accord an important role to such event representations in cognitive development. Nelson (1981, p. 101) referred to scripts as "generalized event schemas"; scripts provide "a basic level of knowledge representation in a hierarchy of relations that reaches upward through plans to goals and themes." In her work on children's acquisition of event representations, Nelson highlighted other important properties of scripts as artifacts. First, such event schemas serve as guides to action. When individuals participate in novel events, they must seek out an answer to the question, "What's going on here?" For example, once a person has even a crude idea of what the appropriate actions associated with going to a restaurant are, she or he can enter the flow of the particular event with partial knowledge, which gets enriched in the course of the event itself, facilitating later coordination. "Without shared scripts, every social act would need to be negotiated afresh" (Nelson, 1981, p. 109). Nelson also pointed out that children grow up within contexts controlled by adults and hence within adult scripts. By and large, adults arrange the conditions for children's actions, including the culturally appropriate goals, rather than engage in direct teaching. In effect, they use their notion of the appropriate script to provide constraints on the child's actions and allow the child to fill in the expected role activity in the process. In this sense, "the acquisition of scripts is central to the acquisition of culture" (Nelson, 1981, p. 110).

According to Bruner (1990), scripts are best considered constituents of a narrative. In his view, it is narrative, the linking of events over time, that lies at the heart of human thought. The re-presentation of experience in narratives provides a frame ("folk psychology") that enables humans to interpret their experiences and each other. If it were not for such narrative framing, "we would be lost in a murk of chaotic experience and probably would not have survived as a species in any case" (Bruner, 1990, p. 56). Luria's (1974) notion of kinetic melody further illustrates how, like narrative, the purposive aspect of action organizes and forms an integral part of movement. A kinetic melody represents not only the coordination of various afferent and efferent neural systems, but also the amalgamation of these with meaningful, skilled movements learned over time that allow one to interact with and act on the world. A kinetic melody, therefore, embodies the interpenetration of the cultural and the neural, providing an interwoven, dynamic unit of analysis that transcends reductionism and opens the way to analysis of the ecological complexity of human experience.

We have spent the bulk of this discussion on the concept of culture because it is central to the purpose of this chapter, but similar complexities apply to the notions of cognition and development. Generally, the term cognition applies to the process of acquiring knowledge or the products of that process designated by such terms as perceiving, attending, remembering, reasoning, linguistic ability, and so on. Equally generally, development applied to human beings refers to changes over time (generally, "growth" over time in a variety of capacities). Each of these concepts, no less than the concept of culture, is thoroughly saturated with theoretical commitments. For present purposes, we background such considerations to highlight the role of culture in the process of cognitive development, treated in as neutral a fashion as possible.

Culture and Cognitive Development: Universal Processes

Because of evidence for the presence of culture among the hominid precursors of modern humans for many hundreds of thousands, if not millions, of years prior to the emergence of *Homo sapiens*, it is not appropriate to juxtapose human biology and human culture. The human brain and body have co-evolved over a long period of time with our species' increasingly complex cultural environment (Richerson and Boyd, 2005). The implications of the co-evolution of human culture and human biology have been succinctly summarized by Geertz (1973, p. 68) who argued that, as a result of their tangled relations in the course of human phylogeny, culture and biology are equally tangled in the course of human ontogeny:

> Rather than culture acting only to supplement, develop, and extend organically based capacities logically and genetically prior to it, it would seem to be ingredient to those capacities themselves. A cultureless human being would probably turn out to be not an intrinsically talented though unfulfilled ape, but a wholly mindless and consequently unworkable monstrosity.

At the time, Geertz was arguing from scanty data, but contemporary studies of hominization have made clear the general principle that the contemporary human brain co-evolved with the accumulation of culture. Based on contemporary neuroscientific evidence, Quartz and Sejnowski (2002, p. 58) declared that culture "contains part of the developmental program that works with genes to build the brain that underlies who you are." Donald (2001, p. 23) made the same point in slightly different terms: "Culture actually configures the complex symbolic systems needed to support it by engineering the functional capture of the brain for epigenesis."

According to this same logic, culture does not act independently of biological processes during the child's development. Rather, to use a currently fashionable phrase, one needs to speak of "bio-cultural constructivism" (Li, 2006). Both culture, the historically accumulated artifacts that constitute the human-made part of the environment that greets a newborn at birth, *and* biological processes with a long phylogenetic history operate simultaneously in ontogeny to create the conditions for all of development, including its cognitive aspects.

With these considerations in mind, it should be clear that culture plays a central role in cognitive development, regardless of which particular culture a child is born into by virtue of the common history of *Homo sapiens*. Culture's role is complementary to the role of biological processes during ontogenetic development that are heavily constrained by infants' long phylogenetic history.

First, and most obviously, culture provides a vast storehouse of partial solutions to problems that human beings have frequently encountered and solved previously. Put differently, culture provides a vast storehouse of "tools to think and act with." Although such tools/solutions routinely need modification because humans must constantly deal with changing environmental, technological, and social circumstances, human infants do not encounter a world created de novo just for them. Rather, it is a world culturally "pre-pared" to provide them with cognitive resources, just as phylogeny has "pre-adapted" them to require and acquire such resources.

Second, the world that greets the newborn is a social world, populated by persons who have already acquired a great deal of the cultural knowledge that the child is going to have to acquire and whose behavior is itself shaped by this knowledge. The entire pattern of the child's early experiences of the world takes place in an intricately choreographed set of events, mediated by the artifacts that embody the society's cultural heritage. These cultural resources include means for organizing babies' experiences so that the babies will, in turn, come to occupy the same role in the social group that their parents and older kin are currently playing, and they will take their turn at organizing the experience of a next generation of children who will make possible the social group's continuation.

Our emphasis on culture as preceding the child and as a set of resources/experiences arranged for the child by adults who are heavily invested in the child's development provides the background for a third way in which culture plays an essential role in children's development. It requires the active efforts of children to acquire the necessary cultural knowledge to become competent members of the social group, thus reducing their dependence on the ministrations of others and maximizing their own potential to conduct their lives on their own terms. In short, children must learn to mediate their own behavior through the same cultural resources that their elders use to enable them to continue as members of the social group. From this perspective, cognitive development is a process of children learning to control the world and themselves by appropriating the cultural resources made available to them at birth by their families and community; if the process is successful, they will eventually change and perchance add to that set of cultural resources under the unforeseeable conditions of their own adult lives.

In summary, when considering the universal features of culture in human development, what one sees is a three-sided process in which the social inheritance of the past is made available to children at birth in an ongoing process of enculturation that requires that both the social world and the child actively engage with their social inheritance to enable the child to become a competent adult member of the social group.

Cultural Contributions to Cognition in Biological Context

What the earlier account leaves out is the initial biological state of the newborn when the child emerges into the culturally organized postnatal environment. As summarized in Cole and Hatano (2007), a number of developmentalists have converged around the idea that a full account of cognitive development requires synthesis of information about phylogenetic/biological and cultural constraints present at birth, both of which change dynamically over time during ontogenesis. Early-appearing phylogenetic contributions are of two kinds. The first are psychological processes that are organized in terms of "core" or "privileged" domains or "skeletal constraints" with identifiable precursors in nonhuman primates. Such processes display characteristic domain boundaries and task specificity. Each represents a particular class of entities for a particular set of purposes (Spelke, 2000). Widely accepted candidates for such core domains providing skeletal constraints for cognitive development include naive physics, mathematics, psychology (theory of mind), and biology (Wellman and Gelman, 1998). In these privileged domains, humans are genetically prepared to acquire knowledge systems that depend on essential physical features of the world, as well as competencies evident in embryonic form in common ancestor species such as language and number.

In addition to such domain-specific constraints, researchers have also identified powerful general learning mechanisms. Even infants possess the ability to identify sequential dependencies in the speech stream (Saffran, Aslin, and Newport, 1996) or in the mechanical movement that occurs when one object collides with another (Baillargeon, 1994). Moreover, humans are conceptual learners from early on. To mention a few such processes, they are able to (1) build concepts coherent within a larger system (Mandler, 2004); (2) understand a set of antecedent-consequent pairs in terms of unobservable, mediating forces (Tomasello, 1999); and (3) "bootstrap" (i.e., create a new system of representation that is more powerful than those present; Carey, 2004).

These general learning mechanisms are also products of evolution, but not in response to task-specific adaptation. They are heavily dependent on enlarged frontal and prefrontal cortices that may have evolved through uniquely human ways of living, such as posing and solving complex interpersonal and social problems, learning and using culturally inherited artifacts, and adapting the natural environment to their needs (Quartz and Sejnowski, 2002).

Whatever the phylogenetic constraints that characterize knowledge acquisition in core domains, such knowledge is woefully inadequate to fully explain normal adult human functioning; they are skeletal, not structurally complete (Gelman, 2000). Ontogenetic development of the human mind also requires repeated participation in culturally organized practices. Cultural practices are a bridge between phylogeny and ontogeny. On the one hand, the cultural history of a child's social group provides the kinds of practices that are available, their relative frequency, and their accessibility as proximal environments for development. On the other hand, developing individuals have increasing ability to choose the practices they enter into and to change their own features through participation. However, even when participants have no choice but to participate in a cultural practice and have no desire to actively improve their skills, repeated participation enhances the cognitive skills needed to perform well in these practices. This simple principle of neuro-associative learning suggests a possible mechanism for the perpetuation of core cultural practices and how such practices may take root within the individual.

Practices vary greatly both within and between social groups. In some cases, people acquire skills to perform competently only in a specific practice, whereas in other cases, they acquire a rich and well-structured body of knowledge and associated skills. Among these knowledge-rich domains, they may further acquire conceptual knowledge, based on which they can modify known procedures flexibly, invent new procedures, and employ their knowledge in a wide variety of practices. Moreover, for some domains of human activity, gaining cognitive competence may require years of experience in solving problems in the domain, experience that often takes the form of "deliberate practice" requiring sustained concentration (Ericsson, Krampe, and Tesch-Romer, 1993); alternatively, it may be achieved readily and promptly, based on a small number of experiences.

The amount of time and effort required to gain expertise in a given cultural practice or with respect to a particular cognitive domain (depending on whether one is dealing with a core domain and its skeletal principles or a domain of social practice for which no obvious skeletal principles appear) is currently uncertain. It seems plausible that in core domains, acquisition to a level broadly characteristic of the adult population should be relatively rapid and effortless, whereas acquisition of cultural practices that bear no clear relation to any known core domain would be slower and more effortful and require specialized arrangements for their acquisition. So, for example, natural languages appear to be acquired rapidly without any explicit instruction (in fact, young language learners may acquire a natural language even when doing so is discouraged, as in the case of deaf children placed in oralist schools run by hearing people; Padden and Humphries, 1988). By contrast, learning to read English or fly an airplane is rarely accomplished without explicit instruction and a great deal of practice. Human beings evolved to acquire natural languages. It required tens of thousands of years for them to invent written languages or to construct and fly airplanes, and to this day, such knowledge is not universal.

The Level of Large Populations: Culture Styles of Cognition

By far the most frequently studied level of culture–cognition relations involves comparisons between populations, often associated with an entire society or nation and sometimes even entire civilizations (such as Nisbett and colleagues contrasting the cognitive properties of societies descended from the Greek tradition with those of East Asian origin; Nisbett and Masuda, 2003).

A key assumption of many who conduct research at this level of cultural generality was famously formulated by the anthropologist Benedict (1934, p. 53):

> A human society must make for itself some design for living. It approves certain ways of meeting situations and certain ways of sizing them up. People in that society regard these solutions as foundations of the universe. They integrate them no matter what the difficulties. Men who have accepted a system of values by which to live cannot without courting inefficiency and chaos keep for long a fenced-off portion of their lives where they think and behave according to a contrary set of values. They try to bring about more conformity. They provide themselves with some common rationale and some common motivations. Some degree of consistency is necessary or the whole scheme falls to pieces.

Benedict's belief in the coherent patterning of psychological life by the cultural environment was expanded during the last half of the twentieth century into a large program of cross-cultural work that has been termed an "eco-cultural" psychology (Berry, 1976; Greenfield, Keller, Fuligni, and Maynard, 2003; Whiting and Whiting, 1975). The basic logic of this approach is to relate cultural patterns on the one hand to the physical circumstances of the group on the other. These ecological circumstances are assumed to give rise to configurations of economic activity/technology and social organization (kinship and the divisions of labor of adults), which in turn influence childrearing practices that shape the psychological characteristics of the children. The children, as a result of the patterned process of socialization they have undergone, are assumed to internalize the characteristics of their elders, and in this way, given cultural patterns are maintained over generations, allowing for changes in circumstances that can be expected, at a greater or lesser rate, to instigate cultural changes that will in turn lead to patterned cognitive changes referred to as "cognitive styles" (often thought of as the preferred way a person processes information). In principle, cognitive styles (unlike abilities) are conceived of in terms of bipolar dimensions, so that having a particular cognitive style refers to a tendency to behave in a certain manner.

A variety of terms has been used to characterize cognitive styles associated with cultural patterns. Berry et al. (1986) used the contrast terms "field dependent" and "field independent."

More recent research in this tradition has used such contrasts as "individualism/collectivism," "analytic/holistic," and "independent/interdependent (Kitayama and Cohen, 2007). Although the specifics of the different approaches vary, as reflected in the various tasks that they use to assess their core cognitive styles, they all agree that cognitive styles apply across a wide spectrum of traditional psychological categories including perception, attention, reasoning, categorizing, self-construal, social inferences about others, and so on. This extended understanding of culturally linked cognitive styles has led to a large literature of individualism and collectivism (e.g., independence/interdependence), which further suggests that as a person matures in a particular cultural and historical context, she or he develops a different way of relating to others by either giving primacy to the group the person is a part of (i.e., collectivist) or to herself or himself as an individual separate from the group (i.e., individualist). As a result, the person's self-construal (i.e., how she or he relates to self, others, and the environment) can either be individualistic and field independent or collectivist and field dependent.

The early work of Berry, Witkin, and their colleagues focused on the idea of a cultural/cognitive relation based on the idea that some people are more "field dependent" than others (e.g., some people are more heavily influenced by the context in which stimuli are presented or events occur than others who are considered "field independent;" Berry, 1976). Field dependence in the perceptual and cognitive realms was operationally defined and experimentally tested using the Rod and Frame Test (RFT) and the Embedded Figures Test (EFT). The RFT consists of a rod inside a frame, both of which are moveable, and the participant must adjust the rod to a true vertical position as the position of the frame is changed. Degree of error (the number of degrees away from 90 degrees) provides the measure of field dependence. The higher the score, the more field dependent the participant is considered to be. The EFT requires finding simple forms that are embedded in larger figures. The score is the average time in seconds to detect the simple forms, as well as the total number of correctly disembedded figures within a fixed amount of time. Greater time and more incomplete tasks reflect greater difficulty in analyzing a part separately from a wider pattern (an object from its context) or, alternatively, a greater tendency to perceive complete patterns rather than their separate components. In the social realm, it was assumed that field-independent people also experience themselves as separate and distinct from others, depend on internal referents, and are more autonomous in their social relationships relative to field-dependent people, or, in more recent terminology, that people's reasoning about themselves and others is either more focused on an autonomous agent or an agent whose actions are importantly contingent on the social group.

Berry tested his ideas by gathering data from 18 subsistence societies ranging from West Africa to Northern Canada and Australia as well as 3 industrialized groups. He used data from the Human Relations Area Files to code information about ecological, acculturative, and cultural elements to obtain evidence concerning key elements of the eco-cultural model. He administered tests of cognitive style in the cognitive and social domains to assess cognitive style. Then, the relations between variables were calculated using correlational, analysis of variance, and multiple regression techniques. The results were interpreted as strong evidence in favor of his eco-cultural model relating environment, social structure, cultural practices, and cognitive style.

However, this work encountered skepticism based on a variety of methodological factors, and a large-scale test of the model designed to overcome these objections failed to support the model (Berry et al., 1986), so for some years, the general idea of cognitive styles related to cultural configurations languished. However, the basic idea was subsequently revised and has become one of the most widely encountered approaches to studying culture and cognition currently in use (see Kitayama and Cohen, 2007).

Nisbett, Peng, Choi, and Norenzayan (2001) have focused on the idea that differences in cognitive style can be observed by comparing the performance of Asian and European Americans in a variety of experiments that capitalize on this difference in self-construal or cognitive style. They found that it is relatively more difficult for European Americans to detect changes in the background of scenes, suggesting that they are less field dependent, whereas it is more difficult for Asians to detect changes within objects in the foreground of a scene, suggesting that they are more field dependent. Simons and Levin (1997) also demonstrated that Asians more accurately detect change in the environment or context, whereas European Americans selectively detect changes in objects in the foreground using the "change blindness" paradigm. When an object in the background was removed or added after a brief delay, Asians were aware of the change more often, whereas European Americans did not notice changes in the background. Other research has attempted to explain these findings by suggesting that different cultures show different patterns of attention, with some incorporating more contextual information relative to others in their decision-making processes (Ji, Peng, and Nisbett, 2000; Masuda and Nisbett, 2001). More specifically, Asians tend to focus their attention on the interrelations between objects and the contexts in which they are embedded in visual space, whereas European Americans attend primarily to the object in the foreground and its salient characteristics, echoing previous studies on differential level of perceptual field dependency. Experimental evidence for this includes the fact that, when objects are taken out of the original context in which they were presented, European Americans have little difficulty identifying the object as familiar whether it is presented in isolation or with a new background, whereas Asians have greater difficulty identifying these same objects when they are presented with a novel background as opposed to in isolation (Ji et al., 2000; Masuda and Nisbett, 2001). Other researchers, making no mention of the demographic makeup of their sample, have suggested that, although semantic congruency between objects in the foreground and background increases accuracy, a bias toward processing objects in the foreground exists in the way humans perceive and categorize stimuli (Davenport and Potter, 2004). Nisbett and colleagues, nevertheless, contend that Asians do not simply fail to process the object in the foreground, but rather that they incorporate the spatial context and somehow bind it to their representation of the object.

For example, a recent study showed that patterns in eye movements correlate with observed differences in cognitive style (Chua, Boland, and Nisbett, 2005). Specifically, the eye movements of American (the ethnic makeup of this sample was not specified) and Chinese participants were measured while they viewed photographs of a focal object superimposed on a complex background. Examination using eye-tracking equipment revealed that American participants fixated more on focal objects and tended to fixate on the focal object more quickly after initial presentation of the photograph. By contrast, Chinese participants made more saccades to the background than did the Americans and took longer to direct their gaze specifically toward the focal object. Thus, cultural differences can be observed both at the behavioral level of performance and on a measurable physiological level.

A functional magnetic resonance imaging (fMRI) study (Grön, Schul, Bretschneider, Wunderlich, and Riepe, 2003) showed that, although behavioral performance (i.e., total recall and learning slope) was identical between European Americans and Chinese on a visual learning task that required repetitive memorization of geometric patterns and repetitive active recall, the two groups demonstrated different patterns of neuronal activation. Specifically, initial learning within the Chinese group activated bilateral frontal and parietal areas (i.e., the dorsal stream for analysis of spatial features), whereas the European American group recruited posterior ventral regions, especially the fusiform gyrus and hippocampal complex (i.e., the ventral stream for object identification). Later in learning, a crossover effect was observed such that European Americans began to exhibit dorsal activation and Chinese participants began to exhibit ventral activation before returning to the initially observed baseline pattern. The authors interpreted these results as demonstrating that differences in cultural upbringing influenced participants to initially approach stimuli in their default attentional style (i.e., trying to encode the geometric figures as a whole for the European Americans and trying to encode the visuospatial lay of the land in Chinese). The shift in processing strategy observed midway through the learning process seems to represent an attempt to more fully consolidate the percept to be learned by engaging the complimentary analyzer (i.e., either the ventral or dorsal stream). Once the memorization of the figures had been stabilized in long-term memory, participants returned to their default attentional style.

The fact that both European American and Chinese groups are able to recruit both the ventral and dorsal streams in different ways suggests a certain amount of flexibility in how culture comes into play when processing visual information. It is not the case, for example, that the more individualist culture always engages the ventral stream and the more collectivist culture always engages the dorsal stream. In like manner, Hong, Morris, Chiu, and Benet-Martínez (2000) have shown that cultural style alone cannot fully explain the dynamic nature of differences both between and within cultural groups. Through a series of priming studies aimed at bicultural individuals, they demonstrated that a group's cultural style can be manipulated by manipulating the cultural artifacts available to them. As a result, they suggest a more mediational account of cultural cognition and make the case for a culture by situation interaction model that they coined a "dynamic constructivist approach to culture" (Hong and Mallorie, 2004).

In summary, despite some inconsistencies in the data and the continued presence of critics and skeptics, there is accumulating evidence to support the idea that members of different cultures perform differently on cognitive tasks in a patterned manner consistent with the idea of a culturally linked cognitive style. Moreover, there appear to be differences in how members of different cultures recruit different neural systems when performing the same tasks.

Cultural Practices as the Source of Variations in Cognition

The third level at which it has proven productive to study the relation of culture and cognition is the level of cultural practices—"actions that are repeated, shared with others in a social group, and invested with normative expectations and with meanings or significances that go beyond the immediate goals of the action" (Miller and Goodnow, 1995, p. 7). Cultural practices can be thought of as the proximal units of culturally organized experience. This idea is expressed by Shweder et al. (1998, p. 871) when they wrote that whatever universal cognitive characteristics humans share as a species, these features "only gain character, substance, definition and motivational force…when they are translated and transformed into, and through, the concrete actualities of some particular practice, activity setting, or way of life."

Authors who emphasize the idea of cognitive styles associated with cultural patterns characteristic of large populations also assert the importance of cultural practice. So, for example, Nisbett and Masuda (2003, p. 11169) assert that "the differences in attention, perception, and cognition that we have shown are driven by differences in social structure and social practices." Elsewhere, Nisbett and Norenzayan (2003, p. 28) noted that, "Societies differ in the cultural practices that they promote, affording differential expertise in the use of a cognitive strategy, or differential knowledge about a domain." However, they do not directly study cultural practices; rather their experimental studies model the presumed generalized cognitive outcomes of cultural practices described by others.

By contrast, those who do directly study cultural practices as the proximal locus of culture–cognition relations are more likely to combine direct ethnographic descriptions with experimental methods that model the practice they observe (Cole, 1996; Greenfield, 2004; Mejia-Arauz, Rogoff, and Paradise, 2005). For example, Greenfield and Childs (1977) went to a Mayan community in the state of Chiapas, Mexico, where they studied the cognitive and social consequences of learning to weave. Their work included careful descriptions of the weaving process engaged in by women and young girls who were being apprenticed into weaving. They analyzed the patterns of the weaving products produced as well as experimental tests of children's ability to reproduce weaving patterns using sticks of varying width and color using a model of the traditional loom. In the 1990s, they returned to the same village and conducted parallel observations of parents (former child subjects) inducting their children into weaving and the consequences of the changed weaving practices and products that had arisen over the years (Greenfield, 2004). In contrast to the late 1960s, by the mid-1990s, this Mayan community had shifted from an economy based primarily on subsistence agriculture and relatively secluded from the modern state to one based more heavily on involvement in the money economy and trade and much more frequent interaction with people and trade from outside of the village and the local region, including trade in woven cloth and the profusion of new patterns to which they were exposed. The instructional mode characterizing the mother–child weaving sessions in the 1960s and 1970s consisted of mothers hovering close by and guiding the children with their own hands and bodies, using little verbal instruction. The entire system appeared to focus on maintenance of the "one right way" of the weaving tradition, which consisted of a limited, relatively simple set of weaving patterns. In the 1990s, mothers who were more involved in the modern economy (for example, women who wove products for sale) instructed their children verbally from a distance, sometimes using older siblings to take over instruction, and the children learned by a process characterized by a good deal more trial and error and self-correction of errors. At this later date, there was no longer a small set of simple, "correct" patterns, but an efflorescence of patterns, indicating the increased respect paid to individual innovation that comes with a trial-and-error approach to learning. This proliferation in turn depended on, and contributed to, changes in weaving practices.

Accompanying these historical changes in economic practices and complexity of woven products were changes in the way children represented weaving patterns in the experimental task that used sticks of varying width and color to reproduce weaving patterns. For example, instead of using three white sticks to represent a broad band of white cloth, a single broad white stick was more likely to be used in the later historical period, and those who attended school were more likely to be able to create novel patterns. These historical changes were accompanied by an unchanging pattern of representational development related to age; older children in both historical periods were more able than younger children to represent more complex visual patterns, a fact that Greenfield interpreted as an indication of universal developmental processes accompanying culturally contingent ones.

Scribner and Cole (1981) studied the cognitive consequences of literacy and schooling among the Vai, a tribal group residing along the northwest coast of Liberia. Although standard ethnographies of the Vai made them appear to be similar in most respects to their neighbors, they were remarkable because they had been using a writing system of their own invention for more than 100 years. Their literacy was acquired without any formal schooling.

The research was carried out in three overlapping phases. First, to understand the local organization of literacy, members of the research team conducted a survey of the social correlates of literacy and schooling that spanned all of Vai country and the Vai section of the capital, Monrovia, and conducted an ethnography of daily life in a single Vai village. They added a battery of psychological tests that had produced evidence of schooling effects on cognitive development to the survey to answer the most straightforward question one might pose: Does Vai literacy substitute for schooling in producing improved cognitive performance on learning, classification, and problem-solving tasks?

From this preparatory research, they learned that three kinds of literacy are to be found among the Vai: literacy in Vai, literacy in Arabic (mostly, but not entirely, to read from the Qur'an), and literacy in English, which was acquired in school. Neither Vai nor Qur'anic literacy substituted for schooling with respect to psychological test performance; in general, those who had been to school performed better on the test battery, especially when asked to explain the basis of their performance (metacognitive awareness). The survey and ethnographic observations indicated that, unlike literacy acquired in school, Vai literacy involves no mastery of esoteric knowledge or new forms of institutionalized social interaction. It also does not prepare the learner for a variety of new kinds of economic and social activity in which mediation of action through print is essential. It is used primarily for keeping records and writing letters to kin living in other parts of the country. Learning is almost always a personal affair carried out in the course of daily activities (most often, when a friend of relative agrees to teach the learner to read and write letters).

In the second round of research, instead of seeking evidence of "cognitive change in general," the investigators sought to test the widespread notion that practice in reading and writing changes a person's knowledge of the properties of language itself. The tasks in this "metalinguistic survey" included the ability to define words, to engage in syllogistic reasoning, to distinguish between an object and its name, to make judgments about the grammaticality of various utterances, and to explain what was wrong in the case of ungrammatical utterances. Only the grammaticality task yielded a positive influence of Vai literacy. From observations of Vai literates engaged in their daily activities, the researchers knew that discussions of whether a phrase contained in a correspondence letter was in "proper Vai" or not were common, so it seemed most plausible to attribute Vai literates' skill in this area to their practices when writing and reading letters. But the investigators wanted to find a variety of everyday tasks where people used written Vai to carry out culturally valued activities. From an analysis of a large corpus of letters, they discovered that, although the contents were likely to be relatively routine and hence easy to interpret, they nonetheless contained various "context setting" devices to take into account the fact that the reader was not in face-to-face contact with the writer. They reasoned that extended practice in letter writing to people in other locales ought to promote a tendency to provide fuller descriptions of local events that might be needed for interpretation. This notion was tested by creating a simple board game similar to games common in the area but different enough to require rather explicit instructions. Vai literate and nonliterate people learned the game and then described it, either to another person face-to-face or by dictating a letter to someone in another village in enough detail for that person to be able to play the game based on the instructions alone. Vai literates were far better at this task than nonliterates, and among Vai literates, the degree of experience in reading/writing was positively associated with performance.

Vai literates also excelled at analyzing spoken words into syllables and at synthesizing syllables into meaningful words and phrases (for example, the word for chicken [tiye] and paddle [laa] when combined yield the word waterside), so by combining pictures, it was possible to make entire "sentences." The same kind of result was found when tasks were modeled on Qur'anic literacy practices, wherein children learned to recite the Qur'an by adding one word at a time to the first word of a passage. In an "incremental recall" task in which lists of words are built up by starting with a list length of one item and adding one item per trial, Qur'anic literates excelled. By contrast, when the order of the items changed from trial to trial (free recall), school literates performed better than Qur'anic literates.

Because this research included experimental procedures modeled on alternative literacy practices and schooled people performed more poorly than Vai literates in certain key cases, a richer understanding of the role of literacy in cognitive development offered itself. Formal schooling is constituted as a set of practices including the use of written texts no less than Vai or Vai forms of Qur'anic literacy. There is no more reason to attribute cases where schooled people excelled at tasks to their ability to read and write per se than there is in the cases where Vai or Qur'anic literates excelled. For example, the fact that schooling promotes skill in the verbal explanation of problem-solving processes seems most naturally explained by noting that such skills are demanded by typical teacher–pupil dialogue in classrooms (Griffin and Mehan, 1980). Teachers often require students to respond to questions and demands such as, "Why did you give that answer?" or "Go to the blackboard and explain what you did."

A third example of cross-cultural research that focuses on the level of cultural practice has been carried out by Rogoff and her colleagues who have focused on the proclivity of children from many low-technology, traditional cultures to learn by carefully observing what their peers and elders are doing (Rogoff, Paradise, Meija-Arauz, Correa-Chávez, and Angelillo, 2003). In a typical study, the researchers arranged for 6- to 8-year-old children to observe a 10-year-old child being instructed on how to accomplish an origami paper folding task by a bilingual experimenter (Mejia-Arauz et al., 2005). The children were either from Mexican heritage or European American heritage homes living in a coastal town in California. Half of the Mexican heritage children had mothers with less than a high school education, whereas half of them had mothers with more than a high school education. All of the European American heritage children had mothers with more than a high school education. Based on evidence from many traditional (indigenous) societies, Mexican heritage children were expected to observe more intently and ask for fewer explanations than their European heritage counterparts. This was confirmed, at least, for the Mexican heritage children whose mothers had attained lower levels of education. However, those Mexican heritage children whose mothers had gone beyond high school behaved more like their European American counterparts than their peers. They did not engage in as much intent observation, and they asked for a good deal more verbal explanation. These results led Mejia-Arauz et al. (2005, p. 290) to conclude that:

> Participation in school may socialize specific practices that then gradually become part of indigenous and indigenous–heritage people's own ways of doing things when former schoolchildren become parents, supplanting a traditional emphasis on learning by observation.

A final example of how cognitive skills develop when a society creates artifacts and cultural practices to support more complex cognitive achievements comes from studies of involvement in the use of an abacus in Japan (Hatano, 1997). An abacus is an external memory and computational device. It can register a number as a configuration of beads, and one can find the answer to a given calculation problem, in principle, by manipulating the beads. People can learn how to operate an abacus in an elementary but serviceable manner in a few hours when they participate in deliberate instruction. Advanced training is geared almost entirely to accelerating the speed of the operations involved. Values respecting the speed of calculation are shared among abacus operators.

As a result of extensive training, abacus operation tends to be gradually interiorized to such a degree that most abacus masters can calculate accurately and even faster without a physical abacus present than with the instrument itself. During mental calculation, it appears that they can represent an intermediate, resultant number on their "mental abacus" in the form of a mental image of the configuration of beads, onto which (mentally) they enter, or from which they remove, the next input number. In other words, abacus experts can solve calculation problems by mentally manipulating the mental representation of abacus beads. The interiorization of the operation is an important mechanism for accelerating the speed of calculation because the mental operation is not constrained by the speed of muscle movement. Thus, expert abacus operators use the real abacus only when they calculate very large numbers that cannot be represented on their mental abacus. Abacus operators calculate extraordinarily rapidly (Hatano, 1997). When mixed addition and subtraction problems are presented in print, experts manipulate 5 to 10 digits per second. Remarkable speed is also observed for multiplication and division.

The case of gaining expertise in abacus operation (both material and mental) exemplifies the sociocultural nature of expertise (Hatano, 1997). Pupils who attend abacus classes are usually first sent there by their parents while in elementary school. The parents often believe that the exercise will foster children's diligence and punctiliousness as well as enhance their calculation and estimation ability. Young pupils are motivated to learn abacus skills to get parental praise, especially by passing an exam for qualification.

The students' motivation changes when they join an abacus club at school or become a representative of the abacus school, in other words, when the operation is embedded in a different kind of practice. Abacus enthusiasts compete in matches and tournaments, as tennis or chess players do. Also like these players, abacus club members not only engage in exercise at least a few hours every day, but also seek knowledge of how to improve their skills. Their learning is strongly supported by the immediate social context of the club and the larger community of abacus operators.

Abacus operators are also socialized in terms of their values, for example, regarding the importance of abacus skills and their status in general education, as well as their respect for the speed of calculation mentioned earlier. In fact, the community of abacus educators and players constitutes a strong pressure group in the world of education in Japan. In this sense, gaining expertise is far from purely cognitive; it is a social process (Lave and Wenger, 1991), and it involves changes in values and identities (Goodnow, 1990). The experts' values and identities are undoubtedly forms of "culture in mind," acquired through internalization. They serve as the source of motivation for experts to excel in the target domain.

Expertise in mental abacus operation also induces changes at neural levels. For example, using event-related fMRI, Tanaka, Michimata, Kaminaga, Honda, and Sadato (2002) showed that, whereas ordinary people retain series of digits in verbal working memory (revealed as increased activation in the corresponding cortical areas including the Broca's area), mental abacus experts hold them in visuospatial working memory, showing activations in bilateral superior frontal sulcus and superior parietal lobule. Hanakawa, Honda, Okada, Fukuyama, and Shibasaki (2003) demonstrated, also using fMRI, that the posterior-superior parietal cortex was significantly more activated while mental additions were performed among mental abacus experts than nonlearners of abacus.

Conclusion

These are only bare outlines of contemporary approaches to culture and cognitive development. It now seems well established that culture is more than an "add on" to a phylogenetically determined process of cognitive development. Culture matters. In Geertz's terms, it is an "ingredient to the process" of cognitive development because the biological and cultural heritages of human beings have been part of the same process of hominization for millions of years. Claims for this interdependence are bolstered by modern brain imaging techniques that amply demonstrate that culturally organized experience, whether organized at the level of societies as a whole or at the level of cultural practices, has clear influences on brain organization and functioning.

An issue that requires a good deal more thought concerns the connections among cultural patterns, cognitive styles, and cultural practices. On this point, there is as yet no firm agreement among scholars. Many adhere to the notion that broad cognitive styles, although acquired in specific cultural practices, are based on society-wide, historically accumulated designs for living, so that it makes good sense to speak of East Asian versus European or American cognitive styles that shape human cognition in virtually all domains of human experience from conceptions of the self to forms of perception, attention, problem solving, and social interaction. Even some who focus on cultural practices as the proximal locus of cultural influences on cognition believe that such practices are significantly shaped by overall cultural patterns that can be contrasted in terms of overarching binary oppositions such as interdependent versus independent cultural/cognitive styles.

Others place more emphasis on cultural practices as the primary locus of cultural variations in cognitive development and take the view that the degree to which patterns of behavior learned in specific cultural practices become general in a cultural group is the result of the linkages between cultural practices that are never totalizing in their effects. Thus, for example, the range of literacy practices among the Vai is restricted relative to the range of practices associated with literacy in technologically advanced societies. The reasons for this restricted range among the Vai may be many, including absence of a technology of mass production, legal restrictions placed by the central government on the use of Vai script in civil affairs, adherence to a religion that uses a completely different writing system and a foreign language, and so on. Scribner and Cole's (1981) activity-based, cultural practice approach emphasized that, if the uses of writing are few, the skill development they induce will also be limited to accomplishing a narrow range of tasks in a correspondingly narrow range of activities and content domains.

However, when technological, social, and economic conditions create many activities where reading and writing are instrumental, the range of literacy skills can be expected to broaden and increase in complexity. In any society where literacy practices are ubiquitous and complexly interrelated, the associated cognitive skills will also become more widespread and complexly related, giving the (false) impression that engagement in schooling induces generalized changes in cognitive development.

With respect to the differences between Mexican heritage and European American heritage children's proclivity to learn through intent observation, formal, literacy-based schooling is usefully considered as a complex set of cultural practices. Involvement in those practices induces practice-specific learning, but it may also "seep into" practices of the home and community. Hence, one sees changes in children's proclivities to engage in learning through intent observation, not because of a society-wide difference in cognitive style that shapes their involvement in specific practices (folding paper to make objects) but because of the interconnection of home and school practices in the lives of their parents, whose own lives were changed by the practices they engaged in as youngsters. As Rogoff and Angelillo (2002) describe their approach, their aim is to examine a pattern of approaches to learning that relates to a constellation of cultural practices. This approach to culture, focusing on multifaceted and coherent cultural practices rather than on variables "independent" of each other, allows examination of cultural patterns that would be obscured if all but a few differences between communities were "controlled."

The challenge for students of culture and cognitive development is to work out more systematically the degree of generality of cultural patterns across practices, their sources, and their consequences for cognition. This work has been put on a firmer foundation as a result of the research carried out in recent decades, but there is still a long way to go before we can claim a firm understanding of the intricate ways in which culture and cognitive development relate to each other.

Acknowledgments

Preparation of this manuscript was supported in part by funds provided to Michael Cole by the University of California in his capacity as a university professor and in part by support provided by the National Institutes of Health to Xavier Cigagas.

References

Baillargeon, R. (1994). How do infants learn about the physical world? *Current Directions in Psychological Science, 3,* 133–140.
Bartlett, F. C. (1932). *Remembering.* Cambridge, United Kingdom: Cambridge University Press.

Benedict, R. (1934). *Patterns of culture.* New York: Houghton Mifflin.
Berry, J. W. (1976). *Human ecology and cultural style.* New York: Sage-Halstead.
Berry, J. W., Van de Koppel, J. M., Sĭnŭchal, C., Annis, R. C., Bahuchet, S., Cavalli-Sforza, L. L., et al. (1986). *On the edge of the forest: Cultural adaptation and cognitive development in Central Africa.* Lisse, The Netherlands: Swets and Zeitlinger.
Bruner, J. S. (1990). *Acts of meaning.* Cambridge, MA: Harvard University Press.
Carey, S. (2004). Bootstrapping and the origins of concepts. *Daedalus,* 59–68.
Chua, H. F., Boland, J. E., and Nisbett, R. E. (2005). Cultural variation in eye movements during scene perception. *Proceedings of the National Academy of Sciences 102,* 12629–12633.
Cole, M. (1996). *Cultural psychology.* Cambridge, MA: Harvard University Press.
Cole, M., and Hatano, G. (2007). Cultural-historical activity theory: Integrating phylogeny, cultural history, and ontogenesis in cultural psychology. In S. Kitayama & D. Cohen (Eds.), *Handbook of cultural psychology* (pp. 109–135). New York: Guilford Press.
D'Andrade, R. (1986). Three scientific world views and the covering law model. In D. Fiske and R. Shweder (Eds.), *Meta-theory in the social sciences.* Chicago: University of Chicago Press.
D'Andrade, R. (1996). Culture. In *Social Science Encyclopedia* (pp. 161–163). London: Routledge.
Davenport, J. L., and Potter, M. C. (2004). Scene consistency in object and background perception. *Psychological Science, 15,* 559–564.
Donald, M. (2001). *A mind so rare: The evolution of human consciousness.* New York: W. W. Norton and Co.
Ericsson, K. A., Krampe, R. T., and Tesch-Romer, C. (1993). The role of deliberate practice in the acquisition of expert performance. *Psychological Review, 100,* 363–406.
Geertz, C. (1973). *The interpretation of cultures.* New York: Basic Books.
Gelman, R. (2000). Domain specificity and variability in cognitive development. *Child Development, 71,* 854–856.
Goodenough, W. (1994). Toward a working theory of culture. In R. Borowsky (Ed.), *Assessing cultural anthropology* (pp. 262–273). New York: Mc-Graw Hill.
Goodnow, J. J. (1990). Using sociology to extend psychological accounts of cognitive development. *Human Development, 33,* 81–107.
Greenfield, P. M. (2004). *Weaving generations together: Evolving creativity in the Maya of Chiapas.* Santa Fe, NM: School of American Research.
Greenfield, P. M., and Childs, C. P. (1977). Weaving, color terms and pattern representation: Cultural influences and cognitive development among the Zinacantecos of Southern Mexico. *Inter-American Journal of Psychology, 11,* 23–28.
Greenfield, P. M., Keller, H., Fuligni, A., and Maynard, A. (2003). Cultural pathways through universal development. *Annual Review of Psychology, 54,* 461–490.
Griffin, P., and Hugh M. (1981). Sense and ritual in classroom discourse. In F. Coulmas (Ed.), *Conversational Routine: Explorations in standardized communication situations and prepatterned speech.* (pp. 187–213) The Hague: Mouton Press.
Grön, G., Schul, D., Bretschneider, V., Wunderlich, A. P., and Riepe, M. W. (2003). Alike performance during nonverbal episodic learning from diversely imprinted neural networks. *European Journal of Neuroscience, 18,* 3112–3120.
Hanakawa, T., Honda, M., Okada, T., Fukuyama, H., and Shibasaki, H. (2003). Neural correlates underlying mental calculation in abacus experts: A functional magnetic resonance imaging study. *NeuroImage, 19,* 296–307.
Hatano, G. (1997). Commentary: Core domains of thought, innate constraints, and sociocultural contexts. In H. M. Wellman and K. Inagaki (Eds.), *The emergence of core domains of thought: Children's reasoning about physical, psychological, and biological phenomena* (pp. 71–78). San Francisco: Jossey-Bass.
Herskovitz, M. (1948). *Cultural dynamics.* New York: A. Knopf.
Hong, Y.-Y., Morris, M. W. Y., and Benet-Martínez, V. (2000). Multicultural minds: A dynamic constructivist approach to culture and cognition. *American Psychologist, 55,* 709–720.
Hong, Y.-Y., and Mallorie, L. A. M. (2004). A dynamic constructivist approach to culture: Lessons learned from personality psychology. *Journal of Research in Personality, 38,* 59–67.
Ji, L., Peng, K., and Nisbett, R. E. (2000). Culture, control, and perception of relationships in the environment. *Journal of Personality and Social Psychology, 78,* 943–955.
Kitayama, S., and Cohen, D. (2007). *The handbook of cultural psychology.* New York: Guilford Press.
Lave, J., and Wenger, E. (1991). *Situated learning. Legitimate peripheral participation.* Cambridge, United Kingdom: University of Cambridge Press.

Li, S.-C. (2006). Biocultural co-construction of lifespan development. In P. B. Baltes, P. A. Reuter-Lorenz, and F. Rösler (Eds.), *Lifespan development and the brain: The perspective of biocultural co-constructivism* (pp. 40–57). New York: Cambridge University Press.

Luria, A. R. (1974). *The working brain*. London: Penguin.

Mandler, J. M. (2004). A synopsis of *The foundations of mind: Origins of conceptual thought*. New York: Oxford University Press. *Developmental Science, 7*, 499–505.

Masuda, T., and Nisbett, R. E. (2001). Attending holistically vs analytically: Comparing the context sensitivity of Japanese and Americans. *Journal of Personality and Social Psychology, 81*, 922–934.

Mejia-Arauz, R., Rogoff, B., and Paradise, R. (2005). Cultural variation in children's observation during a demonstration. *International Journal of Behavioural Development, 29*, 283–291.

Miller, P. J., and Goodnow, J. J. (1995). Cultural practices: Toward an integration of development and culture. In J. J. Goodnow, P. J. Miller, and F. Kessel (Eds.), *Cultural practices as contexts for development. New directions for children development* (Vol. 67, pp. 5–16). San Francisco: Jossey-Bass.

Nelson, K. (1981). Cognition in a script framework. In J. H. Flavell and L. Ross (Eds.), *Social cognitive development*. Cambridge, United Kingdom: Cambridge University Press.

Nisbett, R., and Masuda, T. (2003). Culture and point of view. *Proceedings of the National Academy of Sciences, 100*, 11163–11170.

Nisbett, R. E. & Norenzayan, A. (2002). Culture and cognition. In H. Pashler & D. Medin (Eds.) *Steven's handbook of experimental psychology: Memory and cognitive processes* (Vol. 2, pp. 561–597). Hoboken, NJ: John Wiley & Sons Inc.

Nisbett, R. E., Peng, K., Choi, I., and Norenzayan, A. (2001). Culture and systems of thought: Holistic versus analytic cognition. *Psychological Review, 108*, 291–310.

Padden, C., and Humphries, T. (1988). *Deaf in America*. Cambridge, MA: Harvard University Press.

Quartz, S. R., and Sejnowski, T. J. (2002). *Liars, lovers, and heroes: What the new brain science reveals about how we become who we are*. New York: William Morrow.

Richerson, P. J., and Boyd, R. (2005). *Not by genes alone: How culture transformed human evolution*. Chicago: University of Chicago Press.

Rogoff, B., and Angelillo, C. (2002) Investigating the coordinated functioning of multifaceted cultural practices in human developent. *Human Development, 45*, 211–225.

Rogoff, B., Paradise, R., Meija-Arauz, R., Correa-Chávez, M., and Angelillo, C. (2003). Firsthand learning through intent participation. *Annual Review of Psychology, 54*, 175–203.

Saffran, J. R., Aslin, R. N., and Newport, E. L. (1996). Statistical learning by 8-month old infants. *Science, 274*, 1926–1928.

Scribner, S., and Cole, M. (1981). *The psychology of literacy*. Cambridge, MA: Harvard University Press.

Shweder, R. A., Goodnow, J., Hatano, G., LeVine, R. A., Markus, H., and Miller, P. (1998). The cultural psychology of development: One mind, many mentalities. In R. M. Lerner (Ed.), *Handbook of child psychology. Volume 1: Theoretical models of human development* (pp. 865–938). New York: Wiley.

Simons, D. J., and Levin, D. T. (1997). Change blindness. *Trends in Cognitive Sciences, 1*, 261–267.

Spelke, E. S. (2000). Core knowledge. *American Psychologist, 55*, 1233–1243.

Tanaka, S., Michimata, C., Kaminaga, T., Honda, M., and Sadato, N. (2002). Superior digit memory of abacus experts: An event-related functional MRI study. *NeuroReport, 13*, 2187–2191.

Tomasello, M. (1999). *The cultural orgins of human cognition*. Cambridge, MA: Harvard University Press.

Wartofsky, M. (1973). *Models*. Dordrecht, The Netherlands: D. Reidel.

Wellman, H. M. & Gelman, S. A. (1998). Knowledge acquisition in foundational domains. In W. Damon (Ed.). *Handbook of child psychology: Cognition, perception, and language* (Vol. 2, pp. 523–573). Hoboken, NJ: John Wiley & Sons Inc.

Whiting, B. B., and Whiting, J. W. M. (1975). *Children of six cultures: A psycho-cultural analysis*. Cambridge, MA: Harvard University Press.

7
Language

ELENA LIEVEN and SABINE STOLL

Introduction

Only human beings have language in the sense of a system of signs that allows them to express communicative intentions in an unlimited variation. Both biological and environmental factors play a role in acquiring a language. However, the exact balance of nature and nurture, especially which biological features are relevant for language acquisition, has been hotly debated. In studying language acquisition cross-linguistically, we learn about the range of capacities required for language learning. Children can learn any language even though languages vary extremely in their structures. Every normally developing child will learn the language or, as is the case in most cultures of the world, the languages of their community in the first years of their lives, including children brought up with a sign language.* How do children learn such complex and variable systems? In all of the languages studied, children follow approximately the same timetable in the major landmarks of development such as babbling, first words, and first complex utterances. But how do children learn the structures of their languages and is there uniformity in the strategies they use even if they are learning languages with completely different structures? To assess the task of the language learner and discover the strategies children employ, it is important to study the acquisition of as wide a range of languages as possible and to conduct systematic cross-linguistic comparisons of acquisition strategies.

In this chapter, we first consider some historical and demographic issues in cross-linguistic developmental research. In the next section, we point out that a central problem in this field is that only a tiny number of languages and of linguistic features have been studied for how children learn them; this severely limits the conclusions that can be drawn about language learning. We then turn to a consideration of the major theoretical divide in the field, namely between those who think that an innate specifically linguistic, universal grammar must exist to account for language learning and those who, although accepting that language is unique to humans, think that grammar can be built out of more general human cognitive capacities. One important focus of this section is the structure of the language environment and how this interacts with children's learning. Next follows a section covering the key classical and modern studies in cross-linguistic research on language acquisition; here we consider precursors to language development in the first year of life, major cross-linguistic studies that have been carried out, the relationship between language and cognition, approaches that compare closely related languages, and finally, the learning of the major argument roles of verbs. Before the concluding section, we raise a number of practical issues.

---

* In this chapter, we confine the discussion to what is known about monolingual first language acquisition, but it is important to remember that many children in the world grow up learning more than one language.

Historical and Demographic Issues in Cross-Linguistic Developmental Research

An interest in how children can learn language goes back many centuries. The private teacher of Louis XIII noted down the language development of his pupil in a diary. However, language acquisition became a systematic field of research only in the late nineteenth century. At that time, researchers of various European languages began to record extensive diaries about the development of their children (e.g., for German: Leopold, 1948; Lindner, 1885, 1898; Preyer, 1882; Stern and Stern, 1928/1965; for Russian: Gvozdev, 1949; for French: Grégoire, 1937; and for Polish: Zarebina, 1965). These diaries gave major insights into the overall course of these children's language development. The diary method, however, is only really feasible in the early stages of language acquisition, and researchers can apply it only very selectively at later, more complex stages of development because the child simply talks too much and in sentences that are too complex. It is thus impossible to note down verbatim what is said if the diary is not restricted to very specific questions (e.g., the development of personal pronouns or a particular type of complex sentence structure).

With the rise of behaviorism and the use of empirical methods in psychology in the first half of the twentieth century, the data sources for language acquisition studies changed radically. Researchers collected large samples of data from a great number of children in specific age bands, largely with a view to working out norms for milestones of language acquisition. Naturalistic studies also became more systematic, and experiments began to address specific issues in language development.

The use of experiments in cross-linguistic research is constrained by a number of factors. There is the problem general to cross-cultural comparisons—the fact that the whole context of experiments derives from a particular cultural background—and therefore, it is very difficult to know what factors are responsible when different outcomes are obtained in different cultures. The more technologically advanced and similar to urban Western culture, the more likely it is that experiments can be run and the results treated as comparable, even if the comparisons are being made across widely different typological families (e.g., children learning English and Japanese).

The other main data source employed in modern studies of language acquisition is systematic recordings of the development of individual children over an extended period. The goal of such longitudinal recordings is to obtain a representative sample of the child's speech and the speech addressed to the child. However, this data source only became possible in the second half of the twentieth century with the development of technology that is necessary for such recordings. In these studies, children were audiotaped and, later in the century, also videotaped at regular intervals over an extended period, often several years. The data were then transcribed and grammatically coded and analyzed.

Currently, there are longitudinal studies on approximately 28 languages available that are openly accessible to the research community through the Child Language Data Exchange System (CHILDES) project (http://childes.psy.cmu.edu/) initiated by MacWhinney and Snow. CHILDES is the major resource for child language research. It also provides tools to transcribe and analyze language corpora.

If we take all the acquisition studies together (experiments and longitudinal studies), we know something about the acquisition of approximately 70 to 80 languages (i.e., approximately 1% of all the languages spoken today). This 1% of languages also includes languages for which only one acquisition study of a single feature exists (for instance, the use of word order, subject and object case marking, or the development of the passive). Given the fact that there are approximately 7,000 languages spoken in the world with approximately 400 language families, this is a rather small sample (www.uni-leipzig.de/~autotyp). Languages do not only differ widely in structure, but they are also spoken in a huge variety of different cultures with different traditions of parenting. However, most of the studies available are on the major Indo-European languages of Northwestern Europe, such as English, German, French, and Spanish. This geographical area is known to be typologically very unusual with rare features such as interrogative word order in questions requiring "yes" or "no" as an answer, relative pronouns in subject relative clauses (e.g., "The man *who* is walking down the street is nice"), and so forth (Cysouw, 2002; Dahl, 1990; Haspelmath, 2001).

There are mostly practical reasons for the bias to this one geographic area. To conduct a study of language acquisition, considerable resources of time and labor are necessary. Therefore, it is easier for researchers to study acquisition as close as possible to home. Furthermore, undertaking language acquisition research in a range of different cultures and languages requires a major interdisciplinary effort, using methods from psychology, linguistics, and social anthropology, at the least. Researchers need to have an unusual combination of expertise and considerable funding to conduct such a study. For instance, the authors are involved in a project documenting the learning of Chintang, an endangered Sino-Tibetan language of Eastern Nepal. To carry out this project, preliminary work in the culture by a team that includes three linguists, two anthropologists, and two developmental psycholinguists together with a large team of local research assistants was essential (www.mpi.nl/DOBES/projects/chintang).

However, if we want to make cross-linguistic comparisons that cover all kinds of different variables found in the languages of the world, we have a serious sampling problem because we know very little about languages of other families and even less about endangered languages or languages spoken by rather few people. These can sometimes reveal features that have been deemed impossible for a human language on theoretical grounds. An example of such a feature is the recent discovery that certain prefixes on the verb can be freely ordered in Chintang, without any consequence for meaning (Bickel et al., 2007). In all of the languages previously studied, the ordering of prefixes is fixed; this was thought to be a linguistic universal.

Given these sampling issues, it is currently very difficult to make general statements about child language acquisition. At best, we can make claims about the acquisition of individual languages or features within closely related languages (e.g., within a language family within or across subbranches).

Central Issues in Cross-Linguistic Developmental Research

One of the central reasons why language acquisition is studied from a cross-linguistic perspective is that, if we want to make claims about language acquisition in general and not only about an individual language, we need to find out first what learners have to be able to master in learning different languages. Because languages differ so widely in their phonological, morphological, and syntactic structure, what has to be learned will vary considerably, and we might expect differences in acquisition strategies as a result of the specific linguistic variables languages exhibit.

This variation can occur on all linguistic levels. We illustrate just a few examples here. If we take the sound systems of languages, learners are confronted with very different tasks. Rotokas (West Bougainville), a language of Papua New Guinea, has only 6 consonants, whereas !Xóõ, a Southern Khoisan language spoken in Botwsana and Namibia, has 122 consonants, which include a large number of clicks (Maddieson, 2005a). The most typical consonant inventories have approximately 22 consonants. Thus, English with 24 consonants is about average. Variation in vowels is much smaller and ranges from 2 to 14 (Maddieson, 2005b); the average number of vowels is 6. Structural diversity is also very prominent in word formation, and we find big differences across languages. Some languages are analytic, which means that syntactic units—words—contain only few meaning units (i.e., the ratio of morphemes per word is very low). The fewer morphemes per word, the more analytic a language is (e.g., Vietnamese is an extremely analytic language, with no productive affixes or other morphological units combining with words). Other languages (called synthetic) exhibit the opposite pattern. They express a lot of grammatical information per word unit, such as Turkish, so the ratio of morphemes per word is very high. The most extremely synthetic languages are sometimes called "polysynthetic" and can be exemplified by such languages as Koasati (Bickel and Nichols, 2005). Languages vary considerably not only in the structure of words but also in how words are combined. Most languages show a preferred word order pattern, that is, an ordering of subject (S), verb (V), and object (O). For instance, in some languages, word order is predominantly SVO, and in others, it is SOV. Some languages, however, do not show such a preferred pattern at all; for example, in Nunggubuyu (Gunwinyguan, northern Australia; Heath, 1984), all word order patterns are possible and common. In many cases, however, even if word order is flexible, there is a correlation between, for example, discourse patterns, length of constituents, and word order patterns. In addition to this formal variation in grammar, there is also diversity in what kind of world knowledge the use of these grammatical markers presupposes. This means that children cannot use the markers productively until they have acquired the relevant world knowledge. For instance, Martuthunia, an Australian language, has verb suffixes registering the kinship relations of the people involved in an event. Children learning this language have to learn that there is a distinction in grammatical marking when talking about somebody of the same generation (i.e., brother, sister, grandfather) versus about somebody in an alternating generation (father, mother, great grandmother) (Dench, 1987; Evans, 2003). Thus, in this language, children need to acquire the relevant world knowledge before they can become fully competent in even simple sentences. These are only a few examples from the huge range of features by which languages differ in their *conceptual* and *formal* complexities. The question then arises whether some of these features are more difficult to learn than others and whether the strategies children employ in learning them are the same across languages.

Theories in Language and Cross-Linguistic Developmental Research

The major controversy in language acquisition studies has been about what is innate to enable a child to learn a language. First, we briefly review some aspects of different theoretical approaches because they are relevant to cross-linguistic variability. Then, we address how these approaches interact with ideas about the nature of the child's language learning environment.

Nativist-Linguistic Theory

Nativist-linguistic theories hold that there are innate, universal principles that constitute a universal grammar (UG; e.g., Chomsky, 1965, 1981). These are principles that apply to every language, and these principles constitute the so-called core grammar. The core grammar is taken to be a system for operating on abstract entities in an essentially algebraic way. Children's task is to use UG in interaction with what they hear to work out fundamental aspects of how the grammar of their language works. Within nativist-linguistic approaches, one solution to the issue of how children use the hypothesized UG to work out the syntactic particularities of their input language is to suggest that they have to set a range of parameters as the result of hearing a small number of utterances in the target language (the Principles and Parameters [P&P] theory; Hyams, 1994). An example is the "head direction parameter," which determines how children identify the input language as being "left or right branching" (i.e., the order of words in noun phrases and prepositional phrases together with the order of verb and object). Once this is set, children should know how to order words and constituents across a range of structures. The success of the P&P approach in its own terms depends on the number of parameters being relatively small and on agreement among researchers as to how the specified settings can account for the range of relevant phenomena in language development (Fodor, 2001; Valian, 1991).

Another approach arising from nativist-linguistic theories is to hypothesize that, if UG is innate, some parts of the system are on a later maturational timetable, and this can account for some of the early error patterns shown by children. Two well-known accounts that use this approach are Borer and Wexler's (1987) attempt to explain the late use of full eventive passives by English-speaking children and Wexler's Agreement-Tense Omission Model (ATOM; Wexler, 1998). In the first, the authors suggest that children are late with eventive passives (e.g., "The horse was kicked by the dog") because "argument-linking chains" are a late biological maturation. This theory, however, cannot account for the fact that full passives emerge early in some languages (e.g., Demuth, 1990; Pye and Quixtan Poz, 1988). Here is an example of how the study of a wider range of languages can have a major impact on either falsifying a theory or providing supportive evidence for it.

The ATOM model is intended to account for patterns of incorrect finiteness marking found in young children's speech across a range of languages (e.g., saying "It go there" instead of "It goes there"). Wexler (1998) argues that, because they are in a prematurational stage, children are subject to "the unique checking constraint" and will only be able to check either for tense or for agreement and thus will sometimes fail to mark for finiteness in languages for which subjects are present that also require agreement with the verb. However, it seems that a simple learning model that operates from the ends of utterances in child-directed speech (CDS) can model these cross-linguistic differences equally well, making unnecessary the postulate that children know about tense and agreement innately (Freudenthal, Pine, Aguado-Orea, and Gobet, 2007).

Emergentist and Usage-Based Theories

The opposing position, which has become known as usage-based and constructivist (Tomasello, 2003) or emergentist (Elman et al., 1997), argues that language acquisition can be explained by other more general human cognitive abilities. According to this view, children learn the use of symbols with the help of innate abilities, which emerge in human ontogeny around 9 to 12 months of age (see section on "Sociocognitive Development"). Unlike the algorithmic, UG approach, these approaches assume that there is no clear break between rules and other more idiosyncratic constructions, and what the child needs to learn is a set of constructions that map form to meaning. Abstraction arises through processes of pattern finding and analogy. Because constructions vary significantly across languages, one of the goals of the usage-based account is work out the different strategies children use in learning these constructions. The implications of this approach are that children learn language by identifying patterns in what they hear and mapping those patterns to meaning. For instance, a child might have abstracted a schema, "Where's X gone?", but have no representation for the underlying syntax of *wh*-questions, of auxiliary syntax (*'s* = "has"), or of tense marking. The meaning abstracted may also be limited. In a usage-based approach, the form–meaning mappings become more complex (i.e., gain more parts) and more abstract (i.e., have less concrete form) over time. Emergentist and usage-based approaches are therefore concerned with the details of how much input children hear and what the relative type and token frequencies of different forms are in this input. These, in turn, lead to predictions about how different cues to form–meaning mappings may be more or less available to the language-learning child. Both of these issues are taken up in somewhat more detail later.

Cross-linguistic research is an extremely important testing ground for these different theoretical approaches. On the one hand, applying the theory to a new language requires almost always much more careful specification of the proposals being made. On the other hand, cross-linguistic research can actually falsify a well-specified proposal.

The Structure of Language Environment

Because languages vary so widely and children's utterances reflect many language-specific features from the very beginning, it is obvious that children learn their language or languages from their environment. Beyond this, there are very different views of how important the environment is. All acknowledge the importance of learning for morphology and the lexicon, but at one extreme, theorists suggest that only a small number of sentences in the input are enough to guide the development of language-specific syntax because, in the main, the syntax of any individual language is derived from an innate UG. An alternative perspective claims that children learn entirely from what they hear, using their sociocognitive knowledge to match form to meaning and subsequently to build up the more abstract representations of the grammar they are learning. To the nativist-linguists, if all children learn to talk on roughly the same timescale under very different environmental conditions, this is support for the limited role of the language environment in the development of syntax. For constructivists, it is important to show that the language environment affords learning in terms of salience, frequency, and the presentation of relatively accessible form–meaning mappings. In the limit, constructivists must accept that, if there are relevant differences in the language environment, children should learn differently either qualitatively or quantitatively (i.e., faster or slower). Thus, everything comes down to what is a "relevant difference."

The cultural backgrounds in which children are reared clearly vary widely. The children usually studied in research on first language acquisition seem to spend a lot of time alone with one person. In other cultures, such as many rural societies, children are surrounded and cared for by more people including siblings, extended families, other children, and adults (see Lieven, 1994, for an overview). Factors like climate may also be relevant; in a more moderate climate where people spend most of their day outside, interlocutors may vary more than in a cold climate where one does not leave the house much.

We do not have to go far to find that quantitative and qualitative differences in the ways that adults talk to children affect children's language development. There are numerous studies showing that the amount of CDS is correlated with rate of language learning (Barnes, Gutfreund, Satterly, and Wells, 1983; Hart and Risley, 1995). In addition, there are correlations between the rate of noun use in CDS and the relative proportions of nouns in children's own vocabularies (Pine, 1992) and between the proportion of utterances with complex syntax used to children by their parents and teachers and those children's own use of complex syntax (Huttenlocher, Vasilyeva, Cymerman, and Levine, 2002).

However, one could argue that the cultural differences documented in these studies are not so great and that we have to sample much wider variation to safely assess the role of the environment. Unfortunately, with very few exceptions, the further away that the research conducted is from the technological, urban environments in which most children have been studied, the more anecdotal and hard to assess the data become. There are good reasons for this. Researchers in these circumstances are often anthropologists or linguists working with more qualitative than quantitative methodologies; it is not at all easy to set up the kind of longitudinal recording studies that allow quantitative assessment of development to be made. It is harder still to conduct experiments with children and adults for whom the idea of playing these sorts of games, let alone being tested, is entirely alien. Therefore, we still know rather little about the structure and the amount of input children receive in most cultures and whether there are significant cross-cultural differences.

On the one hand, many studies have shown that speech addressed to children shows similar characteristics across a number of different cultures. One such modification is the use of higher pitch and the use of wider intonation contours in CDS (see Clark, 2003; Ferguson, 1964; Fernald et al., 1989). Across many cultures, CDS also consists of shorter, clearer, and more grammatical utterances than utterances in speech between adults. CDS also tends to be highly repetitive and very largely located in the "here and now." Furthermore, the speech addressed to young infants has more and longer pauses, and it is more grammatical with fewer false starts than adult to adult speech (Snow, 1995). A major further issue is the repetitions typically found in CDS (Brown, 1998a). It has been shown for English (Cameron-Faulkner, Lieven, and Tomasello, 2003) and also for German and Russian that there is a lot of repetition at the beginning of utterances in CDS (even though, as we would expect from their grammatical structure, they show less than English) (Stoll, Abbot-Smith, and Lieven, 2009). Most of these features probably derive from the attempt by competent speakers to communicate with less competent ones, and therefore, we cannot assume that they are deliberately adapted to teach language, but they may nevertheless serve as a useful basis for making generalizations on which to build up a grammar of the language.

However, there are reports of cultures that do not show some or all of these features of CDS. In a study of children's acquisition of Quiche Mayan, Ratner and Pye (1984) reported that small infants are not spoken to with the prosodically higher pitch that characterizes CDS found elsewhere. Thus, on the one hand, exaggerated contours in the speech that children hear may help them segment aspects of the speech stream, but on the other hand, it seems not to be the case that this type of speech characterizes speech to children the world over from birth.

There are also some reports of cultures in which adults do not seem to talk to infants much, if at all. Schieffelin (1985) reported that Kaluli of Papua New Guinea believe that children have to be weaned away from babbling and baby talk because it reflects their nearness and vulnerability to the animistic world. Thus, only when children start to talk themselves do adults start talking to them, and when they do so, they try to teach them what to say. Heath (1983) also reported that for one of three groups in her study located in the Piedmont Carolinas of the United States—the group she called "Trackton"—adults did not tend to talk to infants and young children. Here, there was a strong ideology that children had to learn for themselves and that was against addressing them with CDS. Children made their own way in conversation initially by "forcing their way in." Status hierarchies in Samoa mean, according to Ochs (1982), that the idea of adjusting speech to the child (in the form of CDS) is alien because it would mean someone of higher status adjusting to someone of lower status. Thus, adults tend to tell older children how to deal with infants, and it is these older children who largely do the talking to the infants.

One interesting point that arises from all these studies is that the way in which adults think children should be spoken to is, not surprisingly, closely linked to their ideologies of childrearing. It seems almost certain to be true that, compared to the one-on-one mother–child dyads who are the usual participants in child language research, most children in the world are spending more time in mixed groups of adults and children and are being looked after and therefore spoken to more by other children. However, from the point of language development, the important question is what the outcome is in terms of what children actually hear and how they build their language from it.

Because all children must make mappings between the forms they hear and meaning, with or without assistance from innate linguistic or cognitive universals, the question is how this is done if the amount or type of CDS varies so widely. Of course, one possibility is that these differences are not as extreme as the previously mentioned studies would suggest and that the researchers are picking up only one small part of the child's life. De León (1998) pointed out that children in the Tzotzil culture engage in dyadic conversational exchanges similar to those documented in previous studies of CDS (often with their grandmothers rather than their busy mothers) but that these conversations rarely go on outside the house in the presence of the researcher. Certainly, in many of these nontechnological cultures, spaces will exist in which adults and children interact that are unlikely to be very accessible to a researcher from another world. A second possibility is that, as a result of rather more mixed input, children may learn to talk on a somewhat slower timetable. This is certainly supported by the correlations reported earlier between the amount of talk addressed to children and their speech of vocabulary and syntax acquisition (Hart and Risley, 1995; Huttenlocher et al., 2002). It might, in fact, be better to describe middle-class children in technological societies as learning to talk ahead of a more natural cultural timetable.

Finally, we should note that just because the ways in which children are spoken to in other cultures vary does not mean that the children are in receipt of an almost unparsable input. There are a limited number of ways in which one can interact with a small child, and there is likely to be a high degree of repetitiveness associated with these event schemas. In addition, when people speak to young children, they are almost always monitoring the infants' attentional gaze. In both cases, then, utterances do not come "out of the blue." An example is Schieffelin's (1985) reports of the "*elema*" strategy that Kaluli mothers use to teach their children how to behave communicatively. The mother holds up the child facing toward the interlocutor, and then she tells the child verbatim what to say with the always same construction *elema* "Say X." However, she does this when she sees that the child has something to communicate about, for instance, when the baby is protesting about stolen food. Thus, the utterance is being taught in close conjunction with the child's focus of attention.

Imperatives are reported to be used extensively to children by both adult and child caregivers in cultures where there seems to be less dyadic and child-centred CDS (Nwokah, 1987; Ochs, 1982). In fact, the relation of imperatives to rate of language learning in technological cultures is quite complex. Early studies suggested a negative correlation between imperatives and rate of language development and a positive one for child-contingent speech (in the sense of elaborations of what the child had said; Cross, 1977). However, a number of these studies confounded the form of the utterance and its pragmatic use. When imperatives per se were separated from noncontingent speech (i.e., speech that did not follow the child's focus of attention), there were studies that suggested that child-contingent imperatives to young children were also correlated with early language advance (Barnes et al., 1983; Pine, 1994). Imperatives are often relatively syntactically simple, and they almost by definition map onto whatever the infant is currently doing (i.e., his or her attentional state).

This example indicates the complexity of the task of assessing what aspects of CDS are important in language learning and how frequent they need to be. We have to analyze the form of the utterance, its relation to the critical features of the language that children learn first, and also the developmental stage of the child. Imperatives may be helpful at early stages when the child is not producing much speech; they may be less helpful later as the child is able to put more into the utterance itself, affording adults the opportunity to say more that is contingent on what the child has actually said. Finally, we have to try to collect quantitative data that are sensitive to the cultural framework in which children are learning to talk.

Key Classical and Modern Studies in Cross-Linguistic Developmental Research

Developmental Prerequisites for Language Acquisition

To learn a language, a child needs to have some general abilities that are most likely innate. Obviously, infants must have adequate hearing or sight (for learning a sign language).* There is a clear path of development during the first 12 to 18 months of life; as children's experience with language develops, so do their segmentation, word recognition, and pattern recognition skills. Research of the last decades has made clear that children are sensitized very early on to the language(s) of their environment. Studies with newborns hearing different languages have shown that infants are able to distinguish their language from a language that is foreign to

---

* We treat language acquisition as if it was based on sound, although we refer to the acquisition of sign languages at various points. Sign language acquisition has to be included in a complete account of the cross-linguistic study of acquisition but raises many complex issues in terms of culture, learning, and notation that we cannot deal with adequately in the space of this chapter.

them 4 days after birth (Mehler et al., 1988). Infants' ability to discriminate the sounds of languages other than those they are hearing reduces over the first year of life (Werker and Tees, 1984), an interesting example of how the environment can shape the child's prelinguistic skills. Experiments with English, Japanese, and French infants ages 6 to 10 months have shown that they can discriminate words that they have heard before from those that they have not heard even when the words were embedded in speech (Jusczyk, 1997). Finally, using experiments with simple artificial languages, experiments have shown that, depending on the structure of the artificial grammar, infants between 7½ and 17 months of age are able to recognize patterns in strings of repeated syllables with the same ordering rules but with different "vocabulary" after a short exposure (Gómez and Gerken, 1999; Marcus, Vijayan, Bandi Rao, and Vishton, 1999). They probably do this by relying on the patterns of repeating and alternating "words" in the input strings. We should note that, although these skills are central to the child's ability to parse the input, they depend on the infant discriminating one stimulus from another. Children do not have to understand or use the stimuli in communication or connect them to any meaning in the environment. The linking of identifiable sequences in the input to meaning, which starts from approximately 9 months, is almost certainly related to the child's developing sociocognitive skills.

Early Production

Children start babbling at approximately 6 months and can start to produce their first word any time from 10 months on, although much depends on how a "word" is defined and word production usually starts later. There is a complex interaction both in babbling and in early word production between the constraints on the infant's articulatory apparatus and the characteristics of the ambient language, particularly in terms of consonant–vowel sequencing and the syllable length of words.

Vihman and Croft (2007) report that, although the ambient language influences the sounds that infants produce in babbling and their first words, there is considerable cross-linguistic similarity in these early productions as a result of the physical constraints on infant articulators.* They argue that after these initially rather similar first 5 to 10 words, which are "selected" to match what the child can produce and are therefore rather similar across different languages, children start to match the syllable pattern of their language and developing individual templates to which they assimilate their perception of the word. This pattern accounts for the difficulty in distinguishing children's early words from each other and for the fact that children themselves can hear the difference between two words without being able to produce it.

Sociocognitive Development

Infants make huge developmental strides in their cognitive and social development during the first 12 months of life. Cognitively, infants (probably from birth) have clear expectations about the ways in which objects will behave, and these develop in sophistication over the first year of life. From 3 months, they can form perceptual categories of objects, and by 7 to 11 months, they show evidence of categorization at the level of superordinate categories (Mandler, 2000). By 11 to 12 months, they show surprise if a familiar sequence of actions (e.g., preparing something to eat) does not go in the right order or ends with a "surprising" outcome (Baldwin, Baird, Saylor,

---

* Optimality theory, by contrast, deals with these issues by hypothesizing a set of universal cognitive-linguistic constraints in production that are ranked differently for different languages (Prince and Smolensky, 2004). The most important of these are faithfulness constraints (trying to match what is heard) and markedness constraints (which constrain the possible range of correct forms for a particular language). The question of whether there is any need to postulate these innate constraints has been the subject of much debate.

and Clark, 2001). This research has been almost exclusively carried out in English-speaking, urban environments, but although differences in the objects and situations that surround the child may result in differences in the types of categories or action schemas abstracted, there is little reason to think that these cognitive abilities would fundamentally differ between infants reared in different cultures.

Probably the most striking changes during the first year of life are the major developments in sociocognitive skills between 9 and 12 months: using interpersonal context to inform others and to work out their intentions. These are almost certainly universal and, at least in the combination and degree shown by infants, unique to human beings (Tomasello, Carpenter, Call, Behne, and Moll, 2005). Thus, as far as we know, pointing develops universally from approximately the age of 9 months and is used for the same range of functions worldwide: requesting, drawing attention, and informing. There is, however, a great deal more work to be done to see how this species-unique behavior is modulated by differences in childrearing environments across the world.

Thus, by the time children are 12 months old, they have developed the species-unique skills that underpin intentional communication and the ability to understand the communication of others. The sounds and patterns of the language that surround them have also become separable and identifiable. If we assume that this is true for all human infants growing up without developmental problems, the question that is important in cross-linguistic research is how children equipped with these skills break into the very different languages that they are hearing and whether they use the same strategies in learning and producing linguistic structures independent of the structure being learned. To study this requires a deep understanding of the typological differences between languages as well as of the developmental characteristics of the child at this stage. Slobin's path-breaking research, which started with his first cross-linguistic project (Slobin and Bever, 1982), fulfils these requirements.

Slobin's Cross-Linguistic Project

The continuation, and most elaborate development, of Slobin's project was the publication of a series of volumes documenting cross-linguistic language acquisition (Slobin, 1985a, 1985b, 1992, 1997a, 1997b). This included 23 languages from several language families and a chapter on American sign language. In the five volumes of this series, the acquisition of these languages was described by leading specialists within a uniform scheme to enable comparisons of acquisition strategies.

One of the main tenets of this approach was "patterns of acquisition VARY from language to language, while they are determined by common principles of a higher order" (Slobin, 1985a, p. 5). Two conclusions came out of this research. First, language acquisition can be explained by so-called "operating principles" (OPs). Second, the child comes endowed with a "basic child grammar." OPs constitute very general strategies every child uses in learning a language. The function of OPs is to organize and store the input. An example of a general OP is the OP about the interpretation of the function of elements: "OP (Review): Limited Functions. At first apply a solution to the smallest motivated category and do not extend it without evidence" (Slobin, 1985b, p. 1199). Other OPs are more specific, such as the "OP (Mapping): ANALYTIC FORM: If you discover that a complex notion can be expressed by a single, unitary form (synthetic expression) or by a combination of several separate forms (analytic expression), prefer the analytic expression" (Slobin, 1985b, p. 1229). This approach, which is based on innate processing strategies (either cognitive or specifically language-based), was a counter proposal to formal and content-based universals as proposed in generative approaches in the tradition of Chomsky. Thus, according to this approach, formal structure is acquired without the help of innate syntactic rules, but it is guided by processing strategies. The second conclusion was formulated in

"Basic Child Grammar," which claims that the child is endowed with a "prestructured space" that influences and sometimes even predetermines the acquisition of grammatical markers. This would lead children learning very different languages to look more similar at the outset of language learning because it was suggested that, initially, these prestructured concepts provide the basis for form–meaning mappings. One example of this is the idea that, as a result of the salience of objects in the child's environment, it may be easier to learn words for objects than for other categories.

Are Nouns Easier to Learn?

Research that seems to support the idea of cognitive underpinnings to language universals is Gentner's (1982) analysis of the composition of early vocabulary in English, German, Japanese, Kaluli, Mandarin, and Turkish. Gentner found a noun bias in early word use in all the surveyed languages, and she argued that this bias is a result of the more complex structure of verbs. Nouns in early child language are usually concrete and refer to "naturally individuated referents" (Gentner, 2006, p. 544). Verbs are more complex because they relate a participant to a certain action or event in contrast to nouns, which lack this relational component. Some subsequent research challenges these findings, with researchers reporting a verb bias for languages like Tzeltal and Korean (e.g., Brown, 1998b; Choi and Gopnik, 1995). However, to properly compare these various results is problematic because of the different methods applied (Clark, 2003). Some studies use maternal checklists, whereas others use spontaneous speech samples, and thus, the results from such different methods and speech contexts are difficult to compare. Furthermore, because early one-word utterances are difficult to interpret, it is far from clear whether parts of speech can straightforwardly be assigned to words (i.e., whether a "noun" used by a child also has the meaning of a noun; Clark, 2003). More controlled studies such as by Bornstein et al. (2004), however, support the finding of a strong noun bias in early language acquisition for Spanish, Dutch, French, Hebrew, Italian, Korean, and American English, using the same vocabulary checklists. By contrast, a study comparing Mandarin and English verb/noun ratios by Tardif, Gelman, and Xu (1999) using the exact same methods and data sets for both languages showed that even though across all measures Mandarin-speaking children used more verbs and fewer nouns than English-speaking children, the distributions in various contexts varied significantly. In a book-reading context, children of both languages used more nouns than verbs, but not in a free-play situation. Other factors like urban versus rural setting need to be controlled for as well (Bornstein and Cote, 2005). Thus, to resolve this issue, more studies on a variety of different languages using the same method, data sets, and contexts are needed.

Linguistic Influences on Conceptual Structure

Development in infancy and early childhood is obviously relevant to the complex issue of the relation between language and thought. Do children start with universals of cognition, which are reflected in their early language, only later refining the language to fit the semantic distinctions that it makes? Or do children observe the semantic distinctions of the language they are learning from the outset? One major area of research into this issue has been concerned with whether there are conceptual predispositions in the structuring and expression of spatial relations. In a cross-linguistic study on English, Italian, Serbo-Croatian, and Turkish, Johnston and Slobin (1979) found similar sequences of development in these languages, and they took this as evidence that conceptual development determines the order of emergence of grammatical forms, here spatial expressions. The assumption was that children's ability to conceptualize spatial relations develops from simple to more complex relations. However, how exactly these relations look and whether they are indeed universal has been debated. As shown by Bowerman (1985), semantic space is more flexible than was postulated for "Basic Child Grammar," and a more relativistic view seems to be warranted. The variation in structuring space and the influence of the individual language on the conception of space becomes especially obvious in Bowerman and Choi's work (Bowerman, 1996; Bowerman and Choi, 2001; Choi and Bowerman, 1991) on cross-linguistic differences in expressing and conceptualizing space in Korean and English. English uses mainly prepositions, whereas Korean uses verbs. The crucial distinction, however, is what kind of spatial relations are important in the two languages. The main feature for English is the distinction of putting a "figure" into contact with the surface of a ground object ("on") and putting a "figure" into some kind of enclosure ("in"). In Korean, by contrast, the features tight fit (*kkita*, "interlock, fit tightly") versus loose fit (*nehhta*, "put loosely in or around") are important, which are irrelevant for spatial expressions in English. Furthermore, English children do not have to distinguish between spontaneous and caused motion, whereas Korean children must. Results show that, when asked to refer to particular actions and events, children of both languages from the start do so along the distinctions made by the language they are learning. Thus, at least once children are starting to make form–meaning mappings between language and the world, there does not seem to be an initial developmental stage in which children show language-independent conceptualization.

"Thinking for Speaking"

Exactly this kind of influence of language-specific features on conceptualization became a focus of Slobin's later research (Slobin, 1996). In his "thinking for speaking" hypothesis, he proposed that online thinking is strongly influenced by the type of categories expressed in the language used. This was investigated in a large-scale cross-linguistic project on event structuring in narratives (Berman and Slobin, 1994). The languages studied in this project were English, German, Spanish, Hebrew, and Turkish, and the goal was to find out whether and how typological differences bear out in narratives. To test this, a picture book without words, *Frog, Where Are You?* (Mayer, 1969), was used as the stimulus. In a study of motion events, Slobin (1997b) classified the languages into a binary typology on the means of expressing the path of a movement. Languages were divided into verb-framed languages in which the verb expresses the path (e.g., *entrar* "enter") and satellite-framed languages in which the path is expressed by a satellite (e.g., *go in*; Talmy, 1985, 1996). Systematic differences in the packaging of events depending on language type were found. There is a clear tendency for a speaker of a satellite-framed language like English to include information about the path of a motion event in a single verb. In a verb-framed language like Spanish, information about the path is either completely omitted or the path description is simplified or divided up by several verbs. In a continuation of the project (Strömqvist and Verhoeven, 2004), which included languages from a wider range such as Warlpiri, Tzeltal, West-Greelandic, Basque, Thai, and several other languages, this binary typology needed revision, and equipollently framed languages needed to be included as a third category. Furthermore, the expression of path turns out to be only one factor among many, such as online processing of forms, cultural practices and perspectives, and communicative aims of the speaker (Slobin, 2004).

"Intratypological Approaches"

One of the key issues in cross-linguistic language acquisition studies has been what makes languages or a feature of a specific language difficult or easy to learn? In other words, what controls early learning versus later learning? These questions can best be addressed with what Slobin called the intratypological approach. The intratypological approach focuses on variation in languages that belong to one typological grouping and are genetically related (Slobin, 1997b). Fine-grained differences between similar languages can be studied. The advantage of this approach is that one can hold most factors constant while investigating one factor in which the languages vary systematically. An illustration of such intralinguistic research is the study by Strömqvist et al. (Strömqvist, Peters, and Ragnarsdóttir, 1995; Strömqvist, Ragnarsdottir, et al., 1995) on the acquisition of verb–particle constructions in Swedish, Danish, and Norwegian. All three languages have verb–particle constructions; however, they differ systematically in prosody and word order. The Swedish and Danish particles are stressed, but only in Swedish is the particle contiguous to the verb. Danish and Norwegian also differ minimally. The Danish particle is prosodically prominent, whereas the Norwegian particle is not. However, in both of the languages, the particle is separated from the verb. This is an ideal situation to test the role of prosodic prominence and the position of the particle with respect to the verb. Strömqvist, Ragnarsdottir, et al. (1995) predicted that acquisition is conditioned by two general principles. First, prosodically more prominent features are easier to attend to in the speech flow, and second, semantically close elements should be placed closely together syntactically. Their results showed that the acquisition patterns for these three languages differ. In Danish, the postposed particle is learned very early as a one-word utterance (i.e., as an individual word). In Swedish, the emergence of these particles is a later development, and they occur attached to the verb. In Norwegian, where there is neither prosodic prominence nor contingency to the verb, it seems that the verbs occur first in isolation and the particles are a later development.

Learning Argument Structure

In this context, a major theme has been how children learn to mark the arguments of verbs (e.g., agents and patients). Children's ability to express and understand who did what to whom represents an important milestone in their development of language, and the transitive construction almost always shows some of the most fundamental features of how a language works.*
Languages basically use three methods of marking major arguments either alone or in combination: word order (e.g., English), case marking on nouns (e.g., Turkish), and agreement marking on verbs (e.g., subject–verb agreement in Italian). English uses word order exclusively, although some pronouns are also case marked ("He ate him"). "The cat ate the mouse" means something very different than "The mouse ate the cat." German uses case marking on determiners (*der Zug* "the train" nominative subject, *den Zug*, accusative object) and allows a greater variety of word orders; French, like English, only has case marking on pronouns but changes the word order when the object of the verb is a pronoun rather than a noun (*Marie pousse Jean; Marie lui pousse*: "Mary pushes/is pushing John," "Mary pushes/is pushing him").

In a language like Turkish with highly regular case marking, children appear to start marking the arguments of verbs at least as early or earlier than do children in languages where word order is the predominant method (Slobin and Bever, 1982). This shows that there is nothing inherently more complicated about learning case marking than learning syntactic word order.

A major issue in trying to understand which cues might be easier to learn is that cues often go together in a language. To separate out the effect of each cue, researchers design experiments where children act out sentences, some of which are not fully grammatical. For example, in English, subjects of transitives tend to be animate and patients inanimate. If a child is presented with "Table eat doggie," will the child follow the word order (which would mean that they have a grasp of word order syntax), or will the child go with animacy and make the dog eat the table? A series of experiments in nine languages investigating, among other things, case, animacy, word order, and subject–verb agreement indicates that children, on the one hand, follow the clearest and most available cue and, on the other, do not always behave as adults would (summarized in

---

* All of the experimental research that we discuss here involves so-called nominative-accusative languages in which the subjects of transitives and intransitives receive the same marking. The types of experiments discussed have not been carried out with ergative languages in which the subject of an intransitive verb is marked in the same way as the object of a transitive verb.

Bates and MacWhinney, 1989; and Tomasello, 2003, p. 138). Out of the results of these experiments, Bates and MacWhinney developed their "competition model" to try to quantify the ways in which cues within a language interacted and competed (Bates and MacWhinney, 1987; Kempe and MacWhinney, 1998). One problem with these experiments, which introduces a major confound, is that almost all of them used verbs familiar to the children. There have been a few attempts to run the same sort of experiment but using novel verbs (e.g., Dittmar, Abbot-Smith, Lieven, and Tomasello, 2008; Naigles, Gleitman, and Gleitman, 1993; Wittek and Tomasello, 2005).

It seems clear that children are able to learn the ways in which cues such as word order, case marking, and agreement mark agent and patient roles relatively early (at least by the end of their third year), but the speed with which they do this depends on the relative frequency of the cues, how transparent they are distributionally and semantically, and how they are interrelated with other cues.

Practical Issues in Cross-Linguistic Developmental Research

We have raised a number of practical issues throughout; here we summarize and add additional points. Generalizations about language acquisition are still very limited by the scarcity of data available. Presently, our knowledge is dominated by the acquisition of some Indo-European languages. We clearly need many more detailed longitudinal studies of children's language development that move beyond the confines of children growing up in urban surroundings in industrialized cultures learning a rather small range of languages. Data alone, however, are not enough, and there is much to do on the level of methodology. To quantitatively compare data of completely different structures, we need structure-sensitive methods. For instance, if we want to compare the development of utterance length in an analytic and a synthetic language, we cannot use the same measurement. A popular way of comparing children by calculating their mean length of utterance at a particular age is of no use; one word or morpheme in one language can mean something similar to many words and morphemes in another language. Another no less important issue is the role of CDS. To judge the order of development and what has to be acquired, we need to know how adults talk to children, and this implies that it is critically important that the actual language that children hear be well documented. This can only be studied if we have recorded the actual conversations of children and their caregivers. A linguist's description of the grammatical principles of a language is no substitute for recorded data addressed to the child. We know that genre, frequency in the use of particular constructions, and the immediate context, to name only a few factors, are crucially important for the acquisition process. This information is usually entirely absent in grammars.

The enterprise of studying language in widely different cultures requires a truly multidisciplinary effort. Linguists are essential to working out the structure of the language, anthropologists are essential to understanding the culture and ideologies of childrearing, and psychologists are essential to design culture-sensitive but robust methods of gathering replicable data. Finally, we need to think carefully about the implications of the multilingual situations in which many children grow up and to develop methods of incorporating this fact into our theories of language development.

Conclusion

We have attempted to give some idea of the challenges that any child would face learning any of the world's languages and of the theoretical issues that are raised when attempting to account for how children undertake this task of language learning. Whether or not children come with pregiven and linguistically specific skills, the main burden of language learning clearly has to be in interaction with what they are hearing; this is where the specifics of phonology, morphology, syntax, semantics, and pragmatics come from, and it is these that vary so much from language to language and from culture to culture. One important conclusion to draw is that English is not a very good basis for understanding how children learn this wide range of languages because it has a number of characteristics that make it a poor exemplar. Two of the most important are very fixed syntactic word order and impoverished morphology. A second important conclusion is that we need to study not only a wider range of languages, but also a wider range of language learning environments. This includes not only children growing up in less one-on-one environments than those children normally studied, but also the many children in the world who grow up learning, or at least hearing, more than one language.

In terms of theories of language development, it is clear that studying children learning different languages is critical to developing an understanding of the relationship between cognition and language and of how this may change with development. It is also important to the main theoretical divide in the literature—that between a nativist-linguistic approach to language development and an emergentist–constructivist approach. Theories that postulate a universal grammar that provides children with the basis for breaking into language need to be able to support claims of early linguistic abstraction and of the biological maturation of later emerging structures by reference to a range of different languages. On the other hand, because constructivist theories depend to a considerable extent on the relative frequencies of different structures in what children are hearing, they too should be looking to a much wider variety of input situations as a test for their positions.

Clearly, the study of language development in typologically different languages and in a wide variety of cultural situations is fundamental to coming up with a psychologically realistic theory of how language is learned.

Acknowledgments

We thank Balthasar Bickel and Michael Tomasello for their comments on an earlier version.

References

Baldwin, D. A., Baird, J. A., Saylor, M. M., and Clark, A. M. (2001). Infants parse dynamic action. *Child Development, 7,* 708–717.

Barnes, S., Gutfreund, M., Satterly, D., and Wells, G. (1983). Characteristics of adult speech which predict children's language development. *Journal of Child Language, 10,* 65–84.

Bates, E., and MacWhinney, B. (1987). Competition, variation, and language learning. In B. MacWhinney (Ed.), *Mechanisms of language acquisition* (pp. 157–193). Hillsdale, NJ: Erlbaum.

Bates, E., and MacWhinney, B. (1989). Functionalism and the competition model. In B. MacWhinney and E. Bates (Eds.), *The crosslinguistic study of sentence processing.* New York: Cambridge University Press.

Berman, R., and Slobin, D. (1994). *Relating events in narrative: A crosslinguistic developmental study.* Hillsdale, NJ: Erlbaum.

Bickel, B., Banjade, G., Gaenszle, M., Lieven, E., Paudyal, N., Rai, I. P., et al. (2007). Free prefix ordering in Chintang. *Language, 83,* 1–31.

Bickel, B., and Nichols, J. (2005). Inflectional synthesis of the verb. In M. Haspelmath, M. S. Dryer, D. Gil, and B. Comrie (Eds.), *World atlas of language structures* (pp. 94–97). Oxford, United Kingdom: Oxford University Press.

Borer, H., and Wexler, K. (1987). The maturation of syntax. In T. Roeper and E. Williams (Eds.), *Parameter setting* (pp. 123–173). Dordrecht, The Netherlands: D. Reidel.

Bornstein, M., and Cote, L. (2005). Expressive vocabulary from language learners from two ecological settings in three language communities. *Infancy, 7,* 299–316.

Bornstein, M., Cote, L., Maital, S., Painter, K., Park, S.-Y., and Pascual, L. (2004). Cross-linguistic analysis of vocabulary in young children: Spanish, Dutch, French, Hebrew, Italian, Korean, and American English. *Child Development, 75,* 1115–1139.

Bowerman, M. (1985). What shapes children's grammars? In D. I. Slobin (Ed.), *The crosslinguistic study of language acquisition: Theoretical issues* (Vol. 2, pp. 1257–1319). Hillsdale, NJ: Erlbaum.

Bowerman, M. (1996). Learning how to structure space for language: A cross-linguistic perspective. In P. Bloom, M. Peterson, L. Nadel, and M. Garret (Eds.), *Language and space* (pp. 385–436). Cambridge, MA: MIT Press.

Bowerman, M., and Choi, S. (2001). Shaping meanings for language: Universal and language-specific in the acquisition of spatial semantic categories. In M. Bowerman and S. C. Levinson (Eds.), *Language acquisition and conceptual development* (pp. 475–511). Cambridge, United Kingdom: Cambridge University Press.

Brown, P. (1998a). Children's first verbs in Tzeltal: Evidence for an early verb category. *Linguistics, 36*, 713–753.

Brown, P. (1998b). Conversational structure and language acquisition: The role of repetition in Tzeltal adult and child speech. *Journal of Linguistic Anthropology, 8*, 197–221.

Cameron-Faulkner, T., Lieven, E., and Tomasello, M. (2003). A construction based analysis of child directed speech. *Cognitive Science, 27*, 843–873.

Choi, S., and Bowerman, M. (1991). Learning to express motion events in English and Korean—The influence of language-specific lexicalization patterns. *Cognition, 41*, 83–121.

Choi, S., and Gopnik, A. (1995). Early acquisition of verbs in Korean: A cross-linguistic study. *Journal of Child Language, 22*, 497–529.

Chomsky, N. (1965). *Aspects of the theory of syntax*. Cambridge, MA: MIT Press.

Chomsky, N. (1981). *Lectures on government and binding*. Dordrecht, The Netherlands: Foris.

Clark, E. (2003). *First language acquisition*. Cambridge, United Kingdom: Cambridge University Press.

Cross, T. G. (1977). Mother's speech adjustments: The contribution of selected child listener variables. In C. E. Snow and C. A. Ferguson (Eds.), *Talking to children: Language input and acquisition* (pp. 151–188). Cambridge, United Kingdom: Cambridge University Press.

Cysouw, M. (2002). Interpreting typological clusters. *Linguistic Typology, 6*, 49–93.

Dahl, Ö. (1990). Standard average European as an exotic language. In J. Bechert, G. Bernini, and C. Buridant (Eds.), *Towards a typology of European languages* (pp. 3–8). Berlin: Mouton de Gruyter.

de León, L. (1998). The emergent participant: Interactive patterns in the socialization of Tzotzil (Mayan) infants. *Journal of Linguistic Anthropology, 8*, 131–161.

Demuth, K. (1990). Subject, topic and Sesotho passive. *Journal of Child Language, 17*, 67–84.

Dench, A. (1987). Kinship and collective activity in the Ngayarda languages of Australia. *Language in Society, 16*, 321–339.

Dittmar, M., Abbot-Smith, K., Lieven, E., and Tomasello M. (2008) German children's comprehension of word order and case marking in causative sentences. *Child Development, 79*, 1152–1167.

Elman, J., Bates, E., Johnson, M., Karmiloff-Smith, A., Parisi, D., and Plunkett, K. (1997). *Rethinking innateness: A connectionist perspective on development*. Cambridge, MA: The MIT Press.

Evans, N. (2003). Context, culture, and structuration in the languages of Australia. *Annual Review of Anthropology, 32*, 13–40.

Ferguson, C. (1964). Baby talk in six languages. *American Anthropologist, 66*, 103–114.

Fernald, A., Taeschner, T., Dunn, J., Papousek, M., Boysson-Bardies, B. D., and Fuko, I. (1989). A cross-language study of prosodic modifications in mothers' and fathers' speech to preverbal infants. *Journal of Child Language, 16*, 477–501.

Fodor, J. (2001). Setting syntactic parameters. In M. Baltin and C. Collins (Eds.), *The handbook of contemporary syntactic theory* (pp. 730–767). Oxford, United Kingdom: Blackwell.

Freudenthal, D. J., Pine, J. M., Aguado-Orea, J., and Gobet, F. (2007). Modelling the developmental patterning of finiteness marking in English, Dutch, German, and Spanish using mosaic. *Cognitive Science, 31*, 311–341.

Gentner, D. (1982). Why nouns are learned before verbs: Linguistic relativity versus natural partitioning. In S. Kuczaj (Ed.), *Language development* (pp. 301–334). Hillsdale, NJ: Erlbaum.

Gentner, D. (2006). Why verbs are hard to learn. In K. Hirsh-Pasek and R. M. Golinkoff (Eds.), *Action meets words: How children learn verbs* (pp. 544–564). Oxford, United Kingdom: Oxford University Press.

Gómez, R. L., and Gerken, L. A. (1999). Artificial grammar learning by 1-year-olds leads to specific and abstract knowledge. *Cognition, 70*, 109–135.

Grégoire, A. (1937). *L'apprentissage du langage: Volume 1. Les deux premieres annees*. Paris: Droz.

Gvozdev, A. N. (1949). *Formirovaniya u rebenka grammaticheskogo stroya russkogo yazyka*. Moscow: Akad. Pedag. Nauk RSFSR.

Hart, B., and Risley, T. R. (1995). *Meaningful differences in the everyday experience of young American children*. Baltimore: Paul Brookes Publishing.

Haspelmath, M. (2001). The European linguistic area: Standard average European. In M. Haspelmath, E. König, W. Oesterreicher, and W. Raible (Eds.), *Language typology and language universals: An international handbook* (pp. 1492–1510). Berlin: Mouton de Gruyter.

Heath, J. (1984). *A functional grammar of Nunggubuyu*. Atlantic Highlands, NJ: Humanities Press.

Heath, S. B. (1983). *Ways with words*. New York: Cambridge University Press.
Huttenlocher, J., Vasilyeva, M., Cymerman, E., and Levine, S. (2002). Language input and child syntax. *Cognitive Psychology, 45*, 337–374.
Hyams, N. (1994). Non-discreteness and variation in child language: Implications for principle and parameter models of language development. In Y. Levy (Ed.), *Other children, other languages* (pp. 11–40). Hillsdale, NJ: Lawrence Earlbaum.
Johnston, J., and Slobin, D. I. (1979). The development of locative expressions in English, Italian, Serbo-Croatian and Turkish. *Journal of Child Language, 6*, 529–545.
Jusczyk, P. W. (1997). *The discovery of spoken language*. Cambridge, MA: MIT Press.
Kempe, V., and MacWhinney, B. (1998). The acquisition of case marking by adult learners of Russian and German. *Studies in Second Language Acquisition, 20*, 543–587.
Leopold, W. F. (1948). The study of child language and infant bilingualism. *Word, 4*, 1–17.
Lieven, E. (1994). Crosslinguistic and crosscultural aspects of language addressed to children. In C. Gallaway and B. J. Richards (Eds.), *Input and interaction in language acquisition*. Cambridge, United Kingdom: Cambridge University Press.
Lindner, G. (1885). Zum studium der kindersprache. *Kosmos, 9*, 161–173, 241–259.
Lindner, G. (1898). *Aus dem naturgarten der kindersprache: Ein beitrag zur kindlichen sprach-und geistesentwicklung in den ersten vier lebensjahren*. Leipzig, Germany: Grieben.
Maddieson, I. (2005a). Consonant inventories. In M. Haspelmath, M. S. Dryer, D. Gil, and B. Comrie (Eds.), *The world atlas of language structures* (pp. 10–14). Oxford, United Kingdom: Oxford University Press.
Maddieson, I. (2005b). Vowel quality inventories. In M. Haspelmath, M. S. Dryer, D. Gil, and B. Comrie (Eds.), *The world atlas of language structures* (pp. 14–18). Oxford, United Kingdom: Oxford University Press.
Mandler, J. M. (2000). Perceptual and conceptual processes in infancy. *Journal of Cognition and Development, 1*, 3–36.
Marcus, G. F., Vijayan, S., Bandi Rao, S., and Vishton, P. M. (1999). Rule learning by seven-month-old infants. *Science, 283*, 77–80.
Mayer, M. (1969). *Frog, where are you?* New York: Dial Books.
Mehler, J., Jusczyk, P., Lambertz, G., Halsted, N., Bertoncini, J., and Amiel-Tison, C. (1988). A precursor of language acquisition in young infants. *Cognition, 29*, 143–178.
Naigles, L., Gleitman, L., and Gleitman, H. (1993). Children acquire word meaning components from syntactic evidence. In E. Dromi (Ed.), *Language and cognition: A developmental perspective* (pp. 104–140). Norwood, NJ: Ablex.
Nwokah, E. (1987). Maidese versus motherese: Is the language input of child and adult caregivers similar? *Language and Speech, 30*, 213–237.
Ochs, E. (1982). Talking to children in Western Samoa. *Language in Society, 11*, 77–104.
Pine, J. M. (1992). Maternal style at the early one-word stage: Re-evaluating the stereotyping of the directive mother. *First Language, 12*, 169.
Pine, J. (1994). The language of primary caregivers. In C. Gallaway and B. J. Richards (Eds.), *Input and interaction in language acquisition* (pp. 13–37). Cambridge, United Kingdom: Cambridge University Press.
Preyer, W. (1882). *Die seele des kindes: Beobachtungen über die geistige entwicklung des menschen in den ersten lebensjahren*. Leipzig, Germany: Schaefer.
Prince, A., and Smolensky, P. (2004) *Optimality theory: Constraint interaction in generative grammar*. Oxford: Blackwell.
Pye, C., and Quixtan Poz, P. (1988). Precocious passives and antipassives. *Papers and Reports on Child Language Development, 27*, 71–80.
Ratner, N. B., and Pye, C. (1984). Higher pitch in bt is not universal: Acoustic evidence from Quiche Mayan. *Journal of Child Language, 11*, 515–522.
Schieffelin, B. B. (1985). The acquisition of Kaluli. In D. I. Slobin (Ed.), *The crosslinguistic study of language acquisition. Volume 1: The data* (pp. 525–593). Hillsdale, NJ: Erlbaum.
Slobin, D. I. (Ed.). (1985a). *The crosslinguistic study of language acquisition. Volume 1: The data*. Hillsdale, NJ: Lawrence Erlbaum.
Slobin, D. I. (Ed.). (1985b). *The crosslinguistic study of language acquisition. Volume 2: Theoretical issues*. Hillsdale, NJ: Lawrence Erlbaum Associates.
Slobin, D. I. (Ed.). (1992). *The crosslinguistic study of language acquisition*. Hillsdale, NJ: Lawrence Erlbaum Associates.
Slobin, D. I. (1996). From "Thought and language" to "thinking for speaking." In J. J. Gumperz and S. C. Levinson (Eds.), *Rethinking linguistic relativity* (pp. 70–96). Cambridge, United Kingdom: Cambridge University Press.

Slobin, D. I. (Ed.). (1997a). *The crosslinguistic study of language acquisition.* Mahwah, NJ: Lawrence Erlbaum Associates.
Slobin, D. I. (Ed.). (1997b). *The crosslinguistic study of language acquisition. Volume 5: Expanding the contexts.* Mahwah, NJ: Lawrence Erlbaum Associates.
Slobin, D. I. (2004). Many ways to search for a frog: Linguistic typology and the expression of motion events. In S. Strömqvist and L. Verhoeven (Eds.), *Relating events in narrative: Typological and contextual perspectives* (Vol. 2, pp. 219–259). Mahwah, NJ: Lawrence Erlbaum Associates.
Slobin, D. I., and Bever, T. G. (1982). Children use canonical sentence schemes: A crosslinguistic study of word order and inflections. *Cognition, 12,* 229–265.
Snow, C. E. (1995). Issues in the study of input: Finetuning, universality, individual and developmental differences, and necessary causes. In P. Fletcher and B. MacWhinney (Eds.), *The handbook of child language* (pp. 180–193). Cambridge, MA: Blackwell.
Stern, W., and Stern, C. (1928/1965). *Die kindersprache: Eine psychologische und sprachtheoretische untersuchung [Child language: A psychological and linguistic study].* Darmstadt, Germany: Wissenschaftliche Buchgesellschaft.
Stoll, S., Abbot-Smith, K., and Lieven, E. (2009). Lexically restricted utterances in Russian, German and English child directed speech. *Cognitive Science, 33,* 75–103.
Strömqvist, S., Peters, A., and Ragnarsdóttir, H. (1995). *Particles and prepositions in Scandinavian child language development: Effects of prosodic spotlight?* Paper presented at the Proceedings of the 13th International Congress of Phonetic Sciences, Stockholm, Sweden.
Strömqvist, S., Ragnarsdottir, H., Engstrand, O., Jonsdottir, H., Lanza, E., Leiwo, M., et al. (1995). The inter-Nordic study of language acquisition. *Nordic Journal of Linguistics, 18,* 3–29.
Strömqvist, S., and Verhoeven, L. (Eds.). (2004). *Relating events in narrative: Typological and contextual perspectives* (Vol. 2). Mahwah, NJ: Lawrence Erlbaum Associates.
Talmy, L. (1985). Lexicalization patterns: Semantic structure in lexical forms. In T. Shopen (Ed.), *Language typology and syntactic description. Volume 3* (pp. 57–149). Cambridge, United Kingdom: Cambridge University Press.
Talmy, L. (1996). The windowing of attention in language. In M. Shibatani and S. Thompson (Eds.), *Grammatical constructions* (pp. 235–287). Oxford, United Kingdom: Oxford University Press.
Tardif, T., Gelman, S. A., and Xu, F. (1999). Putting the "noun bias" in context: A comparison of English and Mandarin. *Child Development, 70,* 620–635.
Tomasello, M. (2003). *Constructing a language: A usage-based theory of language acquisition.* Harvard, MA: Harvard University Press.
Tomasello, M., Carpenter, M., Call, J., Behne, T., and Moll, H. (2005). Understanding and sharing intentions: The origins of cultural cognition. *Behavioral and Brain Sciences, 28,* 675–735.
Valian, V. (1991). Syntactic subjects in the early speech of American and Italian children. *Cognition, 40,* 21–81.
Vihman, M., and Croft, W. (2007). Phonological development: Toward a 'radical' templatic phonology. *Linguistics, 45,* 683–725.
Werker, J. F., and Tees, R. C. (1984). Cross-language speech perception: Evidence for perceptual reorganization during the first year of life. *Infant Behaviour and Development, 7,* 49–63.
Wexler, K. (1998). Very early parameter setting and the unique checking constraint: A new explanation of the optional infinitive stage. *Lingua, 106,* 23–79.
Wittek, A., and Tomasello, M. (2005). German-speaking children's productivity with syntactic constructions and case morphology: Local cues help locally. *First Language, 25,* 103–125.
Zarebina, M. (1965). *Ksztaltowanie sie̜ systemu jezykowego dziecka.* Cracow, Poland: Polish Academy of Science.

8
Literacy

DANIEL A. WAGNER

Introduction

Literacy has been equated with freedom, economic development, and even civilization. Literacy comes with many different definitions, historical trends, and serious implications for individuals and societies all over the world. The study of literacy combines all social science disciplines, including psychology, linguistics, history, anthropology, sociology, and demography, but the field itself broadens beyond research to both policy and practice, from childhood through adulthood. Literacy, at its core, refers to the composite set of abilities needed to comprehend and produce written forms of language.

Within a cross-cultural developmental science perspective, literacy invokes a band of research that includes the intersection of both cognitive and social inputs to literacy development across the life span, along with contextual, cultural, and linguistic variations that shape literacy acquisition around the world. It would be convenient to be able to say that there is a consensus that ties together the various ways that social scientists view literacy, but such is not the case. Every subfield of literacy research has its own internal debates, and the disciplinary variants on literacy work assure that such debates, even over the meaning of literacy itself, will continue into the future. It needs to be kept in mind too that in industrialized countries, literacy acquisition begins and is completed largely in childhood and early adolescence, but that in poor and developing countries, literacy acquisition may take place in later adolescence and adulthood. The present analysis takes into account a breadth of research from early childhood through adolescence and into adulthood, while trying to give a sense of cross-cultural variation. This chapter begins with broad historical brushstrokes and then moves into several key domains of literacy work today, eventually focusing on policy and practice considerations for the future. As we shall see in later sections, the varieties of literacy used today, of which school-based literacy tends to be the most prominent, mirror the increased social complexity in rapidly changing societies.

Historical Perspectives on Literacy

The history of literacy has been the subject of a considerable number of scholarly studies in recent years (see Wagner, Venezky, and Street, 1999). Historical research indicates that literacy was often transmitted and practiced outside of what we now call "formal schooling." For example, as early as the sixteenth century, reading was widespread in Sweden on account of family and church efforts to teach Bible reading at home (Johansson, 1987). In nineteenth century Liberia, the Vai created an indigenous script and have used it ever since for economic and personal written communication (Scribner and Cole, 1981). Likewise, the Native American Cree of northern

Canada maintain the use of their syllabic script as a source of cultural identity (Bennett and Berry, 1987). And, of course, literacy was used in the Near East, India, and China more than 2,000 years ago largely as part of religious texts (Goody and Watt, 1963).

These illustrations outside of formal schooling represent only a few of the many cases of literacy development across time and geography. More importantly, such examples point to a new perspective in literacy research and current literacy efforts. Literacy is a *cultural* phenomenon, and it is practiced in a variety of settings and contexts. Literacy, for most children in today's world, is primarily taught in the classroom, but achievement levels are often determined as much by the out-of-school determinants (such as literacy of parents, availability of home reading) as by school factors, such as teacher training or textbook quality. Literacy skills as taught in schools all over the globe tell only part of the literacy story because literacy is practiced in far more varied ways outside of school contexts. It is essential to keep this fact in mind because literacy development depends on a sensitive understanding of how literacy and culture relate to one another (Wagner, 1992).

The varieties of literacy in schooling in today's world have expanded greatly since the advent of modern public education. More languages are written each year, with scripts, dictionaries, and newspapers to support them.* More individuals have increasingly varied literacy skills, as requirements for using and producing written language have changed. For example, there has been a dramatic increase in the use of new information technologies, which has produced an array of requirements including typing, cutting and pasting, image-word multimedia, and texting and "acronyming" ("Be right back" as BRB) on cell phones (Wagner and Kozma, 2005). Simply put, the world can no longer be characterized as a place where the literate elites dominate the masses of unschooled illiterates, as was once the case. There are relatively few "naïve" illiterates (who know absolutely nothing about scripts or print), but there are many individuals with quite limited or restricted literacy skills, such that their own governments might list them as illiterate or functionally illiterate for census purposes. The varieties of literacy, of which school-based literacy tends to be the best understood, mirror the increased social complexity within rapidly changing societies (Resnick and Resnick, 1990).

Beyond academic research, major international agencies (like the World Bank and the United Nations Educational, Scientific and Cultural Organization [UNESCO]) have also been concerned about literacy from an economic perspective. To provide worldwide statistical comparisons, such agencies have relied almost entirely on data provided by their member countries. According to the most recent UNESCO statistics (Table 8.1), world illiteracy rates have dropped from 25% to less than 20% over the last two decades, apparently primarily because of increases in primary school enrollments. Yet these data also indicate that the actual number of persons labeled as "illiterate" (approximately one billion persons today) has remained relatively constant because of population growth. It was once assumed that increased efforts to achieve universal primary schooling would lead to near-zero adult illiteracy around the world. These optimistic views are no longer widely held for a variety of reasons, including continued increases in population growth in developing countries, declining quality of basic education where rapid expansion has taken place, upward changes in the skill standards for literacy, both in developing and industrialized countries, and improved measurement of literacy through surveys that show that previous estimates of literacy (based on school grade levels achieved) often overestimated actual basic learning competencies (Wagner, 2000).

---

* This evolution comes despite "language death," where some languages in very small ethno-linguistic populations cease to be able to keep a critical mass of native speakers given the advent of schooling and literacy in more dominant languages (Crystal, 2000).

Table 8.1. Global and regional trends in Adult Literacy Rates, 1950 to 2000–2004

	Adult literacy rates (%)						Increase in literacy rates (%)		
	1950	1960	1970	1980	1990	2000–2004	1970 to 1980	1980 to 1990	1990 to 2000–2004
World	55.7	60.7	63.4	69.7	75.4	81.9	9.9	8.2	8.5
Developing countries	–	–	47.7	58.0	67.0	76.4	21.6	15.6	14.0
Developed and transition countries	–	–	94.5	96.4	98.6	99.0	2.0	1.8	0.5
Selected regions									
Sub-Saharan Africa	–	–	27.8	37.8	49.9	59.7	36.0	32.1	19.6
Arab States	–	18.9	28.8	39.2	50.0	62.7	36.1	27.7	25.3
East Asia and the Pacific	–	–	57.5	70.3	81.8	91.4	22.3	16.4	11.7
South and West Asia	-	–	31.6	39.3	47.5	58.6	24.4	20.8	23.5
Latin America and the Caribbean	-	–	73.7	80.0	85.0	89.7	8.5	6.3	5.5

Sources: United Nations Educational, Scientific and Cultural Organization, *Global monitoring report on literacy*, United Nations Educational, Scientific and Cultural Organization, Paris, 2006.

Literacy Development: Four Key Themes

Literacy development can be seen from a number of perspectives. Following is a review that focuses on four intersecting themes. First, we consider the various ways that literacy can be operationally defined. Second, the acquisition of literacy in formal and informal settings is considered, across human development in ontogenetic time. Third, we review some of the major sociocultural parameters that significantly support or constrain literacy development. Finally, research on the consequences of becoming literate is reviewed. Taken together, these four themes begin to provide a coherent picture of literacy development.

Defining Literacy: A Moving Target

> A person is functionally literate when he has acquired the knowledge and skills in reading and writing which enable him to engage effectively in all those activities in which literacy is normally assumed in his culture or group. (Gray, 1956, p. 19)

> …[L]iteracy is a characteristic acquired by individuals in varying degrees from just above none to an indeterminate upper level. Some individuals are more literate or less literate than others, but it is really not possible to speak of literate and illiterate persons as two distinct categories. (UNESCO, 1957, p. 18)

> It appears that a functional competence [in literacy] has been defined so that it is merely sufficient to bring its possessor within the reach of bureaucratic modes of communication and authority. (Levine, 1982, p. 261)

> Literacy [is] not simply…a set of isolated skills associated with reading and writing, but more importantly…the application of those skills for specific purposes in specific contexts.… There is no single measure or specific point on a single scale that separates the "literate" from the "illiterate." …[B]ecoming fully literate in a technologically advanced society is a lifelong pursuit, as is sustaining good health. …[Like] the physical health of every individual, there is no single action or step, that if taken, will ensure that every individual will become fully literate. (Kirsch and Jungeblut, 1986, p. 67)

As noted earlier, most specialists today would agree that the term "literacy" connotes reading and writing (although some would add basic math and even computer skills).* Where major debates continue, it is often around such issues as what specific abilities count most as literacy and what "levels" can and should be defined for measurement, or as "standards," in a given society. Thus, UNESCO, an organization that has devoted much energy and resources to promoting literacy, opted for the rather general notion of "functional literacy," as defined earlier by Gray (1956). If the phrase functional literacy has appeal because of its implied adaptability to a given cultural context, it is also inadequately defined for measurement purposes. For example, it is unclear in an industrialized nation like Great Britain what level of literacy should be required of all citizens; does a coal miner have functionally different needs than a barrister? Similarly, in a developing country, does an illiterate woman need to learn to read and write to take her prescribed medicine correctly, or is it more functional (and cost effective) to have her school-going son read the instructions to her? The general use of the term functionality, based on norms of a given society, fails precisely because adequate norms are so difficult to establish.

What might be an adequate definition of literacy? Is it, as implied earlier by Levine (1982), a competency that permits the individual to be controlled (and propagandized) by government media and bureaucracies? Based on the earlier 1957 UNESCO statement, the work of Kirsch and colleagues in literacy measurement (Kirsch and Jungeblut, 1986; Kirsch, Jungeblut, Jenkins, and Kolstad, 1993), and efforts by UNESCO (2006) in its *Global Monitoring Report on Literacy*, literacy competency may be defined as a continuum of abilities that range from zero to some undefined upper limit, whose desired level may vary across societies. Because dozens of orthographies for hundreds of languages with innumerable cultural variations exist, it would seem ill-advised to select a universal operational definition of competence required, either at minimum or maximum, to "succeed" in a given society. In some countries today, the use of newspaper reading skills as a functional baseline may seriously underestimate literacy if the emphasis is on comprehension of text (especially if the text is in a national language not well understood by the individual). Such tests may overestimate literacy competency if the individual, as is often the case in national censuses, is asked simply either whether she or he can read and write in a quick self-assessment procedure or (less often) to read aloud a short text, with little or no attempt to measure comprehension.

At least part of the controversy in defining literacy lies in how literacy has been studied in the first place. Anthropologists provide in-depth ethnographic accounts of single communities, while trying to understand how literacy is woven into the fabric of community cultural life (e.g., Street, 1999). In this work, the focus is on the social meanings of literacy, to the individual and to the society, and relatively little attempt is made at quantifying levels of particular literacy abilities. This approach has led to an epistemological shift toward thinking of literacy as a plural, as *literacies*. Anthropologists typically use qualitative description, whereas psychologists and educators tend to use psychometrics and inferential statistics to substantiate claims beyond a

---

* This author was once informed that in Zimbabwe, a citizen was considered "literate" if he or she could recite a few lines of President Robert Mugabe's most recent annual speech to the nation.

numerical level of uncertainty; this approach is often favored by those who need to test for skill levels (e.g., UNESCO, 2006). As might be expected, even within the quantitative subfield of literacy assessment, there are various views as to which methodology is suitable for which purpose (see, for example, Wagner, 2003, on "quick" assessments for use in program development in developing countries).

Literacy Acquisition

> Six stages (of reading) are hypothesized…, from a kind of pseudo-reading to reading that is highly creative…. Individuals vary in their progression, yet most who are educated in typical schools tend to progress largely through the stages within (certain) age limits…. Among adult illiterates, the typical time periods for each of the stages is uncertain. Hypothetically they, too, tend to follow largely the same course of development, although like others with special needs, they have more success with some stages (of reading) than with others. (Chall, 1983, p. 9)

> Children growing up in literate societies, surrounded by the printed word, begin to read and write long before they start school. They become aware of many of the uses of written language, they develop a sense of the written forms, and they begin to make sense of print and to experiment with communication through writing. Until recently, this growth into literacy has not been expected or appreciated, even by professional educationists. (Goodman, 1985, p. 57)

> …[T]he mistrust which blacks [in the United States] have toward the school and the conflict between them and these schools reduce the degree to which black parents and their children are able to accept the goals, standards, and instructional approaches of the schools as legitimate, and hence, their internalization or convictions of the need to cooperate with the school and follow their rules of behavior for achievement [of literacy] as conceived by and required by the schools. (Ogbu, 1980, p. 26)

> …[L]iteracy development is multiply determined; successful reading and writing in the later elementary and secondary grades is not possible without high levels of language proficiency, access to large stores of knowledge, and control over the local cultural norms of communication. (Snow and Kang, 2006)

The study of literacy acquisition remains heavily biased in favor of research undertaken in the industrialized world. Much of this research might better be termed the acquisition reading and writing skills, with an emphasis on the relation between cognitive skills, such as perception and memory, and reading skills, such as decoding and comprehension (Kamil, Mosenthal, Pearson, and Barr, 2000). Most of this work has been carried out with school-aged children, rather than with adolescents or adults. Even today, there is a relative dearth of research on literacy acquisition undertaken in non-Western parts of the world and in the huge variety of the world's languages and scripts, and much that has been done has focused more on adult acquisition of literacy than on children learning to read (perhaps a result of the significant emphasis by international organizations to promote adult literacy in the developing world).

Nonetheless, work has increased on children's literacy acquisition in diverse languages, some in minority groups in countries like the United States, where children from these groups often have poor school achievement, and among researchers who are interested in cross-cultural variation in language and literacy development. The subfield of comparative reading acquisition was begun by Downing (1973), who surveyed the acquisition of reading skills across a wide variety of languages and orthographies. Mastery of the spoken language is a typical prerequisite for fluent reading comprehension in a language, although many exceptions exist. For example, some Islamic scholars can read and interpret the Qur'an, even though they cannot speak classical Arabic, the language in which the Qur'an is written (Wagner, 1993); and, of course, many individuals can read and write languages that they may not speak fluently. Chall (1983) identified universal stages through which individuals seems to progress in achieving fluency and becoming a comprehending reader, ranging from word decoding to understanding the intent of the person who wrote the passage. If some would take issue with Chall's precise stages, most specialists agree that there is a variety of cognitive and linguistic skills that need to be acquired as a basis for literacy acquisition in a given written language and that a good proportion of these skills must be mastered before fluent reading can be accomplished (Snow and Kang, 2006).

The issue of reading skills acquisition has been the subject of a "great debate" (Chall, 1967) in the United States (in particular), with specific abilities (such as the "phonics" approach to decoding of text) thought by some to be at the center of cognitive growth in reading. Those associated with a more linguistic-cultural context approach have claimed, by contrast, that literacy is more like language in the sense that specific abilities do not need to be learned; rather, an individual must be able to interact with a "literate environment" (a term that is itself often ill-defined; Goodman, 1985). This latter approach stems in part from the popular perception of a high correlation between literate parents and children in many societies but, as such, does not imply direct causation. It is likely that literate parents provide a variety of additional opportunities for their children to learn reading abilities, including book reading practice at home, but they also afford their children better schools, more textbooks, and the attitudes and values that help children learn in school. Over the past decade, research reviews have sought to evaluate the empirical evidence in this debate and came down squarely in favor of a more phonics-based, skill-based approach to literacy acquisition as an optimal pathway for children's reading in alphabetic scripts (National Reading Panel, 2000; Snow, Burns, and Griffin, 1998). Additional support for this perspective has now come from a variety of other languages, such as Spanish (Dickenson, McCabe, Clark-Chiarelli, and Wolf, 2004), Turkish (Oney and Durgunoglu, 1997), and Arabic (Abu-Rabia and Siegel, 2002); for a general theoretical review, see Ziegler and Goswami (2005). However, this empirical conclusion does not undermine the importance of cultural variables; it only posits that, when these can be controlled (within, say, a homogeneous sample of learners), phonics skill learning proves to be a crucial part of school-based instruction.

In what ways is reading acquisition similar or different between children and adults? Strikingly little can be said in response to this question. In both developing and industrialized countries, there is a real need for this type of research, which would provide useful insights concerning the relation between cognitive and knowledge-based skills on the one hand and social factors and reading achievement on the other. Because adults have a much more complete repertoire of cognitive and linguistic skills and general knowledge than most beginning readers of primary school age, it ought to be possible to tease apart the range of cognitive and social prerequisites to learning to read. Little research has been undertaken along these lines (but see, for example, Durgunoglu and Oney, 2002; Greenberg, Ehri, and Perin, 2002). Such comparisons have been accompanied by an important increase in research on adult literacy in industrialized countries (e.g., Organisation for Economic Co-operation and Development [OECD] and Statistics Canada, 2000; Tuijnman, Kirsch, and Wagner, 1997; Wagner and Venezky, 1999).

Sociocultural Context, Literacy, and Literacies

> …[T]here is no real sense in which a level of education in the active population of a country can be said to be technically 'required' to permit the achieved level of economic growth of that country. That sort of argument grossly exaggerates the contribution of manipulative and cognitive skills in the performance of economic functions, and ignores the fact that such skills are largely acquired by on-the-job training. (Blaug, 1985, p. 25)

...[T]he single most compelling fact about literacy is that it is a *social* achievement; individuals in societies without writing systems do not become literate. (Scribner, 1984, p. 7)

Literacy is not just a set of uniform 'technical skills' to be imparted to those lacking them – the 'autonomous' model – but rather there are multiple literacies in communities and literacy practices are socially embedded (p. 2). The alternative, ideological model... offers a more culturally sensitive view of literacy practices as they vary from one context to another; it posits instead that literacy is a social practice.... It is about knowledge: the ways in which people address reading and writing are themselves rooted in conceptions of knowledge, identity and being. (Street, 2001, p. 7)

Focusing on the plurality of literacies means recognizing the diversity of reading and writing practices and the different genres, styles and types of texts associated with various activities, domains or social identities.... In multilingual contexts, different languages, language varieties and scripts add other dimensions to the diversity and complexity of literacies. (Martin-Jones and Jones, 2000, p. 5)

Since World War II, perhaps the most compelling argument for human resources development is that literacy and schooling normatively lead to economic growth in countries that are able to make a sufficient investment. Anderson and Bowman (1965), for example, went so far as to estimate that an 80% national adult literacy rate would be necessary for rapid economic development, but at least a 40% literacy rate would be required for a minimal amount of economic development. Naturally, this type of claim makes use of aggregated data across many countries of the world, based on a significant correlation between gross national product and literacy rates. Claiming causality using such correlations is hazardous of course. One would probably be equally correct in claiming that literacy rates, like infant mortality rates, are prime indicators of the degree of economic development in most countries. If social and economic progress is being attained, then one usually finds that literacy rates climb and infant mortality rates decline. Blaug (1985) came to the conclusion (cited earlier) that neither years of schooling nor specific literacy rates have a direct effect on economic growth. Yet, today there are few national policy makers who do not act as if literacy levels are one of the most important drivers of social and economic progress. One of the endemic problems in the sociocultural domain is whether to continue to view literacy as the "possession" or trait of the individual or whether literacy is more socially constructed as a relative phenomenon within a social group.

Within the domain of social context and in the 1980s, specialists took a fresh look at national literacy programs and at the singular concept of literacy. Some were psychologists with a cross-cultural perspective. For example, Scribner (1984; Scribner and Cole, 1981), working in Liberia, suggested that researchers should resist making broad statements about literacy and its consequences (economic or cognitive) because there exists a variety of social literacy practices that are crucial in understanding both the inputs made into promoting literacy and the outcomes of literacy programs and activities (Wagner et al., 1999).

Among the first to adopt the multiple *literacies* perspective and formalize it through ethnographic research was Street (1984). Street developed a bimodal distinction for conceptualizing literacy: one that considered literacy as a tool (or set of skills) for producing and understanding written text, which he called the *autonomous* model of literacy, and one that considered literacy in its fullest cultural context, which he called the *ideological* model of literacy. Based on his initial field work in prerevolutionary Iran in the 1970s, Street found that the official Farsi literacy used in the Iranian government campaign and in formal schooling conformed to the autonomous model, but the Arabic language literacy learned in Islamic schools and that was used for a variety of everyday tasks, including small business enterprises, conformed to the ideological model. Because Arabic and Farsi literacy differed from one another, Street claimed that they should be called different literacies, as distinct from, but related to, the social practice perspective of Scribner and Cole.

The term *literacies* has been adopted by many who were frustrated by the singular notion of literacy as a unique skill or set of cognitive skills that is or is not possessed by individuals to varying degrees. From the perspective of anthropologists such as Street, literacy in the singular is something appropriated by cognitivists, school pedagogues, and reading specialists whose principal goal, it is said, seems to be the purveyance of efficient formal schooling on the one hand and formalized adult literacy programs on the other. Because many individuals whose literacy falls below par in terms of statistical standards are from ethno-linguistic minority groups, anthropologists and ethnographers often attribute this "deficit" description to a lack of cultural sensitivity in those pursuing the autonomous model. Thus, Street claimed that the meanings and practices of literacy are necessarily contested; particular versions and interpretations of literacy are "always rooted in a particular world-view and a desire for that view to dominate and to marginalize others" (Street, 2001, p. 8). The literacies movement not only challenges the cognitive tradition, but also even more directly challenges those doing literacy work in developing countries where issues of dominance, hierarchy, and power are more central to policy discourse.

Individual Consequences

> What does illiteracy mean to the illiterate? …[T]he map of illiteracy closely coincides with the maps of poverty, malnutrition, ill-health, infant mortality, etc. Hence, in the typical case, the illiterate is not only unable to read and write, but he—or more usually she—is poor, hungry, (and) vulnerable to illness…. In these circumstances, does his or her literacy really matter? Would he or she even list illiteracy among life's major problems? (Gillette and Ryan, 1985, p. 21)

> An individual needs a minimum level of mastery in order to "pass" as literate in public and keep intact his or her self-respect; as schools and literacy programs become more effective in equipping their students with these skills, the effective threshold of acceptability will be raised accordingly. There is, quite simply, no finite level of attainment, even within a specific society, which is capable of eliminating the disadvantages of illiteracy or semi-literacy by permitting the less literate to compete on equal terms for employment and enjoy parity of status with the more literate. (Levine, 1982, p. 260)

> …[A]dopting different criteria [for literacy] for different regions and communities would ensure the perpetuation of educational inequalities and the differential access to life opportunities with which these standards are associated. (Scribner, 1984, p. 10)

> [L]iteracy proficiency…has a substantial effect on earnings, a net effect that is independent of the effects of education. (OECD and Statistics Canada, 2000, p. 84)

These quotations are perspectives typical of the two opposing sides of the arguments concerning the necessity of literacy for every individual, but each perspective leaves out an essential ingredient. Gillette and Ryan (1985) admit that other problems might have a higher salience and importance than literacy to the world's poor but nonetheless claim that literacy can somehow be part of the remedy, without specifying what the real linkage is between literacy and other types of benefits, such as health. In contrast, Levine (1982) treats literacy like intelligence quotient (IQ) scores in that, as the latter is a normed average, it is impossible to raise the national IQ because it will always stay at 100, even if many individuals obtain more correct answers in a given year. In the same way, by improving national literacy rates, one is simply putting the norm at a higher level, which, on the whole, maintains most individuals at their same relative level compared to others. Levine's argument, of course, denies the real possibility that literacy ability might have some concrete utility beyond one's social status relative to his or her neighbor or classmate. However, international surveys convincingly demonstrate that individual literacy levels are strong predictors of income in adults (OECD and Statistics Canada, 1995, 2000).

Does either perspective truly represent the real problems of individuals living in situations where a change from low to high literacy will make a concrete difference in life? The only way to reach a satisfactory answer is to undertake more ethnographic and case studies that explore the actual lives of individuals. Looking at the "average literacy rate" and comparing this with other estimated health indicators or estimating "employability" is akin to flying over a given area at 20,000 feet in the air—it can give a high-level idea but lacks detail on the ground. Work in rural low-literate Morocco has demonstrated that people with higher literacy tend to be better off economically, but also that an increasing number of parents believe that more education and more literacy will not necessarily lead to greater wealth because more and more school graduates have not found work (Wagner, 1993). A common perception is that both some literacy and some level of education are needed by some individuals in every family (or extended family) to meet the tasks required by government bureaucracy in Morocco, but not everyone needs to be literate to accomplish such tasks (Wagner, 1993). Similar mixed views and beliefs about the advantages of literacy and disadvantages of illiteracy have been found in studies in the United States (e.g., Wagner and Venezky, 1999) and in the domain of technological literacy (Wagner and Kozma, 2005).

In sum, the four intersecting themes described in the previous sections provide a sense of the complexity of literacy. The first two themes (on definition and acquisition) have been the most common battleground for academics because they are both linked to how policy makers will need to make decisions. The second two themes (on sociocultural parameters and individual consequences) essentially call into question the first two themes by asking whether literacy can be a singular concept (or not) and by asking the degree to which it really matters to become literate.

Cross-Cultural Research and Developmental Theory in Literacy

If one were to engage in a substantive Internet-based search of publications in the field of reading today, the outcome would surely show millions of articles, books, and chapters. The vast majority of these would be in only a handful of languages, largely contained within a dozen major languages of the world (perhaps mirroring, to some real extent, the distribution of languages on the Web itself). This statistic would leave the remaining 2,000 to 3,000 languages most commonly used in the world with near-zero research as to how literacy is acquired or utilized. As with other developmental phenomena, such as language, motor skills, and personality, one might (indeed should) ask the legitimate question of how much of a global sample of humanity is necessary before we can reach generalizable conclusions about a particular domain of behavior. For decades (even centuries), developmentalists have not bothered very much about whether their conclusions might apply to peoples in faraway places or even ethnic groups much closer to home. Hence, we have seen that the end of the twentieth century has brought a rise in the number of cross-cultural and comparative studies across developmental science.

Still, it is not clear how much this cross-cultural research has directly affected child and human development theory, broadly speaking, or literacy development, more specifically. No doubt, there has been impact, yet there is also little doubt that the main tendency in reading research has been to focus on how to improve children's reading achievement in advanced industrialized countries. One area of literacy development research that is growing rapidly reflects changes in such societies, namely in countries subject to important ethno-linguistic population changes as a result of immigration. Many of these cross-linguistic population contexts are now well known and even well studied, such as the United States and Spanish–English communities, Holland (Dutch–Arabic), France (North African Arabic–French), and England (Urdu–English). Both ethnographic and cognitive research has shown that ethno-linguistic minority groups in these situations fare less well than the dominant (majority) groups in reading achievement in the school years, although some intervention programs hold promise of improvements (for a review, see Snow and Kang, 2006). The available evidence suggests that cultural dimensions of the majority culture must be mastered if minority children are to catch up in school. Because this is a matter of politics and social dynamics, it is clear that even the best reading program will have difficulty in helping minority ethnic-linguistic group children reach parity in reading achievement in a second language.

Future Directions in Research and Policy in Literacy

The year 2015 is the target by which the United Nations' Millennium Development Goals should be reached, including that of universal basic education and literacy.* What are the prospects for attaining this goal, or even coming close? To have a realistic policy goal of increasing literacy, we need to have a clearer understanding of it as a sociocultural phenomenon. Those who would promote short-term media-oriented campaigns with only modest adaptations to the local contexts for literacy have two major problems to contend with: first, campaigns are typically top-down government-sponsored approaches where citizens may have at least an ambivalent relation with central authorities; second, the notion of short-term programming, although convenient for ideologues, runs counter to the notion that adaptation and flexibility in programming will be critical for success and fails to recognize that literacy is a cultural phenomenon that cannot be imposed or maintained through short-term interventions.

As noted earlier, much of the research on literacy in Western-type school settings has been largely irrelevant to those interested in the promotion of literacy around the world. One prime reason for this paradox (as in other areas of Third World research inquiry) is that researchers have been motivated more by theoretically derived questions than by questions based on policy needs (Wagner, 1986). The picture began to change at the turn of the twenty-first century, as publications on literacy have proliferated. Policy makers should not simply decide that everyone must be literate by such and such date, but rather (it is hoped), they should be informed by the best research not only on normative learning in Western schools, but also on issues such as first and second language/literacy learning, the roles of literacy in diverse societies, and other areas such as those discussed earlier.

European and American studies have made the case for teaching early reading using the phonics (decoding) approach to acquisition, along with an important dose of reading support by parents and teachers in and out of school. There is little in this Western approach to reading achievement to suggest that non-Western countries should treat this developmental approach as fundamentally lacking in substance. However, languages and scripts vary greatly around the world. We can be less sure of our experimental interventions or hierarchical regressions when the context changes dramatically. For example, in nonalphabetic scripts, such as Chinese, a strictly constrained decoding approach will be of little value (Taylor, 1999). When letters have multiple forms (such as in Telugu and Kanada in South India), then emphases on earlier letter discrimination become important (Daswani, 2001). Finally, although the use of new technologies in education is expanding rapidly, we have only a few examples of its use for literacy programs in the developing world (e.g., in India; see Wagner and Daswani, 2006).

---

* The actual target is to reduce by 50% the rates of illiteracy in each nation worldwide. Given the wide variety of definitions of literacy mentioned above, actual investments in literacy promotion and achievement will vary widely (United Nations, 2002).

In the policy arena, it is crucial to understand the pros and cons of language of instruction in schools as a determinant of literacy achievement. Often the decision on national or official language(s) is based on such factors as major or dominant linguistic groups, colonial or postcolonial history, and the importance of a given language to the interests of economic development. Official languages are typically those most commonly used in primary and secondary school, although there may be differences between languages used in beginning schooling and those used later on. Furthermore, there may be important differences between language policy in primary schooling and that of nonformal education and adult education. For example, in Senegal, French is used exclusively in primary school, but local Senegalese languages are used in adult literacy programs nationwide. The use of mother tongue instruction in primary and adult education remains a topic of continuing debate (Alidou et al., 2006; Engle, 1975; Wagner, 1992).

There is usually general agreement that all official languages ought to be assessed in a national literacy survey (e.g., English in the United States; English and French in Canada; and German, French, Italian, and Romanch in Switzerland), but there may be disagreement over the assessment of literacy in nonofficial or semiofficial languages, where these have a recognized and functional orthography (e.g., Athabaskan in Canada, or Hungarian in Romania). In many countries, there exists a multitude of local languages that have varying relations and status with respect to the official language(s). How these languages and literacies may be included in a national literacy survey can be a matter of serious debate. For example, in predominantly Muslim countries in sub-Saharan Africa (e.g., Senegal or Ghana), the official language of literacy might be French or English, but Arabic, which is taught in Islamic schools and used by a sizable population for certain everyday and religious tasks, is usually excluded from official literacy censuses. Similarly, literacy in Chinese, Spanish, Cherokee, and other written languages has generally been ignored in literacy assessments in the United States.*

Conclusion

Cross-cultural developmental science constitutes a general lifespan approach to the development of human behavior. Literacy development has begun down the same road and certainly has a stronger empirical base now compared with a decade or two ago. National and international agencies have evidenced greater interest in literacy as well. Yet, with population growth taken into account, little real progress can be claimed in reducing the illiteracy rates of most countries, especially in the developing world, and despite the 2015 United Nations' Millennium Development Goals. This observation should come as no surprise because the problems of illiteracy, low literacy, literacy, and multiple literacies are embedded in the sociocultural fabric of each society. With population migration continuing along with globalization of other parts of our societies, a multiply variegated world of ethnolinguistic complexity seems to be our societal destiny. As a consequence, policy decisions about language and literacy will become ever more relevant and more complicated, even as our knowledge base about literacy continues to increase. To keep pace with changes in societies today, as well as with a global economy that requires ever more skills in a competitive market place, we will no doubt have to keep the study and promotion of literacy on the research front burner for years to come.

---

* In addition to English, the recent National Assessment of Adult Literacy survey (United States Department of Education, 2007) systematically included Spanish language literacy assessment for the first time; other languages, however, were excluded.

Acknowledgments

Support for the writing of this chapter was provided in part by grants from the Spencer Foundation, the Lumina Foundation for Education, and the JP Morgan Chase Foundation. Thanks are due to the excellent editing work on an earlier version of this chapter. Naturally, all remaining errors are those of the author.

References

Abu-Rabia, S., and Siegel, L. S. (2002). Reading, syntactic, orthographic, and working memory skills of bilingual Arabic-English speaking Canadian children. *Journal of Psycholinguistic Research, 31*, 661–678.
Alidou, H., Boly, A., Brock-Utne, B., Diallo, Y. S., Heugh, K., and Wolff, H. E. (2006). *Optimising learning and education in Africa: The language factor.* Paris: ADEA, GTZ, Commonwealth Secretariat.
Anderson, C. A., and Bowman, M. J. (1965). *Education and economic development.* London: Frank Cass.
Bennett, J. A. H., and Berry, J. (1999). The future of Cree syllabic literacy in Northern Canada. In Wagner, D. A. (Ed.), *The future of literacy in a changing world* (revised ed., pp. 271–290). Cresskill, NJ: Hampton.
Blaug, M. (1985). Where are we now in the economics of education? *Economics of Education Review, 4*, 17–28.
Chall, J. S. (1967). *Learning to read: The great debate.* New York: McGraw-Hill.
Chall, J. S. (1983). *Stages of reading development.* New York: McGraw-Hill.
Crystal, D. (2000). *Language death.* London: Cambridge University Press.
Daswani, C. J. (2001). *Language education in multilingual India.* Delhi: United Nations Educational, Scientific and Cultural Organization.
Dickenson, D. K., McCabe, A., Clark-Chiarelli, N., and Wolf, A. (2004). Cross-language transfer of phonological awareness in low-income Spanish and English bilingual preschool children. *Applied Psycholinguistics, 25*, 323–347.
Downing, J. (1973). *Comparative reading.* New York: Macmillan.
Durgunoglu, A. Y., and Oney, B. (2002). Phonological awareness in literacy acquisition: it's not only for children. *Scientific Studies of Reading, 6*, 245–266.
Engle, P. L. (1975). Language medium in early school years for minority language groups. *Review of Educational Research, 45*, 283–325.
Gillette, A., and Ryan, J. (1985). Eleven issues in literacy for the 1990's. *Assignment Children, 63/64*, 19–44.
Goodman, K. S. (1985). Growing into literacy. *Prospects, 15*, 57–65.
Goody, J., and Watt, I. (1963). The consequences of literacy. *Comparative Studies in Society and History, 5*, 304–345.
Gray, W. S. (1956). *The teaching of reading and writing.* Paris: United Nations Educational, Scientific and Cultural Organization.
Greenberg, D., Ehri, L. C., and Perin, D. (2002). Do adult literacy students make the same word-reading and spelling errors as children matched for word-reading age? *Scientific Studies of Reading, 6*, 221–243.
Johansson, E. (1987). Literacy campaigns in Sweden. In R. F. Arnove and H. J. Graff (Eds.), *National literacy campaigns.* New York: Plenum.
Kamil, M. L., Mosenthal, P. B., Pearson, P. D., and Barr, R. (Eds.). (2000). *Handbook of reading research: Volume III.* Mahwah, NJ: Erlbaum.
Kirsch, I., and Jungeblut, A. (1986). *Literacy: Profiles of America's young adults. Final report of the National Assessment of Educational Progress.* Princeton, NJ: ETS.
Kirsch, I. S., Jungeblut, A., Jenkins, L., and Kolstad, A. (1993). *Adult literacy in America: A first look at the results of the National Adult Literacy Survey.* Washington, DC: National Center for Educational Statistics, United States Department of Education.
Levine, K. (1982). Functional literacy: Fond illusions and false economies. *Harvard Educational Review, 52*, 249–266.
Martin-Jones, M., and Jones, K. (2000). *Multilingual literacies: Reading and writing in different worlds.* Philadelphia: John Benjamins.
National Reading Panel. (2000). *Teaching children to read: An evidence based assessment of the scientific research literature on reading and its implications for reading instruction.* Publication No. 00-4769. Washington, DC: National Institutes of Health.
Ogbu, J. U. (1980). Literacy in subordinate cultures: The case of black Americans. Paper presented at the Literacy Conference of the Library of Congress, Washington, DC.

Oney, B., and Durgunoglu, A. Y. (1997). Beginning to read in Turkish: A phonologically transparent orthography. *Applied Psycholinguistics, 18*, 1–15.

Organisation for Economic Co-operation and Development and Statistics Canada. (1995). *Literacy, economy and society.* Paris: Organisation for Economic Co-operation and Development.

Organisation for Economic Co-operation and Development and Statistics Canada. (2000). *Literacy in the information age.* Paris: Organisation for Economic Co-operation and Development.

Resnick, D. P., and Resnick, L. B. (1990). Varieties of literacy. In A. E. Barnes and P. N. Stearns (Eds.), *Social history and issues in human consciousness: Some interdisciplinary connections* (pp. 171–196). New York: New York University Press.

Scribner, S. (1984). Literacy in three metaphors. *American Journal of Education, 93*, 6–21.

Scribner, S., and Cole, M. (1981). *The psychology of literacy.* Cambridge, MA: Harvard University Press.

Snow, C. E., Burns, S., and Griffin, P. (Eds.). (1998). *Preventing reading difficulties in young children.* Washington, DC: National Academy Press.

Snow, C. E., and Kang, J. Y. (2006). Becoming bilingual, biliterate, and bicultural. In K. A. Renninger, I. E. Sigel, W. Damon, and R. M. Lerner (Eds.), *Handbook of child psychology: Volume 4. Child psychology in practice* (6th ed., pp. 75–102). New York: Wiley.

Street, B. V. (1984). *Literacy in theory and practice.* London: Cambridge University Press.

Street, B. V. (1999). The meanings of literacy. In D. A. Wagner, R. L. Venezky, and B. V. Street (Eds.), *Literacy: An international handbook.* Boulder, CO: Westview Press.

Street, B. V. (2001). *Literacy and development: Ethnographic perspectives.* London: Routledge.

Taylor, I. (1999). Literacy in China, Korea and Japan. In D. A. Wagner, R. L. Venezky, and B. V. Street (Eds.), *Literacy: An international handbook* (pp. 423–429). Boulder, CO: Westview Press.

Tuijnman, A., Kirsch, I., and Wagner, D. A. (Eds.). (1997). *Adult basic skills: Innovations in measurement and policy analysis.* Cresskill, NJ: Hampton Press.

United Nations. (2002). United Nations Literacy Decade: Education for All. International Plan of Action: Implementation of General Assembly Resolution 56/116. New York: United Nations.

United Nations Educational, Scientific and Cultural Organization. (1957). *World illiteracy at mid-century.* Paris: United Nations Educational, Scientific and Cultural Organization.

United Nations Educational, Scientific and Cultural Organization. (2006). *Global monitoring report on literacy.* Paris: United Nations Educational, Scientific and Cultural Organization.

United States Department of Education. (2007). *National assessment of adult literacy: Literacy in everyday life.* NCES480. Washington, DC: Institute of Educational Sciences.

Wagner, D. A. (1986). Child development research and the Third World: A future of mutual interest? *American Psychologist, 41*, 298–301.

Wagner, D. A. (1992). *Literacy: Developing the future. UNESCO Yearbook of Education, 1992, Volume 43.* Paris: United Nations Educational, Scientific and Cultural Organization.

Wagner, D. A. (1993). *Literacy, culture and development: Becoming literate in Morocco.* New York: Cambridge University Press.

Wagner, D. A. (2000). Literacy and adult education. Global thematic review prepared for the United Nations World Education Forum, Dakar, Senegal. Paris: United Nations Educational, Scientific and Cultural Organization.

Wagner, D. A. (2003). Smaller, quicker, cheaper: Alternative strategies for literacy assessment in the UN Literacy Decade. *International Journal of Educational Research, 39*, 293–309.

Wagner, D. A., and Daswani, C. J. (2006). Bridges to the Future Initiative in India: Research update. Technical Report, International Literacy Institute, University of Pennsylvania, Philadelphia, PA.

Wagner, D. A., and Kozma, R. (2005). *New technologies for literacy and adult education: A global perspective.* Paris: United Nations Educational, Scientific and Cultural Organization.

Wagner, D. A., and Venezky, R. L. (1999). Adult literacy: The next generation. *Educational Researcher, 28*, 21–29.

Wagner, D. A., Venezky, R. L., and Street, B. V. (Eds.). (1999). *Literacy: An international handbook.* Boulder, CO: Westview Press.

Ziegler, J., and Goswami, U. (2005). Reading acquisition, developmental dyslexia, and skilled reading across languages: A psycholinguistic grain size theory. *Psychological Bulletin, 131*, 3–29.

9
Emotions and Temperament

JEROME KAGAN

Introduction

There is a natural relation among the concepts of temperament, emotion, and culture because a primary feature of a temperamental bias is a vulnerability to particular feeling states that, following cognitive appraisals influenced by the cultural setting, become emotions.

The Concept of Emotion

There is no current consensus on the meaning of the abstract concept of emotion. Hence, any scholar entering this arena must begin with the definitions that happen to enjoy accord among a majority of scholars during this particular historical era. The article by Cacioppo and Gardner (1999) on emotion in a 1999 issue of *Annual Review of Psychology* exemplifies the uncertainty surrounding the definition of emotion. The authors never defined this concept, leaving the decision up to each reader, and treated biological, behavioral, and semantic evidence as equivalently useful indexes of an emotion. This laissez-faire stance is reminiscent of the 11 emotions posited by Alexander Bain (1859), the fierce nineteenth century advocate of associationism, which is a potpourri of sensations (a sweet taste), motives (a desire for power), and strong feelings (terror).

A majority of contemporary psychologists regard a human emotion as a superordinate, value-free construct involving a cascade of four different imperfectly related phenomena: (1) a change in brain activity to select incentives, (2) a consciously detected change in feeling that has sensory qualities, (3) cognitive processes that interpret and/or name the feeling with a word or phrase, and (4) a preparedness for, or display of, a behavioral response. This chapter will use the term *feeling* for the consciously detected change in feeling and *emotion* for the interpretation and semantic labeling of the feeling, although the author acknowledges that others hold different definitions of these terms.

Investigators vary in the significance they award to each of these four components and in their assumptions of the strength of the associations among them. This distinction among the separate components of emotion is shared with Scherer (2004) and Buck (1999), although Buck regards the four phenomena as more closely related. Neuroscientists who call a brain profile an emotion (for example, calling activation of the amygdala to an angry face a fear state) when the neural activity is not accompanied by a detected change in feeling or motor reaction must acknowledge that every concept has a special meaning when a brain state is the only referent. The meaning of the concept of anxious ascribed to strains of mice that fail to explore a brightly lit alley, presumably because of a change in their brains, should not be equated with the meaning attributed to adults who have just learned they have a malignant tumor of the pancreas (Holmes, Parmigiani, Ferrari, Palanza, and Rodgers, 2000). Although feelings, their interpretations, and any behaviors that follow have a foundation in brain activity, each of the four components can occur without the others. For example, the detection of a brief feeling of dizziness does not need to be labeled or followed by an action. An action, such as a brief smile, does not need to be accompanied by a detected change in feeling or any symbolic interpretation (Sperli, Spinelli, Pollo, and Seeck, 2006). And a change in brain activity does not need to provoke any change in conscious feeling or behavior (Fairclough and Venables, 2006; Hoehn-Saric and McLeod, 2000).

Temperament

The sense meaning of a temperamental bias, as contrasted with the referential or operational meaning, is a biologically based foundation for a cluster of feelings and actions that appear during early childhood, although not always in the opening weeks or months. This biological state is sculpted by the environment into a large, but nonetheless limited, combination of traits that defines a personality. The personality traits called extraversion, conscientiousness, and impulsivity are joint products of a personal history and a temperamental bias developing in a particular cultural setting (Heinrichs et al., 2006). It is assumed, but not yet proven, that the biological foundations of many, but certainly not all, of the human temperaments are heritable neurochemical profiles. This hypothesis, which had been anticipated 75 years ago (McDougall, 1908; Rich, 1928), was present in an early form in the writings of the ancient Greeks who posited that the melancholic, sanguine, choleric, and phlegmatic temperamental types derived from the balance among the four body humors.

A small number of neurochemical profiles that can be the foundations of temperaments are not strictly heritable. For example, a female fetus lying next to her fraternal twin brother is influenced by the androgens secreted by the latter and is likely, as an older child, to have a higher pain threshold (Morley-Fletcher, Polanza, Parolaro, Vigaro, and Laviola, 2003). More relevant to this Handbook is the fact that the season of conception has a modest predictive relation to behaviors and moods that can be regarded as derivatives of a temperament, and this effect is more salient in cultures located at extreme latitudes than in those close to the equator. Early fall conceptions in the Northern Hemisphere (conceptions in February through April of the Southern Hemisphere) predict extreme shyness in children (Gortmaker, Kagan, Caspi, and Silva, 1997), the development of an affective disorder (Joiner, Pfaff, Acres, and Johnson, 2002; Pjrek et al., 2004), and differential dopamine turnover in the brain (Chotai and Adolfsson, 2002). Melatonin, which is secreted by the pineal gland, is a likely contributor to these outcomes. All humans secrete larger amounts of melatonin when the hours of daylight are decreasing. Eight-week-old infants who had been conceived in October had the highest concentrations of melatonin metabolites in their urine (Sivan, Laudon, Tauman, and Zisapel, 2001). A pregnant mother's secretion of high levels of melatonin can affect fetal brain growth in diverse ways because this molecule binds to receptors in many sites, including the hypothalamus (Thomas, Purvis, Drew, Abramovich, and Williams, 2002), contributes to cell death (Ciesla, 2001), and suppresses both the release of dopamine (Zisapel, 2001) and the production of cortisol (Torres-Farton et al., 2004). It is conceivable, therefore, that a fetus's genetic vulnerability to a temperamental bias could be potentiated by a conception that occurred during the months when the hours of daylight were decreasing.

However, the immaturity of our current understanding of the relations among genes, brain chemistry, postnatal experience, and behavior frustrates a confident prediction of a relation between a particular gene or physiological profile and a temperamental bias. As a result, every current definition of a temperament is based primarily on emotional and behavioral reactions, observed directly or described by an informant or the individual on a questionnaire. Although future investigators will add biological measures to behavioral ones in defining a temperamental bias, a psychological component will always be a part of the definition because temperament is a psychobiological concept.

Rothbart (1989) has suggested that infant temperamental biases affect two relatively independent, but primary, dimensions. One refers to the reactivity to particular incentives; the second refers to variation in the ability to regulate the state produced by an incentive. The contrast between reactivity and regulation has always been a primary issue in writings on emotion, ancient and modern, because of the concern with each individual's ability to control strong feelings. It is necessary, however, to specify the cause of the reactivity by noting the type of incentive (a sweet taste or a loud noise) as well as the form the reactivity takes (motor, autonomic, or brain reaction). A sweet liquid produces a decrease in heart rate and a smile in infants; a loud noise is followed by an increase in heart rate and, on occasion, crying. The bases for reactivity and the regulatory reaction change with development and vary across culture.

Although future research will reveal a very large number of temperamental biases, the most extensive research has been devoted to the temperamental biases that affect the young child's reaction to unfamiliar events. The simplest unexpected or unfamiliar event perturbs the chemistry of the genes within neurons (Kandiel, Chen, and Hillman, 1999; Moncada and Viola, 2006). Unexpected events that are familiar are quickly assimilated, but unexpected events that are unfamiliar are not, and event-related potential waveforms within the first 300 milliseconds differentiate these two categories of events (Kagan and Snidman, 2004).

The unfamiliarity or unexpectedness of an event always depends on the context in which it appears. For example, the unexpected presentation of a face with a fearful expression usually activates the amygdala. However, when the fear faces are presented along with unexpected scenes representing fearful events, the latter, but not the former, activate the amygdala because the fear faces lost their salience when presented in the context of the scenes (Schafer, Schienle, and Vaitl, 2005). The approach of a stranger is more likely to produce a cry in 8-month-olds if the setting is an unfamiliar laboratory room rather than the infant's familiar bedroom. There are few consistent consequences of any foreground event; there are only consequences of events in specific contexts.

Historical, Cultural, and Demographic Influences on Emotion

The historical era and cultural setting have had, and will always have, a profound influence on the classification and evaluation of emotional states. Greek and Roman writers confronted with the cascade that begins with an incentive and proceeds to a pattern of brain activity, a conscious feeling, an interpretation, and a possible action focused on the later appraisal process because these societies were especially concerned with the individual's ability to restrain actions provoked by an emotion that might disrupt the community. Most Greek philosophers assumed that this control was possible because, unlike Freud and some students of evolution, they believed that nature was benevolent. If individuals lived in accord with what felt natural, they would be able to regulate their passions (Cooper, 1999). It is not a coincidence that the large number of essays and books on emotion almost competes with the number devoted to morality. The idea that links these two domains is the need for and concern with maintaining social harmony. Thus, it is not surprising that the first factor in Aristotle's list of 14 emotions contrasted ethically good with bad emotional states.

A subtle ethical judgment also permeates the currently popular contrast between positive and negative affect, with anger, fear, and sadness nominated as prototypes for the latter category because of the implicit premise that negative affect interferes with happiness and health. It can be suggested, however, that Medieval Christians committed to their faith would have reported a feeling of positive affect that existed simultaneously with the presence of justified anger at Muslims, Jews, and atheists; a fear of God's punishment for the commission of a sin; and sadness over the death of a young child. Thus, the specific emotions judged as positive or negative vary with time and culture. They are ethical categories linked to the constructs good and bad and are not fixed biological or mental states that remain the same across history or place. Hence, it is not obvious that they are useful as scientific terms that refer to particular brain or psychological states across time and culture.

Thomas Aquinas's division of the soul's passions into states of arousal modulated by states of restraint retained an evaluative connotation; note the similarity to Rothbart's concepts of reactivity and regulation. This opposition was preserved through the nineteenth century in the contrast between uncontrollable emotions and deliberate reason until Freud turned the tables on the past by arguing that the restraint dictated by reason, in the form of repression, was the cause of, rather than the cure for, unhappiness and mental illness (Smith, 1992). It is not surprising that Aristotle and Aquinas would be preoccupied with the consequences of an imbalance between the socially dangerous emotions of excessive anger, greed, lust, and ambition, which were difficult to suppress and disrupted community life, and benevolent states that engendered a feeling of virtue and preserved social harmony. Modern readers who celebrate the emotions of exuberant joy, intense love, and justified anger might find it hard to believe that less than 75 years ago, P. T. Young (1936) resurrected the nineteenth century's dark view of these emotions by writing that they were always accompanied by a disintegration of behavior.

Darwin's ideas were a significant watershed in discussions of emotion because, prior to his writing, most commentators regarded emotions as primarily a human phenomenon requiring an awareness of a change in bodily states. Darwin's treatises on evolution and emotion introduced two ideas missing from most essays written during the prior two centuries. Darwin suggested that there were profound biological continuities between animals and humans; hence, scientists could illuminate the mystery of human affects by observing and performing experiments on animals. The second suggestion was that emotional states found expression in the distinct arrangements of facial muscles provoked by a "nerve force." This notion implied that emotions were potentially localizable in brain activity. Both assumptions are alive and well in contemporary reports that attribute select emotions to animals (for example, anxiety in mice, fear in rats, anger in monkeys, empathy in chimpanzees) and nominate particular brain circuits as the biological foundation of emotions (e.g., fear mediated by the amygdala and disgust by the insula and orbitofrontal cortex).

Freud's conception of anxiety added a significant element to Darwin's theses. Freud inserted an undifferentiated state of anxiety between brain and symptom and implied that this state could range from mild to intense. Hence, anyone was vulnerable to developing a phobia, depression, or delusion. Historical changes added an evaluation of excessive timidity, caution, and concern with the opinions of others as maladaptive traits in an increasingly competitive, mobile, industrialized urban society, compared with the more desirable evaluation of these qualities two centuries earlier in the rural economies of villages and towns. As a result, anxiety over the adequacy of self's skills, status, sociability, appearance, and sexual pleasures ascended to the position of the alpha emotion in the hierarchy of human affects, replacing anger, lust, shame, guilt, and an insatiable desire for power as the enemies of happiness.

Almost a century later, when biological measurements were becoming more routine, neuroscience was flourishing, and sociobiological ideas were popular, scientists turned their attention to the initial phase of the emotional state that involved brain activity. Ekman and Davidson (1994) edited essays on emotion written by 23 social scientists. The nodes of disagreement centered on three issues: (1) the utility of positing a small set of basic, compared with a larger set of less basic, emotions; (2) debate over whether unconscious brain states should be treated as emotions; and (3) debate over whether emotions should be restricted to states that have consequences. None of these questions explicitly engaged the ancient preoccupation with good versus bad emotional states or the importance of controlling overpowering feelings to preserve community harmony.

The most significant historical change in the conceptualization of emotion by Western commentators has been a replacement of the implications of an agent's feelings for the integrity of, and their relation to, their family and community as a criterion for classifying emotions with the individual's pleasures and biological fitness. Instead of celebrating the emotions that sustained courage, restraint, honesty, cooperation, loyalty, and modesty, the feelings that maintained sexual arousal, justified anger, seeking of sensory delights, and dominance were nominated as being in closer accord with human biology. No sociobiologist would agree with Plato's claim that each person should try to maximize his or her wisdom, courage, temperance, and sense of justice. A tipping point occurred in one of the generations between Locke and Wilson when feeling happy because the self's sensory pleasures and potency were enhanced replaced feeling happy because the self was respected by friends and neighbors.

Nonetheless, considerable controversy remains. Eleven contemporary theorists had different opinions regarding the states that should be treated as emotions. Only 7 of the 11 nominated guilt, shame, or surprise, and surprisingly, 5 theorists did not think that the emotion accompanying sexual feelings toward a beloved partner warranted distinct status (Gonzaga, Turner, Keltner, Campos, and Altemus, 2006). These scholars should reread Homer's *Odyssey*, which contains almost as many references to sexual desire as to anger and sadness.

Language and Emotions

The most powerful effect of culture on emotions is on the semantic concepts that label the products of the appraisal process. Most of these concepts can be assigned a position in one of four quadrants created by crossing a valence dimension (pleasant versus unpleasant) with a salience or intensity dimension. Joy has a pleasant valence and high salience; whereas serenity has a pleasant valence combined with low salience. Boredom has an unpleasant valence but low salience; fear has an unpleasant valence and high salience. Most emotional words in English, Chinese, Japanese, Indonesian, and Dutch languages fit this scheme (Fontaine, Poortinga, Setiadi, and Markham, 2002). However, this simple semantic structure cannot be applied to states that are emotional blends. The state of many college seniors as June approaches combines the emotion of intense joy with some sadness over leaving their campus. This state cannot be assigned a location in one of the four quadrants (Larsen, McGraw, and Cacioppo, 2001).

Furthermore, members of all cultures use the dimensions of valence and salience to classify people, objects, and events that have little or no relation to emotions (potholes are bad and of low salience) (Osgood, Suci, and Tannenbaum, 1957; Saucier, 2003). Even adults who cannot experience any autonomic feedback from body to brain and patients with lesioned amygdalae rely on valence and salience when they classify emotional events with language (Wiens, 2005).

Apparently, humans are biased to organize semantic terms and propositions in accord with their position on the dimensions of good to bad and high to low salience. The former dimension reflects the irrepressible human tendency to evaluate experience with respect to each individual's ethical beliefs. The salience dimension reflects the equally pervasive urge to classify experiences with respect to their power to intrude into or alter a state of consciousness. Humans remain continually preoccupied with the answers to two questions: Am I a good person? Am I able to control my thoughts, feelings, and actions?

However, the evaluative dimension is far less significant for the perceptual representations, or schemata, derived from the sensory experiences that represent the natural events to which the words refer. Most adults use the sensory qualities of odorants, rather than the semantic categories of desirable or undesirable, when they judge the perceived similarity of two olfactory stimuli (Chrea, Valentin, Sulmont-Rosse, Nguyen, and Abdi, 2005). Perceptual schemata are only categorized as good or bad following a symbolic appraisal that ignores their sensory properties.

There is an important difference between feelings and the semantic categories that name them. Feelings are dynamic, fleeting sensory experiences, whereas semantic concepts freeze-frame these states into static concepts with core properties resembling Plato's geometric forms. Languages invite an either/or categorization of experience and throw away a great deal of information to construct a tidy package. Feelings, by contrast, vary in quality, duration, and intensity. Thus, from the perspective of an experiencing agent, an emotion is a dynamic event, but from the perspective of an investigator asking an informant to describe his or her emotions, the verbal replies are treated as static categories. Bohr's concept of complementarity between waves and particles may be useful. An emotion is a dynamic event (that is, like a wave) in the subjective frame of the experiencing agent but a category (that is, a particle) in the objective frame of the scientist. Words for emotional states, like the photograph of a dancing woman, transform an inherently dynamic event into one frozen in time and space. The moment a woman announces that she is happy after reading a letter informing her of a promotion, her emotional state has already begun to change.

Many words for emotions are embedded in distinct semantic networks among the members of different cultures. The word in the center of the network—called the prototype of the concept—is related through an intricate set of semantic and schematic links to observations at the edge of the web of representations. Contemporary North American college students regard a mother's love, not love of God, as a prototype for the concept love (Fehr and Russell, 1991). Medieval monks and nuns would have reversed this profile. The German term angst refers to an uncomfortable feeling that accompanies the inability to know the future (Wierzbicka, 1992). Because all future events are unknowable, only a culture that found this psychological state distressing would have invented this concept. The prototype for the Greek term *philia* is a mutuality of affection between two people. The English concept of affection for a friend refers to the feeling of one person toward another, without requiring a reciprocal emotion on the part of the other. Americans treat the words happy and excited as more similar in meaning than the Japanese; Chinese informants regard shame and fear as closer in meaning than the Japanese (Moore, Romney, Hsia, and Rusch, 1999).

An emotional term can represent a personality trait or the feelings, origins, or consequences of an emotion depending on the network in which it is embedded. An analysis of 113 Chinese words related to *shame* revealed terms for a shy personality, blushing, acts that violated community norms, anger toward those responsible for the feeling, and individuals who are shameless (Li, Wang, and Fischer, 2004). Both the culture and its vocabulary influence the features of a feeling that will be awarded a privileged status in a description. Speakers of English select terms that refer to the quality and valence of a private state; the terms anxious, happy, and sad are examples. Other languages bias agents to emphasize the bodily origins of their emotion (e.g., dizzy, headache, racing heart), and a few languages emphasize the origin of the feeling. The Chinese have five distinct terms for shame or guilt that specify its origin and whether or not an agent's action injured another (Frank, Harvey, and Verdun, 2000).

The extraordinary variation in the semantic networks for emotional categories implies that investigators cannot assume that a word or sentence has the same meaning across speakers from different cultures. The phrase "I love you" provides an example. Americans use this phrase far more often than members of most societies (Wilkins and Gareis, 2006), and it usually does not have the salience it possesses for others. Bilingual adults who know both English and a native language find it much easier to say "I love you" in the former than in the latter language because this phrase implies a deeper emotional relationship in the native language. These stubborn facts mean that it is probably impossible to translate some emotional words from one language into another (Russell, 1991).

When the fourth century Christian philosopher Augustine reflected on the differences between his feelings and the states he believed God wished him to have, he was forced to use several words to describe his emotion: "How foul I was and how crooked and sordid, bespotted and ulcerous" (cited in Jones, 1969, p. 106). Most contemporary Americans could not have experienced Augustine's state because it required strong beliefs in the existence of God and the devil and absolutely sinful acts that condemned the soul to purgatory. God and the devil were not regarded as inventions of the mind. Thus, the feeling of humiliation vis-à-vis God differed from the state of humiliation experienced by a person in the presence of a stronger or wiser individual. The emotion felt by medieval men during sexual intercourse probably differed from the experience of moderns making love because the former believed that because semen originated in the brain, every orgasm depleted the body's reservoir of vital energy (Jacquart and Thomasset, 1988). The Ifaluk of Micronesia used the word *fago* to describe the emotion evoked when a friend dies, as well as the state of a person in the presence of someone who is admired (Lutz, 1982). There is no English word that comes close in meaning to the concept of fago.

These robust facts imply that investigators should follow A. N. Whitehead when writing about emotions and use full sentences that specify the event, its presumed origin, the target of the feeling, and the context in which the event occurs. There is no anger without a target because a person is angry at something or some person. If, as is likely, some targets occur only in particular cultural settings, it will be impossible to map all of the emotional concepts in one society onto those from every other culture.

Developmental Constraints

Different concepts will be required for the emotional states of human infants less than 12 months old who cannot impose symbolic interpretations on their feeling states. One-week-old infants swaddled in a blanket cry when someone opens the blanket to expose them to the cooler temperature of the room. This cry should not be regarded as a sign of a fear or angry state because it is a biologically prepared reaction to the change in temperature. Nor should we call the 6-month-old who cries after dropping her rattle angry because anger presumes knowledge of the cause of a distress state. Although some psychologists attribute fear to 7-month-olds who cry to the approach of a stranger as well as to 40-year-olds who notice clotted blood in their saliva, the states of these two agents cannot be the same because of the profound biological and psychological differences between 7-month-olds and adults. The infants' behavioral reactions to incentives are either biologically prepared responses or acquired habits. Their behaviors are signs of a change in internal state, but one that is free of appraisal.

The structural immaturity of the infant brain means that the emotions that require thought, such as guilt, pride, despair, shame, and empathy, cannot be experienced in the first year because the cognitive abilities necessary for their actualization have not yet developed. The restriction on possible emotions extends beyond infancy. Children under age 4 years find it difficult to retrieve the past and relate it to the present and, as a result, cannot experience the emotions of regret or nostalgia (Levine, 2004). Preadolescents, 8- to 12-years-old, have some difficulty manipulating several representations simultaneously in a working memory circuit because of incomplete maturation of the connectivity of the dorsolateral prefrontal cortex to other sites (Crone, Wendelken, Donohue, van Leijenhorst, and Bunge, 2006). This fact implies that preadolescents are protected, to some degree, from the emotions that emerge from a thoughtful examination of the logical inconsistencies among personal beliefs. Older adolescents are susceptible to the uncertainty that follows recognition of the inconsistency between their experiences and childhood premises referring to sexuality, loyalty, God, or the infallibility of their parents. The desire to repair the semantic inconsistency requires some alteration in their earlier beliefs and the subsequent evocation of emotions that are denied to younger children. The cognitive immaturity of preadolescent children means that they are protected from concluding that they have explored every possible coping response to a crisis and no adaptive action is available. As a result, they cannot experience the hopelessness that often leads to a suicide attempt. Hence, we need a vocabulary for the repertoire of emotional states experienced by infants and young children. Remember, embryologists invented distinct terms, such as zygote and gastrulation, for the temporary structures and processes present during the opening weeks of embryological growth.

In addition to cultures preparing their members for select emotions, the social class in which a person was reared over the first dozen years creates a profile of preparedness for variation in intensity and frequency of anxiety and depression (Simm and Nath, 2004; Wang, Du, Liu, Liu, and Wang, 2002), as well as the form of physiological reaction to challenges (Manuck, Flory, Ferrell, and Muldoon, 2004; Steptoe, Kunz-Ebrecht, Wright, and Feldman, 2005). Social class is a far better predictor of the development of an anxiety or depressive disorder among Americans and Europeans than their genes or ethnicity (Johnson, Cohen, Dohrenwend, Link, and Brook, 1999). The frequency of reports of sadness, anger, and fear among adults living in 1 of 13 foraging-farming villages in the Bolivian Amazon was correlated with the degree of income inequality in the village (Godoy et al., 2006). The greater the inequality, the more frequent was the report of these emotions. The recognition in contemporary societies that one is economically less privileged than one's neighbors implies a compromise in the expectation of the respect and dignity others hold or will display toward self. Many medieval citizens who were not pious Christians felt a similar emotion. When class position is correlated with ethnicity, as is true in many nations, the emotional consequences are often more dramatic. Muslim youth from poor families living in England feel more marginalized than poor Presbyterian youth living in rural Scotland.

Gender, too, generates a preparedness for the frequency and quality of emotions that is the product of different cultural norms for males and females and/or a combination of these norms with select biological differences between males and females. Members of same-sex college crew teams displayed different emotions to the same impending competition. Although both men and women showed an increase in cortisol before the competition, the magnitude of the increase was associated with different emotional states in males and females. The men who had large increases in this hormone reported a more intense desire to win to feel personally more potent. The women with equally large cortisol increases were concerned with strengthening the emotional bond with their teammates by not disappointing them (Kivlighan, Granger, and Booth, 2005). Most societies have promoted the notion that females are more prone to fear and anxiety than males, and school-age children have already learned, implicitly, that females are weaker than males. Seven-year-old children asked to indicate whether a frightened rabbit or a bold tiger was more appropriate for their mother or their father assigned the rabbit to the mother and the tiger to the father, even if the father happened to be passive and the mother the dominant member of the dyad (Kagan, 1984).

Culture and Temperament

Variation in ethnicity, class, gender, and culture prepares individuals for different emotional hierarchies. Temperamental biases, on the other hand, affect the frequency and salience of detected feelings resulting from spontaneous brain states or visceral feedback from the body (Stabell et al., 2004). Human populations that have been reproductively isolated for thousands of years possess temperamental biases with implications for emotions. Although only 0.02% of all human nucleotides distinguish reproductively separated human populations from each other, this small proportion represents approximately 600,000 nucleotides resulting from reproductive isolations that have lasted for at least 1,500 generations. This number is large enough to create temperamental variations among Europeans, Africans, and Asians (Jones and Perlis, 2006).

To illustrate, Caucasian infants and young children display more frequent smiles than children born to Chinese parents, whether the latter were born in the United States or the People's Republic of China (Camras, Chen, Bakeman, Norris, and Cain, 2006; Freedman, 1974; Kagan, Kearsley, and Zelazo, 1978; Kagan et al., 1994). Caucasian infants are also more easily provoked than Chinese infants to high levels of arousal accompanied by vigorous motor activity and frequent crying (Kagan and Snidman, 2004).

Many commentators have noted that Asians celebrate a low level of arousal as an ideal state. Buddhist philosophy, which did not appeal to Europeans, regards a serene feeling, in which the individual desires nothing and has severed intense emotional attachments, as the ideal state of nirvana each individual should try to attain. By contrast, European Americans regard the arousal associated with the excitement that accompanies sexual relationships, visiting new places, and engagement in new activities as the perfected state. It is possible that temperamental differences between Asians and Caucasians make a small contribution to these cultural preferences.

Asian and European American populations differ in several alleles (Redd et al., 2006). One such allele is in the promoter region of the gene for the serotonin transporter molecule, which affects the excitability of the amygdala (Marui et al., 2004). If Caucasians were biologically prepared for more arousing emotions because of their genome, a philosophy that promoted calm serenity as the ideal would appear to be both less attainable and less valid than it would to Asians whose biology biased them for a lower state of arousal. It is difficult to persuade a person to work toward a goal they do not believe they can attain.

The suggestion that Japanese, Chinese, and Koreans differ temperamentally from European Caucasians is supported by evidence on the functions of the serotonin transporter molecule during embryological development. Soon after the neural tube forms, within the first weeks after conception, a cluster of cells called the neural crest migrates to become the bones of the face, autonomic nervous system, adrenal medulla, part of the aortic arch, and the pigment cells of the iris and skin. The serotonin transporter molecule influences the structural differentiation of these neural crest cells. As a result, polymorphisms of the gene for the serotonin transporter molecule could affect the crest cells and, by inference, the tissues they become later in development (Hansson, Mezey, and Hoffman, 1999). Asians are more likely than Caucasians to inherit the short allele (Gelernter, Kranzier, and Cubelis, 1997; Gelernter, Cubelis, Kidd, Pakstis, and Kidd, 1999), which is associated with less effective transcription of the gene and, therefore, a slower reabsorption of serotonin from the synapse.

Some of the neural crest cells migrate to become bones of the face, and human populations vary in the prominence of the chin and the nose. One consequence of the domestication of mammals (for example, horse, cattle, and fox) is a shortening of the components of the snout. Silver fox bred for tameness have both shorter snouts and higher levels of serotonin than wild silver fox (Trut, 1999). It is of interest, therefore, that most Asians have flatter faces than most Caucasians and also have a less labile cardiovascular profile. These facts imply genetic differences in the structure of the migrating neural crest cells as a result, in part, of polymorphisms of the serotonin transporter gene. All of the evidence implies that the psychological and biological differences between Asians and Caucasians might have a small temperamental component that traces its origin to differences in the serotonin transporter gene and neural crest differentiation within the first months of embryological growth.

However, a person's biology never determines a particular personality type. Rather, the biology places limits on the ease with which certain moods can be sustained and the frequency of particular acute emotions. Genes, and the biology they promote, limit the actualization of certain outcomes, while not guaranteeing any one particular profile. An infant girl born with two short alleles in the promoter region of the serotonin transporter gene could develop any one of a large number of personalities. However, the probability that she will not be an extremely sociable, spontaneous, bold woman is greater than it would be for an infant born with two long alleles. The genetic differences between Caucasian Europeans and Americans, one the one hand, and Asians, on the other, do not deny the more powerful contributions of culture, but they suggest that perhaps both biology and culture, acting together, influence the preferred philosophical orientations and emotional patinas of these two populations.

Central Issues in Emotions and Temperament

Three questions assume primacy at the present time. The first refers to whether a brain state that does not result in a consciously detected feeling should be regarded as an emotional state. The second puzzle involves the role of the cultural setting on the varied outcomes of temperamental biases. The third question refers to the influences of maturation and postnatal experience on the emotional hierarchies that develop from a particular temperamental bias.

Consider a hypothetical example of the joint contribution of temperament, culture, and development on the emotional profiles of children and adolescents. Some infants inherit a temperamental bias to become highly aroused by unfamiliar events (Kagan and Snidman, 2004). This bias is displayed in all 16-week-old infants in vigorous motor activity and crying to unfamiliar stimuli and in an initially restrained, cautious posture to unfamiliar people, objects, locations, and challenges in later childhood. However, cultures differ in the frequency and type of unfamiliarity they present to children as they grow. American children in cities encounter many strangers and new places; hence, those with this bias will experience uncertainty in crowds and appear shy to observers. By contrast, strangers and new locations are less common in isolated, rural settings, and therefore, 5-year-olds with the same bias are less likely to be shy but might display their temperament in uncertainty toward and avoidance of new foods. By adolescence, when maturation of the frontal lobe permits youth to control avoidant reactions, American youth are likely to worry over their school performance, whereas the isolated adolescents might worry over violating the local standards for their gender. Furthermore, cultures differ in the tendency to accept or to discourage restrained, avoidant reactions in their children. American parents, especially well-educated ones, are likely to encourage their shy, timid children to control their uncertainty and cope with the targets they fear; Japanese parents are more accepting of their child's restrained behavior (Kagan et al., 1978).

Is a Brain State an Emotion?

Some scientists argue that an emotional state is automatically generated when a specific brain circuit is activated by a relevant class of releasing stimuli. The strongest argument has been made for the emotion of fear (Öhman and Wiens, 2004). In the case of fear, the releasing events imply danger, with snakes and spiders nominated as the prototypic incentives. There are two problems with this biologically deterministic position. First, most human infants fail to show any signs of fear to realistic toy versions of snakes or spiders. Second, most of the components of the circuit activated by snakes and spiders are also activated by the unexpected appearance of unfamiliar events that are perfectly harmless. Spider phobics exposed to forms of spiders show greater neuronal activity in the right dorsolateral prefrontal cortex than in the amygdala probably because they are trying to control their fear (Paquette et al., 2003).

A study of graduate students preparing for the oral defense of their Ph.D. dissertation—an event that generates a high level of anxiety over performance failure—reveals not only the extraordinary specificity of biological reactions, but also the lack of a relation between a person's biology and their subjective emotional state. Self-ratings of degree of experienced stress, several biological measures, and reports of somatic complaints were gathered on three occasions: 6 to 8 weeks before the oral examination, on the day of the examination, and several days after the examination. The same data were gathered on students who were not preparing for any examination. Both the men and women preparing for the examination reported more frequent headaches, sore throats, and fatigue 2 months before the exam but showed no distinct change in immune function and did not report feeling more stressed than the students who were not going to be examined. Furthermore, the women anticipating an oral exam, but not the men, showed increased cortisol secretion on the day of the exam, but not 6 to 8 weeks earlier. Finally, there were no significant correlations among the several biological measures or between these measures and self-reported stress (Lacey et al., 2000). These data reveal why the concept of *stress* is meaningless unless the investigator specifies the threatening event and the gender of the individual.

Brain profiles have a limited power to illuminate many human emotions, at least at the present time, because it is impossible to create the appropriate conditions in the artificial setting of the laboratory. The circuits that accompany most human emotions as they occur in ecologically natural settings cannot be measured in the scanner because the noise, restricted supine posture, and social context (the individuals are aware the experimenter is sitting nearby evaluating them) can alter a person's psychobiological state in unknown ways (Allen, Blascovich, Tomaka, and Kelsey, 1991; Pripfl, Robinson, Leodolter, Moser, and Bauer, 2006).

More seriously, different measures of brain activity to the same incentive often lead to divergent conclusions. Not surprisingly, adult men rated female nudes as more pleasant than male nudes. However, the event-related potential waveform and the magnetic fields produced by these pictures required different inferences. The waveforms were larger for female than for male nudes, but the magnetic fields were similar to both the male and female nudes (Costa, Braun, and Birbaumer, 2003).

At the moment, the hope of finding a well-defined biological pattern of blood flow or glucose utilization that always accompanies a particular emotion, as experienced by an individual or a group of individuals, has not been realized (Nair, 2005; Peper, 2006). However, should scientists discover such a profile, it will have to be described with a biological, not a psychological, vocabulary. Individuals expecting an electric shock showed the usual increase in neural activity in the somatosensory cortex. The scientists who conducted this experiment concluded that the brain profile was the foundation of the emotion *dread* (Berns et al., 2006). However, because the same cortical areas are activated by events unrelated to the anticipation of pain, the scientists should have invented a new term to describe the correlation between the anticipated shock and the neural pattern. The amygdala, insular cortex, and anterior cingulate, which are interconnected, are activated in adults exposed to an aversive event, as well as in adult men experiencing penile erections while watching erotic films (Ferretti et al., 2005). Hence, a scientist could not know what emotion was being experienced by examining the brain profile in these areas because the brain's reaction is a function of a person's private interpretation of an event and there is usually variation in that appraisal (Kim et al., 2004).

In sum, scientists must invent distinct terms for changes in brain activity, whether spontaneous or produced by an external incentive or thought—for example, the medulla-amygdala-striatal circuitry to an aversive event or the locus ceruleus-mediotemporal-prefrontal circuit to an unfamiliar event. Biologists do not call a drop in blood sugar hunger because this biological state can occur for reasons other than a lack of food.

Equally important, different brain states can be accompanied by similar consciously reported emotions. The first exposure to faces displaying fear or disgust evoked a clear profile of activation combined with a report of very high arousal. Although the presentation of the same pictures a week later was accompanied by a dramatic reduction in brain activation, there was no difference in the participants' verbal descriptions of the intensity of their psychological arousal (Stark et al., 2004).

Most 20-year-olds living in affluent homes in industrialized nations report a stronger feeling of emotional well-being than adults over age 65 years whose bodies are beginning to show signs of wear. Yet a team of scientists who used only brain activity to faces with different expressions as the measure of well-being arrived at the counterintuitive conclusion that "emotional well-being improves over seven decades in the human life span" (Williams et al., 2006). This example should persuade readers that the meanings of concepts that refer to emotional states change seriously when brain states are the only source of evidence. The scientists who believe that a well-defined brain state always implies a particular emotion resemble fourteenth century Jewish scholars who were convinced that each of the 22 consonants of the Hebrew language had a numerical value. The letter, *shin*, for example, had a value of 300, and one could discern the meaning of a Biblical passage by adding up its numbers. For example, if the sum were 4,400, the passage represented the summoning of the angel Samael (Ball, 2006).

The Influence of Culture and Maturation on the Outcomes of a Temperamental Bias

Kagan and colleagues have studied two temperamental biases that are defined by the frequency and intensity of motor activity and crying to unfamiliar stimuli in 4-month-old infants. Approximately 20% of large samples of 4-month-olds showed high levels of motor activity and distress to unfamiliar moving mobiles, tape-recorded speech, and olfactory stimulation. These infants are called *high-reactive* and are likely to show avoidant behavior to unfamiliar events in the second year of life. Approximately 40% of the same sample, who showed minimal motor activity and minimal crying, are called *low-reactive*, and these infants are biased to be sociable and bold in the second year (Kagan et al., 1994).

These two groups were followed through adolescence. The youths who had been high-reactive as infants were more likely to be subdued when interacting with unfamiliar adults and to report unrealistic sources of worry about the future and unfamiliar places (Kagan and Snidman, 2004). We believe this is because they are vulnerable to frequent occurrences of unpredictable visceral feedback that they interpret as anxiety over future unfamiliar challenges. This interpretation could be a function of culture. American youths are biased to interpret the feeling evoked by a racing heart, excessive perspiration, or muscle tension as implying that they are worried about their inability to cope with a future or novel encounter, in part, because strangers, novel challenges, and new places are the most frequent novelties in their lives, and the folk theory they learned implies that their uncertainty is a result of a compromise in their psychological characteristics. Members of other cultures might impose different interpretations on the same visceral feedback. For example, Cambodian refugees living in Massachusetts interpret an unexpected bout of tachycardia as implying the possession of a weak heart caused by a loss of energy as a result of lack of sleep or a diminished appetite (Hinton, Pich, Safren, Pollack, and McNally, 2005).

High-reactive youths are especially vulnerable to limbic arousal to unfamiliar events, and strangers and new places are the primary sources of unfamiliarity in North American and European cultures. However, if the source of unfamiliarity were the colors, tastes, and viscosities of liquids with a bitter taste, rather than strangers and new places, adults who had been high-reactive might worry about drinking liquids with a novel color or viscosity, and psychiatrists would have created a category of drinking disorder. Clinicians are familiar with individuals with phobias of particular foods.

Social anxiety is more frequent in our culture than anxiety over drinking an unfamiliar liquid because strangers and new places are more common. Pious medieval Christians who suffered a misfortune after violating an ethical norm worried that their unpleasant emotion was the result of God's wrath. John Calvin, the strict Protestant reformer from Geneva, worried continually over God's disapproval of his actions (Bouwsma, 1984). The Saulteaux Indians of Manitoba worry about contracting a serious disease because illness implies that they have violated an ethical norm on sexual, aggressive, or sharing behavior (Hallowell, 1941). Social anxiety is a natural phenomenon, but it is especially salient in societies, like our own, where encounters with strangers and new places are frequent sources of uncertainty and social acceptance is a primary goal. There is a temperamental bias that renders individuals especially vulnerable to some form of uncertainty; history and culture supply the specific target of this emotional family. In contemporary America, occupational and social failure have replaced the traditional sins of pride, anger, avarice, sloth, gluttony, and lust as the basis for anxiety or guilt. Members of other cultures would be uncertain over the malevolent actions of a witch, the curse of a dead ancestor, the gossip of neighbors, shrinking of the genitals, or famine.

The members of every society are potentially vulnerable to a state of uncertainty over the validity of their ethical beliefs. When historical changes in economy or demography alter the certainty of traditional norms, the individuals who wish to remain loyal to the older mores are motivated to support a counter-reformation that restores the traditional ideology. The witch craze in fifteenth century Europe was brought on, in part, by the desire among some men to restore women, who were beginning to enter the workforce, to their traditional roles as home-makers and mothers. Ideological uncertainty can, in certain cultural contexts, lead to increased violence. Gould (2003) notes that homicides in Corsica peaked during periods of political unrest when the social rank of many individuals became ambiguous.

New ideas with ethical implications are as powerful incentives for human anxiety or anger as unexpected or unfamiliar events are for animals, but we suspect that the physiological mechanisms are different. Worry over the abortions performed on unmarried adolescents does not require the amygdala; a rat's acquisition of conditioned freezing to a tone that signaled electric shock does. Thus, scientists should not treat classically conditioned responses in animals as an appropriate model for all human anxieties (see Mineka and Zinbarg, 2006, and Phelps, 2006, for a different view). Classical conditioning might be a useful model for human phobias of animals, but it is less likely to illuminate the reasons for anxiety over a plane trip to Europe, a party with strangers, or becoming ill because one violated an ethical imperative to share food with a relative.

Theoretical Considerations in Emotions and Temperament

Two important unresolved theoretical issues refer to the biological bases of the large number of temperaments and whether the source of evidence for an emotion imposes different meanings on emotional concepts.

Genes, Neurochemistry, and Temperament

Research over the past few decades has provided a preliminary scaffolding for some of the genetic bases for human temperaments. There are at least 150 different molecules that, along with the density and location of their receptors, have the potential to influence the emotions and behaviors that define the large number of human temperaments. These molecules include nor-epinephrine, dopamine, epinephrine, serotonin, corticotropin-releasing hormone, glutamate, gamma-aminobutyric acid (GABA), opioids, vasopressin, oxytocin, prolactin, monoamine oxi-dase (MAO), neuropeptide S, and the sex hormones androgen and estrogen (Hartl and Jones, 2005).

The genes that represent the foundation of these molecules and their receptor distributions have a number of polymorphisms (that is, variation in the DNA sequence sometimes called an allele) in one or more of the gene's exons or in the regulatory sequences contiguous with the exons, called promoters and enhancers. Promoters control the effectiveness of the transcription of the exon into messenger RNA; whereas, the enhancers determine where and when the transcription, which will eventuate in amino acids and proteins, occurs.

Recent research invites a skeptical view of the older concept of a gene as a discrete entity with a particular structure and a deterministic contribution to a phenotype. Each gene is now regarded as a flexible entity with borders defined by its location and its responsivity to particular signals (Dillon, 2003). If each gene that influenced brain chemistry had an average of five polymorphisms, there would be at least 3^{750} possible neurochemical combinations that could contribute to a temperamental bias (Irizzary and Galbraith, 2004). Even if a majority of these neurochemical profiles had no relevance for temperament, the very large number of remaining patterns implies that future scientists will discover many neurochemical bases for temperaments that currently are hidden. One reason why reported relations between genes and psychological variables are often inconsistent across laboratories is that most scientists measure only one polymorphism, rather than several, and it is the combination that determines the temperamental bias (Arbelle et al., 2003).

Because the postnatal environment is always influential, interactions between genes and experience are to be expected. For example, upper middle-class adults with two or five, rather than seven, repeats of the gene for the DRD4 receptor were high on novelty seeking. However, surprisingly, individuals from economically disadvantaged backgrounds with the same polymorphism were not novelty seeking (Lahti et al., 2006). Other studies report that a combination of a harsh childhood environment and a shorter number of repeats in the MAO A allele predicted antisocial behaviors (Caspi et al., 2002; Nilsson et al., 2005). However, adolescent boys with the shorter number of repeats who grew up in economically advantaged homes had very low criminality scores. Thus, the combination of a disadvantaged background and maltreatment was a more significant predictor of later criminality than the MAO A polymorphism. Investigators trying to predict criminality, depression, or anxiety would do far better by relying on demographic features than genetic markers, even though the combination of genetic markers and psychological features predicts criminality or depression with greater accuracy for a small group. Because historical events alter the prevalence of poverty and childhood abuse within a society, the relation between genes and psychological outcomes will vary across time and culture.

If each gene that contributes to a temperamental bias is regarded as a word in a long sentence whose letters could be rearranged (analogous to a polymorphism), and the meaning of a sentence is analogous to a temperament, then there will be many opportunities for a rearrangement that will change the meaning of the sentence. Some alterations such as "ran" for "run" will have little effect on meaning, but spelling "hate" as "mate" or "rape" as "race" would change meaning more seriously. Current laboratory assays exist for only a very small proportion of the large number of possible polymorphisms (D'Souza and Craig, 2006). Thus, contemporary scientists trying to find the genetic contributions to emotions or psychopathology resemble children who can only recognize six words trying to read a Harry Potter novel. It is likely that when investigators can measure more of the alleles that reflect mood and behavior, they will discover that combinations of genes and rearing environments are always the best predictors of psychological variations that define human temperaments and personalities.

The Source of Evidence

The existing corpus of information reveals that the meaning of every emotional term varies with whether the source of evidence for an emotion is verbal self-report, observed behavior, or a brain state. This fact implies the utility of categorizing emotions with respect to combinations of origin (external event, thought, or spontaneous brain activity), brain state, subjective judgments of the valence and salience of a feeling, and the semantic label imposed on the feeling in a particular setting. A change in any one of these features could represent a distinct emotion. For example, an unexpected criticism from a parent in the context of the home that evoked a particular brain profile, a salient and unpleasant perception of an increase in heart rate, a furrowing of the forehead muscles, and an interpretation that the criticism was motivated by the parent's wish to help the adolescent develop better character would represent an emotion different from the state evoked if all of these features were the same, except the adolescent interpreted the comment as unjust and motivated by parental hostility. A third emotion would be realized if the origin were an episodic memory of the above incident, and a fourth state would emerge if the parental criticism had been expected. The reluctance to acknowledge the extreme specificity of emotional phenomena is retarding theoretical progress. Scientists bothered by this suggestion should examine any recent textbook that describes the extraordinary complexity of the biochemistry of a cancer cell.

Some scientists believe it is advantageous to regard all instances of amygdala activation to unpleasant pictures of war as an index of the same emotional state, even though the biological and behavioral signs of emotion evoked by a photograph of a bloodied soldier differ from the profile generated by a picture of a cobra with exposed fangs (Bernat, Patrick, Benning, and Tellegen, 2006). Put plainly, the features that define an emotional state cannot be fixed at the present time because they depend on the investigator's interest. Cows are classified with soybeans for the commodities investor, with alligators for the shoe manufacturer, with bison for evolutionary biologists, with fish for the grocer arranging foods, and with gods for religious Hindus. Every natural event can be assigned to more than one theoretical category. Emotions, like motor habits, are such a pervasive component of daily life that it is unlikely that a single theoretical organization will serve the interests of all.

Clinicians award special weight to the consequences of emotions because their central concern is with the influence of a patient's emotions on their functioning and the therapeutic effect of drugs or psychotherapy on those states. Although both outcomes might vary with the origins of the emotion, the current assumption that a drug's effectiveness in reducing anxiety or depression is independent of the reasons for the patient's emotion turns clinicians' interests away from origins, whether historical experiences or temperamental biases. This indifference to origins is unwarranted. Patients with posttraumatic stress disorder who report chronic feelings of shame over events in their past history fail to show improvement on the drug risperidone, whereas those free of that mood did improve (Petty et al., 2006). Depressed patients who failed to respond to a selective serotonin reuptake inhibitor antidepressant were more likely to show right frontal activation in the electroencephalogram, whereas those with left frontal activation were helped by the drug (Bruder et al., 2006). Thus, clinicians might prescribe treatment that is more effective if they attended to the origins of their patients' states and gathered biological information.

Neuroscientists who wish to localize the sites that make an emotion possible select the biological features of the feelings provoked by specific incentives. However, they should be interested in the salience of an emotion, which is always influenced by the unexpectedness or unfamiliarity of the incentive or change in feeling because of the relation between perceptual salience and brain activity (McGaugh and Cahill, 2003). Investigators committed to evolutionary theory emphasize the consequences of emotions that have implications for inclusive fitness; hence, they award significance to fear of physical harm, sexual arousal, and anxiety over threats to kin. Psychologists concerned with personality are interested in the historical conditions that produced emotions. Philosophers have traditionally focused on the valence of an emotion because of its implications for morality and the extensiveness of the information on targets and agents implied by the semantic form that names the emotion. Anthropologists are concerned with the words members of different cultures use to name emotional states, but their inquiries would profit from attention to the unfamiliarity of the detected feeling and the incentive.

In sum, the features scholars select for categorizing emotions depend on the questions they wish to answer and the premises they bring to the evidence. The immaturity in our current understanding implies that scientists should resist a premature insistence on one particular way to categorize emotions. Chemists classify matter into the categories of atoms and molecules; physicists rely on the heady constructs of quarks, leptons, and gluons. Evolutionary biologists debate the best way to classify animal groups; geneticists argue over the most frequent categories for DNA strings; and astrophysicists remain uncertain as to how many types of energy exist in the cosmos. Some reduction in the current level of frustration will occur when scientists have gained greater insight into the relations of incentives, brain states, feelings, and their symbolic appraisals.

Conclusion

There are two major goals the next cohort of scientists must try to achieve. They must determine the relations among the components of the cascade that includes specific incentives, brain states, detected feelings, appraisals of the feelings, and semantic labels imposed on the appraisal. The advances in the physical sciences over the past century have taught us that all any investigator has are observations that require selecting one interpretation from a set of alternatives. The task is to discover the sets of probabilities indicating that certain observations will follow a class of incentive, a brain state, a feeling, or an appraisal. For example, what is the probability that the unexpected appearance of a picture of a snake on a screen will activate the amygdala and the orbitofrontal cortex more than an unexpected picture of an antelope in 100 snake phobics compared with 100 nonphobics? These probabilities are unusually modest at the present time. The discovery of a statistically significant difference between the snake phobics and the controls in the mean level of activation does not mean that 70% to 80% of the phobics displayed greater activation than any nonphobic. Usually a significant difference is produced by less than 30% of the sample. Thus, the current reliance on differences in mean values exaggerates the confidence in the predictability of a biological or behavioral reaction to an incentive.

Second, we must learn more about the biological bases for varied temperaments and how development and cultural setting sculpt a personality type from a particular temperament. For example, adolescent boys who were high-reactive infants growing up in contemporary New England were much shyer than adolescent girls with the same infant temperament and developmental setting. One reason is that adolescent boys in this culture are critical and rejecting of boys who appear timid, but adolescent girls are gentler with equally shy-timid girls. As a result, the former are more socially anxious than the latter. This difference might not be actualized in Chinese villages.

This chapter provides only a scaffolding for understanding human emotions and their temperamental contributions. Despite the many options for classification, the core phenomena, analogous to phonemes in speech, are consciously detected changes in feeling that vary in origin, quality, salience, expectedness, and familiarity. If one removes this class of events, the concept of emotion dissolves into proposals for semantic terms, behaviors, and profiles of brain activation, each with a metric and structure different from those appropriate for feelings and each possible without the presence of any conscious feeling.

In light of the evidence pointing to the utility of examining the specific relations among the components of emotion, it is appropriate to ask why social scientists and biologists have been reluctant to descend deeper into the empirical trenches to ferret out the facts necessary for advances. Two factors seem relevant. Social scientists do not have methods sensitive enough to measure all of the relevant phenomena, but acknowledging that fact would generate cognitive dissonance. Second, the fragmentation of specializations has created a state of affairs in which investigators expert at measuring brain activity are less skilled at quantifying behaviors or semantic products, and many who know how to measure and analyze behaviors and questionnaire data are not expert at gathering information on the brain. Thus, each group continues to do what it knows best. The primary message in this chapter is a suggestion that all declarations about emotions append the source of evidence for the conclusion and acknowledge that the meaning of a conclusion based on one class of information is restricted to that evidence. Psychologists and neuroscientists should begin to write about emotional processes with full sentences rather than continuing to rely on solitary predicates.

Acknowledgments

Preparation of this chapter was supported, in part, by a grant from the Bial Foundation and the Metanexus Institute. I thank Nancy Snidman for her continuing collaborative wisdom

References

Allen, K. M., Blascovich, J., Tomaka, J., and Kelsey, R. M. (1991). Presence of human friends and pet dogs as moderators of autonomic responses to stress in women. *Journal of Personality and Social Psychology, 61*, 582–589.

Arbelle, S., Benjamin, J., Golin, M., Kremer, I., Belmaker, R. H., and Ebstein, R. P. (2003). Relation of shyness in grade school children to the genotype for the long form of the serotonin transporter promoter region polymorphism. *American Journal of Psychiatry, 160*, 671–676.

Bain, A. (1859). *The emotions and the will.* London: Parker.

Ball, P. (2006). *The devil's doctor.* London: Heinemann.

Bernat, E., Patrick, C. J., Benning, S. D., and Tellegen, A. (2006). Effective picture content and intensity on affective physiological responses. *Psychophysiology, 43*, 93–103.

Berns, G. S., Chapellow, J., Cekic, M., Zink, C. F., Pagnoni, G., and Martin-Skurski, M. E. (2006). Neurobiological substrates of dread. *Science, 312*, 754–758.

Bouwsma, W. J. (1984). John Calvin's anxiety. *The Proceedings of the American Philosophical Society, 128*, 252–256.

Bruder, G. E., Sedoruk, J. P., Tenke, C. E., Stewart, J. W., McGrath, P. J., and Quitkin, F. M. (2006). Regional hemisphere activity predicts clinical response to an SSRI antidepressant. *Biological Psychiatry Supplement, 59*, 136S.

Buck, R. (1999). The biological affects: A typology. *Psychological Review, 106*, 301–336.

Cacioppo, J. T., and Gardner, W. L. (1999). Emotion. *Annual Review of Psychology, 50*, 191–234.

Camras, L. A., Chen, Y., Bakeman, R., Norris, K., and Cain, T. R. (2006) Culture, ethnicity, and children's facial expressions. *Emotion, 6*, 103–114.

Caspi, A., McClay, J., Moffitt, T. E., Mill, J., Martin, J., Craig, I., et al. (2002). Evidence that the cycle of violence in maltreated children depends on genotype. *Science, 297*, 851–854.

Chotai, J., and Adolfsson, R. (2002). Converging evidence suggests that monoamine neurotransmitter turnover in human adults is associated with their season of birth. *European Archives of Psychiatry and Clinical Neuroscience, 252*, 130–134.

Chrea, C., Valentin, D., Sulmont-Rosse, C., Nguyen, D. H., and Abdi, H. (2005). Semantic typicality and odor representation: a cross-cultural study. *Chemical Senses, 30*, 37–49.

Ciesla, W. (2001). Can melatonin regulate the expression of prohormone convertase 1 and 2 gene via monomeric and dimeric forms of RZR/ROR nuclear receptor, and can melatonin influence the processes of embryogenesis or carcinogenesis by disturbing the proportion of cAMP and cGMP concentrations? Theoretic model of controlled apoptosis. *Medical Hypotheses, 56*, 181–193.

Cooper, J. M. (1999). *Reason and emotion.* Princeton, NJ: Princeton University Press.

Costa, M., Braun, C., and Birbaumer, N. (2003). Gender differences in response to pictures of nudes. *Biological Psychology, 63*, 129–147.

Crone, E. A., Wendelken, C., Donohue, S., van Leijenhorst, L., and Bunge, S. A. (2006). Neurocognitive development of the ability to manipulate information in working memory. *Proceedings of the National Academy of Science, 103*, 9315–9320.

Dillon, N. (2003). Positions, please.... *Nature, 425*, 457.

D'Souza, U. M., and Craig, I. W. (2006). Functional polymorphisms in dopamine and serotonin pathway genes. *Human Mutation, 27*, 1–13.

Ekman, P., and Davidson, R. J. (Eds.). (1994). *The nature of emotion.* New York: Oxford.

Fairclough, S. H., and Venables, L. (2006). Prediction of subjective states from psychophysiology: A multivariate approach. *Biological Psychology, 71*, 100–110.

Fehr, B., and Russell, J. A. (1991). The concept of love viewed from a prototype perspective. *Journal of Personality and Social Psychology, 60*, 425–438.

Ferretti, A., Caulo, M., Del Gratta, C., Di Matteo, R., Merla, A., Montorsi, F., et al. (2005). Dynamics of male sexual arousal. *Neuroimage, 26*, 1086–1096.

Fontaine, J. R. J., Poortinga, Y. H., Setiadi, B., and Markham, S. S. (2002). Cognitive structure of emotion terms in Indonesia and the Netherlands. *Cognition and Emotion, 16*, 61–87.

Frank, H., Harvey, O. J., and Verdun, K. (2000). American responses to five categories of shame in Chinese culture. *Personality and Individual Differences, 28*, 887–896.

Freedman, D. G. (1974). *Human infancy: An evolutionary perspective*. New York: Halsted Press.

Gelernter, J., Cubelis, J. F., Kidd, J. R., Pakstis, A. J., and Kidd, K. K. (1999). Population studies of polymorphisms of the serotonin transporter protein gene. *American Journal of Medical Genetics, 88*, 61–66.

Gelernter, J., Kranzier, H., and Cubelis, J. F. (1997). Serotonin transporter protein (SLC6A4) allele and haplotype frequencies and linkage disequilibria in African- and European-American and Japanese populations and in alcohol-dependent subjects. *Human Genetics, 101*, 243–246.

Godoy, R. A., Reyes-Garcia, V., McDade, T., Huanca, T., Leonard, W. R., Tanner, S., et al. (2006). Does village inequality in modern income harm the psyche? Anger, fear, sadness, and alcohol consumption in a pre-industrial society. *Social Science and Medicine, 63*, 359–372.

Gonzaga, G. C., Turner, R. A., Keltner, D., Campos, B., and Altemus, M. (2006). Romantic love and sexual desire in close relationships. *Emotion, 6*, 163–179.

Gortmaker, S. L., Kagan, J., Caspi, A., and Silva, P. A. (1997). Daylength during pregnancy and shyness in children. *Developmental Psychobiology, 31*, 107–114.

Gould, R. V. (2003). *Collision of wills*. Chicago: University of Chicago Press.

Hallowell, A. I. (1941). The social function of anxiety in a primitive society. *American Sociological Review, 6*, 869–891.

Hansson, S. R., Mezey, E., and Hoffman, B. J. (1999). Serotonin transporter messenger RNA expression in neural crest-derived structures and sensory pathways of the developing rat embryo. *Neuroscience, 89*, 243–265.

Hartl, D., and Jones, E. W. (2005). *Genetics* (6th ed.). Boston: Jones and Bartlett.

Heinrichs, N., Rapee, R. M., Alden, L. A., Bogels, S., Hoffmann, S. G., Oh K. J., et al. (2006). Cultural differences in perceived social norms and social anxiety. *Behaviour Research and Therapy, 44*, 1187–1197.

Hinton, D. E., Pich, V., Safren, S. A., Pollack, M. H., and McNally, R. J. (2005). Anxiety sensitivity in traumatized Cambodian refugees. *Behaviour Research and Therapy, 43*, 1631–1643.

Hoehn-Saric, R., and McLeod, D. R. (2000). Anxiety and arousal. *Journal of Affective Disorders, 61*, 217–224.

Holmes, A., Parmigiani, S., Ferrari, F., Palanza, P., and Rodgers, R. J. (2000). Behavioral profile of wild mice in the elevated plus-maze for anxiety. *Physiology and Behavior, 71*, 509–516.

Irizarry, Y., and Galbraith, S. J. (2004). Complex disorders reloaded: causality, action, reaction, cause and effect. *Molecular Psychiatry, 9*, 431–432.

Jacquart, D., and Thomasset, C. (1988). *Sexuality and medicine in the middle ages*. Princeton, NJ: Princeton University Press.

Johnson, J. G., Cohen, P., Dohrenwend, B. P., Link, B. G., and Brook, J. S. (1999). A longitudinal investigation of social causation and social selection processes involved in the association between socioeconomic status and psychiatric disorders. *Journal of Abnormal Psychology, 108*, 490–499.

Joiner, T. E., Pfaff, J. J., Acres, J. G., and Johnson, F. (2002). Birth month and suicidal and depressive symptoms in Australians born in the Southern vs. the Northern Hemisphere. *Psychiatry Research, 112*, 89–92.

Jones, W. T. (1969). *The medieval mind* (2nd ed.). New York: Harcourt, Brace and World.

Jones, D. S., and Perlis, R. H. (2006). Pharmacogenetics, race, and psychiatry. *Harvard Review of Psychiatry, 14*, 92–108.

Kagan, J. (1984). *The nature of the child*. New York: Basic Books.

Kagan, J., Arcus, D., Snidman, N., Yufeng, W., Hendler, J., and Green, S. (1994). Reactivity in infants: A cross national comparison. *Developmental Psychology, 30*, 342–345.

Kagan, J., Kearsley, R. B., and Zelazo, P. R. (1978). *Infancy: Its place in human development*. Cambridge, MA: Harvard University Press.

Kagan, J., and Snidman, N. (2004). *The long shadow of temperament*. Cambridge, MA: Harvard University Press.

Kandiel, A., Chen, S., and Hillman, D. E. (1999). c-fos gene expression parallels auditory adaption in the adult rat. *Brain Research, 839*, 292–297.

Kim, H., Somerville, L. H., Johnstone, T., Polis, S., Alexander, A. L., Shin, L. M., et al. (2004). Contextual modulation of amygdala responsivity to surprised faces. *Journal of Cognitive Neuroscience, 16*, 1730–1745.

Kivlighan, K. T., Granger, D. A., and Booth, A. (2005). Gender differences in testosterone and cortisol response to competition. *Psychoneuroendocrinology, 30*, 58–71.

Lacey, K., Zaharin, M. D., Griffiths, J., Ravindran, A. V., Merali, Z., and Anisman, H. (2000). A prospective study of neuroendocrine and immune alterations associated with the stress of an oral academic examination among graduate students. *Psychoneuroendocrinology, 25*, 339–356.

Lahti, J., Raikkonen, K., Ekelund, J., Peltonen, L., Raitakari, O. T., and Keltikangas-Jarvinen, L. (2006). Sociodemographic characteristics moderate the association between DRD4 and novelty seeking. *Personality and Individual Differences, 40*, 533–543.

Larsen, J. T., McGraw, A. P., and Cacioppo, J. T. (2001). Can people feel happy and sad at the same time? *Journal of Personality and Social Psychology, 81*, 684–696.

Levine, B. (2004). Autobiographical memory and the self in time. *Brain and Cognition, 55*, 54–68.

Li, J., Wang, L., and Fischer, K. W. (2004). The organization of Chinese shame concepts? *Cognition and Emotion, 18*, 767–797.

Lutz, C. (1982). The domain of emotional words in Ifaluk. *American Ethnologist, 9*, 113–128.

Manuck, S. B., Flory, J. D., Ferrell, R. E., and Muldoon, M. F. (2004). Socio-economic status covaries with central nervous system serotonergic responsivity as a function of allelic variation in the serotonin transporter gene-linked polymorphic region. *Psychoneuroendocrinology, 29*, 651–668.

Marui, T., Hashimoto, O., Nanba, E., Kato, C., Tochigi, M., Umekage, T., et al. (2004). Gastrin-releasing peptide receptor (GRPR) locus in Japanese subjects with autism. *Brain and Development, 26*, 5–7.

McDougall, W. (1908). *Introduction to social psychology*. London: Methuen.

McGaugh, J. L., and Cahill, L. (2003). Emotion and memory. In R. J. Davidson, K. R. Scherer, and H. H. Goldsmith (Eds.), *Handbook of affective science* (pp. 93–116). New York: Oxford.

Mineka, S., and Zinbarg, R. (2006). A contemporary learning theory perspective on the etiology of anxiety disorder. *American Psychologist, 61*, 10–26.

Moncada, D., and Viola, H. (2006). Phosphorylation state of CREB in the rat hippocampus: A molecular switch between spatial novelty and spatial familiarity? *Neurobiology of Learning and Memory, 86*, 9–18.

Moore, C. C., Romney, K., Hsia, T. L., and Rusch, C. D. (1999). The universality of the semantic structure of emotion terms: Methods for the study of inter- and intra-cultural variability. *American Anthropologist, 101*, 529–546.

Morley-Fletcher, S., Polanza, P., Parolaro, D., Vigaro, D., and Laviola, G. (2003). Intra-uterine position has long term influences on brain mu-opioid receptor densities and behavior in mice. *Psychoneuroendicrinology, 28*, 386–400.

Nair, D. G. (2005). About being BOLD. *Brain Research Reviews, 50*, 229–243.

Nilsson, K. W., Sjoberg, R. L., Dambey, M., Leppert, J., Ohrvik, J., Alm, P. O., et al. (2005). Role of monoamine oxidase A genotype and psychosocial factors in male adolescent criminal activity. *Biological Psychiatry, 59*, 121–127.

Öhman, A., and Wiens, S. (2004). The concept of an evolved fear module and cognitive theories of anxiety. In A. S. R. Manstead, N. Frijda, and A. Fischer (Eds.), *Feelings and emotions* (pp. 58–80). New York: Cambridge University Press.

Osgood, C. E., Suci, G. J., and Tannenbaum, P. H. (1957). *The measurement of meaning*. Urbana, IL: University of Illinois Press.

Paquette, V., Levesque, J., Memsour, B., Leroux, J. M., Beaudoin, G., Bourguin, T., et al. (2003). "Change the mind and you change the brain." *Neuroimage, 18*, 401–410.

Peper, M. (2006). Imaging emotional brain functions. *Journal of Physiology-Paris, 99*, 293–307.

Petty, F., Padala, P. R., Ramaswamy, S., Almeida, M., Monnahan, M., and Wilson, D. R. (2006). Predictors of treatment response in PTSD: Childhood trauma, social rank, defeat, and entrapment. *Biological Psychiatry Supplement, 59*, 156S.

Phelps, E. A. (2006). Emotion and cognition. *Annual Review of Psychology, 57*, 27–53.

Pjrek, E., Winkler, D., Heiden, A., Praschak-Rieder, N., Willeit, M., Konstantinidis, A., et al. (2004). Seasonality of birth in seasonal affective disorder. *Journal of Clinical Psychiatry, 65*, 1389–1393.

Pripfl, J., Robinson, S., Leodolter, U., Moser, E., and Bauer, H. (2006). EEG reveals the effect of fMRI scanner noise on noise-sensitive subjects. *Neuroimage, 31*, 332–341.

Redd, A. J., Chamberlain, V. F., Kearney, V. F., Stover, D., Karafet, T., Calderon, K., et al. (2006). Genetic structure among 38 populations from the United States based on 11 U.S. core Y chromosome STRs. *Journal of Forensic Science, 51*, 580–585.

Rich, G. J. (1928). A biochemical approach to the study of personality. *Journal of Abnormal and Social Psychology, 23*, 158–179.

Rothbart, M. K. (1989). Temperament in childhood. In J. A. Kohnstamm, J. E. Bates, and M. K. Rothbart (Eds.), *Temperament in childhood* (pp. 59–76). New York: Wiley.

Russell, J. A. (1991). Culture and the categorization of emotions. *Psychological Bulletin, 110*, 426–450.
Saucier, G. (2003). Factor structures of English-language personality type-nouns. *Journal of Personality and Social Psychology, 85*, 695–708.
Schafer, A., Schienle, A., and Vaitl, D. (2005). Stimulus type and design influence hemodynamic responses towards visual disgust and fear elicitors. *International Journal of Psychophysiology, 57*, 53–59.
Scherer, K. R. (2004). Feelings integrate the central representation of appraisal-driven response organization in emotion. In A. S. R. Manstead, N. Frijda, and A. Fischer (Eds.), *Feelings and emotions* (pp. 136–157). New York: Cambridge University Press.
Simm, R. W., and Nath, L. E. (2004). Gender and emotion. *American Journal of Sociology, 109*, 1137–1176.
Sivan, Y., Laudon, M., Tauman, R., and Zisapel, N. (2001). Melatonin production in healthy infants: Evidence for seasonal variations. *Pediatric Research, 49*, 63–68.
Smith, R. (1992). *Inhibition*. Berkeley, CA: University of California Press.
Sperli, F., Spinelli, L., Pollo, C., and Seeck, M. (2006). Contralateral smile and laughter, but no mirth, induced by electrical stimulation of the cingulate cortex. *Epilepsia, 47*, 440–443.
Stabell, K. E., Andreson, S., Bakke S. J., Bjornaes, H., Borchgrevink, H. M., Heminghyt, E., et al. (2004). Emotional responses during unilateral amobarbitol anesthesia: Differential hemispheric contributions? *Acta Neurologica Scandinavia, 110*, 313–321.
Stark, R., Schienle, A., Walter, B., Kirsch, P., Blecker, C., Ott, U., et al. (2004). Hemodynamic effects of negative emotional pictures- a test-retest analysis. *Neuropsychobiology, 50*, 108–118.
Steptoe, A., Kunz-Ebrecht, S. R., Wright, C., and Feldman, P. J. (2005). Socioeconomic position and cardiovascular and neuroendocrine responses following cognitive challenge in old age. *Biological Psychology, 69*, 149–166.
Thomas, L., Purvis, C. C., Drew, J. E., Abramovich, D. R., and Williams, L. M. (2002). Melatonin receptors in human fetal brain: 2-[(125)I] iodomelatonin binding and MT1 gene expression. *The Journal of Pineal Research, 33*, 218–224.
Torres-Farton, C., Richter, H. G., Germain, A. M., Valenzuela, G. J., Campino, C., Rojas-Garcia, P., et al. (2004). Maternal melatonin selectively inhibits cortisol production in the primate fetal adrenal gland. *The Journal of Physiology, 554*, 841–856.
Trut, L. N. (1999). Early canid domestication. *American Scientist, 87*, 160–169.
Wang, W., Du, W., Liu, P., Liu, J., and Wang, Y. (2002). Five-factor personality measures in Chinese university students: Effects of one-child policy? *Psychiatry Research, 109*, 37–44.
Wiens, S. (2005). Interoception in emotional experience. *Current Opinion in Neurology, 18*, 442–447.
Wierzbicka, A. (1992). Talk about emotions: Semantics, culture, and cognition. *Cognition and Emotion, 6*, 285–319.
Wilkins, R., and Gareis, E. (2006). Emotion expression and the locution "I love you": A cross-cultural study. *International Journal of Intercultural Relations, 30*, 51–75.
Williams, L. M., Brown, K. J., Palmer, D., Liddell, B. J., Kemp, A. H., Olivieri, G., et al. (2006). The mellow years?: Neural basis of improving emotional stability over age. *The Journal of Neuroscience, 26*, 6422–6430.
Young, P. T. (1936). *Motivation of behavior*. New York: John Wiley.
Zisapel, N. (2001). Melatonin-dopamine interactions: from basic neurochemistry to a clinical setting. *Cell Molecular Neurobiology, 21*, 605–616.

10
Self and Personality

ROSS A. THOMPSON and ELITA AMINI VIRMANI

Introduction

The influence of culture on self and personality development has a long and venerable history. For more than 75 years, scholars in cultural anthropology, personality, developmental psychology, and education have debated how cultural practices help to create the characteristics and self-referential beliefs in its members that enable cultures to function. Included in this rich legacy are the classic ethnographic studies of culture and personality by Ruth Benedict, Margaret Mead, and their colleagues; the psychoanalytically oriented explorations of culturally based early experiences and the formation of adult personality; the Six Culture Study by Whiting and Whiting (1975) and other culturally comparative field studies of childrearing practices and beliefs; and more recent research on parent ethnotheories of children and development, the developmental niche, acculturation, and globalization and child development (see Harkness and Super, 2002, for a review). In all of these literatures, culture and the development of self and personality loom large because these developments are central to understanding how cultures create persons.

The view that cultural practices contribute to the social construction of personalities that mesh well with cultural values is provocative. In recent years, however, with growing interest in biological influences on development, studies of culture and personality have increasingly had to consider species-typical universals in developmental processes. One example is the literature on attachment and culture. Attachment theory has traditionally emphasized the deeply rooted biological incentives for infants to develop secure attachments in response to sensitive care (Bowlby, 1982). But a large research literature reveals that there is considerable cultural variability in how the sensitivity of care is associated with attachment security and in the outcomes of a secure or insecure attachment (see Thompson, 2006). To some commentators, this means that the claims of attachment theory concerning parental care and personality development must be reworked for each cultural setting in which attachment is studied (see Rothbaum, Weisz, Pott, Miyake, and Morelli, 2000). An alternative conclusion, however, is that although relational security and parental responsiveness are probably universal requirements for healthy psychological development, how security develops and how sensitivity is conveyed (and assessed) are likely to vary cross-culturally according to local developmental ethnotheories, cultural needs, and ecological constraints. This alternative view reflects the importance of incorporating species-typical influences into an understanding of culture and development, especially when early developmental processes are concerned.

This orientation guides this chapter. Our goal is to profile research on the development of self and culture, a topic of considerable recent research interest because of its importance to personality development. Our analysis focuses on the earliest and most fundamental elements of self-understanding that emerge in infancy and early childhood, and the influence of cultural practices on the emergence of self is discussed. In doing so, the question is asked of how basic (and probably universal) achievements in early self-awareness are affected by practices and values of the culture in which children grow up. By focusing on developments early in life that are biologically and culturally shaped, we are interested in how early and significantly the self becomes enculturated.

This chapter begins with a short reflection on the nature of culture to expand conventional portrayals of the dimensions of cultural variability that might be most influential in the development of self. Then, considered in turn are several critical early achievements in the growth of the self: the initial emergence of subjective self-awareness, the growth of self-recognition, the development of self-regulation, the emergence of the conceptual self, and finally, autobiographical self-awareness. In each case, the goal is to understand cultural variability in practices that shape each of these advances. Of particular interest are studies that connect cultural values, culturally specific care practices, and self-related outcomes in infants and young children.

Conceptualizing Culture in Relation to Self and Personality

When considering the development of self within a cultural context, researchers have typically portrayed cultural conceptions of self according to two dimensions; independent (or individualist) cultures are contrasted with interdependent (or collectivist) cultures (e.g., Markus and Kitayama, 1991; Shweder et al., 1998; Triandis, 1989). Markus and Kitayama (1991), for example, portray self-construal in independent cultures as emphasizing separateness from the social context, internal attributes, and the ability to assert oneself as unique and self-contained. By contrast, the self in interdependent cultures is portrayed as emphasizing connectedness, external roles, self in relation to others, and the ability to forego one's own desires in the interest of group goals. In general, the United States and Western European societies are assumed to reflect the independent orientation, and certain Asian, South American, and African cultures are considered to be interdependent.

Critics of this approach have pointed out the remarkable heterogeneity of cultural approaches to the self within each orientation, as well as the changes that societies undergo intergenerationally and with the impact of globalization. Furthermore, this approach neglects cultural systems that span the independent–interdependent distinction. Kagitcibasi (1996, 2005) has proposed, for example, that a third orientation bridges the preceding two and is associated with a sense of self that is both autonomous (agentic) and relational. She argues that this orientation is found most often in collectivist societies that are experiencing increased urbanization and industrialization and in which psychological interdependence is valued while material dependence among family members is lower than in interdependent societies.

These dimensions of cultural variability are important for our analysis only if they are associated with differences in family practices and childrearing behaviors that influence developing self and personality in children. In general, cultural psychologists argue that these orientations are indeed transmitted to children, beginning early in life, in parenting practices, family customs, and the broader structure of family life (e.g., Harkness and Super, 2002; Keller, 2007; Rogoff, 2003; Shweder et al., 1998). According to this view, interdependent cultures are associated with parenting practices emphasizing child obedience through control-oriented (e.g., authoritarian) parenting methods, close relationships, and other practices supporting a self that is high in relatedness and compliance and low in autonomy. By contrast, independent cultures are associated with greater affection and more child-centered, permissive parenting practices promoting self-reliance and personal privacy. Kagitcibasi (1996, 2005) argues that families in societies with an autonomous-relational orientation are more likely to enlist practices involving both parental control and child self-determination in which relational connectedness is also emphasized (such as authoritative parenting). Keller (2007) notes that from early in life, caregivers from interdependent systems are more likely to exhibit close physical contact with young offspring, face-to-face interaction, and other practices emphasizing relational closeness, whereas those from independent cultures are more likely to emphasize object stimulation, contingent responsiveness (fostering a sense of agency), and sensitivity to infant signals across a distance.

The following section examines research exploring whether these practices can be observed in different cultural systems and, equally importantly, whether they are associated with the development of self in young children.

Culture and the Development of Self

How does the "self" develop? One conclusion from the research literature is that the "development of self" is not a singular achievement but rather a gradual process as different features of self-awareness emerge in the early years. According to Thompson (2006), an early foundation of the development of self is the emergence of *existential or subjective self-awareness* (James's [1890] "I-self") during the first year as the result of certain perceptual affordances, contingency awareness, and the experience of agency. These experiences provide infants with a basic subjective self-awareness that helps to organize their experiences and perceptions. By the end of the first year, extended episodes of social interaction combined with a dawning awareness of others' perceptions, intentions, and emotions contribute to the emergence of the *intersubjective self*. *Featural self-recognition* (James's [1890] "me-self"), which is most commonly manifested in mirror self-recognition, is an achievement of the second year. The second year also witnesses the beginning of *self-regulation* as toddlers acquire the skills for managing their behavior in relation to a standard; this process continues for several years. Later, as young children begin to think self-referentially and as theory of mind informs their understanding of themselves and others, early childhood witnesses the emergence of the *conceptual self* by which children think about and refer to their inner experiences, characteristics, and traits. By ages 4 and 5 years, a new capacity for *autobiographical self-awareness* emerges as young children memorially "tag" certain past experiences as meaningful to the self in the present. Other aspects of self-awareness continue to emerge as young children become capable of thinking of themselves in a temporal context and in increasingly complex ways, underscoring that the "development of self" is an extended process of psychological growth.

Not all of these features of the developing self have been studied in a culturally comparative context, but the results of recent studies reviewed in the following sections suggest that culture is an important developmental context for emergent self-understanding.

Subjective Self-Awareness and Intersubjectivity

How do young infants develop an initial sense of self—that is, an implicit subjective frame of reference for organizing their interactions with the social and nonsocial world? Early experiences of contingency, in which the infant's behavior reliably elicits an environmental response, are likely to be an important influence (Gergely and Watson, 1999). Indeed, whether contingent responding derives from a nonsocial crib mobile (that moves when babies kick their legs) or a social partner (who smiles in response to the baby's smiles), it elicits a young infant's interest and pleasure probably because it provides some of the earliest experiences of agency and consolidates a sense of the self as a potent actor on environmental events.

Keller (2007) argues that in face-to-face interaction with young infants, parents from independent and interdependent cultural systems respond differently because of their different values concerning infant development. More specifically, parents from independent cultures are more likely to respond contingently to infant cues because of their attention the child's unique emotional expressions and to support the baby's experience of agency and self-efficacy. In a study of mothers with their 3-month-old infants from German and Greek urban middle-class families, Keller et al. (2003) observed mothers and infants in free play episodes lasting 15 minutes, and subsequently, they conducted a detailed analysis of the video records. German families were assumed to reflect their culture's independent orientation, and Greek families were assumed to reflect the autonomous-relational orientation identified by Kagitcibasi. The researchers found, as expected, that whereas Greek mothers exhibited more smiling and warmth in their interactions, German mothers were more contingently responsive to infant signals.

Although there were no assessments of infant self-awareness in this study, a companion study by Keller, Kärtner, Borke, Yovsi, and Kleis (2005) found similar differences between German middle-class mothers and mothers from the rural Nso community in Cameroon, who are members of an interdependent culture. German mothers were more contingently responsive to their 3-month-olds, and when children's mirror self-recognition was subsequently assessed at 18 to 20 months, German children were more likely to recognize themselves than were Cameroonian toddlers. Moreover, infants in both cultural groups whose mothers had been more contingent in their interactive behavior at 3 months tended to exhibit greater self-recognition at the follow-up assessment. Although these findings are suggestive, it will be important in future research to assess early self-awareness as a function of maternal contingent responding and to explore later maternal behaviors that may also promote featural self-recognition in toddlers.

Other researchers have also examined early mother–infant interaction in different cultures in ways potentially relevant to the development of intersubjective self-awareness. In a series of studies, Bornstein and his colleagues analyzed observations of the interactions of mothers with their 5-month-olds in Tokyo and New York (Bornstein, Azuma, Tamis-LeMonda, and Ogino, 1990; Bornstein, Toda, Azuma, Tamis-LeMonda, and Ogino, 1990; see also Bornstein et al., 1992). Although similarities between mothers in the different cultural contexts were more prominent than differences, different patterns of maternal responsiveness emerged with respect to infant attention. Specifically, when Tokyo 5-month-olds looked toward their mothers, mothers tended to encourage infants to attend to the environment, but when infants were gazing at objects or events in the environment, mothers encouraged infants to look at them. By contrast, New York mothers tended to encourage their infants to look in whatever directions the infant chose. The authors interpreted these differences to reflect broader cultural patterns, with the American emphasis on fostering independent initiative and exploratory competence contrasted with the Japanese emphasis on controlling children's exploration and guiding it interpersonally. These differences could be relevant to the development of intersubjectivity during the first year, particularly as Japanese mothers insinuate themselves into infant orientation to the environment to promote *sunaosa*, or receptivity to adult behavior (Bornstein, Toda, et al., 1990).

This study was not designed to include an independent assessment of infant self-awareness or social responsiveness to determine whether these differences in maternal behavior influenced early intersubjectivity, and such an inquiry is a worthwhile topic for future research. This is especially so because the first year is when, in some communal cultures such as the Gusii of Kenya and Marquesas Islanders, infants become oriented toward others as well as the caregiver in everyday social activities (Tamis-Lemonda, Uzgiris, and Bornstein, 2002).

Self-Recognition

To many developmental scientists in Western countries, the ability to recognize one's mirror image by 18 to 24 months is the hallmark of the development of self. This criterion reflects the orientation of Western cultures toward the independent, autonomous child whose capacity to identify her or his unique physical features, independent of the social context, is a critical indicator of self-awareness. As Rogoff (2003) and other developmental cultural scientists have noted, mirrors are not familiar cultural tools in all societies, and more fundamentally, physical self-recognition may be a more important marker of individuality and self-awareness in Western than non-Western contexts. This is an important interpretive framework for research on cultural practices and the development of mirror self-recognition in toddlers.

As noted earlier, Keller et al. (2005) found that at 18 to 20 months, toddlers from German urban middle-class families were significantly more likely to recognize their mirror images than were toddlers from rural Nso Cameroonian farming families. Furthermore, mirror self-recognition was marginally associated with the contingency of maternal responsiveness during interactions with the infant at 3 months; infants who experienced greater interactive contingency tended to subsequently exhibit greater self-recognition at 18 to 20 months. A companion study extended these findings by comparing Nso toddlers with toddlers from Greek urban middle-class families (presumed to reflect an integrated autonomous-relational orientation) and toddlers from Costa Rican middle-class families, who were expected to be in between the Nso and Greek samples in their independent–interdependent orientation (Keller et al., 2004). Greek toddlers exhibited the greatest rate of mirror self-recognition, and Nso toddlers exhibited the least, as expected, with the Costa Rican toddlers midway between the other two groups. The frequency of object-oriented stimulation during mother–infant free play at 3 months, which was highest among Greek families, and mutual eye contact were significant predictors of individual differences in subsequent toddler self-recognition. The researchers interpreted these findings to reflect how characteristics of the interactive style of mothers in more independent cultures, including an emphasis on object-oriented stimulation to promote curiosity and exploration and the contingency of responding that is manifested in mutual gazing, facilitate the development of independent agency that is especially manifested in featural self-recognition.

A short-term follow-up study of these children found that during the 6 weeks after the mirror assessment, the rate of self-recognition of Nso toddlers increased dramatically, even though they still lagged behind German toddlers at the end of the follow-up period (Keller, 2007). These findings raise questions concerning the significance of differential rates of acquisition of physical self-recognition in toddlers from different cultural contexts and whether these differences have long-term significance for self-understanding.

Self-Regulation

The development of self-regulation is another advance in the growth of self because it reflects young children's ability to apply an evaluative standard to themselves. As Kopp's (1982) analysis shows, self-regulation has an extended developmental timetable because its constituent achievements, such as the growth of behavioral self-control, representations of evaluative standards, and self-monitoring, are slowly developing in early childhood. With respect to culture and the developing self, researchers have been particularly interested in differences in self-regulation manifested in children's compliance with a parental request rather than a self-generated standard. This is important because compliance to a parent reflects the child's willingness to preference a caregiver's request over the child's own desires (such as in a toy clean-up task), in contrast with alternative approaches in which self-regulation is indexed by the child's independent initiative (e.g., a delay of gratification task). Culture may be differentially relevant to each kind of self-regulatory activity.

In the study by Keller et al. (2004) described earlier, 18- to 20-month-olds from Greek, Costa Rican, and Cameroonian Nso families were also observed at home in procedures designed to assess self-regulation. These included assessments of compliance to maternal requests (mother asking the child to bring objects and to put them away) and of compliance to the experimenter's prohibition (resisting a forbidden treat in the mother's presence). The researchers found that in both assessments, Nso toddlers showed significantly greater rates of "internal regulation" (i.e., compliance without reminders), especially compared with the Greek toddlers who were more likely to be noncompliant. Toddlers from Costa Rican families were between the other two groups. In predicting individual differences in compliance across cultural groups based on observations of mother–infant play at 3 months, the researchers found that the amount of close body contact between mother and baby (which was highest for Nso families) was the strongest predictor of later differences in internal regulation. They interpreted these findings to reflect the early cultivation of relational closeness by parents in interdependent societies as a motivational foundation for the child's subsequent obedience. By contrast, in more independent societies, there are fewer cultural incentives to foster obedience because even a child's noncompliance, although annoying to parents, is often regarded as a healthy expression of autonomy and self-determination.

This conclusion is supported by other cultural studies of compliance and self-regulation. Chen et al. (2003) observed Chinese and Canadian 2-year-olds with their mothers in a laboratory play session followed by assessments of child compliance during a mother-initiated clean-up task and the experimenter's request that the child not play with an attractive toy in the mother's presence. Chinese toddlers most often exhibited "committed compliance" (enthusiastic and self-regulated cooperation), whereas Canadian toddlers more often displayed "situational compliance" (cooperative with maternal prompts) or overt protest. Independent self-reported assessments of maternal childrearing attitudes were used to predict individual differences in toddlers' compliance and also revealed cultural differences. Whereas maternal warmth and inductive reasoning were positively associated with committed compliance (and negatively associated with situational compliance) for Chinese families, reasoning was associated only with situational compliance for Canadians. Maternal punishment orientation was positively associated with situational compliance in Chinese toddlers, but not Canadian toddlers. These findings suggest, as the researchers argue, that different forms of child self-regulation have different meanings for parents within different cultural systems. Consistent with the values of an interdependent culture, Chinese mothers expect cooperation from their children and enlist socialization efforts to foster it through relational activity, such as warmth and reasoning (as well as punishing behavior that is not fully cooperative). Canadian mothers, however, place a greater value on the child's independence and self-assertion, which may be manifested in the kind of compliance that requires adult monitoring and reminders. This view is supported by a companion report analyzing maternal and child behavior during a play session in an expanded sample. Chinese mothers devoted a relatively greater proportion of their play time to "connectedness" behavior (e.g., cooperative play, sitting close to the child, communicating frequently), whereas Canadian mothers were higher in "autonomy" behavior (e.g., encouragement of independent initiative or decision making), and their children exhibited similar differences in their play behavior (Liu et al., 2005).

The development of self-regulation thus appears to become associated with different motivational foundations for young children from independent and interdependent societies. In some Asian cultures, parental practices cultivating relational closeness heighten the child's compliance by tying cooperation to the maintenance of relational harmony. In some Western societies, by contrast, cultural values prize young children's independent initiative as well as obedience, and consequently, children are likely to be more self-interested in their motivation to cooperate with adult goals.

Conceptual Self

Parents begin thinking about their offspring as distinct, unique persons from the child's birth, if not before. They draw conclusions about the child's temperament and personality qualities and evaluate these qualities based on their careful observations of the child's behavior. But children do not derive insight into their own character so early. It is not until late in the second year and early in the third that toddlers exhibit initial indications of psychological forms of self-awareness that can be described as the emergence of the conceptual self. They refer explicitly to themselves (e.g., "Me big!"), for example, and label internal experiences such as their feelings and desires. They assert their competence by refusing assistance, assert ownership, and categorize themselves by gender and size and in other manifest ways. Young children also become sensitive to how their actions are evaluated by others, and self-referential emotions like pride, guilt, shame, and embarrassment begin to appear (see Thompson, 2006, for a review). These advances in psychological self-awareness derive, in part, from the dawning psychological insights accompanying the growth of theory of mind that enable children to understand how their internal experience of desires, intentions, feelings, thoughts, goals, and beliefs differ from those of others (Thompson, 2006). Young children begin to appreciate not only that they have internal characteristics that they can mentally conceptualize, but also that their internal characteristics differ from those of others. By ages 4 or 5 years, moreover, children can explicitly describe themselves using psychological as well as physical and behavioral attributes (Measelle, Ablow, Cowan, and Cowan, 1998).

As young children acquire the capacity to conceptualize themselves in multidimensional ways, the characteristics they attribute to themselves are likely to have social origins. Consistent with Mead's (1934) concept of the "looking glass self," there is considerable evidence that young children appropriate descriptions of themselves that they overhear from (or are directly told by) adults and that their earliest experiences of pride, guilt, and shame derive from how they are evaluated by caregivers (Measelle et al., 1998; Nelson and Fivush, 2004; Stipek, Recchia, and McClintic, 1992; see review by Thompson, 2006). Although young children have multiple sources of information for learning about and evaluating their personal characteristics, parental influences are central (Stipek et al., 1992).

Culture can influence the development of self, therefore, as young children appropriate their parents' evaluations of their characteristics and behaviors because parents' evaluations are influenced by the beliefs and ethnotheories of their culture (see also Kagan, Chapter 9, in this volume). Behavioral inhibition is a characteristic commonly observed in young children that illustrates this culturally based evaluation. Behavioral inhibition describes a pattern of anxious or withdrawn behavior in response to new situations or stimuli, and in Western contexts, it is regarded as psychologically and socially maladaptive and as a risk factor for the development of internalizing disorders and other psychological problems (Rubin, Bukowski, and Parker, 2006). However, in Chinese society, reflecting an interdependent cultural orientation, behavioral inhibition is instead viewed as reflecting mature capacities for self-restraint, obedience, and accommodation to the group (Chen et al., 1998). To the extent that these cultural belief systems are adopted by parents, they are likely to influence how adults evaluate the characteristics of their offspring and reinforce certain attributes rather than others. Behavioral inhibition, among other characteristics, may be appraised much differently in Chinese and Western cultures.

In a study of behavioral inhibition in response to a standardized laboratory assessment, Chen et al. (1998) found that Chinese 2-year-olds displayed significantly more reticence than did Canadian toddlers; they spent significantly more time in physical contact with their mothers and showed greater latency to approach a stranger and a novel toy robot. Maternal responses to an inventory of childrearing beliefs showed that Chinese mothers scored significantly higher than Canadian mothers on items related to the encouragement of achievement, protection and concern, punishment orientation, and rejection, and they scored significantly lower than Canadian mothers on acceptance. This is the constellation of attitudes, emphasizing child obedience, adult direction, and control, that might be expected from mothers of an interdependent cultural system. However, when individual differences in toddlers' behavioral inhibition were associated with these childrearing beliefs, cultural differences were profound. Controlling and rejecting parenting is typically associated with behavioral inhibition in Western samples (Rubin, Hastings, Stewart, Henderson, and Chen, 1997), but punishment orientation and maternal rejection were significantly *negatively* correlated with behavioral inhibition in the Chinese sample. Maternal attitudes of acceptance, encouragement of achievement, and encouragement of independence were positively associated with behavioral inhibition in Chinese toddlers. None of these associations was apparent in the Canadian sample; instead, maternal punishment orientation was significantly *positively* associated with behavioral inhibition, and inhibition was negatively associated with maternal acceptance and encouragement of achievement (Chen et al., 1998). Behavioral inhibition was, in short, associated with a constellation of positive parenting attitudes (acceptance, encouragement, and lack of punitiveness) in the Chinese sample but with more negative maternal attitudes (punitiveness and lack of acceptance) in the Canadian sample (see Bornstein, 1995).

These conclusions are consistent with other studies of parenting practices in Chinese families (Chao and Tseng, 2002), although further research involving direct observations of parent–child interaction at home would help to confirm and enrich this portrayal of parenting. Pending further study, this research suggests that in their affirmative, punitive, encouraging, and critical behaviors toward offspring, parents respond to children's characteristics in ways that reflect broader cultural values and that may therefore shape children's behaviors in the direction of culturally approved qualities. There are other ways, moreover, that parents convey cultural attitudes about personal characteristics and dispositions to young children. One way is through the language that parents share in conversation with young children from early in life.

As a means of representing and sharing knowledge about their inner psychological experiences, language has a revolutionary impact on young children's thinking for several reasons (Thompson, 2006; Thompson, Laible, and Ontai, 2003). First, language lexicalizes psychological experience to specify and provide common referents to the young child's conceptions of emotions, motives, intentions, goals, thoughts, desires, and other internal qualities in themselves and others. As young children acquire words to describe these qualities and verbalize them to others, they become tutored in how these characteristics are represented by the social world in which they live. Second, as language is enlisted into simple conversations with caregivers about shared experiences, young children's direct representations of these experiences confront the different interpretations and inferences of the adult. Because adults approach the experiences they share with young children in a psychologically more sophisticated manner, their representations of events are likely to be highly influential on the child's own thinking about and memory for those experiences. Third, because language incorporates cultural values and beliefs, young children's use of language in their representations of experience enfranchises them into cultural belief systems (Nelson, 1996). Taken together, these influences of language in the context of parent–child conversation reflect both the content and quality of language; it is not only *what* is said, but also *how* it is said that is likely to be influential.

When Chinese and American mothers were observed talking about recent events with their 3-year-olds, cultural differences in the content and the style of maternal discourse were apparent. American mothers were more interactive and elaborative, focusing on the child's preferences and opinions as they co-constructed a shared narrative. By contrast, Chinese mothers were more directive, posing factual questions and using the narrative to underscore moral rules and behavioral standards. In this respect, conversations about events in the recent past served somewhat different purposes for American and Chinese mothers, offering the former an opportunity to help children develop a sense of themselves and providing the latter a context for socializing proper conduct, consistent with broader cultural goals for child development (Wang and Fivush, 2005; Wang, Leichtman, and Davies, 2000). Other researchers have reached similar conclusions. Miller, Wiley, Fung, and Liang (1997), for example, compared the personal storytelling of American and Taiwanese parents with their 2½-year-olds and found that Chinese caregivers were more likely to use storytelling to convey moral and social standards, whereas Americans used stories as a means of entertainment and affirmation. In these contexts, for example, when mothers recalled the child's earlier misbehavior, Chinese mothers emphasized the shame inherent in misconduct, whereas mothers in the United States tended to attribute child misbehavior to spunk or mischievousness (see also Miller, Fung, and Mintz, 1996).

It is not surprising that the content and structure of language in the conversations that parents share with young children should reflect cultural belief systems. After all, adults have represented their experiences according to these belief systems for most of their lives, so it would be natural that these values would also color their conversations with offspring. More importantly, these conversations become a regular feature of parent–child interaction at exactly the period in development when young children are beginning to think of themselves in terms of inner dispositions, characteristics, and traits. This underscores the need for more research that directly relates these cultural differences in adult discourse style to children's emergent conceptual selves. There is little research of this kind. One study, however, found that when Chinese and American young children (preschool through second grade) were asked to describe themselves and recount four autobiographical events, American children described themselves positively, using a richer variety of personal attributes and inner traits, and they provided more elaborate memories focusing on their personal qualities (e.g., roles, preferences, emotions). Chinese children described themselves more modestly and in terms of social roles and characteristics, describing behaviors that were specific to particular contexts. They also provided accounts that centered more on social interactions and daily routines (Wang, 2004, 2006a).

Autobiographical Self

Another important advance in self-understanding emerges during the preschool years with the growth of autobiographical memory. Although infants and toddlers are capable of retaining specific episodic memories over modest periods of time, it is not until age 3½ or 4 years that preschoolers become capable of mnemonically representing certain events as personally significant and relevant to their present selves. As such, the emergence of autobiographical memory builds on the development of a sense of self, knowledge representation, and an awareness of the temporal connections between past and present events (Thompson, 2006).

This is a considerable conceptual achievement, and according to one influential theory, young children become capable of doing so because of the representational assistance of parent–child conversation. Nelson and Fivush (2004) argue that in conversations with caregivers about the recent past, preschoolers are assisted in representing past experiences in a coherent and meaningful manner, understanding the significance of these events for themselves, and conceptualizing how these events relate to their present experience. In their conversations with young children, in other words, parents not only help children understand themselves but also scaffold their memory of the personal past and add narrative content to these personal representations to make them memorable.

Cultural beliefs and values are likely to be incorporated into children's autobiographical memories as parents insinuate into their shared narratives of the child's experiences their own moral judgments, attributional biases, emotional inferences, and other evaluations drawn from the adult's cultural membership. This is illustrated in the studies earlier described that indicate how mothers in China and the United States discuss events in the recent past in different ways. What is the significance of this for the development of autobiographical memory? In one study, Chinese and American 6-year-olds were asked to recount a series of recent memories as well as to tell stories prompted by pictures and verbal leads. The accounts of Chinese children showed greater social engagement, a greater focus on moral correctness and proper behavior, and a heightened concern with authority. By contrast, the stories of American children exhibited a greater autonomous orientation involving more frequent reference to the protagonist's personal preferences, evaluations, and self-determination (Wang and Leichtman, 2000). Similar differences have been found when American children's autobiographical accounts were compared with those of Korean as well as Chinese children, suggesting that these differences in autobiographical narrative may reflect a broader independent–interdependent cultural difference (Han, Leichtman, and Wang, 1998).

Another way of inquiring into the impact of culture on autobiographical memory is to study the earliest autobiographical memories of adults from different cultures. In the studies that have done so, similar differences in the content and style of autobiographical narrative have emerged, with Americans providing long, self-focused, and emotionally elaborate memories focused on personal attributes and Chinese adults providing briefer narratives focused on social activities and routines and emotionally neutral events (Wang, 2001, 2006b). Thus, although much more research is needed that directly relates parent–child conversation to young children's independent autobiographical narratives (see, e.g., Wang, 2006c), these studies suggest that different styles of autobiographical self-reference are apparent in children and adults in Asian societies and in the United States that are consistent with the interdependent and independent cultural values of these societies.

Conclusion

The development of autobiographical memory does not conclude the development of self. In the years that follow, children acquire a more sophisticated grasp of the continuity of self over time, evaluate their strengths and weaknesses across many domains of competency, and create a conception of their enduring personality characteristics. Each of these subsequent advances in self-understanding is also affected by cultural values, but our reason for focusing on the earliest accomplishments of self-awareness is because these are foundational. The initial emergence of subjective self-awareness and intersubjectivity and the early development of self-recognition, self-regulatory ability, the conceptual self, and autobiographical memory are likely to be universal elements of the process by which children worldwide begin to understand who they are. The fact that even these initial developments are significantly affected by cultural beliefs and values, mediated by the practices of caregivers, attests to how early and fundamentally young children become enculturated.

The parental practices through which culture influences the development of self are multifaceted. This research review highlights the importance in infancy of the contingency of parental responsiveness, the warmth and support of close body contact, the parent's responsiveness to the direction of infant attention, and the enlistment of object-oriented stimulation and social stimulation in face-to-face play as some of the means by which babies become enlisted into systems of relational connectedness and interdependency or systems of individual uniqueness and independence (see also Bornstein, Tamis-LeMonda, Hahn, and Haynes, 2007). Somewhat later, as young children become psychologically more sophisticated, parental practices such as inductive reasoning, punitiveness or acceptance, warmth, control, and the co-construction of shared understanding in the context of parent–child conversation become equally potent cultural influences on the development of self. These practices are important not only because they influence how young children implicitly and explicitly begin to understand themselves, but also because they influence how children perceive their temperamental individuality, how children are motivated to exert self-control, and many other aspects of personality development. In these ways, the cultural developmental processes affecting the growth of self-awareness are also broader influences on the development of personality.

This portrayal of the cultural construction of the person is provocative, but this literature is thin, and throughout the chapter, several directions have been offered for much needed further research. A broader concern is that most of the research in this field is correlational, which, even in longitudinal studies, can be interpretively challenging. It can be difficult to know, for instance, whether the association between maternal practices in infancy and subsequent dimensions of self-awareness in toddlerhood are causal or are mediated by other unmeasured aspects of parent–child interaction. The problems of correlational research are enhanced when groups are compared based on differences in "culture" (broadly defined), when group differences or similarities in socioeconomic status, urban or rural residency, education, or exposure to certain cultural tools might accentuate or diminish group differences in parent–child interaction or children's self-reports. These potential confounds are notoriously difficult to control in research of this kind, which makes the replication of patterns of results across different samples particularly important. Finally, it is impressive that researchers who study the development of self in culturally comparative studies are guided by Western portrayals of the development of self, and we have commented on the suitability of mirror self-recognition or compliance with maternal requests as universally appropriate indexes of self for comparative study. We need greater exploration of the nature of indigenous portrayals of the development of self in non-Western societies and how they might illuminate features of the growth of self-awareness that have thus far been unexplored.

Most broadly, of course, it is also valuable to consider whether current research highlights differences between cultural systems at the expense of their commonalities. Consider, for example, the following portrayal of the development of young children's motivation to self-regulate to comply with parental requests:

> Some parent-child dyads establish a mutually responsive orientation (MRO), a relationship that is close, mutually binding, cooperative, and affectively positive…. Children growing up with parents who are responsive to their needs and whose interactions are infused with happy emotions adopt a willing, responsive stance toward parental influence and become eager to embrace parental values and standards for behavior. (Kochanska, 2002, p. 191)

In light of the discussion of this chapter, one might anticipate that this description is based on studies of parent–child interaction in Japan or another interdependent culture. Instead, it is a summary of an influential program of research on early conscience development in middle-class Iowa families. It is not surprising to find that this kind of relationally oriented approach to fostering young children's responsiveness to adult standards would be apparent in United States families, and it highlights how easily culturally comparative studies can exaggerate cultural differences that exist.

The important contribution of these studies, however, is that they underscore how essentially culture is part of the developing self and the multifaceted ways that children become enculturated members from early in life.

Acknowledgments

We are deeply grateful to Dr. Xiangkui Zhang of the Department of Psychology of Northeast Normal University in China for conversations that illuminated this discussion of culture and self.

References

Bornstein, M. H. (1995). Form and function: Implications for studies of culture and human development. *Culture and Psychology, 1*, 123–137.

Bornstein, M. H., Azuma, H., Tamis-LeMonda, C., and Ogino, M. (1990). Mother and infant activity and interaction in Japan and in the United States: I. A comparative macroanalysis of naturalistic exchanges. *International Journal of Behavioral Development, 13*, 267–287.

Bornstein, M. H., Tamis-LeMonda, C. S., Hahn, C.-S., and Haynes, O. M. (2007). Maternal responsiveness to young children at three ages: Longitudinal analysis of a multidimensional, modular, and specific parenting construct. Unpublished manuscript, Child and Family Research, National Institute of Child Health and Human Development, Washington, DC.

Bornstein, M. H., Tamis-LeMonda, C. S., Tal, J., Ludemann, P., Toda, S., Rahn, C. W., et al. (1992). Maternal responsiveness to infants in three societies: The United States, France, and Japan. *Child Development, 63*, 808–821.

Bornstein, M. H., Toda, S., Azuma, H., Tamis-LeMonda, C., and Ogino, M. (1990). Mother and infant activity and interaction in Japan and in the United States: II. A comparative microanalysis of naturalistic exchanges focused on the organization of infant attention. *International Journal of Behavioral Development, 13*, 289–308.

Bowlby, J. (1982). *Attachment and loss: Volume 1. Attachment* (2nd ed.). New York: Basic.

Chao, R., and Tseng, V. (2002). Parenting of Asians. In M. H. Bornstein (Ed.), *Handbook of parenting: Volume 4. Social conditions and applied parenting* (2nd ed., pp. 59–93). Mahwah, NJ: Erlbaum.

Chen, X., Hastings, P. D., Rubin, K. H., Chen, H., Cen, G., and Stewart, S. L. (1998). Child-rearing attitudes and behavioral inhibition in Chinese and Canadian Toddlers: A cross-cultural study. *Developmental Psychology, 34*, 677–686.

Chen, X., Rubin, K. H., Liu, M., Chen, L., Wang, L., Li, D., et al. (2003). Compliance in Chinese and Canadian toddlers: A cross-cultural study. *International Journal of Behavioral Development, 27*, 428–436.

Gergely, G., and Watson, J. (1999). Early socio-emotional development: Contingency perception and the social-biofeedback model. In P. Rochat (Ed.), *Early social cognition* (pp. 101–136). Mahwah, NJ: Erlbaum.

Han, J., Leichtman, M., and Wang, Q. (1998). Autobiographical memory in Korean, Chinese, and American children. *Developmental Psychology, 34*, 701–713.

Harkness, S., and Super, C. M. (2002). Culture and parenting. In M. H. Bornstein (Ed.), *Handbook of parenting: Volume 2. Biology and ecology of parenting* (2nd ed., pp. 253–280). Mahwah, NJ: Erlbaum.

James, W. (1890). *The principles of psychology*. New York: Henry Holt.

Kagitcibasi, C. (1996). The autonomous-relational self: A new synthesis. *European Psychologist, 1*, 180–186.

Kagitcibasi, C. (2005). Autonomy and relatedness in cultural context: Implications for self and family. *Journal of Cross-Cultural Psychology, 36*, 403–422.

Keller, H. (2007). *Cultures of infancy*. Mahwah, NJ: Erlbaum.

Keller, H., Kärtner, J., Borke, J., Yvosi, R., and Kleis, A. (2005). Parenting styles and the development of the categorical self: A longitudinal study on mirror self-recognition in Cameroonian Nso and German families. *International Journal of Behavioral Development, 29*, 496–504.

Keller, H., Papaligoura, Z., Kuensemueller, P., Voelker, S., Papaeliou, C., Lohaus, A., et al. (2003). Concepts of mother-infant interaction in Greece and Germany. *Journal of Cross-Cultural Psychology, 34*, 677–689.

Keller, H., Yovsi, R., Borke, J., Kärtner, J., Jensen, H., and Papaligoura, Z. (2004). Developmental consequences of early parenting experiences: Self-recognition and self-regulation in three cultural communities. *Child Development, 75*, 1745–1760.

Kochanska, G. (2002). Mutually responsive orientation between mothers and their young children: A context for the early development of conscience. *Current Directions in Psychological Science, 11*, 191–195.

Kopp, C. B. (1982). Antecedents of self-regulation: A developmental perspective. *Developmental Psychology, 18*, 199–214.

Liu, M., Chen, X., Rubin, K., Zheng, S., Cui, L., Li, D., et al. (2005). Autonomy- vs. connectedness-oriented parenting behaviours in Chinese and Canadian mothers. *International Journal of Behavioral Development, 29*, 489–495.

Markus, H. R., and Kitayama, S. (1991). Culture and the self: Implications for cognition, emotion, and motivation. *Psychological Review, 98*, 224–253.

Measelle, J., Ablow, J., Cowan, P., and Cowan, C. (1998). Assessing young children's views of their academic, social, and emotional lives: An evaluation of the self-perception scales of the Berkeley Puppet Interview. *Child Development, 69*, 1556–1576.

Mead, G. H. (1934). *Mind, self, and society*. Chicago: University of Chicago Press.

Miller, P., Fung, H., and Mintz, J. (1996). Self-construction through narrative practices: A Chinese and American comparison of early socialization. *Ethos, 24*, 237–280.

Miller, P. J., Wiley, A. R., Fung, H., and Liang, C.-H. (1997). Personal storytelling as a medium of socialization in Chinese and American families. *Child Development, 68*, 557–568.

Nelson, K. (1996). *Language in cognitive development: The emergence of the mediated mind*. New York: Cambridge.

Nelson, K., and Fivush, R. (2004). The emergence of autobiographical memory: A social-cultural developmental theory. *Psychological Review, 111*, 486–511.

Rogoff, B. (2003). *The cultural nature of human development.* New York: Oxford University Press.

Rothbaum, F., Weisz, J., Pott, M., Miyake, K., and Morelli, G. (2000). Attachment and culture: Security in the United States and Japan. *American Psychologist, 55*, 1092–1104.

Rubin, K. H., Bukowski, W. M., and Parker, J. G. (2006). Peer interactions, relationships, and groups. In W. Damon and R. M. Lerner (Eds.), N. Eisenberg (Vol. Ed.), *Handbook of child psychology: Volume 3. Social, emotional, and personality development* (6th ed., pp. 571–645). New York: Wiley.

Rubin, K. H., Hastings, P. D., Stewart, S. L., Henderson, H. A., and Chen, X. (1997). The consistency and concomitants of inhibition: Some of the children, all of the time. *Child Development, 68*, 467–483.

Shweder, R. A., Goodnow, J. J., Hatano, G., LeVine, R. A., Markus, H. R., and Miller, P. J. (1998). The cultural psychology of development: One mind, many mentalities. In W. Damon and R. M. Lerner (Eds.), R. M. Lerner (Vol. Ed.), *Handbook of child psychology: Volume 1. Theoretical models of human development* (6th ed., pp. 716–792). New York: Wiley.

Stipek, D., Recchia, S., and McClintic, S. (1992). Self-evaluation in young children. *Monographs of the Society for Research in Child Development, 57*, 1–98.

Tamis-LeMonda, C., Uzgiris, I., and Bornstein, M. (2002). Play in parent-child interactions. In M. H. Bornstein (Ed.), *Handbook of parenting: Volume 5. Practical issues in parenting* (2nd ed., pp. 221–241). Mahwah, NJ: Erlbaum.

Thompson, R. A. (2006). The development of the person: Social understanding, relationships, self, conscience. In W. Damon and R. M. Lerner (Eds.), N. Eisenberg (Vol. Ed.), *Handbook of child psychology: Volume 3. Social, emotional, and personality development* (6th ed., pp. 24–98). New York: Wiley.

Thompson, R. A., Laible, D. J., and Ontai, L. L. (2003). Early understanding of emotion, morality, and the self: Developing a working model. In R. V. Kail (Ed.), *Advances in child development and behavior* (Vol. 31, pp. 137–171). San Diego, CA: Academic.

Triandis, H. (1989). The self and social behavior in differing cultural contexts. *Psychological Review, 96*, 506–520.

Wang, Q. (2001). Culture effects on adults' earliest childhood recollection and self-description: Implications for the relation between memory and the self. *Journal of Personality and Social Psychology, 81*, 220–233.

Wang, Q. (2004). The emergence of cultural self-constructs: Autobiographical memory and self-description in European American and Chinese children. *Developmental Psychology, 40*, 3–15.

Wang, Q. (2006a). Culture and the development of self-knowledge. *Current Directions in Psychological Science, 15*, 182–187.

Wang, Q. (2006b). Earliest recollections of self and others in European American and Taiwanese young adults. *Psychological Science, 17*, 708–714.

Wang, Q. (2006c). Relations of maternal style and child self-concept to autobiographical memories in Chinese, Chinese immigrant, and European American 3-year-olds. *Child Development, 77*, 1794–1809.

Wang, Q., and Fivush, R. (2005). Mother-child conversations of emotionally salient events: Exploring the functions of emotional reminiscing in European-American and Chinese families. *Social Development, 14*, 473–495.

Wang, Q., and Leichtman, M. D. (2000). Same beginnings, different stories: A comparison of American and Chinese children's narratives. *Child Development, 71*, 1329–1346.

Wang, Q., Leichtman, M., and Davies, K. (2000). Sharing memories and telling stories: American and Chinese mothers and their 3-year-olds. *Memory, 8*, 159–178.

Whiting, B. B., and Whiting, J. W. M. (1975). *The children of six cultures: A psychocultural analysis.* Cambridge, MA: Harvard University Press.

11
Gender

DEBORAH L. BEST

Introduction

Sex is often used to refer to biological differences between males and females, and gender is often used to refer to learned behaviors and expectations. Yet, in truth, it is impossible to separate the biological and social influences on the development of cultural and self-perceptions of male and female roles and identity. Using separate terms for gender and sex sets up an arbitrary, unnecessary dichotomy between biological and environmental influences (Fausto-Sterling, 2000; Hoyenga and Hoyenga, 1993). Human beings are products of both biology and environment, past and present, simultaneously and inseparably. From conception to death, gender directs and influences how children are reared and what roles they learn and carry out.

Sex typing, the development of gender-related differences in children, changes with age and is a multidimensional process (Huston, 1983). To examine the various dimensions, Ruble and Martin (1998) created a sex-typing matrix of six areas (biological gender, activities and interests, personal-social attributes, gender-based social relationships, stylistic and symbolic content, and gender-related values) and four content aspects (beliefs, self-perceptions, preferences or attitudes, and behavioral tendencies). Gender differences are found in all areas, but few studies have looked at interrelationships among them (e.g., the exception is Cheung Mui-ching's [1986] examination of gender stereotypes and self- and ideal self-descriptions of adolescents). Most of the cross-cultural research has dealt with differences in socialization, gender roles, and sex stereotypes, and these will be the focus of this chapter.

Historical and Demographic Considerations on Gender, Development, and Culture

In the earliest human societies in prehistory (circa 40,000 to 4,000 years before the present), among Neanderthals, there was practically no sexual dimorphism, that is, no sex-associated differences in body size or robustness suggesting no routinized division of labor. Among the Upper Paleolithic peoples approximately 12,000 years ago, formalized division of labor based on skill, not sex, began to appear. By the Mesolithic era, it is likely that gender served as a principle structuring much of everyday life. Approximately 4,000 years ago, craft specialization was in full swing, and much of the work was divided along gender lines, such as corn processing and beer making by women in Mexico, textile production by men in China, and metal work by men in central and eastern Europe (Dobres, 2004).

There is historical and anthropological evidence from societies around the world where gender was not based on morphology or chromosomes but on a person's role in reproduction, religious rituals, or production of food and other necessities (Meade and Wiesner-Hanks, 2004). In most cultures, adults have been gendered male and female, in the usual binary sex schemata.

However, in some indigenous cultures, children, older adults, or transgendered individuals were considered to be a third or fourth gender (e.g., *bissu* of Southeast Asia, two-spirit people among some Native American groups), and one's gender could change across the life span (Andaya, 2004; Williams, 1992).

Gender was salient in social identity and served as an organizing principle long ago as well as in the modern world, although it is likely that gender was quite different from today. Gender meaningfulness, organization of relationships, practices, and impact on work, status, and values has certainly evolved over time. Major shifts in gender configuration and beliefs were likely involved both in changes in everyday life and in wholesale cultural transformations that have taken place across human history (Dobres, 2004).

Central Issues in Gender, Development, and Culture

Examining the roles of biology and socialization, the long-standing nature–nurture controversy in developmental science is critical for understanding gender development.

Nature: The Biological Aspects of Gender

Even though gender and sex are usually treated as categorical variables, in measuring many biological differences between males and females, most attributes are on a continuum rather than falling into a clear dichotomy or typology. For example, people differ in levels of testosterone with some at the higher end of the continuum with most males, others at the lower end with most females, and others ranging across the middle with levels below the typical male but above the typical female. However, with most biological definitions of gender, chromosomes, hormones, gonads, and external anatomy are the determinative factors.

Biological Determinism   Similarities in gender differences across cultures are often used as support for the role of genes and hormones, suggesting genetic or biological determinism. Biological determinism assumes that any biological influence or bias always leads to an irreversible sex difference. Thus, biology is both the necessary and sufficient cause of sex differences. However, biology is neither.

Sex chromosomes and sex hormones do not cause behaviors; they simply change the probability of occurrence of various behaviors (Hoyenga and Hoyenga, 1993; Stewart, 1988). The gene–behavior pathway is bidirectional (Gottlieb, 1983), and similar to how people inherit genes, they may also "inherit" environments by living close to parents and family.

Probabilistic Epigenesis   Genes and environment may act similarly on the developmental process, which reflects the impact of both. Thus, a particular phenotype may come from a gene or from a cultural environment or both (Cairns, Gariépy, and Hood, 1990; Gottlieb, 1997). Genes and environments tend to influence the same developmental processes with equivalent outcomes that work through different mechanisms. As a result, life history strategies (evolutionary patterns of adaptation that differ by developmental stage) can be altered by both genes and developmental environments (Hoyenga and Hoyenga, 1993). Both genes and environment affect brain anatomy and the child's intellectual abilities and traits, and both can lead to stability and change. Indeed, in the sexually dimorphic process, gender is the added factor that may affect the form of the interaction between genes and environmental context.

Nurture: The Psycho-Socio-Cultural Aspects of Gender

Even though biological factors may impose restrictions and predispositions on gender development, sociocultural factors are important determinants of development (Best and Williams,

1993; Munroe and Munroe, 1975/1994; Rogoff, Gauvain, and Ellis, 1984). Culture has profound effects on gender-related behavior, prescribing how babies are delivered, how children are socialized, how children are dressed, what is considered intelligent behavior, what tasks children are taught, and what roles adult men and women will adopt. Even behaviors that are considered biologically determined are governed by culture. Cultural universals in gender differences are often explained by similarities in socialization practices, whereas cultural differences are attributed to differences in socialization.

Children grow up in the context of other people's scripts, which guide their actions long before the children themselves can understand or carry out the culturally appropriate actions. Gender should be examined not only in relation to culture (e.g., social systems, practices, myths, beliefs, rituals), but also in the context of the history and economics of the society (Mukhopadhyay and Higgins, 1998). Mechanisms within a culture that are responsible for developmental changes in gender-related behaviors must account for variation between individuals within the cultural group as well as variation between cultures.

Across time, the interaction between a child's biological makeup and the social world in which he or she lives results in behaviors that sometimes differ by gender. From the moment of birth (e.g., Is it a boy, or is it a girl?), parents interpret the child's biological sex characteristics. The cultural practices they invoke shape the child to fit into his or her particular circumstances.

Theories of Gender Role Development

Most theories recognize the role of gender information readily available in the child's culture. Although maturational theories are no longer in vogue, assumptions about the importance of biological influences have been incorporated into more current theories of sex role development such as evolutionary theory and social role theory.

Evolutionary Theories

Evolutionary theories grew out of early nineteenth century evolutionary thinking (e.g., Darwin, Spencer, Haeckel, Lamarck; see Dixon and Lerner, 1999) and suggest that natural selection shapes the morphology of an organism, which in turn shapes behavioral and psychological tendencies (Kenrick and Luce, 2000). Animals and humans inherit bodies, brains, and behavioral mechanisms that are ready to adapt to their environments and to solve recurring problems from their ancestral past. The measure of evolutionary success is reproductive success, not survival. Sexual selection (e.g., attracting a mate; Geary, 1998) and differential parental investment in offspring (e.g., provision of food, protection from predators; Trivers, 1985) may account for some of the sex differences found throughout the animal kingdom.

Physical and reproductive sex differences are related to sex differences in social behaviors, such as mate preferences (Buss, 1989; Kenrick and Keefe, 1992), aggression (Daly and Wilson, 1988), sexuality (Daly and Wilson, 1988), and childcare (Geary, 1998). Some evolutionary theorists assume that cultural variation in behavior results from a flexible genetic program that unfolds in different environments (Kenrick and Luce, 2000). Öhman (1986) describes an open genetic program in which a cultural pool of information structures learning episodes for members of the social group.

Concerning gender, evolutionary theorists have borrowed the experimental psychology notion of preparedness that originated from research with animal taste aversion (e.g., poison) and with the development of human phobias (e.g., predatory defense system—fear of snakes, spiders; Rozin and Kalat, 1971; Seligman, 1971). Males and females are presumed to enter the world biologically prepared to experience their environments differently, and their experiences shape sex-appropriate behaviors. This is an interesting notion, but presently, there are no data to support such an extension of the preparedness mechanism.

Indeed the broad outline of evolutionary theory may be correct, but the propositions are difficult to test. The precise developmental mechanisms by which gender-differentiated values and norms are transmitted to individuals within a cultural group have not been identified.

Social Role Theory

Differences between male and female behaviors are presumed to result from the different social roles they play, which in turn are a function of the sexual division of labor. The division of labor and the gender power/status hierarchy result from differences in reproductive behaviors and the physical size and strength of women and men, with differences usually favoring men (Wood and Eagly, 2002). The dissimilar social positions of men and women lead to differential gender roles, beliefs (descriptive norms), and expectations about what males and females do. Cultural stereotypes (Ross, 1977) reflect differential social roles. Thus, women are more frequently associated with the domestic role, and the characteristics thought to represent homemakers are ascribed to women in general. Similarly, characteristics thought to exemplify providers are ascribed to men in general (Wood and Eagly, 2002). Cultural expectations promote conformity to gender roles and influence how people think about themselves, their perceptions of masculinity and femininity, and child socialization practices. Gender stereotypes often become the rationalizations that justify differential sex role distributions (Hoffman and Hurst, 1990; Williams and Best, 1982/1990).

Physical sex differences, however, are not the whole story. There is no explanation of why social structures, such as the sexual division of labor and gender hierarchy, are found in most cultural groups. Furthermore, the theory does not identify the mechanisms by which social structures exert their influence on individuals and groups within various cultural settings.

Perhaps Van Leeuwen's (1978) ecological model sheds light on cultural variations. In sedentary, high-food-accumulating societies, socialization differs greatly, with females being trained to be nurturant and compliant. In low-food-accumulating societies (e.g., hunting societies), there is little division of labor by sex; both males and females contribute to subsistence, so socialization is similar for females and males. Cross-cultural variations in gender-related behaviors are likely a product of socialization practices that vary in the degrees of compliance training for girls and boys.

Social Learning Theory

Sears and his colleagues (Sears, Maccoby, and Levin, 1957; Sears, Rau, and Alpert, 1965) revised Freud's conceptions of sex role development by incorporating learning theory's principles of reinforcement and modeling. According to social learning theory, socialization of sex-typed behaviors resulted from differential parenting behaviors—warmth and emotional support from mothers and control and discipline from fathers. Bandura (Bandura, 1969; Bussey and Bandura, 1984) and Mischel (1970) expanded the cognitive aspects of social learning theory, emphasizing the importance of modeling and expectations in the differential treatment of boys and girls.

Observational learning demonstrates how sex typing and gender stereotypes can be passed from parent to child, from one generation to the next, and from one child to another (Hoyenga and Hoyenga, 1993). Girls see fewer same-sex models with power and prestige than do boys, which certainly influences the development of stereotypes.

There is substantial cross-cultural evidence that social learning plays an important role in gender role learning. However, by itself, social learning is not a sufficient explanation. Differential treatment of boys and girls shows wide cross-cultural variation and is not consistently related to differential behavior (Bronstein, 1984; Lamb, Frodi, Hwang, Frodi, and Steinberg, 1982; Sagi Lamb, Shoham, Dvir, and Lewkowicz, 1985). Task assignment and models provide differential cultural learning opportunities for boys and girls and encourage different behaviors. Indeed, peer group socialization within child culture may be more influential in social change than are parents.

Cognitive Stage Theories

Although Piaget embraced biological concepts, such as reflexes, assimilation, and accommodation, his theory went beyond maturation. For Piaget, the invariant stages of cognitive development are not genetically prewired. As they interact with their environments, children actively construct increasingly more sophisticated ways of thinking, schemes, or action structures, for dealing with their environments (Ginsberg and Opper, 1969). The environment has both physical and social interaction effects, which are interactive with one another (Ginsberg and Opper, 1969).

Building on Piagetian theory, Kohlberg (1966) developed a cognitive theory of gender development. Children's understanding of gender develops through a series of stages from gender identity or labeling (achieved by 2½ years), through gender stability (by 3½ years), and finally, gender consistency or constancy (by 4½ to 5 years). The influence of children's experiences on their gender-role orientation is determined by the child's developing cognitive structure.

Cognitive developmental theory was examined by Munroe, Shimmin, and Munroe (1984) in a cross-cultural study with children in American Samoa, Belize, Kenya, and Nepal. They expected gender classification to be more salient for children in the cultures that emphasized gender in their socialization practices (e.g., Kenya, Nepal). Later stages of gender development are dependent on cognitive structures, so they were predicted to appear at about the same time for all groups and to reflect little cultural differences. Children's stages of gender development were consistent with those found in the United States, but unexpectedly, the culture-specific predictions were not supported. Attainment of gender classification capabilities was not related to the salience of gender differentiation within the culture.

Certainly cognitive factors are important in gender development, but it has been difficult to find a relation between stages of gender identity and sex-typed behaviors (Bussey, 1983). Children seem to learn sex-appropriate behaviors before they can translate such behaviors into words. Moreover, the process seems to differ for boys, who show a two-process model (acceptance of masculine behavior and rejection of feminine behavior), and girls, who show a one-process model (acceptance of same-sex behavior only). It would be illuminating to examine further the gender identity acquisition processes across cultures.

Gender Schema Theories

Gender schema theory assumes that notions about gender organize and bias behavior, thinking, and attention to information in one's environment. Environmental information about being male or female leads to the creation of gender schemas that facilitate gender-related processing of new information (Martin, 2000). Accumulated social experiences activate gender schemas and lead to automatic use of gender-related knowledge. Consequently, children come to see themselves and others in terms of gender differences (e.g., boys versus girls, females versus males, masculinity versus femininity). Gender concepts are cognitive constructions that are used to evaluate the appropriateness of behaviors.

Cognitive developmental theory proposes a multidimensional model (Huston, 1983; Ruble and Martin, 1998) of gender-related constructs (e.g., gender identity, gender stereotypes, gender scripts, self-perceptions of masculinity and femininity, expectations about gender-appropriate behaviors). Although interrelationships among these constructs have been hypothesized, only a few have been tested developmentally or cross-culturally. Even fewer have been related to gendered behaviors (e.g., interaction styles, segregation of play groups; Maccoby, 1998).

Pancultural Model of Gender Development

Williams and Best (1982/1990; Best, 2004; Best and Williams, 2001) propose that biological differences set the stage (e.g., females bear children, males have greater physical strength) and lead to a division of labor, with women mainly responsible for childcare and other domestic activities and men primarily responsible for providing and protection. Gender stereotypes that evolve as a rationale for this division of labor assume that each sex has or can develop characteristics congruent with the assigned role. Once established, stereotypes become socialization models that encourage boys to become masculine (adventurous and independent) and girls to become feminine (nurturant and affiliative). Consistent with the ecocultural framework (Berry, Poortinga, Segall, and Dasen, 1992) that recognizes biological influences and cultural influences at both the population and individual level, this model demonstrates how widely different cultures come to associate one set of characteristics with men and another set with women, with only minor variations around these central themes.

Key Classical and Modern Research Studies in Gender, Development, and Culture

Culture and the Socialization of Boys and Girls

The Six Cultures Study   The classic Six Cultures Study (Edwards and Whiting, 1974; Minturn and Lambert, 1964; Whiting, 1963; Whiting and Edwards, 1973) begun in 1954 by teams of social scientists from Harvard, Yale, and Cornell and its sequel, *Children of Different Worlds* (Whiting and Edwards, 1988), represent the first systematic cross-cultural data sets collected in multiple cultures using standard methods. The data focused on child and family life observed over 20 years in communities undergoing immense economic, political, and cultural changes. Mothers and their 3- to 11-year-old children were observed in India, Kenya, Mexico, Okinawa, the Philippines, and the United States, and gender differences were examined in behaviors such as aggression, nurturance, responsibility, and help- and attention-seeking. Findings from these studies will be discussed later in the chapter.

Stereotyping of Toys and Play   Gender roles and behaviors develop within the context of cultural stereotypes about male–female differences. In the United States, as early as age 2 years, children stereotype objects as masculine or feminine (Weinraub et al., 1984), and by age 3 to 4 years, children correctly use stereotypic labels with toys, activities, and occupations (Edelbrock and Sugawara, 1978). In Africa, similar gender stereotyping of toys occurs with girls playing with dolls and boys constructing vehicles and weapons (Bloch and Adler, 1994). By age 4 to 5 years, Sri Lankan village children display gender differences in play, similar to those found with British children (Prosser, Hutt, Hutt, Mahindadasa, and Goonetilleke, 1986). Cultural factors determine the content of children's play (e.g., sword fights versus fashioning cars of wire), and role play allows children to prepare for adult roles, especially for girls, who show more of it than boys (Edwards, 2000).

Gender Trait Stereotypes   For children in the United States, stereotypes about traits associated with men and women are learned somewhat later than stereotypic knowledge of toys and occupations (Best et al., 1977; Reis and Wright, 1982; Williams and Best, 1982/1990). Williams and Best (1982/1990) assessed children's knowledge of adult-defined stereotypes (e.g., women are emotional and gentle, and men are strong and dominant). European American children's knowledge of sex-trait stereotypes increased from kindergarten through high school, with the most dramatic gains during elementary school years. African American children's knowledge of stereotype traits also increased with age but at a slower rate, suggesting that different ethnic or national groups within one country may vary in their stereotype knowledge. Stereotypes become more differentiated with age (Biernat, 1991) and often incorporate gender-incongruent information (e.g., expressive attributes in males, instrumental attributes in females; Hanover, 2000).

Williams and Best (1982/1990) also examined sex stereotypes of 5-, 8-, and 11-year-old children in 25 countries. Although countries varied in learning rates, there was a general developmental pattern of stereotype acquisition beginning prior to age 5, accelerating during the early school years, and becoming complete during adolescence. *Strong, aggressive, cruel, coarse,* and *adventurous* were consistently associated with men by all age groups. *Weak, appreciative, softhearted, gentle,* and *meek* were consistently associated with women. Relative to the other countries studied, stereotype scores were unusually high in Pakistan and relatively high in New Zealand and England. Scores were atypically low in Brazil, Taiwan, Germany, and France. In the more urbanized countries where education is heavily emphasized, children appear to learn stereotypes that are more global and are quite similar to the pancultural ones. Indeed, at age 8 years, high degrees of urbanization facilitated learning the female stereotypes. By the adult level, after "fine-tuning" by the culture, urban and educational influences have less effect on the stereotype traits that have been learned.

Similarities found across diverse cultures with different measures (Albert and Porter, 1986; Intons-Peterson, 1988) suggest that sex stereotypes are universal. However, culture modifies the rate of learning as well as some aspects of content.

Cultural Influences and Agents

Cultural Transmission   Across time, socially useful belief systems are incorporated into cultural practices and traditions. Beliefs concerning the qualities of women and men are absorbed into religion and myth, oral history, and written literature. Heroes and heroines, real or imaginary, embody the stereotypic characteristics of the sexes and may serve as potent models for sex-appropriate characteristics. Central components of the male and female stereotypes are woven into the fabric of every culture and serve to reinforce stereotypic views of the psychological makeup of the sexes. There is considerable variation, from culture to culture, in the particular vehicles that carry the stereotypes. Clearly, within the larger cultural context, the distal influences, as well as more immediate socialization practices that are proximal, interact across the lifespan of the individual and result in gender-related beliefs, attitudes, and role behaviors.

Parental Influences   One of the first influences on the development of gender comes from parents. "Baby X" studies (e.g., sex of the infant is not known to study participants) in the United States have shown that parents and young adults treat infants differently depending on whether they think they are interacting with a girl or a boy (Seavey, Katz, and Zalk, 1975; Sidorowicz and Lunney, 1980). Boys are described as big and strong and are bounced and handled more physically than girls, who are described as pretty and sweet and handled more gently. Even before birth after finding out their child's sex via ultrasound, parents described girls as "finer" and "quieter" than boys, who were described as "more coordinated" than girls (Sweeney and Bradbard, 1989). Parental presumptions such as these reflect the impact of culture on parents' memories of their own past and their assumptions about their child's future. However, culture is a dynamic influence that changes across time. In the United States, parents of the 1950s would never have assumed their daughters would grow up to be soccer players in college, but many parents today would certainly have this expectation.

Such parental expectations are not peculiar to the United States. Greenfield and her colleagues (Greenfield, Brazelton, and Childs, 1989) report that shortly after birth, Zinacanteco babies in Mexico are given objects that are gender appropriate. A father reported giving his son "three green chilies to hold so that it would know to buy chili when it grew up." According to the

Zincanteco saying, "in the newborn baby is the future of our world." Parents assume that things in the future will be as they have been in the past, an assumption of continuity.

Behavioral differences between girls and boys are often attributed to differences in socialization. Barry, Bacon, and Child (1957) examined socialization practices in over 100 societies and found that, generally, boys are reared to achieve and to be self-reliant and independent, whereas girls are reared to be nurturant, responsible, and obedient. However, when Hendrix and Johnson (1985) reanalyzed these data, they found no evidence of a general sex differentiation in socialization, and instead of being polar opposites, the instrumental-expressive components were orthogonal, unrelated dimensions with similar emphases in the training of girls and boys. For both male and female socialization factors, self-reliance and independence had strong positive loadings, and nurturance loaded negatively.

In a meta-analysis, Lytton and Romney (1991) examined 158 North American studies of socialization and found the only significant effect was for the encouragement of sex-typed behaviors. In 17 additional studies from other Western countries, there was a significant sex difference for physical punishment, with boys receiving a greater portion than girls. Differential treatment of boys and girls decreased with age, particularly for disciplinary strictness and encouragement of sex-typed activities.

Overall, socialization studies suggest that there may be subtle differences in how parents treat boys and girls. These differences are only occasionally significant, perhaps because of the ways the behaviors are measured or which parent is being observed. Fathers play an especially important role in signaling the types of behaviors they consider appropriate, particularly for their sons, who have fewer accessible male role models and for whom deviations are considered more undesirable (Jacklin, DiPietro, and Maccoby, 1984). Even if parents do not differentiate between daughters and sons, the same parental treatment may affect girls and boys differently. Research in the United States suggests that gender lessons are finely focused on specific behaviors and that learning often occurs during transitional periods in development when new abilities first emerge, particularly during the toddler period and during adolescence (Beal, 1994).

Parents' behaviors communicate the importance of gender via their reactions to their children's behavior and by the organization of activities within the family. Parent behaviors as well as those of peers, teachers, and other socialization agents help shape sex-appropriate behaviors, toy choices, playmates, and other activities. Peers, task assignment, caregiving, and the educational environment are among the cultural influences that help to socialize children's gender role behaviors.

Peer Influences   Throughout childhood and adolescence, peers play an important role in socialization. In some cultures, boys and girls are separated by the end of infancy (Whiting and Edwards, 1988), and in others, children play freely within mixed age and gender groups (Rogoff, 1990). Peer influence increases as children grow older, helping to structure the transition between childhood and adulthood (Edwards, 1992). Maccoby (1998) suggests that peers may play as important a role as parents, if not more so, in the socialization of gender roles.

Maccoby (1998) has identified three major gender-linked phenomena in children's social development: gender segregation, differentiation of interaction styles, and group asymmetry. Both with American children and cross-culturally (Whiting and Edwards, 1988), as early as age 3 years, there is a powerful tendency for children to seek out playmates of their own sex and to avoid children of the other sex. This tendency strengthens throughout grade school. These segregated playgroups differ in their interaction styles and activities. Boys strive for dominance, play rough, take risks, "grandstand," and are reluctant to reveal weaknesses to each other. In contrast, girls self-disclose more, try to maintain positive social relationships, and avoid open conflict. Same-sex playgroups provide children with useful socialization experiences and the venue for construction of social norms, but there is an asymmetry in these groups. Compared with girls' groups, boys' groups are more cohesive, more exclusionary, and more separate from adult culture.

Maccoby (1998) has found that behavioral compatibility, avoidance of aggression or rough-and-tumble play, and matching activity levels cannot by themselves account for gender segregation of playgroups. She proposes an interplay between biology (differences in metabolic rate, activity level, arousability, maturation rates of language and inhibitory mechanisms, and prenatal hormones), socialization (role of fathers, more emotion talk with girls, role of peer group, and cultural practices), and cognition (self-identity, cultural stereotypes, and scripts). Segregation of playgroups leads to different activities and toy choices, which in turn may lead to differences in intellectual and emotional development (Block, 1983).

Examination of peer interactions of 2- to 10-year-olds from the Six Cultures Study and from six additional samples (Edwards, 1992; Edwards and Whiting, 1993) showed a robust, cross-culturally universal same-gender preference that emerges after age 2 years. By middle childhood, gender segregation is found frequently, perhaps in part motivated by a desire for self-discovery (Edwards, 1992). Agemates who resemble the child in abilities and activity preferences also provide the greatest opportunity for competition and conflict.

Moreover, gender segregation results from culturally prescribed adolescent initiation rites that are found in many cultures. Initiation rites are designed to separate initiates from their families; to socialize them to culturally appropriate sexuality, dominance, and aggression; to create peer group loyalty; and to solidify political ties. Collective rituals, more common for boys than girls, are found more frequently in warrior societies that emphasize gender differences in adult activities (Edwards, 1992). Western education has begun to change initiation rites, but vestiges remain in many cultures.

Task Assignment Examining children's learning environments in various cultures shows how cultural differences in socialization processes affect the development of gender roles. Learning environments were investigated in the Six Cultures Study (Edwards and Whiting, 1974; Minturn and Lambert, 1964; Whiting and Edwards, 1973), which examined aggression, nurturance, responsibility, and help- and attention-seeking behaviors of children ages 3 to 11 years in Okinawa (Japan), Mexico (the Mixtecans), the Philippines, India, Kenya (the Gusii), and the United States. Fewer gender differences were found in the three groups (United States, the Philippines, and Kenya) where both boys and girls cared for younger siblings and performed household chores. In contrast, more differences were found in the samples (India, Mexico, and Okinawa) where boys and girls were treated dissimilarly, with girls assuming more responsibility for siblings and household tasks. Indeed, the fewest gender differences were found between American girls and boys who were assigned few childcare or household tasks.

Bradley (1993) examined children's labor in 91 Standard Cross-Cultural Sample cultures (Murdock and White, 1969) and found that children younger than age 6 years perform little work, whereas children older than 10 years perform work similar to that of same-gender adults. Both boys and girls do women's work (e.g., fetching water) more frequently than men's work (e.g., hunting), and children tend to do chores that adults consider demeaning or unskilled. Women monitor children's work while simultaneously socializing with their daughters. These joint tasks provide help for the mother, which she also needs. Parents report that along with providing care in parents' old age, children's labor is an important benefit of having children.

Caregiving Analyzing data from 186 societies, Weisner and Gallimore (1977) found that in most cases, mothers, female adult relatives, and female children are the primary caregivers of infants. However, when those infants reach early childhood, both sex peers share caregiving responsibilities. Sibling caregivers play an important socialization role in societies where 2- to 4-year-olds spend more than 70% of every day with their child nurses. Because mothers in such societies spend much of their time in productive activities, they are not devoted exclusively to mothering (Greenfield, 1981; Minturn and Lambert, 1964), even though children in all cultures see mothers as responsible for children.

Moreover, in 20% of 80 cultures surveyed (Katz and Konner, 1981), fathers were rarely or never near their infants. Father–infant relationships were close in only 4% of the cultures, but even when close, fathers spent only 14% of their time with their infants and only gave 6% of the actual caregiving. In most societies, paternal interactions with children are characterized by play (Munroe and Munroe, 1975/1994).

Fathers pay less attention to female offspring than to males and promote sex-typed activities more than mothers (Lytton and Romney, 1991). Mothers are equally involved in the caregiving of sons and daughters, but fathers tend to be more involved as caregivers of sons (Rohner and Rohner, 1982). Mackey (Mackey, 1981, 1985; Mackey and Day, 1979) observed parents and children in public places in 10 different cultures and found that girls were more often in groups with no adult males, whereas boys were frequently found in all-male groups, and these differences increased with age.

Education Educational settings also greatly influence the development of children's gender roles. Observations of Japanese and American fifth graders indicate that teachers in both countries paid more attention to boys, particularly negative attention, and the greater attention was not a result of off-task or bad behavior (Hamilton, Blumenfeld, Akoh, and Miura, 1991).

Parents' beliefs about academic performance can also have a profound impact on children's achievements. Serpell (1993) found that education was considered to be more important for Zambian boys than girls, and fathers made schooling arrangements for boys even though mothers were primarily responsible for childcare. In China, Japan, and the United States, mothers expect boys to be better at mathematics and girls to be better at reading (Lummis and Stevenson, 1990), even though they perform equally well in some aspects of both disciplines.

Conclusion

Gender differences have fascinated social scientists for decades, and with the growing interest in culture, questions regarding the joint effects of these variables should continue to intrigue researchers for years to come. It is remarkable to see that pancultural similarities in sex and gender greatly outweigh the cultural differences that are found. Indeed, the ways in which male–female relationships are organized are remarkably similar across social groups. With the many technological advances that have shrunk the world, longitudinal studies within societies undergoing rapid socioeconomic development should address concomitant changes in gender roles and behaviors.

Despite the fact that males and females are biologically more similar than different, persons in traditional or modern, industrialized societies can expect to live qualitatively different lives based on their gender. The relatively minor biological differences between the sexes can be expanded or reduced by cultural practices and socialization, resulting in gender differences in roles and behaviors that are generally modest but in some cases culturally important. Furthermore, few researchers have studied the relation between cultural practices, such as initiation rites—a typical anthropological topic—and the development of the individual, a topic usually confined to the psychological domain.

The range of variation and diversity in familial and peer relationships seen across cultural groups provides an exceptional opportunity for examining gender-related social development. Future studies of gender roles across cultural groups should address how social relationships and behaviors change with age to identify the mechanisms that contribute to the development of gendered behaviors. Cross-cultural researchers have only begun to explore these social and behavioral issues with children in diverse societies.

References

Albert, A. A., and Porter, J. R. (1986). Children's gender role stereotypes: A comparison of the United States and South Africa. *Journal of Cross-Cultural Psychology, 17*, 45–65.

Andaya, B. W. (2004). Gender history, Southeast Asia, and the "World Regions" framework. In T. A. Meade and M. E. Wiesner-Hanks (Eds.), *A companion to gender history*. Malden, MA: Blackwell.

Bandura, A. (1969). Social learning theory of identificatory process. In D. A. Goslin (Ed.), *Handbook of socialization theory and research* (pp. 213–262). Chicago: Rand McNally.

Barry, H., III, Bacon, M. K., and Child, I. L. (1957). A cross-cultural survey of some sex differences in socialization. *Journal of Abnormal and Social Psychology, 55*, 327–332.

Beal, C. R. (1994). *Boys and girls: The development of gender roles*. New York: McGraw-Hill.

Berry, J. W., Poortinga, Y. H., Segall, M. H., and Dasen, P. R. (1992). *Cross-cultural psychology: Research and applications*. New York: Cambridge University Press.

Best, D. L. (2004). Gender roles in childhood and adolescence. In U. P. Gielen and J. L. Roopnarine (Eds.), *Childhood and adolescence in cross-cultural perspective*. Westport, CT: Greenwood Press/Ablex.

Best, D. L., and Williams, J. E. (1993). Cross-cultural viewpoint. In A. E. Beall and R. J. Sternberg (Eds.), *Perspectives on the psychology of gender* (pp. 215–248). New York: Guilford.

Best, D. L., and Williams, J. E. (2001). Gender and culture. In D. Matsumoto (Ed.), *Handbook of culture and psychology* (pp. 195–219). New York: Oxford University Press.

Best, D. L., Williams, J. E., Cloud, J. M., Davis, S. W., Robertson, L. S., Edwards, J. R., et al. (1977). Development of sex-trait stereotypes among young children in the United States, England, and Ireland. *Child Development, 48*, 1375–1384.

Biernat, M. (1991). Gender stereotypes and the relationship between masculinity and femininity: A developmental analysis. *Journal of Personality and Social Psychology, 61*, 351–365.

Bloch, M. N., and Adler, S. M. (1994). African children's play and the emergence of the sexual division of labor. In J. L. Roopnarine, J. E. Johnson, and F. H. Hooper (Eds.), *Children's play in diverse cultures* (pp. 148–178). Albany, NY: State University of New York Press.

Block, J. H. (1983). Differential premises arising from differential socialization of the sexes: Some conjectures. *Child Development, 54*, 1335–1354.

Bradley, C. (1993). Women's power, children's labor. *Cross-Cultural Research, 27*, 70–96.

Bronstein, P. (1984). Differences in mothers' and fathers' behaviors toward children: A cross-cultural comparison. *Developmental Psychology, 20*, 995–1003.

Buss, D. M. (1989). Sex differences in human mate preferences: Evolutionary hypotheses tested in 37 cultures. *Behavioral and Brain Sciences, 12*, 1–49.

Bussey, K. (1983). A social-cognitive appraisal of sex-role development. *Australian Journal of Psychology, 35*, 135–143.

Bussey, K., and Bandura, A. (1984). Influence of gender constancy and social power on sex-linked modeling. *Journal of Personality and Social Psychology, 47*, 1292–1302.

Cairns, R. B., Gariépy, J. L., and Hood, K. E. (1990). Development, microevolution, and social behavior. *Psychological Review, 97*, 49–65.

Cheung Mui-ching, F. (1986). Development of gender stereotypes. *Educational Research Journal, 1*, 68–73.

Daly, M., and Wilson, E. O. (1988). *Sex, evolution, and behavior* (2nd ed.). Belmont, CA: Wadsworth

Dixon, R. A., and Lerner, R. M. (1999). History and systems in developmental psychology. In M. H. Bornstein and M. E. Lamb (Eds.), *Developmental psychology: An advanced textbook* (pp. 3–45). Mahwah, NJ: Erlbaum.

Dobres, M.-A. (2004). Digging up gender in the earliest human societies. In T. A. Meade and M. E. Wiesner-Hanks (Eds.), *A companion to gender history*. Malden, MA: Blackwell.

Edelbrock, C., and Sugawara, A. I. (1978). Acquisition of sex-typed preferences in preschool-aged children. *Developmental Psychology, 14*, 614–623.

Edwards, C. P. (1992). Cross-cultural perspectives on family-peer relations. In R. D. Parke and G. W. Ladd (Eds.), *Family-peer relationships: Modes of linkages* (pp. 285–315). Mahwah, NJ: Erlbaum

Edwards, C. P. (2000). Children's play in cross-cultural perspective: A new look at the Six Cultures Study. *Cross-Cultural Research, 34*, 318–338.

Edwards, C. P., and Whiting, B. B. (1974). Women and dependency. *Politics and Society, 4*, 343–355.

Edwards, C. P., and Whiting, B. B. (1993). "Mother, older sibling, and me": The overlapping roles of caretakers and companions in the social world of 2-3 year olds in Ngeca, Kenya. In K. MacDonald (Ed.), *Parent-child: Descriptions and implications* (pp. 305–329). Albany, NY: State University of New York Press.

Fausto-Sterling, A. (2000). *Sexing the body: Gender politics and the construction of sexuality*. New York: Basic Books.

Geary, D. C. (1998). *Male, female: The evolution of human sex differences*. Washington, DC: American Psychological Association.

Ginsberg, H., and Opper, S. (1969). *Piaget's theory of intellectual development: An introduction*. Englewood Cliffs, NJ: Prentice-Hall.

Gottlieb, G. (1983). The psychobiological approach to development. In P. H. Mussen (Ed.), M. M. Haith, and J. J. Campos (Vol. Eds.), *Handbook of child psychology. Volume 2: Infancy and developmental psychobiology* (pp. 1–26). New York: Wiley.

Gottlieb, G. (1997). *Synthesizing nature-nurture: Prenatal roots of instinctive behavior*. Mahwah, NJ: Erlbaum.

Greenfield, P. M. (1981). Child care in cross-cultural perspectives: Implications for the future organization of child care in the United States. *Psychology of Women Quarterly, 6*, 41–54.

Greenfield, P. M., Brazelton, T. B., and Childs, C. P. (1989). From birth to maturity in Zinacantan: Ontogenesis in cultural context. In V. Bricker and G. Gosen (Eds.), *Ethnographic encounters in southern Mesoamerica: Celebratory essays in honor of Evon Z. Vogt* (pp. 177–216). Albany, NY: Institute of Mesoamerican Studies, State University of New York.

Hamilton, V. L., Blumenfeld, P. C., Akoh, H., and Miura, K. (1991). Group and gender in Japanese and American elementary classrooms. *Journal of Cross-Cultural Psychology, 22*, 317–346.

Hanover, B. (2000). Development of the self in gendered contexts. In T. Eckes and H. M. Trautner (Eds.), *The developmental social psychology of gender* (pp. 177–206). Mahwah, NJ: Erlbaum.

Hendrix, L., and Johnson, G. D. (1985). Instrumental and expressive socialization: A false dichotomy. *Sex Roles, 13*, 581–595.

Hoffman, C., and Hurst, N. (1990). Gender stereotypes: Perceptions or rationalization? *Journal of Personality and Social Psychology, 58*, 197–208.

Hoyenga, K. B., and Hoyenga, K. T. (1993). *Gender-related differences: Origins and outcomes*. Boston, MA: Allyn & Bacon.

Huston, A. C. (1983). Sex-typing. In P. H. Mussen (Ed.), *Handbook of child psychology* (4th ed., Vol. 4, pp. 387–467). New York: Wiley.

Intons-Peterson, M. J. (1988). *Gender concepts of Swedish and American youth*. Hillsdale, NJ: Erlbaum.

Jacklin, C. N., DiPietro, J. A., and Maccoby, E. E. (1984). Sex typing behavior and sex typing pressure in child/parent interaction. *Archives of Sexual Behavior, 13*, 413–425.

Katz, M. M., and Konner, M. J. (1981). The role of the father: An anthropological perspective. In M. E. Lamb (Ed.), *The role of the father in child development* (pp. 155–185). New York: Wiley.

Kenrick, D. T., and Keefe, R. C. (1992). Age preferences in mates reflect sex differences in human reproductive strategies. *Behavioral and Brain Sciences, 15*, 75–91.

Kenrick, D. T., and Luce, C. L. (2000). An evolutionary life-history model of gender differences and similarities. In T. Eckes and H. M. Trautner (Eds.), *The developmental social psychology of gender* (pp. 35–63). Mahwah, NJ: Erlbaum.

Kohlberg, L. (1966). A cognitive-developmental analysis of children's sex-role concepts and attitudes. In E. E. Maccoby (Ed.), *The development of sex differences* (pp. 82–173). Palo Alto, CA: Stanford University Press.

Lamb, M. E., Frodi, A. M., Hwang, C. P., Frodi, M., and Steinberg, J. (1982). Mother- and father-infant interaction involving play and holding in traditional and nontraditional Swedish families. *Developmental Psychology, 18*, 215–221.

Lummis, M., and Stevenson, H. W. (1990). Gender differences in beliefs and achievement: A cross-cultural study. *Developmental Psychology, 26*, 254–263.

Lytton, H., and Romney, D. M. (1991). Parents' differential socialization of boys and girls: A meta-analysis. *Psychological Bulletin, 109*, 267–296.

Maccoby, E. E. (1998). *The two sexes: Growing up apart, coming together*. Cambridge, MA: Belnap Press.

Mackey, W. C. (1981). A cross-cultural analysis of adult-child proxemics in relation to the Plowman-Protector Complex: A preliminary study. *Behavior Science Research, 3/4*, 187–223.

Mackey, W. C. (1985). *Fathering behaviors: The dynamics of the man-child bond*. New York: Plenum.

Mackey, W. C., and Day, R. (1979). Some indicators of fathering behaviors in the United States: A cross-cultural examination of adult male-child interaction. *Journal of Marriage and the Family, 41*, 287–299.

Martin, C. L. (2000). Cognitive theories of gender development. In T. Eckes and H. M. Trautner (Eds.), *The developmental social psychology of gender* (pp. 91–121). Mahwah, NJ: Lawrence.

Meade, T. A., and Wiesner-Hanks, M. E. (2004). Introduction. In T. A. Meade and M. E. Wiesner-Hanks (Eds.), *A companion to gender history*. Malden, MA: Blackwell.

Minturn, L., and Lambert, W. W. (1964). *Mothers of six cultures: Antecedents of child rearing*. New York: Wiley.

Mischel, W. (1970). Sex-typing and socialization. In P. H. Mussen (Ed.), *Carmichael's manual of child psychology* (Vol. 2, pp. 3–72). New York: Wiley.

Mukhopadhyay, C. C., and Higgins, P. J. (1998). Anthropological studies of women's status revisited: 1977-1987. *Annual Review of Anthropology, 17*, 461–495.

Munroe, R. H., Shimmin, H. S., and Munroe, R. L. (1984). Gender understanding and sex role preference in four cultures. *Developmental Psychology, 20*, 673–682.

Munroe, R. L., and Munroe, R. H. (1975/1994). *Cross-cultural human development*. Prospect Heights, IL: Waveland Press.

Murdock, G. P., and White, D. R. (1969). Standard cross-cultural sample. *Ethnology, 8*, 329–369.

Öhman, A. (1986). Face the beast and fear the face: Animal and social fears as prototypes for evolutionary analysis of emotion. *Psychophysiology, 23*, 123–145.

Prossner, G. V., Hutt, C., Hutt, S. J., Mahindadasa, K. J., and Goonetilleke, M. D. J. (1986). Children's play in Sri Lanka: A cross-cultural study. *British Journal of Developmental Psychology, 4*, 179–186.

Reis, H. T., and Wright, S. (1982). Knowledge of sex-role stereotypes in children aged 3 to 5. *Sex Roles, 8*, 1049-1056.

Rogoff, B. (1990). *Apprenticeship in thinking: Cognitive development in social context*. New York: Oxford University Press.

Rogoff, B., Gauvain, M., and Ellis, S. (1984). Development viewed in its cultural context. In M. H. Bornstein and M. E. Lamb (Eds.), *Developmental psychology: An advanced textbook* (pp. 533–571). Hillsdale, NJ: Erlbaum.

Rohner, R. P., and Rohner, E. C. (1982). Enculturative continuity and the importance of caretakers: Cross-cultural codes. *Behavior Science Research, 17*, 91–114.

Ross, L. (1977). The intuitive psychologist and his shortcomings: Distortions in the attribution process. In L. Berkowitz (Ed.), *Advances in experimental social psychology* (Vol. 10, pp. 173–220). New York: Academic Press.

Rozin, P., and Kalat, J. W. (1971). Specific hungers and poison avoidance as adaptive specializations of learning. *Psychological Review, 78*, 459–486.

Ruble, D. N., and Martin, C. L. (1998). Gender development. In W. Damon (Series Ed.) and N. Eisenberg (Vol. Ed.), *Handbook of child psychology. Volume 3: Social, emotional, and personality development* (5th ed., pp. 933–1016). New York: Wiley.

Sagi, A., Lamb, M. E., Shoham, R., Dvir, R., and Lewkowicz, K. (1985). Parent-infant interaction in families on Israeli Kibbutzim. *International Journal of Behavioral Development, 8*, 273–284.

Sears, R. R., Maccoby, E .E., and Levin, H. (1957). *Patterns of child rearing*. Palo Alto, CA: Stanford University Press.

Sears, R. R., Rau, L., and Alpert, R. (1965). *Identification and child rearing*. Palo Alto, CA: Stanford University Press.

Seavey, C. A., Katz, P. A., and Zalk, S. R. (1975). Baby X: The effect of gender labels on adult responses to infants. *Sex Roles, 1*, 103–110.

Seligman, M. E. P. (1971). Phobias and preparedness. *Behavior Therapy, 2*, 307–320.

Serpell, R. (1993). *The significance of schooling: Life-journeys in an African society*. New York: Cambridge University Press.

Sidorowicz, L. S., and Lunney, G. S. (1980). Baby X revisited. *Sex Roles, 6*, 67–73.

Stewart, J. (1988). Current themes, theoretical issues, and preoccupations in the study of sexual differentiation and gender-related behaviors. *Psychobiology, 16*, 315–320.

Sweeney, J., and Bradbard, M. R. (1989). Mothers' and fathers' changing perceptions of their male and female infants over the course of pregnancy. *Journal of Genetic Psychology, 149*, 393–404.

Trivers, R. L. (1985). *Social evolution*. Menlo Park, CA: Benjamin/Cummings.

Van Leeuwen, M. S. (1978). A cross-cultural examination of psychological differentiation in males and females. *International Journal of Psychology, 13*, 87–122.

Weinraub, M., Clemens, L. P., Sockloff, A., Etheridge, R., Gracely, E., and Myers, B. (1984). The development of sex role stereotypes in the third year: Relationships to gender labeling, gender identity, sex-typed toy preferences, and family characteristics. *Child Development, 55*, 1493–1503.

Weisner, T. S., and Gallimore, R. (1977). My brother's keeper: Child and sibling caretaking. *Current Anthropology, 18*, 169–190.

Whiting, B. B. (1963). *Six cultures: Studies of child rearing*. Oxford, England: Wiley.
Whiting, B., and Edwards, C. P. (1973). A cross-cultural analysis of sex differences in the behavior of children aged 3 to 11. *Journal of Social Psychology, 91*, 171–188.
Whiting, B. B., and Edwards, C. P. (1988). *Children of different worlds: The formation of social behavior*. Cambridge, MA: Harvard University Press.
Williams, J. E., and Best, D. L. (1982/1990). *Measuring sex stereotypes: A multination study* (Rev. ed., 1990). Newbury Park, CA: Sage.
Williams, W. L. (1992). *The spirit and the flesh: Sexual diversity in American Indian culture* (Rev. Ed.). Boston: Beacon Press.
Wood, W., and Eagly, A. H. (2002). A cross-cultural analysis of the behavior of women and men: Implications for the origins of sex differences. *Psychological Bulletin, 128*, 699–727.

12
Peers

KENNETH H. RUBIN, CHARISSA CHEAH, and MELISSA M. MENZER

Introduction

Children spend much of their time in the company of their peers, and they do so within cultural contexts that play a significant role in their peer relationships (Rubin, Bukowski, and Parker, 2006). For example, cultural beliefs and norms help interpret the acceptability of individual characteristics and the types and ranges of interactions and relationships that are likely or permissible (Rubin et al., 2006). Yet, the vast majority of studies pertaining to children's peer relationships have focused primarily on Western European and North American samples. Today, researchers examine peer relationships from a cultural perspective; emerging data suggest that there is considerable cultural variability in children's peer experiences (Chen, French, and Schneider, 2006). Thus, in this chapter, we review the extant cultural and cross-cultural psychological literature on children's peer interactions, relationships, and groups.

Theory

In this chapter, we borrow heavily from the writings of Hinde (1987), who proposed that in any consideration of the social world, one must regard, simultaneously, contributions from several levels of social complexity—individual characteristics, social interactions, social relationships, groups, and culture. Importantly, events and processes at each level constrain and influence events and processes at other levels.

Individuals bring to social exchanges relatively stable social orientations, temperaments that dispose them to be more or less physiologically aroused to social stimuli, and a repertoire of social skills for social perception, cognition, and social problem solving. Other observable individual characteristics, such as sex, ethnicity, and race, can also play important roles in children's interactions and relationships. Children's *interactions* with others over the short term vary in form and function in response to fluctuations in the parameters of the social situation, such as the partner's individual characteristics, overtures, and responses. The flow of interactions between children can be described as generally (1) positive and/or prosocial; (2) negative and agonistic; or (3) asocial and/or nonsocial. In the latter case, children may refrain from interacting with others or choose to remove themselves from social company.

Most interactions are embedded in longer term *relationships* and thus are influenced by past and anticipated future interactions. Moreover, the nature of a relationship is defined partly by the characteristics of its members and its constituent interactions. Over the long term, the kinds of relationships individuals form depend on their history of interactions and on the relationships they had earlier formed with significant others. For example, it has been proposed that the quality of children's friendships depends, in part, on the interactions that the partners have had with each other as well as on the quality of each partner's relationships with primary caregivers.

At the highest level of social complexity, individual relationships are embedded in *groups* or networks of relationships with more or less clearly defined boundaries (cliques, teams, or school classes). Groups are more than mere aggregates of relationships; through emergent properties, such as norms or shared cultural conventions, groups help define the type and range of relationships and interactions that are likely or permissible.

In this chapter, we use the successive levels of social complexity in children's experiences with peers as a framework. We suggest that an understanding of each social "level" is determined with reference to the "highest" level of Hinde's framework—culture.

Central Issues and Key Research Studies

Culture

Culture can be defined as "the set of attitudes, values, beliefs, and behaviors shared by a group of people, communicated from one generation to the next" (Matsumoto, 1997, p. 5). Given that the majority of the world's children do not reside in culturally Westernized countries, cross-cultural research on peer interactions, relationships, and groups requires special attention.

Importantly, the *form* that behaviors take (the way things look) may appear identical from culture to culture (Whiting and Child, 1953), yet, given that cultures vary in their customs and belief systems (Harkness and Super, 2002), any particular form (e.g., a behavior or an interaction) may be interpreted differently across cultures. Put another way, the psychological "meaning" attributed to any given social behavior is, in large part, a function of the ecological niche in which it is produced and exhibited (Bornstein, 1995). Furthermore, it is likely that any behavior that is viewed, within a culture, as adaptive will lead to its encouragement by significant others including peers; in contrast, if a behavior is perceived to be maladaptive or abnormal, significant others will attempt to discourage its growth and development. Moreover, the means by which the given behavior is encouraged or discouraged may be culturally determined and defined. For example, in some cultures, the response to an aggressive act may be to explain to the child why the behavior is unacceptable; in others, physical discipline may be the accepted norm; in yet others, aggression may be ignored or perhaps even reinforced (for discussions, see Bornstein and Cheah, 2006). In some cultures, parents and adult figures remain the most important judges of acceptable behaviors throughout childhood; in other cultures, the peer group becomes an increasingly important adjudicator of acceptable behavior and relationships with increasing age.

Another central issue pertaining to culture is the degree to which peer interactions and relationships are encouraged or even allowed. In Western cultures, for example, children are generally encouraged to interact with peers and form relationships with them. It is believed that the development of close, extrafamilial relationships augers well for the child's future well-being. However, in kin-based societies, peer interactions may be discouraged because parents fear the potential for competition and conflict (Edwards, 1992). In addition, interactions and relationships with siblings may take the place of peers in many kin-based societies (e.g., Gaskins, 2006).

Individual Characteristics

We first consider children's individual characteristics that may be interpreted or responded to in different ways in different cultures.

Temperament Temperament can be broadly defined as the biological basis for the affective arousal, expression, and regulatory components of personality (Goldsmith et al., 1987). Three broad groups of temperamental traits are differentially associated with children's social functioning in the peer group. The first group is related to *resistance to control* and encompasses lack of attention, low agreeableness, and strong attention to rewarding stimuli. In the peer group, such children tend to have poorer social skills and are more likely to "act out" and display other externalizing problems (Coplan, Bowker, and Cooper, 2003). The second broadly defined group of temperamental traits is focused on negative emotional *reactivity* and difficulty in *regulating* negative affect (Rothbart and Bates, 2006). Highly reactive and poorly regulated children are easily angered, frustrated, and provoked by peers and do not adequately control the expression of these negative emotions. One might expect that these two constellations of dispositionally based behaviors would mark children for peer rejection in most cultural contexts. The third group of temperamental traits constitutes shyness/behavioral inhibition and involves wary responses to social situations and novelty as well as a seemingly quiet, reserved demeanor (Rubin, Burgess, and Coplan, 2002).

Dispositional expressivity, reactivity, and regulation are judged as acceptable and adaptive or unacceptable and maladaptive depending on the culture within which the child develops. For example, behavioral inhibition has been the focus of study in many different countries, such as Canada, China, England, Germany, India, Sweden, and the United States (Asendorpf, 1991; Broberg, Lamb, and Hwang, 1990; Chen et al., 1998; Fox, Henderson, Rubin, Calkins, and Schmidt, 2001; Prakash and Coplan, 2007; Rubin, Burgess, and Hastings, 2002). Researchers have reported that inhibition is more prevalent among Chinese and Korean toddlers than among American, Italian, and Australian toddlers (Rubin, Hemphill, et al., 2006). In this regard, the form taken by inhibited-shy behavior is the same across cultures. However, the meaning and interpretation of the behavior varies from culture to culture. Thus, a shy-inhibited child in Western culture is seen as fearful, lacking in social confidence, and socially incompetent and immature (Rubin, Burgess, and Coplan, 2002). However, in East Asian cultures, Confucian and Taoist philosophies consider behavioral inhibition and self-restraint as indices of social maturity, accomplishment, and mastery (King and Bond, 1985); thus, shy, reserved behavior may be more prevalent because it is more valued and encouraged in Asian than in Western cultures. For example, shy children in China are greeted with positive, supportive responses such as approval, cooperation, and compliance when initiating interactions with their peers, whereas the social initiations of shy North American children are more likely to result in rejection and neglect (Chen, Wang, and DeSouza, 2006). Moreover, peers are more likely to initiate such positive interactions as sharing and helping with shy children in China than in North America.

Sex, Ethnicity, and Race Other individual characteristics that appear to have some bearing on children's peer interactions and relationships are sex, ethnicity, and race. We examine these individual characteristics, where relevant to culture, in sections that follow.

Peers: Interactions

Social Participation Rubin and colleagues (Rubin, Fein, and Vandenberg, 1983) have argued that whether alone, near others, or with others, children may produce simple sensorimotor behaviors (functional play; e.g., aimlessly bouncing a ball), construct structures from blocks or draw with crayons (constructive play), or engage in some form of pretense (dramatic play). These cognitive forms of play, when examined in their social context, reveal developmental trends. Solitary sensorimotor behaviors become increasingly rare over the preschool years, whereas the prevalence of solitary constructive or exploratory play remains stable. Sociodramatic play and games with rules also increase with age. Taken together, the extant data from Western cultures reveal age differences only for particular forms of solitary and group behavior.

Observational studies of cultural differences in social participation are unfortunately rare. To begin with, from extensive observations, age "norms" can be established for the production of particular forms of social behavior. From these "norms," procedures may be developed to identify children who deviate from their agemates. Instead, most cross-cultural studies of children's social participation and interaction rely on parent, teacher, or peer assessments developed by Western scientists. Some exceptions do exist. For example, Farver and Lee-Shin (2000) examined the extent to which Korean American and European American preschoolers engaged in parallel and sociodramatic play. They reported that Korean children of highly acculturated mothers were just as likely to engage in sociodramatic play as their non-Korean agemates. However, Korean children whose mothers maintained their traditional values engaged in less sociodramatic play and more parallel play than their more acculturated peers and their European American agemates. Farver and Shin (1997; Farver and Lee-Shin, 2000) argued that these findings reflect the notion that culturally assimilated Korean mothers, like European American mothers, think positively about the benefits of pretense, whereas more traditional Korean mothers believe that sociodramatic activities are superfluous and not particularly relevant for academic accomplishment.

Prosocial Behavior   In general, helping and sharing behaviors with peers are observed to increase across childhood (Benenson, Markovits, Roy, and Denko, 2003). This developmental change is likely the result of increasing social-cognitive abilities, which tend to increase children's willingness to consider conflicting perspectives. Research in non-Western cultures suggests that societies vary greatly in the development and prevalence of prosocial and cooperative behaviors. Stevenson, Chen, Lee, and Fuligni (1991) reported that the observed incidence of sharing, comforting, and helping is higher among Taiwanese and Japanese kindergarteners than American kindergarteners. Keller, Edelstein, Schmid, Fang, and Fang (1998) found that, for moral conflict and friendship dilemmas, Chinese youth were more likely to use altruistic behaviors than Icelandic youth. These researchers suggest that many Asian populations believe that they are obliged to be prosocial toward others due to collectivist (interdependent) values. In support of this contention, Cheah and Rubin (2003) found that Chinese mothers of preschoolers were more likely than European American mothers to indicate that they wanted their preschool children to share and help other children for social conventional reasons (e.g., to fit in with the group and function well in Chinese society). Among Western, industrialized countries such as Germany, Russia, Australia, and the United States, cross-national studies of sharing or helping have reported few consistent differences (e.g., Kienbaum and Trommsdorff, 1999).

Politeness may be considered another facet of prosocial behavior. Farver and Lee-Shin (2000) reported that when Korean American preschoolers converse with peers, they are more likely than European American children to make statements of agreement and polite requests. European American children use more directives and are more likely to make statements pertaining to peer rejection than their Korean American counterparts.

Cooperation/Competition   Whereas competition can damage group harmony, cooperation is seen as a necessary component to maintaining close relationships (Schneider, Woodburn, Soteras-de Toro, and Udvari, 2005). Children from collectivistic or traditional, rural communities are more cooperative and less competitive than those from individualistic, urban, or Westernized cultures (Schneider et al., 2005).

Within collectivist cultures, competition and cooperation appear to coexist. For example, Kim, Triandis, Kagitcibasi, Choi, and Yoon (1994) reported that among many Asian collectivist cultures, cooperation occurs more often within friend and family relationships, whereas competition occurs more often within education and work contexts. Moreover, generational differences appear to exist within traditionally collectivistic cultures. For example, third-generation Mexican Americans are more competitive than their second-generation counterparts (Knight and Kagan, 1977). Consistent with this finding, de Guzman and Carlo (2004) reported a negative association between acculturation and Latino adolescents' prosocial behaviors.

Moving Against Peers: Aggression and Bullying Long before verbal aggression is first displayed, physical aggression emerges and peaks. During middle childhood, verbal aggression (insults, derogation, threats, and gossip) gradually replaces physical aggression. Furthermore, relative to preschoolers, the aggressive behavior of 6- to 12-year-olds is less frequently directed toward possessing objects or occupying specific territory and more specifically directed toward others (Dodge, Coie, and Lynam, 2006). The focus on *relational* aggression provides a point of contrast to physical aggression (Crick and Grotpeter, 1995). Relational aggression is defined as behavior in which a perpetrator seeks to harm others through "purposeful manipulation and damage of their peer relationships" (Crick and Grotpeter, 1995, p. 711). Similar constructs in the literature include indirect aggression (Lagerspetz, Björkqvist, and Peltonen, 1988) and social aggression (Xie, Swift, Cairns, and Cairns, 2002).

Culture and Aggression The forms of aggression mentioned earlier exist in many cultures. For example, physical, verbal, and relational aggression have been identified as distinct entities during middle childhood and adolescence in Australia (Owens, 1996), China (Nelson et al., 2006), Finland (Lagerspetz et al., 1988), Indonesia (French, Jansen, and Pidada, 2002), and Italy (Tomada and Schneider, 1997). Nelson, Hart, Yang, and Jin (2007) found that all forms of aggression appear to be significant social liabilities in Chinese culture.

The costs of aggression appear consistent from culture to culture. For example, physical aggression is associated with peer *rejection* in most countries (e.g., Attili, Vermigli, and Schneider, 1997; Cillessen, van IJzendoorn, van Lieshout, and Hartup, 1992; French et al., 2002; Hart et al., 2000; Kereteš and Milanovic, 2006; Prakash and Coplan, 2007; Xu, Farver, Schwartz, and Chang, 2004). In China, aggressive children experience feelings of loneliness and depression, whereas aggressive children in North America, Brazil, and Italy do not (Chen et al., 2004). This latter finding may emanate from the strict prohibition of disruptive and aggressive behavior among Chinese youth; in North America, the "Queen Bee" and those middle schoolers viewed as dominant by way of their meanness and aggressiveness seem to be viewed as popular by their peers (Prinstein and Cillessen, 2003). Bergeron and Schneider (2005) conducted a meta-analysis to examine cross-national differences in peer-directed aggression among children living or attending school in urban areas on 36 studies including 28 different countries. In general, cultures characterized by collectivistic values, high moral discipline, a high level of egalitarian commitment, and high uncertainty avoidance and that emphasized values that are heavily Confucian showed lower levels of aggression toward peers than their counterparts. Thus, values emphasizing the social order and the importance of the creation of responsible and dedicated individuals, egalitarianism, voluntary cooperation, and moral restraint appear to contribute to lower levels of aggression.

Culture, Bullying, and Victimization Another form of interaction emerging fully blown during middle childhood and early adolescence is *bullying*. Bullying refers to the attainment of power and control in relationships through acts of verbal, physical, and indirect aggression that are chronic and directed toward particular peers (victims) (Pepler et al., 2006). Bullying accounts for a substantial portion of the aggression that occurs in the peer group and has been found to be most prevalent during adolescence (Pellegrini and Long, 2002). Strikingly, bullies generally do not experience much resistance to their aggressive acts.

Surveys in many countries around the world show that bullying is a significant problem for large numbers of children across many countries, including Australia, Austria, Canada, China, Denmark, England, Finland, France, Germany, Greece, Iceland, Ireland, Italy, Japan, The Netherlands, Norway Portugal, Spain, Sweden, and Thailand (Eslea et al., 2004; Pepler et al., 2006; Rigby, 2005; Smith et al., 2002). Children who are at greatest risk for victimization are those who are either aggressive or socially withdrawn. The strong, positive association between aggressiveness and victimization appears to be culturally universal in Australia (Slee, 1995), North America (Hanish and Guerra, 2004), Europe (Smith et al., 2002), Southern Asia (Khatri and Kupersmidt, 2003), and East Asia (Schwartz, Farver, Chang, and Lee-Shin, 2002).

Anxious and socially reticent children are often victims of bullying behavior (Olweus, 1993), perhaps because withdrawn children are easy and nonthreatening prey who are unlikely to retaliate when provoked (e.g., the construct of "whipping boy"; Olweus, 1978). A cultural view of victimization asserts that children who do not promote the basic group goals of coherence, harmony, and evolution are targets of bullying. Accordingly, aggressive and withdrawn children do not promote these positive aspects of group functioning and are victimized as a result (Eslea et al., 2004). Victims of bullying in North America, Europe, and Asia report having few friends and are typically rejected by the peer group at large (e.g., Eslea et al., 2004). In summary, the costs of being victimized by bullies appear to be negative and culturally universal.

Moving Away From Peers: Social Withdrawal   Rubin, Burgess, and Coplan (2002) suggested that social withdrawal may result from a biologically based trait that pits a motivation to avoid others with a similarly strong motivation to engage others in interaction (behavioral inhibition; shyness). For example, there is increasing evidence that behavioral inhibition is a developmental precursor of social reticence, withdrawal, and anxiety proneness in childhood. Rubin, Burgess, and Hastings (2002) reported that toddlers who were temperamentally inhibited and socially wary are more likely to display reticent behavior during free play 2 years later. This finding has also been reported in China (Sun, Chen, and Zheng, 2006).

Insofar as the prevalence of socially restrained behavior is concerned, it has been reported that Southeast Asian children produce more socially passive and reticent behaviors than do their North American counterparts (Farver and Howes, 1988; Weisz, Suwanlert, Chaiyasit, and Walter, 1987). Hart et al. (2000) found that Chinese children were rated by teachers as engaging in significantly less sociable play than American children.

The demonstration of socially withdrawn and wary behavior has been linked to all manner of difficulty in Western youth. For example, withdrawal has been associated with negative self-esteem, loneliness, and depression in such Western cultures as Brazil, Canada, Italy, and the United States (e.g., Chen et al., 2004; Rubin, Chen, McDougall, Bowker, and McKinnon, 1995). Social withdrawal is also associated with poor performance on individual, face-to-face exams with the teacher and general academic achievement in Great Britain and Greece (Crozier and Hostettler, 2003).

In traditional Chinese culture, shyness and reservedness are interpreted as representing well-regulated and appropriate behavior. Whereas shy-inhibited children in Western countries experience social and psychological difficulties, shy children in China are well adjusted in the school environment and less likely than nonshy children to report loneliness and depression (Chen, Rubin, Li, and Li, 1999; Chen, Rubin, and Sun, 1992). Other aspects of social withdrawal, however, such as spending time alone when in social company or expressing social disinterest, are discouraged in Chinese children. These behaviors are incompatible with a collectivistic orientation (Cheah and Rubin, 2004).

Because social assertiveness and competitiveness are increasingly required in market-oriented China, research on the construct of shyness-social wariness demonstrates that it is now a significant correlate of some indices of maladjustment (e.g., school problems, depression). Chen, Cen, Li, and He (2005) examined three cohorts (1990, 1998, and 2002) of elementary school children. Whereas shyness was associated positively with social and academic achievement in the 1990 cohort, the associations became weaker or nonsignificant in the 1998 cohort. Furthermore, shyness was associated with school difficulty and depression in the 2002 cohort. These results show how social and cultural changes may affect the meanings of individual behaviors differently across societies and over time (Oyserman, Coon, and Kemmelmeier, 2002).

Peer Relationships: Friendship

In the following sections, we discuss the functions, prevalence, and stability of friendship in childhood as well as children's understanding of friendship, the process of friendship formation, and similarities between friends.

Functions of Friendship Friendship is often referred to as a close, mutual, and voluntary dyadic relationship. The voluntary nature of friendships means that children are able to initiate, maintain, and relinquish friendships that meet their expectations and/or needs. However, the notion that friendship is a voluntary, freely chosen relationship may not be the case in all cultures. In some cultures, friendship is considered a permanent pact between individuals that may be assigned at birth (Krappmann, 1996).

Friendships serve to provide (1) support, self-esteem enhancement, and positive self-evaluation; (2) emotional security; (3) affection and opportunities for intimacy; (4) consensual validation of interests, hopes, and fears; (5) instrumental and informational assistance; and (6) prototypes for later romantic, marital, and parental relationships. Perhaps most importantly, friendships offer children an extrafamilial base of security from which they may explore the effects of their behaviors on themselves, their peers, and their environments (Rubin, Bukowski, et al., 2006).

From a Western perspective, Parker and Gottman (1989) have argued that friendship serves different functions for children at different points in development. Young children's friendships serve to maximize excitement and amusement levels in play and to aid in the organization of behavior. During middle childhood, friendships aid in the learning of behavioral norms and the necessary skills for successful self-presentation and impression management. Finally, in adolescence, friends assist in identity development and self-exploration. Little is known, however, about the developmental course of the functions of friendship across cultures. Moreover, the functions and nature of friendship appear to vary across cultures. In cultures within which friendships are considered one of very few relationships guaranteeing societal success, both intimacy and exclusivity should be regarded as the most important aspects of a friendship (Triandis, Bontempo, Villareal, and Asai, 1988). Reflecting this idea, researchers have found that intimacy is more important in the friendships of children in Korea (French, Lee, and Pidada, 2006) and Cuba (Gonzalez, Moreno, Schneider, 2004) than in those of North American children. And yet, differences within putatively collectivistic cultures also exist. Children in collectivist Indonesia did not differ from North American children with respect to intimacy (French, Pidada, and Victor, 2005); Indonesian children were also more inclusive rather than exclusive in their friendships. Sharabany (2006) highlighted within–collectivistic culture variation in Arab and Israeli children's relationships. Arab culture values kin-based over nonkin-based friendships and believes in a patriarchal organization of the community. The Israeli children resided in kibbutzim (small collective communities in which property and responsibilities are shared). Sharabany found that Israeli children disclosed more intimacy and reported lower conflict with their best friends than did their Arab counterparts.

Given that friends tend to spend more time with each other than nonfriends, it should not be surprising that friend dyads are more likely to engage in conflict than nonfriend dyads

(Newcomb and Bagwell, 1995). Indeed, conflict with friends, if appropriately resolved, has been viewed as a positive force in social and cognitive developmental growth (Hartup and Laursen, 1995). Researchers have found that conflict is equally prevalent among friends in collectivistic and individualistic cultures (French, Pidada, Denoma, McDonald, and Lawton, 2005). Although a similar rate of conflict may occur between friends, methods of conflict resolution differ. Whereas American children use negotiation to resolve conflict, Indonesian children disengage from conflict to decrease the tension. Thus, Americans may move toward each other to resolve conflicts, whereas those from Eastern cultures may withdraw from each other. However, differences in friendship conflict prevalence have also been found *within* Western cultures. For example, Schneider, Fonzi, Tani, and Tomada (1997) found that Italian children had fewer conflicts with their friends than their Canadian counterparts. The authors suggested that this difference may be attributed to better communication among Italian than Canadian children.

The majority of North American friendship research has involved only European American children and adolescents. Yet, most Western cultures comprise multiracial or multiethnic communities. Friendships of minority and majority children differ in quality (e.g., Hamm, Brown, and Heck, 2005; Way, Cowal, Gingold, Pahl, and Bissessar, 2001). For example, in the United States, African American boys have been found to have more intimate friendships than European American boys (DuBois and Hirsch, 1990). Among low-income minority children (African, Latin, and Asian American), Way and Chen (2000) reported that the gender gap in intimate self-disclosure favoring girls is only found among Latina children.

Friendship Prevalence, Stability, and Homophily   Approximately 75% to 80% of Western children have a mutual best friendship (Rubin, Bukowski, et al., 2006). Once mutual friendships are formed, friendships at all ages show remarkable stability. Triandis et al. (1988) argued that friendships are more stable in non-Western, more collectivistic cultures than in individualistic cultures, where friendships are supposedly more fluid. However, the individualistic culture dimension appears inadequate to explain within-collectivistic variability in friendship prevalence and stability. For example, the friendships of South Korean children are both more stable and exclusive than those of Indonesian children (French et al., 2006). Within individualistic cultures, Schneider et al. (1997) found that Italian children, particularly girls, report more stable friendships than Canadian children. With regard to prevalence, French, Jansen, Riansari, and Setiono (2003) found that Indonesian and North American children have the same number of friendships.

From an early age, most children form friendships with those who are like themselves in observable characteristics, such as age, sex, race, ethnicity, and behavioral proclivities. Children are more likely to choose same-race or -ethnic peers with whom to interact and form friendships than would be expected by chance (e.g., Howes and Wu, 1990; Kao and Joyner, 2004). The tendency to form same-race friendships has been documented from the preschool through high school years, with a peak in intensity during the developmental periods of middle and late childhood (Aboud and Mendelson, 1998).

Dashiell, Wojslawowicz Bowker, Rubin, Booth-LaForce, and Rose-Krasnor (2006) examined prevalence, stability, behavioral homophily, and quality in African American and European American children's friendships in diverse schools. They found that European and African American young adolescents were equally likely to possess a mutual and stable best friendship. Moreover, the friendships of these young adolescents did not differ qualitatively. Significantly, the friendships of both African and European American young adolescents were largely homophilous. That is, both African and European American young adolescents and their mutual best friends were similar in terms of their aggressive and prosocial behaviors and their sociability.

The Peer Group

Children spend much of their time in group settings where membership is not defined solely by friendship. Here we explore structural and functional characteristics of the peer group.

The Peer Group as a Social Context   In many cultures, young children are regularly found playing together in the classroom, the schoolyard, or the neighborhood. However, when young children are observed together, the majority of their behaviors are independently oriented, and their concerns are with their own immediate ends. Somewhere in middle childhood, however, a transformation occurs from a group of peers to a peer group. In both Western and Eastern cultures, cliques usually range in size from 3 to more than 10 children, with an average of 5 or 6 members, and mostly comprise same-sex peers (Chen, Chang, and He, 2003; Kindermann, McCollom, and Gibson, 1995). In childhood, participation in smaller, more intimate cliques predominates but then declines in adolescence. During adolescence, affiliation with larger crowds becomes a salient feature of social life (Brown, Eicher, and Petrie, 1986).

The characteristics of a group are not reducible to the characteristics of the individuals who comprise the group (Cairns and Cairns, 1994; Chen, Chen, and Kaspar, 2001). Unlike such dyadic social relationships as friendship, the peer group represents a social context that is developed through the collective functioning of members based on group norms and values. As a result, the "social character" of the group functions as a context for social interactions and individual behaviors.

In Western cultures, group affiliation is viewed as fulfilling individual psychological needs, such as the development of self-identity and the enhancement of self-worth. In Asian cultures, such as in China, however, social values and norms are presumed to discourage the formation of small groups or cliques because they threaten the broader collective and may lead to intergroup disharmony. For example, Xu et al. (2004) found that in fifth and sixth grade classrooms, Chinese children were not members of cliques; the majority of the groups were defined based on the sex of the members.

Peer Group Functions   Fine (1987) argued that peer groups teach children (1) how to engage in cooperative activity aimed at collective rather than individual goals, (2) about social structures, (3) the skills associated with leading and following others, (4) the control of hostile impulses toward fellow members, and (5) how to mobilize aggression in the service of group loyalty by directing it toward "outsiders." In addition, social networks and emotional connections that children establish and maintain with other members may constitute a major source of social support for children to cope with stress and adjustment difficulties. In short, frequent contact, common activities, and interpersonal affective connectedness among group members may make children's groups a strong socialization influence (Kindermann et al., 1995). Whereas experiences with friends may be specific to dyadic social situations, peer groups may have pervasive impact on individual social, emotional, and behavioral functioning and adjustment in larger social settings (Cairns and Cairns, 1994). For example, whereas natural peer groups might be formed based on children's motivational factors, the profile of peer networks predicts subsequent changes in individual motivation in school (Kindermann et al., 1995). Similar findings have been reported, in both North America and China, with reference to the contributions of peer groups to such matters as school dropout, teenage pregnancy, and delinquency (Chen et al., 2001; Xie, Cairns, and Cairns, 2001).

Peer Acceptance and Rejection

Popularity is the experience of being liked and accepted by the peer group. In the following sections, we examine the relations between peer status and children's social behaviors across various cultures.

Behavioral Correlates of Peer Acceptance   Children who are liked and accepted by their peers are typically skilled at initiating and maintaining qualitatively positive relationships. They are also viewed as cooperative, friendly, sociable, and sensitive by peers, teachers, and behavioral observers. Studies conducted in North America indicate that children who engage in friendly/amicable behavior and who are prosocial in their helping, sharing, and comforting behaviors are typically better adjusted to school, less aggressive and withdrawn, less prone to psychosocial problems, and better accepted by peers (Rubin, Bukowski, et al., 2006). Sociable behavior appears to be highly adaptable in most cultural settings. For example, children who engage in friendly and outgoing behavior are more likely to be accepted by peers in China (Chang, 2003; Chen et al., 2002), Greece (Hatzichristou and Hopf, 1996), Italy (Casiglia, Lo Coco, and Zappulla, 1998), and Russia (Hart et al., 2000).

Peer Rejection   A high level of heterogeneity exists among the behavioral characteristics of rejected children. Some rejected children are immature, whereas others are rejected because they are socially unskilled, aggressive, or socially wary and withdrawn. For example, instrumental and relational aggression, as well as bullying, are strongly related with peer rejection in North America (Crick and Grotpeter, 1995) as well as China (Xu et al., 2004), Croatia (Kerestes̆ and Milanovic, 2006), Greece (Hatzichristou and Hopf, 1996), India (Prakash and Coplan, 2007), Italy (Tomada and Schneider, 1997), Indonesia (French et al., 2002), The Netherlands (Haselager, Cillessen, van Lieshout, Riksen-Walraven, and Hartup, 2002), and Russia (Hart et al., 2000).

In cultural contexts within which such individual characteristics as assertiveness, expressiveness, and competitiveness are valued and encouraged (Triandis, 1990), withdrawal has been linked to peer rejection. Thus, in such countries as Argentina, Canada, Greece, Italy, The Netherlands, and the United States (Casiglia et al., 1998; Cillessen et al., 1992; Rubin, Chen, and Hymel, 1993; Schaughency, Vannatta, Langhinrichsen, and Lally, 1992), socially wary and withdrawn children are largely rejected by their peers. Although previous research indicated that shy, wary children were accepted by peers in China (Chen et al., 1999), more recent findings reveal that socially withdrawn and wary Chinese children are also rejected by the peer group (Chang et al., 2005; Chen et al., 2005). These findings have been replicated in South Asia (India) as well (Prakash and Coplan, 2007).

The correlates of peer acceptance and rejection across cultures appear to be more similar than different. Both aggressiveness and wary withdrawal are associated with rejection. Kind, helpful, sharing, caring behavior is linked with peer acceptance across cultures.

Conclusion

In this chapter, we have reviewed literature concerning children's peer interactions, relationships, and groups. It must be noted, however, that most cross-cultural work on peer interactions and relationships has been dominated by an etic framework; Western (mostly North American) researchers have assumed that the constructs measured have relevance across all cultural communities. However, this biased perspective may cause researchers to overlook or miss social conventions that are related to a specific construct in one culture but are completely unrelated in another culture. Assume that social competence, as a construct, is etic. That is, it is universally recognized and required across cultures for the development of rich, strong peer relationships. This assumption may be entirely incorrect; nevertheless, the assumption can be empirically verified. To do so would require a belief that social competence is probably best defined within culture and that some aspects of competence may be universally held and others not.

An example is the construct *ren*, or forbearance. According to Xu, Farver, Chang, Yu, and Zhang (2006), when Chinese children use the *ren* strategy in response to peer animosity, they refrain from arguing or confronting their peers. However, this strategy is unlike problem-focused avoidance because Chinese children who use *ren* are not avoiding or running away from the situation. When Chinese children choose *ren* as a coping strategy, they do not participate in confrontation but directly attempt to elicit *ren* from the peers with whom they are interacting. This method of coping is used to encourage social harmony and group orientation. Measures developed in the West may overlook this social convention and, thus, could inaccurately assess social competence in Chinese culture. Given that *ren* is an integral component of Chinese culture, it makes sense to ask questions pertaining to the development of *ren*, the importance of temperament and parenting in *ren*, and the outcomes for children who fail to display *ren* with regard to the development of their peer relationships.

Western researchers who have interests in cross-cultural studies of children's peer interactions and relationships would do well to incorporate into their research programs the expertise of collaborators from other cultures. Only through conversations with their collaborators will there develop a better understanding of the constructs that truly matter in the lives of children and their peers.

Acknowledgments

The writing of this chapter was supported, in part, by a grant from the National Institute of Mental Health (no. MH58116) to Kenneth H. Rubin.

References

Aboud, F., and Mendelson, M. (1998). Determinants of friendship selection and quality: Developmental perspectives. In W. Bukowski and A. Newcomb (Eds.), *The company they keep: Friendship in childhood and adolescence* (pp. 87–112). New York: Cambridge University Press.

Asendorpf, J. (1991). Development of inhibited children's coping with unfamiliarity. *Child Development, 62*, 1460–1474.

Attili, G., Vermigli, P., and Schneider, B. (1997). Peer acceptance and friendship patterns among Italian schoolchildren within a cross-cultural perspective. *International Journal of Behavioral Development, 21*, 277–288.

Benenson, J. F., Markovits, H., Roy, R., and Denko, P. (2003). Behavioural rules underlying learning to share: Effects of development and context. *International Journal of Behavioural Development, 27*, 116–121.

Bergeron, N., and Schneider, B. (2005). Explaining cross-national differences in peer-directed aggression: A quantitative synthesis. *Aggressive Behavior, 31*, 116–137.

Bornstein, M. (Ed.). (1991). *Cultural approaches to parenting*. Hillsdale, NJ: Lawrence Erlbaum Associates, Inc.

Bornstein, M. H. (1995). Form and function: Implications for studies of culture and human development. *Culture & Psychology, 1*, 123-137.

Bornstein, M. H., and Cheah, C. S. L. (2006). The place of "culture and parenting" in the ecological contextual perspective on developmental science. In K. H. Rubin and O. Boon Chung (Eds.), *Parental beliefs, parenting, and child development in cross-cultural perspective* (pp. 3–33). London: Psychology Press.

Broberg, A., Lamb, M., and Hwang, P. (1990). Inhibition: Its stability and correlates in sixteen- to forty-month-old children. *Child Development, 61*, 1153–1163.

Brown, B. B., Eicher, S. A., and Petrie, S. (1986). The importance of peer group ("crowd") affiliation in adolescence. *Journal of Adolescence, 9*, 73–96.

Cairns, R. B., and Cairns, B. D. (1994). *Lifelines and risks: Pathways of youth in our time*. Cambridge, United Kingdom: Cambridge University Press.

Casiglia, A. C., Lo Coco, A., and Zappulla, C. (1998). Aspects of social reputation and peer relationships in Italian children: A cross-cultural perspective. *Developmental Psychology, 34*, 723–730.

Chang, L. (2003). Variable effects of children's aggression, social withdrawal, and prosocial leadership as functions of teacher beliefs and behaviors. *Child Development, 74*, 535–548.

Chang, L., Lei, L., Li, K. K., Liu, H., Guo, B., Wang, Y., et al. (2005). Peer acceptance and self-perceptions of verbal and behavioural aggression and social withdrawal. *International Journal of Behavioral Development, 29*, 48–57.

Cheah, C. S. L., and Rubin, K. H. (2003) European-American and mainland Chinese mothers socialization beliefs regarding preschoolers' social skills. *Parenting: Science and Practice, 3*, 1–21.

Cheah, C. S. L., and Rubin, K. H. (2004). A cross-cultural examination of maternal beliefs regarding maladaptive behaviors in preschoolers. *International Journal of Behavioral Development, 28*, 83–94.

Chen, X., Cen, G., Li, D., and He, Y. (2005). Social functioning and adjustment in Chinese children: The imprint of historical time. *Child Development, 76*, 182–195.

Chen, X., Chang, L., and He, Y. (2003). The peer group as a context: Mediating and moderating effects on the relations between academic achievement and social functioning in Chinese children. *Child Development, 74*, 710–727.

Chen, X., Chen, H., and Kaspar, V. (2001). Group social functioning and individual socio-emotional and school adjustment in Chinese children. *Merrill-Palmer Quarterly, 47*, 264–299.

Chen, X., French, D., and Schneider, B. (2006). Culture and peer relationships. In X. Chen, D. French, and B. H. Schneider (Eds.), *Peer relationships in cultural context* (pp. 3–20). New York: Cambridge University Press.

Chen, X., Hastings, P., Rubin, K. H., Chen, H., Cen, G., and Stewart, S. L. (1998). Childrearing attitudes and behavioral inhibition in Chinese and Canadian toddlers: A cross-cultural study. *Developmental Psychology, 34*, 677–686.

Chen, X., He, Y., De Oliveira, A. M., Lo Coco, A., Zappulla, C., Kaspar, V., et al. (2004). Loneliness and social adaptation in Brazilian, Canadian, Chinese, and Italian children: A multi-national comparative study. *Journal of Child Psychology and Psychiatry, 45*, 1373–1384.

Chen, X., Liu, M., Rubin, K., Cen, G., Gao, X., and Li, D. (2002). Sociability and prosocial orientation as predictors of youth adjustment: A seven-year longitudinal study in a Chinese sample. *International Journal of Behavioral Development, 26*, 128–136.

Chen, X., Rubin, K. H., Li, D., and Li, Z. (1999). Adolescent outcomes of social functioning in Chinese children. *International Journal of Behavioral Development, 23*, 199–223.

Chen, X., Rubin, K. H., and Sun, Y. (1992). Social reputation and peer relationships in Chinese and Canadian children. *Social Development, 3*, 269–290.

Chen, X., Wang, L., and DeSouza, A. (2006). Temperament, socioemotional functioning, and peer relationships in Chinese and North American children. In X. Chen, D. French, and B. H. Schneider (Eds.), *Peer relationships in cultural context* (pp. 123–147). New York: Cambridge University Press.

Cillessen, A. H., van Ijzendoorn, H. W., van Lieshout, C. F., and Hartup, W. W. (1992). Heterogeneity among peer-rejected boys: Subtypes and stabilities. *Child Development, 63*, 893–905.

Coplan, R., Bowker, A., and Cooper, S. (2003). Parenting daily hassles, child temperament, and social adjustment in preschool. *Early Childhood Research Quarterly, 18*, 376–395.

Crick, N. R., and Grotpeter, J. K. (1995). Relational aggression, gender, and social-psychological adjustment. *Child Development, 66*, 710–722.

Crozier, W., and Hostettler, K. (2003). The influence of shyness on children's test performance. *British Journal of Educational Psychology, 73*, 317–328.

Dashiell, E. N., Wojslawowicz Bowker, J. C., Rubin, K. H., Booth-LaForce, C., and Rose-Krasnor, L. (2006, July). Friendships of African-American children: Does similarity matter? In E. N. Dashiell, and J. Chung (Chairs), *Children's peer relationships: The role of ethnicity and culture*. Symposium conducted at the biennial meeting of the International Society for the Study of Behavioral Development, Melbourne, Australia.

de Guzman, M., and Carlo, G. (2004). Family, peer, and acculturative correlates of prosocial development among Latino youth in Nebraska. *Great Plains Research, 14*, 182–202.

Dodge, K., Coie, J., and Lynam, D. (2006). Aggression and antisocial behavior in youth. In N. Eisenberg, W. Damon, and R. M. Lerner (Eds.), *Handbook of child psychology. Volume 3: Social, emotional, and personality development* (6th ed., pp. 719–788). New York: Wiley.

DuBois, D., and Hirsch, B. (1990). School and neighborhood friendship patterns of blacks and whites in early adolescence. *Child Development, 61*, 524–536.

Edwards, C. P. (1992). Cross-cultural perspective on family-peer relations. In R. D. Parke and G. W. Ladd (Eds.), *Family-peer relationships: Modes of linkage* (pp. 285–316). Hillsdale, NJ: Lawrence Erlbaum Associates, Inc.

Eslea, M., Menesini, E., Morita, Y., O'Moore, M., Mora-Merchan, J. A., Pereira, B., and Smith, P. K. (2004). Friendship and loneliness among bullies and victims: Data from seven countries. *Aggressive Behavior, 30*, 71–83.

Farver, J., and Howes, C. (1988). Cross-cultural differences in social interaction: A comparison of American and Indonesian children. *Journal of Cross-Cultural Psychology, 19*, 203–215.

Farver, J., and Lee-Shin, Y. (2000). Acculturation and Korean-American children's social and play behavior. *Social Development, 9*, 316–336.

Farver, J., and Shin, Y. (1997). Social pretend play in Korean- and Anglo-American preschoolers. *Child Development, 68*, 544–556.

Fine, G. A. (1987). *With the boys: Little league baseball and preadolescent culture*. Chicago: University of Chicago Press.
Fox, N., Henderson, H., Rubin, K., Calkins, S., and Schmidt, L. (2001). Continuity and discontinuity of behavioral inhibition and exuberance: Psychophysiological and behavioral influences across the first four years of life. *Child Development, 72*, 1–21.
French, D., Jansen, E., and Pidada, S. (2002). United States and Indonesian children's and adolescents' reports of relational aggression by disliked peers. *Child Development, 73*, 1143–1150.
French, D., Jansen, E., Riansari, M., and Setiono, K. (2003). Friendships of Indonesian children: Adjustment of children who differ in friendship presence and similarity between mutual friends. *Social Development, 12*, 606–621.
French, D., Lee, O., and Pidada, S. (2006). Friendships of Indonesian, South Korean, and U.S. Youth: Exclusivity, intimacy, enhancement of worth, and conflict. In X. Chen, D. French, and B. H. Schneider (Eds.), *Peer relationships in cultural context* (pp. 379–402). New York: Cambridge University Press.
French, D., Pidada, S., Denoma, J., McDonald, K., and Lawton, A. (2005). Reported peer conflicts of children in the United States and Indonesia. *Social Development, 14*, 458–472.
French, D., Pidada, S., and Victor, A. (2005). Friendships of Indonesian and United States youth. *International Journal of Behavioral Development, 29*, 304–313.
Gaskins, S. (2006). The cultural organization of Yucatec Mayan children's social interactions. In Chen, X., French, D. C., and Schneider, B. H. (Eds.), *Peer relationships in cultural context* (pp. 283–309). New York: Cambridge University Press.
Goldsmith, H. H., Buss, A., Plomin, R., Rothbart, M. K., Thomas, A., Chess, S., Hinde, R. A., et al. (1987). What is temperament? Four approaches. *Child Development, 58*, 505–529.
Gonzalez, Y., Moreno, D., and Schneider, B. (2004). Friendship expectations of early adolescents in Cuba and Canada. *Journal of Cross-Cultural Psychology, 35*, 436–445.
Hamm, J., Brown, B., and Heck, D. (2005). Bridging the ethnic divide: Student and school characteristics in African American, Asian-descent, Latino, and White adolescents' cross-ethnic friend nominations. *Journal of Research on Adolescence, 15*, 21–46.
Hanish, L., and Guerra, N. (2004). Aggressive victims, passive victims, and bullies: Developmental continuity or developmental change? *Merrill-Palmer Quarterly, 50*, 17–38.
Harkness, S., and Super, C. M. (2002). Culture and parenting. In M. H. Bornstein (Ed.), *Handbook of parenting. Volume 2: Biology and ecology of parenting* (2nd ed., pp. 253–280). Mahwah, NJ: Lawrence Erlbaum Associates, Inc.
Hart, C. H., Yang, C., Nelson, L. J., Robinson, C. C., Olsen, J. A., Nelson, D. A., et al. (2000). Peer acceptance in early childhood and subtypes of socially withdrawn behaviour in China, Russia and the United States. *International Journal of Behavioral Development, 24*, 73–81.
Hartup, W. W., and Laursen, B. (1995). Conflict and context in peer relations. In C. H. Hart (Ed.), *Children on playgrounds* (pp. 44–84). Ithaca, NY: State University of New York Press.
Haselager, G. J. T., Cillessen, H. N., van Lieshout, C. F. M., Riksen-Walraven, J. M. A., and Hartup, W. W. (2002). Heterogeneity among peer-rejected boys across middle childhood: Developmental pathways of social behavior. *Child Development, 73*, 446–456.
Hatzichristou, C., and Hopf, D. (1996). A multiperspective comparison of peer sociometric status groups in childhood and adolescence. *Child Development, 67*, 1085–1102.
Hinde, R. A. (1987). *Individuals, relationships, and culture*. Cambridge, United Kingdom: Cambridge University Press.
Howes, C., and Wu, F. (1990). Peer interactions and friendships in an ethnically diverse school setting. *Child Development, 61*, 537–541.
Kao, G., and Joyner, K. (2004). Do race and ethnicity matter among friends? Activities among interracial, interethnic, and intraethnic adolescent friends. *Sociological Quarterly, 45*, 557–573.
Keller, M., Edelstein W., Schmid, C., Fang, F.-X., and Fang, G. (1998). Reasoning about responsibilities and obligations in close relationships: A comparison across two cultures. *Developmental Psychology, 34*, 731–741.
Kereteš, G., and Milanovic, A. (2006). Relations between different types of children's aggressive behavior and sociometric status among peers of the same and opposite gender. *Scandinavian Journal of Psychology, 47*, 477–483.
Khatri, P., and Kupersmidt, J. (2003). Aggression, peer victimization, and social relationships among Indian youth. *International Journal of Behavioral Development, 27*, 87–95.
Kienbaum, J., and Trommsdorff, G. (1999). Social development of young children in different cultural systems. *International Journal of Early Years Education, 7*, 241–248.

Kim, U., Triandis, H. C., Kagitcibasi, C., Choi, C., and Yoon, G. (1994). *Individualism and collectivism: Theory, methods, and applications.* Thousand Oaks, CA: Sage.

Kindermann, T. A., McCollom, T. L., and Gibson, E., Jr. (1995). Peer networks and students' classroom engagement during childhood and adolescence. In K. Wentzel and J. Juvonen (Eds.), *Social motivation: Understanding children's school adjustment* (pp. 279–312). New York: Cambridge University Press.

King, A. Y. C., and Bond, M. H. (1985). The Confucian paradigm of man: A sociological view. In W. Tseng and D. Y. H. Wu (Eds.), *Chinese culture and mental health* (pp. 29–46). Orlando, FL: Academic Press.

Knight, G., and Kagan, S. (1977). Acculturation of prosocial and competitive behaviors among second- and third-generation Mexican-American children. *Journal of Cross-Cultural Psychology, 8*, 273–284.

Krappmann, L. (1996). Amicitia, drujba, shin-yu, philia, freundschaft, friendship: On the cultural diversity of a human relationship. In W. M. Bukowski, A. F. Newcomb, and W. W. Hartup (Eds.), *The company they keep: Friendship in childhood and adolescence* (pp. 19–40). New York: Cambridge University Press.

Lagerspetz, K., Björkqvist, K., and Peltonen, T. (1988). Is indirect aggression typical of females? Gender differences in aggressiveness in 11- to 12-year-old children. *Aggressive Behavior, 14*, 403–414.

Matsumoto, D. (1997). *Culture and modern life.* Pacific Grove, CA: Brooks/Cole.

Nelson, D. A., Hart, C. H., Yang, C., and Jin, S. (2007). Aggression subtypes in the U.S. and Chinese preschoolers: Cultural equivalence, statistical distinctiveness, and peer outcomes. Manuscript submitted for publication.

Newcomb, A., and Bagwell, C. (1995). Children's friendship relations: A meta-analytic review. *Psychological Bulletin, 117*, 306–347.

Olweus, D. (1978). *Aggression in the schools: Bullies and whipping boys.* Oxford, England: Hemisphere.

Olweus, D. (1993) Victimization by peers: Antecedents and long-term outcomes. In K. H. Rubin and J. B. Asendorf (Eds.), *Social withdrawal, inhibition, and shyness in childhood.* Hillsdale, NJ: Lawrence Erlbaum Associates, Inc.

Owens, L. D. (1996). Sticks and stones and sugar and spice: Girls' and boys' aggression in schools. *Australian Journal of Guidance and Counseling, 6*, 45–55.

Oyserman, D., Coon, H., and Kemmelmeier, M. (2002). Rethinking individualism and collectivism: Evaluation of theoretical assumptions and meta-analyses. *Psychological Bulletin, 128*, 3–72.

Parker, J., and Gottman, J. (1989). Social and emotional development in a relational context: Friendship interaction from early childhood to adolescence. In T. J. Berndt and G. W. Ladd (Eds.), *Peer relationships in child development* (pp. 95–131). Oxford, England: John Wiley and Sons.

Pellegrini, A., and Long, J. (2002). A longitudinal study of bullying, dominance, and victimization during the transition from primary school through secondary school. *British Journal of Developmental Psychology, 20*, 259–280.

Pepler, D., Craig, W., Connolly, J., Yuile, A., McMaster, L., and Jiang, D. (2006). A developmental perspective on bullying. *Aggressive Behavior, 32*, 376–384.

Prakash, K., and Coplan, R. (2007). Socioemotional characteristics and school adjustment of socially withdrawn children in India. *International Journal of Behavioral Development, 31*, 123–132.

Prinstein, M., and Cillessen, A. (2003). Forms and functions of adolescent peer aggression associated with high levels of peer status. *Merrill-Palmer Quarterly, 49*, 310–342.

Rigby, K. (2005). Bullying in schools and the mental health of children. *Australian Journal of Guidance and Counseling, 15*, 195–208.

Rothbart, M. K., and Bates, J. E. (2006). Temperament. In N. Eisenberg (Vol. Ed.) and W. Damon and R. Lerner (Series Eds.), *Handbook of child psychology. Volume 3: Social, emotional, and personality development* (6th ed., pp. 99–166). Hoboken, NJ: Wiley.

Rubin, K., Bukowski, W., and Parker, J. (2006). Peer interactions, relationships, and groups. In N. Eisenberg, W. Damon, and R. M. Lerner (Eds.), *Handbook of child psychology. Volume 3: Social, emotional, and personality development* (6th ed., pp. 571–645). New York: Wiley.

Rubin, K., Burgess, K., and Coplan, R. (2002). Social withdrawal and shyness. In P. K. Smith and C. H. Hart (Eds.), *Blackwell handbook of childhood social development* (pp. 330–352), Malden, MA: Blackwell Publishing.

Rubin, K. H., Burgess, K. B., and Hastings, P. D. (2002). Stability and social-behavioral consequences of toddlers' inhibited temperament and parenting. *Child Development, 73*, 483–495.

Rubin, K. H., Chen, X., and Hymel, S. (1993). Socioemotional characteristics of withdrawn and aggressive children. *Merrill-Palmer Quarterly, 39*, 518–534.

Rubin, K. H., Chen, X., McDougall, P., Bowker, A., and McKinnon, J. (1995). The Waterloo longitudinal project: Predicting internalizing and externalizing problems in adolescence. *Development and Psychopathology, 7*, 751–764.

Rubin, K. H., Fein, G., and Vandenberg, B. (1983). Play. In P. H. Mussen (Series Ed.) and E. M. Hetherington (Vol. Ed.), *Handbook of child psychology. Volume 4: Socialization, personality and social development* (4th ed., pp. 693–774). New York: Wiley.

Rubin, K. H., Hemphill, S. A., Chen, X., Hastings, P., Sanson, A., Lo Coco, A., et al. (2006). A cross-cultural study of behavioral inhibition in toddlers: East-West-North-South. *International Journal of Behavioral Development, 30,* 219–226.

Schaughency, E., Vannatta, K., Langhinrichsen, J., and Lally, C. (1992). Correlates of sociometric status in school children in Buenos Aires. *Journal of Abnormal Child Psychology, 20,* 317–326.

Schneider, B., Fonzi, A., Tani, F., and Tomada, G. (1997). A cross-cultural exploration of the stability of children's friendships and predictors of their continuation. *Social Development, 6,* 322–339.

Schneider, B., Woodburn, S., Soteras-de Toro, M., and Udvari, S. (2005). Cultural and gender differences in the implications of competition for early adolescent friendship. *Merrill-Palmer Quarterly, 51,* 163–191.

Schwartz, D., Farver, J., Chang, L., and Lee-Shin, Y. (2002). Victimization in South Korean children's peer groups. *Journal of Abnormal Child Psychology, 30,* 113–125.

Sharabany, R. (2006). The cultural context of children and adolescents: Peer relationships and intimate friendships among Arab and Jewish children in Israel. In X. Chen, D. French, and B. H. Schneider (Eds.), *Peer relationships in cultural context* (pp. 452–478). New York: Cambridge University Press.

Slee, P. (1995). Bullying in the playground: The impact of inter-personal violence on Australian children's perceptions of their play environment. *Children's Environments, 12,* 320–327.

Smith, P. K., Cowie, H., Olafsson, R. F., Liefooghe, A. P. D., Almeida, A., Araki, H., et al. (2002). Definitions of bullying: A comparison of terms used, and age and gender differences, in a fourteen-country international comparison. *Child Development, 73,* 1119–1133.

Stevenson, H. W., Chen, C., Lee, S., and Fuligni, A. J. (1991). In L. Okagaki and R. J. Sternberg (Eds.), *Directors of development: Influences on the development of children's thinking* (pp. 243–268). Hillsdale, NJ: Lawrence Erlbaum Associates, Inc.

Sun, L., Chen, H. C., and Zheng, S. J. (2006). The subtypes of social withdrawal and temperament in early childhood. *Chinese Mental Health Journal, 20,* 288–290.

Tomada, G., and Schneider, B. H. (1997). Relational aggression, gender, and peer acceptance: Invariance across culture, stability over time, and concordance among informants. *Developmental Psychology, 33,* 601–609.

Triandis, H. C. (1990). Cross-cultural studies on individualism and collectivism. In J. J. Berman, (Ed.), *Nebraska Symposium on Motivation, 1989: Cross-cultural perspectives* (pp. 41–133). Lincoln, NE: University of Nebraska Press.

Triandis, H., Bontempo, R., Villareal, M., and Asai, M. (1988). Individualism and collectivism: Cross-cultural perspectives on self-ingroup relationships. *Journal of Personality and Social Psychology, 54,* 323–338.

Way, N., and Chen, L. (2000). Close and general friendships among African American, Latino, and Asian American adolescents from low-income families. *Journal of Adolescent Research, 15,* 274–301.

Way, N., Cowal, K., Gingold, R., Pahl, K., and Bissessar, N. (2001). Friendship patterns among African American, Asian American, and Latino adolescents from low-income families. *Journal of Social and Personal Relationships, 18,* 29–53.

Weisz, J., Suwanlert, S., Chaiyasit, W., and Walter, B. (1987). Over- and undercontrolled referral problems among children and adolescents from Thailand and the United States: The wat and wai of cultural differences. *Journal of Consulting and Clinical Psychology, 55,* 719–726.

Whiting, J., and Child, I. (1953). *Child training and personality: A cross-cultural study.* New Haven, CT: Yale University Press.

Xie, H., Cairns, B. D., and Cairns, R. B. (2001). Predicting teen motherhood and teen fatherhood: Individual characteristics and peer affiliations. *Social Development, 10,* 488–511.

Xie, H., Swift, D., Cairns, B., and Cairns, R. (2002). Aggressive behaviors in social interaction and developmental adaptation: A narrative analysis of interpersonal conflicts during early adolescence. *Social Development, 11,* 205–224.

Xu, Y., Farver, J., Schwartz, D., and Chang, L. (2004). Social networks and aggressive behavior in Chinese children. *International Journal of Behavioral Development, 28,* 401–410.

Xu, Y., Farver, J., Chang, L., Yu, L., and Zhang, Z. (2006). Culture, family contexts, and children's coping strategies in peer interactions. In X. Chen, D. French, and B. H. Schneider (Eds.), *Peer relationships in cultural context* (pp. 264–280). New York: Cambridge University Press.

13
Socialization

MARY GAUVAIN and ROSS D. PARKE

Introduction

Children do not develop on their own. The process of human development is supported and guided by teams of individuals and groups. Moreover, this process is not haphazard. Over the course of development, children are steered along a particular path. This path is defined by many factors including, perhaps most significantly, the culture in which the child lives and is expected to function as a competent and contributing member, albeit in different ways at different ages. Socialization is the term used to describe the process of development along a culturally prescribed path. More specifically, it is the process through which children acquire the beliefs, values, practices, skills, attitudes, behaviors, ways of thinking, and motives of their culture that together help children develop into effective and contributing members of the group.

Socialization is a natural feature of human development. No healthy human beings exist outside of culture, and it is, therefore, reasonable to assume that the socialization of young members into the cultural group is a human imperative. Socialization is also a pervasive feature of human development, as LeVine (1982, p. 62) stated, "children absorb culture in every aspect of their experience." A central function of socialization is its role in maintaining culture across generations. Through cross-generational transmission, the accumulated wisdom of the group is sustained in a process of cumulative cultural evolution (Tomasello, 1999). New cultural members adopt and adapt practices and tools devised by prior generations to support intelligent action, a process referred to as "the ratchet effect" (Tomasello, Kruger, and Ratner, 1993). Thus, socialization supports individual human development, while at the same time, it sustains culture, both by maintaining the practices and tools that support valued activities in the community and by making way for modifications in these social forms as environmental conditions and cultural resources change.

Over the last century, socialization has been conceptualized in many ways. In historical treatments, research largely concentrated on how parents and kin trained children to use culturally appropriate behaviors (Berry, Poortinga, Segall, and Dasen, 2006). Contemporary research recognizes the contributions of a broader range of social forces, including peers, adults other than kin, and cultural tools and symbol systems. Additionally, in many early conceptualizations, the child was viewed as the passive recipient of the socialization efforts of adults. For instance, Margaret Mead (1964) considered socialization the process whereby culture is communicated to children through childrearing and that results in an adult personality type that reflects the pattern of the culture. In contrast, contemporary approaches see children as playing active roles in socialization, which is viewed as dynamic and socially constructed. Socialization occurs through human transactions as children are exposed to and develop behaviors and ways of understanding that reflect their culture. Children contribute to this process through their interests, needs, and abilities. Neither the shape of socialization nor its endpoint is predetermined. Both the specific social processes and the goals that guide socialization at any point in time are subject to local conditions. Thus, human socialization is inherently flexible, and as such, the content, procedures, and participants vary across cultural settings and reflect the time, place, and needs of individuals and the community.

In this chapter, we discuss the process of child socialization in cultural context. We describe the main social agents involved and the common and diverse goals and strategies of socialization across cultural settings that have been identified by research. However, we first take a closer look at the socialization process along with current developmental perspectives we find useful for examining this process.

The Socialization Process

Socialization is the means by which children become members of a cultural group. A culture is a unique type of social group. For our discussion, we define culture as a species-typical way of life of a group of human beings of mixed ages and relatedness whose behaviors and activities are guided by shared meaning, practices, and purpose that have been transmitted across generations through various social means. Socialization occurs over a long period of time via myriad transactions between the child and the culture in which the child lives. These transactions are multidimensional. They involve a host of partners and experiences, and they exist in many forms, including interpersonal contact; participation in cultural routines, rituals, and institutions; and during solitary activity when children work on problems or with materials derived from the culture. Although socialization is organized largely by more experienced cultural members, the process is reciprocal. It builds on the capabilities of the human child that are present at birth, including a vast potential for learning, a bias toward social processes and experience, and the capacity to form strong emotional ties. Throughout development, children and their more experienced partners jointly create and regulate the socialization process. With increasing age, as children's skills and interests change, the nature of their participation in culture, along with expectations pertaining to their participation, change accordingly (Rogoff, 2003).

The pervasive, multidimensional, and reciprocal nature of socialization attests to its importance in the development of the individual and the culture. The need for children to be part of culture and the need for culture to maintain and build on its cumulative accomplishments across generations vis-à-vis its members are complementary and generative forces (Tomasello, 1999). These forces are evident whether one examines the process from a contemporary or an evolutionary vantage point. From an evolutionary perspective, several characteristics of the human species underlie the socialization process. The immaturity of human beings at birth, the protracted period of dependence on mature members of the species, the ability to create strong emotional ties from the beginning of life, early and powerful learning capabilities, and the gradual specialization of human intelligence to local circumstances ensure that childhood is marked by extensive learning in the company of people who already know much of what the child needs to learn and who are invested in the child physically and emotionally (Bjorklund and Pellegrini, 2002). This entourage, which includes caregivers, siblings, peers, and other members of the community, provides sustenance for healthy development. These individuals, through their own behavioral tendencies and actions, function as representatives of the culture and, thereby, as agents of socialization. In their interactions with children, agents of socialization communicate the expectations and goals of the culture to children.

To reach adult levels of competence, children have to learn a lot about the culture. To this end, cultural members rely on many social learning processes, including observation, imitation, attention regulation, demonstration, instruction, rehearsal, shaping, scaffolding, guided participation, and trial and error (Berry et al., 2006). In every culture there are also many established settings of learning that support socialization, including formal institutions, such as school, and less formal settings, including specialized and intentional arrangements like apprenticeships and more incidental opportunities for learning about culture, such as observation of and participation in routines and rituals (Serpell and Hatano, 1997).

Because of the complexity of culture, the importance of cultural learning, and the developing needs and abilities of the child, socialization transpires over a long period of time. Several factors regulate the frequency and manner in which socialization occurs. Cultures differ in what knowledge they consider important to pass on to children, how this knowledge is conveyed, and when children should acquire it (Goodnow, 1990). Human maturity is not reached until puberty, and even at this point, many cultures continue to endorse close ties between adults and youth (Schlegel and Barry, 1991). Such ties permit the honing of skills along specialized cultural lines either in apprenticeships or more advanced formal training in societal institutions. Although formal and informal arrangements of socialization differ on many counts, they are similar in that they include sets of actions that are shared by and have meaning to cultural members (Greenfield and Lave, 1982). They are repeated and, thereby, function as part of the regular cultural fabric (Goodnow, Miller, and Kessel, 1995), and they include expectations that extend beyond the immediate circumstance and help guide later behavior (Valsiner and Lawrence, 1997). Thus, through participation in cultural arrangements of learning, human behavior becomes increasingly aligned with the behaviors and practices of the cultural group.

The recognition of cultural variability in socialization does not mean that there are no universal aspects of this process. Socialization builds on universal characteristics of the child, including innate capabilities to use language, communicate with others, and participate in social relationships (LeVine et al., 1994). Socialization is also constrained by human capabilities that define the information to which human beings attend and how this information is processed (Elman et al., 1996). Both innate capabilities and constraints of the human processing system facilitate cultural learning in that certain forms of experience or environmental input are given priority over other forms. For instance, the social bias that is evident in early perceptual development directs children's attention toward conspecifics in ways that optimize learning about the world from other people from the very early years of life (Gauvain, 2001).

Universal features of the human system do not predetermine either the pattern or outcome of the socialization process. Rather, they represent a broad set of parameters that define the species-typical or average expected environment in which human development occurs (Bjorklund and Pellegrini, 2002). Culturally specific patterns of socialization emerge from the dynamic and bidirectional interaction of these universal characteristics with historical and ecological features of culture. In other words, children acquire cultural understanding and beliefs within the limits that are established by processes of development, including cognitive capabilities, which are common across the species (Greenfield and Bruner, 1969). Variations in socialization across cultures are derived from the different ways that cultures use these innate and species-general capacities to address the "human dilemmas and human ambiguities" (Kessen, 1991, p. 188) unique to their time, place, and history. Thus, socialization is at the same time a universal and a culturally specific process, and understanding this process requires attention to both of these contributions and their interrelation over time.

In this chapter, theoretical perspectives that help to capture the dynamic nature of the socialization process over ontogenetic and historical time, the multiple systems and institutions of culture that are involved, and the individual transactions that form the bases of socialization are used to discuss this process in more detail. It is also important to identify common cultural contexts of human development that can provide researchers with a window into the universal and culturally specific aspects of socialization. To reach these goals, this chapter relies on several current developmental theories or perspectives and provides illustrations of the socialization process from both cross-cultural and within-culture analyses.

As our guides, we use the perspectives of Dynamic Systems approaches (Thelen and Smith, 2006), Ecological Systems Theory (Bronfenbrenner and Morris, 2006), sociocultural approaches (Shweder et al., 2006), and the idea of the developmental niche (Super and Harkness, 1986). Each of these views offers unique insight for studying the socialization process. In addition, they avoid two assumptions inherent to many contemporary views of development that present problems to understanding socialization. First, many contemporary theories adopt an individualistic stance in which the child is the unit of study, individual functioning is the outcome of development, or the primary role of culture is its influence on individual performance (or vice versa) (Kessen, 1979; Rogoff, 2003). An individualism assumption overlooks a key aspect of socialization, specifically that individual development and the sociocultural context of development are mutually constituted. Therefore, separating these components either theoretically or empirically undermines examination of the process.

A second assumption in many contemporary theories that presents problems to understanding socialization is that development is seen as directed toward a particular outcome, typically "represented by finished adult forms, the thought of the rational adult" (Kessen, 1984, p. 422). As Kessen pointed out, this assumption, which is rarely questioned in research, suggests that human psychological growth has a predetermined course and endpoint. However, flexibility in response to environmental demands is a hallmark of human functioning (Greenough, Black, and Wallace, 1987). Such flexibility played a critical role in human evolution (Bjorklund and Pellegrini, 2002), and it remains a key force in the socialization process. Although one might be able to provide a rough description of the type of adult that a child should grow into at a particular point in a culture's history, how development unfolds is subject to many factors, and it is rooted in actual human experience. The activities that compose socialization are targeted toward local solutions, such as solving a particular problem or carrying out a social practice. The outcome of socialization is the product of these solutions, and this product is arrived at in a nonlinear and complex way. In other words, socialization is a composition; it is made up of many discrete yet related activities in which children engage over a long period of time—a time during which children are growing and changing. In addition, this process is not unique to a child; it resonates among a cohort of children and represents a historically based set of solutions.

As a consequence, in any particular activity, the link between the activity and long-range socialization goals may not be evident. Such links may only be apparent in the concerted nature of activities over time, with the final adult form emerging from these moments. In other words, socialization is fleshed out over a long period of time via the activities in which children engage, the skills that adults pass onto children, the expectations for when and how children are involved in activities, and children's participation in the process (Rogoff, 2003). Given this course, it is important that socialization be both overdetermined and underdefined. It is overdetermined in that the pervasive nature of culture ensures that children are enmeshed in the activities, tools, and social practices of the culture. This reality makes socialization to culture an unavoidable aspect of normal human development (LeVine, 1982). Socialization is also underdefined; its path and outcomes are painted in broad rather than narrow brush strokes. This permits the maintenance of culturally valued ways of living across generations while at the same time allowing for flexibility and openness, which are essential for innovation and change.

To summarize, socialization follows a path that is sensitive to the biological states of the organism and the historical features of the culture, while at the same time, it is subject to the overarching rules and local conditions of the environment. A universal and deterministic function drives all human development forward in time, but it is the culture's unique history that sets the stage for what information gets transmitted and how it gets transmitted across generations.

Because human beings and the socialization process through which development occurs are flexible and responsive to environmental conditions, there is no predetermined course or endpoint of socialization at a particular time in a culture's history. Changes in local conditions give different arcs to the socialization process both across cultural contexts and within a single cultural setting over historical time. Because human development is, by and large, pretty stable, small perturbations are not likely to alter the socialization process of a culture very much. However, large perturbations may change the process considerably. Variations in socialization across and within cultures over time stand as evidence of the creativity, flexibility, and diversity of the human system. These variations helped support, perhaps even made way for, the viability of the species across a large span of evolutionary history. In addition, most importantly for present purposes, these variations are expressed in the process of human development. This suggests that examination of cultural variation in the socialization process may increase understanding of the potential and limitations of the human system itself.

Guiding Theoretical Perspectives on Socialization

In this section, we outline some of the early efforts to study socialization from a cultural vantage and describe some recent societal and demographic trends that impinge on socialization. Following this discussion, we describe several theoretical perspectives that are useful for understanding socialization in cultural context. We then illustrate how these perspectives shed light on socialization with select examples from cross-cultural and intracultural research. Because research on socialization is reviewed in many sources (see Berry, Dasen, and Saraswathi, 1997; Bugental and Grusec, 2006), including a recent handbook on the topic (Grusec and Hastings, 2007), it is not necessary to review this body of work here.

A Brief History of Culturally Based Research on Child Socialization

Research on socialization has been conducted for over a century by investigators from a range of disciplines, including anthropology, sociology, linguistics, and psychology. One of the early and most influential scholars in the study of socialization was Margaret Mead (1930) who argued that much could be learned about human development by studying natural variations in childrearing and development across different cultural settings. Mead introduced some of the core questions about socialization that remain today, including whether universal features of development exist and, if they do, how different cultures support these features, and whether and how biological inheritance contributes to the socialization process.

By the mid-twentieth century, socialization was a primary focus of social science research, and although interest in the topic waned in the 1970s, it did not entirely disappear. Several important studies on cultural socialization were conducted during this period (e.g., LeVine et al., 1994; Whiting and Whiting, 1975). Research also appeared that took a narrower focus than Mead envisioned but nonetheless advanced understanding of the relation between childrearing and development in specific areas of growth. Research by Stevenson and colleagues (see Stevenson and Stigler, 1992) on the contributions of cultural practices to the development of academic skills exemplifies this direction of study.

The research on socialization that has been conducted over the past century has been guided by a variety of theoretical and research perspectives including learning theory, human ethology, biosocial and ecocultural approaches, sociocultural views, and child development in minority populations (Bugental and Grusec, 2006; Harkness, 1992; Saraswathi, 2003; Werner, 1979). Many of the early views of socialization in cultural context that used a psychological perspective were founded on psychoanalytically oriented theories that, in turn, led to a view of the mother as the major socialization agent. Because this view was consistent with assumptions in developmental psychology at the time, chiefly represented in attachment theory, the characterization of socialization that emerged in the mid-twentieth century both in anthropology and developmental psychology was one in which the process was largely the province of parents, especially mothers. This view also suggested that because socialization is rooted in universal properties of the human organism, cross-cultural study of this process would be useful for the evaluation of theories, such as Freudian theory, that include such assumptions.

A significant shift in theory and research on socialization from a psychological perspective occurred in the 1970s when John and Beatrice Whiting (1975) and a team of collaborators studied socialization in six different cultures around the world: East Africa, India, Okinawa, the Philippines, Mexico, and the United States. Investigators lived in traditional communities in these regions and conducted research that yielded similar and, therefore, comparable information. This research was based on the psycho-cultural model of human development introduced by Whiting and Child (1953), which conceptualized child socialization as the link between societal-cultural features and the psychology of adults in the culture. Culture was defined in broad terms and included characteristics of the natural environment, the history of the group, and subsistence patterns and other institutionalized practices. Extensive behavioral observations of childrearing practices and child behavior were used to probe the relations between cultural experience and human development. The aim of this research was to connect large-scale cultural dimensions directly with the child's learning environment. The researchers attempted to link the settings that children occupied and the activities and caregivers with whom children engaged with adult personality types depicted in projective and expressive systems such as religious beliefs, rituals, and art. For these researchers, child socialization was the crucial link between societal and cultural factors and the psychology of adults in a culture.

Findings from this research illustrated a diverse range of childrearing practices across the six cultures. They supported the view that different learning environments lead to different child behaviors, which led Beatrice Whiting (1980) to define culture as a "provider of settings" and parents as the "organizers of settings" for human development. However, establishing clear and defining links between the ecocultural context, child socialization, and adult personality was difficult (Frijda and Jahoda, 1966). This research has been criticized for failing to view the child as an active agent in the socialization process and for ignoring influences on child socialization that come from beyond the culture, like media-based images, or that have been imported into the culture, such as Western schooling (Werner, 1979). Despite these criticisms, this research represented an important step in the examination of the relations between large-scale ecological and sociocultural factors and child socialization. It influenced later studies of socialization including the idea of the developmental niche (Super and Harkness, 1986), discussed later, and research that examines children's activity settings, household organization and responsibilities, patterns of infant and childcare, and socialization practices (Munroe and Munroe, 1971; Seymour, 1988; Tronick, Morelli, and Ivey, 1992; Weisner, 1984).

In the late twentieth century, changing demographics of children and the experiences of childhood, including societal and cultural changes that affect how children are socialized, have introduced new approaches to this area of study. For instance, changes in family size and the availability of social, economic, educational, and health resources have had substantial effect on child socialization in the United States (Hernandez, 1995). From an international perspective, many factors often grouped together under the term globalization, such as rural to urban and international migration, rapid social change, contact among distant cultures through media and various forms of direct experience (e.g., travel, military occupation, international health agencies, relief work), and processes associated with modernization (e.g., increased literacy rates and commerce, availability of electricity and other amenities that reorganize how people use time), have had tremendous impact on child socialization worldwide. Such changes raise questions about children's daily experiences, including how economic, political, and social forces may conflict with established socialization practices and, as a result, affect psychological development. For instance, Kagitçibasi (1995) pointed out that in developing nations, increasing numbers of poor children are being sent to school in the hope that they will support the changing economic and social system of a country. However, these children often enter school lacking the type of early cognitive stimulation that research conducted in developed nations has identified as critical to school readiness and academic success. Proposing modifications to early socialization practices that help to prepare children for school could enhance children's success in school. Yet such efforts raise many questions about cultural values and ethnocentrism. To address these concerns, research has showed that culturally sensitive methods of supporting parents and children in communities undergoing widespread cultural change, as in the Turkish Early Enrichment Project (Kagitçibasi, 1993), can benefit families, children, and society.

Contemporary Developmental Theories and Culturally Based Research on Child Socialization

In our view, four theoretical approaches in contemporary developmental science are useful for studying the process of socialization. These perspectives are Dynamic Systems approaches, Ecological Systems Theory, sociocultural approaches, and the idea of the developmental niche.

Dynamic Systems Approaches Dynamic Systems approaches to child development, including transactional views, concentrate on changes over time and consider these changes the result of the coordination of elements of a complex, integrated system (Fogel, 1993; Sameroff, 1989, 1994; Thelen, 1995). This view attempts to describe how development arises from the system as a whole, not from any single factor. Contemporary research in this area covers a wide range of topics, including motor development, early relationships, emotional functioning, and development in the family system. The term *dynamic* underscores the constant interaction and mutual influence of elements of the system. Several specific principles are used to describe this dynamic relation. The principle of complexity suggests that each part of a system is unique but at the same time related to one or more of the other parts of the system (e.g., a culture contains individual members as well as related members and subgroups). The principle of wholeness and organization stresses that the system is organized and contains more than just the sum of its parts (e.g., to understand a culture, it is important to study the members, the relationships between them, the organization of the relationships, and the entire culture as an interacting unit). The principle of identity suggests that no matter how a system may change, the identity of the system remains intact (e.g., a culture continues even when new members join it and old members die). Stability refers to the maintenance of the system over time (e.g., the socialization process and the physical and emotional ties among cultural members maintain the culture as a system). The principle of morphogenesis refers to change; systems, such as a culture, must be able to adapt to internal and external changes. The principle of equifinality holds that most individuals reach essentially the same end state (e.g., maintenance of human culture can be met by multiple means and, therefore, diverse pathways or methods of socialization both across cultures and within a culture over historical time are expected).

The emphasis in Dynamic Systems approaches on the processes and transactions among elements of the system is useful for examining the nature, purpose, and course of socialization in cultural context. A culture and its members change in relation to ongoing interactions and demands within the system. The socialization process, which mirrors these changes, is constrained but not wholly predetermined in course or outcome.

Ecological Systems Theory Ecological Systems Theory (Bronfenbrenner and Morris, 2006) stresses the importance of understanding not only the relationships between the child and various environmental systems, such as the family and the community, but also the relationships among environmental systems. It provides a description of the many layers of human social and psychological experience that make up development in cultural context. In addition, Ecological Systems Theory views children as active participants in creating their own environments and considers children's subjective experiences of their relationships and their surroundings as important as the objective aspects of these phenomena.

This approach describes the layers of environment that impact child development and are intricately tied to the socialization process. In this view, child development is embedded in a set of nested contextual influences that range from the most immediate settings (the microsystem), such as the family or peer group, to more remote contexts of the child's life, such as the culture's systems of values and rules (exo- and macrosystems). The mesosystem comprises the interrelations among the components of the microsystem (e.g., parents interact with caregivers and teachers). The chronosystem reflects that these systems change over time and both the child and the environment undergo change. From the perspective of Ecological Systems Theory, socialization in cultural context involves the interaction of a changing child with the changing ecological and cultural context in all of its complexity.

Sociocultural Approaches The sociohistorical or sociocultural approach, which traces much of its roots to the writings of Lev S. Vygotsky (1978), emphasizes the role of the social and cultural context in human development. Social interaction, in particular, is seen as a critical force. In social interaction, children learn about themselves, their social partners, and their culture, including cultural activities and tools that support intelligent action. In this way, social and cultural experiences mediate individual development and transform the child's innate psychological abilities, such as perceptual and memory skills, into more complex, higher order psychological functions that are suited to the needs and interests of the culture.

By emphasizing the socially mediated nature of psychological development, this approach offers a useful way of conceptualizing and investigating the day-to-day interactions that make up socialization. In this approach, the particular ways in which adults support and direct child development are influenced by culture, such as in the values and practices that organize what and how adults and children think and work together in the course of everyday activities. Sociocultural approaches also emphasize the psychological activities and tools children use to understand the world. These activities and tools, which are devised by culture, take a variety of forms and include goal-directed actions, language, mathematical notation, mnemonic devices, art, literacy, and technology. As children develop, different activities and tools help children to function more effectively in solving problems and understanding the world. Thus, the practices and products of culture are embedded in socialization and are evident in the ways in which children learn to think about and solve problems alone and with others.

The Developmental Niche Super and Harkness (1986) proposed the concept of the developmental niche as a means of considering simultaneously psychological and cultural contributions to human development. Super and Harkness adapted a concept from biological ecology, the ecological niche, and used it to describe the relation between organisms and their cultural environments. The developmental niche is similar to its counterpart in biology in that the physical and social environment is a defining feature of an organism and its development. For humans, this ecological setting is the cultural system that provides children with regulation and direction for development. This view of development directs attention away from the solitary organism or the environment as a unit of study and toward the continuing and changing fit between regularities in the cultural system and those in the organism over the course of growth.

Super and Harkness identified three subsystems of the developmental niche that connect human development directly to culture. These subsystems are the physical and social settings of development, customs of childcare, and the psychology of caregivers. These subsystems simultaneously emphasize the psychological contributions of the participants and the context of development. The concept of the developmental niche can help to identify subsystems that are critical to the socialization process and therefore universal. At the same time, it permits examination of the unique form that these universal requirements take in any particular cultural and historical context. The idea of the developmental niche resonates with Ecological Systems Theory; however, in the latter, the focus is the broad range of proximal and distal features of children's experience that affect development. The developmental niche approach concentrates on how the everyday environment or microenvironment of the child is regulated by the culture.

In summary, each of these four theoretical approaches provides inroads for addressing aspects of the socialization process. Dynamic Systems approaches offer a way of conceptualizing socialization as a process that emerges over the course of development and is derived from the capabilities and constraints of the organism in conjunction with the rules and local conditions of the culture and the environment. Ecological Systems Theory recognizes that socialization is embedded in multiple, interacting systems that have both unique and mutual patterns of influence on human development. Sociocultural approaches describe processes that mediate psychological functioning and underlie socialization, such as social interaction and the use of activities, tools, and symbol systems to support thinking. Finally, the idea of the developmental niche can be used to identify subsystems of a culture that directly impinge on child socialization.

Central Issues in the Study of Socialization

In this section, we discuss socialization practices more explicitly by focusing on the people who serve as major agents of socialization, the socialization goals embedded in children's experiences with these agents, and various strategies that are used by more and less experienced cultural members to communicate about and negotiate socialization information. In this discussion, we integrate ideas and techniques of study offered by the four theoretical perspectives outlined previously, with the aim of showing how these perspectives provide unique and complementary views of the socialization process. By way of illustration, we discuss research findings regarding cultural variations in the agents and processes of socialization.

Agents, Goals, and Strategies of Socialization to Culture

We adopt a multiagent view of socialization that flows from the theoretical perspectives outlined previously. The roles that different people assume and the manner in which they contribute to socialization vary substantially across cultures. This variation attests to the flexibility of the socialization process in meeting its overall aim of integrating children, the new members of the community, into the practices and values of the group.

Dynamic Systems Approaches Instead of mothers being the central socialization agent, a dynamic family systems perspective recognizes that multiple family and community members such as fathers, siblings, and other kin and nonkin community members play interrelated roles in the socialization effort. Although each of these agents plays a distinctive role—one that is largely prescribed by cultural values and practices—they operate together in ways not fully understood to influence children's socialization into culture. Examining the various partners involved in socialization activities as a dynamic and transactional system can help in identifying the unique and collective contributions of different agents of socialization to the process.

Consistent with the levels of analysis assumption inherent in the dynamic systems approach (Sameroff, 1994), it is recognized that dyadic relationships, such as parent–child or sibling relationships, are merely one level of organization within the family, along with triadic (mother–father–child, father–sibling–sibling) and extended kin units (grandparents–parents–siblings) and family and community levels (cohesion, identity, rituals, routines) (see Fiese, 2006; Parke and Buriel, 2006). The properties, functions, and effects of the family unit cannot necessarily be inferred from smaller units of analysis. In addition, families change in response to changes in the individual members, life circumstances, and scheduled and unscheduled transitions. Families develop distinct "climates" (Moos and Moos, 1981), "styles" of responding to events (Reiss, 1989), and "boundaries" (Boss, 1999), which provide differing socialization contexts for the developing child. Various social agents contribute to socialization, and culture determines who these agents are and what children learn from these encounters.

Research on children's play, which functions as a major avenue of socialization to culture (Göncü and Gaskins, 2007), illustrates these points. Play can provide children with exposure to and practice with many different types of cultural behaviors and expectations that are valued in a culture (Gaskins, Haight, and Lancy, 2007). In all cultures, play provides children with a particular kind of access to various members of the community, along with information about the roles and responsibilities that these members have in the culture and towards each other. For instance, parent–child play can introduce children to the values and routine adult activities of the culture, which are critical components of socialization.

Play can be conceptualized along the various dimensions outlined by Dynamic Systems Theory. It is complex and involves many aspects and agents of socialization, ranging from the various play partners children have, the types of play in which children engage, the developmental capabilities that are integrated with and perhaps emerge from play, and the mapping of play onto the short- and long-range expectations that the culture has for the child. These contributions can be examined in relation to their unique contributions, but in terms of socialization, it is their wholeness and organization that are important.

The contribution of play to socialization is more than the sum of its parts; it conveys many messages about the culture in a form that is accessible and motivating to children and that entails their active participation. Various social agents engage in play with children in ways that help sustain cultural identity as expressed in the psychology of its members (e.g., in role play, children attempt to simulate the emotions, thoughts, and actions of other people; Harris, 2000). From a broad perspective, play, as a ubiquitous feature of childhood, demonstrates the principle of equifinality. Cultural variation in the form and frequency of play illustrates diversity within the common method of socialization. Finally, play experiences transfer across social contexts and partners (e.g., playful exchanges with mother influence how children play with other social partners and vice versa). This mutual influence illustrates the principles of complexity and morphogenesis via the interdependence of subsystems that are connected to broader cultural values and practices (Göncü and Gaskins, 2007). Whereas European American parents emphasize independence and self-expression in pretend play with their young children, Taiwanese parents focus on harmonious social interactions and understanding of and respect for rules (Gaskins et al., 2007). In an Australian study (Russell and Russell, 1987), parents were involved in play interactions with their 6- to 7-year-old children that reproduced conventional parenting roles (e.g., fathers were involved in physical/outdoor play interactions such as fixing things around the house and garden). Even in cultures where children play very little, important messages about cultural values are embedded in these practices (Gaskins, 1999).

In some cultures, different play partners, such as mothers and fathers, provide distinctively different socialization experiences for children (see Bornstein and Lansford, Chapter 14, in this volume). In North American families, fathers, regardless of ethnicity (European American, African American, or Hispanic American), spend a greater percentage of their time with their infants in play than mothers, although in absolute terms, mothers spend more time than fathers in play with their children (Yeung, Sandberg, Davis-Kean, and Hofferth, 2001). The quality of play across mothers and fathers differs, too. For infants and toddlers, mothers tend to play more conventional motor games or toy-mediated activities and are more verbal and didactic. This type of play provides information about routine cultural practices such as social interaction, body movement, and object manipulation (Parke, 1996, 2002). In contrast, fathers tend to play more physical and arousing games, which provide children with opportunities to experience heightened emotions in a safe encounter and, thereby, facilitate the development of emotion regulation skills. However, findings from several cultures indicate that physical play may not be a central part of the father–infant relationship. For instance, Chinese Malaysian, Indian, Aka (Central Africa), and Italian fathers display affection and engage in close physical contact with their children, but these parents rarely engage in physical play with their children (Hewlett, 2004; New and Benigni, 1987; Roopnarine, 2004).

Siblings also make important contributions to socialization in their roles as playmates (Larson and Richards, 1994). Play with siblings provides a context for the expression of a range of positive social behaviors as well as conflictual encounters and experiences with conflict resolution (Dunn, 1993). Furthermore, this array of interactions between siblings is typified by greater emotional intensity than the behavioral exchanges that characterize other relationships. In these exchanges, children can learn about culturally accepted expressions of positive and negative affect as well as conventional patterns of affiliation. Through their interactions with siblings, children develop interaction patterns and social understanding skills that generalize to relationships with other children (see Rubin, Cheah, and Menzer, Chapter 12, in this volume).

In sum, according to the Dynamics Systems perspective, various agents contribute in dynamic ways and as an organized system to the socialization process. Through these transactions, children learn the beliefs and norms of their culture.

Ecological Systems Theory   Under the guidance of Ecological Systems Theory (Bronfenbrenner and Morris, 2006), agents of socialization include the range of individuals located in the variety of extrafamilial settings, such as schools, recreational contexts, religious institutions, neighborhoods, and even the mass media and the cyber world of the Internet. Links between individuals and across these levels as well as societal presses at a given point in a culture's history are recognized as part of the socialization process (see Elder and Conger, 2000; Elliott, Menard, Rankin, Elliott, and Wilson, 2006; Greenfield, 1994). For instance, parents influence socialization not only through their direct interactions with their children, but also as managers of their children's social lives (Furstenberg, Cook, Eccles, Elder, and Sameroff, 1999; Parke et al., 2003). In many cultures, parents make choices about neighborhoods and schools as well as the formal and informal activities in which their children participate, which include access to and the nature of interaction with peers—decisions that can influence children's social and academic outcomes (Ladd and Pettit, 2002). Thus, Ecological Systems Theory aids in the examination of socialization because it does not view any particular agent of socialization as acting alone.

Consideration of the multiple and mutual influences of various agents of socialization does not mean that these agents have equivalent force or impact on the process. For example, studies find evidence of "neighborhood effects" across a range of developmental outcomes in both children and adolescents, but these effects are modest after taking into account family effects (Elliott et al., 2006; Leventhal and Brooks-Gunn, 2000). The effects of neighborhoods on children's outcomes are often mediated by parenting practices such as supervision and monitoring. When parents perceive their neighborhoods as dangerous and low in social control, they place more restrictions on their children's activities (O'Neil, Parke, and McDowell, 2001). Child outcomes, such as social competence with peers, for children who live in neighborhoods that parents perceive to be dangerous are mediated by parental regulatory strategies, including the consistency of disciplinary practices (Hill and Herman-Stahl, 2002).

The ecological context also prescribes the activities and institutions that compose socialization, which includes when and how children participate in these activities and institutions. The goals and strategies of socialization are instantiated in everyday activities, including spontaneously generated events, informal routines, and more formalized behaviors in the institutions and rituals of a culture. The influence that an activity or institution has on socialization may extend beyond the actual activity or institution. For instance, the institution of compulsory schooling not only affects how children are socialized in the school setting, but also affects experiences children have before they enter school. Preschoolers in cultures with compulsory formal schooling engage in interactions with parents that mimic school-related practices, such as adult-designed lessons and patterns of discourse (e.g., asking children questions to which the child knows that the adult knows the answer, which is a regular routine in school; Rogoff, 2003). In these cultures, children are more likely to play both inside and outside of school with agemates rather than with children from a range of ages, a pattern that is more common in cultures without formal schooling or where the availability of children is limited as a result of community size.

The experiences that agents of socialization have outside of their interactions with children may influence how they socialize children. Research has demonstrated that stressful experiences at the workplace can interfere with parenting (Repetti, 1994), that experiences with discrimination can regulate how minority parents prepare their children as they venture into the broader social community (Coard and Sellers, 2005), and that the nature of children's play is influenced by aspects of the broader ecological context including economics and other environmental factors (Bornstein, 2007). Children also exert influence in socialization experiences across levels of the ecological system. For instance, there is evidence that children's success and difficulty in school in both social and academic domains influence the nature of the parent–child interaction at home (Repetti, 1996).

The macrosystem is the level in Ecological Systems Theory that contains the dominant beliefs and ideologies of the culture. The system has direct bearing on child socialization through parental and community beliefs that range from ideas concerning the purpose of children and childhood to conceptions of age-related capabilities to the existence and participation of formal rituals and institutions emblematic of these beliefs and ideologies. As a result, the macrosystem includes the most identifiable and pervasive expression of the goals and strategies of the culture. The macrosystem often operates on socialization through the other levels of the ecological system (e.g., in the United States, when both parents participate in religious practices and institutions on a regular basis, children are more likely to be involved in religious organizations; Elder and Conger, 2000). Children's involvement in religious organizations is associated with endorsement of school, good grades, and—especially for boys—community activities. Religiously involved youth and their friends are less involved in deviant behaviors and exhibit fewer externalizing problems in early adolescence (Brody, Stoneman, and Flor, 1996).

Ecological Systems Theory reminds us that a wide set of agents embedded in a range of contexts beyond the family, such as the neighborhood, religious institutions, schools, and workplaces, operates together in the socialization process. Recognition that there are both direct and indirect ways that agents in these various contexts influence each other and ultimately children is one of the strengths of this perspective in examining socialization.

Sociocultural Theory Sociocultural theory (Cole, 1996; Rogoff, 2003) provides insight in the processes of learning as children participate with others in the activities of culture that form the basis of socialization. It also draws attention to the active role of the child in socialization. The ultimate aim in socialization is that children come to embody cultural values, practices, and understanding rather than merely mimic them. Therefore, in learning situations that contribute to socialization, an essential component is the activity of the child. For instance, during scaffolding, the process of learning is both learner focused and guided (Wood, Bruner, and Ross, 1976). Assistance by the more experienced partner is contingent on the learner's immediate needs, with the aim of developing the learner's competence in a specific knowledge base or skill. The learner communicates these needs through his or her involvement and competence in the activity.

For socialization to be effective, children have much to learn, and both formal and informal learning are important. Cultural members rely on many social learning processes, including observation, imitation, attention regulation, demonstration, instruction, rehearsal, shaping, scaffolding, guided participation, and trial and error. Implicit and gradual learning opportunities that occur as children participate in the activities of their community alongside more experienced partners may be relied on for the socialization of routine behaviors and practices that are readily observable (Rogoff, 1990). Didactic instruction may be likely when adults transmit rules and codes of conduct to children (Lancy, 1996). Scaffolding may be more common for developing skills that are important to carry out mostly or entirely error free, such as knowledge linked to economic viability (Greenfield, 1984). In contrast, trial and error learning may be more likely when cost does not matter or innovation is desired. Research on the process of learning to weave among 10- to 12-year-old boys in the Dioula community in Côte d'Ivoire (Tanon, 1994) supports this view. In this community, weaving is economically important, and competent execution is critical. Tanon observed careful scaffolding in the beginning stages of learning to weave, such as setting up the loom, and when apprentices learned traditional patterns, which are valued for skilled representation of the patterns. However, innovative patterns are also highly valued, especially by tourists, and Tanon observed more trial and error learning once a youth had mastered the basics of weaving and began working on these types of patterns.

Different points of development may also influence the topics and forms of learning that are used in socializing children. Instruction pertaining to information that may protect children in their environment is especially important when children enter middle childhood and start to venture beyond the immediate homestead on their own or with other children (Berry et al., 2006). Such unsupervised adventures can carry risk to the individual and the group. Although all potential dangers cannot be anticipated, it may be important to teach children about those that can be foreseen so that, if they arise, children can identify them and respond effectively. Research on the acquisition of environmental knowledge, such as which plants are edible, medicinal, protected, and poisonous in a Q'eqhi' Maya community in Belize, suggests that child socialization related to this type of knowledge entails a range of learning approaches, including observation, imitation, and deliberate instruction (Zarger, 2002).

Theoretical views and research techniques derived from sociocultural approaches and that focus explicitly on children's learning of cultural knowledge can make important contributions to our understanding of socialization. The sociocultural perspective also reminds us that cultural activities and tools, including formal and informal arrangements of learning, goal-directed activities, literacy, and even the mass media and newer technological tools like computers and the Internet, play major socializing roles (Comstock and Scharrer, 2006). Although there is continuing debate about the positive and negative effects of well-established cultural tools and more recent innovations, the important point is that these tools and the activities they support are products of culture and are socially managed by adults, especially early in children's development. Even in adolescence when there is less parental monitoring of technology and media use, family values, norms, and beliefs continue to shape the selection of cultural tools that are made by adolescents. The sociocultural perspective also underscores the active role that the child plays in conjunction with more culturally knowledgeable others in the socialization process. A wide range of socialization processes is highlighted by this perspective, and research based on this perspective shows the interdependence between the acquisition of cognitive skills and the social and cultural experiences that children have.

Developmental Niche The development niche approach is concerned with the cultural underpinnings of common or universal circumstances of socialization, such as the physical and social settings of development, customs of childcare, and the psychology of caregivers (Super and Harkness, 1986). Agents of socialization abound in the developmental niche; in fact, they determine and orchestrate the settings in which socialization occurs. The developmental niche draws attention to a critical feature of socialization, the psychology and beliefs of caregivers, which are often referred to as ethnotheories (Harkness and Super, 1996). Ethnotheories about children and their development guide agents of socialization in the activities they provide for and the manner in which they interact with children. When caregivers interact with children, the caregiver's behaviors are not only guided by the activity, they are also influenced by expectations as to when the child will be able to carry out this activity on his or her own and more long-range goals such as how this activity will help establish a future place for a child in the society (LeVine, 1974).

Illustrations of the developmental niche and its relation to socialization can be found in practices of childcare. In the United States, parents choose the type and quality of daycare and elementary schools that their children attend. These choices make a difference to children's socialization experiences and later development. As studies of childcare have shown, the quality of and, to some extent, the amount of time in care are linked to children's cognitive and social development (Clarke-Stewart and Allhusen, 2005). In many cultures, siblings provide much of the care for young children. In African, Polynesian, and Mexican cultures, children, especially girls, become involved in sibling caregiving and teaching activities at a relatively early age (Weisner, 1993). Patterns of sibling interaction in New England families suggest that formal caregiving responsibilities by siblings may not be as common in American culture as in other cultures (Edwards and Whiting, 1993). However, Bryant (1989) suggested that, although parents may not formally assign caregiving duties to children, children frequently voluntarily assume the role of caregiver of younger siblings and make unique contributions to the socialization of young children.

The developmental niche viewpoint provides an important addition to our thinking about socialization by its emphasis on cultural contexts of socialization. This approach also stresses the role of ethnotheories, or sets of culturally based beliefs, in the socialization process (Harkness and Super, 1996). These ethnotheories serve a central role in organizing the behaviors of agents of socialization and, as a result, help ensure that the skills that are necessary for successful adaptation to a particular cultural context are acquired by children during development.

Conclusion

Several theoretical suggestions and methodological innovations relevant to the study of socialization are implied in our discussion. Our hope is to encourage a revitalization of research on socialization from a cultural perspective among developmental scientists.

New Directions to Theory

In terms of theoretical issues, the study of socialization from a cultural point of view would benefit from more integration of extant developmental theories. In our discussion, we outline four approaches to this topic and illustrate how each can be useful for generating questions about and understanding of how children are socialized over the course of development to meet the expectations and goals of the culture in which they live. A fusion of these perspectives could be useful and perhaps yield a new and more comprehensive theoretical approach to socialization. Such a view might reconcile research on cultural socialization with research in related areas of social development, which concentrate largely on socialization within cultures, primarily the United States. The Ecological and Dynamic Systems theoretical perspectives provide frameworks for organizing the multiple nested and layered contexts of socialization. The sociocultural and developmental niche perspectives provide insight into and identification of socialization processes such as ethnotheories or cultural beliefs and interactional exchanges between children and socializing agents.

One of the main limitations in our current theories, including the theories we outline, is their relative inattention to developmental issues. Despite Maccoby's (1984) plea, we still are only beginning to map changes in socialization practices to the developmental status of the child. This issue is particularly significant when examining socialization processes across cultures. Although age is a primary organizing dimension in developmental psychology, this "metric of development," as Rogoff (2003) points out, is deeply connected to cultural practices, values, and goals. Examining socialization to culture in developmental, rather than age-specific, terms will be critical. Such efforts may not only clarify the intricate relations among broader cultural practices and expectations and children's socialization experiences, but they may also deepen our understanding of the process of development in relation to child age.

To understand socialization, it will be important to focus not only on children's development, but also on adult development. The point in the developmental life course that adults are located when they have responsibility for socialization can profoundly influence their socialization choices (Elder, 1998; Parke, 1988). Moreover, we need a fuller appreciation of how different cultures conceptualize development and how these beliefs determine the culturally controlled social agenda that dictate the nature and timing of the child's entry into various social, training, or occupational settings such as school or apprenticeship and when a child is permitted to begin socializing with children of the other gender or participate in adult work. These suggestions, of course, flow directly from the sociocultural and developmental niche perspectives. Research indicates that these two aspects of development—the child's developmental status and the culturally determined developmental agenda—interact in shaping children's reactions to changes in the life course. For example, the extent to which the onset of menarche is linked with school-related transitions, such as the shift from elementary to junior high school, has profound implications for adolescent adjustment (Wigfield, Eccles, Schiefele, Roeser, and Davis-Kean, 2006). Revisiting cultural transitions, such as major school transitions or initiation ceremonies, in conjunction with measures of physical, cognitive, emotional, and social development would help illuminate the interplay between these different aspects of development.

Our review of contemporary theories suggests that we have moved beyond unidirectional views of the socialization process and recognize the mutual influence between adults and children. However, we need to take a broader view and examine the mutual influence process between cultures. We should explore not only how Western cultural experiences can influence child socialization in non-Western cultures (e.g., through cultural changes associated with modernization and globalization), but also assess the lessons that we can learn from other cultures. Although there is a great deal of attention to the effects of immigration and acculturation in Western cultures such as Europe, North America, and Australia, tracking the processes and consequences of cultural change in countries that are undergoing rapid modernization should be a priority and a welcome opportunity for theory testing. The process of modernization is a natural experiment that permits an evaluation of how socialization practices shift in response to new demands and conditions (Greenfield, 2004). Only by reducing ethnocentric barriers will we be open to new socialization strategies that have proven useful in other cultures such as the diffusion of responsibility for socialization by the use of extended family networks and community-based childrearing arrangements. These concepts are highly compatible with the theoretical perspectives that have guided our discussion. Finally, we need to recognize intracultural variability to avoid oversimplifying generalizations about socialization practices in any particular culture, a lesson that has been learned in studies of ethnic groups in North America (Parke and Buriel, 2006).

Methodological Innovations

A variety of methodological innovations is suggested by our discussion. First, new statistical techniques such as hierarchical linear modeling allow more adequate testing of complex models such as the nested contexts suggested by Ecological and Dynamic Systems theories. Similarly, the role of mediating and moderating processes that are so critical to understand if we are going to move beyond description in cross-cultural research can be addressed by recent advances in path analysis and structural equation modeling (MacKinnon, Lockwood, Hoffman, West, and Sheets, 2002; Muthén and Muthén, 2005). For example, such approaches make investigating the direct and indirect paths among culture rituals, kin networks, marital relationships, family rituals, and socialization more feasible. Similarly, to better capture the dyadic character of socialization processes, use of social relations models (Kenny, Kashy, and Cook, 2006) that allow examination of actor, partner, and relationship effects would be valuable approaches to examining socialization in different cultures. Application of these advances in design and statistical analyses to cross-cultural studies would permit more sophisticated testing of the contemporary theoretical models that we have proposed.

Second, it is important to recognize the need for additional construct validity studies of measurement equivalence among different cultural groups. Often in cross-cultural studies, the validity and meaningfulness of imported measures from the researcher's home culture are unknown and need to be evaluated. At the same time, scholars have cautioned against sole reliance on similar methods for different cultural groups and argue that such a strategy can obscure rather than illuminate the comparisons (Rogoff, 1990). For example, Greenfield (1997), in a study of Mexican children's understanding of kin terms, modified the questions to reflect the fact that, in this culture, older and younger siblings have separate terms. Without this change, the questions asked would not have been meaningful. One challenge is to develop better guidelines for when comparability of measurement across cultures helps and when it hinders understanding.

One of the lessons from cross-cultural research is the recognition that both qualitative and quantitative approaches are useful. Researchers in this tradition have strived to avoid the binary thinking that often characterizes research in Western social science that suggests that one must choose between quantitative and qualitative approaches. Research in other cultures under the guiding hand of the anthropological tradition is more likely to avoid this dichotomous trap and utilize a wide range of methods from qualitative to quantitative at various stages in the research program. As interest grows in both cross- and intracultural comparisons among Western scholars, this multimethod approach is a valuable model to emulate.

By following these theoretical and methodological guidelines, our understanding of the diversity and integrity of socialization strategies across cultures will improve (Kessen, 1991). In addition, these efforts will broaden our understanding of human adaptation as it is expressed in child socialization experiences. Finally, these efforts will expand our appreciation of the various ways that cultures invest in childhood, an investment in the context of socialization that is best conceptualized as mutually constituted goals shared by children and other members of the community.

Acknowledgments

We thank Robert L. Munroe and Scott Coltrane for several helpful discussions as we were writing this chapter.

References

Berry, J. W., Dasen, P. R., and Saraswathi, T. S. (1997). *Handbook of cross-cultural psychology, Volume 2: Basic processes and human development.* Boston: Allyn and Bacon.

Berry, J. W., Poortinga, Y. H., Segall, M. H., and Dasen, P. R. (2006). *Cross-cultural psychology: Research and applications* (2nd ed.). Cambridge, United Kingdom: Cambridge University Press.

Bjorklund, D. F., and Pellegrini, A. D. (2002). *The origins of human nature: Evolutionary developmental psychology.* Washington, DC: American Psychological Association.

Bornstein, M. H. (2007). On the significance of social relationships in the development of children's earliest symbolic play: An ecological perspective. In A. Göncü and S. Gaskins (Eds.), *Play and development: Evolutionary, sociocultural, and functional perspectives* (pp. 101–129). Mahwah, NJ: Erlbaum.

Boss, P. (1999). *Ambiguous loss: Learning to live with unresolved grief.* Cambridge, MA: Harvard University Press.

Brody, G. H., Stoneman, Z., and Flor, D. (1996). Parental religiosity, family processes and youth competence in rural two-parent African American families. *Developmental Psychology, 32,* 696–706.

Bronfenbrenner, U., and Morris, P. A. (2006). The bioecological model of human development. In W. Damon and R. M. Lerner (Series Eds.), and R. M. Lerner (Vol. Ed.), *Handbook of child psychology. Volume 1: Theoretical models of human development* (6th ed., pp. 793–828). New York: Wiley.

Bryant, B. K. (1989). The child's perspective of sibling caretaking and its relevance to understanding social-emotional functioning and development. In P. G. Zukow (Ed.), *Sibling interaction across cultures: Theoretical and methodological issues* (pp. 143–164). New York: Springer-Verlag.

Bugental, D. B., and Grusec, J. E. (2006). Socialization processes. In W. Damon and R. M. Lerner (Series Eds.), and N. Eisenberg (Vol. Ed.), *Handbook of child psychology. Volume 3: Social, emotional, and personality development* (6th ed., pp. 366-428). New York: Wiley.

Clarke-Stewart, K. A., and Allhusen, V. (2005). *What we know about childcare.* Cambridge, MA: Harvard University Press.

Coard, S. I., and Sellers, R. M. (2005). African American families as a context for racial socialization. In V. C. McLoyd, N. E. Hill, and K. A. Dodge (Eds.), *African American family life* (pp. 264–284). New York: Guilford.

Cole, M. (1996). *Cultural psychology: A once and future discipline.* Cambridge, MA: Harvard University Press.

Comstock, G., and Scharrer, E. (2006). Media and pop culture. In W. Damon and R. E. Lerner (Series Eds.), and K. A. Renninger and I. Sigel (Vol. Eds.), *Handbook of child psychology. Volume 4: Child psychology in practice* (pp. 817–863). New York: Wiley.

Dunn, J. (1993). *Young children's close relationships: Beyond attachment.* Thousand Oaks, CA: Sage.

Edwards, C. P., and Whiting, B. B. (1993). "Mother, older sibling and me": The overlapping roles of caregivers and companions in the social world of 2- to 3-year-olds in Ngeca, Kenya. In K. MacDonald (Ed.), *Parent-child play: Descriptions and implications* (pp. 305–329). Albany, NY: State University of New York Press.

Elder, G. H., Jr. (1998). The life course as developmental theory. *Child Development, 69,* 1–12.

Elder, G. H., Jr., and Conger, R. D. (2000). *Children of the land: Adversity and success in rural America.* Chicago: University of Chicago Press.

Elliott, D. B., Menard, S., Rankin, B., Elliott, A., and Wilson, W. J. (2006). *Good kids from bad neighborhoods.* New York: Cambridge University Press

Elman, J. L., Bates, E. A., Johnson, M. H., Karmiloff-Smith, A., Parisi, D., and Plunkett, K. (1996). *Rethinking innateness: A connectionist perspective on development.* Cambridge, MA: MIT Press.

Fiese, B. H. (2006). Family routines and rituals: Family transactions and individual health. In D. Snyder, J. Simpson, and I. N. Hughes (Eds.), *Emotional regulation in families.* Washington, DC: American Psychological Association.

Fogel, A. (1993). *Developing through relationships: Origins of communication, self, and culture.* Chicago: University of Chicago Press.

Frijda, N., and Jahoda, G. (1966). On the scope and methods of cross-cultural research. *International Journal of Psychology, 58,* 67–89.

Furstenberg, F. F., Jr., Cook, T. D., Eccles, J., Elder, G. H., Jr., and Sameroff, A. (1999). *Managing to make it: Urban families and adolescent success.* Chicago: University of Chicago Press.

Gaskins, S. (1999). Children's daily lives in a Mayan village: A case study of culturally constructed roles and activities. In A. Göncü (Ed.), *Children's engagement in the world* (pp. 25–61). New York: Cambridge University Press.

Gaskins, S., Haight, W., and Lancy, D. F. (2007). The cultural construction of play. In A. Göncü and S. Gaskins (Eds.), *Play and development: Evolutionary, sociocultural, and functional perspectives* (pp. 179–202). Mahwah, NJ: Erlbaum.

Gauvain, M. (2001). *The social context of cognitive development.* New York: Guilford.

Göncü, A., and Gaskins, S. (Eds.). (2007). *Play and development: Evolutionary, sociocultural, and functional perspectives.* Mahwah, NJ: Erlbaum.

Goodnow, J. J. (1990). The socialization of cognition: What's involved? In J. W. Stigler, R. A. Shweder, and G. Herdt (Eds.), *Cultural psychology* (pp. 259–286). Cambridge, United Kingdom: Cambridge University Press.

Goodnow, J. J., Miller, P. J., and Kessel, F. (1995). *Cultural practices as contexts for development.* San Francisco: Jossey-Bass.

Greenfield, P. M. (1984). A theory of the teacher in the learning activities of everyday life. In B. Rogoff and J. Lave (Eds.), *Everyday cognition: Its development in social context.* Cambridge, MA: Harvard University Press.

Greenfield, P. M. (1994). Independence and interdependence as developmental scripts: Implications for theory, research, and practice. In P. M. Greenfield and R. R. Cocking (Eds.), *Cross-cultural roots of minority child development* (pp. 1–37). Hillsdale, NJ: Erlbaum.

Greenfield, P. M. (1997). Culture as process: Empirical methodology for cultural psychology. In J. W. Berry, Y. H. Poortinga, and J. Pandey (Eds.), *Handbook of cross-cultural psychology. Volume 1: Theory and method* (2nd ed., pp. 301–346). Boston: Allyn and Bacon.

Greenfield, P. M. (2004). *Weaving generations together: Evolving creativity in the Maya of Chiapas.* Santa Fe, NM: SAR Press.

Greenfield, P. M., and Bruner, J. S. (1969). Culture and cognitive growth. In D. Goslin (Ed.), *Handbook of socialization theory* (pp. 653–657). Chicago: Rand McNally.

Greenfield, P. M., and Lave, J. (1982). Cognitive aspects of informal education. In D. A. Wagner and H. W. Stevenson (Eds.), *Cultural perspectives on child development* (pp. 181–207). San Francisco: Freeman.

Greenough, W. T., Black, J. E., and Wallace, C. S. (1987). Experience and brain development. *Child Development, 58,* 539–559.

Grusec, J. E., and Hastings, P. D. (Eds.). (2007). *Handbook of socialization: Theory and research.* New York: Guilford.

Harkness, S. (1992). Human development in psychological anthropology. In T. Schwartz, G. M. White, and C. A. Lutz (Eds.), *New directions in psychological anthropology* (pp. 102–121). New York: Cambridge University Press.

Harkness, S., and Super, C. M. (1996*). Parents' cultural belief systems: Their origins, expressions, and consequences.* New York: Guilford.

Harris, P. L. (2000). *The work of the imagination.* Oxford, United Kingdom: Blackwell.

Hernandez, D. J. (1995). *America's children: Resources from family, government, and the economy.* New York: Russell Sage Foundation.

Hewlett, B. S. (2004). Fathers in forager, farmer, and pastoral cultures. In M. E. Lamb (Ed.), *The role of the father in child development* (4th ed., pp. 182–195). New York: Wiley.

Hill, N. E., and Herman-Stahl, M. A. (2002). Neighborhood safety and social involvement: Associations with parenting behaviors and depressive symptoms among African-American and Euro-American mothers. *Journal of Family Psychology, 16,* 209–219.

Kagitçibasi, Ç. (1993). A model of multipurpose non-formal education: The case of the Turkish Early Enrichment Project. In L. Eldering and P. Leseman (Eds.), *Early intervention and culture* (pp. 253–268). The Hague, The Netherlands: UNESCO.

Kagitçibasi, Ç. (1995). Is psychology relevant to global human development issues? *American Psychologist, 50,* 293–300.

Kenny, D. A., Kashy, D. A., and Cook, W. L. (2006). *The analysis of dyadic data.* New York: Guilford.

Kessen, W. (1979). The American child and other cultural inventions. *American Psychologist, 34,* 815–820.

Kessen, W. (1984). Construction, deconstruction, and reconstruction of the child's mind. In C. Sophian (Ed.), *Origins of cognitive skills* (pp. 419–429). Hillsdale, NJ: Erlbaum.

Kessen, W. (1991). Commentary: Dynamics of enculturation. In M. H. Bornstein (Ed.), *Cultural approaches to parenting* (pp. 185–193). Hillsdale, NJ: Erlbaum.

Ladd, G., and Pettit, G. (2002). Parenting and the development of children's peer relationships. In M. H. Bornstein (Ed.), *Handbook of parenting. Volume 5: Practical issues in parenting* (2nd ed., pp. 269–309). Mahwah, NJ: Erlbaum.

Lancy, D. F. (1996). *Playing on the mother-ground: Cultural routines for children's development*. New York: Guilford.
Larson, R., and Richards, M. H. (1994). *Divergent realities: The emotional lives of mothers, fathers, and adolescents*. New York: Basic Books.
Leventhal, T., and Brooks-Gunn, J. (2000). The neighborhoods they live in: The effects of neighborhood residence on child and adolescent outcomes. *Psychological Bulletin, 126,* 309–337.
LeVine, R. A. (1974). Parental goals: A cross-cultural view. *Teachers College Record, 76,* 226–239.
LeVine, R. A. (1982). *Culture, behavior, and personality* (2nd ed.). New York: Aldine.
LeVine, R., Dixon, S., LeVine, S., Richman, A., Leiderman, P. H., Keefer, C. H., et al. (1994). *Childcare and culture: Lessons from Africa*. Cambridge, United Kingdom: Cambridge University Press.
Maccoby, E. E. (1984). Socialization and developmental change. *Child Development, 55,* 317–328.
MacKinnon, D. P., Lockwood, C. M., Hoffman, J. M., West, S. G., and Sheets, V. (2002). A comparison of methods to test mediation and other intervening variable effects. *Psychological Methods, 7,* 83–104.
Mead, M. (1930). *Growing up in New Guinea*. New York: William Morrow.
Mead, M. (1964). *Continuities in cultural evolution*. New Haven, CT: Yale University Press.
Moos, R. H., and Moos, B. S. (1981). *Family environment scales manual*. Palo Alto, CA: Consulting Psychologists Press.
Munroe, R. H., and Munroe, R. L. (1971). Household density and infant care in an east African society. *Journal of Social Psychology, 83,* 9–13.
Muthén, B., and Muthén, L. (2005). *Mplus users manual version 3.12*. Los Angeles, CA: Muthén & Muthén.
New, R., and Benigni, L. (1987). Italian fathers and infants: Cultural constraints on paternal behavior. In M. E. Lamb (Ed.), *The father's role: Cross-cultural perspectives* (pp. 139–167). Hillsdale, NJ: Erlbaum.
O'Neil, R., Parke, R. D., and McDowell, D. J. (2001). Objective and subjective features of children's neighborhoods: Relations to parental regulatory strategies and children's social competence. *Journal of Applied Developmental Psychology, 22,* 135–155.
Parke, R. D. (1988). Families in life-span perspective: A multi-level developmental approach. In E. M. Hetherington, R. M. Lerner, and M. Perlmutter (Eds.), *Child development in life-span perspective* (pp. 159–190). Hillsdale, NJ: Erlbaum.
Parke, R. D. (1996). *Fatherhood*. Cambridge, MA: Harvard University Press.
Parke, R. D. (2002). Fathers and families. In M. H. Bornstein (Ed.), *Handbook of parenting. Volume 3: Being and becoming a parent* (2nd ed., pp. 27–73). Mahwah, NJ: Erlbaum.
Parke, R. D., and Buriel, R. (2006). Socialization in the family: Ethnic and ecological perspectives. In W. Damon and R. M. Lerner (Series Eds.), and N. Eisenberg (Vol. Ed.), *Handbook of child psychology. Volume 3: Social, emotional, and personality development* (6th ed., pp. 429–504). New York: Wiley.
Parke, R. D., Killian, C. M., Dennis, J., Flyr, M. V., McDowell, D. J., Simpkins, S., et al. (2003). Managing the external environment: The parent and child as active agents in the system. In L. Kuczynski (Ed.), *Handbook of dynamics in parent-child relations* (pp. 247–270). Thousand Oaks, CA: Sage.
Reiss, D. (1989). The represented and practicing family: Contrasting visions of family continuity. In A. J. Sameroff and R. N. Emde (Eds.), *Relationship disturbances in early childhood: A developmental approach* (pp. 191–220). New York: Basic Books.
Repetti, R. L. (1994). Short-term and long-term processes linking job stressors to father-child interactions. *Social Development, 3,* 1–15.
Repetti, R. L. (1996). The effects of perceived daily social and academic failure experiences on school-age children's subsequent interactions with parents. *Child Development, 67,* 1467–1482.
Rogoff, B. (1990). *Apprenticeship in thinking: Cognitive development in social context*. New York: Oxford University Press.
Rogoff, B. (2003). *The cultural nature of human development*. Oxford, United Kingdom: Oxford University Press.
Roopnarine, J. (2004). African-American and African Caribbean fathers: Level, quality, and meaning involvement. In M. E. Lamb (Ed.), *The role of the father in child development* (4th ed., pp. 58–97). Hoboken, NJ: Wiley.
Russell, G., and Russell, A. (1987). Mother-child and father-child relationships in middle childhood. *Child Development, 58,* 1573–1585.
Sameroff, A. J. (1989). General systems and the regulation of development. In M. R. Gunnar and E. Thelen (Eds.), *Systems and development* (Vol. 22, pp. 219–235). Hillsdale, NJ: Erlbaum.
Sameroff, A. J. (1994). Developmental systems and family functioning. In R. D. Parke and S. G. Kellam (Eds.), *Exploring family relationships with other social contexts: Family research consortium—Advances in family research* (pp. 199–214). Hillsdale, NJ: Erlbaum.

Saraswathi, T. S. (2003). *Cross-cultural perspectives on human development.* New Delhi, India: Sage.
Schlegel, A., and Barry, H., III (1991). *Adolescence: An anthropological inquiry.* New York: Free Press.
Serpell, R., and Hatano, G. (1997). Education, schooling, and literacy. In J. W. Berry, P. R. Dasen, and T. S. Saraswathi (Eds.), *Handbook of cross-cultural psychology. Volume 2: Basic processes and human development* (pp. 339–376). Boston: Allyn and Bacon.
Seymour, S. (1988). Expressions of responsibility among Indian children: Some precursors of adult status and sex roles. *Ethos, 16,* 355–370.
Shweder, R. A., Goodnow, J. J., Hatano, G., LeVine, R. A., Markus, H. R., and Miller, P. J. (2006). The cultural psychology of development: One mind, many mentalities. In W. Damon and R. M. Lerner (Series Eds.), and R. M. Lerner (Vol. Ed.), *Handbook of child psychology. Volume 1: Theoretical models of human development* (6th ed., pp. 716–792). New York: Wiley.
Stevenson, H. W., and Stigler, J. W. (1992). *The learning gap: Why our schools are failing and what we can learn from Japanese and Chinese education.* New York: Summit Books.
Super, C. M., and Harkness, S. (1986). The developmental niche: A conceptualization at the interface of child and culture. *International Journal of Behavioral Development, 9,* 545–569.
Tanon, F. (1994). *A cultural view on planning: The case of weaving in Ivory Coast.* Tilburg, The Netherlands: Tilburg University Press.
Thelen, E. (1995). Motor development: A new synthesis. *American Psychologist, 50,* 79–95.
Thelen, E., and Smith, L. (2006). Dynamic systems theory. In W. Damon and R. M. Lerner (Series Eds.), and R. M. Lerner (Vol. Ed.), *Handbook of child psychology. Volume 1: Theoretical models of human development* (6th ed., pp. 258–312). New York: Wiley.
Tomasello, M. (1999). *The cultural origins of human cognition.* Cambridge, MA: Harvard University Press.
Tomasello, M., Kruger, A. C., and Ratner, H. H. (1993). Cultural learning. *Behavioral and Brain Sciences, 16,* 495–511.
Tronick, E. Z., Morelli, G. A., and Ivey, P. K. (1992). The Efe forager infant and toddler's pattern of social relationships: Multiple and simultaneous. *Developmental Psychology, 28,* 568–577.
Valsiner, J., and Lawrence, J. A. (1997). Human development in culture across the life span. In J. W. Berry, P. R. Dasen, and T. S. Saraswathi (Eds.), *Handbook of cross-cultural psychology. Volume 2: Basic processes and human development* (pp. 69–106). Boston: Allyn and Bacon.
Vygotsky, L. S. (1978). *Mind in society.* Cambridge, MA: Harvard University Press.
Weisner, T. S. (1984). A cross-cultural perspective: Ecocultural niches of middle childhood. In A. Collins (Ed.), *The elementary school years: Understanding development during middle childhood* (pp. 335–369). Washington, DC: National Academy Press.
Weisner, T. S. (1993). Overview: Sibling similarity and difference in different cultures. In C. W. Nuckolls (Ed.), *Siblings in south Asia: Brothers and sisters in cultural context* (pp. 1–17). New York: Guilford Press.
Werner, E. E. (1979). *Cross-cultural child development: A view from the planet Earth.* Monterey, CA: Brooks Cole.
Whiting, B. B. (1980). Culture and social behavior: A model for the development of social behavior. *Ethos, 8,* 95–116.
Whiting, B. B., and Whiting, J. W. M. (1975). *The children of six cultures: A psychocultural analysis.* Cambridge, MA: Harvard University Press.
Whiting, J. W. M., and Child, I. (1953). *Child training and personality.* New Haven, CT: Yale University Press.
Wigfield, A., Eccles, J. S., Schiefele, U., Roeser, R. W., and Davis-Kean, P. (2006). Development of achievement motivation. In W. Damon and R. M. Lerner (Series Eds.), and N. Eisenberg (Vol. Ed.), *Handbook of child psychology. Volume 3: Social, emotional, and personality development* (6th ed., pp. 933–1002). New York: Wiley.
Wood, D. J., Bruner, J. S., and Ross, G. (1976). The role of tutoring in problem solving. *Journal of Child Psychology and Psychiatry, 17,* 89–100.
Yeung, W. J., Sandberg, J. F., Davis-Kean, P. E., and Hofferth, S. L. (2001). Children's time with fathers in intact families. *Journal of Marriage and the Family, 63,* 136–154.
Zarger, R. K. (2002). Acquisition and transmission of subsistence knowledge by Q'eqchi' Maya in Belize. In J. R. Stepp, F. S. Wyndham, and R. K. Zarger (Eds.), *Ethnobiology and biocultural diversity* (pp. 593–603). Athens, GA: University of Georgia Press.

14
Parenting

MARC H. BORNSTEIN and JENNIFER E. LANSFORD

Introduction

Parents throughout the world are the first and primary individuals entrusted with childcaring, the important task of rearing children to be culturally competent mature members of their respective society. From a parent's point of view, after reproduction, survival is achieved through protection of the infant and provision of food, but also through social and didactic processes that involve sharing information and inculcating culture (Wilson, 1975). All cultural groups foster particular characteristics that are deemed advantageous or essential to their members, and all cultural groups stint other characteristics as inappropriate or detrimental to adequate functioning within the group. Cross-cultural studies show that culture shapes parenting by providing models of childrearing that include which parenting cognitions and practices are acceptable, normative, or optimal vis-à-vis when and how to care for children and what traits in children are desirable and to be encouraged or undesirable and to be discouraged. Some demands on parents are culturally universal. For example, parents in all societies are expected to nurture and protect young children (Bornstein, 2002, 2006). Other demands vary greatly across cultural groups. For example, parents in some societies speak to babies and see them as interactive partners, whereas parents in other societies think that it is nonsensical to talk to infants before infants are capable of speech (Dixon, Keefer, Tronick, and Brazelton, 1982; Ochs, 1988; Richman, Miller, and LeVine, 1992). Some parenting practices are consistently associated with similar child outcomes. In a study of 11 countries, including at least one each from Africa, Asia, Europe, the Middle East, North America, and South America, virtual unanimity was observed in the direction and significance of associations of parental monitoring with less, and psychological control with more, adolescent antisocial behavior (Barber, Stolz, and Olsen, 2005). However, other parenting practices have different effects on child outcomes depending on the specific cultural, and even intracultural, context. Parental supervision and consistency of discipline are negatively related to delinquency among European Americans but unrelated among Mexican Americans (Smith and Krohn, 1995), and corporal punishment is associated with externalizing problems in European American but not African American children (Deater-Deckard, Dodge, Bates, and Pettit, 1996).

Cultures consist of distinctive patterns of norms, ideas, values, conventions, behaviors, and symbolic representations about life that are widely shared by a collection of people, persist over time, guide and regulate daily living, and constitute the valued competencies communicated to new members of the group. Thus, culture helps to construct children and is transmitted by influencing parental cognitions about childrearing that in turn influence parental practices (Bornstein, 1991; Cole, 2005; McGillicuddy-De Lisi and Subramanian, 1994). Variations in culture make for subtle as well as manifest, but always meaningful, differences in patterns of parent–child interaction. Thus, variation in cultures of parenting can be striking. Mothers in rural Thailand do not know that their newborns can see (only 1.7% believe their babies can see at 1 week, 14.7% at 1 month), and often during the day, they swaddle infants on their backs in a fabric hammock that allows the baby only a narrow slit view of ceiling or sky (Kotchabhakdi, Winichagoon, Smitasiri, Dhanamitta, and Valyasevi, 1987). Central to a concept of culture, therefore, is the expectation that different peoples possess different beliefs and behave in different ways with respect to their parenting. Experiencing differences in parenting is a principal reason that individuals in different cultures are who they are and often differ so from one another. Cultural expectations regarding what is acceptable development, and what is not, shape parents' caregiving cognitions as well as their rearing practices and, ultimately, children's experiences. In turn, children's experiences with their parents within a cultural context scaffold them to become culturally competent members of their society (Morelli and Rothbaum, 2007). Beyond nurturance, an important function of parents is to socialize children in what beliefs and behaviors are expected and acceptable versus not within their cultural group. Thus, culture becomes embedded in children's own beliefs and behaviors. Culture shapes parenting cognitions and practices even before children are born. For example, an investigation of knowledge of developmental timetables in new mothers of Australian versus Lebanese extraction arrived at the conclusion that cultural differences influenced parental expectations more than other prominent factors, such as mothers' experiences observing their own children, comparing them to other children, and receiving advice from friends and experts (Goodnow, Cashmore, Cotton, and Knight, 1984).

Parents' cognitions about how to rear children as well as their actual childrearing practices (apart from those that are affected by children or by parents' own unique personological characteristics) are influenced by several culturally conditioned forces, including prevailing advice about childrearing, suggestions from family and friends, and direct observations of parenting practices of their own and others' parents. All of these forces contribute to the cultural construction of parenting. Of course, culture-specific patterns of childrearing can be expected to adapt to each specific society's setting and needs. It is likely that cultural variation in childrearing philosophies, values, and beliefs mediates differences in childrearing practices vis-à-vis the local and larger physical and social environments. So, parents in different cultures may structure their environments differently, make experiences of one sort or another available, and interpret the meaning, usefulness, and so forth of different aspects of their environments differentially based on their culture. The ways that culture influences child development can be found at all levels of the ecological systems model (Bronfenbrenner and Morris, 1998).

The immediate settings and forces that mold children's daily lives have been conceptualized as encompassing three groups of factors (Super and Harkness, 1986). The first includes the physical and social settings in which children live. The types of dwellings and expected activities of members of their cultural group determine the boundaries of children's experiences as well as embody cultural meanings associated with them. For example, the physical and social experiences of a child in a contemporary Western culture, reared in a nuclear family and cared for at home predominantly by one or two adults, differ dramatically from the experiences of a child of nomadic hunter-gatherers who spends each day in a large group of peers being looked after by a group of adults. The point has been made that perhaps the most important single thing that a parent does for a child is to determine into which culture that child is born (Weisner, 2002).

The second group of factors includes parents' cognitions (e.g., expectations about ages at which children will achieve particular developmental milestones). Parents in different cultures possess different ideas about childrearing and child development. For example, European American mothers of 12- to 15-month-olds emphasize the development of individual autonomy, whereas Puerto Rican mothers focus on maternal–child interdependence and connectedness (Harwood, Schoelmerich, Schulze, and Gonzalez, 1999). These differences relate to mothers' actual behavior, with European American mothers using suggestions (rather than commands) and other indirect means of structuring their children's behavior, and Puerto Rican mothers using more direct means of structuring, such as commands, physical positioning and restraints, and direct attempts to recruit their children's attention.

The third group of factors includes specific childrearing practices (e.g., how much freedom the child has to explore, how nurturing caregivers are). Marked variations in this regard have been recorded even between different preindustrial, non-Western "small-scale" cultures. For example, infants still in the first half-year of life among the nomadic hunter-gatherer Aka are more likely to be held and fed in close proximity to their caregivers than are Ngandu infants from farming cultures who are more likely to be left alone, even though both of these traditional groups may be found living cheek by jowl in central African settings (Hewlett, Lamb, Shannon, Leyendecker, and Schoelmerich, 1998). Aka parents appear to maintain closer proximity to infants because they move in search of food more frequently than do Ngandu parents. Cultural differences related to settings, suggestions, and practices frame the activities and routines that instantiate themes that matter to the principal agents of socialization and thereby communicate consistent cultural messages (Quinn and Holland, 1987). Thus, the same ideas and images tend to recur in the meanings that are inherent in settings and activities. All three of these cultural sources filter through parenting.

Cultural influences on how parenting cognitions and practices relate to children's adjustment occur in a small variety of interlinked ways. They may be moderated by the cultural contexts in which parenting practices occur; they may be mediated by children's appraisals of them, which could be affected by cultural views regarding their use; and they may be similar across cultural contexts suggesting broad developmental principles. Although much theoretical and empirical emphasis is now placed on cross-cultural differences, many developmental milestones, parenting strategies, and family processes are likely to be similar across cultures. In the end, all parents want physical health, social adjustment, educational achievement, and economic security for their children. Moreover, social and economic development and information globalization present parents today in different cultural groups with many increasingly similar socialization issues and challenges (e.g., Internet safety, prevention of abuse).

In a nutshell, parental goals are aligned with cultural context and are manifested in different socialization strategies. The central purpose of this chapter is to provide an overview of historical and demographic considerations that lead to the nexus of culture and parenting, to review some of the central issues that define the field of culture and parenting, and to illustrate them with reference to some telling variation in parenting cognitions and practices. We then turn to discuss form (or behavior) versus function (or meaning) in parenting as expressed in culture, some of the principal mechanisms of parenting, and how parenting articulates with prevailing ecological contextual views of development. We conclude with some practical considerations and brief reflections on culture and parenting.

Historical and Demographic Considerations in Culture and Parenting

Throughout history, parents have been concerned with how to influence their offspring in desired ways as well as how their neighbors do so, just as the Athenians expressed interest in Spartan childrearing practices (Herodotus, 1996). Social anthropological inquiry has almost always, as a matter of course, included reports of child life and parenting. Mead (1928) understood that the world's cultures essentially represent "experimental conditions" of sorts for rearing children and that social science could advance an understanding of parenting and child development by evaluating the effects of such different cultural and environmental conditions. Mead's (1935) studies of the influence of childrearing patterns on the socialization of sex roles and Benedict's (1938) studies of the mechanisms by which cultural customs, beliefs, and knowledge are transmitted across generations are representative of landmark early efforts.

Yet, historically, three limitations related to culture have impeded a comprehensive understanding of parenting (Serpell, 1990). First, samples in most empirical research have been drawn predominantly from middle-class North American or Western European backgrounds. Second, most authors of empirical research have come from these same demographic circumstances. Third, the intended audiences of most scientific investigation have been likewise restricted sociodemographically. These limitations have led to many critiques of single-culture perspectives and motivated consistent calls for more cross-cultural study (Arnett, 2008; Bornstein, 1980, 1991, 2001; Kennedy, Scheirer, and Rogers, 1984; Moghaddam, 1987; Russell, 1984; Segall, Lonner, and Berry, 1998; Tomlinson and Swartz, 2003). Thus, researchers increasingly recognize the need to expand the scope of parenting inquiry to include more culturally diverse samples. Heeding these calls is important to avoid misperceptions of universality as well as biases that can arise from monocultural study.

The history of the study of children's psychomotor development illustrates some key drawbacks to a monocultural approach to parenting and child development. Gesell (e.g., Gesell and Amatruda, 1945) originally conceptualized infants' psychomotor development as being controlled by biology. Through detailed observations, he constructed "atlases" completely detailing the features of normative psychomotor growth in the first years (see Bornstein, 2001). However, Gesell studied only infants from middle-class European American families. Subsequent research conducted with different cultural groups challenged Gesell's assumptions of biological determinism. For example, African, Iranian, and Balinese infants were observed to differ with respect to the stages and timing of motor development in early childhood compared to the middle-class European American infants Gesell had studied. Specifically, Ghanda and Wolof infants tend to be more advanced (Ainsworth, 1967; Geber, 1956, 1958), Iranian orphanage-reared infants tend to be delayed (Dennis, 1960), and Balinese infants transit a different series of stages as they learn to walk (Mead and MacGregor, 1951). Dutch infants, who are stimulated less than U.S. American infants, score lower on scales of psychomotor development (Rebelsky, 1967, 1972). When Ghanda and Kipsigis infants are reared using practices favored by European Americans, they no longer showed the psychomotor advances of their peers who were reared using traditional practices (Geber, 1958; Super, 1976). This body of research suggests that psychomotor development in infants is not driven exclusively by biological forces but rather is shaped systematically by parenting practices that vary by culture. Even domains of child development under seeming biological control must be regarded as plastic, within limits, to parenting and culture.

In many societies, the caregiving role is assumed primarily by mother and father. However, children in other societies spend large amounts of time with nonparental caregivers such as siblings, grandparents, and other adults, all of whom may share caregiving responsibilities with parents. Despite the involvement of other caregivers, biological mothers (or sisters or female relatives) almost universally assume ultimate responsibility for young children within nuclear or extended families (Geary, 2000; Leiderman, Tulkin, and Rosenfeld, 1977; Weisner and Gallimore, 1977). Compared to fathers, for example, mothers spend, on average, between 65% and 80% more time in direct one-to-one interaction with young children (Parke et al., 2005). Fathers generally remain helpers rather than assuming primary responsibility for young children. Mothers and fathers also typically interact with and care for children in complementary ways (e.g., mothers in providing direct care and fathers in serving as playmates; Barnard and Solchany, 2002; Parke, 2002). In addition, fathers indirectly affect their children's development through the supportiveness of mothers (Parke et al., 2005). In the remainder of this chapter, we refer to parenting as a broad and inclusive construct, but we acknowledge important within-culture as well as between-culture variations in the respective roles of mothers, fathers, and children's other caregivers.

Parenting Across Cultures

Children are born into many different types of worlds, and it is the hope as well as the objective of their parents to prepare, or socialize, them to adapt to those worlds. In its most general sense, socialization constitutes preparation of the young to manage the tasks of life. It involves the continuous interplay between biological mechanisms that facilitate receptivity and motivation to acquire competencies within the experienced environment and the mechanisms by which the culture and environment shape and strengthen those competencies. Within this system, biological and social-cultural factors mutually reinforce one another in a recursive fashion. The child appears to expect these experiences, and the human brain is prepared for socialization (Greenough, Black, and Wallace, 1987). Parenting modifies not only the cognitive, socioemotional, and behavioral competencies of the developing individual, but also the design of the brain. Culture has a significant moderating impact on the effect of parent-provided experiences. What parenting is and how it works depend on cultural context.

Parenting has benefits as well as costs for offspring. Positive parenting promotes children's success in managing their lives, and socialization influences children's motivation and ability to acquire culturally shared emotional, social, and cognitive competencies. Poor parenting places those same goals in jeopardy, especially among parents who lack the knowledge, investment, or competencies to rear their young so as to augment the individual and common good alike (Bugental and Grusec, 2006). Parents and their offspring also coexist in biological and social conflicts, as for example, when first toddlers and later adolescents seek autonomy or when the priorities of parents and their children diverge.

Parenting incorporates cultural models, meanings, and practices into basic psychological processes that reciprocally maintain or change the culture (Bornstein, 2001; Fiske, Kitayama, Markus, and Nisbett, 1998). Context and meaning are central to socialization. Parenting transmits values in the form of cultural adages about what is important. Cultural prescriptives for parenting practices likewise derive from and maintain cultural models: A parental armamentarium of negotiation, compromise, and reason indicates that maintaining positive relationships is a goal of social interactions in one culture, whereas parental power assertion tells children that obedience is a desirable and important outcome in another.

Some Central Issues in Culture and Parenting

The move to encompass a culturally richer understanding of parenting has given rise to a set of important questions about parenting (Bornstein, 2001). What is normative parenting for a culture, and to what extent does parenting vary across cultures? Is it possible to identify historical, economic, social, or other sources of cultural differences in parenting? How do cultural beliefs translate into parenting cognitions and practices? In what ways do diverse parenting strategies relate to children's short- and long-term developmental accommodation to culture?

Culture and Parenting Cognitions

Culture expresses itself through parenting cognitions and practices. One key question is how culture relates to parents' cognitions and practices and, in turn, to the enculturation and development of children. An illustrative example comes from comparative work on parental responses to inhibition in children (Chen et al., 1998). Some children appear relatively relaxed when confronted with an unfamiliar situation and manifest little distress. Other children react to novel situations with anxiety: They do not readily explore new objects or easily interact with unfamiliar people. This pattern of actions signals behavioral inhibition. Traditional Chinese mothers view behavioral inhibition in their toddlers as a positive trait. Behavior inhibition is associated with maternal acceptance; those Chinese mothers of inhibited children harbor warm and loving attitudes toward them. In contrast, Canadian parents of European descent regard behavioral inhibition in a poor light; it is negatively associated with maternal acceptance and encouragement of children's achievement. Among Canadian families, children who display behavioral inhibition have mothers who are likely to believe that physical punishment is the best way to discipline them and are likely to feel angry toward them. In short, behavioral inhibition in children is associated with positive attitudes in traditional Chinese mothers and negative ones in Canadian mothers, as conditioned by culture. In school, such shy Chinese children achieve academically, and their teachers and peers rate them more positively; by contrast, shy Canadian children fare worse in school in general as well as with their peers (Chen, Rubin, Li, and Li, 1999; Chen, Rubin, and Li, 1995; for insight into historical changes in this domain, see Chen and French, 2008). Shyness and inhibition in children are regarded by parents and teachers in Western cultures as signs of incompetence and immaturity requiring protection, intervention, and sometimes reprimand, whereas they are viewed by traditional Chinese parents, children, and teachers as desirable characteristics and are linked to better adjustment.

Culture-based expectations about developmental norms and milestones (when a child is expected to achieve a particular developmental skill, for example) affect parents' appraisals of their child's development. Hopkins and Westra (1989, 1990) surveyed English, Jamaican, and Indian mothers living in the same city and found that Jamaican mothers expected their children to sit and to walk earlier, whereas Indian mothers expected their children to crawl later. In each case, children's actual attainment of developmental milestones accorded with their mothers' expectations.

Interrelatedness and autonomy are important in all cultures, but the ways in which parents foster them in children vary as a function of the values and goals that exist in particular cultures (e.g., Greenfield, Suzuki, and Rothstein-Fisch, 2006; Morelli and Rothbaum, 2007). U.S. American infants derive security from using mothers as a base from which to explore the world, and Japanese infants derive security from their mothers' indulgence of their needs; this contrast is reflected in greater distal eye contact by American mothers and greater proximal body contact by Japanese mothers (Barratt, Negayama, and Minami, 1993). In essence, then, relationships are central in both cultures, but they assume different forms as a function of different cultural emphases on individuation and accommodation. Hence, the force of cultural representations involves the implicit meanings and obvious understanding of culture, parenting, and childhood. Children bring certain proclivities to their interactions with parents, and parents interpret even similar characteristics in children within their culture's frame of reference; parents either encourage or discourage the continuation of features of their children's development depending on the meaning culture attaches to it. Culturally unifying forces typically work through parental beliefs or attitudes, called "ethnotheories" (Harkness and Super, 2002). Ethnotheories represent culturally homogenizing influences on parents. Cultures provide their members with implicit or explicit models of childrearing that engender uniform ethnotheories. They include when and how to care for children, what child characteristics are desirable, orientations toward family versus work, maternal employment, and childcare, as well as which parenting practices are accepted or expected.

Culture and Parenting Practices

The realization of parenting cognitions and attainment of parenting goals are achieved through parenting practices. At the dinner table, Japanese American families discuss group activities and shared experiences, whereas European American families focus on individual children's activities and experiences (Martini, 1996). U.S. American children are encouraged to discuss their own feelings and those of others as a way of increasing their understanding of emotion and ability to regulate it; Chinese families encourage attunement to the feelings of others but restraint in the expression of one's own feelings as key to group harmony (Chao, 1995). Chinese parents are likely to remind children of their past transgressions, using storytelling, for example, as a way to teach social norms and behavioral standards and to engender a sense of shame over bad behavior. In contrast, U.S. American parents avoid stories of transgression so as not to damage their children's self-esteem (Miller, Fung, and Mintz, 1996; Miller, Wiley, Fung, and Liang, 1997). European American parents are more likely to engage in authoritative parenting that emphasizes the growth of separation and autonomy within a supportive and responsive relationship, whereas Asian American, Latin American, and African American parents tend to engage in authoritarian parenting with its greater emphasis on obedience and conformity (Steinberg, Mounts, Lamborn, and Dornbusch, 1991).

In the cultural approach, some of the basic tenets of attachment—the meaning of sensitivity, competence, and the function of the caregiver as a secure base for exploration—assume culture-specific forms. In contrast, the universals of attachment—pursuit of proximity and protection and distress at separation—remain unchanged. The different goals that characterize different cultures shape parenting practices, so that anticipatory or immediate reactions to infant distress signals, close body contact, and disapproval of mother–child separation feature in one sort of (collectivist) cultural context as a way of fostering early close relationships in contrast to different practices in another sort of (individualist) culture (Greenfield et al., 2006). Maternal behavior in the protective care domain offers a detailed example of how different cultural values are mirrored in the ways that caregivers construe the tasks of parenting. Rothbaum, Weisz, Pott, Miyake, and Morelli (2000) analyzed how sensitivity in mother–infant interactions manifests itself in different cultural settings. They focused on Japanese and American cultures that contrast independence and interdependence and how each reveals itself in the way mothers respond to distress and bid for infant attention. Sensitivity is expressed to American infants in encouragement of expression of emotion, whereas sensitivity is expressed to Japanese infants through muting emotional expression. Sensitivity occurs in anticipation of children's signals in the Japanese context and in response to children's signals in the American context, and sensitivity fosters exploration and autonomy in the latter and emotional closeness in the former. Secure attachment promotes social competence, but competence differs in the two cultures—exploration, autonomy, willingness to express emotion, and a positive self-concept are valued in the U.S. American context, whereas dependence, emotional restraint, self-effacement, and indirect expression of feelings are valued in the Japanese context (Morelli and Rothbaum, 2007).

Theory in Culture and Parenting

Form Versus Function

Understanding parenting cognitions and practices and their meaning requires situating them in their cultural context (Bornstein, 1995). A particular parenting cognition or practice can have the same or different meanings in different cultural contexts, just as different parenting cognitions or practices can have the same or different meanings in different cultural contexts. Culture informs not only about quantitative aspects but also about the qualitative meaning of parents' beliefs and behaviors. These constructs cannot be understood without knowledge of the cultural meaning they have and the cultural contexts in which they are embedded. One of the most powerful moderators of the impact of experience on children's development is the cultural context in which the experience occurs. It is context that gives meaning to a belief or behavior. Thus, the same attitude or action may yield different outcomes in different cultural contexts because it assumes a different meaning in each. Understanding culture augments understanding the mechanisms of parenting by demonstrating the roles of cognitions and practices that are influenced by culture, as well as identifying those cognitions and practices that cross-cut culture. It helps address questions such as why it is that authoritarian parenting leads to negative outcomes in one culture and not in another, or whether autonomy and separation can be universal features of psychological functioning independent of the context in which they are exhibited.

When a particular parenting cognition or practice connotes the same meaning and serves the same function in different cultures, it probably constitutes a cultural universal. For example, caregivers in (almost) all cultures routinely adjust their speech to children, making it simpler and more redundant, presumably to support early language acquisition. Child-directed speech constitutes a cultural universal that is even difficult to suppress (Papoušek and Bornstein, 1992). Likewise, parental psychological control of adolescents appears to have negative correlates across a wide variety of cultural contexts (Barber et al., 2005).

The same parenting cognition or practice can also assume different meanings or functions in different cultural contexts. For example, in some cultural groups, mutual eye contact sets the stage for interpersonal communication and social interaction (Trevarthen, 1998; Tronick, Als, and Brazelton, 1977), but in other cultural groups, mutual eye contact can signal disrespect and aggression (Attneave, 1987; Brazelton, 1972; Mitchum, 1989). Differences attached to the meaning of particular behaviors can cause problems for children whose parents expect them to behave in one way that is encouraged at home (e.g., avoiding eye contact to show deference and respect) when children find themselves in a context where adults attach a different (often negative) meaning to the same behavior (e.g., appearing disinterested and unengaged with a teacher at school).

Conversely, different parenting cognitions and practices may connote the same meaning or serve the same function in different cultural contexts. For example, in some cultural groups, parents show affection predominately through their tone of voice, whereas in other cultural groups, parents demonstrate their affection physically. These different displays serve the same function of making children feel loved, valued, and approved of by parents in their respective societies. As another example, even gestures as apparently simple as moving one's head to indicate assent or dissent are not culturally universal. In some cultural groups, the form that showing assent takes is an up and down nod, whereas in other cultural groups, the form that showing assent takes is shaking the head from side to side (a gesture that indicates dissent elsewhere), but the function of these different forms is to communicate assent with what a speaker is saying (McClave, Kim, Tamer, and Mileff, 2007). By modeling the appropriate cultural forms of communication for their children, parents socialize them to be competent members of the society whose communication will function in the desired way in a given cultural context.

When different parenting cognitions or practices connote different meanings or serve different functions in different settings, this provides evidence for cultural specificity. Cultures differ in the value they place on different parenting practices that will promote desirable qualities and behaviors in children (Mistry, Chaudhuri, and Dietz, 2003). For example, mothers in China and India use authoritative and authoritarian parenting practices in ways that relate to relative differences in their goals of social and emotional development and family honor (Rao, McHale, and Pearson, 2003).

Neither parenting forms nor functions within cultural groups are presumed to remain static across child development. For example, parents do not rely on the same rewards to encourage adolescents' good behavior that they used to encourage good behavior in their toddlers (Darling and Steinberg, 1993; Maccoby and Martin, 1983), even if the desired goal across development is a consistent one—to praise and support children. Instead, to maintain a proactive, sensitive parenting style over time likely requires that parents alter particular cognitions and practices to adjust to children's developing physical, cognitive, emotional, and social capabilities (Bradley,

2002). On this argument, too, it is possible for the parenting practices of different cultural groups to look similar during infancy but diverge during childhood or adolescence.

Mechanisms of Parenting

What are the mechanisms parents employ with their children to promote their cultural competence and ensure they become mature and adjusted members of society? Several theoretical frameworks position parents as mediators between the wider cultural context and the development of children's culturally grounded beliefs and behaviors (Kağitçibaşi, 2007). For example, learning theorists emphasize the roles that conditioning and modeling play as children acquire associations or make observations that subsequently form the basis for their culturally constructed selves. Through observational learning, for example, children later come to imitate behaviors they have previously encoded by watching or listening to others who are already embedded in the culture (Rogoff, 2003). Attachment theorists propose that children develop internal working models of social relationships through interactions with their primary caregivers early in life (Bowlby, 1969) and that these models shape children's future social relationships with, and expectations of, others (Sroufe and Fleeson, 1986).

Although parents and other caregivers clearly influence children's development as learning and attachment theorists would suggest, children also play an active role in co-constructing their parenting experiences. For example, sensitive parents are able to assess children's current levels of competence and interact with children at a level that is just beyond what children would be able to accomplish alone (Vygotsky, 1978). In this way, children come to think and act like their more experienced caregivers who guide them to more advanced and adapted levels of cultural functioning. Wood, Bruner, and Ross (1976) described these types of interactions as "scaffolds" or temporary aids parents put in place to facilitate the child's development. Sensitive caregivers adjust their scaffolding strategies as children grow to accommodate children's developing competencies (Bornstein, 2006).

Children's appraisals of their parents play a mediating role in the association between parenting and child adjustment. Rohner's (1986) parental acceptance–rejection theory suggests that, if children interpret their parents' behavior as rejection, it will have deleterious effects on their adjustment. Children's perceptions of the harshness versus justness of their parents' physical punishment does not exert direct effects on their own psychological adjustment; instead, these effects are fully mediated by children's perceptions of their parents' acceptance and rejection (Rohner, Bourque, and Elordi, 1996).

Even if specific parenting gambits differ across cultures, the mechanisms through which they affect children's adjustment might be universal. The theory would be that parenting exerts effects on child outcomes through the meaning (i.e., the emotional implications and cognitive interpretations) that they communicate to children and that this meaning is only understood in the cultural context in which the parenting occurs. This theory implies testable hypotheses that cultural normativeness in parenting moderates the association between parenting and children's adjustment; the association between parenting and children's adjustment is conditioned by the broader affective quality of the parent–child relationship; and cognitive and emotional appraisals of parenting (which are affected by cultural context) mediate the association between parenting and children's adjustment.

Ecological Theory, Culture, and Parenting

Bioecological theory involves four basic nuclei: process, person, context, and time (Bronfenbrenner, 1999; Bronfenbrenner and Morris, 1998). Process, which is basic to understanding human development, is viewed as the mediator between individual and context. Proximal processes constitute the typically occurring practices to which the child is exposed and link individual to context. Human development takes place through processes of progressively more complex reciprocal interaction between an active, evolving biopsychological human organism and the persons, objects, and symbols in the person's proximal-to-distal external environments. "The form, power, content, and direction of the proximal processes affecting development vary systematically as a joint function of the characteristics of the developing person; of the environment—both immediate and remote—in which the processes take place; the nature of the developmental outcomes under consideration; and the social continuities and changes occurring over time throughout the life course and the historical period during which the person has lived" (Bronfenbrenner and Morris, 1998, p. 996). Proximal processes thus constitute the link between the distal environment (culture) and children's everyday activities with more competent members of the community (parents). This idea of process points to typically occurring activities and interactions in which people engage, while at the same time assessing how those proximal processes are themselves influenced both by characteristics of the individuals involved and by aspects of the broader context. The person in development is an active individual, capable of discovering, maintaining, or transforming his or her environment of opportunities.

Context is characterized by a series of systems, defined hierarchically, from most proximal to the individual to the most distal. A microsystem is a pattern of activities, social roles, and interpersonal relationships experienced by the developing person in a given face-to-face setting with particular physical, social, and symbolic features that invite, permit, or inhibit engagement in sustained, progressively more complex interaction with, and activity in, the immediate environment. The mesosystem comprises the linkages and processes taking place between two or more settings containing the developing person. The exosystem comprises the linkages and processes taking place between two or more settings, at least one of which does not contain the developing person, but in which events occur that indirectly influence processes within the immediate setting in which the developing person lives. The macrosystem consists of the overarching pattern of micro-, meso-, and exosystems characteristic of a given culture or subculture, with particular reference to the belief systems, bodies of knowledge, material resources, customs, lifestyles, opportunity structures, hazards, and life course options that are embedded in each of these broader systems (Bronfenbrenner and Ceci, 1994). Parent–child interactions with the cultural environment occur at multiple levels, and all constitute effective cultural environmental stimulants to individual child development.

Illustrative Cross-Cultural Studies of Parenting

The anthropological literature archives a rich history of childrearing cognitions and practices across cultural groups. Notably, Whiting and Whiting's Six Cultures project incorporated observations of children, interviews with mothers, and ethnographic notes to understand parenting practices and children's behavior in India, Japan, Kenya, Mexico, the Philippines, and the United States (Whiting, 1963; Whiting and Whiting, 1960). Many researchers of varying academic stripes have investigated how different cultural niches influence parents' cognitions and practices in rearing their children and how effective they may be depending on the cultural context in which they are situated (Garcia Coll and Pachter, 2002). Cultural influences on parenting (and child development) begin long before children are born, and they shape fundamental decisions about which behaviors parents should promote in their children and how parents should interact with their children (Benedict, 1938; Bornstein, 1991; Caudill and Frost, 1972; Caudill and Weinstein, 1974; Erikson, 1950; Whiting, 1963). Although the United States and Japan are both child-centered modern societies with high standards of living, as we have recounted, American and Japanese parents harbor very different childrearing goals, which they express in different ways (Azuma, 1986; Bornstein, 1989; Morelli and Rothbaum, 2007). American mothers try to promote autonomy, assertiveness, verbal competence, and self-actualization in their children, whereas Japanese mothers try to promote emotional maturity, self-control, social courtesy, and interdependency within the mother–child dyad. Mothers' responsiveness to infants (Bornstein et al., 1992) reflects these contrasting parenting styles. American mothers are more likely to respond when their children orient to the environment, whereas Japanese mothers are more likely to respond when their children orient socially. American mothers try to direct their children's attention to the environment; Japanese mothers try to direct their children's attention to themselves. Overall, American mothers behave in ways that promote independence, whereas Japanese mothers behave in ways that promote interdependence (Befu, 1986; Bornstein, Azuma, Tamis-LeMonda, and Ogino, 1990; Hess, Chang, and McDevitt, 1987; Kojima, 1986). American parents threaten to ground their disobedient children inside the home, whereas Japanese parents threaten to banish theirs outside the home (Johnson, 1993).

Different parenting styles appear to be adaptive for different cultural groups depending on family characteristics, assimilation experiences, broader cultural contexts, or other factors (Bulcroft, Carmody, and Bulcroft, 1996; Ogbu, 1993). For example, Baumrind (1989) found that, although an authoritative parenting style leads to the most positive outcomes for European American school children, an authoritarian parenting style leads to the most positive outcomes for African American school children; moreover, the association between authoritative parenting and academic achievement is stronger for European American than for African American adolescents (Darling and Steinberg, 1993). Authoritarianism is positively related to externalizing problems among European Americans but is unrelated among Mexican Americans (Lindahl and Malik, 1999); indeed, authoritarian parenting has positive effects on adolescents' school performance among Chinese in Hong Kong (Leung, Lau, and Lam, 1998).

Studies of parents' use of physical discipline are further illustrative. An analysis of ethnographies from 186 preindustrial societies revealed that parents' use of physical punishment is most likely to be found in societies high in social stratification, political integration, undemocratic political decision making, and higher levels of violence (Ember and Ember, 2005). However, it might be that the cultural climate in which discipline occurs is more important than discipline per se in predicting effects on children's development (Gunnoe and Mariner, 1997). In an empirical test of the role of cultural normativeness on parent–child relationships, the moderation link between mothers' use of physical discipline and children's adjustment was studied in six countries. Multilevel modeling revealed that countries differed in the reported use and normativeness of physical discipline and in the way that physical discipline related to children's adjustment (Lansford et al., 2005). Perceived normativeness of physical discipline, particularly children's perceptions, moderated the association between experiencing physical discipline and child aggression and anxiety. More frequently experiencing physical discipline was associated with higher levels of anxiety regardless of whether physical discipline was perceived as being normative, and children who perceived the use of physical discipline as being normative expressed higher levels of aggression, regardless of whether they personally experienced high or low levels of physical discipline. However, culture significantly moderated the strength of this relation. More frequent use of physical discipline was less strongly associated with adverse child outcomes in conditions of greater perceived normativeness. Thus, the association between mothers' use of physical discipline and child adjustment appears to be moderated by the cultural normativeness of physical discipline. However, at the individual level, physical discipline also has negative effects regardless of its cultural normativeness, and at a societal level, more frequent use of corporal punishment with children is related to higher prevalence of adult violence and endorsement of violence (Lansford and Dodge, 2008).

Cultural contexts may moderate the association between parents' behavior and children's adjustment to the extent that they influence children's construal of parents' behaviors. For example, it is possible that children in one culture regard spanking as a legitimate, albeit painful, parenting practice that is carried out with their best interests at heart, whereas children in another culture view spanking as a frightening experience in which their parents are out of control. Graziano and Hamblen (1996) found that the vast majority of the middle-class, primarily European American parents reported experiencing moderate to high levels of anger, remorse, and agitation when physically disciplining their children. Furthermore, Straus (1996) found that more than half of mothers reported that more than half of the times they resorted to physical discipline, it was the wrong strategy to have used. Cultural differences in the meaning that children attach to being disciplined help to explain why physical discipline is related differently to their subsequent externalizing behavior. If cultural normativeness and acceptance of a discipline practice contribute to children's perceptions of their parents' use of it as being indicative of "good" and caring parenting, there may be no association between that type of discipline and children's adjustment problems. However, if children do not perceive that that type of discipline is indicative of good parenting (perhaps because it is not culturally normative), they may associate being disciplined with being rejected by their parents, which could be related to later higher levels of problem behavior.

Cultural normativeness also conditions whether a particular caregiving style promotes the effective transmission of values. Parenting styles that are congruent with cultural norms appear to be more effective in transmitting values from parents to children, perhaps because parenting practices that are more culturally normative result in a childrearing environment that is more positive and predictable and that facilitates children's accurate perceptions of parents' values. Furthermore, if parents behave in culturally normative ways, their children are also likely to encounter similar values in settings outside the family (e.g., in religious institutions, in the community). Repeatedly encountering consistent beliefs and behaviors in different settings helps to organize children's development around culturally acceptable norms (Quinn and Holland, 1987). Thematicity (the repetition of the same cultural idea across mechanisms and contexts) has special importance in culture *qua* an organizer of behavior (Schank and Abelson, 1977). Every culture is characterized and distinguished from others by thoroughgoing, deep-rooted, and consistent themes that inculcate what one needs to feel, think, and do as a functioning member of the culture. So, for example, in the United States, personal choice is closely bound up with how individuals think of themselves and make sense of their lives. Personal choice is firmly rooted in principles of liberty and freedom and is a persistent and significant psychological construct in the literature on U.S.-born children (Deci, Ryan, and Koestner, 1999; Tamis-LeMonda and McFadden, Chapter 16, in this volume).

How firmly are cultural cognitions and practices related to parenting? Studies of immigrant families suggest that some beliefs about parenting that are inculcated in parents reared in one culture may endure even after those parents relocate to cultures that espouse different parenting beliefs. For example, Bornstein and Cote (2001; Cote and Bornstein, 2000, 2001) found that Japanese immigrant mothers' cognitions remained close to the cognitions of mothers in Japan or were intermediate between those of Japanese and European American mothers, whereas their behaviors changed to resemble those of European American mothers more closely than those of Japanese mothers. However, otherwise similar immigrant mothers from South America shared more cognitions and practices with U.S. American mothers in their culture of destination than mothers in their cultures of origin. Pachter and Dworkin (1997) asked mothers from minority (Puerto Rican, African American, and West Indian/Caribbean) and majority cultural groups about normal ages of attainment of typical developmental milestones during the first 3 years of life. Although all responses fell within a normative developmental range, significant differences emerged among ethnic groups for more than one-third of developmental milestones assessed. Thus, cognitions of the majority group are not always readily adopted, and culturally significant parenting beliefs and norms often also resist change (e.g., LeVine, 1988; Ngo and Malz, 1998).

Moreover, different immigrant groups adopt and retain culture-specific cognitions and practices differently (Lin and Fu, 1990).

Practical Considerations in Culture and Parenting

Particular parental practices are perceived as being abusive in some cultural contexts, but in others, the same behaviors are thought not to be harmful to children's adjustment. For example, parenting practices in some cultural contexts include folk remedies that are meant to help children recover from illness but that leave burns or other marks in the process (Hansen, 1997; Risser and Mazur, 1995). These parenting practices become problematic only when parents use them outside of their normative context (e.g., after immigrating to another culture when these behaviors conflict with definitions of child maltreatment; Levesque, 2000). Legal cases involving these types of scenarios sometimes invoke cultural evidence (for a review, see Coleman, 2007). For example, a judge dismissed a case in which a mother made small cuts on the cheeks of her two sons to signify that the sons were initiated into the native tribe of her ancestors (Fischer, 1998). Ear piercing is an example of a parenting practice that is normative in one culture (the United States) and that may physically hurt children in the short term and permanently alter their appearance; nevertheless, parenting that countenances ear piercing is not defined as abusive, and there is no presumption that it has long-term negative effects on children's adjustment. However, some parenting practices may be detrimental to children even if they are sanctioned by the cultural group. Female circumcision is an example of a practice that has been widely criticized as being abusive and having long-term negative effects on the adjustment of girls and women, despite its normativeness in certain cultural contexts (Ali, 2007; Coleman, 2007). The global community has increasingly taken a stand that children have particular rights regardless of where they live and that it is sometimes necessary to intervene with parents to prevent serious harm.

Straus's (2004) criminogenic theory of corporal punishment posits that some forms of violence are readily accepted in contexts in which corporal punishment is frequent and that the use of corporal punishment increases the probability that children will engage in violent behaviors during adulthood. Supportive evidence has been found in contexts where large proportions of youth who had experienced corporal punishment were also the contexts in which a large proportion of students reported assaulting or injuring a dating partner. The cultural spillover theory of violence likewise suggests that individuals are more likely to resort to violence in the future (either for socially legitimate or criminal purposes) if the society in which they live condones violence for legitimate purposes such as rearing children. In other words, violence in one domain tends to generalize (spill over) into other domains. For example, war, homicide, assault, combative sports, and severe punishment of criminals jointly characterize cultures of violence. Corporal punishment of children may be part of this more general culture of violence. Societies vary greatly in the degree to which they recognize corporal punishment as a legitimate parenting practice. In 1990, the United Nations Convention on the Rights of the Child placed the protection of children's rights at the forefront of the international community. This is an example of how the global community may, at times, adopt a position that is meant to alter parenting worldwide.

Conclusion

This is an exciting time for cultural studies of parenting. Researchers are no longer satisfied simply to document exotic cultural differences. Instead, research is increasingly focused on when and why links between parenting cognitions and practices and children's development are culturally general versus culturally specific, as well as which aspects of culture moderate parenting cognitions and practices and how they do so. These new directions move the field toward a deeper understanding, not just of whether parenting practices and children's development differ across cultures, but of why differences arise, in whom, and under which conditions.

Culture influences some parenting cognitions and practices (and, in turn, child development) from a very early age through such pervasive factors as what parents expect of children, when and how parents care for children, and which behaviors parents appreciate, emphasize, and reward. Parents are influenced by conventionalized images of what is and what ought to be in the domains of childrearing, and so they (even unconsciously) seek to implement an agendum derived from culture-specific concepts characteristic of their milieu.

Human cultures have different adaptive goals, and societies have developed different institutions and structures to instantiate parental cognitions about childrearing and to instigate parental practices. Parents provide childhood experiences and populate the environments of childhood that shape their children's development. Major domains of cross-cultural parenting inquiry include nurturance, social interactions, didactic exchanges, speech to children, and orchestration of the child's environment (Bornstein, 2002). Insofar as parents belong to a culture and subscribe to particular conventions of that culture, they likely follow prevailing "cultural scripts" in childrearing. Human beings acquire understandings of what it is to parent by living in a culture. Generational, social, and media images of parenting, children, and family life that are handed down or ready-made play significant roles in helping people form their parenting cognitions and guide their parenting practices (Holden and Buck, 2002; Sigel and McGillicuddy-De Lisi, 2002). Inasmuch as culture is organized information, parenting consists of mechanisms for transmitting that information and development in childhood of processing that information. Both parent and child then select, edit, and refashion cultural information. Through parenting, cultural information is not solely transmitted from parents to children. Rather, children are active participants in a bidirectional process in which they selectively attend to and assimilate as well as interact with cultural information from their parents and also elicit new information and responses from them. Cultural psychologists contend that cultures can be understood as created, sustained, and communicated in everyday practices and behavioral routines (Goodnow, Miller, and Kessel, 1995) and that development occurs through participation in cultural activities as well as the acquisition of cultural knowledge and skills (Rogoff, 2003). Parents of each generation are charged with the particular and continuing task to enculturate the next generation—that is, to prepare it for the physical, economic, and psychosocial situations that are characteristic of their culture. Thus, parenting occupies a central node in the nexus between culture and human development.

Acknowledgments

This chapter summarizes selected aspects of our research, and portions of the text have appeared in previous scientific publications cited in the references. Research was supported by the Intramural Research Program of the National Institutes of Health, *Eunice Kennedy Shriver* National Institute of Child Health and Human Development. We thank T. Taylor.

References

Ainsworth, M. (1967). *Infancy in Uganda*. Baltimore: Johns Hopkins University Press.
Ali, A. H. (2007). *Infidel*. New York: The Free Press.
Arnett, J. J. (2008). The neglected 95%: Why American psychology needs to become less American. *American Psychologist*, 63, 602–614.
Attneave, C. L. (1987). Practical counseling with American Indian and Alaska native clients. In P. Pedersen (Ed.), *Handbook of cross-cultural counseling and therapy* (pp. 135–140). New York: Greenwood Press.
Azuma, H. (1986). Why study child development in Japan? In H. W. Stevenson, H. Azuma, and K. Hakuta (Eds.), *Child development and education in Japan* (pp. 3–12). New York: Freeman.

Barber, B. K., Stolz, H. E., and Olsen, J. A. (2005). Parental support, psychological control, and behavioral control: Assessing relevance across time, culture, and method. *Monographs of the Society for Research in Child Development, Serial No. 282, 70*, 1–137.

Barnard, K. E., and Solchany, J. E. (2002). Mothering. In M. H. Bornstein (Ed.), *Handbook of parenting. Volume 3: Status and social conditions of parenting* (2nd ed., pp. 3–25). Mahwah, NJ: Erlbaum.

Barratt, M., Negayama, K., and Minami, T. (1993). The social environments of early infancy in Japan and the United States. *Early Development and Parenting, 2*, 51–64.

Baumrind, D. (1989). Rearing competent children. In W. Damon (Ed.), *Child development today and tomorrow* (pp. 349–378). San Francisco: Jossey-Bass.

Befu, H. (1986). Social and cultural background for child development in Japan and the United States. In H. W. Stevenson, H. Azuma, and K. Hakuta (Eds.), *Child development and education in Japan* (pp. 13–27). New York: Freeman.

Benedict, R. (1938). Continuities and discontinuities in cultural conditioning. *Psychiatry, 1*, 161–167.

Bornstein, M. H. (1980). Cross cultural developmental psychology. In M. H. Bornstein (Ed.), *Comparative methods in psychology* (pp. 231–281). Hillsdale, NJ: Erlbaum.

Bornstein, M. H. (1989). Cross-cultural developmental comparisons: The case of Japanese–American infant and mother activities and interactions. What we know, what we need to know, and why we need to know. *Developmental Review, 9*, 171–204.

Bornstein, M. H. (Ed.). (1991). *Cultural approaches to parenting*. Hillsdale, NJ: Erlbaum.

Bornstein, M. H. (1995). Form and function: Implications for studies of culture and human development. *Culture and Psychology, 1*, 123–137.

Bornstein, M. H. (2001). Some questions for a science of "culture and parenting" (…but certainly not all). *International Society for the Study of Behavioural Development Newsletter, 1*, 1–4.

Bornstein, M. H. (2002). Parenting infants. In M. H. Bornstein (Ed.), *Handbook of parenting: Volume 1: Children and parenting* (2nd ed., pp. 3–43). Mahwah, NJ: Erlbaum.

Bornstein, M. H. (2006). Parenting science and practice. In W. Damon (Series Ed.) and K. A. Renninger and I. E. Sigel (Vol. Eds.), *Handbook of child psychology. Volume 4: Child psychology in practice* (6th ed., pp. 893–949). New York: Wiley.

Bornstein, M. H., Azuma, H., Tamis-LeMonda, C. S., and Ogino, M. (1990). Mother and infant activity and interaction in Japan and in the United States: I. A comparative macroanalysis of naturalistic exchanges. *International Journal of Behavioral Development, 13*, 267–287.

Bornstein, M. H., and Cote, L. R. (2001). Mother-infant interaction and acculturation I: Behavioral comparisons in Japanese American and South American families. *International Journal of Behavioral Development, 25*, 549–563.

Bornstein, M. H., Tamis-LeMonda, C. S., Tal, J., Ludemann, P., Toda, S., Rahn, C. W., et al. (1992). Maternal responsiveness to infants in three societies: The United States, France, and Japan. *Child Development, 63*, 808–821.

Bowlby, J. (1969). *Attachment and loss* (Vol. 1). New York: Basic Books.

Bradley, R. H. (2002). Environment and parenting. In M. H. Bornstein (Ed.), *Handbook of parenting. Volume 2: Biology and ecology of parenting* (2nd ed., pp. 281–314). Mahwah, NJ: Erlbaum.

Brazelton, T. B. (1972). Implications of infant development among the Mayan Indians of Mexico. *Human Development, 15*, 90–111.

Bronfenbrenner, U. (1999). Environments in developmental perspective: Theoretical and operational models. In S. L. Friedman and T. D. Wachs (Eds.), *Measuring environment across the life span: Emerging methods and concepts* (pp. 3–28). Washington, DC: American Psychological Association.

Bronfenbrenner, U., and Ceci, S. J. (1994). Nature-nurture reconceptualized in developmental perspective: A bioecological model. *Psychological Review, 101*, 568–586.

Bronfenbrenner, U., and Morris, P. A. (1998). The ecology of developmental processes. In W. Damon (Series Ed.) and R. M. Lerner (Vol. Ed.), *Handbook of child psychology. Volume 1: Theoretical models of human development* (5th ed., pp. 993–1028). New York: Wiley.

Bugental, D. B., and Grusec, J. E. (2006). Socialization processes. In W. Damon (Series Ed.) and N. Eisenberg (Vol. Ed.), *Handbook of child psychology. Volume 3: Social, emotional, and personality development* (6th ed., pp. 366–428). New York: Wiley.

Bulcroft, R. A., Carmody, D. C., and Bulcroft, K. A. (1996). Patterns of parental independence giving to adolescents: Variations by race, age, and gender of child. *Journal of Marriage and the Family, 58*, 866–883.

Caudill, W., and Frost, L. (1972). A comparison of maternal care and infant behavior in Japanese-American, American, and Japanese Families. In U. Bronfenbrenner (Ed.), *Influences on human development* (pp. 329–342). Hinsdale, IL: Dryden.

Caudill, W. A., and Weinstein, H. (1974). Maternal care and infant behavior in Japan and America. In T. S. Lebra and W. P. Lebra (Eds.), *Japanese culture and behavior* (pp. 226–276). Honolulu, HI: University of Hawaii Press.

Chao, R. (1995). Chinese and European-American cultural models of the self reflected in mothers' child-rearing beliefs. *Ethos, 23*, 328–354.

Chen, X., and French, D. C. (2008). Children's social competence in cultural context. *Annual Review of Psychology, 59*, 591–616.

Chen, X., Hastings, P., Rubin, K. H., Chen, H., Cen, G., and Stewart, S. L. (1998). Childrearing attitudes and behavioral inhibition in Chinese and Canadian toddlers: A cross-cultural study. *Developmental Psychology, 34*, 677–686.

Chen, X., Rubin, K. H., and Li, Z. (1995). Social functioning and adjustment in Chinese children: A longitudinal study. *Developmental Psychology, 31*, 531–539.

Chen, X., Rubin, K. H., Li, B., and Li, D. (1999). Adolescent outcomes of social functioning in Chinese children. *International Journal of Behavioral Development, 23*, 199–223.

Cole, M. (2005). Culture in development. In M. H. Bornstein and M. E. Lamb (Eds.), *Developmental science: An advanced textbook* (pp. 45–101). Mahwah, NJ: Erlbaum.

Coleman, D. L. (2007). The role of the law in relationships within immigrant families: Traditional parenting practices in conflict with American concepts of maltreatment. In J. E. Lansford, K. Deater-Deckard, and M. H. Bornstein (Eds.), *Immigrant families in contemporary society* (pp. 287–304). New York: Guilford.

Cote, L. R., and Bornstein, M. H. (2000). Social and didactic parenting behaviors and beliefs among Japanese American and South American mothers of infants. *Infancy, 1*, 363–374.

Cote, L. R., and Bornstein, M. H. (2001). Mother-infant interaction and acculturation II: Behavioral coherence and correspondence in Japanese American and South American families. *International Journal of Behavioral Development, 25*, 564–576.

Darling, N., and Steinberg, L. (1993). Parenting style as context: An integrative model. *Psychological Bulletin, 113*, 487–496.

Deater-Deckard, K., Dodge, K. A., Bates, J. E., and Pettit, G. S. (1996). Physical discipline among African American and European American mothers: Links to children's externalizing behaviors. *Developmental Psychology, 32*, 1065–1072.

Deci, E. L., Ryan, R. M., and Koestner, R. (1999). A meta-analytic review of experiments examining the effects of extrinsic rewards on intrinsic motivation. *Psychological Bulletin, 125*, 627–668.

Dennis, W. (1960). Causes of retardation among institutional children: Iran. *Journal of Genetic Psychology, 96*, 47–59.

Dixon, S., Keefer, C., Tronick, E., and Brazelton, T. B. (1982). Perinatal circumstances and newborn outcome among the Gusii of Kenya: Assessment of risk. *Infant Behavior and Development, 5*, 11–32.

Ember, C. R., and Ember, M. (2005). Explaining corporal punishment of children: A cross-cultural study. *American Anthropologist, 107*, 609–619.

Erikson, E. H. (1950). *Childhood and society*. New York: Norton.

Fischer, M. (1998). The human rights implications of a cultural defense. *Southern California Interdisciplinary Law Journal, 6*, 663–702.

Fiske, A. P., Kitayama, S., Markus, H. R., and Nisbett, R. E. (1998). The cultural matrix of social psychology. In D. T. Gilbert, S. T. Fiske, and G. Lindzey (Eds.), *The handbook of social psychology* (Vols. 1 and 2, 4th ed., pp. 915–981). New York: McGraw-Hill.

Garcia Coll, C. T., and Pachter, L. M. (2002). Ethnic and minority parenting. In M. H. Bornstein (Ed.), *Handbook of parenting. Volume 4: Applied parenting* (2nd ed., pp. 1–20). Mahwah, NJ: Erlbaum.

Geary, D. C. (2000). Evolution and proximate expression of human paternal investment. *Psychological Bulletin, 126*, 55–77.

Geber, M. (1956). Development psychomoteur de l'enfant Africain. *Courrier, 6*, 17–28.

Geber, M. (1958). The psycho-motor development of African children in the first year, and the influence of maternal behavior. *Journal of Social Psychology, 47*, 185–195.

Gesell, A. L., and Amatruda, C. S. (1945). *The embryology of behavior: The beginnings of the human mind*. New York: Harper.

Goodnow, J. J., Cashmore, J. A., Cotton, S., and Knight, R. (1984). Mothers' developmental timetables in two cultural groups. *International Journal of Psychology, 19*, 193–205.

Goodnow, J. J., Miller, P. J., and Kessel, F. (Eds.). (1995). *Cultural practices as contexts for development*. San Francisco: Jossey-Bass.

Graziano, A. M., and Hamblen, J. L. (1996). Subabusive violence in child rearing in middle-class American families. *Pediatrics, 98*, 845–848.

Greenfield, P. M., Suzuki, L. K., and Rothstein-Fisch, C. (2006). Cultural pathways through human development. In W. Damon (Series Ed.) and K. A. Renninger and I. E. Sigel (Vol. Eds.), *Handbook of child psychology. Volume 4: Child psychology in practice* (6th ed., pp. 655–699). New York: Wiley.

Greenough, W. T., Black, J. E., and Wallace, C. S. (1987). Experience and brain development. *Child Development, 58,* 539–559.

Gunnoe, M. L., and Mariner, C. L. (1997). Toward a developmental-contextual model of the effects of parental spanking on children's aggression. *Archives of Pediatrics and Adolescent Medicine, 151,* 768–775.

Hansen, K. K. (1997). Folk remedies and child abuse: A review with emphasis on caida de mollera and its relationship to shaken baby syndrome. *Child Abuse and Neglect, 22,* 117–127.

Harkness, S., and Super, C. M. (2002). Culture and parenting. In M. H. Bornstein (Ed.), *Handbook of parenting. Volume 2: Biology and ecology of parenting* (2nd ed., pp. 253–280). Mahwah, NJ: Erlbaum.

Harwood, R. L., Schoelmerich, A., Schulze, P. A., and Gonzalez, Z. (1999). Cultural differences in maternal beliefs and behaviors: A study of middle-class Anglo and Puerto Rican mother-infant pairs in four everyday situations. *Child Development, 70,* 1005–1016.

Herodotus. (1996). *The histories.* New York: Penguin.

Hess, R. D., Chang, C. M., and McDevitt, T. M. (1987). Cultural variations in family beliefs about children's performance in mathematics: Comparisons among People's Republic of China, Chinese-American, and Caucasian-American families. *Journal of Educational Psychology, 79,* 179–188.

Hewlett, B. S., Lamb, M. E., Shannon, D., Leyendecker, B., and Scholmerich, A. (1998). Culture and early infancy among central African foragers and farmers. *Developmental Psychology, 34,* 653–661.

Holden, G. W., and Buck, M. J. (2002). Parental attitudes toward childrearing. In M. H. Bornstein (Ed.), *Handbook of parenting. Volume 3: Status and social conditions of parenting* (2nd ed., pp. 537–562). Mahwah, NJ: Erlbaum.

Hopkins, B., and Westra, T. (1989). Maternal expectations of their infants' development: Some cultural differences. *Developmental Medicine and Child Neurology, 31,* 384–390.

Hopkins, B., and Westra, T. (1990). Motor development, maternal expectations, and the role of handling. *Infant Behavior and Development, 13,* 117–122.

Johnson, F. A. (1993). *Dependency and Japanese socialization: Psychoanalytic and anthropological investigations into amae.* New York: New York University Press.

Kağitçibaşi, C. (2007). *Family, self, and human development across cultures: Theory and applications.* Mahwah, NJ: Erlbaum.

Kennedy, S., Scheirer, J., and Rogers, A. (1984). International education in psychology: The price of success—Our monocultural science. *American Psychologist, 39,* 996–997.

Kojima, H. (1986). Japanese concepts of child development from the mid-17th to mid-19th century. *International Journal of Behavioral Development, 9,* 315–329.

Kotchabhakdi, N. J., Winichagoon, P., Smitasiri, S., Dhanamitta, S., and Valyasevi, A. (1987). The integration of psychosocial components in nutrition education in northeastern Thai villages. *Asia-Pacific Journal of Public Health, 1,* 16–25.

Lansford, J. E., Chang, L., Dodge, K. A., Malone, P. S., Oburu, P., Palmérus, K., et al. (2005). Cultural normativeness as a moderator of the link between physical discipline and children's adjustment: A comparison of China, India, Italy, Kenya, Philippines, and Thailand. *Child Development, 76,* 1234–1246.

Lansford, J. E., and Dodge, K. A. (2008). Cultural norms for adult corporal punishment of children and societal rates of endorsement and use of violence. *Parenting: Science and Practice, 8,* 257–270.

Leiderman, P. H., Tulkin, S. R., and Rosenfeld, A. (Eds.). (1977). *Culture and infancy: Variations in the human experience.* New York: Academic Press.

Leung, K., Lau, S., and Lam, W. (1998). Parenting styles and academic achievement: A cross-cultural study. *Merrill-Palmer Quarterly, 44,* 157–172.

Levesque, R. J. R. (2000). Cultural evidence, child maltreatment, and the law. *Child Maltreatment, 5,* 146–160.

LeVine, R. A. (1988). Human parental care: Universal goals, cultural strategies, individual behavior. In R. A. LeVine and P. M. Miller (Eds.), *Parental behavior in diverse societies. New directions for child development* (No. 40, pp. 3–12). San Francisco: Jossey-Bass.

Lin, C. C., and Fu, V. R. (1990). A comparison of child-rearing practices among Chinese, immigrant Chinese, and Caucasian-American parents. *Child Development, 61,* 429–433.

Lindahl, K. M., and Malik, N. M. (1999). Marital conflict, family processes, and boys' externalizing behavior in Hispanic American and European American families. *Journal of Clinical Child Psychology, 28,* 12–24.

Maccoby, E. E., and Martin, J. A. (1983). Socialization in the context of the family: Parent-child interaction. In P. H. Mussen (Series Ed.) and E. M. Hetherington (Vol. Ed.), *Handbook of child psychology. Volume 4: Socialization, personality, and social development* (4th ed., pp. 1–101). New York: Wiley.

Martini, M. (1996). "What's new?" at the dinner table: Family dynamics during mealtimes in two cultural groups in Hawaii. *Early Development and Parenting, 5*, 23–34.

McClave, E., Kim, H., Tamer, R., and Mileff, M. (2007). Head movements in the context of speech in Arabic, Bulgarian, Korean, and African-American Vernacular English. *Gesture, 7*, 343–390.

McGillicuddy-De Lisi, A. V., and Subramanian, S. (1994). Tanzanian and United States mothers' beliefs about parents' and teachers' roles in children's knowledge acquisition. *International Journal of Behavioral Development, 17*, 209–237.

Mead, M. (1928). *Coming of age in Samoa: A psychological study of primitive youth for Western civilization.* New York: Morrow.

Mead, M. (1935). *Sex and temperament in three primitive societies.* New York: Morrow.

Mead, M., and MacGregor, F. C. (1951). *Growth and culture.* New York: Putnam's Sons.

Miller, P. J., Fung, H., and Mintz, J. (1996). Self-construction through narrative practices: A Chinese and American comparison of early socialization. *Ethos, 24*, 237–280.

Miller, P. J., Wiley, A. R., Fung, H., and Liang, C.-H. (1997). Personal storytelling as a medium of socialization in Chinese and American families. *Child Development, 68*, 557–568.

Mistry, J., Chaudhuri, J. H., and Dietz, V. (2003). Ethnotheories of parenting: At the interface between culture and child development. In R. M. Lerner, F. Jacobs, and D. Wertlieb (Eds.), *Handbook of applied developmental science* (Vol. 1, pp. 233–258). Thousand Oaks, CA: Sage.

Mitchum, N. T. (1989). Increasing self-esteem in Native-American children. *Elementary School Guidance and Counseling, 23*, 266–271.

Moghaddam, F. M. (1987). Psychology in three worlds. *American Psychologist, 42*, 912–920.

Morelli, G. A., and Rothbaum, F. (2007). Situating the child in context: Attachment relationships and self-regulation in different cultures. In S. Kitayama and D. Cohen (Eds.), *Handbook of cultural psychology* (pp. 500–527). New York: Guilford Press.

Ngo, P. Y. L., and Malz, T. A. (1998). Cross-cultural and cross-generational differences in Asian Americans' cultural and familial systems and their impact on academic striving. In H. I. McCubbin and E. A. Thompson (Eds.), *Resiliency in family series. Volume 2: Resiliency in Native American and immigrant families* (pp. 265–274). Thousand Oaks, CA: Sage.

Ochs, E. (1988). *Culture and language development.* Cambridge, United Kingdom: Cambridge University Press.

Ogbu, J. U. (1993). Differences in cultural frame of reference. *International Journal of Behavioral Development, 16*, 483–506.

Pachter, L. M., and Dworkin, P. H. (1997). Maternal expectations about normal child development in 4 cultural groups. *Archives of Pediatrics and Adolescent Medicine, 151*, 1144–1150.

Papoušek, H., and Bornstein, M. H. (1992). Didactic interactions: Intuitive parental support of vocal and verbal development in human infants. In H. Papoušek, U. Jürgens, and M. Papoušek (Eds.), *Nonverbal vocal communication: Comparative and developmental approaches* (pp. 209–229). Cambridge, United Kingdom: Cambridge University Press.

Parke, R. D. (2002). Fathers and families. In M. H. Bornstein (Ed.), *Handbook of parenting. Volume 3: Status and social conditions of parenting* (2nd ed., pp. 27–73). Mahwah, NJ: Erlbaum.

Parke, R. D., Dennis, J., Flyr, M. L., Morris, K. L., Leidy, M. S., and Schofield, T. J. (2005). Fathers: Cultural and ecological perspectives. In T. Luster and L. Okagaki (Eds.), *Parenting: An ecological perspective* (2nd ed., pp. 103–144). Mahwah, NJ: Erlbaum.

Quinn, N., and Holland, D. (1987). Culture and cognition. In D. Holland and N. Quinn (Eds.), *Cultural models in language and thought* (pp. 1–40). New York: Cambridge University Press.

Rao, N., McHale, J. P., and Pearson, E. (2003). Links between socialization goals and child-rearing practices in Chinese and Indian mothers. *Infant and Child Development, 12*, 475–492.

Rebelsky, F. G. (1967). Infancy in two cultures. *Nederlands Tijdschrift voor de Psychologie, 22*, 379–385.

Rebelsky, F. G. (1972). First discussant's comments: Cross-cultural studies of mother-infant interaction. *Human Development, 15*, 128–130.

Richman, A. L., Miller, P. M., and LeVine, R. A. (1992). Cultural and educational variations in maternal responsiveness. *Developmental Psychology, 28*, 614–621.

Risser, A. L., and Mazur, L. J. (1995). Use of folk remedies in a Hispanic population. *Archives of Pediatric and Adolescent Medicine, 149*, 978–981.

Rogoff, B. (2003). *The cultural nature of human development.* New York: Oxford University Press.

Rohner, R. P. (1986). *The warmth dimension: Foundations of parental acceptance-rejection theory.* Thousand Oaks, CA: Sage.

Rohner, R. P., Bourque, S. L., and Elordi, C. A. (1996). Children's perceptions of corporal punishment, caretaker acceptance, and psychological adjustment in a poor, biracial southern community. *Journal of Marriage and the Family, 58*, 842–852.

Rothbaum, F., Weisz, J., Pott, M., Miyake, K., and Morelli, G. (2000). Attachment and culture: Security in the United States and Japan. *American Psychologist, 55,* 1093–1104.

Russell, R. (1984). Psychology in its world context. *American Psychologist, 39,* 1017–1025.

Schank, R., and Abelson, R. (1977). *Scripts, plans, goals and understanding: An inquiry into human knowledge structures.* Hillsdale, NJ: Erlbaum.

Segall, M. H., Lonner, W. J., and Berry, J. W. (1998). Cross-cultural psychology as a scholarly discipline: On the flowering of culture in behavioral research. *American Psychologist, 53,* 1101–1110.

Serpell, R. Audience, culture and psychological explanation. *Quarterly Newsletter of the Laboratory of Comparative Human Cognition, 12,* 99-132.

Sigel, I. E., and McGillicuddy-De Lisi, A. V. (2002). Parental beliefs and cognitions: The dynamic belief systems model. In M. H. Bornstein (Ed.), *Handbook of parenting. Volume 3: Status and social conditions of parenting* (2nd ed., pp. 485–508). Mahwah, NJ: Erlbaum.

Smith, C., and Krohn, M. D. (1995). Delinquency and family life among male adolescents: The role of ethnicity. *Journal of Youth and Adolescence, 24,* 69–93.

Sroufe, L. A., and Fleeson, J. (1986). Attachment and the construction of relationships. In W. Hartup and Z. Rubin (Eds.), *Relationships and development* (pp. 51–71). Hillsdale, NJ: Erlbaum.

Steinberg, L., Mounts, N. S., Lamborn, S. D., and Dornbusch, S. M. (1991). Authoritative parenting and adolescent adjustment across varied ecological niches. *Journal of Research on Adolescence, 1,* 19–36.

Straus, M. A. (1996). Spanking and the making of a violent society. *Pediatrics, 98,* 837–842.

Straus, M. A. (2004). *The primordial violence: Corporal punishment by parents, cognitive development, and crime.* Walnut Creek, CA: Alta Mira Press.

Super, C. M. (1976). Environmental effects on motor development: The case of "African infant precocity." *Developmental Medicine and Child Neurology, 18,* 561–567.

Super, C. M., and Harkness, S. (1986). The developmental niche: A conceptualization at the interface of child and culture. *International Journal of Behavioral Development, 9,* 545–569.

Tomlinson, M., and Swartz, L. (2003). Imbalances in the knowledge about infancy: The divide between rich and poor countries. *Infant Mental Health Journal, 24,* 547–556.

Trevarthen, C. (1998). The concept and foundations of infant intersubjectivity. In S. Braten (Ed.), *Intersubjective communication and emotion in early ontogeny* (pp. 15–46). New York: Cambridge University Press.

Tronick, E. D., Als, H., and Brazelton, T. B. (1977). Mutuality in mother-infant interaction. *Journal of Communication, 27,* 74–79.

Vygotsky, L. (1978). *Mind in society.* Cambridge, MA: Harvard University Press.

Weisner, T. S. (2002). Ecocultural understanding of children's developmental pathways. *Human Development, 45,* 275–281.

Weisner, T. S., and Gallimore, R. (1977). My brother's keeper: Child and sibling caretaking. *Current Anthropology, 18,* 169–190.

Whiting, B. B. (Ed.). (1963). *Six cultures: Studies of child rearing.* New York: Wiley.

Whiting, J. W. M., and Whiting, B. B. (1960). Contributions of anthropology to the methods of studying child rearing. In P. Mussen (Ed.), *Handbook of research methods in child development* (pp. 918–944). New York: Wiley.

Wilson, E. O. (1975). *Sociobiology.* Cambridge, MA: Harvard University Press.

Wood, D. J., Bruner, J. S., and Ross, G. (1976). The role of tutoring in problem solving. *Journal of Child Psychology and Psychiatry, 17,* 89–100.

15
Religion

GEORGE W. HOLDEN and BRIGITTE VITTRUP

> Religion and culture and everything, they combine together to make the person that you really are.
>
> McEvoy et al., 2005, p. 146

Introduction

The theme for this chapter was uttered by an immigrant mother from Kosovo living in the United States (McEvoy et al., 2005). It illustrates one parent's recognition of the mutual importance of religion and culture for development. Although culture has long been recognized as a key determinant of development, considerably less attention has been paid to religion. That is now changing. Social scientists are increasingly documenting the ways in which religion, along with culture, can have a profound effect on the way children are perceived and reared by their parents and in turn develop and experience their world.

Since the earliest days of psychological research in the United States, the role of religion in human development has been a topic of intermittent interest. G. Stanley Hall (1891) led the way with his essay, "The Moral and Religious Training of Children and Adolescents." Subsequently, many intellectual leaders of psychology have written about the role of religion in development, including William James, Sigmund Freud, Alfred Adler, Carl Jung, Gordon Allport, and Abraham Maslow. Erik Erikson (1959) considered religion to be a central influence on personality development because it provides a mechanism by which culture promotes positive development.

Despite the attention devoted to the topic by our intellectual forefathers, the study of religion in development was virtually ignored for about a 30-year period until the mid-1950s. With the publication of Gorsuch's (1988) *Annual Review of Psychology* chapter, the study of religion regained acceptance as a legitimate subject to study in psychology. Since then, the revival has continued to gain momentum. The role of religion as a determinant of parental cognitions and behaviors as well as an influence in children's development and outcomes is now a topic of serious intellectual inquiry in psychology and sociology, as marked by the publication of handbooks and encyclopedias on religion and spirituality, such as *The Handbook of Spiritual Development* (Roehlkepartain, King, Waggoner, and Benson, 2006) and the *Encyclopedia of Religious and Spiritual Development* (Dowling and Scarlett, 2006).

Scholarly recognition of the role of religion in *cross-cultural* research has lagged. Until recently, religion was largely forgotten as an important variable within cultures. For example, in a study of parental values for their children conducted in eight countries, including Indonesia, Korea, the Philippines, Singapore, Taiwan, Thailand, Turkey, and the United States, Hoffman (1988) hypothesized that the social and economic structure of each society would influence parental values. Religion went unmentioned. Similarly, Goodnow and Collins (1990), in a review of sources of parental ideas and values, which included studies from many countries, failed to consider the role of religion. This neglect of religion when studying development from a cross-cultural perspective is problematic because religion may be a prime source of variation. Similarly, researchers who have examined racial/ethnic group differences may have actually identified, although left unmentioned, religious influences.

Cross-cultural investigations into the role of religion in child development lies at the intersection of three topics: child development, religion, and culture. Relations among those topics can be conceptualized in various ways. Around the world, human development is typically nested within religions, which are, in turn, nested within a culture, as is illustrated in the top diagram in Figure 15.1. However, research efforts have all too frequently approached the topics separately as depicted in the Venn diagram on the bottom of Figure 15.1. Although cross-cultural research into child development has been increasing, as this *Handbook* so clearly documents, surprisingly little attention has been devoted to exploring the union of these three research domains. This union is the focus of this chapter.

One explanation for the neglect of this three-topic intersection is that it is not an easy domain to study. Both culture and religion are ambiguous, imprecise, and intertwined concepts (Sander, 1996). Although individuals may identify themselves as belonging to a particular religious faith, that identification may not be a meaningful influence on their cognitions or behaviors. Alternatively, living in a culture infused with a particular religious worldview can dramatically influence an individual. The domain is also challenging to study because separating the influence of religion from that of culture can be difficult. Given that religions have been a central part of cultures for thousands of years, religious ideologies have blended with culture. For the predominately Muslim Malays, religion and culture are inseparable (Keats, 2000). In such cultures, distinctions between secular and spiritual cannot be made: "the spiritual life involves the whole of life" (Mattis, Ahluwalia, Cowie, and Kirkland-Harris, 2006, p. 293). In other countries, multiple religious and cultural influences have resulted in a unique mélange.

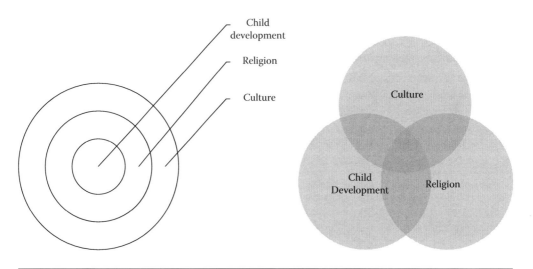

Figure 15.1 Diagrams of two ways of thinking about child development, religion, and culture.

Haitian Catholicism is an admixture of African religions, European Catholicism, and indigenous Caribbean Indian cultural practices. Hence, in many societies, divisions between religion and culture are fluid and complex. Another complicating factor are the interethnic, intercultural, and interreligious (or heterogamous) marital unions or family backgrounds. Adolescents in Tanzania identify themselves simultaneously as Christian, Muslim, and adherents of traditional religion (Mattis et al., 2006). In addition, immigration and acculturation add a dynamic quality to the study of religion and culture (Bornstein and Cote, Chapter 27, in this volume).

In some religiously and ethnically pluralistic societies, divisions between religious groups and their culture offer ripe opportunities for cross-cultural research. The short-lived fundamentalist Islam rule of the Taliban in Afghanistan (1996 to 2001) provided a vivid example of how a small religious sect can dramatically alter a cultural landscape. While the Taliban were in power, girls were forbidden to attend school, and women could not vote, hold jobs, or even reveal their faces in public. In the United States, despite an historically underlying Judeo-Christian influence, the concept of "separation of church and state" helps to formalize boundaries and divisions between religion and culture. Distinctions can also readily be drawn between certain religious denominations that hold different views, such as fundamentalists and liberal Protestants. In Iraq, the sectarian split between Shia and Sunni Muslims has, tragically, become well known. Diverse ethnic/cultural groups (e.g., Arabs, Kurds, Mennonites) as well as religious divisions among the Jews (e.g., Orthodox, Hassidic, Reformed, nonreligious) can be found living virtually side by side in Israel.

The cross-cultural study of the role of religion in development patently warrants attention because religion has powerful effects on behavior. Its influences may also be studied through the impact of sacred writings, including the Tanakh (Judaism), the Bible (Christianity), the Qur'an (Islam), the Vedas (Hindu), the Tipitaka (Theravada Buddhist), the Analects (Confucianism), and the Tao Te Ching (Taoist). These writings have given rise to a set of beliefs (norms and values), behaviors, and prescriptions for ways of interacting. Religions specify the roles of men and women, as well as rituals, rites of passage, and holy days (Marks, 2004). However, formalized religion does not have uniform influences, as individual adherence to religious values, beliefs, and practices is varied (Holden, 2001). Nevertheless, the role of religion in development is vital to study because, as the next section indicates, religion is a fundamental force of human development for most of the world's population.

In this chapter, a discussion of the research related to religion, culture, and development will be presented in five sections. First, a brief review of the historical role of religion and the statistics about the centrality of religion in the lives of most people is provided. Next, key issues in the investigation of religion, culture, and development will be identified. Theoretical orientations utilized are then considered. The main body of the chapter consists of a review of the key research studies. These are divided into four topics: the influence of religion at the cultural level, and associations between religion and the family context, childrearing, and child development. Finally, several directions for future research are outlined.

Historical and Demographic Considerations of Religion, Culture, and Development

In most cultures, religion has been an integral part of life for thousands of years. Hinduism, considered the oldest organized religion still practiced today, is centered around the Vedas, written around 1500 BCE. The Torah, part of the Jewish holy text, was recorded in 1400 BCE. Founders of the Oriental religions, including Lao Tzu (Taoism), Siddhartha Gautama (Buddhism), and Confucius (Confucianism) all were born between 604 and 551 BCE. The two other world religions are younger: Christianity emerged around 30 CE, and Islam started in 610 CE.

Worldwide, 86% of people claim that they identify with a particular religious group. The three largest religions are Christianity (32% of the world population), Islam (19%), and Hinduism (13%). In addition, there are 16 other world religions, and religious groups can further be divided into approximately 270 groups, denominations, or sects (Barnett, Kurian, and Johnson, 2001). Although some religions like Islam and the Church of Jesus Christ of Latter-day Saints (Mormons) are showing dramatic increases in adherents, evidence suggests a sharp decline in membership in mainline Protestant denominations (Methodist, Lutheran, Episcopal, Presbyterian) in North America and especially in Western Europe (Altemeyer, 2004).

In the United States, the majority of people (76%) consider themselves Christians. Approximately 13% are "nonreligious" (atheist, agnostic, nonbelievers), 1.3% affiliate with Judaism, and less than 1% are adherents of Islam, Buddhism, or Hinduism (Adherents, n.d.). The largest Christian denominations in the United States are Catholic (25%), Baptist (16%), Methodist (7%), and Lutheran (5%) (Barnett et al., 2001). However, with the increase of nondenominational congregations across the United States, the religious landscape is changing, and it is now more difficult to measure religiosity simply through denominational labels.

Approximately 85% of Americans state that they believe in God, and approximately 72% report that they pray at least once a week (Baylor Institute for the Study of Religion, 2006). Close to 50% of Americans attend church at least once a month. However, church attendance is not an accurate measure of religious commitment. As discovered by the Baylor researchers, unaffiliated people are not necessarily nonbelievers. In fact, a majority (63%) of Americans who are unaffiliated with a religious tradition report that they believe in God or a higher power, and almost one-third of them pray at least occasionally.

Religion for parents appears to be particularly important. Most (95%) of all married couples and parents report a religious affiliation (Mahoney, Pargament, Tarakeshwar, and Swank, 2001), and 90% want their children to have some religious training (Gallup and Castelli, 1989, cited in Mahoney et al., 1999). Young people are likely to embrace religion as well. For example, the majority (87%) of adolescents in the United States affiliate with some religious group or tradition. Most (67%) report religious beliefs similar to their parents, but they also claim that they attend religious services because they want to, not only because their parents make them. Approximately half of adolescents attend religious services on a regular basis (Smith, Denton, Farris, and Regnerus, 2002).

Central Issues in Religion, Culture, and Development

Given the limited research on this topic, the current central issues are methodological. How does one best study the influence of religion on child development from a cross-cultural perspective? A fundamental aspect of this question concerns how religion and culture are conceptualized and operationalized. In some studies, participants simply report their religious identity. In other efforts, multidimensional indices of religion and faith are collected. Culture is generally defined by the "social address" or location where the participant lives (e.g., rural or urban area, or a particular country) (Goodnow, Chapter 1, in this volume).

Four types of methodological designs, using both qualitative and quantitative approaches, predominate this research domain. The simplest approach has been to examine one religion within one culture. This method, which can be labeled the "Mono-Religion, Mono-Culture" model, is useful for providing an initial investigation into possible relations between religion and culture. For example, a study by Brody, Stoneman, and Flor (1996) examined the role of religiosity in how well families were functioning and adolescents were behaving in a sample of African American families in the rural south. One of their central findings was that parents who were more religious enjoyed more cohesive family relationships than other parents.

Religion • 283

A second approach that involves an actual comparison of religions can be labeled the "Religions within Culture" model (Figure 15.2). Here, the focus is on differences between two or more religious orientations within a culture. An example from the developing world comes from Nsamenang and Lamb (1995) who investigated parental values in rural Cameroon. Among other issues, they compared parents of young children who were Muslim, Christian, or the indigenous African religion. Religion was found to be associated with parental attitudes about discipline and parental authority. A study by Gershoff, Miller, and Holden (1999) provides another example. Contrasts were made among attitudes and disciplinary practices of conservative Protestant, mainline Protestant, and Catholic mothers and fathers of 3-year-old children from one community in the southwest United States. Conservative Protestant parents differed from the other groups of parents in their beliefs and reliance on corporal punishment as an instrumental disciplinary technique. This approach focuses on religious differences within one cultural context.

The third approach can be labeled the "Religion across Cultures" model (Figure 15.3) and highlights the role of the culture while holding religion constant. One of the first examples of

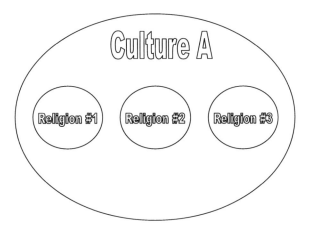

Figure 15.2 The "Religions within Culture" model.

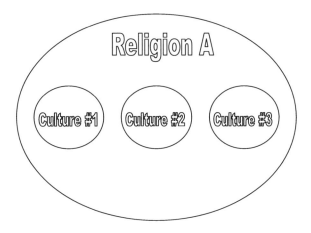

Figure 15.3 The "Religion across Cultures" model.

this approach was a study by Smith, Weigert, and Thomas (1979), who examined the relation between religiosity and self-esteem in almost 2,000 adolescents from 12 samples of Catholic youth who lived in the United States, Puerto Rico, Mexico, Spain, and West Germany. Across cultures, they found that religiosity was positively associated with self-esteem. A modest interaction between gender and location was also detected; females from the Latin samples tended to have higher self-esteem than males. A second example of a "Religion across Cultures" study included about 2,900 Arab adolescents in eight African and Middle Eastern countries (Dwairy et al., 2006). Reports by the youth about their parents' childrearing style indicated considerable differences within and between Arab cultures. In particular, children who reported the most controlling parents were children from Saudi Arabia, the most conservative authoritarian Arab society, and Palestinian children living in the occupied territories, who were living in a war zone.

The final approach used to study this domain can be labeled the "Religions by Cultures" model (Figure 15.4) and is the only complete way to contrast the influence of different religions across different cultures. We could locate only one study that approximated this model. Kelley and De Graaf (1997) analyzed data from almost 20,000 individuals from 15 nations. Although they did not directly compare different religions, they contrasted national religious beliefs, individual family religiosity, and Catholics versus Protestant beliefs. Their findings, described later, provide a good example for insights that can be gained from such a comprehensive analytic model.

Each of the four approaches has certain strengths and limitations for revealing the role of religion and culture in human development (van de Vijver, Hofer, and Chasiotis, Chapter 2, in this volume). The "Mono-Religion, Mono-Culture" model is the simplest and most common. Although the approach provides a feasible initial effort at identifying possible relations, by definition, it does not allow for comparisons. Both the "Religions within Culture" approach and the more expensive and difficult approach of "Religion across Cultures" provide comparative data but only systematically vary one dimension. Not surprisingly, the cross-cultural research that is available is often limited by small samples and the use of qualitative methods. Nevertheless, there is enough research to begin to generate hypotheses about how religion influences human development. After a brief discussion of theory, we review examples of research findings into four basic questions from all four approaches.

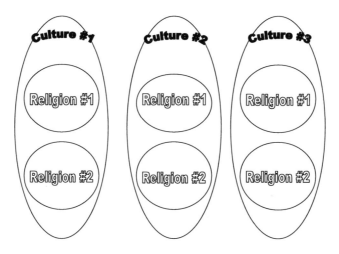

Figure 15.4 The "Religions by Cultures" model.

Theory in Religion, Culture, and Development

To date, cross-cultural research into the role of religion in children's lives is best characterized as descriptive. Although a few studies rely on a cognitive-constructionist framework (Takriti, Barrett, and Buchanan-Barrow, 2006) or social capital theory (King and Furrow, 2004), most available studies are, at least on the surface, atheoretical. However, when a theoretical orientation can be gleaned, it is most likely to be based around an ecological contextual perspective.

Ecological models, such as the well-known model by Bronfenbrenner (Bronfenbrenner and Morris, 1998), are particularly useful for cross-cultural examination of the role of religion on development. The model captures multiple types of influences on the developing child within different environments by identifying four levels or layers of influence (microsystem, mesosystem, exosystem, and macrosystem), how those change over time (chronosystem), and their interrelations. An implicit example of this theory can be found in Kelly and De Graaf's (1997) multinational study. They evaluated beliefs within two types of religious environments: a generalized, national normative belief about religion and individual family religiosity. This approach illustrated the concept of nested layers of contexts: family religious beliefs were evaluated along with the religious beliefs held by the society as a whole.

Another useful conceptual approach to understanding culture is Super and Harkness's (1986; Harkness and Super 2006) concept of the *developmental niche*. Emerging from their cross-cultural research into childrearing, it draws attention to three basic features of the childrearing context: (1) the physical and social environment in which a child lives; (2) customs of childcare and childrearing; and (3) parents' individual "ethnotheories" (or values and beliefs) pertaining to childrearing. Religion can influence each of those features—whom the child interacts with, the child's religious rituals and practices, and parental childrearing beliefs. These two perspectives—developmental niche and ecological systems—provide useful frameworks for better understanding the relations of culture and religion to children's development. Future investigations should take greater advantage of them.

Key Classical and Modern Research Studies in Religion, Culture, and Development

Given that this topic is in its own formative stages of development, it is too soon to identify key studies, let alone classic efforts. Indeed, many of the available studies are qualitative and provide a basis for hypothesis generation rather than testing. Still, there is enough empirical work to allow a brief review of research into the four central issues. First, what is the relation between religion and culture vis-à-vis development? Second, what are the associations between religion and family relationships? Third, how does religion influence parenting? Finally, how is religion related to child and youth development?

The Influence of Religion at the Cultural Level

Religion and religious institutions provide powerful agencies for socialization into particular world views. At the most global levels (Bronfenbrenner's macrosystem and exosystem), religion can influence laws, cultural institutions, cultural norms, transmission of moral values, regulation of sexuality, and even general interpersonal orientations (Browning, Green, and Witte, 2006; Parrinder, 1996). Religions prescribe culturally sanctioned pathways for development to occur, with rites of passage, such as baptism, and signals of the passage into adulthood, such as *bar* and *bat mitzvahs*, confirmations, and turban ceremonies. Toward that end, children are reared with religiously sanctioned spiritual guides, who provide social capital to children and families. These individuals include priests, pastors, rabbis, gurus, ayatollahs, mullahs, swamis, sages, and youth ministers, as well as the more informal "godparents" (Mattis et al., 2006).

The best example of how an ethical system of thought can influence cultural orientations toward parent–child relationships can be found in the influence of Confucianism. In Japan and other parts of Asia, Confucian ideology permeates society. Following its principles, the family is considered the fundamental unit of society, and there is a strict hierarchical order to human relationships. Thus, children are expected to show family loyalty, filial piety, and elder respect. It is the role of parents and elders to train and discipline youth in these cultural norms (Chao, 1994). When Asian countries become westernized, as in the case of South Korea, conflict between religiously imputed socialization values and new ideas can be detected (Park and Cheah, 2005).

Associations Between Religion and the Family Context

Links between religion and how families function have been an increasing focus of sociological and psychological research. All three of the world's largest deistic religions (Christianity, Judaism, and Islam) share an emphasis on the family and encourage parents to devote considerable time and attention to their children. Family matters concern approximately one-third of the injunctions in the Qur'an (Ashan, 1995, cited in Frosh, 2004). It follows then that religious parents, compared to nonreligious parents, hold different values, allocate time differently, and involve their children in social networks associated with a religious community (Bartkowski et al., 2008; Wilcox, 2002).

To date, the role of religion has been investigated most frequently in four marital domains, as reviewed by Mahoney et al. (2001). Although most of the work has been in North America and limited to Christian or Mormon samples, the findings are consistent. Religion is positively associated with marital satisfaction, commitment, and communication but negatively associated with verbal conflict, physical aggression, and divorce rates. Brody et al. (1996) found that religious African American parents had more cohesive family relationships and fewer problems with their children than did other African American parents. Religious involvement has also been shown to have an inverse relation to domestic violence, at least in the United States (Ellison and Anderson, 2001).

At the same time, religious involvement can be a source of family conflict. Heterogamous couples are more likely to experience marital problems than are partners who share the same faith (Mahoney et al., 1999). Parental religious beliefs and practices can also clash with children's desires and the larger culture. In a qualitative study, Marks (2004) interviewed Christian, Jewish, Mormon, and Muslim parents of children age 5 to 13 years. Parents recognized that their religion promoted family connections and closeness but also could be a source of conflict both within the family (i.e., children resistant to religious participation) and with the larger community. A Jewish mother observed, "Because our faith is not the faith of the nation, we have conflicts with the general community…. There is a lot of conflict in terms of when you need to observe [the Sabbath and other holy days] when other things are going on" (Marks, 2004, p. 227).

In summary, although there are few studies that clearly delineate how religion has influenced the family context, it is plausible that children of religious parents experience a qualitatively different family context and social environment than what other children experience.

Associations Between Religion and Childrearing

It is now well recognized that culture provides a fundamental contextual influence on how parents think about childrearing and their children (Bornstein, 1991; Bornstein and Cheah, 2006; Bornstein and Lansford, Chapter 14, this volume). So does religion. Religions frame long-term parenting goals through specifying desirable behavior, both in childhood and adulthood. Consequently, many religions, or the interpreters of the sacred texts, have specific prescriptions for how to attain those childrearing goals. Muslim women, according to one interpreter, may work outside the home "as long as it does not interfere with her first duty as a mother, the one who first trains her children in the Islamic call. So her first, holy, and most important mission is to be mother and wife" (Stewart et al., 1999, p. 751). Cross-cultural research into the associations between religion and childrearing can be divided into investigations on childrearing cognitions and childrearing practices.

Childrearing Cognitions Fundamentally, religion is about what is to be valued in life. Several cross-cultural studies have examined relations between religion or religiosity and adult values. In a meta-analytic review of research across cultures and religious groups, Saroglu, Delpierre, and Dernelle (2004) found that religious people shared the values of kindness, tradition, and conformity, whereas they disdained hedonism. Inglehart and Baker (2000), in an analysis of 63 societies, discovered that across religions, those adults who were more religious were also more likely to value tradition, obedience, respect for authority, and religious faith in their children, rather than independence and self-determination. A smaller, qualitative interview study of immigrant parents—from 27 countries and many faiths—residing in New York City replicated many of those findings. In addition to childrearing values of respecting elders, revering family, and recognizing the importance of faith and spirituality for their children's positive development, the parents also valued successfully managing the conflict between cultural heritage and assimilation (McEvoy et al., 2005).

The tension between religiously inspired cultural values and Westernized values has been the topic of much investigation. Cross-cultural investigators have also examined more specific childrearing attitudes of Asian, Asian American, and European American mothers. The view is that Oriental values, strongly influenced by Confucius's teachings, have permeated Asian societies but get diluted once exposed to Western values. Confucius emphasized filial piety ("parents are always right"), respect for elders, interdependence, group identification, harmony, self-discipline, and achievement (Chiu, 1987; Lin and Fu, 1990). Sexuality is de-emphasized, and aggression is suppressed. These values are reflected in childrearing attitudes. Chinese mothers have been found to have the most restrictive childrearing attitudes, compared to European American mothers who were most permissive and Chinese American mothers who were in the middle (Chiu, 1987). Other researchers have found similar patterns (Lin and Fu, 1990).

Islam also values respect for parents, but it differs by emphasizing the importance of family honor. Maintaining family *izzat* (pride, honor, self-respect) is an important goal and determinant of behavior in Islamic families (Stewart et al., 1999). *Izzat* can be easily damaged by inappropriate behavior, especially by female family members, and thereby provides a religious justification for restricting behavior and punishment. Thus, Muslim girls have been murdered by their family members simply for the appearance of impropriety.

In addition to values and attitudes, there are many historical and cross-cultural examples of ways in which religion shapes parenting cognitions. An historical example comes from the Puritan Americans, who formed their beliefs about children based, in part, on John Calvin's reformist theology. Children were conceived as born with "original sin," and parents were instructed by their ministers to "break the will" of children to socialize them into faithful adults (Greven, 1977). In contrast, both Confucianism and Islam espouse the view (one also promulgated by the Catholic Jean Jacques Rousseau in 1762) that children are inherently good and that parents play an important role in promoting children's healthy development (Stewart et al., 1999).

A very different religious belief about the nature of children can be found in many African, South Asian, and Native North American cultures. For many inhabitants in those societies, children are believed to be reincarnations of ancestral spirits. Consequently, a child's personality, luck, spiritual journey, and fate are largely a consequence of that inherited spirit (Gottlieb,

2006; Mattis et al., 2006). Another religiously inspired conviction, one that highlights the potential pernicious role of the environment in development, can be found in parents who subscribe to a belief in the "evil eye." The evil occurs when someone excessively admires an infant with a direct and extended look or with lavish praise and compliments. This belief, still held in Latin America, Caribbean countries, Northern Africa, Europe, and South Asia, reveals parental assumptions about the spiritual vulnerability of children (Mattis et al., 2006).

Parental disciplinary beliefs have been a popular topic of inquiry because they reveal how religion can influence childrearing attitudes. In particular, Christian denominations in the United States that espouse literalist interpretations of the Bible (or more accurately, the six applicable Proverbs in the Old Testament) have been studied. Conservative Protestants (e.g., Baptist, Nazarene, Pentecostal) accept as God's word such statements as "Do not withhold discipline from a child; if you punish him with the rod, he will not die" (Proverbs 23:13 New International Version). These parents report more positive attitudes toward (and more frequent use of) physical punishment than other Christians (e.g., Roman Catholic, Presbyterian, Methodist) or adherents of other religions (Ellison, 1996; Gershoff et al., 1999). At least one study in another country has replicated these findings: Conservative Protestant mothers in Holland are more likely to value obedience, restrict autonomy, and favor physical punishment than are Catholic, Dutch Reform, or unaffiliated mothers (de Roos, Iedema, and Miedema, 2004).

Disciplinary attitudes have been compared in two cross-religion studies. In Cameroon, Christian and Muslim parents shared harsher attitudes toward discipline than parents who adhere to traditional African religions, where children are considered a divine gift and ancestors will punish those who are cruel to them (Nsamenang and Lamb, 1995). In India, the childrearing attitudes of Hindu, Muslim, and Christian mothers were compared (Ojha and Pramanick, 1992): Hindu mothers had the least restrictive attitudes, and Christian mothers the most. However, Christian mothers had warmer and more protective attitudes than did the Muslim mothers.

Childrearing Practices   Religions and religious beliefs have also been linked to parenting practices in both mono- and multicultural research. This is not surprising, given the prevalence of religiously based childrearing articles and manuals. In the United States, bookstores are stocked with dozens of Christian parenting books, including bestselling authors like James Dobson (Dobson, 1970, 1996) who has sold more than 3.5 million copies of his *Dare to Discipline* books. For Jews, the *Hadassah Magazine* frequently publishes articles that inform and prescribe how Jewish parents should rear their children (Bell, 1989). Similarly, childrearing manuals based on the Qur'an are readily available for Muslim parents (Husain, 1979; Sabiruddin, 1990). Childrearing advice stemming from Buddhism can even be found. In line with the Buddhist orientation toward selflessness and living in the present comes the concept of "mindful parenting." This refers to moment-to-moment, nonjudgmental awareness that encourages parents to go beyond their automatic thoughts and feelings. In that way, parents can be more intentional in their childrearing and grounded in the present moment (Kabat-Zinn and Kabat-Zinn, 1997).

Research has empirically linked religion to several areas of parenting behavior. In terms of involvement and the quality of social relationships, both religious mothers and fathers in North America have been found to exhibit more supervision of, be warmer toward (e.g., praise, hug), and enjoy more positive relationships with their children than do less religious parents (Bartkowski and Wilcox, 2000; Dollahite, 1998; King and Furrow, 2004; Pearce and Axinn, 1998). Religiosity has been observed to be negatively associated with maternal authoritarian behavior but unrelated to father behavior (Gunnoe, Hetherington, and Reiss, 1999). It should be pointed out that the relation between religion and parenting can be bidirectional; the onset of fatherhood can prompt more religious involvement (Palkovitz and Palm, 1998).

Infant feeding practices have been linked to religious involvement. In a cross-religion study comparing the practices of Indian Hindu, Muslim, and Christian mothers, several group differences were found. Only approximately one-half of the Hindu mothers breastfed their infants, in contrast to 75% of the other mothers. Hindu mothers also were likely to wean earlier (before 12 months) than other mothers (Ojha and Pramanick, 1992).

Religion has been linked to at least one other area of parental behavior—that of parental coping with child medical or developmental problems (Mahoney et al., 2001). For instance, Skinner, Correa, Skinner, and Bailey (2001), in a qualitative study of Mexican and Puerto Rican parents living in the United States, found that organized religion and individual faith served as important coping mechanisms for parents of young children who were mentally handicapped or developmentally delayed.

The Influence of Religion on Children's Development

Despite G. S. Hall's early efforts, relatively little attention has been devoted to studying the influence of religion on development. As Bartkowski et al. (2008) phrased it, such research is "sorely lacking" (p. 2). Even less consideration has been given to cross-cultural investigations of development. Nevertheless, a body of literature is beginning to accumulate on how religion is associated with child and adolescent development. The areas that have received some cross-cultural attention are children's spiritual, emotional, and identity development and the role of religion in social/behavioral adjustment.

Spiritual, Emotional, and Identity Development   One approach to studying how child development is influenced by religion has been to examine several different domains of children's development. Not surprisingly, the most common topic of inquiry has been children's spiritual development, including their conceptions of God. This subject has been studied in monocultural efforts both in the United States (Dickie et al., 1997) and other countries. For example, in a study with Dutch preschoolers and their mothers, maternal religious affiliation was linked to children's conceptions about God (de Roos et al., 2004). Children of conservative Protestant mothers viewed God to be more powerful than did children of Catholic, Dutch Reform, or unaffiliated mothers. Studies of children's beliefs about the supernatural have been conducted with Mexican children (Knight, Sousa, Barrett, and Atran, 2004). Other descriptions and qualitative research about spiritual development in African, Asian, and Middle Eastern countries can be found in Yust, Johnson, Sasso, and Roehlkepartain (2006).

The single largest cross-cultural study of religious beliefs in adolescents was conducted by Kelley and De Graaf (1997). They analyzed data from almost 20,000 individuals from 15 nations. Although different religions were not compared, they did contrast Catholics with Protestants. Their findings provide a good example of the insights that can be gained from a comprehensive analytic model. They found that in relatively secular nations (e.g., Norway, Australia), family religiosity strongly shapes children's religious beliefs. In contrast, in relatively religious nations (e.g., Ireland, Poland), normative religious beliefs play a stronger role in influencing youths' spirituality than do variations in family religiosity.

A cross-cultural approach to the role of religion in emotional development has also been investigated. Cole, Bruschi, and Tamang (2002) compared emotional reactions of two groups of children from small villages in Nepal and a third group of children from a farming community in the United States. One village consisted of high-caste Hindus, called Brahman. Brahman culture promotes individual achievement and tolerates expressions of anger. In contrast, children from the other village were reared by indigenous Tibetan parents who practiced Buddhism, where traditional Buddhist values of egalitarianism and maintaining a calm demeanor are valued. The children revealed distinct ways of appraising and acting on emotions in difficult interpersonal situations that reflected both the intertwined religious and cultural differences in their communities.

Religion and identity formation have also been studied from a cross-religion perspective. In a qualitative study of children's identity conducted in London, Muslim (both Arab and Asian), Christian, and Hindu children between the ages of 5 and 11 years were interviewed. Despite the young ages of some of the children, all reported that religion was a very important aspect of their identity (Takriti et al., 2006).

Social and Behavioral Adjustment Another approach to examining the effects of religion on children has been to examine their social and behavioral adjustment. In "Mono-Religion, Mono-Culture" studies, a number of benefits have been associated with children and adolescents who regularly attend church. Compared with children reared in nonreligious households, religious children are better adjusted socially and emotionally, have higher self-esteem and social responsibility, and show lower levels of internalizing and externalizing behavior problems (Bartkowski et al., 2008; Brody et al., 1996; Gunnoe et al., 1999; King and Furrow 2004; Regnerus and Elder 2003).

Religion has been documented to be a protective factor for adolescents, "inoculating" them against delinquency (Elder and Conger, 2000; Johnson, Jang, Larson, and Li, 2001; Regnerus, 2003), drug use (e.g., Wills, Yager, and Sandy, 2003), and early sexual activity (Doswell, Kouyate, and Taylor, 2003). Although most of these studies were conducted in North America, some cross-religion comparisons from Western Europe have also appeared (Engs and Mullen, 1999).

The importance of conducting cross-religious and cross-cultural studies was highlighted by a study conducted on preadolescents in Scotland. Abbotts, Williams, Sweeting, and West (2004) examined associations between church attendance and the behavior problems of 11-year-old children. A main effect for religious involvement was found: Children who attended church each week were less aggressive. However, an interaction with denomination was also observed on emotional problems (i.e., depression, anxiety): Catholic children fared better than those affiliated with the Church of Scotland. The effect, according to the authors, was likely a result of a third variable: normative experiences. Regular church attendance, expected within the Catholic peer group but not for the others, resulted in differential peer treatment.

Future Directions in Religion, Culture, and Development

Cross-cultural research into the role of religion in child development is still in its early stages. Despite the challenges inherent in trying to separate out the contributions of religion and culture to development, such investigations promise to provide insights. In general, more work is needed to expand on each of the four central questions we have identified and discussed. Those efforts would benefit greatly from utilizing the "Religion across Cultures" model (Figure 15.3) to understand religious influences and their interactions within cultures.

Future research would also benefit from a focus on four central questions. First, in what ways do different religions have similar as well as unique influences on child development? Given that the major organized religions share certain values such as caring for others, helping the needy, and combating hedonistic orientations (Roccas, 2005), to what extent are religions successful in effecting these values and behaviors? A related question is to what extent do religions differentially influence children's development? For example, Islamic parents use shame as a training technique, whereas that practice is no longer in favor among Christian parents (Stewart et al., 1999). On the other hand, a distinctive feature of Christian doctrine is its focus on forgiveness. Thus, a reasonable question to evaluate would be how does the practice of forgiveness in families influence how a child develops?

A second key question concerns the religious mechanisms that may influence a child's development. What is it about familial involvement in religious practices and beliefs that might modify how a child develops? What are the "active ingredients" in religious influences on development—do they include an emphasis on the family, daily practices, types of peer networks, positive adult influences (i.e., social capital), promotion of moral development and values, teaching of self-regulation, or differential identity formation (Hood, Spilka, Hunsberger, and Gorsuch, 1996)? In turn, how are these different types of developmental influences manifested in different cultures?

Future research must also take into account social change. Recognizing and tracking the dynamic nature of cultural and religious beliefs (Bronfenbrenner's chronosystem) is more important than ever. For example, Alwin (2001) found that the gap in beliefs that once characterized the Catholic–Protestant division in the United States has seen a convergence in terms of parental childrearing values. Given immigration and the religious diversity found in most countries, a child's development must be considered within the larger ecological context and in light of such developmental issues as acculturation as well as religious and ethnic identity.

A fourth research question concerns the possible negative effects of religion. A comprehensive understanding of religion, culture, and development requires it. For instance, as mentioned earlier, religiously heterogamous marriages can be a source of marital conflict, which, in turn, can have negative consequences on children (Bartkowski et al., 2008; Mahoney, 2005). A second example occurs when religion is used in a misguided way, such as to promote religious extremism in Pakistani madrasses or as a misguided rationale for abusive or neglectful parenting behavior (Bottoms, Shaver, Goodman, and Qin, 1995). These and other negative consequences of religion need to be explored.

Conclusion

The role of religion in development has not been adequately recognized or studied in cross-cultural investigations. This is ironic for several reasons. First, early developmental research recognized the importance of religion, but subsequent interest has been intermittent. Second, given the historic nature, prevalence, and salience of religion in many people's lives, religion should be recognized as a central influence, but it has not.

There are now indications that academics are waking up and increasingly coming to the realization that the union between religion, cultures, and development is an important one to study. The inclusion of a chapter on religion in this handbook is one example, as is the edited book on the development of children's spirituality from a cross-cultural perspective (Yust et al., 2006). By including religion in our research, new insights can be attained to better understand determinants of parenting behavior as well as influences on children's development outcomes.

Admittedly the topic is a challenging one to study. Four different research models have been used. The simplest one, a mono-religion, mono-culture approach, can be labeled the "Religion within Culture" model. Other approaches include looking at one religion across two or more cultures (the "Religion across Cultures" model), examining multiple religions within one culture (the "Religions within Culture" model), and studying multiple religions across multiple cultures (the "Religions across Cultures" model). Although the first three models each can provide useful information, it is the latter model that provides the richest understanding of the interplay of religion and culture on development.

In the work that is available, it is clear that religion has multiple levels of influence on children and youth. Religion influences the very fabric of many societies through the inculcation of religious values. Furthermore, a number of studies have shown that religiosity is associated with family functioning, childrearing, and child adjustment, although the mechanisms are unclear. Cross-culture research has revealed that religious influences may not necessarily have main effects but instead may interact with the larger social context in which the child is developing. In sum, as the immigrant mother from Kosovo so perceptively recognized, religion and culture are two integral elements in the mix that forms human development.

In our increasingly diverse, mobile, and "flat" world (Friedman, 2006), religion continues to be a powerful force for most of the world's population. Given the importance of spiritual beliefs to adults and its intergenerational transmission, the significant role that religion plays in family life will not diminish. In addition, evidence is accumulating that religion has positive effects on children and youth. Those are reasons enough to warrant cross-cultural studies in the role of religion on children. Current events provide an additional and compelling rationale for the study of this topic. If nations are to combat xenophobia, reduce sectarian hatred and violence, and promote tolerance (Silberman, Higgins, and Dweck, 2005), then an understanding of the role of religion in development from a cross-cultural perspective is essential.

Acknowledgments

This work was supported, in part, by National Institutes of Health grant no. R03 HD044674-01A1. Several colleagues provided assistance in locating research and/or commenting on drafts of this chapter. We thank Rev. Dr. Anne Cameron and Drs. Wendy Domjan, Carol Hawk, Annette Mahoney, and Mark Regnerus for their assistance.

References

Abbotts, J. E., Williams, R. G. A., Sweeting, H. N., and West, P. B. (2004). Is going to church good or bad for you? Denomination, attendance and mental health of children in West Scotland. *Social Science & Medicine, 58*, 645–656.

Adherents (n.d.). Largest religious groups in the United States. Retrieved January 4, 2007, from http://www.adherents.com/rel_USA.html.

Altemeyer, B. (2004). The decline of organized religion in western civilization. *International Journal for the Psychology of Religion, 1*, 77–89.

Alwin, D. F. (2001). Parental values, beliefs, and behavior: A review and promulga for research into the new century. In S. L. Hofferth and T. J. Owens (Eds.), *Children at the millennium: Where have we come from, where are we going?* (pp. 97–139). New York: JAI Press.

Barnett, D. B., Kurian, G. T., and Johnson, T. M. (2001). *World Christian encyclopedia: A comparative survey of churches and religions in the modern world.* New York: Oxford University Press.

Bartkowski, J. P., and Wilcox, W. B. (2000). Conservative Protestant child discipline: The case of parental yelling. *Social Forces, 79*, 265–290.

Bartkowski, J.P., Xu, X., and Levin, M.L. (2008). Religion and child development: Evidence from the Early Childhood Longitudinal Study. *Social Science Review, 37*, 18–36.

Baylor Institute for the Study of Religion (2006). *American piety in the 21st century: New insights into the depth and complexity of religion in the U.S.* Baylor, TX: Baylor University.

Bell, R. (Ed.). (1989). *The Hadassah Magazine Jewish parenting book.* New York: Free Press.

Bornstein, M. H. (Ed.). (1991). *Cultural approaches to parenting.* Hillsdale, NJ: Erlbaum.

Bornstein, M. H., and Cheah, C. S. L. (2006). The place of "culture and parenting" in the ecological context perspective on developmental science. In K. H. Rubin and O. B. Chung (Eds.), *Parenting beliefs, behaviors, and parent-child relations: A cross-cultural perspective* (pp. 3–33). New York: Psychology Press.

Bottoms, B. L., Shaver, P. R., Goodman, G. S., and Qin, J. (1995). In the name of God: A profile of religion-related child abuse. *Journal of Social Issue, 51*, 85–111.

Brody, G. H., Stoneman, Z., and Flor, D. (1996). Parental religiosity, family processes, and youth competence in rural, two-parent African American families. *Developmental Psychology, 32*, 696–706.

Bronfenbrenner, U., and Morris, P. A. (1998). The ecology of developmental processes. In R. M. Lerner (Ed.) and W. Damon (Series Ed.), *Handbook of child psychology. Volume 4: Theoretical models of human development* (pp. 993–1028). New York: Wiley.

Browning, D. S., Green, M. C., and Witte, J., (Eds.). (2006). *Sex, marriage, and family in world religions.* New York: Columbia University.

Chao, R. K. (1994). Beyond parental control and authoritarian parenting style: Understanding Chinese parenting through the cultural notion of training. *Child Development, 65*, 1111–1119.

Chiu, L.-H. (1987). Child-rearing attitudes of Chinese, Chinese-American, and Anglo-American mothers. *International Journal of Psychology, 22*, 409–419.
Cole, P. M., Bruschi, C. J., and Tamang, B. L. (2002). Cultural differences in children's emotional reactions to difficult situations. *Child Development, 73*, 983–996.
De Roos, S. A., Iedema, J., and Miedema, S. (2004). Influence of maternal denomination, God concepts, and child-rearing practices on young children's God concepts. *Journal for the Scientific Study of Religion, 43*, 519–535.
Dickie, J. R., Eshleman, A. K., Merasco, D. M., Shepard, A., Vander Wilt, M., and Johnson, M. (1997). Parent-child relationships and children's images of God. *Journal for the Scientific Study of Religion, 36*, 25–43.
Dobson, J. (1970). *Dare to discipline*. New York: Bantam Books.
Dobson, J. (1996). *The new dare to discipline*. New York: Bantam Books.
Dollahite, D. C. (1998). Fathering, faith, and spirituality. *Journal of Men's Studies, 7*, 3–15.
Doswell, W. M., Kouyate, M., and Taylor, J. (2003). The role of spirituality in preventing early sexual behavior. *American Journal of Health Studies, 18*, 195–202.
Dowling, E. M., and Scarlett, W. G. (Eds.). (2006). *Encyclopedia of religious and spiritual development*. Thousand Oaks, CA: Sage.
Dwairy, M., Achoui, M., Abouserie, R., Farah, A., Sakhleh, A. A., Fayad, M., et al. (2006). Parenting styles in Arab societies: A first cross-regional research study. *Journal of Cross-Cultural Psychology, 37*, 230–247.
Elder, G. H., and Conger, R. D. (2000). *Children of the land: Adversity and success in rural America*. Chicago: University of Chicago.
Ellison, C. G. (1996). Conservative Protestantism and the corporal punishment of children: Clarifying the issues. *Journal for the Scientific Study of Religion, 35*, 1–16.
Ellison, C. G., and Anderson, K. L. (2001). Religious involvement and domestic violence among U.S. couples. *Journal for the Scientific Study of Religion, 40*, 269–286.
Engs, R. C., and Mullen, K. (1999). The effect of religion and religiosity on drug use among a selected sample of post secondary students in Scotland. *Addiction Research, 7*, 149–170.
Erickson, E. H. (1959). *Identity and the life cycle*. New York: International Universities Press.
Friedman, T. L. (2006). *The world is flat: A brief history of the twenty-first century*. New York: Farrar, Straus, and Giroux.
Frosh, S. (2004). Religious influences on parenting. In M. Hoghughi and N. Long (Eds.), *Handbook of parenting: Theory research for practice* (pp. 98–109). Thousand Oaks, CA: Sage.
Gershoff, E. T., Miller, P. C., and Holden, G. W. (1999). Parenting influences from the pulpit: Religious affiliation as a determinant of parental corporal punishment. *Journal of Family Psychology, 13*, 307–320.
Goodnow, J. J., and Collins, A. (1990). *Development according to parents: The nature, sources, and consequences of parents' ideas*. Hillsdale, NJ: Erlbaum.
Gorsuch, R. L. (1988). Psychology of religion. *Annual Review of Psychology, 39*, 201–221.
Gottlieb, A. (2006). Non-western approaches to spiritual development among infants and young children: A case study from West Africa. In E. C. Roehlkepartain, P. E. King, L. Wagener, and P. L. Benson (Eds.), *The handbook of spiritual development in childhood and adolescence* (pp. 150–162). Thousand Oaks, CA: Sage.
Greven, P. (1977). *The Protestant temperament: Patterns of child-rearing, religious experience, and the self in early America*. New York: Knopf.
Gunnoe, M. L., Hetherington, E. M., and Reiss, D. (1999). Parental religiosity, parenting style, and adolescent social responsibility. *Journal of Early Adolescence, 19*, 199–225.
Hall, G. S. (1891). The moral and religious training of children and adolescents. *Pedagogical Seminary, 1*, 196–210.
Harkness, S., and Super, C. M. (2006). Themes and variations: Parental ethnotheories in western cultures. In K. H. Rubin and O. B. Chung (Eds.), *Parenting beliefs, behaviors, and parent-child relations: A cross-cultural perspective* (pp. 61–79). New York: Psychology Press.
Hoffman, L. W. (1988). Cross-cultural differences in childrearing goals. Parental behavior in diverse societies. In R. A. LeVine, P. M. Miller, and M. M. West (Eds.), *New Directions for Child Development, 40*, 99–122.
Holden, G. W. (2001). Psychology, religion, and the family: It's time for a revival. *Journal of Family Psychology, 15*, 657–662.
Hood, R. W. J., Spilka, B., Hunsberger, B., and Gorsuch, R. (1996). *The psychology of religion: An empirical approach*. New York: Guilford.
Husain, A. (1979). *Muslim parents: Their rights and duties*. Karachi, Pakistan: International Islamic Publishers.

Inglehart, R., and Baker, W. E. (2000). Modernization, cultural change, and persistence of traditional values. *American Sociological Review, 65*, 19–51.

Johnson, B. R., Jang, S. J., Larson, D. B., and De Li, S. (2001). Does adolescent religious commitment matter? A reexamination of the effects of religiosity on delinquency. *Journal of Research in Crime and Delinquency, 38*, 22–43.

Kabat-Zinn, M., and Kabat-Zinn, J. (1997). *Everyday blessings: The inner work of mindful parenting.* New York: Hyperion.

Keats, D. M. (2000). Cross-cultural studies in child development in Asian contexts. *Cross-Cultural Research, 34*, 339–350.

Kelley, J., and De Graaf, N. D. (1997). National context, parental socialization, and religious belief: Results from 15 nations. *American Sociological Review, 62*, 639–659.

King, P. E., and Furrow, J. L. (2004). Religion as a resource for positive youth development: Religion, social capital, and moral outcomes. *Developmental Psychology, 40*, 703–713.

Knight, N., Sousa, P., Barrett, J. L., and Atran, S. (2004). Children's attributions of beliefs to humans and God: Cross-cultural evidence. *Cognitive Science, 28*, 117–126.

Lin, C.-Y. C., and Fu, V. R. (1990). A comparison of child-rearing practices among Chinese, immigrant Chinese, and Caucasian-American parents. *Child Development, 61*, 429–433.

Mahoney, A. (2005). Religion and conflict in marital and parent-child relationships. *Journal of Social Issues, 61*, 689–706.

Mahoney, A., Pargament, K. I., Jewell, T., Swank, A. B., Scott, E., Emery, E., et al. (1999). Marriage and the spiritual realm: The role of proximal and distal religious constructs in marital functioning. *Journal of Family Psychology, 13*, 321–338.

Mahoney, A., Pargament, K. I., Tarakeshwar, N., and Swank, A. B. (2001). Religion in the home in the 1980s and 1990s: A meta-analytic review and conceptual analysis of links between religion, marriage, and parenting. *Journal of Family Psychology, 15*, 559–596.

Marks, L. D. (2004). Sacred practices in highly religious families: Christian, Jewish, Mormon, and Muslim perspectives. *Family Process, 43*, 217–231.

Mattis, J. S., Ahluwalia, M. K., Cowie, S.-A. E., and Kirkland-Harris, A. M. (2006). Ethnicity, culture, and spiritual development. In E. C. Roehlkepartain, P. E. King, L. Wagener, and P. L. Benson (Eds.), *The handbook of spiritual development in childhood and adolescence* (pp. 283–296). Thousand Oaks, CA: Sage.

McEvoy, M., Lee, C., O'Neill, A., Groisman, A., Roberts-Butelman, K., Dinghra, K., et al. (2005). Are there universal parenting concepts among culturally diverse families in an inner-city pediatric clinic? *Journal of Pediatric Health Care, 19*, 142–150.

Nsamenang, A. B., and Lamb, M. E. (1995). The force of beliefs: How the parental values of the Nso of northwest Cameroon shape children's progress toward adult models. *Journal of Applied Developmental Psychology, 16*, 613–627.

Ojha, H., and Pramanick, M. (1992). Religio-cultural variation in childbearing practices. *Psychological Studies, 37*, 65–72.

Palkovitz, R., and Palm, G. (1998). Fatherhood and faith in formation: The developmental effects of fathering on religiosity, morals, and values. *Journal of Men's Studies, 7*, 33–51.

Park, S., and Cheah, C. S. L. (2005). Korean mothers' proactive socialisation beliefs regarding preschoolers' social skills. *International Journal of Behavioral Development, 29*, 24–34.

Parrinder, G. (1996). *Sexual morality in the world's religions.* Oxford, England: Oneworld.

Pearce, L. D., and Axinn, W. G. (1998). The impact of family religious life on the quality of mother-child relations. *American Sociological Review, 63*, 810–828.

Regnerus, M. D. (2003). Linked lives, faith, and behavior: Intergenerational religious influence on adolescent delinquency. *Journal for the Scientific Study of Religion, 42*, 189–203.

Regnerus, M. D., and Elder, G. H. (2003). Staying on track in school: Religious influences in high- and low-risk settings. *Journal for the Scientific Study of Religion, 42*, 633–649.

Roccas, S. (2005). Religion and value systems. *Journal of Social Issues, 61*, 747–759.

Roehlkepartain, E. C., King, P. E., Waggoner, L., and Benson, P. L. (Eds.). (2006). *The handbook of spiritual development in childhood and adolescence.* Thousand Oaks, CA: Sage.

Sabiruddin (1990). *A Muslim husband and wife.* New Delhi, India: Kitab Bhavan.

Sander, A. (1996). Images of the child and childhood in religion. In C. P. Hwang, M. E. Lamb, and I. E. Sigel (Eds.), *Images of childhood* (pp. 14–26). Mahwah, NJ: Erlbaum.

Saroglu, V., Delpierre, V., and Dernelle, R. (2004). Values and religiosity: A meta-analysis of studies using Schwartz's model. *Personality and Individual Differences, 37*, 721–734.

Silberman, I., Higgins, E. T., and Dweck, C. S. (2005). Religion and world change: Violence and terrorism versus peace. *Journal of Social Issues, 61,* 761–784.

Skinner, D. G., Correa, V., Skinner, M., and Bailey, D. B. (2001). Role of religion in the lives of Latino families of young children with developmental delays. *American Journal on Mental Retardation, 106,* 297–313.

Smith, C., Denton, M. L., Faris, R., and Regnerus, M. (2002). Mapping American adolescent religious participation. *Journal for the Scientific Study of Religion, 41,* 597–612.

Smith, C. B., Weigert, A. J., and Thomas, D. L. (1979). Self-esteem and religiosity: An analysis of Catholic adolescents from five cultures. *Journal for the Scientific Study of Religion, 18,* 51–60.

Stewart, S. M., Bond, M. H., Zaman, R. M., McBride-Chang, C., Rao, N., Ho, L. M., et al. (1999). Functional parenting in Pakistan. *International Journal of Behavioral Development, 23,* 747–770.

Super, C. M., and Harkness, S. (1986). The developmental niche: A conceptualization at the interface of child and culture. *International Journal of Behavioral Development, 9,* 545–569.

Takriti, R. A., Barrett, M., and Buchanan-Barrow, E. (2006). Children's understanding of religion: Interviews with Arab-Muslim, Asian-Muslim, Christian and Hindu children aged 5-11 years. *Mental Health, Religion and Culture, 9,* 29–42.

Wilcox, W. B. (2002). Religion, convention, and paternal involvement. *Journal of Marriage and Family, 64,* 780–792.

Wills, T. A., Yager, A. M., and Sandy, J. M. (2003). Buffering effect of religiosity for adolescent substance use. *Psychology of Addictive Behaviors, 17,* 24–31.

Yust, K. M., Johnson, A. N., Sasso, S. E., and Roehlkepartain, E. C. (Eds.). (2006). *Nurturing child and adolescent spirituality: Perspectives from the world's religious traditions.* New York: Rowman and Littlefield.

Part II
Development in Different Places on Earth

16
The United States of America

CATHERINE S. TAMIS-LEMONDA and KAREN E. MCFADDEN

Introduction

The beliefs, norms, and practices of cultural communities are rooted in their economic, social, and political histories (Super and Harkness, 2002). As such, a chapter on the children of the United States of America must begin with consideration of the cultural forces that have shaped the country's history from its start to the present. The core principles laid down by the Founding Fathers encompass liberty, freedom, and equality, and these have remained unifying concepts throughout the nation's history. Citizens of the United States have the liberty to make choices; the freedom to pursue those choices; and equality in their pursuits, as reflected in the phrase "life, liberty and the pursuit of happiness" in the Declaration of Independence. These ideals apply not only to the individual, but also to the market economy. Markets are free to vary according to capitalistic forces rather than hegemonic economic decisions. In theory, all Americans, having been created equal, have equal opportunity in the marketplace and thereby an equal chance to share in the American Dream.

The principles of liberty, freedom, and equality, together with the opportunities provided in U.S. capitalistic society, have provided fertile ground for many shared beliefs and practices concerning ways to effectively promote children's development. For the most part, children are taught that hard work, optimism, and perseverance are the means to material prosperity and life satisfaction. Parents celebrate their children's individuality by permitting them to choose their friends, clothes, hobbies, careers, and partners. Parents and educators alike espouse the importance of children's positive self-image, and use stickers, praise, trophies, certificates, and pictures displayed on refrigerators and bulletin boards to bolster children's self-esteem. In school settings, girls and boys from all ethnic backgrounds are expected to receive equal opportunities for learning and school activities, and as children transition to adolescence and young adulthood, they expect equal treatment and financial compensation in the workforce.

However, in the context of these shared national ideals, enormous variation exists in the actual experiences and developmental trajectories of children in the United States. For the most part, this variation is rooted in economic and cultural differences among families. In terms of *economic variation*, geographic regions of the United States (e.g., rural versus urban) have historically experienced significant resource disparities, as have children and families from certain ethnic and racial groups. In terms of *cultural variation*, the promise of upward mobility in the free market has attracted new immigrants to the United States throughout its history. The result has been a dynamic kaleidoscope of cultural traditions in dress, food, music, holidays, languages, and childrearing practices. Diversity is the fabric of U.S. society, and economic and cultural variations are powerful influences in the lives of children growing up in America.

Two main themes, therefore, are woven throughout this chapter. The first focuses on the ways that the *shared* national principles of liberty, freedom, and equality, as well as a strong market economy and workplace opportunities, have shaped the experiences and development of children in the United States. The second theme speaks to economic and cultural *variation* in the experiences and development of these same children. To frame these dual themes, the chapter begins with a historical overview of forces that have affected U.S. society more broadly and parenting and child development more specifically. Next, the chapter focuses on the ways that opportunities and shared ideals have shaped contemporary life of children in the United States. A fundamental outgrowth of the American legacy is the ubiquitous characterization of U.S. parenting and child development as "individualistic" (see Goodnow, Chapter 1, this volume; Harwood, Schoelmerich, Schulze, and Gonzalez, 1999; Hofstede, 1980; Kohn, 1969; Markus and Kitayama, 1991; Triandis, 1988; 1995; Triandis, Bontempo, Villareal, Masaaki, and Lucca, 1988). Evidence is provided in support of the idea that children in the United States are encouraged to develop into autonomous individuals who: (1) strive to attain their full potential, (2) make their own choices, and (3) are equal in their rights to pursue their goals. However, in line with the chapter's emphases on both cultural similarity and variation, the final section highlights economic and cultural differences around themes of personal achievement, choice, and equality in children and families from different subgroups of the nation's population. As such, emphasis is placed on the dynamic heterogeneity of child development and parenting in the United States.

Historical Forces in Contemporary American Life

Even before its birth as a nation, America was a land of immigrants. As any school-aged child can recount, the narrative that survives as our collective remembrance of the first Thanksgiving, when Native Americans and English Pilgrims together shared a harvest meal, conveys the ideals of peace, equality, and abundance to children in classrooms across the country. Many other time-honored versions of American history likewise reflect the country's cultural ideals. Stories surrounding early colonialism are often marked by a collective view of American history that begins with the arrival of the *Mayflower* at Plymouth Rock and Pilgrims' search for religious freedom. Although the first permanent colony in America was established somewhat earlier in Jamestown, Virginia for what were perhaps less idealistic purposes, it is historical narratives of freedom and equality that have come to represent the colonial history of America (Jernegan, 1959). Such shared national values likewise permeate accounts of the Revolutionary War, during which patriots sacrificed their lives to preserve the personal and political liberties they had come to seek in the new world. The Boston Tea Party, the signing of the Declaration of Independence, and Patrick Henry's cry "Give me liberty, or give me death!" live on in national narratives and collectively exemplify the early roots of U.S. ideals.

In the following century, new workplace opportunities created by industrial growth meant that children were now required to learn the skills that would prepare them for future careers. Whereas during the early 1800s, 70% of U.S. children lived in farming families and worked by the sides of their parents as active participants in adult life (Hernandez, 1994), growing industries in the United States led to a decline in children's involvement in work at home. In tandem with educational reform movements, the institutionalization of schools brought about another major change in children's lives. Childhood was rendered a time of preparation for, rather than involvement in, work, and formal schooling became a core means to this end (Morelli, Rogoff, and Angelillo, 2003). With the widespread availability of formal educational training, more children could now pursue economic opportunities offered by a wealthy nation that was founded on the ideals of liberty, freedom, and equality.

Variation in Opportunity

The prosperity generated across the roughly 250 years of U.S. history, coupled with the American tradition of democratic ideals, resulted in favorable conditions for many children growing up in the United States—one of the top five wealthiest nations in the world (World Bank, 2005, 2006). Children have universal access to public education and the freedom to pursue the occupation of their choice. At the same time, however, the ideals of liberty, freedom, and equality and the economic opportunities afforded by a free market have not always played out as intended in reality. Large-scale inequalities among cultural groups have a history in the legacy of slavery in the United States, during which Africans were brought to this country to labor in agrarian enterprises and did not share in the benefits of the great wealth they generated. Additionally, the prosperity brought about by the industrial revolution was unevenly distributed across geographic regions. The growth of cities and relative isolation of rural areas led to an unequal distribution of wealth in the United States.

The disparities of the industrial revolution continue through the present. In comparing states in terms of wealth, the top 10 on a number of measures are those featuring major American cities like New York, Chicago, and Los Angeles, whereas states that are large in geographic size but more isolated from these areas, like Montana or North Dakota, typically fall near the bottom. At the same time, in urban centers with concentrations of wealth, poverty is widespread. For instance, in New York City, approximately 700,000 people have individual net worths of a million dollars or more, but twice that number of families with children (approximately 1.5 million of the city's 8 million residents) live below the federal poverty level, and 18,000 children sleep in homeless shelters every night. New York is one of America's richest cities, and yet its borough of The Bronx is the poorest urban county in the nation (Herbert, 2007a).

Children in the United States also inherit disparities associated with racial and ethnic groups. Of the 73 million children under 18 years old living in America, approximately 60% are European American, 16% are African American, 19% are Latin American, 4% are Asian American, and 1% are classified as "other," which includes Native American and multi-racial/ethnic children (Federal Interagency Forum on Child and Family Statistics, 2006). Yet the distributions of children living in poverty do not reflect overall population percentages. Whereas 17% of children live below the official poverty line, African American and Latin American children are approximately three times more likely than their European American counterparts to live in families characterized as poor (Federal Interagency Forum on Child and Family Statistics, 2006; Flanagan and West, 2004). This economic divide mirrors educational inequities in America.

Such statistics are in flux, however, and projections for the next 20 years estimate sharp declines in the percentage of European American children in the United States, accompanied by marked increases in the percentage of Latin American and multiracial children. Immigration accounts for a major part of this momentum; one in five of all children in the United States today are immigrants or children of immigrants, hailing from hundreds of countries all over the globe (Hernandez and Charney, 1998). Outcomes for immigrant children are diverse, as they sometimes outperform, sometimes match, and sometimes achieve below their native-born peers (Rumbaut and Portes, 2001; Suarez-Orozco and Suarez-Orozco, 2001). Yet the children of immigrants, as well as those of less educated and less resourced parents, often experience diminished opportunities to apply their education to a profession.

Summary

The United States is founded on the principles of liberty, freedom, and equality, which have been cultural magnets for immigrants from across the globe for over 200 years. Many families and children have prospered in the land of opportunity, yet many others have experienced educational and income disparities that can be traced back to the days of slavery and uneven growth across geographic regions. These realities do not lessen the impact of prosperity or American democratic ideals on the development of children in the United States, but rather present a backdrop to understanding the great diversity that characterizes contemporary American family life. The next section presents a closer look at the ways in which the founding ideals and relative affluence of the United States affect the experiences of children today.

Child Development in the Contemporary United States

The social and political histories of the United States have shaped contemporary beliefs and practices surrounding children's development in countless ways. In this chapter, focus is on three main themes that reflect these cultural influences. First, the historical legacy of U.S. economic success (together with freedom and liberty) is directly reflected in the theme of *Personal Achievement*, as expressed in the view that children should maximize opportunities available to them by developing into relatively autonomous, accomplished individuals. Children in the United States are encouraged to strive to reach their full potential, and parents in the United States are ubiquitously portrayed as the purveyors of individualistic goals (e.g., Harkness and Super, 2002). Second, the ideals of liberty and freedom live on in the theme of *Personal Choice*. In the United States, individuals have the right to make choices in matters ranging from the election of political leaders to decisions surrounding religion, partners, and food. Personal choice is cherished, and children are expected to pursue their goals unencumbered by interference from others. Finally, the ideal of *Equality* is a theme that cuts across both personal achievement and personal choice. Equality reflects the shared view that all children, regardless of gender, creed, or race, have the right to choose and pursue their own life paths and will benefit from equal opportunities in school and the workforce, as well as equal protection under the legal system.

Personal Achievement

The economic prosperity of the United States is a vital force in the experiences of the nation's children, and the focus on personal achievement echoes the nation's capitalistic ideals of freedom, hard work, and economic opportunity (Weber, 1904-1905/1958). The seeds of personal achievement are rooted in the notion of "Economic Freedom." Four markers of worldwide economic freedom were identified in the first major report on the subject: (1) personal choice rather than collective choice, (2) voluntary exchange coordinated by markets rather than allocation via the political process, (3) freedom to enter and compete in markets, and (4) protection of persons and their property from aggression by others (Gwartney, Lawson, and Norton, 2008). Those nations high on indicators of freedom outperform nonfree nations on measures of economic growth, life expectancy, and health (Gwartney et al., 2008). The United States ranked third of all nations on indicators of economic freedom and also ranked among the highest on all indicators of economic prosperity. For example, the United States boasts the highest gross national product in the world, with a per capita income of over $34,000 (World Desk Reference, 2004) and has been assigned an Education Index of 99.9 from the United Nations, tied for the highest score among all nations in the world. Approximately 85% of the population graduates from high school, and close to one-third (27.2%) of people have earned a college bachelor's degree or higher. Moreover, although the United States continues to be a country of immigrants, the basic literacy rate is 99% for the population over age 15 years (United Nations Development Programme, 2006).

These statistics help frame an understanding of the nation's emphasis on personal achievement. Children in the United States have access to enormous resources compared to the majority of children from other parts of the world. The vast majority of U.S. children have access to health care, universal education, housing, and food; most make widespread use of media, computers, and technology; and many children carry cell phones and digital cameras, drive cars, frequent restaurants, and join their families on annual vacations—opportunities and resources that in turn provide the means to personal achievement. Children are expected to strive to reach their full potential and to remain positive and optimistic in their pursuit of the American Dream.

The theme of personal achievement is echoed throughout Western psychological literature, as in Maslow's (1948) notion of "self-actualization," White's (1959) construct of "effectance motivation," and Erikson's (1968) stage of "self-identity formation." These theories share an emphasis on the child as an independent agent in the world, a philosophy that is thought to be rooted in the cultural pattern of segregating children from the adult workplace and sending them to schools where they are encouraged to find and follow a unique life path (Morelli et al., 2003). The American emphasis on personal achievement and individualistic goals permeates children's lives virtually from birth. This cultural characterization has been contrasted with that of Asian, Latino, and indigenous cultures, which are often referred to as "collectivistic." By definition, collectivist cultures prioritize relatedness, and children are socialized to value the harmony, wishes, and betterment of the larger group (see Harwood et al., 1999; Hofstede, 1980; Kohn, 1969; Markus and Kitayama, 1991; Oyserman, Coon, and Kemmelmeier, 2002; Sampson, 1977; Triandis, 1988, 1995).

In infancy, the signature example of the U.S. emphasis on autonomy and personal achievement begins with the sleeping patterns of families. Infants in the United States, unlike the vast majority of cultures around the world, are expected to sleep through the night away from their parents and often in their own rooms, soon after birth. Although some newborns sleep in their parents' room for the first few months, typically in a separate crib or bassinette, some parents never share a room even with their infants (Keener, Zeanah, and Anders, 1988), and in nearly all cases, the majority of middle-class European American parents in the United States expect their children to eventually sleep in a space that is physically removed from parents. Reflecting on this practice, U.S. European American mothers typically report that this custom provides an important foundation for children's development of "independence" (Morelli, Rogoff, Oppenheim, and Goldsmith, 1992). Moreover, co-sleeping is associated with more sleeping problems in the United States than in countries where co-sleeping is normative and part of the interdependence cultural complex, such as Japan (Latz, Wolf, and Lozoff, 1999).

The move toward personal achievement in the United States is also reflected in the view that infants should separate from their primary caregivers so as to independently explore and learn about their worlds. Cultural communities that place more value on independence are thought to emphasize early orientation to the nonsocial world of objects (Greenfield, Keller, Fuligni, and Maynard, 2003). Building on this emphasis, studies reveal a high prevalence of didactic behaviors in U.S. mothers during naturalistic, everyday engagements with their infants (Bornstein and Tamis-LeMonda, 1990). Not only do mothers frequently encourage their infants to attend to objects in the outside world already at 2 months of age (and even before), but these early parenting behaviors are stable over the infancy period. In one study, didactic interactions (those that emphasized infants' attention to objects and events outside the dyad) were compared to social interactions (those that emphasized infants' attention to mother) in middle-income U.S. and Japanese mothers and their 4- to 5-month-old infants. U.S. mothers displayed higher levels of didactic engagement, whereas Japanese mothers displayed higher levels of social engagement (Bornstein, Azuma, Tamis-LeMonda, and Ogino, 1990). By the time infants turned 13 months, U.S. mothers were more likely to prompt their toddlers to engage in independent, constructive play, such as placing blocks in shapesorters, whereas Japanese mothers were more likely to prompt their toddlers to engage in other-directed symbolic play, for example by feeding or bowing to dolls (Tamis-LeMonda, Bornstein, Cyphers, Toda, and Ogino, 1992).

Similarly, core ideas about the foundations of interpersonal relationships are based on the idea that infants' healthy development hinges on the ability to separate from caregivers and explore the world on their own (Bowlby, 1980, 1988). Ironically, children considered "securely attached" to their primary caregivers are those who can physically separate from their mothers so as to explore unfamiliar environments (Ainsworth, Blehar, Waters, and Wall, 1978). These children are thus thought to be more open to opportunities to experience their environments, whereas children who remain within the immediate physical vicinity of their caregivers are thought to be limiting their learning experiences and are consequently labelled as "insecure."

Furthermore, U.S. European American mothers highlight the importance of young children's achievement and independence across a range of everyday contexts, and their descriptions of an ideal child consistently emphasize the importance of children developing independence in the service of reaching their full potential and growing into individuals who could "make goals and reach for them" (Harwood, Schoelmerich, Ventura-Cook, Schulze, and Wilson, 1996; Harwood et al., 1999; Schulze, Harwood, and Schoelmerich, 2001). Based on these findings, the term "self-maximization" was used to refer to U.S. parents' goals for their young toddlers. Not only do European American mothers talk about valuing self-maximization in their children, but they also structure their toddlers' everyday experiences in line with these goals. U.S. mothers expect their toddlers to feed themselves earlier than do Puerto Rican mothers and also believe that their toddlers should learn to entertain themselves in play (Harwood et al., 1996; Schulze et al., 2001). They are also less likely to physically structure their infants' actions than Puerto Rican mothers, more likely to use suggestions rather than commands to encourage their infants' activities, and more likely to praise their infants' efforts and encourage them to do things on their own (Harwood et al., 1999). U.S. European American mothers believe that infants should be able to drink from a cup at 9 months and use utensils by 12 months, and they place cups and spoons on their child's highchair for independent use at these ages. In contrast, Puerto Rican mothers continue to assist their infants with eating as babies sit on their laps (Harwood et al., 1999; Schulze et al., 2001). Consequently, in these studies, more than 80% of European American children learned to feed themselves by 12 months compared to less than 5% of Puerto Rican infants (Schulze et al., 2001).

In the childhood years, the push for personal achievement is reflected in common parlance about the importance of the "Whole Child" (Zigler, 2004). Children in the United States are expected to be "well rounded" (successful across multiple areas), and parents and educators alike should support children's development across multiple domains. For example, when middle-income European American parents are probed about the qualities that make an ideal child, they talk about curiosity, assertiveness, diligence, compassion, academic success, and getting along with others to name a few (Tamis-LeMonda, Wang, Koutsouvanou, and Albright, 2002; Wang and Tamis-LeMonda 2003). Similarly, a well-adjusted adolescent in contemporary U.S. society is defined as someone who excels at school, is socially competent or popular, has a range of interests and hobbies, and volunteers in community service. Thus, personal achievement includes both goals of independence/autonomy and social connection.

In the United States, the concepts of optimism and self-esteem are integrally tied to personal achievement and viewed as critical precursors to children's success, happiness, and well-being, as well as buffers to later risky behaviors. Parents and teachers go to great lengths to keep children optimistic, by offering rewards or praise for children's efforts. Indeed, in America, overly positive self-evaluations, rather than "realistic" or "accurate" ones, are more strongly associated with psychological well-being (Taylor and Brown, 1988), and thus, parents in the United States may benefit their children through their emphasis on positivity. Because the concept of self-esteem is so ingrained in the popular discourse, it is easy to assume its universal relevance. However, the construct of self-esteem is culturally embedded. In many ways, the promotion of children's self-esteem is a largely U.S. (or Western) phenomenon that may not be as pronounced in the goals of parents outside these cultures. European American parents place greater value on children's self-esteem compared with parents from Japan, China, Puerto Rico, and Taiwan (e.g., Harwood et al., 1995, 1999; Miller, Wang, Sandel, and Cho, 2002; Stevenson and Stigler, 1992; Tamis-LeMonda et al., 2002).

The U.S. emphasis on optimism and self-esteem begins early and continues throughout the childhood and adolescent years. Moreover, many U.S.-based developmental theories suggest that the benefits of positive parenting on adolescent outcomes are mediated by improved self-esteem in children (e.g., Jackson, Pratt, Hunsberger, and Pancer, 2005). For the most part, these studies indicate that low self-esteem is related to a wide range of negative outcomes, including school drop out, delinquency, early pregnancy, and poor body image, just as high self-esteem or self-worth is associated with a wide range of positive outcomes, including academic achievement and quality of friendships (e.g., Crocker, 2001; Crocker, Luhtanen, and Sommers, 2005; DuBois et al., 2002; Galambos, Barker, and Krahn, 2006; Trzesniewski et al., 2006).

The economic prosperity of the United States has been a vital force behind the nation's emphasis on personal achievement. A core aspect of personal achievement is children's development of autonomy, which begins for many infants at birth. Studies with European American families reveal that many infants are expected to sleep on their own, feed themselves, and venture beyond the secure base of primary caregivers to explore the object world. The psychological underpinnings to personal achievement include optimism and self-esteem. Children are expected to feel good about themselves, "make goals and reach for them" (Harwood, 1992), and persist in the pursuits of their dreams.

Personal Choice

Personal choice is firmly rooted in the principles of liberty and freedom and is one of the most salient psychological constructs in the literature on U.S.-born children (see Deci, Ryan, and Koestner, 1999, for review). Liberty is the freedom to act without being constrained by necessity or force. With liberty comes the right to make higher level organizational choices (e.g., political representatives), broader lifestyle choices (e.g., neighborhoods to live in or schools to attend), and everyday routine choices (e.g., what to wear or eat). Choice is the pillar of the U.S. democracy and its system of elections. The welfare of children is protected and provided for by the state and through elections, whether it is a school board, the state legislature, or the president. Moreover, parents function as advocates for children and have the power to act if the system does not reflect their children's best interests.

At the level of the family, parents make choices about children's lives on a daily basis. Parents choose where, how, and according to what principles they will live and rear their children. They can decide in what church and religion they will rear their child or whether or not they will expose children to organized religion at all. Parents may also select among a wide range of educational options for their children, from home school to boarding school and, within reason, can decide to hold their children back a year from starting school (a trend that is on the rise as parents hope to maximize their children's school and sports achievements by gaining a developmental edge). Parents also make choices of their own, and it is not uncommon for parents to change careers, neighborhoods, partners, or lifestyles.

As primary witnesses to their parents' choices, children soon learn the value of personal choice in their everyday lives. For the most part, children decide what to wear, what to eat, and the toys with which to play. Children select the sports, hobbies, classes, and majors to pursue and are later expected to follow career paths that reflect their individual talents and passions.

Choice is an unspoken value that underlies children's interactions with others from their first days of life.

Choice is reflected in the tendency of many U.S. parents to view their infants as "intentional agents" soon after birth. Parents treat infants as conversational partners, and interpret their early gestures and vocalizations as attempts to communicate their wishes (Hemphill and Snow, 1996). Soon after birth, infants are assumed to be making choices. U.S. American parents are quick to ascribe meaning when infants look, turn their heads, swipe their arms, and babble. According to parents, infants avert their gaze because they are bored, annoyed, or unhappy, and they coo to express their likes and dislikes. This interpretation of early mother–infant interaction is one in which the infants' presumed intentions drive social exchanges, and the parents' role is to figure out their babies' intentions and to respond accordingly.

The U.S. view of infants as intentional agents is also reflected in the value that is placed on parents' "responsiveness." Responsiveness is defined as a parent's prompt, contingent, and appropriate reaction to a child's behaviors, as reflected in the three-term sequence of "infant act–parent react–effect on child" (Bornstein, Tamis-LeMonda, Hahn, and Haynes, 2008). U.S. mothers display relatively high levels of responsiveness by "waiting" for their children to decide what to look at, touch, and play with, and then "following" their lead with prompt and supportive actions and words. Parents also quickly adjust their behaviors when infants are distressed.

As infants grow into toddlers, the term "terrible 2s" crops up, referring to young children's stubborn desire to "do their own thing" rather than accommodate to the will of others. Parents perceive toddlers' expressions of negativism as linked to the development of autonomy and choice, both of which are strongly encouraged. Consequently, when a parent bemoans a toddler's outbursts, it is often with implicit pride, pointing out that the child wants to "do everything himself" or that "she won't listen to anything I say!" Indeed, researchers have proposed that a limited amount of child noncompliance is healthy and positive in that it serves an important function by supporting children's development of autonomy (Kuczynski, Kochanska, Radke-Yarrow, and Girnius-Brown, 1987). Consequently, many U.S. parents aim to master the fine art of socializing proper behavior in their children without asserting their own will too strongly. To do so, parents often seek compliance in their toddlers and preschoolers by gently encouraging acceptable behavior through suggestions, explanations, and if necessary, bargaining, which itself reflects parents' acknowledgement of children's rights and autonomy. For the most part, U.S. parents use "gentle" discipline that deemphasizes parental power and encourages children's internalization of parental intentions, for example, asking rather than telling children to put away their toys or lightly guiding children's hands toward the intended goal (Kochanska, 1997; Kochanska, Aksan, and Nichols, 2003; Kuczynski et al., 1987).

Similarly, when disciplining their older children, parents frequently use explanatory requests accompanied by reasoning (e.g. "I'd like you to do this because…") rather than commands or assertions of power (e.g., "Put it away!"), perceiving the need to appeal to children's cognitive understanding of the logic behind parental management strategies (Critchley and Sanson, 2006; Gershoff, 2002). In fact, parental assertions of power markedly decrease over time, and parents are most likely to use commands only when children are about 1 year of age or younger, when they are less likely to understand more complex reasoning (Kochanska et al., 2003). Indeed, parents in the United States believe that it is the *reasoning* behind behavioral requirements, rather than the requests themselves, that promote children's internalization of proper behavior and moral standards (Grusec and Goodnow, 1994; Hoffman, 1979). Such ideas have a reality beyond just beliefs, in that U.S. studies have documented links between parental power assertions and children's behavior problems. Such behavior problems are thought to emerge in response to the threat to children's developing autonomy posed by unilateral parental authority (Deater-

Deckard, Dodge, Bates, and Petit, 1990; Grusec and Goodnow, 1994). In contrast, the value of choice is implicitly reflected in typical indirect parental management strategies; appropriate behavior in children is insufficient on its own; rather, children must themselves *want to* engage in the appropriate behavior. Choice ultimately resides with the child. Moreover, as children become adults, many U.S. parents want them to spend time with their parents by choice, not obligation (Poasa, Mallinckrodt, and Suzuki, 2000).

Regardless of the extent to which children are permitted to make choices at home, when they enter public schools in the United States (and many private schools as well), their teachers have often received training that emphasizes the importance of autonomy and choice in their young students (Bredekamp, 1987; DeVries and Zan, 1994). Although teachers of young children often underscore classroom rules and the fact that it is unacceptible to pursue desires in ways that violate class rules (e.g., grabbing toys from others), outside of the moral domain, children's personal decisions are generally respected (Killen and Smetana, 1999; Lagattuta, 2005). This includes presenting children with a range of choices about where they will sit, what snacks they will eat, and which activities they will engage in. Specifically, "activity time," "lunch time," and "circle time" have been identified as settings that provide fitting opportunities to provide preschool children with choice and thus nurture children's developing sense of self (DeVries and Zan, 1994). These ideas are exemplifed in a study of 3-, 4-, and 5-year-old preschoolers and their teachers (Killen and Smetana, 1999). Teachers voiced the opinion that it is "very important to provide children with choice" and, in turn, frequently presented children with choices, such as "Do you want to play with blocks or draw pictures?" For their part, children responded to classroom opportunities by expressing their wishes, as in "I want juice, not milk."

In the United States, choice is associated with positive developmental outcomes. The act of making a personal choice provides children with needed opportunities to assert personal preferences and establish a unique identity and is also linked to high levels of motivation and performance (Iyengar and Lepper, 1999; Ryan and Deci, 2000). The benefits of choice are clearly illustrated in a set of studies in which choice was experimentally manipulated, followed by assessments of children's motivation and achievement (Iyengar and Lepper, 1999). The authors manipulated the choices of European American children (and Asian American children, discussed later) attending schools in San Francisco. Specifically, children were presented with anagrams or asked to play a space-quest math game on computers; these tasks were either chosen by themselves, an experimenter, or their mothers (or, by valued in-group members). European American children showed the highest levels of motivation, enjoyment, and performance in tasks where they made personal choices versus those in which choices were made for them. Research has similarly linked parental behaviors that prohibit children's ability to choose with negative child outcomes such as higher levels of aggression and conduct problems in school (Deater-Deckard et al., 1990; Dodge, Petit, and Bates, 1997). Thus, opportunities for children to choose provide many U.S. children the experiences that undergird the potential to achieve.

Personal choice reflects the ideals of liberty and freedom on which the United States was founded and permeates the everyday lives of the nation's children. From infancy, parents view children as intentional agents and respond to infants' initiatives as though their babies are already making choices about what to communicate and what they want. Parents engage in forms of discipline that accommodate children's needs, and they affirm children's rights to make choices as a pathway to children's growing autonomy. In classroom settings, teachers encourage children to make their own decisions as a way to foster children's autonomy. Thus, both families and schools are core channels through which children are exposed to the value of personal choice.

Equality

Following the Civil War, the Fourteenth Amendment of the U. S. Constitution made various provisions to protect the equal rights of all citizens of the United States, as reflected in the clause: "nor shall any state deprive any person of life, liberty, or property, without due process of law; nor deny to any person within its jurisdiction the equal protection of the laws." This valuing of equal rights for all citizens—across race, creed, religion, and gender—is fundamental to U.S. society and is the foundation for ideals about equality more broadly.

At a national level, equal rights means that every citizen above the age of 18 years, regardless of gender, race, or creed, has the right to cast an equal vote that in aggregate determines a democratic system of representation for all people in the government. Moreover, the emphasis on equal representation extends beyond government officials to laws that govern peoples' rights in social institutions such as school and the workplace. In the workforce, laws mandate the fair and equitable treatment of employees regardless of background in terms of pay scale, benefits, and so forth. Hiring practices are likewise guided by rules governing equal treatment of prospective employees, such that no qualified person can be denied a position based on gender, ethnicity, race, or age. All children in the United States have equal rights to a publicly funded education from kindergarten through high school (with universal pre-K being currently considered as well), and school systems are guided by legislation that requires the allocation of resources to students in need of extra support or who speak languages other than English.

At the level of family life, at least in recent years, women are increasingly represented in the workforce, and there is movement toward a fairer distribution of household labor. Many contemporary fathers bathe and feed infants, and although they continue to be primary breadwinners in many households, there is clear recognition that fathers should contribute in meaningful ways to the rearing of their children (Lamb and Tamis-LeMonda, 2004).

For children, the U.S. ideal of equality affects many aspects of life at home, school, and in neighborhoods. The ways that equality shapes children's lives takes two main forms: (1) equality across social groups (i.e., that children should have equal rights and opportunities across gender, ethnicity, and race) and (2) equality in the structure of social relationships (i.e., that children's relationships with others are characterized by relatively balanced power).

Equality Across Social Groups

In terms of equality across social groups, the ideals of U.S. society call for the righting of historical inequities and equal treatment and opportunity for all children, regardless of gender, ethnicity, race, or creed. As one salient example, the ideal of gender equity permeates many beliefs and practices in the United States. In infancy, girls can play with trucks, and boys can play with dolls. Parents are often thoughtful about the toys they buy their children, and some studies indicate that they tend to purchase more gender-neutral rather than gender-stereotyped toys, such as children's books or creative toys like art supplies (Robinson and Morris, 1986; Robinson, Watson, and Morris, 1984). And if girls request more dolls or boys request more toy vehicles in their holiday letters to Santa Claus, it is increasingly the case that they are equally likely to ask for sports equipment, clothing, and male dolls (Marcon and Freeman, 1996). Gender equality is so ingrained in the minds of parents in the United States that, even though countless studies show that parents actually treat their girls and boys differently, parents deny such differences, and most adamantly voice the importance of fair and equitable treatment for boys and girls. Gender equality lives on as an ideal in the United States, even when its practice falls short.

As children in the United States get older and enter schools, equal opportunity policies, such as Title IX, work to increase the availability of equivalent experiences for boys and girls. In accordance with Title IX's provisions, American high schools have started girls' programs in traditionally male sports like ice hockey, and traditionally female athletics like cheerleading today often include boys in their squads, all of whom cheer equally for girls' and boys' sports programs (Haggerty, 2005; Hu, 2007). Mandated gender equity carries over into the big business of collegiate sports, and any college or university receiving federal dollars must offer equal scholarships, dedicate equal resources, and spend equal funds on women's and men's programs.

Equality in children's lives is highlighted in more than just gendered situations. Local, state, and federal governmental systems require all public programs, services, and resources to be available to everyone regardless of race/ethnicity or socioeconomic status. Children must have equal access to resources necessary for survival, and programs like Food Stamps, Women, Infants, and Children, Section 8, and Medicaid were established to bring necessities like nutrition, shelter, and health care to all American children regardless of their parental incomes. The American institution of public education likely features numerous examples of measures aimed at providing children with equal experiences, such as the landmark U.S. Supreme Court decision on the *Brown v. Board of Education* case of 1954. Although recent court rulings have somewhat modified this precedent, *Brown* established that the school reforms promising public education for all in the mid-1800s would not be realized while schools were still segregated because separate educational systems based on race were deemed to be "inherently unequal" and children attending racially segregated schools were "deprived of the equal protection of the laws guaranteed by the Fourteenth Amendment" (Chief Justice Earl Warren, quoted in Williams, 1987, p. 44). As a result of *Brown* and the momentous Civil Rights Act of 1964 in the next decade, increasing measures of equity were brought to American schools. The following year, Head Start was established to bring early childhood education to disadvantaged communities, where such experiences would not otherwise be available for preschoolers (Ripple and Zigler, 2003; Zigler, 2004).

Policy makers continue to work to increase equality across social groups by strengthening measures that ensure parity in the experiences of American children, especially in regard to education. New initiatives provide parents with school vouchers in an effort to equalize the availability of different educational options to all children, and district buses provide equal access to schools that children might otherwise be unable to attend. When children seek to enter institutions of higher learning, Affirmative Action policies were designed with the promise that even if economic inequities associated with race or ethnicity may not allow for the college preparatory experiences more advantaged children receive, all children have an equal chance to attend universities.

Equality in Social Structure

In terms of equality in the structure of social relationships, power hierarchies are, in certain ways, less pronounced in the lives of U.S. children than in certain other regions of the world. Consequently, children's relationships with other people are more likely to be characterized by horizontal than vertical social structures and, hence, equality (Hofstede, 1980; Smetana, 2002). Even American English does not have formal and informal pronouns for addressing others, as is common in most other languages (e.g., "tu" versus "lei" in Italian, "tu" versus "usted" in Spanish, "vy" versus "ty" in Russian). Thus, children who speak English address peers and adults alike by using the pronoun "you."

Such subtle but pervasive aspects of culture have a powerful effect on the structures of human relationships. Even when children are toddlers, mothers maintain a certain amount of equality in their interactions with children, as expressed through child-focused exchanges in which parents take on the role of "peer" to their children. Adults in the United States engage young children as peers in child-focused conversations on child-related topics; they enter into children's play as playmates, accommodating their speech to facilitate children's involvement in conversations; they respect the right of their young children to determine what activity will be played together; they use adult–child play to create special learning situations; and they involve children in "lessons" that are responsively focused on children's interests and attention (Haight and Miller, 1993; Heath, 1982; Nucci and Weber, 1995; Rogoff, 1990; Schieffelin and Ochs, 1986; Snow, 1977; Whiting et al., 1988).

This child-focused, relatively power-balanced style of parent–child interactions is thought to emerge out of the societal arrangement of separation between the adult world of work and children's preparation for that world (Morelli et al., 2003). Children attend school in preparation of entry into the prosperous, opportunity-rich U.S. marketplace. During these years, while children are largely excluded from the everyday work lives of their parents, adults create specialized settings that center on children's activities and prepare children for later experiences in the adult world (Morelli et al., 2003). This form of adult–child relationship can be contrasted with those that develop in environments where children participate in the adult world and the work of the family, where conversations are not geared to children, adults do not modify their speech to "meet" the child's level, and adults' play with children as peers is rare (Heath, 1982).

Differences in horizontal versus vertical relationship structures are exemplified in a study comparing U.S. parent–child relationships and interactions with those of parents and children from non-American indigenous societies (Morelli et al., 2003). The authors looked at two middle-class European American communities, one outside of Boston and the other in Salt Lake City. These communities were contrasted with those of the Efe foragers of the Democratic Republic of Congo (formerly Zaire) and San Pedro, a Mayan town in Guatemala. In both Efe and Mayan communities, but not the American ones, children begin to participate responsibly in the work activities of their communities by age 5 years (Morelli and Verhoef, 1999). In the two U.S. groups, adults participated in high levels of play with children of 2 to 3 years and also involved them in more conversations with adults. American adults often engaged children in child-directed topics by asking questions about children's activities and feelings, such as "Tell me what you did in preschool today?" or "Did you have a nice time playing on the swings?" In contrast, parents did not engage in child-focused questioning in the Efe and San Pedro communities, and teaching was rarely observed. The authors argued that it would be superfluous for parents to use specialized child-focused activities to prepare children for a world in which they already participate.

Over the course of development, European American parents' treatment of children's opinions as equivalent to those of adults increases, and in cases of disputes, adults will often compromise and allow input from children (Nucci and Smetana, 1996; Nucci and Weber, 1995). Young children likewise express an understanding that they should retain control of their personal decisions both at home and in school (Killen and Smetana, 1999; Nucci and Weber, 1995). As noted earlier, in school settings, teachers allow children to make personal decisions and reinforce children's equal rights in the classroom (Killen and Smetana, 1999).

In adolescence especially, there is a conscious valuing of balanced parent–adolescent power, such that adolescents and parents alike agree that adolescents should make more of their own decisions (Smetana, 1988; Smetana, Campione-Barr, and Metzger, 2006; Youniss and Smollar, 1985). Although teenagers may wish for more personal jurisdiction over a wider range of issues than their parents are willing to grant, U.S. parents typically give even their young adolescents the right to make decisions about personal issues (whom to befriend or what social events to attend), yet retain authority over moral issues (lying to parents) and conventional issues (not keeping parents informed of their whereabouts) (Smetana, 1988). Moreover, parents of older adolescents often yield to adolescents' wishes, even in situations where adolescents' choices may violate parental or community norms, for example, in style of dress (Smetana and Daddis, 2002).

In addition to the increased power parents are willing to grant their adolescents in acknowledgement of adolescents' increasingly equal status, youth are simultaneously provided with more independence and responsibility in their schools and communities. A systematic review of youth programs indicates that organizations that allow adolescents the freedom to make real decisions and take leadership roles help promote positive youth outcomes (Eccles and Gootman, 2002). In addition, organizations that are centered on a specific philosophy, cause, or ideology appear to infuse adolescent participation with meaning (Flanagan, 2004; Youniss, McLellan, and Yates, 1999). The informal, less hierarchically organized environment of youth organizations fosters adolescents' affective ties to their community (Flanagan, 2004) and provides an environment where at-risk youth may feel efficacious and respected by adults (Kahne et al., 2001).

In peer groups, American culture also engenders egalitarian relationships among children. Social equality characterizes the vast majority of friendships in childhood and adolescence, and children expect mutual understanding and loyalty from their friends (Hartup, 1989). Equality in peer relationships is also demonstrated by the fact that children not only value their own autonomy and intentions, but also respect those of their peers, seeking to achieve their own goals without impeding the goals of others (Crockenberg and Litman, 1990; Laupa and Turiel, 1986).

Thus, both children and adolescents experience equality in relationships across a multitude of contexts as they grow and develop in the United States. Parents, teachers, and community members all reinforce the importance of developing independence and autonomy in children by bestowing even toddlers with discretion over personal issues and increasing the range of matters over which children have authority as they grow older. This relative balance of power in children's relationships with adults, if not evenly distributed across social and ethnic/racial groups, nonetheless widely characterizes the experiences of U.S. children.

Equality is a U.S. ideal that is reflected in the legal protections and rights provided to all social groups in the United States. Opportunities and choices ranging from education and sports participation to their future careers are expected to be equally available to children from all backgrounds. Moreover, equality is evidenced in the relatively horizontal structure of social relationships experienced by many children in the United States. Many parents engage children as equal partners in everyday interactions, such as talking to children at their level and engaging in child-focused conversations and play, and this equality also exists in peer relationships.

Variation in Developmental Experiences of Children in the United States

Despite the economic prosperity of the United States, opportunities for children are unevenly distributed and, in turn, so are children's chances for personal achievement, choice, and equality. Additionally, the cultural heterogeneity of the United States means that parents vary in their beliefs and practices in ways that affect children's experiences around these U.S. ideals.

Economic Variation

Although capitalism has been beneficial for many as it is practiced in the United States, it is not an economic system that evenly distributes resources and opportunities. Indeed, income in the United States is distributed less equally than in similar developed nations such as Austria or Sweden (http://imf.org/external/pubs/ft/weo/2007/01). These disparities have consequences for children's health as well as their cognitive, social, and emotional growth. Empirically, poverty is linked to diminished self-evaluation and lowered persistence on tasks (e.g., Dweck, 1975, 1986; Evans, 1998, 2003; Evans, Saegert, and Harrid, 2001; Paschall and Hubbard, 1998; Repetti,

Taylor, and Seeman, 2002). Children who live in chaotic, crowded situations may experience a loss of control in social interactions, which in turn increases their susceptibility to learned helplessness. For example, neighborhood poverty affects African American male adolescents' propensity for violence through influences on family stress, conflict, and adolescents' sense of self-worth (Paschall and Hubbard, 1998). Additionally, the adverse life circumstances surrounding poverty, including chronic overcrowding and low resources, often create psychological vulnerabilities to lowered self-esteem and a sense of learned helplessness (Evans, 1998). As such, poverty can perpetuate inequities by hampering children's motivation and personal achievement.

Similarly, adverse economic conditions can foreclose children's abilities to make everyday *choices* (e.g., children can only choose the food or clothing that their family can afford); limit more meaningful, long-term choices (e.g., children's educational goals may be eclipsed by the need for early employment to meet the family's financial needs); and also affect children's perception of choices. Children growing up in disadvantaged homes typically have a restricted range of choices in both home (e.g., toys to play with or books to read) and neighborhood settings (e.g., parks or places to visit safely, access to libraries or museums) (Jencks and Mayer, 1990; Leventhal and Brooks-Gunn, 2000).

The range of choices available to children is typically limited in poorer neighborhoods in comparison with more advantaged ones, even when accounting for the resources of individual families. The neighborhoods in which children live dictate the schools they attend and the programs in which they may become involved. Parents may deem it necessary to restrict their children's freedom and rights to make certain choices when living in dangerous neighborhoods. Children may not be able to decide for themselves where to "hang out" or play and may be given less latitude in choosing their friends. Indeed, parental monitoring and discipline strategies vary as a function of neighborhood safety. Mothers in more high-risk neighborhoods are more restrictive and use more authoritarian discipline strategies with their children regardless of ethnic background (Gonzales, Cauce, Friedman, and Mason, 1996; Hill and Herman-Stahl, 2002).

It is not only the choices that are available that matter for developmental outcomes, but perhaps more so children's perceptions of available choices. As the findings of Iyengar and Lepper (1999) emphasize, American children may function optimally under conditions in which they perceive personal choice. However, for children living in poverty, options for educational and employment pursuits may be limited or even unrecognized (Ogbu, 1991; Paulter and Lewko, 1987; Willis, 1977), perhaps because of the lack of adult role models and/or economic limitations on the actual choices themselves (Mincy, 2006; Orfield, Losen, Wald, and Swanson, 2004). If youth do not recognize the choices that would be available to them if they were to complete school, they may instead drop out to pursue more immediate financial returns.

Finally, economic circumstances influence children's experiences with equality. Although a wide range of provisions is in place to address disparities in equality across gender, race, and ethnicity, the extent to which resources are distributed, available, or enforced remains varied. Public support for policies that give extra provision to the disadvantaged is uneven, and provisions in the tax code granting social services to poor children have partially eroded (Krugman, 2007; Steiner, 1981). Thus, although many social service programs for children exist, a lack of publicity, education, and funding often make them unavailable to many children who might otherwise benefit. Efforts to bring food, shelter, and health care to the disadvantaged are not always supported or enacted (Albee, 1986; Ripple and Zigler, 2003). Head Start, for example, despite 40 years of expansion, is still only partially funded (Ripple and Zigler, 2003). Medicaid coverage has been scaled back, and eight million children in the United States have no health coverage at all. These realities have resulted in child death in many cases that could have been prevented by inexpensive and routine medical visits (Herbert, 2007b; Krugman, 2007).

Additionally, despite continuing efforts to ensure equality in the educational experiences of American children in public schools, pervasive large-scale disparities exist in available school resources, supplementary educational programs in sports and the arts, and the quality of instruction in school districts across the country. Education is considered to be the main route to achievement and out of poverty, and yet because public schools are funded by local taxes in the United States, schools in low-income neighborhoods receive lower amounts of financial support. As a result, they are typically evaluated as providing lower quality education than schools in more affluent areas and are also often physically deteriorating and overcrowded (Levanthal and Brooks-Gunn, 2000; Lopez, 2003; Massey and Denton, 1993). Furthermore, instruction levels, as well as the standards to which children are held, may be substandard (Lopez, 2003).

These economic effects disproportionately apply to minority children (Massey and Denton, 1993). Even within schools attended by children from a variety of economic backgrounds, many ethnic minority students are less prepared for the rigors of better academic programs. Many minority children are "tracked" into lower level programs featuring "dumbed-down" curricula (Bowles and Gintis, 1976; Lopez, 2003; Oakes and Guiton, 1995). This engenders a self-perpetuating cycle in which children receiving subpar educational experiences are unable to transition into more demanding college preparatory courses (Fine, 1994).

Finally, beyond inequities evidenced in the lives of minority and poor children, gender divides also persist in children's experiences, leading to unequal treatment of boys versus girls in many arenas. As an example, although Title IX was enacted to provide equity in the resources for girls and boys in schools, in reality, boys' sports like football and basketball generate vastly greater revenue, especially at the collegiate level. Loose interpretations of principles surrounding equality can lead to practices that work against equity, as when money gets funneled from certain boys' sports to enhance the budgets of high-profile sports like football or when surveys with poor response rates are used to demonstrate low levels of interest in women's athletics and to justify lack of effort at increasing women's athletics participation (Fuchs, 2005; Hu, 2007).

Cultural Variation

Significant cultural variation exists in ideas and practices in families and communities, which likewise engenders variation in children's experiences with personal achievement, choice, and equality. These differences are often framed by the consideration of various ethnic minority groups as more collectivistic, including East Asian, Latin American, and African American communities (Cortes, 1995; Fuligni, Tseng, and Lam, 1999; Spencer and Dornbusch, 1990). Constructs such as "familism" among Latin American families, "family obligation" and "filial piety" among Asian American families, and "extended kin" among African American families each encompasses feelings of closeness, allegiance, and mutuality among family members, as well as notions of the self as an extension of the family (e.g., Cortes, 1995; Gonzalez-Ramos, Zayas, and Cohen, 1998; Sabogal, Marin, Otero-Sabogal, and Marin, 1987). In its broader application, connection to the family also extends to other people with whom an individual shares close relationships, termed "relational collectivism" (Brewer and Chen, 2007).

These obligations to family may shape children's personal achievement in a number of ways. Children from Asian and Latin American families in the United States may be expected to take part in a range of household chores, be present at family meals, and spend time with family elders, such as grandparents, which may interfere with the time they have available to focus on personal goals (Fuglini et al., 1999; Caplan, Choy, and Whitmore, 1991; Chao, 1995; Mordkowitz and Ginsburg, 1987). Additionally, in immigrant families, the burden of dealing with the outside, English-speaking world may fall to children who must interpret political, financial, and logistical exchanges for their parents (Bornstein and Cote, 2006; Lansford, Deater-Deckard, and Bornstein, 2007; Zhou, 1997). Such familial duties often persist over the life course, as children are expected to build their lives around that of their families by continuing to live close to and assist their parents even in adulthood (Uba, 1994).

Yet familial duty in immigrant families may in some cases bolster children's personal achievement efforts, as many students say that a desire to please their parents motivates them to do well in school (Suarez-Orozco and Suarez-Orozco, 2001). Many children of immigrants are aware of the sacrifices their parents made to immigrate to the United States and seek to make something of the opportunities their parents opened to them (Chao, 1995). However, the effects of familial duties also vary; moderate levels of obligation may allow for academic achievement, whereas high levels of household duties may interfere with school success (Fuglini et al., 1999). Thus, links between "autonomy" and "personal achievement" that are often found in European American U.S. populations may be specific to the cultural values and expectations of that group.

The cultural heterogeneity of the United States also affects views and practices surrounding choice. In some families, parents feel that are they are better equipped to make choices that serve the best interests of their children, and in such cultural contexts, choice may not reap the same benefits as it does for other children and families. For example, communication patterns that assume intentionality and choice in infants and in which infants are treated as conversational partners are far from the norm in certain cultures within the United States. Among African American families in rural Louisiana, children are expected to figure out the rules of social exchanges if they are to participate in conversations with others; they are expected to listen and follow orders rather than initiate conversations and actions of their own choosing (Schieffelin and Eisenberg, 1984; Schieffelin and Ochs, 1986). Consequently, much of language learning develops through overheard conversations rather than engagement of the child in adult–child conversations (Ahktar, 2005).

Variation around choice can partly be ascribed to different cultural emphases on the self as an individual versus the self as connected to others, as reviewed earlier. For example, in Latin American cultures, where family or group goals receive purportedly greater emphasis, children may be expected to respect others and display greater obedience to authority. The emphasis on obedience and respect carries with it the understanding that parents and elders of the community can make decisions for the young (Kagitcibasi, 1996; Keller, 2003; Triandis, 1995). Consequently, disciplinary practices of parents from certain U.S. communities may not contain the same levels of inductive reasoning often displayed by European American parents and may emphasize "vertical" rather than "horizontal" power distributions in parent–child relationships, where parents make decisions for their children (and believe such decisions to be in their children's best interests), rather than children making decisions autonomously.

Greater parental control and exercise of authority and less encouragement of autonomy and personal choice characterize South Asian Indian, Filipino, Japanese, Vietnamese, and Chinese families, as well as various Asian communities in the United States, as compared to European American families (Chao and Tseng, 2002). For example, when children's choices were experimentally manipulated such that game options were chosen by the children, an experimenter, or children's mothers, Asian American children were more intrinsically motivated when choices were made for them by their mothers or respected others (Iyengar and Lepper, 1999). The value of personal choice may not be an essential human characteristic but rather a cultural preference (Kim and Sherman, 2007; Petrova, Cialdini, and Sills, 2007).

Yet children from diverse cultures growing up in the United States may also experience choice in certain specific contexts, both within the family and within classrooms in American schools. For instance, immigrant parents may consider it their responsibility to make many choices for their children, but they may view decisions surrounding personal matters as appropriate for children to make themselves. Specifically, there is evidence that, when they come to the United States, immigrant parents give their children jurisdiction over whether they will identify as, for example, Dominican, Dominican American, or simply American (Waters, 1990). Additionally a trend among some (particularly Asian American) immigrant families is to permit their children to choose an "American" name for use in school.

Cultural beliefs and practices also affect equality, both across social groups as well as within social structures. Families from different ethnic and religious backgrounds have different views and practices surrounding equality, and as a result, there may be greater disparities in parents' rearing of boys versus girls (for example), as well as in the balance of power between adults and children. For example, views about gender equality may differ in newly arriving immigrants who tend to hold more traditional views about the roles of males and females in family life. In families where fathers are the main providers and mothers are viewed as primary caregivers and nurturers, boys and girls will be exposed to different role models and stronger gender-based stereotypes. Even in the United States, young Latin American boys may positively value "machismo," whereas girls may be more likely to notice female role models who take care of children and do not work outside the home, thereby making the cultural value of "respeto" (respect) more salient for them. This would especially be the case among less acculturated families and more recent immigrant groups.

Not only do children have different experiences with parents as gender role models depending on cultural context, but also parents from different cultures living in the United States often have different ideas about how boys and girls should be socialized. For example, there is evidence that African American mothers use more authoritarian parenting styles and harsh discipline with their boys than their girls as a result of perceptions about the hard world of African American males in America. In South Asian Indian American families, mothers typically must prepare girls for roles as wives in a patriarchal community and guard their daughters against the dominant American culture often perceived to be promiscuous and especially dangerous for girls (Espin, 1995). South Asian Indian mothers in the United States particularly monitor what their girls wear and the friends with whom they associate (Dasgupta, 1998; Kallivayalil, 2004).

Children's experiences of equality in relationships with adults also depend on cultural context. For instance, Asian American parents may expect high levels of obedience and therefore engender more hierarchical relationships with their children as compared to the more equal status that American children may experience with adults (Yau and Smetana, 1996; Yew, 1987). Similarly, South Asian Indian American adolescents are not granted as much jurisdiction over personal decisions as European American U.S. adolescents. What may be considered personal by European American U.S. parents may be considered duty by Asian American parents (Miller and Bersoff, 1992). The extent to which children contest these inequalities in their relationships with parents varies with acculturation, and more acculturated ethnically diverse adolescents approach the perceptions of mainstream American teens (Phinney, Kim-Jo, Osorio, and Vilhjalmsdottir, 2005). Although children generally voice a desire for more of a power balance than parents are willing to grant, Mexican, Chinese, and Filipino youth in the United States report greater respect for their parents' authority than European Americans (e.g., Fuglini et al., 1999).

Conclusion

From the earliest days of the United States, economic prosperity and the ideals of liberty, freedom, and equality have shaped family life and child development. These pillars of U.S. society are reflected in themes of personal achievement, personal choice, and equality across social groups and social structures. The emphases on personal achievement, personal choice, and equality are evidenced across a range of developmental areas, including attachment, infants' sleeping and feeding patterns, children's play, parent–child conversations, parental discipline, parents' expectations and goals for children, children's sports, and the structure of peer relationships and youth organizations.

However, diversity lies at the heart of U.S. society and is reflected in both the economic and cultural backgrounds of U.S. children and families. Therefore, even in the context of shared ideals, personal achievement, choice, and equality can play out quite differently in the lives of U.S. children. In some families, children's opportunities and choices are limited by economic circumstances, which in turn pose a threat to the U.S. ideal of equality. Attempts to rectify these disparities continue to be at the forefront of U.S. policy, as reflected in federal laws, programs, and state and local initiatives such as Title IX, Head Start, and school voucher systems. These efforts represent noteworthy attempts to "level the playing field" for children and families in the United States who confront numerous obstacles to pursuing their goals.

In terms of cultural variation, parents from different communities uphold different beliefs about the importance of personal achievement and personal choice, with some parents emphasizing children's relatedness and family obligations more than autonomy and individual success. Moreover, the benefits of autonomy and choice may be culturally bound, with some children taking pride in making independent decisions and others taking pride in the opportunity to carry forth the wishes of others. In terms of cultural perspectives on equality, parents from different ethnic and religious backgrounds may rear children in more gender-specialized ways and may also vary in their practices regarding the balance of power in parent–child relationships.

What is noteworthy about the cultural variation of the United States is that differences in views and practices within and across communities function to further enhance the ideals of freedom, choice, and equality on which the nation was founded. Children and families in the United States are exposed to a range of life styles and experience different cultural worlds on a daily basis. These encounters with different foods, clothing, beliefs, values, languages, religions, and political ideologies are both borne of and feed back into the national ideal of "liberty for all." Heterogeneity means that personal choice will become even more salient as children are continually faced with opportunities to decide among the paths to follow over the course of their lives. Moreover, the process of navigating different cultural communities challenges children to be psychologically and behaviorally flexible in their thinking and acting. Therefore, it is not surprising that the cultural views and practices of families within the United States change from moment to moment, across situations, and over developmental and historical time (Tamis-LeMonda et al., 2008). This dynamic quality of U.S. life provides the foundation for equality—in the context of freedom and choice, no single way of thinking or acting reigns superior to others. As such, the rich differences that exist in the lifestyles of U.S. families are a natural outgrowth of the nation's shared ideals.

Acknowledgments

The National Science Foundation, grant BCS 0218159, which funds New York University's Center for Research on Culture, Development and Education, supported Catherine S. Tamis-LeMonda.

References

Ahktar, N. (2005). Is joint attention necessary for early word learning? In B. D. Homer and C. S. Tamis-LeMonda (Eds.), *The development of social cognition and communication*. Mahwah, NJ: Lawrence Erlbaum Associates.

Ainsworth, M. D., Blehar, M. C., Waters, E., and Wall, S. (1978). *Patterns of attachment: A psychological study of the strange situation*. Hillsdale, NJ: Erlbaum.

Albee, G. W. (1986). Toward a just society: Lessons from observations on the primary prevention of psychopathology. *American Psychologist, 41*, 891–898.

Bornstein, M. H., Azuma, H., Tamis-LeMonda, C. S., and Ogino, M. (1990). Mother and infant activity and interaction in Japan and the United States: I. A comparative macroanalysis of naturalistic exchanges. *International Journal of Behavioral Development, 13*, 267–287.

Bornstein, M. H., and Cote, L. R. (2006). *Acculturation and parent-child relationships: Measurement and development*. Mahwah, NJ: Lawrence Erlbaum Associates.

Bornstein, M. H., and Tamis-LeMonda, C. S. (1990). Activities and interactions of mothers and their firstborn infants in the first six months of life: Covariation, stability, continuity, correspondence, and prediction. *Child Development, 61*, 1206–1217.

Bornstein, M. H., Tamis-LeMonda, C. S., Hahn, C-S., and Haynes, M. (2008). Maternal responsiveness to young children at three ages: Longitudinal analysis of a multidimensional, modular, and specific parenting construct. *Developmental Psychology, 44*, 867–874.

Bowlby, J. (1980). *Attachment and loss.* New York: Basic Books.

Bowlby, J. (1988). *A secure base: Parent-child attachment and healthy human development*. New York: Basic Books.

Bowles, S., and Gintis, H. (1976). *Schooling in capitalist America: Educational reform and the contradictions of economic life*. New York: Basic Books.

Bredekamp, S. (1987). *Developmentally appropriate practice in early childhood education programs serving children from birth through age 8*. Washington, DC: National Association for the Education of Young Children.

Brewer, M. B., and Chen, Y. (2007). Where (who) are collectives in collectivism? Toward conceptual clarification of individualism and collectivism. *Psychological Review, 114*, 133–151.

Caplan, N., Choy, M. H., and Whitmore, J. K. (1991). *Children of the boat people: A study of educational success*. Ann Arbor, MI: University of Michigan Press.

Chao, R. K. (1995). Chinese and European American cultural models of the self reflected in mothers' childrearing beliefs. *Ethos, 23*, 328–354.

Chao, R., and Tseng, V. (2002). Parenting of Asians. In M. H. Bornstein (Ed.), *Handbook of parenting. Volume 4: Social conditions and applied parenting* (pp. 59–93). Mahwah, NJ: Lawrence Erlbaum Associates.

Cortes, D. E. (1995). Variations in familism in two generations of Puerto Ricans. *Hispanic Journal of Behavioral Sciences, 17*, 249–255.

Critchley, C. R., and Sanson, A. V. (2006). Is parent disciplinary behavior enduring or situational? A multilevel modeling investigation of individual and contextual influences on power assertive and inductive reasoning behaviors. *Applied Developmental Psychology, 27*, 370–388.

Crockenberg, S., and Litman, C. (1990). Autonomy as competence in 2-year olds: Maternal correlates of child defiance, compliance, and self-assertion. *Developmental Psychology, 26*, 961–971.

Crocker, J. (2001). Contingencies of self-worth. *Psychological Review, 108*, 593–623.

Crocker, J., Luhtanen, R. K., and Sommers, S. R. (2005). Contingencies of self-worth: Progress and prospects. *European Review of Social Psychology, 15*, 133–181.

Dasgupta, S. (1998). Gender roles and cultural continuity in the Asian Indian immigrant community in the U.S. *Sex Roles, 38*, 953–974.

Deater-Deckard, K., Dodge, K. A., Bates, J. E., and Petit, G. S. (1990). Physical discipline among African American and European American mothers: Links to children's externalizing behaviors. *Developmental Psychology, 32*, 1065–1072.

Deci, E. L., Ryan, R. M., and Koestner, R. (1999). A meta-analytic review of experiments examining the effects of extrinsic rewards on intrinsic motivation. *Psychological Bulletin, 125*, 627–668.

DeVries, R., and Zan, B. (1994). *Moral classrooms, moral children*. New York: Teachers College Press.

Dodge, K. A., Petit, G. S., and Bates, J. E. (1997). How the experience of early physical abuse leads children to become chronically aggressive. In D. Cicchetti and S. Toth (Eds.), *Developmental perspectives on trauma: Theory, research, and intervention*. Rochester, NY: University of Rochester Press.

DuBois, D. L., Burk-Braxtn, C., Swenson, L. P., Tevendale, H. D., Lockerd, E. M., and Moran, B. L. (2002). Getting by with a little help from self and others: Self-esteem and social support as resources during early adolescence. *Developmental Psychology, 38*, 822–839.

Dweck, C. S. (1975). The role of expectations and attributions in the alleviation of learned helplessness. *Journal of Personality and Social Psychology, 31*, 674–685.

Dweck, C. S. (1986). Motivational processes affecting learning. American Psychologist. *Special Issue: Psychological Science and Education, 41*, 1040–1048.

Eccles, J. S., and Gootman, J. A. (Eds.). (2002). *Community programs to promote youth development*. Washington, DC: National Academy Press.

Erikson, E. (1968). *Identity: Youth and crisis*. New York: Norton and Co.

Espin, O. (1995). Race, racism, and sexuality in the life narratives of immigrant women. *Feminism and Psychology, 5*, 223–238.

Evans, G. (1998). Chronic residential crowding and children's well-being: An ecological perspective. *Child Development, 69*, 1514–1523.

Evans, G. (2003). A multimethodological analysis of cumulative risk and allostatic load among rural children. *Developmental Psychology, 39*, 924–933.

Evans, G., Saegert, S., and Harrid, R. (2001). Residential density and psychological health among children in low-income families. *Environment and Behavior, 33*, 165–180.

Federal Interagency Forum on Child and Family Statistics (2006). *America's children: Key national indicators of well-being 2006*. Washington, DC: U.S. Government Printing Office.

Fine, M. (1994). *Chartering urban school reform: Reflections on public high schools in the midst of change*. New York: Teachers College Press.

Flanagan, C. A. (2004). Institutional support for morality: community-based and neighborhood organizations. In T. A. Thorkildsen and H. J. Walberg (Eds.), *Nurturing morality: Issues in children's and families' lives* (pp. 173–183). New York: Kluwer Academic.

Flanagan, K., and West, J. (2004). *Children born in 2001: First results from the base year of the Early Childhood Longitudinal Study, Birth Cohort (ECLS-B)* (NCES 2005-036). Washington, DC: U.S. Department of Education, National Center for Education Statistics.

Fuchs, M. (2005, July 31). For women's athletics, a tempest over a survey. *The New York Times,* Section 14WC, p. 2.

Fuligni, A. J., Tseng, V., and Lam, M. (1999) Attitudes toward family obligations among American adolescents from Asian, Latin American, and European backgrounds. *Child Development, 73*, 306–318.

Galambos, N. L., Barker, E. T., and Krahn, H. J. (2006). Depression, self-esteem, and anger in emerging adulthood: Seven-year trajectories. *Developmental Psychology, 42*, 350–365.

Gershoff, E. (2002) Corporal punishment by parents and associated child behaviors and experiences: A meta-analytic and theoretical review. *Psychological Bulletin, 128*, 539–579.

Gonzales, N. A., Cauce, A. M., Friedman, R. J., and Mason, C. A. (1996). Family, peer and neighborhood influences on academic acheivement among African-American adolescents. *American Journal of Community Psychology, 24*, 365–387.

Gonzalez-Ramos, G., Zayas, L. H., and Cohen, E. (1998). Child-rearing values of low-income, urban Puerto Rican mothers of preschool children. *Professional Psychology: Research and Practice, 29*, 377–382.

Greenfield, P. M., Keller, H., Fuligni, A., and Maynard, A. (2003). Cultural pathways through universal development. *Annual Review of Psychology, 54*, 461–490.

Grusec, J. E., and Goodnow, J. J. (1994). Impact of parental discipline methods on the child's internalization of values: A reconceptualization of current points of view. *Developmental Psychology, 30*, 4–19.

Gwartney, J. D., Lawson, R., and Norton, S. (2008). *Economic Freedom of the World, Annual Report* 2008. http://www.freetheworld.com/2008/economicfreedomoftheworld2008.pdf.

Haggerty, N. (2005, December 4). Girls with their eyes on a goal, and a puck. *The New York Times,* Section 14WC, p. 1.

Haight, W., and Miller, P. J. (1993). *Pretending at home: Early development in a sociocultural context*. SUNY series, Children's Play in Society. Albany, NY: State University of New York Press.

Harkness, S., and Super, C. M. (2002). Culture and parenting. In M. H. Bornstein (Ed.), *Handbook of parenting. Volume 2: Biology and ecology of parenting* (2nd ed., pp. 253–280). Mahwah, NJ: Lawrence Erlbaum Associates.

Hartup, W. W. (1989). Social relationships and their developmental significance. *American Psychologist, 44*, 120–126.

Harwood, R. L. (1992). The influence of culturally derived values on Anglo and Puerto Rican mothers' perceptions of attachment behavior. *Child Development, 63*, 882–839.

Harwood, R. L., Schoelmerich, A., Schulze, P. A., and Gonzalez, Z. (1999). Cultural differences in maternal beliefs and behaviors: A study of middle-class Anglo and Puerto Rican mother-infant pairs in four everyday situations. *Child Development, 70*, 1005–1016.

Harwood, R. L., Schoelmerich, A., Ventura-Cook, E., Schulze, P. A., and Wilson, S. P. (1996). Culture and class influences on Anglo and Puerto Rican mothers' beliefs regarding long-term socialization goals and child behavior. *Child Development, 67*, 2446–2461.

Heath, S. B. (1982). What no bedtime story means: Narrative skills at home and school. *Language in Society, 11*, 49–76.

Hemphill, L., and Snow, C. (1996). Language and literacy development: Discontinuities and differences. In D. R. Olson and N. Torrance (Eds.), *The handbook of education and human development: New models of learning, teaching and schooling* (pp. 173–201). Malden, MA: Blackwell Publishing.

Herbert, B. (2007a, May 19). Young, ill and uninsured. *The New York Times,* Section A, p. 13.

Herbert, B. (2007b, May 22). American cities and the great divide. *The New York Times,* Section A, p. 23.

Hernandez, D. J. (1994) Children's changing access to resources: A historical perspective. *Social Policy Report, VIII*, 1–23.

Hernandez, D. J., and Charney, E. (1998). *From generation to generation: The health and well-being of children in immigrant families.* Washington, DC: National Academy Press.

Hill, N. E., and Herman-Stahl, M. A. (2002). Neighborhood safety and social involvement: Associations with parenting behaviors and depressive symptoms among African American and Euro-American mothers. *Journal of Family Psychology, 16*, 209–219.

Hoffman, M. L. (1979). Development of moral thought, feeling and behavior. *American Psychologist, 34*, 958–966.

Hofstede, G. H. (1980). *Culture's consequence: International differences in work-related values.* Beverly Hills, CA: Sage.

Hu, W. (2007, January 14). Equal cheers for boys and girls draw some boos. *The New York Times,* Section 1, p. 1.

Iyengar, S. S., and Lepper, M. R. (1999). Rethinking the value of choice: A cultural perspective on intrinsic motivation. *Journal of Personality and Social Psychology, 76*, 349–366.

Jackson, L. M., Pratt, M. W., Hunsberger, B., and Pancer, S. M. (2005). Optimism as a mediator of the relation between perceived parental authoritativeness and adjustment among adolescents: Finding the sunny side of the street. *Social Development, 14*, 273–304.

Jencks, C., and Mayer, S. (1990). The social consequences of growing up in a poor neighborhood. In L. E. Lynn and M. F. H. McGeary (Eds.), *Inner-city poverty in the United States* (pp. 111–186). Washington, DC: National Academy Press.

Jernegan, M. W. (1959). *The American Colonies, 1492-1750: A study of their political, economic and social development.* New York: F. Ungar Publishing Co.

Kagitcibasi, C. (1996). *Family and human development across cultures: A view from the other side.* Mahwah, NJ: Erlbaum.

Kahne, J., Nagaoka, J., Brown, A., O'Brien, J., Quinn, T., and Thiede, K. (2001). Assessing after-school programs as contexts for youth development. *Youth and Society, 32*, 421–446.

Kallivayalil, D. (2004). Gender and cultural socialization in Indian immigrant families in the United States. *Feminism and Psychology, 14*, 535–559.

Keener, M. A., Zeanah, C. H., and Anders, T. F. (1988). Infant temperament, sleep organization, and parental interventions. *Pediatrics, 81*, 762–771.

Keller, H. (2003). Socialization for competence: Cultural models of infancy. *Human Development, 46*, 288–311.

Killen, M., and Smetana, J. G. (1999). Social interactions in preschool classrooms and the development of young children's conceptions of the personal. *Child Development, 70*, 486–501.

Kim, H. S., and Sherman, D. K. (2007). "Express yourself": Culture and the effect of self-expression on choice. *Journal of Personality and Social Psychology, 92*, 1–11.

Kochanska, G. (1997). Multiple pathways to conscience for children with different temperaments: From toddlerhood to age 5. *Developmental Psychology, 33*, 228–240.

Kochanska, G., Aksan, N., and Nichols, K. E. (2003). Maternal power assertion in discipline and moral discourse contexts: Commonalities, differences, and implications for children's moral conduct and cognition. *Developmental Psychology, 39*, 949–963.

Kohn, M. L. (1969). *Class and conformity: A study in values.* Chicago: The University of Chicago Press.

Krugman, P. (2007, April 27). Gilded once more. *The New York Times,* Section A, p. 27.

Kuczynski, L., Kochanska, G., Radke-Yarrow, M., and Girnius-Brown, O. (1987). A developmental interpretation of young children's noncompliance. *Developmental Psychology, 23*, 799–806.

Lagattuta, K. H. (2005). When you shouldn't do what you want to do: Young children's understanding of desires, rules, and emotions. *Child Development, 76*, 713–733.

Lamb, M., and Tamis-LeMonda, C. S. (2004). The role of the father: An introduction. In M. E. Lamb (Ed.), *The role of the father in child development* (4th ed., pp. 1–31). Hoboken, NJ: John Wiley & Sons Inc.

Lansford, J., Deater-Deckard, K. K., and Bornstein, M. H. (2007). *Immigrant families in contemporary society.* New York: Guilford Press.

Latz, S., Wolf, A. W., and Lozoff, B. (1999). Cosleeping in context: sleep practices and problems in young children in Japan and the United States. *Archives of Pediatric and Adolescent Medicine, 153*, 339–346.

Laupa, M., and Turiel, E. (1986). Children's conceptions of adult and peer authority. *Child Development, 57*, 405–412.

Leventhal, T., and Brooks-Gunn, J. (2000). The neighborhoods they live in: The effects of neighborhood residence on child and adolescent outcomes. *Psychological Bulletin, 126*, 309–337.

Lopez, N. (2003). *Hopeful girls, troubled boys: Race and gender disparity in urban education*. New York: Routledge.

Marcon, R. A., and Freeman, G. (1996). Linking gender-related toy preferences to social structure: Changes in children's letters to Santa since 1978. *Journal of Psychological Practice, 2*, 1–10.

Markus, H. R., and Kitayama, S. (1991). Culture and the self: Implications for cognition, emotion, and motivation. *Psychological Review, 98*, 224–253.

Maslow, A. H. (1948). "Higher" and "lower" needs. *Journal of Psychology: Interdisciplinary and Applied, 25*, 433–436.

Massey, D. S., and Denton, N. A. (1993). *American apartheid: Segregation and the making of the underclass*. Cambridge, MA: Harvard University Press.

Miller, J. G., and Bersoff, D. M. (1992). Culture and moral judgment: How are conflicts between justice and interpersonal responsibilities resolved? *Journal of Personality and Social Psychology, 62*, 541–554.

Miller, P. J., Wang, S., Sandel, T., and Cho, G. E. (2002). Self-esteem as folk theory: A comparison of European American and Taiwanese mothers' beliefs. In C. S. Tamis-LeMonda and R. Harwood (Guest Eds.), *Special Issue of Parenting: Science and Practice: Parental Ethnotheories: Cultural Practices and Normative Development, 2*, 209–239.

Mincy, R. B. (2006). *Black males left behind*. Washington, DC: Urban Institute Press.

Mordkowitz, E. R., and Ginsburg, H. P. (1987). Early academic socialization of successful Asian-American college students. *The Quarterly Newsletter of the Laboratory of Comparative Human Cognition, 9*, 85–91.

Morelli, G. A., Rogoff, B., and Angelillo, C. (2003). Cultural variation in young children's access to work or involvement in specialized child-focused activities. *International Journal of Behavioral Development, 27*, 264–274.

Morelli, G. A., Rogoff, B., Oppenheim, D., and Goldsmith, D. (1992). Cultural variation in infant's sleeping arrangements: Questions of independence. *Developmental Psychology, 28*, 604–613.

Morelli, G. A., and Verhoef, H. (1999). Who should help me raise my child? A cultural approach to understanding nonmaternal child care decisions. In L. Balter and C. S. Tamis-LeMonda (Eds.), *Child psychology: A handbook of contemporary issues* (pp. 491–509). New York: Psychology Press.

Nucci, L. P., and Smetana, J. G. (1996). Mothers' conceptions of young children's personal domain. *Child Development, 67*, 1870–1886.

Nucci, L. P., and Weber, E. K. (1995). Social interactions in the home and the development of young children's conceptions of the personal. *Child Development, 66*, 1438–1452.

Oakes, J., and Guiton, G. (1995). Matchmaking: The dynamics of high school tracking decisions. *American Education Research Journal, 32*, 3–33.

Ogbu, J. U. (1991). Minority coping responses and school experience. *Journal of Psychohistory, 18*, 433–456.

Orfield, G., Losen, D., Wald, J., and Swanson, C. B. (2004). *Losing our future: How minority youth are being left behind by the graduation rate crisis*. Cambridge, MA: Harvard Education Press.

Oyserman, D., Coon, H. M., and Kemmelmeier, M. (2002). Rethinking individualism and collectivism: Evaluation of theoretical assumptions and meta-analyses. *Psychological Bulletin, 128*, 3–72.

Paschall, M. J., and Hubbard, M. L. (1998). Effects of neighborhood and family stressors on African American male adolescents. *Journal of Consulting and Clinical Psychology, 66*, 825–831.

Paulter, K. J., and Lewko, J. H. (1987). Children's and adolescents' views of the work world in times of economic uncertainty. In J. H. Lewko (Ed.), *How children and adolescents view the world of work* (pp. 21–31). San Francisco: Jossey-Bass.

Paz, O. (1961). *The labyrinth of solitude: Life and thought in Mexico*. New York: Evergreen Books.

Petrova, P. K., Cialdini, R. B., and Sills, S. J. (2007). Consistency-based compliance across cultures. *Journal of Experimental Social Psychology, 43*, 104–111.

Phinney, J. S., Kim-Jo, T., Osorio, S., and Vilhjalmsdottir, P. (2005). Autonomy-relatedness in adolescent-parent disagreements: Ethnic and developmental factors. *Journal of Adolescent Research, 20*, 8–39.

Poasa, K. H., Mallinckrodt, B., and Suzuki, L. A. (2000). Causal attributions for problematic family interactions: A qualitative, cultural comparison of Western Samoa, American Samoa, and the United States. *Counseling Psychologist, 28*, 32–60.

Repetti, R. L., Taylor, S. E., and Seeman, T. E. (2002). Risky families: Family social environments and the mental and physical health of offspring. *Psychological Bulletin, 128*, 330–366.

Ripple, C. H., and Zigler, E. (2003). Research, policy, and the federal role in prevention initiatives for children. *American Psychologist, 58*, 482–490.

Robinson, C., and Morris, J. T. (1986). The gender-stereotyped nature of Christmas toys received by 36-, 48-, and 60-month-old children: A comparison between nonrequested vs requested toys. *Sex Roles, 15*, 21–32.

Robinson, C. C., Watson, J. A., and Morris, J. T. (1984). An examination of fundamental sex-role behavioral change: Mothers' toy purchasing behavior. *Parenting Studies, 1,* 61–66.

Rogoff, B. (1990). *Apprenticeship in thinking: Cognitive development in social context.* New York: Oxford University Press.

Rumbaut, R. G., and Portes, A. (2001). *Ethnicities: Children of immigrants in America.* Los Angeles: University of California Press.

Ryan, R. M., and Deci, E. L. (2000). Self-determination theory and the facilitation of intrinsic motivation, social development, and well-being. *American Psychologist, 55,* 68–78.

Sabogal, F., Marin, G., Otero-Sabogal, R., and Marin, B. V. (1987). Hispanic familism and acculturation: What changes and what doesn't? *Hispanic Journal of Behavioral Sciences, 9,* 397–412.

Sampson, E. E. (1977). Psychology and the American ideal. *Journal of Personality and Social Psychology, 35,* 767–782.

Schieffelin, B. B., and Eisenberg, A. R. (1984). Cultural variation in children's conversations. In R. L. Schiefelbusch and J. Pickar (Eds.), *The acquisition of communicative competence.* Baltimore: University Park Press.

Schieffelin, B. B., and Ochs, E. (1986). Language socialization. *Annual Review of Anthropology, 15,* 163–191.

Schulze, P. A., Harwood, R. L., and Schoelmerich, A. (2001). Feeding practices and expectations among middle-class Anglo and Puerto Rican mothers of 12 month old infants. *Journal of Cross-Cultural Psychology, 32,* 397–406.

Smetana, J. G. (1988). Adolescents and parents' conceptions of parental authority. *Child Development, 59,* 321–335.

Smetana, J. G. (2002). Culture, autonomy, and personal jurisdiction. In R. Kail and H. Reese (Eds.), *Advances in child development and behavior* (Vol. 29, pp. 52–87). Amsterdam: Academic Press.

Smetana, J. G., Campione-Barr, N., and Metzger, A. (2006). Adolescent development in interpersonal and societal contexts. *Annual Review of Psychology, 57,* 255–284.

Smetana, J. G., and Daddis, C. (2002). Domain-specific antecedents of parental psychological control and monitoring: The role of parenting beliefs and practices. *Child Development, 73,* 563–580.

Snow, C. E. (1977). The development of conversation between mothers and babies. *Journal of Child Language, 4,* 1–22.

Spencer, M. B., and Dornbusch, S. M. (1990). Challenges in studying minority youth. In S. S. Feldman and G. R. Elliott (Eds.), *At the threshold: The developing adolescent* (pp. 123–146). Cambridge, MA: Harvard University Press.

Steiner, G. (1981). *The futility of family policy.* Washington, DC: Brookings Institution.

Stevenson, H. W., and Stigler, J. W. (1992). *The learning gap: Why our schools are failing and what we can learn from Japanese and Chinese education.* New York: Summit Books.

Suarez-Orozco, C., and Suarez-Orozco, M. M. (2001). *Children of immigration.* Cambridge, MA: Harvard University Press.

Super, C. M., and Harkness, S. (2002). Culture structures the environment for development. *Human Development, 45,* 270–274.

Tamis-LeMonda, C. S., Bornstein, M. H., Cyphers, L., Toda, S., and Ogino, M. (1992). Language and play at one year: A comparison of toddlers and mothers in the United States and Japan. *International Journal of Behavioral Development, 15,* 19–42.

Tamis-LeMonda, C. S., Wang, S., Koutsouvanou, E., and Albright, M. (2002). Childrearing values in Greece, Taiwan, and the United States. *Parenting: Science and Practice, 2,* 185–208.

Tamis-LeMonda, C. S., Way, N., Hughes, D., Yoshikawa, H., Kahana-Kalman, R., and Niwa, E. (2008). Parents' goals for children: The dynamic co-existence of collectivism and individualism. *Social Development, 17,* 183–209.

Taylor, S. E., and Brown, J. D. (1988). Illusion and well-being: A social psychological perspective on mental health. *Psychological Bulletin, 103,* 193–210.

Triandis, H. C. (1988). Collectivism and development. In D. Sinha and H. S. R. Kao (Eds.), *Social values and development: Asian perspectives* (pp. 285–303). Thousand Oaks, CA: Sage Publications, Inc.

Triandis, H. C. (1995). *Individualism and collectivism.* Boulder, CO: Western Press.

Triandis, H. C., Bontempo, R., Villareal, M. J., Masaaki, A., and Lucca, N. (1988). Individualism and collectivism: Cross-cultural perspectives on self in group relationships. *Journal of Personality and Social Psychology, 54,* 323–338.

Trzesniewski, K. H., Donnellan, B. M., Moffitt, T. E., Robins, R. W., Poulton, R., and Caspi, A. (2006). Low self-esteem during adolescence predicts poor health, criminal behavior, and limited economic prospects during adulthood. *Developmental Psychology, 42,* 381–390.

Uba, L. (1994). *Asian Americans: Personality patterns, identity, and mental health.* New York: Guilford Press.
United Nations Development Programme (2006). 2006 Annual Report: Global partnership for development. Retrieved February 16, 2009 from http://www.undp.org/publications/annualreport2006/index.shtml.
Wang, S., and Tamis-LeMonda, C. S. (2003) Do child-rearing values in Taiwan and the United States reflect cultural values of Collectivism and Individualism? *Journal of Cross-Cultural Psychology, 34,* 629–642.
Waters, M. C. (1990). *Ethnic options: Choosing identities in America.* Berkeley, CA: University of California Press.
Weber, M. (1958). *The Protestant ethic and the spirit of capitalism (T. Parsons, Trans.).* New York: Charles Scribner's Sons. (Originally published as two separate essays, 1904–1905)
White, R. W. (1959). Motivation reconsidered: The concept of competence. *Psychological Review, 66,* 297–333.
Whiting, B. B., Edwards, C. P., Ember, C. R., Erchak, G. M., Harkness, S., Munroe, R. L., et al. (1988). *Children of different worlds: The formation of social behavior.* Cambridge, MA: Harvard University Press.
Williams, J. (1987). *Eyes on the Prize: America's Civil Rights Years, 1954-1965.* New York: Viking Penguin Inc.
Willis, P. (1977). *Learning to labor: How working class kids get working class jobs.* New York: Columbia University Press.
World Bank (2005). World Development Report 2005: A better investment climate for everyone. Available at: http://web.worldbank.org/WBSITE/EXTERNAL/EXTDEC/EXTRESEARCH/EXTWDRS/EXTWDR2005/0,,menuPK:477681~pagePK:64167702~piPK:64167676~theSitePK:477665,00.html.
World Bank (2006). World Development Report 2006: Equity and development. Available at: http://web.worldbank.org/WBSITE/EXTERNAL/EXTDEC/EXTRESEARCH/EXTWDRS/EXTWDR2006/0,menuPK:477658~pagePK:64167702~piPK:64167676~theSitePK:477642,00.html.
World Desk Reference (2004). United States: World ranking. Retrieved February 16, 2009 from http://dev.prenhall.com/divisions/hss/worldreference/US/worldranking.html.
Yau, J., and Smetana, J. G. (1996). Adolescent-parent conflict among Chinese adolescents in Hong Kong. *Child Development, 67,* 1262–1275.
Yew, W. (1987). Immigrant families. *Challenger, 26,* 1–3.
Youniss, J., McLellan, J. A., and Yates, M. (1999). Religion, community service, and identity in American youth. *Journal of Adolescence, 22,* 243–253.
Youniss, J., and Smollar, J. (1985). *Adolescents' relations with mothers, fathers, and friends.* Chicago: University of Chicago Press.
Zhou, M. (1997). Growing up American: The challenge confronting immigrant children and children of immigrants. *Annual Review of Sociology, 23,* 63–95.
Zigler, E. (2004). Moving Head Start to the states: One experiment too many. *Applied Developmental Science, 8,* 51–55.

17
Central and South America

RODOLFO DE CASTRO RIBAS, JR.

Introduction

Cross-cultural developmental studies involving participants from Central and South America, a geopolitical region characterized by great cultural diversity, have contributed to our understanding of both universal and culture-specific aspects of human development. The study of Posada et al. (2002) on maternal caregiving and infant security is an example of this contribution. The generality of the link between sensitive caregiving and infant security has been consistently reported in the literature. However, few studies have been conducted in developing countries, and evidence from South America is even scarcer. Among other aspects, Posada et al. investigated the adequacy of the conceptualization of caregiving and the cross-cultural generality of the sensitivity–security link in a study with Colombian and U.S. mother–infant dyads from urban (Bogotá and Denver) middle-class backgrounds. Using an ethnographic methodology, Posada et al. concluded that the domains of maternal behavior related to the attachment security provide a suitable framework to describe Colombian mothers' behavior. In addition, analyses revealed that Colombian and U.S. mothers did not differ in maternal sensitivity, and consistent with previous research, positive associations were observed between maternal sensitivity and infant security in both groups. Nonetheless, Posada et al. (2002) also identified discrete differences between the Colombian and U.S. groups. For instance, although mothers of both groups tended to be more cooperative than intrusive, Colombian mothers were perceived as less interfering and more active and animated in interactions with their babies, whereas American mothers were perceived as more active in creating interesting environments. In sum, the findings provide support for the universality of the importance of the early care and also indicate some cross-cultural variations in maternal caregiving.

Central and South American countries have significant economic and social problems that have directly impacted families (Kaslow, 2001). Among these problems, poverty is probably the more deleterious threat for children and adolescents because it dramatically reduces opportunities to a healthy development. In Central and South America, approximately one-fourth of those under 18 live in poverty (Economic Commission for Latin America and the Caribbean [ECLAC], 2005).

Cross-cultural developmental studies have also detected the impact of these problems and provided information that can be useful for intervention programs (Harkness and Keefer, 2000). For example, also using the attachment theory and research framework, Valenzuela (1997) evaluated the universality and the applicability of concept of maternal sensitivity for designing intervention programs for children and families at risk in a developing country. The study involved two groups of Chilean mothers living in a context of urban poverty; one group had chronically underweight children, whereas the other had adequate weight-for-age children. All mothers had similar access to medical care and to supplementary feeding programs. Valenzuela investigated associations between several variables (e.g., family total income, mother's age, and education) and the nutritional status of the children. Positive associations between maternal sensitivity and children's weight-for-age and security were identified. Furthermore, maternal sensitivity emerged as the only significant predictor of the children's weight-for-age. Maternal education, maternal weight, maternal height, and marital satisfaction were identified as predictors of maternal sensitivity. Valenzuela argued that the findings stressed the importance of the maternal sensitivity that would act as a mediator between biological, social, and psychological variables influencing child development and that intervention strategies should go beyond nutritional supplementation programs and help caregivers provide sensitive care for their children.

The main objective of this chapter is to provide a review of contributions of cross-cultural developmental studies involving participants from Central and South America to our understanding of the human development. The potential importance of this knowledge for the implementation of intervention programs is discussed. The chapter is organized in four sections. In the first section, some aspects of Central and South American history and culture are briefly discussed, and key sociodemographic information relevant for the interpretation of findings or for the implementation cross-cultural developmental studies in the region is provided. Next, a bibliometric portrait of the cross-cultural research involving Central and South American participants is offered. The third section presents a review of studies in five areas: poverty and street children, parenting, mother–infant interaction, cognitive development, and social behavior. In the final section, a concise evaluation of trends and contributions of cross-cultural developmental studies conducted in Central and South America is offered.

Historic, Cultural, and Demographic Considerations about Central and South America

Central and South America comprise basically the mainland area in the western hemisphere south of the United States. According to the United Nations standard country classification (Table 17.1), the area is geopolitically divided into 20 independent countries, a French overseas department (French Guiana), and an overseas territory of the United Kingdom (Falklands Islands). In 2006, approximately 881 million people lived in the Americas; 58% of this total, approximately half a billion, lived in Central and South America. Nearly 38% of the Central and South America population (156 million people) are less than 15 years of age (United Nations Statistics Division, 1999, 2006). The situation of these Central and South America countries and the peoples inhabiting them are briefly discussed. Special attention is paid to specific topics (e.g., language, formal education, urbanization, socioeconomic status, religious affiliation, ethnicity) that have outstanding relevance for the implementation of cultural and cross-cultural developmental studies (Betancourt and Lopez, 1993; Bornstein and Lansford, Chapter 14, in this volume; Bradley and Corwyn, 2002; Conger and Donnellan, 2007; Goodnow, Chapter 1, in this volume; Holden and Vittrup, Chapter 15, in this volume; Keller and Greenfield, 2000; Marsella, 1998; Segall, Lonner, and Berry, 1998; van de Vijver, Hofer, and Chasiotis, Chapter 2, in this volume; Wagner, Chapter 8, in this volume).

By the end of the fifteenth century, Spain and Portugal were trying to establish sea routes between Europe and Asia. Sponsored by Catholic monarchs of Aragon and Castile in Spain, Christopher Columbus (1451–1506) sailed west from Europe aiming for India but discovered new lands and claimed them for Spain in October 1492. Columbus believed he had reached islands off the eastern coast of Asia and called the inhabitants of the New World *indigenous* (*indios*, a Latin word employed to designate inhabitants of India). Later, the navigator and cartographer Americus Vespucius (1454–1512) pointed out that an entirely new continent or a New World had been discovered. In this period, Spain and Portugal signed several treatises to avoid

Table 17.1 Central and South America: Selected Social Indicators

Countries and Dependencies	Total Population (Thousands)[a] 2006	Urban Population (%)[a] 2005	Population under 15 Years (%)[a] 2005	Adult (15+) Illiteracy Rate (%)[a] 2000–2004 Men	Adult (15+) Illiteracy Rate (%)[a] 2000–2004 Women	Per Capita GDP (US$)[a] 2004	Roman Catholics (%)[b] 2006	Indigenous Population (Thousands)[b] 2000–2002	Indigenous Population (%)[c] 2000–2002	Predominant Ethnic Composition[b] 2006 Group	Predominant Ethnic Composition[b] 2006 %
Central America											
Belize	275.1	48.3	36.8	23.3	22.9	3,594	50	—	—	Mestizo	49
Costa Rica	4,398.8	61.7	28.4	4.3	4.1	4,325	91	65.5	1.7	European	77
El Salvador	6,998.7	59.8	34.0	17.6	22.9	2,301	79	—	—	Mestizo	88
Guatemala	12,911.1	47.2	43.2	22.7	37.5	2,157	73	4,433.2	39.5	Mestizo	64
Honduras	7,362.3	46.5	39.2	20.2	19.8	1,046	83	440.3	7.2	Mestizo	87
Mexico	108,326.9	76.0	31.0	7.4	11.3	6,397	87	7,619.0	7.9	Mestizo	64
Nicaragua	5,599.8	59.0	38.9	23.2	23.4	820	81	—	—	Mestizo	63
Panama	3,287.5	70.8	30.4	7.5	8.8	4,269	71	285.2	10.0	Mestizo	58
South America											
Argentina	39,134.3	90.1	26.4	3.0	3.0	3,988	80	—	—	European	86
Bolivia	9,353.8	64.2	38.1	6.9	19.3	935	88	5,358.1	66.2	Amerindian	65
Brazil	188,882.8	84.2	27.9	13.8	13.5	3,225	74	734.1	0.4	European	54
Chile	16,465.4	87.6	24.9	4.2	4.4	5,838	70	692.2	4.6	Mestizo	72
Colombia	46,279.4	72.7	31.0	7.9	7.8	2,130	96	—	—	Mestizo	47
Ecuador	13,418.6	62.8	32.4	7.7	10.3	2,302	94	830.4	6.8	Mestizo	42
Falkland Islands (Malvinas)	2.9	90.2	15.0	—	—	—	—	—	—	—	—
French Guiana	191.5	75.6	34.4	—	—	—	80	—	—	Mulatto	38
Guyana	751.9	28.2	29.3	—	—	1,037	10	—	—	Indo-Pakistani	46
Paraguay	6,300.8	58.5	37.6	6.9	9.8	1,168	89	87.6	1.7	Mestizo	86
Peru	28,380.3	72.6	32.2	8.7	19.7	2,439	86	—	—	Amerindian	47
Suriname	452.0	73.9	30.1	—	—	2,475	22	—	—	Indo-Pakistani	37
Uruguay	3,486.5	92.0	24.3	2.7	1.9	3,842	78	—	—	European	94
Venezuela	27,216.4	93.4	31.2	6.7	7.3	4,260	89	—	—	Mestizo	64

Sources:
[a] Data from United Nations Statistics Division, Demographic and Social Statistics. Retrieved September 10, 2006 from unstats.un.org/unsd/demographic. With permission.
[b] Data from World Data, Encyclopaedia Britannica On Line. Retrieved September 12, 2006 from http://www.britannica.com.
[c] Data from Economic Commission for Latin America and the Caribbean, *Challenges*, 1, 4–9. Retrieved March 17, 2007. from http://www.cepal.org.

Notes: GDP, gross domestic product; —, not available.

disputes over lands newly discovered. The terms of the Treaty of Tordesillas of 1494, for example, stated that the New World would be divided between the Spaniards and Portuguese along a meridian 370 leagues (1,550 km) west of the Cape Verde islands. That meridian cut through the easternmost part of the South American continent. The lands lying west would belong to Spain and the lands east (today part of Brazil) to Portugal (Treaty of Tordesillas, 2006). Also aiming for India, the Portuguese navigator Pedro Alvarez Cabral (circa 1467–1520) sailed south and, in April 1500, reached the northeastern coast of South America, where Brazil is today, and claimed it for Portugal (Flint, 2006; Robinson, 2005).

These agreements and events in part determined the division of the Central and South America into two main spheres of influence, the Portuguese in Brazil and the Spanish in the rest of the region. From their initial bases in the Caribbean Islands, the Spaniards colonized large areas in Central America as far as south of the United States and the west of South America. The Portuguese did not strictly enforce agreements and occupied areas originally granted to Spain, expanding Brazilian territory to nearly one-half of South America. Later, other European countries (France, United Kingdom, and The Netherlands) settled relatively small areas in the north of South America (today French Guiana, Guyana, and Suriname) and Belize in Central America (Flint, 2006; Latin America, 2006). The regions that were not colonized by Spaniards and Portuguese have had a diverse historical development and differ from the rest of the continent in many aspects (e.g., language).

During the eighteenth century, the Spanish and Portuguese powers declined significantly. Different historical movements (e.g., enlightenment, liberalism) and especially Napoleon's invasion of the Iberian Peninsula in 1808 compelled American elites, mostly Iberian-born person or Iberian descendents, to advocate independence. By the end of the 1820s, all mainland Spanish and Portuguese colonies had become independent states. The British and Dutch colonies obtained their independence later in the 1970s and 1980s (Robinson, 2005).

These European conquerors profoundly influenced the region. The Iberians who were militarily superior subjugated native peoples and imposed on them their language, legal system, and culture. Today, Spanish is the official language in all countries that gained their independence from Spain, whereas the Portuguese is the official language in Brazil. In a few South American countries (e.g., Bolivia, Ecuador, Peru), pre-Columbian languages (e.g., Aymara, Quechua, Shuar) are also officially recognized as national languages.

The Roman Catholic Church became a major political and economic power during the colonization. Catholic clergymen not only acted as spiritual leaders converting Native Americans to Catholicism, but also held governing positions, served as bankers, and were the important landholders (Robinson, 2005). Today, the Roman Catholic Church dominates the religious scene in the region. The percentage of followers of Roman Catholicism varies from 70% to 96% in Spanish and Portuguese America (Table 17.1), although other Christian (e.g., Pentecostalism) and non-Christian religious sects (e.g., African-descendant religions such as Umbanda and Candomblé) are also popular (Stewart-Gambino, 2001).

Approximately 85% of the native population of the Americas was decimated by epidemic diseases bought by the Europeans (e.g., smallpox, typhus, influenza). Most of those who survived became slaves in plantations and mines (Robinson, 2005). However, this aspect of colonization was not homogenous across countries. Data from national censuses (Table 17.1) indicate that Native American peoples, normally inferred operationally from maternal language, self-identification, or geographical position, almost disappeared in countries like Brazil but still represent a significant proportion of the populations, for instance, in Bolivia, Guatemala, and Mexico (ECLAC, 2006). It is also important to note that different Native American indigenous peoples (e.g., Quechua, Aymara, Maya) diverge significantly in many cultural aspects. For example, approximately 160 different Amerindian languages or dialects are spoken by communities of

10,000 or more speakers (Gonzalez, 1995; United Nations Children's Fund, 2004). Furthermore, to complement the Native American labor force, a large number of enslaved African laborers were imported by the Iberians especially to Brazil and the Caribbean Islands. These slavers, brought from different regions of Africa, also represented diverse cultures and societies (ECLAC, 2006).

Relatively few Iberian women came to the New World during the colonization period, and intermarriage between Iberians, Native Americans, and Africans was very common. The people of mixed Native American and European ancestry were called *mestizos*, whereas the people of mixed African and European ancestry were called *mulattoes*. Today, mestizos represent the majority of the population in several countries of the region (Table 17.1). Some South American countries (e.g., Argentina, Uruguay, Brazil) absorbed large numbers of immigrants from Europe (e.g., Spaniards, Portuguese, Italians, Germans) and the Middle East and Asia (e.g., Lebanese, Syrians, Japanese) in the late nineteenth and early twentieth centuries. Today, this region has a majority of people of European ancestry. In the same period, Guyana and Suriname, two British and Dutch colonies, received a significant number of immigrants from India, and today Indo-Pakistani descendants, most Hindus and Muslim, represent significant proportions of the population in these countries (Latin America, 2006).

In their review of the psychology in Latin America, Sosa and Valderrama Iturbe (2001) commented that, despite sharing cultural and historical elements, the countries in the region have very different levels of economic, scientific, and human development. In fact, although there are no rich countries in Central and South America and approximately one-third of the households are poor (Bulmer-Thomas, 2001), indexes like urban population, adult illiteracy rate, and gross domestic product per capita (Table 17.1) vary greatly from country to country. The levels of poverty and illiteracy, for instance, represent important challenges to researchers. In the next sections, it is argued that topics like homelessness and poverty have frequently been investigated in Central and South American studies of human development.

It is also useful to mention that terms such as *Latino families*, *Latin Americans*, or *Hispanics* frequently used to designate inhabitants of countries that developed from Spanish and Portuguese colonies imply a sense of cultural homogeneity and supranational identity that should be viewed with great caution. Stanislawski (1959, p. 4), for example, stressed that "a Portuguese is not a Spaniard. No Portuguese would say otherwise and probably few foreigners who know both nations would disagree." In this direction, the American Psychological Association (2001) recognized the relevance of providing, among other aspects, more specific information about participants (e.g., nation or region of origin). Furthermore, despite the great influence of the Iberians, significant aspects of Native American and African cultures (e.g., language, religion, customs, lifestyle, music) survived and coexist with the colonizers' official language and cultural system (Gonzalez, 1995), so that expressions like *cultural diversity* and *blend of cultures* (see, e.g., Robinson, 2005) have usually been used to describe Central and South America. Rumbaut (2001, p. 845) pointed out that "immigration is a transformative force, producing profound and unanticipated social changes in both sending and receiving societies" (see also, Cote and Bornstein, 2000; Bornstein and Cote, Chapter 27, in this volume).

Cross-Cultural Developmental Psychology in Central and South America: A Bibliometric Evaluation

In the previous section, some aspects of the Central and South American history and culture were briefly discussed. Updated sociodemographic information was also provided. Special attention was paid to topics that can be useful to interpret findings or even to guide the implementation of cross-cultural developmental studies in the region. In this section, a portrait of the cross-cultural developmental psychology in Central and South America is presented.

The procedures used to trace this portrait were similar to those used in other bibliometric studies (Brouwers, van Hemert, Breugelmans, and van de Vijver, 2004; Robins, Gosling and Craik, 2000) and included, among other aspects, a systematic analysis of records stored in the PsycInfo database (http://psycnet.apa.org/).

A search was initially conduced in PsycInfo in June 2006 to identify entries of developmental articles (i.e., articles labeled as Developmental Psychology, Cognitive and Perceptual Development, and Psychosocial and Personality Development by the PsycInfo) published from 1986 to 2005. The entries of developmental articles were then retrieved if they included the name of a Central or South American country or dependency (Table 17.1) in at least one of five PsycInfo database fields (Location, Title, Abstract, Key Concepts, and Index Terms). Entries of articles on Gerontology were systematically discarded. The retrieved entries (developmental articles involving Central or South America) were then classified as cross-cultural if they involved participants from two or more countries (i.e., more than one country name in the Location field) or included words with the stem "cultur" in the Title, Abstract, Key Concepts, or Index Terms. This procedure permitted the identification of entries that included terms like *culture*, *cross-cultural*, *socio-cultural*, and *acculturation*. The cross-cultural developmental entries involving Central or South America were subsequently analyzed by two independent reviewers. It is worth noting that the procedures used certainly did not identify all cross-cultural developmental psychological studies involving Central and South American participants, but did identify a reasonable sample of studies published in internationally recognized journals. A summary of the findings of the bibliometric analysis follows.

A total of 58,733 entries of developmental articles published from 1986 through 2005 were identified in PsycInfo. From this total, 1,045 (1.8%) involved Central and South American countries. The percentage of annually published developmental articles involving Central and South American participants increased slowly from 1.5% in 1986 to 1.9% in 2005. Consistent with the van de Vijver et al. (Chapter 2, this volume) and Smith (2001) evaluations, these findings indicate that the region has been underrepresented in the literature.

Approximately 30% of the development entries involving Central and South American countries ($n = 317$) were identified as cultural. From this total, 34 were discarded because they did not focus primarily on children and adolescents or involve Central or South American participants (e.g., participants were from New Mexico or the United States). These findings are consistent with previous studies. Salazar (1997), for example, reported that approximately 48% of the articles published from 1967 to 1996 in the *Interamerican Journal of Psychology*, an official publication of the Interamerican Society of Psychology, reported comparisons between cultural groups or made direct or indirect reference to cultural differences. According to Salazar, social psychology, psychometrics, and developmental psychology were the three most frequently studied areas. Other studies (e.g., Ardila, 2004; Sosa and Valderrama Iturbe, 2001) have pointed out that cross-cultural psychology and developmental psychology have been main areas of interest for Latin American psychologists. Furthermore, the percentage of annually published developmental articles involving Central and South America that were also classified as cultural nearly doubled from 18% in 1986 to 37% in 2005. Following a major tendency in developmental psychology (Dasen and Mishra, 2000), developmental studies involving Central and South America are becoming more and more culturally oriented.

According to the PsycInfo Classification Code, approximately half of the articles focused on psychosocial and personality development, one-fourth focused on cognitive and perceptual development, and nearly one-tenth focused on scale development or evaluation. Approximately 88% of the cross-cultural developmental articles involving Central and South America reported empirical investigations. Approximately 53% of the empirical entries reported cross-national comparisons, 23% reported intranational comparisons (e.g., urban versus rural, upper middle class versus slum dwellers), 8% involved both cross-national and intranational comparisons, and 16% were replications or not comparative studies. Nearly 65% of the cross-national studies recruited participants from two countries, 14% involved three countries, and 9% involved four countries. Approximately 47% of the studies used self-report instruments (e.g., questionnaires), 24% used interviews, 27% used observation, 20% used nonexperimental tasks, and 3% used experimental tasks. The predominance of empirical articles, studies on psychosocial topics, studies involving two cultures, and the use of self-reports is consistent with the Brouwers et al. (2004) evaluation of publications in the *Journal of Cross-Cultural Psychology*.

Approximately 91% of the empirical studies were conducted in urban contexts, and 17% were conducted in rural contexts. Approximately 27% of the empirical studies involved Mexicans participants, 26% involved Brazilians, and 11% involved Colombians. Nearly 63% of all empirical studies involved participants from these three countries, whereas 14% involved participants from Argentina, Guatemala, Peru, and Chile. Of course, these studies also involved non–Central and South American participants. For example, nearly 29% involved North Americans, 8% involved Spanish, 5% involved Canadians, 5% involved Italians, and 4% involved British. Native American participants were included in 13% ($n = 33$) of the studies. From these 33 studies, 17 studied Mayan groups in Guatemala ($n = 8$), Mexico ($n = 8$), and Belize ($n = 1$), 5 studied Quechua groups in Peru, and 4 studied Brazilian indigenous groups (e.g., Karajá, Terena, Wari). The seven remaining studies were conducted in six different countries (Bolivia, Colombia, Ecuador, Nicaragua, Panama, and Paraguay). In line with previous research (e.g., Öngel and Smith, 1994; Smith, 2001), these results provide some evidence about the influence of the North American psychology. This influence may, in part, explain distribution of countries and indigenous groups studied. The contribution of the U.S. researchers to the study of Mayan groups in Guatemala and Mexico, for example, is clear.

Classical and Modern Developmental Research in Central and South America

The foregoing bibliometric analysis offered a profile of the cross-cultural research involving Central and South American participants published between 1986 and 2005. The analysis also revealed some topics more frequently investigated and particularly relevant for the development of basic and applied research. In this section, some of these topics are examined. More specifically, research focusing on poverty and street children, parenting, mother–infant interaction, cognitive development, and social behavior is presented.

Before the presentation of these topics, two preliminary observations are in order. First, researchers are increasingly aware of theoretical and methodological challenges for cross-cultural research (van de Vijver et al., Chapter 2, in this volume; van de Vijver and Leung, 2000). As a result, the quality and complexity of the studies (e.g., theoretical frameworks, methodological concerns, data analytic plans, number of citations) have improved over time. For example, it is of some historical significance to note that the first issue of *Child Development* presented a cross-cultural study on responses (e.g., Babinski reflex) of European American, African American, and Mexican newborns (Bryan, 1930). Although Bryan reported several differences between groups, the findings are difficult to interpret because relevant information about the participants and procedures was not presented and the sample was relatively small (e.g., nine Mexican newborns were tested). In another study, Billig, Gillin, and Davidson (1948) employed the Rorschach test to evaluate aspects of the personality of adolescents and adults in an indigenous community in Guatemala. Based on a U.S. standardized procedure to interpret the Rorschach responses, the authors concluded, among other aspects, that "the adult Indians as a group would show a somewhat limited understanding for everyday life problems" and "intellectual limitations - either inabilities or deep-seated frustrations" (Billig et al., 1948, pp. 331, 332).

Today it is well known that several steps are needed to produce psychologically acceptable instruments for use across cultural and linguistic groups and that there is a growing need for translated and validated psychological instruments in cross-cultural comparisons (van de Vijver and Hambleton, 1996). In fact, the bibliometric analysis presented in the last section revealed that approximately 10% of the developmental studies published between 1986 and 2005 focused the development or evaluation of scales (e.g., Child Behavior Checklist, Coppersmith Self-Esteem Inventories, Minnesota Multiphasic Personality Inventory, Raven's Progressive Matrices) in Central and South America.

In his review of cross-cultural research on child animism published on the 1930s, 1940s, and 1950s, Jahoda (1958) examined probable causes of divergence in results of cross-cultural studies. Among these causes, Jahoda indicated sampling, linguistics factors (e.g., utilization of participants' native languages in interviews), forms of problem presentation, methods of administration (e.g., oral versus written material), and the personal influence of the investigator (e.g., a European adult investigator interviewing an indigenous little child). Fortunately, those problems have increasingly been acknowledged and overcome by developmental researchers. For example, in a study about eidetic imagery with the Bororo, a Brazilian indigenous group, Levak (1969) noticed that the participants were anxious during the test administration and that standard explanations did not calm them. She reported that participants kept asking about the purposes of the study: "Are you not measuring our vision; is this a way to find out who is going to die?" (Levak, 1969, p. 137). In a study on recognition memory with 5-, 8-, and 11-year-old urban-dwelling U.S. American and isolated village-dwelling Guatemalan children, Kagan, Klein, Haith, and Morrison (1973) reported that memory improved with age in both groups, but the performance of the 5- and 8-year-old U.S. children was superior to the Guatemalan children. Several possible explanations for these differences were discussed, and posterior observations made by the first author on a similar population revealed that many of the 5- to 8-year-old Guatemalan children seemed frightened and confused during test administration.

The second observation to be made refers to the cultural groups living in Central and South America. If on the one side, cross-cultural developmental psychology has changed, on the other, many Central and South American cultural groups have experienced significant transformations, and developmental researchers have registered or even witnessed these changes. For example, Posada et al. (2002) pointed out that social roles of men and women are changing in Colombian society and that these changes are transforming family relations.

In a two-decade follow-up study in Zinacantan, a Maya community in Mexico, Greenfield (1999) observed how an historical change, the transition from agricultural subsistence to an entrepreneurial cash economy, has been accompanied by several cultural and cognitive changes. She pointed out, for example, that experimentation and innovation were not valorized in the traditional Zinacantec agricultural subsistence economy, and as a result, the weaving was limited to a small stock of patterns. The transition to a commercial economy stimulated changes in the way weaving was taught to young girls (e.g., valorization of innovative creation and independence), which, in turn, led to changes in the production of weaving artifacts so that the number of figurative and geometrical patterns grew immensely. According to Greenfield, the study provided empirical support to the sociohistorical perspective proposed by Vygotsky (1896–1934).

Keller, Borke, Yovsi, Lohaus, and Jensen (2005) investigated stability and variability of patterns of parenting in three cultural environments (German middle-class families, Cameroonian Nso farmers, and Costa Rican urban families) assuming that these three groups differed with respect to their cultural socialization models (primarily independent goals, primarily interdependent goals, and autonomous relational goals, respectively). In each cultural environment, Keller et al. assessed parenting interaction patterns of mothers of 3-month-old babies twice, with an interval of 4 to 6 years between assessments. As predicted, differences in parenting style between groups were observed. German middle-class families more often demonstrated a distal parenting style (more face-to-face contact and object play and less body contact and body stimulation) and differed from the Nso farmers (proximal parenting style with more body contact and body stimulation and less face-to-face contexts and object play) and from the Costa Rican urban families (a more proximal parenting style with object stimulation and less body contact). Furthermore, Keller et al. predicted and detected variations across time in parenting styles toward a more independent cultural model in the German and Costa Rican cultural environments. These changes were associated with macro-level societal changes, such as globalization.

In summary, it is desirable to take into account the fact that developmental psychology and Central and South America cultural groups have experienced significant changes in recent years. Next, a review of cross-cultural investigations in five areas (poverty and street children, parenting, mother–infant interaction, cognitive development, and social behavior) is presented.

Poverty and Street Children

The impact of the poverty on children and adolescents has been a popular topic of developmental studies. Associations between poverty and brain maturation (inferred from electroencephalograms) in 4-year-old Mexicans were reported by Otero (1997) who reported that economically, socially, and culturally disadvantaged environments are major predictors of lags in brain maturation. The long-term synergistic effect of food supplementation and maternal tutoring in cognitive and social stimulation on the physical growth of Colombian children living in a context of urban poverty was reported by Super, Herrera, and Mora (1990). These findings are consistent with the associations between maternal sensitivity and children's nutritional status observed in the Valenzuela (1997) study, which was discussed in the introduction.

Researchers have also investigated children and adolescents living in streets, or the "street children" phenomenon (le Roux and Smith, 1998). In their review of investigations conducted in Brazil, Hutz and Koller (1997) pointed out that, although street children are exposed to high levels of stress and personal and social risk, they do not differ significantly from other lower socioeconomic groups of children in levels of subjective well-being, depression, and trauma (see also Aptekar, 1989). Raffaelli and Koller (2005) evaluated expectations about the future in a group of Brazilian street children and adolescents and concluded that the life on the streets shaped and constrained how the youngsters see their future. For example, when asked "What do you think will happen to you when you're 18 years old?", approximately 30% of the participants answered "I don't know." Two-fifths of the boys answered that they expected to be doing military service. Military service is mandatory for 18-year-olds in Brazil. This service offers a small income and some hope of a career.

Poverty and related problems have been investigated from different perspectives. Enesco and Navarro (2003), for example, investigated the development of the conception of socioeconomic mobility in middle-class Mexican and Spanish children. Overall, comparisons identified similarities between groups. For example, regardless of age and group, when asked "How do people get rich?", 70% to 100% of the children answered "working." However, Enesco and Navarro also reported that children's ideas about work changed with age. Older children more often reported qualified jobs, individual qualities, and education as sources of social mobility.

Parenting

Investigations conducted in Central and South America have consistently provided evidence about links between parenting and social and cultural variables. Tudge et al. (2006), for example, studied everyday activities of 3-year-old children from four cultural groups (European Americans, African Americans, Kenyan Luo, and European-descent Brazilians) from middle- and working-class backgrounds. Tudge et al. pointed out that an intersection between the cultural and social variables explained the observed variations in children's activities. For example, overall, middle-class children engaged more in lessons than working-class children. However, the frequency of different types of activity (e.g., lessons, work, play, conversation) varied across cultural groups. Brazilian children, for instance, engaged in fewer lessons, whereas working-class Kenyan children engaged in more work (household activities). In the same direction, Morelli, Rogoff, and Angelillo (2003) investigated cultural variation in 2- to 4-year-old children's access to work or involvement in specialized child-focused activities in four communities: two middle-class European American communities, Efe foragers of the Democratic Republic of Congo, and Guatemalan Mayas. As predicted, middle-class European American children had less frequent access to work and were more frequently involved in specialized child-focused activities when compared with Efe and Mayan children. Morelli, Rogoff, Oppenheim, and Goldsmith (1992) investigated the practices of Highland Mayan and middle-class U.S. parents regarding sleeping arrangements during their child's first 2 years. All of the Mayan children slept in their mothers' beds into toddlerhood, whereas none of the U.S. infants did so on a regular basis. Mayan parents explained their sleeping arrangements in terms of the value of closeness with infants, whereas U.S. parents explained their sleeping arrangements in terms of the value of independence for infants.

Every year, millions of children sustain serious unintentional injuries (www.safekids.org). Unintentional and preventable injuries (e.g., burns, falls, drowning, poisoning, suffocation) are a leading cause of hospitalization, disability, and death for children worldwide (Bartlett, 2002). Studies have indicated that cultural factors have significant influence on home safety. Mull, Agran, Winn, and Anderson (2001), for example, studied Mexican, Mexican American, and European American families in the United States and reported that although Mexican families were poorer, less educated, and lived in more hazardous and crowded conditions than the other families, their children benefited from strong family bonds, lower levels of parental dysfunction, and a cultural tradition in which older children supervise their younger siblings. Vaughan, Anderson, Agran, and Winn (2004) reported that less acculturated Hispanic mothers expressed greater difficulty in preventing injury and also a greater demand for information about injury prevention when compared with more acculturated Hispanic and European American mothers.

Ribas and Bornstein (2005) investigated parenting knowledge (knowledge about child development, health and safety, and strategies to meet the physical, biological, socioemotional, and cognitive needs of children) in a group of Brazilian mothers and fathers. This type of knowledge is vital to parents' evaluation of their children's behaviors and development and to guide everyday decisions about childcare. Mothers had more parenting knowledge than fathers, whereas differences between parents of boys and girls were not observed. Mothers and fathers in the same family were correlated in their parenting knowledge. For mothers, education and child age predicted parenting knowledge, but for fathers, only education emerged as a predictor. The study indicated the influence of education and everyday activities for parenting knowledge. Ribas, Tymchuk, and Ribas (2006) evaluated parenting knowledge about home dangers and safety precautions in a group of Brazilian mothers and reported that mothers had considerable difficulty in identifying home dangers and even more difficulty in providing suitable precautions for prevention or remediation of those dangers. The study provided information that has been used to guide intervention programs with mothers and daycare center workers in Brazil.

Mother–Infant Interaction

Keller et al.'s (2005) investigation, which has been previously mentioned, and other similar studies conducted in Central and South America have identified both universal and culture-specific patterns of mother–infant interaction. Bornstein, Haynes, Pascual, Painter, and Galperin (1999), for instance, investigated exploratory, symbolic, and social play and interaction in 20-month-old Argentine and U.S. babies and their mothers. Similarities and differences between groups were observed. For example, in both cultural groups, boys engaged in more exploratory play than girls, and girls engaged in more symbolic play than boys. In the same direction, mothers of boys engaged in more exploratory play than mothers of girls, and mothers of girls engaged in more symbolic play than mothers of boys. It was observed that U.S. children and their mothers engaged in more exploratory play, whereas Argentine children and their mothers engaged in more symbolic play. Furthermore, Argentine mothers engaged in more social play and verbal praise than U.S. mothers. Bornstein et al. argued that differences between Argentine and U.S. dyads indicate different styles of exploration, representation, and interaction and that these differences are rooted in broader cultural concerns prevalent in the two societies: The Argentines are more allocentric or collectivist, whereas the U.S. Americans are more idiocentric or individualist.

Keller, Scholmerich, and Eibl-Eibesfeldt (1988) analyzed early communications in adult–child interactions with 2- to 6-month-old babies in two Western (West Germany and Greece) and two non-Western (Yanomami Indians and Trobriand Islanders) societies. Their findings corroborate assumptions about universal interactional structures. For example, positive vocalizations occurred mostly during eye contact, infants did not produce vocalizations during adult talking, and adults responded to positive and negative vocalizations differently. Leyendecker, Lamb, Scholmerich, and Fracasso (1995) explored the everyday experiences of 8- to 12-month-old babies from families who migrated recently from Central America (El Salvador, Nicaragua, and Guatemala) and from U.S. middle-class families of European American background. The groups differed, for example, in the opportunities for interaction with multiple people, which are relatively frequent in the social world of the Central American infants (Leyendecker, Harwood, Lamb, and Scholmerich, 2002).

Bornstein et al. (1992) investigated the maternal speech to infants in three Western cultures and one Eastern culture (Argentine, French, Japanese, and United States) to evaluate the influence of infant age and cultural background on the contents of the speech. Mothers were videotaped in naturalistic free play interactions at home with their 5- and 13-month-olds. Similarities across cultures were observed. For example, independent of culture, mothers spoke more to older infants, and mothers of 5-month-old infants favored affect over information in speaking, whereas mothers of 13-month-old infants favored information over affect. However, differences in content were also observed. Argentine mothers, for instance, displayed higher frequencies of direct statements than mothers in the other three cultures. This finding was linked to the authoritative traditional child-rearing orientation prevalent in Argentina. These findings provided evidence about universal aspects of maternal speech to infants as well as the influence of cultural forces in shaping aspects of this speech.

Cognitive Development

Cross-cultural studies focusing on cognitive development conducted in Central and South American countries have frequently reported similarities across cultures in developmental trends. In addition, the influence of social contexts and the importance of methodological designs have also been reported.

For example, Barrett and Behne (2005) investigated children's understanding of death as the cessation of agency in Ecuadorian Shuar and German children and found that, by age 4 years, causal cues to death bar agency attributions to animals and people, whereas cues to sleep do not. Consistent with the hypothesis of a living/dead discrimination mechanism as part of core cognitive architecture, no differences in developmental trajectories were observed across cultures. Callaghan et al. (2005) tested children's ability to pass false-belief tasks in five cultures (Canada,

India, Peru, Samoa, and Thailand) to evaluate the onset of a theory of mind. A synchrony was observed in the onset of mentalistic reasoning. Overall, independent of culture, 5-year-olds crossed the false-belief milestone. These studies provide some indication about the universality of basic aspects of the early mental state reasoning.

Brewis, Schmidt, and Casas (2003) compared the developmental trajectory of attention and impulse control of U.S. and Mexican children using a computerized test (Test of Variable Attention). In line with previous research on attention (e.g., Finley, Kagan, and Layne, 1972), similarities in the developmental trajectory across groups were observed. However, it was also reported that Mexican children made significantly more errors when compared to the U.S. children, indicating higher levels of inattentive and impulsive behaviors. Although Brewis et al. were not conclusive about probable causes of these differences (e.g., testing, cultural characteristics of the Mexican culture), the findings are especially relevant because some researchers have suggested that inattention and impulsivity in attention deficit hyperactivity disorder may be explained by delays in typical developmental trajectory for attention and impulse control. Worldwide attention deficit hyperactivity disorder is one of the most prevalent child mental disorders (Faraone, Sergeant, Gillberg, and Biederman 2003).

Several studies have investigated cognitive development, particularly mathematical skills, with children with limited or no schooling who make a living on the streets, especially in Brazil (e.g., Guberman, 1996; Nunes, Schliemann, and Carraher, 1993; Saxe, 1988). Saxe (1988), for example, compared the mathematical understandings of 10- to 12-year-old Brazilian street candy vendors with little or no schooling with those of nonvendors matched for age and schooling living in urban and rural settings. Saxe observed that both vendors and nonvendors developed nonstandard means to represent large numerical values. However, most vendors, in contrast to nonvendors, developed suitable strategies to solve arithmetic and ratio problems involving large numerical values. Usually, these investigations have stressed the relevance of everyday cultural practices for the development of cognitive abilities. Nonetheless, these studies have also documented the effects of poverty and the existence of children making their living on the streets in countries where fundamental education is supposed to be universal and compulsory.

Roazzi (1986) investigated the influence of natural and formal settings in class-inclusion reasoning tasks with 6- to 9-year-old children from two socioeconomic backgrounds (middle class and lower class). Children participated in sales transactions that embedded a class-inclusion task in natural and formal settings. As predicted, middle-class children performed better in formal settings, whereas lower class children performed better in informal settings. In line with these findings, Dias, Roazzi, O'Brien, and Harris (2005) studied the effect of the mode of problem presentation (make-believe fantasy or standard verbal) on reasoning about valid conditional syllogisms in three groups of 5-year-old children: English school children from middle-class families, Brazilian school children from middle-class families, and Brazilian children from lower class families who had never gone to school. Overall, the performance of the children was greatly improved in the make-believe mode. English and Brazilian children who were enrolled in school did not differ from one another, but both groups performed better than unschooled Brazilian children.

Maynard and Greenfield (2003) presented sets of preoperational and concrete operational spatial problems (from weaving domains, adapted from previous Piagetian research) to 4- to 13-year-old Zinancantec Mayan Mexican and U.S. children. It was reported that the sequence of operational development was invariant across domains and both cultures. However, Mayan children were more precocious with weaving problems, whereas U.S. children were more precocious with spatial problems. These findings provided support for an implicit ethnotheory of cognitive development in the Zinancantec weaving tools and their developmental sequencing.

Social Behavior

Topics like social behavior, attitudes, social representations, self-concepts, and self-perceptions have also been frequently studied in Central and South Americans (e.g., Valdez Medina, Mondragon, and Morelato, 2005). These studies have focused on a wide range of subjects. Like other studies, similarities and differences across cultural groups and links with societal characteristics have been identified. Pilgrim and Rueda Riedle (2002) investigated prosocial behavior of first-grade children in two countries usually classified as collectivist (Colombia) and individualist (United States). Overall, both U.S. and Latin children shared more with friends than with other classmates. U.S. children were more likely to take candy from another child without permission, but contrary to expectations, U.S. children also shared more than Colombian children did. Pilgrim and Rueda Riedle pointed out that friendship between children was a better predictor of prosocial behavior than was their classification into the collectivist–individualist dichotomy. Chen et al. (2004) investigated associations between self-perceptions of social and scholastic competence in a sample of Brazilian, Canadian, Chinese, and Italian children. Similarities and differences in the patterns of associations between self-perceptions and social and school adjustment across countries were observed. For example, self-perceptions of social competence were positively associated with academic achievement in Canadian and Chinese children, but not in Brazilian and Italian children. Self-perceptions of social competence were negatively associated with shyness in Brazilian, Canadian, and Italian children, but not in Chinese children. These findings are consistent with the societal values prevalent in each culture.

Conclusion

This chapter provided psychologically relevant information about the formation of the South and Central American countries and the people in the region. The rich cultural diversity of regional groups, which is usually overlooked and masked by the use of monolithic terms like "Latin American," was discussed. A bibliometric analysis offered several indicators about cross-cultural developmental psychology in Central and South America. Analyses indicated, for example, that the region has been underrepresented in developmental science. Furthermore, it was reported that the proportion of developmental studies involving Central and South America that can be classified as cultural or cross-cultural increased consistently between 1986 and 2005. The predominance of empirical articles, studies on psychosocial topics, studies involving two cultures, and the use of self-reports is a profile frequently associated with cross-cultural psychology. Nonetheless, it is worth noting that researchers (e.g., Keller and Greenfield, 2000; van de Vijver et al., Chapter 2, in this volume) have pointed out that findings from two-culture studies are usually harder to interpret because of rival hypotheses and because the use of self-reports tends to limit data collection to more privileged samples. The analysis also revealed topics more frequently investigated and particularly relevant for the development of basic and applied research.

A review of developmental studies involving participants from Central and South America was presented. Because of space limitations, a selected number of areas (poverty and street children, parenting, mother–infant interaction, cognitive development, and social behavior) were highlighted. These developmental investigations have not only contributed to our understanding of both culture-general and culture-specific aspects of human development, but also documented the impact of significant social issues and provided information that can be useful for intervention programs.

Although Central and South American countries differ significantly in levels of economic, scientific, and human development, all of these countries have significant economic and social problems that have negatively affected children and their families. It is evident that more information is needed to help these people, and cross-cultural developmental psychology can provide most of this information. It is also important to acknowledge that conducting research in Central and South America is not an easy task. The levels of illiteracy and poverty, for instance, present important challenges that researchers need to overcome. In this respect, the growth in the number of cross-cultural developmental investigations in Central and South America is good news.

Acknowledgments

Preparation of this work was partly supported by the Fundação José Bonifácio, FUJB, Brazil. I thank Marc H. Bornstein and Adriana F. P. Ribas for helpful comments on earlier drafts of this work and Roberto Nicolas Pimmingstorfer Gimena for assistance in the database construction. I also thank Clarice Moreira Portugal, Ludmilla Tassano Pitrowsky, Maicon Pereira da Cunha, Midori Takanaca de Decco, and Pamela Ramos Blanco for their research assistance.

References

American Psychological Association (2001). *Publication manual* (5th ed.). Washington: American Psychological Association.
Aptekar, L. (1989). Characteristics of the street children of Colombia. *Child Abuse and Neglect, 13*, 427–437.
Ardila, R. (2004). A psicologia Latinoamericana: El printer media siglo. [Latin American psychology: The first half century.] *Interamerican Journal of Psychology, 38*, 317–322.
Barrett, H. C., and Behne, T. (2005). Children's understanding of death as the cessation of agency: A test using sleep versus death. *Cognition, 96*, 93–108.
Bartlett, S. N. (2002). The problem of children's injuries in low-income countries: A review. *Health Policy and Planning, 17*, 1–13.
Betancourt, H., and Lopez, S. R. (1993). The study of culture, ethnicity, and race in American psychology. *American Psychologist, 48*, 629–637.
Billig, O., Gillin, J., and Davidson, W. (1948). Aspects of personality and culture in a Guatemalan community: Ethnological and Rorschach approaches. Part II. *Journal of Personality, 16*, 326–368.
Bornstein, M. H., Haynes, O. M., Pascual, L., Painter, K. M., and Galperin, C. (1999). Play in two societies: Pervasiveness of process, specificity of structure. *Child Development, 70*, 317–331.
Bornstein, M. H., Tal, J., Rahn, C., Galperin, C. Z., Pecheux, M., Lamour, M., et al. (1992). Functional analysis of the contents of maternal speech to infants of 5 and 13 months in four cultures: Argentina, France, Japan, and the United States. *Developmental Psychology, 28*, 593–603.
Bradley, R. H., and Corwyn, R. F. (2002). Socioeconomic status and child development. *Annual Review of Psychology, 53*, 371–399.
Brewis, A., Schmidt, K. L., and Casas, C. A. S. (2003). Cross-cultural study of the childhood developmental trajectory of attention and impulse control. *International Journal of Behavioral Development, 27*, 174–181.
Brouwers, S. A., van Hemert, D. A., Breugelmans, S. M., and van de Vijver, F. J. R. (2004). A historical analysis of empirical studies published in the *Journal of Cross-Cultural Psychology*: 1970-2004. *Journal of Cross-Cultural Psychology, 35*, 251–262.
Bryan, E. S. (1930). Variations in the responses of infants during first ten days of post-natal life. *Child Development, 1*, 56–77.
Bulmer-Thomas, V. (2001). Latin American studies: Economics. In N. J. Smelser and P. B. Baltes (Eds.), *International encyclopedia of the social and behavioral sciences* (pp. 8400–8405). New York: Elsevier Science.
Callaghan, T., Rochat, P., Lillard, A., Claux, M. L., Odden, H., Itakura, S., et al. (2005). Synchrony in the onset of mental-state reasoning. Evidence from five cultures. *Psychological Science, 16*, 378–384.
Chen, X., Zappulla, C., Coco, A. L., Schneider, B., Kaspar, V., De Oliveira, A. M., et al. (2004). Self-perceptions of competence in Brazilian, Canadian, Chinese and Italian children: Relations with social and school adjustment. *International Journal of Behavioral Development, 28*, 129–138.
Conger, R. D., and Donnellan, M. B. (2007). An interactionist perspective on the socioeconomic context of human development. *Annual Review of Psychology, 58*, 175–199.
Cote, L. R., and Bornstein, M. H. (2000). Acculturation. In L. Balter (Ed.), *Parenthood in America: An encyclopedia* (pp. 11–14). Denver, CO: ABC-CLIO.
Dasen, P. R., and Mishra, R. C. (2000). Cross-cultural views on human development in the third millennium. *International Journal of Behavioral Development, 24*, 428–434.

Dias, M.G. B. B., Roazzi, A., O'Brien, D. P., and Harris, P. L. (2005). Logical reasoning and fantasy contexts: Eliminating differences between children with and without experience in school. *Revista Interamericana de Psicologia, 39,* 13–22.

Economic Commission for Latin America and the Caribbean (2005). Child poverty in Latin America. *Challenges, 1,* 4–9. Retrieved March 17, 2007. from http://www.cepal.org.

Economic Commission for Latin America and the Caribbean (2006). Pueblos indígenas y afrodescendientes de América Latina y el Caribe. Documento de Proyecto. Series CEPAL, 72. Retrieved September 10, 2006, from http://www.eclac.cl.

Enesco, I., and Navarro, A. (2003). The development of the conception of socioeconomic mobility in children from Mexico and Spain. *Journal of Genetic Psychology, 164,* 293–317.

Faraone, T. V., Sergeant, J., Gillberg, C., and Biederman, J. (2003). The worldwide prevalence of ADHD: Is it an American condition? *World Psychiatry, 2,* 104–113.

Finley, G. E., Kagan, J., and Layne, O. (1972). Development of young children's attention to normal and distorted stimuli: A cross-cultural study. *Developmental Psychology, 6,* 288–292.

Flint, V. I. J. (2006). Christopher Columbus. Encyclopædia Britannica. Retrieved November 24, 2006, from http://www.britannica.com/eb/article-223123.

Gonzalez, M. L. (1995). How many indigenous people? In G. Psacharopolous and H. A. Patrinos (Eds.), *Indigenous People and poverty in Latin America: An empirical analysis* (pp. 21–39). Washington, DC: World Bank. Retrieved September 10, 2006, from http://www.worldbank.org/indigenous.

Greenfield, P. M. (1999). Historical change and cognitive change: A two-decade follow-up study in Zinacantan, a Maya community in Chiapas, Mexico. *Mind, Culture, and Activity, 6,* 92–108.

Guberman, S. R. (1996). The development of everyday mathematics in Brazilian children with limited formal education. *Child Development, 67,* 1609–1623.

Harkness, S., and Keefer, C. H. (2000). Contributions of cross-cultural psychology to research and interventions in education and health. *Journal of Cross-Cultural Psychology, 31,* 92–109.

Hutz, C. S., and Koller, S. H. (1997). Issues regarding the development of street children. *Estudos de Psicologia, 2,* 175–197.

Jahoda, G. (1958). Child Animism: I. A critical survey of cross-cultural research. *Journal of Social Psychology, 47,* 197–212.

Kagan, J., Klein, R. E., Haith, M. M., and Morrison, F. J. (1973). Memory and meaning in two cultures. *Child Development, 44,* 221–223.

Kaslow, F. W. (2001). Families and family psychology at the millennium: Intersecting crossroads. *American Psychologist, 56,* 37–46.

Keller, H., Borke, J., Yovsi, R., Lohaus, A., and Jensen, H. (2005). Cultural orientations and historical changes as predictors of parenting behaviour. *International Journal of Behavioral Development, 29,* 229–237.

Keller, H., and Greenfield, P. M. (2000). History and future of development in cross-cultural psychology. *Journal of Cross-Cultural Psychology, 31,* 52–62.

Keller, H., Scholmerich, A., and Eibl-Eibesfeldt, I. (1988). Communication patterns in adult-infant interactions in Western and non-Western cultures. *Journal of Cross-Cultural Psychology, 19,* 427–445.

Latin America. (2006). Wikipedia, the Free Encyclopedia. Retrieved June 14, 2006, from http://en.wikipedia.org.

le Roux, J., and Smith, C. S. (1998). Causes and characteristics of the street child phenomenon: A global perspective. *Adolescence, 33,* 683–688.

Levak, M. D. (1969). Eidetic images among the Bororo of Brazil. *Journal of Social Psychology, 79,* 135–137.

Leyendecker, B., Harwood, R. L., Lamb, M. E., and Scholmerich, A. (2002). Mothers' socialisation goals and evaluations of desirable and undesirable everyday situations in two diverse cultural groups. *International Journal of Behavioral Development, 26,* 248–258.

Leyendecker, B., Lamb, M. E., Scholmerich, A., and Fracasso, M. P. (1995). The social worlds of 8- and 12-month-old infants: Early experiences in two subcultural contexts. *Social Development, 4,* 194–208.

Marsella, A. J. (1998). Urbanization, mental health, and social deviancy: A review of issues and research. *American Psychologist, 53,* 624–634.

Maynard, A. E., and Greenfield, P. M. (2003). Implicit cognitive development in cultural tools and children: Lessons from Maya Mexico. *Cognitive Development, 18,* 489–510.

Morelli, G. A., Rogoff, B., and Angelillo, C. (2003). Cultural variation in young children's access to work or involvement in specialised child-focused activities. *International Journal of Behavioral Development, 27,* 264–274.

Morelli, G. A., Rogoff, B., Oppenheim, D., and Goldsmith, D. (1992). Cultural variation in infants' sleeping arrangements: Questions of independence. *Developmental Psychology, 28,* 604–613.

Mull, D. S., Agran, P., Winn, D. G., and Anderson, C. L. (2001). Injury in children of low-income Mexican, Mexican American, and non-Hispanic white mothers in the USA: A focused ethnography. *Social Science and Medicine, 52*, 1081–1091.

Nunes, T., Schliemann, A.-L., and Carraher, D. (1993). *Street mathematics and school mathematics.* New York: Cambridge University Press.

Öngel, Ü., and Smith, P. B. (1994). Who are we and where are we going? JCCP approaches its 100th issue. *Journal of Cross-Cultural Psychology, 25,* 25–53.

Otero, G. A. (1997). Poverty, cultural disadvantage and brain development: A study of pre-school children in Mexico. *Electroencephalography and Clinical Neurophysiology, 102,* 512–516.

Pilgrim, C., and Rueda Riedle, A. (2002). The importance of social context in cross-cultural comparisons: First graders in Colombia and the United States. *Journal of Genetic Psychology, 163,* 283–295.

Posada, G., Jacobs, A., Richmond, M. K., Carbonell, O. A., Alzate, G., Bustamante, M. R., et al. (2002). Maternal caregiving and infant security in two cultures. *Developmental Psychology, 38,* 67–78.

Raffaelli, M., and Koller, S. H. (2005). Future expectations of Brasilian street youth. *Journal of Adolescence, 28,* 249–262.

Ribas, R. C., Jr., and Bornstein, M. H. (2005). Parenting knowledge: Similarities and differences in Brazilian mothers and fathers. *Interamerican Journal of Psychology, 39,* 5–12.

Ribas, R. C., Jr., Tymchuk, A. J., and Ribas, A. F. P. (2006). Brazilian mothers' knowledge about home dangers and safety precautions. An initial evaluation. *Social Science and Medicine, 63,* 1979–1888.

Roazzi, A. (1986). Implicações metodológicas na pesquisa transcultural: A influencia do contexto social em tarefas lógicas [Methodological implications of transcultural research: The influence of social context on logical tasks]. *Arquivos Brasileiros de Psicologia, 38,* 71–91.

Robins, R. W., Gosling, S. D., and Craik, K. H. (2000). Trends in psychology: An empirical issue. *American Psychologist, 55,* 276–277.

Robinson, D. J. (2005). Latin América. Microsoft Encarta Online Encyclopedia. Retrieved April 18, 2006, from http://encarta.msn.com.

Rumbaut, R.G. (2001). Latin American studies: Economics. In N. J. Smelser and P. B. Baltes (Eds.), *International encyclopedia of the social and behavioral sciences* (pp. 845–849). New York: Elsevier Science.

Salazar, J. M. (1997). La investigacion transcultural en 30 anos de la *Revista Interamericana de Psicologia* [Cross-cultural research in 30 years of the *Interamerican Journal of Psychology*]. *Interamerican Journal of Psychology, 31,* 169–184.

Saxe, G. B. (1988). The mathematics of child street vendors. *Child Development, 59,* 1415–1425.

Segall, M. H., Lonner, W. J., and Berry, J. W. (1998). Cross-cultural psychology as a scholarly discipline: On the flowering of culture in behavioral research. *American Psychologist, 53,* 1101–1110.

Smith, P. B. (2001). Cross-cultural psychology: Where next? *Psychology and Developing Societies, 13,* 141–151.

Sosa, J. J. S., and Valderrama Iturbe, P. (2001). Psychology in Latin America: Historical reflections and perspectives. *International Journal of Psychology, 36,* 384–394.

Stanislawski, D. (1959). *The individuality of Portugal: A study in historical-political geography.* Austin, TX: University of Texas Press.

Stewart-Gambino, H. W. (2001). Latin American studies: Religion. In N. J. Smelser and P. B. Baltes (Eds.), *International encyclopedia of the social and behavioral sciences* (pp. 8426–8430). New York: Elsevier.

Super, C. M., Herrera, M. G., and Mora, J. O. (1990). Long-term effects of food supplementation and psychosocial intervention on the physical growth of Colombian infants at risk of malnutrition. *Child Development, 61,* 29–49.

Treaty of Tordesillas (2006). Wikipedia, the Free Encyclopedia. Retrieved September 24, 2006, from http://en.wikipedia.org.

Tudge, J. R. H., Doucet, F., Odero, D., Sperb, T. M., Piccinini, C. A., and Lopes, R. S. (2006). A Window into different cultural worlds: Young children's everyday activities in the United States, Brazil, and Kenya. *Child Development, 77,* 1446–1469.

United Nations Children's Fund (2004). Ensuring the rights of indigenous children. *Innocenti Digest,* 11. Florence, Italy: UNICEF Innocenti Research Centre.

United Nations Statistics Division (1999). Standard country or area codes for statistical use. Retrieved September 10, 2006, from http://millenniumindicators.un.org.

United Nations Statistics Division (2006). Demographic and social statistics. Online data files Retrieved September 10, 2006, from http://unstats.un.org/unsd/demographic/.

Valdez Medina, J. L., Mondragon, J. A., and Morelato, G. S. (2005). El autoconcepto en ninos Mexicanos y Argentinos [The self concept in Mexican and Argentinean children]. *Revista Interamericana de Psicologia, 39*, 253–258.

Valenzuela, M. (1997). Maternal sensitivity in a developing society: The context of urban poverty and infant chronic undernutrition. *Developmental Psychology, 33*, 845–855.

van de Vijver, F., and Hambleton, R. K. (1996). Translating tests. Some practical guidelines. *European Psychologist, 1*, 89–99.

van de Vijver, F. J. R., and Leung, K. (2000). Methodological issues in psychological research on culture. *Journal of Cross-Cultural Psychology, 31*, 33–51.

Vaughan, E., Anderson, C., Agran, P., and Winn, D. (2004). Cultural differences in young children's vulnerability to injuries: A risk and protection perspective. *Health Psychology, 23*, 289–298.

World Data (2006). Encyclopædia Britannica. Retrieved September 12, 2006, from http://www.britannica.com.

18
European Union

MARTIN PINQUART and RAINER K. SILBEREISEN

Introduction

As of 2007, the European Union (EU) consists of 27 member states, and approximately 80 million people age 0 to 14 years and another 62 million people age 15 to 24 years live in the EU (European Commission, 2006). Although many scientists refer to young people from Western countries, such as those that constitute the EU, as one general group, we have to be aware that there are similarities in the development of young people in the EU (e.g., based on similar economic conditions, common traditions, and programs of the EU targeted at children and adolescents) as well as differences, both among and within the EU countries.

Based on the focus of this handbook on cross-cultural developmental science, the present chapter focuses on these similarities and differences by comparing conditions of growing up and psychological development of young people from the 27 EU states. Because of space limitations, we do not focus on comparisons between EU countries and other parts of the world, such as non-Western countries. We start with some general comments on the history and structure of the EU, followed by data on contexts for the development of young people (family, peer group, childcare, school, and work) and by research on attitudes, psychosocial transitions, subjective well-being, physical health, and problem behavior. Finally, we discuss new demands and resources needed for young people's mastery of future challenges in a changing EU. We rely mainly on statistics from the United Nations, the EU, and the United Nations Children's Fund (UNICEF) and on data from large cross-national studies, such as Health Behavior in School-aged Children (HBSC; Currie et al., 2004), the European School Survey Project on Alcohol and other Drugs (ESPAD; Hibell et al., 2004), the Programme for International Student Assessment (PISA; Organisation for Economic Co-operation and Development [OECD], 2004), and the Euronet study (Alsaker and Flammer, 1999). In the case of studies that collected cross-sectional data at more than one time period (HBSC, ESPAD, and PISA), we mainly focus on the last available survey. However, we also report selected comparisons across repeated surveys. Here, although a focus on longer intervals would provide additional insights, because of space limitations and lack of comparative data, we focus on the last two decades, a time that has witnessed much social change in Europe and in Eastern Europe in particular. If no data from large cross-national studies are available for a variable of interest, we also include data from smaller studies that compare some but not all European countries. Furthermore, our focus is on data about young people from the present 27 EU countries, irrespective of whether the country in question was already a member of the EU at the time of data collection.

The present chapter focuses on cross-national similarities and differences. When comparing data from different countries, we use the term "cross-national" rather than "cross-cultural" because there is a lot of cultural diversity within the European countries (e.g., based on different ethnic backgrounds). In the EU, the percentage of foreigners among people younger than 20 years old varies between 44% in Luxembourg and less than 1% in most Eastern EU members (European Commission, 2006).

Cross-national studies may focus on positioning effects (whether differences in the mean levels of variables are observed between countries) or patterning effects (whether the size of associations of variables varies between nations; Feldman and Rosenthal, 1994). Because available studies were usually restricted to positioning effects and because in the few other studies almost no national differences in the size of associations were observed, the main focus of the chapter will be on positioning effects.

Cross-national studies are susceptible to measurement artifacts. Sources of bias may exist on the level of the construct under investigation, on the method level, and on the item level. For example, even in otherwise well-planned studies, observed national differences may, in part, result from a lack of comparability of the samples (e.g., because of inevitable differences in the educational system) or from inadequate item translation (van de Vijver and Leung, 1997). Because of space limitations, we do not report measures taken by the authors of the reviewed studies for securing equivalence of the samples and measures. However, if serious methodological doubts arose regarding the quality of a cross-national study, we did not include it here.

History and Membership of the European Union

The historical roots of the EU lie in the aftermath of World War II and the determination of Europeans to prevent such killing and destruction from ever happening again. In the early years, cooperation among the EU countries was mainly about trade and economic aspects. In 1957, Belgium, West Germany, Luxembourg, France, Italy, and The Netherlands signed the Treaties of Rome, creating the European Economic Community (EEC). The EU has grown in size with successive waves of accessions. Denmark, Ireland, and the United Kingdom joined in 1973 followed by Greece in 1981, Spain and Portugal in 1986, and Austria, Finland, and Sweden in 1995. The EU welcomed 10 new countries in 2004: Cyprus, the Czech Republic, Estonia, Hungary, Latvia, Lithuania, Malta, Poland, Slovakia, and Slovenia. Bulgaria and Romania followed in 2007, and Croatia and Turkey began membership negotiations. In 2007, the EU embraced 27 countries and approximately 480 million people. Starting with a common economic market, the EU has developed common policies in a very wide range of fields, such as finance, environment, culture, and social politics.

From political, linguistic, and religious points of view, Europe can be divided along a north–south line. Northern European countries share a culture and mentality that is characterized by political liberalism, Protestantism, and related values. Southern and many central European countries have a different cultural background that is characterized by certain types of conservatism, Catholicism, an emphasis on family ties, and Romanic language. In addition, EU members can be divided along an east–west line. The new Eastern EU members had socialist/communist regimes for decades, whereas Western Europe maintained a capitalist market economy. In addition, most new Eastern EU members share a basis in the Slavic culture and languages, and the Orthodox Church has a strong influence in Bulgaria and Romania. Between the fall of the Iron Curtain and the admission to the EU, the amount of political and economic change varied considerably between the Eastern European countries. For example, Hungary had been experimenting with modified market principles for 15 years prior to the political changes of 1989, so that subsequent market reforms were less drastic than those experienced in other Eastern European countries. In addition, countries with advanced industry before the political transition, such as the Czech Republic, had better infrastructure for successful market transformation.

Despite some common traditions and values, each EU member has its own history, culture, and institutional structure. The countries differ from each other in a number of important respects, including economically, legally, politically, and socially. For example, large differences emerge in socioeconomic indicators, such as the per capita gross domestic product (GDP). Whereas in 2005, Luxembourg and Ireland had a GDP in purchasing power standard (PPS) of more than 30,000, Bulgaria and Romania had a GDP of less than 10,000 (European Commission, 2006). Note that the PPS is an artificial currency unit that reflects differences in national price levels that are not taken into account by exchange rates. The EU countries also differ on a number of less tangible and measurable social qualities. For example, The Netherlands is very tolerant with respect to different lifestyles and fundamental values (e.g., abortion, drugs, and so forth), whereas Southern European EU members are much more conservative in this regard. These differences may impact the development and the lives of young people.

Contexts of the Development of Young People in the European Union

Human development is embedded in contexts. National differences in family structure and processes, peer relations, nonparental childcare, schools, and neighborhoods may explain, at least in part, observed national differences in the mean levels of indicators of child development. Thus, the following section gives an overview of national differences and similarities in important contexts of the development of children and adolescents, namely the family, peer relations, nonparental childcare, and schools.

The Family

Many studies on child and adolescent development have shown that parental socioeconomic status, growing up in a complete family, positive parent–child relationships, high levels of authoritative parenting, and availability of cultural goods are important predictors of psychological and physical health and of success in school (Clarke-Stewart and Dunn, 2006). Available cross-national studies have focused on parental socioeconomic status and family structure.

In the EU, there is growing concern about poverty among children and among families with children. Economic differences across EU members clearly relate to differences in the socioeconomic conditions of growing up. For example, when defining family affluence by car ownership, frequency of traveling away for family holidays, computer ownership, and whether a child has his or her own bedroom, the highest percentages of 11- to 15-year-olds living in families with a low level of affluence are observed in Eastern EU members (except Slovenia), ranging from 55.9% in Latvia to 38.7% in Hungary (World Health Organization [WHO], 2005). Low levels of affluence are also more often observed in Southern Europe (ranging from 22.4% in Italy to 28.8% in Portugal) compared to Western and Northern European countries (9.0% in The Netherlands to 19.1% in Belgium). Data concerning the percentage of children less than 18 years old living in relative poverty (as defined by household income of less than 50% of the national median income) were available from 18 EU members (data were lacking for the Baltic states, Bulgaria, and Romania). The relative poverty rates were highest in Southern Europe and the United Kingdom (e.g., Italy, 16.6%; Portugal, 15.6%; United Kingdom, 15.4%) and lowest in the Nordic countries (Sweden, 4.2%; Finland, 2.8%; Denmark, 2.4%), reflecting regional differences in economic conditions and social policy (WHO, 2005).

In most countries, increased family affluence is associated with positive health behaviors such as exercising regularly and eating more fruit. In addition, perception of family wealth is associated with children's happiness and feeling of confidence in all countries (Mullan and Currie, 2000).

Similar to other Western countries, *families* in the EU have changed markedly in the last decades, and terms such as "modern childhood" and "children of postmodernity" are used in the sociological literature for describing changing conditions of growing up (Scott, 2004). For example, high rates of workforce participation are observed for European mothers, which are also associated with high utilization of extrafamiliar daycare. Similarly, low and declining birth rates in EU countries are associated with a rise in the number of children growing up without siblings. In addition, an increasing number of children grow up with single mothers or in patchwork families, although the divorce rate of almost all EU countries is lower than in the United States. The highest increases in divorce rates and numbers of single-parent families are observed in EU countries where constraints by religious values are weak. In the HBSC study, the percentage of young people living with both parents was highest in Southern Europe (Malta, 93%; Greece, 91%; Italy, 90%) and lowest in England (67%), Wales (69%), Denmark (69%), and Sweden (70%). Stepfamilies are more common in Northern and Northwestern Europe, whereas the proportion of single-parent families is highest in Eastern Europe (e.g., Latvia, 19%; Currie et al., 2004).

In the PISA study, the availability of possessions and activities related to "classical culture," such as classic literature, books of poetry, or works of art, was related to better student test performance (OECD, 2004). The participating Eastern European countries (Latvia, Slovakia, Hungary, Czech Republic, and Poland) scored above the median, whereas some Western countries, such as The Netherlands, Belgium, and Ireland, scored below the median. However, availability of computers in the home is still lower in some Eastern EU members than in the other countries. For example, in the 2001/2002 HBSC study, 64% of adolescents from Lithuania, 51% from Latvia, and 41% from Estonia reported that there was no computer in their family home. The average of all countries participating in that study was 23% (Currie et al., 2004).

Children from EU countries give, on average, quite positive judgements about their families. For example, the majority of 11- to 15-year-olds from all EU countries found it easy to talk to their mothers and fathers. The percentages were highest in Slovenia (88%) and Poland (85%) and lowest in Belgium (63%) and Lithuania (66%) (Petersen et al., 2004). Similarly, a comparative study of 13- to 16-year-olds from 12 European cities (East Berlin, West Berlin, and Frankfurt/Oder, Germany; Slubice and Warsaw, Poland; Moscow, Russia; Prague, Czech Republic; Ioannina and Corfu, Greece; Budapest, Hungary; Bratislava, Slovakia; and Sofia, Bulgaria) from 1991 found that the great majority of adolescents evaluated the emotional climate in their family favorably. In that study, only 5% judged their family climate to be poor or very poor (Steiner, 1995). Above-average levels were found in Warsaw, Moscow, Budapest, Ioannina, Prague, Bratislava, and Corfu, and below average levels appeared in Sofia and Berlin.

Nonetheless, a less positive picture emerges from the Young Voices poll from 2000/2001 (UNICEF, 2001) about experiences of shouting and hitting within the family. Although the participating 9- to 17-year-olds described relationships with parents in strongly positive terms, approximately 69% of the children from Central European states (Czech Republic, Hungary, Poland, and Slovakia) experienced shouting or hitting, compared to 63% of children and adolescents from the Baltic States and 54% of those from Western Europe. Not surprisingly, verbal aggression was three times more common than physical aggression. In addition, hitting was more common in lower income families (16%) and was proportionately highest in Central Europe (21%). Higher levels of physical punishment in some Eastern European countries may reflect greater distress in parents as a result of rapid social change (e.g., associated unemployment) and/or differences in parenting styles. For example, a comparative study of Polish and German adolescents from the early 1990s showed that 80% of Polish adolescents compared to 40% of their German peers agreed that children should learn discipline and obedience as early as possible (Melzer, Lukowski, and Schmidt, 1991). However, these East–West differences may have declined with increased opening of Central and Eastern European countries to the West.

Vazsonyi and Belliston (2006) asked approximately 7,000 adolescents from Hungary, The Netherlands, Switzerland, and the United States to fill out a self-report measure of perceived family and parenting processes and measures of anxiety and depressive symptoms. In general, the young reported moderate to high levels of positive parenting behavior and low to moderate levels of conflict with their parents. Hungarian fathers were perceived as more controlling and less supportive than Dutch and Swiss fathers, and Hungarian mothers were perceived as less supportive than mothers from Switzerland and the United States. Although these differences indicate lower levels of authoritative parenting in Hungary than in the Western countries, national differences were generally small (less than 0.4 standard deviation units). Vazsonyi and Belliston next analyzed predictors of anxiety and depression in the four samples. The patterns of associations between individual parenting processes and internalizing symptoms were highly similar across the cultural contexts. High levels of parental support and low levels of conflict predicted low symptom levels in all samples, thus indicating that key parenting processes worked in a similar manner in the four countries.

Finally, in a comparative study of concepts about parenting of mothers from three Western EU members (Belgium, France, and Italy) and four non-EU countries (Argentina, Israel, Japan, and the United States), Bornstein et al. (1998) found few cross-national differences. Nonetheless, French mothers rated their investment in parenting and the importance of effort to parenting success as relatively low, which may, in part, be explained by high availability and use of a very modern infant and childcare system (in which almost 100% of 4-year-olds are enrolled).

Friendships and Peer Groups

Being linked to and accepted by peers is crucial to the healthy development of children and adolescents. In the HBSC study, approximately 60% to 90% of European adolescents reported having three or more friends of the same gender (Currie et al., 2004). However, national differences were observed in the way young people chose friends. Young people from the United Kingdom and the Scandinavian countries were most likely to have three or more friends (frequencies of approximately 80% to 90%), and those from Mediterranean and Eastern European countries were least likely to have three or more friends, with proportions of 70% or less.

After school, a substantial amount of adolescents' time is spent among peers and friends, such as playing sports or hanging around. The percentages of adolescents reporting spending time with friends on four or more afternoons per week also varies widely between the countries, in part depending on whether school hours were extended to the afternoon. For example, more than 60% of 13-year-olds in Malta reported meeting their friends after school on a regular base, compared to less than 30% in the French part of Belgium, Greece, and Sweden. In all countries, peer contact increased from early to middle adolescence. In Southern European countries, boys were more likely than girls to socialize in the evening. This may reflect their higher freedom and the fact that girls spent more time on homework (Currie et al., 2004). In the Euronet study, the amount of daily time spent in hanging around with peers differed between 0.22 hours in Germany and 1.64 hours in Finland (Flammer, Alsaker, and Noack, 1999).

Spending time with friends seemed to become more important over time in the Eastern European countries. For example, data from three waves (1993/1994, 1997/1998, and 2001/2002) of the HBSC study were available on the percentage of adolescents who reported spending time with their friends after school four to five times a week. These numbers increased in the Eastern European samples from 33.5% to 36.5% and 41.8%, whereas a small decline was observed in their Western peers (from 38.7% to 35.2%; Currie et al., 2004; King et al., 1996; Settertobule, 2000).

Not surprisingly, the Western youth culture has become widespread in Eastern Europe (Roberts and Fagan, 1999). The fall of the Iron Curtain and the integration of Eastern European countries in the EU were associated with high curiosity of Eastern European adolescents about the life of their Western peers. For example, in the Euronet study, youth from Eastern Europe had strong preferences for meeting their peers from Western Europe. This interest, however, was not reciprocated by their Western peers shortly after the fall of the Iron Curtain (Flanagan and Botcheva, 1999).

Participation in formal civic associations is considered a key activity in establishing social integration. In Nordic countries, an ample majority of youth belong to at least one association, as opposed to a minority in Southern European countries (Instituto di Ricerca, 2001). For example, 82% of young people from Sweden and 77% of their peers from Denmark reported belonging to such an organization, compared to 40% of young people from Portugal, 38% from Spain, and 36% from Greece. In general, young people most often belonged to sport associations. Membership in youth organizations varied from 18% in The Netherlands and Italy to 2% in Belgium and Greece.

Nonparental Child Care

The officially defined general objectives for pre-primary education focus on the development of children's independence, well-being, self-confidence, citizenship, and preparation for life and learning in school (European Commission, 2005). By the age of 4 years, most children from the EU are enrolled in pre-primary educational institutions, although numbers of hours of enrollment and childcare quality vary considerably (Tietze and Cryer, 1999), and attendance is not compulsory. The participation rate exceeds 60% in nearly all countries. For example, in 2001/2002, almost 100% of 4-year-olds attended childcare in Belgium, France, Italy, Luxembourg, Spain, and the United Kingdom. However, low rates persist in Poland (33%) and Finland (44%) (European Commission, 2005).

Between 1979 and 2002, the participation rates of 4-year-olds in pre-primary education increased in most European countries, with countries having lower levels initially showing the greatest increases. For example, participation rates more than quadrupled in Portugal (from 18% to 79%) and more than doubled in Sweden (from 28% to 78%) and Finland (from 18% to 44%). Increases were also observed in most Eastern European countries. Between 1989 and 2003, participation rates increased from 57% to 78% in Latvia, from 56% to 76% in Slovenia, from 62% to 81% in Estonia, from 67% to 75% in Bulgaria, and from 62% to 72% in Romania. Relatively stable rates were observed in the Czech Republic, Hungary, Poland, and Slovakia.

In the PISA study, children who attended preschool for more than 1 year showed an advantage in the test for mathematical abilities (OECD, 2004). However, the effects of nonparental childcare on child development also depend on the quality of the care. For example, recommended maximum numbers of 4-year-old children per adult in pre-primary education varies between 7 in Finland and 30 in Northern Ireland, Ireland, and Greece (European Commission, 2005). Deynoot-Schaub, Gevers, and Riksen-Walraven (2005) observed a decline in childcare quality in the Netherlands between 1995 and 2001, probably reflecting insufficient financial support by the local communities, a shortage of qualified caregivers, and increased workload within the daycare centers. In addition to providing sufficient funding for high-quality childcare services, further efforts are needed for providing adequate services for children under 3 years of age (Tietze and Cryer, 1999).

A minority of children live without their parents because the parents lack the means to care for their children appropriately, the children have been abandoned by their parents, or the parents have died. A survey by the WHO regional office for Europe reported high use of institutional care for young children in need. For example, in 2002, rates per 10,000 children under 3 years old in institutional care varied from less than 1 in the United Kingdom to 88 in Bulgaria (Browne, Hamilton-Giachritsis, Johnson, and Ostergren, 2006). The overall rate of institutionalization in

Europe (including non-EU members) was 14.4. Higher rates were observed in Eastern than in Western Europe. In fact, between 1989 and 2003, increases in the proportion of children ages 0 to 3 years in infant homes were observed in many Eastern European countries (Estonia, +86%; Latvia, +54%; Romania, +56%; Slovakia, +44%; Lithuania, +25%; Bulgaria, +23%; and Poland, +6%), in part based on increasing poverty. However, proportions declined in the Czech Republic (–18%), Hungary (–25%), and Slovenia (–42%) (UNICEF, 2005).

Therapeutic foster care and rehabilitation services have been introduced in some EU members, such as Slovenia and the United Kingdom, to prevent institutional care for children. Although in 1990 the world was shocked by the conditions found in Romanian orphanages where the worst homes left children living in subhuman conditions, all of the large Ceausescu-era institutions have now been closed down in favor of alternatives such as foster care, adoption, and small state-run homes.

The School System

Compulsory education begins between the age of 4 years in Luxembourg and Northern Ireland and the age of 7 years in Denmark, Finland, Sweden, and Estonia and ends between ages of 14 and 18 (European Commission, 2005). For example, compulsory school attendance covers 8 years in Lithuania and Romania; 9 years in Austria, Belgium, Bulgaria, the Czech Republic, Denmark, Estonia, Finland, Germany, and Sweden; 10 years in France, Poland, and Spain; 11 years in Latvia, Malta, Luxembourg, and most parts of the United Kingdom; 12 years in The Netherlands and Northern Ireland; and 13 years in Hungary.

Countries vary in the amount of wealth spent on education. Whereas in 2001 EU members spent, on average, 5.1% of their GDP for education, the percentages varied between 3.8% (Luxembourg) and 8.5% (Denmark). In 2003, the ratio of pupils to teaching staff in primary education varied between 10.6 (Italy) and 19.9 (United Kingdom). In secondary education, the pupil to teaching staff ratio varied between 7.5 (Portugal) and 21.6 (United Kingdom). Note that classroom sizes are often larger. In most EU countries, the average number of 15-year-old pupils per computer in public-sector schools was less than 10. However, in Slovakia, this number was 35 (European Commission, 2005).

School systems of EU countries vary considerably depending on national educational policy and resources available for schools. In some EU countries, parents have to choose a particular branch or type of schooling for their children at the beginning of lower secondary education. This happens at the age of 10 years in the majority of regions in Germany and Austria and at the age of 12 years in Luxembourg, the Czech Republic, Hungary, and Slovakia. In most countries, secondary education is divided into two levels (lower and upper secondary school with a college-bound track and a vocational school track).

Except for courses in foreign languages, information and communication technology, and religion, the primary education curricula consist of the same compulsory subjects in all EU countries (e.g., reading, mathematics, sports, arts; European Commission, 2005).

As a response to increasing problems in the labor market, young people in Europe, as in many other countries, strive for more education. During the period of 1998 to 2002, the number of students in tertiary education increased steadily in the EU. Average annual growth rates were 2%, with a 5-year increase of 16%. Growth in the new member states was even greater than the EU average. The increase exceeded 50% in Latvia, Lithuania, Luxembourg, Poland, and Romania. However, following the introduction of tuition fees in tertiary education, Austria and Bulgaria experienced a decrease in the student population.

In 2007, approximately 60% of all young people aged 15 to 24 years were enrolled in some form of education or training. Education enrollment rates among this age group are lower in Eastern than in Western European countries, and below average rates are found in Malta (39%),

Romania (51%), and Bulgaria (54%). As in other parts of the world, adolescents from ethnic minorities, poor families, and rural areas are overrepresented among out-of-school youth. The number of years of education that a 5-year-old child can expect to receive during his or her lifetime ranges from 14 years in Cyprus, Luxembourg, and Malta to 19 years in Belgium, Finland, Sweden, and the United Kingdom (European Commission, 2005).

A good school environment and psychosocial climate is an important condition for good academic performance. Data on whether young people in Europe like their schools are available from the HBSC study. In 2001/2002, similar to other Western countries, such as Canada and the United States, only approximately 25% to 50% of European 11-year-olds and 10% to 20% of the 13- to 15-year-olds reported that they liked school a lot. Lowest rates for 11- to 15-year-olds were reported in Finland (8%), Estonia (11%), and the Czech Republic (12%). The most positive evaluations of the schools were found in Austria (36%) and Malta (34%). With increasing age, liking school declined in all European countries (Currie et al., 2004). Feeling pressured by schoolwork was highest in Lithuania and Malta and lowest in The Netherlands, Austria, and Belgium. The percentages of students who spend long weekday hours doing homework varied between 2% (Finland) and 60% (Greece). Data were similar on weekends (Finland, 2%; Greece, 54%) (Currie et al., 2004).

In the PISA study, 15-year-olds were asked whether school has taught them things that could be useful in a job. Between 53% (Luxembourg) and 86% (Portugal) agreed with that statement. Agreement was slightly higher in students from Eastern European EU members (75%) than in their Western peers (70%). However, between 17% (Latvia) and 49% (Luxembourg) of the students thought that school had done little to prepare them for adult life, and between 4% (Latvia, Portugal) and 11% (Belgium, The Netherlands, Poland) perceived school as a waste of time (OECD, 2004). Negative school attitudes were slightly more prevalent in the Western than the Eastern part of the EU. In line with this, another study of 9- to 17-year-olds found that performing well in school was cited as a source of happiness by significantly fewer Western European children and adolescents (33%) than by their peers from Central/Eastern Europe (45%) (UNICEF, 2001).

Comparative data on school-related performance of 15-year-olds are available from the PISA study (OECD, 2004). In the 2003 wave, 12 EU countries scored above the average on the mathematics scale, and eight countries scored below. Similar results were found for natural science, reading, and problem-solving abilities. Finland came out top in the PISA study of learning skills, with high performances in all fields matching those of top-ranking Asian school systems in Hong Kong-China, Japan, and Korea. Within the participating EU members, lowest scores were found in students from Greece (mathematics and problem-solving abilities), Portugal (natural sciences), and the Slovak Republic (reading). With regard to the students from five participating Eastern EU countries, only those from one country were above the average in mathematics and reading performance, and only those from two countries were above average in natural sciences and problem solving. This reflects the general picture that overall, wealthier countries tend to do better in educational terms than poorer nations. As in most other countries, migration background was a risk factor for low school-related performance, especially if the child did not speak the language of the host culture.

Work and Employment

In the EU, youth unemployment is a major challenge. After the breakdown of communism, rapid economic reform translated into high rates of youth employment in the new Eastern EU members. Here, unemployment rates peaked in the late 1990s or early 2000s and declined slightly thereafter. In most West European EU countries, however, youth unemployment declined between 1996 and 2002. When dividing the EU along a north–south line, youth unemployment rates are higher in southern Europe than in Northern Europe (Lagree, 1995).

In the EU in 2002, approximately 20% of 15- to 24-year-olds who had left education were without a job (European Commission, 2005). Unemployment rates were highest in Poland (42%), Slovakia (38%), and Bulgaria (36%) and lowest in The Netherlands (5%), Austria (7%), and Denmark (7%). On average, youth unemployment rates are approximately twice as high as adult unemployment rates. Many Western European countries provide government-sponsored jobs for young people to avoid youth long-term unemployment. If this were not the case, unemployment rates among young people would be even higher as a result of the fact that older workers have better protection against losing their job.

The Development of European Children and Adolescents

In 2000, approximately 106 million young people under the age of 20 lived in the EU. Declining fertility rates have led to a decrease in the number of children and adolescents in every European country. For example, in countries that were EU members in 2000, the number of young people under the age of 20 declined by 21.5% between 1975 and 2000 (European Union, 2005). However, the effect of declining birth rates on the total number of young people in the EU has been compensated by the inclusion of new countries. In 2005, Ireland had the highest percentage of young inhabitants (20.7% were younger than 15 years old), and Bulgaria had the lowest percentage (13.8%).

Attitudes and Values

In 2005, approximately 3,800 young people ages 15 to 24 years from the 25 EU countries were asked about their attitudes regarding the EU (Tham, 2006). Approximately 63% of respondents had a positive view of the EU membership of their country, and 56% showed a generally positive attitude toward the EU; only 10% reported a negative attitude. Approximately 55% of the respondents were satisfied with the EU, and higher satisfaction was found in the new EU countries (62%) compared with the old EU countries. The young population from the new EU countries was more enthusiastic about the EU offering freedom to travel and opportunities to study and working in every country of the EU (76% versus 59% of young from the old EU countries). On a question regarding priority actions of the EU, 52% of the youth mentioned fight against unemployment, 45% mentioned overcoming poverty and social exclusion, and 31% mentioned peace and security. The fight against unemployment was more important for young people from new EU members, and 68% of all respondents worried that EU membership may be associated with increasing unemployment as a result of shifting jobs to other EU members with lower costs.

In Eastern Europe, for many decades, a positive valuation of collectivism, equality, conformity, and dependency was forced on people by the political system. Based on the former history of these countries, lower standards of living, and lower rates of urbanization, traditional collectivistic and material values are more prevalent in Eastern European adolescents than in Western European adolescents. For example, in the Euronet study, young people from Eastern Europe (Poland, Hungary, Bulgaria, and Romania) emphasized the importance of social responsibility (taking responsibility for their parents and being useful to their country) more than those from three Western European countries (France, Switzerland, and Germany; Nurmi, Liiceanu, and Liberska, 1999). In addition, Melzer et al. (1991) observed that self-realization was perceived as more important in German adolescents than in their Polish peers, whereas protection against unemployment was more important for Polish and East German adolescents than for adolescents in West Germany. An economic crisis may have strengthened the importance of this issue in adolescents from the former Communist Bloc. With regard to materialistic values, Nurmi et al. (1999) observed that being successful (becoming rich, famous, or professional) was perceived as more important in Eastern European adolescents (Romania, Poland, Bulgaria, and Russia) than in Western European adolescents (Switzerland, Finland, France, Germany, and Norway).

Young people from Western European countries emphasized the importance of social pleasure more than those from Eastern Europe.

Declining East–West differences in values may be expected with increasing similarity of living conditions and political integration of Eastern European countries into the EU. For example, Reitzle and Silbereisen (2000) observed that shortly after German unification, young people from East Germany put more emphasis on collectivist values, such as family safety, whereas their Western peers were more likely to endorse individualistic values (e.g., social power, freedom, and inner harmony). Five years later, attitudes of same-aged persons had come closer, but only in those younger East Germans who were still exposed to the socialization of the (new, Western-style) education system that was introduced after the fall of the Berlin Wall.

Psychosocial Transitions

A main topic of cross-national research is identifying which aspects of psychological development are influenced by societal conditions and which show no national differences. With regard to the timing of psychosocial transitions, Silbereisen and Wiesner (2002) hypothesized that the more private or personal the transition (e.g., building the first romantic relationship), the less influential different societal conditions, such as school and labor market conditions, are likely to be. To test this assumption, they compared the timing of psychosocial transitions of people from East and West Germany 2 years after the fall of the Berlin Wall (1991) and of an equivalent replication sample in 1996. In their first survey (for 1991), they expected to find East–West differences only with regard to transitions that had been influenced by societal institutions (e.g., developing vocational preferences, becoming financially self-sufficient), and this is exactly what was found. For example, based on statewide vocational counseling in East German schools and on fewer available places on the academic school track, East Germans made vocational choices 18 months earlier than their Western peers. In addition, as could be expected from the West German institutional system being introduced into the East after reunification, the timing of the less private transitions of young East Germans was more similar to their Western peers in 1996 than in 1991.

Similarly, the study by Motola, Sinisalo, and Guichard (1998) showed how national differences in the educational system influence the timing of development of vocational preferences. French adolescents have to choose between 5 academic and 16 technical programs or enter a vocational high school or apprenticeship at the age of 16 years. In contrast, Finnish adolescents stay together in a comprehensive school until age 16 years and are then tracked into either an upper secondary school or a vocational school. However, no decisions about a specific occupation are required before leaving vocational school or entering university. Thus, not surprisingly, French eleventh graders were three times as likely as their Finnish peers to have a clear idea of their future occupation (58% versus 19%).

Psychological Health

Perceptions of psychological health and satisfaction with life reflect the balance between the level of stress that young people experience and their positive experiences, such as the attainment of their life goals. Given the higher level of stressors as a result of the transformation of the former Eastern European communist societies to Western democracies, it could be expected that children and adolescents from the East would show lower levels of psychological health than their Western peers. In line with this, the Euronet study found that young people living in Western Europe (Germany and Finland) had, on average, higher self-esteem and higher general psychological well-being than those living in former socialist countries (Bulgaria, Poland, Hungary, Czech Republic, and Romania; Grob, Little, Wanner, Wearing, and Euronet, 1996). In that study, only French adolescents had low levels of self-esteem similar to those of their Eastern European peers.

In the 2001/2002 HBSC study, most young people were satisfied with their lives in all European countries, and on average, more than 80% of the 11- to 15-year-olds scored above the mean on a scale of life satisfaction. Nonetheless, there were substantial national differences, with highest scores in The Netherlands (94% above the mean of the scale), Finland (92%), and Greece (92%) and lowest scores in Estonia (77%), Latvia (77%), and Lithuania (75%) (Currie et al., 2004). In another study, Wardle et al. (2004) found lower life satisfaction and higher levels of depressive symptoms in students from Eastern European countries (e.g., Slovakia, Poland, Bulgaria) than in Western Europe. For example, 16% of Western European students, compared to 22% of Eastern European peers, had low life satisfaction ratings. Reports about loneliness in adolescence are available from the PISA study. Although loneliness was generally low, more adolescents from Eastern European EU member countries felt lonely (8%) compared with their Western peers (6%) (OECD, 2004). In a smaller study, Vazsonyi and Belliston (2006) found higher levels of depressive symptoms but lower levels of anxiety symptoms in Hungarian adolescents compared with their Swiss and Dutch peers.

Feeling helpless is characterized by a sense of being vulnerable and powerless to influence the direction of one's life. Comparative data on the frequency of perceived helplessness have been published from the 1993/1994 survey of the HBSC study. Rates of feeling helpless always or often were lowest in the Scandinavian countries (Denmark, 5%; Sweden, 4%; and Finland, 3%). Higher rates were reported in Lithuania (12%), Hungary (10%), and Poland (10%). However, even higher rates emerged in France (27%) and the French part of Belgium (22%). The authors interpreted these unexpectedly high rates as a problem with translation because there are four different French words for the term "helplessness" with different meanings (e.g., lacking in strength, powerlessness), which probably relate to differences in response rates. In another question on self-confidence, rates were highest in Spain (48% always felt confident) and France (37%) and lowest in Estonia (12%), Slovakia (14%), and the Czech Republic (18%) (King et al., 1996). In the Euronet study, more Eastern European adolescents believed that they would not have control over their future workplace or over school subjects than their Western European peers (Grob and Flammer, 1999). No such differences regarding perceived control over personality development were observed. In addition, lower levels of general internal locus of control have been reported in Eastern European than in Western European students (Wardle et al., 2004).

In summary, these data indicate that most young people in the EU have high levels of psychological well-being and feel that their life is under their control, but rates of well-being and perceptions of control are lower in the new Eastern European members of the EU. However, East–West differences in psychological well-being are generally small. This probably indicates an adaptation of standards for evaluating one's life to the present condition, so that national differences in psychological well-being become smaller than might be expected from national differences in objective living conditions (see, for example, the set point theory of life satisfaction; Fujita and Diener, 2005).

Despite high average rates of psychological well-being, a minority of young people are highly distressed. This is, amongst other indicators, reflected in youth suicide rates (WHO, 2007). In 2004, the suicide rate for children and adolescents younger than 25 years in the EU countries was 10.3 per 10,000 (similar to the incidence of 10.5 in the United States). However, higher rates were observed in former members of the Communist Bloc (13.0) than in Western countries (8.8). Suicide rates were highest in Lithuania (27.1), Finland (22.5; in part explained by high levels of private gun ownership), and Estonia (21.7) and lowest in the Southern European countries that are strongly influenced by the Orthodox or Roman Catholic Church (Greece, 2.4; Portugal, 3.7; Italy, 4.3; and Spain, 4.6).

After the fall of the Iron Curtain, increases in suicide rates in young people were observed in many Eastern European countries, although official statistics from communist times may often not be valid. For example, suicide rates of 15- to 19-year-old female adolescents peaked in Slovakia in 1993, in Bulgaria in 1995, in Poland in 1997, in Estonia in 1999, in Lithuania in 2000, and in the Czech Republic in 2002. In male adolescents, suicide rates peaked in 1992 in Hungary and Latvia, in 1993 in Bulgaria, in 1995 in the Czech Republic, in 1998 in Slovenia, in 1999 in Estonia and Poland, and in 2000 in Romania (UNICEF, 2005). Loss of social cohesion, breakdown of traditional family structure, growing economic instability, unemployment, and a disparity between increasing stressors and lacking resources probably explain increasing suicide rates (Gailiene, 2005). Declining suicide rates in the late 1990s and early 2000s may be explained by the fact that the economic recession, high unemployment, and insecurity regarding the future that followed the breakdown of the Communist Bloc bottomed out in the mid to late 1990s.

Physical Health

Although infant mortality is decreasing in all new Eastern European members of the EU, at the beginning of the new millennium, it is still twice as high as the average EU level (10.3 versus 5.1 per 1,000 live births), with particularly high rates in Bulgaria (20.6) and Romania (26.4) (Central Intelligence Agency, 2006). Perinatal conditions are responsible for approximately 50% of infant deaths. Low birth weight increases the risk for ill physical health and for cognitive impairments. In 2002, the percentages of children born with low birth weight (<2,500 g) were lowest in France, Finland, Sweden, and Lithuania (4% each) and highest in Bulgaria (10%) and Hungary (9%), which may reflect effects of higher poverty rates and of problems in reorganizing the former communist health care system (WHO, 2005).

Generally positive evaluations of physical health have been observed in European adolescents. For example, in the HBSC study, only approximately 17% of 11- to 15-year-olds perceived their health as fair or poor. Within the EU, the percentages were highest in Lithuania (32%) and Latvia (27%) and lowest in Spain (9%), Greece (10%), and Finland (11%). Nonetheless, from a list of eight health complaints, approximately one-third of the adolescents surveyed reported more than one complaint. Adolescents from Southern Europe were most likely to experience two or more health complaints (Italy, 47%; Greece, 46%; and Spain, 42%), and adolescents from Germany (19%) and Austria (22%) were least likely to do so. Contrary to other indicators of psychological and physical health, scores of Eastern European adolescents were modest (Currie et al., 2004).

Based on the HBSC data from 1997/1998, Torsheim et al. (2004) reported a strong positive correlation between the economic wealth of the country (as indicated by the GDP) and country level of subjective health among 11-year-olds ($r = .67$). Weaker correlations were found for the 13- and 15-year-olds ($r = .50$ and $r = .31$). Within the countries covered, the HBSC study showed a decreasing proportion of adolescents reporting poor health and daily health complaints as family affluence increased (Currie et al., 2004).

Externalizing Problem Behavior

Few European cross-national studies are available on global measures of externalizing problem behavior. The 2001/2002 wave of the HBSC study collected data on bullying (Currie et al., 2004), which is the assertion of interpersonal power through aggression involving negative physical and verbal action that has hostile intent. Approximately one-third of the 11- to 15-year-olds reported bullying others during the past couple of months. Austria, Estonia, Germany, Latvia, and Lithuania were in the top quartile of all assessed age groups, and the Czech Republic, Ireland, Scotland, Slovenia, Sweden, and Wales were in the lowest quartile. Based on the same data set, Pickett et al. (2005) analyzed the frequency of physical fighting during the previous 12 months. Data ranged from 37% (Finland) to 69% (the Czech Republic) of boys being involved in at least one physical fight and from 13% (Finland) to 32% (Hungary) of girls. The observed high level of violence in the Czech boys probably indicates a lack of social control (Eisner, 2002). In a smaller study, Vazsonyi, Hibbert, and Snider (2003) found that Dutch male and female adolescents reported higher levels of school misconduct than their peers from Hungary.

National statistics show that young people from Eastern European countries are, for the most part, less likely to get into conflict with the law than their peers from Western countries (UNICEF, 2000). However, when they come in conflict with the law, they are at a greater risk of being given a custodial sentence, often under harsh conditions. In the 1990s, an increase in youth crime rates was observed in many Eastern European countries. With regard to the new EU members, highest youth crime rates were found in Slovenia and Bulgaria, although these rates are still lower than those of many Western countries, such as the United States.

Several comparative studies have focused on adolescent substance use. The prevalence of harmful levels of alcohol use and illegal substance use among European countries is a challenge to health professionals. Alcohol abuse and drug use among young people are frequent in highly urbanized, highly affluent contexts where lifestyles are leisure-time oriented. In the most recent wave of the HBSC study, the highest rates of weekly alcohol consumption were found in 11- to 15-year-olds from England (31%), The Netherlands (26%), and Italy (25%); the lowest rates were observed in France, Ireland, Portugal, Latvia, and Finland (9% each). Similarly to other countries, boys drank more than girls, and alcohol consumption increased with increasing age (Currie et al., 2004). Countries can be clustered according to their traditions in alcohol use. In wine-producing, predominantly Catholic or Orthodox, Mediterranean countries, adolescents had a relatively late onset of drinking and a low proportion of drunkenness. In the Scandinavian EU members, drunkenness had a rather early onset and was widespread in young people (Denmark in particular). A relatively early onset of drunkenness and high percentages of weekly drinkers among 15-year-olds were also observed in Western Europe, such as in Belgium and England. Finally, Eastern European countries have a more spirits-oriented drinking culture among adults but did not show elevated levels of alcohol use among adolescents.

In the ESPAD study with 16-year-olds, lifetime alcohol use of more than 40 times was most often observed in Denmark, Austria, the Czech Republic, The Netherlands, and the United Kingdom (43% to 50%) and least often observed in Portugal (14%) and Sweden (17%). Similarly, the highest prevalence rates of drunkenness (defined as more than 20 times in the lifetime) were observed in Denmark, Ireland, the United Kingdom, Estonia, and Finland (26% to 36%); the lowest rates were found in Cyprus, France, Greece, and Portugal (2% to 5%) (Hibell et al., 2004).

During times of socialism, families were protected against some negative consequences of single parenthood, for example, by cheap childcare facilities, so that growing up with a single mother had less negative consequences on child development (Sharma and Silbereisen, 2007). Some protective factors seemed to have survived the breakdown of socialism; whereas living with a single parent was associated with higher alcohol use in 10 Western countries, no such association was found in Eastern European countries (Bulgaria, Estonia, Hungary, Lithuania, Romania, Slovenia, and Slovakia), except in the Czech Republic and Estonia (Hibell et al., 2004).

Between 1995 and 2003, the prevalence rates of alcohol consumption were relatively unchanged in many countries under investigation. Nonetheless, an increase was observed in Bulgaria, the Czech Republic, Estonia, Hungary, Italy, Latvia, Lithuania, and Slovakia, most of which are Eastern European EU members, which probably reflects declining social control (Silbereisen, Robins, and Rutter, 1995). A decrease in alcohol use was only observed in three Western countries (Denmark, the United Kingdom, and Greece; Hibell et al., 2004).

Cannabis is the most widely used illegal drug for adolescents. In the 2001/2002 HBSC study, more than 30% of 15-year-olds from England, Scotland, and Spain reported having used cannabis in the previous 12 months. In contrast, prevalence rates were much lower in Eastern Europe (e.g., Latvia, 8%; Lithuania, 6%), Malta (6%), and Sweden (5%). Experimentation and occasional use were far more common in that age group than heavy use. Nonetheless, approximately 7% of 15-year-olds from England were classified as heavy users (≥40 times; Currie et al., 2004).

In a Eurobarometer survey, 29% of 15- to 24-year olds from 15 EU countries said that they had already used cannabis, and 9% stated that they already had tried other drugs. Cannabis consumption was most prevalent in Denmark (45%), Spain (44%), and France (40%) and least prevalent in Finland (18%), Sweden (14%), and Greece (7%) (EOS Gallup Europe, 2004). In the ESPAD study, more than one-quarter of the 16-year-olds had experience with cannabis. Highest levels of lifetime users were found in the Czech Republic (44%), Ireland (39%), and France (38%). Low prevalence rates were observed in Romania (3%), Cyprus (4%), and Greece (6%) (Hibell et al., 2004).

Recent use of ecstasy was most prevalent in 15- to 24-year-olds from the Czech Republic (11%) and Estonia (6%) and least prevalent in France, Italy, Poland, and Portugal (1% each; European Monitoring Centre for Drugs and Drug Addiction, 2005).

Because availability of illegal drugs was, on average, lower in the times of communism than in the Western European countries, politicians and practitioners in the social field worried whether there would be a strong increase in Eastern Europe. Based on data from three waves of the ESPAD study, we computed the average percentage of lifetime experience of any illegal drug in 16-year-olds from the Eastern European EU countries (Bulgaria, Czech Republic, Estonia, Hungary, Latvia, Lithuania, Poland, Romania, Slovenia, and Slovakia) and from 11 Western European EU countries (Denmark, Cyprus, Greece, Finland, France, Ireland, Italy, Malta, Portugal, Sweden, and United Kingdom). Unfortunately, data were lacking for the other Western countries. In 1995, the lifetime use of illegal drugs in Eastern Europe had reached approximately 10% from near zero in 1989, but this rate was still much lower than in Western European countries. A further catch up was observed in 1999, and average rates were slightly higher in the East than in the West in 2003 (Hibell et al., 2004). However, there are exceptions to the rule: A decrease in lifetime users was observed in Latvia and Romania between 1999 and 2003. Although Eastern European societies can count on fewer practical experiences in the field of prevention of illegal substance use, effective efforts are needed in the field of prevention and promoting healthy adolescent development.

Conclusion

Available empirical evidence shows that most European children and adolescents do well, as indicated by good psychological and physical health, low levels of problem behavior, and academic success at least in the expected range. Differences in wellness of the families and in psychological well-being still exist along the East–West divide, with lower levels in the former Eastern European communist countries. Fewer differences emerge along the North–South line, such as higher percentages of young people living with both parents in Southern European countries, which is probably based on the impact of the Catholic Church. National differences in living conditions and child health are expected to decline with a further convergence of living conditions, but it is probably unlikely that all differences will be eliminated.

National differences were most often observed in the mean levels of variables, whereas few studies found differences in the patterning of the interrelationship of these variables. Thus, and actually not surprisingly, influences on the development of children and adolescents were found to be similar across the EU countries. Unfortunately, most available studies restricted their focus to identifying national differences, rather than testing which specific conditions mediated these effects. For example, for developing European intervention strategies, it would be important to test whether national differences in social control explain observed differences in delinquent behavior and substance use. In addition, up to now, we have mainly comparative data on sociostructural characteristics of children's living conditions, such as rates of daycare use and of growing up in two-parent families. However, comparative data from all EU countries are also needed on more qualitative aspects, such as parenting styles and quality of daycare. These kinds of studies call for interdisciplinary research including developmental psychologists, sociologists, specialists from the field of education, and others.

Although the conditions for healthy development are, on average, quite good for most children and adolescents in the EU, efforts are needed to overcome some widespread problems, such as making quality childcare available for children under 3 years of age, reducing parental poverty, supporting single parents, improving linguistic abilities of migrant children, securing a drug-free environment, offering community-based services for children in need, and overcoming youth unemployment.

In addition, the opening of the EU to Eastern Europe and social change in general exert new demands on Europe's youth. Based on the mobility of the labor force in the EU, an increasing number of young people can expect to be trained, study, or work outside their native country. Here, intercultural competencies, such as knowledge of foreign languages and psychological openness to new experiences, are needed.

Rapid changes of the labor market and a growing pluralization of biographical trajectories (e.g., when and whether to marry and to have children; Bertram and Kreher, 1996) call for capabilities for coping with uncertainty, belief in one's own abilities, and self-regulation, such as setting personal goals, as well as tenacious and flexible goal pursuit. Efforts are needed from families, schools, and youth organizations to support the development of psychological resources, such as self-efficacy beliefs and abilities for setting and pursuing realistic goals. For example, in a study of adolescents facing German unification, we observed that students with higher self-efficacy beliefs were more successful in mastering the rapid social change by finding an adequate apprenticeship, avoiding unemployment, and bolstering their psychological health against stressors (Pinquart, Juang, and Silbereisen, 2003).

Furthermore, based on rapid technological development and the shrinking traditional labor market, young people with low qualifications will have little or no chance to find their way into regular work. For example, Titma and Tuma (2005) observed that educational attainment became a stronger predictor for career success in young people from successors of the Soviet Union showing faster progress to a market economy (the Baltic States) than in other transition countries. Thus, efforts to reduce early school leaving and to ensure that an increasing number of students complete upper secondary education have to be intensified.

References

Alsaker, F. D., and Flammer, A. (Eds.). (1999). *The adolescent experience: European and American adolescents in the 1990s.* Mahwah, NJ: Erlbaum.

Bertram, H., and Kreher, S. (1996). Lebensformen und lebensverläufe in diesem jahrhundert. [Life designs and life courses of this century]. *Politik und Zeitgeschichte, B 42,* 18–29.

Bornstein, M., Haynes, O. M., Azuma, H., Galperin, C., Maital, S., Ogino, M., et al. (1998). A cross-national study of self-evaluations and attributions in parenting: Argentina, Belgium, France, Israel, Italy, Japan, and the United States. *Developmental Psychology, 34,* 662–676.

Browne, K., Hamilton-Giachritsis, C., Johnson, R., and Ostergren, M. (2006). Overuse of institutional care for children in Europe. *British Medical Journal, 332,* 485–487.

Central Intelligence Agency (2006). *CIA world factbook 2006.* Washington, DC: Author.

Clarke-Stewart, A. and Dunn, J. (Eds.). (2006). *Family count: Effects on child and adolescent development.* New York: Cambridge University Press.

Currie, C., Roberts, C., Morgan, A., Smith, R., Settertobule, W., Samdal, O., et al. (Eds.). (2004). *Young people's health in context*. Copenhagen, Denmark: World Health Organization.

Deynoot-Schaub, M. J., Gevers, J. M. and Riksen-Walraven, J. M. (2005). Child care under pressure: The quality of Dutch centers in 1995 and 2001. *Journal of Genetic Psychology, 166*, 280–296.

Eisner, M. (2002). Crime, problem drinking, and drug use: Patterns of problem behavior in cross-national perspective. *Annals of the American Academy of Political and Social Science, 580*, 201–225.

EOS Gallup Europe (2004). *Flash Eurobarometer 158: Young people and drugs*. Author.

European Commission (2005). *Key data on education in Europe*. Luxembourg: Office for Official Communications of the European Communities.

European Commission (2006). *Key figures on Europe*. Luxembourg: Author.

European Monitoring Centre for Drugs and Drug Addiction (2005). *Annual report 2005: The state of the drugs problem in Europe*. Lisbon, Portugal: Author.

Feldman, S. S., and Rosenthal, D. A. (1994). Culture makes a difference or does it? A comparison of adolescents in Hong Kong, Australia, and the United States. In R. K. Silbereisen and E. Todt (Eds.), *Adolescence in context: The interplay of family, school, peers, and work in adjustment* (pp. 99–124). New York: Springer.

Flammer, A., Alsaker, D. D., and Noack, P. (1999). Time use by adolescents in an international perspective I: The case of leisure activities. In F. D. Alsaker and A. Flammer (Eds.), *The adolescent experience: European and American adolescents in the 1990s* (pp. 33–60). Mahwah, NJ: Erlbaum.

Flanagan, C., and Botcheva, L. (1999). Adolescents' preferences for their homeland and other countries. In F. D. Alsaker and A. Flammer (Eds.), *The adolescent experience: European and American adolescents in the 1990s* (pp. 131–144). Mahwah, NJ: Erlbaum.

Fujita, F., and Diener, E. (2005). Life satisfaction set point: Stability and change. *Journal of Personality and Social Psychology, 88*, 158–164.

Gailiene, D. (2005). Uzburtame rate: Savizudybiu paplitimas Lietuvoje po nepriklausomybes atkurimo [Vicious circle: Suicides in Lithuania after the independence]. *Psichologija, 31*, 7–15.

Grob, A., and Flammer, A. (1999). Macrosocial context and adolescents' perceived control. In F. D. Alsaker and A. Flammer (Eds.), *The adolescent experience: European and American adolescents in the 1990s* (pp. 99–113). Mahwah, NJ: Erlbaum.

Grob, A., Little, T. D., Wanner, B., Wearing, A. J., and Euronet (1996). Adolescents' well-being and perceived control across fourteen sociocultural contexts. *Journal of Personality and Social Psychology, 71*, 785–795.

Hibell, B., Andersson, B., Bjarnasson, T., Ahström, S., Balakireva, O., Kokkevi, A., et al. (2004). *The ESPAD report 2003: Alcohol and other drug use among students in 35 European countries*. Stockholm: Swedish Council for Information on Alcohol and Drugs.

Instituto di Ricerca (2001). *Study on the state of young people and youth policy in Europe*. Milan: Author.

King, A., Wold, B., Tudor-Smith, C., and Harel, Y. (1996). *The health of youth: A cross-national survey*. Copenhagen: WHO.

Lagree, J. C. (1995). Young people and employment in the European community: Convergence or divergence? In L. Chisholm, L. P. Buchner, H. H. Kruger, and M. du Bois-Reymond (Eds.), *Growing up in Europe: Contemporary horizons in childhood and youth studies* (pp. 61–72). New York: de Gruyter.

Melzer, W., Lukowski, W., and Schmidt, L. (1991). *Deutsch-Polnischer jugendreport* [*German-Polish youth report*]. Weinheim, Germany: Juventa.

Motola, M., Sinisalo, P., and Guichard, J. (1998). Social habitus and future plans. In J. Nurmi (Ed.), *Adolescents, cultures, and conflicts* (pp. 43–73). New York: Garland.

Mullan, E., and Currie, C. (2000). Socioeconomic inequalities in adolescent health. In C. Currie, K. Hurrelmann, W. Settertobule, R. Smith, and J. Todd (Eds.), *Health and health behaviour among young people* (pp. 65–72). Copenhagen, Denmark: World Health Organization.

Nurmi, J. E., Liiceanu, A., and Liberska, H. (1999). Future-oriented interests. In F. D. Alsaker and A. Flammer (Eds.), *The adolescent experience: European and American adolescents in the 1990s* (pp. 85–98). Mahwah, NJ: Erlbaum.

Organisation for Economic Co-operation and Development (2004). *Learning for tomorrow's world: First results from Pisa 2003*. Paris: Author.

Petersen, M., Alcón, M. C., Rodriguez, C. M., and Smith, R. (2004). Family. In C. Currie, C. Roberts, A. Morgan, R. Smith, W. Settertobule, O. Samdal, and V. B. Rasmussen (Eds.), *Young people's health in context* (pp. 26–33). Copenhagen: WHO.

Pickett, W., Craig, W., Harel, Y., Cunningham, J., Simpson, K., Molcho, M., et al. (2005). Cross-national study of fighting and weapon carrying as determinants of adolescent injury. *Pediatrics, 116*, 855–863.

Pinquart, M., Juang, L. P., and Silbereisen, R. K. (2003). Self-efficacy and successful school-to-work transition: A longitudinal study. *Journal of Vocational Behavior, 63*, 329–346.

Reitzle, M., and Silbereisen, R. K. (2000). Adapting to social change: Adolescent values in eastern and western Germany. In J. Bynner and R. K. Silbereisen (Eds.), *Adversity and challenge in life in the new Germany and in England* (pp. 123–152). Houndmills, United Kingdom: Macmillan.

Roberts, K., and Fagan, C. (1999). Young people and their leisure in the former communist countries: Four theses examined. *Leisure Studies, 18*, 1–17.

Scott, J. (2004). Children's families. In J. Scott and J. Treas (Eds.), *The Blackwell companion to the sociology of families* (pp. 109–125). Malden, MA: Blackwell.

Settertobule, W. (2000). Family and peer relations. In C. Currie, K. Hurrelmann, W. Settertobule, R. Smith, and J. Todd (Eds.), *Health and health behaviour among young people* (pp. 39–48). WHO Copenhagen.

Sharma, D., and Silbereisen, R. K. (2007). Revisiting an era in Germany from the perspective of adolescents in mother-headed single-parent families. *International Journal of Psychology, 42*, 46–58.

Silbereisen, R. K., Robins, L., and Rutter, M. (1995). Secular trends in substance use: Concepts and data on the impact of social change on alcohol and drug abuse. In M. Rutter and D. J. Smith (Eds.), *Psychosocial disorders in young people: Time trends and their origins* (pp. 490–543). Chichester, United Kingdom: Wiley.

Silbereisen, R. K. and Wiesner, M. (2002). Lessons from research on the consequences of German unification: Continuity and discontinuity of self-efficacy and the timing of psychosocial transitions. *Applied Psychology, 51*, 291–317.

Steiner, I. (1995). Growing up in 12 cities: The families in which pupils live. In L. Chisholm, P. Buchner, and H. H. Kruger (Eds.), *Growing up in Europe: Contemporary horizons in childhood and youth studies* (pp. 73–82). New York: de Gruyter.

Tham, B. (2006). *Einstellungen, erwartungen und befürchtungen jugendlicher gegenüber der Europäischen Union und ihrer politik im Jahr 2005*. München, Germany: Centrum für Angewandte Politikforschung.

Tietze, W., and Cryer, D. (1999). Current trends in European early child care and education. *Annals of the American Academy of Political and Social Sciences, 563*, 175–193.

Titma, M., and Tuma, N. B. (2005). Human agency in the transition from communism: Perspectives on the life course and aging. In W. Schaie and G. H. Elder (Eds.), *Historical influences on lives and aging* (pp. 108–143). New York: Springer.

Torsheim, T., Currie, C., Boyce, W., Kalnins, I., Overpeck, M., and Haugland, S. (2004). Material deprivation and self-rated health: A multilevel study of adolescents from 22 European and North American countries. *Social Science and Medicine, 59*, 1–12.

United Nations Children's Fund (UNICEF) (2000). *Young people in changing societies*. Florence, Italy: UNICEF Innocenti Research Centre.

United Nations Children's Fund (UNICEF) (2001). *Young voices opinion survey of children and young people in Europe and Central Asia*. Geneva, Switzerland: Author.

United Nations Children's Fund (UNICEF) (2005). *TransMonee 2005: Data, indicators, and features on the situation of children in the CEE/CIS and Baltic States*. Florence, Italy: Author.

van de Vijver, F., and Leung, K. (1997). *Methods and data analysis for cross-cultural research*. Thousand Oaks, CA: Sage.

Vazsonyi, A. T., and Belliston, L. M. (2006). The cultural and developmental significance of parenting processes in adolescent anxiety and depression symptoms. *Journal of Youth and Adolescence, 35*, 491–505.

Vazsonyi, A. T., Hibbert, J. R. and Snider, J. B. (2003). Exotic enterprise no more? Adolescent reports of family and parenting processes from youth in four countries. *Journal of Research on Adolescence, 13*, 129–160.

Wardle, J., Steptoe, A., Gulis, G., Sartory, G., Sek, H., Todorova, I., et al. (2004). Depression, perceived control, and life satisfaction in university students from Central Eastern and Western Europe. *International Journal of Behavioral Medicine, 11*, 27–36.

World Health Organization (2005). *Public health action for healthier children and populations*. Copenhagen, Denmark: Author.

World Health Organization (2007). Suicide rates 1955-2004. Retrieved February 16, 2009, from http://www.who.int/mental_health/prevention/suicide/country_reports/en/index.html.

19
North Africa and the Middle East

RAMADAN A. AHMED

Introduction

History tells us that developmental issues have attracted several Arab and Muslim scholars since the ninth century (Ahmed and Gielen, 1998). Arab literature reflects a wide and deep interest in a variety of developmental issues, socialization, the parent–child relationship, and the education of children. This interest in studying developmental issues has many reasons, including their relations to socialization and education of children and adolescents and the facts that children and adolescents constitute approximately 40% of the Arab population and Islam, as a dominant religion in this region, emphasizes that parents are responsible for their offspring. Islam asks parents to choose good names for their children and provide their children with the best possible care. To understand children and youth in the Arab countries, religious, sociocultural, and traditional issues should be taken into consideration. To provide the reader with a clear picture of the development of children and youth in Arab countries, the present chapter starts with a historical and demographic overview of the development of Arab children and youth, followed by a discussion of central issues concerning the development of Arab children and youth. Then, the chapter discusses key classical and modern studies on Arab children and youth. The chapter also covers some practical information about the children and youth and sheds light on the future directions of theory and research on child and youth development in the Arab countries.

Historical and Demographic Considerations for Developmental Science in North Africa and the Middle East

North Africa and the Middle East encompass the Arab world (consisting of 22 countries in which live more than 320 million people), Turkey (71 million inhabitants; Celen and Cok, 2007), Iran (68 million inhabitants; Sondaite, 2007), and Israel (6.87 million inhabitants; Seginer and Shoyer, 2007). Including countries as geographically disparate as North Africa and the Middle East stretches the Arab world from the Atlantic Ocean to central Asia, from the Black to the Mediterranean Seas, and to the Horn of Africa. This territory is a vast realm of enormous historical and cultural complexity. It lies at the crossroads where Europe, Asia, and Africa meet, and it is part of all three. On the Mesopotamian Plain, between the Tigris and Euphrates rivers and the banks of the Egyptian Nile, the very earliest civilizations arose. In this territory, walked the religious prophets Moses, Jesus, and Mohammed, whose teachings are still followed by hundreds of millions of people. In this territory, in the twentieth and twenty-first centuries, the most bitter and dangerous conflicts on earth have occurred, conflicts that could still provoke far-reaching armed confrontations (Ahmed, 2005a, 2005b).

Income per capita in North Africa and Middle East countries varies dramatically. Statistics for 2005 show that Qatar, United Arab Emirates (UAE), and Kuwait were the highest, whereas Mauritania, Djibouti, Yemen, and the Sudan were the lowest (Al-Qabas, 2007). Illiteracy levels in North Africa and Middle East countries also vary widely. In some of the richest countries such as Kuwait and Turkey, illiteracy is only 5.4% (Al-Seyassah, 2008) and 6.0%, respectively, whereas illiteracy in countries such as Egypt has decreased to 29.6%, with higher percentages among rural and female populations. In countries such as the Sudan, Somalia, Mauritania, Djibouti, and Comoros, illiteracy is still 80% or higher (United Nations Children's Fund [UNICEF], 2005).

Although the North Africa and Middle East countries differ in language and sociocultural level, they share many similarities. One is the high rate of unemployment, especially among youth and young adults. For example, Al-Qabas (2008) reported that 25.6% of Iranian youth and young adults aged 15 to 24 years are unemployed (29.9% in urban areas and 19.4% in rural areas). Another similarity that characterizes North Africa and Middle East countries is that approximately one-half of their populations are under age 20 years. For example, 37.7% of the Egyptian population is less than 15 years of age; 32% is between 10 and 24 years of age (Ahmed, 2007a).

All three religions emphasize that parents should fulfill their responsibilities in rearing and caring for children. For example, Islam is the dominant religion in the North Africa and Middle East countries. The Holy Koran (trans. 1981), which contains the infallible word of Allah as revealed to the Prophet Mohammed, still provides the basic rules of conduct fundamental to the Muslim way of life; it includes many suras, which determine parents' duties toward their children.

Luqman admonished his son. "My son," he said "serve no other god instead of Allah, for idolatry is an abominable sin." (31:13)

"My son, be steadfast in prayer, enjoin justice, and forbid evil. Endure with fortitude whatever befalls you. That is a duty incumbent on all." (31:17)

"And when they have reached the age of puberty, let your children still ask your leave as their elders do. Thus Allah makes plain to you His revelations: He is wise and all-knowing." (24:59)

Prophet Mohammed advised Muslim men to choose their wives not only for their beauty but also and for their morality, honesty, and kindness. Unsurprisingly, religiosity and religious feeling and their development received early attention from researchers in Arab countries, especially Egypt. El-Meliugi (1951) studied the development of religious feeling in children and adolescents. A study using Muslim youth from Egypt found that those who were higher on intrinsic religious orientation showed negative attitudes toward violence and reflected healthier personality traits, compared with those who expressed extrinsic religious orientations (Ghalab and El-Dousseki, 1994). Results of Ghalab and El-Dousseki (1994) received support from Al-Khatib's (2002) study, which showed: (1) Al-Azher University (an Islamic university in Cairo, Egypt) students had higher religious commitment, compared with other secular universities' Muslim students; (2) males, compared with their female peers, were higher on religious practices; and (3) a negative correlation was obtained between religiosity and depression. Other research studies have focused on the relation between religiosity and personality traits among children and youth in North Africa and Middle East countries. One study was conducted by Abdalla (1989) on the relation between prejudicial attitudes and neuroticism, prejudice, rigidity, social conformity, aggressiveness, dogmatism, dominance, and overall tendency toward an extreme response and value system in 800 secondary school and university Egyptian Muslim and Christian students. Muslim children were more prejudicial than their Christian counterparts. Moreover, a strong positive correlation emerged between prejudicial religious attitudes and measured personality traits. Moussa (1992) found that the highly religious Al-Azhar University students were less depressed than less religious students.

In most North Africa and Middle East countries, the concepts of childhood and adolescence are rooted in Islamic traditions and the Islamic legal point of view (Celen and Cok, 2007; Sondaite, 2007). According to these traditions, individuals are deemed to be responsible for their actions when they reach puberty. By puberty, Muslims are asked to fulfill all pillars of the faith. These pillars include the obligation to pray five times a day and keep the fast at Ramadan. Legally, individuals are considered responsible for their actions after the age of 21 years; prior to that age, they are considered juveniles (Ahmed, 2007a). Legally, the age distribution in most countries is structured in five major groups: 0 to 14 years, 15 to 20 years, 21 to 39 years, 40 to 60 years, and 60 years and older (Ahmed, 2007a). Some North Africa and Middle East countries (such as Egypt in June 2008) raised the age of marriage for the females to reduce the high rate of fertility and to encourage girls to obtain more education (Al-Ahram, 2008). In Egypt alone, two million children and adolescents are involved in paid work, although the law prohibits work of any person age less than 14 years. Baza (2003) estimated that working children and adolescents constitute approximately 7% of the total Egyptian labor force. Similar percentages can be also found in countries such as Turkey and Iran (Celen and Cok, 2007; Sendaite, 2007).

There is no clear-cut definition for adolescence in most North Africa and Middle East countries. Adolescence in these countries is generally characterized by physiological and psychological changes. No ceremonies or rites are used to mark its beginning or end. The psychological dimensions of adolescence in North Africa and Middle East countries are not fully appreciated. One reason is that adolescence is viewed as pertaining to the realm of family and thus varies according to cultural orientation, gender, religion, and sociocultural status. Adolescents' rebellion and autonomy, typically observed in Western countries, are not core features in North Africa and Middle East countries. Very few male adolescents, and even fewer females, leave the family household to study, work, and live on their own before marriage (Ahmed, 2007a). The collective nature of social life in Arab countries (and in both Turkey and Iran) and family members' central role shape the values and self-conceptions of individuals. Young people typically live at home until they are married and remain dependent on older family members for financial and emotional support as young adults. One implication of this arrangement is that the adolescents' experiences in the North Africa and Middle East countries is less likely to be characterized by rebellion or social distancing from parents than is the case in Western societies (Mensch, Ibrahim, Lee, and El-Gibaly, 2000). "Young Egyptians [and in my opinion, the young people in North Africa and Middle East countries] may experience adolescence more as a time of refining interpersonal skill than as a period in which to achieve separation or autonomy" (Mensch et al., 2000, p. 3).

In North Africa and Middle East countries, substantial differences are seen in the ways adolescent boys and girls occupy themselves. Whereas for girls puberty leads to a greater restriction on mobility; for boys, the amount of time devoted to work outside the home and to community involvement is expected to increase. Schooling has had a major impact on these patterns, extending the ages when girls are able to be out in public and increasing contact between boys and girls. However, the academic year in the region is much shorter than that of most other countries, and double-shift schools are common (especially in some Arab countries such as Egypt). Mensch et al. (2000) analyzed time-use data in Egypt and reported that both boys and girls are expected to help at home during childhood and early adolescence, although higher expectations in this regard are placed on girls. As they age, boys gradually withdraw from domestic responsibilities, which is consistent with the notion of consolidating the adult male's position by his distancing himself from the tasks of children and women.

The activity profile that emerges by late adolescence reflects expected patterns for Middle Eastern societies: Boys have considerably more free time than girls, and in contrast with their sisters, boys tend to spend that time outside home engaged in sports or visiting friends. Work roles become gradually segregated, with boys being more likely to participate in paid labor and girls participate in domestic work within the household (Mensch et al., 2000).

In traditional societies in North Africa and Middle East countries, sexual issues are considered as taboo. However, some Arab countries such as Egypt and Syria have recognized the importance of gender education, especially among youth. Media and schooling systems have begun to display and discuss sexual issues (Al-Seyassah, 2008).

Education in most of the North Africa and Middle East countries needs dramatic and significant changes to prepare and qualify children and youth to live in the era of globalization (Abdel-Hamid, 1990; Gregg, 2005). "Access to education and the amount of schooling completed are believed to be powerful predictors of many subsequent behaviors and attitudes. Moreover, differential access to education is thought to be an important indicator of gender inequality in a society. Whereas school enrollment for boys is nearly universal in Egypt (and in most of North Africa and Middle East countries), girls have been disadvantaged relative to boys in their likelihood of entering school (95% of 10- to 19-year-old boys in 1997 in Egypt had attended school, compared with 84% of girls). However, once a girl is enrolled, the probability that she will remain in school is almost equal to that of a boy. To the extent, then, that a gender gap exists in educational attainment among young people in Egypt (and also in some North Africa and Middle East societies), the difference is attributable to girls' not entering school at the same rate as boys. It is not a consequence of a gender difference in the propensity to drop out" (Mensch et al., 2000, p. 4).

Some North African and Middle East countries have passed laws and legislation to protect children and adolescents. One example is Egypt, which passed a law for motherhood and childhood in 2000 by which new procedures and measures have been established to protect both mothers and children. At present, the Egyptian Parliament is reviewing a child law for further protection of children that includes banning female circumcision, parents' responsibility for the abuse of children, confronting the "street child" phenomenon, and changing the age of marriage, especially for girls. Although laws in most of the North Africa and Middle East countries grant that all people, males and females, have to register in voting records when they reach 18 years of age and, by law, they must participate in the electoral processes, and although no obstruction could be found concerning female participation in the political life, political participation of adolescents and young adults, and especially females, is very weak. As a result, the number of young (and female) representatives in various legislatures is very small (Ahmed, 2007a; Ahmed and Al-Khawajah, 2007).

Central Issues About Developmental Science in North Africa and the Middle East

Islam is the guiding force in child development in North Africa and Middle East countries. The conceptual base of Islam consists of the following: the Koran, the *Sunna* or *Hadith* (sayings and traditions of the Prophet Mohammed), and the Shari'a law. Islam emphasizes the complementary nature of the sexes and dictates their roles accordingly. Women are placed under male guardianship to ensure the safeguarding of morality. Marriage is considered a contract between a man and a woman, and a woman must give her consent (through her father/brother/uncle if she is less than 18 years old and in the case of first marriage) for a marriage to occur. Divorce is a prerogative of men. Females are entitled to inheritance rights and ownership of property, but they inherit one-half the portion that men inherit. These rules are being challenged daily by women, and religious leaders also argue over these dictates. Real change, however, has been slow in coming.

Like many of their counterparts in other parts of the world, parents in the Arab world prefer sons. It is said that a man with a son is immortal, whereas a girl is brought up to contribute to someone else's family tree. Young women typically leave their family to join their husband's family at marriage, whereas young men, especially in the rural (in countries such as Egypt) or Bedouin areas (in countries such as the six Arab Gulf oil-producing states: Kingdom of Bahrain, Kuwait, Sultanate of Oman, Qatar, Kingdom of Saudi Arabia, and the UAE), stay at home and bring their new wife into their family. There are many compelling economic reasons why parents prefer a boy. For example, at least 70% of Egypt is rural. Here, sons are indispensable as a built-in workforce. Unlike girls, boys do not have to be supervised very closely because their sexual behavior cannot dishonor the family or compromise their chance for marriage (Ahmed, 2007a).

Greater numbers of Arab youth tend to join theoretical, social sciences, and humanitarian disciplines, but fewer numbers tend to join applied sciences specializations. An example is youth in Egypt. A 2008 survey (Al-Ahram, 2008) showed that approximately a million university students are enrolled in colleges for social sciences and humanities. Public authorities have raised serious concern about work opportunities for this number of youth.

Key Classical and Modern Research Studies on Developmental Science in North Africa and the Middle East

Researchers in North Africa and the Middle East have shown since the early twentieth century a gradually increasing interest in investigating topics related to developmental science, especially childhood and adolescence. In most cases, developmental scientists in the North Africa and Middle East countries have depended on imported tools to assess psychological aspects and dimensions, although some researchers have tried to develop their own tools. Debais (1997) in Saudi Arabia developed and used a scale for rating aggressive behavior of children with mild mental retardation. Another local scale is the Ain Shams Scale for Aggressive Behaviors (Egypt), which was developed and used by Hafez and Kasem (1993b). In addition, Saleh (1995) developed and used an Index for Observing Aggressive Behavior among Egyptian Preschool Children. The fourth locally developed scale is the Violence and Aggression Phenomenon Scale, which was developed in Egypt by S. Y. Al-Aser (Ahmed, 2005a, 2005b). A fifth scale is the Scale of the Irrational Beliefs among Children and Adolescents (Abdalla and Abdel-Rahman, 1996/1997). Research interests cover a great variety of topics such as socialization, cognitive development, identity formation and identity disorders, moral development, political attitudes, socialization, participation, drug abuse, happiness, violence, religious prejudice and extreme behavior, the effects of crowding, and Internet use. In the following sections, examples of these studies are briefly discussed.

Socialization, Parental Behavior, and Treatment

Socialization and parental treatment became a subject of Arab research interest in the early 1960s (Nagaty, 1962, 1963). Some studies (Melikian, 1965) showed that the type of socialization followed in Arab families is authoritative (see also Gregg, 2005, for more detailed information). During the last four decades, more than 500 research studies have been conducted in Arab countries aimed at investigating children's and adolescents' perceptions of their parents' behavior in countries such as Egypt, Kuwait, Saudi Arabia, Bahrain, Qatar, UAE, Yemen, Algeria, Jordan, and the Sudan. Among these studies, approximately 100 have been conducted using Rohner's Parental Acceptance-Rejection Questionnaire. Other research studies have employed other scales and measures such as Schaefer, Baumrind, Embu, and Rigio (cited in Ahmed, 2007b, 2008; Ahmed and Gielen, 2006b). Perceptions of mother/father rejection correlate with negative personality dispositions, aggressive/violent behavior, low academic achievement and achievement motivation, low levels of aspiration, negative self-concept and self-esteem, juvenile delinquency, peer rejection, aggression, and identity disorders (foreclosure and diffusion). Children's perceptions of parental acceptance correlate with positive personality dispositions, creative and critical thinking, higher levels of aspiration, healthy self-concept/self-esteem, psychological security, altruism, identity status (achievement), higher levels of achievement and achievement motivation, psychological security, critical thinking, and moral development. Moreover, results of these studies show that males and older children more often tend to perceive their parents as being accepting compared with their female counterparts. In addition, very few studies sought to investigate the relations between perception of parental acceptance/rejection, perceived parental corporal punishment, and personality dispositions in children and youth (Abou-el-Kheir, 1995, in Egypt; Ahmed and Gielen, 2006a, in Kuwait). Results revealed significant correlations between perception of parental rejection, harshness and severity of punishment, and unhealthy personality dispositions. An Israeli study (Lavi and Slone, 2008) compared Jewish and Arab families and children between age 7 and 13.5 years. Results showed that levels of parental warmth and control were very high and similar in both Jewish and Arab families. However, Arab families reported a higher level of authoritative control compared with Jewish families. In both Jewish and Arab families, parental warmth had a direct relation with children's self-esteem.

Other studies have tried to assess the impact of education and work on mothers' socialization practices (Al-Mazeruoi, 2006; Bedani, 1995). Whereas Bedani's (1995) study found a positive correlation between mother's work and children's and adolescents' social maturity, Al-Mazeroui's (2006) study found that noneducated and nonworking Saudi mothers tend to breastfeed their babies more and tend to use socialization styles and practices that encourage forgiveness and acceptance in their children, whereas educated and working mothers tend to use socialization practices characterized by control and encouraging independence in their children. Other studies (Habib, 1995) focus on the relations between parental treatment and family size as early determinants of children's extreme responses.

Values, Needs, and Problems of Youth

Values, needs, and psychological problems of youth have been repeatedly investigated in North Africa and the Middle East since the early 1960s (Hana, 1965). A study on values and locus of control in Egyptian and Saudi youth (El-Zayyat, 1990) showed a similarity between two national samples in ranking theoretical, economic, aesthetic, and political values; religious values were ranked first by Egyptians and second by Saudis, whereas social values were ranked first by Saudis and second by Egyptians. Only one study (S. K. Ahmed, 1992) reported significant value changes among Egyptian families (parents and their children) who returned to Egypt after staying several years in other Arab countries, especially the Arab Gulf oil-producing states. Some other studies (Abdel-Hamid, 1992) sought to investigate the impact of rural family immigration to urban areas and reported changes in families' socialization practices and children's value systems.

As for needs, an early study (Gaber, 1968) found that the similarities in needs structure (measured by Edwards Personal Preference Schedule) between the Egyptian and Iraqi samples surpassed the similarities between Egyptian and Iraq samples and the American sample. Both Arab samples scored higher than Americans on needs for order, succorance, nurturance, endurance, and aggression but lower on the needs for exhibition, affiliation, introspection, and heterosexuality. Ali and Ewidaih (1994) focused on the gender differences in needs among university students. Another study (Ahlawat, 1991) sought to investigate the differences/similarities in students' general structure underlying the two for personal importance and personal satisfaction in Jordan, China, Japan, and Switzerland. In general, results of the four nations showed similar patterns of degrees of satisfaction, rank order correlations, and differences in average amount of satisfaction. A fourth study (Dousseki, 1992) used the Thematic Apperception Test to assess youth problems and relations with personality characteristics and social values. Khaleefa (cited in Ahmed, 2007b and 2008) found significant correlations between perceptions of parental rejection and incidence (prevalence) of psychological problems among Qatari children. Finally, Al-Shamy (2008) investigated the psychological problems that characterized gifted intermediate-school students in the Kingdom of Bahrain.

Socioemotional Development

Several studies have focused on internal-external locus of control in children and youth residing in North Africa and Middle East countries (Hedia, 1994; Ibrahim and Abdel-Hamid, 1994; Abou-Shideed and Naser, 2002, on Egyptian youth; Jacoup and Makableh, 1994, in Jordan; Al-Khawajah and Ahmed, 1996/1997, on Kuwaiti and Sudanese youth; Soliman and Abdel-Hamid, 1994, on Saudi university students). Results of these studies showed that educated, higher socioeconomic status, and urban participants tended to report more internal locus of control compared with female, non- to lower educated, lower socioeconomic status, and rural participants. A Lebanese study (Abou-Shideed and Naser, 2002) sought the relation between locus of control and Muslim, Christian, and Druze University male and female students' attitudes toward peace with Israel. Results showed a positive correlation between internal locus of control and positive attitudes toward a peace process. No impact of social class and religious affiliation on participants' attitudes has been reported. Females, compared with their male counterparts, were more consistent in their political attitudes toward peace. Finally, participants reported that current social and political institutions are not capable of facing the challenges of peace.

Whereas very few Arab studies have dealt with children's perception of supports and reinforcements, an example is the study by Hewaidy and Al-Yameni (1995), who investigated the common reinforcements among primary school children in Bahrain. In addition, other studies have tried to assess the development of social competence among young adults (Naser, 1996). Some studies have dealt with attitudes of respondents from different ages and settings toward modernization (Badri, 1965, on Sudanese children; Naser, 1997; Abou-Zaid, 2003, on Egyptian youth), the future (Abou-Zaid, 1992; Ibrahim, 2003, on Egyptian youth), social responsibility (Kurdy, 2003, on Egyptian youth; Kaffafi and Al-Naial, 1994, on Qatari youth), and conservatism–liberalism (Ibrahim, 1992, on Egyptian adolescents). Other studies have investigated Egyptian adolescents' assertiveness between submission and hostility toward authority (Abdel-Kader, 2000), the relation between attitudes toward social problems and manifestation of alienation among Egyptian adolescents (Abou-el-Enien, 1995), gender differences in perception of the stressful life events (Youssef, 1994), and terrorism as seen by youth in Egypt (Ali, 1994). Ibrahim's (1992) study focused on conservatism–liberalism among technical secondary school students in Egypt and reported a tendency toward conservatism among participants. However, female and younger students showed more conservative tendencies compared with their male and older counterparts. This result could be a reflection of conservative tendencies dominant in the family. Few studies have been conducted to investigate orientation toward forgiveness among Arab youth (Ahmed, Azar, and Mullet, 2007; Eid, 2002b). The study by Ahmed et al. (2007) aimed to investigate the impact of the Iraqi invasion on orientations toward forgiveness among Kuwaiti adolescents and adults. Results showed that the levels and dimensions of forgiveness among Kuwaiti participants do not differ from those of other investigated societies. In addition, some studies conducted in Israel showed that Jewish adolescents and Jewish and Israeli Arab female adolescents were less conservative than Arab adolescents and Jewish and Arab male adolescents (Seginer and Shoyer, 2007). Other Israeli studies showed that "despite political and cultural differences, the constructed future space of Jewish, Arab, and Druze adolescents is partly similar" (Seginer and Shoyer, 2007, p. 493).

Studies that focus on risk perception among Arab respondents (Ahmed, Macri, and Mullet, 2006; Ahmed and Mullet, 2008; Sabry, 1989) show that, whereas Egyptian and Kuwaiti adolescents and young adults are almost identical in their perceptions of risky items, they differ from Europeans (i.e., French) in the perception of environmental risk. The overall means in both Egyptians and Kuwaitis were almost the same. The liner association between Egyptian and French ratings and also between Kuwaiti and French ratings was moderate, but the association between Egyptian and Kuwaiti ratings was high. Results generally indicate that, despite great socioeconomic differences between both Arab nations, they perceive societal risk in a common way, a way that differs from the way Western respondents perceive risk.

Some studies have investigated participants' perceptions of family members (blood relatives, such as mother, father, and brother, and in-laws, such as mother-in-law and father-in-law) in Sudanese, Kuwaiti, and Egyptian adolescents and young adults compared with American and Indian counterparts (Adler, et al., 1998; Adler, Davis, and Ahmed, 1988; Adler et al., 1989; Adler, Denmark, and Ahmed, 1989, 1991; Adler et al., 1992). Results showed consistent schemata, despite the wide economic, social, and cultural differences, that participants see their blood relatives as closer than their in-laws.

Several Arab studies have focused on investigating psychosocial development/maturity using Erikson's theory as a framework. Abdel-Moety (1991b) reported a significant positive correlation between university students' psychosocial maturity and moral development. Some studies have focused on identity formation, identity disorders, and ego identity (Abdel-Moety, 1991a, 1991b, 1993; Abdel-Rahman, 1998b; Ahmed and Megreya, 2008; Al-Otaibi, 2005; Eid, 2002a; Mohammed, 2000a, 2000b), whereas others (Morsy, 2002) investigated the need for psychological counseling to confront identity crisis among adolescents. Abdel-Moety (1991a) found that, whereas positive parental treatment correlated with identity achievement, negative parental treatment correlated with identity diffusion in Egyptian university students. Similar results have been reported by Al-Otaibi (2005) in Kuwaiti adolescents and young adults. Finally, a positive correlation between identity achievement and both academic achievement and academic adjustment has been found. Abdel-Moety's (1991b) results received support from studies conducted by Mohammed (2000a, 2000b) in Egypt. A third study by Abdel-Moety (1991b) reported a correlation between psychosocial development and moral maturity. Results of Abdel-Rahman's study (1998b) on Egyptian youth showed that, whereas identity achievement correlated significantly with dominance, boldness, self-discipline, emotional stability, and conformity, the identity statuses of moratorium, foreclosure, and diffusion correlated with sensitivity, insecurity, tension, and suspiciousness. Ahmed and Megreya (2008) compared identity disorders in samples of Egyptian and Kuwaiti adolescents and young adults and found that Egyptians outnumbered Kuwaitis on identity achievement, but Kuwaitis were higher than their Egyptian peers on the following three identity disorders (statuses): foreclosure, moratorium, and diffusion. An explanation for these results is the difference between the two countries in economic situation and lifestyle, which could strengthen achievement motivation among Egyptians. In the same context, Henry (2007) asked Egyptian undergraduate psychology female students to write about their reactions to the topic of gender development. Youth used what they learned about gender roles and identity to reflect on women's status in Egypt. They reflected considerable efforts to examine the relation between their own psychological functioning and gender expectations/roles. Understanding about gender influenced their reactions to many psychological topics such as moral, emotional, and sexual development and parenting and marriage. Finally, they integrated religious beliefs with many principles of psychology.

Several studies have focused on social skills, social isolation, and/or alienation among children, adolescents, and young adults (Abdel-Rahman, 1998a; Al-Anwar, 2002; Mohammed, 2000c, 2000d). In Abdel-Rahman's study (1998a), the aim was to assess the relation between social skills and depression and hopelessness in samples of Egyptian urban and rural boys and girls with mean age of 11 years. Results showed a significant negative correlation between social skills and both depression and hopelessness. Moreover, girls and older and rural children had significantly higher social skills and lower depression and hopelessness compared with boys and younger and urban children. In Egypt, Mohammed (2000c) found that male university students experienced higher alienation compared with their female counterparts. Moreover, the interaction between gender and gender role had a significant impact on the level of alienation. In Al-Anwar's (2002) study of Egyptian adolescents, alienation correlated positively with lower scores on sociability and emotional stability and with higher scores on psychological insecurity and tension. Moreover, males, compared with their female counterparts, scored lower on sociability and emotional stability but higher on psychological insecurity and tension. One study employed Jordanian youth (summarized by Benat and Salama, unpublished); alienation correlated negatively with religiosity. Finally, in a study by El-Dabaa and Al-Saud (2008), approximately 25% of their sample of university female students reported higher scores (than the average) on alienation.

A survey conducted in Dubai, UAE (Al-Qabas, 2008) on happiness in 7,434 youths and adults from different Arab countries showed that the Sultanate of Oman had the highest rate of happiness (61%), followed by Saudi Arabia (57%), Qatar (56%), Bahrain (54%), Kuwait (53%), UAE (52%), Jordan (47%), Egypt (46%), Syria (46%), Morocco (44%), and Lebanon (35%). Males and females reported similar levels of happiness. Older participants (46 years and older) reported higher levels of happiness compared with youth (age 18 to 35 years). Figley, Ashkanani, Chapman, and Al-Nasser (2008) studied Kuwaiti male and female adults; they showed that less educated, less wealthy, and unmarried individuals reported higher levels of Raha (comfort). Respondents who indicated that they were healthier, had less wealth, and had more stringent religious beliefs reported higher Raha scores.

Intelligence and Cognitive Development

Several studies have been conducted on intelligence, critical thinking, creative thinking, and creativity among children, adolescents, and young adults in North Africa and Middle East countries (Al-Sharkawy, 2005; Behagat, 2005; Ibrahim, 2006, in Egypt; Ameziane, 2004, in Morocco; Al-Zeqay, 2001, in Algeria; Al-Emam and El-Zeraigat, 2005; Al-Mustafa, 2006, in Jordan). Behagat (2005) reported that exposing gifted primary school children in Egypt to enriched activities led to a significant improvement in their scholastic performance. Ibrahim (2006) focused on critical thinking and its components in samples of male and female university students. No significant differences emerged in the components of critical thinking as a result of differences in gender (males versus females), academic specialization (science versus literature), or place of residence (urban versus rural areas).

By the late 1970s, North Africa and Middle East researchers showed a gradually increasing interest in investigating cognitive styles (especially field dependence versus field independence and impulsivity versus reflectivity) and related variables in different age group participants. One of these studies (Ahmed, 1993) found that Sudanese adolescents, compared with their Kuwaiti counterparts, were more reflective and tended to score more mistakes. Another study (Ameziane, 2002) found a positive relation between reflectivity and both intelligence and problem solving among Moroccan children.

Piagetian theory and research have been known in many of the North Africa and Middle East countries since the early 1950s (Karam el-Din, 1998). In the Arab countries alone, more than 80 research studies based on Piagetian theory and work were conducted between the early 1950s and the mid-1990s and dealt with a variety of concepts such as animism, space, quantity, number, causality, and reasoning concepts and, to lesser extent, formal operations. A great number of these studies has been conducted in Egypt. These studies, whether related to the general stages of cognitive development or to specific developmental stages such as conservation, causality, time, formal operations, or moral development, have shown that the cognitive development of Arab children and adolescents follows the same course and sequence of stages found among Swiss children as described by Piaget. In general, however, Arab children and adolescents reached the various stages of cognitive development at a later age than their Swiss counterparts. The developmental lag ranged between 1 to 4 years depending on the area of cognitive development studied. These findings were confirmed in the few cross-cultural studies that simultaneously compared cognitive development in Arab and Western samples (Ahmed, 1981, 1989; Gaber et al., 1981; Hyde, 1970).

Arab Piagetian studies have reported a strong positive correlation between cognitive development and intelligence in the psychometric sense and language. A similar correlation was found between children's cognitive development and their academic achievement, especially in specific areas such as arithmetic, which correlated significantly with children's conservation of number. A study of the development of quantity among Saudi Arabian Bedouin primary school children ages 7 to 15 years (Sendioni and Abdalla, 2001) showed that Piaget's three stages of development could be clearly distinguished. Results also showed that the percentage of children achieving conservation of each age level increased from 14.5% at age 7, to 33% age 8, 48% at age 9, 69% at age 10, 72% at age 11, 93% at age 12, and 100% at age 13. The researchers indicated that these results were in line with those of Hyde (1970), who reported that Arab, Indian, and Somali children living in Aden, Yemen, showed the same types of responses as those described by Piaget, often giving explanations in Arabic that were almost word-for-word translations of the explanations given by Swiss children.

Most Arab Piagetian studies have not found systematic gender differences in rates of cognitive development (Karam el-Din, 1998). The relation between cognitive development and family background has not been studied frequently. Yet, the few Arab research studies that investigated this relation reported nonsignificant correlations. In contrast, Arab studies focused on the urban/rural differences in cognitive development have reported faster rates of cognitive development among urban children and adolescents compared with their rural counterparts.

Moral Development

Several studies have been conducted in North Africa and Middle East countries focused on the development of moral judgment/thinking/reasoning using Piaget's tasks (Haraby, 1948), Kohlberg's interview, J. Rest's Defining Issues Test (DIT) (Ahmed, Gielen, and Avellani, 1987, in Sudan; Gielen, Ahmed, and Avellani, 1992, in Kuwait; Abdel-Moety, 1991b, in Egypt), Gibbs' Social Reflection Measure-Short Form (SRM-SF) (H. Al-Ghamdi, 1996, on Saudi Arabian adolescents, cited in Ahmed and Gielen, 2002), or even locally developed measures and scales in children, adolescents, and young adults from Egypt, Algeria, Kuwait, Saudi Arabia, and Sudan. Results using the DIT (Abdel-Moety, 1991b; Ahmed and Gielen, 2002) showed that Arab adolescents and young adults, compared with American and South Asian peers, tend to prefer conventional arguments (stages 3 and 4) to preconventional (stage 2) and postconventional arguments (stages 5 and 6). Those Arab studies that used consistency checks showed high rates of inconsistency among Arab respondents (between 20% and 55%). The last few decades have witnessed some attempts to study moral development in children and youth from an Islamic point of view (Hasan and Al-Thafery, 2006).

Religiosity, Religious Feelings, and Attitudes

The first study to address the development of religious feeling was conducted by El-Meliugi (1951) using Egyptian children and adolescents. Since the late 1970s, several studies were conducted in North Africa and Middle East and dealt with religiosity, religious feelings, and attitudes. One study (Torki, 1980, cited in Moussa, El-Dousseki, and Ahmed, 1998) on youth from Kuwait found that, whereas religiosity correlated with flexibility, no correlation between religiosity and neuroticism, introversion–extroversion, self-confidence, and achievement motivation was found. Another study (Al-Mestikawy, 1982, cited in Moussa et al., 1998) on rural and urban male and female Egyptian university students found that students exhibiting moderate religious attitudes scored higher on scales of neuroticism, self-assertiveness, introversion–extroversion, dominance–submissiveness, social participation, and adjustment. In contrast, students with extreme religious attitudes scored higher on a scale of self-esteem. In a sample of Kuwaiti university students, Al-Tai (1992, cited in Moussa et al., 1998) found (1) a correlation between more intense religious attitudes and several adaptive personality traits as measured by the Personality Inventory and Minnesota Multiphasic Personality Inventory; (2) that more religious students were characterized by more normal and acceptable personality traits compared with the less religious students; and (3) that the psychological profile of the more religious students was more "normal" than the psychological profile of the less religious students. Another study (Ghalab and El-Dousseki, 1994) tested the link between violence/aggression or extreme behavior and religiosity in samples of religious Muslim and Christian university students in Egypt. Results showed significant differences between higher intrinsic and extrinsic religious orientations. Higher extrinsic religious orientation youth, especially males from both religions, reported more positive attitudes toward violence, neuroticism, rigidity, and anxiety, whereas intrinsic youth had higher self-assertiveness. Muslim extrinsic females showed more neuroticism, rigidity, and dominancy compared with their Christian counterparts.

Political Attitudes

Surprisingly few studies have dealt with political attitudes of youth in North Africa and Middle East countries. One study (Al-Madhoun, 1998) of students at Al-Azhar University, Gaza Strip, reported positive correlations (1) between radical political attitudes and neuroticism, (2) between extroversion, social attractiveness, and perception of parental acceptance and conservatism, and (3) between liberal political attitudes and extroversion, social attractiveness, and parents' encouragement of independence in their children. Another study (E. A. Ahmed, 1992) investigated the relation between image of authority and perceived parental treatment in university students in Egypt and found that (1) perceived parental rejection correlated with participants' rebellious tendencies and (2) males, urban students, and students of humanitarian and social sciences colleges reported more rebelliousness toward authority compared with females and students of science and applied colleges. A third study (Zoqan, 1997) investigated the impact of Palestinian Intifada (uprising) on children's play. Children tended to choose military, violent, and group play more, with a clear tendency among boys to choose leadership positions. Several studies have been conducted on political alienation among Egyptian, Saudi Arabian, Jordanian, Palestine, and Kuwaiti youth (cited in Benat and Salama, unpublished) and in Morocco (El-Seddik, 2006). In general, results showed a preference for political alienation among respondents (approximately 20% to 25%). No significant effect for age, gender, socioeconomic status, and educational level on respondents' alienation was found.

To assess the impact of the Iraqi invasion (August 1990 to February 1991) on Kuwaiti psychological well-being, more than 100 studies have been conducted between 1991 and 2000 (summarized by Ahmed, 2000; see also the study by Awadh, Vance, El-Beblawi, and Pumariega, 2004) and showed negative impacts on personality traits, cognitive aspects, values, and beliefs among the Kuwaitis, especially children and youth. Concerning Palestinian youth, "By 2001, 70 percent of 1.000 [Palestinian] nine- to sixteen-year-olds interviewed by the psychologist Fadal Abu-Hin said they wanted to be martyrs" (Gregg, 2005, p. 40).

Collectivism Versus Individualism

Few Arab research studies have investigated individualism/collectivism in Arab respondents (Al-Youssefi, 1999; Darwish and Huber, 2002, in Egypt; Khaleefa, Al-Mustafa, Al-Bailey, and Al-Ghreniah, 2007, in Bahrain). Darwish and Huber (2002) showed that, whereas Egyptian university students scored higher on collectivism, their German counterparts scored higher on individualism. In both nations, females scored significantly higher than their male counterparts on vertical and horizontal collectivism; however, gender differences were more clear-cut in the case of the German respondents.

Drug Abuse and Cigarette Smoking in Children and Youth

Drug consumption, abuse, and addiction (including hashish) and cigarette smoking have attracted psychologists from North Africa and the Middle East since the late 1950s. The Lasting Program of Drug Abuse led by M. I. Soueif (1998a) resulted in several epidemiological research studies dealing with drugs, psychoactive substances, and cigarette smoking among Egyptian youth. The percentage of drug addicts among secondary school students was higher than among university students. Factors that correlated with drug abuse were the presence of a drug addiction culture, the presence of addicts among family members or friends, and the strong negative influence of the media. In one study, 18% of adolescents reported that they had smoked cigarettes; 5.22% used tranquilizers; 5.75% used psychoactive drugs; and 5% used sedative or hypnotic drugs. A great number reported that they had tried hashish, beer, opium, and alcohol. The majority had favorable attitudes toward psychoactive substances and believed that such substances have a useful effect.

Another Egyptian study (Mohammed, 1994) focused on the dynamics of attitudes toward drug addiction among Egyptian male and female youth in relation to variables such as family size, perception of parental acceptance/rejection, dependency, self-esteem, self-adequacy, and world view. Results showed a significant positive relation between perceptions of parental rejection and positive attitudes toward drug addiction and a significant negative relation between perceptions of parental acceptance and positive attitudes toward drugs addiction. Youth who reported positive attitudes toward drug addiction were more dependent, were more negative in self-esteem, had higher feelings of negative self-adequacy, and had a more negative world view.

The Lasting Program of Drugs Consumption inspired several Egyptian and Arab psychologists to conduct studies on drugs/psychoactive substances (Ali and Sabry, 1997; Habib, 1992, 1994). As an example, in Egypt, Ali and Sabry (1997) investigated addicted and nonaddicted children. Drug addiction among children correlated with parents' (especially fathers) unemployment, lack or absence of the ideal figure in the family context, and maladjustment in the relationship between parents and the parent–child relationship.

A Sudanese study (El-Hilo, 2001) investigated the prevalence of drug abuse among secondary school male and female students (ages 14 to 19 years) in Khartoum. Results revealed that 45% (31% males and 14% females) reported use of tobacco; 11.2% used smokeless tobacco (toombak); 3% used a water pipe (shesha); 27.6% used medical drugs as prescribed by their physicians; 6.7% used alcohol; 6.5% used bango (cannabis); 4% used heroin; 5.9% used solvents and gases; and 2% used amphetamines. A report (Al-Qabas 2008) showed that 28% and 14% of Kuwaiti males and females, respectively, between the ages of 13 and 15 years were identified as cigarette smokers. In agreement with the earlier mentioned results, Israeli reports show that the average age of starting cigarette smoking is 13 years, at which age 12% and 8% of Jewish and Arab boys, respectively, smoke at least one cigarette per day (Seginer and Shoyer, 2007). Similarly, some Turkish studies reported that 11% of adolescents (age 15 years) were active smokers. Other Turkish findings revealed that between 45.9% and 63.8% of high school students were identified as regular cigarette smokers (Celen and Cok, 2007). As for alcohol use, reports showed that more than 60% of adolescents tried alcohol between 17 and 18 years (Celen and Cok, 2007). In Iran, 22.3% of 12- to 14-year-olds experienced drugs, alcohol, or tobacco one or more time during their lives: "tobacco 17.5%, alcohol 6.8%, opium 0.6%, heroin 0.4%, and hashish 0.2%," and "8.3% of students were substance dependent, 6.2% were tobacco dependent and 2.8% were alcohol dependent" (Sondaite, 2007, p. 476).

Violence in Children and Youth

Several studies have focused on violence/aggression and extreme responses among children and youth in the North Africa and Middle East countries (Abou-Maraq, 1997; Ali, 2001; Azab, 2002; Soueif, 1958, 1959; and Bader, 2001, cited in Ahmed, 2007b, 2008). In one study, Ali (2001) aimed to investigate the relation between violence and social variables in a sample of Egyptian adolescents. Males and lower socioeconomic status individuals were more violent than females and medium and higher socioeconomic status counterparts, and lower socioeconomic status males reported more verbal violence than their higher socioeconomic status peers.

Children's and adolescents' violent/aggressive behavior correlates significantly and positively with perceptions of parental behavior as characterized by violence, aggression, hostility, neglect, indifference, and rejection (Faied, 1996; Gabr and Haredy, 2003, in Egypt; Bader, 2001, cited in Ahmed, 2007b, 2008; Azab, 2002, in Saudi Arabia; Taher, 2005, in Kuwait, cited in Ahmed, 2007b, 2008). Kamel (2002) sought to study abuse and neglect and related variables among children and adolescents age 10 to 19 years in Egypt and found that abuse and neglect victims came from families characterized by broken homes, parents with negative psychological characteristics, and illiterate or poorly educated parents. Moreover, 38.8% reported that they were subjects of severe verbal insult, 37.8% mentioned that they had been beaten badly, and 26% to 44.2% reported that were abused at work.

Street Children

The twenty-first century has witnessed a dramatic increase in the number of street children in North Africa and Middle East countries, leading to societal problems and consequences. In countries such as Egypt, street children are estimated to number one million (Abdalla and Hussein, 2001; Baza, 2003; Ghoniemah, 2003; Hamza, 1996/1997; Ismail, 2002; Wahdan, Al-Ater, Abdel-Ghany, and Elias, 1999). Broken homes, child abuse, school dropout (which could be estimated to be between 10% to 15% of all primary school in Egypt; Baza, 2003), and economic hardships are the main reasons for this phenomenon. Another similar phenomenon is the leaving (escape) of children and adolescents (Farag, 2003), which became the subject of great concern for authorities and academicians, especially in light of the increasing numbers of girls who escape or leave their family. Broken homes (absent one or both parents), child abuse, and economic hardship are considered the reasons underlying such societal problems.

Prevalence of Psychological Disturbances

Very few studies have sought the prevalence of psychological disturbances among youth. Examples include Ouwaida and Ali (1992) and Ahmed and Khalil (2004) in Egypt and Ahmed and Al-Khawajah (2008) in Kuwait. These three studies revealed a correlation between age and the prevalence of psychological disturbances and also reported higher levels of psychological disturbances (such as depression, hostility, anxiety, and phobia) among intermediate and secondary school male and female students between the ages of 11 and 20 years. Female, Egyptian rural, and Kuwaiti Bedouin youth showed higher levels of psychological disturbances compared with males and Egyptian and Kuwaiti urban youth.

Effects of Crowding on Child and Youth Behavior

Kamel and El-Fakhrany (2002) investigated the effect of crowding as an environmental variable on hostility and assertiveness in Egyptian male and female students (mean age, 19 years). High levels of crowding were associated with higher levels of hostility and lower levels of assertiveness, and males outnumbered their female counterparts on hostility. Finally, males reported higher levels of direct hostility, but females, compared with males, reported higher levels of hostility toward others. An Algerian study by F. Nacuer (2001, cited in Ahmed, 2005b) showed that the type of built environment correlated positively with children's aggressive behavior.

Since the mid-1990s, a large number of Internet cafes have appeared in North Africa and Middle East countries, especially in larger cities such as Cairo and Alexandria (Egypt), Rabat (Morocco), Amman (Jordan), Khartoum (Sudan), and Istanbul (Turkey) and, to a lesser extent, in the richer countries such as the oil-producing Arab Gulf states (Saudi Arabia, Bahrain, Kuwait, Qatar, Sultanate of Oman, and the UAE), where most adolescents and young adults possess their own computers. These cafes are attended by young males and (to a lesser extent) females (Ahmed, 2007a; Ahmed and Al-Khawajah, 2007). In one Arab study by Taie (2000, cited in Ahmed, 2007a), the aim was to explore use of the Internet by youth in five Arab countries (Egypt, Saudi Arabia, the UAE, Kuwait, and Bahrain). It showed that 72% of youth use the Internet regularly. The average time spent per week was 2 hours in Egypt, 3 hours in the UAE, 4 hours in both Kuwait and Bahrain, and 6 hours in Saudi Arabia. Moreover, males, compared with females, tended to use the Internet more extensively. Finally, youth tend to use the Internet more intensively at night.

Practical Information About Developmental Science in North Africa and the Middle East

During the last two decades, researchers have tried to develop programs to modify children's and adolescents' behavior. Among these attempts, Mohammed (1999) investigated the efficiency of a behavioral training program in reducing aggressive behavior in a sample of autistic and normal Egyptian children age 7 to 13 years. Results showed a significant reduction (decline) in the autistic children's aggressive behavior as a result of participating in the training program. Ibrahim and Soliman (2002) successfully tested the efficiency of a special program to develop mental, cognitive, and linguistic aspects of preschool children in Egypt. Other researchers have developed programs for improving self-concept in children (Abdel-Latif, Al-Mushref, and Al-Saway, 2006). Examples of other new practical topics include extensive investigations of violence, including domestic violence, violence in school and university (Abdalla, 2005), personality and demographic variables related to violence (Al-Mestikawy, 2005), the relation between families' violence and aggressive behavior in adolescents (Al-Motwa, 2008), and violence as viewed by adolescents, youth, and intellectuals (Ghanam, 1998, 2003, 2005). Other topics also include university students' attitudes toward some forms of abnormal gender behavior (Al-Mestikawy, 2006) and variables characterized by perpetrators of traffic accidents and violations (Abdalla and Radwan, 2005).

A steadily increasing number of Arab research studies have aimed at developing intervention programs to eradicate psychological/behavioral problems, such as reducing aggression/violence or reducing psychological disturbances among children and adolescents (R. E. Ahmed, 2006; Hafez and Kasem, 1993a; Saigh and Omar, 1983; A. M. H. Saleh, 1995; S. Kh. Saleh, 1998); to help adolescents face identity crises (Morsy, 2002); and to improve social and psychological skills and abilities such as improving self-confidence, problem-solving methods, and creative and critical thinking among the young. Some other intervention programs aim at improving social skills in blind (Ali, 2002) or mentally retarded children (Keshaf, 2002). In addition, some intervention programs focus on discovering gifted and creative school children (Mensy and El-Bana, 2002).

Several countries in North Africa and the Middle East established institutions and centers to secure suitable care for offspring. Examples include the National Council for Motherhood and Childhood (established in 2000 in Cairo) and the Kuwait Foundation for Advancement of Arab Childhood (established in the early 1980s in Kuwait). Moreover, some Arab universities have established institutes devoted to the study of children and adolescents; an example is the Institute of Higher Studies on Childhood at Ain Shams University (which was established in Cairo, Egypt in the early 1980s). "The scant literature on adolescent socialization in developing countries [such as North Africa and Middle East countries] focuses mainly on the roles of family, peers, and the media. Systematic research is lacking on the ways in which the process and content of formal schooling affect the maturation of girls and boys. Indeed, the specific mechanism through which education exerts its influences on young people are inculcated with norms and values and exposed to new ideas. The curriculum and textbook content, interpersonal interactions within and outside the classroom (including teacher-student and student-student interaction), extracurricular activities, and formal administrative rules and regulations are obvious vehicles through which messages regarding gender and other social norms are transmitted. Formal schooling may also impart a set of skills related to personal efficacy, problem-solving, and social negotiation" (Mensch et al., 2000, p. 2).

Conclusion

Previous review of the Arab psychological literature shows that developmental issues have been widely investigated (Ahmed and Gielen, 1998). After reviewing the Arab literature in psychology, Soueif (1998b) concluded that this literature could be categorized in seven broad areas spanning developmental topics, education and creativity, personality, social and organizational psychology, biological psychology and experimentation, clinical efforts, and cross-cultural investigations. As Soueif (1998b) stated, Arab psychologists showed early interest in Piagetian theory. Cognitive styles, especially field dependency/independency and impulsivity/reflectivity, have been extensively investigated in their relation to a variety of variables such as temperamental characteristics, intellectual abilities (fluid intelligence and spatial ability), professional specialization, academic achievement, children's drawings, learning processes, and problem-solving methods (Soueif, 1998b).

The last two decades have witnessed a significant shift in the Arab research interest in developmental issues. Researchers tried to expand their focus of interest to include new developmental issues such as violence. Social perception constitutes another new developmental topic, including positivism and self-actualization among students (Eid, 2002c, 2002d); adolescents' and youth's view toward the future (Abou-Zaid, 1992); gender differences in citizenship (Al-Ali, 2008); emotional intelligence and related variables (Abou-Nashy, 2002); ideal and good example for the secondary school students (Ghanam, 2000); effect of globalization on value systems among university students (Alduaij and Al-Salameh, 2007); youths' attitudes toward secret (consensual) marriage (Abdel-Wahab and Munieb, 2003); perceptions/attitudes toward globalization, modernization, and environment (Naser, 1997); perception of family members' and university students' concept of personal commitment (Naser, 2003); the relation between physical movement and perceptual motor abilities (Al-Mustafa, 2006; Abdel-Wahid et al., 2004); risk perception and orientation toward forgiveness (Ahmed, Macri, and Mullet, 2006; Ahmed and Mullet, 2008; Ahmed et al., 2007; Eid, 2002b); and social attitudes as measured through children's drawings (Gibbons, Ahmed, Van den Broeck, and Brown, 2008).

The majority of Arab developmental research studies have been conducted and also published in Egypt. Also, a great number of Arab developmental studies have employed children in late childhood, adolescence, and youth, and only a few studies have used infants and preschool children. Most Arab developmental research studies have focused on investigating topics related to social and personality development more than intelligence and cognition. Despite significant progress in studying developmental issues in the Arab world, especially during the last two decades, there is still much room for further efforts, such as investigating properly the impact of education on young people's capabilities and increasing the intervention psychological programs and training among children and youth. Such programs are much needed to help children cope with the new demands of globalization.

References

Abdalla, J. B., and Hussein, N. (2001). Psycho-social adjustment of street children. *Arab Psychologist* (Egypt), 2, 61–71.

Abdalla, M. S. (1989). *Prejudice*. Kuwait: Alem el-Maarifah Series No.137.

Abdalla, M. S. (2005). *Violence in the university life: Its reasons, manifestations, and suggested solutions to treat it*. Cairo, Egypt: Publications of the Center of Psychological Research and Studies, Faculty of Arts, Cairo University.

Abdalla, M. S., and Abdel-Rahman, M. E. (1996/1997). Developing a scale of irrational beliefs for children and adolescents. *Journal of Psychology* (Egypt), 11, 124–140.

Abdalla, M. S., and Radwan, S. G. (2005). Personality characteristics among perpetrators of traffic accidents and violations. *Annals of the Center of Psychological Studies, Faculty of Arts, Cairo University*, Cairo, Egypt, Annals No. 1, Monograph No. 4, October.

Abdel-Hamid, M. I. (1992). *The relationship between family's immigration from rural settings to city settings and the change in styles of children's socialization: A field study*. Unpublished master's thesis, Institute of Higher Studies on Childhood, Ain Shams University, Cairo, Egypt.

Abdel-Hamid, T. (1990). *Producing compelling: A study in education and social control*. Cairo, Egypt: Sinai for Publishing.

Abdel-Kader, A. A. (2000). Assertiveness between submission and hostility (aggression) toward authority: A comparative study of adolescents in rural and urban areas. In *Proceedings of the 7th International Conference of the Centre of Counseling "Developing Man for a Better Society," Ain Shams University* (pp. 313–348). Cairo, Egypt, November 5-7, 2000.

Abdel-Latif, F. I., Al-Mushrefy, I. I., and Al-Saway, I. Z. (2006). The efficiency of a suggested program based on life activities in improving child's self-concept. *Arab Journal of Contemporary Psychology* (Egypt), 2, 77–107.

Abdel-Moety, H. M. (1991a). Family socialization and its impact on identity formation among university youth. *Journal of the Faculty of Education, Tanta University* (Egypt), 14, 233–277.

Abdel-Moety, H. M. (1991b). The relationship between psychosocial development and the development of moral thinking among adolescents and adults. *Journal of the Faculty of Education, Tanta University* (Egypt), 14, 312–368.

Abdel-Moety, H. M. (1993). A study of some academic variables related to identity formation among university youth. *Journal of Psychology* (Egypt), 7, 6–36.

Abdel-Rahman, M. E. (1998a). Social skills and their relation with depression and hopelessness in children. In M. E. Abdel-Rahman (Ed.), *Studies in mental health, socialization, social skills, psychological dependency, and identity* (Vol. 2, pp. 9–81), Cairo, Egypt: Dar Ghareeb.

Abdel-Rahman, M. E. (1998b). Personality traits and their relation with ways of confronting identity crisis among secondary school and university students. In M. E. Abdel-Rahman (Ed.), *Studies in mental health, social skills, psychological independency, and identity* (Vol. 2, pp. 389–470), Cairo, Egypt: Dar Ghareeb.

Abdel-Wahab, A. A., and Munieb, T. O. (2003). Youth attitudes towards secret (consensual) marriage and their relationship with family climate: A comparative study between rural and urban areas and a suggested program to reduce the phenomenon. *Egyptian Journal of Psychological Studies* (Egypt), 13, 141–192.

Abdel-Wahid, A., Al-Fyez, G., Harville, M., Arikawa, H., Temeo, M. E., Templer, D. I., et al. (2004). Comparative prevalence of isolated sleep paralysis in Kuwaiti, Sudanese, and American students. *Psychological Reports*, 95, 317–32322.

Abou-el-Enien, A. F. I. (1995). *The relationship between attitudes towards contemporary social problems and manifestations of alienation in the light of socioeconomic status.* Unpublished master's thesis, Department of Psychology, Faculty of Arts, Ain Shams University, Cairo, Egypt.

Abou-el-Kheir, M. M. S. (1995). *Physical punishment and patterns of parental control and their relation with psychological characteristics in children and adolescents.* Unpublished doctoral dissertation, Faculty of Arts, Zagazig University, Zagazig, Egypt.

Abou-Maraq, G. Z. (1997). Aggressive behavior among primary school students: A cross-cultural study in Saudi Arabia, Egypt, and Algeria. *The Journal of Research in Education and Psychology, Minia University* (Egypt), *1*, 112–134.

Abou-Nashy, M. S. (2002). Emotional intelligence and its relation with general intelligence, social skills, and personality traits. *The Egyptian Journal of Psychological Studies* (Egypt), *12*, 145–188.

Abou-Shideed, K. A., and Naser, R. N. (2002). Internal and external controls and their relations with university students' attribution for the reason of peace with Israel. *Journal of Psychology* (Egypt), *16*, 88–97.

Abou-Zaid, N. A. A. (1992). Future view among university male and female youth: A survey. *Journal of Psychology* (Egypt), *6*, 48–61.

Abou-Zaid, N. A. A. (2003). Psychological and social motives related to use modern communication sets (apparatus) among adolescents. *Journal of Psychology* (Egypt), *17*, 72–91.

Adler, L. L., Clark, S. P., Denmark, F. L., Ahmed, R. A., Kim, T., de Silva, S. S., et al. (1998, February). *Similarities and differences of attitudes in cross-cultural comparisons.* Paper presented at the 27th Annual Meeting of the Society for Cross-Cultural Research, St. Petersburg, FL.

Adler, L. L., Davis, W.H., and Ahmed, R. A. (1988, February). *The perceptions of middle age and old age in cross-cultural perspective.* Paper presented at the 17th Annual Meeting of the Society for Cross-Cultural Research, El-Paso, TX.

Adler, L. L., Davis, W. H., Ahmed, R. A., Mrinal, N. R., Mukherji, R., and Morgan, N. (1989). The perception of mother-in-law and father-in-law in cross-cultural perspective. *International Journal of Group Tensions, 19*, 245–254.

Adler, L. L., Denmark, F. L., and Ahmed, R. A. 1989). Attitudes toward mother-in-law and step-mother: A cross-cultural study. *Psychological Reports, 65*, 1194.

Adler, L. L., Denmark, F. L., and Ahmed, R. A. (1991). A critical evaluation of attitudes toward mother-in-law and stepmother: A cross-cultural study. In W. Oxman-Michelli and M. Weinstein (Eds.), *Conference 1989 Proceedings: Critical Thinking Focus on Social and Cultural Inquiry* (pp. 427–434). Upper Montclair, NJ: Montclair State College.

Adler, L. L., Denmark, F. L., Miao, E. S. C. Y., Ahmed, R. A., Takooshian, H., Adler, H. E., et al. (1992). Cross-cultural comparisons of projected social distances toward family members: A programmatic study. In U. P. Gielen, L. L. Adler, and N. A. Milgram (Eds.), *Psychology in international perspective: 50 Years of the International Council of Psychologists "ICP"* (pp. 260–270). Amsterdam, The Netherlands: Swets and Zeitlinger.

Ahlawat, K. S. (1991, July). *Cross-cultural comparison of human needs in China, Japan, Jordan, and Switzerland: A search for common structure.* Paper presented at Regional Meeting of the International Association for Cross-Cultural Psychology, Debrecen, Hungary.

Ahmed, E. A. (1992). *Image of authority among university students and its relation with parental socialization.* Unpublished master's thesis, Department of Psychology, Faculty of Arts, Ain Shams University, Cairo, Egypt.

Ahmed, R. A. (1981). *Zur Ontogenese der Begriffskompetenz bei aegyptishen Kindern in Abhangigkeit von sozalen und kulturellen Entwicklungsbedingungen.* Unpublished doctoral dissertation, Leipzig University, Leipzig, Germany.

Ahmed, R. A. (1989). The development of number, space, quantity, and reasoning concepts in Sudanese school children. In L. L. Adler (Ed.), *Cross-cultural research in human development: Focus on life-span* (pp. 17–23). New York: Praeger.

Ahmed, R. A. (1993, August). *Perceptual tempo in Sudanese, Kuwaiti, and non-Kuwaiti intermediate school students.* Paper presented at the 51st Annual Meeting of the International Council of Psychologists, Montreal, Quebec, Canada.

Ahmed, R. A. (2000). *Psychology of captivity and war prisoner.* Kuwait: Kuwait National Guard.

Ahmed, R. A. (2005a). Manifestations of violence in Arab schools and procedures for reducing it. In F. L. Denmark, H. H. Krauss, R. W. Wesner, E. Midlarsky, and U. P. Gielen (Eds.), *Violence in schools: Cross-national and cross-cultural perspectives* (pp. 207–236). New York: Springer Science and Business Media, Inc.

Ahmed, R. A. (2005b). A critical review of Arab research studies on violence/aggression and extreme behavior. In L. L. Adler and F. L. Denmark (Eds.), *Violence around the world* (pp. 1–25). New York: Greenwood Press.

Ahmed, R. A. (2007a). Egypt. In J. J. Arnett (Ed.), *International encyclopedia of adolescents* (Vol. 1, pp. 255–2680). New York: Routledge, Taylor and Francis Group.

Ahmed, R. A. (2007b). Arab studies on parental acceptance-rejection. *Interpersonal Acceptance (International Society for Interpersonal Acceptance and Rejection), 1,* 4, 8–10.

Ahmed, R. A. (2008). Review of Arab research on parental acceptance-rejection. In F. Erkman (Ed.), *Acceptance: The essence of peace: Selected papers from the First International Congress on "Interpersonal Acceptance and Rejection,"* held in Istanbul, Turkey, June 22-24, 2006 (pp. 201–224). Istanbul, Turkey: Turkish Psychology Association, Istanbul Branch.

Ahmed, R. A., and Al-Khawajah, J. M. (2007). Kuwait. In J. J. Arnett (Ed.), *International encyclopedia of adolescents* (Vol. 1, pp. 562–573), New York: Routledge.

Ahmed, R. A., and Al-Khawajah, J. M. A. (2008, February). *Prevalence of psychological disturbances among intermediate and secondary school students in Kuwait.* Paper presented at the 37th Annual Meeting of the Society for Cross-Cultural Research. New Orleans, LA.

Ahmed, R. A., Azar, F., and Mullet, E. (2007). Interpersonal forgiveness among Kuwaiti adolescents and adults. *Conflict Management and Peace Science, 24,* 159–170.

Ahmed, R. A., and Gielen, U. P. (1998). Psychology in the Arab world. In R. A. Ahmed and U. P. Gielen (Eds.), *Psychology in the Arab countries* (pp. 3–48). Menoufia, Egypt: Menoufia University Press.

Ahmed, R. A., and Gielen, U. P. (2002). A critical review of studies on moral judgment development using the Defining Issues Test in Arab countries. *Arab Journal for the Humanities* (Kuwait), *20,* 261–281.

Ahmed, R. A. and Gielen, U. P. (2006a, February). *The relationships between corporal punishment, parental acceptance-rejection, and personality dispositions in Kuwaiti students.* Paper presented at the 35th Annual Meeting of the Society for Cross-Cultural Research (SCCR), Savannah, GA.

Ahmed, R. A., and Gielen, U. P. (2006b, June). *A critical review of Arab studies on parental behavior.* Paper presented at the 1st International Congress of the International Society for Interpersonal Acceptance and Rejection, Istanbul, Turkey.

Ahmed, R. A., Gielen, U. P., and Avellani, J. (1987). Perceptions of parental behavior and the development of moral reasoning in Sudanese students. In C. Kagitcibasi (Ed.), *Growth and progress in cross-cultural psychology: Selected papers from the 8th international Conference of the International Association for Cross-Cultural Psychology* (pp. 196–206). Amsterdam, The Netherlands: Swets and Zeitlinger.

Ahmed, R. A., and Khalil, E. A. (2004). Prevalence of psychological disturbances among intermediate and secondary school male and female students in Menoufia Governorate, Egypt. *The Egyptian Journal of Psychological Studies* (Egypt), *11,* 30–65.

Ahmed, R. A., Macri, D., and Mullet, E. (2006). Societal risk perception among Egyptian adolescents and young adults. *The Journal of North African Studies, 11,* 307–318.

Ahmed, R. A., and Megreya, A. M. (2008, February). *Identity disorders in Egypt and Kuwait: A cross-cultural study.* Paper presented at the 37th Annual Meeting of the Society for Cross-Cultural Research. New Orleans, LA.

Ahmed, R. A., and Mullet, E. (2008). Societal risk perception in Arab countries: the case of Kuwait. *Human and Ecological Risk Assessment, 14,* 1291–1305.

Ahmed, R. E. (2006). The efficacy of relaxation with visualization and biofeedback training in reduce the levels of generalized anxiety disorder among sample of university students. *Arab Journal of Contemporary Psychology* (Egypt), *2,* 99–126.

Ahmed, S. K. (1992). Common (prevailing) and desired values in Egyptian families returned back from immigration countries. *Journal of Psychology* (Egypt), *6,* 24–37.

Al-Ahram (2008). An Egyptian daily newspaper. March 25, 2008; June 8, 2008.

Al-Ali, M. M. (2008). *The differences between the genders in the citizenship among secondary school students: A cross-cultural study between State of Kuwait and Czech Republic.* Paper presented at the Forum for Individuals with Special Needs in the 21st Century: Aspirations and Accomplishments, Department of Sociology and Social Work, College of Social Sciences, Kuwait University, Kuwait.

Al-Anwar, M. A. (2002). Psychological alienation and personality variables. *Journal of Psychology* (Egypt), *16,* 154–174.

Alduaij, H. S., and Al-Salameh, I. M. (2007). The effect of globalization on values from the point of view of University of Jordan and Kuwait University. *Journal of Social Sciences* (Kuwait), *35,* 13–40.

Al-Emam, M. A. S., and El-Zeraigat, I. A. F. (2005). The effect of a suggested instructional program based on drawing on developing creative thinking skills among deaf children. *Arab Journal on Childhood* (Kuwait), *6,* 8–24.

Ali, A. A. M. (2002). The impact of a counseling program on the development of blind child's social skill. *The Egyptian Journal of Psychological Studies* (Egypt), *12*, 67–102.

Ali, A. R. (2001). The relationship between students' violence and some social variables. In *Proceedings of the 8th International Conference of the Center of Counseling, Ain Shams University* (pp. 569–602). Cairo, Egypt.

Ali, S. A. (1994). Terrorism phenomenon as seen by a sample of youth: A psychological survey. *Journal of Psychology* (Egypt), *8*, 48–76.

Ali, S. A., and Ewidaih, M. A. (1994). Psychological needs of university students: A comparative psychological study. *Journal of Psychology* (Egypt), *8*, 96–118.

Ali, S. A., and Sabry, E. M. (1997). Inhalants abuse in children: A pilot socio-psychological study. *Journal of Psychology* (Egypt), *11*, 92–124.

Al-Khatib, R. A. (2002). Religiosity and its relation with depression among male and female students at Al-Azhar University and other universities. *Journal of Psychology* (Egypt), *16*, 6–21.

Al-Khawajah, J. M. A., and Ahmed, R. A. (1996/1997). Sex role typing and I. E. locus of control. *Bulletin of the Faculty of Arts, Alexandria University* (Egypt), *46*, 83–100.

Al-Madhoun, A. S. (1998). *A study of some social and social variables and their relation with political attitudes among students of Al-Azhar University, Gaza Strip*. Unpublished master's thesis, Faculty of Education, Al-Azhar University, Gaza Strip, Palestine.

Al-Mazeruoi, L. A. A. (2006). *Socialization in Saudi mothers*. Cairo, Egypt: Dar al-Qaheira.

Al-Mestikawy, T. A. (2005). Aggressive behavior and its relationship with some demographic variables and personality traits among secondary school students. *Annals of the Center of Psychological Studies, Faculty of Arts, Cairo University*, Cairo, Egypt, Annals No. 1, Monograph No. 3, October.

Al-Mestikawy, T. A. (2006). Attitudes of university students and their behaviors towards some forms of abnormal sexual behavior. *Annals of the Center of Psychological Studies, Faculty of Arts, Cairo University*, Cairo, Egypt, Annals No. 2, Monograph No. 2, June.

Al-Motwa, M. B. A. (2008). The relationship between the family violence towards children and their aggressive behavior: A field study on a sample of secondary stage students in Riyadh City. *Journal of the Social Sciences* (Kuwait), *36*, 49–101.

Al-Mustafa, A. A. (2006). The effect of physical movement on developing perceptual motor abilities in preschool children. *Arab Journal on Childhood* (Kuwait), *6*, 43–55.

Al-Otaibi, D. R (2005). *Perception of parental acceptance-rejection and its relation to identity disorders, ego-strength, and single mindedness*. Unpublished master's thesis, Department of Psychology, College of Social Sciences, Kuwait University, Kuwait.

Al-Qabas (2007). A Kuwaiti daily newspaper. November 30, 2007.

Al-Qabas (2008). A Kuwaiti daily newspaper. April 22, 2008; May 13, 2008; June 11, 2008; July 14, 2008.

Al-Seyassah (2008). A Kuwaiti daily newspaper. April 20, 2008; July 29, 2008.

Al-Shamy, J. M. (2008). *Psychological problems characterized gifted students at the intermediate school in the Kingdom of Bahrain*. Paper presented at the Forum for Individuals with Special Needs in the 21st Century: Aspirations and Accomplishments, Department of Sociology and Social Work, College of Social Sciences, Kuwait University, Kuwait.

Al-Sharkawy, A. M. (2005). Creativity among children in Arab research and studies: Research topics and results' directions. In *Proceedings of the Conference on Education in Society of Knowledge* (pp. 207–272). Cairo, Egypt: The Supreme Council of Culture.

Al-Youssefi, M. A. (1999). Individualism/collectivism as a predictor of teacher's adjustment. In *Proceedings of the 6th Annual Conference of the Counseling Center, Ain Shams University "Quality of Life"* (pp. 447–515). Cairo, Egypt.

Al-Zeqay, N. M. (2001). Ability of creative thinking in its relation with values and some psychological and social variables in a sample of students at the Institute of Psychology, University of Oran, Algeria. *Journal of Humanities, University of Monterey* (Algeria), *15*, 35–58.

Ameziane, M. (2002). Reflectivity-impulsivity and its relation with intelligence and problem solving. *Arab Journal on Childhood* (Kuwait), *3*, 38–54.

Ameziane, M. (2004). Multiple intelligences and problem-solving among preschool Moroccan children. *Arab Journal on Childhood* (Kuwait), *5*, 8–26.

Awadh, A. M., Vance, B., El-Beblawi, V., and Pumariega, A. J. (2004). Effects of trauma of the Gulf War on Kuwaiti children. *Journal of Child and Family Studies*, *7*, 493–498.

Azab, H. M. (2002, December). *The efficiency of an integrative, neogative and therapeutic program to overcome violent behaviors in adolescents*. Paper presented at the 9th Annual Conference of the Psychological Center, Ain Shams University, Cairo, Egypt.

Badri, M. B. (1965). Influence of modernization on Goodenough quotients of Sudanese children. *Perceptual and Motor Skills, 20,* 931–932.

Baza, A. A. M. (2003). *At risk children and adolescents.* Cairo, Egypt: The Anglo-Egyptian Bookshop.

Bedani, A. K. M. (1995). *Socialization of working and non-working mothers and its relation to social maturity in their male and female children at the intermediate educational level.* Unpublished master's thesis, College of Girls, Ain Shams University, Cairo, Egypt.

Behagat, R. M. (2005). *Enrichment and critical thinking: An experimental study on gifted primary school children.* Cairo, Egypt: Alem el-Fikr.

Benat, B., and Salama, B. (unpublished). Political alienation in Palestinian refuges and its relation with some variables. Retrieved April 2, 2009, from http://www.minshawi.com/node/180.

Celen, N., and Cok, F. (2007). Turkey. In J. J. Arnett (Ed.), *International encyclopedia of adolescents* (Vol. 2, pp. 1010–1024). New York: Routledge.

Darwish, A. E., and Huber, J. L. (2002). Individualism-collectivism in different cultural societies: A cross-cultural study. *Journal of Psychology* (Egypt), *16,* 152–162.

Debais, S. A. (1997). Dimensions of aggressive behavior in children with mild mental retardation in terms of age and place of residence. *Psychological Studies* (Egypt), *7,* 353–385.

Dousseki, I. M. (1992). The projected image of youth problems as appeared on the T.A.T. and its relation with personality characteristics and social values. *Journal of Psychology* (Egypt), *6,* 6–25.

Eid, M. I. (2002a). Identity. In M. I., Eid (Ed.), *Identity, anxiety, and creativity* (pp. 9–71). Cairo, Egypt: Dar el-Qahraa.

Eid, M. I. (2002b). Forgiveness and its relation with dogmatism among university students. In M. I. Eid (Ed.), *Identity, anxiety, and creativity* (pp. 73–122). Cairo, Egypt: Dar el-Qahraa.

Eid, M. I. (2002c). Positiveness. In M. I. Eid (Ed.), *Identity, anxiety, and creativity* (pp. 123–197). Cairo, Egypt: Dar el-Qahraa.

Eid, M. I. (2002d). Self-actualization. In M. I. Eid (Ed.), *Identity, anxiety, and creativity* (pp. 199–254). Cairo, Egypt: Dar el-Qahraa.

El-Dabaa, S. Y., and Al-Saud, A. Bint Fahed (2008). A factorial study on alienation problem in the light of globalization era in a sample of university female Saudi students. Retrieved July 15, 2008, from http://www.ksu.edu.sa/sites/colleges/arabic.

El-Hilo, B. M. M. (2001). Prevalence of drug abuse among secondary school students in Khartoum State [Sudan]. *Arab Psychologist* (Egypt), *2,* 43–60.

El-Meliugi, A. (1951). *The development of religious feeling in children and adolescents.* Unpublished master's thesis, Cairo University, Cairo, Egypt.

El-Seddik, N. (2006, April 11). Political alienation phenomena in Morocco. *Civilized Dialogue* (Morocco), *29.* Available at http://www.ahewar.org/search/Dsearch.asp?nr=1517.

El-Zayyat, F. M. (1990). The relationship between value system, locus of control and achievement in samples of male students at Mansoura University (Egypt) and Umm el-Qura University (Saudi Arabia): An analytical study. *Proceedings of the 6th Annual Convention on Psychology in Egypt, The Egyptian Association for Psychological Studies, Part 2* (pp. 543–571). Cairo, Egypt.

Faied, H. A. (1996). Dimensions of the aggressive behavior among university students. In *Proceedings of the 3rd international conference of the Center of the Psychological Counseling,* (pp. 135–182). Cairo, Egypt: Ain Shams University.

Farag, T. S. M. (2003). Female adolescents' leaving out (escape) the family: A psychological view. In T. S. M. Farag (Ed.), *Social and communicative skills: psychological research studies* (pp. 295–348). Cairo, Egypt: Dar Ghareeb.

Figley, C. R., Ashkanani, H. R., Chapman, P., and Al-Nasser, F. (2008). In the shadows of Saddam: A household survey of mental health in Kuwait. *International Journal of Psychology.* Manuscript submitted for publication.

Gaber, G. A. (1968). Needs of Egyptian, Iraqi, and American students teachers: A cross-cultural study. *The National Review of Social Sciences* (Egypt), *5,* 455–458.

Gaber, G. A., et al. (1981). *The development of some concepts in samples of Qatari and non-Qatari kindergarten children in Doha, Qatar.* The Center for Educational Research, University of Qatar, Qatar, No. 22.

Gabr, G. M., and Haredy, A. M. (2003). The motives and levels of violence practice with reference to the demographic aspects. *Egyptian Journal of Psychological Studies* (Egypt), *13,* 85–159.

Ghalab, M. A., and El-Dousseki, M. I. (1994). A comparative psychological study between extrinsic religious orientations and intrinsic religious orientations in attitudes toward violence and some personality traits. *Psychological Studies* (Egypt), *4,* 327–374.

Ghanem, M. H. (1998). Violence phenomenon in the eyes of a sample of Egyptian intellectuals. *Journal of Psychology* (Egypt), *12*, 80–90.

Ghanem, M. H. (2000). Ideal and good example for the secondary school students: A psychological pilot study. *Journal of Psychology* (Egypt), *14*, 132–149.

Ghanem, M. H. (2003). Addicts' dreams: A cross-cultural survey. *Journal of Psychology* (Egypt), *17*, 134–147.

Ghanem, M. H. (2005). A*ddiction: Negative impacts, theories, and treatment: A cross-cultural study on addicts in Egypt and the Arab Gulf states*. Cairo, Egypt: Dar Gahreeb.

Ghoniemah, H. A. M. (2003). The psycho-social needs of streets' children in the light of sex (gender) and place of residence. *Egyptian Journal of Psychological Studies* (Egypt), *13*, 363–426.

Gibbons, J. L., Ahmed, R. A., Van den Broeck, C. T., and Brown, C. M. (2008, February). *Traditional dress in Kuwaiti adolescents' drawings: Relation to social attitudes*. Paper presented at the 37th Annual Meeting of the Society for Cross-Cultural Research, New Orleans, LA.

Gielen, U. P., Ahmed, R. A., and Avellani, J. (1992). The development of moral reasoning and perceptions of parental behavior in students from Kuwait. *Moral Education Forum*, *17*, 20–37.

Gregg, G. S. (2005). *The Middle East: A cultural psychology*. New York: Oxford University Press.

Habib, M. A. (1992). Non medical addiction of alcohol among secondary school students. *Journal of Psychology* (Egypt), *6*, 96–109.

Habib, M. A. (1994). Extremeness, ambiguity intolerance, rigidity, dogmatism, conformity, and non decisive response as predictions of psychological tension. *Journal of Psychology* (Egypt), *8*, 44–69.

Habib, M. A. (1995). Styles of parental treatment and family size as early determinants of children's extreme responses. *Journal of Psychology* (Egypt), *9*, 98–127.

Hafez, N., and Kasem, N. F. (1993a). A suggestive counseling program for reducing aggressive behavior among children in the light of some variables. *Journal of Counseling* (Egypt), *1*, 143–177.

Hafez, N., and Kasem, N. F. (1993b). *Ain Shams scale for aggressive behavior forms in children*. Cairo, Egypt: The Anglo-Egyptian Bookshop.

Hamza, J. M. (1996/1997). Children's work: A psychological view. *Journal of Psychology* (Egypt), *11*, 150–157.

Hana, A. M. (1965). A cross-cultural study of values. In L. K. Melieka (Ed.), *Readings in social psychology in the Arab countries* (Vol. 1, pp. 602–613). Cairo, Egypt: The National House for Printing and Publishing.

Haraby, M. Kh. (1948). *Moral development and socialization in six to twelve year old Egyptian children*. Unpublished master's thesis, Faculty of Arts, Cairo University, Cairo, Egypt.

Hasan, A. S., and Al-Thafery, S. B.-S. (2006). Islamic moral values and their relation with self-control among Sultan Qaboos University students. *Journal of Psychology* (Egypt), *19*, 38–61.

Hedia, F. M. A. (1994). A study of internal-external control among male and female adolescents. *Journal of Psychology* (Egypt), *8*, 82–95.

Henry, H. (2007, August). *Gender discussion in psychology courses and young Egyptian women's empowerment*. Paper presented at the 65th Annual Convention of the International Council of Psychologists (ICP), San Diego, CA.

Hewaidy, M., and Al-Yameni, S. (1995). Common reinforcements among primary school children in Bahrain. *Journal of Psychology* (Egypt), *9*, 52–82.

Hyde, D. M. G. (1970). *Piaget and conceptual development*. London: Holt, Rinehart, and Winston.

Ibrahim, A. S. (1992). A study of the conservatism-liberation tendency among technical secondary education students. *Journal of Contemporary Psychology* (Egypt), *2*, 19–47.

Ibrahim, A. S., and Abdel-Hamid, M. N. (1994). Aggression/hostility and its relation with locus of control and self-esteem in a sample of male students at Imam Mohammed Ibn Saud Islamic University, Kingdom of Saudi Arabia. *Journal of Psychology* (Egypt), *8*, 38–58.

Ibrahim, F. F., and Soliman, A. S. (2002). Psychological and social basis of mental, cognitive, and linguistic program for preschool child (aged between 3-6 years): A suggestive program. In F. F. Ibrahim and A. S. Soliman (Eds.), *Studies in the developmental psychology: Childhood and adolescence* (Vol. 1, pp. 137–188). Cairo, Egypt: Zahraa el-Shark.

Ibrahim, I. M. (2003). Level of orientation toward future and its relation with some psychological disturbances among university youth: A comparative study between Egyptian and Saudi samples. *Egyptian Journal of Psychological Studies* (Egypt), *13*, 33–83.

Ibrahim, M. A. (2006). *Critical thinking and contemporary society issues*. Cairo, Egypt: The Anglo-Egyptian Bookshop.

Ismail, E. M. S. (2002). Houses' maids: A psychosocial studies. *Journal of Psychology* (Egypt), *16*, 82–111.

Jacoup, I. M., and Makableh, N. Y. (1994). Locus of control and its relation with some variables among university students. *Journal of Psychology* (Egypt), *8*, 119–128.

Kaffafi, A. M., and Al-Naial, M. A. (1994). Birth order and its relation with social responsibility: A psychometric study in a sample of Qatar University male and female students. *Journal of Psychology* (Egypt), 8, 26–37.

Kamel, A. M. (2002). Children's abuse and neglect. In A. M. Kamel (Ed.), *Research in psychology: Field and experimental studies* (pp. 357–385). Cairo, Egypt: Dar el-Nahada al-Mesria.

Kamel, A. M., and El-Fakhrany, Kh. I. (2002). The effect of crowding as [an] environmental variable on hostility and assertiveness. In A. M. Kamel (Ed.), *Research in psychology: Field and experimental studies* (pp. 209–246). Cairo, Egypt: Dar el-Nahada al-Mesria.

Karam el-Din, L. A. E. (1998). Piagetian research. In R. A. Ahmed and U. P. Gielen (Eds.), *Psychology in the Arab countries* (pp. 51–75). Menoufia, Egypt: Menoufia University Press.

Kashef, E. F. (2002). The efficiency of based-computer programs in improving learning some skills among mentally retarded children. *The Egyptian Journal of Psychological Studies* (Egypt), 12, 103–143.

Khaleefa, O. H., Al-Mustafa, M. Y., Al-Bailey, M., and Al-Ghreniah, F. (2007). Collectivism and individualism in Bahrain and United Arab Emirates: Cross-cultural study. *Arab Journal of Contemporary Psychology* (Egypt), 3, 47–66.

Koran (1981). An English translation by N. J. Dawood. London: Penguin Books.

Kurdy, S. A. M. (2003). Social responsibility and its relation with achievement motivation among Faculty of Education female students in Al-Taef. *Journal of Psychology* (Egypt), 17, 110–140.

Lavi, I., and Slone, M. (2008). Parental warmth, parental control, and children's resilience: Cross-cultural aspects. In F. Erkman (Ed.), *Acceptance, the essence of peace: Selected papers from the First International Congress on International Acceptance and Rejection* (pp. 133–156). Istanbul, Turkey: Turkish Psychological Society, Istanbul Branch.

Melikian, L. H. (1965). Authoritarianism and some related variables in two cultural groups. In L. K. Melieka (Ed.), *Readings in social psychology in the Arab countries* (Vol. 1, pp. 572–589). Cairo, Egypt: The National House for Printing and Publishing.

Mensch, B. S., Ibrahim, B. L., Lee, S. M., and El-Gibaly, O. (2000, March). *Socialization to gender roles and marriage among Egyptian adolescents*. Paper presented at the Annual Meeting of the Population Association of America. Los Angles, CA.

Mensy, M. A., and El-Bana, A. A. (2002). Preparing programs for discovering gifted and creative preschool children from Kindergarten level to university education. *The Egyptian Journal of Psychological Studies* (Egypt), 12, 29–65.

Mohammed, A. A. (1999). Efficacy of a behavioral training program of different group activities in reducing aggressive behavior in autistic children. *Journal of the Faculty of Arts, Menoufia University* (Egypt), 38, 41–67.

Mohammed, A. M. (1994). *Dynamics of attitudes towards drugs addiction: A psychosocial study*. Unpublished doctoral dissertation, Faculty of Arts, Zagazig University, Zagazig, Egypt.

Mohammed, A. M. (2000a). Ways of confronting identity crisis among university youth. In A. M. Mohammed (Ed.), *Studies in mental health: Identity, alienation, and psychological disturbances* (pp. 11–53). Cairo, Egypt: Dar el-Rashad.

Mohammed, A. M. (2000b). A comparative study on self-esteem among university youth with different ways of confronting identity crisis. In A. M. Mohammed (Ed.), *Studies in mental health: Identity, alienation, and psychological disturbances* (pp. 44–91). Cairo, Egypt: Dar el-Rashad.

Mohammed, A. M. (2000c). Sex- roles and alienation among university students. In A. M. Mohammed (Ed.), *Studies in mental health: Identity, alienation, and psychological disturbances* (pp. 93–144). Cairo, Egypt: Dar el-Rashad.

Mohammed, A. M. (2000d). Some psychological characteristics related to social isolation among university youth. In A. M. Mohammed (Ed.), *Studies in mental health: Identity, alienation, and psychological disturbances* (pp. 189–292). Cairo, Egypt: Dar el-Rashad.

Morsy, A. M. M. (2002). *Identity crisis in adolescence and the need for psychological counseling*. Cairo, Egypt: El-Nahada el-Mesria Bookshop.

Moussa, R. A. (1992). The influence of religiosity on psychological depression. In *Proceedings of the 8th Annual Convention of the Egyptian Association for Psychological Studies (EAPS)* (pp. 113–134). Cairo, Egypt.

Moussa, R. A., El-Dousseki, M. M. S., and Ahmed, R. A. (1998). Psychology of religion. In R. A. Ahmed and U. P. Gielen (Eds.), *Psychology in the Arab countries* (pp. 303–319). Cairo, Egypt: Menoufia University Press.

Nagaty, M. O. (1962). *Youth's attitudes and problems: A cross-cultural study of youth in Egypt, Lebanon, Iraq, Syria, Jordan, and the USA: The first report: Research aim and methodology*. Cairo, Egypt: Dar el-Nahada al-Arabia.

Nagaty, M. O. (1963). *Modernization and parental permissiveness: A cross-cultural research of youth in Egypt, Lebanon, Iraq, Syria, Jordan, and the USA*. Cairo, Egypt: Dar el-Nahada al-Arabia.

Naser, A. G. K. (1996). A longitude study on the development of social competence among young adults. In *Proceedings of the 3rd International Conference of the Counseling Centre, Ain Shams University "Counseling in Changing World"* (Vol. 2, pp. 671–699). Cairo, Egypt.

Naser, A. G. K. (1997). Youth's attitudes towards modernization and their relation with youth's psychosocial adjustment. *Journal of Psychology* (Egypt), *11*, 110–157.

Naser, A. G. K. (2003). The concept of personal commitment in a sample of university students. *Journal of Psychology* (Egypt), *17*, 142–156.

Ouwaida, M. A., and Ali, S. A. (1992). Information from an Egyptian societal sample on the prevalence of psychological disturbances. *Journal of Psychology* (Egypt), *6*, 42–53.

Sabry, Y. E. (1989). Risk behavior among juvenile delinquents and its relation to intelligence. *Contemporary Education* (Egypt), *13*, 133–149.

Saigh, P. A., and Omar, A. M. (1983). The effects of a good behavior game on the disruptive behavior of Sudanese elementary school students. *Journal of Applied Behavior Analysis, 16*, 329–344.

Saleh, A. M. H. (1995). Efficiency of reward-punishment reinforcement package and peers' pressure in modifying the aggressive behavior in preschool children: An experimental study. *Educational Studies* (Egypt), *10*, 17–56.

Saleh, S. Kh. (1998). *Strategies for confronting violence among secondary school students: A critical view and empirical study*. Cairo, Egypt: Dar Ghreeb.

Seginer, R., and Shoyer, S. (2007). Israel. In J. J. Arnett (Ed.), *International encyclopedia of adolescents* (Vol. 1, pp. 490–509). New York: Routledge.

Sendioni, F., and Abdalla, J. (2001). Piaget among the Bedouins. *Arab Psychologist* (Egypt), *2*, 1–8.

Soliman, A. E., and Abdel-Hamid, M. N. (1994). Hostility and its relation with locus of control and self-esteem in a sample of Imam Mohammed Ibn Saud Islamic University male students, Saudi Arabia. *Journal of Psychology* (Egypt), *9*, 28–59.

Sondaite, J. (2007). Iran. In J. J. Arnett (Ed.), *International encyclopedia of adolescents* (Vol. 1, pp. 470–480). New York: Routledge.

Soueif, M. I. (1958). Extreme response sets in a sample of juvenile delinquents: I. *National Review of Criminal Science* (Egypt), *1*, 24–28.

Soueif, M. I. (1959). Extreme response sets in a sample of juvenile delinquents. II. *National Review of Criminal Science* (Egypt), *2*, 89–95.

Soueif, M. I. (1998a). Drug use, abuse, and dependence. In R. A. Ahmed and U. P. Gielen (Eds.), *Psychology in the Arab countries* (pp. 494–516), Menoufia, Egypt: Menoufia University Press.

Soueif, M. I. (1998b). Conclusion. In R. A. Ahmed and U. P. Gielen (Eds.), *Psychology in the Arab countries* (pp. 569–582), Menoufia, Egypt: Menoufia University Press.

United Nations Children's Fund (2005). *Children's situation in the world*. An Arabic translation. Amman, Jordan: United Nations Children's Fund.

Wahdan, A., Al-Ater, F., Abdel-Ghany, M., and Elias, I. (1999). *The new patterns of exposed to deviant behavior among children: Street children: A pilot study*. Cairo, Egypt: The National Center for Sociological and Criminal Research.

Youssef, G. S. (1994). Differences between males and females in perception of the stressful life events. *Journal of Psychology* (Egypt), *8*, 60–74.

Zoqan, G. F. T. (1997). *The impact of Intifada (Uprising) on Palestinian children's play*. Unpublished master's thesis, Faculty of Graduate Studies, Al-Nagah National University, Nabulus, Palestine.

20
Afrique Noire

A. BAME NSAMENANG and JOSEPH L. LO-OH

Introduction

This chapter approaches developmental science from an African perspective. It is written from a stance that most contemporary perspectives persist in a single model of humanity as a template for comparative norms (Saraswathi, 1998) in a world marked by huge human diversity. African theories of the universe and the developmental ethos that follow from them differ from, but are not absolutely inconsistent with, those that drive the dominant paradigms of developmental science. This perhaps accounts for why researchers (e.g., MacGaffey, 1981) have failed to identify exact equivalences between Western epistemologies and developmental norms and those of African cultures. Africa's developmental grids are largely uncharted, but they are coherent and purposeful, at least to Africa's peoples. Indeed, Africans "have already successfully practiced childrearing within the framework of an African culture for centuries" (Callaghan, 1998, p. 31).

Human development is context bound. It unfolds within the limits of an individualized biological potentiality not in vacuity but within the meaning systems of a specific culture in a given ecology. The evidence of passive, evocative, and active genotype-environment effects (Scarr and McCartney, 1983) underline the value of nature–nurture interaction to output developmental outcomes. Although development is genetically wired, it is a context-sensitive process. Human beings have the capacity to organize their environment and life according to their cultural meaning systems (Cole, 1999). In addition, every culture possesses a theory within which to organize lifespan development and children's learning. In this light, the reciprocal processes by which culture and psyche co-construct one another result in divergences in the praxes, intelligences, and desirable child outcomes that are valued and promoted by different peoples in different times and societies (Shweder, 1995). In this sense, the type of adult a child grows up to become depends much on how nurture in terms of enculturation and socialization, especially parental and formal education and the peer culture, channels his or her biology.

Worldwide, children are embedded in varied ecologies and cultural niches. "The culture of a particular society surrounds children from the beginning of life, enveloping them like the air they breathe and without which they could not grow into viable human beings" (Sharan, 1988, p. 1). For every child, the processes of development, socialization, education, and acculturation proceed hand-in-hand with the child's social and physical settings (Hinde and Stevenson-Hinde, 1990). As ecology and culture, the developmental environment is central to human psychosocial differentiation. Of course, African ecocultures canalize human ontogenesis and psychic differentiation in patterns that "had not been imagined in developmental theories" (LeVine, 2004, p. 163).

This chapter exposes an Afrocentric perspective to developmental science. It charts human ontogenesis and psychosocial differentiation within an African theory of the universe. It also engenders how that theory disposes African children and their families to receive the intervention of their status and circumstances. An African perspective contains caveats that could enrich and extend the frontiers of developmental science because the African ecoculture "provides opportunities for learning and development which simply do not exist in the West and therefore are not considered by the predominant theories" (Curran, 1984, p. 2). In addition, a great deal of African developmental knowledge exists in indigenous practices, folklores, idioms, spatial use of cues, touch, garden metaphors, and participatory processes (Nsamenang, 1992a; Ojiaku, 1974), which current developmental tools and techniques neither aptly access nor appropriately measure. These learning opportunities and knowledge sources have not gained entry into the dominant narratives.

The chapter begins with an overview of the origin and development of scientific psychology in Africa, with special focus on the evolution of developmental psychology. The grounding of the chapter on a historical perspective is essential given the status of scientific psychology as a European American "article of export" (Danziger, 2006, p. 271) that now coexists with Africa's centuries-old indigenous developmental science, which awaits "discovery." A portrait of the context in which human development and research occur is an important elaboration from a historical record. Understanding that contemporary Africa has a hybrid developmental context (Nsamenang and Dawes, 1998) provides the basal knowledge on which to critique the developmental research that has been undertaken or ongoing in Africa. It is regrettable that the appraisal is undertaken from limited access to the broadest scope of that knowledge base. The next section articulates one version of developmental science that is emerging from an African theory of the universe and the theoretical issues it evokes. Strands of relevant reigning theories and how African theoretical precepts and processes fit into or diverge from the dominant narratives frame the discourse. The focus of the fourth section is on the major challenges to developmental research and discipline development in Afrique Noire (Black Africa). Finally, a conclusion to the chapter proposes how the contemporary developmental science could transform into a visionary discipline inclusive of developmental trajectories of all cultures in their vibrant global diversity.

Africa is not the native soil of either scientific psychology or its developmental subfield. The rest of this chapter identifies and endeavors to substantiate each theme invoked here in the chapter's brief preview with available science-based evidence.

Emergence and Growth of Psychology in Sub-Saharan Africa

Developmental science, like scientific psychology, is an "export" commodity evolved from European Enlightenment (Berry, 2006). It arrived in Africa with colonization in the context of services development, including evangelism (Nsamenang, 2008) and anthropological research (Peltzer and Bless, 1989). Like every colonial import into Africa, it has retained an extraverted identity (Owusu-Bempah and Howitt, 1995) in the sense that its theories and tools are still Eurocentric and its primary focus is on topics that reflect this externalized orientation. As such, psychology largely loses "sight of the soil out of which the existing [African] society has grown and the human values it has produced" (D. Westermann, cited in Kishani, 2001, p. 37).

LeVine (2004) intimated that developmentally appropriate practices have been crafted and proselytized in the semblance of science-based knowledge in a formula based heavily on European American cultural ideology. Thus, the orienting values and scientific methods that frame a "modernizing" developmental science in sub-Saharan Africa are imported European American conceptual and intellectual systems into Africa. Both African and expatriate scholars favor these imported systems over Africa's uncharted indigenous value systems and procedures and techniques. Thus, in one sense, this chapter represents "a struggle" within a narrative that is saturated with European American developmental metaphors and ethos.

The foregoing perhaps constitutes a major rationale why the state of scientific psychology in general and developmental science in particular in Afrique Noire (Black Africa) is inchoate (Nsamenang, 1993), except in South Africa where psychology, at least in its legislation and ethical codes, is purported to be "relatively well developed, compared with most European countries, second only perhaps to the USA and Canada" (Wassenaar, 1998, p. 142). In reality, Afrique Noire occupies an outlier position in the knowledge base of developmental science. This is despite another reality that the East African countries of Kenya and Uganda contributed the seminal cross-cultural data for some influential developmental theories—attachment theory (Ainsworth, 1967, 1977) and developmental niche framework (Super and Harkness, 1986). Although developmental psychology is slowly evolving into an academic discipline, it still occupies the fringes of academia and society in much of Africa. For example, few members of Africa's governing classes and policy planners know the meaning and potential applications of psychology (Eze, 1991), and many more are ignorant of the role and value of developmental science. Worse still, Africa has a low generative capacity to produce and disseminate its own developmental knowledge. The value of this chapter comes to the fore in the face of the potential dangers of guiding child development and grounding services in Africa on the basis of "received knowledge" and of Africa being a net importer of psychological principles.

The evolution and growth of psychology in Africa has not been uniform. Variation exists across and within African countries, regions, and language blocks in the orienting models, resources, conditions for training, research, and applications, as well as in the number of psychologists and their integration into research, policy, and human services. Whereas countries like Cameroon, Chad, and Gabon have been "struggling" to establish the discipline of psychology, formal psychology institutions and service programs at various stages of implantation already exist in Ethiopia, Ghana, Kenya, Liberia, Namibia, Nigeria, Senegal, South Africa, Uganda, Zambia, and Zimbabwe. Only in South Africa has professional psychology reached a level of development comparable with Australia and the United States (Manganyi and Louw, 1986), although the research publication output of the discipline in South Africa is relatively low (Mauer, Marais, and Prinsloo, 1991). Psychology seems to be more "advanced" in English-colonized Africa than French-, Portuguese-, or Spanish-colonized countries, a state of the field that reflects the mindsets of its European and American exporters and their Anglo-driven values (Nsamenang, in press).

The next section paints in broad strokes the various facets of the contexts in which child and youth development occurs in Africa.

Contexts of Child and Youth Development in Afrique Noire

Our geopolitical scope is not the entire African continent, but Afrique Noire (Black Africa), which is that part of the African continent that tends to be detached from northern Africa (Ahmed, Chapter 19, in this volume), which is more readily identified with the Arab world than with Africa south of the Sahara. Afrique Noire stretches from the northern borders of Mauritania eastward across the Sudan to the horn of Africa and the Indian Ocean islands and down to its southerly border, the Cape of Good Hope in South Africa. Afrique Noire or sub-Saharan Africa comprises 48 nation states that display diversity in flora and fauna, topography, political regimes, demographic profile, ethno-linguistic composition, and status of scientific and service disciplines like psychology and developmental science.

Africa is a continent of bewildering diversity and extraordinary dynamism (Olaniyan, 1982). With all of these variations, how can one justifiably write about the subject of childbearing and childrearing in Africa as a unified experience? The justification of such an attempt cannot be based on the many visible differences that exist across Africa and its peoples, but the commonalities shared among them (Chibwana, 2007). An understanding of cultural commonalities and theory of the universe is essential and fundamental to any attempt at recognizing and explaining African life-journeys (Serpell, 1993) and how an African identity and psyche is shaped and becomes differentiated.

The Cultural Commonalities That Underlie Africa's Diversity

A history of African societies reveals population movements and the adjustments of cultural patterns and adaptations to the ecology to evolve "common political and social institutions with only slight variations" (Nkwi, 1983, p. 102). There also exist peculiarly African ideas, practices, and issues that contrast those of cultures loosely known as Western (Serpell, 1992). As a result, Diop (1960) perceived a cultural unity in Black Africa's visible diversity. Maquet (1972, p. 3) felt "a certain common quality" emerging from Africa's similar patterns of ecological adaptations, institutional structures, and historical traumas from slavery, colonization, and their fallouts.

Many aspects of life and culture are similar among most ethnicities in Africa. Mphahlele argues that "Africans could be called one on the basis of their beliefs in ancestry, existence of a supreme being, and the value they attach to the extended family" (as cited in Mwamwenda, 1996, p.421). On his part, Durojaiye states, "an individual in the traditional African society considers himself [or herself] fulfilled only if he [or she] is in symbiotic relationship with the extended family" (as cited in Mwamwenda, 1996, p. 413). That aspect of collectiveness and interdependence is typical of the values with which children are brought up in Africa. African ideas, issues, and practices have coalesced into a worldview or theory of the universe that frames views on desirable child states and how to attain them through care, socialization, and education.

An African Theory of the Universe

An African theory of the universe constitutes "a very different *psychological frame of reference* from that which informs contemporary Western developmental psychology" (Serpell, 1994, p. 18). It is holistic and theocentric in nature. An African theory envisions human destiny in three unbroken lifecycle periods of an existential self and two metaphysical phases of selfhood. The theory highlights "the interplay of social, religious, and political roles, working together to ensure the well-being of the people" (Bongmba, 2001, p. 7). Africa's theocentric theory acknowledges everyone's humanity, imputes spirituality into human life, and positions the child not in his or her sovereignty but as socially integrated in a human community. This fact of African culture emits pronatalist reproductive ideologies and a psychology that focuses on socializing the meaning of life, self-definition, and identity within the socio-affective field rather than into sovereign individualism (Holdstock, 2000; Nsamenang, 2004).

The social capital that flows from Africa's theory of the universe engenders strengths that prime adaptability and resilience, but they are more often discounted than recognized and enhanced. For instance, had sub-Saharan African communities not relied on sibling caregiving, which eased children's transition into adult roles after their parents' death (Nsamenang, 2007a), but had waited on donor responses, its crisis from acquired immunodeficiency syndrome (AIDS) deaths would have been more devastating than it has turned out to be. Bare statistics have not conveyed the countless examples of domestic heroism by AIDS-affected families in Afrique Noire. Research in countries such as Kenya, Malawi, Rwanda, and Zambia suggests that family structures in sub-Saharan Africa are more resilient than the international development field had expected (Joint United Nations Programme on HIV/AIDS [UNAIDS], 2006). Yet most interventions in Afrique Noire continue to bypass such strengths and achievements, as the intervention of Africa's awful state is framed by mindsets and strategies of replacement rather than enhancement. One of Africa's unused strengths is human resources in terms of demography and social capital.

World Demographic and Social Trends Affecting Africa's Children and Youth

The world population is estimated at 6,571,414,237 (United Nations Population Fund [UNFPA], 2007). By 2050, Africa's population will surge from its present estimated 900 million to almost 2 billion, whereas South Asia's population will swell from 1.6 billion to nearly 2.5 billion (Population Reference Bureau, 2000). According to current data, sub-Saharan Africa remains the region with the highest fertility (Smith, 2004). The West African fertility rate ranges from 4.5 children per woman in Cameroon to 7.0 children in most countries of the region (Ware, 1983). "Nigerians experience fertility transition paradoxically, simultaneously acknowledging the potential benefits of smaller numbers of children while lamenting the pressures to curtail fertility" (Smith, 2004, p. 222). Africans thus perceive pressures to limit fertility as related to economic hardship, but also link having fewer children to economic development and progress. It is critical to note that childbearing Africans do not conceptualize their reproductive ideas and practices in the language or formulas of demography (Smith, 2004).

The age structure of the world population is 1.8 billion people under age 15 years (27.4%), 4.3 billion people age 15 to 64 years (65.2%), and 483 million people age 65 years and over (7.4%). Approximately 45% of sub-Saharan Africa's population was under 15 years of age in 1998, rendering Africa the youngest continent. In fact, of the 18 countries whose population of people 0 to 14 years of age is 45% or more, 14 are African (World Factbook, 2006). In many African countries, child and youth cohorts make up approximately 70% of the total population (Nsamenang, 2002).

Infant mortality declined in Africa to 105 per 1,000 live births in 1997 but is still the highest in the world. Although child survival is increasing in Africa, the children are not thriving optimally. Of the children who survive through age 6 years, nearly 30 million (or one-third) of the children are chronically malnourished, weighing only three-fourths of the weight standard for their age. Approximately 35% of the children are stunted following persistent malnutrition before they reach the age of 3 years. Mental and reproductive health services are remarkable for their scarcity or disorganized and youth-unfriendly nature.

The precarious situation of Africa's children and youth is exacerbated by a devastating AIDS epidemic that left over 11 million orphans by the end of 2001, nearly 80% of the world total (United Nations Children's Fund [UNICEF], 2003). A Uganda survey exemplifies the scenario, revealing that every fourth household hosts a child to parents who have died of AIDS (Baguma, 2006). By 2010, the number of orphans in Afrique Noire is expected to grow to 20 million, comprising approximately half of all orphans in the subcontinent. In general, approximately 15% of orphans are 0 to 4 years old, 35% are 5 to 9 years old, and 50% are 10 to 14 years old (Monasch and Boerma, 2003). Wars and civil conflict within states also increased the number of African refugees from internal displacement and out-of-country flight to 35 million in 1999. At least 85% of the displaced persons were children and women. A raging phenomenon of youth flight has hyped a yet to be assessed number of Africa's young people, who pose serious immigration problems worldwide.

Today, 20% of sub-Saharan Africa's total population of children below 6 years of age is seriously at risk. Whereas life expectancy is longest in Japan at 82 years, followed by Iceland and Switzerland at 80 years, children can expect to live just 36 years in Zimbabwe, 38 years in Zambia, and 40 years in Malawi as a result of the AIDS epidemic. In fact, all countries (29 of them) with the lowest life expectancy (under 50 years) are African, except for Afghanistan. Furthermore, Africa is home to 34 of the world's 49 least developed countries (UNFPA, 2007). Sub-Saharan Africa has the worst performance of any region of the world on virtually any measure of living standards, including per capita income, access to clean water, life expectancy, infant mortality, and prevalence of diseases, particularly human immunodeficiency virus (HIV)/AIDS (Nsamenang, 2002). Most countries of Africa, paradoxically, are rich in natural resources such as petroleum, gold, diamonds, timber, wildlife, and much more.

Africa: Rich in Natural and Human Resources but an Impoverished Continent

Africa is richly endowed with natural resources and human capital, but it cannot afford to finance its human development services or fund research of its developmental contexts without foreign aid. Instead, Africa's resources are a risk factor that underlie its difficult, if not impossible, transition into its own generative spirit and sustainable development trajectory because "Western expertise and technologies loudly dictate the fate of Africa's vast resources" (Nsamenang, 2007a, p. 23). In brief, Africa's resources and human capital have been, since the scramble for Africa, open to exploitation by Western countries. The rush for Africa's resources has not ended but merely transformed into neocolonial intrigues.

Arnett (2004) laments how the exploitation of Africa's natural resources by the West, followed by corruption, waste, and war, has not translated to economic prosperity for Africans. Rather than benefiting from the value of their natural wealth, destitute African populations have set into conflict and internecine wars, which have produced a large population of children and youth as soldiers in different regions of the rich but impoverished continent. It is difficult to imagine why a rights-driven world should acquiesce to external demands for resources from such a rich continent like Africa, leaving it unable to garner the means to support a decent standard of living for its peoples and to lay a strong foundation for its next generations. Perhaps the extreme levels of poverty in Afrique Noire symbolize social Darwinism in its starkest form (Nsamenang, 2007a). The unfairness inherent in exploiting vast resources and bringing pittances of the huge profits in relief funds to liberate the Dark Continent is captured in Frederick Masinde's insight: "If Africa could be granted an additional 1% share in global trade, she would earn for herself much more than she is currently being given in foreign aid" (cited in Barsby, 2006, p. 52).

The African Family

Africa's theocentric theory of the universe primes pronatalist values and attitudes and inserts childbearing into African lifestyles. Infertility is a loathsome possibility because childlessness in Ghana, as elsewhere in Afrique Noire, is "felt by both men and women as the greatest personal tragedies and humiliations" (Fortes, 1950, p. 262). The desire to become a parent of many children is in the hearts of both men and women. But Nigerians, like most Africans, "must navigate a paradoxical political-economic and cultural landscape wherein they face powerful pressures both to limit their fertility and to have large families" (Smith, 2004, p. 221). Regardless of this trend, individuals, couples, and families spare neither effort nor resources to establish, restore, or prove fertility in a fervent wish to be immortalized with offspring.

The legitimate way to have socially integrated children is to limit procreation and childrearing to the marital couple (Feldman-Savelsberg, 1994). The conjugal pair is the pivot of African societies. The marital contract ramifies relationships beyond the spouses to interconnect their two families into extended or joint family systems (Nsamenang, 2000, 2005a). Spouses and their children are usually not the only members of the household. Adult kin and friends are sometimes part of the household. In some cases, a man's or woman's children from a previous marriage, premarital childbearing, or the so-called "outside" partner are also bona fide members of the household (Ellis, 1978). In addition to the biological offspring, some households also assist in rearing and educating the children of relatives (Hake, 1972). Taken together, all of the children and adult members of a household give the picture of a large family. The contemporary African family is best seen "as an intergenerational, multilocal, psychosocial community linked to local, national, and global economies and polities" (Bradley and Weisner, 1997, p. xxvi).

Although alternate family forms such as single-parent and child-headed families are emerging as a result of the AIDS epidemic, the typical African adult is uncomfortable imagining the family in its nuclear version. Substantial historical, cultural, socioeconomic, and technological changes have affected the African family. Most notable in its magnitude and its diabolic, dehumanizing, generational intention and effects are the slave trade and the colonization that marked Africa's partition (Chibwana, 2007). These events shattered the patterns of the African family but did not entirely eliminate African familism. It bears mention here that, as a continent, Africa has never recovered from this brutality and its aftermath (see Nsamenang, 2004; Smith, 1999).

The extended African family as the primary institution responsible for organizing the socialization, education, and development of children predates colonial times. In fact, the cultural values and belief systems concerning the purpose and meaning of life, which are reflected in the way Africans view children, provide for them, and rear them, have survived to this day (Callaghan, 1998; Chibwana, 2007). Although largely uncharted, that reservoir of knowledge, values, and practices persists even after the people of Africa have been subjected to colonialism as well as westernization, urbanization, and formal education. Africans have produced and sustained "strategies of survival for infants and children, strategies reflecting environmental pressures from a more recent past encoded in customs rather than in genes and transmitted socially rather than biologically" (LeVine, 1974, p. 227). Evidence indicates that African fathers are important to their children, even when physically absent (Nsamenang, 1987, 2000). But Aka fathers in the central African forest zone provide more direct care and are near their infants more than fathers in any other human population (Hewlett, 1992).

Socialization theories and methods, however, have oriented research to parental caregiving but limited attention on nonparental caregivers (see Lamb, Sternberg, Hwang, and Broberg, 1992; LeVine et al., 1994; Weisner and Gallimore, 1977).

Nonparental Childcare and Institutional Education

Deciding how to care for children is an old problem to which individuals and societies have developed a large repertoire of solutions (Lamb and Sternberg, 1992). The variety and diversity of these solutions illustrate the ways in which historical, economic, ideological, and demographic realities shape or constrain childbearing and childrearing policies and practices across nations. The demand for childcare far outstrips the available supply in almost every country and community. When African mothers left home during the day to go to the farm or market or to work outside the home, extended family members or older siblings, especially female children, were readily available to care for infants and preschool children. There also were situations in polygamous homes where older wives delegated the care of the home and younger children to younger wives (Ogbimi and Alao, 1998). In this way, it was possible for infants and toddlers to be taken care of in the traditional setup until they were old enough to take care of themselves. The traditional kin group of childcare assistance, especially sibling caregiving, is no longer as readily available or has become inadequate since children are expected to attend school.

It is clear from various lines of research (e.g., Harkness, 1987; Kaye, 1962; Nsamenang, 1992a; Ohuche and Otaala, 1981; Uka, 1966; Wober, 1975) that African societies receive newborns with largely positive attitudes, even under conditions of domestic strain and economic hardship. Zimba (2002, p. 94) referred to the "indigenous network of support" that is reserved for newborns and their mothers in southern Africa. The "deep and comforting sense of tradition and community" and sense of "sacred duty" to which Nsamenang (1992b, p. 427) refers provide part of the emotional force sustaining the perception of a new infant as, according to Harkness and Super

(1992, p. 446), "a precious treasure…nurtured, and enjoyed by the whole family." Africans back up their positive disposition to childbearing with shared caregiving (e.g., Harkness and Super, 1992; Nsamenang, 1992b; Weisner, 1987). Childrearing is a social enterprise wherein children also receive attention and care from the early months of life from grandmothers, other members of the extended family, including older siblings, and sometimes neighbors. Such a shared caregiving landscape contrasts with the image in the literature of the woman as the primary caregiver. Given the ubiquity of sibling caregiving in African cultures, the portrayal of the "typical" African early childhood development worker as almost always a mother or grandmother, a sister or an aunt, a cousin, or a neighbor (e.g., Bernard van Leer Foundation, 1994) is a mistaken picture. In most HIV/AIDS-devastated communities, increasing numbers of orphaned children are heading families (UNICEF, 2003).

Caregiving facilities have frequently been used to facilitate acculturation and ideological indoctrination. Caregivers in African traditions have had no formal training or accreditation in professional early childhood development; they were and still are natural caregivers who have provided care to young children since time immemorial (Bernard van Leer Foundation, 1994). But today, public early childhood development services are advocated as "a good start in life involving nurturing, care and a safe environment" for children 0 to 8 years old (Ministers and Representatives of Ministers, 2005). Childcare in daycare settings and preschools has become popular throughout Africa because it provides early childhood education to preschool children and plays a custodial role for mothers who are at work. "The Nigerian urban working mother," for example, "is able to play the dual roles of being a mother and an employee successfully due to availability of child care services such as housemaids, nannies, day care centres, nursery schools and kindergartens" (Ogbimi and Alao, 1998, p. 48).

Therefore, formal education or schooling is only one element of childrearing. Understanding indigenous life-journeys is "an essential adjunct to the adaptation of exogenous institutions for endogenous progress in the field of education" in Africa (Serpell, 1993, xii). Unfortunately, many values and norms that are cherished in the shared childcare and participatory education of African family traditions are relatively ignored in the curricula of most schools in Africa (Serpell, 1993). All children face the developmental task of entering into interpersonal relationships with adults and with their peers at home, in school, in the community, and on a lifelong basis.

Friendships and Peer Groups

From an early age, children rapidly learn to become birds of a feather flocking together. This is a process about affiliation, common interests, and peer influence and friendship (Hartup and Moore, 1990). The peer group is a ubiquitous institution in sub-Saharan Africa. It is generally constituted by age, gender, interest/activity, or neighborhood. In some societies, peers "mature" out of one pivot activity setting to another, sometimes with a rite of passage. "Liberal" parental attitudes "thrust" children from earlier than toddlerhood into more interaction and "productive" activities within the free spirit of the African peer culture than with parents or other adults. A commonplace scenario is that of a multiage "gang" of children of walking age along with older siblings coming under the care and supervision of two or more pubescent teenagers, who monitor their safety and welfare while parents are engaged in activities outside the home (Nsamenang, 1992b). Schooling has not eliminated peer group activities but modified configurations of peer grouping. Pupils and students of all ages and levels of education can be observed functioning in peer networks for various purposes in all educational institutions and in nonschool settings.

Although the peer culture is a world of its own, children's relations do not happen in a world of their own; they are linked to, or are even embedded in, other relationship systems

(Bukowski, Newcomb, and Hartup, 1996). Peer relationships occur not in a vacuum but in a context provided not only by various human needs that relationships satisfy and that direct relational behaviors, but also by exterior elements that impinge on people's choices and freedom to exercise them, such as the prevailing cultural rules (Duck, 1988). The peer group is effective in Africa because a mechanism of self-regulation is brought into the peer culture by "the word of the adult, whose direct intervention is no longer needed" (Zempleni-Rabain, 1973, p. 233). Thus, parental values and expectations play a directive role in shaping the developmental niche and, consequently, the development of children's behavior. Among the Nso of northwest Cameroon, the "masters" of the apprenticeship type of peer group collegiality who mentor younger siblings are older peers (Nsamenang and Lamb, 1995). Like Maya children, African peers teach and interstimulate one another, under the guidance and mentorship of older peers (Maynard, 2002). Once children join the peer culture, they must carve out their own niche in the "bunch" in terms of secure and reliable friends through whom to abstract a sense of security, acceptable rules and norms, and livelihood lessons.

The first and perhaps longest-lived relationship is the parent–child bond. From parents, children learn their earliest and, for most people, the most memorable lessons in interpersonal connectedness. The early learning engendered in the ecosystem of the family may well define how a child eventually engages socially with other adults and children in extrafamilial settings. Intrafamilial relationships contribute to the processes of individuation and identity formation. In sub-Saharan African cultures, for example, children are humanized to "gain significance from and through their relationships with others" (Ellis, 1978, p. 6). Children equally learn prosocial and organizational skills from peer friendliness and activities, which contribute immensely to their identity development and the processes of social competence and social integration. Personal well-being is also served by active social contacts (Carson, Butcher, and Mineka, 1998). The power of social connectedness led Erik Erikson (1902–1994) to highlight the interpersonal aspects of psychoanalytic theory, while Harry Stack Sullivan (1892–1949) espoused the meaning of personality only in relation to interpersonal processes. Consistent with these theorists, Africans promote sociogenic values of systematic incorporation into the community of other humans at critical ontogenetic stations of life through such procedures as naming, initiation, marriage, and death, among others. An important concern with such ontogenesis is responsible and productive engagement, particularly involvement in family work.

Work and Employment

African governments have adopted the school as a source of enlightenment and an emancipatory tool to achieve equality and reduce poverty. More specifically, the African Union (2006, p. 2) has rightly positioned the school as a frontline strategy that should enable Africa to "take its rightful place in the global community and the knowledge economy." But schooling means different things to different people (Serpell, 1996), most of all in Africa where the cultural curricula of indigenous education coexist intrusively into the dominant impervious curricula, to the chagrin of the development community whose unvoiced motive, apparently, is to subtly policy Africa's systems into obsolescence and extinction. The dire need is to adapt the school to Africa's theory of the universe, agrarian livelihoods, and participatory pedagogy. One grand hypothesis, which should not be interpreted as censure of the school, is that the most profound and most utilizable learning for most Africans occurs from an early age in African family traditions and is rehearsed and extended within peer cultures outside the school (Nsamenang, 1992b, 2004).

Fretful children and youth are sensitized to pursue an elusive "modernity" through academic pipelines (Cooper, 2001), bypassing viable alternative pathways that could be enhanced into culturally meaningful productive citizenship. It is not at all difficult to perceive the directive attitude and orientating values to interventions of the African condition as one intolerant of indigenous African childrearing ideas and praxes and aversive of African life-journeys (Serpell, 1993).

Accordingly, all levels of the education systems of most African countries prepare graduates for Western-type careers in Africa's predominantly agrarian economies that are bereft of such vocational paths and opportunities. It is perhaps for this reason that Durojaiye (1973) reported Nigerian youth as not adequately guided into the vocational requirements and opportunities in their countries. Many young people in the school systems are even unable to indicate a choice of an occupation because they have not been exposed to the national labor market. Like Nigerians, Africans choose careers from a narrow range of occupations and select careers either above or below their measured abilities (Durojaiye, 1973).

With education in African family traditions, all the occupations in which children and youth participated were complementary to those of adults of the same gender. It was reported that the profitability of women's trades, especially among the Hausa of Northern Nigeria, varied directly with the women's utilization of child/adolescent workers who were either the women's own or fostered children (Hake, 1972). Child work is common across Africa. In Burundi, a 2000 UNICEF-sponsored study revealed that 25% of children less than 14 years of age were used in various sectors, including agriculture, cattle rearing, commerce, construction, catering, and transportation (Bangurambona, 2006). The children reared in extended families ensured that younger children had ample opportunities to go along with and learn from working older ones. By the time these adolescents began to work on their own, they had imbibed technical and attitudinal requirements of their work and were adapted physically and mentally to the environment of work such that they knew how to handle work problems. The apprenticeship system has placed Africa's youth productively in motor mechanics, iron/metal or wood works, driving, cloth weaving or tailoring, hairdressing, catering, information and communication technologies, and creative sports, amongst other crafts and trades.

To ponder Africa's education quandary and the shape education, as envisioned in the African Union's (2006) *Draft Plan of Action*, should take, it seems rational to juxtapose indigenous African ideas and praxes against the imported liberatory education in sub-Saharan Africa, which produces experts, most of whom are alienated from and somehow ignorant of the countries and agrarian livelihoods their education is meant to serve. In consequence, youth unemployment is unprecedented throughout Afrique Noire. Between 1985 and 1987, unemployment rates in Nigeria, for instance, were in excess of 40% (Philips, 1988). Although the majority of youth from middle and high socioeconomic backgrounds enter tertiary institutions, most poor youth drop out of the educational system and end up in vocational training or the apprenticeship systems mentioned earlier (Okojie, 1994).

One spin off of unemployment is street trading. Oloko (1998) reported an increasing trend in the proportion of students in Lagos of Nigeria who engaged in street vending after school hours as one out of four in 1979, two out of four in 1988, and two out of three in 1997. The proportion of young vendors who worked all day without respite was 21.2% in 1998. Adeagbo (1997) reported that 57.5% of street traders in selected neighborhoods of Ibadan in southwest Nigeria were young adolescents and youth. Some children attended school and vended wares as an after-school activity (Bekombo, 1981). Apart from street vending, other works that adolescents are involved in include begging, car washing, shoe shining, and scavenging.

Perhaps the African Union (2006) is still to realize that Eurocentric education, beginning with early childhood care and education programs, initiates Africa's children into an educational process by which they, from one developmental stage to another, increasingly gain in unfamiliar knowledge and skills but disturbingly dip into alienation and ignorance of their cultural circumstances and agrarian livelihoods by service programs and education curricula that are deficient on local content and insensitive of national skills demands (Nsamenang, 2005b).

It is worth noting that, as national governments throughout sub-Saharan Africa are grappling with slim budgets, their education systems are churning out masses of marginally literate school leavers and graduates, increasing numbers barely able to scratch a living (Nsamenang, 2005b). Education in much of Africa apparently is more suitable for foreign than national labor markets because it does not focus on generating national and local career paths. Furthermore, present systems of education in much of Afrique Noire mature African children into citizens who are ignorant of their own realities. The excessively externalized curricula deprive African youth of the empowering value of their own knowledge and skills, especially their right to understand and develop insight into their own humanity and dreadful state. Perhaps in tacit support of the unprecedented phenomenon of youth flight, most educational institutions have recently reoriented not to training for self-employment and local job development but more to training for the global workforces.

A Bartered Hybrid Developmental Niche

The African developmental niche, identified in its classical components of (1) physical and social settings, (2) cultural traditions of childcare and childrearing, and (3) a psychology of caregivers, includes shared caregiving and sibling caregivers, early childhood development practitioners, and teachers. This is a cultural mélange of a triple heritage (Mazrui, 1986) of Eastern and Western cultural fragments in coexistence with deeply ingrained Indigenous African developmental ideas and praxes, such as garden metaphors and participatory learning processes.

The many factors behind the changing status of the contemporary African family include poverty, war and family disruption, overcrowding, inadequate housing and food supply, and disease, among many others. The erosion of traditional family structures, for instance, is caused mainly by the increasing participation of women in the labor force, increasing demands on farms, urbanization, economic- and conflict-related migration, AIDS death or incapacity, and the increasing number of nuclear and single-parent families. As rapid change and unceasing crises continue to outpace social security responses for Africa's youngsters, Sharp's (1970, p. 20) caution "against destroying too abruptly the traditional background of the African" child, which is still "the best guarantee of the child's welfare and education," stands relevant today. Appropriately, then, the heart of the psychosocial care for vulnerable children is to be found in the African family and home, and it is here that the main thrust of external efforts to improve the well-being of Africa's children in difficult circumstances must be directed (Richter, Foster, and Sherr, 2006).

It is obvious from the foregoing paragraphs that in the sub-Saharan developmental contexts, both local and foreign factors and psychologies now live together in the same individuals and communities. In one sense, African children and youth, like their parents, grope in confusion in search of an identity and modicum of an elusive certainty from their marginal existence within the fringes of multiple cultural imperatives. This chapter, therefore, is an attempt to tease out from Africa's hybridism the indigenous developmental ideas and practices of parents and caregivers who "have been caught up in the web of cultural transition where there are no longer clearly defined values and moral codes of behavior that should be instilled in children and young people" (Cohen, 2001, p. 6).

The next section charts trends in developmental science, which reveal increasing sensitivity to the value of the developmental context, indigenous precepts, and situated developmental phenomena and processes of psychosocial differentiation.

Developmental Research in Afrique Noire

Four periods are discernible in developmental research in African societies. This section identifies the periods and attempts an overview of the nature of developmental ideas and practices and/or the main thrust of the research characteristic of each period.

First, rudiments of developmental psychology arrived in Africa in the apron strings of colonial services of governance, education, health, evangelism, social work, and more. The elements of the developmental science that arrived in Africa allied to colonialism met an unfamiliar and uncharted indigenous developmental science. But both the "native" and expatriate disciples of the imported bits and pieces of European American science did not acknowledge indigenous developmental psychology, which submerged and still immerses the "new" science. In the course of colonial history, psychology in general and developmental science in particular began to implant from research in the colonial services but more definitely from anthropological research to domesticate the savage mind (Goody, 1977) and understand stagnated development in the Dark Continent (Forde, 1963; Kidd, 1906/1969).

Most of the dispensers of the earliest elements of developmental science were not psychologists but colonial agents mandated with services development and consolidation of the colonial clutch on Africa. The European American voyagers or sojourners who rejected or reviled Africa's knowledge systems, modus vivendi, and forms of intelligence published the earliest racist literature on Africa. In brief, Ellis (1978) writes of European voyagers, merchants, missionaries, and colonial agents who referred to the irrationality and gullibility of the African, who bartered food, cattle, and other necessities for a few pieces of European iron and silver frippery. Africa's resources still suffer this fate today—hence, Africa's abject poverty and inability to cater for and support its children.

A developmental topic that attracted early research attention was curiosity about the precocity of physical development of the African child compared to that of the Western child. Wober (1975) overviewed research on accelerated physical (but not mental) development of African children, which was attributed to excessive contact/comfort and physical handling that began to lag behind the European American child as the children were abruptly weaned at the birth of the next sibling. The shape of developmental science implanting as a fledging scientific discipline in Africa today was determined then by the orientating attitude adopted in reporting research. The African data were never presented as integral or contributory to the developmental knowledge base but as failing to conform to or as poor templates of developmentally appropriate European American norms (LeVine, 2004). Thus, reports of the substantive cross-cultural research on Africa have tacitly rejected and still largely disdain African patterns of child life and development.

But although developmental science is well under way in Afrique Noire, it is not yet as far along in ecological and social relevance as it should be. Wober (1975) sensitively predicted that Western psychology would not successfully implant and thrive in Africa without anchor in the local reality. The rest of this section reveals gradual accentuation of Wober's (1975) spark of the discourse of indigenous versus scientific psychology in the provocation that psychological research would be different in the hands of native-born Africans. The indigenization movement is sustained by increasing realization that the bulk of printed research about Africa was authored by itinerant non-Africans and embodied the cultural imprints and vested interests the foreigners brought to Africa.

The second period of disciplinary development in Africa was marked by a gradual shift from interest in specific abilities and personality profiling in comparison with Western standards to focus on the developmental impact of the cultural setting. In her *Six Cultures, Studies of Child Rearing*, B.B. Whiting (1963) moved the field of psychological anthropology toward a more systematic, measurement-oriented approach to human abilities and psychological characteristics. On their part, Cole, Gay, and Sharp (1971) expanded and enriched the field by comparing performance on cognitive tests between Liberian and American respondents and concluded that performance outcomes on cognitive tasks was more dependent on situational factors than on underlying differences in cognitive abilities.

The 1970s and 1980s were indeed a watershed period in cross-cultural research on human abilities and development of cognitive and social competencies. The Whitings (Whiting and Whiting, 1975) provided the roadmap for the role of culture on child development in *Children of Six Cultures*, whereas Berry (1976) sketched the ecology of cognitive styles and, along with colleagues (Berry et al., 1986), demonstrated the role of acculturation on cognitive development with respect to figure-ground perceptual abilities with a central African subsample. The Munroes (Munroe and Munroe, 1975) published the first textbook on cross-cultural developmental research, with influential data from their childrearing research in East Africa. Mundy-Castle (1975) offered an important distinction between academic or technological and social intelligence in African children. Dasen, Inhelder, Lavallee, and Retschitzki (1978) published an influential monograph on the "birth" of intelligence in the Baoule child in Cote d'Ivoire based on their research on Piagetian theory. In the same year, Erny (1978) offered an educational perspective on the African child and his/her developmental setting.

Collaborating with B.B. Whiting, the Munroes (Munroe, Munroe, and Whiting, 1981) published the first comprehensive handbook on cross-cultural human development, which integrated anthropological and psychological research, including insightful glimpses from databases obtained from across Africa. Serpell's (1984) critique of cognitive development research and psychological testing in Africa revealed that, ab initio, the studies were designed to determine how well African children performed the "tricks" of Western schooling rather than to understand Afrocentric abilities and the conditions under which they were actualized. The differences observed in test scores between African children and Western comparative samples were interpreted as "developmental lags." A "deficiency" interpretation was thus imputed into African children's abilities, rather than attributing differences in cultural and schooling experiences between African and Western children.

Regarding social development, LeVine (1973; LeVine and LeVine, 1963) hinted that Gusii parents in Kenya tend not to be overtly affectionate with their infants and toddlers, and Ainsworth (1967) described lack of face-to-face interactions between Bagandan (Ugandan) mothers and their infants. Similarly, Goldschmidt (1975) purported a pattern of "idle hands and absent eyes" in mothers' interactions with infants among the Sebei of Kenya and Uganda. On the other hand, the Kilbride and Kilbride (1974, 1975) studies among the Baganda corroborated findings by Super and Harkness (1974) that East African parents influenced the social behavior of their infants through smiling and talking to the infants. Two African psychologists, Ohuche and Otaala (1981), provided broad strokes of the developmental context of African children. Cognizant of the divergences in perspectives to cultural research, Super and Harkness (1986), with data from East Africa and the Boston area of the United States, published a classic article of a sociological–anthropological framework with which to understand children and psychosocial differentiation in cultural context in which they outlined a three-component "developmental niche," referred to earlier.

A movement away from cross-cultural comparisons toward efforts to understand Africans as Africans and not in the throes of European American images is the signpost of the third phase of developmental research in Africa. For this phase, Nsamenang (1992a, 1992b) emphasized a contextual viewpoint and the contributions that indigenous African scholars could introduce to the science. LeVine et al. (1994) reported an interdisciplinary research project on childrearing among the Gusii, a high-fertility, polygynous society of Kenya, as "Lessons from Africa." It is instructive that LeVine (2004, p. 149) revisited this data set a decade later to acknowledge sub-Saharan African mothers as having "a practical understanding of infant care and development contrasting sharply with expert knowledge in the child development field." To be specific, "Gusii mothers raised [sic] their infants and toddlers according to a different set of standards" (LeVine, 2004, p. 159) than the developmentally appropriate practices promoted as derived from science/evidence that is derived from the European American cultural ideology (LeVine, 2004). On their part, the edited volume by Dawes and Donald (1994) mapped out several dimensions of the psychosocial consequences of adversity on childhood and adversity from South African research. On their part, Weisner, Bradley, and Kilbride (1997) devoted an edited volume to the African family as a flexible and adaptive childrearing agency in which various chapters appraised different facets of Africa's family in a "crisis of social change."

The fourth milestone in developmental research, which is not orderly but at various stages of Azuma's (1984) five-tier process of adapting psychology across the continent, is an indigenization movement. This movement represents attempts by African scholars to evolve a psychology that makes sense in their cultural circumstances and by which they can gain understanding of their mindset, subjectivity, intersubjectivity, and modus vivendi.

A majority of children in rural sub-Saharan Africa are more familiar with clay or other local materials as mediums of expression than they are with pencil and paper or commercially prepared toys. Furthermore, familiarity with 'intelligent behavior' in sub-Saharan Africa reveals that primacy is placed on social rather than mentalistic or cognitive intelligence, per se. Serpell (1977) initiated research into African forms of intelligent behavior by charting the perceptions of intelligence in a rural community in eastern Zambia. This eventually led Kathuria and Serpell (1999) to develop a language-reduced test suitable for use by children in rural Africa—the *Panga Muntu Test* (Make-A-Person Test). The test presents children with wet clay, and the children are asked to "make" a person with the clay. The children's figures are then quantitatively scored for accurate representation of human physical characteristics. Sternberg et al. (2001) studied the relationship between academic and practical intelligence in Kenya. They developed a Test for Tacit Knowledge for Natural Herbs with Luo children of a rural Kenyan community (Sternberg et al., 2001). The test sampled from common illnesses in the Luo community and standard herbal treatments for those illnesses in that community. Given the significance of schooling and the adoption of European languages for school instruction in much of Africa (Serpell, 1993), concerns have focused on the interfaces of African mother tongues and the learning of European languages in Cameroon (Fai, 1996; Kishani, 2001), Namibia (Veii and Everatt, 2005), and Zambia (Chamvu, 2006; Kaani, 2006), to cite a few.

The significance of these studies is that they depart from normative comparisons and represent genuine attempts to recognize, respect, and describe indigenous mindsets and intellectual values by using ecologically meaningful, local materials and media to focus on indigenous psychosocial processes (Mpofu, 2002). They also demonstrate the appropriate application of psychometric procedures with indigenous materials and for the purpose of supporting local educational activities or practices in other sectors. Although promising beginnings have been recorded in indigenizing the measurement of human intelligence in sub-Saharan Africa, much remains to be achieved in terms of programmatic research in this and other areas.

Systematic research may endeavor to improve on Tape's (1993) work on cognition with Ivorian adolescents, which Dasen (1993, p. 156) recognized as "a good beginning of the development of a truly African psychology." A truly developmental approach is Nsamenang's (1992a) sociogenic explication of human ontogenesis in the cultural context of Africa that Serpell (1994, p. 18) judged as offering a different "theoretical focus from the more individualistic account proposed by Freud, Erikson and Piaget." Ngaujah (2003) recommends Nsamenang's theoretical approach for education and missionary work. For pedagogy, it highlights the affective nature of the environment on children's cognitive and social learning possibilities. Missionaries can take from it "a healthy respect for the people of Africa" (Ngaujah, 2003, p. 9).

Developmental Science Within an African Theory of the Universe

A Lifecycle Developmental Trajectory

An Afrocentric vision of human ontogenesis transcends that of developmental science by identifying phases of the human lifecycle, which scientific psychology invokes but has not articulated. An African theory of the universe recognizes a cyclical human ontogenesis or lifecycle nexus wherein the newborn is taking on a social selfhood into an existing human community, while the dying person is at the verge of taking on an ancestral cum spiritual selfhood into the world of the "living-dead" (Mbiti, 1990) on his or her biological death. An African theory of the universe visualizes a lifecycle developmental trajectory in three phases of selfhood, namely, social selfhood or the experiential self and the metaphysical phases of spiritual selfhood and ancestral selfhood.

A universal but mostly inferred recognition of the metaphysical phases of human selfhood is discernible in the intentions and connotations of funeral rites and the signification of the forms of memorabilia people in all cultures hold of their *loving dead* (Nsamenang, 2005a) decades, even centuries, after they died. Developmental science, however, excludes them from its focal content, but they are issues of intimate attention for most people. For instance, people in all cultures loathe death perhaps because most can never be truly ready for it or they dread to imagine their transition into the spiritual world of evil or loving-dead ancestors in their afterlife. To the extent that Africans, like everyone else, cognize the implications of the metaphysical phases of the human lifecycle, the concerns constitute an essential component of their psychosocial being and functioning, which stand in the face of the science to develop the capacity to operationalize and the tools to capture and measure. It might be noticed that some people sometimes deploy more time and resources into anticipation of their afterlife than to children's needs and welfare.

Within the experiential or social selfhood, the forte of developmental science, African social ontogeny posits seven ontogenetic stages, which add to the two metaphysical phases to give a total of nine distinctive periods of the human lifecycle. They include the neonatal period, social priming, social apprenticeship, social entrée, social internment, adulthood, old age/death, and ancestral and spiritual selfhoods (see Nsamenang, 1992a, 2005a). Each ontogenetic stage is marked by distinctive developmental tasks, defined within the framework of the culture's conception of child, family, and their welfare. An essential task that traverses all stages is responsibility training, which begins from an early age. Within the African worldview, responsibility is more valued than cognition, per se, in the sense that one cannot be responsible without cognizing, whereas some people are cognitively alert but irresponsible. Africans cherish cognition not as an end in itself but as a means to social ends or as it is subordinated to servicing or enhancing human needs. Cultures differ in the manner in which they guide children's development and organize developmental learning.

Developmental Learning

In African cultures, children also develop through their own initiative, taking an active role in managing their own learning. Some cultures instruct intelligence, whereas others permit children to develop their intelligences mainly by themselves as they engage with the world or as they interstimulate one another within the freedom of the peer culture with little to no adult intervention. The seminal concept of Afrocentric developmental thinking is sociogenesis, which does not discount biology but incorporates it by tacitly implicating genotype as underwriting social ontogenesis. What social ontogeny stresses is not physical development, which is not disregarded, but the fact that human development occurs in a sociological garden. In Africa's developmental garden, there are members of different demographic cohorts and mixed abilities who share roles in nurturing children and performing familial and societal duties.

Consistent with Afrocentric construal of functional shrewdness, intelligence is construed practically as that human quality that outputs from biological embedding into, or genetic interactionism with, life circumstances. Through lifetime interaction between children's biological systems and lifespan conditions, children increasingly become competent and responsible as they acquire and grow into or transcend (in superior intellect or as geniuses) the knowledge and skills that exist "already in their culture, which needs them" (Ogbu, 1994, p. 365). Intelligent behavior thus implicates adaptability to or transcendence of experienced circumstances and lifetime changes.

The handy principle within the African worldview that permits unfettered attainment of intelligent capacities is not instruction but participatory pedagogy. In this sense, children's developmental lessons are not derived from instruction or didactic processes. They exist to be extracted, depending on ontogenetic (indeed intellectual) ability, from family routines, ethnic languages, institutional structures, cultural practices, economic activities, imagined or spatial cues, and social encounters, particularly those of the peer culture. The concept of developmental learning (Nsamenang, 2004) implies that children are not born with the knowledge and cognitive skills with which to make sense of and face the world; they learn or grow into them as they develop. Accordingly, Africans assign sequential tasks to their culturally perceived ontogenetic stages. The core learnings are achieved without "the usual sense of classrooms and schools" (Bruner, 1996, p. ix).

Of course, participatory learning is liable to abuse because it sometimes degenerates into child labor. However, in its indigenous version, participatory learning or child work is not abusive but an African mode of social integration and responsibility training that fits into Piaget's (1952) theory of interactional–extractive learning. It deserves incorporation into the school curricula (Lo-oh, 2005) and guidance to avoid its abuse rather than substitution with the didactic modes of institutional education, as the development community wrongly advocates. Its integration into school curricula could permit more competent African children, like their Mayan peers, to mentor and "tutor" their conspecifics (Maynard, 2002). We feel the urge to juxtapose Africa's early responsibilization of children with the concern voiced by Ellis (1978, p. 50) that "whether in Britain too little is expected of children, their activities being restricted almost entirely to play."

Developmental Processes and Principles

African theories represent development in garden metaphors of *seed* and *plant* (Erny, 1968; Nsamenang, 1992a), among others, to underscore an inherent potentiality for self-generated development and learning. The metaphors engender developmental genetics. Developmental learning can be enhanced through processes of "cultivation," nurturing, socialization, education, and mentoring. Garden metaphors also connote nursing to maturity, as from seeding through planting into fruit bearing. Without at least an own child, a typical African feels unfulfilled, hence African pronatalist values. Unborn children are "buds of hope and expectation" (Zimba, 2002, p. 94), and newborns are "entirely geared toward the future" in a gradual "becoming" (Erny, 1968, p. 21) into socialized agents of the cultural community. The cultural capital supports positive reproductive values, as some practices "subject pregnant women and their spouses to behavioral taboos that guide sexual intercourse, specific food items and emotional distress, among others, in order to promote the health of the unborn child and mother" (Zimba and Otaala, 1995, p. 43).

The image of the African childrearing garden is that of polycropping, not monoculture. Such visualization excludes lonesome sovereignty and embraces relational integration. African ethnotheories prime individuation, identity formation, and intellectual development mainly from socio-affective premises, in the light of Vygotsky (1978). For instance, "children's cognitive development must be understood not only as taking place with social support in interaction with others, but also as involving the development of skills with socio-historically developed tools that mediate intellectual activity" (Rogoff, 1990, p. 35).

African cultures transcend Vygotsky, however, by priming children from an early age to seek out others and to extract "intelligences" and define self within a dense sociological field of kin, siblings, peers/friends, and neighbors. The school and other social institutions expand the human networks. Zimba (2002) refers to the South African Zulu as nurturing *umuntu umuntu ngabantu*, which is literally translated as "a person is only a person with other people." Obiechina (1975) interpreted the West African novel as portraying individual African characters, not through their private psychological profiles, but as reflecting communitarian motives and activities of a social nature. A relational self is virtuous within the African worldview, but this does not disqualify the individual as a distinct entity (Nsamenang, 2004). Identity begins to differentiate from an early age as children are increasingly subjected to learning their cultural content beginning with interaction with multiple caregivers and gradual introduction to and involvement in family routines. Often, children "teach" their cultural curriculum to themselves within the peer culture far more than do parents or other adults. Thus, the African child is exposed to more attachment figures than European American children on whom attachment theory has been embellished, despite its being founded on Ainsworth's (1967) seminal attachment research in the African nation of Uganda.

In much of Africa, an unwritten curriculum is wedged into the daily routines of family and society and sequenced to fit into the developmental stages of the school of life (Moumouni, 1968). Child caregiving is integral to this curriculum as a social enterprise in which siblings provide the bulk of the care to toddlers and younger siblings, while mothers or other adults are available not as full-time care providers but only as partial caregivers and "managers" of such care (Nsamenang, 1992b). "Liberal" parental values permit and create participative spaces that allow children to spend more time within the peer culture than in interactions with parents or in adult company. The peer culture engages children in friendly as well as antagonistic sociability, anticipatory socialization, and interstimulation. The assignment of livelihood duties to children, most of them completed as peer group activities, trains not only responsibility but also organizational and productive skills (Ogunaike and Houser, 2002). The free spirit of the peer culture reinforces parental injunctions, therein sharpening prosocial and moral values, cognitive abilities, and leadership skills.

Participatory pedagogy recognizes early markers of affectionate bonding and gradually matures an infant into an accredited child-participant in domestic chores and, thereafter, into an adolescent, who eventually graduates into more mature interactional networks and transactional roles. The guidance of human development as progressive social integration differs from the individualistic, mechanistic conceptual perspectives that dominate European American theories. The notable difference between the Afrocentric and Eurocentric perspectives strikes a chord as to the existence of an alternative trajectory that sharply contrasts the promotion of sovereign individualism and not relational connectedness as humanity's sole path to individuation, personal identity, and intellectual functioning. The possibility of such alternatives poses not just daunting challenges but also compelling opportunities.

Challenges and Opportunities

Children mature progressively toward the adult images and roles of their cultures. This fact of human ontogenesis heightens the importance of knowing what children need today to usefully tailor this unfolding process into preparing young people to better face the challenges of a turbulent, future adulthood. Such a concern, in practice, translates into anxiety about whether Afrique Noire "is equipping her next generations with responsible values and the right techno-cognitive orientation to cope with and make progress in a competitive, knowledge-driven world in continuous transition" (Nsamenang, 2004, p. 7).

Children are contextual beings. African children are "situated" in a sociological garden of mixed abilities to which research, education, policies, and services are best directed with the objective of generating innovative strategies tuned to child and youth development in participatory communities (Lanyasunya and Lesolayia, 2001). The challenge as well as the opportunity is to extract authentic Afrocentric developmental principles from the communitarian and participatory processes and social capital of African life paths, rather than persist in efforts to nudge and adjust Africans to the universe as envisioned by Western civilization (Nsamenang and Dawes, 1998). Africa's input into developmental science could extend the frontiers of the discipline "If we could continue to listen to, and learn from, the African worldview, seeing a holistic and integrated way of looking at the family and the universe" (Callaghan, 1998, p. 32); we might see children and their ontogenesis in a new and more inclusive way.

Western developmental science tends to be used as the template against which to verify the essence and adequacy of African folk epistemology, developmental ethos, and procedures, which, although largely unexplored, are coherent within an African theory of the universe. European American evaluative criteria are unjustified in view of the obvious differences in social realities and cognitive values between indigenous African and European American circumstances. Imagine, for example, the implications and heuristic significance of the fact that sub-Saharan African mothers understand infant care and development in ways "that had not been imagined in developmental theories" (LeVine, 2004, p. 163). For Ngaujah (2003), such evidence constitutes the impetus to look at Africa and its developmental realities from other-than-European American frames of reference. One expectation is that the psychology community in general and the developmental science family in particular use such insights to enrich and extend the frontiers of the discipline. In fact, the social capital and lifecycle trajectory engendered in Africa's theory of the universe offers opportunities to extend theoretical vistas, open novel analytical frames, and inspire inclusive methodological techniques. But this expectation is unlikely to fructify unless a learning posture (Agar, 1986) is adopted within an inclusivity, diversity paradigm (Nsamenang, 2005b).

Progress with Afrocentric developmental science can come through revolutionizing the education of African psychologists and allied professionals not solely in the theories, methods, and languages of Europe and North America, as is the case with the impervious curricular models in situ, but more so in those of their indigenous psychologies. Such a revolution transcends the often posited development of culturally sensitive education curricula to contextualizing and infusing trainees with keen sensitivity to the multicultural contents reflective of the hybridism and globalism of Africa's developmental contexts. This is a daunting task indeed in the sense that education was imported into Africa as "a source of enlightenment and liberation" (Serpell, 1996, p. 5) to the detriment of designing it to understand the mindsets and circumstances of Africa's children; the education and its related services, like early childhood development programs (Nsamenang, 2007b), were and still are devised and intended to uplift and emancipate. Africa is preparing its children and youth to achieve the vision of "an integrated, peaceful, prosperous Africa" (African Union, 2006) against chronic scarcity of financial resources and dependence on foreign aid, while its enormous natural resources are being exploited by foreign interests. Furthermore, in contextualizing developmental science, it is essential not to ignore its public interest domain that could undertake research and tailor human services to "contribute to an improvement of the life circumstances of African children" (Nsamenang and Dawes, 1998, p. 74). In this direction, Dawes' (2006; Dawes and Donald, 2000) research in South Africa incites reflection on child development research that can make a difference. The nature of the "difference" that research is making in a multiracial South Africa itself merits research attention. Is the research mother-centered, or does it incorporate fatherhood and others?

The protracted and deep-seated economic crisis that has gripped every country in sub-Saharan Africa since the early 1980s has had a profoundly negative impact on the well-being of the large majority of the population, particularly youth (Bennell, 2000). With a deepening poverty, family and other social safety nets have become increasingly strained. Nigerians, like other Africans, "must navigate a paradoxical political-economic and cultural landscape wherein they face powerful pressures both to limit their fertility and to have large families" (Smith, 2004, p. 221). Although young people growing up in the midst of Africa's crises of survival and development have been particularly badly affected, the resourcefulness with which they maneuver through their precarious circumstances has yet to be researched. Economic opportunities in the formal sector have contracted sharply, while the "popular economy" is burgeoning in the hands of youth and women. But instead of appreciating and understanding the extent to which most youth, having no opportunities and perceiving no alternatives, eke out an existence on small farms and urban streets, the governing class and political elite classes have alienated the young, acted in their own corporate interests, and imposed barriers that stifle creativity and proscribe productive youth activities. A focal case is the enactment of laws by most sub-Saharan governments to outlaw the street economy (Nsamenang, 1998) instead of understudying to understand and shrewdly formalize it as youth creativity in efforts not to be irresponsible and unproductive.

Conclusion

Callaghan (1998, p. 33) visualizes "the future of the African child" within the hub of Africa's social capital–the extended family–whose "rich cultures and wisdom of her timeless traditions… is reflected" in successful childrearing for centuries. Regrettably, scholars and interventionists of the continent's appalling condition tacitly condemn and stealthily circumvent or out-phase this most robust resource from research agendas, school curricula, service programs, and policy development. In this sense, ostensible empowering interventions turn out to instead disempower most African communities. Programs and services are more appropriately mounted on the reality that most children's needs are best "met through everyday activities in their families, supported by communities and assisted by government [and other sources of] services" (Richter, Foster, and Sherr, 2006, p. 10).

The developmental field deserves to be informed of how the African ecoculture impacts children's psychosocial differentiation. An Afrocentric developmental perspective can flesh out how shades of Africa's hybridism map out on to various domains of human development. Exclusion of African developmental precepts and processes alongside the imposition of foreign models accentuates the misunderstanding of Africa and estranges children and youth from the security of their familiar home turfs. The missionary rather than enhancement flavor of most policies and programs and the values they engender unwittingly transmit the message to children and their families that their cultural life is "clandestine." This induces a high dose of shame and alienation whose net effect dispels any intervention benefits to instead stunt development, hence the unrequited development in Africa. This point is consistent with Vandenbroeck's (1999) intimation that many youngsters around the world "hide" parts of their personalities because current early childhood development services, for example, render them ashamed to expose their differentness.

In one sense, this chapter represents a silent call for a paradigm shift from a restrictive dominant discourse to a more inclusive, diversity paradigm accommodative of all narratives, particularly the African. Given the *science's* difficulty, if not incapacity, to access the bulk of its African content, the paradigm shift becomes a compelling imperative. It is absurd that the bulk of a discipline's knowledge should persist outside its reigning narratives and assessment tools.

Some factors that shape the discipline in Afrique Noire are also constraining as they hold a great potential to extend the field. First, schooling that systematically transforms Africans into

Eurocentric literate citizens exposes most African children and scholars to multiple cultural worlds that increase their acceptance and tolerance of human diversity. Paradoxical achievements (Nsamenang, 2004) and the cognitive tolerance of otherwise opposing values and role demands (Carr and MacLachlan, 1994) also expand the cognitive systems of Africans. For instance, Africans, even in the same household, are at peace with Christianity, Islam, and African theodicy, as well as the requirements of ethnomedicine and biomedicine. These and many other processes bestow multicultural cognitive repertoires on Africans, which could extend the frontiers of the discipline if an enabling environment is created for African developmentalists and allied scholars to properly research and disseminate them.

Second, innovative theorization is required to capture the contemporary braid of developmental ideas and praxes in Africa's hybrid ecocultures that no existing theory fittingly explains. Sensitivity to the dualism and openness to the unmeasured resilience and resourcefulness within Africa's developmental ethos disqualify a simplistic adjustment of Western models, epistemologies, and techniques for use in Africa. Objective research attention on what the convolutions of developmental realities mean and are outputting in developmental outcomes can illumine perspectives beyond current molds. Africa's hybrid developmental ecoculture can thus edify creative theorization and inspire innovative methodologies to adroitly craft, synthesize, and enhance a blend of imported and indigenous developmental legacies into a visionary theoretical package that unites and is inclusive of disparate developmental realities that hitherto have been little contemplated or theorized about.

Acknowledgments

We sincerely acknowledge the editor of this landmark *Handbook* for his insightful editorial inputs.

References

Adeagbo, D. (1997). *Monograph 10: Physical and socio-economic impact of street trading: Case study of Ibadan.* Ibadan, Nigeria: N.I.S.E.R.

African Union (2006). *Second decade of education for Africa (2006-2015): Draft plan of action.* Addis Ababa, Ethiopia: African Union, Department of Human Resources, Science and Technology.

Agar, M. H. (1986). *Speaking of ethnography.* Newbury Park, CA: Sage.

Ainsworth, M. D. S. (1967). *Infancy in Uganda: Infant care and the growth of love.* Baltimore: John Hopkins University Press.

Ainsworth, M. D. S. (1977). Infant development and mother-infant interaction among Ganda and American families. In P. H. Leiderman, S. R. Tulkin, and A. Rosenfield (Eds.), *Culture and infancy* (pp. 119–148). New York: Academic Press.

Arnett, J. J. (2004). Adolescence in the twenty-first century: A worldwide survey. In U. P. Gielen and J. Roopnarine (Eds.), *Childhood and adolescence: Cross-cultural perspectives and applications* (pp. 277–294). Westport, CT: Praeger.

Azuma, H. (1984). Psychology in a non-Western country. *International Journal of Psychology, 19*, 45–55.

Baguma, P. (2006, November). *Psychosocial problems among children orphaned by AIDS: Case study of Uganda.* Keynote Paper Presented at the 7th ISSBD Africa Region Workshop, Johannesburg, South Africa.

Bangurambona, J. (1994). *Le rôle de la tante paternelle à travers les rondes populaires.* Bujumbura, Burundi: Université du Burundi: Mémoire de Licence.

Barsby, J. (2006). Fair trade: What cost a cup of coffee? *The Traveler Msafiri, 57*, 50–54.

Bekombo, M. (1981). The child in Africa: Socialization, education and work. In G. Rodgers and G. Standing (Eds.), *Child work, poverty, and underdevelopment* (pp. 113–129). Geneva, Switzerland: International Labor Organization.

Bennell, P. (2000). *Improving youth livelihoods in Sub-Saharan Africa.* Ottawa, Canada: IDRC.

Bernard van Leer Foundation. (1994). *Building on people's strengths: Early childhood in Africa.* The Hague, The Netherlands: Bernard van Leer Foundation.

Berry, J. W. (1976). *Human ecology and cognitive style.* Beverly Hills, CA: Sage.

Berry, J. W. (2006). Origins and development of indigenous psychologies in Canada. In C. M. Allwood and J. W. Berry (Eds.), Origins and development of indigenous psychologies: An international analysis. *International Journal of Psychology, 41*, 260–261.

Berry, J. W., van de Koppe, J. M. H., Annis, R. C., Senechal, C., Bahuchet, S., Sforza-Cavali, L. L., et al. (1986). *On the edge of the forest: Cultural adaptation and cognitive development in central Africa*. West Chester, PA: Swets, North America Inc.

Bongmba, E. K. (2001). *African witchcraft and otherness: A philosophical and theological critique of intersubjective relations*. New York: New York University Press.

Bradley, C., and Weisner, T. S. (1997). Introduction. In T. S. Weisner, C. Bradley, and C. P. Kilbride (Eds.), *African families and the crisis of social change*. Westport, CT: Bergin & Garvey.

Bruner, J. (1996). *The culture of education*. Cambridge, MA: Harvard University Press.

Bukowski, W. M., Newcomb, A. F., and Hartup, W. W. (1996). *The company they keep: Friendship in childhood and adolescence*. Cambridge, United Kingdom: Cambridge University Press.

Callaghan, L. (1998). Building on an African worldview. *Early Childhood Matters, 89*, 30–33.

Carr, S. C., and MacLachlan, M. (1994, July). *Psychology for the developing world*. Paper presented at the International Congress of Applied Psychology, Madrid, Spain.

Carson, R. C., Butcher, J. N., and Mineka, S. (1998). *Abnormal psychology and modern life*. New York: Longman.

Chamvu, F. (2006, November). *Analysis of the psychometric properties of the Zambia Achievement Test: Reading recognition*. Poster presented at 7th ISSBD Africa Region Workshop on Enhancing Research Capacity in Human Development, Johannesburg, South Africa.

Chibwana, K. (2007). *Community-based childcare resource assessment: The case of Zomba District in Malawi*. Master of Arts Thesis in Child and Youth Care, Faculty of Human and Social Development, University of Victoria, Victoria, British Columbia, Canada.

Cohen, R. N. (2001). Foreword. In A. Njenga and M. Kabiru (Authors), *In the web of cultural transition: A tracer study of children in Embu District of Kenya*. The Hague, The Netherlands: Bernard van Leer Foundation.

Cole, M. (1999). Culture in development. In M. H. Bornstein and M. E. Lamb (Eds.), *Developmental psychology: An advanced textbook* (pp. 73–123). Mahwah, NJ: Erlbaum.

Cole, M., Gay, J. A., and Sharp, D. W. (1971). *The cultural context of learning and thinking: An exploration in experimental anthropology*. New York: Basic Books.

Cooper, C. R. (2001). Bridging multiple worlds: Inclusive, selective, and competitive programs, Latino youth, and pathways to college. Affirmative development of ethnic minority students. *The CEIC Review: A Catalyst for Merging Research, Policy, and Practice, 9*, 14–15, 22.

Curran, H. V. (1984). Introduction. In H. V. Curran (Ed.), *Nigerian children: Developmental perspectives*. London: Routledge and Kegan Paul.

Danziger, K. (2006). Comment (pp. 269–275): Special issue on indigenous psychologies. *International Journal of Psychology, 41*, 241–320.

Dasen, P. R. (1984). The cross-cultural study of intelligence: Piaget and the Baoule. *International Journal of Behavioral Development, 19*, 407–434.

Dasen, P. R. (1993). Theoretical/conceptual issues in developmental research in Africa. *Journal of Psychology in Africa, 1*, 151–158.

Dasen, P. R., Inhelder, R., Lavallee, M., and Retschitzki, J. (1978). *Naissance de l'intelligence chez l'enfant Baoule de Cote d'Ivoire* [Birth of intelligence among Baoule children of Ivory Coast]. Berne, Germany: Hans Huber.

Dawes, A. (2006). *Doing child development research that aims to make a difference: South African reflections*. A Keynote Address Presented at the ISSBD Biennial Meetings, Melbourne, Australia.

Dawes, A., and Donald, D. (1994). *Childhood and adversity: Psychological perspectives from South African research*. Cape Town, South Africa: David Philip.

Dawes, A., and Donald, D. (2000). Improving children's chances: Development theory and effective interventions in community contexts. In D. Donald, A. Dawes, and J. Louw (Eds.), *Addressing childhood adversity* (pp. 1–25). Cape Town, South Africa: David Philip.

Diop, C. A. (1960). *L'universe culturelle de l'Afrique Noire* [The Black African cultural world]. Paris: Presence Africaine.

Durojaiye, M. O. A. (1984). The impact of psychological testing on educational and personnel selection in Africa. *International Journal of Psychology, 19*, 135–144.

Ellis, J. (1978). *West African families in Great Britain*. London: Routledge.

Erny, P. (1968). *L'enfant dans la pensee traditionnelle d'Afrique Noire* [The child in traditional African social thought]. Paris: Le Livre Africain.

Erny, P. (1973). *Childhood and cosmos: The social psychology of the Black African child.* New York: New Perspectives.
Erny, P. (1978). *L'enfant et son milieu en Afrique noire* [The child and his environment in Black Africa]. Paris: L'Harmattan.
Eze, N. (1991). The progress and status of psychology in Africa. *Journal of Psychology in Africa, 1,* 27–37.
Fai, P. J. (1996). *Loan adaptations in Lamnso' and effects on the teaching of English.* DISPES II Memoir of Ecole Normale Superieure, University of Yaounde, Yaounde, Cameroon.
Feldman-Savelsberg, P. (1994). Plundered kitchens and empty wombs: Fear of infertility in the Cameroonia grassfields. *Social Science and Medicine, 39,* 463–474.
Forde, C. D. (1963). *African worlds: Studies in the cosmological ideas and social values of African peoples.* Oxford, United Kingdom: Oxford University Press.
Fortes, M. (1950). Kinship and marriage among the Ashanti. In A. R. Radcliffe Brown and D. Forde (Eds.), *African systems and kinship and marriage.* Oxford, United Kingdom: Oxford University Press.
Goldschmidt, W. (1975). Absent eyes and idle hands: Socialization for low affect among the Sebei. *Ethos, 3,* 157–163.
Goody, J. (1977). *The domestication of the savage mind.* Cambridge, United Kingdom: Cambridge University Press.
Hake, J. M. (1972). *Childrearing practices in Northern Nigeria.* Ibadan, Nigeria: University of Ibadan Press.
Harkness, S. (1987). The cultural mediation of postpartum depression. *Medical Anthropology Quarterly, 1,* 194–209.
Harkness, S., and Super, C. M. (1992). Shared child care in East Africa: Sociocultural origins and developmental consequences. In M. E. Lamb, K. J. Sternberg, C.-P. Hwang, and A. G. Broberg (Eds.), *Child care in context* (pp. 441–459). Hillsdale, NJ: Erlbaum.
Hartup, W. W., and Moore, S. G. (1990). Early peer relations: Developmental significance and prognostic implications. *Early Childhood Research Quarterly, 5,* 1–17.
Hewlett, B. S. (1992). Husband-wife reciprocity and the father-infant relationship among Aka Pygmies. In B. S. Hewlett (Ed.), *Father-child relations: Anthropological and biosocial perspectives* (pp. 153–176). New York: Aldine de Gruyter.
Hinde, R. A., and Stevenson-Hinde, J. (1990). Attachment: Biological, cultural and individual desiderata. *Human Development, 33,* 62–72.
Holdstock, T. L. (2000). *Re-examining psychology: Critical perspectives and African insights.* London: Routledge.
Joint United Nations Programme on HIV/AIDS (UNAIDS) (2006). *Report on the global AIDS epidemic.* Geneva, Switzerland: UNAIDS.
Kaani, B. (2006, November). *Nature and prevalence of reading difficulties among school-dropouts: A case of selected areas in Chipata Distric, Zambia.* Poster presented at the 7th ISSBD Africa Region Workshop on Enhancing Research Capacity in human Development, Johannesburg, South Africa.
Kathuria, R., and Serpell, R. (1999). Standardization of the Panga Muntu Test: A nonverbal cognitive test developed in Zambia. *Journal of Negro Education, 67,* 228–241.
Kaye, B. (1962). *Bringing up children in Ghana.* London: Allen and Unwin.
Kidd, D. (1906/1969). *Savage childhood.* New York: Negro Universities Press.
Kilbride, P. L., and Kilbride, J. E. (1974). Sociocultural factors and the early manifestation of sociability behavior among Baganda infants. *Ethos, 2,* 296–314.
Kilbride, J. E., and Kilbride P. L. (1975). Sitting and smiling behavior of Baganda infants: The influence of culturally constituted experience. *Journal of Cross-Cultural Psychology, 6,* 88–107.
Kishani, B. T. (2001). On the interface of philosophy and language in Africa: Some practical and theoretical considerations. *African Studies Review, 44,* 27–45.
Lamb, M. E., and Sternberg, K. J. (1992). Sociocultural perspectives in nonparental child care. In M. E. Lamb, K. J. Sternberg, C.-P. Hwang, and A. G. Broberg (Eds.), *Child care in context* (pp. 1–23). Hillsdale, NJ: Erlbaum.
Lamb, M. E. Sternberg, K. J., Hwang, C.-P., and Broberg, A. G. (Eds.). (1992). *Child care in context* (pp. 441–459). Hillsdale, NJ: Erlbaum.
Lanyasunya, A. R., and Lesolayia, M. S. (2001). *El-barta Child and Family Project: Working papers in early childhood development, No. 28.* The Hague, The Netherlands: Bernard van Leer Foundation.
LeVine, R. A. (1973). Patterns of personality in Africa. *Ethos, 1,* 123–152.
LeVine, R. A. (1974). Child rearing as cultural adaptation. *Teachers College Record, 76,* 226–239.
LeVine, R. A. (2004). Challenging expert knowledge: Findings from an African study of infant care and development. In U. P. Gielen and J. Roopnarine (Eds.), *Childhood and adolescence: Cross-cultural perspectives and applications* (pp. 149–165). Westport, CT: Praeger.

LeVine, R. A., Dixon, S., LeVine, S., Richman, A., Leiderman, P. H., Keefer, C. H., et al. (1994). *Child care and culture: Lessons from Africa.* Cambridge, United Kingdom: Cambridge University Press.

LeVine, R. A., and LeVine, B. B. (1963). Nyansongo: A Gusii community in Kenya. In B. Whiting (Ed.), *Six cultures: Studies of child rearing* (Vol. 2). New York: Wiley.

Lo-oh, J. L. (2005). An emerging Africentric educational thought and praxis. Book review of Nsamenang, A. B. (2004): Teaching-learning transaction. Bamenda, Cameroon: HDRC Series. *Journal of Psychology in Africa, 15,* 115–116.

MacGaffey, W. (1981). African ideology and beliefs: A survey. *African Studies Review, 24,* 227–274.

Manganyi, N. C., and Louw, J. (1986). Clinical psychology in South Africa: A comparative study of emerging professional trends. *Professional Psychology, 3,* 171–178.

Maquet, J. (1972). *Africanity.* New York: Oxford University Press.

Mauer, K. F., Marais, H. C., and Prinsloo, R. J. (1991). Psychology: The high road or the low road. *South African Journal of Psychology, 21,* 90–97.

Maynard, A. E. (2002). Cultural teaching: The development of teaching skills in Maya sibling interactions. *Child Development, 73,* 969–982.

Mazrui, A. A. (1986). *The Africans.* New York: Praeger.

Mbiti, J. S. (1990). *African religions and philosophy.* Oxford, United Kingdom: Heinemann Educational.

Ministers and Representatives of Ministers of Education (2005). Communiqué on early childhood development by African ministers or their representatives. Third African Conference on ECD, Accra, Ghana, May 30–June 2, 2005.

Monasch, R., and Boerma, J. T. (2003). Orphaned and childcare patterns in sub-Saharan Africa: An analysis of national surveys from 40 countries. *AIDS, 18*(Suppl. 2), S55–S65.

Moumouni, A. (1968). *Education in Africa.* New York: Praeger.

Mpofu, E. (2002). Indigenization of the psychology of human intelligence in Sub-Saharan Africa. In W. J. Lonner, D. L. Dinnel, S. A. Hayes, and D. N. Sattler (Eds.), *Online readings in psychology and culture* (Unit 5, Chapter 2). Retrieved February 23, 2009, from http://www.ac.wwu.edu/~culture/Mpofu.htm.

Mundy-Castle, A. C. (1975). Social and technological intelligence in western and non-western cultures. In I. Pilowsky (Ed.), *Culture in collision* (pp. 344–348). Adelaide, Australia: Australian National Association for Mental Health.

Munroe, R. L., and Munroe, R. H. (1975). *Cross-cultural human development.* Prospect Heights, IL: Waveland Press.

Munroe, R. L., Munroe, R. H., and Whiting, B. B. (1981). *Handbook of cross-cultural human development.* New York: Garland STPM Press.

Mwamwenda, T. S. (1996). *Educational psychology: An African perspective.* Durban, South Africa: Buttersworth.

Ngaujah, D. E. (2003, Fall). *An eco-cultural and social paradigm for understanding human development: A (West African) context.* Graduate Seminar Paper (supervised by Dr. Dennis H. Dirks), Biola University, La Mirada, CA.

Nkwi, P. N. (1983). Traditional diplomacy, trade and warfare in the 19th century Western Grassfields. *Science and Technology Review, 1,* 101–116.

Nsamenang, A. B. (1987). Fatherhood: A West African perspective. In M. E. Lamb (ed.), *The father's role: Cross-Cultural perspectives* (pp. 273–293). Hillsdale, NJ: Erlbaum.

Nsamenang, A. B. (1992a). *Human development in cultural context: A Third World perspective.* Newbury Park, CA: Sage.

Nsamenang, A. B. (1992b). Early childhood care and education in Cameroon. In M. E. Lamb et al. (Eds.), *Day care in context: Socio-cultural perspectives.* Hillsdale, NJ: Erlbaum.

Nsamenang, A. B. (1993). Psychology in sub-Saharan Africa. *Psychology and Developing Societies, 5,* 171–184.

Nsamenang, A. B. (1998). Work organization and economic management in sub-Saharan Africa: From a Eurocentric orientation toward an Afrocentric perspective. *Psychology and Developing Societies, 10,* 75–97.

Nsamenang, A. B. (2000). *Fathers, families, and child well-being in Cameroon: A review of the literature.* Philadelphia: NCOFF

Nsamenang, A. B. (2002). Adolescence in sub-Saharan Africa: An image constructed from Africa's triple inheritance. In B. B. Brown, R. W. Larson, and T. S. Saraswathi (Eds.), *The world's youth: Adolescence in eight regions of the globe* (pp. 61–104). Cambridge, United Kingdom: Cambridge University Press.

Nsamenang, A. B. (2004). *Cultures of human development and education: Challenge to growing up African.* New York: Nova.

Nsamenang, A. B. (2005a). African culture, human ontogenesis within. In C. Fisher and R. Lerner (Eds.), *Encyclopedia of applied developmental science* (pp. 58–61). Thousand Oaks, CA: Sage.

Nsamenang, A. B. (2005b). Educational development and knowledge flow: Local and global forces in human development in Africa. *Higher Education Policy, 18*, 275–288.

Nsamenang, A. B. (2007a). A critical peek at early childhood care and education in Africa. *Child Health and Education, 1*, 14–26.

Nsamenang, A. B. (2007b). Origins and development of scientific psychology in Afrique Noire. In M. J. Stevens and D. Wedding (Eds.), *Psychology: IUPsyS global resource*. London: Psychology Press.

Nsamenang, A. B. (2008). (Mis)Understanding ECD in Africa: The force of local and global motives. In M. Garcia, A. Pence, and J. Evans (Eds.), Africa's future, Africa's challenge: Early childhood care and development in sub-Saharan Africa (pp. 135–149). Washington, DC: World Bank.

Nsamenang, A. B., and Dawes, A. (1998). Developmental psychology as political psychology in sub-Saharan Africa: The challenge of Africanisation. *Applied Psychology: An International Review, 47*, 73–87.

Nsamenang, A. B., and Lamb, M. E. (1995). The force of beliefs: How the parental values of the Nso of Northwest Cameroon shape children's progress towards adult models. *Journal of Applied Developmental Psychology, 16*, 613–627.

Obiechina, E. N. (1975). *Culture, tradition and society in the West African novel*. Cambridge, United Kingdom: Cambridge University Press.

Ogbimi, G. E., and Alao, J. A. (1998). Developing sustainable day care services in rural communities of Nigeria. *Early Child Development and Care, 145*, 47–58.

Ogbu, J. U. (1994). From cultural differences to differences in cultural frames of reference. In P. M. Greenfield and R. R. Cocking (Eds.), *Cross-cultural roots of minority child development* (pp. 365–391). Hillsdale, NJ: Erlbaum.

Ogunaike, O. A., and Houser, R. F. Jr. (2002). Yoruba toddler's engagement in errands and cognitive performance on the Yoruba Mental Subscale. *International Journal of Behavioral Development, 26*, 145–153.

Ohuche, R. O., and Otaala, B. (1981). *The African child in his environment*. Oxford, United Kingdom: Pergamon.

Ojiaku, M. O. (1974). Traditional African social thought and Western scholarship. *Presence Africaine, 90*, 2nd Quarterly.

Okojie, C. E. (1994). Poor housing and the integration and employment of youth in Nigeria. In I. Albert, J. Adisa, I. Agbola, and G. Heranlt (Eds.), *Urban management and urban violence in Africa* (pp. 179–190). Ibadan, Nigeria: French Institute for Research in Africa (IFRA).

Olaniyan, R. (1982). African history and culture: An overview. In R. Olaniyan (Ed.), *African history and culture* (pp. 1–14). Lagos, Nigeria: Longman.

Oloko, S. B. A. (1998). *Protection and violation of child right in Nigeria: An overview*. Child Protection in Nigeria, UNICEF Report Volume 4. New York: United Nations Children's Fund.

Owusu-Bempah, J., and Howitt, D. (1995). How Eurocentric psychology damages Africa. *The Psychologist: Bulletin of the British Psychological Society*, October, 462–465.

Peltzer, K., and Bless, C. (1989). History and present status of professional psychology in Zambia. *Psychology and Developing Societies, 1*, 51–64.

Philips, O. (1988). *The performance of the Nigerian economy under SAP*. Ibadan, Nigeria: N.S.S.E.R.

Piaget, J. (1952). *The origins of intelligence in children*. New York: International Universities Press.

Population Reference Bureau (2000). *Population Services International. Social marketing for adolescent sexual health: Results of operations research projects in Botswana, Cameroon, Guinea, and South Africa*. Washington, DC: The Population Reference Bureau.

Richter, L., Foster, G., and Sherr, L. (2006). *Where the heart is: Meeting the psychosocial needs of young children in the context of HIV/AIDS*. The Hague, The Netherlands: Bernard van Leer Foundation.

Rogoff, B. (1990). *Apprenticeship in thinking: cognitive development in social context*. New York: Oxford University Press.

Saraswathi, T. S. (1998). Many deities, one God: Towards convergence in cultural psychology. *Culture and Psychology, 4*, 147–160.

Scarr, S., and McCartney, K. (1983). How people make their own environments: A theory of genotype-environment effects. *Child Development, 54*, 424–435.

Serpell, R. (1977). Estimates of intelligence in a rural community of Eastern Zambia. In F.M. Okatcha (Ed.), *Modern psychology and cultural adaptation* (pp. 179–216). Nairobi, Kenya: Swahili Language Consultants and Publishers.

Serpell, R. (1984). Research on cognitive development in sub-Saharan Africa. *International Journal of Behavioral Development, 7*, 111–127.

Serpell, R. (1992, April). *Afrocentrism: What contribution to science of developmental psychology*. Paper presented at the First ISSBD Africa Region Workshop on Child Development and National Development in Africa, Yaounde, Cameroon.

Serpell, R. (1993). *The significance of schooling: Life-journeys into an African society.* Cambridge, United Kingdom: Cambridge University Press.
Serpell, R. (1994). An African social ontogeny: Review of A. Bame Nsamenang (1992): Human development in cultural context. *Cross-Cultural Psychology Bulletin, 28,* 17–21.
Serpell, R. (1996). Commentary on Freitag's lead article: The role of the school in child development. *ISSBD Newsletter, 1,* 5.
Sharan, P. (1988). One view of the cultural context for the study of child-rearing in India. *ISSBD Newsletter, 1,* 1–3.
Sharp, E. (1970). *The African child.* Westport, CT: Negro University Press.
Shweder, R. A. (1995). The ethnographic aims of cultural psychology. *ISSBD Newsletter, 1/95,* 2–4.
Smith, D. J. (1999). *Having people: Fertility, family and modernity on Igbo-speaking Nigeria.* Ph.D. dissertation, Department of Anthropology, Emory University, Atlanta, GA.
Smith, D. J. (2004). Contradictions in Nigeria's fertility transition: The burdens and benefits of having people. *Population and Development Review, 30,* 221–238.
Sternberg, R. J., Nokes, C., Geissler, P. W., Prince, R., Okatcha, F., Bundy, D. A., et al. (2001). *The relationship between academic and practical intelligence: A case study in Kenya.* Unpublished manuscript.
Super, C. M., and Harkness, S. (1974). Patterns of personality in Africa: A note from the field. *Ethos, 2,* 377–381.
Super, C. M., and Harkness, S. (1986). The developmental niche: A conceptualization at the interface of child and culture. *International Journal of Behavioral Development, 9,* 545–569.
Tape, G. (1993). *Milieu africain et developpement cognitive: Une etude du raisonnement experimental chez l'adolescent Ivorien* [Cognitive development in an African context: An experimental study of reasoning in Ivorian adolescents]. Paris: L'Harmattan.
Uka, N. (1966). *Growing up in Nigeria culture.* Ibadan, Nigeria: Ibadan University Press.
United Nations Children's Fund (2003). *Africa's orphaned generations.* New York: UNICEF.
United Nations Population Fund (2007). *State of world population 2007: Sub-Saharan Africa.* Retrieved on December, 3, 2007, from http://www.unfpa.org/swp/.
Vandenbroeck, M. (1999). *The view of the Yet: Bringing up children in the spirit of self-awareness and knowledge.* The Hague, The Netherlands: Bernard van Leer Foundation.
Veii, K., and Everatt, J. (2005). Predictors of reading among Herero-English bilingual Namibian school children. *Bilingualism: Language and Cognition, 8,* 239–254.
Vygotsky, L. (1978). *Mind in society: The development of higher psychological processes.* Cambridge, United Kingdom: Cambridge University Press.
Ware, H. (1983). Male and female life cycles. In C. Oppong (Ed.), *Male and female in West Africa* (pp. 6–31). London: Allen & Unwin.
Wassenaar, D. R. (1998). A history of ethical codes in South African psychology: An insider's view. *South African Journal of Psychology, 28,* 135–145.
Weisner, T. S. (1987). Socialization for parenthood in sibling caretaking societies. In J. B. Lancaster, J. Altman, A. S. Rossi, and L. R. Sherrod (Eds.), *Parenting across the lifespan: Biosocial dimensions* (pp. 237–270). Hawthorne, NY: Aldine de Gruyter.
Weisner, T. S., and Gallimore, R. (1977). My brother's keeper: Child and sibling caretaking. *Current Anthropology, 18,* 169–190.
Weisner, T. S., Bradley, C., and Kilbride, C. P. (Eds.). (1997). *African families and the crisis of social change.* Westport, CT: Bergin & Garvey.
Whiting, B. B. (1963). *Six cultures, studies of child rearing.* New York: John Wiley and Sons.
Whiting, B. B., and Whiting, J. W. M. (1975). *Children of six cultures: A psycho-cultural analysis.* Cambridge, MA: Harvard University Press.
Wober, M. (1975). *Psychology in Africa.* London: International African Institute.
World Factbook (2006). World population: Age structure. Retrieved July 5, 2007, from http://www.cia.gov/cia/publications/factbook/index.html.
Zempleni-Rabain, J. (1973). Food and strategy involved in learning fraternal external exchange among Wolof children. In P. Alexander (Ed.), *French perspectives in African studies* (pp. 221–233). London: Oxford University Press.
Zimba, R. F. (2002). Indigenous conceptions of childhood development and social realities in southern Africa. In H. Keller, Y. P. Poortinga, and A. Scholmerish (Eds.), *Between cultures and biology: Perspectives on ontogenetic development* (pp. 89–115). Cambridge, United Kingdom: Cambridge University Press.
Zimba, R. F., and Otaala, B. (1995). *The family in transition: A study of child rearing practices and beliefs among the Nama of the Karas and Hardap regions of Namibia.* Windhoek: UNICEF Namibia and the University of Namibia.

21
Russia

DAVID A. NELSON, CRAIG H. HART,
EMILY K. KEISTER, and KARINA PIASSETSKAIA

Introduction

Through the turn of the twentieth century, Russians lived through a difficult transition as their society adapted to political, economic, and social challenges following the collapse of the Union of Soviet Socialist Republics (USSR). Changes were particularly dramatic in Russia's largest cosmopolitan cities, which have embraced Western-style capitalism, spurred by a heavy influx of capital. In Moscow and St. Petersburg, the current generation is witnessing evidence of significant wealth creation. At the same time, many Russians are experiencing poverty and economic difficulty, because not all have been positively affected by the economic transformation. Expectable social challenges also abound in the face of considerable economic and political tumult. It is in this context that the current chapter focuses on childhood, adolescence, and, to some degree, emerging adulthood in modern-day Russia.

In pursuing this task, we first acknowledge the limited information that exists. Before perestroika, few data on Russian child psychology or family studies were collected as a result of Soviet repression of the social sciences. Following the demise of the Soviet Union, opportunities to collect such data were, in theory, more readily available but severely limited by the chaotic state of Russian academia (Kerig, 1991, 1995). Accordingly, it will likely be some years before a definitive picture of Russian childhood emerges. Nonetheless, extant data are useful in assembling a broad outline, and this information is presented in three sections in this chapter. First, we examine the turmoil of the recent past and attempt to document current demographic trends that affect children and also reflect, in part, current societal attitudes toward family and childrearing. Second, we consider the nature of the Russian family, past and present. We also present recent data documenting some of the ways in which Russian children are affected by family influence. Finally, we review extant research regarding the nature of Russian childhood across developmental periods (infancy/early childhood, middle childhood, and adolescence/emerging adulthood). Particularly in adolescence, we focus on trends in social-psychological adjustment indices as well as the nature of the peer group, schooling, and other environmental contributors to development.

Modern Russia: A Story of Societal Upheaval

To say that Russians have recently experienced tremendous social, political, and economic change is an understatement. The societal turbulence also makes it more difficult for developmental scientists to document what current trends in Russian child development are reflective of native culture or, alternatively, the product of societal turmoil or the introduction of Western influence. In the years prior to the decline of the Soviet Union, Bronfenbrenner (1970) deemed the cultural contrast between childhood in the United States and the USSR to be so significant that he spoke of "two worlds of childhood." The current generation of Russian children, however, is not experiencing the same world that Bronfenbrenner described, as is apparent in the sections that follow.

As it became evident in the late 1980s that Soviet-era communism could not endure, Mikhail Gorbachev initiated reforms well known as *perestroika* (restructuring) and *glasnost* (openness). Perestroika was focused on the creation of a pluralistic parliamentary democracy, where the communist party no longer maintained complete control. Glasnost focused on candor and truth about the past and the present and allowed Soviet citizens for the first time to hear what had been kept from them—the disarray of the USSR and the incompetence of past and present leadership. These reforms hastened the demise of the USSR.

Following a failed coup by hard-line communists in August, 1991, the union collapsed, and Boris Yeltsin led the country into a protracted period of uncertainty, instability, and dissatisfaction. Russians experienced a profound identity crisis (Billington, 2004). In particular, Russians mourned the loss of their country's superpower status, and most, especially outside of the major urban areas, found few personal benefits in emergent democracy and capitalism. The Yeltsin era was characterized by corruption and persistent economic shocks that led people to view democracy as synonymous with chaos and upheaval rather than opportunity (Baker and Glasser, 2005). Many Russians saw a marked decline in their living standards as Russia moved from a centrally planned economy to a member of the global market. The resulting economic adjustment has been long and arduous. Many Russian parents have also been distressed by the cultural changes, often ascribed to negative Western influence, that flooded Russian society during the Yeltsin era. Although many Russians valued greater freedom of speech, many also found it distasteful that such freedom also allowed for the import of Western media, which glorified violence, pornography, and liberal sexuality.

Accordingly, in 2003, only one-third of Russians considered themselves democrats, and an equal number favored a quick return to authoritarianism (Gerber and Mendelson, 2003). In particular, the older generation longs for the relative well-being of the Soviet period. Some observers have accordingly concluded that President Vladimir Putin has taken cues from Russian society and launched a counterrevolution that has slowly turned back the clock on market and political reform (Baker and Glasser, 2005). Therefore, the long-term stability of Russian democracy and capitalism is unclear, and accordingly, the sociocultural environment of today's Russian children may yet undergo further dramatic change.

Demographic Trends in Modern-Day Russia

The upheaval has produced a number of disturbing demographic trends that threaten to undermine the family and, by extension, influence child development. Eberstadt (2005) referred to Russia as the "sick man of Europe." Eberstadt (2004, p. 11) also described the most significant trend—toward depopulation—as bearing "all the trappings of a 'demographic shock,' reflecting abrupt and violent changes in the nation's vital rates in the immediate wake of a momentous, system-shattering, historical event." Such was the fall of the Soviet Union. These societal trends are briefly detailed in sections that follow.

Family Economic Well-Being

In any culture, a harbinger of successful child development is the ability of families to economically subsist. Communist doctrine implicitly recognized this reality and focused on the establishment of a "classless" society in which all citizens were equally assured of life's essentials. Consistent with official Soviet propaganda that depicted poverty as a hallmark of capitalism, communist public policy was designed to eradicate poverty. However, Russians joke that under communism, they were indeed of one class—the lower class. Today, the average Russian continues to have a lower standard of living in comparison with citizens of other industrialized countries, with a gross domestic product (GDP) per person that is one-third of typical European standards.

However, the typical Russian family enjoys a much higher standard of living than those living in truly impoverished countries of the world. Most Russians have a domicile; access to heat, water, and electricity; the use of many modern appliances; decent public transportation; health care; and free education (Stetsenko, 2002). Furthermore, as capitalism has flourished in some of the largest cities like Moscow, enhanced economic opportunity has emerged for many Russians. There is evidence that an urban, Russian middle class has emerged that enjoys luxuries that would have been considered unimaginable for all but the elite during the Soviet period (such as vehicle ownership; Baker and Glasser, 2005).

Nonetheless, a significant number of Russians have seen their economic well-being fall to levels far short of what they were accustomed to during communist times. At the peak of the 1999 financial crisis, 16.4% of Russians were living below the poverty line. As economic conditions have improved, the poverty rate has dropped. A World Bank report (2005) shows that, as of 2002, 6.3% of Russians were living in absolute deprivation. In these estimates, poverty is defined as those who subsist on less than US$2.15 per person per day, with an additional classification of "economic vulnerability" for subsistence between US$2.15 and US$4.30 per person per day. Economic vulnerability describes those who are not abjectly poor but are vulnerable to poverty. Significantly, 33% of Russians in 2002 were below the economically vulnerable level, down from a high of 51.9% in 1999.

World Bank (2005) statistics also show that 26.7% of Russian children (under 16 years of age) were living in poverty in 2002, and poverty was most likely for families with more children. In particular, 20.3% of families with one child were living in poverty compared with 48.9% of families with three or more children. Thus, a greater number of Russian children in today's generation will face the challenges of poverty that are so well-documented in other cultures such as the United States (e.g., Ackerman, Kogos, Youngstrom, Schoff, and Izard, 1999; Brooks-Gunn, Linver, and Fauth, 2005). Furthermore, economic difficulties likely contribute to many of the other disturbing demographic trends noted in the following sections.

Marriage Trends

The health of marriage is also an important indicator of family stability for children, and there is evidence that the nature of marriage in Russia is changing. Although age of first marriage is rising in Russia as young people are increasingly accepting of cohabitation and delayed marriage (Zakharov, 2005), marriage is still common at a young age. Economics and parental expectations are cited as reasons for the high number of early marriages. In particular, young Russians are exposed to Western media and mores and are increasingly likely to embrace more liberal sexual attitudes. However, because most young couples are forced by economic circumstances to live with parents, who may not sanction sexual relations outside marriage, they may marry to have a regular sex life (Zubkov, 2007). Marriage is also a tradition in Russia, regardless of the sexual attitudes of the young couple or their parents, and this also promotes early marriage. However, these young adults are often emotionally immature and socially and economically dependent on their parents, a combination that unfortunately leaves many prone to short-lived marriage (Abdullaev, 2004). Early marriage and, by extension, divorce among Russians well outpaces such trends in other former Soviet countries (Abdullaev, 2004; Stetsenko, 2002). In 2002, for example, the marriage rate was 7.1 couples per 1,000 people, and the divorce rate was 5.9 couples per 1,000 people (83% of the marriage rate; Russian Federal State Statistics Service, 2007). As of 2007, the divorce rate had tempered somewhat to 54% of the marriage rate. Nonetheless, the divorce rate remains high, and children in these situations face additional challenges.

Economic constraints also uniquely affect the course of divorce as the inability to afford separate housing arrangements often compels couples to continue to live together after the divorce (Daw, 2002). Accordingly, children may continue to experience significant interparental conflict, which predicts many child and adolescent psychosocial adjustment problems in Western studies (e.g., Amato, 2006).

Decline of the Two-Parent Family

Since the end of the Soviet period, the two-parent family has been in rapid decline. A 2002 report found that 75.1% of Russian children live with two biological parents, with 16.9% in single-parent families and 6.8% in stepfamilies (Pedersen, Alcon, Rodriguez, and Smith, 2002). In contrast, approximately 60% of American children live with two biological parents. The increase in Russian single parents is partly a result of the greater incidence of divorce but also a result of childbearing outside of marriage (Klugman and Motivans, 2001). In 1987, approximately 13% of children were born out of wedlock. By 2001, the proportion had more than doubled to nearly 29% (Eberstadt, 2004). Unique to Russia, a higher level of premature death of parents is also contributing to the incidence of single parenthood. In fact, a United Nations Children's Fund (UNICEF) report reported that death of a parent is as common as out-of-wedlock births in contributing to the rise of single parenthood (Motivans, 2001; Swafford, Artamonova, and Gerassimova, 2001). This is an often overlooked consequence of the population decline currently gripping Russia (covered in more detail in the next section).

During Soviet times, the state provided single parents with full employment, free childcare, and other subsidies to help them manage. Those supports are now gone, and single-parent families are vulnerable. Accordingly, single parenthood in modern Russia is associated with greater risk for poverty, morbidity, and lower child educational attainment (Coudouel and Foley, 2001; Klugman and Kolev, 2001). Adolescents in single-parent households are also more likely to drink, smoke, become pregnant, and drop out of school (Coudouel and Foley, 2001). These findings mirror those obtained with U.S. samples (e.g., Ackerman et al., 1999; Brooks-Gunn et al., 2005). In seeking to adjust to new realities, at least half of single mothers in Russia are relying on grandparents or other family members to take care of their children while they work. This is a critical support because part-time work is much less common in Russia, thereby necessitating full-time care for children (Klugman and Kolev, 2001).

Fertility Rate and Population Decline

The typical Russian family consists of one or two children, with only 15% of families having more than two children (Rouchkin, 1997). These statistics parallel the current total fertility rate. Any discussion of total fertility rates often cites the standard replacement rate for a population to maintain itself to be 2.1 children per woman. Russia maintained levels near this range until the collapse of the Soviet Union. Since then, the fertility rate plummeted to a low of 1.17 in 1999 but has rebounded slightly to 1.41 (Central Intelligence Agency of the United States, 2009). This pattern generally holds across the entire territorial expanse of Russia, not just the urban centers.

Concomitant with this plunge in fertility rate is a significant decrease in life expectancy for Russian men. Estimates show the average life expectancy for a Russian male to be 59.3 years of age, the lowest life expectancy of any country in Europe (CIA, 2009). Russian male life expectancy is 5 years shorter than what was expected in 1990. In comparison, male life expectancy in the United States is approximately 75 years of age. The life expectancy of Russian women, at 73.1 years, has not declined significantly but still ranks among the very lowest of European countries.

The decreasing age of male life expectancy is consistent with a catastrophic surge in death rate, with deaths far outnumbering births. The current U.S. death rate is approximately 8.3 per 1,000 people, and the birth rate is 14.2 per 1,000 people. In stark contrast, the 2008 Russian death rate was 16.1 per 1,000 people, and the birth rate was only 11.0 per 1,000 people, corresponding with a net population decline (CIA, 2009). The rate will also accelerate as fewer women of childbearing age will be available in the coming generation. Estimates suggest that the current population of 140.1 million may drop by nearly one-third to approximately 100 million by 2050 (DaVanzo and Farnsworth, 1996).

Many factors have led to the surging death rate. Russia's cardiovascular disease rate is more than four times higher than the next highest European country (Cockerham, 2007). The death rate as a result of injury and violence is similarly pronounced. Pervasive smoking, poor diets, sedentary lifestyles, increasing social disintegration, the special economic stresses, and a weak medical system are oft-cited reasons for the vast increase in the death rate. Eberstadt (2004) also cites the prominent effect of the "Russian love affair with vodka." The 1994 per capita level of alcohol intake was three times as high as in 1913, before the Soviet period (Eberstadt, 2004). Furthermore, from 1990 to 2002, alcohol consumption among Russian males doubled as they sought to cope with the societal disruption of this period (Daw, 2002). Beyond the physical health effects, alcohol consumption also affects family processes, as will be discussed later.

This population decline, if unabated, will leave Russia vulnerable to considerable economic and political difficulties in the near future. In particular, low birth rates place strain on any society as the lower number of working people relative to retired people makes it difficult for the state to raise adequate revenue through taxes to support retirement benefits and geriatric medical care. Lower tax revenue also negatively impacts the ability of the state to provide support to children and families, particularly the most vulnerable populations. As noted earlier, more single-parent families are also resulting from premature parent death, and few state supports are available to these families. Extended family support will also be increasingly limited as families shrink in size and fewer grandparents, particularly grandfathers, are available to lend support.

The severity of the crisis led President Putin on May 10, 2006, to announce an incentive plan in which women who bear a second child receive a large cash bonus, extended maternity leave, monthly support allowances, and larger subsidies for childcare ("Vladimir Putin," 2006). These incentives began in January, 2007. At the close of his speech, President Putin called for a return to family values: "We cannot resolve the problem of the low birth rate without changing the attitudes within our society to families and family values. Academician Likhachev once wrote that 'love for one's homeland, for one's country, starts with love for one's family.' We need to restore these time-honoured values of love and care for family and home (p. 389)."

Characteristics of the Russian Family: Then and Now

The previously mentioned demographic trends make it clear that life in modern Russian society is stressful for most Russian children and their families. This contrasts markedly with depictions of Russian family life during the Soviet period. In his well-known treatise comparing childhood in the United States versus the USSR, Bronfenbrenner (1970) dwelt on the many faults of American society and childrearing and contrasted them with what he considered to be ideal methods in Soviet collective upbringing. In particular, Bronfenbrenner praised, "the high priority given to children in Soviet society" (pp. xi–xii). The book cover gives the following synopsis of Bronfenbrenner's description of the two societies:

> The Soviet child, both in and out of school, grows up in an environment that encourages him to look beyond his own gratification to the needs and expectations of Soviet society. By contrast, the American child, exposed to a process of development by which he is

actually brought up by his peers, is shaped by an atmosphere of subtle opposition to the standards of adult society, and by televised values which significantly contribute to his personality and behavior.

Bronfenbrenner (1970) cited the deliberately open and supportive connection between Soviet society and family and contrasted it with the emphasis in American society on the family as largely independent of society. Conformity, loyalty, group-mindedness, and unquestioning acceptance of and obedience to government authority were important values in Soviet Russia (Ispa, 1994; Shipler, 1983). In the upbringing of children, a collectivistic ideology was developed to facilitate the socialization of those values. To make this point, Bronfenbrenner (1970, pp. xi–xii) quoted Makarenko (1954), who defined Soviet family life in this manner:

> Our family is not a closed-in collective body, like the bourgeois family. It is an organic part of Soviet society, and every attempt it makes to build up its own experience independently of the moral demands of society is bound to result in a disproportion, discordant as an alarm bell. Our parents are not without authority either, but this authority is only the reflection of social authority. In our country the duty of a father toward his children is a particular form of his duty toward society. It is as if our society says to parents:… you have given birth to new people. A time will come when these people will cease to be only a joy to you and become independent members of society. It is not at all a matter of indifference to society what kind of people they will be…the Soviet state demands from you correct upbringing of future citizens. Particularly it relies…on your parental love. If you wish to give birth to a citizen and do without parental love, then be so kind as to warn society that you wish to play such an underhanded trick. People brought up without parental love are often deformed people…

However, the fall of the Soviet Union dramatically altered this relation between Russian families and society, with the latter no longer providing crucial supports. In particular, as hyperinflation and economic depression emerged, the Russian government could not afford to provide much support. Alternative socialization experiences for children or diversions for parents were significantly curtailed by the economic disruption. Today, the private sector has, to some degree, filled in gaps left by the disappearance of state-funded institutions, at least in the larger cities. But because these activities are rarely subsidized, they tend to be for those who can afford such enrichments for their children. Hence, the Russian family appears to be increasingly independent of greater society, a trend that Bronfenbrenner (1970) once condemned in American family life. It remains to be seen whether, with economic expansion, Russian society may yet rebound to better support the family and children as in Soviet times.

Russian Parenting

Returning to Makarenko's statement, it is clear that the family was always considered central to Soviet childrearing. Stetsenko (2002) also clarified that Russians continue to view the family as the most important institution in society. In contrast, other institutions, associated with the deception of compulsory communist ideology, have long been a focus of mistrust. In addition, Russians clearly value children, as a 1994 poll found that 80% of Russians considered children to be an essential component of marital happiness (Curtis, 1996). Furthermore, some experts suggest that economic tumult has had the effect of focusing Russians on family ties to sustain themselves through difficult times. Family life is perhaps the most stable of all societal institutions, as Russian families tend to display an impressive resiliency (Zubhov, 2007).

Given the value of the Russian family, there has been consistent direction on how Russian parents should provide caregiving. From the writings of Makarenko (1967), a highly influential

Soviet educator, down to the present (e.g., Azarov, 1983), Russian parents have generally been encouraged to be warm, responsive, and nurturing and to use reasoning and persuasion (Bronfenbrenner, 1970). By the early 1990s, the major theme in Russian educational writing appeared to endorse democratic childrearing approaches that encourage initiative and independent problem solving in children (Ispa, 1994; Tudge, 1991). Some of this counsel even appears to border on indulgence and permissiveness (Ispa, 1993). In addition, parental use of corporal punishment has historically been discouraged as a means for fostering conformity to societal values (Ispa, 1994). Accordingly, Russian parents have often been encouraged to adhere to more authoritative forms of childrearing, with the implicit acknowledgment that authoritarian and permissive practices are common. Indeed, similar to other cultural contexts (see Nelson, Nelson, Hart, Yang, and Jin, 2006, for a review), these parenting styles have been empirically identified in Russian cultural samples of preschoolers and adolescents (Grigorenko and Sternberg, 2000; Hart, Nelson, et al., 2000).

Furthermore, Grigorenko and Sternberg (2000) have documented many factors that predict Russian parenting styles with adolescents. First, style varies by parent and child gender. Russian fathers tend to be more authoritarian, whereas mothers are more authoritative or indulgent with their adolescents. Russian parents are also more accepting of daughters than sons. Parenting together (in intact families rather than divorced or widowed situations) was also associated with more demandingness with offspring. Furthermore, the characteristics of the parents matter, with college-educated parents being less accepting and controlling than their less-educated counterparts. Older parents are also more accepting and demanding than younger parents. Parents who consume more alcohol are significantly more likely to be authoritarian. Finally, it is easier for parents to be more accepting and less demanding when parents have established higher levels of family cohesion.

One premise underlying research on parenting styles is that the various styles are expected to promote varied child outcomes. In the years since the dissolution of the Soviet Union, few studies have assessed Russian childrearing and its linkages to child developmental outcomes. Nonetheless, as has been found in other cultures (see Nelson, Nelson, et al., 2006), extant Russian data suggest that, for young children, authoritarian parenting is associated with more child aggression and disruptive behavior with peers. Responsive, patient, playful, and easygoing parent–child interaction styles (particularly involving fathers) are also linked to fewer child behavior problems with peers (Hart, Nelson, Robinson, Olsen, and McNeilly-Choque, 1998). Accordingly, child outcomes associated with authoritarian or authoritative dimensions, at least in nursery school, appear consistent with outcomes found across diverse cultures (Nelson, Nelson, et al., 2006). However, little is known about how permissive parenting plays out in measures of adjustment for Russian children of any age (Hart, Nelson, et al., 2000).

During the Soviet period, Bronfenbrenner (1970) documented the central place of love withdrawal in Russian childrearing, particularly in response to child disobedience. This "love-oriented" discipline has also been studied in North American and other cultural contexts (Barber, Stolz, and Olsen, 2005; Nelson, Hart, Yang, Olsen, and Jin, 2006). It is currently considered to be an important component of psychological control, a form of control in which parents seek to manipulate and exploit the parent–child bond in their bid to gain child compliance. Love withdrawal is often used by Russian parents to manipulate young children into a particular course of action (Subbotskii, 1992). Similar to findings in other cultures, this parenting practice has been associated with aggressive/disruptive and internalizing behavior in Russian preschool-age children (Hart et al., 1998; Nelson, Yang, and Hart, 2005; Olsen, et al., 2002).

Finally, overprotective parenting, as reflected in parents being overly anxious to step in and solve their children's problems, has also been found to be associated with Russian children being more victimized by their aggressive peers (Hart, Nelson, et al., 2000). Beyond this type of work focused on studying peer group behavioral outcomes associated with parenting, little is known about ways that Russian parenting is associated with other aspects of development. This is particularly the case in studies of older children. In short, we have much to learn about how Russians socialize their children.

Family Processes

Western research also makes clear that a number of family processes, either negative or positive, can significantly impact child development. Little data exist, however, to document these patterns in Russia. The extant data suggest that more marital conflict is associated with heightened engagement in aggression in preschool, particularly for boys (Hart, Nelson, et al., 1998). More family conflict and less family cohesion (indicated by little support and time spent together) are also related to more child behavior problems. In particular, in a preschool sample, these markers of family difficulty were associated with aggressive/disruptive behavior in some children and victimization in others (Hart, Nelson, et al., 2000). However, little is known about how these variables are associated with older children's adjustment, and the salutary effects of positive family functioning have not been considered.

Evidence cited earlier shows that societal transitions have influenced changes in Russian family structure. Negative trends in family processes, evident during the Soviet period, have also been exacerbated by the turmoil. In particular, domestic violence continues to be rampant in Russian society, with at least one in five women consistently facing the threat or actual infliction of injury by their husbands or partners (Bodrova and David, 2001, as cited in Zakirova, 2005). In this disturbing family trend, alcoholism is presumed to be an important contributor. Societal attitudes also play a role, as many women believe that "If he beats me, it means he loves me," and authorities consider the problem to primarily be a "private family affair" and not a criminal issue (Zakirova, 2005). In addition, Russian women may tolerate violence because of their economic dependence on their husbands. As noted earlier, parents often continue to live together following a divorce, so true separation may often seem impossible. Children are also trapped in these situations, and Western research demonstrates that they suffer severe psychological consequences as they witness domestic violence between parents (e.g., Ellis, Dulmus, and Wodarski, 2003).

Another manifestation of family instability is the prevalence of child abuse. Few studies have documented the prevalence of child abuse in modern-day Russia, where it has only recently been recognized in all its forms (i.e., neglect, physical abuse, emotional abuse, and sexual abuse). Family law is still being formulated in response (Berrien, Safonova, and Tsimbal, 2001). A study conducted during the Yeltsin era (Berrien, Aprelkov, Ivanova, Zhmurov, and Buzhicheeva, 1995) asked 375 early and mid-adolescent children in a Siberian city to self-report abuse they experienced. Results showed that 28.9% of adolescents reported abuse experience, and 3.8% suffered serious injuries that required medical attention. Like domestic violence, adult alcohol consumption is likely a risk factor for child abuse in Russia (e.g., Freisthler, Merrit, and LaScala, 2006).

Support and intervention services for both victims and perpetrators of abuse have yet to be fully developed in Russia. The primary method of managing child abuse has been to separate children from their parents (Berrien et al., 2001). In addition, a significant number of street children may have run away from home to escape abuse. Statistics also suggest that parent–child separation is disturbingly common. A UNICEF study found that the number of Russian children deprived of parental care is the largest among former Soviet countries (Abdullaev, 2004). One in 70 Russian children under the age of 17 live in infant homes, orphanages, or boarding schools.

Infancy and Early Childhood in Russia

It is also enlightening to consider the nature of Russian childhood by developmental period. To begin with, there are important demographic and societal trends that particularly concern the well-being of infants and young children in today's Russia. In particular, the infant mortality rate tends to be much higher than in other industrialized countries. As of 2007, statistics showed that 9.4 out of every 1,000 Russian infants died before their first birthday (Russian Federal State Statistics Service, 2007). This mortality rate is two to four times higher than in the United States or most of the developed countries in Europe (UNICEF, 2007). Surprisingly, this high infant mortality rate has actually significantly improved since the beginning of the Yeltsin era in 1992, when the rate was 29.2 per 1,000 infants.

Many negative health trends, such as smoking and drinking, deleteriously impact maternal health and certainly contribute to pregnancy complications and compromise the health of infants. A 2002 Russian Health Ministry report showed that approximately 30% of births have complications, and every third newborn discharged from a maternity clinic has health problems (Yablokova, 2002). In all of these health challenges, the ability of the state-run medical care system to respond has been compromised because of low funding. In addition, prenatal care is often not a high priority for mothers because it is considered necessary only when something seems to be going wrong (Evanikoff, 1996). Societal trends toward single parenting also present potential obstacles for optimal infant care because fewer resources exist for such families.

Early Childcare and Education

Historically, expectations and goals for childrearing have been quite different for home and school. As noted earlier, warmth and supportiveness have always been encouraged in home environments. In contrast, educational traditions persisting from czarist Russia have embodied restrictiveness, structure, sternness, and emotional distance in the teacher–child relationship (Ispa, 1993). However, significant educational reforms have been implemented as part of the recent democratic revolution. There is now less emphasis on collectivist upbringing and more emphasis on individual-oriented outcomes (Ispa, 2002). Early childhood teachers increasingly value characteristics such as inquisitiveness and creativity and the importance of happiness and self-esteem (Ispa, 1995, 2002). Teachers are also more likely to emphasize the role parents play in their child's scholastic development as well (Ispa, 2002). Nonetheless, Russian nursery schools still value the positive collectivist traits, such as concern for others (Ispa, 1994).

Accordingly, early childcare programs appear to be increasingly more appropriate for the individualized needs of young children. However, with the collapse of the economy and diminished government funding, academic institutions have struggled to survive. Teaching continues to be one of the most underpaid professions. The dedication of Russian nursery school teachers and administrators in the face of such challenge is admirable. In short, they have continued to provide for children as best they can and seem to do remarkably well.

Beyond many of these indirect indicators, it is difficult to know the exact nature of early childhood in Russia. Particularly in comparison to later age periods, few studies have focused on infants or nursery school children. In our own work, we have focused on social development outcomes in nursery school and identified some of the family factors that contribute to these outcomes. The earlier section regarding the nature of Russian parenting has already highlighted some of this work. It is also clear that many Russian parents are concerned about their children's social development, as evidenced in the next section.

Parent–Peer Group Linkages

To begin with, significant peer interaction opportunities already exist in Russian nursery schools. In comparison with their U.S. peers, who spend, on average, approximately 27 hours a week in childcare (Institute of Child Health and Human Development, 2006), our data, collected in 1995, suggested that many Russian children spent 45 hours a week (9 hours per day) in nursery school (Hart et al., 1998). In addition, data gathered in the early 1990s indicated that more Russian children were attending early childhood programs than in any of the other former Soviet republics (Maddock, Hogan, Antonov, and Matskovsky, 1994), with attendance peaking at 86% of children ages 2 to 7 years in 1993 (Ispa, 1994).

Beyond the school context, children may also enjoy family or neighborhood relationships that provide social opportunities. But it is up to parents to provide such opportunities in early childhood. Western studies over the past few decades generally suggest that parents who facilitate these social opportunities outside of school tend to promote their children's social competence (e.g., Bryant, 1985; Bryant and DeMorris, 1992; Hart, Newell, and Olsen, 2003; Ladd and Hart, 1992). In Russia, play groups outside of school are mostly composed of neighborhood friends rather than relatives or friends from daycare/nursery school (Hart, Yang, et al., 1998). They are also more likely to be composed of same-sex, same-age peers. Our data also indicate that more association with peers outside of school corresponds with less socially withdrawn behavior at school for Russian boys. Russian girls were also more accepted by peers at school if they spent more time together with peers outside of school. Similar to other cultures, young Russian boys and girls who are more anxious and withdrawn from peers at nursery school are also less accepted by them (Hart, Yang, et al., 2000).

Hart, Yang, et al. (1998) also found that Russian mothers were more involved in initiating and managing their child's nonschool peer group activities when their children were rated by teachers as being more anxious/withdrawn and less cooperative with peers at school. These findings suggest that Russian mothers are conscientious about helping less socially adept preschoolers develop social skills through remedial socialization opportunities with peers outside of formal early childhood settings.

Middle Childhood in Russia

Our review of the literature found very few studies that address the nature of middle childhood in Russia. Of what exists, the primary focus is a general description of the peer group and schooling experience. Although family is arguably one of the most important influences in a child's life, peer groups also play a major role in all cultures, especially in children's social development (Chen, French, and Schneider, 2006). This is particularly true as children move into middle childhood. To children reared in the former Soviet Union, peers were everything (Bronfenbrenner, 1970). Unlike U.S. culture, for example, which expected the family to be the main socialization agent in children's lives, the collectivist approach to childrearing in the Soviet Union shifted the focus to peers, also known as the *children's collective*. This societal trend had roots stemming from the early Bolshevik years (Kirschenbaum, 2001).

Russian governmental standards also mandate that children in Russia attend school for 9 years starting at age 6 (Kouptsov and Tatur, 2001; Stetsenko, 2002). However, the typical student graduates with not just 9 but 11 years of schooling. Traditionally, classes of 20 to 30 students progress through school as a relatively intact peer group for the entire 9 years (Stetsenko, 2002). This fact likely impacts the influential effect of peers in quite a different way from U.S. children, who generally do not experience such a stable or continuous peer experience. However, there is also evidence that the stability of the peer group in Russia is changing as greater family mobility and educational options make the prospect of remaining in the same school over time less likely.

Regardless, more focus is needed to define the nature of middle childhood for Russian children. It is expected that many of the same social and academic issues that are the focus of current Western research will be relevant to the Russian context as well.

Adolescence and Emerging Adulthood in Russia

Compared to previous age periods addressed in this chapter, there is significantly more research attention to adolescence and emerging adulthood in modern-day Russia. Although the data are not extensive, they do suggest some tentative conclusions. Stetsenko (2002, pp. 243–244) has given the most recent synopsis of Russian adolescent life and aptly summarized it in this manner:

> Today's adolescents in Russia grew up in an unusually turbulent and dynamic sociocultural and political context. It is today's adolescents who have suffered most because of the worsening conditions in schools due to lack of funds for education. But it is also they who grew up in freedom and can now appreciate an unprecedented access to information and diverse education, can plan more varied career paths due to the emerging, more dynamic job market, and can generally enjoy advantages brought about by democracy. It is also they for whom the right to elect a president is as self-evident and indisputable as it is for their Western counterparts. The outcomes of today's reforms will and already does shape the life course of Russia's young generation.

In contrast with older generations who would like to return to Soviet-era communism, today's young people appear determined to hold onto the political and financial reforms that have transpired. In particular, even in the midst of the turbulent 1990s, young people showed that they had predominately accepted the market economy, with 70% seeing it as the only way forward. In contrast, a scant 10% rejected capitalism (Saliev, 1997). This is not to say that young people are completely satisfied with the nature or results of ongoing reforms; they simply see today's life as relatively better than the communist past. Observers have also noted, however, that Russian youth have generally avoided political or social involvement, instead choosing to focus on more carefree pursuits, such as *kife* (fun), rock music, clothing, and hanging out with friends (Markowitz, 1999; Pilkington, 1994). This may change, however, as youth become accustomed to democratic freedoms and the new political process.

Stetsenko (2002) referred to the Russian family as a "filter" that mediates the impact of many of the socioeconomic changes surrounding their adolescents. As a result of high divorce rates, however, some estimate that approximately 15% of adolescents will spend at least part of their life in a single-parent home (Iasnaia and Magun, 1999). These homes are expected to struggle more to provide a filtering influence. Nonetheless, the filtering effect of the family is expected to endure well into adulthood for many adolescents. As a result of housing shortages, many young people will continue to live with one or both of their parents well into their 30s and, as noted earlier, even after they elect to marry. Parents often provide extended financial assistance as well.

That said, there is increasing evidence that some emerging adults who become involved in the market sector of the Russian economy (e.g., banking, computers, business) may earn a living such that they can afford to support their parents and perhaps their own apartment (Stetsenko, 2002). In contrast, many worthy occupations continue to be underpaid and may therefore limit enthusiasm for such occupations. In particular, many of the "working poor" are found in education, culture, science, and health, occupations that are at least middle class in the West (Stetsenko, 2002).

These extended family living situations are part of the Russian culture of family ties. Accordingly, Russian adolescents tend to be more cognizant of their responsibilities to care for parents than their counterparts in most Western European countries (Nurmi, Liiceanu, and Liberska, 1999). The need for the elderly to be cared for by their children is especially pronounced, given shortages in care institutions for the elderly. This feeling of responsibility is not solely driven by economic concerns either. There is also evidence that Russian adolescents tend to have close ties to their parents (Markowitz, 1999). Compared to adolescents in other countries, young Russian adolescents are no different in the feeling of easiness they find in conversations with their mothers about matters of concern (King, Wold, Tudor-Smith, and Harel, 1996). Moreover, Russian adolescents were more likely than their counterparts in other countries to report that conversations with their fathers were also relatively easy (70% of boys, 78% of girls).

During the tumult of the 1990s, Russian youth clearly needed the filtering effect of the family to accommodate to massive societal changes impinging on their lives. Studies conducted during the early 1990s found that Russian youth reported lower psychological well-being than their American counterparts (Balatsky and Diener, 1993; Grob, Little, Wanner, Wearing, and Euronet, 1996). Jose et al. (1998) asked Russian and American adolescents in 1993 to report their stress levels, depression, and coping mechanisms. Sources of everyday stress varied considerably across these groups. American adolescents described more stress emerging from sibling arguments, boredom, concerns with weight, racism, fast pace of life, and gangs. In contrast, Russian adolescents felt more stress from health issues, sufficient food, family worries and concerns (including the prospect of war), not spending enough time with parents, and crowded living conditions. Furthermore, Russian adolescents reported significantly more depression than American adolescents. In the midst of significant stress and depression, Russians were also more likely to cite the use of more productive coping strategies such as problem solving (e.g., trying to change something about oneself or the situation) or seeking social support. In contrast, American adolescents were more likely to report externalizing behavior as a coping mechanism (e.g., yelling, fighting with others, breaking things). Nonetheless, social support was a significant buffer for stress related to depression in both countries.

Gender Roles

One of the apparently significant impacts of Russian societal change is that attitudes about gender roles appear to be shifting from the more egalitarian expectations of women in the workforce during the Soviet era to a more traditional focus on homemaking (Stetsenko, 2002). Although the espoused gender equality of the Soviet era was more myth than fact, older women appear more likely than younger women to embrace self-reliance and career orientation as desirable for women. In contrast, younger women profess a greater focus on childrearing and home life. Youth expectations of family life during the 1990s also focused on the father as breadwinner and mother as homemaker (Attwood, 1996). This may partially reflect a reaction to the Soviet system, wherein some Russian women felt that they did not have the choice to stay home with their children (du Plessix Gray, 1990; Jancar, 1978). Today's generation appears to want to make a choice, and for some, it may be a traditional pattern of family life (Markowitz, 1995).

However, professed desires may not correspond with other realities. In particular, given economic stress, the option of not having to work is a luxury few women enjoy. In addition, young girls also appear ambivalent because they desire both a traditional female sex role identity as well as a career (Kotovskaia and Shalygina, 1996; Murcott and Feltham, 1996). Accordingly, young women's actions may not match what they claim their priorities otherwise to be. In fact, it is very common for young mothers to leave children in a grandmother's care while they return to work and their careers.

School and Peer Group Characteristics

There are few studies to document the nature of the peer group and the school environment for Russian adolescents and emerging adults. Extant evidence suggests, however, that there are important differences from what is experienced in the United States. In particular, American adolescents are often immersed in large schools with a culture of cliques and crowds, wherein students with similar interests congregate. Unlike American high schools, Russian students are more likely to remain in the same class that they have been in since elementary school, progressing through school as an intact social group. This is consistent with the collectivist focus of Soviet upbringing, with the intent that "strong group consciousness and bonds of affiliation" will result (Stetsenko, 2002). Furthermore, schools do not have sports programs like American schools (at least in the sense of sports teams that compete against one another). Accordingly, crowds like jocks and cheerleaders, for example, are not a fixture in Russian schools. The small size of a Russian class (i.e., 20 to 30 students) also tends to preclude the development of school-based crowds.

However, Russian students still seek those with similar interests in after-school programs or other environments. In recent years, a slang term *tusovka* has been used to identify "mutually exclusive social circles, for example, those of football fans or hippies and 'hard-metal' rock fans, which provide a sense of identity to their members" (Stetsenko, 2002, p. 267; see also Curtis and Leighton, 1996). Tusovki (pl.) have been previously regarded as groups on the outskirts of society (e.g., punks, hippies). Curtis and Leighton (1996) described them as decadent groups composed of risk takers and trend followers. However, the term appears increasingly used to describe mainstream social interactions. This is perhaps best illustrated by the popularity of a social networking Internet site using the term (www.tusovka.ru). Thus, it appears that tusovki may be the equivalent of adolescent crowds, with the critical distinction being that many of these associations are not school based. Markowitz (2000, p. 130) also described the meaning of the term, *guliat'*, a "uniquely Russian word that means to take a stroll, to party, or to hang around." Many teenagers describe this as their favorite leisure activity. Accordingly, Russian adolescents are no different from their peers in other areas of the world in their liking for "hanging out" with friends.

A comparative study of adolescents and their peer relationships in many European countries, including Russia, was conducted in 1993 to 1994 and gives more clues about peer relationships in Russia for 11- to 15-year-olds (King et al., 1996). At that time, Russian adolescents were among the least likely to view their classmates as kind and helpful. Only approximately 40% of Russian 11-year-olds saw their classmates positively, compared to 80% of their counterparts in Denmark. The results also suggested that rates of bullying were high in Russia, with 68% of girls and 75% of boys reported being a victim at least once in the current school term (compared with approximately 20% of Swedish adolescents who responded similarly). Russian adolescents also reported physical fighting with other students and more frequent engagement in bullying other students than adolescents in most other nations. However, by age 15, rates of bullying and victimization dropped significantly (Craig and Harel, 2002). A study also found that only 14% of Russian students reported problems significant enough to disrupt peer relationships (Andriushina, 2000). In the King et al. (1996) study, Russian adolescents were also among the least likely to say that it was easy to make new friends, which may reflect high standards for friendship (Stetsenko, 2002).

Friendships, once formed, are of central importance. For example, a comparative study (reported in Settertobulte and de Matos, 2002) found that 11-year-old Russian girls reported spending 50% of their after-school free time with friends. In contrast, U.S. girls reported spending 33% of their after-school time with friends. Furthermore, Russian youth are consistently among the top countries whose adolescents report spending 4 or more days and evenings a week with friends after school. Russian youth also report using electronics (i.e., telephones, email) to keep in touch with friends more than other youth in most of the other 33 countries included for comparison in the study (although these trends are most applicable in the major urban centers).

Furthermore, even in troubled economic times, the state has continued to support youth programs in sports and the arts, and these provide additional peer interaction opportunities.

Educational Opportunities

In the context of schooling, previous studies suggest that education continued to be highly valued during the 1990s, and most young people understand the necessity of education to secure a good job. Russian adolescents have also moved beyond collectivist values to embrace materialism, with wealth and fame being critical considerations in their choice of profession (Nurmi et al., 1999). Accordingly, higher education is in high demand. The Russian approach to education also seems effective as Russian students demonstrate higher levels of self-efficacy in regard to academic achievement than their Western counterparts (Little, Oettingen, Stetsenko, and Baltes, 1995; Stetsenko, Little, Oettingen, and Baltes, 1996). Russian parents also accentuate the importance of education, evidenced in part by the fact that at least one-third of Moscow adolescents have a computer in their home (Stetsenko, 2002).

Nonetheless, many Russian teenagers are sober in their expectations of life change tied to emerging education and career opportunities. Although higher education and new professions are more available, Russian youth are also pragmatic in understanding that high grades, significant financial resources, and personal connections often determine access to opportunity. Thus, as in Soviet times, young people often make education and career decisions based on their parents' preferences and connections (Markowitz, 1999).

Religious and Western Influences

Religion is in resurgence among Russian youth. Whereas religious faith was uncommon among youth during the Soviet period, today's young Russians often report a religious affinity. In particular, two-thirds of Russian youth self-describe as believers, and many embrace the Russian Orthodox faith. Only 3% claim to be atheist (Stetsenko, 2002). However, faith does not correspond with church attendance, as few attend regularly. Markowitz (2000) suggests that one reason for low church attendance is that religion is considered a more internalized and private experience for today's Russian youth.

When Bronfenbrenner (1970) compared Soviet and American youth, he found that the collective upbringing served to buffer Soviet adolescents against inappropriate behavior. In contrast, the youth culture since perestroika is described as one defined by "non-conformist dress, music, and antiestablishment stance," similar to that observed in the West (Stetsenko, 2002). Evidence suggests that, in several ways, today's Russian youth are embracing Western mass culture and behavioral trends or at least adopting adult trends at earlier ages. For example, sexual attitudes are becoming more liberal, with much greater acceptance of premarital sex (Zubhov, 2007). A 2002 study of Russian 15-year-olds showed that 16.4% of girls and 40.9% of boys reported that they had had sexual intercourse (Ross, Godeau, and Dias, 2002). Adolescents are also having their first sexual experience at increasingly earlier ages, although evidence also suggests that Russian adolescents still wait longer than their Western counterparts (Stetsenko, 2002; Markowitz, 2000).

Physical Health

In regard to physical health, dramatic increases in sexually transmitted infections have accompanied the greater sexual liberality. Adolescents' smoking habits have also increased, corresponding with an expanding tobacco habit in the greater population. The average age that young adolescents begin smoking has decreased to 11.3 years for boys and 13.5 years for girls (Akopyan, Kharchenko, and Mishiev, 1999). Alcohol consumption also tends to be problematic, with reports indicating that more than 60% of Russian youth have at least tried alcohol. For some adolescents, habitual use of alcohol starts early. In 2002, a significant number of Russian 13-year-olds (10% of girls, 16.5% of boys) reported that they drank beer on a weekly basis (Schmid and Gabhainn, 2002). Illicit drug use among youth, much less common in Soviet times, has dramatically increased but is still well shy of levels in other industrialized countries. For example, among 15-year-olds, only 5.1% of females and 12.4% of males in Russia report recent cannabis use. In contrast, 30.4% of females and 41.6% of males in the United States fit this category of cannabis use (ter Bogt, Fotiou and Gabhainn, 2002). The number of Russian youth receiving treatment for drug addiction increased more than 10-fold from 1992 to 1996 (Stetsenko, 2002). Drug abuse has also been one of the primary reasons why acquired immunodeficiency syndrome (AIDS), which first appeared in Russia in 1987, has dramatically expanded in scope, and youth are among its carriers. The Russian medical care system struggles to confront many of these health challenges.

Conclusion

Despite many challenging trends in Russian society, studies also suggest that Russian youth tend to be hopeful and optimistic about their futures, and this trend has increased over time as their society has stabilized (Kolesnikov 1997; Rouchkin, 1997). Accordingly, one can hope that, as Russian society further stabilizes, the younger generation will have the foundation to contribute to significant cultural change that will improve the daily lives of Russian citizens. It is of empirical interest to document how youth respond to tumultuous and social change and perhaps lead the way to more productive social change. Accordingly, it is hoped that a greater number of investigators will emerge to document the course of change in Russian child and youth development in coming decades.

The evidence reviewed in this chapter also suggests that many Russian families have shown tremendous resilience in the face of significant social upheaval. Nonetheless, it is also clear that Russian society has changed significantly since Soviet times, and fewer supports are now available to help parents to successfully raise their children. Current social trends are also worrisome as they present new challenges with potentially severe consequences for children and adolescents. It is encouraging, however, that Russian society has long been invested in what children need to succeed. For example, soviet educators have consistently pressed parents to be more authoritative in their childrearing. Limited evidence also suggests that authoritative parenting is likely the most effective form of parenting in Russia, consistent with Western findings.

It is also clear, however, that we know relatively little about child and adolescent development in contemporary Russia. The dearth of research is most disturbing, given the very real need for informed public policy to help Russian families and their children to adjust to a changing environment. However, with the fall of communism, conditions are now more suitable for investigators to engage in appropriate research. In particular, Gorbachev's reforms marked the end of socialist realism, which depicted, in Soviet media and propaganda, a reality manufactured by the communist party. Not surprisingly, this version of reality was often at odds with reality. A clearer picture of societal trends should now be available for researchers to document. Hopefully, social science research will help Russians to clarify what they can do to make their society more sensitive to the needs of children and their families so that upcoming generations may contribute to a stronger and healthier society.

It is also readily apparent that the diversity of childhood experience that exists for subpopulations in Russia will need to be captured in future research. Although the majority of people living in Russia are ethnic Russian (83%), more than 100 different nationalities are represented in the country. The scope of this chapter has been primarily limited to the experience of ethnic Russians, particularly those who live in large urban centers. There are almost no data available on Russians living in provincial areas and the remaining ethnic groups. During the Soviet era, children were educated in a school system that considered the religious and cultural history of minorities to be irrelevant to citizenship. Since the fall of the Soviet Union, many ethnic and cultural groups have experienced a resurgence of interest in their ethnic identity, native language, and traditional customs (Butovskaya and Vorotnikova, 2004). We might expect qualitatively different paths of development for many of these groups. This is particularly relevant in considering those who live in war-torn areas like Chechnya. Different faith traditions, such as the Muslim faith, are also the source of significant differences in life experience for many Russians in the southern reaches of the country.

Acknowledgments

Funding for this chapter was provided by the College of Family, Home, and Social Sciences, the Camilla Eyring Kimball Endowment, the Brigham Young University Family Studies Center, and the Zina Young Williams Card Professorship awarded to Craig H. Hart.

References

Abdullaev, N. (2004, December 8). Russians: Quickest to marry and divorce. *Moscow Times*. Retrieved December 7, 2006, from http://lists101.his.com/pipermail/smartmarriages/2004-December/002583.html.

Ackerman, B. P., Kogos, J., Youngstrom, E., Schoff, K., and Izard, C. (1999). Family instability and the problem behaviors of children from economically disadvantaged families. *Child Development, 35*, 258–268.

Akopyan, A. S., Kharchenko, V. I., and Mishiev, V. G. (1999). *Sostojanie zdorovja I smertnosti detej i vzroshlih reproduktivnogo vozrasta v sovremmenoj Rossi* [Health and mortality of children and adults of reproductive age in contemporary Russia]. Moscow: Supplement to the Statistical Issues.

Amato, P. (2006). Marital discord, divorce, and children's well-being: Results from a 20-year longitudinal study of two generations. In A. Clarke-Stewart and J. Dunn (Eds.), *Families count: Effects on child and adolescent development* (pp. 179–202). New York: Cambridge University Press.

Andriushina, E. V. (2000). The family and the adolescent's health. *Russian Education and Society, 42*, 61–87.

Attwood, L. (1996). Young people's attitudes toward sex roles and sexuality. In H. Pilkington (Ed.), *Gender, generation, and identity in contemporary Russia* (pp. 132–151). London: Routledge.

Azarov, Y. (1983). *A book about bringing up children*. Moscow: Progress Publishers.

Baker, P., and Glasser, S. (2005). *Kremlin rising: Vladimir Putin's Russia and the end of revolution*. New York: Scribner.

Balatsky, G., and Diener, E. (1993). Subjective well-being among Russian students. *Social Indicators Research, 28*, 225–243.

Barber, B. K., Stolz, H. E., and Olsen, J. A. (2005). Parental support, psychological control, and behavioral control: Assessing relevance across time, culture, and method. *Monographs of the Society for Research in Child Development, 70*, 1–137.

Berrien, F. B., Aprelkov, G., Ivanova, T., Zhmurov, V., and Buzhicheeva, V. (1995). Child abuse prevalence in Russian urban population: A preliminary report. *Child Abuse and Neglect, 19*, 261–264.

Berrien, F. B., Safonova, T. Y., and Tsimbal, E. I. (2001). Russia. In B. M. Schwartz-Kenney, M. McCauley, and M. A. Epstein (Eds.), *Child abuse: a global view* (pp. 195–207). Westport, CT: Greenwood Publishing Group.

Billington, J. H. (2004). *Russia in search of itself*. Baltimore: The Johns Hopkins University Press.

Bronfenbrenner, U. (1970). *Two worlds of childhood: U.S. and U.S.S.R.* New York: Simon and Schuster.

Brooks-Gunn, J., Linver, M. R., and Fauth, R. C. (2005). Children' competence and socioeconomic status in the family and neighborhood. In A. J. Elliot and C. S. Dweck (Eds.), *Handbook of competence and motivation* (pp. 414–435). New York: Guilford Publications.

Bryant, B. K. (1985). The neighborhood walk: Sources of support in middle childhood. *Monographs of the Society for Research in Child Development, 50*, 1–122.

Bryant, B. K., and DeMorris, K. A. (1992). Beyond parent-child relationships: Potential links between family environments and peer relations. In R. D. Parke and G. W. Ladd (Eds.), *Family-peer relationships: Modes of linkage* (pp. 159–189). Hillsdale, NJ: Erlbaum.

Butovskaya, M., and Vorotnikova, O. (2004). Social behavior among Kalmyk primary school children: An observational study. Retrieved March 8, 2007, from http://www.noldus.com/site/content/files/case_studies/pu_psych_butov.pdf.

Central Intelligence Agency (CIA) of the United States (2009). The world factbook: Russia. Retrieved April 6, 2009, from http://www.cia.gov/library/publications/the-world-factbook/geos/rs.html.

Chen, X., French, D. C., and Schneider, B. H. (2006). *Peer relations in cultural context*. New York: Cambridge University Press.

Cockerham, W. C. (2007). Health lifestyles and the absence of the Russian middle class. *Sociology of Health and Illness, 29*, 457–473.

Coudouel, A., and Foley, M. (2001). Family structure and child welfare outcomes. In J. Klugman and A. Motivans (Eds.), *Single parents and child welfare in the new Russia* (pp. 191–224). New York: Palgrave.

Craig, W. M., and Harel, Y. (2002). Bullying, physical fighting, and victimization. In C. Currie, C. Roberts, A. Morgan, R. Smith, W. Settertobulte, O. Samdal, et al. (Eds.), *Young people's health in context: Health Behaviour in School-aged Children (HBSC) study: International report from the 2001/2002 survey* (WHO Health Policy for Children and Adolescents No. 4, pp. 133–144). Copenhagen, Denmark: World Health Organization.

Curtis, G. E. (Ed). (1996). Russia: A country study. Federal Research Division, Library of Congress. Retrieved January 20, 2007, from http://lcweb2.loc.gov/frd/cs/rutoc.html.

Curtis, G. E., and Leighton, M. (1996). Social stratification. In G. E. Curtis (Ed.), *Russia: A country study*. Federal Research Division, Library of Congress. Retrieved January 24, 2007, from http://lcweb2.loc.gov/cgi-bin/query/r?frd/cstdy:@field(DOCID+ru0092).

DaVanzo, J., and Farnsworth, G. (1996). Russia's demographic "crisis." Rand Corporation. Retrieved January 6, 2007, from http://www.rand.org.

Daw, J. (2002). Struggling to build a practice: Russian psychology fights to bring psychotherapy to a needy but wary public. *APA Monitor on Psychology, 33*. Retrieved December 15, 2006, from http://www.apa.org/monitor/jun02/russia.html.

du Plessix Gray, F. (1990). *Soviet women: Walking the tightrope*. New York: Doubleday.

Eberstadt, N. (2004). Russia's demographic straightjacket. *SAIS Review, 24*, 9–25.

Eberstadt, N. (2005, Winter). Russia, the sick man of Europe. *The Public Interest, 158*.

Ellis, R. A., Dulmus, C. N., and Wodarski, J. S. (2003). *Essentials of child welfare*. Hoboken, NJ: John Wiley and Sons, Inc.

Evanikoff, L. J. (1996). Russians. In *Culture and nursing care: A pocket guide*. San Francisco: University of California.

Freisthler, B., Merritt, D. H., and LaScala, E. A. (2006). Understanding the ecology of child maltreatment: A review of the literature and directions for future research. *Child Maltreatment, 11*, 263–280.

Gerber, T. P., and Mendelson, S. E. (2003, November). Up for grabs: Russia's political trajectory and Stalin's legacy. *PONARS Policy Memo, 296*.

Grigorenko, E. L., and Sternberg, R. J. (2000). Elucidating the etiology and nature of beliefs about parenting styles. *Developmental Science, 3*, 93–112.

Grob, A., Little, T. D., Wanner, B., Wearing, A. J., and Euronet. (1996). Adolescents' well-being and perceived control across 14 sociocultural contexts. *Journal of Personality and Social Psychology, 71*, 785–795.

Hart, C. H., Nelson, D. A., Robinson, C. C., Olsen, S. F., and McNeilly-Choque, M. K. (1998). Overt and relational aggression in Russian nursery-school-age children: Parenting style and marital linkages. *Developmental Psychology, 34*, 687–697.

Hart, C. H., Nelson, D. A., Robinson, C. C., Olsen, S. F., McNeilly-Choque, M. K., Porter, C. L., et al. (2000). Russian parenting styles and family processes: Linkages with subtypes of victimization and aggression. In K. A. Kerns, J. M. Contreras, and A.M. Neal-Barnett (Eds.), *Family and peers: Linking two social worlds* (pp. 47–84). Westport, CT: Praeger Publishers.

Hart, C. H., Newell, L. D., and Olsen, S. F. (2003). Parenting skills and social-communicative competence in childhood. In J. O. Green and B. R. Burleson (Eds.), *Handbook of communication and social interaction skills* (pp. 753–797). Mahwah, NJ: Erlbaum.

Hart, C. H., Yang, C., Nelson, L. J., Robinson, C. C., Olsen, J. A., Nelson, D. A., et al. (2000). Peer acceptance in early childhood and subtypes of socially withdrawn behavior in China, Russia, and the United States. *International Journal of Behavioural Development, 24*, 73–81.

Hart, C. H., Yang, C., Nelson, D. A., Jin, S., Bazarskaya, N., Nelson, L. J., et al. (1998). Peer contact patterns, parenting practices, and preschoolers' social competence in China, Russia, and the United States. In P. Slee and K. Rigby (Eds.), *Children's peer relations* (pp. 3–30). London: Routledge.

Iasnaia, L. V., and Magun, V. S. (1999). The parental home and its influence on the aspirations and life strategies of young men and women. *Russian Education and Society, 41*, 43–64.

Ispa, J. M. (1993, March). *A comparison of the child-rearing ideas of Russian mothers and child care center teachers.* Paper presented at the Society for Research in Child Development meetings, New Orleans, LA.

Ispa, J. M. (1994). Child rearing ideas and feelings of Russian and American mothers and early childhood teachers. *Advances in Early Education and Day Care, 6,* 235–257.

Ispa, J. M. (1995). Ideas about infant and toddler care among Russian child care teachers, mothers, and university students. *Early Childhood Research Quarterly, 10,* 359–379.

Ispa, J. M. (2002). Russian child care goals and values: From perestroika to 2001. *Early Childhood Research Quarterly, 17,* 393–413.

Jancar, B. W. (1978). *Women under communism.* Baltimore: Johns Hopkins University Press.

Jose, P. E., D'Anna, C. A., Cafasso, L. L., Bryant, F. B., Chiker, V., Gein, N., et al. (1998). Stress and coping among Russian and American early adolescents. *Developmental Psychology, 34,* 757–769.

Kerig, P. K. (1991). Perestroika of the soul: Soviet psychology and the Russian psyche. *Canadian Psychological Association Section on Developmental Psychology Newsletter, 10,* 15–20.

Kerig, P. K. (1995). Transition to where? The new Russia. *Canadian Psychological Association Section on Developmental Psychology Newsletter, 14,* 7–12.

King, A., Wold, B., Tudor-Smith, C., and Harel, R., (1996). The health of youth: A cross-national survey. *WHO Regional Publications,* European series No. 69.

Kirschenbaum, L. A. (2001). *Small comrades: Revolutionizing childhood in Soviet Russia, 1917-1932.* New York: Routledge Falmer.

Klugman, J., and Kolev, A. (2001). The welfare repercussions of single-parenthood in Russia in transition. In J. Klugman and A. Motivans (Eds.), *Single parents and child welfare in the new Russia* (pp. 153–190). New York: Palgrave.

Klugman, J., and Motivans A. (Eds.). (2001). *Single parents and child welfare in the new Russia.* New York: Palgrave.

Kolesnikov, J. S. (1997). Stanovlenije rinochnikh standartov povedenija studentov [Development of market-oriented forms of students' behavior]. In B. A. Rouchkin (Ed.), *Molodezh 1997; Nadezhdi i razocharovanija* [*Youth 1997: Hopes and disillusionments*] (pp. 176–183). Moscow: Research Center at the Institute of Youth Policy Press.

Kotovskaia, M., and Shalygina, N. (1996). Love, sex, and marriage: The female mirror. Value orientations of young women in Russia. In H. Pilkington (Ed.), *Gender, generation, and identity in contemporary Russia* (pp. 121–131). London: Routledge.

Kouptsov, O., and Tatur, Y. (2001). *Quality assurance in higher education in the Russian Federation.* Retrieved January 23, 2007, from http://www.cpes.ro/publications/pdf/ quality_russian.pdf.

Ladd, G. W., and Hart, C. H. (1992). Creating informal play opportunities: Are parents' and preschoolers' initiations related to children's competence with peers? *Developmental Psychology, 28,* 1179–1187.

Little, T. D., Oettingen, G., Stetsenko, A., and Baltes, P. B. (1995). Children's action-control beliefs and school performance: How do American children compare with German and Russian children? *Journal of Personality and Social Psychology, 69,* 686–700.

Maddock, J. W., Hogan, M. J., Antonov, A. A., and Matskovsky, M. S. (1994). *Families before and after Perestroika: Russian and U.S. perspectives.* New York: Guilford Press.

Makarenko, A. S. (1954). *A book for parents [Kniga dlya roditelei].* Moscow: Foreign Language Publishing House.

Makarenko, A. S. (1967). *The collective family: A handbook for Russian parents* (R. Dagglish, Trans.). New York: Anchor Books (Original work published 1937).

Markowitz, F. (1995). Striving for femininity; (Post-) Soviet unfeminism. *Canadian Woman Studies; Les Cahiers de la Femme, 16,* 38–42.

Markowitz, F. (1999). "To live well, to live at ease": Reflections on life by post-Soviet Russian teenagers. *Adolescence, 34,* 339–350.

Markowitz, F. (2000). *Coming of age in post-soviet Russia.* Chicago. University of Illinois.

Motivans, A. (2001). Family formation, stability, and structure in Russia. In J. Klugman and A. Motivans (Eds.), *Single parents and child welfare in the new Russia* (pp. 27–51). New York: Palgrave.

Murcott, A., and Feltham, A. (1996). Beliefs about reproductive health: Young Russian women talking. In H. Pilkington (Ed.), *Gender, generation, and identity in contemporary Russia* (pp. 152–168). London: Routledge.

National Institute of Child Health and Human Development. (2006). *The NICHD study of early child care and youth development: Findings for children up to age 4 1/2 years (05-4318).* Washington, DC: U.S. Government Printing Office.

Nelson, D. A., Hart, C. H., Yang, C., Olsen, J. A., and Jin, S. (2006). Aversive parenting in China: Associations with child physical and relational aggression. *Child Development, 77,* 554–572.

Nelson, D. A., Nelson, L. J., Hart, C. H., Yang, C., and Jin, S. (2006). Parenting and peer-group behavior in cultural context. In X. Chen, B. Schneider, and D. French (Eds.), *Peer relations in cultural context* (pp. 213–246). New York: Cambridge University Press.

Nelson, D. A., Yang, C., and Hart, C. H. (2005, April). Dimensions of parental psychological control: Connections with physical and relational aggression in Russian preschoolers. In M. K. Underwood (Chair), *Family relationships and children's social/relational aggression.* Symposium conducted at the biennial meetings of the Society for Research in Child Development, Atlanta, GA.

Nurmi, J. E., Liiceanu, A., and Liberska, H. (1999). Future-oriented interests. In F. Alsaker and A. Flammer (Eds.), *The adolescent experience: European and American adolescents in the 1990s* (pp. 85–98). Mahwah, NJ: Lawrence Erlbaum.

Olsen, S. F., Yang, C., Hart, C. H., Robinson, C. C., Wu, P. Nelson, D. A., et al. (2002). Mothers' psychological control and preschool children's behavioral outcomes in China, Russia, and the United States. In B. K. Barber (Ed.), *Intrusive parenting: How psychological control affects children and adolescents* (pp. 235–262). Washington, DC: American Psychological Association.

Pedersen, M., Alcon, M. C. G., Rodriguez, C. M., and Smith, R. (2002). Family. In C. Currie, C. Roberts, A. Morgan, R. Smith, W. Settertobulte, O. Samdal, et al. (Eds.), *Young people's health in context: Health Behaviour in School-aged Children (HBSC) study: International report from the 2001/2002 survey* (WHO Health Policy for Children and Adolescents No. 4, pp. 26–33). Copenhagen, Denmark: World Health Organization.

Pilkington, H. (1994). *Russia's youth and its culture: A nation's constructors and constructed.* London: Routledge.

Ross, J., Godeau, E., and Dias, S. (2002). Sexual health. In C. Currie, C. Roberts, A. Morgan, R. Smith, W. Settertobulte, O. Samdal, et al. (Eds.), *Young people's health in context: Health Behaviour in School-aged Children (HBSC) study: International report from the 2001/2002 survey* (WHO Health Policy for Children and Adolescents No. 4, pp. 153–160). Copenhagen, Denmark: World Health Organization.

Rouchkin, B. A. (1997). Molodezh in stanovlenije novoj Rossii [Youth and the emergence of a new Russia]. In B. A. Rouchkin (Ed.), *Molodezh 1997; Nadezhdi i razocharovanija* [*Youth 1997: Hopes and disillusionments*] (pp. 16–30). Moscow: Research Center at the Institute of Youth Policy Press.

Russian Federal State Statistics Service. (2007). *Russia in figures: Population.* Retrieved January 8, 2007, from http://www.gks.ru/wps/portal/english.

Saliev, R. Z. (1997). Ideologiya i tsennostnye orientatsii molodyozhi [Ideology and value orientations of youth]. *Sotsiologicheskie Issledovaniya* [*Sociological Studies*], *21,* 30–43.

Schmid, H., and Gabhainn, S. N. (2002). Alcohol use. In C. Currie, C. Roberts, A. Morgan, R. Smith, W. Settertobulte, O. Samdal, et al. (Eds.), *Young people's health in context: Health Behaviour in School-aged Children (HBSC) study: International report from the 2001/2002 survey* (WHO Health Policy for Children and Adolescents No. 4, pp. 73–83). Copenhagen, Denmark: World Health Organization.

Settertobulte, W., and de Matos, M. G. (2002). Peers. In Currie, C., Roberts, C., Morgan, A., Smith, R., Settertobulte, W., Samdal, O., et al. (Eds.), *Young people's health in context: Health Behaviour in School-aged Children (HBSC) study: International report from the 2001/2002 survey* (WHO Health Policy for Children and Adolescents No. 4, pp. 34–38). Copenhagen, Denmark: World Health Organization.

Shipler, D. K. (1983). *Russia: Broken idols, solemn dreams.* New York: New York Times Books.

Stetsenko, A. (2002). Adolescents in Russia: Surviving the turmoil and creating a brighter future. In B. B. Brown, R. W. Larson, and T. S. Saraswathi (Eds.), *The world's youth: Adolescence in eight regions around the globe* (pp. 243–275). Cambridge, United Kingdom: Cambridge University Press.

Stetsenko, A., Little, T. D., Oettingen, G., and Baltes, P. B. (1995). Control, agency and means-ends beliefs about school performance in Moscow children: How similar are they to beliefs of Western children? *Developmental Psychology, 31,* 285–299.

Subbotskii, E. V. (1992). Moral socialization of the child in the Soviet Union from birth to age seven. In J. L. Roopnarine and D. B. Carter (Eds.), *Parent-child socialization in diverse cultures* (pp. 89–105). Norwood, NJ: Ablex.

Swafford, M., Artamonova, E., and Gerassimova, S. (2001). The living arrangements of Russian children. In J. Klugman and A. Motivans (Eds.), *Single parents and child welfare in the new Russia* (pp. 53–85). New York: Palgrave.

ter Bogt, T., Fotiou, A., and Gabhainn, S. N. (2002). Cannabis use. In C. Currie, C. Roberts, A. Morgan, R. Smith, W. Settertobulte, O. Samdal, et al. (Eds.), *Young people's health in context: Health Behaviour in School-aged Children (HBSC) study: International report from the 2001/2002 survey* (WHO Health Policy for Children and Adolescents No. 4, pp. 84–89). Copenhagen, Denmark: World Health Organization.

Tudge, J. (1991). Education of young children in the Soviet Union: Current practice in historical perspective. *The Elementary School Journal, 92*, 121–133.

United Nations Children's Fund. (2007). *The state of the world's children*. Retrieved December 19, 2006, from http://www.unicef.org/sowc07/docs/sowc07.pdf.

Vladimir Putin on raising Russia's birth rate. (2006). *Population and Development Review, 32*, 385–389.

World Bank Report. (2005). *Russian Federation: Reducing poverty through growth and social reform*. (Report No. 28923-RU). Retrieved January 20, 2009 from http://194.84.38.65/mdb/upload/PAR_020805_eng.pdf.

Yablokova, O. (2002, October 22). Birthrate continuing upward trend. *The St. Petersburg Times*. Retrieved March 7, 2007, from http://www.sptimes.ru/index.php?action_id=2&story_id=8429.

Zakharov, S. (2005, July). *Recent trends in first marriage in Russia: Retarded second demographic transition*. Paper presented at the International Population Conference of the International Union for the Scientific Study of Population, Tours, France.

Zakirova, V. (2005). War against the family: Domestic violence and human rights in Russia—A view from the Bashkortostan Republic. *Current Sociology, 53*, 75–91.

Zubkov, V. (2007). Russian families: Historical and contemporary perspectives on problems and strengths. *Marriage and Family Review, 41*, 361–392.

22
China

XINYIN CHEN and LI WANG

Introduction

Developmental scientists have been interested in child development in China not only because Chinese children represent approximately one-fifth of the population of children in the world, but also because they live in an environment with distinct social and cultural features. Since the 1980s, a number of studies have examined socioemotional and cognitive functions in Chinese children from cultural and cross-cultural perspectives. The findings indicate that the Chinese cultural values and social and ecological circumstances may affect children's behavior and development in various areas and thus support the argument that human development should be understood in social and cultural contexts (e.g., Bornstein, 1991; Vygotsky, 1978). In this chapter, we review these studies with a particular focus on the role of contextual factors in development.

To understand Chinese children, we first provide some background information about the society in which they live and grow. Next, we review the work on a salient aspect of cognitive functioning in Chinese children, academic achievement, and discuss the school practices and family environment that contribute to academic achievement. In the following section, we focus on children's socioemotional functioning, including early dispositional characteristics, social behaviors, and peer relationships. Then, we review the literature on Chinese socialization patterns, such as parenting goals, styles, and strategies, and their relations with child behaviors. We also discuss the implications of the one-child policy for child development. Researchers have conducted some studies examining the impact of macro-level social, economic, and cultural changes in China on socialization and child behaviors. We review the findings of these studies in the next section. Our chapter concludes with a discussion of future directions in Chinese developmental science.

Historical, Demographic, Cultural, and Social Background of Children in China

The distinct features of socialization and child development in China are derived from its unique historical, socioecological, and cultural conditions. Among various contextual factors, cultural beliefs and values concerning interpersonal relationships, social and economic circumstances, and the structure and organization of the family appear to be particularly relevant to socioemotional and cognitive development in Chinese children.

Historical and Demographic Background

As a country with one of the most sophisticated ancient civilizations, China has more than 4,000 years of recorded history. Various waves of migration, amalgamation, and development during thousands of years generated a distinctive social, political, economic, and cultural system. Like many other nations, China passed through the stages of primitive, slave, and feudal societies in many dynasties. The founding of the People's Republic in 1949 marked China's entry into its current socialist stage.

China currently has a population of over 1.3 billion people, the largest in the world. There are approximately 265 million children (20.3% of the total population) aged 0 to14 years (National Bureau of Statistics of China, 2006). A large proportion of the population (57.1%) lives in rural areas. There are 56 ethnic groups in China, with the Han nationality the most populace, representing approximately 91% of the population. The largest minority nationalities, such as Zhuang, Man, Hui, Miao, and Uygur, are located mostly in Western provinces of the country including Guangxi, Sichuan, Yunnan, and Tibet.

Cultural Background

Chinese society is relatively homogenous in its cultural background, with Confucianism serving as a predominant ideological guideline for social activities. Confucius (551–479 B.C.) was born at the time of transition from slave society to feudal society, which was full of conflicts and disputes. Confucius was concerned with recovering social order and harmony. He believed that, to reach this goal, it was important to establish a set of moral standards and social rules to guide interpersonal interactions and individual behaviors in daily life (Luo, 1996). The highest social-moral standards in the Confucian system include 仁 or *ren* (benevolence, humanity), 义 or *yi* (righteousness), 礼 or *li* (propriety, proper conduct), 智 or *zhi* (wisdom and knowledge), and 信 or *xin* (trustworthiness). To reach these standards, individuals in different roles should follow specific social rules. For example, the doctrine of 孝 or *Xiao* (filial piety) stipulates that, in the family, children must pledge obedience and reverence to parents. In turn, parents are responsible for "governing" (i.e., teaching, disciplining) their children. Social relationships, even those between friends, are constructed in hierarchical patterns (Liang, 1987). In this hierarchical, holistic cultural framework, the expression of individual needs or striving for autonomous behaviors is considered socially unacceptable. Behaviors that threaten the hierarchical structure of the group are strictly prohibited. Confucian principles concerning individual behaviors and relationships have been endorsed by most rulers of the country in its history and have had remarkable influences on socialization and child development in China.

Taoism is another indigenous belief system in Chinese culture that has significantly influenced the lifestyles of the Chinese people. Taoism advocates passive attitudes and behaviors in daily life activities to pursue internal harmony. It is believed that pursuing external material possessions leads to desires and confusions, which cause psychoemotional disturbances. According to Taoism, softness, tenderness, and weakness are the desirable attributes of life, whereas firmness, strength, and stiffness are undesirable concomitants of death. Thus, it is beneficial to remain flexible and take "no action" in dealing with challenges and adversities (Wang, 2006).

Social and Economic Conditions

China has been an agricultural society for thousands of years. Due to relatively limited resources, most people have lived under poor conditions during most periods of its history. The living standard in China did not improve substantially until the early 1980s. Since then, China has carried out massive reforms toward a market economy. The initial phase of the reforms was the "internal vitalization" in rural areas and the "open-door" movement in some Southern regions. Full-scale reforms were expanded to cities and other parts of the country in the early 1990s. In the past decade, the centrally planned command economy has rapidly been transformed into a market economy, which led to dramatic growth of domestic and foreign private enterprises and joint ventures. The economy in China is currently the fourth largest in the world and growing at the rate of approximately 10% a year.

According to the National Bureau of Statistics of China (2006), in comparison to the annual per capita income of 100 and 50 Yuan for urban and rural areas, respectively, in 1949, the annual per capita income was 10,493 Yuan (approximately US$1,312) for urban residents and 3,255 Yuan (approximately US$406) for rural residents in 2005. The total poverty-stricken population was 250 million in 1978 but dropped to 43 million in 1998. There are substantial regional differences within China in social and economic development, particularly between urban and rural areas. Since the early 1990s, a large number of rural people, mostly young adults, has moved to cities to seek opportunities. Internal migrations and the social and psychological experiences of migrant families and children have become an important issue in the society (Cui, 2003).

Family Structure and Organization

A traditional Chinese family is usually a large family, consisting of three or four generations. In the feudal period of China, families were authoritarian, with the dominance of elders and men. The structure and organization of Chinese families have changed over the past 50 years. The number of large families has decreased, and the number of small nuclear families has increased. There are still many medium-sized families in China in which three generations (parents of husband or wife, husband and wife, and children) live together. Four- or five-generation families are rare (<0.3%). The average family size was 4.79, 3.58, and 3.13 persons in 1985, 1999, and 2005, respectively (3.27 and 2.97 in rural and urban regions, respectively, in 2005; National Bureau of Statistics of China, 2006).

Women's social, political, and economic statuses in the family and the society have substantially improved since the 1950s. Almost all adult women work outside the home and have almost the same salary levels as men. In 1997, for example, approximately 90% of women between the ages of 20 and 49 years in urban areas were employed (Ni, 2000). In the family, women are now involved in decision making on major activities (Xu and Ye, 1999). The divorce rate is generally low but is growing (below 5% in 1980, 11.4% in 1995, and 13% in 1997; Ni, 2000), especially in major cities (25% in 1997; Ni, 2000). Consequently, the number of single-parent families is increasing.

Since the late 1970s, China has implemented the one child per family policy. This policy has been highly successful in population control in urban areas. As a result, more than 95% of children in the urban areas have no siblings (Chen and He, 2004). A "four-two-one" family structure (four grandparents, two parents, and one child) is the norm in urban areas. Although the one-child policy has not been so successful in rural areas, it is the case that most families do not have as many children today as traditional families used to have in the past.

Chinese sociocultural and family conditions are likely to exert pervasive influences on child cognitive and social development. Among cognitive functions, researchers have examined such issues as moral development, theory of mind, and language development (e.g., Li and Cen, 1999; McBride-Chang, Shu, Zhou, Wat, and Wagner, 2003; Miao, 2001; Tardif and Wellman, 2002). Many studies have been conducted to test whether the Western theories can be generalized to China. Findings seem to be largely consistent with the Western literature. Nevertheless, a particular area that has received much attention from researchers as well as educators is academic achievement in Chinese children. Therefore, we focus on academic achievement and factors that contribute to achievement in the next section. Researchers have also examined various aspects of socioemotional functioning in Chinese children including early dispositional characteristics, social behaviors, and social relationships. The findings indicate that Chinese cultural context may affect the exhibition and developmental patterns of socioemotional functioning.

Academic Achievement in Chinese Children

China is working toward 9-year compulsory education. By the end of 2004, the program had covered approximately 94% of school-aged children in the country. The enrollment rate was 98.95% at elementary or primary school level and 92.7% at middle school level (China Education and Research Network, 2005). Almost all schools from kindergarten to university are public schools. However, private schools at all levels are increasing in number.

Since the 1990s, cross-cultural researchers have found that Chinese children outperform their counterparts in the United States and many other countries in academic areas (e.g., Harmon et al., 1997; Kwok and Lytton, 1996). For example, Stevenson, Chen, and Lee (1993) conducted a series of studies comparing children's academic performance in the United States and China. Chinese children scored consistently higher than their American peers in mathematics and reading. Moreover, the differences persist throughout the elementary and high school years.

Factors Contributing to Academic Achievement in Chinese Children

Cultural Values and Social Pressure   One of the most important factors believed to account for academic excellence in Chinese children is traditional values of achievement in the Chinese culture (Stevenson et al., 1990). According to Li (2003, 2004), learning is considered a process of seeking knowledge and cultivating personal virtue in Chinese culture. At the same time, success in school is often directly associated with attainment of a high level of education, which in turn leads to high social and occupational status in China. As a result of limited opportunities to receive a higher education, there is strong competition among students in the school; children are constantly pressured by parents and teachers to perform optimally on academic work. That pressure is particularly marked in the final years of junior and senior high school because acceptance to senior high schools and colleges/universities is based almost completely on scores in examinations. Chinese students spend most of their time in school and most of their school time on academic work. High schools are often open for self-learning or tutorial sessions in the morning from 6:00 AM and in the evening until 10:00 to 11:00 PM.

School Practices   The high achievement of Chinese children and adolescents may also be associated with effective strategies of classroom instruction (Stevenson and Stigler, 1992; Stigler and Hiebert, 1999). The curriculum, established by the State Educational Bureau, is identical in all schools in the country, and the schedule of courses and other activities is typically identical for students in the same class. Despite large class sizes, teachers in Chinese schools normally know their students well and actively promote student involvement in classroom instruction (Stevenson et al., 1990). There is a designated head teacher in each class who normally stays with the class for multiple years. The head teacher keeps close contact with students' families and often visits students' homes. The head teacher system allows the school and teachers to be involved extensively and effectively in students' activities that are organized to facilitate academic achievement (Chang, 2003).

Parental Socialization Beliefs and Involvement   Some familial factors may be associated with the overall high level of academic achievement in China (Chen and He, 2004). These factors include parental beliefs about the role of effort in achievement and parental monitoring of children's academic work. Whereas U.S. American parents believe academic achievement is largely determined by innate abilities, Chinese parents believe that it is mainly based on diligence and effort (Biggs, 1996; Stevenson et al., 1990). Parental beliefs are likely to affect children's attitudes. Li (2004) found that, whereas U.S. children showed a heightened awareness of the mind/task attributes of the learner (e.g., ability, task attempting, and strategy use), Chinese children perceived more the learner's dispositional qualities of diligence, persistence, and concentration. The different beliefs and attitudes of parents and children likely affect learning processes and academic outcomes.

Significance of Academic Achievement for Social and Psychological Adjustment

Given the importance of academic achievement in China, it is not surprising that it contributes significantly to socioemotional development. Academic achievement predicts leadership status and social competence (e.g., Chen, Rubin, and Li, 1997). In contrast, academic failure and learning problems predict peer rejection and school-related social problems. Academic achievement also plays an important role in peer group functioning. For example, children often form groups based on similar academic interest and achievement. Moreover, academic achievement serves as an important norm that regulates group organization in Chinese children and adolescents (Chen, Chang, and He, 2003; Sun, 1995).

Finally, academic achievement is associated with psychological adjustment such as feelings of loneliness, social insecurity, and depression in Chinese children (Chen, Rubin, and Li, 1995a, 1995b). Children who have low academic achievement are likely to report negative perceptions of cognitive competence and general self-worth. It is possible that academic difficulties result in frustration and negative attitudes toward self, others, and the school and eventually contribute to a variety of social and psychological problems (e.g., Chen et al., 1997).

Socioemotional Functioning and Peer Relationships in Chinese Children

Research on socioemotional functioning often focuses on dispositional characteristics such as reactivity to novel social situations in the early years. As children become increasingly active in interaction with others, especially outside the family, in childhood and adolescence, the behaviors that children display in the social setting may determine, in part, their social relationships, school performance, and psychological adjustment. Cross-cultural developmental researchers have found that Chinese children may differ from their Western counterparts in early socioemotional characteristics, social behaviors, and the patterns of peer relationships. The group-oriented cultural norms and values seem to be an important factor in regulating socioemotional functioning in Chinese children.

Early Socioemotional Characteristics

Chinese children differ from their Western counterparts with respect to some early socioemotional characteristics including emotional expressivity (Camras et al., 1998), sociability (Chen, DeSouza, Chen, and Wang, 2006), and impulsivity (Ho, 1986). For example, Camras et al. (1998) reported that Chinese infants and toddlers were more emotionally restrained than North American children in the laboratory setting. The relatively low level of early emotional expressivity in Chinese children seems also to relate to their emotion communication skills and emotion knowledge in the later years (e.g., Wang, 2003).

Social Initiative and Self-Control The differences between Chinese and Western children in the early years may be characterized largely by two fundamental dimensions of socioemotional functioning in social situations, initiative and self-control (Chen, Wang, and DeSouza, 2006). Whereas social initiative represents the tendency to initiate and maintain social interactions, which is often indicated by children's reactivity to challenging situations, self-control or self-regulation represents the ability to modulate behavioral and emotional reactivity to promote the appropriateness of socioemotional activities during social interactions (Asendorpf, 1990; Rothbart and Bates, 2006). Chinese children appear to have a lower level of social initiative than do their North American counterparts (Chen et al., 1998; Freedman and Freedman, 1969;

Kagan, Kearsley, and Zelazo, 1978). In an observational study of behavioral inhibition in a variety of activities including free play and interaction with a stranger, Chen et al. (1998) found that, compared with Canadian toddlers, Chinese toddlers were more vigilant and reactive. They stayed closer to their mothers and were less likely to explore the environment. They also displayed more anxious and fearful behaviors in interacting with the stranger and were reluctant to approach the stranger and the toys. Similarly, compared with Canadian children, Chinese children displayed more nonsocial behaviors in peer interactions (Chen, DeSouza, et al., 2006).

Chinese and North American children also differ on self-control in early childhood. Chen, Rubin, et al. (2003) found that Chinese toddlers displayed more committed and internalized control on a series of compliance and prohibition tasks than their Canadian counterparts. In contrast, Canadian children were likely to maintain control based on situational requirements such as parental requests. Consistent with this study, Sabbagh, Xu, Carlson, Moses, and Lee (2006) found that Chinese preschoolers performed better than their U.S. counterparts on executive function tasks assessing self-control abilities.

Children's Socioemotional Functioning and Adult and Peer Evaluations and Responses Unlike Western cultures that emphasize autonomy and assertiveness, social initiative is not so highly appreciated or valued in Chinese society. This may be because social initiative does not bear much relevance to mutual support and cohesiveness in the group. To maintain group harmony, children are encouraged to restrain personal desires for the benefits and interests of the collective (Greenfield, Suzuki, and Rothstein-Fisch, 2006; Oyserman, Coon, and Kemmelmeier, 2002). As a result, self-control is emphasized in a consistent and absolute manner; children are taught to exert self-control from a very early age (Ho, 1986; Luo, 1996; Yang, 1986; Zhou, Eisenberg, Wang, and Reiser, 2004).

The cultural norms and values concerning socialization goals may be reflected in parental childrearing attitudes (Bornstein, 1995, 2006). Chen et al. (1998), for example, found that, whereas reactive and inhibited behavior in Canadian children was associated with parental punishment orientation, disappointment, and rejection, it was associated with parental warm and accepting attitudes in China. Cultural values are also reflected in different parental attitudes toward self-control. Chinese parents expect a higher level or more mature form of self-control in children than North American parents. When a child failed to display committed self-control, Canadian parents expressed understanding and acceptance toward the child. However, Chinese parents were clearly disappointed and tended to respond negatively (Chen, Rubin, et al., 2003).

Cultural influence over social attitudes is also evident in children's peer interactions. In a study concerning how children responded to shy–inhibited behaviors, Chen, DeSouza, et al. (2006) found that, when making passive low-power social initiations, shy–inhibited children were less likely than others to receive positive responses and more likely than others to receive rejection from peers in Canada. However, this was not the case in China; shy–inhibited children were more likely to receive positive responses from peers when they made low-power initiations.

Chen and French (2008) have proposed a contextual–developmental model focusing on how social evaluation and response and the active participation of the child in interactions play a mediating role in cultural influence on individual socioemotional development. According to this model, cultural norms and values serve as a basis for the social processes in which adults and peers evaluate and respond to specific characteristics. Social processes, in turn, regulate child behaviors and developmental patterns. The child actively participates in social interactions through interpreting, processing, and reacting to social influence and through regulating interaction processes. Thus, social processes are bidirectional and transactional in nature. Through these processes, personal characteristics, socialization, and cultural factors collectively shape the child's social behaviors and psychoemotional adjustment as well as the social relationships that the child establishes.

Social Behaviors and Adjustment in Childhood and Adolescence

Cultural values of social initiative and self-control are likely reflected in the developmental patterns of social behaviors formed on the basis of these two dimensions (Chen, Wang, et al., 2006). In the following sections, we discuss major forms of social functioning in Chinese children, including prosocial and sociable behaviors (based on relatively high social initiative and high self-control), aggression-disruption (high social initiative and low self-control), and shyness-sensitivity (low initiative and adequate control to constrain reactivity toward self).

Prosocial and Sociable Behaviors Sociability and prosocial orientation represent two main aspects of social competence in children (e.g., Chen, Li, Li, Li, and Liu, 2000; Rydell, Hagekull, and Bohlin, 1997). Whereas sociability focuses more on motivation and capacity to engage in social interactions, prosociality and cooperation, including helping, cooperating, and caring or taking responsibility for another, tap children's attitudes and behaviors that are based on the consideration of the interests of others in social interactions. Sociable and prosocial behaviors are valued differently in Chinese society (Chen, Li, et al., 2000). Prosocial–cooperative behavior is considered essential to collective functioning and thus is highly encouraged. In Chinese schools, children are often required to participate in extensive extracurricular activities that are organized by student organizations such as the Young Pioneers and the Class Committee. During these activities, children are encouraged to cooperate with each other and display prosocial behaviors. Compared with Western children, Chinese children tend to display more prosocial and cooperative behaviors (e.g., Orlick, Zhou, and Partington, 1990; Rao and Stewart, 1999). Moreover, prosocial behaviors are predictive of social and school adjustment outcomes, including peer acceptance, leadership status, and school achievement in Chinese children (Chen, Li, et al., 2000).

Compared with prosocial behavior, sociability is regarded as relatively unimportant in Chinese culture. It does not predict social and school outcomes after its overlap with prosocial behavior is controlled (Chen, Li, et al., 2000). Despite the neglect of sociability in Chinese culture, however, the active participation of sociable children in social interactions has been found to be conducive to psychoemotional adjustment. Chen et al. (2002) found that sociability in childhood is associated positively with perceived self-worth and negatively with internalizing symptoms such as loneliness and depression in late adolescence. It appears that sociable children are able to form social support systems, which help them cope with adjustment difficulties, particularly under adverse circumstances.

Aggression–Disruption Because of their potential threat to collective harmony, aggressive and defiant behaviors are strictly prohibited in China. Children are required to learn how to control or suppress their impulsivity, frustration, anger, and defiance (Yang, 1986). Materials such as illegal drugs and guns that can be used in antisocial behaviors are generally unavailable to children and adolescents. As a result, Chinese children and adolescents seldom engage in extreme forms of antisocial behaviors such as drug use, theft, murder, and robbery. Violent or delinquent behaviors in the form of large groups or gangs are extremely rare. Nevertheless, it is the case that antisocial and violent behaviors have increased in China (e.g., "Adolescent delinquency," 1999).

Although serious delinquent behaviors are uncommon, aggressive and disruptive behaviors are relatively common in Chinese children and adolescents. However, aggressive children in China tend to experience extensive social and psychological difficulties, including low social status and poor quality peer relationships (Chen et al., 1995a). Unlike their North American counterparts who typically do not experience internalizing problems (Asher, Parkhurst, Hymel, and Williams, 1990), aggressive children in China perceive themselves negatively and report a high level of loneliness and depression (Chen et al., 1995a). This may be because children's social behavior and performance are regularly and publicly evaluated by teachers, peers, and self in Chinese schools, which makes it difficult for aggressive children to develop inflated or "inaccurate" self-perceptions of their social competence.

Shyness–Sensitivity Shy–sensitive behavior is conceptualized as reflecting internal fearfulness and lack of self-confidence (Rubin, Bukowski, and Parker, 2006). Because children are generally expected and socialized to be increasingly assertive and self-directed in Western cultures, shy, wary, and sensitive behaviors are often viewed as socially incompetent, immature, and deviant (Rubin, Burgess, and Coplan, 2002). Consistently, it has been found in the West that shyness and social wariness in childhood and adolescence are associated with peer rejection, school maladjustment, and psychoemotional problems (Rubin et al., 2002). In traditional Chinese culture, shy–sensitive behavior is associated with virtuous qualities, such as modesty and cautiousness. Socially sensitive and restrained behaviors are regarded as indications of accomplishment, mastery, and maturity; shy–sensitive children are perceived as well behaved and understanding (e.g., Ho, 1986; Liang, 1987). The cultural endorsement may help shy children obtain social support in interactions, develop self-confidence, and achieve positive adjustment outcomes. Indeed, unlike their counterparts in the West who experience extensive difficulties, shy–sensitive children in China are accepted by peers, perceived as competent by teachers, and perform well in academic areas (Chen, Rubin, and Sun, 1992; Chen et al., 1995b). Shy children are more likely than others to achieve leadership status and the award of the distinguished studentship in the school (e.g., Chen et al., 1995b). Finally, shy Chinese children do not feel lonely and depressed or develop negative perceptions of their competence (Chen et al., 1995a; Chen, Zappulla, et al., 2004).

Peer Relationships

A primary function of peer relationships in Western cultures is to serve as social resources for fulfilling individual psychological needs such as the formation of self-identity and the development of positive self-regard (e.g., Rubin et al., 2006; Sullivan, 1953). This function is not highly appreciated in Chinese culture. Chinese culture emphasizes the socialization function of peer relationships in helping children learn social standards and develop socially acceptable behaviors (Sun, 1995). Thus, particular attention has been paid to the *nature* of peer relationships in terms of whether peer social activities are guided by the "right" social goals and whether these activities are beneficial to children's social and school achievement (Luo, 1996). Children who have "good" relationships, which may be considered "instrumental" in Western cultures, encourage and help each other to improve social and school performance (Sun, 1995). Chen, Kaspar, Zhang, Wang, and Zheng (2004) conducted a study in China and Canada to investigate the functional roles of friendships based on children's self-reports. The results showed that, whereas the enhancement of self-esteem was regarded as important in Canadian children, it was not salient in Chinese children. In contrast, Chinese children were more likely than Canadian children to emphasize the value of their friendships in social and school achievement. Chinese children had relatively higher scores on instrumental assistance than Canadian children. Both Chinese and Canadian children reported that companionship and intimate disclosure were more important than instrumental assistance in their friendships. Thus, playfulness and emotional closeness may be fundamental features of children's friendships.

Similar to their Western counterparts (e.g., Cairns and Cairns, 1994), the majority of school-age children in China are affiliated with a peer group (Chen, Chang, et al., 2003; Sun, 1995).

Peer groups among Chinese children comprise mostly same-sex members, with the average group size of four to six members. Groups are often formed and organized on similar academic interest and achievement (Chen, Chang, et al., 2003). Groups that function on academic norms have more positive impact on children's social and psychological adjustment than groups consisting of academically poor members. In addition to academic norms, peer groups among Chinese children vary on prosocial–cooperative and antisocial–destructive dimensions (e.g., Chen, Chang, He, and Liu, 2005). The social norms of the peer group also exert significant influence through directing group activities on children's social behaviors and school achievement. Moreover, whereas prosocial–cooperative groups serve to facilitate parental socialization effort to help children develop social and school competencies, antisocial–destructive groups tend to undermine the contributions of supportive parenting to child development (Chen, Chang, et al., 2005).

Socialization Goals and Practices in Chinese Childrearing

Socioemotional and cognitive characteristics in Chinese children are likely associated with the socialization beliefs and practices in Chinese childrearing. Compared with Western parents, Chinese parents may have different expectations and use different approaches and strategies in childrearing. An important issue is how childrearing beliefs and practices may lead to child outcomes in Chinese culture. Scholars and researchers have been debating on whether the Western-based theories concerning the major parenting categories, such as authoritative and authoritarian parenting styles, can be generalized to the Chinese context.

Childrearing Beliefs and Practices in China

In traditional Chinese culture, children are socialized mainly to develop relatedness and interdependence. Specific socialization goals may include connection to the family, orientation to the larger group, and obedience to the authority (Tamis-LeMonda et al., in press). As required by the socialization goals, the main task of parents is to train children to control individualistic behaviors and to display cooperative–compliant behaviors. To help children learn collectivistic norms and group-oriented behaviors, maintaining parental authority is believed to be essential in childrearing (Luo, 1996). Thus, the culture endorses parental use of high-power, directive, and restrictive childrearing practices (e.g., Chao, 1994; Ho, 1986).

Compared with Western parents, Chinese parents are more concerned with training children on behavioral and emotion control and less with encouraging children to be independent and exploratory (Ho, 1986; Liu et al., 2005). Regarding parenting strategies, Chinese parents are more controlling and power assertive and are less likely to use reasoning and inductive methods (e.g., Chao, 1994; Wu, 1981). Chinese parents are also less responsive and affectionate toward their children than North American parents (Chen et al., 1998). Despite the cross-cultural differences, however, most Chinese parents, especially those with a higher education, still use responsive and inductive, rather than power-assertive and punitive, parenting in childrearing (e.g., Chen, Liu, Li, Cen, and Chen, 2000). Many parents believe that warmth and induction are important for children's social and emotional development.

Parenting and Child Behaviors

What are the relations between parental beliefs and practices and child behaviors in Chinese culture? Researchers have argued that such parenting constructs as parental warmth and parental authoritarianism, initially developed for Western cultures, may not be relevant to social, cognitive, and psychological functioning in Chinese children (Chao, 1994; Steinberg, Dornbusch, and Brown, 1992). Inconsistent with this argument, however, these fundamental parenting dimensions and categories are associated with child outcomes in a virtually identical fashion in Chinese and Western cultures (e.g., Chang, Schwartz, Dodge, McBride-Chang, 2003; Chen, Liu, and Li, 2000; Nelson, Hart, Jin, Yang, and Olsen, 2006). Whereas authoritarian and power assertive parenting is associated with adjustment problems, authoritative and inductive parenting is associated with indexes of social competence and school achievement (Chen, Liu, Li, Cen, and Chen, 2000; Nelson et al., 2006). Thus, despite the cultural endorsement of parental authority and control in Chinese society, coercive and prohibitive strategies that authoritarian parents use may lead to the child's negative emotional and behavioral reactions such as fear, frustration, and anger, which in turn are associated with developmental problems. In contrast, explanation, guidance, and communication of affect that authoritative parenting uses may help children develop feelings of confidence in the exploration of the world and positive parent–child relationships, which in turn are associated with children's social and cognitive competencies.

Maternal and paternal parenting styles may play different roles in children's adjustment in specific areas. In the Chinese family, the mother is regarded as important for providing care and affection to the child, whereas the role of the father is mainly to help children achieve in academic areas, learn societal values, and develop appropriate behaviors (Ho, 1986; Shwalb, Nakazawa, Yamamoto, and Hyun, 2003). Chen, Liu, and Li (2000) have found that, whereas maternal warmth significantly predicts later *emotional* adjustment, such as feelings of insecurity and loneliness, paternal support significantly predicts later *social and school* adjustment, including peer social status, social competence, and academic achievement.

The "Only Child" Issue

An important issue in Chinese childrearing is how the one-child policy has affected socialization patterns and children's social and cognitive development. Many parents and educators in China are concerned about whether only-children are "spoiled" in the family (Jiao, Ji, and Jing, 1980). Early reports suggested that only-children may have more negative behavioral qualities and social and school problems such as impulsiveness, aggressiveness, selfishness, and poor peer relationships (Jiao et al., 1980; Tao and Chiu, 1985). In a study concerning parenting styles and their effects on only-children, Chen, Liu, and Li (2000) found that paternal indulgence, but not maternal indulgence, had significant and negative effects on children's social behaviors and academic achievement. It is possible that children who have indulgent fathers may have inadequate opportunities to learn the social, behavioral, and cognitive skills such as self-control that are required for successful social and school performance.

A number of studies, particularly recent ones, have shown that only children and adolescents as a group may not differ significantly from, or even show certain advantages over, sibling children (e.g., Chen, Rubin, and Li, 1994; Tao, Qui, Zeng, Xu, and Goebert, 1999). According to Falbo and Poston (1993), where differences are present, only-children are taller and weigh more than siblings children, and only-children have better verbal abilities (see also Rosenberg and Jing, 1996). The different results in early and recent studies may be related to changes in childrearing and childcare conditions in China. Increasing numbers of children receive preschool education and daycare, particularly in urban areas. Many children go to public nursery centers at a very young age because most parents work outside the home. Almost all children now enter kindergarten at the age of 4 or 5 years and primary school at the age of 7 years. The same early out-of-home care experiences may weaken the different parental influences on only-children and sibling children. In addition, participation in a variety of collective activities in public settings may compensate, to some extent, for the lack of sibling interactions for only-children.

The Impact of Social and Cultural Changes on Socialization and Child Development in China

Chinese society has changed dramatically since the early 1980s. During this period, the full-scale reforms toward a market economy have resulted in increased variations in individual and family income, massive movement of the population, decline in the government control of social welfare and protection, and rapid rise in unemployment rate and competition. The dramatic changes in social structure and organization inevitably have substantial implications for socialization and child education. In the new market-oriented society that emphasizes personal initiative and competitiveness, it is important for parents and educators to help children learn assertive and autonomous skills. Indeed, Chinese schools have expended their education goals to include helping children develop social and behavioral qualities that are required for adaptation in competitive society such as expression of personal opinions, self-direction, and self-confidence (Yu, 2002). A variety of strategies facilitates the development of these qualities (e.g., encouraging students to engage in public debate and to propose and implement their own plans about extracurricular activities). In a study concerning socialization goal-oriented behaviors, Liu et al. (2005) found that, although Chinese mothers had higher scores on encouragement of relatedness and lower scores on autonomy support than Canadian mothers, mothers in both samples had significantly higher scores on encouragement of autonomy than on encouragement of relatedness. Similarly, Chen et al. (1998) found that Chinese parents were likely to encourage child independence. Chinese mothers may have realized that, to function adequately and achieve success in the competitive environment, children need to learn independent and assertive skills.

The impact of the social and cultural changes on children's socioemotional functioning is evident in many studies (e.g., Chang, 2003; Chen, Cen, Li, and He, 2005; Hart et al., 2000). Chen, Cen, et al. (2005), for example, examined relations between shyness–inhibition and adjustment in Chinese children in three cohorts (1990, 1998, and 2002) that represented different phases of the societal transition. Shyness was positively associated with peer acceptance, leadership, and academic achievement in the 1990 cohort. However, shyness was negatively associated with peer acceptance and teacher-rated competence and positively associated with peer rejection and depression in the 2002 cohort. The patterns of the relations between shyness and peer relationships and adjustment variables were nonsignificant or mixed in the 1998 cohort.

Therefore, the extensive changes toward the capitalistic system and the introduction of Western individualistic ideologies may have led to the decline in the adaptive value of shy–inhibited behavior. In the new competitive environment, shy, anxious, and inhibited behavior that may impede self-expression, active social communication, and exploration may no longer be regarded as adaptive and competent. An interesting finding in Chen, Cen, et al.'s study (2005) was that shyness was positively associated with both peer acceptance and peer rejection in the 1998 cohort; they were liked and disliked by peers at the same time. These results indicated mixed attitudes of peers toward shy–inhibited children, which, to some extent, may reflect the cultural conflict between imported Western values of social initiative and individual autonomy and traditional Chinese values of self-control.

As China becomes more market-oriented economically and individualistic ideologically, social initiative and other social skills are required to adapt to the changing demands of contemporary society. To help children develop these skills, parents and educators need to adopt a more inductive and child-centered approach in childrearing and education. During this process, however, they should not abandon all socialization goals and practices that are traditionally endorsed in Chinese culture, especially those proven to be conductive to child development such as values of self-control and parental high involvement in child education (e.g., Chen, Rubin, et al., 2003; Stevenson et al., 1990). How to maintain a balance between traditional, largely group-oriented goals and new child-centered parenting styles and how to effectively integrate diverse values and strategies will challenge socialization agents in China.

Future Directions in Chinese Developmental Science

Researchers have been increasingly interested in child and adolescent development in Chinese culture. Some studies with Chinese children (e.g., Stevenson et al., 1993) have made significant contributions to understanding cultural involvement in human development. In general, however, there have been inadequate systematic research programs in China. Many important issues, such as children's abilities and skills to cope with stress in the changing context, remain to be explored. Moreover, many studies in China have been conducted without a culturally relevant theoretical foundation. Researchers have proposed some frameworks such as the contextual-development perspective (e.g., Chen, Wang, et al., 2006) to describe developmental processes and patterns in Chinese children. However, these frameworks need to be elaborated at the theoretical level and tested empirically in various domains.

There are substantial regional differences in social and economic development within China, particularly between urban and rural areas. The market economy, such as the opening of stock markets, has been largely limited to cities. Families in rural China have lived mostly agricultural lives, and rural children do not have as much exposure as urban children to the influence of the market economy (Cui, 2003). As a result of practical difficulties, research on Chinese children has been carried out largely in urban areas. It will be a challenging but important task to investigate child development in rural areas. Relatedly, as more and more rural people move to cities and stay there for years or permanently, it will be important to study the experiences and adjustment difficulties of children from migrant families (Chen, Wang, and Wang, in press).

Conclusion

For many years, most, if not all, of the research on human development has been conducted in North America and Western Europe. As a result, our understanding of children's social and cognitive functions has been based mainly on European American cultures. The findings from research in China indicate that, as a distinct belief and value system, Chinese culture has pervasive influence on socialization and child development in various areas including academic achievement, social functioning, and social relationships. Moreover, studies show that the macro-level changes in Chinese society have considerable implications for family organization and children's socioemotional and psychological adjustment. These studies provide valuable information, not only about Chinese children, but also about the developmental processes and the role of context in the processes in general.

China is a large country with unbalanced social and economic development in different regions. Children across these regions live under different circumstances. Moreover, the distinct social and cultural backgrounds of ethnic minority nationalities in China are likely to affect children in these nationalities. Consequently, these children may develop in ways that differ from those of Han Chinese children. Social, cultural, and demographic diversities within China provide challenges as well as opportunities for theorists and researchers to study how various personal and contextual factors contribute to socioemotional and cognitive development. Obviously, continuous exploration is essential for achieving a thorough understanding of children and adolescents in China.

Acknowledgments

The writing of this chapter was supported by grants from the Social Sciences and Humanities Research Council of Canada. We are grateful to the children, parents, and teachers who participated in some of the research projects that were described in this chapter.

References

Adolescent delinquency in urban areas. (1999, January). *Guang Ming Daily*, 1.

Asendorpf, J. (1990). Beyond social withdrawal: Shyness, unsociability, and peer avoidance. *Human Development, 33*, 250–259.

Asher, S., Parkhurst, J. T., Hymel, S., and Williams, G. A. (1990). Peer rejection and loneliness in childhood. In S. R. Asher and J. D. Coie (Eds.), *Peer rejection in childhood* (pp. 253–273). New York: Cambridge University Press.

Biggs, J. B. (1996). Learning, schooling, and socialization: A Chinese solution to a Western problem. In S. Lau (Ed.), *Growing up the Chinese way: Chinese child and adolescent development* (pp. 147–168). Hong Kong: Chinese University Press.

Bornstein, M. H. (1991). Approaches to parenting in culture. In M. H. Bornstein (Ed.), *Cultural approach to parenting* (pp. 3–19). Hillsdale, NJ: Lawrence Erlbaum.

Bornstein, M. H. (1995). Form and function: Implications for studies of culture and human development. *Culture and Psychology, 1*, 123–138.

Bornstein, M. H. (2006). Parenting science and practice. In K. A. Renninger and I. E. Sigel (Eds.), *Handbook of child psychology. Volume 4: Child psychology in practice* (pp. 893–949). New York: Wiley.

Cairns, R. B., and Cairns, B. D. (1994). *Lifelines and risks: Pathways of youth in our time*. Cambridge, United Kingdom: Cambridge University Press.

Camras, L. A., Oster, H., Campos, J., Campos, R., Ujiie, T., Miyake, K., et al. (1998). Production of emotional facial expressions in European American, Japanese, and Chinese infants. *Developmental Psychology, 34*, 616–628.

Chang, L. (2003). Variable effects of children's aggression, social withdrawal, and prosocial leadership as functions of teacher beliefs and behaviors. *Child Development, 74*, 535–548.

Chang, L., Schwartz, D., Dodge, K. A., and McBride-Chang, C. (2003). Harsh parenting in relation to child emotion regulation and aggression. *Journal of Family Psychology, 17*, 598–606.

Chao, R. K. (1994). Beyond parental control and authoritarian parenting style: Understanding Chinese parenting through the cultural notion of training. *Child Development, 65*, 1111–1119.

Chen, X., Cen, G., Li, D., and He, Y. (2005). Social functioning and adjustment in Chinese children: The imprint of historical time. *Child Development, 76*, 182–195.

Chen, X., Chang, L., and He, Y. (2003). The peer group as a context: Mediating and moderating effects on the relations between academic achievement and social functioning in Chinese children. *Child Development, 74*, 710–727.

Chen, X., Chang, L., He, Y., and Liu, H. (2005). The peer group as a context: Moderating effects on relations between maternal parenting and social and school adjustment in Chinese children. *Child Development, 76*, 417–434.

Chen, X., DeSouza, A., Chen, H., and Wang, L. (2006). Reticent behavior and experiences in peer interactions in Canadian and Chinese children. *Developmental Psychology, 42*, 656–665.

Chen, X., and French, D. (2008). Children's social competence in cultural context. *Annual Review of Psychology, 59*, 591–616.

Chen, X., Hastings, P., Rubin, K. H., Chen, H., Cen, G., and Stewart, S. L. (1998). Childrearing attitudes and behavioral inhibition in Chinese and Canadian toddlers: A cross-cultural study. *Developmental Psychology, 34*, 677–686.

Chen, X., and He, H. (2004). The family in mainland China: Structure, organization, and significance for child development. In J. L. Roopnarine and U. P. Gielen (Eds.), *Families in global perspective* (pp. 51–62). Boston: Allyn and Bacon.

Chen, X., Kaspar, V., Zhang, Y., Wang, L., and Zheng, S. (2004). Peer relationships among Chinese and North American boys: A cross-cultural perspective. In N. Way and J. Chu (Eds.), *Adolescent boys in context* (pp. 197–218). New York: New York University Press.

Chen, X., Li, D., Li, Z., Li, B., and Liu, M. (2000). Sociable and prosocial dimensions of social competence in Chinese children: Common and unique contributions to social, academic and psychological adjustment. *Developmental Psychology, 36*, 302–314.

Chen, X., Liu, M., and Li, D. (2000). Parental warmth, control and indulgence and their relations to adjustment in Chinese children: A longitudinal study. *Journal of Family Psychology, 14*, 401–419.

Chen, X., Liu, M., Li, B., Cen, G., and Chen, H. (2000). Maternal authoritative and authoritarian attitudes and mother-child interactions and relationships in China. *International Journal of Behavioral Development, 24*, 119–126.

Chen, X., Liu, M., Rubin, K. H., Cen, G., Gao, X., and Li, D. (2002). Sociability and prosocial orientation as predictors of youth adjustment: A seven-year longitudinal study in a Chinese sample. *International Journal of Behavioral Development, 26*, 128–136.

Chen, X., Rubin, K. H., and Li, B. (1994). Only children and sibling children in urban China: A re-examination. *International Journal of Behavioral Development, 17*, 413-421.

Chen, X., Rubin, K. H., and Li, B. (1995a). Depressed mood in Chinese children: Relations with school performance and family environment. *Journal of Consulting and Clinical Psychology, 63*, 938–947.

Chen, X., Rubin, K. H., and Li, Z. (1995b). Social functioning and adjustment in Chinese children: A longitudinal study. *Developmental Psychology, 31*, 531–539.

Chen, X., Rubin, K. H., and Li, D. (1997). Relation between academic achievement and social adjustment: Evidence from Chinese children. *Developmental Psychology, 33*, 518–525.

Chen, X., Rubin, K. H., Liu, M., Chen, H., Wang, L., Li, D., et al. (2003). Compliance in Chinese and Canadian toddlers. *International Journal of Behavioral Development, 27*, 428–436.

Chen, X., Rubin, K. H., and Sun, Y. (1992). Social reputation and peer relationships in Chinese and Canadian children: A cross-cultural study. *Child Development, 63*, 1336–1343.

Chen, X., Wang, L., and DeSouza, A. (2006). Temperament and socio-emotional functioning in Chinese and North American children. In X. Chen, D. French, and B. Schneider (Eds.), *Peer relationships in cultural context* (pp. 123–147). New York: Cambridge University Press.

Chen, X., Wang, L., and Wang, Z. (in press). Shyness-sensitivity and social, school, and psychologiical adjustment in rural migrant and urban children in China. *Child Development.*

Chen, X., Zappulla, C., Alida, L. C., Schneider, B., Kaspar, V., Oliveira, A. M. D., et al. (2004). Self-perceptions of competence in Brazilian, Canadian, Chinese and Italian children: Relations with social and school adjustment. *International Journal of Behavioral Development, 28*, 129–138.

China Education and Research Network (2005, March). *China sees progress in six aspects of education.* China Education and Research Network: Education in China, News and Events.

Cui, C. (2003). Adapting to the city and adjusting rural-urban relations: A study of migrant children's school and live circumstances in Beijing. In B. Li (Ed.), *The peasant worker: An analysis of social and economic status of Chinese rural-to-urban migrants.* Beijing, China: Social Sciences and Documentation Publishing House.

Falbo, T., and Poston, D. L. (1993). The academic, personality, and physical outcomes of only children in China. *Child Development, 64*, 18–35.

Freedman, D. G., and Freedman, M. (1969). Behavioral differences between Chinese-American and American newborns. *Nature, 224*, 1227.

Greenfield, P. M., Suzuki, L. K., and Rothstein-Fisch, C. (2006). Cultural pathways through human development. In K. A. Renninger and I. E. Sigel (Eds.), *Handbook of child psychology. Volume 4: Child psychology in practice* (pp. 655–699). New York: Wiley.

Harmon, M., Smith, T. A., Martin, M. O., Kelly, D. L., Beaton, A. E., Mullis, I. V. S., et al. (1997). *Performance assessment in IEA's Third International Mathematics and Science Study (TIMSS).* Chestnut Hill, MA: Boston College, Center for the Study of Testing, Evaluation, and Education Policy.

Hart, C. H., Yang, C., Nelson, L. J., Robinson, C. C., Olson, J. A., Nelson, D. A., et al. (2000). Peer acceptance in early childhood and subtypes of socially withdrawn behaviour in China, Russia and the United States. *International Journal of Behavioral Development, 24*, 73–81.

Ho, D. Y. F. (1986). Chinese pattern of socialization: A critical review. In M. H. Bond (Ed.), *The psychology of the Chinese people* (pp. 1–37). New York: Oxford University Press.

Jiao, S., Ji, G., and Jing, Q. (Ching, C. C.). (1986). Comparative study of behavioural qualities of only children and sibling children. *Child Development, 57*, 357–361.

Kagan, J., Kearsley, R. B., and Zelazo, P. R. (1978). *Infancy: Its place in human development.* Cambridge, MA: Harvard University Press.

Kwok, D. C., and Lytton, H. (1996). Perceptions of mathematics ability versus actual mathematics performance: Canadian and Hong Kong Chinese children. *British Journal of Educational Psychology, 66*, 209–222.

Li, B. S., and Cen, G. Z. (1999). *Moral development and the model of moral education.* Shanghai, China: East China Normal University Press.

Li, J. (2003). U. S. and Chinese cultural beliefs about learning. *Journal of Educational Psychology, 95*, 258–267.

Li, J. (2004). Learning as a task or a virtue: U.S. and Chinese preschoolers explain learning. *Developmental Psychology, 40*, 595–605.

Liang, S. (1987). *The outline of Chinese culture.* Shanghai, China: Shanghai Teachers' University Press, Xue Lin.

Liu, M., Chen, X., Rubin, K. H., Zheng, S., Cui, L., Li, D., et al. (2005). Autonomy- vs. connectedness-oriented parenting behaviors in Chinese and Canadian mothers. *International Journal of Behavioral Development, 29,* 489–495.

Luo, G. (1996). *Chinese traditional social and moral ideas and rules.* Beijing, China: The University of Chinese People Press.

McBride-Chang, C., Shu, H., Zhou, A., Wat, C. P., and Wagner, R. K. (2003). Morphological awareness uniquely predicts young children's Chinese character recognition. *Journal of Educational Psychology, 95,* 743–751.

Miao, X. C. (2001). Research on language comprehension and child language. In Chinese Psychological Society (Ed.), *Current Chinese psychology* (pp. 288–293). Beijing, China: People's Educational Press.

National Bureau of Statistics of China (2006, March). *Data of the national survey of 1% of the population in 2005.* Beijing, China: National Bureau of Statistics of China.

National Bureau of Statistics of China (2006, February). *Bulletin of China's economic and social development in 2005.* Beijing, China: National Bureau of Statistics of China.

Nelson, D. A., Hart, C. H., Jin, S., Yang, C., and Olsen, J. A. (2006). Aversive parenting in China: Associations with child physical and relational aggression. *Child Development, 77,* 554–572.

Ni, S. (2000). How should we revise the Marriage Law? *The People's Daily (Oversea Edition),* November 3, 5.

Orlick, T., Zhou, Q. Y., and Partington, J. (1990). Co-operation and conflict within Chinese and Canadian kindergarten settings. *Canadian Journal of Behavioral Science, 22,* 20–25.

Oyserman, D., Coon, H. M., and Kemmelmeier, M. (2002). Rethinking individualism and collectivism: Evaluation of theoretical assumptions and meta-analyses. *Psychological Bulletin, 128,* 3–72.

Rao, N., and Stewart, S. M. (1999). Cultural influences on sharer and recipient behavior: Sharing in Chinese and Indian preschool children. *Journal of Cross-Cultural Psychology, 30,* 219–241.

Rosenberg, B. G., and Jing, Q. (1996). A revolution in family life: The political and social structural impact of China's one child policy. *Journal of Social Issues, 52,* 51–69.

Rothbart, M. K., and Bates, J. E. (2006). Temperament. In N. Eisenberg (Ed.), *Handbook of child psychology. Volume 3: Social, emotional, and personality development* (pp. 99–166). New York: Wiley.

Rubin, K. H., Bukowski, W., and Parker, J. G. (2006). Peer interactions, relationships, and groups. In N. Eisenberg (Ed.), *Handbook of child psychology. Volume 3: Social, emotional, and personality development* (pp. 571–645). New York: Wiley.

Rubin, K. H., Burgess, K. B., and Coplan, R. J. (2002). Social withdrawal and shyness. In P. K. Smith and C. H. Hart (Eds.), *Blackwell handbook of childhood social development* (pp. 330–352). Malden, MA: Blackwell Publishers.

Rydell, A. M., Hagekull, B., and Bohlin, G. (1997). Measurement of two social competence aspects in middle childhood. *Developmental Psychology, 33,* 824–833.

Sabbagh, M. A., Xu, F., Carlson, S. M., Moses, L. J., and Lee, K. (2006). The development of executive functioning and theory of mind: A comparison of Chinese and U.S. preschoolers. *Psychological Science, 17,* 74–81.

Shwalb, D. W., Nakazawa, J., Yamamoto, T., and Hyun, J. H. (2003). Fathering in Japanese, Chinese, and Korean cultures: A review of the research literature. In M. E. Lamb (Ed.), *The role of the father in child development* (4th ed., pp. 146–181). New York: Wiley.

Steinberg, L., Dornbusch, S., and Brown, B. B. (1992). Ethnic differences in adolescent achievement: An ecological perspective. *American Psychologists, 47,* 723–729.

Stevenson, H. W., Chen, C., and Lee, S. (1993). Mathematics achievement of Chinese, Japanese, and American children: Ten years later. *Science, 259,* 53–58.

Stevenson, H. W., Lee, S., Chen, C., Stigler, J. W., Hsu, C., and Kitamura, S. (1990). Contexts of achievement. *Monographs of the Society for Research in Child Development, 55,* Serial no. 221.

Stevenson, H. W., and Stigler, J. W. (1992). *The learning gap.* New York: Simon and Schuster.

Stigler, J. W., and Hiebert, J. (1999). *The teaching gap: Best ideas from the world's teachers for improving education in the classroom.* New York: Free Press.

Sullivan, H. S. (1953). *The interpersonal theory of psychiatry.* New York: Norton.

Sun, S. L. (1995). *The development of social networks among Chinese children in Taiwan.* Unpublished doctoral dissertation, University of North Carolina at Chapel Hill, Chapel Hill, NC.

Tamis-LeMonda, C. S., Way, N., Hughes, D., Yoshikawa, H., Kalman, R. K., and Niwa, E. (in press). Parents' goals for children: The dynamic co-existence of collectivism and individualism in cultures and individuals. *Social Development.*

Tao, G., Qiu, J., Li, B., Zeng, W., Xu, J., and Goebert, D. (1999). A longitudinal study of psychological development of only and non-only children and families: A 10-year follow-up study in Nanjing. *Chinese Mental Health Journal, 13,* 210–212.

Tao, K., and Chiu, J. (1985). The one-child-per-family policy: A psychological perspective. In W. Tseng and D. Y. H. Wu (Eds.), *Chinese culture and mental health* (pp. 153–165). New York: Harcourt Brace Jovanovich, Academic Press.

Tardif, T., and Wellman, H. M (2002). Acquisition of mental state language in Mandarin- and Cantonese-speaking children. *Developmental Psychology, 36*, 25–43.

Vygotsky L. S. (1978). *Mind in society: The development of higher psychological processes.* Cambridge, MA: Harvard University Press.

Wang, B. (2006). *The philosophy of Zhuangzi.* Beijing, China: Peking University Press.

Wang, Q. (2003). Emotion situation knowledge in American and Chinese preschool children and adults. *Cognition and Emotion, 17*, 725–746.

Wu, D. H. (1981). Child abuse in Taiwan. In J. E. Korbin (Ed.), *Child abuse and neglect: Cross-cultural perspectives* (pp. 139–165). Los Angeles: University of California Press.

Xu, A., and Ye, W. (1999). *Research on marital quality in China.* Beijing, China: Social Sciences Publication House.

Yang, K. S. (1986). Chinese personality and its change. In M. H. Bond (Ed.), *The psychology of the Chinese people* (pp. 106–170). New York: Oxford University Press.

Yu, R. (2002). On the reform of elementary school education in China. *Educational Exploration, 129*, 56–57.

Zhou, Q, Eisenberg, N., Wang, Y., and Reiser, M. (2004). Chinese children's effortful control and dispositional anger/frustration: Relations to parenting styles and children's social functioning. *Developmental Psychology, 40*, 352–366.

23
East and Southeast Asia: Japan, South Korea, Vietnam, and Indonesia

DAVID W. SHWALB, BARBARA J. SHWALB, JUN NAKAZAWA,
JUNG-HWAN HYUN, HAO VAN LE, and MONTY P. SATIADARMA

Introduction

This chapter summarizes our knowledge about the development of children and adolescents in Japan, South Korea (hereafter, Korea), Vietnam, and Indonesia. We focus on three research areas of shared significance to developmental scientists in all four societies: (1) relationships in the family, (2) peer relationships, and (3) problem behavior and values. A fourth section presents findings on culture-specific issues of importance in each respective culture. Comparisons between the four cultural groups are made difficult by a lack of cross-cultural research data and also by the multiple developmental paths and contextual influences found within each culture. For example, similar to India (Saraswathi and Dutta, Chapter 24, in this volume), diversity is a central feature of Indonesian culture, which has 300 ethnic groups, 740 dialects spoken, numerous religions, and a motto of *Bhinneka Tunggal Ika* (Unity in Diversity).

Cultural Contexts

Current demographic statistics for the four cultures are presented in Table 23.1 and show both population similarities and differences as of 2008. It is also notable that in all four countries, population density is high, fertility rates and infant/child mortality rates are declining, and life expectancy, urbanization, per capita income, and use of technology are increasing. Yet there are other important differences between the four populations; for example, approximately one-third of the population in Indonesia and Vietnam consists of children or adolescents, a much higher fraction than is the case in the rapidly aging populations of Japan and Korea.

Traditional values and normative family dynamics in Japan, Korea, and Vietnam reflect a shared Chinese, East Asian, and Confucian heritage (see Chen and Wang, Chapter 22, in this volume), that distinguishes them from Indonesia. Japan and Korea are more commonly paired as distinct from the other two cultures in terms of Westernization, economic development, and social problems associated with postmodern life. They are also reaching a state of negative population growth and have near universal education through secondary school. In contrast, Vietnam and Indonesia are experiencing different types of social, historical, and economic changes more characteristic of developing nations, resulting in critical problems in health and education that significantly affect the lives of children and adolescents.

Table 23.1 Demographic Characteristics of Four Cultures

	Japan	Korea	Vietnam	Indonesia
Population (millions)	128	48	86	228
Population of children/adolescents (millions)	21	10	30	77
Population density (per km^2)	336	498	254	117[a]
Fertility rate (births per woman)	1.3	1.2	1.9	2.4
Life expectancy (years)	82	78	74	70
Infant mortality rate (under 1)	3	5	16	30
Under 5 mortality rate	4	5	19	38
Percent enrolled in school (primary/secondary)	99/99	100/90	95/73	90/70
Gross national income per capita (in US$)	38,410	17,690	690	1,420
Population urbanized (percent)	67	81	26	47
Number/100 population (phones, Internet use)	115,48	124, 61	9, 4	13,4

Source: www.unicef.org.

[a] Population density of Java/Bali/Madura islands = 799/km^2.

Vietnam has a young population, with more than half of its population under the age of 30 years and born after the 1975 national unification. It has improved economic and health services greatly in the last 20 years, and the government allocates 4% of its budget to health. However, the poverty rate in rural Vietnam (45%) is more than double that of urban areas (18%). The percentage of low birth weight babies in Vietnam (9% in 2000) is about average among Southeast Asian cultures, but 32% of children under age 5 are moderately or severely underweight. In rural areas, child labor rates are as high as 23%, and the child marriage rate (arranged by adults before the legal age) is 18%. Malnutrition is still a major problem for Vietnamese children who are poor, rural, or belong to ethnic minorities, despite the recent growth of the national economy (Thang and Popkin, 2003).

Indonesian public health problems gained international attention after the December 2004 tsunami claimed over 150,000 lives, but had already been a major social dilemma. For example, malaria poses a growing crisis, and the threat of malaria currently affects 20% of Indonesians. More than 100 million Indonesians lack adequate sanitation and health facilities, and inadequate sex and health education is associated with growing human immunodeficiency virus (HIV) rates. Approximately 30% of Indonesians do not receive adequate immunizations. Its child labor rate of 5% is a lower rate than that of Vietnam, yet it involves three million Indonesian children. Approximately one-third of children in rural areas are subject to child marriage, compared to one-seventh in urban settings. Finally, many women and children endure sexual and physical exploitation from human trafficking.

Developmental Science

In all four cultures, almost all research on human development is published in their respective native languages (i.e., inaccessible to international readers). There are also cultural disparities in the depth and breadth of developmental science; Japan has more developmental scientists than any country outside the United States and Europe, but Vietnam and Indonesia have no distinct developmental scientific field.

Japan Membership in the Japan Society of Developmental Psychology (founded in 1989) exceeded 4,000 in 2008. Approximately 180 universities offer master's degrees in psychology, and approximately 50 universities offer a psychology (including developmental) doctorate. Developmental research is published in the *Japanese Journal of Developmental Psychology*, *Japanese Journal of Psychology*, *Japanese Journal of Educational Psychology*, *Annual of Educational Psychology in Japan*, and *Japanese Psychological Research* (the latter is in English). Despite the maturity and quality of Japanese developmental science, a language barrier still limits publication of this research literature outside of Japan (Shwalb, Nakazawa, and Shwalb, 2005).

Korea Developmental psychology is required in the teacher training and counseling curricula of universities and junior colleges. As a result, many specialists in developmental science teach at the college level. Membership in the Korean Society for Developmental Psychology, founded in 1975, has now reached 1,600 members. Research on development is published in the *Korean Journal of Developmental Psychology*, *Korean Journal of Psychology*, *Korean Journal of Educational Psychology*, and *Korean Journal of Clinical Psychology*.

Vietnam Most teacher training colleges in Vietnam include a very general study of developmental psychology focusing mainly on childhood and adolescence, and there are approximately 180–200 instructors of the subject nationwide. Few do research, however, so it is doubtful that one may describe a "field" of developmental science in Vietnam. To our knowledge, no university in Vietnam currently grants a degree in the developmental sciences.

Indonesia Only about 600 of the 8,000 members of the Indonesian Psychological Association are registered as developmental psychologists. Developmental psychology degrees are commonly granted at the master's level, and students may also focus on developmental psychology in their doctoral studies. There is no developmental psychology journal in Indonesia, where official academic journals are generally very limited.

Relationships in the Family

Japan

The percentage of the overall population younger than 15 years old in 2005 was 13.7% (lowest among comparable nations; Cabinet Office, 2006), and the percentage of people older than 65 years of age was 21%. According to the National Institute of Population and Social Security Research (2006), the percentage of households with parents and children was 40%; the percentage with grandparents, parents, and children was 14.2%; the percentage with a mother and children was 5.6%; and the percentage with a father and children was 1%. An understanding of child and adolescent development must be placed in the context of these demographics. Japanese developmental research originated with studies on parent–child relationships (Shwalb and Shwalb, 1996). For example, one influential Japanese study of mother–infant relationships using the Strange Situation found no A-type infants (avoidant) and more C-type (ambivalent) infants than in previous Western research (Takahashi, 1990). Mainstream attachment theory derives from a developmental view that emphasizes children's independence, individualization, and exploration. But Miyake (1992) interpreted Takahashi's findings by noting that the Strange Situation procedure may not be valid in Japan because mother–child relationships are particularly close, physical, and emotional.

Mother–child relationships have traditionally been considered central to Japanese family life, and a folk belief called the "3-year-old myth" stated that a mother must take care of her children at home for at least the first 3 years of life. However, Sugawara (2005) showed in longitudinal research of over 13 years that the 3-year-old myth was unfounded and that maternal employment has no harmful effects on children. There has also been extensive Japanese research on father–child relationships (Shwalb, Nakazawa, Yamamoto, and Hyun, in press), although until recently many fathers were said to have little direct contact with children and were characterized as psychologically detached or physically absent. A division of labor persisted until recently in Japan whereby husbands worked outside the home and wives performed housekeeping, childrearing, and care of elder parents. However, many Japanese fathers' orientations are becoming decidely child-centered and family-centered.

As a result of a trend toward increased incidence of child psychopathology in Japan, growing numbers of professionals serve as school counselors and child clinicians. Specifically, the number of consultations for child abuse brought to Japanese Child Guidance Centers increased from 1,101 cases in 1990 to 17,725 cases in 2000 and 34,451 cases in 2005. Early mother–child separation for low birth weight children, the child's difficult temperament, unwanted pregnancy, lack of maternal nurturing behavior, the parents' own past abused experience, unstable marital relationships, and unstable economic situations have all been associated in Japan with child abuse (Shoji, 2005). Meanwhile living facilities that provide stable support for abused children only recently began to proliferate in Japan (Kaneko, 2004).

Korea

With a predominance of nuclear families, the percentage of Korean families with a grandparent-parent-child structure has now fallen below 10% (Korea National Statistical Office, 2005). In this context, filial piety (효도, or *hyodo*) toward parents, grandparents, and ancestors, which was once a pillar of Korean family relaions, has weakened (Yim and Janelli, 2001). Whereas in the past children lived with and supported their elderly parents unconditionally, the current trend is for nuclear families to live separately from grandparents (Cho and Lee, 2004). However, some families live separately from yet within the same apartment complex as the aging parents and take care of them. Divorce in Korea has also become more common, and according to the annual report of the Korea Bureau of Statistics, there were 316,000 marriages and 124,590 divorces in 2007 (Korea National Statistical Office, 2007). With increased incidence of divorces, single parents, remarriages, and blended or bicultural families, there is a growing Korean interest in research on parent–child relationships (K. H. Lee, 2001).

Developmental research in Korea, as in Japan, has centered on family contexts. In Korean culture, there is a deep-rooted consciousness of parent and child as unified in "body and soul" (일심동체 or *ilshim dongche*; Choi, 2000), whereby the joys and sorrows of many children and parents are thought to be identical (Lee and Choi, 2003). The purpose of family life is unity (Kim, Kim, and Park, 2000; Park, Kim, Kim, You, and Lee, 2000), and the value of family unity extends across generations (Choi, Park, and Kim, 2003). As a result of their intense child-centeredness (G.W. Kim and Park, 2004), many parents believe that they exist to sacrifice for their children. This orientation may have been reflected in reports of Korean mothers as indulgent in cross-cultural studies of mother–infant relationships (e.g., Honig and Chung, 1989).

Parental self-sacrifice and devotion are also associated with feelings of appreciation and respect from children (Park and Kim, 2003). In the socialization of children (Park and Cheah, 2005), Korean parents may transmit cultural values of concern for others and self-sacrifice more by setting an example than through direct teaching or behavioral control of children. Parent–child relationships based on parental *and* children's self-sacrifice are prototypes for relationships in Korea. As a result, nothing is more important than self-sacrifice in relationships between teacher–student, husband–wife, or coworkers.

Other research has shown that relationships with parents strengthen children's academic performance and feelings of academic efficacy (Park and Kim, 2004), predict overall life satisfaction and satisfaction at school (Park, 2005), and influence the emotional problems of adolescents (Lee and Lee, 2005). In addition, quality of attachment with the parent appears to have a significant influence on the incidence of problem behaviors in children (Han, 2002) and on the formation of children's self-concepts (Moon and Park, 2005).

Many nuclear families and children are now isolated and deprived of relationships with extended family and neighbors. In this context, there are also diminishing opportunities to experience sibling relationships (Yang and Choi, 2005). Social isolation has contributed to maternal anxiety about childrearing (Hyun, 2004), and the incidence of child abuse is increasing. According to the Child Abuse Prevention Center, reported abuse cases increased by 35.7% between 2001 and 2003 alone. This incidence peaked in early and middle childhood, 80% of abusers were parents, and 77.5% of the abusing parents were age 30 to 40 years (Nam, 2005).

Vietnam

Traditional Normative Parent–Child Relationships   According to Toan (1992), the fetus is "educated" by its mother during the prenatal period. This phenomenon is called womb education (*thai giao*), and the Vietnamese believe that the thoughts, feelings, and actions of the pregnant woman influence the fetus. Socialization begins in early infancy, for example when a 6- to 7-month-old baby is taught to use polite language such as *da* to express respect for elders and adults and *xin* (thank you) when someone gives him or her something (Le and Vuong, 1999). Parents and other family members are gentle in childrearing during this developmental period.

When the baby begins to speak, listen, and understand what adults tell him or her, parents become stricter in discipline. For example, the popular expression, "Loving, one hits. Not loving, one is sweet" meant that severity was an expression of affection. The father in a Vietnamese family traditionally played the role of *nghiem phu* (severe father) in relation to children, whereas the mother looked after the family and children in the role of *tu mau* (tender mother) (Nguyen, 1994). This same Confucian-based distinction was once observed throughout East Asia in the expression "strict father, kind mother" (in Korean, *umbu- jamo* - 嚴父慈母; Shwalb et al., in press), although it is perhaps becoming obsolete in postmodern societies. In terms of power within the family, patrilineal authority (a Chinese influence) combines with matriarchy, an indigenous Southeast Asian influence.

Parent–child relationships play a central role in the traditional family as "the very core of Vietnamese culture dominating everything else" (Jamieson, 1993, p. 17). But unlike the traditional Chinese father who was said to have absolute rights over his children and wife, the Vietnamese father shared with his children collective and bilateral responsibility in legal, moral, and spiritual terms (Tran, 2001). Le and Vuong (1999) reported that severe discipline was common in the past, for example in beating children by whipping on the buttocks. Although beating and scolding are less common in modern Vietnam, recent studies show that physical and emotional punishment of children in Vietnam are still widespread (Save the Children Sweden, Plan, and United Nations Children's Fund [UNICEF], 2006). Family socialization traditionally fostered dependency between parents and children who relied on each other for security, and it was characterized by love for the children and respectful care for the elderly (Le, 1996). According to Te (1962, p. 99), a Vietnamese proverb described parental love and sacrifice for their children as "immense as the sky and ocean."

Modern Parent–Child Relationships   Since the early twentieth century, childrearing in Vietnam evolved from sacrificing the individual for the sake of the family toward respecting the individuality of the child (Dao, 1938/1998). Meanwhile, the strictness of the old system of education, both at home and school, gave way to a more flexible and liberal style (Vu, 2002). Over the past 33 years following national unification, families have also become more heterogeneous and modern (Nguyen, 1995). Contrary to their Confucian and Chinese heritage, nuclear families are more common than extended families in contemporary Vietnamese society (Hirschman and Vu, 1996). By the early 1990s, only 32% of Vietnamese families were extended families (Belanger, 1995).

A study on childrearing by Oudenhoven and Nhom Chan Troi Moi (1999) found that most Vietnamese parents reported that they loved their children, knew what was best for them, and were able to give them the care they needed. However, young Vietnamese increasingly assert their identities, encouraged by dramatic socioeconomic reforms and globalization (Ministry of Health, General Statistics Office, UNICEF, and World Health Organization, 2005). Young people generally have expressed the hope for a good loving family, but many students report conflicts with parents about matters like school, housework, coming home late, hairstyle, and relationships with friends of the same and opposite sex (Le, 2001). According to Le, urban students (32%) were more likely than rural students (22%) to report such conflicts.

Boys are still preferred by many parents and grandparents, particularly in rural and remote areas. The reason for this preference, observable in the past throughout East and Southeast Asia (Pong, 1994), was that only males could perpetuate the family name and carry out ancestor worship. Boys tend to have more freedom than girls in housework, friendships, and play. Conversely, there is some evidence that Vietnamese parents are harsher with females than males (Luu, 2005a, 2005b).

Indonesia

There have been few empirical studies of children or adolescents in Indonesian family settings, although descriptive reports are available about normative family life. Nuclear families are the most common structure in the modern urbanized portions of Indonesia. Because they lack daily contact with extended family members, parents in these families typically rear their own children. But some affluent and modern families can pay helpers and hire servants and nannies. Under these conditions, a child may be reared more by the nanny than by the parents, resulting in attachment to the nanny and emotional detachment from the parents. In the less modern sectors populated by a majority of Indonesians, families may also include grandparents, great-grandparents, uncles, aunts, nephews, and cousins (Koentjaraningrat, 1998).

The typical Indonesian family system is a patriarchy (Koentjaraningrat, 1998). Thus, the boy has a key responsibility to continue the family line, and in most Indonesian families, boys receive more attention than girls from parents. Females also have important roles in housework and childrearing, yet a girl has less status and rights in the family than a boy. Birth order is another important factor in family relationships; normally, the older child has more responsibility than the younger child. When the older child is not superior in ability to the younger child, both children may experience great stress, particularly if the older child is a boy and the younger child is a girl. Personal names reflect birth order, such as *Wayan*, *Putu*, or *Gde* for first child; *Made* or *Kadek* for the second child; *Nyoman*, *Nengah*, or *Komang* for the third child, and so forth.

Among the Javanese, the largest ethnic group in Indonesia, social rank is determined by ancestral origin; Balinese are influenced by Hinduism and its castes: *Brahmana* (spiritual leaders), *Ksatrya* (warriors), *Waisya* (traders), and *Syudra* (low-class society). When a child's ancestor is from a certain caste (primarily the *Brahmana* or *Ksatrya*), another title is included in the name. For example, if the child is a boy, he normally is given the name "I" (pronounced "ee"), and if the child is a girl, she takes the name "Ni" (pronounced "nee"). Children's rights, opportunities, and responsibilities are all influenced by their ancestral origins.

Javanese cultural norms may enable siblings, more than mothers, to facilitate play with children. Farver and Wimbarti (1995) found that play with siblings was characterized more by pretend play with objects and cooperative social pretend play than mothers' play with children. In addition, older siblings (4½ to 6 years) were more likely to actively join in playing with younger siblings (18 to 36 months) than were mothers. Unfortunately, this type of objective study of Indonesian family relationships has been rare.

Peer Relationships

Japan

As Japanese children adjust to group life in kindergarten, they experience a transition from a close and dependent relationship with mothers at home to peer relationships at school (Tobin, Hsueh, Karasawa, 2009). Peak (1991) identified two factors that enable this smooth transition. First, parents promote a positive image of kindergarten, and children enter school with positive expectations. Second, kindergarten teachers provide children with a daily schedule and establish customs and attitudes toward group life from the beginning of kindergarten, by modeling and providing individual support. Kindergarten children learn how to be independent and behave as "good children" (LeVine and Shimizu, 2000), and peers also act as school children's socialization agents (Hosaka, 2009).

Sumida (1995) compared elementary school children's everyday play activities of 1954 and 1985. He found that the contents of children's play changed from traditionally physical (jump-rope, tag) and less active (playing house) outdoor play with peers in the 1950s to physical outdoor peer group sports (baseball, football, dodge ball), less active indoor peer group play (video games with peers, chatting), and less active indoor personal play (watching television or videos, playing piano or video games) in the 1980s. In another comparison between cohorts, a survey of fourth to sixth graders by Nippon Hoso Kyokai (1991) showed that between 1984 and 1989, the percentage that had "friends in different grades" decreased from 86% to 75%, and the percentage of children who had "friends only in the same grade" increased from 14% to 24%. Thus, some children lost the opportunity to play with and gain information from older friends and to learn social skills through interactions with different-age children. Similar to the findings of Sumida (1995), Nippon Hoso Kyokai found that children's outdoor play decreased and indoor play increased historically.

A study on the development of Japanese adolescent peer relationships from junior high school through college revealed different developmental paths for males and females (Enomoto, 2003). In this study, male students started with play activities with friends emphasizing shared activities, and then play developed into activities of mutual understanding and respect for differences with others. Female students began in junior high school with intimacy-seeking activities emphasizing similarity to peers, later developed close activities in close relationships and rejected others who were different, and finally based their activities on mutual understanding.

Korea

Throughout Choi's (2000) book on Korean psychology, the emotional heart (심정 or *shim jung*) is the most important concept for understanding interpersonal relationships. In viewing child and adolescent peer relationships, we must view Korea as a relationship-centered society. Specifically, human relationships are formed in groups from the standpoint of "we" (in Korean, *uri*; Choi, 1997). In a "we-centered" culture, an individual who belongs to a group or organization should not surpass the group, and group values and standards are more important than those of the individual. In daily life, the word "we" is used often to express one's relationship with other people or one's group affiliations. Therefore, rather than "my mother" or "my school," it is more natural to say "our mother" and "our school." Expressing oneself as "we" enables Koreans to experience feelings of intimacy, mutual receptiveness, and tranquility.

The Korean proverb "sell the parent and buy the friend" reflects a growing importance of peer relationships in childhood and adolescence. In the past, parents clearly had a greater influence than peers, but the proverb is indicative of a cultural change by which both parents and peers are both influential. Hwang (2006) compared the roles of parents and friends in adolescents' daily lives and found that adolescents expected friends to be more empathetic and emotional than their parents. However, Baek and Seo (1993) observed other important factors in adolescents' friendships, including a sense of humor, a positive attitude by parents and teachers toward the friend, academic achievement, and one's physical appearance. Research on elementary school children (Kim, 2005) has shown that with age, exchanges of feelings and harmonious communication become more characteristic of friendships than proximity of one's home or physical attributes.

Other studies of Korean adolescents have shown that in adolescence, Internet communications influence adolescent peer relationships, as the digital age has influenced youth culture. According to a survey by Doh (2004), adolescents used the Internet 2 to 3 hours daily, about double the amount of time they spent playing with friends. According to a report by the Korean Network Information Center (2003), 91.3% of children between the ages of 6 and 19 use the Internet. A research study by Marketing Insight (www.mktinsight.co.kr) also revealed the following rates of student usage of cellular phones: elementary school = 10.2%, junior high school (ages 13 to 15 years) = 55.3%, high school (ages 16 to 18 years) = 83%, and college = 97.3%. Thus, with age, technology becomes increasingly important for communication with peers.

Vietnam

As reflected in a Vietnamese proverb, "if we play with ink we will be darkened, if we stay by a lamp we will have light," young people's personalities and reputations are said to be shaped by their personal associations. For example, a UNICEF, Ministry of Education and Training, and Population Council (1997) report on adolescents in Quang Ninh and Kien Giang documented patterns in sexual and social relationships. According to the report, relationships with the opposite sex included unprotected premarital sex by ages 16 to 18 years. Adolescents who were attending school spent Sundays and holidays at the beach, restaurants, skating rinks, cafes, and soccer fields. By comparison, adolescents who did not attend school went to the same locales but tended for economic reasons to spend more time at home, at work, or in household labor. Teenagers in this study spent more time with their friends than did young people in the past and were exposed to considerable peer pressure.

Le (2000) showed that strong friendships were the most commonly cited experiences at school for 16- to 18-year-old students. Almost 70% of Le's sample reported having good friends, and for many students, friendships were of enormous importance. Most students, 99% in rural areas and 91% in cities, reported that they had close friends; only 2.5% said that they had no close friends. In addition, 33% of students had close friends of the same sex, 65% had close friends of both sexes, and only 2% had only opposite sex close friends. According to the Ministry of Health et al. (2005), 88% of Vietnamese youth (age 14 to 25) reported that they had a group of friends with whom they often met; 9% of males and 15% of females stated that they did not belong to a friendship group.

Indonesia

As in other countries, play was traditionally the essence of Indonesian children's world (Mulyadi, 1998). The contents of Indonesian play were documented by the Ministry of Education and Culture (Departemen Pendidikan dan Kebudayaan, 1983), which compiled a list of 100 traditional ethnic play activities in five provinces. Children played with close family members, with family members they had never met, and with others in their neighborhood. Each example of traditional play was unique and associated with an ethnic group (e.g., using a tribal language or based on a particular belief system). Most traditional Indonesian play involved physical exercise such as running, chasing, throwing, or dancing, whereas in other traditional play, children would count, guess, or role play. Mulyadi (1998) reported that 72 out of the 100 games were for children (ages 8 to 11 years), 19 were for adolescents, and the other 9 were for adults. Children also interacted with adolescents and adults in a few traditional games. In some forms of play, participants learned to follow rules or develop emotional connections with others. Unfortunately, in the context of a developing society with social and economic problems, many children and adolescents in modern Indonesia now have limited opportunities to play.

In a rare systematic study of Indonesian children's social and emotional development, Eisenberg, Liew, and Pidada (2004) reported gender differences in how Indonesian children develop between third and sixth grade. They found that sixth grade boys' positive functioning was associated with emotional regulation in third grade, and that by sixth grade, girls were generally more socially competent and self-regulated than boys.

French and his colleagues examined Indonesian (mostly Javanese) children's peer relations in several studies and replicated studies of Western children using sociometrics, achievement data, and teacher ratings. As in the West, Indonesian children with fewer friends had certain characteristics (aggressive, withdrawn, lower academic achievement, and lower sociometric ratings), and friends had more similar scores on the preceding measures than nonfriends (French, Jansen, Riansari, and Setiono, 2003). Elsewhere, French, Pidada, Denoma, McDonald, and Lawton (2005) compared American and Indonesian 9- and 11-year-olds and found different styles of conflict resolution, whereby Indonesian children used disengagement from conflict and American children used negotiations to resolve conflict. French, Siansari, Pidada, Nelwan, and Buhrmester (2001) showed both differences and similarities between Indonesian and American children in the supportive functions of their friends and family. Specifically, they revealed that elementary and junior high school Indonesian students rated family members higher and friends lower for companionship and satisfaction than did American students, but students in both societies rated friends as their primary source of intimacy. Finally, French, Jansen, and Pidada (2002) reported gender differences in types of aggression among 11- and 14-year-old children. Their descriptions of disliked peers showed that relational aggression was cited more often by girls than boys in both Indonesia and the United States. Overall, French and his team found many similarities in American and Indonesian peer relationships and interpreted the cultural differences mainly in terms of individualistic American versus collectivistic Indonesian orientations.

Problem Behavior and Values

Japan

Since World War II, the crime rate of Japanese adolescents peaked four times, in 1951, 1964, 1983, and 1998. In 2005, the percentage of 14- to 20-year-olds who committed crimes was 1.6%, and the percentage of adolescent crimes among all crimes was 32.0%; this was the second lowest percentage in the past 32 years (National Police Agency Juvenile Division, 2006).

In Hosaka's (2005) view, peers exert pressure in early adolescence for conformity because of cultural values placed on group togetherness and harmony. He examined connections between Japanese adolescents' peer relationships, relatively infrequent externalizing problems (delinquency and bullying), and more common internalizing problems (school nonattendance). In 2005, 0.32% of children in elementary school and 2.75% in middle school were absent for 30 days or more. Three causes of nonattendance in elementary school, according to Hosaka, in order of importance, were children's personality (anxiety, apathy, nervousness), relationships in the family (marital strife, opposition to parents, changing family circumstances from divorce or relocation), and school contexts (bullying, conflict with peers or teachers, academic failure). But in middle school, this order of causal importance changed to school, personality, and lastly family (Ministry of Education, Culture, Sports, Science and Technology, 2006).

Korea

Kim and Kim (2005) reported a gender difference in the behavior of delinquent Korean adolescents. As found previously in the West, female delinquency is increasing and becoming more violent, although it is still less prevalent than in males. Also as in previous Western studies, females tended more toward internalizing (depression) behavior, whereas males tended toward externalizing behavior (antisocial personality, alcohol and drug abuse). The greatest predictor of delinquency among females was alcohol/drug abuse, whereas age and antisocial personality were predictors for males, i.e., an increasing delinquency rate with age among male adolescents. Kim and Kim (2005) also reported family dynamics as causes of delinquency for both genders. One of the clearest trends in the values of Korean adolescents is the gradual disappearance of the traditional mentality of filial piety. Associated with this tendency is a notable increase in elder abuse and abandonment of support of elderly parents. In addition, whereas in the past the eldest son would normally look after his elderly parents, in recent years whoever is capable of supporting the parents, including daughters, may contribute to this support (Cho and Lee, 2004).

Vietnam

Traditional values placed on parental authority and filial obedience have been challenged by processes of economic and social reform (United Nations Development Programme, 1998). Vietnamese family unity is under strain by adjustment to these reforms, with apparent increases in the incidence of family breakups, homeless or abandoned children, alcoholism, drug abuse, HIV/acquired immunodeficiency syndrome (AIDS), domestic violence, street crime, begging, prostitution, and trafficking in women and children. In particular, the rate of children in conflict with the law has risen in urban areas (UNICEF, 2005).

Deviant behavior among adolescents in Vietnam is a problem for educators and families alike. These behaviors include school dropouts, runaways, truancy, cheating on tests, refusal to do homework, disrespect for teachers, fighting, and alcohol use (Luu, 2005a). In the study of 532 students in Hanoi (ages 13 to 15 years), 97.6% of students reported committing some form of misbehavior in the past year, including "told lies" (82.3%), "did not complete school work or assignments" (65.6%), "swore" (42.9%), and "made a disturbance or noise in the classroom" (32.1%). Of greater interest to parents and professionals were the reported rates of more serious misbehavior such as "smoked" (3%), "drank alcohol" (4.7%), and "ran away from home" (2.1%). Male students generally reported more misbehavior than did female students.

Studies on troubled adolescents and youth in Vietnam have identified parenting styles, parent–child relationships, and family environments that were related to types of moral and deviant behavior. Interviews with 550 adolescents in rehabilitation centers (Nguyen, 2000) revealed that antisocial behavior was correlated with family relationships where parents were in conflict, used authoritarian or even cruel parenting styles, or were highly permissive. Research on peer relationships and peer pressure for conformity among troubled minors revealed another aspect of problem behavior in Vietnamese youth (Dang, 2006). In Dang's study, 61% of respondents reported that they were more influenced by friends than by their families, and 53% listened to their friends' advice more often than to their parents. Yet delinquency in Vietnam is relatively uncommon. For example, in Haiphong, Vietnam's third largest city with over 500,000 youth ages 14 to 25 years, only 363 minors were tried in court in 2005.

Indonesia

The basic traditional principle of Indonesian society for centuries has been called "*gotong-royong*," which means togetherness. In the larger cities like Jakarta, people apparently seem relatively unaware of the influence of collectivism, but in most areas of Indonesia, this form of togetherness forms a central social bond (Koentjaraningrat, 1998). In multiethnic Indonesia, there are two forms of we-ness: *kita* and *kami* (Hassan, 1975). Kita exists when the people include others within their group. Kami exists when the person and the group are unified and exclude others and can even lead to interracial and intercultural conflicts. Unfortunately, many parents foster *kami* we-ness in their children by preventing their children from interacting with children of another race, religion, or culture. Hidayat (2004) found a positive correlation between mother's physical abuse and the aggressive behavior of adolescents, but Helen (2002) showed that students who fought at school were influenced primarily by their peer groups and violent films.

In the world's most populous Muslim-majority nation (86% Islamic), religion and religious values may now have a stronger and more widespread influence over social relationships in Indonesia than in Japan, Korea, or Vietnam. For example, in Indonesian Muslim society, prior to the fasting month, people go to cemeteries to place flowers on gravesites and recollect about their ancestors, and some believe that such behavior will ensure spiritual support from their ancestors during the entire month of fasting. This and other practices are passed down from the older generation to children and adolescents, who learn about rituals and mysticism rather than just a religious group identification.

Culture-Specific Issues

Japan

Literacy   Japanese society attaches great importance to educational background and to academic achievement. Its literacy rate is 99.9%, and most children can read and write before they enter elementary school. This system consists of two types of syllabaries, *hiragana* (for most Japanese words) and *katakana* (mainly for foreign words and onomatopoeia), and *kanji* characters derived from Chinese (Akita, 2005). *Hiragana* is the basic writing system of 71 letters, including 5 voiced and 66 consonant-vowel combinations. One characteristic of Japanese *hiragana* is the one-to-one correspondence between phoneme elements (morae) and grapheme elements (letters). Japanese children can easily learn *katakana* letters after learning *hiragan*a, and their high rate of literacy is related to orthographic characteristics of Japanese language system. This literacy is the basis for high levels of academic achievement fron childhood through adolescence.

After-School Education   There are many after-school activities in Japan (Sugie, Shwalb, and Shwalb, 2006). *Naraigoto* (lessons) and *kyoshitsu* (classrooms) teach sports (e.g., swimming school, football, or baseball), music (e.g., piano or violin), drawing, and dance. *Juku* (academies) teach academic skills like mathematics, English, abacus, or calligraphy. *Yobikoh* (preparatory schools) trains students to pass examinations for admission to college. Typically, lower (grades 1 to 2) and middle (grades 3 to 4) elementary school children attend *naraigoto* or *kyoshitsu*, mainly upper elementary school children (grades 5 to 6) and junior high school students attend *juku*, and high school students attend *yobikoh*. One study by the Cabinet Office (2005) indicated that more than 70% of parents of junior high school students gave more credit to *juku* and *yobikoh* for their children's academic achievement than to the formal school system. Shwalb, Sugie, and Yang (2005) compared students who attended abacus *juku* with students not attending the *juku* and found that abacus *juku* students reported having higher mental calculation abilities (corroborated by teacher ratings) and higher confidence in their calculation abilities. Children who studied abacus also reported having higher motivation and achievement for regular school mathematics, showing a connection between learning and motivation at school and in an after-school program.

Technology and Media   Media and information technology are widely available to Japanese children. Among the media, video games and *manga* (Japanese comics) now are popular not only with Japanese children but also outside of Japan. Sakamoto (2005) reported longitudinal panel data on the effects of video games on children, showing the impact of video games on aggressiveness to be influenced by game content (i.e., degree of realism and rewarding nature of games). His data did not connect video game activity with the level of social adjustment of students younger than college age, but university students' video game play was related to lower empathy. According to Sakamoto, university students generally played video games less often than did adolescents, and those who did play may have isolated themselves from other people and become less empathic. Video game activities also appeared to affect the cognitive abilities and academic skills of children.

Nakazawa (2005) examined another popular medium of Japanese child culture: *manga* comics. According to Nakazawa, exposure to *manga* was associated with superior human-drawing skills and other information-processing skills of elementary school children. *Manga* reading comprehension was based on "panel reading literacy" and "context reading from panel sequences literacy."

Korea

School Achievement   Like the Japanese, Koreans value a person's educational background, and educational attainment affects one's occupational status and personal relationships (Park and Kim, 2002). The historical origin of this emphasis on academic achievement was in Confucian values that emphasize the importance of teaching and learning. This value was shown in a study of children and adolescents (Park, Kim, and Tak, 2002) in which 65% expressed the belief that academic success was their proudest achievement. According to government statistics, 82.1% of Korean high school students entered college in 2005, compared to 33.2% in 1990 (Korean Educational Development Institute, 2005); this rate is now the highest in the world. In fact, more than 98% of Korean parents want their children to go to college, and 20% to 30% want their children to study at the doctoral level (Park and Kim, 2002).

Intense societal and parental interest in education has brought about societal problems. The first is the considerable burden that Korean families bear in paying for private tuition and other educational costs. Second, a survey has shown that 84.1% of parents also enroll their children in *haak won* (after-school academies like Japanese *juku*) for supplemental studies. According to McMahon (2002), South Korea spends a greater proportion of its Gross Domestic Product on education than do most modern nations. A majority of Korean children and adolescents were reported as under severe pressure to achieve (Korea National Statistical Office, 2000). Because of the high cost of education in Korea, some families send children or adolescents to study abroad. Children cannot live independently, and so they usually travel overseas with the mother while the father remains in Korea working to pay for their expenses. Such a father is called the "father of a wild goose" because a pattern of divided families is actually common among geese, and the cultural image of wild geese is one of loneliness. Under such conditions, problems arise from the separation of the father from both child and wife.

Educational pressures also affect early childhood education. Many Korean parents emphasize children's education over their development early in life (Woo, 2004). According to K. S. Lee's (2001) survey, as many as 84% of parents begin teaching children the Korean language and other academic materials before they are 2 years old. Besides language, classes are now popular before age 2 in music, art, English, piano, and mathematics (Choi, 2003). This exposure prior to age 2 is especially intense among affluent families; education in music, Korean language, mathematics, and English is common for the general population after children enter preschool. Some children are stressed by this early education, as reflected by a rapid increase in psychiatric disorders such as alopecia (hair loss) among children (Shin, 2002).

Vietnam

Filial Piety   Although mediated by indigenous Vietnamese culture, Confucianism for centuries had a great influence on society and families (Dao, 1937/1994), and filial piety was the ethical foundation of traditional parent–child relationships. Lan (cited by Truong, 2002), in a study of childrearing among 300 extended families in Hanoi, reported that the two traits parents and grandparents most wanted to instill in children and grandchildren were honesty and attentiveness to others' needs (according to parents) and honesty and filial piety (according to grandparents). In the rural areas of Thai Binh Province in 1984, however, the most desirable characteristic of children was their "value as economic contributors." By 1994, in the same rural sample, economic value of children was ranked third, after "reliability when I become old" and "maintaining continuity of the family line" (Truong, 2002). It is widely assumed in Vietnam that when parents become old, the younger generation is obligated to support them. This family support is critical in a country with such rudimentary welfare infrastructure as Vietnam, especially in rural areas.

Vietnamese parent–child relationships normally involve long-term mutual dependence. A popular saying is *Tre cay cha, gia cay con* ("When young one relies on the father, when old one relies on the children"). This mutual dependence promotes psychological security between the older and younger generations and a strong, coherent, and durable family. According to Le (2000), more than 90% of 17- to 18-year-olds agreed with the statement that "no matter what the circumstances, I shall support my parents when they become old." Only 4% responded, "my parents will support themselves or go on social welfare," consistent with Vietnamese tradition.

Despite a growing desire to lead more independent lives and even in the context of globalization, Vietnamese adolescents still have great respect for their elders. Compared with other East Asian cultures in the World Value Survey of 1995 to 1998, Russell et al. (2002) reported that Vietnamese ranked highest with regard to their respect for parents. Filial piety gives parent–child relationships a warm, affectionate, and permanent quality, although in some cases the youth may become so docile as to lack initiative and be passive.

Indonesia

Impact of Poverty on Childhood Socialization   Ancestral origin, the family, collectivism, religion, traditional play, formal education, the peer group, and overall cultural changes all influence the socialization of children and adolescents in Indonesia. MuhammedAlly, Fellow, and Coursen-Neff (2004) from Human Rights Watch have reported that Indonesian children face many serious problems. Poverty is the greatest problem, as evidenced by limited resources to support child development and low survival rates. Poverty forces children to work to support their families. Significantly more girls than boys have to give up the life of childhood and forego opportunities for education to contribute to households at a very young age. Many young people migrate from villages to big cities in hope of a better life, but they ultimately face various limitations, receive a low salary, and may even be abused, exploited, or forced into prostitution. Those who are able to gain proper work, for more affluent families, may also have opportunities for education and other life experiences. For example, some children are adopted by the families for whom they work and gradually become part of their new families. But even in these cases, they are still unlikely to obtain full rights. For example, adopted children may not be permitted by the host family to study at a day school, but rather, they must attend after work. Such exploitation precludes children from normal experiences and development.

Urbanization   In urban life, some parents are too busy to take care of family matters. Many affluent families thus employ professionals or have volunteers to tend children, and their children may lack parental love and attention. These children become emotionally starved, and because parents do not fulfill their needs the children turn to peer groups (especially in adolescence) and behave accordingly. Some urban peer groups are creative and productive, but more often they impart negative values. Soekanto (1990) explained that during adolescence some urban youth lack parental guidance or support. They may not internalize social values and have to accommodate alternative peer group values incongruent with general ethnic or societal values.

Conclusion

One must consider historical, ideological, and economic influences on the development of children and adolescents. For example, as we reviewed the literature across the four cultures, it was apparent that there are a great number of cross-cultural similarities among the three societies that may have originated from their shared Confucian heritage. Several other similarities were notable between the affluent and geographically East Asian Japanese and Koreans and between the less affluent and geographically Southeast Asian Vietnamese and Indonesian cultural groups.

Family Relationships

Prenatal or early childhood development was emphasized in the Vietnamese, Japanese, and Korean research literatures. For example, the Vietnamese expression of "womb education" has equivalent terms in Japanese and Korean. This emphasis on early influence was also illustrated by the behavior of some Korean parents who reportedly teach children piano and English before age 2 years. Many Japanese parents to expose their children to early instruction (e.g., swimming, music), and in both Japan and Korea there is currently controversy over whether this emphasis on training has cut into children's opportunities for play.

Another similarity, across all four cultures, was the preference for male children, as they are called on to perpetuate the family line. This tendency has gradually weakened in Japan and Korea in the context of an aging and declining population. Some of these parents now actually prefer girls because they are believed to be easier to raise and may be more capable of caring for aged parents later in life.

A third important example of a similarity across the four cultures was the declining birth rate. This trend may be felt most strongly in Japan and Korea because these societies are approaching negative population growth. For example, in the context of very small families, there is a trend toward increasingly permissive and less strict childrearing in Japan. As Indonesian and Vietnamese populations continue in their trend toward lower birth rates, it will be interesting to see whether their traditional parenting styles also change.

Peer Relationships

Peer groups become more influential as children and adolescents become independent of their parents. But as noted in this chapter, this normative tendency and the strength of peer influences depend on changing cultural norms and values. In Japan, Korea, Vietnam, and Indonesia, as throughout Asia, we have seen that the family and parents generally retain a strong and primary influence despite the tendency for modernization and globalization to weaken family traditions and values.

Problem Behavior and Values

Problem behavior and delinquency are still relatively uncommon throughout East and Southeast Asia, partly because of the legacy of collectivistic ideologies that value group harmony over the desires of the individual. In Japan, Korea, and Vietnam, one reason for the strong pressure on young people to conform to cultural expectations is that each of these cultures has a single predominant ethnic group once rooted in a traditional Confucian code of ethics. In the case of multiethnic Indonesian culture, Islamic beliefs provide the impetus for social integration. We predict that deviance and psychopathology will continue to increase in incidence, as a reflection of societal change stressors across the four cultures. Culturally based problem behaviors and delinquent behaviors were also of interest. For example, Japanese children display more internalizing rather than externalizing of problems, such as school nonattendance and "shut-in" adolescents who refuse to leave their rooms or homes. Future research should study these culture influences on problems of youth.

Culture-Specific Issues

Cultural similarities were apparent even when we tried to identify particular issues of concern in each culture. For example, Japanese and Korean children and adolescents were all reported to have a strong motivation to excel in highly competitive educational systems. Young people in these two affluent societies were also reported to be strongly influenced by their usage of the Internet, computer games, and other types of technology. Confucian filial piety was identified as a key historical influence on lifespan development in Vietnam, Korea, and Japan, but its influence is changing rapidly in each culture. With modernization, fewer children contribute to the family's finances, and the percentages of multigenerational families that live together are in decline. Despite these similarities, the expression of filial piety in each society depends on culture-specific values, degree of modernization, and changing family processes and structures. In our opinion, the strongest degree of filial piety generally seems to remain in Vietnam, followed by Korea, and with the Japanese now expressing the weakest level of filial piety.

General Conclusions

We have observed at various points that Japanese, Korean, Vietnamese, and Indonesian cultures all emphasize group harmony and conformity. In this post-modern era of globalization, the clash of their traditional tendencies with modernization and economic development complicates life in all four cultures. In Indonesia and Vietnam, many children and adolescents still face widespread poverty along with the stress of social instability and economic growth. Progress in the health sciences has been one benefit of modernization and has significantly increased life expectancy in all four societies. But health and economic advancements have also led to an increase in population density and an aging population (most notably in Japan and Korea), placing new strains on these societies. Meanwhile, scientific progress in less affluent nations (e.g., Vietnam and Indonesia) has significantly increased the survival rate of infants. As a result, increasing numbers of citizens require government services (health, education, etc.) as children and adolescents and homes and jobs as adults. In Indonesia and Vietnam, public and educational infrastructures have not improved at the same rate as technology and science, causing new life stresses. In sum, social change has caused both positive and negative changes in the worlds of children and adolescents.

Finally, we conclude that family relationships remain the primary influence on the development of children and adolescents in Japan, Korea, Vietnam, and Indonesia. In our opinion, developmental science can and should contribute to the welfare of families and enable future generations of these Asian children and adolescents to enjoy a higher quality of life while maintaining their cultural heritage.

Acknowledgments

Every coauthor made a huge contribution to the writing of this chapter. We also acknowledge the support of Seisoh Sukemune, Tetsuji Itoh, and the Southern Utah University Psychology Department. This chapter is dedicated to Boris Ruslan Franz, David Joseph Shwalb, Kikue Nakazawa, Mar-Sun Lee, Kha'nh and Trung, Tb.Budisatiadarma, and Dian Satiani.

References

Akita, K. (2005). Developmental processes of literacy in Japan. In D. W. Shwalb, J. Nakazawa, and B. J. Shwalb (Eds.), *Applied developmental psychology: Theory, practice, and research from Japan* (pp. 137–153). Charlotte, NC: Information Age.

Baek, K. L., and Seo, D. I. (1993). Seongbyeol gwa haknyeon e ttareun cheongsonyeon ui chingu gwangye [Adolescent boys and girls of peer-relations by sex and grade]. *Journal of Korean Institute for Youth Development, 15*, 45–63.

Belanger, D. (1995). *Household structure and family formation patterns*. Hanoi, Vietnam: Social Sciences Publishing House.

Cabinet Office (2006). *Shoshika shakai hakusho*. [White paper on birthrate: Declining society]. Retrieved from http://www8.cao.go.jp/shoushi/whitepaper/index-w.html.

Cho, Y. J., and Lee, S. H. (2004). Daehaksaeng janyeo ga jigakhan bumo waui jeongseojeok gwangye wa bumo buyang uisik [College students' perception of emotional tie with their parents and attitudes toward parent caregiving]. *Journal of Korean Home Management Association, 22*, 63–74.

Choi, E. (2003). Sahoe idong e daehan chameul su eopneun yokmang [Aspirations for social mobility: Globalization, educational interest, parent-school relations]. Korean Educational Development Institute. *RM 2003-22*, 32–46.

Choi, G. S., Park, Y. S., and Kim, E. C. (2003). *Hwamokhan gajeong eul wihan gajok ui yeokhal e daehan tochak simrihakjeok bunseok* [Conception of harmonious family life and family role: Indigenous psychological analysis of parents and educators]. Paper presented at the Congress of Korean Psychological Association, Seoul, Korea.

Choi, S. J. (1997). *Dangsaja simrihak gwa je 3ja simrihak: Ingwan gwangye jomang ui du gaji teul* [The psychology of the person and third person: Two aspects of personal relations]. Paper presented at the Congress of Korean Psychological Association in Autumn Symposium, Seoul, Korea, 131–143.

Choi, S. J. (2000). *HanGukIn SimRihak* [Korean psychology]. Seoul, South Korea: Chung-Ang University Press.

Dalton, R., Pham, H. M., Pham, N. T., and Ong, N. N. (2002). Social relations and social capital in Vietnam. *Nghien cuu con nguoi (Human Studies), 2*.

Dang, T. B. (2006). Xa hoi hoa tre em o nong thon mien nui thong qua lao dong trong gia dinh (nghien cuu truong hop xa Cat Thinh, huyen Van Chan, tinh Yen Bai) [Socialization of rural children through housework in mountainous areas (The case of Cat Thinh Commune, Van Chan District, Yen Bai Province)]. *Sociology, 1*, 64–72.

Dao, D. A. (1937/1994). Influence of Confucianism in Vietnam. *Vietnamese Studies, 1*, 23–25.

Dao, D. A. (1938/1998) *Vietnam van hoa su cuong* [Brief history of Vietnamese culture]. Dong Thap, Vietnam: Dong Thap Publishing.

Departemen Pendidikan dan Kebudayaan [The Indonesian Ministry of Education and Culture] (1983). *Traditional children's play in Indonesia: Aceh, Jambi, East Kalimantan, Central Java, and Irian Jaya*. Jakarta, Indonesia: Departemen Pendidikan dan Kebudayaan.

Doh, H. S. (2004). Digital sidae ui cheongsonyeon munhwa, bumo-janyeo gwangye mit sahoe jeongseo baldal [Adolescent culture, parent-child relationships, and socioemotional development in a digital era]. *Journal of Human Ecology, 2*, 47–63.

Eisenberg, N., Liew, J., and Pidada, S. U. (2004). The longitudinal relations of regulation and emotionality to quality of Indonesian children's socioemotional functioning. *Developmental Psychology, 40*, 790–804.

Enomoto, J. (2003) *Seinenki no yujinkankei no hattatuteki henka* [Developmental change of friendship among adolescents]. Tokyo: Kazama Shoboh.

Farver, J. M., and Wimbarti, S. (1995). Indonesian children's play with their mothers and older siblings. *Child Development, 66*, 1493–1503.

French, D., Jansen, E. A., and Pidada, S. (2002). United States and Indonesian children's and adolescents' reports of relational aggression by disliked peers. *Child Development, 73*, 1143–1150.

French, D., Jansen, E. A., Riansari, M., and Setiono, K. (2003). Friendships of Indonesian children: Adjustment of children who differ in friendship presence and similarity between mutual friends. *Social Develoment, 12*, 605–621.

French, D., Pidada, S., Denoma, J., McDonald, K., and Lawton, A. (2005). Reported conflicts of children in the United States and Indonesia. *Social Development, 14*, 458–472.

French, D. C., Siansari, M., Pidada, S., Nelwan, P., and Buhrmester, D. (2001). Social support of Indonesian and U.S. children and adolescents by family members and friends. *Merrill-Palmer Quarterly, 47*, 377–394.

Han, Y. O. (2002). Eomeoni ui aechak yuhyeong i adong haengdong munje e michi neun yeonghyang [The effect of a maternal attachment style on child behavioral problem: A cross-cultural study of Korea and America]. *The Korean Journal of Clinical Psychology, 21*, 361–376.

Hassan, F. (1975). *Kita dan kami: An analysis of the basic modes of togetherness*. Jakarta, Indonesia: Bratara.

Helen, M. (2002). *Pengaruh mikorsistem terhadap perilaku tawuran pelajar* [The impact of microsystem on students who engage in school fights]. Graduate research, Department of Psychology, Tarumanagara University, Jakarta, Indonesia.

Hidayat, S. (2004). Hubungan perilaku kekerasan fisik ibu pada anaknya terhadap munculnya perilaku agresif pada anak SMP [Relationship between mothers' physical abuse on children and aggressive behavior in junior high school students]. *Provitae, 1*, 83–92.

Hirschman, C., and Vu, L. M. (1996) Family and household structure in Vietnam: Some glimpses from a recent survey. *Pacific Affairs, 69*, 229.

Honig, A. S., and Chung, M. (1989). Child-rearing practices of urban poor mothers of infants and three-year-olds in five cultures. *Early Child Development and Care, 50*, 75–97.

Hosaka, T. (2005). School absenteeism, bullying, and loss of peer relationships in Japanese children. In D. W. Shwalb, J. Nakazawa, and B. J. Shwalb (Eds.), *Applied developmental psychology: Theory, practice, and research from Japan* (pp. 283–299). Charlotte, NC: Information Age.

Hwang, C. S. (2006). Chogi cheongsonyeongi ui bumo mit ttorae aechak gwa aechak ui byeonhwa [Parent- and peer-attachments of early adolescents and the transition of attachment functions]. *Studies on Korean Youth, 17*, 201–225.

Hyun, J. H. (2004). Chwieopmo ui adonggwan mitboyuk taedo, eomeoni yeokhal ui insik e daehan yeon-gu [A study on one's sense of view on infancy, bringing up and awareness of mother's role]. *Korean Journal of Child Education and Care, 4*, 235–248.

Jamieson, N. (1993). *Understanding Vietnam*. Berkeley, CA: University of California Press.

Kaneko, R. (2004). *Kizutsuita inochi wo hagukumu: Gyakutai no rensa wo fusegu aratana shakaiteki yougo* [Support the hurting life: New social care preventing the cycle of abuse]. Tokyo: Seisinshobo.

Kim, E. C., and Park, Y. S. (2004). The basis of trust in relationships: Indigenous psychological analysis of adolescents and their parents. *Korean Journal of Psychological and Social Issues, 10*, 103–137.

Kim, G. W., and Park, K. (2004). Cheongsonyeon gwa bumo ui ingan gwangye reul tonghae bon sinroe uisik: Tochak simrihakjeok jeopgeun [Informatization and the Korean youth's viewpoint of the family values]. *Korean Journal of Information Society, 6*, 1–32.

Kim, H. S., and Kim, H. S. (2005). Gender differences in delinquent behavior among Korean adolescents. *Child Psychiatry and Human Development, 35*, 325–345.

Kim, M. J. (2005). Chodeung hakgyo ui gyou gwangye hyeongseong yoin e gwanhan yeongu [A study of the factors influencing on peer-relations among elementary school children]. Master's thesis, The Graduate School of Sook-Myung Women's University, Seoul, South Korea.

Kim, M. U., Kim, E. C., and Park, Y. S. (2000). Cheongsonyeon gwa seongin ganui sedae chai wa usaseong [Intergenerational differences and similarities between adolescents and adults]. *Korean Journal of Psychological and Social Issues, 6*, 181–204.

Koentjaraningrat, R. (1998). *Pengantar antropologi: Pokok-pokok etnografi* [Introduction to anthropology: Basic ethnography]. Jakarta, Indonesia: Rineka Cipta.

Korean Educational Development Institute (2005). *OECD gyoyuk jipyo, tonggye jaryo* [An index of education in OECD]. Statistics Data: SM2000-1.

Korea National Statistical Office (2000). *Hanguk ui sahoe jipyo* [Indices of Korean society]. Retrieved from http://www.nso.go.kr/.

Korea National Statistical Office (2005). *Chulsan ryul* [Fertility rate]. Retrieved from http://www.nso.go.kr/.

Korea National Statistical Office (2007). *Ihon ryul* [Divorces rates]. Retrieved from http://www.nso.go.kr/.

Korea Network Information Center (2003). *2003 sangbangi jeongbohwa siltae josa* [2003 survey about realities of information society for the first half-year]. Seoul, South Korea: Ministry of Information and Communication.

Le, H. V. (2000). *Vietnamese youth value. beyond Doi Moi: Tradition, continuity and change in culturally shared outlooks on the family, education, leisure and community*. Master's thesis, RMIT University, Melbourne, Australia.

Le, H. V. (2001). Quan he cha me- con cai la thanh nien: bat dong va ung xu [Parent-child relations: Clashes and dealings]. *Psychology, 4*, 28–35.

Le, T. (1996). Gia dinh Viet Nam hien nay nhung van de dang dat ra. In T. Le (Ed.), *Gia dinh Vietnam ngay nay* [Vietnam today's family]. Hanoi, Vietnam: Social Sciences Publishing House.

Le, T. T. N., and Vuong, T. X. (Eds.). (1999). *Reproductive culture in Vietnam*. Hanoi: Gioi Publishing.

Lee, J. J., and Choi, S. J. (2003). Bujauchin seonjeong cheokdo ui jejak gwatadanghwa yeongu [The construction and validation of parent-adolescent affective bonding scale]. *Korean Journal of Psychological Association: Society and Personality, 17*, 87–104.

Lee, K .H. (2001). Sahoe byeonhwa wa bumo janyeo gwangye [Social change and relationships between parents and children]. *Korean Parent-Child Health Journal, 4*, 43–55.

Lee, K. S. (2001). *ChangUiJeok IGo JeonInJeok* [Human resources for childrearing, and early childhood education]. Ministry of Education and Human Resources Development. Political Task for Education of Infant, 2001-24.

Lee, S. E., and Lee, J. C. (2005). Daehaksaeng ui aechak uhyeong, bumo ttorae aechak, geurigo jeongseojeok teukseong gwa ui gwangye [The relationships among attachment style, parent-peer attachment, and emotional characteristics in college students]. *The Korean Journal of Counseling and Psychotherapy, 17,* 947–963.

LeVine, R. A., and Shimizu, H. (2000). *Japanese frames of mind: Cultural perspectives on human development.* New York: Cambridge University Press.

Luu, H. S. (2005a). *Hanh vi lech chuan cua hoc sinh trung hoc co so va moi tuong quan giua no voi kieu quan hecha me con cai* [Deviant behavior of lower secondary school students in correlation to parent child relation types]. Unpublished doctoral thesis, psychology. National Institute of Psychology, Hanoi, Vietnam.

Luu, H. S. (2005b). Relations between parents and children of lower secondary school age. *Psychology, 8,* 17–24

Marketing Insight. Retrieved January 15, 2007, from http://www.mktinsight.co.kr.

McMahon, W. W. (2002). *Education and development: Measuring the social benefits.* New York: Oxford University Press.

Ministry of Education, Culture, Sports, Science and Technology (2006). *Gakkou kihon chosa* [Fundamental survey of school education in Japan]. Retrieved from http://mext.go.jp/bnenu/toukei/001/06080115/index.htm.

Ministry of Health, General Statistics Office, United Nations Children's Fund, and World Health Organization (2005). *Survey assessment of Vietnamese youth.* Hanoi, Vietnam: Author.

Miyake, K. (1992). *Nyuyouji no jikakukeisei to bosikankei* [Personallity development and child-mother relationships]. Tokyo: The University of Tokyo Press.

Moon, Y. S., and Park, I. S. (2004). Yeodaesaeng i jigak han bumo-janyeo gwangye ga bumo-janyeo aechak gwajaa gaenyeom e michineun yeonghyang [The relationship between perceived parent-child relationship, parent-child attachment and self-conception of women college students]. *Korean Parent-Child Health Journal, 8,* 75–88.

MuhammedAlly, S., Fellow, A., and Coursen-Neff, Z. (2004). *Ringkasan* [Summary]. Human Rights Watch. Retrieved October 26, 2006, from http://www.hrw.org/indonesian/reports/2005/indonesia0605/2.htm.

Mulyadi, S. (1998). Traditional children's play in Indonesia. *Arkhe, 5,* 87–95.

Nakazawa, J. (1996). *Shakaitekikoudou niokeru nintiteiseigyono hattatu.* [Development of cognitive regulation for social behavior]. Tokyo: Taga Shuppan.

Nakazawa, J. (2005). Development of *manga* (comic book) literacy in children. In D. W. Shwalb, J. Nakazawa, and B. J. Shwalb (Eds.), *Applied developmental psychology: Theory, practice, and research from Japan* (pp. 23–42). Charlotte, NC: Information Age.

Nam, J. R. (2005). Adong hakdae munje ui choegeun siltae wa haegyeol gwaje [The recent realities and problems of child abuse]. *Social Development and Policy Research, 20,* 113–195.

National Institute of Population and Social Security Research (2006). *Daigo-kai setai doukou chosa* [Fifth survey of household dynamics in Japan]. Retrieved from http://www.ipss.go.jp/.

National Police Agency Juvenile Division (2006). *Shonen hikou no gaiyou.* [Situation of juvenile Delinquency in Japan in 2005]. National Police Agency. Retrieved from http://www.npa.go.jp/safetylife/syonen30/20060805.pdf.

Nguyen, G. K. (1995). Di tim nhung quan he moi giua xa hoi va gia dinh [In research of new relations between society and family]. In T. Le (Ed.), *Gia dinh Viet Nam ngay nay* [Vietnam today's family]. Hanoi, Vietnam: Social Sciences Publishing House.

Nguyen, L. H. (2000). Anh huong cua gia dinh toi hanh vi vi pham phap luat cua tre em vi thanh nien [Influence of family on law violated behaviors of minors]. *Psychology, 6,* 39–42.

Nguyen, T. X. (1994). The Vietnamese family moral code. In *Vietnamese Studies in a Multicultural World.* Melbourne, Australia: Vietnamese Language and Culture Publications.

Nippon Hoso Kyokai (1991). *Gendai shogakusei no seikatu to ishiki* [Life and opinion of modern elementary school children]. Tokyo: Meiji Tosho.

Oudenhoven, N. V., and Nhom Chan Troi Moi [New Horizons Group]. (1999). *Prospect for Vietnam's rural children: A Study on early children care. The voice of major stakeholders.* Hanoi, Vietnam: United Nations Children's Fund.

Park, N. (2005). Life satisfaction among Korean children and youth: A developmental perspective. *School Psychology International, 26,* 209–223.

Park, S.-Y., and Cheah, C. S. L. (2005). Korean mothers' proactive socialization beliefs regarding preschoolers' social skills. *International Journal of Behavioral Development, 29*, 24–34.

Park, Y. S., and Kim, E. C. (2003). Hanguk cheongsonyeon ui seongchwi e daehan bumo janyeo gwangye ui yeonghyang [The influence of parent-child relationship on achievement motivation, and academic achievement among Korean adolescents: Indigenous psychological analysis]. *Korean Journal of Youth Studies, 10*, 139–165.

Park, Y. S., and Kim, E. C. (2004). *Hangukin ui bumo janyeo gwangye* [The relationship between parents-child in Korea]. Seoul, South Korea: Kyo Yook-Books.

Park, Y. S., Kim. E. C., and Tak, S. Y. (2002). Imf sidae ihu Hanguk haktaeng gwa seongi ui seonggong e daehanuisik [The effect of economic crisis on success attribution among Korean students and adults: An indigenous psychological analysis]. *Korean Journal of Psychological and Social Issues, 8*, 103–139.

Park, Y. S., Kim, M. U., Kim, E. C., You, H. C., and Lee, G. U. (2000). Cheongsonyeon, seongin, noin sedae ui chai wa saenghwal manjokdo [Intergenerational differences and life satisfaction: Comparative analysis of adolescents, adults, and the elderly]. *Korean Journal of Health Psychology, 5*, 119–145.

Park, Y. S., and Kim, U. C. (2002). Hanguk sahoe ui gyoyukjeok seongchwi: Hyeonsang gwa simrijeok giban [The nature of educational achievement in Korea: Psychological, indigenous, and cultural perspectives]. *The Korean Journal of Educational Psychology, 16*, 325–351.

Peak, L. (1991). *Learning to go to school in Japan*. Berkeley, CA: University California Press.

Pong, S.-L. (1994). Sex preference and fertility in Peninsular Malaysia. *Studies in Family Planning, 25*, 137.

Russell, J. D., Pham, M. H. Pham, T. N., and Ong, T. N. N. (2002). Social relations and social capital in Vietnam: WVS 2001. *Nghien cuu con nguoi (Human Studies), 2*.

Sakamoto, A. (2005). Video games and the psychological development of Japanese children. In D. W. Shwalb, J. Nakazawa, and B. J. Shwalb (Eds.), *Applied developmental psychology: Theory, practice, and research from Japan* (pp. 3–21). Charlotte, NC: Information Age.

Save the Children Sweden, Plan, and United Nations Children's Fund. (2006). *Educating or abusing? Physical and emotional punishment of children in Vietnam*. Hanoi, Vietnam: Author.

Shin, U. J. (2002). *Jogi gyoyuk gwa baldal byeongrijeok munje. Hanguk jogi gyoyuk ui hyeonhwang gwa gwaje* [Early education and developmental pathology: Problems and realities of Korean early education]. Paper presented at the Autumn Congress of Korean Association of Child Studies, Seoul, Korea, 29–42.

Shoji, J. (2005). Child abuse in Japan. In D. W. Shwalb, J. Nakazawa, and B. J. Shwalb (Eds.), *Applied developmental psychology: Theory, practice, and research from Japan* (pp. 261–279). Charlotte, NC: Information Age.

Shwalb, D. W., Nakazawa, J., and Shwalb, B. J. (Eds.). (2005). *Applied developmental psychology: Theory, practice, and research from Japan*. Charlotte, NC: Information Age.

Shwalb, D. W., Nakazawa, J., Yamamoto, T., and Hyun, J.-H. (in press). Fathering in Japanese, Chinese, and Korean cultures: Changing images and reality. In M. E. Lamb (Ed.), *The role of the father in child development* (5th ed., pp. 146–181). Hoboken, NJ: John Wiley and Sons.

Shwalb, D. W., and Shwalb, B. J. (Eds.). (1996). *Japanese childrearing: Two generations of scholarship*. New York: Guilford.

Shwalb, D., Sugie, S., and Yang, C. (2005). Motivation for abacus studies and school mathematics: A longitudinal study of Japanese 3rd-6th graders. In D. W. Shwalb, J. Nakazawa, and B. J. Shwalb (Eds.), *Applied developmental psychology: Theory, practice, and research from Japan* (pp. 109–135). Charlotte, NC: Information Age.

Soekanto, S. (1990). *Sosiologi: Suatu pengantar* [Sociology: An introduction]. Jakarta, Indonesia: Raja Grafindo Persada.

Sugawara, M. (2005). Maternal employment and child development in Japan. In D. W. Shwalb, J. Nakazawa, and B. J. Shwalb (Eds.), *Applied developmental psychology: Theory, practice, and research from Japan* (pp. 225–240). Charlotte, NC: Information Age.

Sugie, S., Shwalb, D. W., and Shwalb, B. J. (2006). Respect in Japanese childhood, adolescence, and society. *New Directions for Child and Adolescent Development, 114*, 39–52.

Sumida, M. (1995). *Kodomono nakamashudan no kenkyu* [Children's peer groups]. Fukuoka, Japan: Kyushu University Press.

Takahashi, K. (1990). Are the key assumptions of the "Strange Situation" procedure universal? A view from Japanese research. *Human Development, 33*, 23–30.

Te, H.D. (1962). Vietnamese cultural patterns and values as expressed in proverbs. Ph.D. dissertation, Columbia University, New York, NY.

Thang, N. M., and Popkin, B. (2003). Child malnutrition in Vietnam and its transition in an era of economic growth. *Journal of Human Nutritional Dietetics, 16*, 233–244.

Toan, A. (1992). *Phong tuc Viet Nam. Nep cu gia dinh* [Vietnamese custom: Family traditions]. Hanoi, Vietnam: Thanh Nien Publishing House.
Tobin, J., Hsueh, Y., and Karasawa, M. (2009). *Preschool in three cultures revisited: China, Japan, and the United States*. Chicago: University of Chicago Press.
Tran, T. N. (2001). *Tim hieu ban sac van hoa Vietnam* [Discovering the identity of Vietnamese Culture]. Ho Chi Minh City, Vietnam: Ho Chi Minh City Publishing House.
Truong, T. X. (2002). Mot so van de nhan thuc va hanh vi cham soc suc khoe sinh san cua nguoi nong dan vung chau tho song Hong [Issues of reproductive health care awareness and practice of farmers in Red River Delta]. In Mai Quynh Nam (Ed.), *Gia dinh trong tam guong xa hoi hoc* [Family in the sociological mirror]. Hanoi, Vietnam: Social Sciences Publishing.
United Nations Children's Fund (2005). *Report on assessment and analysis of juvenile delinquents and juvenile justice system in Hai Phong*. Hanoi, Vietnam: Author.
United Nations Children's Fund, Ministry of Education and Training, and Population Council (1997). *A narrative study of decision making for health and HIV/AIDS prevention in Vietnamese youth in Kien Giang and Quang Ninh Provinces*. Hanoi, Vietnam: Author.
United Nations Development Programme (1998). *Expanding choices for the rural poor, human development in Vietnam*. Hanoi, Vietnam: Author.
Vu, K. (2002). Gia dinh Viet Nam tren con duong cong nghiep hoa va hien dai hoa [Vietnamese family on the road to industrialization and modernization]. In Mai Quynh Nam (Ed.), *Gia dinh trong tam guong xa hoi hoc* [Family in the sociological mirror]. Hanoi, Vietnam: Social Sciences Publishing House.
Woo, N. H. (2004). Adong ui gwonri wa Hanguk ui jogi gyoyuk [Children's rights and early education in Korea]. *Journal of Korean Council for Children's Rights, 8*, 189–207.
Yang, J. H., and Choi, K. Y. (2005). 5 se ua ui bumo wa hyeongje gwangye e daehan IHae [Young children understanding of parent and sibling relationships]. *The Journal of Korea Open Association for Early Childhood Education, 10*, 365–397.
Yim, D. H., and Janelli, R. L. (2001). Hanguk hyo munhwa ui byeonyong [Transformations of filial piety in Korea]. *Korean Cultural Anthropology, 34*, 3–30.

24
India

T. S. SARASWATHI and RANJANA DUTTA

Introduction

It is a challenge to address development and socialization of "Indian" children and youth in a country that is an intricate mosaic of religions, castes, family types, languages, and many regional variations in cultural practices. Cultural complexity in India is best represented by the kaleidoscope patterns made by 28 states (and 7 union territories); 15 languages (1,652 language groups including dialects), not counting English (Ramanujam, 1994, cited in Chaudhry and Sharma, in press.); four religions (Hinduism, Islam, Christianity, and Sikhism) with several denominations; four traditional social castes (Brahmin, Kshatriya, Vaishnava, and Shudra) with hundreds of culturally and hierarchically distinct subsects within each; four family types (patriarchal and matriarchal, either joint or nuclear) with several variations; and a wide range of socioeconomic classes from the "street urchins" to the "Silicon Valley millionaires" (Verma and Saraswathi, 2002). Add to these variations the North–South divide of India, rural–urban differences, and so forth, and the combinations would slow down a supercomputer!

So what does it mean to be Indian? Does the 15-year-old illiterate mother in rural India or the former Prime Minister of India, Mrs. Indira Gandhi, represent Indians? Are Indians represented by the street urchin peddling drugs in the alleys of Mumbai or by Lakshmi Mittal, the steel king shaking the European steel market? Based on ethnographic work in South India, Trawick (1990, pp. 257–258) warned "we cannot find 'the key' to Indian culture or to any one of its boundless domains, or even to one of its individuals.... It may help if we learn to accept the reality and the power of chaos…the unpredictable, the uncontrollable, the contradictory, the illogical, the unexplainable." If so, should one not make generalizations about the representative Indian?

Or could one focus on the commonality that allows the world to perceive Indians as distinct from the Chinese and Japanese in the East and the Arabs or the Europeans in the West? This commonality may seem elusive, but it arises from shared history and cultural evolution over 5,000 years. Roots of this community can be traced by historical analysis of the Indian "chronosystem" as done by Thapar (2004). Going beyond the sterile chronology of historical events, her accounts reveal the "social lived history" of the people of India and evolution of plural local cultural identities in India based on political, intellectual, and economic power differentials. Her descriptions provide a rare view into the dynamic and complex nature of cultural change. Historical events often have uneven impact in large heterogeneous societies and further accentuate diversity. This is witnessed by the uneven impact of technological globalization in India. For example, the Indian information technology revolution has created a tremor in the United States as a result of transfer of Business Product Outsourcing (BPO), yet Indian census reveals massive illiteracy. The best Indian schools are world beacons in technology, yet universal primary education remains a distant dream. However, the power of historical events in producing shared culture and cohort effects cannot be ignored or undermined. Just as a poorly clad uneducated street vendor can surprise us by pulling out a cell phone to do business, we continue to be charmed by the cultural commonalities that show up among the diverse groups of Indians. Lastly, as developmental scientists, we recognize the role of national policies in shaping developmental outcomes.

Given the scope of this chapter, we aim to provide an overview of the socialization of children and adolescents in the common and pervasive Indian cultural context. Our goal is to give an insight into the dynamics of the developmental context by reporting key studies to highlight the state of developmental science research and application. We do this by setting the stage with a brief demographic profile of India followed by a section on the central issues that plague the emergence of developmental sciences in India as a robust discipline. Some of the key research studies in infancy, childhood, and adolescence are reviewed next, after which, a brief section provides insight into intervention programs and issues pertinent to applied developmental science in India. The chapter concludes with a few pointers for future directions and concluding comments on the contributions that developmental sciences in India can make to the understanding of cultural universalities and specificities, with further refinement in perspectives on theory and research. Given space limitations, this chapter is not meant to be a comprehensive review, and we urge the reader to peruse other sources of developmental research in India (Pandey, 2000, 2001, 2004; Saraswathi, 1999).

Demographic Considerations in Indian Youth Development

India is the second most populous country in the world. The current population is 1,103.4 million, and the growth rate is 1.6% per year (United Nations Statistical Yearbook, 2005). Currently, 30.8% of the population is less than 15 years old, and 7.5% is over 60 years old (U.S. Central Intelligence Agency, 2006). This pyramid structure of population holds promise of high domestic productivity, provided the nation invests in health and education of the young.

India, although late in initiating fertility control (Fussell and Greene, 2002, Table 2.1, pp. 23–24), has shown a decline in fertility (from average birth rate of 33.9 in 1981 to 22.0 in 2006; U.S. Central Intelligence Agency, 2006). Adolescent marriages and fertility rates are high despite legal sanctions on early marriage and aggressive family planning programs. Nearly 70% of the population is rural, although urban migration has steadily increased (United Nations Development Programme [UNDP], 2005).

There has been a marked decrease in infant mortality rate from 96 per 1,000 live births in 1991 to 55 per 1,000 in 2006, but the rate is still higher than most countries (UNDP, 2005). Unsafe drinking water and poor environmental sanitation contribute to morbidity and mortality and are preventable. The nationwide network of Primary Health Centers has had a positive impact on disease prevention despite economic constraints.

Despite the increase in school enrollment, India has the largest concentration of children and adolescents not enrolled in school and the largest numbers of nonliterate adults between the ages of 15 and 35 (De and Dreze, 1999; UNDP, 2005). Gender disparities are marked in both literacy rates and school completion rates, and adult literacy (over 15 years old) is 70% for males and 48% for females. Although the open economy of the 1990s has expanded employment opportunities for educated youth, there are few opportunities for youth with little skill or training. Child labor continues to be a controversial issue, as is the widening gap in wealth distribution (despite an overall positive Gini Index; Fussell and Green, 2002, Table 2.2, pp. 45–46) and inequity in distribution of household income favoring male children.

In sum, India's demographic profile presents optimism regarding the potential of a youthful population. However, despite considerable progress, there are concerns about falling short on the promises of health and education for all by the year 2010.

Central Issues in Studying Indian Youth

Much of the research on human development in India has been plagued by inappropriate transplanting of the European American theories and methods of social science disciplines like psychology (Sinha, 1986, 1997). For example, psychology, which purports to understand, explain, and predict human development in its cultural context, has been practiced in India with Western cultural constructs, language, and metaphors alien to the Indian ecology (Saraswathi, 1999). Western training received by Indian scholars and the adoption of English as the medium of instruction in Indian universities (Saraswathi, 1999; Saraswathi and Dutta, 1988a) have been impediments in the revival of indigenous constructs expounded in Indian philosophical and intellectual traditions written in Sanskrit, Hindi, Tamil, and other languages, which better explain behaviors and emotions in the Indian context. A number of these constructs are not easily translated into English, and a dearth of psychologists fluent in Sanskrit and other Indian languages has led to abandonment of cultural constructs in favor of those "in vogue" in the politics of academic funding, research, and publication. Similarly, the established epistemological methodologies of long hours of introspection and meditation for psychological understanding, holistic synthesis, and pithy conclusions of basic human psychological nature based on observation and self-study in traditional treatises have been replaced by empirical study of "objective" psychology by studying others' behaviors and verbal expositions.

In tracing the history of Indian psychology, Sinha (1986) described four phases: (1) pre-independence (before 1947), when "Indian psychology remained tied to the apron strings of the West" (p. 36); (2) early post-independence (1947–1960), when Western concepts were indiscriminately replicated in India in an effort to standardize many Western psychometric measures on Indian samples; (3) late post-independent phase (1960–1970), when Indian psychologists shifted to research on real issues and problems in the social, political, and economic realities in India; and (4) an indigenization phase (1970–present), wherein psychologists delve into Indian theories and models to study Indian psychology in an attempt to forge a new identity. As a result, psychology today reflects vestiges of all of the last three phases, although the last is becoming dominant, especially in developmental, social, and clinical psychology (Sinha, 1986, 1997).

On a methodological front, Indian psychologists historically leaned on and adopted Western tools and techniques, many of which were inappropriate for the largely illiterate rural population of India (Mohanty and Prakash, 1993; Saraswathi and Dutta, 1988a). More recently, the tide is shifting to using indigenously developed measures and qualitative methods.

External generalizability of studies conducted in India continues to be a cause for concern. Psychology in India is still predominantly the study of the privileged few (Kaur, 1993). Typically, participants are urban, upper-middle class, school- or college-going children and youth who represent approximately 40% of the population. The remaining 60%, who constitute the less privileged (rural, poor, tribal, nonschooled), seldom form participants for study. In some ways, this situation is no different from that seen worldwide where poor, non–English-speaking, homeless, and traditional communities are underrepresented in psychological research. From another perspective, the latter segment constitutes the majority and may be more representative of "untarnished Indian-ness" because it is less affected by Western cultural influences (through the Western model of education, recreation, and travel). Aware of this shortcoming, academic programs in developmental sciences have shifted their emphasis to community participation to enhance students' exposure to the masses. The resultant outcome is new research addressing questions with wider relevance, including issues of the nonprivileged urban and rural children and youth.

There are other deterrents to rich contribution of Indian psychology, such as limited sustained funding and recognition of its value by the state (Kaur, 1993). Unlike the physical and natural sciences, which enjoy tremendous patronage from the state, basic research in the social sciences, particularly psychology, suffers from both inadequate and unsustained funding. As a result, there is lack of concerted effort on the part of scholars to work systematically in a select area over a period of time to build a sound knowledge and database. Applied research is considered more relevant in developing countries like India with many unrelenting ground-level problems in need of urgent solutions. Unfortunately, such research tends to be driven more by passion than by sound research design and theoretical conceptualization, resulting in limited generalizability and policy development.

In sum, the central issues of the study of human development in India are: (1) revival of indigenous constructs in a way so they make contribution to the field of psychology; (2) operationalization of these constructs in culturally appropriate measures; and (3) research on socially relevant topics and methodological studies using multiple methods to build a body of knowledge in the field of human development, such that there is a dynamic exchange between Western and Indian psychology and developmental science at large.

Theory in Indian Developmental Science

The dominant tendency in all branches of psychology has been to test the applicability of Western theories to the Indian situation rather than to evolve indigenous theories. In this section, we summarize select contributions of relevance to the field of developmental psychology made by Indian scholars.

The contributions of Kakar (1979, 1982) deserve special attention because his work drew from the Indian philosophical tradition, heritage, and folklore. "Adopting a largely psychoanalytic and Eriksonian stance.... But keeping within the realm of Indian cultural heritage, Kakar (1979) describes the interplay between the universal processes of development and the specific forces of Indian social reality surrounding the growing child, such as the religious ideals, historical traditions, and social institutions that are unique to the Indian scene" (Sinha, 1997, p. 149). Kakar's work in the area of clinical psychology is also noteworthy and has relevance for human development in the cultural context. In India, many folk healing traditions exist, and all involve participation by the family and relatives along with the affected individual in the healing process and are usually associated with elaborate religious rituals often in the temple premises. In contrast to the individualized therapy in the West, these indigenous practices emphasize "...that faith and surrender to the power beyond the individual are better than individual effort and struggle, that the source of human strength lies in a harmonious integration with one's group, in the individual's affirmation of the community's values and its given order, in his obedience to the community's goods and his cherishing of its traditions" (Kakar, 1982, p. 88).

Kakar's theme of "interdependence" reverberated in the area of organizational management. Sinha (1980) argued that management styles such as "nurturant task leadership" work better in Indian organizational settings because they resemble the prevalent family relationships in India, especially the perceived role of the father. "It suggests an indigenous style of management in which the leader cares for the subordinates, shows affection, takes personal interest in their well-being, and above all is committed to their growth" (Sinha, 1997, p. 156). This kind of leadership is characteristic of authoritarian yet caring and affectionate family relationships seen in most Indian families. Hence, it is seen as more appropriate than the participatory style of Western management that emphasizes individual initiative and independence. Indian employees need to be resocialized for adopting the latter style practiced in most multinational corporate companies.

Finally, work in the area of self (Paranjpe, 1987; Saraswathi, 2005) and, most significantly, D. Sinha's lifetime contributions to raising awareness of cultural and context specificity in human development need special mention. Besides the development of indigenous theories in the coming years, the meaningful utilization of Vygotskian and other sociocultural theories to interpret human development in India may pay even richer dividends in the light of community practices that will help account for both similarities and variations observed within the Indian subcontinent.

Key Substantive Contributions in Indian Psychology

Infancy and Early Childhood

In this section, we address the context in which children are born and develop during infancy and early childhood (0 to 5 years). Vedic philosophical tradition demarcated the first phase of life (Brahmacharya) from childhood to youth (before marriage), during which the main developmental task was education. Initiation of this phase occurred around 5 years of age, before which there are no prescribed tasks.

Even today, children are considered God's gift, and people look forward to starting a family. The procreative function of marriage is more salient than actualization of a romantic self. The concept of not wanting to have children is quite alien, and inability to have children, termed barrenness, is negatively perceived. The number of live children per woman/family has decreased from five or six two generations ago to less than three in recent years (U.S. Central Intelligence Agency, 2006) thanks to interventions designed for family planning. Pregnancy announcement (especially the first) calls for celebration and becomes an extended family affair. There are elaborate rituals and ceremonies during the second and third trimesters of the first pregnancy. Pregnancy may perhaps be the only time when most women (even in the lowest socioeconomic classes) enjoy the privilege of being treated with care and consideration (Saraswathi and Pai, 1997).

Traditionally, women spent 4 to 6 months in their parents' home, from the third trimester to 40 days after childbirth. This way they got care and rest to prepare for childbirth. Indirectly, this arrangement also facilitated child spacing as a result of postpartum taboos and breast feeding. With increase in women's employment, the mother or mother-in-law provides extensive support to the expectant parents. Special foods are prepared to enrich maternal nutrition and later for lactation. The pregnant mother is indulged by extended family, visiting kin, and neighbors, as food cravings are believed to be the unborn baby's desires.

After birth, the mother and newborn were traditionally quarantined to a separate room and rested for 40 days. Except for one prime caregiver, nobody (not even the spouse) was allowed to touch the mother and child during that time. The confinement prevented exposure of mother and infant to infections in addition to providing recovery from the stress of childbirth. The mother or mother-in-law assisted the new mother in caring for the baby and encouraged and supported breast feeding. Issues with breast feeding or lactation rarely surfaced. Postpartum depression has been a culturally alien concept until recent times. With women's workforce participation, the strictness of taboos associated with the 40-day confinement has been relaxed in most urban areas.

Preference for a male child cuts across all social classes (Dube, 1988; Shah, 2005). It is believed that sons continue the family name, contribute to family income, take care of aging parents, and above all, enable the release of the parents' soul. Ironically, in practice, it is often daughters who take care of elderly parents as a result of male emigration for work and because parents are more comfortable with their daughters than daughters-in-law! This marked preference for the male child is of grave concern because of gender inequity in distribution of household income and because it leads to amniocentesis, feticide, and infanticide in some regions of the country (Agnihotri, 2003; Griffiths, Hinde, and Mathews, 2001).

In conditions of extreme poverty, the picture is rather dismal, and the women can well be described as poor, pregnant, and powerless with little or no support. Despite the wide network of Primary Health Centers and the nationwide Integrated Child Development Services (ICDS; integrating nutritional, educational, prenatal, and neonatal services), women in this group are severely malnourished and suffer from deficiencies like anemia (United Nations Children's Fund [UNICEF], 2006). Less than 50% of the births occur in presence of trained personnel (UNDP, 2005), and approximately 30% of babies are of low birth weight (UNDP, 2005). Marked variations in childcare practices prevail as a correlate of low socioeconomic status, such as high infant mortality, caregivers other than mother, community involvement, and multiparty care rather than dyadic interactions. With 25% of the Indian population below poverty line (U.S. Central Intelligence Agency, 2006), this situation may not be alleviated soon.

Landers (1989) showed that infants with low birth weights catch up with appropriate family and public health intervention in the early months. Landers' study followed 30 term Indian babies in Kerela from birth to 3 months and showed a dramatic increase in birth weight with no additional intervention other than mothers' breast feeding on demand. Landers argued that the inherent biologic capacity or catch-up growth is augmented by maternal proximity and demand feeding. In extremely dire circumstances, the outcome is likely to be less encouraging.

The interdependent nature of the Indian social setting is reflected in its ethnotheories and childcare practices (Abels et al., 2005; Keller et al., 2005; Sharma, 2003; Sharma and LeVine, 1998). Almost 50% of households are characterized as joint or extended (D'Cruz and Bharat, 2001). Childcare is typically the joint responsibility of several caregivers including older siblings. However, the mother remains the primary caregiver especially during the first year of the infant's life. In fact, "The Indian mother's psychosocial commitment to her child emerges out of an extended family system which instructs, rewards, and supports her in these efforts" (Landers, 1989, p. 203). The image of the grandmother with a baby on her lap seated in the central courtyard of the house or a school-age girl playing hop-scotch with an infant/toddler on her hip is very real and contemporary.

Working mothers in urban areas prefer to employ in-home childcare providers. Daycares are sought only in situations when no grandparent or family member can assist. The quality of care offered by most daycare centers and crèches is suspect because there is no government regulation (Datta, 1995; Sriram, 1994). There has been, however, a rise in the number of private, good quality daycare centers in areas with professional working women. The father's role is also undergoing change in urban working-class families. Childcare traditionally was regarded as a woman's job (Ramu, 1987), but fathers are beginning to take a more active part. Roopnarine and Suppal (2003) noted that Indian fathers as well as other adult male members observed in studies by Saraswathi and her associates (Saraswathi, 1994) engaged in childcare and are capable of cuing into infants' signals and responding appropriately.

Until 5 or 6 years of age, children are indulged (Kakar, 1979; Saraswathi and Dutta, 1988b) not only by the mothers and immediate family members, but also by neighbors and visiting kin. Breast feeding lasts for 10 to 12 months or longer in rural areas. Infants co-sleep with the mother initially and then share a bed and later a room with siblings. Toilet training is relaxed, although started and completed earlier than in the United States. Seymour (1976, 1999) observed that Indian children are not usually pushed to do things on their own at an early age. Parental ethnotheories support the idea of early indulgence (Keller et al., 2005; Saraswathi and Ganapathy, 2002) and foster interdependence. Several ethnographic studies based on small samples in different regions of India (Abels et al., 2005; Keller et al., 2005; Landers, 1989; Seymour, 1976) acknowledged the paucity of maternal vocalizations and eye-to-eye contact directed toward the infants. Yet cultural practices in general, particularly in nonpoverty settings, highlight the rich fund of region-specific lullabies, rhymes, and games that foster tactile and kinesthetic stimulation of the infant through dyadic or multigroup interactions with the mother and extended family members.

Indian infants are clearly precocious in motor development compared to Western babies. Though somewhat dated (Landers, 1989; Phatak, 1970; Werner, 1972), this finding deserves mention because of the consistency of results from cross-sectional and longitudinal studies of rural and urban infants from the lower and upper classes. Genetic, climatic, and cultural factors may account for the accelerated development. These include small body size (hence greater mobility), less restrictive clothing, freedom to move on firm ground, stimulation through oil massage, and so forth. This earlier advantage is counterbalanced often by a decline in motor performance when compared with Western babies after the 10th month (when weaning), and thereafter, Western babies tend to excel both in motor and mental performance on the Bayley Scale of Infant Development. This difference is particularly marked in the lower classes, where supplementary foods are nutritionally inadequate and the presence of poor environmental sanitation leads to infection and morbidity (Werner, 1972).

In sum, children are valued and cherished by the family and society. Women's status is raised by motherhood, and families and society make an effort to accommodate children's needs. Traditionally, children less than 5 years old are likened to flowers in a garden and nurtured with affection with not many cognitive, affective, or social demands. Siblings assist considerably with childcare and socializing infants. To some degree, this psychological advantage can offset physical and material disadvantages of limited resources.

Childhood

Three major social contexts that dominate life experiences during Indian childhood from 5 to 12 years of age are described in this section. These are family relationships and parenting styles, education and schooling, and child labor.

Family Relationships and Parenting Styles   The vast majority of households, especially in rural India (70% of population is rural), are multigenerational or housing extended family members (UNDP, 2005). Urbanization is characterized by more nuclear family units, but they too typically maintain close ties with the extended family. Parenting processes and parent–child relationships can be more complex in such a context than typically encountered in Western studies. Age and seniority in family hierarchy are important features of family structure affecting the process of decision making for all major events. Even in modern nuclear units, advice is solicited from senior family members, and when given unasked, it is seen not as invasion into personal privacy but as reflecting "jointness" and concern (Saraswathi and Pai, 1997). Questions of parenting theories, control, involvement, and disciplinary practices thus need to be articulated with respect to family structure because presence of other family members modifies parenting processes and impact.

In general, children are socialized to respect parents and elders. Parental involvement and control of all aspects of children's lives is very high, especially among the educated middle-class families. Parents set high career aspirations for their children and become active participants in their children's achievements often at great personal sacrifice in terms of money and time. This type of strict parental control in childhood and then adolescence, combined with a high degree of parental responsiveness and closeness, is called a "traditional parenting style" (Baumrind, 1987). The parenting style outwardly appears authoritarian and controlling but does not carry the same connotations associated with poor parental responsiveness (Baumrind, 1971). Hence, children perceive the control as "care" (and not as imposition of adult "will" as reported in

Western literature). There is greater use of power assertion among the lower classes and more use of induction in the middle and upper classes (Saraswathi and Sundaresan, 1980). Trends of increased education, women's employment, and reduced family size coincide with authoritative parent–child relationships.

Family roles are considered very important (moral duty), and solidarity and interdependence are fostered by rituals and family gatherings. In the patriarchal Indian family, growing up as a girl carries with it the connotation of inferior status and lesser privileges (Dube, 1988; Kakar, 1979). From early childhood, across social classes, girls are encouraged to develop an interdependent and even sacrificial self and prepare for their future roles as wives and mothers (Saraswathi, 1999). In many homes, daughters may be treated with special affection because they are considered as temporary residents who will move to their conjugal homes. The onus of family obligations lies on sons, and they are made aware early in life that they will care for parents in their old age, educate younger siblings if parents are unable to, and support and protect their sisters before and after marriage as needed. Regardless of gender, parental beliefs regarding childrearing reflect the traditional emphases on familism, interdependence, and respect for the elders (Saraswathi and Ganapathy, 2002).

The mother is the primary socializing agent between 5 and 12 years of age as well. The father's role is to provide and discipline (Saraswathi and Pai, 1997). Because older siblings become caregivers to younger ones at an early age and play a nurturing role (Whiting and Edwards, 1988), they also become key attachment figures.

Sibling relationships remain close even in large families. The brother–sister bond has special significance in Indian families. It is ritualistically renewed every year in most parts of India through the observance of a festival where the interdependence of sister to brother and his promise of protection is reaffirmed (see Sinha-Kerkhoff, 2003, for detailed discussion).

Elementary Education Caste, class, location, gender, and religion frame parents' educational expectations and aspirations for their children. The indigenous education system of "gurukula" (residential school with close and nurturing guru–pupil relationship) was based on the oral tradition for boys of upper caste families before it was displaced by the formal education system introduced by the British using English as the "medium" of textbook instruction and mass examination system (Kumar, 1991). The dominance of the privileged middle and upper classes in the educational system has been a result of the perception of English as a language of prestige and power, a legacy that has outlived colonial domination and struggles for language supremacy in a multilingual society (Manjrekar, cited in Verma and Saraswathi, 2002).

Presently, India has the largest school system in the world. In addition, the state has constitutional commitment to universal, free, and compulsory elementary education; however, large numbers of children and adolescents are still not enrolled in school (De and Dreze, 1999; UNDP, 2005). There are marked rural–urban and male–female disparities in school attendance favoring urban and male children. Educational inequalities form a pyramidal structure of relative disadvantage with the rural, tribal, and low-caste girls in the most economically depressed regions (UNDP, 2000, 2005).

Policies of affirmative action to provide incentives to socially and economically disadvantaged groups, including girls, have not alleviated the situation. More than 16% of children enrolled in grade 1 drop out by grade 5 (UNDP, 2005), and 57% drop out by grade 8 (Government of India [GOI]/Ministry of Human Resource Development [MHRD], 1999–2000). Dropout rates are even higher for children from the scheduled castes and tribes (identified by the Indian Constitution as the most deprived and targeted for affirmative action; Nambissan and Sedwal, 2002). The poorest children from the poorer regions drop out the earliest from school. Saraswathi, Manjrekar, and Pant (2003) point out several reasons for dropout, which are home related (low priority given by parents to education, especially for girls), poverty related (earning wages or relieving the mother from earning wages), school related (poor access, unfriendly teachers, and inability to cope with school demands), and systemic (disconnect between education and employment). A model of full-day school is not ecologically suitable for the large majority of parents coping with immediate economic needs.

There are marked regional variations to all of these generalizations. As stated succinctly by Dreze (2003, p. 974, cited in Chaudhry and Sharma, 2006): "India's proverbial diversity applies in particular to literacy and education. On one end of the scale, remaining uneducated is almost unthinkable for a Tamil Brahmin or Bengali Kayastha or Goan Christian; at the other end, literacy rates in 1981 were as low as 2.2 percent among the Musahars of Bihar and 2.5 percent among the Kalbelias of Rajasthan" (and have not changed much since).

During the 1980s and 1990s, several initiatives supported by government and voluntary agencies have addressed the needs of more than 40 million children out of school (Govinda, 2002) through innovative non-formal education programs, which have been successful albeit limited in outreach (see Population Council, 1999, case studies). Elementary education programs currently suffer from insufficient funds, a situation not likely to get better because public expenditure on education has further reduced under policies of economic liberalization (Tilak, 1999). The strains of transition to a market economy are being passed on to children via competitive access to quality education at high cost. Overcoming the colonial legacy of education that is not culturally embedded and that does not have meaning in the daily lives of many children is indeed a Himalayan task.

Child Labor   Child labor is an exploitative version of the historical tradition of apprenticeship for adult roles, especially for boys to learn their father's trade (Dube, 1981). India has the largest number of working children in the world. The 2000 yearbook of the Institute of Applied Manpower Research (2001) estimated that 10 million children between 0 and 14 years old were out of school and working. The actual figures are probably higher because labor in informal family settings or the street economy often remains unremunerated and undercounted. Burra (1995) estimated that children constitute 10% to 33% of total industrial workers.

There are several reasons for the continued prevalence of child labor on the Indian subcontinent. Poverty, urgent need for money to survive, and the failure and disillusion with schools often push parents to make children early wage earners. School dropout, in turn, results in poor future employment prospects and curtailment of upward social mobility (Kanbargi, 1988). Migration of families, broken homes, and parental abuse and abandonment provide additional reasons for children to join the workforce (Fonseka and Malhotra, 1994, cited in Verma and Saraswathi, 2002). Employers often prefer child workers because they are cheap, obedient, and productive (Burra, 1995). Arguments legitimizing child labor, suggesting that children usually work as apprentices, acquire skills for adult employment, and contribute to family income, are used as part of family labor and sustain India's handicraft industries but were not borne out empirically (Burra, 1995). Furthermore, Burra cautioned that devaluation of girls relative to boys is exacerbated by child labor.

Policy makers in the Indian government consider child labor a necessary evil. In addition, the Child Labor Prohibition and Regulation Act (GOI, 1986) does not completely ban child labor, but only seeks to "protect" working children from exploitation. The National Policy for Education (GOI, 1986) supported the continuation of nonformal education for child workers who cannot be enrolled in schools but need education. The policy was amended in 1996 with clarifications for protection from hazardous occupations and bonded labor. In 2006, there was a resurgence of interest in implementing the policy banning child labor, causing much furor in public debates and disruption in the lives of working children. The ban is a catch 22 situation and a mixed blessing for those concerned.

Some of the remedial measures undertaken by states and nongovernment organization to improve the lives of working children include provision of nonformal education, supplementary nutrition, basic health care, recreational services, monitoring and regulation of work conditions, provision of on-the-job training and safety measures, and provision of social intervention in family and community settings (Fonseka and Malhotra, 1994, cited in Verma and Saraswathi, 2002). There will be no easy solutions to the problem of child labor in India until there is overall improvement in socioeconomic conditions and quality of life.

Adolescence and Youth

The differential socialization based on gender and social class becomes more distinct in adolescence. Variations in the timing of puberty, ultimate body size, and most significantly, the educational and career trajectories available and chosen are governed by gender and class (Saraswathi, 1999). In this section, we address three topics of central importance to the lives of Indian adolescents. These are mate selection and sexuality, education, and employment. Information on other topics such as adolescent peer relations, substance abuse, and community participation may be gleaned from Verma and Saraswathi (2002).

Mate Selection and Sexuality   Traditionally, Indian marriages were "arranged" by family elders after scrutinizing family background, assessing compatibility of family values, and examining physical appearance and chastity of women and economic potential of men (Buss et al., 1990). Marriage was and continues to be viewed with a biological perspective as "sowing the seeds of a thousand years." Today, the mate selection process has many variants in addition to the traditionally arranged process where youth may have a greater voice in this decision. Romantic love and self-selection take a back seat, and parents' choice is considered appropriate and preferred by many (Phathak, 1994; Uplaonkar, 1995, cited in Verma and Saraswathi, 2002), and even those who select their own mate will typically do so with family approval and blessings.

Studies show that in urban areas, premarital sex among adolescents is on the rise. Statistics on premarital sexual activity vary by region and gender. Twenty to thirty percent of all unmarried males (17 to 24 years) are reported as sexually active (Goparaju, 1993, cited in Verma and Saraswathi, 2002; Sharma and Sharma, 1995). Self-report figures for females are much lower at 6% to 9% (Bhende, 1994, and Savara and Sridhar, 1994, cited in Verma and Saraswathi, 2002). An exceptionally high incidence of 40% is reported in the case of tribal girls in one unique study by Bang et al. (1989) who used direct clinical examination of all adolescent girls (not self-reports as is usually done) in the tribal belt of Maharashtra. Males are less critical of premarital sexual activity for themselves, have more opportunities, and engage in premarital sex more frequently, while disapproving of girls' freedom to engage in sexual activity (Bhende, 1994, cited in Verma and Saraswathi, 2002; Jejeebhoy, 1996). Females echo the double standard.

Use of contraceptives and accurate information of their use are minimal among the sexually active (Sharma and Sharma, 1995) as well as the general population of youth (Deb, 2005; Tikoo, Bollman, and Bergen, 1995). Increase in sexual activity, clinical abortions in unmarried adolescents, and prevalence of sexually transmitted diseases and human immunodeficiency virus (HIV)/acquired immunodeficiency syndrome (AIDS) point to the pitfalls of parent and teacher reluctance to talk freely about sex (Deb, 2005).

Post-Elementary Education   The 1998 to 1999 National Family Health Survey (International Institute of Population Sciences and ORC Macro, 2000) revealed that only 18% of children completed middle school and only 9% complete high school, which shows a further drop from the 29%

who completed primary school. Social discrimination and economic deprivation translate into low participation of the lower caste and tribal youth in schooling (Nambissan and Sedwal, 2002).

University education, which caters to the age group of 18 to 24+ years, is highly subsidized by the government. Only 5% of high school graduates opt for vocational courses (Tilak, 1999), even while thousands of commerce and arts graduates join the ranks of the educated unemployed every year (Visaria, 1998). Since the 1980s, privatization of higher education, especially for professional courses, has steadily increased, benefiting the economically and socially advantaged.

Gender and other social disparities continue in higher education as well. Women make up to 24% to 50% of class enrollment on average, but numbers in the sciences and engineering are small (33% in the sciences and 7% in engineering; Karlekar, 2000). In contrast, women make up more than 50% of students in education and psychology. The positive effect of affirmative action is seen in the case of male students from scheduled castes and tribes but less so in the case of female students from these subgroups (Chanana, 2000). (Scheduled castes and tribes are identified by the Indian Constitution as the most deprived and targeted for affirmative action.)

Employment   Child labor issues discussed earlier translate to employment issues in the late teens. Besides the 10 million children categorized as child laborers (Institute of Applied Manpower Research, 2001), there are an estimated additional 11 million street children and youth in urban slums who fend for themselves (Phillips, 1992) and do not figure in the labor statistics. UNICEF studies across major Indian cities reveal that street youth come from households chronically ailing from unemployment, criminality, family discord, health crises, and alcoholism. The situation often leads to engagement in antisocial activities by the youth (Institute of Psychological and Educational Research, 1991). They resort to rag picking, begging, shoe shining, and vending. Harassed by street thugs and policemen, they resort to thieving, drug peddling, and pimping (Panikar and Nangia, 1992, cited in Verma and Saraswathi, 2002). Adolescent girls are typically more protected by families but, in dire situations, run away from home and are lured or forced into prostitution.

By contrast, the employment outlook is far more optimistic for adolescents and youth from the educated middle classes. Many factors contribute to this difference in opportunity structure. Here, parents value education as a means for upward mobility and make enormous personal sacrifices to educate their children, especially boys. There is greater awareness of resources such as educational loans and school scholarships. Furthermore, the ethos of literacy in these homes contributes to supervision, support, and modeling.

The higher educational environment is very competitive. Adolescents from the lower-middle class opt for vocational training after school (boys train as mechanics, electricians, plumbers, carpenters, and similar skilled occupations; girls train as paraprofessionals in health and education, seamstresses, beauticians, and recently, as computer programmers or retail agents). Entry is less competitive for a college degree in arts and commerce, preparing them for white-collar jobs as accountants, clerks, or sales persons. The upper-middle class and upper class youth compete for professional degrees such as in medicine, engineering, computer sciences, finance, and management offered by prestigious institutions, with a back up of second-tier quality institutions. Seats are limited and competition is stiff, and so preparation begins early with supports such as after-school tutors and private programs. The highest quality institutions prepare Indian youth for lucrative jobs in national and multinational corporations or qualify them for admissions in universities abroad opening up worldwide opportunities. The odds of advancement in education and employment favor the upper castes.

Applied Human Development

In this section, we outline a few exemplars of the major large-scale intervention programs designed to facilitate development by way of health and educational services. Even a brief description or review of the major programs would take up more space than provided for this chapter; hence, we only highlight a few with the intention to give a sense of the scale of these interventions and provide insight into challenges of applied developmental science in India rather than to describe or review them. The interested reader may refer to publications listed in the Websites of the National Institute of Public Corporation and Child Development (NIPPCD), Population Council, and the Voluntary Health Association of India (VHAI).

India has an estimated 1.2 million nongovernment organizations (NGOs) initiating programs to improve the lives of children and youth (PRIA, 2002). Each initiative has a different focus and targets different potentials for growth. The quality of the programs also ranges widely. India's large and diverse population poses a serious challenge to outreach services for the community. No single strategy or effort can serve all.

The Integrated Child Development Scheme (ICDS), initiated by the government since mid-1970s, is one of the world's largest ongoing early child development programs. It aims at addressing the needs of children younger than 6 years, especially from the disadvantaged sectors of the population. Services are delivered through "Anganwadis," which are village-based centers. In 2004, there were 6,500 blocks (1 block = 100 centers; each center serves 1,000 people) serving 650 million people. The target is to have 100% coverage by 2007 (GOI/MHRD, 2004–2005). This program supports holistic development of children and provides many services such as health, nutrition, and education by way of regular health checkups and referrals, immunization, growth monitoring, and treatment for children and antenatal and postnatal checkups for women. An additional component focusing on adolescent girls' nutrition, health awareness, and skill development was added in the year 2000. Reviews indicate that the program has successfully reduced malnutrition and increased enrollment in schools (UNICEF, 2004).

In response to maternal and fetal undernutrition, an additional multisectoral National Nutrition program for mothers and young children was initiated in 1993. It aimed to reduce undernutrition and deficiency disorders. The National Immunization program against polio, measles, tuberculosis, diphtheria, and tetanus has contributed to a decrease in the incidence of preventable diseases (GOI/Ministry of Women and Child Development, 2005; UNICEF, 2006).

Besides these massive nationwide programs, several community-based programs have innovatively addressed local maternal and child health needs in disadvantaged, small, rural, and remote communities, thus reducing infant, child, and maternal mortality. These interventions address health, education, and child labor in poverty contexts (see the interesting series of case studies by Ford Foundation, India and the Voluntary Health Association of India, 1980–current).

In keeping with India's mission to achieve free and compulsory elementary education by 2015, several interventions target formal education such as Sarva Shikshan Abhiyan (Education for All), District Primary Education Program, and Operation Black Board. To specifically target young girls' development, an innovative strategy is used by the Mahila Samakhya Program. With the belief that young girls will benefit most when they have educated, enlightened, and empowered mothers as role models, this programs operates via women's groups called Mahila Sanghas, where women are provide educational and economic skills and support. This program is currently implemented in more than 10 states, covering more than 9,000 villages (Government of India, 1997).

The needs of youth are addressed by the Ministry for Health and Family Welfare and the Department of Youth Affairs and Sports. The focus of their initiatives is youth empowerment achieved by engaging youth in community service (National Service Scheme), offering vocational training via youth clubs (Nehru Yuvak Kendra Sangathan), and fostering interaction, inclusion, and integration of isolated border and tribal youth (Rashtriya Sadbhavana Yojana, National Reconstruction Corps; Government of India, Ministry of Youth Affairs and Sports,

2005). The government has also initiated the Employment Guarantee Scheme (2004–2005) with a focus on rural population. At the local levels in urban slums and rural and tribal districts, several initiatives have generated community-based solutions and integrated the needs of youth in program services. They include training in modern agricultural practices for employment generation; handling social issues such as de-addiction, life skills training, sex education, and HIV/AIDS awareness; and providing a platform for entertainment and sports (Ford Foundation, India, and the Voluntary Health Association of India, 1980–current; UNICEF, 2005) The outreach and effectiveness of delivery of services rest on operational factors such as existence of international pressure, availability of funds and infrastructure, individual leadership and commitment, and knowledge of local cultures and practices on the part of program implementers. In the Indian context, dealing with large numbers and widely disparate geographic, economic, and sociocultural conditions presents the greatest challenge.

Future Trends in Indian Developmental Science

In this section, we outline current trends and potential directions that would make developmental science more meaningful in the Indian context. We base these on trends gleaned in the literature and hopes of anticipated robust contributions by Indian psychologists in the future.

Many social scientists, including developmental psychologists, have called for greater indigenization of psychosocial constructs in future research in India (see Berry, Mishra, and Tripathi, 2003; Pandey, 2004). This can be done by drawing ideas from the complex sociocultural reality of the Indian subcontinent. For example, observational studies on language socialization reveal the complex cognitive strategies children are expected to deploy for effective communication in a multilingual and hierarchically stratified context (see Mohanty's chapter in Berry et al., 2003; and in Pandey, 2000). Saraswathi (see chapter in Berry et al., 2003) provides many insightful developmental questions from the Indian sociocultural reality that can enrich understanding of development in the Indian context.

Ideas could also be drawn from grounded theory and observed cultural practices, folklore, ethnotheories, and philosophies that shape daily lives of Indians. Examining the effects of belief in "selfless karma," temporality of human existence, humility, meditation, and introspection on relevant concepts like perceived control, achievement motivation, tolerance, self-regulation, and attention would be examples of this approach. Similar questions have been addressed by Shweder (2003) regarding cultural meanings of sleeping patterns in a traditional Hindu setting; by Menon and Shweder (1994) on the meaning of emotions in different Indian contexts; by Miller (1981) on regional differences in the status of women and female infants based on ethnographic records and Indian census data; and by Stork (1980) on cultural significance of preference for the male child from original Sanskrit scriptures. Misra (see chapter in Berry et al., 2003) articulates 14 salient features from diverse but shared philosophical traditions that describe Indians. Empirical inquiry using such descriptions would enrich Indian developmental science as well as cross-cultural psychology.

The extant diversity in India has also been used by developmental researchers in innovative ways. Brouwers, Mishra, and van de Vijver (2006) conducted a naturalistic experiment to disentangle the confounding effects of chronological and educational age and of schooling and socioeconomic status to study the cognitive consequences of schooling, something that is difficult to do in most other developed countries. Lamm and Keller (2007) have studied more than one community within India to examine intracultural variation in socialization goals and response styles vis-à-vis other cultures to elucidate theoretical and methodological factors (response style) affecting parenting. We believe this type of inquiry is just beginning and that such extension of ideas born from local "emic" meanings to derived "etics" and vice versa, when done in ecologically valid ways, will contribute significantly to developmental science worldwide.

A shift to adopting a sociocultural or sociohistorical perspective may also resolve the current malaise of imposed "etic" based on Western models. Discerning regularities in cultural practices may provide a turning point to cultural and cross-cultural developmental psychology. Rogoff (2003) conceptualized cultural practices as the configuration of routine ways of doing things in any community's approach to living. These practices are not piecemeal but make a meaningful configuration across domains and contexts and are linked to the overarching goals of the cultural community. India provides a fertile ground to test this conceptualization. For example, a study of the Brahmin community (historically the highest caste in India) would reveal that their practices of everyday life ritualistically weave in instances of learning, cleanliness, piety, study of religious texts, and appreciation of fine arts and performing arts. Growing up in such a niche is advantageous to children in acquiring academic skills and hence entry into prestigious and intellectual occupations. It may be productive to examine how a set of cultural practices fit together to create alternative pathways in development that provide common grounds to understand Indians rather than the use of diverse social categories and groups. Such an understanding can also guide intervention for change.

Indigenous psychological understanding would help differentiate Indian worldviews not only from the West but also from the Confucian Eastern traditions of countries like Japan, Korea and China. Confucian thought is different from Hindu ideology, and they translate into different child socialization goals for parents and childrearing practices (Rao, McHale, and Pearson, 2003). There are multiple points of departures of socialization in India vis-à-vis these other Eastern nations that are equally important to explore.

Although indigenization of theories and constructs is much discussed, relatively less attention has been paid to methodological issues in doing developmental studies in India. Cultures differ in their self-presentational styles, honesty, acquiescence, and social desirability on self-reports and interviews. Multiple methods to validate the data help, but methodological studies to establish validity of methods specific to the Indian context are also warranted.

These trends and future directions imply a radical change in the existing graduate curriculum in the fields of psychology and human development. Prominence would need to be given to culture-sensitive ideas along with focus on Indian literature, and there would need to be greater emphasis on cross-cultural rather than mainstream Euro-American psychology and greater weight to field placements to sensitize students from educated urban backgrounds to the wider Indian reality. Such changes in program would also likely result in more meaningful and positive collaborative research with non-Indian researchers. In fact, such changes are likely to increase the accountability and survival of the developmental sciences rather than the current restrictive approach of using Indian samples solely for comparisons in multinational studies.

Conclusion

In this chapter, we have provided an overview of socialization of Indian children and adolescents within their historical and current sociocultural milieu, giving an unfamiliar reader a sketch of the state of developmental science in India and the special challenges it faces. With roots in an ancient and highly evolved and stratified social structure, a long history of invasions and colonization, and a relatively short 60 years since independence, India provides a rare, dynamic, and rich cultural landscape of several pluralistic subcultures within which socialization of Indian youth takes place. Developmental scientists grapple with its diversity and large populous while working with other social scientists to develop national, political, economic, and educational policies that would facilitate development in each of the subcultures. Amidst much political upheaval, economic and technological change, and tight budgets, they struggle to prioritize issues of survival (physical growth, nutrition, poverty, education, and employment) and those of theory and research.

Despite the challenges of size and diversity, all demographic indicators show a steady improvement in quality of life in India. Large-scale intervention programs and applied developmental research have delivered beneficial outcomes, despite meager and inconsistent funds. However, progress is slow, and there is room for improvement when it comes to universal education, eradicating poverty, and providing a good quality of life for all.

The present economic growth has further widened the gap between the "haves" and the "have-nots." Growing up in the lower social classes in contrast to growing up in the middle and upper classes creates two worlds of childhood (and thereafter) with very different outlooks. The middle and upper classes are characterized by higher education, upward mobility in employment, late marriage, low fertility, and low infant mortality and morbidity. Consequently, the focus is on the promotion of overall development. This visible novae riche, educated elite in urban metropolis areas represents only less than half of the Indian population. In this subculture, traditional gender differences in roles have been reduced, and women have become educationally and economically independent. Economic well-being is mirrored by conspicuous consumption contrary to the Indian tradition of simplicity and moderation. Joint families have given way to nuclear units, and as a result, there are changes in number of children, parenting roles, and childrearing practices. Akin to Western families, they are world citizens but pay the price of hectic lifestyles with stress and alienation as a result of lack of time to sustain family and community relations. Development in this group contrasts sharply with that in poverty settings characterized by low prenatal care, poor nutrition, higher infant morbidity and mortality, low education, early entry into the labor market, early marriage, and high fertility. Child survival and health remain the focus of parents and of government policies addressing this stratum

The big hurdle for Indian developmental and social science is to redefine its identity. There is a large chasm between the growing mainstream (Western) knowledge base of developmental science concepts and methods (taught via textbooks and journals) and indigenous concepts and remnant cultural philosophies that guide behavior and are not easily translated in the English language. Lack of sustained funding for large-scale cross-sectional or longitudinal studies further undermines developmental research. As a result, developmental theory articulation in the Indian context is very weak. The task ahead for Indian developmental scientists is to define and empirically document how development in India is different from not only the West but also from the "East" (i.e., Japan, China, and Korea) with which it is often grouped.

While researchers struggle to juxtapose traditional theories and modern notions of development, the populous itself forges ahead, embracing technology and change. Some emulate the West, some heed to tradition and ancient wisdom striving for balance, and some are blind sighted by extant worldviews, but all participate continually in changing cultural communities to strive for survival and personal gain. This is the reality that is easy to grasp but challenging to get in step with to articulate good questions and translate to meaningful research. To the aspiring developmental scientist with a cultural or cross-cultural bend, the Indian sociocultural setting presents a microcosm of rich opportunities to understand development in situ and examine the forces that facilitate, resist, and modify developmental trajectories.

Acknowledgments

We gratefully acknowledge the contribution of Meera Oke to the preparation of the section on applied child development. Our sincere thanks to Jayanthi Mistry, Heidi Keller, Farida Khan, Saun Strobel, and Marc Bornstein who critically read the earlier drafts of the manuscript and offered useful comments both for the present chapter and future work. Access to search facilities and secretarial assistance was made possible by the Primary Education Department at Bogacizi University, Istanbul, during the first author's residence there in summer 2006.

References

Abels, M., Keller, H., Mohite, P., Mankodi, H., Shastri, J., Bhargava, S., et al. (2005). Early socialization contexts and social experiences of infants in rural and urban Gujarat, India. *Journal of Cross-Cultural Psychology, 36*, 717–738.

Agnihotri, S. B. (2003). Survival of the girl child: Tunneling out of the chakravyuha. *Economic and Political Weekly, 41*, 4351–4360.

Bang, R. A., Bang, A. T., Batule, M., Choudhary, Y., Sarmukaddam, S., and Tale, O. (1989). High prevalence of gynecological diseases in rural Indian women. *Lancet, 1*, 85–88.

Baumrind, D. (1971). Current patterns of parental authority. *Developmental Psychology Monograph, 4* (1, Pt 2).

Baumrind, D. (1987). A developmental perspective on adolescent risk-taking behavior in contemporary America. In C. E. Irwin, Jr. (Ed.), *Adolescent social behavior and health (New directions for child development)*. San Francisco: Jossey-Bass.

Berry, J. W., Mishra, R. C., and Tripathi, R. C. (2003). *Psychology in human and social development: Lessons from diverse cultures: A festschrift for Durganard Sinha*. New Delhi, India: Sage Publications.

Brouwers, S. A., Mishra, R. C., and van de Vijver, F. J. R. (2006). Schooling and everyday cognitive development among Kharwar children in India: A natural experiment. *International Journal of Behavioral Development, 30*, 559–567.

Burra, N. (1995). *Born to work: Child labour in India*. Delhi, India: Oxford University Press.

Buss, D. M., Abbott, M., Angleitner, A., Asherian, A., Biaggio, A., Blanco-Villasenor, A., et al. (1990). International preferences in selecting mates: A study of 37 cultures. *Journal of Cross-Cultural Psychology, 21*, 5–47.

Chanana, K. (2000). Treading the hallowed halls: Women in higher education in India. *Economic and Political Weekly, 35*, 1012–1022.

Chaudhry, N., and Sharma, N. (2006). Adolescence in India. In J. J. Arnett, with R. Ahmed, N. Galombos, B. Nsamenang, T. S. Saraswathi, and R.K. Silbereisen (Eds.), *International encyclopedia of adolescence, 2 Volumes* (pp. 442–459). New York: Routledge.

Chaudhry, N., and Sharma, N. (in press). Review of research in developmental psychology. In G. Misra (Ed.), *Survey of researches in psychology*. New Delhi: Pearson.

Datta, V. (1995). Home away from home: Family day care in Bombay. *Suraksha Monograph Series No. 1*. Madras, India: M.S. Swaminathan Research Foundation (MSSRF).

D'Cruz, P., and Bharat, S. (2001). Beyond joint and nuclear: The Indian family revisited. *Journal of Comparative Family Studies, 32*, 167–194.

De, A., and Dreze, J. (1999). *Public report on basic education for India*. New Delhi, India: Oxford University Press.

Deb, S. (2005). Knowledge, attitude and perception of adolescents about different aspects of reproductive health: A cross sectional study. *Social Science International, 21*, 70–92.

Dube, L. (1981). The economic roles of children in India: Methodological issues. In G. Rodgers and G. Standing (Eds.), *Child work, poverty, and underdevelopment* (pp. 179–213). Geneva, Switzerland: International Labour Organization.

Dube, L. (1988). On the construction of gender: Hindu girls in patrilineal India. In K. Chanana (Ed.), *Socialization, education and women: Explorations in gender identity* (pp. 166–192). New Delhi, India: Orient Longman.

Ford Foundation, India and The Voluntary Health Association of India (1980–current). *Anubhav series (Experiences in community health)*. New Delhi, India: Author.

Fussell, M. E., and Greene, M. E. (2002). Demographic trends affecting youth around the world. In B. B. Brown, R. W. Larson, and T. S. Saraswathi (Eds.), *The world's youth: Adolescence in eight regions of the globe* (pp. 21–60). New York: Cambridge University Press.

Government of India (1997). *We can change our world: The Mahila Samakhya experience*. New Delhi, India: Author.

Government of India (1986). *Child labour (prohibition and regulation act)*. New Delhi, India: Ministry of Labor.

Government of India, Ministry of Human Resource Development (1999–2000). *Ministry of human resource development annual report*. New Delhi, India: Author.

Government of India, Ministry of Human Resource Development. (2001). *Sarva shikshan abhiyan* [Education for all.] New Delhi, India: Author.

Government of India, Ministry of Human Resource Development (2004–2005). *Ministry of human resource development annual report (2004–2005)*. New Delhi, India: Author.

Government of India, Ministry of Women and Child Development (2005). *Ministry of women and child development report (2005–2006)*. New Delhi, India: Author.

Government of India, Ministry of Youth Affairs and Sports (2005). *Ministry of youth affairs and sports. annual report (2005–2006)*. New Delhi, India: Author.

Govinda, R. (Ed.). (2002). *India education report: A profile of basic education.* New Delhi, India: Oxford University Press.

Griffiths, P., Hinde, A., and Matthews, Z. (2001). Infant and child mortality in three culturally contrasting states of India. *Journal of Biosocial Science, 33,* 603–622.

Institute of Applied Manpower Research (2001). *Manpower profile India year book 2000.* New Delhi, India: Author.

Institute of Psychological and Educational Research (1991). *A composite report of the situational analysis of urban street children in India. Study report of six major cities in India.* Calcutta, India: Author.

International Institute of Population Sciences and ORC Macro. (2000). *National family health survey (NFHS-2) 1998-99: İndıa.* Mumbai, India: Author.

Jejeebhoy, S. J. (1996) *Adolescent sexual and reproductive behavior. A review of the evidence from India.* International Center for Research on Women (ICRW). Working paper No. 3. Washington, DC: ICRW.

Kakar, S. (1979). *Indian childhood: Cultural ideals and social reality.* Delhi, India: Oxford University Press.

Kakar, S. (1982). *Shamans, mystics and doctors: A psychological inquiry into India and its healing traditions* (Indian ed.). Bombay, India: Oxford University Press.

Kanbargi, R. (1988). Child labor in India: The carpet industry of Varanasi. In A. Bequele and J. Boyden (Eds.), *Combating child labor* (pp. 93–108). Geneva, Switzerland: International Labour Organization.

Karlekar, M. (2000). Women's studies and women's development. In M. S. Gore (Ed.), *Third survey of research in sociology and anthropology* (pp. 117–220). New Delhi, India: Indian Council of Social Science Research.

Kaur, B. (1993). An agenda for future theory building, research, and action. In T. S. Saraswathi and B. Kaur (Eds.), *Human development and family studies in India: An agenda for research and policy* (pp. 317–335). New Delhi, India: Sage.

Keller, H., Abels, M., Lamm, B., Yovsi, R. D., Voelker, S., and Lakhani, A. (2005). Ecocultural effects on early infant care: A study in Cameroon, India, and Germany. *Ethos, 33,* 512–541.

Kumar, K. (1991). *Political agenda of education: A study of colonialist and nationalist ideas.* New Delhi, India: Sage.

Lamm, B., and Keller, H. (2007). Understanding cultural models of parenting: The role of intracultural variation and response style. *Journal of Cross-Cultural Psychology, 38,* 1–8.

Landers, C. (1989). A psychobiological study of infant development in South India. In J. K. Nugent, B. M. Lester, and T. B. Brazelton (Eds.), *The cultural context of infancy* (pp. 169–208). Norwood, NJ: Ablex.

Menon, U., and Shweder, R. A. (1994). Kali's tongue: Cultural psychology and the power of "shame" in Orissa, India. In S. Kitayama and H. R. Markus (Eds.), *Emotion and culture: Empirical studies of mutual influence* (pp. 241–282). Washington, DC: American Psychological Association.

Miller, B. D. (1981). *The endangered sex. Neglect of female children in rural North India.* Ithaca, NY: Cornell University Press.

Mohanty, A. K., and Prakash, P. (1993). Theoretical despairs and methodological predicaments of developmental psychology in India: Some reflections. In T. S. Saraswathi and B. Kaur (Eds.), *Human development and family studies in India: An agenda for research and policy* (pp. 104–121). New Delhi, India: Sage.

Nambissan, G. B., and Sedwal, M. (2002). Education for all. The situation of Dalit children in India. In R. Govinda (Ed.), *India education report. A profile of basic education* (pp. 72–86). New Delhi, India: Oxford University Press.

Pandey, J. (Ed.). (2000). *Psychology in India revisited: Developments in the discipline. Volume 1: Physiological foundation and human cognition.* New Delhi, India: Sage.

Pandey. J. (Ed.). (2001). *Psychology in India revisited: Developments in the discipline. Volume 2: Personality and health psychology.* New Delhi, India: Sage.

Pandey. J. (Ed.). (2004). *Psychology in India revisited: Developments in the discipline. Volume 3: Applied social and organizational psychology.* New Delhi, India: Sage.

Paranjpe, A. C. (1987). The self beyond cognition, action, pain, and pleasure: An Eastern perspective. In K. Yardley and T. Honess (Eds.), *Self and identity: Psychosocial perspectives* (pp. 27–40). New York: Wiley.

Phatak, P. (1970). Motor growth patterns of Indian babies and some related factors. *Indian Pediatrics, 7,* 619–624.

Phathak, R. (1994). The new generation. *India Today.* January 31, 72–87.
Phillips, W. S. K. (1992). *Street children of Indore.* New Delhi, India: Child Labour Cell.
Population Council (1999). *Adolescents in transition: Program and practices in India.* New Delhi, India: Author.
PRIA. (2002) *Invisible yet widespread: The non-profit sector of India.* Author.
Ramu, G. N. (1987). Indian husbands: Their role, perceptions and performance in single- and dual-earner families. *Journal of Marriage and the Family, 49,* 903–915.
Rao, N., McHale, J. P., and Pearson, E. (2003). Links between socialization goals and child-rearing practices in Chinese and Indian mothers. *Infant and Child Development, 12,* 475–492.
Rogoff, B. (2003). *The cultural nature of human development.* New York: Oxford University Press.
Roopnarine, J. L., and Suppal, P. (2003). Kakar's psychoanalytic interpretation of Indian childhood: The need to emphasize the father and multiple care-givers in the socialization equation. In D. Sharma (Ed.), *Childhood, family and sociocultural change in India: Reinterpreting the inner world* (pp. 115–137). New Delhi, India: Oxford University Press.
Saraswathi, T. S. (1994).Women in poverty contexts. Balancing economic needs and child care needs. In R. Borooah, K. Cloud, S. Seshadri, T. S. Saraswathi, J. T. Peterson, and A. Verma (Eds.), *Capturing complexity. An interdisciplinary look at women, households and development* (pp. 163–178). New Delhi, India: Sage.
Saraswathi, T. S. (Ed.). (1999). *Culture, socialization, and human development: Theory, research and applications in India.* New Delhi, India: Sage.
Saraswathi, T. S. (2005). Hindu worldview in the development of selfways: The "Atman" as the real self. In L. A. Jensen and R. W. Larson (Eds.), *New horizons in developmental theory and research: New directions for child and adolescent development, No. 109.* (pp. 43–50). San Francisco: Jossey-Bass.
Saraswathi, T. S., and Dutta, R. (1988a). Current trends in developmental psychology: A life span perspective. In J. Pandey (Ed.), *Psychology in India. The state-of-the-art. Personality and mental processes* (Vol. 1, pp. 93–152). New Delhi, India: Sage.
Saraswathi, T. S., and Dutta, R. (1988b). *Invisible boundaries: Grooming for adult roles.* New Delhi, India: Northern Book Center.
Saraswathi, T. S., and Ganapathy, H. (2002). Indian parents' ethnotheories as reflections of the Hindu scheme of child and human development. In H. Keller, Y. P. Poortinga, and A. Schölmerich (Eds.), *Between culture and biology: Perspectives on ontogenetic development* (pp. 79–88). Cambridge, United Kingdom: Cambridge University Press.
Saraswathi, T. S., Manjrekar, N., and Pant, P. (2003). Education of adolescents in India: Contexts and constraints. In F. Pajares and T. Urdan (Eds.), *International perspectives on adolescence (Adolescence and education series)* (pp. 343–365). Greenwich, CT: Information Age Publishing.
Saraswathi, T. S., and Pai, S. (1997). Socialization in the Indian context. In H. S. R. Kao and D. Sinha (Eds.), *Asian perspectives in psyhology: Cross-cultural research and methodology series* (Vol. 19, pp. 74–92). New Delhi, India: Sage.
Saraswathi, T. S., and Sundaresan, J. (1980). Perceived maternal disciplinary practices and their relation to development of moral judgment. *International Journal of Behavioral Development, 3,* 91–104.
Seymour, S. (1976). Caste/class and child rearing in a changing Indian town. *American Ethnologist, 3,* 783–796.
Seymour, S. C. (1999). *Women, family and child care in India: A world in transition.* New York: Cambridge University Press.
Shah, M. (2005). Son preference and its consequences (A review). *Gender & Behavior, 3,* 269–280.
Sharma, D. (Ed.). (2003). *Childhood, family and socio-cultural change in India: Reinterpreting the inner world.* New Delhi, India: Oxford.
Sharma, D., and LeVine, R. A. (1998). Child care in India: A comparative developmental view of infant social environments. *New Directions for Child Development, 81,* 45–68.
Sharma, V., and Sharma, A. (1995). The letter-box approach: A model for sex eduction in an orthodox society. *The Journal of Family Welfare, 41,* 31–34.
Shweder, R. A. (2003). Who sleeps by whom revisited. In R. A. Shweder (Ed.), *Why do men barbecue? Recipes for cultural psychology* (pp. 46–73). Cambridge, MA: Harvard University Press.
Sinha, D. (1986). *Psychology in a third world country. The Indian experience.* New Delhi, India: Sage.
Sinha, D. (1997). Indigenising psychology. In J. W.Berry, Y. H. Poortinga, and J. Pandey (Eds.), *Handbook of cross cultural psychology: Theory and method* (Vol. 1, 2nd ed., pp. 129–169). Boston: Allyn and Bacon.
Sinha, J. B. P. (1980). *The nurturant task leader.* New Delhi, India: Concept.
Sinha-Kerkhoff, K. (2003). Practising Rakshabhandan: Brothers in Ranchi, Jharkhand. *Indian Journal of Gender Studies, 10,* 431–455.

Sriram, R. (1994). Social support services for women: A delivery system In R. Borooah, K. Cloud, S. Seshadri, T. S. Saraswathi, J. T. Peterson, and A. Verma (Eds.), *Capturing complexity. An interdisciplinary look at women, households and development* (pp. 179–188). New Delhi, India: Sage.

Stork, H. (1980). La naissance d'un fils dans la tradition religieuse de l'inde [The birth of a son in the religious traditions of India]. *Journal de Psychologie Normale et Pathologique, 77,* 151–186.

Thapar, R. (2004). *Early India. From the origins to AD 1300.* Berkeley, CA: University of California Press.

Tikoo, M., Bollman, R., and Bergen, M. B. (1995). Knowledge level of youth in India regarding human sexuality and AIDS. *Journal of Sex & Marital Therapy, 21,* 248–254.

Tilak, J. B. G. (1999). National human development initiative: Education in the union budget. *Economic and Political Weekly, 34,* 614–620.

Trawick, M. (1990). *Notes on love in a Tamil family.* Berkeley, CA: University of California Press.

United Nations Development Programme (2000). *Human development report 2000.* New York: Oxford University Press.

United Nations Development Programme (2005). *Human development report.* New York: Oxford University Press.

United Nations Statistical Yearbook (2005). Forty ninth issue. Series No. 25. Department of Economic and Social Affairs. Retrieved from http://unstats.un.org/unsd/cdb.

United Nations Children's Fund (2004). *State of the world's children 2004: Girls, education and development.* Retrieved from http://www.unicef.org/sowc04/.

United Nations Children's Fund (2005). *State of the world's children 2005: Childhood under threat.* Retrieved from http://www.unicef.org/sowc05/.

United Nations Children's Fund (2006). *State of the world's children 2006: Excluded and Invisible.* Retrieved from http://www.unicef.org/sowc06/.

U.S. Central Intelligence Agency. (2006). *World fact book 2006.* Retrieved July 2006, from http://www.cia.gov/cia/publications/factbook/index.html.

Verma, S., and Saraswathi, T. S. (2002). Adolescence in India: Street urchins or Silicon Valley millionaires? In B. B. Brown, R. W. Larson, and T. S. Saraswathi (Eds.), *The world's youth: Adolescence in eight regions of the globe* (pp. 105–140). Cambridge, United Kingdom: Cambridge University Press.

Visaria, P. (1998). *Unemployment among youth in India: Level, nature and policy implications.* Geneva, Switzerland: International Labour Organization.

Werner, E. E. (1972). Infants around the world: Cross-Cultural studies of psychomotor development from birth to two years. *Journal of Cross-Cultural Psychology, 3,* 111–134.

Whiting, B. B., and Edwards, C. P. (1988). *Children of different worlds: The formation of social behavior.* Cambridge, MA: Harvard University Press.

25
Australia and New Zealand

ANN V. SANSON and JANIS E. PATERSON

Introduction

The journey through life for people living in Australia and New Zealand has many resemblances to life in other countries but in some respects is unique. Both countries are modern, Western, English-speaking industrialized democracies, and hence, human development shares many common features with the rest of the English-speaking world. These two countries (here referred to Australasia[*]) also have important similarities with each other as well as distinctive features. They are geographically dissimilar, but both have indigenous populations, were colonized by the United Kingdom, and experienced subsequent waves of migration from a large, but differing, range of countries. This has resulted in two unique, diverse multicultural societies with markedly different demography.

This chapter seeks to provide an overview of child and youth development in Australasia. It starts with a brief outline of historical and demographic considerations pertinent to human development in Australasia. It then identifies and discusses three central issues that create distinctive contexts for development in these two "down under" countries: indigenous peoples, ethnic diversity, and societal change. Following this, there is discussion of internationally significant longitudinal research in both Australia and New Zealand, which has shed light on the processes and contexts for development. Current trends and likely future directions are then described that might foreshadow human development issues and research over the coming decades.

Historical and Demographic Considerations

Australia and New Zealand were both colonized in the late eighteenth century. However, their precolonization histories, geography, indigenous peoples, the nature of their colonization processes, and their subsequent national development vary substantially.

Australia

Australia is a vast and ancient land, with sparsely populated desert and semi-desert fringed by forests, agricultural land, and cities. Australian Aboriginal people hold the distinction of the oldest continuing culture in the world, dating back at least 40,000 years. Before colonization,

---

[*] The term Australasia is sometimes used to refer to a broader region including New Guinea and neighboring islands north and east of Australia in the Pacific Ocean. The designation is sometimes applied to all the lands and islands of the Pacific Ocean lying between the equator and latitude 47° south. However, here it is used in a more limited sense to refer simply to Australia and New Zealand.

they formed many tribes with a hunter-gatherer lifestyle and sophisticated social system, speaking over 300 distinct languages. Torres Strait Islanders form a second group of indigenous Australians, living on islands between the Australian mainland and Papua New Guinea.

Although Australia was first "discovered" by Portuguese explorers in the sixteenth century, it was not settled by Europeans until the "First Fleet" of convicts and marines arrived near present-day Sydney in 1778. By the mid-nineteenth century, there were six colonies, which in 1901 became the States and Territories of the Commonwealth of Australia (Macintyre, 2004). There have been multiple waves of migration to Australia. A series of gold rushes, starting in the 1850s, brought immigrants from the United Kingdom, Ireland, Europe, North America, and China. A "White Australia policy," aiming to exclude all nonwhite immigrants, was in place from the 1890s to the 1950s. Following World War II, a massive program of European immigration was instigated, in the belief that the country must "populate or perish," bringing more migrants from the United Kingdom and large numbers from Southern and Eastern Europe. Since the 1970s, migrants have arrived from all parts of Asia, North Africa, the Middle East, and elsewhere, radically transforming Australia's demography, culture, and image of itself (Macintyre, 2004). Currently, 24% of the population is overseas born (Australian Bureau of Statistics [ABS], 2005).

With exposure to white people and Western culture, the indigenous people suffered from European diseases, alcohol, poor nutrition, deep cultural dislocation as a result of forced removal from their land onto missions and reserves, and numerous other forms of racism and discrimination, some of which continue to the present day (Sanson et al., 1998). Of particular significance from a developmental point of view, a widespread policy of forced removal of Aboriginal children from their families into foster homes or institutions, which continued up to the late 1960s, resulted in generations of indigenous youth growing up with broken connections to family and culture (now known as the Stolen Generations; Wilson, 1997). Wilson's report details "multiple and profoundly disabling" layers of abuse, leading to a "cycle of damage from which it is difficult to escape unaided" (p. 178). Only in 1965 were all indigenous people given the right to vote (Sanson et al., 1998). In the "Mabo Case" in 1992, the legal fiction that Australia was "terra nullius" (without people) at the time of European settlement was overturned, opening the way to native title land claims. In contrast to New Zealand, the Australian government has made no treaty or formal agreement with its indigenous people.

Indigenous Australians currently make up approximately 2.4% of the population. Life expectancy is approximately 17 years shorter than that of nonindigenous Australians, and the proportion of indigenous 0 to 14 year olds is considerably higher than in the total Australian population (39% versus 20%) (ABS, 2007). Over one-quarter of indigenous Australians live in remote communities, one-quarter live in major cities, and the remainder live in regional areas (ABS, 2003). Indicators of indigenous Australians' well-being are very poor. On the United Nations Human Development Index, Aboriginal Australians are ranked 103rd compared with Australia's overall population, which is ranked 4th. Indigenous children are five times more likely than other Australian children to come to the attention of child welfare authorities and almost six times as likely to be in out-of-home care (ABS, 2003). Rates of tertiary education are low; for example, there are about 25 Indigenous psychologists, compared to 300 if numbers were proportional to population.

In contrast to some popular conceptions, Australia is one of the most urbanized countries in the world, with 84% of the population within the most densely populated 1% of the continent. Well over one-half of the total population of 20 million lives in five capital cities (ABS, 2002a). Australia has a Westminster-style democratic government, with universal suffrage and compulsory voting. Although recent decades have seen a shift toward a "user-pays," market-based economy, reasonably strong social welfare and public education systems still exist. Australia was early to adopt public health measures such as universal child immunization, seatbelt regulations, and compulsory bicycle helmets. It also has regulatory and accreditation systems to ensure that childcare is of adequate quality.

New Zealand

Geographically, New Zealand is of volcanic origin and comprises two main islands and a number of smaller islands. Its diverse landscape includes rich agricultural land and extensive mountain ranges. Maori were the first inhabitants of New Zealand and formed multiple tribes with their own societal rules, family networks, and responsibilities. Although Abel Tasman "discovered" New Zealand in 1642, European contact only started after Captain Cook "rediscovered" it 126 years later. Following this, increasing trade, sealing, whaling, and missionary activity brought Maoris into close contact with Europeans, in particular with British people who started settling the country in 1840 (King, 2003).

The Treaty of Waitangi of 1840 was a formal agreement between Maori and Queen Victoria on behalf of the United Kingdom colonists. The Treaty gave protection to the Maori in return for coming under the Crown's jurisdiction, while maintaining their customary rights. Its signing was followed by two decades of minimal conflict, but during the 1860s, wars between Maori and Pakeha* erupted, fuelled by issues around land confiscation and colonization. Around this time, the Maori population dropped, and it was widely believed that Maoris were headed for extinction (King, 2003). By the 1880s, the country had a representative government, and the years of overt Maori–Pakeha conflict were over. A Native Land Court was established to investigate Maori claims to land, and specific Maori seats were instituted in parliament. The Waitangi Tribunal, established in 1975, continues to investigate claims by Maori about breaches of the Treaty.

From the time of World War II, most Maori families moved from rural communities into towns and cities, resulting in wider educational and employment opportunities but also cultural and emotional dislocation. By the 1970s, many Maori families had lost all connection with Maori language, rituals, and traditions (King, 2003).

New Zealand was the first neo-European country to give voting rights to its indigenous population (in 1867), and in 1893, it became the first sovereign state in the world to give women the vote (King, 2003). Like Australia, New Zealand has a Westminster-style democratic government with universal suffrage and compulsory voting.

During the nineteenth and first half of the twentieth centuries, there was a continuing influx of Europeans, dominated by settlers from the United Kingdom and Ireland. In the late nineteenth century, immigrants also came from China and Australia to work in the goldfields, and in the early twentieth century, another influx came principally from the Netherlands, Ireland, and India (King, 2003). Significant migration from neighboring Pacific islands began during the 1960s, largely in response to labor demands and high economic growth in New Zealand. Since the late 1980s, many migrants of Asian ethnicity have arrived.

These migration events have resulted in one in five of the population of approximately four million New Zealanders being foreign born. Maori make up 15% of the total population, with approximately 25% of these being under 14 years of age. It is projected that one in three New Zealand children will have some Maori heritage by 2051. According to the 2001 Census, 6.5% of New Zealanders were of Pacific ethnicity, and this is expected to grow to 12% by 2051. New Zealanders of Asian descent already make up almost 10% of the total population and are expected to reach 15% by 2010 (Cook, Didham, and Khawaja, 1999). In response to this diversity, New Zealand has made a strong commitment to biculturalism in Maori–Pakeha relationships and to multiculturalism (King, 2003).

---

* Pakeha refers to New Zealanders of predominantly European descent.

Central Issues Impacting on Child Development: Indigenous Peoples, Ethnic Diversity, and Societal Change

Distinctive issues grounded in demography, history, and culture drive our understanding of development in Australia and New Zealand. (1) Indigenous peoples: In both Australia and New Zealand, the processes of colonization and postcolonization outlined earlier have had disastrous negative repercussions for indigenous peoples, occasioning profound concerns about the development of indigenous children and youth today. Hence, a better understanding of the developmental pathways for indigenous children and youth, taking account of risk and protective mechanisms that operate at multiple levels (historical, political, economic, cultural, community, and family) is critically needed. (2) Ethnic diversity: The multicultural and dynamic nature of the Australasian populations has raised a number of issues concerning development. For example, researchers have examined various aspects of the migration experience, and Pacific Island people in New Zealand are using their own frameworks for thinking about human development to shape research questions, design, and methods. (3) Societal changes: Australasian families have experienced similar demographic trends to those in much of the Western world, including high mobility, high divorce rates, increasing variability in family types, delayed childbearing, reduced fertility rates, more variable and unstable employment conditions, greatly increased maternal employment, and rising rates of notifications of child abuse and neglect (de Vaus, 2004; Statistics New Zealand, 2003). Such changes have spurred ecologically oriented research on child and youth development. This includes major broadly based longitudinal studies and more focused research addressing issues including the "child care debate," the impact of family transitions such as divorce, and the impact of modern media. The "new morbidities," such as asthma, obesity, and child and adolescent behavior problems, which have complex etiologies, have elicited calls for interdisciplinary research and closer connections between research, policy, and practice.

Research on these central issues, as well as major research utilizing longitudinal methods, are briefly outlined in the following sections to paint a picture of child development in Australasia.*

Indigenous Children's Development

Early Australasian research with indigenous peoples reflected the biases of the time in adopting paternalistic or outright racist orientations. Recent research tends to be more participatory and respectful and, in New Zealand in particular, is using culturally based research methodologies.

Australia As noted earlier, from the time of first contact with white colonizers, the health, development, and well-being of indigenous Australians has tended to be much poorer than that of nonindigenous people. Yet, despite the multiple challenges, indigenous children and their families and communities have also shown remarkable capacity for survival and resilience. In a critique entitled, "Australian Psychology Has a Black History," Garvey, Dudgeon, and Kearins (2000) noted that indigenous people served as "objects" for early psychological research, much of which would now be regarded as unethical. Early research, driven by social Darwinism, regarded Australia as a scientific opportunity to examine development among "primitive" people in a geographically isolated environment, with assumed genetic and/or cultural inferiority (Davidson, Sanson, and Gridley, 2000). The Cambridge Anthropological Expedition in the early twentieth century studied the sensorimotor functions (e.g., hearing, vision, reaction times) of Torres Strait Islanders in the belief that these functions were highly correlated with intelligence.

---

* A discussion of Australian research following broader Western models in traditional areas of developmental science such as cognition, memory, perception, and language development can be found in Garton (2006).

Few differences were found between the Islanders and educated English people, providing no evidence to support the notion that they were "primitive," although this seems to have had little impact on either popular or scientific opinion. Later research, for example the intelligence testing movement pioneered by Porteus (1959) to screen for educational capacity, continued to assume inferiority.

Such research supported constructions of indigenous adults as poor parents and of indigenous communities as culturally inadequate for the intellectual development of children and hence helped to support the policy of forcibly removing children from their families and communities. It is estimated that around one in three indigenous people have been affected, directly or indirectly, by these policies (Silburn et al., 2006a). The film *The Rabbit Proof Fence* (2002, Director Phillip Noyce) gives a vivid portrayal of the distress and despair of the children who were "taken away" and their bereft families, but also of their resilience.

Much of the research conducted in the 1960s and 1970s continued to reflect societal assumptions that indigenous people were inferior. For example, de Lemos (1973) showed that the performance of Aboriginal children on Piagetian conservation tasks lagged behind that for Western children, leading some to conclude that Aboriginal children were intellectually deficient and would not benefit from education. Later work showed that performance on such tasks was dependent on environmental contexts. For example, Seagrim and Lendon (1980) tested children reared in the isolated Hermannsburg mission in Central Australia on Piagetian tasks and compared them with Aboriginal children reared in towns and white Australian children. The town-reared Aboriginal children performed as well as age- and education-matched white children, whereas those on the mission station performed much more poorly. The results were interpreted in terms of the inadequacies of the mission environment, without consideration of the cultural relevance of the tasks or types of thinking assessed. The results were again used by some to argue that children might be better off if removed from their families (see Davidson et al., 2000).

Drawing from the same project, Kearins (1986) attempted to identify cognitive skills underlying the detailed understanding of the environment that allowed Aboriginal people to survive in an often harsh natural context. Comparing the spatial location and memory skills of Aboriginal and white children and adolescents, she found that the Aboriginal children performed significantly better and concluded that these skills were valued and maintained by the culture. From observing children's behavior during the testing session, she inferred that the Aboriginal children used a visual strategy (sitting still and concentrating on the array of objects) and the white children used a verbal strategy ("muttering"), which was not very effective for these tasks but may be adaptive for other Piagetian tasks (see Garton, 2003, for a fuller discussion).

With the recognition of the role of formal schooling in the development of Piagetian types of thinking, research turned to the examination of the different learning styles of Aboriginal and white children, as well as the differing attitudes and expectations of teachers. For example, Sommerland and Bellingham (1972) observed Aboriginal and non-Aboriginal students at a residential school in Darwin. For the Aboriginal children, school was their first close experience of white culture. These children were more cooperative in group games, and when they did compete, they did so in mutually supportive ways (e.g., allowing the least rewarded child in a previous round to start the next round). This cooperative orientation has been widely observed. The authors also noted that teachers were more pessimistic about Aboriginal children and directed more criticism and shorter explanations to them than to non-Aboriginal children. Harris and Harris (1988) contrasted the typically informal, participatory, and nonverbal Aboriginal learning style with largely verbally mediated school learning, reminiscent of Rogoff's later work on learning styles of children in Guatemala and the United States (Rogoff, Paradice, Mejía Arauz, Correa-Chávez, and Angelillo, 2003; see Goodnow, Chapter 1, in this volume). These studies indicate that education systems need to take account of differences in learning style if they are to foster the cognitive and educational development of all students. The extent to which such findings have been translated into practice is patchy at best.

It is now widely recognized that past developmental research was unhelpful if not downright harmful, a point made in several papers in the first edition of the *Australian Psychologist* that were devoted to indigenous issues (Sanson and Dudgeon, 2000; see also Davidson et al., 2000; Garvey et al., 2000; Sanson et al., 1998). Today, developmental research is typically characterized by consultation and participation by indigenous people and takes a more ecological and culturally sensitive approach. Research has sought to understand the family contexts for development of Indigenous children, without the pejorative or judgmental overtones of earlier research. In an example of studies documenting cultural parenting practices that help children "grow up strong," a group of senior Aboriginal women from central Australia documented their own childrearing practices, which included treating even infants as small adults, granting them much autonomy in choosing what they want, while encouraging them to be generous and compassionate (Waltja Tjutangku Palyapayi Aboriginal Corporation, 2001). Even in the cities, many Aboriginal people still hold strong cultural values, and extended families with shared responsibility for childrearing are normative in both Aboriginal and Torres Strait Islander communities (Batrouney and Soriano, 2001).

A picture of the current status of indigenous children and youth development comes from the Western Australian Aboriginal Child Health Survey (WAACHS). This cross-sectional survey undertaken in 2000 to 2002 involved a representative community sample of more than 5,000 0- to 17-year-old Aboriginal and Torres Strait Islander children and youth in the state of Western Australia. Extensive consultation with Aboriginal communities and agencies preceded the survey, an Aboriginal Steering Committee directed all phases of its development and implementation, and many Aboriginal people were recruited onto the study team. Collecting information from parents, young people, and teachers, it sought to identify factors underlying positive and problematic developmental outcomes including physical health, social and emotional well-being, educational outcomes, and the broader circumstances and capacities of Aboriginal children, families, and communities.

WAACHS data demonstrated that the effects of removal from ancestral lands, separations of families, and institutionalization on reserves or missions continue to be felt and are manifested in the continuing disadvantage experienced by Aboriginal children and youth in all aspects of development. More than one-third of the children had parents or grandparents who had been forcibly "taken away," and these family experiences of separation were associated with poorer mental health in carers and almost one-third of children being at high risk for clinically significant emotional or behavioral problems, compared to 15% of non-Aboriginal children (Silburn et al., 2006b). By the time they started school, 60% were already significantly behind non-Aboriginal children. Investigating why so little improvement has been seen in the health and well-being of Aboriginal children, the authors called for high-quality, high-frequency, early intervention programs to begin to break the intergenerational cycle of disadvantage (Silburn et al., 2006a).

The Longitudinal Study of Indigenous Children (LSIC, or "Footprints in Time"), funded by the Australian Government, is currently in the planning and pilot testing phase. The project is overseen by a Steering Committee with an Aboriginal chair and many indigenous members. The study will be the first national longitudinal study of indigenous children and aims to gather information on all aspects of children's health and development over time and how positive outcomes may be facilitated or hindered over time by aspects of family life, communities, cultural factors, service delivery, and policies. Thus, it reflects a new focus on the strengths and coping capacities, and not merely the problems, of indigenous people. Data collection for the first wave was conducted in 2008 (see http://www.facs.gov.au/internet/facsinternet.nsf/research/ldi-lsic_nav.htm).

New Zealand Over the years, the disadvantaged health profile of Maori in comparison with non-Maori has been well documented (Pomare, Keefe-Ormsby, and Ormsby, 1995). Despite major health and social reforms and the development of specific Maori health and social services, there remains a persistently high Maori mortality rate (Sporle, Pearce, and Davis, 2002) and poorer social and educational outcomes. For example, a continuing issue in the lives of Maori youth is gang organization and domestic violence, as illustrated in the film *Once Were Warriors* (1994, Director Lee Tamahori). However, Maori culture (*taonga*) is being reinvented, and many parts of this vibrant culture are incorporated in ceremonies and other public events. Visiting dignitaries receive a Maori welcome, and the All Black Rugby Team (the national team) performs a *haka* (challenge) before games. The emerging importance of Maori within New Zealand culture is also illustrated by the increasing acknowledgement of Maori symbolism in art and literature (King, 2003).

There is a growing number of well-trained Maori researchers in the human development field. L. T. Smith (1999) noted that typical research is inextricably linked to European imperialism and colonialism and called for the "decolonization" of research methods that use Western conceptions of the individual and society, space and time, and other ways of establishing the superior position of Western knowledge. She set out an indigenous research agenda that encompassed the processes of decolonization, healing, mobilization, and transformation within four community statuses: survival, recovery, development, and self-determination. There are now numerous examples of indigenous research projects in New Zealand. Maori researchers in education, health, and science use a methodological approach to research known as Kaupapa Maori research (L. T. Smith, 1999) that is typically qualitative in nature and involves Maori research leadership and an acceptance and understanding of Maori concepts and constructs.

Since the 1970s, there has been a tremendous effort to revitalize Maori as a language for everyday settings, particularly in the educational context. Te Kohanga Reo or Maori "language nests" commenced in 1982. These community-based early childhood centers draw on marae-based* learning of customs, traditions, and language; most of this program's graduates have gone on to senior school, tertiary education, or employment (Royal Tangaere, 1999). Such immersion education is making an important contribution to the revival of Maori language, and thousands of new Maori words have been created to allow the teaching of compulsory curriculum subjects in the Maori language. Te Puni Kokiri (2004) reported that the numbers of Maori speakers in the Maori population has stabilized over the last 10 years, at approximately 25%, and there is now optimism for the future of the language. Since 1998, there is a compulsory bicultural early education curriculum, Te Whariki.

Developmental Issues for Non–English-Speaking Migrant Children

Australia The ever-increasing ethnic diversity of the Australian population has led to investigation of topics including language and cognitive development, school-related expectations, and identity development among children and adolescents from non–English-speaking backgrounds (see also Bornstein and Cote, Chapter 27, in this volume). Early research examined language development, particularly bilingualism, as it related to cognitive and educational progress. Keats and Keats (1978), in a program of research on bilingual children, studied migrants from Greece, China, and elsewhere and found higher scores and greater gains in conservation tasks when children were trained and tested in their more fluent language of origin than in their new language of English (see Lieven and Stoll, Chapter 7, in this volume). In a similar vein to research with indigenous Australians reported earlier, some research with children from diverse ethnic backgrounds has addressed the impact of cultural norms and expectations on school

---

* Marae is a traditional meeting place for a Maori community.

performance. For example, as part of an extensive program of research on understandings of work and household obligations, Goodnow (1996) compared Anglo-Australian, Lebanese-Australian, and Japanese families and noted how culturally based rules of politeness and expectations for social approval were relevant to academic performance (see Goodnow, Chapter 1, in this volume).

Other research has thrown light on the process of identity development through studying adolescents with diverse backgrounds. Minority group adolescents often have to confront prejudice, discrimination, and structural barriers that limit their aspirations and achievements, but it is argued that a strong, positive, and stable self-identity needs to incorporate a positively valued ethnic identity (Phinney and Rosenthal, 1993). Australian research suggests that social context and family relationships both play a part in such identity formation. For example, Rosenthal and Hrynevich (1985) reported that sense of ethnic identity varied by context: Greek Australian and Italian Australian adolescents reported that, in some social contexts (such as family gatherings), they felt their ethnic identity strongly and, in others (e.g., when with Australian friends), they were more aware of their Australian identity. Later, Rosenthal and Feldman (1992) found that warm, supportive parenting that encouraged independent decision making and open expression of dissenting points of view was associated with strong positive identification with Chinese culture for both Chinese American and Chinese Australian adolescents, suggesting that the quality of the parent–child relationship may be as important to identity development as issues of ethnicity per se (see Thompson and Virmani, Chapter 10, in this volume).

Another area of concern about children's development has arisen from government policy toward refugees and asylum seekers. In an attempt to halt the flow of asylum seekers arriving by boat from various parts of Asia and the Middle East, they have been held in detention centers, often in remote locations or on off-shore islands, for long periods of time. Children have been held in detention for up to 6 years, witnessing widespread distress, depression, self-mutilation, and riots. When added to the traumatic events experienced in their home countries and in their flight to seek asylum, this has given rise to serious concerns about children's well-being and development. Despite difficulties in carrying out research with this population, evidence is accumulating that the concerns are well-placed. For example, Steel et al. (2004) found that all of the refugee children in their study who had been held in detention for more than 2 years met diagnostic criteria for at least one current psychiatric disorder. Similarly, Robinson and Farhadi (2005) found that, whereas most refugee children and their parents who were not detained showed resilience on measures of mental health, refugees who had been detained experienced pervasive mental health problems and lower levels of adjustment.

New Zealand In New Zealand, language has been a major focus of research with migrant communities. A number of non-Maori children attending primary school speak a home language other than English, in most cases a Pasifika (Pacific Island) language (McNaughton, Phillips, and MacDonald, 2003). During the mid-1980s, women from the Pacific Islands, noting the consequences of language loss, began to set up Pacific Island early childhood education centers to ensure that their children maintained their own languages and cultural practices and improved their chances to succeed educationally. Research has shown that on entry to primary school, children who attended these centers had developed control over both their home language and English (Tagoilelagi-Leota, McNaughton, MacDonald, and Farry, 2004; see Lieven and Stoll, Chapter 7, in this volume).

Like Australia, New Zealand presents unique circumstances for young people from non-English backgrounds as they negotiate their identity between the dominant Pakeha culture and their cultural upbringing. Tupuola (1998), a Samoan researcher, describes Pacific teenage girls as "weaving in-between" the Samoan and Western worlds. Such findings highlight the complexities and challenges associated with transitional periods such as adolescence for migrant youth. With the growth of Asian migration to New Zealand, these challenges are likely to be mirrored for Asian teenagers.

Impacts of Societal Changes on Children: Maternal Work, Parental Separation, and Family Diversity

Australia The most dramatic societal changes in recent decades as far as child development is concerned include the sharp increase in out-of-home work for mothers of young children and the concomitant increase in use of nonparental childcare; and increasing family transitions, resulting in many children experiencing parental separation and many living in single-parent, step, or blended families. Australian research has addressed both these issues.

Recent research in childcare is framed not only by the increasing rates of maternal employment, but also by the early return to work by many mothers and shortages in childcare places, especially for infants. Unlike New Zealand and most other wealthy Western countries (but in common with the United States), Australia does not have compulsory paid maternity leave, although it does have provisions for unpaid leave (i.e., job protection) for 12 months. From a government perspective, childcare was initially conceptualized as an aid to maternal employment but is starting to shift to incorporate its role in early education, including its potential as an early intervention for disadvantaged children (Wise, Ungerer, and Sanson, 2002). As noted earlier, the quality of nonparental care is generally reasonably high in Australia as a result of accreditation and regulatory systems (Department of Family and Community Services, 1999).

Longitudinal research has confirmed overseas findings that quality of care is a stronger determinant of impact on children's development than quantity (Love et al., 2003). In comparison to unregulated home-based care, moderate- to high-quality center-based care was associated with enhanced attachment security in infants and better adjustment to the learning and emotional demands of school. More stable care was associated with better social adjustment, but neither stability nor hours of care affected behavior problems. Longer hours, however, were associated with poorer learning outcomes.

Major transitions in family structure have become almost normative experiences for Australian children. It is estimated that almost one-half of Australian children under the age of 18 years are affected by parental divorce or separation (ABS, 2002b), often resulting in experience of financial hardship for children. Drawing from a survey of 650 divorced Australians, Weston and Smyth (2000) found that nearly 60% of older single mothers and their children and close to 45% of younger single mothers were below the poverty line.

There has been a move to encourage more extensive contact between nonresident fathers and their children. This has been driven by several factors, including the "fathers lobby," which has argued for fathers' rights to contact; the connection between paternal payment of child support and father–child contact; and overseas research indicating the importance of fathers in children's lives (King and Sobolewski, 2006). Under recent family law reforms, family lawyers are now required to raise with their clients the possibility of "equal time" (or 50/50) parenting arrangements, even if neither parent introduces this option. Smyth, Caruana, and Ferro (2004) found that equal time arrangements were logistically complex, and the few parents who adopted them were unusual in having access to family friendly workplaces, living in close proximity, the ability to effectively manage conflict in their relationship, and being child-focused. There are no strong Australian data yet available on the impact of such care arrangements on children's development. Thus, attempts to ensure that postseparation parenting arrangements are made in the best interests of children involve a considerable amount of guesswork (see Bornstein and Lansford, Chapter 14, in this volume).

Many separated parents remarry to form step or blended families. Despite the typical increase in family resources involved in such transitions, early research linked living in a stepfamily with negative outcomes, such as reduced self-esteem (Ochiltree, 1990). New research suggests that, like divorce, living in a stepfamily per se is not detrimental to child development. Pryor and Rogers (2001) reviewed a wide range of Australian and international studies and found that there were few overall differences in the outcomes for children from stepfamilies and sole-parent families and that, when differences were observed, these could usually be accounted for by other factors such as parenting style. However, they did identify children who experienced multiple family transitions as at particularly high risk for adverse outcomes, such as criminality and disruptive behavior, poor educational outcomes, and marital problems in adulthood.

New Zealand The two main cultural influences on family structure in New Zealand are the Maori whanau,[*] which reflect a collectivist society, and Pakeha families, which are based on individualistic Western structures (Pryor, 2006). However, recent statistics reveal that one-half of partnered Maori have non-Maori partners (Callister, 2004), introducing a bidirectional cultural influence and adding to the complexity of analyzing family life in New Zealand. The New Zealand Census (Statistics New Zealand, 2006) revealed similar trends in family formation as in Australia. In comparison to earlier decades, couples are more likely to live together before marriage, to have children at older ages, and to experience more family transitions such as parental separation and stepfamily formation. Many children live in de facto households (13.5%). Rigg and Pryor (2007) found that New Zealand children appear to recognize and accept this diversity of family forms. When children were asked to define a family, they most frequently mentioned love and support and only rarely mentioned marriage, household living arrangements, and biological ties. Children endorsed nuclear families, lone-parent families, cohabitating families, and same-sex couples with children as families. These findings suggest that children view families as social and emotional, rather than biological or legal, entities and see love and support as their critical defining features.

In New Zealand, as elsewhere, the 1960s and 1970s saw intense debate about whether nonparental care would harm children when their mothers joined the workforce (Bird and Drewery, 2000). There has been some form of parental leave in New Zealand since the early 1980s, and it now includes 14 weeks of paid maternity leave for employed women (including self-employed), 2 weeks of unpaid leave for fathers, and various other types of unpaid leave that depend on factors such as length of employment. However, even with only 14 weeks of paid parental leave (which is modest in comparison to many European countries), many parents do not use childcare in the first 12 months of their child's life. Although Smith and Van der Vyer (1993) identified sensitivity and responsiveness of staff as a fundamental criterion for childcare quality (along with structural characteristics such as adult/child ratio, group size, and caregivers' training), A. B. Smith (1999) observed a relatively low level of engagement between adults and children in 100 childcare centers throughout New Zealand, with centers being described as too busy to focus on shared attention with young children.

Early childhood services greatly expanded at the end of the twentieth century. New Zealand has a very high rate of participation in early childhood education, which is now seen as an important part of child development: 93% of 4-year-olds, 83% of 3-year-olds, 49% of 2-year-olds, 30% of 1-year-olds, and 13% of infants are in some form of childcare or early education (Davey, 1998).

In the context of high rates of family breakdown and concerns regarding child abuse, there has been intensive research around the accuracy of children's memory of past events, in particular

---

[*] Whanau means extended family.

their ability to give evidence. This is particularly salient because New Zealand has no minimum age requirement for children to serve as witnesses in court and there is no requirement for their evidence to be corroborated. Children interviewed several days after an event report more information and make fewer errors than children interviewed after several weeks or months (Jones and Pipe, 2002). Despite this decline in memory performance, Pipe, Sutherland, Webster, Jones, and LaRooy (2004) found that delayed interviews had a facilitative effect on subsequent long-term recall. When 5-year-old children were interviewed again 1 year after a novel event, those children who had been interviewed initially between 1 and 6 months after the event recalled more than children who had been interviewed within 1 week of the event. Some New Zealand research has also focused on the use of nonverbal techniques to enhance children's memory reports (Pipe, Salmon, and Priestly, 2002), showing that providing children with props from the event increased the amount and accuracy of the information reported. Drawing has also been shown to be an effective technique for enhancing children's reports about neutral and novel events (Gross and Hayne, 1998).

Other New Zealand research has examined the effect of the questioning technique and the language used in the courtroom on the reliability and accuracy of children's evidence. No children changed their stories when questioned by the prosecution lawyer, but at least 76% changed their stories under cross examination. This was irrespective of the accuracy of their original testimony (Zajac and Hayne, 2003). This research indicates that the unfamiliar courtroom, confusing language, and intimidating questioning techniques may create social pressure that increases children's compliance with the lawyers' questions and introduces inaccuracies in evidence that was originally accurate.

Longitudinal Research "Down Under"

Australia and New Zealand each have major longitudinal studies that provide an opportunity to examine the nature and contexts of their development (see Van de Vijver, Hofer, and Chasiotis, Chapter 2, in this volume). Here, we briefly describe three New Zealand and three Australian studies that have tracked children from infancy forward, ordered according to date of initiation of the studies.

The Dunedin Multidisciplinary Health and Development Study (DMHDS) started with a cohort of 1,037 children born in Dunedin[*] in 1972 and 1973. There have been 12 data collection waves, the last being in 2005 when the participants were 32 years of age. This landmark longitudinal study has an extremely high retention rate (97.3% at age 21 years) and now incorporates children born to the original participants. Almost 900 publications across biological, psychosocial, and developmental topics have been produced (Silva and Stanton, 1996). The DMHDS has been at the forefront of gene–environment research, providing evidence suggesting that genotypes can moderate children's sensitivity to environmental insults. Caspi et al. (2002) found evidence that maltreated male children with a genotype conferring high levels of the neurotransmitter-metabolizing enzyme monoamine oxidase (MAOA) were significantly less likely to develop antisocial problems in late adolescence than those without this genotype. These findings may partly explain why some, but not all, maltreated children grow up to exhibit behavioral problems (see http://dunedinstudy.otago.ac.nz/index.html for more details).

The Christchurch Health and Development Study (CHDS) is a longitudinal study of a birth cohort of 1,265 children born in the Christchurch[†] urban region during 1977. In 21 waves of data collection, the cohort has been followed from infancy into childhood, adolescence, and adulthood. The study has resulted in over 280 publications covering topics including addictions,

---

[*] Dunedin is a small city in the south of the South Island of New Zealand.
[†] Christchurch is a middle-sized city in the South Island of New Zealand.

depression, anxiety disorders, and learning disorders. In a paper addressing the diversity of family forms, Nicholson, Fergusson, and Horwood (1999) found that children with stepparents had an increased risk for a number of poor psychosocial outcomes, including substance abuse, early school leaving, early onset of sexual activity, and multiple sexual partners. However, when other variables such as economic status and history of family instability were taken into account, the risk of living in a stepfamily was nonsignificant. They concluded that much of the association between living in a stepfamily and poor child outcomes was spurious and attributable to other antecedent factors. As another example of findings, Fergusson, Boden, and Horwood (2006) demonstrated that regular or heavy cannabis use was associated with an increased risk of using other illicit drugs. During adolescence, the association was very strong but declined significantly with age, suggesting the involvement of developmental processes such as social and biological maturity (see http://www.chmeds.ac.nz/research/chds/index.htmfor more details).

The Australian Temperament Project (ATP) is a longitudinal study of psychosocial adjustment and is unique in its detailed focus on temperament from infancy onwards, along with other individual and contextual variables (Prior, Sanson, Smart, and Oberklaid, 2000; see Kagan, Chapter 9, in this volume). The ATP cohort of 2,443 infants, representative of the population of the Australian state of Victoria, was recruited in 1983 at the child age of 4 to 8 months. Fourteen waves of data have been collected, with parents, nurses, teachers, and, from late childhood onwards, the children themselves as informants. Besides temperament, the domains of development assessed include behavioral and emotional adjustment, academic progress, health, social skills, peer and family relationships, as well as broader family functioning, parenting practices, and the family sociodemographic background.

More than 100 publications have arisen from the project. These have focused on the contribution of temperament to development (e.g., Sanson, Hemphill, and Smart, 2004), problematic aspects of development such as reading problems and antisocial behavior, genetic influences, and positive developmental outcomes such as civic responsibility and social competence (Smart and Sanson, 2003). Path analysis and trajectory analysis have been used to track developmental pathways and influences on them. For example, a series of studies on antisocial behavior has identified early onset, "experimental" and late-onset trajectories and the intrinsic, family, school, and peer influences on them. In particular, a large group of children who were at risk of antisocial behavior at 11 to 12 years showed normal developmental outcomes at the end of adolescence; factors contributing to this resilience included improved self-regulation capacities, improved parent–adolescent relationships, better school adjustment, and, importantly, an absence of relationships with "deviant" peers. The transition to secondary school seemed to be the critical time point for this shift in the resilient group's trajectory (Smart et al., 2005). The project is now focusing on pathways to positive young adult development (see http://www.aifs.gov.au/atp for more details).

The Mater-University of Queensland Study of Pregnancy (MUSP) is an ongoing study of the health of mothers and their children that started with interviews of 8,556 pregnant women attending the Mater Mothers Hospital in Brisbane in 1981 to 1983. There have been five follow-ups to age 21 years. The study's focus is on the interaction of biological and social determinants of physical and emotional well-being, social behavior, and predictors of youth and adult behavior, collecting data on factors including maternal lifestyle (e.g., tobacco and alcohol consumption, prepregnancy physical activity), maternal physical and mental health, marital relationships, childrearing, nutrition, and child health, cognitive development, and behavior. Examples of the 98 publications that have arisen from the project include studies of sex differences in vulnerability to adolescent depression (Eberhart, Shih, Hammen, and Brennan, 2006) and the relations between childhood sexual abuse and early adult cannabis use (Hayatbakhsh et al., 2009) (see http://www.socialscience.uq.edu.au/ for more details).

The Pacific Islands Families (PIF) Study commenced in 2000 and aims to extend understanding of contemporary family life and children's health and development among Pacific Islanders in New Zealand (Paterson et al., 2006). Pacific peoples in New Zealand are a significant but diverse group with different ethnicities, cultures, languages, and interpretations of issues such as childrearing and child discipline. Auckland is the largest Polynesian city in the world, with over 100,000 Pacific people. Pacific peoples tend to dominate some of the more negative national statistics, with lower income, higher unemployment, higher rates of conviction and prosecution, and lower educational qualifications than the general population (Statistics New Zealand, 2002). Of particular concern are the health statistics for Pacific infants. For example, they have a higher rate of late fetal deaths (stillbirths), with 9.6 deaths per 1,000 births compared to 5.9 in the total New Zealand population, and a higher infant death rate, at 7.9 deaths per 1,000 births (Ministry of Health, 1998). Pacific infants also have very high rates of hospitalization, particularly for respiratory illnesses (Bathgate et al., 1994).

The PIF Study is following a birth cohort of 1,398 Pacific children and their families, with assessments at ages 6 weeks, 12 and 24 months, and 4 and 6 years. An important feature is its ability to recognize Pacific ethnic heterogeneity and study between-group variation; for example, Tongan mothers breast feed at significantly lower rates than Samoan mothers (Butler, Williams, Tukuitonga, and Paterson, 2004). Research into such diverse issues as pregnancy planning, middle ear disease, sudden infant death syndrome, immunization schedules, and child injury and child health problems have contributed to a greater understanding of Pacific communities in New Zealand. For example, findings demonstrate that 15.6% of the cohort at preschool age is in the clinical range on the Child Behavior Checklist and 14% is in the borderline range, which are relatively high rates in comparison to international studies. High levels of physical discipline were associated with elevated problem behavior scores, particularly externalizing behavior. Substantial cross-ethnic differences in behavior problem scores illustrate the diversity of the Pacific population (Paterson, Carter, Gao, and Perese, 2007), indicating the influence of specific cultural settings (see http://www.aut-pif.ac.nz for more details).

The Longitudinal Study of Australian Children (LSAC; or Growing Up in Australia) represents the "next generation" of child longitudinal studies in Australia. The first *national* longitudinal study of children's early development, it is funded by the Australian government and implemented by a multidisciplinary research consortium led by the Australian Institute of Family Studies. It is thus characterized by a close partnership between researchers and policy makers (Sanson et al., 2002). Its research questions concern the relations of children's outcomes to their family and community contexts, childcare experiences, health-related behavior and conditions, and learning experiences.

LSAC has a cross-sequential design, with two nationally representative cohorts—5,104 infants and 4,976 4- to 5-year-olds—each followed biennially starting in 2004. It adopts an ecological model of development, seeking to identify direct and indirect influences on development from the "micro" level (e.g., prenatal exposures, family and childcare) to the "macro" level (e.g., work environments, cultural and economic issues). Data on all aspects of children's development (physical, social-emotional, and cognitive) are collected. Multisource information is derived from home interviews, questionnaires for both parents, direct child assessments, child caregiver and teacher questionnaires, and a time-use diary. It also includes linked data to childcare center accreditation ratings, medical service use, immunization status, and geographic indicators of community (dis)advantage. Data are available to all researchers, increasing the probability that the data will be fully exploited and findings taken up by policy makers and practitioners (Sanson et al., 2002).

Wave 2 data collection has achieved over 90% retention. Among findings emerging from Wave 1 data are evidence of strong associations between poor parenting (low warmth, high hostility, and low consistency) and poorer outcomes for both infants and 4- to 5-year-olds (Zubrick et al., 2008); poorer physical outcomes for infants (but not 4- to 5-year-olds) in large group care settings compared to small groups or no nonparental care, likely as a result of increased exposure to contagious illnesses; and strongest learning outcomes for children in the most educationally oriented preschool programs (Wake et al., 2008) (see http://www.aifs.gov.au/growingup for study details).

Future Directions in Australasian Child Development

Crystal ball gazing is always a dangerous endeavor. However, several societal trends can be discerned that are likely to shape the lives of children growing up in Australia and New Zealand over the coming decades. First, the mass movement of people, information, ideas, and materials that characterizes globalization ensures that our societies will become increasingly diverse and that young people will have unprecedented access to information and cultures from around the globe. Along with their highly developed competence with electronic media, concerns are likely to increase about their unregulated exposure to potentially harmful and exploitative material. Concepts such as "the contraction of childhood" are emerging, as children become "worldly wise" at earlier and earlier ages; at the same time, the concept of "delayed adulthood" is gaining currency, as previous markers of maturity such as moving out of the parental home and engaging in full-time work, marriage, and parenthood are postponed to the later 20s or early 30s, with considerable diversity of pathways during this life stage. Australasian research will no doubt contribute to the international literature as we try to understand the developmental implications of these new opportunities and challenges.

Second, there is increasing recognition of the multiple interacting layers of influence on the growing individual, from biological factors, through family and community influences, to the broader policy environment and culture. Similarly, the links between physical, emotional, social, and cognitive development are now clearer. Hence, those attempting to understand development will need to adopt holistic, ecological, and interdisciplinary approaches. For example, the biological sciences will contribute to ongoing examination of the "Barker hypothesis" on the fetal origins of disease and developmental problems, especially among indigenous children, for whom alienation, stress, nutrition, and substance abuse all pose risks. Study of the social determinants of health and well-being will need to recognize trends such as the increasing geographic concentrations of wealth and poverty and the growth in part-time (often casual) work along with increasing work hours for those in full-time employment (Stanley, Richardson, and Prior, 2005). Such studies will need to simultaneously consider economic and policy factors (e.g., unemployment, family support regimes), community level factors (e.g., neighborhood disadvantage), sociocultural factors (e.g., discrimination, exclusion, and isolation), and family factors (e.g., work-life stress and multiple family transitions). In addition, Australasian research is already responding to the extraordinary developments in genetics and neuroscience that are transforming our understanding of developmental processes.

An important feature of future attempts to understand developmental processes is likely to be the increased attention given to knowledge transfer. Governments, funding bodies, and universities are all calling for researchers to put serious effort into ensuring that knowledge acquired from research is relevant for, communicated to, and taken up by the policy, practice, and community sectors. Rather than being a simple "one-way street" from researchers to other audiences, successful uptake of new knowledge in policy and practice appears to require a genuine partnership across these sectors. The Australian Research Alliance for Children and Youth is a collaboration of a large number of practitioners, policy makers, and researchers from multiple disciplines that is trying to improve outcomes for children and youth by building such partnerships (see http://www.aracy.org.au). Such initiatives hold hope that developmental science will not only contribute to the understanding of the development of children and young people in their evolving social contexts, but will also contribute to improving their well-being.

Conclusion

Although child development in Australia and New Zealand shares many features with child development elsewhere, the particular historical, geographic, cultural, and demographic contexts of these countries have raised some particular issues and concerns that have been a focus for research. Hence, although developmental science here is firmly founded on theories and methods derived in mainly English-speaking Western parts of the world, some distinctive contributions have emerged.

Aboriginal and Torres Strait children and youth in Australia and Maori in New Zealand continue to suffer developmental disadvantages. Until recently, there has been poor evidence to support policy changes that can ameliorate these. Research on the development of indigenous children in both countries has reflected changes in social, political, and ethical understandings of indigenous peoples and is now at a stage where new methodologies are emerging that allow for genuine partnerships among indigenous communities, indigenous researchers, and nonindigenous researchers, aimed at addressing issues of significant developmental concern. This new wave of research may be better able to contribute to an improvement in the developmental outcomes of indigenous children.

The multicultural nature of each country has given rise to attempts to understand the role of culture and language in areas including parenting practices, identity formation, and interaction with the school system and the broader society. These not only contribute to the corpus of psychological knowledge, but also have implications for policy development and provision of educational programs and other services for children and youth from diverse cultural backgrounds.

The substantial changes in family life in recent decades have had significant repercussions for children, and research has sought to shed light on their impact, for instance by trying to uncover the critical mechanisms underlying successful and unsuccessful pathways in the context of family breakdown and reformation and identifying the conditions under which nonparental childcare can be a positive developmental influence.

Finally, a number of major, long-running longitudinal studies in Australia and New Zealand have made substantial contributions to our understanding of social, emotional, cognitive, and physical development from infancy to adulthood. The next generation of such studies is likely to add further to knowledge. Recognition of the complexity of influences on a child's development has been one impetus to research that crosses disciplinary and sectoral boundaries, whereas the growing commitment to knowledge transfer is leading to emerging models of communication and partnership among researchers, policy makers, and practitioners, which bodes well for the uptake of new knowledge toward improving children's lives.

With increasing globalization, the similarities in the lives of children in wealthy countries around the world are also likely to increase. Hence, it is unlikely that a completely unique Australasian developmental science will emerge (Garton, 2003). As electronic communication technologies reduce the "tyrannies of distance," Australian and New Zealand researchers will work more with overseas colleagues (including those in the immediate Asia–Pacific region). This is likely to contribute to integrative models that cross national boundaries. At the same time, the particular sociocultural contexts in which Australian and New Zealand young people will grow up will ensure an important continuing role for developmental scientists in understanding and optimizing their development.

Acknowledgments

Ann Sanson would like to acknowledge her many colleagues on the Australian Temperament Project, the Longitudinal Study of Australian Children, and the Australian Research Alliance for Children and Youth, who have all informed the data and thinking behind this paper. She would also like to acknowledge the generosity of Alison Garton in sharing her reviews of the Australian literature and the research assistance of Meredith O'Connor. Janis Paterson would like to thank her Maori, Pacific, and Pakeha colleagues in the National Institute for Public Health and Mental Health Research for assisting with sourcing data on issues facing New Zealand children and families.

References

Australian Bureau of Statistics (2002a). *Measuring Australia's progress*. Catalogue No. 1370.0. Canberra, Australia: Australian Bureau of Statistics.

Australian Bureau of Statistics (2002b). *Australian social trends 2002*. Catalogue no. 4102.0. Canberra, Australia: Australian Bureau of Statistics.

Australian Bureau of Statistics (2003). *The health and welfare of Australia's Aboriginal and Torres Strait Islander peoples*. Canberra, Australia: Australian Bureau of Statistics and Australian Institute of Health and Welfare.

Australian Bureau of Statistics (2005). *Migration, Australia, 2003-04*. Catalogue no.3412.0. Canberra, Australia: Australian Bureau of Statistics.

Australian Bureau of Statistics (2007). *Year Book Australia 2007*. Catalogue No. 1301.0. Canberra, Australia: Australian Bureau of Statistics.

Bathgate, M., Donnell, A., Mitikulena, A., Borman, B., Roberts, A., and Grigg, M. (1994). *The health of Pacific Islands people in New Zealand*. Wellington, New Zealand: Public Health Commission.

Batrouney, T., and Soriano, G. (2001). Parenting in the Torres Strait Islands. *Family Matters, 59*, 48–53.

Bird, L., and Drewery, W. (2000). *Human development in Aotearoa: A journey through life*. Auckland, New Zealand: McGraw Hill.

Butler, S., Williams, M., Tukuitonga, C., and Paterson, J. (2004). Factors associated with non-exclusive breastfeeding among mothers of a cohort of Pacific infants in New Zealand. *New Zealand Medical Journal*. Retrieved from http://www.nzma.org.nz/journal/117-1195/.

Callister, P. (2004). Maori/Non-Maori ethnic intermarriage: A research note. *New Zealand Population Review, 29*, 89–105.

Caspi, A., Sugden, K., Moffitt, T., Taylor, A., Craig, I. W., Harrington, H., et al. (2002). Influence of life stress on depression: Moderation by a polymorphism in the 5-HTT gene. *Science, 301*, 386–389.

Cook, L., Didham, R., and Khawaja, M. (1999). *On the demography of Pacific people in New Zealand*. Wellington, New Zealand: Statistics New Zealand.

Davey, J. (1998). *Tracking social change in New Zealand: From birth to death IV*. Wellington, New Zealand: Victoria University Institute of Public Policy.

Davidson, G., Sanson, A., and Gridley, H. (2000) Australian psychology and Australia's Indigenous people: Existing and emerging narratives. *Australian Psychologist, 36*, 92–99.

Department of Family and Community Services (1999). *Child care in Australia*. Canberra, Australia: Commonwealth of Australia.

de Lemos, M. (1973). The development of conservation. In G. Kearney, P. De Lacey, and G. Davidson (Eds.), *The psychology of Aboriginal Australians*. Sydney, Australia: John Wiley.

de Vaus, D. (2004). *Diversity and change in Australian families: Statistical profiles*. Melbourne, Australia: Australian Institute of Family Studies.

Eberhart, N., Shih, J., Hammen, C., and Brennan, P. (2006). Understanding the sex difference in vulnerability to adolescent depression: An examination of child and parent characteristics. *Journal of Abnormal Child Psychology, 34*, 493–506.

Fergusson, D. M., Boden, J. M., and Horwood, J. L. (2006). Cannabis use and other illicit drug use: Testing the cannabis gateway hypothesis. *Addiction, 101*, 556–569.

Garton, A. F. (2003). Cognitive development. In J. P. Keeves and R. Watanabe (Eds.), *The handbook on educational research in the Asian Pacific region* (pp. 363–375). Dordrecht, The Netherlands: Kluwer.

Garton, A. F. (2006). The origins and development of scientific psychology in Australia. In M. J. Stevens and D. Wedding (Eds.), *Psychology IUPsyS Global Resource*. CD-ROM. Hove, United Kingdom: IUPsyS and Psychology Press.

Garvey, D., Dudgeon, P., and Kearins, J. (2000). Australian psychology has a black history. In P. Dudgeon, D. Garvey, and H. Pickett (Eds.), *Working with Indigenous Australians: A handbook for psychologists* (pp. 231–248). Perth, Australia: Gunada Press.

Goodnow, J. (1996). Collaborative rules: How are people supposed to work with one another? In P. Baltes and U. Staudinger (Eds.), *Interactive minds: Life-span perspectives on the social foundation of cognition* (pp. 163–197). New York: Cambridge University Press.

Gross, J., and Hayne, H. (1998). Drawing facilitates children's verbal reports of emotionally laden events. *Journal of Experimental Psychology: Applied, 4,* 163–179.

Harris, S., and Harris, J. (1988). Aboriginal communication styles, assessment and social change. In G. Davidson (Ed.), *Ethnicity and cognitive assessment: Australian perspectives* (pp. 71–98). Darwin, Australia: DIT Press.

Hayatbakhsh, M., Najman, J., Jamrozik, K., Mamun, A., O'Callaghan, M., and Williams, G. (2009). Childhood sexual abuse and cannabis use in early adulthood: Findings from an Australian birth cohort study. *Archives of Sexual Behavior, 38,* 135–142.

Jones, C. H., and Pipe, M. E. (2002). How quickly do children forget events? *Applied Cognitive Psychology, 16,* 755–768.

Kearins, J. (1986). Visual special memory in Aboriginal and white Australian children. *Australian Journal of Psychology, 38,* 203–214.

Keats, J., and Keats, D. (1978). The role of language in the development of thinking: Theoretical approaches. In J. Keats, K. Collins, and G. Halford (Eds.), *Cognitive development: Research based on a neo-Piagetian approach* (pp. 87–113). Brisbane, Australia: Wiley.

King, M. (2003). *The history of New Zealand.* Auckland, New Zealand: Penguin Books (NZ) Ltd.

King, V., and Sobolewski, J. (2006). Nonresident fathers' contributions to adolescent well-being. *Journal of Marriage and Family, 68,* 537–557.

Love, M., Harrison, L., Sagi-Schwartz, A., van IJzendoorn, M., Ross, C., Ungerer, J., et al. (2003). Child care quality matters: How conclusions may vary with context. *Child Development, 74,* 1021–1033.

Macintyre, S. (2004). *A concise history of Australia.* Melbourne, Australia: Cambridge University Press.

McNaughton, S., Phillips, G., and MacDonald, S. (2003). Profiling teaching and learning needs in beginning literacy instruction: The case of children in low decile schools in New Zealand. *Journal of Literacy Research, 35,* 703–730.

Ministry of Health (1998). *Our children's health. Key findings on the health of New Zealand children.* Wellington, New Zealand: Ministry of Health.

Nicholson, J., Fergusson, D., and Horwood, J. (1999). Effects on later adjustment of living in a stepfamily during childhood and adolescence. *Journal of Child Psychology and Psychiatry, 40,* 405–416.

Ochiltree, G. (1990). *Children in stepfamilies.* New York: Prentice Hall.

Paterson, J., Carter, S., Gao, W., and Perese, L. (2007). Pacific Islands Families Study: Behavioural problems in 2 year old Pacific children living in New Zealand. *Journal of Child Psychology and Psychiatry, 48,* 514–522.

Paterson, J., Tukuitonga, C., Abbott, M., Feehan, M., Silva, P. Percival, T., et al. (2006). Pacific Islands families: First two years of life study – Design and methodology. *The New Zealand Medical Journal.* Retrieved from http://www.nzma.org.nz/journal/119-1228/1814/.

Phinney, J., and Rosenthal, D. (1993). Ethnic identity in adolescence: Process, context and outcome. In G. Adams, R. Montemayor, and T. Gullotta (Eds.), *Adolescent identity formation* (pp. 145–172). London: Sage Publications.

Pipe, M. E., Salmon, K., and Priestly, G. (2002). Enhancing children's accounts: How useful are non-verbal techniques? In H. L. Westcott, G. M. Davies, and R. H. C. Bull (Eds.), *Children's testimony: A handbook of psychological research and forensic practice* (pp. 161–174). Chichester, United Kingdom: John Wiley and Sons.

Pipe, M. E., Sutherland, R., Webster, N., Jones, C. H., and LaRooy, D. (2004). Do early interviews affect children's long-term event recall. *Applied Cognitive Psychology, 18,* 823–839.

Pomare, E., Keefe-Ormsby, V., and Ormsby, C. (1995). *Hauora: Maori standards of ill health 111. A study of the years 1970-1991.* Wellington, New Zealand: Te Ropu Rangahau Hauora a Eru Pomare.

Porteus, S. (1959). *The maze test and clinical psychology.* Palo Alto, CA: Pacific Books.

Prior, M., Sanson, A., Smart, D., and Oberklaid, F. (2000) *Pathways from infancy to adolescence: Australian Temperament Project 1983-2000.* Melbourne, Australia: Australian Institute of Family Studies.

Pryor, J. (2006). New Zealand families: Diversity and change. In J. Low and P. Jose (Eds.), *Lifespan development: New Zealand perspectives* (pp. 158–167). Auckland, New Zealand: Pearson Education.

Pryor, J., and Rogers, B. (2001). *Children in changing families: Life after parental separation.* Oxford, United Kingdom: Blackwell publishers.

Rigg, A., and Pryor, J. (2007). Children's perceptions of families: What do they really think? *Children and Society, 21*, 17–30.

Robinson, J., and Farhadi, S. (2005). *The mental health of child refugees from the Middle-East and their parents: Refugee status and immigration detention*. Paper presented at the 14th Biennial Australasian Human Development Conference, Perth, Australia, July 5-8. Abstract published in *Australian Journal of Psychology, 57*, Supplement, 169–170.

Rogoff, B., Paradise, R., Mejía Arauz, R., Correa-Chávez, M., and Angelillo, C. (2003). Firsthand learning through intent participation. *Annual Review of Psychology, 54*, 175–203.

Rosenthal, D., and Feldman, S. (1992). The relationship between parenting behaviour and ethnic diversity in Chinese-American and Chinese-Australian adolescents. *International Journal of Psychology, 27*, 19–31.

Rosenthal, D., and Hrynevich, C. (1985). Ethnicity and ethnic-identity: A comparative-study of Greek-Australian, Italian-Australian, and Anglo-Australian adolescents. *International Journal of Psychology, 20*, 723–742.

Royal Tangaere, A. (1999). *He Taonga, Te Mokopuna*. First Transitions Seminar: Children's Issues Centre, University of Otago, Otago, New Zealand. Retrieved from http://Royal-Tangaere.notlong.com.

Sanson, A., Augoustinos, M., Gridley, H., Kyrios, K., Reser, J., and Turner, C. (1998). Racism and prejudice: An APS Position Paper. *Australian Psychologist, 33*, 161–182.

Sanson, A., and Dudgeon, P. (2000) Guest editorial: Psychology, indigenous issues, and reconciliation. *Australian Psychologist, 36*, 79–81.

Sanson, A., Hemphill, S. A., and Smart, D. (2004). Connections between temperament and social development: A review. *Social Development, 13*, 142–170.

Sanson, A., Nicholson, J., Ungerer, J., Zubrick, S., Wilson, K., Ainley, J., et al. (2002). *Introducing the Longitudinal Study of Australian Children*. Melbourne, Australia: Australian Institute of Family Studies.

Seagrim, G., and Lendon, K. (1980). *Furnishing the mind*. New York: Academic Press.

Silburn, S., Zubrick, S., De Maio, J., Shepherd, C., Griffin, J., Mitrou, F., et al. (2006a). *The Western Australian Aboriginal Child Health Survey: Strengthening the capacity of Aboriginal children, families and communities*. Perth, Australia: Curtin University of Technology and Telethon Institute for Child Health Research.

Silburn, S., Zubrick, S., Lawrence, D. M., Mitrou, F. G., De Maio, J., Blair, E., et al. (2006b). The intergenerational effects of forced separation on the social and emotional wellbeing of Aboriginal children and young people. *Family Matters, 75*, 10–17.

Silva, P. A., and Stanton, W. R. (Eds.). (1996). *From child to adult: The Dunedin Multidisciplinary Health and Development Study*. Auckland, New Zealand: Oxford University Press.

Smart, D., Richardson, N., Sanson, A., Dussuyer, I., Marshall, B., Toumbourou, J. W., et al. (2005). *Patterns and precursors of adolescent antisocial behaviour: Outcomes and connections*. Melbourne, Australia: Australian Institute of Family Studies.

Smart, D., and Sanson, A. (2003) Social competence in young adulthood, its nature and antecedents. *Family Matters, 64*, 4–10.

Smith, A. B. (1999). Quality childcare and joint attention. *International Journal of Early Years Education, 7*, 85–98

Smith, A. B., and Van der Vyer, R. (1993). *Early childhood Educare: The search for quality*. Videotape, Audiovisual Production Unit, University of Otago, Otago, New Zealand.

Smith L. T. (1999). *Decolonising methodologies: Research and Indigenous peoples*. Dunedin, New Zealand: University of Otago Press.

Smyth, B., Caruana, C., and Ferro, A. (2004). Father-child contact after separation. *Family Matters, 67*, 20–27.

Sommerland, E., and Bellingham, W. (1972). Cooperation-competition: A comparison of Australian European and Aboriginal school children. *Journal of Cross-Cultural Psychology, 3*, 149–157.

Sporle, A., Pearce, N., and Davis, P. (2002). Social class mortality difference in Maori and Non-Maori men ages 15-64 during the last two decades. *New Zealand Medical Journal, 115*, 127–131.

Stanley, F., Richardson, S., and Prior, M. (2005) *Children of the lucky country? How Australian society has turned its back on children and why children matter*. Sydney, Australia: Macmillan.

Statistics New Zealand (2002). *Pacific progress. A report on the economic status of Pacific peoples*. Wellington, New Zealand: Statistics New Zealand.

Statistics New Zealand (2003). *Survey of family income and employment dynamics*. Wellington, New Zealand: Statistics New Zealand.

Steel, Z., Momartin, S., Bateman, C., Hafshejani, A., Silove, D., Everson, N., et al. (2004). Psychiatric status of asylum seeker families held for a protracted period in a remote detention centre. *Australian and New Zealand Journal of Public Health, 28*, 527–536.

Tagoilelagi-Leota, F., McNaughton, S., MacDonald, S., and Farry, S. (2004). *The precious threads: Language and literacy teaching in Pasifika early childhood education centres and bilingual and biliteracy development.* Wellington, New Zealand: Ministry of Education.

Te Puni Kokiri. (2004). *Te Reo i te Hapori: Maori language in the community.* Wellington, New Zealand: Ministry of Maori Development.

Tupuola, A. M. (1998). Fa'aSamoa in the 1990's: Young Samoan women speak. In R. Du Plessis and L. Alice (Eds.), *Feminist thought in Aotearoa New Zealand: Connections and differences* (pp. 51–56). Auckland, New Zealand: Oxford University Press.

Wake, M., Sanson, A., Berthelsen, D., Hardy, P., Misson, S., Smith, K., Ungerer, J. and the LSAC Research Consortium. (2008). *How well are Australian infants and childern aged 4 to 5 doing? FAHCSIA Social Policy Research Paper No. 36.* Canberra, Australia: FAHCSIA. Available online at http://www.fahcsia.gov.an/internet/facsinternet.nsf/research/prps-prps_36.htm.

Waltja Tjutangku Palyapayi Aboriginal Corporation (2001). *Pipirr Wiimaku, 'for the little kids': Innovative childcare report 2000-2001.* Alice Springs, Australia: Waltja Tjutangku Palyapayi Aboriginal Corporation.

Weston, R., and Smyth, B. (2000). Financial living standards after divorce. *Family Matters, 55*, 10–15.

Wilson, R. (1997). *Bringing them home: Report of the National Inquiry into the separation of Aboriginal and Torres Strait Islander children from their families.* Canberra, Australia: Human Rights and Equal Opportunity Commission (HREOC), Commonwealth of Australia.

Wise, S., Ungerer, J., and Sanson, A. (2002). Childcare policy to promote child wellbeing. *The Australian Economic Review, 35*, 180–187.

Zajac, R., and Hayne, M. (2003). I don't think that's what really happened: The effects of cross-examination on the accuracy of children's reports. *Journal of Experimental Psychology: Applied, 9*, 87–195.

Zubrick, S., Smith, P., Nicholson, J., Sanson, A., Jackiewicz, T., and the LSAC Research Consortium. (2008). *Parenting and families in Australia. FAHCSIA Social Policy Research Paper No.34.* Canberra, Australia: FAHCSIA. Available online at http://www.fahcsia.gov.an/internet/facsinternet.nsf/research/prps-prps_34.htm.

26
The HOME Environment

ROBERT H. BRADLEY

Introduction

Using data from 186 societies, Ember and Ember (2001) found that the further away, on average, that fathers slept from their children, the higher the rates of homicide and assault in the society. The effect was stronger in societies where high dominance and aggression is part of the male role. Although these findings are provocative and seemingly straightforward to interpret because of the large sample, it would be foolish to proffer a simple explanation for such findings because human behavior is anything but simple. Nonetheless, the findings suggest that culture is insinuated in the way people organize their living arrangements so that the arrangements are aligned with societal values about interpersonal relationships. Most of the time, those values or arrangements or connections lead to adaptive behaviors for children, but sometimes, adaptive functioning gets caught in the crosshairs, and both child and society are losers.

Culture is a complex system composed of many loosely interlocked, sometimes causally connected elements, including parenting beliefs and practices, family climate, spatial arrangements in dwellings, and the availability and organization of time and materials (D'Andrade, 2001). Culture helps determine how parents both interpret and react to the needs of children. Kitayama (2002) argued that it is difficult to penetrate the distinctive features of a culture because there is a dynamism in how such features are fully instantiated in daily routines, interpersonal rituals, styles of conversation, and relations with social institutions. It is easier to map routines, physical arrangements, and practices than to fully appreciate how they operate within individuals, families, or communities (de Munck, 2001). Part of the dynamism regarding how culture is implicated in children's home life derives from the fact that societal goals represent a fluid blend of what is thought possible and what is deemed desirable. Accordingly, parenting practices in two societies can look remarkably similar when children are infants, only to diverge during middle childhood and adolescence. Likewise, parenting behaviors and household arrangements that align in one society to affect children's development (for good or ill) may not be aligned in a second society (as will be seen throughout this chapter). These differences may reflect cultural values; they may also reflect other aspects of family ecology. In that regard, it is important to remember that little things may mean a lot. It can be instructive to examine how often parents do certain things and how their patterns of behavior function in relation to children's outcomes. By so doing, researchers may derive insights into how culture is implicated in parenting and child development.

For nearly four decades, the Home Observation for Measurement of the Environment (HOME) Inventory (Caldwell and Bradley, 2003), has been extensively used as a measure of the quality and quantity of stimulation and support available to a child in the home environment. It also captures aspects of family organization, routines, and involvement with extended family.

The focus is on the child *in* the environment—child as a recipient of inputs from objects, events, and transactions occurring in connection with family life. The indicators contained in HOME are there because they are deemed salient for children's development. Information needed to score the inventory is obtained during a 45- to 90-minute home visit done during a time when the target child and the child's primary caregiver are present and awake. Other family members, and even guests, can also be present, but their presence is not required. The procedure is a low-key semi-structured observation and interview done so as to minimize intrusiveness and allow family members to act normally. Throughout the course of the visit, observations of parent–child interaction and discussions with the parent and child about objects, events, and transactions that occur are probed and interpreted from the child's point of view. The intent is to understand the child's opportunities and experiences—in essence, to understand what life is like for the particular child in the child's most intimate surroundings. From the outset, it was decided to use an expansive definition of home environment in choosing indicators for the HOME Inventory based on the premise that what a child perceives as part of home life often extends beyond the four walls of a dwelling. For individual parents, too, there is a sense of boundary to the spaces where parenting takes place, but what actually constitutes the boundary varies across parents and time depending on an array of cultural, familial, personal, and child factors (Belsky, 1984; Korosec-Serafty, 1985). In effect, what is appropriated to the idea of the home environment is the meaning of the acts, objects, and places connected to parental caregiving. Different families may use different geographic settings to be part of the parenting environment (e.g., the street beside the house, the backyard, a neighborhood park). Such a capacious definition is consistent with the position of social anthropologists who contend that the social boundaries of household units do not necessarily coincide with the physical boundaries of their dwellings (Altman, 1977). The concept of the home environment as not fully confined to a specific place becomes useful because the role of parent tends to shift as children age from that of direct provider and teacher (most of which may well take place within the family residence) to that of mentor, guide, and arranger of experiences (some of which almost certainly will occur outside the child's residence; Fagot and Kavanaugh 1993; Maccoby and Martin, 1983).

Over the years, researchers and practitioners around the world have offered commentaries on the HOME. Some have been highly technical, sophisticated journal articles, and some have been quite informal—even funny—dealing with practical concerns pertaining to administration, scoring, and interpretation. In this chapter, these diverse sources of information about the HOME will be used to address issues about culture and how it is implicated in children's home experience and how home experience is implicated in children's development. As well, information obtained from research using other means of data gathering will be brought to bear on these discussions in hopes of providing more complete coverage of the dimensions that Whiting and Edwards (1988) contend are important for distinguishing between cultures and for which there is evidence of impact on child adaptive functioning: (1) parental warmth and responsiveness, (2) discipline/control, (3) stimulation/teaching, and (4) household arrangements and community conditions. The data from most societies is sparse, so it will be difficult to draw firm conclusions about cultural differences for some classes of experience and for some patterns of relations with child functioning.

Warmth and Responsiveness

Culture, geography, and general circumstances of daily life affect the organization and expression of emotions (Kagan, Chapter 9, in this volume; Kilbride and Kilbride, 1983; Whiting and Edwards, 1988). Societies can be distinguished in terms of their attention to children's emotional needs. It is assumed that cultures subscribing to an interdependence script rely more on continuous caregiving and parent–child contact (Carlson and Harwood, 2003). For example, Kung infants from Namibia spend many hours a day in direct contact, as do Longoli children in Kenya (Munroe and Munroe, 1980). Likewise, Indian mothers tend to stay close to their infants and score high on emotional responsiveness. This is associated with high levels of proximity seeking and contact maintenance on the part of their children (Agrawal and Gulati, 2005). This contrasts to European American infants, where holding decreases rapidly from the first few weeks of life through age 2 years. For European Americans, tactile contact gives way to other forms of communication (visual, acoustic, and objects based; Bradley, Corwyn, Burchinal, McAdoo, and Garcia Coll, 2001; Valsiner, 2000). Data obtained from Argentine families showed that 70% of children at age 6 months were hugged or kissed by their mothers during the home visit when data were collected. This shrunk to 40% by age 2 years and to 25% by age 5 years. By contrast, speaking to the child rose from 50% at age 6 months to 70% at age 2 and 80% at age 5 (Centro de Estudios sobre Nutricion Infantil, 1996). A similar pattern emerged in Spain: 71% of children were hugged in infancy, and 63% were hugged in early childhood; 69% were spoken to in infancy, and 89% were spoken to in early childhood (Perez and Moreno, 2004).

Data on parental responsiveness from the National Longitudinal Survey of Youth done in the United States show that approximately 90% of all parents spoke to their infants at least twice during the hour-long visit, and 70% to 80% responded verbally to something the infant said (Bradley et al., 2001). Approximately 80% to 85% of nonpoor mothers caressed, kissed, or hugged their infants; the figures for poor mothers were approximately 10% to 15% less, with poor African American mothers having the lowest rate (64%). A study done in Portugal, Germany, Austria, and France also showed socioeconomic differences in indicators of maternal responsiveness, sensitivity, intrusiveness, and remoteness (Gunning et al., 2004). However, scores tended to be high, consistent with the generally low levels of extreme poverty in those countries. Likewise, an analysis done of HOME data from the National Child Development Study in the United Kingdom showed slightly higher scores than were obtained in the United States (Aughinbaugh and Gittleman, 2003).

The situation for preschool-age children in the United States is similar to that for infants. Approximately 90% of mothers conversed with their children at least twice during the 1-hour HOME visit. About the same percentage responded to children's questions. Nearly 60% of nonpoor European American, Latin American, and Asian American mothers caressed, kissed, or hugged their children during the hour-long visit; the figures for African American mothers and for all poor mothers were lower (32% to 48%). Approximately 70% of mothers encouraged their school-age children to talk during the visit, and approximately 85% of mothers answered children's questions. Likewise 80% to 95% of mothers showed generally positive feelings toward the child, with poor mothers lower than nonpoor mothers by 5% to 10%. Approximately 70% of European American and Asian American mothers claimed to have expressed affection to their adolescent children on a daily basis. The figures for Latin Americans and African Americans were approximately 50% and 40%, respectively. Approximately 75% of European American mothers stated that they had praised their children at least three times during the previous week. The figures were approximately 10% less in the other ethnic groups studied. The figures for poor families also tended to be lower than for nonpoor families, most notably among Latin Americans. Studies of the home environments of school-age children in Austria, Germany, Portugal, Hungary, and Spain showed generally high scores on HOME scales that measure maternal warmth and responsiveness, albeit there were socioeconomic differences within each country (Abrue-Lima, n.d.; European Child Care and Education Study Group, 1999; Judit, 2001).

During an hour-long home visit, fewer than 6% of parents (representing five different ethnic groups) made derogatory comments about their adolescent, and more than 80% encouraged the adolescent to contribute to the conversation and responded appropriately to the adolescent's comments and questions (Bradley et al., 2000). Almost 75% spontaneously mentioned a particular strength in the adolescent during the visit. Almost 90% stated that they allowed the adolescent some privacy while at home and stated that they allowed the adolescent to express disagreements without resorting to a harsh reprisal. Only approximately 25% said they had lost their temper with the adolescent during the previous week.

In circumstances of austerity, parents are often less affectionate and responsive. Likewise, in circumstances of danger and scarcity, parents become more discriminating in the care of children (Durbrow, 1999). In Caribbean societies, mothers tend to be less indulgent by the time children are 3; children are assigned household chores, sent on errands, and become caregivers for siblings as they grow older. Parents are sensitive to ways that children are troublesome, and very few parents praise children's qualities or behavior. That said, studies done in Latin America and the Caribbean provide a mixed picture regarding the amount of responsiveness shown to young children. Responsiveness scores on the HOME for children in Paraguay, Argentina, and St. Vincent's were lower than U.S. norms (Blevins-Knabe and Austin, 2000; Centro de Estudios Sobre Nutricion Infantil, 1996; Durbrow, Jones, Bozoky, Jimerson, and Adams 1996), but scores in Jamaica, Costa Rica, and Chile were not much lower (Bulnes, Cajdler, Edwards, and Lira, 1979; Castillo-Durin et al., 2001; Lozoff, Park, Radan, and Wolf, 1995; Lozoff et al., 2003; Tippie, 2003; Walker, Chang, Powell, and Grantham-McGregor, 2004). Performance on certain indicators of responsiveness are particularly revealing regarding cultural differences. Although mean scores in several Latin American countries were not greatly different than U.S. and European samples, it was less common for parents to express overt affection for children or be verbally responsive while the home visitor was present. This likely represents the cultural value of showing deference toward other adults in social situations rather than lack of warmth for the child. In St. Vincent, concerns regarding the way responsiveness was measured by HOME were sufficient so that small adjustments were made to the scale (i.e., the parental praising of children was not considered as central to the construct). This form of spontaneous praise, used to display affection and build self-esteem during middle childhood, appears to be of a different sort than the kind of deliberate praise used to reinforce desired behavior in Cameroon (Nsamenang and Lamb, 1995). In St. Vincent, there is not a strong focus on independence and self-enhancement.

Most studies of African families have concerned infants or preschool-age children. However, Holding (2003) used the Middle Childhood HOME in Kenya. Kenyan parents rarely encouraged children to contribute to conversations during the interview (consistent with the idea that children should be deferent). It was also uncommon for mothers of school-age children to use terms of endearment for children, as is often the case for mothers in Western countries. By contrast, there was a full range of response to the other indicators of responsiveness on the HOME, including the likelihood that parents would respond positively to the visitors' praising of their children and would answer the children's questions during the home visit.

One of the challenges in understanding how culture is implicated in parenting practices pertains to the fact that people from different societies may use somewhat different ways (forms) to accomplish similar goals for children (function) (Bornstein, 1995). Body contact is a near universal form of responsiveness, but it is used with greater frequency in some cultures, less frequency in others. Keller et al. (2004) studied mothers from Cameroon (Nso and Guarati), Greece, Germany, and Costa Rica. Specifically, they observed mothers with their infants in a free-play situation. Almost all of the mothers (a small number of Greek mothers being the exception) used some form of body contact during at least part of the observation period. However, mothers from Cameroon and Costa Rica (where interdependence in social relationships is the norm) maintained that contact for at least 75% of the observation period, whereas Greek and German mothers did so less than 33% of the time. Likewise, almost all mothers had face-to-face contact with their children during the period, but Greek and German mothers maintained such contact for approximately 70% of the time (consistent with a strong focus on education for self-reliance) compared to less than half the time for the other three groups of mothers. In the three groups (German, Greek, and Costa Rican) where great value is ascribed to economic independence, mutual eye contact was maintained throughout almost half the observation period, contrasted to less than 20% of the time for the two groups from Cameroon. Belief in the "evil eye" remains strong in some societies. Where it does, cultural models tend not to include face-to-face engagement as a form of responsiveness (Kilbride and Kilbride, 1983). When Richman et al. (1988) compared the Gusii from Kenya to mothers from Boston, they found that Gusii mothers rarely talked to their infants or even looked at them. This pattern reflects broader cultural conventions concerning conversational interactions. Even so, Gusii mothers held infants more than Boston mothers. The researchers concluded that, "Gusii mothers seek to quiet and soothe their babies, whereas the American mothers pursue a style in which verbal interactions and stimulation of the infant play an important part" (Richman et al., 1988, pp. 616–617).

Aina, Agiobu-Kemmer, Etta, Zeitlin, and Setiloane (1993), in their study of the Yoruba in Nigeria, found that parents are not particularly responsive in a verbal manner. In the course of an hour visit using the HOME, 44% of mothers never spoke to the child, only 26% spoke three times or more, and 88% never responded to the infant's verbalizations. The Yoruba believe that children should be deferential. This follows a general belief that with seniority comes privilege. Unlike adults in many Western countries, Yoruba adults do not view children's comments as having much potential usefulness (i.e., they are not worth paying attention to). They feel that children should heed their elders whose experience leads to knowledge and wisdom. This does not mean that Yoruba parents are totally unresponsive. Aina et al. (1993) observed that 84% of mothers conveyed their positive feelings about the child using tone of voice, 45% spontaneously praised the child, and 52% caressed or kissed the child during the home visit. These HOME findings from Uganda comport with findings from other studies done in Africa. Among the Langoli in Kenya, holding young children and quick responses to distress are prevalent. In the case of the Baganda, the expression of affection toward children takes a form that fits with the Baganda's overall demarcation of what is acceptable for public versus private expressions of emotion. Kilbride and Kilbride (1983) found that Baganda mothers display positive affect toward children but do it in the form of stroking, looking at the child, and putting the child in a face-to-face position rather than in the form of hugs and kisses like American mothers. In Macedonia, where poverty is prevalent and there is less focus on parental responsiveness than survival and building key interpersonal skills, adjustments to scoring were made to HOME indicators of responsiveness, and indicators related to fostering social competence were added.

Rohner (1986) marshaled evidence from several large cross-cultural studies showing that warm, supportive relationships help promote good adjustment, a sense of well-being, good health, and a wealth of other positive developmental outcomes. HOME findings from around the world support this assertion, but findings are mixed. In India, maternal responsiveness was related to infant irritability, but the direction of causality was not made clear in the study (Black et al., 2004). In a second study done in India, responsiveness showed robust associations with several measures of cognitive and adaptive functioning ($r = .36$ to $.49$; Agarwal et al., 1992). Parental nurturance is unrelated to achievement motivation among Indian adolescents but does seem to protect children from having an external locus of control (Basral, Thind, and Jaswal, 2006). Responsiveness is related to social adjustment for Japanese but not American children (Basral, Thind, and Jaswal, 2006). Indicators of affection showed the most divergent relations. In both Brazil and St. Vincent, responsiveness is related to children's mental health problems (Anselmi, Piccinini, Basrros, and Lopes, 2004; Bastos, Almeida-Filho, and Pinho, 1998; Durbrow et al., 1996). Likewise, Zeitlin et al. (1995) observed a relation between maternal affection and a composite measure of child well-being among the Yoruba. HOME studies done in Jamaica,

Argentina, and Nigeria document a relation between responsiveness and measures of competence in early childhood (Aina et al., 1993; Hayes, 1996; Torralva and Cugnasco, 1996). However, Lozoff et al. (1995) did not find associations with Intelligence Quotient (IQ) in Costa Rica, and Drotar et al. (1999) found little relation between a composite derived from the Responsiveness, Parental Involvement, and Organization scales and Bayley Mental Development Index (MDI) scores among Ugandan families.

Part of the challenge in comparing findings pertaining to responsiveness across societies is identifying precisely what complex of parenting behaviors constitutes responsiveness and whether the construct varies by society (Munroe and Munroe, 1980). Whether tactile contact, positive affectivity, and short latency in responding to distress are required in all societies is open to question. Zayas and Solari (1994) also make clear that forms of responsiveness (such as maintaining close physical contact with infants) may not show the same consistency of association with positive child outcomes in all cultures, depending on other parenting practices that are normative in the culture. Adaptations made to HOME for the Yoruba by Aina et al. (1993) and for Koreans by Lee (2002) lend further credence to the idea that to understand parenting requires appreciating how complex behavioral patterns may be organized and expressed differently in different cultures (Bornstein et al., 1992). In the case of the Yoruba, a judgment was made that two Responsiveness items from HOME had limited relevance (allowing children to engage in messy play, and showing a positive response to praising the child). The responsivity scale was recomposed for use with Korean children in middle childhood, and many of the items were eliminated (Lee, 2002). Kurtz, Borkowski, and Deshmukh (1987) also modified the HOME Inventory for use in India. Items pertaining to spontaneous conversation with the child were deleted. Indian children are expected to respect their elders; it is considered irreverent to speak without permission, particularly when visitors are present. Because of Indian tradition, a child who spontaneously talks during a conversation of elders is often not encouraged. That said, others using HOME in India have not selected to change indicators of responsiveness and have found strong correlations with both cognitive and social development (Agarwal et al., 1992).

In overview, there is substantial variability in the frequency with which particular indicators of warmth and responsiveness are observed around the world. The differences appear to reflect differences in cultural belief systems and general socioeconomic conditions. Especially revealing are differences in response to particular indicators (e.g., praising children, overt demonstrations of affection in the presence of other adults, verbal exchanges with the child) and decisions to either drop or add indicators to better capture how responsiveness is enacted in different countries. Relatedly, intercorrelations among indicators of responsiveness tend to vary by culture, suggesting that cultural models of the construct (i.e., what constitutes responsiveness) vary. Despite these differences, responsiveness is consistently associated with measures of socioemotional development and less so with other aspects of well-being. Unfortunately, the samples available in many studies were limited, and there were few controls on key demographic and child variables, making interpretation of findings difficult.

Discipline/Punishment

In societies where self-reliance and autonomy are highly valued, parents tend to demand less compliance with parental directives and are more tolerant regarding displays of disrespect for elders. Parents also tend to use physical forms of child control less frequently. Data from the National Longitudinal Survey of Youth in the United States showed that approximately 25% of African American mothers restricted their infants during the HOME interview, whereas only 12% of Asian mothers did (European American and Latin American mothers were intermediate). Less than 5% of nonpoor European American, Latin American, and Asian American mothers spanked their infants during the visit, compared to 9% of African American mothers.

The figures for poor mothers in every group were 3% to 5% higher. Although the rates of spanking observed during the home visit were relatively low, more than half of the mothers from all ethnic groups reported spanking their children at least once during the previous week. Indeed, approximately 40% of poor European American and poor African American families reported spanking their children at least three times. The figures for Latin American and Asian American families were approximately 10% lower. Sixty to eighty percent of mothers admitted spanking their preschoolers during the previous week; Asian Americans were the least likely and African Americans the most likely to spank. Parents reported spanking school-age children less than preschoolers. More than 60% of European American and Asian American mothers from nonpoor families reported that they had not spanked their children during the past week; for African Americans, approximately 50% said they had spanked their child during the last week (the figures for Latinos were intermediate).

In most African societies, physical punishment is commonplace. In one study done in sub-Saharan Africa, more than 80% of mothers said they spanked children several times a week (Aina et al., 1993). Physical punishment is so common in Uganda that Drotar et al. (1999) decided against using the Acceptance scale from HOME as part of their assessment of the home environment. In adapting the Middle Childhood HOME in Kenya, Holding (2003) modified scoring criteria to allow greater use of punishment. Consistent with the view that children should respect elders, Holding modified the item, "Child can get upset with parent without harsh punishment" to allow an intermediate level of punishment. It is interesting to note that Yoruba mothers did not display other forms of nonacceptance at rates higher than those typically observed in Western countries (e.g., scolding, expressing annoyance). Moreover, such culturally prescribed forms of sternness do not appear to be accompanied by indifference to children's needs or disrespect for children per se. In the case of one indicator ("Parent does not interfere or restrict child more than 3 times"), their rates were lower than in America (1% versus 20%). In Bahrain, where great value is placed on parental authority, scores on the Acceptance scale from the HOME were substantially lower than U.S. norms (Hadeed and Sylva, 1999). The Nso of Cameroon believe that children learn from adversity and need discipline to learn "lessons" about how to act. Respectful behavior is a cornerstone of childhood socialization in Indonesia. Only 42% of Javanese children could express negative feelings without harsh reprisal, compared to 86% of U.S. and 87% of Spanish children; 81% and 53% of U.S. and Spanish children, respectively, could hit a parent without harsh reprisal, whereas only 35% of Javanese children could do so (Zevalkink, 1997).

Although Latino parents are generally more tolerant and indulgent with very young children than is true of European Americans, beliefs in the importance of respect and obedience gradually give way to more restrictive control and punishment, a pattern that contrasts with the reduced use of physical means of control (in favor of reasoning) in families from the United States and Western Europe (Bulcroft, Carmody, and Bulcroft, 1996; Calzada and Eyberg, 2002; Hill, Bush, and Roosa, 2003). As Halgunseth, Ipsa, and Rudy (2006) have noted, the Latino goal of *respeto* gradually moves parents to demand more of their children in terms of following rules and manifesting proper demeanor, with less concern for developing autonomy than is the case for parents in the United States and Western Europe (Durbrow, 1999; Reichel-Dolumatoff and Reichel-Dolumatoff, 1961). In such societies, parents commonly use approaches to control children that are regarded as negative in more technologically advanced Western societies. Displays of annoyance toward children are so common in St. Vincent and Dominica that Durbrow et al. (1996) modified the Middle Childhood HOME to allow parents to lose their tempers more often before losing credit on items that involve expressions of anger. That said, scores on the Acceptance scales from the HOME were not uniformly lower in Latin America and the Caribbean than in the United States and Europe (Blevins-Knabe and Austin, 2000; Bulnes et al.,

1979; Durbrow et al., 1996; Lozoff et al., 1995; Tippie, 2003; Torralva, Esteban, O'Donnell, and Duran, 2000; Walker et al., 2004). In Chile, for example, most parents reported using physical punishment and reprimands routinely, yet their overall scores on Acceptance were not much lower than U.S. scores (Bulnes et al., 1979). As a general rule, Latin American parents were not observed to hit their children more frequently than U.S. and European parents during the visit when the HOME was administered. In addition, parents were not observed to be more intrusive. Moreover, studies of Mayan families show that different cultural models pertaining to child control were obtained in Latin America (Mosier and Rogoff, 2003). Mayans believe that children gradually learn responsible social behavior and that they learn it best if allowed choices early and if positively reinforced for volunteered desirable behavior. In the Mayan cultural model, there is acceptance of children's limited capacity to understand the needs of others or to understand the likely consequences of their actions. In a comparison of Mayan and American mothers on the HOME, none of the Mayan mothers reported punishing their toddlers for misbehavior, whereas approximately one-half the mothers from St. Lake City, Utah, did.

In technologically advanced societies, where personal choice and independence are valued, harsh discipline is used less often than in less industrialized societies. An example of the latter is Macedonia where there is strong emphasis on cooperation and compliance with adult directives. Punishment is so common in Macedonia that adjustments were made to HOME scoring criteria. In India, restrictiveness and punishment are also fairly common (Agrawal and Gulati, 2005). Scores on the HOME Acceptance scale (avoidance of punishment) tend to be high in Canada, the United States, Australia, Japan, and most European countries. A good example is Spain, where less than 20% of mothers expressed annoyance with their children during the HOME visit and only approximately 50% reported spanking their children (Perez and Moreno, 2004). There are exceptions. For example, use of physical punishment is more frequent in Portugal (Abreu-Lima, n.d.). The fact that harsh punishment is used less often in technologically advanced societies does not mean that parents do not value compliance. Nihira, Tomiyasu, and Oshio (1987) argued that, whereas Japanese mothers emphasize affective means to gain child compliance, American mothers tend to rely more on authority, rewards, and punishment.

Although there is controversy regarding the use of punishment, the preponderance of evidence indicates that repeated harsh punishment is inimical to child well-being (Gershoff, 2002; Jaffee, Caspi, Moffitt, and Taylor, 2004). In North America and Europe, scores on the HOME Acceptance scale are often associated with behavior problems (Bradley et al., 2000, 2001; Perez and Moreno, 2004). In the United States, associations begin to emerge during the preschool years with the development of self-regulatory competence (Bradley et al., 2001). Scores on the Acceptance (also called the Avoidance of Punishment) scale tend to be positively correlated with competence and negatively correlated with conduct problems in Latin America and the Caribbean (Durbrow et al., 1996; Hayes, 1996; Lozoff et al., 1995; Toralva et al., 2000).

Granting these general patterns, using physical means to control behavior does not have a consistent negative impact on children's behavior across all societies or across all ethnic groups within societies (Bradley and Corwyn, 2005; Bradley et al., 2001). For example, in India, restrictiveness and punishment is related to diminished contact maintenance and to various measures of social and adaptive functioning during infancy but bears no relation to other attachment behaviors (Agarwal et al., 1992; Agrawal and Gulati, 2005). In Korea, where the items were recomposed to form a broader scale dealing with emotional support and discipline, there was no relation to perceived self-competence is middle childhood (Lee. Super, and Harkness, 2003).

Theory supports a link between harsh punishment and achievement, but the paths appear more complex and thus perhaps less consistent across cultures than is the case for conduct problems (McLoyd, 1998). Part of the reason physical punishment shows an inconsistent relation to behavioral outcomes for children likely results from the fact that using physical means to control children in some societies (most often reflecting values of respect for elders) is not uniformly associated with reduced warmth and sensitivity, as often is the case for technologically advanced Western societies. For example, Latina mothers who display high levels of controlling intrusive behavior frequently are also quite warm and sensitive to their children (Carlson and Harwood, 2003; Ispa, 1994). Likewise, among Haitians, where a blending of Christian and Voodoo traditions inform parenting practice, parents express great overt affection for children while at the same time enforcing strict discipline (McEachern and Kenny, 2002). The joining of physical control with warmth likely accounts for why physical control is positively associated with secure attachment in Puerto Rican, Dominican, and Mexican infants (Carlson and Harwood, 2003; Fracasso, Busch-Rossnagel, and Fisher, 1994).

In some respects, the Chinese notion of *guan* helps clarify why it is difficult to situate the notion of parental control into a universally consistent framework pertaining to the promotion of child well-being. The Chinese idea of guan roughly translates into the English notion of "training" but needs to be distinguished from related notions such as teaching and physical control. Guan includes the idea of parents being directive regarding children's behavior, but research done in the United States, Hong Kong, and Pakistan reveals that guan is more strongly associated with parental warmth than parental domination (Stewart, Bond, Kennard, Ho, and Zaman, 2002). Perhaps because parental directiveness fits well with Chinese and Pakistani cultural values, guan is associated with perceived health, relationship harmony, and life satisfaction in Hong Kong and Pakistan. By contrast, it is not associated with such positive outcomes in the United States, where parents are seen more as facilitators than directors of children's development.

In overview, there is wide variation in the extent to which physical punishment is used to control children's behavior and the situations where physical punishment is deemed appropriate. Where respect for elders is highly valued, physical punishment is more common; however, its use is not necessarily harsh or accompanied by efforts to demean children. Neither is it always accompanied by failure to provide other forms of supportive care. In effect, the degree to which spanking is related to other forms of nonacceptance varies by country. Despite cultural differences in the patterns of punishment, however, its use appears generally associated with negative child outcomes.

Stimulation/Teaching

The deleterious consequences of understimulation were first brought to light in studies of institutionalized children (Dennis, 1973; Skeels and Dye, 1939). Stimulation is important because it shapes the course of development, including neural development. In their penetrating analysis of how children learn, the Committee on Developments in the Science of Learning showed that people learn by actively encountering objects, actions, events, and concepts in their environments (Bransford, Brown, and Cocking, 2000). To move from novice learner to expert in any particular area of knowledge or skill requires substantial (usually structured) experience in that area (meaning much stimulation).

During the last half of the twentieth century, the emphasis on stimulation for children beginning early in life escalated in technologically advanced societies and in societies trying to transition into more market-driven economies. The practice fits with societal goals pertaining to higher order skills and independence. For example, scores on HOME scales such as Learning Materials, Academic Stimulation, Variety of Stimulation, and Parental Involvement tend to be high in Europe, the United States, Canada, Israel, and Japan. However, it is also often associated with providing a generally supportive environment, as witnessed by the positive association between HOME scores and breast feeding in both Dutch and Australian families (Vreugdenhil, Slijper, Mulder, and Weisglas-Kuperus, 2002; Zhou, Baghurst, Gibson, and Makrides, 2007).

Despite the generally high levels of encouragement for learning present in most technologically advanced societies, there are differences in how much parents stimulate children across and within these countries. Consider as an illustration a comparison of U.S. and Israeli school children by Jacobson et al. (1995): 95% of U.S. parents encouraged children to read versus 74% of Israeli parents; 81% of U.S. parents helped children develop motor skills versus 41% of Israeli parents (in Israel it is more often peers); and 59% of U.S. parents included children in their recreational activities versus 20% of Israeli parents. Somewhat similar findings emerged when HOME scores of elementary school children in Hungary, Israel, and the United States were compared (Judit, 2001). Scores on the Learning Materials, Enrichment, and Family Companionship scales were virtually identical for Hungarian and American families, but scores on the latter two (both of which involved parent and child together activities) were a little lower for Israeli households. Even with these differences, the overall emphasis on stimulating achievement is essentially equal in the three countries. HOME findings from the European Child Care and Education Study Group (1997) showed that Spanish mothers are more direct in their encouragement of academic performance than Austrian and German mothers. French and Italian parents tend to perceive child development as depending less on what parents do (see Bornstein et al., 1992, for review). Evidence also suggests that French mothers, compared to North American and Argentine mothers, are less likely to emphasize objects and events in the environment as a way to stimulate children (Bornstein et al., 1996).

Bradley et al. (2001) examined the frequency with which children are exposed to common objects and conditions in the home environment using data from the National Longitudinal Survey of Youth. The data showed that 60% of European American infants had at least 10 books, and 65% had parents who read to them at least three times a week. However, only 25% of Latin American infants living in poverty had parents who read to them at least three times a week. Approximately 33% of infants from all groups had at least three push or pull toys. More than 90% of European American preschoolers had at least 10 books in the home; more than 60% of nonpoor preschoolers from other ethnic groups did as well. In all ethnic and socioeconomic groups, more than 70% of preschool-age children were exposed to at least 3 hours of television per day, and the majority had access to a record or tape player. For 4-year-olds, similar figures on the number of books present in the home and the number of times parents read to children emerged in the National Household Education Survey (NHES). In both surveys, there were differences between poor and nonpoor children in terms of the number of exposures to stimulating objects and events in the home, including direct efforts by parents to teach school-relevant competencies.

Once children became school age, parents reduced the number of times per week they read to children (less than 50% in all groups read to children three times per week). At least 50% of American households contain 10 or more age-appropriate books for school-age children, excepting poor African American and Latin American households. Almost half the European American and Asian American households with incomes above poverty have musical instruments for children of elementary age; and almost half the families in both these groups subscribe to a daily newspaper. Approximately three-fourths of 10- to 15-year-olds have two or more pictures on their bedroom walls, at least two types of reference materials, at least two board games, and at least two pieces of equipment useful for physical development or sports. More than 50% have 20 or more developmentally appropriate books and access to a musical instrument, and more than 40% have home computers. Approximately 70% of the parents stated that they had discussed current events with the adolescent during the previous 2 weeks. Slightly less than half of the adolescents had been to a museum, a live musical or theater performance, or an organized sporting event accompanied by another family member during the previous year. Aughinbaugh and Gittleman (2003) analyzed data from the National Child Development Study in the United Kingdom and found that scores on the HOME Inventory were slightly higher than those reported in the United States. Primarily, there were fewer lower scoring families, perhaps as a result of the fact that there are fewer extremely poor families in Great Britain.

As a general proposition, cultural models of parenting in Arab countries do not place as much emphasis on stimulation of school achievement as is the case for Western democracies and Asian countries like Taiwan, South Korea, and Japan. When the Early Childhood HOME was used in Bahrain, a very broad range of scores emerged (Hadeed and Sylva, 1999). The mean score was approximately one-third standard deviation lower in Bahrain than in the United States and the United Kingdom. Scores on the Physical Environment and Variety of Stimulation scales were noticeably lower. Some of the difference may reflect the fact that houses in Bahrain tend to be small, but there is also less tendency to take children to enriching out-of-home experiences.

In Latin America and the Caribbean, parents tend not to put high emphasis on stimulation and teaching of academic skills, especially early in life, partly because they believe that children attain developmental milestones at a slower pace (Durbrow, Pena, Masten, Sesma, and Williamson, 2001; Pachter and Dworkin, 1997). Mothers in Costa Rica are not highly verbal with children early in infancy and somewhat restrictive with them regarding manipulating objects (Laude, 1999). Likewise, Gaskins (1995) found that Mayan parents believe development is internally generated. The lesser emphasis on direct teaching of academic competencies does not stand in contrast to the general goal of *educacion* in Latin cultures but is reflective of the fact that *educacion* equally refers to training in morality and social responsibility. As an example, Okagaki and Frensch (1998) found that Latin parents feel that developing social skills and motivation are more important to school readiness than developing preacademic skills. They place more importance on socioemotional development than either European American or Asian American parents. Lesser emphasis on stimulation, coupled with generally lower affluence, often means that scores on HOME scales such as Play Materials, Learning Materials, Academic Stimulation, and Variety of Experiences are lower in Latin America and the Caribbean (Blevins-Knabe and Austin, 2000; Bulnes et al., 1979; Durbrow et al., 1996; Lima et al., 2004; Tippie, 2003; Walker et al., 2004).

Partly in response to cultural practice and partly in response to the generally poor living conditions present in Latin America, researchers sometimes relax scoring criteria or eliminate items from HOME (Durbrow et al., 1996). That said, scores on scales representing stimulation are not uniformly lower than in North America (Centro de Estudios Sobre Nutricion Infantil, 1996; Lozoff et al., 1995). Hayes (1997). (1990) observed that pass rates on learning stimulation items for Jamaican families are similar to those in the United States except for two items. Data from Argentina and Chile offer useful illustrations of how opportunities for stimulation in Latin America tend to diverge from the opportunities available in the United States and Europe. In Chile, only approximately one-quarter of parents told children the name of something during the HOME interview, and only approximately one-quarter were credited with consciously encouraging development (Bulnes et al., 1979). In Argentina, only 10% of mothers read to their children at least three times a week during the first year of life (30% at 24 months). Relatively few families bought a daily newspaper (22%) or subscribed to magazines (9%). Only approximately 25% had 10 books, and only 10% of infants had three books (43% at age 2 years). Only approximately 33% of mothers attempted to teach the name of something during the home visit when HOME was administered, increasing to 41% at age 2 years (Centro de Estudios Sobre Nutricion Infantil, 1996). As seen in U.S. samples, children are more likely to have toys that build specific kinds of skills as they move from infancy to middle childhood (Bradley et al., 2001).

It is important to separate what parents do to directly provide stimulation and the amount of materials available for stimulation. The latter often reflects economic well-being. For example, a study done in Pretoria, South Africa, found that only 17% of 5-year-olds have as many as three books in the home, and only 11% have as many as three toys (Liddell, Kvalsvig, Strydom, Qotyana, and Shabalala, 1993). One of the most common adjustments made to home environment measures in less affluent countries is to reduce the number of books and learning materials required to obtain credit for certain items (Aina et al., 1993; Drotar et al., 1999; Grantham-McGregor, Powell, Walker, Chang, and Fletcher, 1995; Holding, 2003; Lima et al., 2004; Lozoff et al., 1995; Richter and Grieve, 1991; Walker et al., 2004; Zeitlin et al., 1995). Such was a major issue in the United Nations Children's Fund (UNICEF) child indicators project. Aina et al. (1993) changed cut-points for some HOME items (requiring 2 rather than 10 books) and included a focus on nonmanufactured objects. Very few Yoruba households have manufactured toys, the most common being a plastic doll (approximately 20%). Only 14% had as many as two children's books. By contrast, the researchers found more evidence for homemade toys (playing with empty tins was especially common, approximately 50%). Moreover, in Africa especially, researchers frequently modify HOME items that reflect access to objects and enriching experiences. For families in Kenya, Holding (2003) deleted items dealing with hobbies, involvement in community organizations, attending theaters, taking trips by plane or train in favor of travel by bus, and attendance at local wedding and cultural celebrations. Likewise, Dubrow et al. (1996) found that children from Jamaica and St. Vincent rarely had access to musical instruments (an item on HOME) and thus made the decision to eliminate the indicator. The cultural implications of these changes in favor of readily available resources are not yet known in that the association between the new items and child outcome measures has not yet been examined. Lower correlations between competence and stimulation at home in poorer countries may also reflect poorer health (as a result of inadequate nutrition and health care and greater exposure to toxins), greater disruptions to family life, or larger amounts of time spent outside the home with siblings and peers. For example, in Bangladesh, infants with low levels of stimulation scored lower on the Bayley MDI and showed poorer growth, but the same infants often showed signs of malnutrition (Black et al., 2004). Health status was also a factor for children in Brazil, as was the adequacy of garbage collections (Lima et al., 2004).

According to Nsamenang and Lamb (1995), cultures vary in the extent to which parents try to organize children's learning. Goldberg (1977) found that mothers from Zambia are not highly concerned with stimulating cognitive and language development. Agiobu-Kemmer (1984) found that Nigerian mothers had to be told to play object games with children to stimulate them. Responses to HOME items among the Yoruba are particularly revealing regarding the tendency of African women to teach language and cognitive skills. Yoruba mothers do not spend much time engaging children in play; only approximately 11% engaged in technical play with toys, and only 27% engaged in sociotechnical play with toys (an adapted item from HOME; Aina et al., 1993). Nearly half reported never talking to children while doing housework, and only approximately 33% structured children's play during the home visit. Although 69% stated that they tried to teach ABCs, only 25% actually pointed to letters or pictures when given a book for their children during the visit. Thirty-eight percent of children were not allowed to touch the book during the visit. Among the Nso of northwest Cameroon, much of the responsibility for learning (mostly nontechnical learning) falls on the children themselves. This does not mean that African parents are incompetent when it comes to teaching children, just that they typically do not spend much time teaching competencies favored in technologically advanced societies.

In much of Africa, rather than preparing children for independent careers and technical jobs, adults teach children practical skills, especially self-care and skills that can be helpful to the family (Whiting and Edwards, 1988). Among the Yoruba, almost every child is taught to run errands and make purchases. Most are taught to wash their own hands and face and to handle certain household duties (Aina et al., 1993). This is part of the larger effort at responsibility training in African communities (Munroe and Munroe, 1980). In some societies, parents spend time directly teaching such practical skills; in others, children are expected to learn by observing. Children from Thailand generally have few learning materials and limited exposure to parental teaching of literacy skills (Williams et al., 2003). Only 11% of Thai parents read to their children at least three times per week (versus 71% in the United States). The authors suggest that the reasons for low scores on these items might be because Thai mothers are introverted, have low income, and have little formal education; thus, they place limited value on academic achievement.

Li and Rao (2000) examined how parents of Chinese preschoolers in Beijing, Hong Kong, and Singapore assisted their children in attaining literacy skills. The majority of parents in all three cities (69% to 83%) believed that reading early was important and that storytelling is a useful way to help children learn Chinese literacy skills. However, most parents in Beijing (68%), Hong Kong (75%), and Singapore (86%) do not set aside a definite time to read to their children, although the majority in each city (56% to 73%) teach their children to read at home. The majority of children in Beijing (66%) and Hong Kong (76%) also have chances to see their parents read each day; the figure for Singapore was 48%. Approximately 60% of parents in all three cities establish reading corners in the house, but there tend to be more children's books available in Beijing households (62% had at least 30) than in Hong Kong (83% had less than 30) or Singapore (76% had less than 30).

There is abundant evidence that exposure to a rich array of objects and stimulating experiences is associated with higher intellectual and academic attainment in the United States (Bradley, 1994). Part reflects the child's opportunity to engage objects and events; part reflects efforts on the parents to provide teaching and guidance. For the most part, studies done throughout the world reveal similar associations (Aina et al., 1993; Aughinbaugh and Gittleman, 2003; Bastos et al., 1998; Chomitz, 1992; Church and Katigbak, 1991; Drotar et al., 1999; Durbrow et al., 1996; Grantham-McGregor, 1991; Grantham-McGregor, Lira, Ashworth, Morris, and Assuncao, 1998; Hamadani, Fuchs, Osendarp, Huda, and Grantham-McGregor, 2002; Jacobson et al., 1995; Jang, 2001; Judit, 2001; Kalmar, Boronkai, and Trefil, 2002; Lee et al., 2003; Marturano, Ferreira, and Bacarji, 2005; Masud, Luster, and Youatt, 1994; McMichael et al., 1988; Misra and Tiwari, 1984; Palti, Otrakkul, Belmaker, Tamair, and Tepper, 1984; Richter and Grieve, 1991; Torralva and Cugnasco, 1996; van Baar, 1991; Wasserman et al., 1992; Zeitlin et al., 1995). However, exposure to stimulating materials and experiences is not always highly correlated with achievement (e.g., Bahrain; Hadeed and Sylva, 1999). That said, it is not altogether clear how best to interpret these findings. They could reflect weaknesses in HOME as a measure of the home environment in Bahrain or weaknesses in outcome measures.

The association between exposure to stimulation and competence emerges in the first year of life and is well established by the end of the second year (Gertner et al., 2002). In some studies, relations hold even with extensive demographic, family context, and health controls. The magnitude of associations varies across studies, and there is some evidence to suggest that the association is strongest in early childhood (after infancy and before early adolescence when schools and peers appear to have increasing impact; Bradley et al., 2001; McCulloch and Joshi, 2001) and for children at biologic risk (Lima et al., 2004). However, studies done in both the United States and Brazil indicate that, if families are involved in stimulating recreational experiences and hobbies together, adolescents perform better in school as well (Bradley et al., 2001; Marturano et al., 2005). Although most studies focus on relatively global intellectual and academic outcomes, several focus on relations between home experience and more specific cognitive processes. These studies show that parents who coach their children to attain higher levels of planfulness and independence in household chores and other daily activities have children who do better on memory tasks. Relatedly, parents who directly instruct their children in strategies to use in homework, housework, or games have children who demonstrate higher levels of recall and better performance on taxonomic-grouping tests (Pierce and Lange, 1996). These parenting strategies are more common in technologically advanced countries where self-reliance is stressed. However, evidence in support of the relation between such parenting efforts and metacognitive processing also exists in non-Western countries, such as India (Kurtz et al., 1987), where there is substantial variability in the availability of toys and learning materials (Agrawal and Gulati, 2005; Kohli, Mohanty, and Kaur, 2005).

HOME scales reflective of learning opportunities tend to be positively associated with cognitive and academic outcomes in most societies. However, a study in the Seychelles showed that higher levels of stimulation also predict the age at which children start walking (Axtell et al., 1998). Harkness and Super (1994) have argued that culturally directed methods of handling and stimulating infants, together with direct teaching of motor skills, accounts for the precocity of motor development in many African children. A study done in both rural and urban communities in India showed that giving children toys, answering their questions, playing with children, and helping them with self-care routines are related to the development of communicative skills, self-care skills, and curiosity (Kapur, Girimaji, Prabhu, Reddy, and Kaliaperumal, 1994). The mother's encouragement of the child to play is an especially strong predictor. That study also showed that there tend to be not only socioeconomic status (SES) differences in parenting practices, but also urban–rural differences, with rural communities often lagging in the amount of stimulation provided for intellectual development.

Observed associations between the level of stimulation in the home and children's social and behavioral outcomes are somewhat less consistent. Nihira et al. (1987) found, for example, that HOME learning stimulation was positively correlated with social adjustment in the United States but not in Japan. Anme and Takayama (1989) added items addressing nonverbal communication to their adapted version of HOME based on the premise that Japanese caregivers want their children to develop sensitivity to the way other people think. Bradley and Corwyn (2005, 2007) examined relations between the stimulation available to children in their homes and children's adaptive functioning in greater detail in two large U.S. samples (the National Longitudinal Survey of Youth and the National Institute of Child Health and Human Development [NICHD] Study of Early Child Care and Youth Development [SECCYD]). In both samples, having greater opportunity for stimulation within the home and having chances for enrichment outside the home reduced the likelihood of externalizing behavior for children in early and middle childhood. In the NICHD SECCYD, the effect was mediated through the development of self-control. This finding is consistent with the notion that parents may foster self-regulatory competence in children by coaching them to reflect on their behavior and make choices designed to achieve goals, a parenting strategy that comports with a cultural value of autonomy and self-reliance. To determine whether the same pattern of relations would emerge in societies that do not place such a strong value in independence, Corapci, Bradley, Castillo, Jimenez, and Lozoff (2006) performed similar analyses on samples from Costa Rica and Chile. In neither country were opportunities for stimulation associated with externalizing behavior. However, in Brazil, more opportunity for stimulation was associated with externalizing behavior in preschool children, even controlling for sociodemographic factors, maternal mental health, and child health (Anselmi et al., 2004). A second study in Brazil showed that the availability of toys and materials, having opportunities to engage in leisure activities, and being involved in recreational pursuits with parents were related to social competence during adolescence (Marturano et al., 2005).

In sum, there is considerable disparity in how much children from different countries are exposed to stimulating materials and parental efforts to teach particular skills. The former at least partly reflects income disparities, but the latter seems more often to reflect cultural values regarding the competencies children need and the parents' role in promoting them. Despite differences in exposure, variability of exposure within countries is generally associated with child competence and less so with social adjustment.

Household Arrangements and Community Conditions

As a general proposition, anthropologists argue that the built environment is recursive—a house is both the medium and the outcome of social practice and cultural belief. As societies become more socio-politically complex and sedentary, there is a great deal more partitioning of space and segregation of activities that occur in particular spaces (Kent, 1991). There tends to be more differentiation on the basis of gender and age. In Europe and America, one often finds separate bedrooms for children and adults, as well as separate spaces for cooking, recreation, various types of work, and so forth. There are often gender-specific rooms, and many activities are performed predominantly or exclusively by one gender. By comparison, in traditional Navajo families, children play throughout the living quarters and adjacent grounds, and activities tend not to be partitioned based on age. Although there is a tendency for men and women to spend most of their time in different sides of the hogan, there is no barrier between the spaces, and each is free to move about the hogan. Gender roles tend to be complementary but not exclusive, and there is no effort to confine activities (including meals) to set times of the day. The Baswara in Botswana live mostly in huts, with lots of their activities occurring outside the hut but with little effort to constrict any type of activity to any particular place inside or outside. Children are essentially allowed to play anywhere they please, and children and adults (of various degrees of relationship) sleep in common areas. Botswanan fathers spend more time with their children than do most American men, and Botswanan children go to sleep when they feel like it. In effect, the more egalitarian the society is, the fewer the separations of space and activity in the household and the fewer the restrictions on children to engage in certain activities in certain places at certain times (Kent, 1991).

What parents tend to do with their children (from play arrangements to sleeping arrangements to the use of control techniques) is partly determined by the physical features of the residence (i.e., size, number of rooms, proximity of certain spaces to others, acoustical properties). The physical and social settings in which families live constitute part of what Harkness and Super (2002) called the *developmental niche*. The developmental niche of families regulates the microenvironment for children. The impact of the developmental niche can be seen in such mundane parental actions as whether babies sleep with their parents or not. The physical environment of cribs and chairs, together with the social environment, sets the structure, opportunities, and incentives for the child's emerging skills. In effect, the setting determines what the child can see, hear, and do. For example, in Kenya, among the Embu, children spend very little time inside their homes, which are situated such that they open onto communal areas. When children become mobile, they join other children from the community outside to play or to perform chores. As a result, children do not tend to be in close proximity to their parents; thus, they are not very likely to engage in verbal exchanges with adults. By contrast, Egyptian homes tend to be quite small, and they are not arranged so that they open onto communal areas. Toddlers spend most of their time within the residence or immediately outside it. Because of their close proximity to adult family members, Egyptian toddlers tend to have their verbalizations responded to with high frequency (Wachs et al., 1992).

Efe foragers of Zaire live in small camps where they typically arrange huts in a semi-circle around the camp's perimeter, creating a communal space where most day-to-day in-camp activities occur. This allows for young children to be cared for by many different members of the community and for mothers and fathers to go about their daily foraging tasks with relative ease (Tronick, Morelli, and Ivey, 1992). Malay and Chinese homes are different, with Malay huts being very small and minimally furnished with rattan mats in the living quarters that are physically separate from storage, work, and cooking facilities. Chinese homes are three times as large on average and more multipurpose. These physical differences give rise to social organizational differences that then influence parenting practices. For example, in contrast to Malay children, Chinese children are twice as likely to be comforted by an alternate caregiver, three times as likely to be held by an alternate caregiver, and twice as likely to be played with by an alternate caregiver (Woodson and Costa-Woodson, 1984). Among the Ache in Eastern Paraguay, parents react to physical hazards by restricting children's locomotion and freedom to explore (Kaplan and Dove, 1987). In Japan, because most families live in close quarters, there is typically very little space contiguous to the house for children to engage in outdoor play. Thus, parents typically have to arrange for children (or permit in the case of older children) to go to parks, playgrounds, and game halls for recreation (Christopher, 1984). Dubrow et al. (1996) found that children from Jamaica and St. Vincent rarely take many trips of greater than 50 miles because of the size and isolation of their homelands.

Climatic conditions affect what parents do and what they believe children should learn. For example, Indian parents tend not to emphasize the attainment of early developmental milestones to the degree most Western parents do. Even so, in Calcutta where the weather is warm, parents have expectations for walking, dressing unaided, self-feeding, and sitting unsupported that are quite similar to Western parents (Goldbart and Mukherjee, 1999). In effect, features of the physical environment can cause adjustments to broader cultural scripts.

In *Native Roots, How the Indians Enriched America*, Weatherford (1991) described how climate, geography, and the available flora and fauna affected almost every aspect of Native American life and how native peoples learned to manage their environments to survive and to prosper. He also demonstrated that European settlers gave up many of the habits drawn from experience in the Old World to survive in the new one, even how they fed and clothed their children and how they organized daily life. This historical lesson, for all intents and purposes, replicates the lessons learned from social scientists: The things that parents do reflect the context in which they live. Much of what is done represents practical accommodations to what the larger environment affords.

Although there is considerable information on how the physical environment affects what children experience as part of their everyday lives, there is limited research on how household arrangements and community conditions affect child well-being. One of the few areas about which a reasonable amount is known pertains to crowding. Crowded conditions in the home often make it difficult for children to organize things for themselves and to make maximum use of persons and objects in the environment. Crowded conditions limit exploration and impede sophisticated play. In the long run, crowding also appears to lower achievement and heighten aggressiveness (Evans, Lepore, Shejwal, and Palsane, 1998). Data from both the United States and the United Kingdom show that less responsive parenting partially mediates the relation between crowding and early cognitive functioning (Evans, Ricciuti, Bradley, Corwyn, and Hazan, submitted), Unfortunately, parents tend to provide less supervision in crowded homes and may involve themselves less intensively with their children (Bradley and Caldwell, 1984; Wachs, 1992). Parents are also more apt to send their children out to play (Gove, Hughes, and Galle, 1979). On the other hand, Bradley et al. (2000) found only a marginal association between household crowding and family efforts to regulate adolescent behavior, perhaps because adolescents are more likely to spend time away from home and separate from their parents than is the case for younger children. Finally, although crowded conditions tend to restrict what parents do with their children and can have inimical effects on children, it is important to remember that most of the crowding research has been done in Western Europe and the United States. In societies where most families live in small dwellings in rural areas and the climate is warm, much of life is lived outdoors. Studies done in countries where small residences are the norm tend not to show such strong relations with crowding, a good example being a study conducted in the rural Philippines (Church and Katigbak, 1991). Likewise, strong relations between factors like crowding and child well-being may be more apt to occur when children are not otherwise at risk for poor development, as is often the case in poor countries where children frequently lack adequate nutrition and are more likely to be exposed to toxins and diseases.

Conclusion

Parenting is influenced by culture, but any notion that parenting is highly constricted by cultural models is partially betrayed by substantial variation observed within and across families from the same society. The United States presents a useful case example. The initial dominant group consisted mostly of Protestant Europeans who espoused autonomy, perseverance, working for the future, individual relationships, and mastery over nature (McEachern and Kenny, 2002). That orientation was merged with Native American ways as a result of needing to survive in unfamiliar surroundings (Weatherford, 1991) and African ways as a result of accommodation to slavery. The press to amalgamate cultural values influenced Native Americans and African Americans as well, as they strove to deal with European dominance in America (see Wilkinson, 2002, for a treatment of the Cherokee). McEachern and Kenny (2002) present case examples of European accommodation to changes in family composition and women's movement into the workforce, the blending of old Catholic and African Yoruba values with modern American workplace values in Cuban Americans, and the blending of Christian, Voodoo, and modern workplace values in Haitian and Jamaican Americans. Sometimes the challenges groups face as they move to a new country (i.e., where they may be of minority status) moves families to adopt a childrearing style that actually conflicts with the dominant cultural values of their country of origin (Valera et al., 2004).

One of the most vexing problems in explicating how culture is implicated in parenting practices, children's experiences at home, and child development is separating what is cultural from the remaining aspects of the macro- and microenvironments. Making comparisons between cultural groups becomes complicated not just because of the blending of cultures that often happens within a society but also because being from a particular culture may also increase the likelihood that one is oppressed, of lower economic status, or resides in a particular geographic locality with its own peculiar affordances. For example, mothers belonging to the Gusii group in Kenya showed responsiveness to infants using holding and touching, whereas American mothers showed responsiveness using verbal and social interaction (Whiting and Edwards, 1988). Because these two groups vary by both cultural setting and SES and because both are known to affect modes of responsiveness, it is hard to determine whether cultural beliefs or affluence may be more instrumental in producing the differences in patterns observed. In dozens of studies in this review, studies spanning all regions examined, significant associations emerged between family SES and HOME scores. Demographic characteristics such as parental education and family income were consistently associated with parent practices and the quality of household and community resources available to children. Thus, whatever cultural models may have contributed to variations in parenting, SES contributed above and beyond. Several findings are interesting in this regard. First, although SES accounted for variance in home environment scores in nearly every society examined, there were variations in the quality of home experience within SES groups every time the issue was examined and in almost every society where data were available (Bradley, Corwyn, and Whiteside-Mansell, 1996). Second, SES is associated with home environment scores despite the average level of affluence present in countries. Third, the specific demographic and family configuration factors contributing most to home environment scores differed by society, indicating that cultural models and other contextual factors affect relations between SES and family practices. A good example is Bahrain. In this nation, birth order is more highly correlated with HOME than the other demographic factors examined. From the literature examined, it appears that access to economic resources (particularly income and education) is a major contributor to what parents do regarding their children. Beyond that, the reasons for relations between SES and HOME are less clear. One mediator of this relation may be traditional versus modern views regarding childrearing. In Europe, Africa, Asia, and the Caribbean, women with more modern views regarding childrearing tended to be more responsive, less punitive, and more stimulating than women with more traditional views (Palacios, Gonzalez, and Moreno, 1992; Zevalkink, Riksen-Walraven, and van Lieshout, 1999). Among Xhosa-speaking families of South Africa, SES is related to parental aspirations, which leads to support for academic performance (Heath, 1995). Likewise, among more educated Mayan women, there is a movement away from privileging of very young children to a greater insistence on equality of privilege even among the young (Mosier and Rogoff, 2003). In each of these instances, there is evidence for evolving models of parenting, all of which were connected to advancing SES.

Because North America is the place where HOME was created, the indicators it contains seem to fit best the dominant cultural values in North America. The current organization of indicators into scales also seems best aligned to the cultural values prevalent in white, middle class America. Qualitative and quantitative analyses have led scholars around the world to (1) change some of the indicators contained in these instruments, (2) rearrange the indicators into somewhat different conceptual groupings, and (3) design culture-specific measures of family environments. Similar issues about the applicability of HOME to specific cultural groups living in North America have emerged as well. Among Hmong immigrants and Eskimos, where there is a strong focus on cooperation and sharing and limited emphasis on individual achievement, children have fewer material possessions or special places to keep them. In addition, the mothers do not spend much time reading to the children. On the other hand, mothers are particularly attentive when feeding infants and when infants are in distress (Harney-Boffman, MacDonald-Clark, and Hjelsel, 1997; MacDonald-Clark and Harney-Boffman, 1994). There is also a published set of supplementary indicators of the HOME designed for use with the urban poor in the United States (Ertem, Forwyth, Avn-Singer, Damour, and Cicchetti, 1997). Among Mexican Americans, there is less emphasis on communication of feelings or assertiveness and self-sufficiency but more emphasis on morality and religion. One sometimes sees less strong predictions to child outcomes in immigrant groups because families are operating from blended, highly dynamic, and constrained value systems that are not fully aligned with the dominant culture and thus are not fully supported by the institutions from within the dominant culture. Those weaker associations also arise because new immigrants are less familiar with all of the strategies longer term residents employ to accomplish particular cultural goals, so they do not as fully and frequently apply the methods of realizing those goals.

The fact that measures such as HOME have been selected for use in quite disparate societies suggests that cultural models of parenting around the world contain some of the same principles regarding what children need from their environments and what parents need to do to prepare children for effective membership in society. Conversely, the fact that questions have been raised about the indicators contained in these instruments and changes have been made in the set of indicators used in every continent says that there are real differences in cultural models at the level where Hui and Triandis (1985) argued they would be—at the level of particular forms (i.e., specific indicators) more so than at the level of broad functions. Culture also reflects itself in how specific behaviors align themselves (covary) in and through time. In North America and Europe, there is a greater tendency for communicative and tactile forms of responsiveness to co-occur than is the case for Africa or poor Caribbean countries. In the more survival-oriented societies, tactile responsiveness (which predominates) appears geared primarily to moving a child from a distressed state to a state of calm. In more well-resourced societies, the combination of tactile and verbal responsiveness appears geared to moving a child from a state of distress to a state of contentment (happiness). It is interesting, nonetheless, that the level of tactile responsiveness (holding) persists longer in some African societies than in the United States, where it drops precipitously over the first few years of life (a crossover pattern between tactile and verbal responsiveness is also recorded in Argentina and Spain). In more technologically advanced societies, the switch to verbal (more distant) forms seems aimed at producing independence (including self-regulatory competence). Likewise, there is early social pressure (scaffolding by direct teaching) of social cooperation (Mosier and Rogoff, 2003). The combination of verbal responsiveness and high general language stimulation appears aimed at more cognitive (as contrasted to behavioral) control/coping strategies. Studies in Costa Rica and Chile, where cultural practice is in flux, make it unclear whether more cognitive approaches can function to improve self-control in transitioning societies, as is the case in more advanced Western societies (Corapci et al., submitted).

Kitayama (2002) argued that a more accurate picture of cultural differences in parenting practice and child behavior can typically be obtained by observing the actions of individuals within specific contexts. The value of direct observation is supported by studies showing contradictions between maternal reports of values and beliefs and their actual behavior in real-world settings (Cote and Bornstein, 2000). However, this chapter shows that differences in cultural models do not lie solely in diversity of form. There are differences in the degree to which certain functions are emphasized too (Stewart and Bond, 2002). Providing the experiences children need for self-care and developing practical skills that can assist family functioning immediately are far more prevalent in Africa than in Europe. Assuring that children will be ready to function effectively in the "white collar" world of work is far more emphasized in affluent, technologically advanced societies.

Although there is evidence that cultural models of parenting vary in terms of emphasis on stimulation of competence, family variations in the amount of stimulation afforded children are associated with measures of competence in almost every society at every age. This is not surprising given the large Western literature showing relations between stimulation and child competence (Bradley and Caldwell, 1995; Kagan, 1984), but its consistency in societies espousing very different models of parenting and having dramatically different average access to resources testifies to its essentially universal value in competence development. Likewise, there is near unanimous support of the salience of parental responsiveness for child well-being. The finding is not surprising, but its applicability in societies where responsiveness may be difficult to enact and where it is not strongly advocated makes its salience for positive adjustment appear near universal. By contrast, the findings pertaining to punishment are less certain, partly because there are fewer studies of harsh punishment and socioemotional development. In countries such as the United States, harsh punishment is consistently related to poor adjustment (Gershoff, 2002; Jaffee et al., 2004). However, a study done in China, India, Italy, Kenya, the Philippines, and Thailand (Lansford et al., 2005) provided evidence that physical punishment is associated less strongly with adverse outcomes in countries where it is normative (i.e., more commonly used).

A major limitation of this chapter is the relative paucity of studies involving school-age children. There is reason to believe that cultural models may have even greater influence on parenting practice during the later stages of childhood, as variations in child personality, societal presses, and economic opportunities lead to greater and greater diversification. A case in point is a study done during middle childhood in St. Vincent. At this age, marked gender differences in patterns of relations emerged, patterns consistent with cultural attitudes toward gender.

Neither the experiences of a child nor the actions of parents are precisely determined by their developmental niches—nor did Harkness and Super (2002) stipulate that they are. Culture and class help to shape and define what parents do and who parents are, but the environment parents create for their children does not exclusively reflect these macro-level ecological factors either. What may sometimes be interpreted as cultural variations in patterns of relations between parenting and child well-being could mask other environmental circumstances (e.g., resources and dangers present in the neighborhood, exposures to trauma or toxic substances). The natural confounding of social and physical conditions appears better appreciated by scientists who study exposures to neurotoxins than social and behavioral scientists generally (Cory-Slechta et al., 2001; Vreugdenhil, Lanting, Mulder, Boersma, and Weisglas-Kuperus, 2002). Moreover, both parent and child are active constructors of their environment as well as responders to what the environment affords (Ford and Lerner, 1992; Wachs, 1992). The actual process of childrearing involves numerous moment-to-moment exchanges between child and environment. Ecological developmental theory suggests that more authoritative and penetrating understanding of how culture is implicated in parenting, daily life, and child development will come as these other environmental influences are more fully incorporated in research designs and statistical analyses.

Acknowledgments

The author wishes to thank those many colleagues from throughout the world who have provided information about their use of HOME and to recognize the many books, articles, and chapters presenting findings pertaining to HOME, many of which were not cited as a result of necessary restrictions pertaining to the length of chapters for this volume.

References

Abreu-Lima, I. M. (n.d.). *Report on the study of the HOME Inventory (preschool form) in a Portuguese sample.* Unpublished manuscript.

Agarwal, D., Awasthy, A., Upadhyay, S., Singh, P., Kumar, J., and Agarwal, K. (1992). Growth, behavior, development and intelligence in rural children between 1-3 years of life. *Indian Pediatrics, 29,* 467–480.

Agiobu-Kemmer, I. (1984). Cognitive and affective aspects of infant development. In H. V. Curran (Ed.), *Nigerian children: Developmental perspectives* (pp. 74–117). London: Routledge and Kegan Paul.

Agrawal, P., and Gulati, J. K. (2005). The patterns of infant-mother attachment as a function of home environment. *Journal of Human Ecology, 18,* 287–293.

Aina, T. A., Agiobu-Kemmer, I., Etta, E. F., Zeitlin, M. F., and Setiloane, K. (1993). *Early child care and nutrition in Lagos State, Nigeria.* Tufts University School of Nutrition and Policy for UNICEF, Boston, MA.

Altman, I. (1977). Privacy regulation: Culturally universal or culturally specific? *Journal of Social Issues, 33,* 66–84.

Anme, T., and Takayama, T. (1989). *The study of evaluation of environmental stimulation for normal and handicapped children and health welfare system in Japan.* Unpublished manuscript. National Rehabilitation Center for the Disabled, Tokyo, Japan.

Anselmi, L., Piccinini, C., Basrros, F., and Lopes, R. (2004). Psychosocial determinants of behavior problems in Brazilian preschool children. *Journal of Child Psychology and Psychiatry, 45,* 779–788.

Aughinbaugh, A., and Gittleman, M. (2003). Does money matter? A comparison of the effect of income on child development in the United States and Great Britain. *The Journal of Human Resources, 38,* 416–440.

Axtell, C., Myers, G., Davidson, P., Choi, A., Cernichiari, E., Sloane-Reeves, J., et al. (1998). Semiparametric modeling of age achieving developmental milestones after prenatal exposure to methylmercury in the Seychelles Child Development Study. *Environmental Health Perspectives, 106,* 559–563.

Basral, S., Thind, S. K., and Jaswal, S. (2006). Relationship between quality of home environment, locus of control and achievement motivation among high achiever urban female adolescents. *Journal of Human Ecology, 19,* 253–257.

Bastos, A., Almeida-Filho, N., and Pinho, L. (1998). *Experilncia iniciało, eventos de vida e ajustamento em adolescentes de um bairro popular de Salvador: Um de follow up.* Unpublished manuscript.

Belsky, J. (1984). The determinants of parenting: A process model. *Child Development, 55,* 83–96.

Black, M., Baqui, A., Zaman, K., Persson, L., Arifeen, S., Le, K., et al. (2004). Iron and zinc supplementation promote motor development and exploratory behavior among Bangladeshi infants. *American Journal of Clinical Nutrition, 80,* 903–910.

Black, M., Suzawal, S., Black, R. E., Kholsa, S., Kumar, J., and Menon, V. (2004). Cognitive and motor development among small for gestational age infants: Impact of zinc supplementation, birth weight, and caregiving practices. *Pediatrics, 113*, 1297–1305.

Blevins-Knabe, B., and Austin, A. (2000, April). *The HOME: Working for cultural validity in rural Paraguay.* Presented at the biennial meeting of the Society for Research in Child Development, Albuquerque, NM.

Bornstein, M. H. (1995). Form and function: Implications for studies of culture and human development. *Culture and Psychology, 1*, 123–137.

Bornstein, M. H., Tamis-LeMonda, C. S., Pascual, L., Haynes, M. O., et al. (1996). Ideas about parenting in Argentina, France, and the United States. *International Journal of Behavioral Development, 19*, 347–367.

Bornstein, M. H., Tamis-LeMonda, C. S., Tal, J., Ludemann, P., Toda, S., Than, C. W., et al. (1992). Maternal responsiveness to infants in three societies: The United States, France, and Japan. *Child Development, 63*, 808–821.

Bradley, R. H. (1994). The HOME Inventory: Review and reflections. In H. Reese (Ed.), *Advances in child development and behavior* (pp. 241–288). San Diego, CA: Academic Press.

Bradley, R. H., and Caldwell, B. M. (1984). The HOME inventory and family demographics. *Developmental Psychology, 20*, 315–320.

Bradley, R. H., and Caldwell, B. M. (1995). Caregiving and the regulation of child growth and development: Describing proximal aspects of caregiving systems. *Developmental Review, 15*, 38–85.

Bradley, R. H., and Corwyn, R. F. (2005). Productive activity and the prevention of behavior problems. *Developmental Psychology, 41*, 89–98.

Bradley, R. H., and Corwyn, R. F. (2007). Externalizing problems in 5th grade: Relations with productive activity, maternal sensitivity and harsh parenting from infancy through middle childhood. *Developmental Psychology, 43*, 1390–1401.

Bradley, R. H., Corwyn, R. F., Burchinal, M., McAdoo, H. P., and Garcia Coll, C. (2001). The home environments of children in the United States. Part 2: Relations with behavioral development through age 13. *Child Development, 72*, 1868–1886.

Bradley, R. H., Corwyn, R. F., Caldwell, B. M., Whiteside-Mansell, L., Wasserman, G. A., and Mink, I. T. (2000). Measuring the home environments of children in early adolescence. *Journal of Research on Adolescence, 10*, 247–289.

Bradley, R. H., Corwyn, R., and Whiteside-Mansell, L. (1996). Life at home: Same time, different places—An examination of the HOME Inventory in different cultures. *Early Education & Parenting, 5*, 251–269.

Bransford, J. D., Brown, A. L., and Cocking, R. R. (Eds.). (2000). *How people learn: Brain, mind, experience, and school.* Washington, DC: National Academy Press.

Bulcroft, R., Carmody, D., and Bulcroft, K. (1996). Patterns of parental independence giving to adolescents: Variations by race, age, and gender of child. *Journal of Marriage and the Family, 58*, 866–883

Bulnes, B., Cajdler, B., Edwards, M., and Lira, M. I. (1979). *Inventario para evaluar el embiente familiar: (HOME). Estudio exporatorio en una muestra de nivel socioeconomic bajo.* Unpublished manuscript. Santiago, Chile.

Caldwell, B. M., and Bradley, R. H. (2003). *Home Observation for Measurement of the Environment: Administration manual.* Little Rock, AR. Available from authors.

Calzada, E., and Eyberg, S. (2002). Self-reported parenting practices in Dominican and Puerto Rican mothers of young children. *Journal of Clinical Child and Adolescent Psychology, 31*, 354–363.

Carlson, V. J., and Harwood, R. L. (2003). Attachment, culture, and the caregiving system: The cultural patterning of everyday experiences among Anglo and Puerto Rican mother-child pairs. *Infant Mental Health Journal, 24*, 53–73.

Castillo-Duran, C., Peralies, C. G., Hertrampf, E. D., Marin, V. B., Rivera, F. A., and Icasa, G. (2001). Effect of zinc supplementation on development of Chilean infants. *Journal of Pediatrics, 138*, 229–235.

Centro de Estudios Sobre Nutricion Infantil (1996). *Proyecto Tierra del Fuego.* Buenos Aires, Argentina: Fundacion Jorge Macri.

Chomitz, V. R. (1992). *Diet of Javanese preschool children: Relationship to household environmental factors and stature.* Unpublished doctoral dissertation, Tufts University, Boston, MA.

Christopher, R. C. (1984). *The Japanese mind.* New York: Fawcett Books.

Church, A. T., and Katigbak, M. S. (1991). Home environment, nutritional status, and maternal intelligence as determinants of intellectual development in rural Philippine preschool children. *Intelligence, 15*, 49–78.

Corapci, F., Bradley, R. H., Castillo, M., Jimenez, E., and Lozoff, B. (2006). The role of parenting and home environment on the emergence of externalizing problems. Does self-regulation act as a mediator in Latin American cultures? Submitted for publication.

Cory-Slechto, D. A., Crofton, K. M., Foran, J. A., Ross, J. F., Sheets, L. P., Weiss, B., et al. (2001). Methods to identify and characterize developmental neurotoxicity for human health risk assessment. I: Behavioral effects. *Environmental Health Perspectives, 109*(Suppl 1), 79–91.

Cote, L., and Bornstein, M. H. (2000). Social and didactic parenting behaviors and beliefs among Japanese American and South American mothers of infants. *Infancy, 1,* 363–374.

D'Andrade, R. (2001). A cognivists's view of the units debate in cultural anthropology. *Cross-cultural Research, 35,* 242–257.

de Munck, V. C. (2001, September). In the belly of the beast: Two incomplete theories of culture and why they dominate the social sciences (part 2). *Cross-cultural Psychology Bulletin,* 5–17.

Dennis, W. (l973). *Children of the creche.* New York: Appleton-Century-Crofts.

Drotar, D., Olness, K., Wiznitzer, M., Maruim, L., Guay, L., Hom, D., et al. (1999). Neurodevelopmental outcomes of Ugandan infants with HIV infection: An application of growth curve analysis. *Health Psychology, 18,* 114–121.

Durbrow, E. H. (1999). Cultural processes in child competence: How rural Caribbean parents evaluate their children. In A. S. Masten (Ed.), *Cultural processes in child development. The Minnesota symposia on child psychology* (Vol. 29, pp. 97–122). Mahwah, NJ: Lawrence Erlbaum.

Durbrow, E. H., Jones, E., Bozoky, I., Jimerson, S., and Adams, E. (1996). *How well does the HOME Inventory predict Caribbean children's academic performance and behavior problems?* Presented at the meeting of the International Society for the Study of Behavioral Development, Quebec City, Canada.

Durbrow, E. H., Pena, L, F., Masten, A., Sesma, A., and Williamson, I. (2001). Mothers' conceptions of child competence in contexts of poverty: The Philippines, St. Vincent, and the United States. *International Journal of Behavioral Development, 25,* 438–443.

Ember, C., and Ember, M. (2001). Father absence and male aggression: A re-examination of comparative evidence. *Ethos, 29,* 296–314.

Ertem, I. O., Forwyth, B. W. C., Avn-Singer, A. J., Damour, L. K., and Cicchetti, D. V. (1997). Development of a supplement to the HOME scale for children living in impoverished urban environments. *Developmental and Behavioral Pediatrics, 18,* 322–328.

European Child Care and Education Study Group (1997). *Final report. European Child Care and Educational Study: Cross national analyses of the quality and effects of early childhood programmes on children's development.* Berlin, Germany: European Child Care and Education Study Group.

European Child Care and Education Study Group (1999). *Final report. School-age assessment of child development: Long-term impact of pre-school experiences on school success, and family-school relationships.* Berlin, Germany: European Child Care and Education Study Group.

Evans, G. W., Lepore, S. J., Shejwal, B. R., and Palsane, M. N. (1998). Chronic residential crowding and children's well being: An ecological perspective. *Child Development, 69,* 1514–1523.

Evans, G. W., Riccuiti, H. N., Bradley, R. H., Corwyn, R. F., and Hazan, C. (submitted). *Crowding and cognitive development: The mediating role of maternal responsiveness among 36 month-old children.* Manuscript submitted for publication.

Fagot, B. I., and Kavanaugh, K. (1993). Parenting during the second year: Effects of children's age, sex, and attachment classification. *Child Development, 64,* 258–271.

Ford, D. H., and Lerner, R. M. (1992). *Developmental systems theory, an integrative approach.* Newbury Park, CA: Sage.

Fracasso, M. P., Busch-Rossnagel, N. A., and Fisher, C. B. (1994). The relationships of maternal behavior and acculturation to the quality of attachment in Hispanic infants living in New York City. *Hispanic Journal of Behavioral Sciences, 16,* 143–154.

Gaskins, S. (1995). How Mayan parental theories come into play. In S. Harkness and C. M. Super (Eds.), *Parents' cultural belief systems: Their origins and consequences* (pp. 345–363). New York: Guilford.

Gershoff, E. T. (2002). Corporal punishment by parents and associated child behaviors and experiences: A meta-analytic and theoretical review. *Psychological Bulletin, 128,* 539–579.

Gertner, S., Greenbaum, C., Sadeh, A., Dolfin, Z., Sirota, L., and Ben-Nun, Y. (2002). Sleep-wake patterns in preterm infants and 6 month's home environment: Implications for early cognitive development. *Early Human Development, 68,* 931–102.

Goldbart, J., and Mukherjee, S. (1999). The appropriateness of Western models of parent involvement in Calcutta, India. Part 1: Parents' views on teaching and child development. *Child: Care, Health, and Development, 25,* 335–347.

Goldberg, S. (1977). Infant development and mother-infant interaction in urban Zambia. In P. Liederman, A. Rosenfeld, and S. Tulkin (Eds.), *Culture and infancy, variations in human experience* (pp. 211–243). New York: Academic Press.

Gove, W. R., Hughes, M., and Galle, V. (1979). Overcrowding in the home: An empirical investigation of its possible pathological consequences. *American Sociological Review, 44,* 59–80.

Grantham-McGregor, S. M. (1991). Nutritional supplementation, psychosocial stimulation, and mental development in stunted children: The Jamaican study. *Lancet, 338,* 1–5.

Grantham-McGregor, S. M., Lira, P. I. C., Ashworth, A., Morris, S. S., and Assuncao, A. M. S. (1998). The development of low birthweight term infants and the effects of the environment in northeast Brazil. *Pediatrics, 132,* 661–666.

Grantham-McGregor, S. M., Powell, C., Walker, S., Chang, S., and Fletcher, P. (1995). The long-term follow-up of severely malnourished children who participated in an intervention program. *Child Development, 65,* 428–439.

Gunning, M., Conroy, S., Valoriani, V., Figueiredo, B., Kammerer, M., Muzik, M., et al. (2004). Measurement of mother-infant interactions and the home environment in a European setting: Preliminary results from a cross-cultural study. *British Journal of Psychiatry, 184*(Suppl 46), E38–E44.

Hadeed, J., and Sylva, K. (1999). Center care and education in Bahrain: Does it benefit children's development? *Early Child Development and Care, 157,* 67–84.

Halgunseth, L. C., Ipsa, J. M., and Rudy, D. (2006). Parental control in Latino families: An integrated review of the literature. *Child Development, 77,* 1282–1297.

Hamadani, J. D., Fuchs, G. J., Osendarp, S. J. M., Huda, S. N., and Grantham-McGregor, S. M. (2002). Zinc supplementation during pregnancy and effects on mental development and behaviour of infants: A follow-up study. *The Lancet, 360,* 290–294.

Harkness, S., and Super, C. M. (1994). The developmental niche: A theoretical framework for analyzing the household production of health. *Social Science and Medicine, 38,* 217–226.

Harkness, S., and Super, C. M. (2002). Culture and parenting. In M. H. Bornstein (Ed.), *Handbook of parenting* (2nd ed., Vol. 2, pp. 253–280). Mahwah, NJ: Lawrence Erlbaum Associates.

Harney-Boffman, J., MacDonald-Clark, N., and Hjelsel, D. (1997). Can NCAST and HOME assessment scales be used with Hmong refugees? *Pediatric Nursing, 23,* 235–248.

Hayes, J. (1996). *Reliability and validity of the HOME preschool inventory in Jamaica.* Unpublished manuscript.

Hayes, J. (1997). Reliability and validity of the HOME Preschool Inventory in Jamaica. *Early Child Development and Care, 136,* 45–55.

Heath, D. T. (1995). Parents' socialization of children. In B. Ingoldsby and S. Smith (Eds.), *Families in multicultural perspective* (pp. 161–186). New York: Guilford.

Hill, N., Bush, K., and Roosa, M. (2003). Parenting and family socialization strategies and children's mental health: Low-income Mexican-American and Euro-American mothers and children. *Child Development, 74,* 189–204.

Holding, P. (2003). *Adaptation and use of the middle childhood HOME Inventory in Kilifi, Kenya.* Unpublished manuscript.

Hui, C. H., and Triandis, H. C. (1985). Measurement in cross-cultural psychology. *Journal of Cross-Cultural Psychology, 16,* 131–153.

Hulgunseth, L. C., Ispa, J. M., & Duane, R. (2006). Parental control in Latino families: An integrated review of the literature. *Child Development, 77,* 1282–1297.

Jacobson, J. L., Jacobson, S. W., Greenbaum, C., Schantz, S., Gornish, K., Ela, S., et al. (1995, July). *Validity of the elementary version of the HOME Inventory in two cultures.* Presented at the meeting of the International Society for the Study of Behavioral Development, Jyvaskyla, Finland.

Jaffee, S. R., Caspi, A., Moffitt, T. E., and Taylor, A. (2004). Physical maltreatment victim to antisocial child: Evidence for environmentally mediated process. *Journal of Abnormal Psychology, 113,* 44–55.

Jang, Y. (2001). An analysis of the children's perceived competence and the related variables. *Journal of Korean Home Economics, 39,* 101–114.

Judit, K. (2001). Az otthonni kornyezet minosegenek szerepe koraszulott gyerekek hosszu tavu ertelmi fejlodeseben. *Magyar Pscichologiai Szemle, 56,* 387–410.

Kagan, J. (1984). *The nature of the child.* New York: Basic Books.

Kalmar, M., Boronkai, J., and Trefil, E. (2002, July). *Long-term prediction of intellectual performance from the HOME Inventory for elementary children.* Presented at the biennial meeting of the International Society for the Study of Behavioral Development, Ottawa, Canada.

Kaplan, H., and Dove, H. (1987). Infant development among the Ache of Eastern Paraguay. *Developmental Psychology, 23*, 190–198.

Kapur, M., Girimaji, S. R., Prabhu, G. G., Reddy, N. N., and Kaliaperumal, V. G. (1994). Home environment and psychosocial development of preschool children in South India. *NIMHANS Journal, 12*, 41–51.

Keller, H., Lohaus, A., Kuensemueller, P., Abels, M., Yovsi, R., Voelker, S., et al. (2004). The bio-culture of parenting: Evidence from five cultural communities. *Parenting: Science and Practice, 4*, 25–50.

Kent, S. (1991). Partitioning space. Cross-cultural factors influencing domestic spatial segmentation. *Environment and Behavior, 23*, 438–473.

Kilbride, P. H., and Kilbride, J. E. (1983). Socialization for high positive affect between mother and infant among the Baganda of Uganda. *Ethos, 11*, 232–245.

Kitayama, S. (2002). Culture and basic psychological processes—Toward a systems view of culture: Comment on Osserman et al., (2002). *Psychological Bulletin, 128*, 89–96.

Kohli, A., Mohanty, M., and Kaur, R. P. (2005). Adaptation of the HOME Inventory for children in simple Hindi. *JIACAM, 1* (article 2).

Korosec-Srafty, P. (1985). Experience and use of the dwelling. In I. Altman and C. Werner (Eds.), *Home environments* (pp. 65–86). New York: Plenum Press.

Kurtz, B. E., Borkowski, J. G., and Deshmukh, K. (1987). Metamemory and learning in Mahrashtrian children: Influences from home and school. *Journal of Genetic Psychology, 149*, 363–376.

Lansford, J. E., Chang, L., Dodge, K. A., Malone, P. S., Oburu, P., Palmérus, K., et al., (2005). Physical discipline and children's adjustment: Cultural normativeness as a moderator. *Child Development, 76*, 1234–1246.

Laude, M. (1999). Assessment of nutritional status, cognitive development, and mother-child interaction in Central American refugee children. *Pan American Journal of Public Health, 6*, 164–171.

Lee, J. (2002). Korean validation of HOME Inventory. *Journal of Korean Home Management Association, 10*, 1–13.

Lee, J., Super, C. M., and Harkness, S. (2003). Self-perception of competence in Korean children: Age, sex and home influences. *Asian Journal of Social Psychology, 6*, 133–147.

Li, H., and Rao, N. (2000). Parental influences on Chinese literacy development: A comparison of preschoolers in Beijing, Hong Kong, and Singapore. *International Journal of Behavioral Development, 24*, 82–90.

Liddell, C., Kvalsvig, J., Strydom, N., Qotyana, P., and Shabalala, A. (1993). An observational study of 5-year-old South African children in the year before school. *International Journal of Behavioral Development, 16*, 537–561.

Lima, M., Eickmann, S., Lima, A., Guerra, M., Lira, P., Huttly, S., et al. (2004). Determinants of mental and motor development at 12 months in a low income population: A cohort study in northeast Brazil. *Acta Paediatrica, 93*, 969–975.

Lozoff, B., Andraca, I., Castillo, M., Smith, J., Walter, T., and Pino, P. (2003). Behavioral and developmental effects of preventing iron-deficiency anemia in healthy full-term infants. *Pediatrics, 112*, 846–854.

Lozoff, B., Park, A., Radan, A., and Wolf, A. (1995). Using the HOME Inventory with infants in Costa Rica. *International Journal of Behavioral Development, 18*, 277–295.

Maccoby, E. E., and Martin, J. A. (1983). Socialization in the context of the family: Parent-child interaction. In P. H. Mussen (Series Ed.) and E. M. Hetherington (Vol. Ed.), *Handbook of child psychology. Volume 4: Socialization, personality, and social development* (4th ed., pp. 1–102). New York: Wiley.

MacDonald-Clark, N., and Harney-Boffman, J. (1994). Using NCAST and the HOME with a minority population: The Alaska Eskimos. *Pediatric Nursing, 20*, 435–516.

Marturano, E., Ferreira, M., and Bacarji, K. (2005). An evaluation scale of family environment of children at risk for school failure. *Psychological Reports, 96*, 307–321.

Masud, S., Luster, T., and Youatt, J. (1994). Predictors of home environment and cognitive competence during early childhood in Pakistan. *Early Child Development and Care, 100*, 43–55.

McCulloch, A., and Joshi, H. (2001). Neighborhood and family influences on the cognitive ability of children in the British National Child Development Study. *Social Science and Medicine, 53*, 579–591.

McEachern, A. G., and Kenny, M. C. (2002). A comparison of family environment characteristics among white (non-Hispanic), Hispanic, and African Caribbean groups. *Multicultural Counseling and Development, 30*, 40–58.

McLoyd, V. C. (1998). Socioeconomic disadvantage and child development. *American Psychologist, 53*, 185–204.

McMichael, A., Baghurst, P., Wigg, H., Vimpani, G., Robertson, E., and Roberts, R. (1988). Port Pirie cohort study: Environmental exposure to lead and children's abilities at the age of four years. *The New England Journal of Medicine, 319*, 468–475.

Misra, G., and Tiwari, B. K. (1984). Environmental correlates of cognitive development. *Indian Journal of Applied Psychology, 24*, 41–52.

Mosier, C. E., and Rogoff, B. (2003). Privileged treatment of toddlers: Cultural aspects of individual choice and responsibility. *Developmental Psychology, 39*, 1047–1060.

Munroe, R. H., and Munroe, R. L. (1980). Infant experience and childhood affect among the Longoli: A longitudinal study. *Ethos, 8*, 295–315.

Nihira, K., Tomiyasu, Y., and Oshio, C. (1987). Homes of TMR children: Comparison between American and Japanese families. *American Journal of Mental Deficiency, 91*, 486–495.

Nsamenang, A. B., and Lamb, M. E. (1995). The force of beliefs: How the parental values of the Nso of northwest Cameroon shape children's progress toward adult models. *Journal of Applied Developmental Psychology, 16*, 613–627.

Okagaki, L., and Frensch, P. (1998). Parenting and children's school achievement: A multiethnic perspective. *American Educational Research Journal, 35*, 123–144.

Pachter, L. M., and Dworkin, P. W. (1997). Maternal expectations about normal child development in four cultural groups. *Archives of Pediatrics and Adolescent Medicine, 151*, 1144–1150.

Palacios, J., Gonzalez, M., and Moreno, C. (1992). Stimulating the child in the zone of proximal development: The role of parents' ideas. In I. Sigel, A. McGillicuddy-DeLisi, and J. Goodnow (Eds.), *Parental belief systems* (pp. 71–94). Hillsdale, NJ: Erlbaum.

Palti, H., Otrakkul, A., Belmaker, E., Tamair, D., and Tepper, D. (1984). Children's home environments: Comparison of a group exposed to stimulation intervention program with controls. *Early Child Development and Care, 13*, 193–212.

Perez, P., and Moreno, C. (2004, September). *Los versions preescolar 7 escolor de la escala HOME: Un setudio longitudinal y un analisis de contenido*. Presented at Congreso Hispano-Portugues de Psicologa, Lisbon, Portugal.

Pierce, S. H., and Lange, B. (1996). The experiential development of memory development in the home environment. *Journal of Genetic Psychology, 157*, 331–347.

Reichel-Dolumatoff, G., and Reichel-Dolumatoff, A. (1961). *The people of Aritama*. London: Routledge and Kegan Paul.

Richman, A. L., LeVine, R. A., New, R. S., Howrigan, G. A., Welles-Nystrom, B., and Levine, S. E. (1988). Maternal behavior to infants in five cultures. In R. A. LeVine, P. M. Miller, and M. M. West (Eds.), *Parental behavior in diverse societies* (pp. 82–97). San Francisco: Jossey-Bass.

Richter, L. M., and Grieve, K. W. (1991). Home environment and cognitive development of black infants in impoverished South African families. *Infant Mental Health Journal, 12*, 88–102.

Rohner, R. (1986). *The warmth dimension*. Beverly Hills, CA: Sage.

Skeels, H., and Dye, H. (l939). A study of the effects of differential stimulation on mentally retarded children. *American Journal of Mental Deficiency, 44*, 114–136.

Stewart, S., and Bond, M. H. (2002). A critical look at parenting research from the mainstream: Problems uncovered while adapting Western research to non-Western cultures. *British Journal of Developmental Psychology, 20*, 379–392.

Stewart, S., Bond, M., Kennard, B., Ho, L., and Zaman, R. (2002). Does the Chinese construct of guan export to the West? *International Journal of Psychology, 37*, 74–82.

Tippie, J. (2003, April). *Psychometrics and cultural modifications of HOME in Chile*. Paper presented at Assessing Home Environment for Children from Diverse Backgrounds, Workshop: Center for Human Growth and Development, University of Michigan, Ann Arbor, MI.

Torralva, T., and Cugnasco, I. (1996) Estudios epidemiologicicos sobre desarrollo infantile. In A. O'Donnell and E. Carmuega (Eds.), *Hoy y manana, Salud y calidad de vida de la ninez Argentina*. Buenos Aires, Argentina: Centro de Estudios Sobre Nutricion Infantil.

Torralva, T., Esteban, C., O'Donnell, A., and Duran, P. (2000). *The HOME Inventory in Argentina*. Unpublished manuscript, Buenos Aires, Argentina.

Tronick, E. Z., Morelli, G. A., and Ivey, P. K. (1992). The Efe forager infant and toddler's pattern of social relationships: Multiple and simultaneous. *Developmental Psychology, 28*, 568–577.

Valera, R. E., Vernberg, E. M., Sanchez-Sosa, J. J., Riveros, A., Mitchell, M., and Mashunkashey, J. (2004). Parenting style of Mexican, Mexican American, and Caucasian non-Hispanic families: Social context and cultural influences. *Journal of Family Psychology, 18*, 651–657.

Valsiner, J. (2000). *Culture and human development*. London: Sage.

Van Baar, A. (1991). *The development of infants of drug dependent mothers*. Amsterdam, The Netherlands: Swets and Zeitlinger.
Vreugdenhil, H., Lanting, C. I., Mulder, P. G., Boersma, E. R., and Weisglas-Kuperus, N. (2002). Effects of prenatal PCB and dioxin background exposure on cognitive and motor abilities in Dutch children at school age. *The Journal of Pediatrics, 140*, 48–56.
Vreugdenhil, H., Slijper, F., Mulder, P., and Weisglas-Kuperus, N. (2002). Effects of perinatal exposure to PCB's and dioxins on play behavior in Dutch children at school age. *Environmental Health Perspectives, 110*, A593–A598.
Wachs, T. D. (1992). *The nature of nurture*. Newbury Park, CA: Sage.
Wachs, T. D., Sigman, M., Bishry, Z., Moussa, W., Jerome, N., Newmann, C., et al. (1992). Caregiver-child interaction patterns in two cultures in relation to nutritional intake. *International Journal of Behavioral Development, 15*, 1–18.
Walker, S. P., Chang, S. M., Powell, C. A., and Grantham-McGregor, S. M. (2004). Psychosocial intervention improves the development of term low-birth-weight infants. *Journal of Nutrition, 134*, 1417–1423.
Wasserman, G., Graziano, J. H., Factor-Litak, P., Popovac, D., Morina, N., Musabegovic, A., et al. (1992). Independent effects of lead exposure and iron deficiency anemia on developmental outcome at age 2 years. *The Journal of Pediatrics, 121*, 695–703.
Weatherford, J. (1991). *Native roots, How the Indians enriched America*. New York: Fawcett Columbine.
Whiting, B., and Edwards, C. (1988). *Children of different worlds: The formation of social behavior*. Cambridge, MA: Harvard University Press.
Wilkinson, D. M. (2002). *Oblivion's altar*. New York: New American Library.
Williams, P., Piamjariyakul, U., Williams, A., Hornboonherm, P., Meena, P., Channukool, N., et al. (2003). Thai mothers and children and the home observation for measurement of the environment (home inventory): Pilot study. *International Journal of Nursing Studies, 40*, 249–258.
Woodson, R., and Costa-Woodson, E. (1984). Social organization, physical environment and infant-caretaker interaction. *Developmental Psychology, 20*, 473–476.
Zayas, L. H., and Solari, F. (1994). Early childhood socialization in Hispanic families: Context, culture, and practice implications. *Professional Psychology: Research and Practice, 25*, 200–206.
Zeitlin, M. F., Megawagni, R., Kramer, E. M., Coletta, N. D., Babatunde, E. D., and Carman, D. (1995). *Strengthening the family, Implications for international development*. Tokyo: United Nations University Press.
Zevalkink, J. (1997). *Attachment in Indonesia: The mother-child relationship in context*. Unpublished doctoral dissertation. University of Nijmegen, The Netherlands.
Zevalkink, J., Riksen-Walraven, J. M., and van Lieshout, C. F. (1999). Attachment in Indonesian caregiving context. *Social Development, 8*, 21–40.
Zhou, S., Baghurst, P., Gibson, R., and Makrides, M. (2007). Home environment, not breastfeeding, predicts Intelligence Quotient of children at four years. *Nutrition, 23*, 236–241.

27
Immigration and Acculturation

MARC H. BORNSTEIN and LINDA R. COTE

Introduction

Immigration and acculturation are major transforming forces on children, parents, and families worldwide. Indeed, migration and adjustment have been facts of the human condition ever since peoples of the African savannah began moving to new lands, not stopping until they had settled virtually all habitable places on earth. Immigration and acculturation are also contemporary global concerns. The International Organization of Migration (http://www.iom.int/jahia/jsp/index.jsp) estimates that approximately 200 million people now live outside the country of their birth or citizenship. Intercountry migration arises as a natural and predictable response to differences in resources and occupational opportunities, demographic growth, climatic change, financial insecurity, and exploitation of human rights. Most modern societies are not culturally homogenous but have repeatedly experienced sociopolitical changes associated with immigration (Cooper and Denner, 1998; Sam and Berry, 2006). Today, for example, nearly 25% of children under the age of 18 years in the United States are either immigrants themselves or the children of immigrants (Hernandez, Denton, and Macartney, 2008). Approximately 10% of all people in The Netherlands belong to immigrant families (Vollebergh et al., 2005).

Immigration and acculturation are disorganizing individual experiences, entailing thoroughgoing changes of social identity and self-image. Immigrants must negotiate new cultures and learn to navigate different systems of speaking, listening, reading, and writing just to communicate effectively in their culture of settlement. Learning those systems requires gaining new knowledge, as well as adjusting responses of engrained life scripts to compensate for cultural differences, language use, and disruption of familiar family roles.

Where immigration implies physical relocation between geographic places, acculturation implies psychological adjustment. Acculturation can be defined as the dual processes of cultural and psychological change that take place as a result of contact between two or more cultural groups and their individual members. Acculturation traditionally included "…those phenomena which result when groups of individuals having different cultures come into continuous first-hand contact, with subsequent changes in the original culture patterns of either or both groups…under this definition, acculturation is to be distinguished from culture change, of which it is but one aspect, and assimilation, which is at times a phase of acculturation" (Redfield, Linton, and Herskovits, 1936, pp. 149–150). In fact, immigration and acculturation are complex processes that occur at both the individual and societal levels, and understanding acculturation is complicated because two sets of individuals and two cultures are involved (Berry, 2006). On the societal plane, acculturation involves changes in social structures and institutions and in cultural practices. On the individual plane (sometimes termed psychological acculturation; Graves, 1967), acculturation involves changes in a person's customs, habits, language, lifestyle, and values (Szapocznik, Scopetta, Kurtines, and Arnalde, 1978). There are two reasons for keeping the cultural and psychological levels of analysis distinct. The first is that cross-cultural psychology views individual human behavior as interacting with the cultural context within which it occurs; hence, separate conceptions and measurement strategies are required at the two levels (Berry, Poortinga, Segall, and Dasen, 2002). The second is that not every individual enters into, participates in, or changes in the same way during acculturation; there is considerable individual variation even among people who live in the same acculturative arena (Sam and Berry, 2006). Thus, even when general acculturation is taking place at the societal level, individuals participate to varying degrees and have different goals.

Culture defines the ways in which a collection of people process and make sense of their experiences, and culture influences a wide array of family functions including roles, decision-making patterns, and cognitions and practices related to childrearing and child development. Intersecting these spheres, immigration and acculturation alter family life, parenting, and child health and development. Immigrants face multiple challenges in acculturating within the existing or mainstream society, including deciding which cultural cognitions or practices to retain from their indigenous culture and which to adopt from their culture of settlement. Acculturation is a process that continues for as long as culturally different groups come into contact. It entails learning each other's languages, sharing cuisine, and accommodating social interactions that are characteristic of each. Sometimes these mutual adaptations take place rather easily, but intercultural interactions can also create acculturative conflict and stress. Evidence suggests that most acculturating individuals are bicultural in some degree; that is, the individual simultaneously adopts cognitions and practices of the new culture while retaining those of the old (e.g., celebrating holidays of one's culture of destination as well as holidays unique to one's culture of origin).

This chapter is concerned with how cultural contexts influence human development among immigrants. Cross-cultural comparisons show that virtually all aspects of human development—cognitions and practices alike—are informed by their cultural framework (Bornstein, 1991, 2006; Bornstein and Lansford, Chapter 14, in this volume). Since the early 1900s, travelers and researchers alike have recognized the thoroughgoing influence of culture on child development and childrearing. Anthropologists were among the first to systematically investigate cultural contributions to family life (Harkness and Super, 2002). From a historical perspective, much research on acculturation has also been anthropological in nature and focused on the migration and adjustment in peoples from undeveloped or developing nations to developed industrial (usually Western) societies (Olmedo, 1979). Despite the increasing numbers of migrants in the twentieth and twenty-first centuries, psychological and developmental research on the influences of acculturation on child development was relatively scarce. The reason for this appears to be the once-dominant assimilationist theory that held that, as immigrants settle in their culture of destination, their beliefs and behaviors come to resemble those of the majority group and they forever relinquish those of their original culture. Indeed, in the past, some governments forced immigrant families (usually children) to adopt mainstream cultural practices (e.g., by requiring children to speak only the dominant language at school). Some early acculturation research nonetheless suggested that some developmental characteristics and socialization in particular resist assimilation (e.g., Masuda, Matsumoto, and Meredith, 1970). In the context of international migration and ethnic relations, a developmental perspective is requisite to understand the psychological processes of continuity and change attendant to immigration and acculturation.

In this chapter, we first review some history and relevant developmental theory about immigration and acculturation and describe possible patterns of acculturation. We then take up central developmental questions that surround child development and parental socialization in the context of immigration and acculturation. Immigration and acculturation raise several practical considerations, three prominent ones being measurement, family separation, and stress. We address those, consider some policy implications, and suggest some profitable future directions in the areas of developmental science and immigration and acculturation.

The focus of our discussion is on immigrants. There are multiple mechanisms through which foreign-born individuals arrive in new cultural settings. The most frequent pathway by far, accounting for approximately two-thirds of permanent immigration to the United States, for example, is through family reunification (Fuligni, 2004). Ninety-five percent of authorized immigration to the United States from Mexico occurs through family reunification, as it does in large measure from India (43%), Taiwan (59%), the Philippines (77%), and Vietnam (68%), the five nations that send the most immigrants to the United States. Other programs that account for the remaining immigrants to the United States include employment-based programs, diversity-based immigration, and humanitarian programs for refugees and asylum seekers. Although both immigrants and refugees (who are driven from their homelands involuntarily by civil wars, ethnic cleansing, or the like) experience acculturation, the experiences of the two groups differ.

Historical and Theoretical Perspectives on Immigration and Acculturation

How do immigrants acculturate? Early theories and research on acculturation were influenced by medicine and psychiatry and examined pathological symptoms thought to accompany "culture shock" (Bornstein, 1971). For many years, it was believed that immigrants inevitably encounter problems and that their experiences result in poor psychological adaptation. Migration can cause stress and increase the risk of mental health problems (anxiety, alienation, psychosomatic symptomatology, and identity diffusion) in youth and their parents alike (Bengi-Arslan, Verhulst, and Crijnen, 2002; Bengi-Arslan, Verhulst, van der Ende, and Erol, 1997; Bhugra and Jones, 2001; Halpern, 1993; Karlsen and Nazroo, 2002). Depression has been observed in children (Rutter, 1971) as well as mothers (Hohn, 1996), and clinical reports indicate that some youth act out in a variety of ways (Burke, 1980; Wilkes, 1992). For example, Turkish children in The Netherlands reportedly manifest internalizing and externalizing problem behaviors (Bengi-Arslan et al., 1997; Janssen et al., 2004; Murad, Joung, van Lenthe, Bengi-Arslan, and Crijnen, 2003). Short of such strong reactions, in "step-wise" immigration (Hondagneu-Sotelo, 1992), family separation is common, and when separations have been protracted, children and parents sometimes report feeling like strangers (Forman, 1993). At the individual level, attachment difficulties have been noted (Wilkes, 1992) because children withdraw from parents with whom they are reunited (Burke, 1980). For their part, parents experience difficulties in reasserting control over children (Arnold, 1991; Boti and Bautista, 1999; Sewell-Coker, Hamilton-Collins, and Fein, 1985). Whereas parents might expect gratitude for their sacrifice, they instead are confronted with children who are ambivalent about migrating (Arnold, 1991; Boti and Bautista, 1999; Chestham, 1972; Sciarra, 1999). Thus, clinical practitioners often encounter immigrants who experience and seek help for psychosocial struggles. Further fallout from this circumstance is that negative stereotypes surrounding acculturation have tended to take root despite evidence of countless cases of positive sociocultural adaptation, such as the successes of immigrant children in American, Australian, and Canadian schools (Fuligni, 1997, 1998; Kwak, 2003).

Contemporary interest in acculturation reflects dynamic changes in demography and social concerns but also grew out of a political climate sensitive to the effects of European domination over indigenous peoples. More recently, work in immigration and acculturation has focused on how ethnocultural groups relate to one other and change as a result of their attempts to live together in multicultural societies. Social-learning theory, derived from social and experimental psychology, emphasizes the role of observation and modeling in the acquisition of culturally appropriate new skills. Variables that facilitate adaptation are general knowledge about the new culture, cultural distance, length of residence, and amount of contact with nationals (e.g., Ward, 1996, 1999; Ward and Kennedy, 1994). In the social-cognition approach, cognitive elements such as expectations, attitudes toward members of the new culture, cultural identity, perceptions, attributions, and changes in values as part of the acculturation process have been investigated (e.g., Kunda, 1999; Wong-Rieger, 1984).

Despite their contemporary prevalence and importance, immigration and acculturation as scientific phenomena remain underresearched and poorly understood. At the aggregate level, immigration and acculturation involve social change in demography, sociology, medicine, and economics in society and affect civic, educational, social service, and legal systems. As a consequence, immigration and acculturation engage multiple perspectives and disciplines (Lansford, Deater-Deckard, and Bornstein, 2007). At the individual level (Bornstein and Cote, 2006a), what little is known about the cognitions and practices of acculturating people suggests that immigrant children may think, feel, and behave differently than majority children on measures of health, well-being, and educational achievement but that, over time and across generations, those differences tend to attenuate (see for example, Committee on the Health and Adjustment of Immigrant Children and Families, 1998; Mendoza, Javier, and Burgos, 2007). For example, second-generation and younger Latin immigrants to the United States adjust more to the majority culture and display weaker family relationships than first-generation and older immigrants (e.g., Sabogal, Marín, Otero-Sabogal, Marín, and Perez-Stable, 1987). Understanding acculturation processes may help to explain and prevent such change.

Immigration and Acculturation: A Task Analysis

The acculturation process can be broadly divided into three parts: acculturation setting conditions, acculturation orientations, and acculturation outcomes.

Acculturation Setting Conditions

The contexts in which acculturation occurs exert a major impact on acculturation (Bourhis, Moïse, Perreault, and Senécal, 1997). At the individual level, setting conditions refer to age, length of settlement, and generational differences; position in the society; personality characteristics (social norms and coping strategies); and situation or social context. People vary within their cultural group (on the basis of their educational or occupational background), and within their families, people vary according to their gender or other status. Individual differences certainly play a role in acculturation; immigrants with a greater sense of control appear to possess personality characteristics that allow them to cope better with the stresses of immigration (Lerner, Kertes, and Zilber, 2005). Relevant setting conditions at the societal level involve the type of migration (temporary versus permanent, voluntary versus involuntary), characteristics of the culture of origin (variation in homogeneity), characteristics of the immigrant group (individualist, collectivist) and the culture of destination (attitudes toward immigrants), and intergroup relationships (social inequality, social distance). For example, knowledge of the motives for migration is essential for understanding how acculturation transpires.

Migrants have been arrayed on a continuum from reactive to proactive, with the former being motivated by factors that are constraining or exclusionary and generally negative in character and the latter being motivated by factors that are facilitating or enabling and generally positive in character these contrasting motives are also referred to as "push/pull" factors. On the push side, for example, immigrants from the former Soviet Union (FSU) to Israel in the 1990s were thought to experience reduced migration-related trauma because their exodus comprised whole families (Florsheim, 1991) who were generally highly educated and professional (Paltiel, Sabatello, and Tal, 1996); moreover, Israeli society is pluralistic and holds generally positive attitudes toward Jewish immigration (Shuval, 1982). On the pull side, some cultural groups are evaluated more negatively than others; the evaluation of ethnic groups according to liking and likeness (social distance) is called the "ethnic hierarchy" (Schalk-Soekar, Van de Vijver, and Hoogsteder, 2004). In The Netherlands, for example, Surinamer and Antillean immigrants are evaluated more positively than Turks and Moroccans.

Acculturation Orientations

Acculturation orientations define how immigrants adapt to intercultural contact and combine culture of origin and culture of destination (e.g., Berry, 1997; Ward, Bochner, and Furnham, 2001). Acculturation orientations link setting conditions to outcomes.

Dimensionality describes the tension between cultural maintenance (what one brings from one's indigenous culture) and cultural adaptation (what one absorbs from one's settlement culture). Maintenance and adaptation are empirically as well as conceptually independent of one another (Ryder, Alden, and Paulhus, 2000); change in adaptation does not require change in maintenance (e.g., Berry, 1997; Hutnik, 1986; Sanchez and Fernandez, 1993). For example, the ability to speak a heritage language is independent of the ability to speak the language of the mainstream society. The independence between cultures of origin and destination predicts four acculturation orientations—integration, assimilation, separation, and marginalization—that involve the relative preference for maintaining one's culture of origin and adapting to one's culture of destination (Berry, Kim, and Boski, 1987). Integration reflects an orientation in which features of the immigrant's indigenous culture are maintained with simultaneous adaptation to elements of the majority culture. Integration potentially affords the best of both worlds. Assimilation refers to the loss of one's culture of origin and complete adaptation to the culture of destination. By contrast, immigrants may continue to cling to their culture of origin, isolating themselves from their new culture of destination; this acculturation strategy is called separation. Finally, when immigrants neither maintain their culture of origin (often for reasons of enforced cultural loss) nor adapt to their culture of destination (often for reasons of exclusion or discrimination), they find themselves in a position of marginalization. This four-fold formulation takes the perspective of the immigrant and is based on the theoretical assumption that immigrants can choose how they will acculturate. However, not all options are always available for personal or for social reasons; moreover, individual differences (e.g., in temperament and personality) come into play. To understand processes of acculturation, it is also meaningful to understand the historical and attitudinal situation faced by immigrants in their culture of destination. Some societies accept pluralism and support the continuation of cultural diversity as a communal resource (Berry and Kalin, 1995); other societies use policies and programs to suppress diversity; and still other societies attempt to segregate or marginalize immigrants (e.g., Lebedeva and Tartarko, 2004).

Berry, Phinney, Sam, and Vedder (2006) studied more than 5,000 immigrant youth who settled in 13 countries and assessed their ethnic and national identities, language knowledge and use, and friendships. Four distinct acculturation profiles emerged from a cluster analysis of their attitudinal and behavioral data. The largest number of youth fell into an integrated cluster; this was defined by positive ethnic and national identities, use of both languages, and a friendship network that included other youth from both cultures. The second largest cluster was an ethnic one, defined by a preference for separation and a rejection of assimilation, a high ethnic and low national identity, predominant use of the ethnic language, and friends drawn mainly from the own ethnic group. The third largest cluster was a national one. These youth preferred the assimilation strategy; they had a positive national identity and a negative ethnic identity, used the national language but not the heritage language, and had friends from the national society but not from their own ethnocultural group. Finally, a diffuse cluster emerged that resembled marginalization and was defined by acceptance of assimilation and separation and a rejection of integration (suggesting an unformed set of acculturation attitudes), low ethnic and national identities (suggesting feelings of nonengagement or nonattachment to either group), high proficiency in the ethnic language (and low proficiency and use of the national language), and high contact with ethnic peers and low contact with national peers.

Integration, the combination of adaptation and maintenance, is the acculturation strategy most preferred and practiced by immigrants and the course thought to be associated with the best mental health outcome (e.g., Berry and Sam, 1997). However, there is considerable variation in what is meant by integration in view of the variety of different possible combinations of cultures. It could mean that immigrants combine or merge cultures in all their behavior or that they switch between cultures. Immigrants could have access to both cultural systems and alternate between them depending on the context; for example, "dual monocultural" individuals may switch between maintenance at home and adaptation outside the home. Integration could also refer to mixing the two cultures, fusing them, or creating a new culture from the old ones that is unique and novel with aspects that are atypical of either original culture per se (Coleman, 1995; Padilla, 1995). For example, Indian immigrant mother–infant dyads in the United States engage in different vocal interaction patterns from Indians in India and from European Americans in the United States, suggesting that the mothers modify their interactive practices as a result of acculturation and that immigrants partake in implicit cultural communicative practices that are specific to their immigration context (Gratier, 2003). Parents constitute the proximal link between immigrant children and their culture of origin. Families that retain some aspects of their original culture appear to fare better in terms of physical health, mental health, and education for the first and second immigrant generations than those who abandon their indigenous culture and language rapidly (Beiser, Dion, Gotowiec, Hyman, and Vu, 1995; Darvies and McKelvey, 1998). "Children are more likely to adjust well to a new culture when they are not isolated from their culture of origin…such social contact provides a secure base for these children from which they can break into a culture that is—at first—alien to them" (Kurtz-Costes and Pungello, 2000, p. 123).

Acculturation Outcomes

All manner of indices are examined as outcomes of immigration and acculturation. Some include objective parameters of adaptation, such as employment, housing conditions, and acquisition of the host language; others are drawn from the intrapsychic realm, such as psychological distress, mood states, feelings of acceptance and satisfaction, and the acquisition of majoritarian beliefs and behaviors. Ward and Kennedy (1994) found that psychological and sociocultural adjustment were related but predicted by different variables and showed different patterns of adjustment over time (i.e., sociocultural problems steadily decrease, whereas psychological distress is more variable).

Domain specificity speaks to immigrants' outcomes as they vary across life categories or situations. Acculturation does not affect all aspects of the psyche in an identical way. For example, immigrants may embrace food habits of the culture of destination but not its religious practices. Nagata's (1994) review of acculturation studies pointed to a decrease in ethnic knowledge and behaviors from the first to the second generations, although attitudes did not significantly change. Domain-specific measures show that different aspects of culture differ in their level of adjustment (e.g., Triandis, Kashima, Shimada, and Villareal, 1986). Immigrants may seek adaptation at work (economic assimilation), speak the languages of origin and destination (linguistic integration), and maintain traditional relationships in the family (separation in private). Generally, the public domain involves activities aimed at participation in the social lives of both culture of origin and culture of destination (e.g., social contacts, following the news, language use), whereas the private domain involves personal, value-related matters (e.g., childrearing and family celebrations; Arends-Tóth and van de Vijver, 2003). Cultural adaptation is often preferred in the public domain, and cultural maintenance is preferred in the private domain. For example, Phalet and Swyngedouw (2003) found that Turkish and Moroccan immigrants in The Netherlands attributed more importance to cultural maintenance in the home and family context (private domain), whereas adaptation was more important in school and work situations (public domain).

Furthermore, domain specificity is moderated by a number of factors, including time. Among FSU immigrants to Israel, for example, positive changes were noted in objective factors 5 years after immigration compared to conditions in the first year. These changes also compared favorably with those reported among immigrants to the United States (Flaherty, Kohn, Galbin, Gaviria, and Birz, 1986; Westermeyer, Neider, and Vang, 1984). However, there was little change in subjective indicators, such as satisfaction with living in Israel and perceived social support (Lerner et al., 2005). Who reports about whom matters as well. For example, parents from immigrant families in The Netherlands report more problems in their daughters than nonimmigrant parents, in contrast to teachers who report lower levels of internalizing, social, and thought problems in immigrant boys but higher levels of externalizing problems in both immigrant boys and girls (Vollebergh et al., 2005).

Developmental Research in Immigration and Acculturation

Two central questions define developmental research in immigration and acculturation. First, to what degree do immigrant parents maintain and instill in their children the cognitions and practices of their culture of origin and adopt those of the culture of destination in acculturation? Second, to what degree do children themselves choose to maintain or adopt the cognitions and practices of their parents' culture of origin or their own new culture of destination once they have achieved sufficient autonomy to decide for themselves? Before these two, the social reality of immigrant parents will be briefly discussed.

Immigrant parents bring with them on their journey conceptual models of the successful adult and how to rear a good child that evolved through generations in their original cultural contexts. When they migrate to a new country, they find that socialization agents in the receiving society, such as other parents, teachers, and social workers, may possess different images of the successful adult and different strategies for childrearing (Roer-Strier, 2001). Thus, parents sometimes experience significant loss in their effectiveness as a result of systemic constraints on their ability to mediate the effects of their new environment on their children and on influencing the environment on behalf of their children (Falicov, 2007). Likewise, immigrant parents are sometimes overwhelmed with immigration-related stress, which curtails their capacity to act as role models for their children. Immigrant parents can attribute their inability to meet their parental obligations to their own limited understanding of institutional rules and resources; lack of language fluency, time, energy, or financial resources; and emotional stress. Immigrant parents often have high educational aspirations for their children (Hernandez and Charney, 1998; Kao, 1999; Rumbaut, 1999) but may know little about the local educational system, particularly if they themselves have completed only a few years of school. Parents with little education may, as a consequence, be less comfortable with the education system, they may not be in a position to help their children with school work, and they negotiate with teachers and education administrators less effectively.

One of the best ways to explore how parents attempt to maintain and instill in their children the cognitions and practices of their culture of origin as well as adopt those of the culture of destination is to observe mothers and children engaged in emerging, universal, developmentally appropriate activities. Some research on acculturating families has employed such an approach.

As will become apparent, most of this research has focused on parents of infants or young children (who are as yet too young to make decisions for themselves about how they wish to incorporate cultural identity into their thinking and behavior).

Caudill and Frost (1974) used a comparative group-level approach by observing mother–infant dyads in Japan, European American mother–infant dyads in the United States, and Japanese immigrants (third-generation Sansei mothers and their fourth-generation Yonsei infants) in naturalistic interactions to determine whether observed differences in the behaviors of mothers and infants in Japan and the United States were attributable to biology or culture. They concluded that there were few differences in mothers' caregiving pertaining to infants' basic needs among the three groups (there were no differences in the frequency with which mothers looked at their infants, for example). They found more differences among these cultural groups with respect to maternal styles of behavior and infant development, however; third-generation Japanese American mothers were more similar to European American mothers than to mothers in Japan, supporting the idea that prior differences found between mothers and infants in the United States and Japan were cultural rather than biological in origin.

Harwood and Feng (2006) compared the parenting values and beliefs of first- and second-generation migrant Puerto Rican mothers of young children. They found that, compared to first-generation mothers, second-generation mothers were more likely to speak English, adopt U.S. values rather than maintain traditional Puerto Rican values, feel more at home in the United States than Puerto Rico, and interact and develop relationships with non–Puerto Ricans. However, despite some adoption of U.S. customs, second-generation mothers kept active attachments to Puerto Rican culture, as indicated, for example, by their tendency to live in multi-generational homes, their identification as predominantly Puerto Rican, and their stated desire for their children to retain a Puerto Rican identity and to feel comfortable in both cultural contexts.

We have studied child development, parenting, and family life longitudinally among three groups of immigrant families—from Japan, Korea, and South America to the United States (Bornstein and Cote, 2006b). We observed mother–child interactions in the home when the children were 5, 13, 20, and 48 months of age and used self-reports to assess maternal demographic background, cultural beliefs, and cognitions about parenting and child development. In groups like these, acculturation does not predict parenting cognitions at the individual level. However, at the societal level, immigrant mothers often differ from mothers of similar socioeconomic circumstances in their cultures of origin and destination. For example, Japanese immigrant mothers' cognitions tend to be more similar to mothers in Japan or intermediate to mothers in Japan and the United States. In contrast, South American mothers' cognitions tend to be more similar to those of European American mothers and different from mothers in South America. Thus, different patterns of results are obtained for Japanese immigrant and South American immigrant mothers even though their cognitions and socioeconomic circumstances are comparable. This may be because North and South America share many Western traditions not shared by Japan. The acculturation of parenting cognitions to U.S. norms may be more relaxed for South American immigrant mothers than for Japanese immigrant mothers, who appear to retain deeply held cultural beliefs about mothering and a woman's social role. These findings accord with other research that has reported that Asian immigrant parents especially tend to maintain traditional childrearing beliefs when in new cultural environments (Chun, 2006; Chun and Akutsu, 2003; Uba, 1994).

As domain specificity would predict, parenting practices appear to acculturate more readily than parenting cognitions (Bornstein and Cote, 2004). Immigrant mothers tend to engage more in behaviors featured by their culture of destination than adopt their beliefs. For example, South American immigrant mothers to the United States, like European American mothers, report more limit setting than mothers in their country of origin; they are also more like European American mothers and less like South American mothers in demonstrating and soliciting exploratory play with their children. Japanese immigrant mothers also tend to play with their children more like European American than like Japanese mothers (e.g., in soliciting less symbolic play). The behaviors of young immigrant children as well tend more closely to resemble those of children in their culture of destination than of children in their culture of origin. Immigrant children to the United States, for example, engage in more exploratory play and less symbolic play than children in cultures of origin that favor symbolic play; their play is similar to that of European American children.

A second central issue in acculturation of interest to developmental scientists is the degree to which youth maintain or adopt cognitions and practices of their parents' culture and/or their new (peer and school) culture once they have achieved sufficient autonomy to decide for themselves. Naturally, most of this research has focused on adolescents' and young adults' cultural identity and developmental outcomes (Phinney and Ong, 2007). Additional research comes from studies of generational conflict between parents and their older children with respect to retaining and adopting cultural beliefs (see p. 542). Israeli society traditionally consisted mostly of East European Jews and their descendents, and expectations for each wave of immigrants have been to assimilate and embrace its national values and norms (Eisenstadt, 1952; Kimmerling, 2001; Lerner et al., 2005). In this connection, research on new immigrants (especially from the FSU and Ethiopia) has revealed diverging acculturation patterns. Despite cultural differences, immigrant adolescents appear more inclined to balance their established cultural identity with their new Israeli identity than to reject one at the expense of the other (Orr, Mana, and Mana 2003). Studies show that less than one-third consider themselves Israelis, whereas the majority consider themselves both Israeli and Russian. Chinese American adolescents feel alienated from their parents and their peers. Alienation from parents is a result of factors such as language barriers, parent work schedules, and high educational expectations; alienation from peers is a result of factors such as language, customs, and discrimination (Qin, Way, and Mukherjee, 2008). Immigrant children's adaptation focuses on how they develop competencies to function in plural society (Berry et al., 2006; Sam, 2004). For example, the mismatch between parents' culturally indigenous belief systems and the beliefs of the culture of settlement has been noted repeatedly in the research literature (Chan and Leong, 1994; Florsheim, 1997). Adolescents often blame their conflicts with their parents on their parents' traditional beliefs. Chinese American adolescents understand that they are a part of two contrasting cultures; America is perceived as idealizing egalitarian relationships between parents and children and open to emotional expression, whereas China is perceived as idealizing parental control and discretion (Qin, 2006, 2008a, 2008b).

Acculturation is a developmentally dynamic process (Sam and Berry, 2006), and it is gendered insofar as women and men and girls and boys acculturate differently. First, a "feminization of migration" has transpired to the extent that the first world's demand for service workers draws mothers from a variety of developing countries to care for "other people's children" (Hondagneu-Sotelo, 1992). Second, males are more likely to respond with distress to humiliating events, such as work-related stress or financial problems, which are common after immigration, whereas women are more distressed by interpersonal events (Farmer and McGuffin, 2003; Vollebergh et al., 2005). Güngör and Bornstein (2008) studied gender differences and similarities in values, adaptation, and perceived discrimination among middle (14 to 17 years) and late (18 to 20 years) second-generation Turk adolescents in Belgium. All adolescents valued openness to change and self-transcendence, but older adolescents attached greater importance to their culture of destination and to conservatism. Girls perceived less discrimination and showed better adaptation than boys. Overall, a larger gender gap in acculturation experiences opened in late than in middle adolescence. Thus, both developmental processes and gender influenced adolescent acculturation.

Individuals within a family may differ with respect to acculturation, which may create tension and conflict within the family. Typically, individuals with the most contact with the dominant culture, by virtue of their participation in the larger community through peers, school, work, or other activities, will acculturate more rapidly and in more domains than individuals with less contact. Given that peers and schools, for example, exert major socializing influences on youth, it is often the case that children become more acculturated than their parents. Because immigrant families straddle two cultures, tension and conflict in the family can arise between parents, who wish to inculcate traditional beliefs of their culture of origin in their children, and children, who wish to conform to and be accepted by peers in the culture of destination (McQueen, Getz, and Bray, 2003). Additionally, school-age children who are fluent in the language and mazeways of the mainstream culture may be required to "language-" or "culture-broker" on behalf of their parents who are not so fluent in the language or comfortable in the ways of the mainstream culture. For example, immigrant children may be thrust into the uncomfortable position of translator at parent–teacher conferences (Buriel, Love, and De Ment, 2006; Chao, 2006). As many as three in four immigrant children act as language brokers for their parents (Hernandez et al., 2008).

In summary, when parents immigrate to a new culture, they carry with them implicit knowledge of childrearing, which includes care practices, communicative styles, and goals for development from their culture of origin, and they encounter a set of new implicit cognitions and explicit practices concerning childrearing in their culture of destination. Therefore, acculturation involves negotiation between the cognitions and practices of the two cultures. Immigrant parents may identify themselves as belonging more to one or another of these cultures or as being bicultural. With respect to parenting and child development, immigrant samples of children and their mothers tend to maintain some mazeways from their culture of origin but also differ from children and mothers in their culture of origin and resemble children and mothers in their culture of destination. Immigrant mothers tend to retain the parenting cognitions of their culture of origin, but parenting practices appear to acculturate more rapidly or easily. Acculturation processes in parenting and child development are also subject to domain specificity—that is, which beliefs or behaviors are evaluated and which cultures are compared. There are large individual and group differences in the ways people go about acculturating, in the degree to which they achieve satisfactory adaptations, and in their types of adaptation. These considerations lead to practical questions that attend immigration and acculturation.

Practical Issues in Immigration and Acculturation

Developmental scientists, policy makers, practitioners, and lay people interested in or experiencing immigration and acculturation confront numerous practical issues. One is measurement. At a societal level, family separation has become a second prominent and perennial topic. At the individual level, the evaluation and promotion of more adaptive strategies to cope constitutes a third challenge. We focus briefly on each.

Measurement

A large number of instruments and designs to measure acculturation have been developed. Successful integration of immigrants in their new country is often measured by objective indicators, such as work, living conditions, language acquisition, and social network. Adaptation thus measured has been found to be positively associated with length of time since arrival in the new country (Scott and Scott, 1989; Scott and Stumpf, 1984; Shuval, 1982). Phinney (2006) usefully distinguished between two types of dependent variables widely used in acculturation research:

markers of time in a new culture, such as generation of immigration or length of time following immigration, and within-person variables that change over time, such as language, identity, and values. Acculturation level has often been equated to generation level. Although many acculturation measures incorporate generation level, even siblings within the same family—who are titularly the same generation level—may not identify with each culture to the same degree. Thus, more precise acculturation measures move beyond demographic descriptors ("social addresses") such as generation level and attempt to capture a psychological feeling of belonging to a particular culture. Proxy measures (e.g., generation level, number of years living in the country) can provide valuable complementary information to direct measures of acculturation but are usually poor stand-alone evaluations. For example, Jain and Belsky (1997) found that demographics (e.g., number of years of settlement in the United States) did not predict immigrant fathers' involvement in their children's lives, whereas direct measures of acculturation orientation (e.g., attitudes) were significant predictors.

Researchers today, therefore, view acculturation as a multidimensional and bidirectional process in which an individual accommodates the cognitions and practices of the culture of origin with those of the culture of destination. Anthropologists have used the concept of the "dual frame of reference" to refer to immigrants' uniquely double lens. Consensus has it that a measure of acculturation is comprehensive only to the extent that it taps aspects of both cultures of origin and destination (Arends-Tóth and van de Vijver, 2006). The use of independent measures of acculturation orientations in a range of different domains and situations achieves this goal. The most reliable acculturation instruments use a "two-item" method that involves separate items to measure maintenance and adaptation in both public and private domains.

Studying variables associated with acculturation separately, rather than combining them into a single scale, also allows researchers to identify the differing roles of various aspects of acculturative change and differing rates of change among acculturation variables. Different generation cohorts (first versus later generations) face different issues vis-à-vis their cultures of origin and destination and thus are likely to have different developmental trajectories to their bicultural identity.

Family Separation

In the process of migration, families typically undergo profound transformations that are often complicated by extended periods of separation among nuclear and extended family members. Levitt (2001) discussed the challenges that attend rearing children transnationally. Focusing on children left behind by their parents, and especially mothers, highlights the emotional consequences, the problems with managing decision making and power sharing between parents and grandparents or other caregivers, and the problems that occur if parents start a new family in their new country. Transnational mothers bear hardships because they are often unable to live up to their own (cultural) expectations of providing care (Parrenas, 2001, 2005; Schmalzbauer, 2004). Children are ambivalent about leaving their home and friends and joining their parents in the new country (Bryceson and Vuorela, 2002; Dreby, 2007). As part of the Longitudinal Immigrant Student Adaptation Study, Suarez-Orozco, Todorova, and Louie (2002) followed 385 early adolescents originating from China, Central America, the Dominican Republic, Haiti, and Mexico; 85% of the participants had been separated from one or both parents for extended periods. Children who were separated from their parents were more likely to report depressive symptoms than children who had not been separated. Chinese tended to migrate as a unit, whereas nearly all Haitians and Central Americans regularly experienced family disruption during migration. Family reunification, which is sometimes not possible for many years, does not automatically address these problems but can intensify stress when parents and children have grown apart or when additional family members are added to the parental household.

Moreover, when children are left in the care of others, such as grandparents or aunts, children must confront two separations—one from the parents and another one from the caregiver to whom the child became attached.

Acculturative Stress

Immigration is a stressful event (Smart and Smart, 1995; Suarez-Orozco and Suarez-Orozco, 2001); immigrants move in large numbers despite the now common knowledge that most risk significant reductions in occupational status and income (Li, 1998, 2003; Reitz, 2001), familial support (Liamputtong, 2001), and social networks (Kilbride, 2000); immigration also deprives children of their familiar environment and supports of extended family and friends (Chan and Leong, 1994; Short and Johnston, 1997).

In psychology, immigrant families are often studied with respect to overcoming traumas in their culture of origin that may have precipitated migration and an "acculturation gap" that sometimes arises between parents and children (Laosa, 1989; Suarez-Orozco and Suarez-Orozco, 2001). Birman (2006) theorized how such acculturation gaps are conceptualized and computed. For example, Chinese immigrant parents in the United States continue to operate on the Chinese cultural model (often dated), comparing their children with children in China or their own experiences growing up, whereas their children increasingly compare their parents' expectations and behaviors to those of American parents of their friends or what they see depicted in U.S. media (Qin, 2006, 2008a, 2008b).

The stress of acculturation has been found to lead to pathogenic processes such as depression, social dysfunction, and delinquency (Berry and Kim, 1988). Learning a new language and culture in an unfamiliar context can generate shearing acculturation stress (Ainslie, 1998; Shuval, 1982; Yeh, 2003). Immigrants from the FSU to Israel experienced psychological distress levels during the first year higher than in the Israeli-born population (Zilber and Lerner, 1996). Marginalization is presumably more stressful, and integration is presumably less stressful; in between are assimilation and separation (Berry, 1997; Berry and Kim, 1988). The distress inherent in immigration is affected by the passage of time and is moderated by other factors, such as postmigration conditions (Beiser, 1990; Shuval, 1982; Zilber and Lerner, 1996), personal (Kuo and Tsai, 1986) and social resources (Beiser, 1990), and the ideological motivation and level of commitment to the new society (Ben Sira, 1997).

Among the many factors that can contribute to well-being in acculturating individuals, the family is particularly important. For a member of the majority group in a society, the family is an integral part of a network of social relationships that constitutes the society, and the family culture is reflective of the mainstream society. The situation for immigrants differs. The family is usually part of another social system and culture. The immigrant family as agent of socialization has a major influence on the acculturation orientations of its members (Nauck, 2001). Good family relationships (especially perceived support) can reduce stress experienced during acculturation (Castillo, Conoley, and Brossart, 2004; Lerner et al., 2005). By contrast, intergenerational discrepancies between immigrant parents and their children likely and often lead to conflicts with the family, thereby threatening the well-being of its members (Kaplan and Marks, 1990; Szapocznik and Kurtines, 1993). Parents of distressed Chinese American adolescents tended to adhere to the importance of education and the hierarchical parental role at home and emphasized superficial, performative levels of traditional Chinese parenting, whereas parents of the nondistressed Chinese American adolescents tended to adapt the broader, general principles and tenets of Chinese parenting (e.g., importance of respect, education, and self-cultivation) into the new American cultural context (Qin, 2006, 2008a, 2008b).

In summary, migration often brings unique challenges, such as parental adaptation difficulty, parental lack of time with their children, and language barriers that tend to destabilize parent–child relationships (Garcia Coll and Magnuson, 1997; Qin, 2006). Portes and Rumbaut (2001, pp. 53–54) describe this as dissonant acculturation—"when children's learning of English and American ways and simultaneously loss of the immigrant culture outstrip their parents." Dissonant acculturation often leads to increasing parent–child conflicts in immigrant families and adaptation challenges for children (Chan and Leong, 1994; Uba, 1994; Ying, 1999). Discrepancies are common in immigrant families because the primary socialization of parents is in their country of origin, whereas, depending on their age of arrival, their children may have received at least some of their primary socialization in the culture of destination. Immigrant children are usually more exposed to the values of the new society through peers and school, contributing to their greater acceptance of those values.

Policy Implications of Immigration and Acculturation

Insofar as systematic relations may exist between how people acculturate and how well they adapt, the possibility exists for the development of some "best practices" in how to promote immigrants' acculturation. The consequence of all these considerations and the increasing numbers of immigrants worldwide make it imperative to learn more about immigration and acculturation so that scientists, educators, and practitioners can effectively enhance immigrant children's development and strengthen their families. With these considerations in mind, we briefly address some prominent policy implications of immigration and acculturation.

Families are economic and legal units as well as social and psychological entities. For example, legal barriers that prevent or delay the migration of dependents in Canada come with a human cost for couples, extended families, and children (Bernhard, Landolt, and Goldring, 2005). Family members are often separated for years while waiting for a decision on their application for family reunification. Dutch immigration policies are no less challenging. Dutch immigration policies rely on notions of "genuine mothers" who provide full-time care (Van Walsum, 2006). These policies assume that, after a certain period of time, no real bond exists between immigrants in The Netherlands and their children abroad and hence no reason for admission on the grounds of family reunification. Single mothers from developing countries are especially affected by these restrictions because it takes them longer to get established in The Netherlands and therefore they are separated from their children longer. Women who appeal to international human rights law receive mixed results.

Immigrant families are sometimes exposed to legal risks that arise from being from cultures that employ childrearing practices that (may) come into direct conflict with majoritarian views regarding childrearing. For example, conflicts can arise from cultural differences in beliefs about parenting practices that may be deemed "neglectful" or "abusive" under laws of the mainstream culture but that are viewed as normative in the migrant's indigenous culture (Ali, 2007; Azar and Cote, 2002). A majority of Korean Americans living in Los Angeles reportedly regard laws concerning physical abuse to be in conflict with their cultural values and childrearing practices (Song, 1986). Similarly, some percentage of Vietnamese parents regard touching children's genitals in certain contexts as acceptable (Gilbert and Ahn, 1990). Such fundamental differences of opinion over normative parenting practices can lead to cultural clashes between foreign-born parents and child protective services systems in the majority culture (Coleman, 2004).

Societies that are supportive of cultural pluralism (that is, with a positive multicultural ideology) provide more positive settlement contexts because they are less likely to enforce cultural change (assimilation) or exclusion (segregation and marginalization) on immigrants, and they are more likely to provide social support both from the institutions of the larger society (e.g., culturally sensitive health care and multicultural curricula in schools) and from the continuing and evolving ethnocultural communities that usually make up pluralistic societies (Lerner et al., 2005; Murphy and Leighton, 1965). However, groups that are less well accepted often experience hostility, rejection, and discrimination, factors that are predictive of poor long-term adaptation.

Differences between cultures have implications beyond legal questions. Conflicts between the values of the majority and those of the immigrant's native culture can play out in profound ways in the lives of foreign-born parents and children. Many challenges present themselves as immigrant youth seek their identities in multiethnic and multicultural societies (Kagitçibasi, 1997). In the context of perceived rejection and loss of status and power, immigrants tend to cling to tenets of their culture of origin, religion, and ethnicity as affirmations of group identity and self-worth. This often occurs even among immigrants who were not particularly religious or ethnic initially. Indeed, strengthening of group identity arises as a consequence of perceived prejudice and xenophobia (Baumgartl, 1994). This situation may render migrants open to influences that turn them inward and cause further separation from the culture of destination. To prevent negative outcomes, thoughtful measures need to be promoted with direct implications for policy. Immigrant parents reportedly see that their role is to get a child to school to which they surrender authority, but schools require greater involvement from immigrant parents. Educators know that active parents are essential to enhancing minority achievement in school (Epstein and Sanders, 2002). Authorities in charge of the well-being of immigrants need to develop effective social, educational, and psychological interventions and professional guides regarding separations and reunions (Guerrero, 2005). For example, the European Union emphasizes the contribution immigrants make to its strategic goals to develop a competitive and dynamic knowledge-based economy and to promote greater social cohesion (Commission of the European Communities, 2003).

Future Research in Immigration and Acculturation

Future directions for a developmental science that contributes to understanding the processes of continuity and change in the context of international migration and acculturation constitute a long agendum. That science needs to differentiate among larger cultural groups to clarify and investigate their commonalities and distinctions. It is incorrect, too, to assume that ideas about child development held by majoritarian families in a society are also held by cultural groups that have newly immigrated. Patterns of parent–child interaction that lead to cognitive and social competencies for immigrant children may not necessarily be the same as those that lead to competence among majority children. Each cultural group is unique and undergoes specific acculturation processes. Language loss provides an informative example (Tienda, 2008). Dutch immigrants in Canada and Australia often lose considerable amounts of their native language. It is not uncommon to find that the third generation has a poor proficiency (if any at all) in the Dutch language. However, Chinese immigrants often maintain knowledge of their first language across generations. Future research also needs to distinguish among immigrants, refugees, and sojourners, all of whom vary with respect to their reasons for migrating (which can affect their psychological profiles and health) and their plans for remaining in the culture of destination (which can affect their motivation to acculturate), to name but a few important ways in which migrants may differ. In addition, because research findings in one cultural area of the world (or even in a few societies) do not readily generalize to others and as our knowledge of international acculturation experiences, ideologies, and sensitivities increases, we need to alter our conceptions and extend the empirical findings that are portrayed in this chapter.

Longitudinal research further enhances the value of the developmental orientation, for example, by providing unique insights into the temporal processes of acculturation for migrants and highlighting intergenerational similarities and differences. Peoples in both sending and receiving countries and cultures are affected by emigration and immigration alike. Migration involves many interconnected family members crossing national borders. It includes those who left, those who remain, and those who come and go. Greater and cheaper travel and communication technologies make it easier for people to move and maintain linkages with the cultures they came from and engage in important transnational activities, such as remittances, phone calls, and visits (Waldinger, 2007). On the one hand, sending countries experience loss in terms of waning population often of entrepreneurial spirit and talent because émigrés are normally highly motivated and resourceful people who possess the élan to start new productive lives in a new context (Gartner, 2005; Whybrow, 2006), and left-behind children may not be able to act as productive citizens of sending countries, and they represent a generation without care. On the other hand, sending countries benefit from remittances (Adams and Page, 2005; Ratha, 2003). On the one hand, receiving countries benefit from the influx of those same resourceful and spirited people, and initial mental health advantages of immigrant children have been attributed to their careful selection as members of healthy, resilient, success-bound families (Beiser, Hou, Hyman, and Tousignant, 2002). On the other hand, in receiving societies, acculturation takes place in the settled and the dominant group as well as in the settling and nondominant group, and when culturally disparate peoples come into continuous contact with each other, the differences between them tend to become salient and can impact cultural patterns of both groups because mainstream cultures and acculturating cultures must mutually accommodate. Although immigration has consequences for both immigrants and members of the receiving society, the former group is usually the more studied. As the way of the world continues, we foresee that theoretical, empirical, and practical perspectives on acculturation will exert major influences on the research community and inevitably insinuate themselves into societal policy as well.

Conclusion

Throughout human history, people have been on the move, and despite increasing numbers of migrating peoples in the twentieth and twenty-first centuries, research on dynamic relations between culture and human development is still relatively scarce. As societies become increasingly diverse and pluralistic, it is imperative that researchers recognize that immigrants do not immediately and forever relinquish the beliefs and behaviors of their cultures of origin and adopt those of their cultures of destination. Acculturation is far more nuanced, dynamic, and thorny than that, and it is more fruitful to study how families, parents, and children reconcile and implement goals, values, and strategies from both cultures and examine the effects of amalgamation on each.

With so much emphasis on our need to examine differences among immigrant peoples more generally, it is easy to forget that nearly all parents—regardless of gender, age, ethnicity, or nationality—seek to lead happy, healthy, fulfilled lives and rear happy, healthy, fulfilled children, grandchildren, and great-grandchildren. Specifically, nearly all parents wish to promote their children's positive development by providing a better economic standard of living for their family, good nutrition, access to health care, a safe living environment, and educational or employment opportunities. This is why parents make great sacrifices for their partners and children, including moving to new regions, nations, and continents—sometimes at great legal jeopardy, economic cost, and physical peril, and sometimes enduring conflicts with and separations from beloved family members for years at a time. Acculturation has both positive (e.g., new opportunities) and negative (e.g., discrimination, separations from loved ones) aspects. The debates about social policies that stem from the examination of differences between people will be well served if we strive also to remember the universal developmental goals shared by families around the world.

Acknowledgments

This research was supported by the Intramural Research Program of the National Institutes of Health, *Eunice Kennedy Shriver* National Institute of Child Health and Human Development. We thank J. T. D. Suwalsky and T. Taylor.

References

Adams, R. H., and Page, J. (2005). Do international migration and remittances reduce poverty in developing countries? *World Development, 33*, 1645–1669.

Ainslie, R. (1998). Cultural mourning, immigration, and engagement: Vignettes from the Mexican experience. In M. M. Suarez-Orozco (Ed.), *Crossings: Mexican immigration in interdisciplinary perspectives* (pp. 283–300). Cambridge, MA: Harvard University Press.

Ali, A. H. (2007). *Infidel*. New York: The Free Press.

Arends-Tóth, J., and van de Vijver, F. J. R. (2003). Multiculturalism and acculturation: Views of Dutch and Turkish-Dutch. *European Journal of Social Psychology, 33*, 249–266.

Arends-Tóth, J., and van de Vijver, F. J. R. (2006). Issues in the conceptualization and assessment of acculturation. In M. H. Bornstein and L. R. Cote (Eds.), *Acculturation and parent-child relationships: Measurement and development* (pp. 33–62). Mahwah, NJ: Erlbaum.

Arnold, E. (1991). Issues of reunification of migrant West Indian children in the United Kingdom. In J. L. Roopnarine and J. Brown (Eds.), *Caribbean families diversity among ethnic groups* (pp. 243–258). Greenwich, CT: Ablex Publishing Corp.

Azar, S. T., and Cote, L. R. (2002). Sociocultural issues in the evaluation of the needs of children in custody decision-making: What do our current frameworks for evaluation parenting practices have to offer? *International Journal of Law and Psychiatry, 25*, 193–217.

Baumgartl, B. (1994). *Xenophobia and racism in Europe*. London: Pinter.

Beiser, M. (1990). Migration, opportunity or mental risk. *Triangle, 29*, 83–90.

Beiser, M., Dion, R., Gotowiec, A., Hyman, I., and Vu, N. (1995). Immigrant and refugee children in Canada. *Canadian Journal of Psychiatry, 40*, 67–72.

Beiser, M., Hou, F., Hyman, I., and Tousignant, M. (2002). Poverty, family process and the mental health of immigrant children in Canada. *American Journal of Public Health, 92*, 220–227.

Bengi-Arslan, L., Verhulst, F. C., and Crijnen, A. A. M. (2002). Prevalence and determinants of minor psychiatric disorder in Turkish immigrants living in the Netherlands. *Social Psychiatry and Psychiatric Epidemiology, 37*, 118–124.

Bengi-Arslan, L., Verhulst, F. C., van der Ende, J., and Erol, N. (1997). Understanding childhood (problem) behaviours from a cultural perspective: Comparison of problem behaviours and competencies in Turkish immigrants, Turkish and Dutch children. *Social Psychiatry and Psychiatric Epidemiology, 32*, 477–484.

Ben Sira, Z. (1997). *Immigration, stress and readjustment*. Westport, CT: Preager.

Bernhard, J. K., Landolt, P., and Goldring, L. (2005). *Transnational, multi-local motherhood: Experiences of separation and reunification among Latin American families in Canada*. Ryerson Working Paper Series. Retrieved from http://www.yorku.ca/cohesion/LARG/PDF/Transantional_Families_LARG_May_05.pdf.

Berry, J. W. (1997). Immigration, acculturation, and adaptation. *Applied Psychology, 46*, 5–68.

Berry, J. W. (2006). Acculturation: A conceptual overview. In M. H. Bornstein and L. R. Cote (Eds.), *Acculturation and parent-child relationships: Measurement and development* (pp. 13–30). Mahwah, NJ: Lawrence Erlbaum Associates.

Berry, J. W., and Kalin, R. (1995). Multicultural and ethnic attitudes in Canada: An overview of the 1991 national survey. *Canadian Journal of Behavioral Sciences, 27*, 301–320.

Berry, J., and Kim, U. (1988). Acculturation and mental health. In P. Dasen, J. W. Berry, and N. Sartorius (Eds.), *Health and cross-cultural psychology: Toward applications*. Newbury Park, CA: Sage.

Berry, J. W., Kim, U., and Boski, P. (1987). Psychological acculturation of immigrants. In Y. Y. Kim and W. B. Gudykunst (Eds.), *International and intercultural communication annual. Volume 11: Cross-cultural adaptation: Current approaches* (pp. 62–89). Newbury Park, CA: Sage Publications.

Berry, J. W., Phinney, J. S., Sam, D. L., and Vedder, P. (2006). *Immigrant youth in cultural transition*. Mahwah, NJ: Erlbaum.

Berry, J. W., Poortinga, Y. H., Segall, M. H., and Dasen, P. R. (2002). *Cross-cultural psychology: Research and applications* (2nd ed.). New York: Cambridge Press.

Berry, J. W., and Sam D. (1997). Acculturation and adaptation. In J. W. Berry, M. H. Segall, and C. Kagitcibasi (Eds.), *Handbook of cross-cultural psychology: Social behavior and applications* (pp. 291–326). Needham Heights, MA: Allyn and Bacon.

Bhugra, D., and Jones, P. (2001). Migration and mental illness. *Advances in Psychiatric Treatment, 7,* 216–223.

Birman, D. (2006). Measurement of the "acculturation gap" in immigrant families and implications for parent-child relationships. In M. H. Bornstein and L. R. Cote (Eds.), *Acculturation and parent-child relationships: Measurement and development* (pp. 113–134). Mahwah, NJ: Erlbaum.

Bornstein, M. H. (1971). Review of *Future Shock* by A. Toffler. *Technology and Culture, 12,* 532–536.

Bornstein, M. H. (1991). Approaches to parenting in culture. In M. H. Bornstein (Ed.), *Cultural approaches to parenting* (pp. 3–19). Hillsdale, NJ: Erlbaum.

Bornstein, M. H. (2006). Parenting science and practice. In K. A. Renninger and I. E. Sigel (Eds.) and W. Damon (Series Ed.), *Handbook of child psychology. Volume 4: Child psychology in practice* (6th ed., pp. 893–949). Hoboken, NJ: Wiley.

Bornstein, M. H., and Cote, L. R. (2004). "Who is sitting across from me?" Immigrant mothers' knowledge of parenting and children's development. *Pediatrics, 114,* e557–e564.

Bornstein, M. H., and Cote, L. R. (Eds.). (2006a). *Acculturation and parent-child relationships: Measurement and development.* Mahwah, NJ: Erlbaum.

Bornstein, M. H., and Cote, L. R. (2006b). Parenting cognitions and practices in the acculturative process. In M. H. Bornstein and L. R. Cote (Eds.), *Acculturation and parent-child relationships: Measurement and development* (pp. 173–196). Mahwah, NJ: Erlbaum.

Boti, M., and Bautista, F. (1999). *When strangers meet.* Toronto, Cananda: National Film Board of Canada.

Bourhis, R. Y., Moïse, L. A., Perreault, S., and Senécal, S. (1997). Towards an interactive acculturation model: A social psychological approach. *International Journal of Psychology, 32,* 369–386.

Bryceson, D. F., and Vuorela, U. (2002). *The transnational family: New European frontiers and global networks.* Oxford, United Kingdom: Berg Publishers.

Buriel, R., Love, J. A., and De Ment, T. L. (2006). The relation of language brokering to depression and parent-child bonding among Latino adolescents. In M. H. Bornstein and L. R. Cote (Eds.), *Acculturation and parent-child relationships: Measurement and development* (pp. 249–270). Mahwah, NJ: Erlbaum.

Burke, A. W. (1980). Family stress and precipitation of psychiatric disorder: A comparative study among immigrant West Indian and native British patients in Birmingham. *International Journal of Social Psychiatry, 26,* 35–40.

Castillo, L. G., Conoley, C. W., and Brossart, D. F. (2004). Acculturation, White marginalization, and family support as predictors of perceived distress in Mexican American female college students. *Journal of Counseling Psychology, 51,* 151–157.

Caudill, W., and Frost, L. (1974). A comparison of maternal care and infant behavior in Japanese-American, American, and Japanese families. In W. P. Lebra (Ed.), *Youth, socialization, and mental health* (pp. 3–15). Honolulu, HI: University of Hawaii Press.

Chan, S., and Leong, C. (1994). Chinese families in transition: Cultural conflicts and adjustment problems. *Journal of Social Distress and the Homeless, 3,* 263–281.

Chao, R. K. (2006). The prevalence and consequences of adolescents' language brokering for their immigrant parents. In M. H. Bornstein and L. R. Cote (Eds.), *Acculturation and parent-child relationships: Measurement and development* (pp. 271–296). Mahwah, NJ: Erlbaum.

Chestham, J. (1972). *Social work with immigrants.* London: Routledge and Kegan Publishing.

Chun, K. M. (2006). Conceptual and measurement issues in family acculturation research. In M. H. Bornstein and L. R. Cote (Eds.), *Acculturation and parent-child relationships: Measurement and development* (pp. 63–78). Mahwah, NJ: Erlbaum.

Chun, K. M., and Akutsu, P. D. (2003). Acculturation among ethnic minority families. In K. Chun, P. B. Organista, and G. Mar (Eds.), *Acculturation: Advances in theory, measurement, and applied research* (pp. 95–114). Washington, DC: American Psychological Association.

Coleman, H. L. K. (1995). Ethnic minorities' ratings of ethnically similar and European American counselors: A meta-analysis. *Journal of Counseling Psychology, 42,* 55–64.

Coleman, P. (2004). When police should say "no!" to gratuities. *Criminal Justice Ethics, 23,* 33–44.

Commission of the European Communities (2003). *The role of the universities in the Europe of knowledge.* Brussels, Belgium: Author.

Committee on the Health and Adjustment of Immigrant Children and Families, Board on Children, Youth, and Families, National Research Council and Institute of Medicine (1998). In D. J. Hernandez and E. Charney (Eds.), *From generation to generation: The health and well-being of children in immigrant families*. Washington, DC: National Academy Press.

Cooper, C. R., and Denner, J. (1998). Theories linking culture and psychology: Universal and community-specific processes. *Annual Review of Psychology, 49*, 559–584.

Darvies, L. G., and McKelvey, R. S. (1998). Emotional and behavioral problems and competencies among immigrant and non-immigrant adolescents. *Australian and New Zealand Journal of Psychiatry, 35*, 658–665.

Dreby, J. (2007). Children and power in Mexican transnational families. *Journal of Marriage and Family, 69*, 1050–1064.

Eisenstadt, S. N. (1952). The process of absorption of new immigrants in Israel. *Human Relations, 5*, 223–246.

Epstein, J. L., and Sanders, M. G. (2002). Family, school, and community partnerships. In M. H. Bornstein (Ed.), *Handbook of parenting. Volume 5: Practical parenting* (2nd ed., pp. 407–437). Mahwah, NJ: Erlbaum.

Falicov, C. J. (2007). Working with transnational immigrants: Expanding meanings of family, community, and culture. *Family Process, 46*, 157–171.

Farmer, A. E., and McGuffin, P. (2003). Humiliation, loss and other types of life events and difficulties: A comparison of depressed subjects, healthy controls and their siblings. *Psychological Medicine, 33*, 1169–1175.

Flaherty, J. A., Kohn, R., Galbin, A., Gaviria, M. B., and Birz, S. (1986). Demoralization and social support in Soviet-Jewish immigrants to the United States. *Comprehensive Psychiatry, 27*, 149–158.

Florsheim, Y. (1991). Immigration to Israel from the Soviet Union in 1990. *Jews and Jewish Topics in the Soviet Union and Eastern Europe, 15*, 5–14.

Florsheim, Y. (1997). Chinese adolescent immigrants: Factors related to psychosocial adjustment. *Journal of Youth and Adolescence, 26*, 143–163.

Forman, G. (1993). Women without their children: Immigrant women in the U.S. *Development, 4*, 51–55.

Fuligni, A. J. (1997). The academic achievement of adolescents from immigrant families: The roles of family background, attitudes, and behavior. *Child Development, 68*, 351–363.

Fuligni, A. J. (1998). The adjustment of children from immigrant families. *Current Directions in Psychological Science, 7*, 99–103.

Fuligni, A. J. (2004). The adaptation and acculturation of children from immigrant families. In U. Gielen and J. Roopnarine (Eds.), *Childhood and adolescence: Cross-cultural perspectives and applications* (pp. 297–318). Westport, CT: Praeger Publishers/Greenwood Publishing Group.

Garcia Coll, C., and Magnuson, K. (1997). The psychological experience of immigration: A developmental perspective. In B. Alan, A. C. Crouter, and N. Landale (Eds), *Immigration and the family* (pp. 91–132). Mahwah, NJ: Lawrence Erlbaum.

Gartner, J. D. (2005). *The hypomanic edge: The link between (a little) craziness and (a lot of) success in America.* New York: Simon and Schuster.

Gilbert, N., and Ahn, H. (1990). *Intimacy and discipline in family life: A cross-cultural analysis with implications for theory and practice in child abuse prevention.* Executive summary, University of California, Berkeley, CA.

Gratier, M. (2003). Expressive timing and interactional synchrony between mothers and infants: cultural similarities, cultural differences, and the immigration experience. *Cognitive Development, 18*, 533–554.

Graves, T. D. (1967). Psychological acculturation in a tri-ethnic community. *Southwestern Journal of Anthropology, 23*, 337–350.

Guerrero, A. (2005). *Repairing Mexican and Central American family bonds: A guide for mental health professionals.* Doctoral dissertation printed as booklet, California School of Professional Psychology, Alhambra, CA.

Güngör, D., and Bornstein, M. H. (2008). Gender, development, values, adaptation, and discrimination in acculturating adolescents: The case of Turk heritage youth born and living in Belgium. *Sex Roles.* Manuscript submitted for publication.

Halpern, D. (1993). Minorities and mental health. *Social Science and Medicine, 36*, 597–607.

Harkness, S., & Super, C. (2002). Culture and parenting. In M. H. Bornstein (Ed.), *Handbook of parenting: Vol. 2. Biology and ecology of parenting* (pp. 253–280). Mahwah, NJ: Lawrence Erlbaum Associates.

Harwood, R. L., and Feng, X. (2006). Studying acculturation among Latinos in the United States. In M. H. Bornstein and L. R. Cote (Eds.), *Acculturation and parent-child relationships: Measurement and development* (pp. 197–222). Mahwah, NJ: Erlbaum.

Hernandez, D. J., and Charney, E. (Eds.). (1998). *From generation to generation: The health and well-being of children in immigrant families.* Washington, DC: National Academy Press.

Hernandez, D. J., Denton, N. A., and Macartney, S. E. (2008). Children in immigrant families: Looking to America's future. Society for Research in Child Development. *Social Policy Report, 22,* 3.

Hohn, G. E. (1996). *The effects of family functioning on the psychological and social adjustment of Jamaican immigrant children.* Unpublished doctoral dissertation, Columbia University, New York, NY.

Hondagneu-Sotelo, P. (1992). Overcoming patriarchal constraints: The reconstruction of gender relations among Mexican immigrant women and men. *Gender and Society, 6,* 393–415.

Hutnik, N. (1986). Patterns of ethnic minority identification and modes of social adaptation. *Ethnic and Racial Studies, 9,* 150–167.

Jain, A., and Belsky, J. (1997). Fathering and acculturation: Immigrant Indian families with young children. *Journal of Marriage and the Family, 59,* 873–883.

Janssen, M. M. M., Verhulst, F. C., Bengi-Arslan, L., Erol N., Salter, C. J., and Crijnen, A. A. M. (2004). Comparison of self-reported emotional and behavioural problems in Turkish immigrant, Dutch and Turkish adolescents. *Social Psychiatry and Psychiatric Epidemiology, 39,* 133–140.

Kagitçibasi, C. (1997). Individualism and collectivism. In J. W. Berry, M. H. Segall, and

C. Kagitçibasi (Eds.), *Handbook of cross-cultural psychology. Volume 3* (2nd ed., pp. 1–49). Boston: Allyn and Bacon.

Kao, G. (1999). Psychological well-being and educational achievement among immigrant youth. In D. J. Hernandez (Ed.), *Children of immigrants: Health, adjustment, and public assistance* (pp. 410–477). Washington, DC: National Academy Press.

Kaplan, M. S., and Marks, G. (1990). Adverse effects of acculturation: Psychological distress among Mexican American young adults. *Social Science Medicine, 31,* 1313–1319.

Karlsen, S., and Nazroo, J. Y. (2002). Relation between racial discrimination, social class, and health among ethnic minority groups. *American Journal of Public Health, 92,* 624–631.

Kilbride, K. M. (2000). *A review of the literature on the human, social and cultural capital of immigrant children and their families with implications for teacher education.* CERIS Working Paper Series No. 13. Toronto, Canada: Joint Centre of Excellence for Research on Immigration and Settlement.

Kimmerling, B. (2001). *The invention and decline of Israeliness: State, society, and the military.* Berkeley, CA: University of California Press.

Kunda, Z. (1999). *Social cognition: Making sense of people.* Cambridge, MA: MIT Press.

Kuo, W. H., and Tsai, Y. M. (1986). Social networking, hardiness and immigrant's mental health. *Journal of Health and Social Behavior, 27,* 133–149.

Kurtz-Costes, B., and Pungello, E. P. (2000). Acculturation and immigrant children: Implications for educators. *Social Education, 64,* 121–125.

Kwak, K. (2003). Adolescents and their parents: A review of intergenerational family relations for immigrant and non-immigrant families. *Human Development, 46,* 115–136.

Lansford, J., Deater-Deckard, K. K., and Bornstein, M. H. (Eds.). (2007). *Immigrant families in contemporary society.* New York: Guilford Press.

Laosa, L. (1989). *Psychological stress, coping, and the development of the Hispanic immigrant child.* Princeton, NJ: Educational Testing Service.

Lebedeva, N., and Tatarko, A. (2004). Socio-psychological factors of ethnic intolerance in Russia's multicultural regions. In B. N. Setiadi, A. Supratiknya, W. J. Lonner, and Y. H. Poortinga (Eds.), *Ongoing themes in psychology and culture* (online ed.). Melbourne, FL: International Association for Cross-Cultural Psychology.

Lerner, Y, Kertes, J., and Zilber, N. (2005). Immigrants from the former Soviet Union, 5 years post-immigration to Israel: Adaptation and risk factors for psychological distress. *Psychological Medicine, 35,* 1805–1814.

Levitt, P. (2001). *The transnational villagers.* Berkeley, CA: University of California Press.

Li, P. (1998). The market value and social value of race. In V. Satzewich (Ed.), *Racism and social inequality in Canada* (pp. 115–130). Toronto, Canada: Thompson Educational.

Li, P. (2003). Initial earnings and catch-up capacity of immigrants. *Canadian Public Policy, 29,* 319–337.

Liamputtong, P. (2001). Motherhood and the challenge of immigrant mothers: A personal reflection. *Families in Society, 82,* 195–201.

Masuda, M., Matsumoto, G. H., and Meredith, G. M. (1970). Ethnic identity in three generations of Japanese Americans. *The Journal of Social Psychology, 81,* 199–207.

McQueen, A., Getz, J. G., and Bray, J. H. (2003). Acculturation, substance use and deviant behavior: Examining separation and family conflict as mediators. *Child Development, 74*, 1737–1750.

Mendoza, F. S., Javier, J. R., and Burgos, A. E. (2007). Health of children in immigrant families. In J. E. Lansford, K. K. Deater-Deckard, and M. H. Bornstein (Eds.), *Immigrant families in contemporary society* (pp. 30–50). New York: Guilford Press.

Murad, S. D., Joung, I. M. A., van Lenthe, F. J., Bengi-Arslan, L., and Crijnen, A. A. M. (2003). Predictors of self-reported problem behaviours in Turkish immigrant and Dutch adolescents in the Netherlands. *Journal of Child Psychology and Psychiatry, 44*, 412–423.

Murphy, J. M., and Leighton, A. H. (Eds.). (1965). *Approaches to cross-cultural psychiatry*. New York: Cornell University Press.

Nagata D. K. (1994). Assessing Asian American acculturation and ethnic identity: The need for a multidimensional framework. *Asian American Pacific Islander Journal of Health, 2*, 108–124.

Nauck, B. (2001). Intercultural contact and intergenerational transmission in immigrant families. *Journal of Cross-Cultural Psychology, 32*, 159–173.

Olmedo, E. L. (1979). Acculturation: A psychometric perspective. *American Psychologist, 34*, 1061–1070.

Orr, E., Mana, A., and Mana, Y. (2003). Immigrant identity of Israeli adolescents from Ethiopia and the former USSR: Culture-specific principles or organization. *European Journal of Social Psychology, 33*, 71–92.

Padilla, A. M. (1995). *Hispanic psychology: Critical issues in theory and research*. Thousand Oaks, CA: Sage.

Paltiel, A. M., Sabatello, E. M., and Tal, D. (1996). Immigrants from the former USSR in Israel in the 1990s: Demographic characteristics and socio-economic absorption. In N. Lewin-Epstein, Y. Ro'I, and P. Ritterband (Eds.), *Russian Jews on three continents* (pp. 284–324). London: Frank Cass.

Parrenas, R. S. (2001). *Servants of globalization: Women, migration and domestic work*. Stanford, CA: Stanford University Press.

Parrenas, R. S. (2005). *Children of global migration: Transnational families and gendered woes*. Stanford, CA: Stanford University Press.

Phalet, K., and Swyngedouw, M. (2003). Measuring immigrant integration: The case of Belgium. *Migration Studies, 152*, 773–803.

Phinney, J. S. (2006). Acculturation is not an independent variable: Approaches to studying acculturation as a complex process. In M. H. Bornstein and L. R. Cote (Eds.), *Acculturation and parent-child relationships: Measurement and development* (pp. 79–95). Mahwah, NJ: Erlbaum.

Phinney, J., and Ong, A. (2007). Conceptualization and measurement of ethnic identity: Current status and future directions. *Journal of Counseling Psychology, 54*, 3.

Portes, A., and Rumbaut, R. (2001). *2001 legacies: The story of the second generation*. Berkeley, CA: University of California Press.

Qin, D. B. (2006). Our child doesn't talk to us any more: Alienation in immigrant Chinese families. *Anthropology and Education Quarterly, 37*, 162–179.

Qin, D. B. (2008a). Doing well vs. feeling well: Understanding family dynamics and the psychological adjustment of Chinese immigrant adolescents. *Journal of Youth and Adolescence, 37*, 22–35.

Qin, D. B. (2008b). The other side of the model minority story. The familial and peer challenges faced by Chinese American adolescents. *Youth and Society, 39*, 480–506.

Qin, D. B., Way, N., and Mukherjee, P. (2008). The other side of the model minority story: The familial and peer challenges faced by Chinese American adolescents. *Youth & Society, 39*, 480–506.

Ratha, D. (2003). *Workers' remittances: an important and stable source of external development finance*. Worldbank. Retrieved from http://www.worldbank.org/prospects/gdf2003/GDF_vol_1_web.pdf.

Redfield, R., Linton, R., and Herskovits, M. J. (1936). Memorandum on the study of acculturation. *American Anthropologist, 38*, 149–152.

Reitz, J. (2001, March). *Immigrant success and changing national institutions: Recent trends in Canada, a U.S. comparison and policy options*. Paper presented at Re-inventing Society in a Changing Global Economy Conference, Toronto, Canada.

Roer-Strier, D. (2001). Reducing risk for children in changing cultural contexts: recommendations for intervention and training. *Child Abuse and Neglect, 25*, 231–248.

Rumbaut, R. G. (1999). Passages to adulthood: The adaptation of children of immigrants in Southern California. In D. J. Hernandez (Ed.), *Children of immigrants: Health, adjustment, and public assistance* (pp. 478–545). Washington, DC: National Academy Press.

Rutter, M. (1971). Parent-child separation: Psychological effects on the children. *Child Psychology and Psychiatry, 12*, 233–260.

Ryder, A. G., Alden, L. E., and Paulhus, D. L. (2000). Is acculturation unidimensional or bidimensional? A head-to-head comparison in the prediction of personality, self-identity, and adjustment. *Journal of Personality and Social Psychology, 79*, 77–88.

Sabogal, F., Marín, G., Otero-Sabogal, R., Marín, B., and Perez-Stable, E. (1987). Hispanic familism and acculturation: What changes and what doesn't? *Hispanic Journal of Behavioral Sciences, 9,* 397–412.

Sam, D. L. (2004). System analysis and modeling. In D. Amyot and A. W. Williams (Eds.), *4th International SDL and MSC Workshop* (pp. 1–301). New York: Springer Publishing Co.

Sam, D., and Berry, J. W. (Eds.). (2006). *Cambridge handbook of acculturation psychology.* Cambridge, United Kingdom: Cambridge Press.

Sanchez, J. I., and Fernandez, D. M. (1993). Acculturative stress among Hispanics: A bidimensional model of ethnic identification. *Journal of Applied Social Psychology, 23,* 654–668.

Schalk-Soekar, S., van de Vijver, F., & Hoogsteder, M. (2004). Attitudes toward multiculturalism of immigrants and majority members in the Netherlands. *International Journal of Intercultural Relations, 28* 533–550.

Schmalzbauer, L. (2004). Searching for wages and mothering from afar: The case of Honduran transnational families. *Journal of Marriage and the Family, 66,* 1317–1331.

Sciarra, D. T. (1999). Intrafamilial separations in the immigrant family: Implications for cross-cultural counselling. *Journal of Multicultural Counseling and Development, 27,* 30–41.

Scott, W. A., and Scott, R. (1989). *Adaptation of immigrants: Individual differences and determinants.* Oxford, United Kingdom: Pergamon Press.

Scott, W. A., and Stumpf, J. (1984). Personal satisfaction and role performance: Subjective and social aspects of adaptation. *Journal of Personality and Social Psychology, 47,* 182–206.

Sewell-Coker, B., Hamilton-Collins, J., and Fein, E. (1985). West Indian immigrants. *Social Casework, 60,* 563–568.

Short, K., and Johnston, C. (1997). Stress, maternal distress, and children's adjustment following immigration: The buffering role of social support. *Journal of Consulting and Clinical Psychology, 65,* 494–503.

Shuval, J. T. (1982). Migration and stress. In L. Goldberger and S. Breznitz (Eds.), *Handbook of stress: Theoretical and clinical aspects* (pp. 677–691). London: The Free Press.

Smart, J. F., and Smart, D. W. (1995). Acculturation stress of Hispanics: Loss and challenge. *Journal of Counseling and Development, 73,* 390–396.

Song, K. (1986). *Defining child abuse: Korean community study.* Unpublished doctoral dissertation, University of California, Los Angeles, CA.

Suarez-Orozco, C., and Suarez-Orozco, M. (2001). *Children of immigration.* Cambridge, MA: Harvard University Press.

Suarez-Orozco, C., Todorova, I. L. G., and Louie, J. M. C. P. (2002). Making up for lost time: The experience of separation and reunification among immigrant families. *Family Process, 41,* 625–643.

Szapocznik, J., and Kurtines, W. M. (1993). Family psychology and cultural diversity: Opportunities for theory, research, and application. *American Psychologist, 48,* 400.

Szapocznik, J., Scopetta, M., Kurtines, W., & Aranalde, M. (1978). Theory and measurement of acculturation. *Revista Interamericana de Psicología, 12,* 113–130.

Tienda, M. (2008). Fragile futures: Immigrant children and children of immigrants. Society for Research in Child Development. *Social Policy Report,* 22, 3.

Triandis, H. C., Kashima, Y., Shimada, E., and Villareal, M. (1986). Acculturation indices as a means of confirming cultural differences. *International Journal of Psychology, 21,* 43–70.

Uba, L. (1994). *Asian Americans: Personality patterns, identity, and mental health.* New York: Guilford.

Van Walsum, S. (2006). Transnational mothering, national immigration policy and the European Court of Human Rights. In P. Shah and W. Menski (Eds.), *Migration, diasporas and legal systems in Europe.* London: Routledge-Cavendish.

Vollebergh, W. A. M., ten Have, M., Dekovic, M., Oosterwegel-Trees Pels, A., Veenstra, R., de Winter, A., et al. (2005). Mental health in immigrant children in the Netherlands. *Social Psychiatry and Psychiatric Epidemiology, 40,* 489–496.

Waldinger, R. (2007). *Between here and there: How attached are Latino immigrants to their native country?* Pew Hispanic Center Report, October 25, 2007. Washington, DC: Pew Hispanic Center. Retrieved May 24, 2008, from http://pewhispanic.org/fi les/reports/80.pdf.

Ward, C. (1996). Acculturation. In D. Landis and R. S. Bhagat (Eds.), *Handbook of intercultural training* (pp. 124–147). Thousand Oaks, CA: Sage.

Ward, C. (1999). Models and measures of acculturation. In W. J. Lonner, D. L. Dinnel, D. K. Forgays, and S. A. Hayes (Eds.), *Merging past, present, and future in cross-cultural psychology: Selected papers from the Fourteenth International Congress of the International Association for Cross-Cultural Psychology* (pp. 221–230). Lisse, The Netherlands: Swets and Zeitlinger B. V.

Ward, C., Bochner, S., and Furnham, A. (2001). *The psychology of culture shock* (2nd ed.). Boston: Routledge Kegan Paul.

Ward, C., and Kennedy, A. (1994). Acculturation strategies, psychological adjustment, and sociocultural competence during cross-cultural transitions. *International Journal of Intercultural Relations, 18*, 329–343.
Westermeyer, J., Neider, J., and Vang, T. F. (1984). Acculturation and mental health: A study of Hmong refugees at 1.5 and 3. 5 years postmigration. *Social Science and Medicine, 18*, 87–93.
Whybrow, P. C. (2006). *American mania: When more is not enough.* New York: Norton.
Wilkes, J. R. (1992). Children in limbo: Working for the best outcome when children are taken into care. *Canada's Mental Health, 40*, 2–5.
Wong-Rieger, D. (1984). Testing a model of emotional and coping responses to problems in adaptation: Foreign students at a Canadian university. *International Journal of Intercultural Relations, 8*, 153–184.
Yeh, C. (2003). Age, acculturation, cultural adjustment, and mental health symptoms of Chinese, Korean, and Japanese immigrant youths. *Cultural Diversity and Ethnic Minority Psychology, 9*, 34–48.
Ying, Y. W. (1999). Strengthening intergenerational/intercultural ties in migrant families: A new intervention for parents. *Journal of Community Psychology, 27*, 89–96.
Zilber, N., and Lerner, Y. (1996). Psychological distress among recent immigrants from the former Soviet Union to Israel: I. Correlates of level of distress. *Psychological Medicine, 26*, 493–501.

Contributors

KAREN E. ADOLPH is Professor of Psychology and Neural Science at New York University. She holds a BA in fine art and psychology from Sarah Lawrence College and a PhD in experimental/developmental psychology from Emory University. She completed a postdoctoral fellowship at Albert Einstein College of Medicine, and Adolph's first faculty position was at Carnegie Mellon University. She received a James McKeen Cattell Sabbatical Award, the Robert L. Fantz Memorial Award from the American Psychological Foundation, the Boyd McCandless Award from the American Psychological Association, the Young Investigator Award from the International Society for Infant Studies, FIRST and MERIT awards from the National Institutes of Health, and is a fellow of the American Psychological Association and the Association for Psychological Science. Supported by grants from the National Institutes of Health, Adolph's research interests focus on learning and development in the context of infant motor skill acquisition. Adolph is author of the SRCD monograph *Learning in the Development of Infant Locomotion* and a chapter on motor development in the *Handbook of Child Psychology*.

RAMADAN A. AHMED is Professor of Psychology in the College of Social Sciences, Kuwait University, Kuwait. He holds university degrees in psychology and law from Cairo University, Egypt, an MA from Alexandria University, Egypt, and a PhD from the University of Leipzig, Germany. Ahmed has taught in Egypt, Sudan, and Kuwait. He is a member of several national, regional, and international associations, including APA, ICP, IACCP, SCCR, and ISIPR, where he was elected Regional Representative for North Africa and the Middle East. Ahmed won Egypt's Incentive Award for Social Sciences, "Psychology." Ahmed's interests include cognitive and moral development, social perception, attitudes toward the family, and the history of psychology, especially in Arab countries. He co-edited the first overview of psychology in the Arab world, *Psychology in the Arab Countries,* which won the Al-Ahram Prize. Ahmed also won the Outstanding International Psychologist Award, Division 52, "International Psychology," of the American Psychological Association.

DEBORAH L. BEST is Dean of the College and William L. Poteat Professor of Psychology at Wake Forest University. She holds a BA and MA in experimental psychology from Wake Forest University and a PhD in developmental psychology from the University of North Carolina at Chapel Hill. Best has been on the faculty at Wake Forest since 1972 and chaired the psychology department for eight years. When named Dean of Wake Forest College, she was the first woman to hold that position. A developmental psychologist by training, Best's research focuses on children's cognitive development and memory strategies. Also a cross-cultural psychologist, she has explored the nature and development of racial, age, and gender stereotypes and attitudes of children and adults around the world. Best received the Wake Forest Excellence in Teaching Award, Excellence in Research Award, and the Schoonmaker Faculty Prize. She served as president of the International Association for Cross-Cultural Psychology and as chair of the Council of Graduate Departments of Psychology and the Association of Heads of Departments of Psychology. Best has published research papers and chapters and authored three books. She has maintained continuous grant support for her research for the past 25 years. She served as editor for several book series, and for the past 10 years she has been associate editor of the *Journal of Cross-Cultural Psychology.*

MARC H. BORNSTEIN is Senior Investigator and Head of Child and Family Research in the Program in Developmental Neuroscience at the *Eunice Kennedy Shriver* National Institute of Child Health and Human Development. He holds a BA from Columbia College, MS and PhD degrees from Yale University, and an honorary doctorate from the University of Padua. Bornstein was a Guggenheim Foundation Fellow, and he received a Research Career Development Award from the NICHD. He also received the Ford Cross-Cultural Research Award, the McCandless Young Scientist Award, a U.S. Public Health Service Superior Service Award, two Japan Society for the Promotion of Science Fellowships, three Awards for Excellence from the American Mensa Education & Research Foundation, the Arnold Gesell Prize from the Theodor-Hellbrügge-Foundation, and an Award of Merit from the National Institutes of Health. Bornstein has held faculty positions at Princeton University and New York University as well as academic appointments in Munich, London, Paris, New York, Tokyo, Bamenda, Seoul, and Trento. Bornstein sits on the Executive Committee of the International Society of Infancy Studies and the Governing Council of the Society for Research in Child Development. Bornstein is editor emeritus of *Child Development* and founding editor of *Parenting: Science and Practice*. He is co-author of *Development in Infancy* (5 editions), *Development: Infancy through Adolescence*, *Lifespan Development*, and *Perceiving Similarity and Comprehending Metaphor*. He is general editor of the Crosscurrents in Contemporary Psychology series (10 volumes) and the Monographs in Parenting series (8 volumes). He also edited the *Handbook of Parenting* and co-edited *Developmental Science: An Advanced Textbook* (5 editions). He is the author of several children's books, videos, and puzzles in The Child's World series and the Baby Explorer series. Bornstein has written scientific papers in the areas of experimental, methodological, comparative, developmental, cross-cultural, neuroscientific, pediatric, and aesthetic psychology.

ROBERT H. BRADLEY is Professor and Director of the Family and Human Dynamics Research Institute at Arizona State University and Adjunct Professor of Pediatrics and Psychiatry at the University of Arkansas for Medical Sciences. His research interests include childcare, early education, fathers, and family factors that affect child well-being. Bradley served on the board of editors for *Child Development* and serves as associate editor of the *Early Childhood Research Quarterly*. He also serves on the editorial boards of *Developmental Psychology*, *Early Education and Development*, *Journal of Marriage and the Family*, *Parenting: Science and Practice*, and the *Journal of Developmental Epidemiology*. He was chair of the Biobehavioral and Behavioral Research Committee for NICHD and the Development and Behavior workgroup for the National Children's Study and was a consultant to the evaluation of Head Start Family Child Care Homes. He serves on technical advisory boards for the Maternal Lifestyle Study, the American Indian/Alaska Native Head Start Research Center, the National Household Education Survey, and the Arkansas Birth Defects Research Center. Bradley is a member of the steering committees for the NICHD Study of Child Care and Youth Development and the Early Head Start National Evaluation Study.

XAVIER E. CAGIGAS is Neuropsychology and Exceptional Abilities Intern at the UCLA Semel Institute for Neurosciences and Human Behavior, transitioning into a postdoctoral fellowship dedicated to the new UCLA Consortium for Neuropsychiatric Phenomics. He holds a BA from Georgetown University, an MS from San Diego State University, and is expecting a PhD from the San Diego State/University of California–San Diego Joint Doctoral Program in Clinical Psychology. Cagigas received the APA Minority Undergraduate Student of Excellence Award, was an NSF Alliance for Graduate Education and the Professoriate doctoral scholar, a University of California Cota-Robles Fellow, and was granted a National Research Service Award from NIMH.

Cagigas has contributed scientific papers in the areas of human cognitive neuropsychology, discursive psychology, and neuroimaging, as well as chapters on the differential diagnosis of dementia and Alexander Luria's contributions to modern methods in neuroimaging and the neurosciences.

ATHANASIOS CHASIOTIS is Associate Professor in Cross-Cultural Psychology at Tilburg University in the Netherlands. He holds a PhD in psychology and biology from the University of Osnabrück in Germany and headed the university's research group in cross-cultural lifespan psychology. His research interests concern the intersection of evolutionary and cross-cultural developmental psychology. Chasiotis has collected data in Europe, Cameroon, Hong Kong, China, and Costa Rica. He published in the fields of evolutionary, cross-cultural, developmental, and personality psychology, as well as in behavioral ecology and evolutionary anthropology. He is co-editor of *Grandmotherhood—The Evolutionary Significance of the Second Half of Female Life*.

CHARISSA CHEAH is Associate Professor of Psychology at the University of Maryland, Baltimore County. She holds a BA in honors psychology from the University of Waterloo, and a PhD in human development from the University of Maryland, College Park. After a postdoctoral fellowship at Yale University, Cheah was an assistant professor in the Culture and Human Development program at the University of Saskatchewan. She received a fellowship from the Foundation for Child Development: Changing Faces of America's Children–Young Scholars Program. Cheah's research interests include the study of the interactions between individual, peer, and family factors in the social and emotional development and health of children. Her scientific papers focus on the exploration of multiple pathways in which cultural factors and contexts contribute to children's development through parenting.

XINYIN CHEN is Professor of Psychology at the University of Western Ontario, Canada. He holds a BA from East China Normal University and an MA and PhD from the University of Waterloo. He received a William T. Grant Scholars Award and several other academic awards. His research interest is mainly in children's and adolescents' socioemotional functioning (e.g., shyness–inhibition, social competence, affect) and social relationships, with a focus on cross-cultural issues. With international collaborators, Chin conducts several large-scale, longitudinal projects in Brazil, Canada, China, Italy, and other countries. He co-edited *Peer Relationships in Cultural Context*; *Social Change and Human Development: Concepts and Results*; and *Socioemotional Development in Cultural Context*. He has published journal articles and book chapters about culture, children's social behaviors and peer relationships, and parental socialization practices.

MICHAEL COLE is University Professor of Communication, Psychology, and Human Development at the University of California, San Diego, and Director of the Laboratory of Comparative Human Cognition. He holds a BA in psychology from UCLA and a PhD from Indiana University as well as honorary doctorates from the Universities of Copenhagen, Helsinki, and Padua. He has held faculty positions at Yale University, the University of California at Irvine, and Rockefeller University. Cole was a recipient of the American Psychological Association Award for Distinguished Contributions to the International Advancement of Psychology and an American Educational Research Association award for Distinguished Contributions to Research and Development in Education. He is a member of the American Academy of Arts and Sciences and the Academies of Education of the United States and Russia. Cole is the founding editor of *Mind, Culture, and Activity* and the *Journal of Russian and East European Psychology*. He is author or co-author of *The Development of Children* (5 editions), *The Cultural Context of Learning and Thinking*, *Culture and Thought*, *The Psychology of Literacy*, and *Cultural Psychology*. He has contributed scientific papers in the areas of human experimental, methodological, comparative, developmental, cross-cultural, and neuroscientific psychology as well as anthropology and communication.

LINDA R. COTE is Assistant Professor at Marymount University in Arlington, Virginia. She holds a PhD from Clark University and did postdoctoral training in the Child and Family Research Section of the *Eunice Kennedy Shriver* National Institute of Child Health and Human Development. Cote is a member of the International Society for Infant Studies, National Council on Family Relations, Society for Research in Child Development, and Zero to Three. She is also a certified family life educator by the National Council on Family Relations. Her research interests include the study of parenting and its effects on immigrant infants' and young children's cognitive and social development.

RANJANA DUTTA is Associate Professor at the Department of Psychology, Saginaw Valley State University, Michigan. She holds an MS in child development from Maharaja Sayajirao University, Baroda, India, and a PhD in individual and family studies from Pennsylvania State University. She has served as postdoctoral research associate at the Department of Psychology, Brandeis University, and assistant professor of psychology at Southwest Missouri State University. She has taught courses in developmental, lifespan, and adult psychology, and is the recipient of the highest award of Excellence in Teaching at SVSU. Dutta has contributed scientific papers in the area of personality rigidity and flexibility and intellectual aging from the Seattle Longitudinal Study, personality and facial appearance from the Oakland Growth Study, and been involved in cross-cultural research in China and India. She has co-authored and co-edited *Invisible Boundaries: Grooming for Adult Roles* and *Developmental Psychology in India 1975–86: An Annotated Bibliography*. Her current areas of interest pertain to cross-cultural differences in socialization and lifespan implications on perceived control, goal pursuit, and wisdom.

MARY GAUVAIN is Professor of Psychology at the University of California, Riverside. She holds a BA from the University of California, Irvine, an MA from Stanford University, and a PhD from the University of Utah. She was a postdoctoral fellow at the City University of New York Graduate Center and at the Oregon Social Learning Center. Gauvain has held faculty positions at Oregon State University and Scripps College and visiting academic appointments at the University of Pennsylvania, University of Melbourne, and University of Hawaii. She has received support for her research from the NIMH, the Spencer Foundation, and the Murray Center at Radcliffe College. Gauvain has served as treasurer and as council representative of the American Psychological Association Division of Developmental Psychology and she has been associate editor of the *Merrill-Palmer Quarterly* and *Child Development*. Her research interests include social and cultural influences on cognitive development, the development of planning skills, and children's spatial cognition. Gauvain is the author of *The Social Context of Cognitive Development* and co-author of *Child Psychology* and *Readings on the Development of Children*.

JACQUELINE J. GOODNOW is Professorial Research Associate at Macquarie University, Sydney, Australia, where she is affiliated with the Institute of Early Childhood. Her interest in cultural contexts reflects educational experiences in both Australia and the United States—a BA in Sydney; a PhD from Harvard University, Department of Social Relations; teaching appointments at George Washington University and Macquarie University—mixed with periods of time in Munich, Hong Kong, and Rome. The author of several books and numerous articles, and associate editor for several journals, Goodnow received awards for distinguished research contributions from the American Psychological Association, the Society for Research in Child Development, and the Australian Psychological Society. Most of her research deals with cognition and cognitive development, increasingly seen from a life span perspective; a view of cognitive and social development as closely interwoven; and the belief that research in this area benefits greatly from attention to everyday tasks and problem-solving, issues of policy and practice as well as theory, and approaches offered by anthropology and sociology as well as psychology.

CRAIG H. HART is Professor of Human Development in the School of Family Life (Department Chair 1998–2004) and Associate Dean in the College of Family, Home, and Social Sciences at Brigham Young University. He holds a PhD from Purdue University and was formerly an associate professor in the School of Human Ecology at Louisiana State University. His interest in cross-cultural developmental science has emerged over the past decade, having published numerous papers from data gathered in Australia, mainland China, Japan, Russia, and the United States. Hart has authored and co-authored scientific articles and book chapters and has presented numerous papers at national and international conferences on parenting and familial linkages with children's social development and on developmentally appropriate practices in early childhood education. His work has appeared in *Child Development* and *Developmental Psychology* and in the *Early Childhood Research Quarterly*. Hart has edited *Children on Playgrounds: Research Perspectives and Applications* and *Integrated Curriculum and Developmentally Appropriate Practice: Birth to Age Eight*. He has served as associate editor for the *Early Childhood Research Quarterly* and is co-editor of the *Handbook of Childhood Social Development*.

JAN HOFER is Postdoctoral Fellow in the Department of Human Sciences (Psychology) at the University of Osnabrück, Germany. He holds a PhD from Friedrich-Alexander University in Erlangen-Nuremberg, Germany, writing his thesis on adolescent development in Zambia. Hofer was a member of a research group on cross-cultural life span psychology at the University of Osnabrück, and he conducts cross-cultural research in collaboration with scholars from Cameroon, Hong Kong, mainland China, and Costa Rica on psychological and behavioral correlates of the implicit motive for power. His research interests include developmental antecedents and behavioral consequences of implicit and consciously represented motives, personality and motives across the life span, identity development, correlates of psychological well-being, and methodological considerations in cross-cultural research.

GEORGE W. HOLDEN is Professor of Psychology at Southern Methodist University. After receiving his BA from Yale University and his PhD from the University of North Carolina at Chapel Hill, he was a member of the psychology faculty at the University of Texas at Austin. Holden's research interests are in the area of social development, with a focus on parent-child relationships. His research on the determinants of parental behavior, parental social cognition, and the causes and consequences of family violence has been supported by grants from the *Eunice Kennedy Shriver* National Institute of Child Health and Human Development, the National Institute of Justice, the Department of Health and Human Services, the Guggenheim Foundation, and the Hogg Foundation for Mental Health. He is the author of numerous scientific articles and chapters, as well as *Parenting: A Dynamic Perspective* and *Parents and the Dynamics of Child Rearing*. In addition, he co-edited *Children Exposed to Marital Violence* and the *Handbook of Family Measurement Techniques*. Holden is a fellow of the American Psychological Society and a member of the Society for Research in Child Development, the American Professional Society on the Abuse of Children, and the Society for Research in Human Development, where he is currently president. He has been or is on the editorial boards of *Child Development, Developmental Psychology, Journal of Emotional Abuse, Journal of Family Psychology,* and *Parenting: Science and Practice.*

JUNG-HWAN HYUN is Professor in the Department of Child Care and Education at Seoul Theological University, where he is also Chief Research Scientist in the Institute of Child Care and Education. He holds a BA from Pukyoung National University, Korea, an MS from Tokyo Gakugei University, and a PhD from Hiroshima University, Japan. He is editor-in-chief of the *Korean Journal of Japanese Education* and a member of the editorial board of the *Korean Journal of Child Education and Care*. Hyun's books include *Children's Freedom, Children's Development,* and *Understanding and Psychotherapy of Children's Abnormal Behavior*. His scientific papers have been on self-efficacy prediction and determinants among preschoolers, and the effects of effort attribution evaluation on children's perceived self-efficacy and academic achievement. Hyun's areas of research are children's cognitive and behavioral development and cross-cultural studies of parental nurturing.

JEROME KAGAN is Professor of Psychology Emeritus at Harvard University. His research has centered on cognitive development in infants, emotional and moral development, and over the past 25 years on temperamental biases in infants and children. Kagan is a member of the Institute of Medicine, a fellow of the American Academy of Arts and Sciences, and recipient of distinguished scientist awards from the American Psychological Association and the Society for Research in Child Development.

LANA B. KARASIK earned her undergraduate degree in biopsychology/cognitive science and sociology, with a concentration in health, aging, and population, from the University of Michigan, and she received her PhD in Developmental Psychology at New York University. Her doctoral research focused on the social context of infants' motor, language, and social development. She examined how mothers communicate to infants about motor action, infants' use of social information in locomotor tasks, and the impact of new motor skills on infants' interactions with the physical and social environment.

EMILY K. KEISTER is a Master's Candidate in the School of Family Life at Brigham Young University, Utah. She holds a BS in child development from Brigham Young University–Idaho. Her research interests include the study of children's peer relationships, with a focus on cross-cultural issues.

JENNIFER E. LANSFORD is Research Scientist in the Center for Child and Family Policy at Duke University. She holds a BA from Duke University and an MA and PhD from the University of Michigan. Lansford has been honored by the American Professional Society on the Abuse of Children for her research on child maltreatment. She is associate editor of *Aggressive Behavior* and serves on the editorial board of the *International Journal of Behavioral Development*. She has edited *Immigrant Families in Contemporary Society* and *Deviant Peer Influences in Programs for Youth*. Lansford is currently principal investigator on a longitudinal study of parenting behavior and children's adjustment in eight countries and investigator on the Child Development Project, a longitudinal study of socialization that has followed youths and their families for over 20 years. Lansford's work has been funded by the National Institute of Mental Health, the *Eunice Kennedy Shriver* National Institute of Child Health and Human Development, and the National Institute on Drug Abuse. She has contributed scientific papers in the areas of aggression and other behavior problems in youth, with an emphasis on how experiences with parents (discipline, physical abuse, divorce) and peers (rejection, friendships) affect the development of children's behavior problems, how influence operates in adolescent peer groups, and how cultural contexts moderate links between parenting practices and children's behavior problems.

HAO VAN LE is Investigator and Head of the Cultural Psychology Department at the Institute of Psychology, Vietnam Academy of Social Sciences, in Hanoi. He holds a BA from Rostov on Done State University, Russia; an MS from Royal Melbourne Institute of Technology, Australia; and a PhD from the Institute of Psychology, Vietnam, where he has served as a researcher since 1992. Le has also worked as a lecturer at the Hanoi School of Public Health and is actively involved in different development and intervention projects, including HIV Education for School Youth and their Families, Poverty Reduction in North Mountainous Provinces, Social Change and Adolescents, Positive Parenting, and Street Children in Hanoi, funded by the European Union, World Bank, United Nations Development Program, and other NGOs. Le is co-author of a number of books and book chapters in Vietnamese, including *Managerial Psychology, Research Methods in Social Psychology, Social Psychology–Theoretical Issues*, and *Individualism and Collectivism in Vietnam*. He has contributed scientific papers in the areas of social and applied, methodological, developmental, and cross-cultural psychology.

ELENA LIEVEN is Senior Research Scientist in the Department of Developmental and Comparative Psychology at the Max Planck Institute for Evolutionary Anthropology, Leipzig. She is director of the Max Planck Child Study Centre, School of Psychological Sciences at the University of Manchester, and holds a professorship there and an honorary professorship at Leipzig University. Her PhD is from the University of Cambridge. She served as editor of the *Journal of Child Language*. Lieven has been centrally involved in the design and collection of naturalistic child language corpora including the Max Planck "Dense databases." She is a member of the Chintang and Puma Documentation Project, a DOBES project funded by the Volkswagen Foundation aiming at the linguistic and ethnographic description of two endangered Sino-Tibetan languages of Nepal. Lieven's principal areas of research involve usage-based approaches to language development, the emergence and construction of grammar, the relation between input characteristics and the process of language development, and variation in children's communicative environments.

JOSEPH L. LO-OH is Part-time Instructor of Human Development, Psychology of Infancy and Childhood, and Psychology of Learning in the Faculty of Education at the University of Buea, Cameroon. He holds a BEd and an MEd from the University of Buea. Lo-oh has taught in secondary education in Cameroon and is a resource person at the British Council (Exams Board), Human Development Resource Centre in Bamenda, and a researcher at the Centre for Research on Child and Family Development and Education in Limbe, Cameroon. Lo-oh received the Young Scholar Award and the Young Scholar Research Grant from the Jacobs Foundation, was nominated as Young Scientist for ARTS, and received Cameroon's Ministry of Higher Education Award for excellence in state universities. Lo-oh has served as guest reviewer for the *Journal of Psychology in Africa*. His research interests are in childhood development of theory of mind with a third world orientation, emerging adulthood in African communities, and transition from school to work.

DAPHNE M. MAURER is Professor in the Department of Psychology, Neuroscience & Behaviour at McMaster University, Canada. She holds an honors BA in anthropology/sociology from Swarthmore College, an MA in psychology from the University of Pennsylvania, and a PhD from the Institute of Child Development at the University of Minnesota. She has received funding for her research on perceptual development from all three federal Canadian research councils, the National Institutes of Health, the Human Frontiers Foundation, and the James S. McDonnell Foundation. Maurer was recognized as Researcher of the Year in Early Child Development, received the Award for Outstanding Service at McMaster University, and is a Fellow of the Royal Society of Canada. Her book, *The World of the Newborn*, co-written with husband Charles Maurer, won the APA Book Award and has been translated into five languages. Maurer's research has documented the different roles that experience plays at different times and for different aspects of perception. Her research has used innovative methodologies to study face processing. Through a collaborative network grant from the James S. McDonnell Foundation, she is testing whether targeted training might reverse deficits from early congenital cataract.

KAREN E. MCFADDEN is a Doctoral Candidate in Developmental Psychology at New York University's Steinhardt School of Culture, Education, and Human Development. She holds an MA in developmental psychology from New York University. McFadden's research focuses on the role of contextual factors on children's development in the years leading up to their entry into formal schooling. Specifically, she examines family processes that support low-income children's preparation for school, especially interactions with mothers and fathers, as well as the ways in which children's early social and emotional development feed into their readiness to learn. McFadden has worked in homes and in schools with children and families in the New York City area on research studies supported by the National Science Foundation, National Institute of Child Development, Administration for Children, Youth and Families, and the Ford Foundation.

MELISSA M. MENZER is a Doctoral Student in the Department of Human Development at the University of Maryland, College Park. She holds a BA in psychology and a BA in studio art from the University of Maryland. Menzer's research interests include the study of children's peer relationships, specifically friendships, and the ways in which culture and ethnicity may influence friendships.

JUN NAKAZAWA is Professor of Developmental Psychology and Associate Dean in the Faculty of Education at Chiba University, and Professor in the Developmental Psychology Doctoral Program at Tokyo Gakugei University, Japan. He holds BA, MA, and PhD degrees from Hiroshima University. He was an instructor at the Research Institute of Early Childhood Education of Hiroshima University and an invited researcher at the Psychology Department of Florida Atlantic University. He was a board member of the Japanese Association of Educational Psychology and is now chief editor of the *Japanese Journal of Educational Psychology*. Nakazawa is the author of *Development of Cognitive Regulation about Social Behavior* (in Japanese), and is co-author and co-editor of *Psychology Manual Series: Observation, Interview, Questionnaire, Factorial Design, and Research Lesson* (five volumes, in Japanese). He is also co-author and co-editor of *Applied Developmental Psychology: Theory, Practice and Research from Japan*. Nakazawa's research interests include child socialization (especially social behavior and cognitive/emotional regulation), fathering, and *manga* (comic) reading literacy.

DAVID A. NELSON is Associate Professor of Human Development in the School of Family Life at Brigham Young University. He holds a PhD in developmental psychology from the Institute of

Child Development at the University of Minnesota. Nelson has contributed scientific papers in the areas of human developmental and cross-cultural psychology published in journals such as *Developmental Psychology* and *Child Development*. His interest in cross-cultural developmental science emerged during his time as an undergraduate student at BYU, when he assisted his mentor, Dr. Craig Hart, in initiating cross-cultural work in Russia, Australia, mainland China, Japan, and the United States. Much of Nelson's cross-cultural work has focused on relational aggression and its correlates (for example, parenting styles and sociometric status). Some of these studies have garnered national and international media attention.

A. BAME NSAMENANG is Associate Professor of Psychology and Counselling at the School of Education of the University of Yaounde, Cameroon. He also directs a child and youth research and service facility, the Human Development Resource Centre in Bamenda, and is research associate in the Child and Family Research Section of the *Eunice Kennedy Shriver* National Institute of Child Health and Human Development. Nsamenang holds a BSc in nursing, an MEd in guidance and counseling, and a PhD in clinical child psychology from the University of Ibadan, Nigeria. Nsamenang was a nurse practitioner and research scientist at Cameroon's Institute of Human Sciences, a Fogarty Fellow at NICHD, a Nehru Chair Visiting Professor at Baroda University, and a research fellow at Stanford University Center for Advanced Study of Behavioral Sciences. His research interest is on Africa's future hope—children and adolescents—and his lifetime commitment is to contribute to an Afrocentric developmental science. Nsamenang received the Paul Harris Fellowship "in appreciation of tangible and significant assistance given for the furtherance of better understanding and friendly relations among peoples of the world." He is an inaugural International Fellow of the Society for Research on Adolescence. Nsamenang has served on the editorial boards of the *Journal of Cross-Cultural Psychology, Journal of Psychology in Africa*, *Human Development,* and *International Journal of Behavioral Development*. He now serves on the editorial boards of the *Journal of Adolescent Research* and the *International Journal of Psychology*. Nsamenang guest-edited the special section of the *International Journal of Psychology* on Culture and Human Development in Africa. He is the author of *Cultures of Human Development and Education: Challenge to Growing up African* and *Human Development in Cultural Context: Third World Perspective,* and co-author of *Africa in Crisis with HIV/AIDS: Best Practices Guide to Cameroon's Frontline Responses with Youth*.

ROSS D. PARKE is Distinguished Professor of Psychology and Director of the Center for Family Studies at the University of California, Riverside. Parke was educated at the Universities of Toronto and Waterloo and previously was affiliated with the Universities of Wisconsin and Illinois and the Fels Research Institute. He has served as president of the Developmental Psychology Division of the American Psychological Association and president of the Society for Research in Child Development. His interests include the relation between families and peers, ethnic variation in families, and the impact of new reproductive technologies on families. He has been editor of *Developmental Psychology* and the *Journal of Family Psychology*, and associate editor of *Child Development*. Parke is the author of *Fathers* and *Fatherhood* and co-author of *Child Psychology* and *Throwaway Dads*.

JANIS E. PATERSON is Senior Investigator and Co-director of the National Institute for Public Health and Mental Health Research at AUT University, Auckland, New Zealand. She holds BA, MA, and PhD degrees from the University of Auckland. Paterson is co-director of the longitudinal Pacific Islands Families (PIF) Study that has been following a birth cohort of

Pacific children and their families over the last six years. Paterson has written scientific papers and chapters based on the PIF database.

KARINA A. PIASSETSKAIA is Assistant to the Director of the Moscow Branch of Deseret International Charities in the Russian Federation. She holds a BS in marketing from Voronezh State University, Russia. She has collaborated with faculty of the BYU School of Family Life to collect data on adolescent social development in Russia.

MARTIN PINQUART is Professor of Developmental Psychology at the Phillips University of Marburg, Germany. He has studied psychology at Friedrich Schiller University and Humboldt University in Berlin and holds a diploma, a PhD, and the German second doctoral degree (Habilitation) from Friedrich Schiller University. He is the secretary of the Task Force on Geropsychology of the European Federation of Psychologists. Pinquart has written a monograph on the self-concept in older adults and has contributed papers in developmental, health, and cross-cultural psychology, and in gerontology.

RODOLFO DE CASTRO RIBAS, JR. is Associate Professor and Head of the Department of General and Experimental Psychology at the Federal University of Rio de Janeiro (UFRJ), Brazil. He holds a bachelor's degree in psychology from the State University of Rio de Janeiro (UERJ), a master's degree in cognitive psychology from the UFRJ, and a doctoral degree in social psychology from the UERJ. He is a licensed psychologist by the Brazilian Federal Council of Psychology. Ribas received a dissertation award and publication grants from the Jacobs Foundation, Switzerland. He is a collaborative investigator to the *Eunice Kennedy Shriver* National Institute of Child Health and Human Development. He has received support from the UFRJ, the José Bonifácio University Foundation (FUJB, Brazil), and NICHD. His research interests include parental psychology, child development, injury prevention, social cognition, psychometrics, bibliometrics, psychological assessment and testing, and cross-cultural psychology. Ribas has contributed scientific papers in the areas of methodological, developmental, parental, pediatric, and cross-cultural psychology.

KENNETH H. RUBIN is Professor of Human Development and Director of the Center for Children, Relationships, and Culture at the University of Maryland, College Park. He holds a BA from McGill University and an MS and PhD from Pennsylvania State University. Rubin is a fellow of the Canadian and American Psychological Associations and the Association of Psychological Science. While at the University of Waterloo, he received both a Killam Research Fellowship (Canada Council) and an Ontario Mental Health Senior Research Fellowship. Rubin was president of the International Society for the Study of Behavioral Development, has twice served as associate editor of *Child Development*, and has been on the editorial boards of numerous professional journals. He has been a member of the *Eunice Kennedy Shriver* National Institute of Child Health and Human Development study section on Human Development and Aging as well as the National Institute of Mental Health study section on Risk and Prevention. Rubin's research interests include the study of children's peer and family relationships and their social and emotional development. He has published books (including *The Friendship Factor*, which won a Gold Award from the National Parenting Publications Awards), chapters, and journal papers. Among the chapters that have appeared in the *Handbook of Child Psychology* are: "Play" and "Peer Interactions, Relationships, and Groups." Rubin is principal investigator for a NIMH-funded longitudinal research project on friendship and psychosocial adjustment in middle childhood and adolescence. He is co-principal investigator for an NICHD-funded project looking at social outcomes in pediatric traumatic brain injury.

ANN V. SANSON is Professor in Paediatrics at the University of Melbourne and Coordinator of the ARC/NHMRC Research Network of the Australian Research Alliance for Children and Youth. She holds a BA from the University of Western Australia and a PhD from La Trobe University. She has held positions in the Department of Psychology at the University of Melbourne and has had terms as deputy director (research) and acting director at the Australian Institute of Family Studies, and as vice president and director of social issues at the Australian Psychological Society (APS). Sanson has convened Psychologists for Peace (an APS Interest Group) and been a member of the Committee for the Psychological Study of Peace of the International Union of Psychological Science. Sanson is principal investigator on the Australian Temperament Project, a 24-year study following children from infancy to adulthood. She was project director of the Longitudinal Study of Australian Children in its early years and is now its principal scientific advisor. Sanson's main research interests revolve around the interplay of intrinsic child characteristics and family and contextual factors in the development of good and poor psychosocial adjustment. She has specifically focused on the nature and contributions of temperament, the development of aggression and antisocial behavior, anxiety and depression, reading problems, and adolescent substance use, as well as positive outcomes such as social competence, conflict resolution skills, and civic responsibility. She also has a strong interest in translating knowledge into evidence-based policy and practice. She has served on the editorial, advisory and consulting boards of the *Journal of Abnormal Child Psychology, International Journal of Psychology, Peace and Conflict,* and *Journal of Peace Psychology*. Sanson is a fellow of the Australian Psychological Society.

T. S. SARASWATHI retired as Senior Professor in Human Development and Family Studies at the Maharaja Sayajirao University of Baroda, India. She is now Associate Fellow at the National Institute of Advanced Studies in Bangalore. She holds a PhD in psychology and child development from Iowa State University where she studied as a Ford Fellow and was a visiting Fulbright Scholar at Cornell University. She has held visiting academic appointments at Tufts University, Child Study Center, De La Salle University in the Philippines, and at Bogacizi University in Istanbul, Turkey. She co-edited *Handbook of Cross-Cultural Psychology* (Volume 2), *The International Encyclopaedia of Adolescence,* and *World Youth: Adolescence in Eight Regions of the World*. Saraswathi's edited volumes in India include *Cross-Cultural Perspectives in Human Development* and *Culture, Socialization, and Human Development*. She has contributed scientific papers in the areas of moral development, culture and socialization, adolescent development, and social policy.

MONTY P. SATIADARMA is Vice Rector of Tarumanagara University in Jakarta, Indonesia, and teaches psychology at Tarumanagara and the University of Indonesia. He was previously Dean of the Department of Psychology at Tarumanagara and coordinator of the Master's Program for Sport Psychology at the University of Indonesia. He holds a BA and PhD from the University of Indonesia; an MS in art therapy from Emporia State University, Kansas; an MFCC degree from Notre Dame de Namur University (formerly the College of Notre Dame) in Belmont, California; and a DCH from the American Institute of Hypnotherapy in Irvine, California. Satiadarma is a board member of the Indonesian Psychological Association, and head of the Indonesian Psychotherapy Association and Indonesian Sport Psychology Association. He has authored books on sport psychology, music therapy, music and child development, extramarital affairs, parental perception of children, and co-authored books on developmental issues and sport psychology. He has presented research at several international congresses and contributed articles to congress proceedings and the *Asian Journal of Social Psychology*.

BARBARA J. SHWALB is Instructor in the Psychology Department at Southern Utah University. She holds BS and MAT degrees from Southeast Missouri State University and a PhD (combined program in education and psychology) from the University of Michigan. She has held faculty positions at the University of Utah, Nagoya University of Business and Commerce, and Southeastern Louisiana University. Shwalb is a research associate of the Japanese Child and Family National Research Center and the Hokkaido University Faculty of Education, and is English abstracts editor for the *Japanese Journal of Developmental Psychology* and the *Japanese Journal of Child Abuse and Neglect*. She was a Japan Ministry of Education Fellow at Tokyo University. She is co-author of *Japanese Childrearing: Two Generations of Scholarship*, *How to Write and Publish Psychology Articles in English* (in Japanese), *Applied Developmental Psychology: Theory, Practice and Research from Japan*, *Internet Communication for Psychologists* (in Japanese), and *Respect and Disrespect: Cultural and Developmental Origins*. She has co-edited special issues of *Evaluation in Education* (Socialization and School Achievement in Japan) and the *International Journal of Educational Research* (Cooperative Learning in Cultural Context). Shwalb is a former public school teacher who has taught at the elementary, junior high, and senior high school levels. She is a Court Appointed Special Advocate serving abused children in Louisiana. Her research interests are cross-cultural developmental and learning issues, meta-analysis, affective and cognitive concept formation, and development of respect and disrespect.

DAVID W. SHWALB is Associate Professor in the Psychology Department at Southern Utah University. He holds a BA degree from Oberlin College and an MA and PhD from the University of Michigan. He has also studied at Waseda University (International Division) and the Tokyo Japanese Language Center. He is past president and webmaster of the Society for Cross-Cultural Research. He has held faculty positions at Westminster College, Koryo Women's College in Japan, Brigham Young University, and Southeastern Louisiana University. Shwalb is a research associate of the Japanese Child and Family National Research Center and the Hokkaido University Faculty of Education, and is English abstracts editor for the *Japanese Journal of Developmental Psychology* and the *Japanese Journal of Child Abuse and Neglect*. He was a *Monbusho* English Fellow at the Hiroshima Board of Educations, Fulbright Dissertation Fellow at Tokyo University, and recipient of a Japanese National Abacus Federation Research Grant. He is co-author of *Japanese Childrearing: Two Generations of Scholarship, How to Write and Publish Psychology Articles in English* (in Japanese), *Applied Developmental Psychology: Theory, Practice and Research from Japan, Internet Communication for Psychologists* (in Japanese), and *Respect and Disrespect: Cultural and Developmental Origins*. He co-edited a special issue of *Journal of Applied Developmental Psychology* (Japanese Developmental Psychology in the 1990s). During eight years in Japan, Shwalb served as a teacher at the preschool, middle school, high school, and college levels. His cross-cultural interests are in parenting, socialization, and personality development in family and school contexts and in the developmental origins of respect and disrespect.

RAINER K. SILBEREISEN is Professor and Chair of the Department of Developmental Psychology at the Department of Psychology at the Friedrich Schiller University of Jena, Germany. He is also director of the Center for Applied Developmental Science and adjunct professor of Human Development and Family Studies at Pennsylvania State University. He holds a diploma in psychology from the University of Muenster and a PhD from the Technical University of Berlin. Silbereisen has held faculty positions at the Technical University of Berlin, the University of Giessen, and at Pennsylvania State University. His scientific work was honored by membership in the European Academy of Sciences (Academia Europaea, London), and in the Akademie gemeinnütziger Wissenschaften, Erfurt, Germany. He received the Fellow Award of the American Psychological Association. Silbereisen was president of the International Society for the Study of Behavioral Development, president of the German Psychological Society and of the Federation of German Psychological Associations, and is a member of the Executive Council of the European Federation of Psychologists and of the International Union of Psychological Science. He is editor of *European Psychologist* and was editor of the *International Journal of Behavioral Development*. He has co-edited more than 20 books, such as *Negotiating Adolescence in Times of Social Change* and *Growing Points in Developmental Science*. His publication list includes research papers on human development across the lifespan, with a particular emphasis on societal and cultural contexts.

SABINE STOLL is Senior Researcher at the Max Planck Institute for Evolutionary Anthropology, Department of Linguistics, Leipzig, and a Dilthey Fellow of the Volkswagen Foundation. She holds a PhD from the University of California, Berkeley. Stoll is a member of the Chintang and Puma Documentation Project, a DOBES project funded by the Volkswagen Foundation aiming at the linguistic and ethnographic description of two endangered Sino-Tibetan languages of Nepal. Her research concentrates on comparative language acquisition focusing on Chintang, Russian, German, and English.

CATHERINE S. TAMIS-LEMONDA is Director of the Center for Research on Culture, Development and Education at New York University (NYU), a project funded by the National Science Foundation that focuses on the cognitive, social, and emotional development of ethnically diverse children. She holds a PhD from NYU in experimental/developmental psychology, and is professor of developmental psychology at NYU's Steinhardt School of Culture, Education, and Human Development. Her research focuses on infants' developing language, cognition, and social understanding across the first three years of life. Tamis-LeMonda's interest in developmental processes highlights the social and cultural contexts of early development, especially the ways in which mothers' and fathers' beliefs and practices relate to children's developmental trajectories in different populations within the United States and internationally. Her research has been funded by the National Science Foundation, National Institute of Child Development, National Institute of Mental Health, Administration for Children, Youth and Families, and the Ford Foundation. She has publications in journals and books and co-edited *Child Psychology: A Handbook of Contemporary Issues* (two editions), *Handbook of Father Involvement: Multidisciplinary Perspectives*, and *The Development of Social Cognition and Communication*.

ROSS A. THOMPSON is Professor of Psychology at the University of California, Davis. He holds a BA from Occidental College and an MA and PhD from the University of Michigan. Thompson has been a visiting scientist at the Max Planck Institute for Human Development and Education at Berlin, a senior National Institute of Mental Health Fellow in Law and Psychology at Stanford University, and a Harris Visiting Professor at the University of Chicago. He received the Boyd McCandless Young Scientist Award for Early Distinguished Achievement from the American Psychological Association and the Ann L. Brown Award for Excellence in Developmental Research. Thompson is a founding member of the National Scientific Council on the Developing Child and was a member of the National Academy of Sciences Committee on Integrating the Science of Early Childhood Development. He has twice been associate editor of *Child Development*. His books include *Preventing Child Maltreatment through Social Support: A Critical Analysis; The Postdivorce Family: Children, Families, and Society; Toward a Child-Centered, Neighborhood-Based Child Protection System; Socioemotional Development* (a Nebraska Symposium on Motivation volume); and *Infant-Mother Attachment*. His research interests are in early parent-child relationships, the development of emotional understanding and emotion regulation, conscience development, and the growth of self-understanding. Thompson is also interested in the applications of developmental research to public policy, including the effects of divorce and custody arrangements on children, child maltreatment prevention, school readiness, research ethics, and early brain development.

FONS J. R. VAN DE VIJVER holds a Chair in Cross-Cultural Psychology at Tilburg University, the Netherlands and is Extraordinary Professor at North-West University, South Africa. He is vice-dean for research of his faculty and co-director of Babylon, an interdisciplinary research center for studies of multicultural societies at Tilburg University. He has studied psychology at Tilburg University in the Netherlands and obtained his PhD from the same university. He was president of Division 2 (Assessment and Evaluation) of the International Association of Applied Psychology. He is editor in chief of the *Journal of Cross-Cultural Psychology* and former editor of the *Bulletin of the International Test Commission*, previously published as part of the *European Journal of Psychological Assessment* and now independently published as the *International Journal of Testing*. He has been a member of the board of editors of *Child Development*. He has written articles, chapters, and books in the field of cross-cultural psychology. Main topics in his research and publications are methodological issues of cross-cultural comparison (bias and equivalence), cross-cultural differences and similarities in cognitive functioning, acculturation (among permanent immigrants, sojourners, exchange students, and refugees), multiculturalism, and large-scale country-level comparisons of psychological test scores. He has collected data in southern Africa, Turkey, and Libya, and has been involved in several large cross-cultural projects.

ELITA AMINI VIRMANI is a Doctoral Student in the Department of Human Development at the University of California, Davis, and a Clinical Intern at the Infant-Parent Program/Day Care Consultants at the University of California, San Francisco. She holds an MS degree in child development from the University of California, Davis. Virmani's research interests focus on caregiver sensitivity among parents and childcare providers. She is also interested in early intervention and prevention efforts that support parents and childcare providers in developing capacities to engage in affectively attuned interactions with the young children in their care.

BRIGITTE VITTRUP is Assistant Professor in Early Childhood Development and Education at Texas Woman's University in Denton, Texas. She holds a BA from Texas State University and BS, MA, and PhD degrees from the University of Texas at Austin. Vittrup specializes in research on parent–child relationships, child discipline, and media influences on children's development.

DANIEL A. WAGNER is Professor of Education and Director of the International Literacy Institute, co-founded by UNESCO and the University of Pennsylvania. He is also director of the National Center on Adult Literacy at the University of Pennsylvania. After undergraduate studies at Cornell University and voluntary service in the Peace Corps (Morocco), he received his PhD in psychology at the University of Michigan, was a two-year postdoctoral fellow at Harvard University, a visiting fellow at the International Institute of Education Planning in Paris, a visiting professor at the University of Geneva (Switzerland), and a Fulbright Scholar at the University of Paris. Wagner has extensive experience in national and international educational issues. In addition to numerous professional publications, he has written or edited the following books: *Literacy: Developing the Future* (now in five languages), *Literacy: An International Handbook*, *Learning to Bridge the Digital Divide*, *New Technologies for Literacy and Adult Education: A Global Review*, and *Monitoring and Evaluation of ICT for Education in Developing Countries*.

LI WANG is Associate Professor of Psychology at Peking University, China. She holds BA, MA, and PhD degrees from Beijing Normal University. She received a research award from the Natural Sciences Foundation of China. Her research interest is in children's emotion and emotion regulation. She has published papers on family interactions and emotional development.

JANET F. WERKER is Professor and Canada Research Chair in the Department of Psychology at the University of British Columbia. She holds a BA from Harvard University and an MSc and PhD from the University of British Columbia. Her first academic position was at Dalhousie University before she returned to the University of British Columbia. Werker has received the Killam Research Prize, the UBC Alumni Prize in the Social Sciences, and Fellowships in the Royal Society of Canada, the Canadian Psychological Association, the Canadian Institutes for Advanced Research, and the American Association for the Advancement of Science. She was awarded the Jacob Bieley Research Prize, UBC's most prestigious award. Werker is on the editorial board of journals spanning cognitive and developmental psychology as well as linguistics and edits the book series, "Essays in Developmental Psychology." Werker has contributed empirical and theoretical papers in the areas of human experimental, methodological, developmental, cross-cultural, and cognitive neuroscience, with her primary focus on the effects of differential language experience on infant speech, perception development, and early language acquisition.

CAROL M. WORTHMAN holds the Samuel Candler Dobbs Chair in the Department of Anthropology, Emory University, where she also directs the Laboratory for Comparative Human Biology. Worthman holds undergraduate degrees in biology and botany from Pomona College and a PhD in biological anthropology from Harvard University. She studied endocrinology at the University of California, San Diego, and neuroscience at the Massachusetts Institute of Technology. She was a Russell Sage Foundation Fellow and has received funding from the National Institutes of Health, the National Science Foundation, the William T. Grant Foundation, the National Geographic Society, the Doris Duke Foundation, and the Spencer Foundation. Worthman has pioneered integration of biological and cultural analysis in the pursuit of comparative interdisciplinary research on human development, reproductive ecology, and bases of differential mental and physical health. She has conducted cross-cultural ethnographic and biosocial research in ten countries, as well as in rural, urban, and semi-urban areas of the United States. Her empirical contributions span cross-cultural human development, reproductive ecology, developmental epidemiology, sleep and state regulation, stress and allostatic load, and the development and application of biomarkers. Her conceptual work includes biocultural anthropology, cultural epidemiology, life history theory, comparative developmental ecology of sleep, and evolutionary medicine.

KATHERINE A. YOSHIDA is a Doctoral Student in the Cognitive Science Programme at the University of British Columbia. She holds a BSc from McGill University. Yoshida is funded by graduate fellowships from the Social Sciences and Humanities Research Council of Canada and the Michael Smith Foundation for Health Research. Her research interests are in language and culture in infancy and adulthood.

Author Index

A

Abbot-Smith, K., 149, 156
Abbotts, J. E., 290
Abdalla, J. B., 368, 371
Abdalla, M. S., 360, 363, 372
Abdel-Ghany, M., 371
Abdel-Hamid, M. I., 364
Abdel-Hamid, M. N., 365
Abdel-Hamid, T., 362
Abdel-Kader, A. A., 365
Abdel-Latif, F. I., 372
Abdel-Moety, H. M., 366, 368
Abdel-Rahman, M. E., 363, 366, 367
Abdel-Wahab, A. A., 373
Abdel-Wahid, A., 373
Abdi, H., 179
Abdullaev, N., 411, 416
Abels, M., 470
Abelson, R., 270
Ablow, J., 201
Abou-el-Enien, A. F. I., 365
Abou-el-Kheir, M. M. S., 364
Abou-Maraq, G. Z., 371
Abou-Nashy, M. S., 373
Abou-Shideed, K. A., 365
Abou-Zaid, N. A. A., 364, 373
Aboud, F., 230
Abraham, G., 99
Abramovich, D. R., 176
Abrue-Lima, I. M., 507
Abu-Rabia, S., 166
Ackerman, B. P., 411, 412
Ackerman, J. M., 106, 107
Acres, J. G., 176
Adamopoulos, J., 26
Adams, B., 99
Adams, E., 508
Adams, R. H., 545
Adams, R. J., 112
Adamson, L., 110
Adeagbo, D., 392
Adler, S. M., 214
Adolfsson, R., 176
Adolph, K. E., 63, 66, 67, 71, 75, 77, 83
Agar, M. H., 400
Agarwal, D., 509, 510
Agarwal, S., 77
Agiobu-Kemmer, I., 509, 516
Agnihotri, S. B., 470
Agran, P., 332

Agrawal, P., 507, 512, 518
Aguado-Orea, J., 147
Ahktar, N., 314
Ahlawat, K. S., 364
Ahluwalia, M. K., 280
Ahmad, O. B., 43f, 44, 47
Ahmed, E. A., 369
Ahmed, R. A., 359, 360, 361, 362, 363, 364, 365, 366, 367, 368, 369, 371, 372, 373
Ahmed, R. E., 372
Ahmed, S. K., 364
Ahn, H., 543
Aina, T. A., 509, 510, 511, 516, 517
Ainslie, R., 542
Ainsworth, M. D. S., 68, 73, 262, 304, 385, 399
Akita, K., 455
Akoh, H., 218
Akopyan, A S., 422
Aksan, N., 306
Akutsu, P. D., 538
Al-Ahram, 361, 363
Al-Ali, M. M., 373
Al-Anwar, M. A., 367
Al-Ater, F., 371
Al-Bailey, M., 370
Al-Emam, M. A. S., 367
Al-Ghreniah, F., 370
Al-Khawajah, J. M. A., 362, 365, 371
Al-Madhoun, A. S., 369
Al-Mazeruoi, L. A. A., 364
Al-Mestikawy, T. A., 369, 372
Al-Motwa, M. B. A., 372
Al-Mushref, I. I., 372
Al-Mustafa, A. A., 367, 373
Al-Mustafa, M. Y., 370
Al-Naial, M. A., 365
Al-Otaibi, D. R., 366
Al-Qabas, 360, 370
Al-Salameh, I. M., 373
Al-Saud, A., 367
Al-Saway, I. Z., 372
Al-Seyassah, 362
Al-Shamy, J. M., 365
Al-Sharkawy, A. M., 367
Al-Thafery, S. B. S., 368
Al-Yameni, S., 365
Al-Youssefi, M. A., 370
Al-Zeqay, N. M., 367
Alao, J. A., 389, 390
Albee, G. W., 312
Albert, A. A., 215

Alberti, K. G, M. M., 53
Albright, M., 304
Alcon, M. C. G., 412
Alden, L. E., 535
Alder, L. L., 366
Alder, N. E., 54
Alduaij, H. S., 373
Ali, A. A. M., 373
Ali, A. H., 271, 543
Ali, A. R., 371
Ali, S. A., 364, 365, 370, 371
Alidou, H., 171
Allen, K. M., 185
Allhusen, V., 252
Almeida-Filho, N., 509
Alohoa, S., 104
Alpert, R., 212
Als, H., 266
Alsaker, F. D., 341, 345
Altemeyer, B., 282
Altemus, M., 179
Altman, I., 506
Alwin, D. F., 291
Amano, S., 96
Amato, P., 412
Amatruda, C. S., 262
Ambady, N., 109, 110
Ameziane, M., 367
Andaya, B. W., 210
Andayani, S., 110
Anders, T. F., 302
Anderson, C., 332
Anderson, C. A., 167
Anderson, C. L., 332
Anderson, K. L., 286
Andriushina, E. V., 421
Angelillo, C., 138, 140, 300, 332, 489
Angold, A., 43
Anme, T., 518
Anselmi, L., 509, 518
Antonov, A. A., 417
Aprelkov, G., 416
Aptekar, L., 331
Arbelle, S., 188
Ardila, R., 328
Arends-Tóth, J., 537, 541
Argenti, A. M., 109
Arimond, M., 51
Armelagos, G. J., 53
Arnett J. J., 262, 388
Arnett Jackson, L., 10
Arnold, E., 533
Artamonova, E., 412
Artreberry, M. E., 112
Asai, M., 229
Asendorpf, J., 225, 433
Asher, S., 436
Ashworth, A., 517

Aslin, R. N., 90, 90f, 94, 99, 114, 131
Assadi, S. M., 6
Assuncao, A. M. S., 517
Atran, S., 289
Attili, G., 227
Attneave, C. L., 266
Attwood, L., 420
Au, J., 438
Au, T. K. F., 97
Aughinbaugh, A., 507, 514, 517
Austin, A., 508, 511, 515
Avellani, J., 368
Avery, R. A., 97
Avn-Singer, A. J., 522
Awadh, A. M., 369
Axinn, W. G., 288
Axtell, C., 518
Azab, H. M., 371
Azar, F., 365
Azar, S. T., 543
Azarov, Y., 415
Azuma, H., 198, 268, 269, 303, 396

B

Babu, B., 64
Bacarji, K., 517
Bacon, M. K., 216
Baddeley, A., 21–22
Badri, M. B., 365
Baek, K. L., 451
Baghurst, P., 513
Baguma, P., 387
Bagwell, C., 229–230
Baharloo, S., 101
Bahrick, L. E., 98
Bailey, D. B., 289
Bailey, F., 65, 78
Baillargeon, R., 131
Bain, A., 175
Baird, J. A., 151–152
Bakeman, R., 110, 183
Baker, P., 410, 411
Baker, S. A., 95
Baker, W. E., 287
Baker-Sennett, J., 11
Balatsky, G., 420
Baldwin, D. A., 151–152
Ball, P., 186
Baltes, P. B., 422
Bandi Rao, S., 151
Bandura, A., 212
Bang, R. A., 474
Bangurambona, J., 392
Bar-Haim, Y., 104
Barber, B. K., 266, 415
Barker, D. J. P., 43, 52
Barker, E. T., 305

Barnard, K. E., 262
Barnes, S., 147, 150
Barnett, D. B., 282
Barnhart, H. X., 52
Baro, M., 51
Baron-Cohen, S., 103
Barr, R. G., 72, 165
Barrat, M., 264
Barrett, H. C., 333
Barrett, J. L., 289
Barrett, M., 285
Barry, H., 216, 241
Barsby, J., 388
Bartkowski, J. P., 288, 290, 291
Bartlett, F. C., 128
Bartlett, S. N., 332
Barton, J. J. S., 104
Basral, S., 509
Basrros, F., 509
Bastos, A., 509, 517
Batchelder, W. H., 5
Bates, E., 156
Bates, J. E., 225, 259, 307, 433
Bathgate, M., 497
Batrouney, T., 490
Bauer, H., 185
Baumgartl, B., 544
Baumrind, D., 269, 471
Baumrind, O., 21
Bautista, F., 533
Bavelier, D., 81
Bayley, N.., 63f, 64, 66
Baza, A. A. M., 361, 371
Beal, C. R., 216
Beard, K., 72
Bedani, A. K. M., 364
Beddor, P., 94
Befu, H., 269
Behagat, R. M., 367
Behne, T., 152, 333
Beiser, M., 536, 542, 545
Bekombo, M., 392
Belanger, D., 450
Bell, R., 288
Bellingham, W., 489
Belliston, L. M., 345, 351
Belmaker, E., 517
Belsky, J., 506, 541
Ben Sira, Z., 542
Bender, M., 24
Benedict, R., 132, 262, 268
Benedikt, R., 7
Benenson, J. F., 226
Benet-Martinez, V., 135
Bengi-Arslan, L., 533
Benigni, L., 249
Bennell, P., 401
Bennett, J. A., 32

Bennett, J. A. H., 162
Benning, S. D., 189
Bensen, J. B., 71
Benson, P. L., 279
Bentley, M. E., 50
Bergen, M. B., 474
Berger, K., 7
Berger, P., 7
Berger, S. E., 66, 67, 72, 75, 83
Bergeron, N., 227
Bergman, T., 102
Berlin, B., 113
Berlin, C. M., 52
Berman, R., 154
Bernat, E., 189
Bernhard, J. K., 543
Berns, G. S., 185
Bernstein, M., 106
Berrien, F. B., 416
Berry, J. W., 28, 31, 32, 132, 133, 162, 214, 239, 241, 243, 251, 262, 324, 384, 395, 477, 531, 532, 535, 536, 539, 542
Bersoff, D. M., 315
Bertenthal, B. I., 66, 67
Bertin, e., 103
Bertinetto, P. M., 97
Bertoncini, J., 93, 98
Bertram, H., 355
Best, C. T., 94, 96, 97
Best, D. L., 210, 212, 214, 215
Betancourt, H., 324
Bever, T. G., 152, 155
Bharat, S., 470
Bhatt, R. S., 103
Bhopal, R., 53
Bhugra, D., 533
Bhutta, Z. A., 45, 51
Bickel, B., 145, 146
Biederman, J., 334
Biernat, M., 215
Biggs, J. B., 432
Bijeljac-Babic, R., 93
Billig, O., 329
Billington, J. H., 410
Birbaumer, N., 185
Bird, L., 494
Birman, D., 542
Birz, S., 537
Bishop, D. V. M., 65
Bjorklund, D. F., 240, 241, 242
Björkqvist, K., 227
Black, J, E., 242, 263
Black, M., 516
Black, R. E., 41, 43, 51
Blake, C. F., 80, 81
Blandin-Gitlin, I., 109
Blanz, V., 108
Blascovich, J., 185

Blaug, M., 166, 167
Blehar, M. D., 304
Bless, C., 384
Blevins-Knabe, B., 508, 511, 515
Bloch, M. N., 214
Block, J. H., 217
Bloem, M. W., 40
Blosser, C. D., 72
Blössner, M., 40, 46, 46f, 47f
Blumenfeld, P. C., 11, 218
Blumstein, S. E., 93
Boas, F., 78
Bochner, S., 535
Boden, J. M., 496
Boerma, J. T., 387
Boersma, E. R., 524
Bogot, T., 423
Bohlin, G., 435
Bohn, O. S., 97
Boland, J. E., 134
Bolinger, D., 97
Bollman, R., 474
Bond, M. H., 22, 23, 225, 513, 523
Bondar, I., 108
Bongmba, E. K., 386
Bonnet, J., 22
Bontempo, R., 229, 300
Booth, A., 182
Booth-LaForce, C., 230
Borer, H., 147
Borghi, E., 46, 46f
Borke, J., 198, 330
Borkowski, J. G., 510
Bornstein, H. G., 78
Bornstein, M. H., 3, 4, 21, 31, 78, 112, 113, 153, 198, 202, 204, 224, 259, 260, 262, 263, 265, 266, 267, 268, 269, 270, 272, 286, 303, 306, 313, 324, 327, 333, 345, 429, 434, 491, 508, 510, 514, 523, 532, 534, 538, 539
Boroditsky, L., 111
Boronkai, J., 517
Bosch, L., 94, 97, 98
Boschi-Pinto, C., 41
Bosker, R., 30
Boski, P., 535
Boss, P., 248
Botcheva, L., 346
Bothwell, R., 105
Boti, M., 533
Bottoms, B. L., 291
Bourdieu, P., 8–9, 10
Bourhis, R. Y., 534
Bourque, S. L., 267
Bouwsma, W. J., 186
Bowerman, M., 153, 154
Bowker, A., 225, 228
Bowlby, J., 195, 267, 304
Bowles, S., 313

Bowman, M. J., 167
Boyd, R., 129
Bozoky, I., 508
Bradley, C., 217, 389, 396
Bradley, R. H., 324, 505, 507, 508, 512, 514, 515, 517, 518, 520, 521, 523
Brady, R. H., 266–267
Braithwaite, J., 13
Bransford, J. D., 513
Braun, C., 185
Bray, J. H., 540
Brazelton, T. B., 64, 65, 215, 259, 266
Bredekamp, S., 307
Brennan, P., 496
Brent, H. P., 103, 104
Bretschneider, V., 134
Breugelman, S. M., 328
Brewer, M. B., 313
Brewis, A., 334
Brigham, J., 105, 108
Bril, B., 61, 67, 68, 68f, 69, 73, 74, 75, 81
Broberg, A., 225
Broberg, A. G., 389
Brody, G. H., 250, 282, 285, 290
Bronfenbrenner, U., 14, 15, 33, 242, 245, 260, 267, 268, 285, 410, 413, 414, 415, 418, 422
Bronstein, P., 212
Brook, J. S., 182
Brooks, J., 72
Brooks-Gunn, J., 249, 312, 313, 412
Brooks-Gunn, M. R., 411
Brossart, D. F., 542
Brouwers, J. A., 32
Brouwers, S. A., 328, 477
Brown, A. L., 513
Brown, B., 230
Brown, B. B., 231, 437
Brown, C. M., 373
Brown, J. D., 304
Brown, K., 41
Brown, P., 149, 153
Brown, P. J., 53
Brown, W. A., 100, 101
Browne, K., 346
Browning, D. S., 285
Bruce, V., 102, 104
Bruder, G. E., 189
Bruner, J. S., 128, 129, 241, 251, 267, 398
Brunstein, J. C., 31
Bruschi, C. J., 289
Bryan, E. S., 329
Bryant, B. J., 252
Bryant, B. K., 418
Bryce, J., 41
Bryceson, D. F., 541
Brye, J., 41
Bryk, A. S., 30
Buchanan-Barrow, E., 285

Buck, M. J., 272
Buck, R., 175
Bugental, D. B., 14, 243, 262
Bukach, C, M., 107
Bukowski, W. M., 201, 223, 229, 230, 232, 390–391, 436
Bulcroft, K. A., 269, 511
Bulcroft, R., 511
Bulcroft, R. A., 269
Bulmer-Thomas, V., 327
Bulnes, B., 508, 511, 512, 515
Bunge, S. A., 181
Burchinal, M., 507
Burgess, K. B., 225, 228, 436
Burghart, R., 67, 68
Burgos, A. E., 534
Buriel, R., 248, 254, 540
Burke, A. W., 533
Burnham, D., 95, 100
Burns, E. M., 100
Burns, S., 166
Burns, T. C., 93, 94
Burra, N., 473
Busch, H., 25, 31
Busch-Rossnagel, N. A., 513
Busey, T., 108
Bush, K., 511
Bushnell, I. W. R., 102
Buss, D. M., 211, 474
Bussey, K., 212, 213
Butler, S., 497
Butovskaya, M., 423, 424
Butte, N., 45
Butterfield, P., 110
Buzhicheeva, V., 416
Byers-Heinlein, K., 93

C

Cacioppo, J. T., 175, 179
Cady, J., 94
Cahill, L., 189
Cain, T. R., 183
Cairns, B., 227
Cairns, B. D., 231, 436
Cairns, R. B., 210, 227, 231, 436
Cajdler, B., 508
Caldera, R., 107
Caldwell, B. M., 505, 520, 523
Call, J., 152
Callaghan, L., 383, 389, 401
Callaghan, T., 333
Callister, P., 494
Calzada, E., 511
Cameron-Falkner, T., 149
Cammuso, K., 100
Campbell, C., 105
Campbell, D. I., 41

Campbell, D. T., 26, 27, 28, 111
Campione-Barr, N., 310
Campos, B., 179
Campos, D., 24, 25, 29, 31
Campos, J., 110
Campos, R. G., 74
Camras, L. A., 183, 433
Caplan, N., 313
Capute, A. J., 64
Carey, S., 102, 103, 104
Carlson, S. M., 24, 434
Carlson, V. J., 507, 513
Carmody, D. C., 269, 511
Carpenter, M., 152
Carr, S. C., 403
Carraher, D., 32, 334
Carroo, A., 108
Carter, S., 497
Caruana, C., 493
Casas, C. A. S., 334
Case, R., 32
Cashmore, J. A., 260
Casiglia, A. C., 232
Caspi, A., 176, 188, 495, 512
Cassia, V. M., 102
Castillo, L. G., 542
Castillo, M., 518
Castillo-Durin, C., 508
Cauce, A. M., 312
Caudill, W., 268, 538
Cavagna, G. A., 76, 76f
Cazden, C., 5, 9
Ceci, S. J., 32, 268
Celen, N., 359, 361, 371
Cen, G., 229, 437, 438, 439
Cen, G. Z., 431
Chaiklin, S., 10
Chaiyasit, W., 228
Chall, J. S., 165, 166
Chamvu, F., 396
Chan, S., 539, 542, 543
Chanana, K., 475
Chance, J., 108
Chandler, M. J., 8
Chang, C. M., 269
Chang, L., 227, 228, 231, 232, 432, 433, 436, 437, 438, 439
Chang, S., 516
Chang, S. M., 508
Chao, R. K., 21, 202, 265, 286, 313, 314, 437, 540
Charney, E., 301, 537
Chasiotis, A., 24, 25, 29, 31, 284, 324
Chaudhry, N., 473
Chaudhuri, J. H., 266
Cheah, C. S. L., 224, 226, 228, 286, 448
Checkley, W., 45, 49
Chee, F., 70
Chen, C., 226, 232, 432

Chen, H., 231, 433, 437, 438
Chen, H. C., 228
Chen, L., 7, 230, 232
Chen, L. C., 50
Chen, S., 177
Chen, X., 200, 201, 202, 223, 225, 227, 228, 229, 231, 232, 263, 264, 335, 418, 431, 432, 433, 434, 435, 436, 437, 438, 439, 440, 445
Chen, Y., 183, 313
Cheng, B. D., 30
Cheour, M., 94, 96
Chestham, J., 533
Cheung, F., 26
Cheung, Y. B., 44
Chew, S., 79, 80
Chiao, J., 106
Chibwana, K., 386, 389
Child, I. L., 216, 244
Child, J., 224
Childs, C. P., 82, 135, 215
Chin, C., 101
Chisholm, J. S., 74
Chiu, J., 438
Chiu, L. H., 287
Cho, G. E., 305
Cho, Y. J., 448, 454
Choi, C., 226
Choi, E., 456
Choi, I., 133
Choi, K. Y., 449, 451
Choi, S., 153, 154
Choi, S. J., 448
Chomitz, V. R., 517
Chomsky, N., 146
Chotai, J., 176
Chowdhury, A. M., 53
Choy, M. H., 313
Chrea, C., 179
Christopher, R. C., 520
Chua, H. F., 134
Chun, K. M., 538
Chung, C. S., 107
Chung, M., 448
Chung, O. B., 15
Church, A. T., 517, 521
Church, T. A., 25, 26
Cialdini, R. B., 314
Cicchetti, D. V., 522
Ciesla, W., 176
Cillessen, A. H., 227
Cillessen, H. N., 232
Cintas, H., 83
Claeson, M., 47
Clark, A. M., 151–152, 153
Clark, D., 51, 70
Clark, E., 148
Clark, H. H., 10, 11
Clark-Chiarelli, N., 166

Clarke-Stewart, K. A., 252, 343
Claypool, H., 106
Clayton, D. F., 99
Clifford, C. W. G., 108
Clifton, R. K., 67
Coard, S. I., 250
Coates, J., 51
Coates, R. J., 52
Cockerham, W.C., 413
Cocking, R. R., 513
Cohen, D., 133
Cohen, E., 313
Cohen, K. M., 70
Cohen, M. M., 95
Cohen, P., 182
Cohen, R. N., 393
Coie, J., 227
Cok, F., 359, 361, 371
Cole, K., 24
Cole, M., 5, 10, 11, 14, 32, 128, 130–131, 135, 136, 140, 161, 167, 250, 259, 383, 394
Cole, P. M., 289
Coleman, D. L., 271
Coleman, P., 536, 543
Collier, G., 64
Collins, A., 280
Collishaw, S. M., 107
Colomzé, A., 97
Coltrane, S., 254
Comstock, G., 251
Conde, W. L., 53
Conger, R. D., 249, 250, 290, 324
Conlisk, A .J., 52
Connolly, K. J., 65
Conoley, C. W., 542
Conway, M., 96
Cook, D. G., 51
Cook, L., 487
Cook, T. D., 13, 249
Cook, W. L., 254
Coon, H., 229
Coon, H. M., 302, 434
Cooper, C. R., 4, 7, 13, 391, 531
Cooper, J. M., 177
Cooper, R. P., 93
Cooper, S., 225
Coplan, R. J., 225, 227, 228, 232, 436
Corapci, F., 518, 523
Corina, D. C., 92
Correa, V., 289
Correa-Chávez, M., 138, 489
Cortes, D. E., 313
Corwyn, R. F., 324, 507, 512, 518, 520, 521
Cory-Slechta, D. A., 524
Costa, A., 97
Costa, M., 185
Costa-Woodson, E., 520
Costello, E. J., 43

Cote, L., 153, 523
Cote, L. M., 270
Cote, L. R., 313, 327, 491, 534, 538, 543
Cotton, S., 260
Coudouel, A., 412
Courage, M. L., 112
Coursen-Neff, N., 457
Cousens, S. N., 41
Cowan, C., 201
Cowan, P., 201
Cowie, S. A. E., 280
Craig, I. W., 188
Craig, W. M., 421
Craik, K. H., 328
Crick, N. R., 227, 232
Crijnen, A. A. M., 533
Crimmins, E. M., 40
Critchley, C. R., 306
Crockenberg, S., 311
Crocker, J., 305
Croft, W., 151
Crone, E. A., 181
Cross, T. G., 150
Crouter, A. C., 14
Crozier, J. B., 101
Crozier, W., 228
Cruickshank, M., 92
Cryer, D., 346
Crystal, D., 162
Csibra, G., 95, 96
Cubelis, J. F., 183
Cueto, S., 44
Cugnasco, I., 510, 517
Cui, C., 431, 440
Cummings, S. R., 81
Cunningham, W., 106
Curran, H. V., 384
Curran, T., 106
Currie, C., 341, 343, 344, 345, 348, 351, 352, 353, 354
Curti, M. W., 64
Curtin, S., 114
Curtis, G. E., 414, 421
Cutler, A., 92, 98
Cymerman, E., 148
Cyphers, L., 303
Cysouw, M., 145

D

Daal, M., 22
Daddis, C., 310
Dahl, O., 145
Dallwitz, A., 72
Daltabuit, M., 74
Daly, M., 211
Damour, L. K., 522
Dana, R. H., 22
D'Andrade, R. G., 8, 113, 127, 158, 505

Dang, T. B., 454
Daniele, J. R., 99
Dantzer, R., 41
Danziger, K., 384
Dao, D. H., 449, 456
Darling, N. E., 6, 21, 266, 269
Darvies, L. G., 536
Darwish, A. E., 370
Dasen, P. R., 214, 239, 243, 328, 395, 396, 532
Dasgupta, S., 315
Dasher, R., 97
Dashiell, E. N., 230
Daswani, C. J., 170
Datta, V., 470
DaVanzo, J., 413
Davenport, J. L., 134
Davey, J., 494
Davey Smith, G., 53
Davidoff, J., 113
Davidson, A. L., 7
Davidson, G., 488, 489, 490
Davidson, R. J., 178
Davidson, W., 329
Davies, I. R. L., 112, 113, 114
Davies, K., 202
Davis, B. E., 72
Davis, P., 491
Davis, W. H., 366
Davis-Kean, P. E., 248, 253
Daw, J., 412, 413
Dawes, A., 384, 400
Day, R., 218
D'Cruz, P., 470
De, A., 466, 472
De Graaf, N. D., 284, 285, 289
de Haan, M., 105
De Heering, A., 102
de Lemos, M., 489
De León, L., 149
de Matos, M. G., 421
De Ment, T. L., 540
de Munck, V. C., 505
de Onis, M., 40, 45, 46, 46f, 47f
de Roos, S. A., 288, 289
de Schonen, S., 102, 103, 104, 109
de Vaus, D., 488
Deal, J. E., 7
Dean, R., 64, 65
Deater-Deckard, K., 259, 306–307, 313, 534
Deaton, A., 48
Deb, S., 474
Debais, S. A., 363
DeCasper, A. J., 93
Deci, E. L., 270, 307
Dediu, D., 101
Dehaene, S., 92
Dehaene-Lambertz, G., 92, 94, 96, 98
Dekkers, H., 30

Delpierre, V., 287
Demetriou, A., 32
DeMorris, K. A., 418
Dench, A., 146
Denko, P., 226
Denmark, F. L., 366
Denner, J., 4, 531
Dennis, M. G., 74
Dennis, W., 61, 71, 74, 262, 513
Denny, M. E., 66
Denoma, J., 453
Denton, M. L., 282
Denton, N. A., 313, 531
Deregowski, J. B., 25
Dernelle, R., 287
Desain, P., 99
Deshmukh, K., 510
Desjardins, R., 95, 101
DeSouza, A., 225, 433, 434
Deubel, T. F., 51
Deutsch, D., 101
Devine, J., 76
deVries, M. W., 50
DeVries, R., 307
Dewey, C., 72
Deynoot-Schaub, M. J., 346
Dhanamitta, S., 260
Diamond, R., 102, 103, 104
Dias, M. G., 334
Dias, S., 422
Dickenson, D. K., 166
Dickie, J. R., 289
Didham, R., 487
Diener, E., 351, 420
Dietrich, C., 96
Dietz, V., 266
Dillon, N., 188
Dion, R., 536
Diop, C. A., 386
DiPietro, J. A., 216
Dittmar, M., 156
Dixon, R. A., 211
Dixon, S., 64, 259
Dobbins, G., 30
Dobres, M. A., 209, 210
Dobson, J., 288
Dodd, B., 95
Dodds, J. B., 64
Dodge, K. A., 227, 259, 269, 307, 438
Doh, H. S., 452
Dohrenwend, B. P., 182
Doi, K., 23
Dollahite, D. C., 288
Dominquez, W., 13
Donald, D., 400
Donald, M., 129
Donohue, S., 181
Dorman, M., 96

Dornbusch, S. M., 21, 265, 313, 437
Dornellan, M. .B., 324
Doswell, W. M., 290
Dousseki, I. M., 365
Dove, H., 71–72, 520
Dowling, E. M., 279
Downing, J., 165
Dowse, G., 53
Drake, A. J., 53
Dreby, J., 541
Drew, J. E., 176
Drewery, W., 494
Dreze, J., 466, 472
Drivonikou, G. V., 114
Drotar, D., 510, 511, 516, 517
D'Souza, V. M., 188
Du, W., 182
du Plessix, Gray, F., 420
Dube, L., 469, 472, 473
Dubois, D., 230
DuBois, D. L., 305
Dudgeon, P., 488, 490
Duff, S., 111
Duhamel, P., 108
Dulmus, C. N., 416
Dunn, J., 249, 343
Dupoux, E., 111
Duran, P., 512
Durbrow, E. H., 508, 509, 511, 512, 515, 516, 517, 520
Durgunoglu, A. Y., 166
Durojaiye, M. D. A., 392
Dutta, R., 467, 470
Dvir, R., 212
Dwairy, M., 284
Dweck, C. S., 292, 311
Dworkin, A., 80
Dworkin, P. H., 270
Dworkin, P. W., 515
Dye, H., 513

E

Eagly, A. H., 212
Easterly, W., 302
Eberhardt, J., 106
Eberhart, N., 496
Eberstadt, N., 410, 412, 413
Ebrey, P., 80, 81
Eccles, J. S., 13, 249, 253, 311
Echeverria, S., 97
Edelbrock, C., 214
Edelstein, W., 226
Edwards, C. P., 214, 216, 217, 224, 252, 472, 506, 516, 521
Edwards, M.., 508
Ehri, L. C., 166
Eibl-Eibesfedt, I., 333

Eichler, S. A., 231
Eid, M. I., 365, 366, 373
Eimas, P. D., 93
Eisenberg, A. R., 314
Eisenberg, N., 434, 453
Eisenstadt, S. N., 539
Eisner, M., 353
Ekman, P., 109, 110, 178
El-Bana, A. A., 373
El-Beblawi, V., 369
El-Dabaa, S. Y., 367
El-Dousseki, M. I., 360
El-Dousseki, M. M. S., 360
El-Fakhrany, Kh. I., 372
El-Gibaly, O., 361
El-Hilo, B. M. M., 370
El-Meliugi, A., 360, 369
El-Seddik, N., 369
El-Zayyat, F. M., 364
El-Zeraigat, I. A. F., 367
Elder, G. H. Jr., 13, 249, 250, 253, 290
Elder, J. A., 50
Eldridge, B., 72
Elfenbein, H., 109
Elia, M., 41
Elias, I., 371
Elliott, D. B., 249
Elliott, E., 108
Ellis, B. B., 26
Ellis, J., 388, 391, 394, 398
Ellis, R. A., 416
Ellis, S., 211
Ellison, C. G., 286, 288
Elman, J., 147
Elordi, C. A., 267
Ember, C. R., 269, 505
Ember, M., 269, 505
Emde, R. N., 110
Endo, M., 105, 106
Enesco, I., 331
Engelhard, G., 26
Engle, P. L., 44, 171
Engs, R. C., 290
Entwistle, D., 109
Epstein, J. L., 544
Ericsson, K. A., 131
Erikson, E. H., 268, 279, 303
Eriksson, J. G., 43, 52
Erkanli, A., 43
Erny, P., 395, 398
Erol, N., 533
Ertem, I. O., 522
Eslea, M., 228
Espin, O., 315
Esteban, C., 512
Etta, E., 509
Evanikoff, L. J., 417
Evans, G. W., 311, 312, 520

Evans, N., 146
Eveleth, P., 40
Everatt, J., 396
Ewidaih, M. A., 364
Eyberg, S., 511
Eze, N., 385

F

Fagan, C., 345
Fahr, J. L., 30
Fai, P. J., 396
Fairclough, S. H., 176
Fais, L., 96
Falicov, C. J., 537
Fang, E-X., 226
Fang, G., 226
Fang, H. S. Y., 79, 80, 81
Farag, T. S. M., 371
Farah, M. J., 102, 104
Faraone, T. V., 334
Farhadi, S., 492
Farmer, A. E., 539
Farmer, P., 50
Farnsworth, G., 413
Farris, R., 282
Farroni, T., 102
Farry, S., 492
Farver, J. M., 226, 227, 228, 232, 450
Fausto-Sterling, A., 209
Fauth, R. C., 411
Fehr, B., 180
Fein, E., 533
Fein, S. A., 225
Feinman, S., 109
Feldman, P. J., 182
Feldman, S. S., 342, 492
Feldman-Savlsberg, P., 388
Fellow, A., 457
Feltham, A., 420
Feng, X., 538
Ferguson, C., 148
Fergusson, D., 496
Fernald, A., 93, 148
Fernandez, D. M., 535
Ferrari, F., 175
Ferreira, M., 517
Ferrell, R. E., 182
Ferretti, A., 185
Ferro, A., 493
Fied, H. A., 371
Fiese, B. H., 15, 248
Fiez, J. A., 96
Fifer, W. P., 93
Finch, C. E., 40
Fine, G. A., 231
Fine, M., 313
Finley, G. E., 334

Fischer, K. W., 180
Fischer, M., 271
Fisher, C. B., 513
Fiske, A. P., 8, 9, 14, 263
Fivush, R., 201, 202, 203
Flaherty, J. A., 537
Flammer, A., 341, 345, 351
Flanagan, C., 346
Flanagan, C. A., 311
Flanagan, K., 301
Fleeson, J., 267
Flege, J. E., 97
Fleming, P., 72
Fletcher, A. C., 6
Fletcher, P., 516
Flint, V. I. J., 326
Flor, D., 250, 282
Florsheim, Y., 534, 539
Flory, J. D., 182
Fodor, J., 146
Fogel, A., 245
Foley, M., 412
Folstein, S. E., 100
Fontaine, J. R. J., 179
Fonzi, A., 230
Ford, D. H., 524
Forde, C. D., 394
Forman, G., 533
Forsén, T., 43, 52
Fortes, M., 388
Forwyth, B. W. C., 522
Foster, G., 393, 401
Fotiou, A., 423
Fox, N., 225
Foy, P., 29
Fracasso, M. P., 333, 513
Frank, H., 180
Frankenberger, T., 51
Frankenburg, W. K., 63f, 64
Franklin, A., 112, 113
Fredrickson, B., 106
Freedland, R. L., 66
Freedman, D. G., 183, 433
Freedman, M., 433
Freeman, G., 308
Freimer, N. B., 101
Freire, A., 103, 104
Freisthler, B., 416
French, D. C., 223, 227, 229, 230, 232, 264, 418, 453
Frensch, P., 515
Freundenthal, D. J., 147
Friedlmeier, W., 25
Friedman, R. J., 312
Friedman, T. L., 292
Frieson, W. V., 109
Frodi, A. M., 212
Frodi, M., 212
Frongillo, E. A., 39, 40, 41, 44, 46, 46f, 47, 47f, 51

Frosh, S., 286
Frost, L., 268, 538
Frost, P. E., 95
Fruechting, L. A., 72
Fu, V. R., 271, 287
Fuchs, G. J., 517
Fuchs, M., 313
Fujita, F., 351
Fukoumoto, M., 50
Fukuyama, H., 139
Fuligni, A. J., 132, 226, 303, 313, 314, 315, 533
Fung, H., 203, 265
Furnham, A., 535
Furrow, J. L., 285, 288, 290
Furstenberg, F. F. Jr., 12, 13, 249
Fussell, M. E., 466

G

Gabbard, C., 64
Gaber, G. A., 364, 368
Gabhainn, S. N., 423
Gabr, G. A., 371
Gabrieli, J., 106
Gailiene, D., 352
Galambos, N. L., 305
Galbin, A., 537
Galbraith, S. J., 188
Galea, M. P., 72
Galle, V., 520
Gallimore, R., 217, 262, 389
Gamba, R. J., 25
Gamble, S. D., 81
Ganapathy, H., 470, 472
Gandour, J., 100
Gangarosa, E. J., 53
Gao, W., 497
Garcia Coll, C., 268, 507, 543
Gardner, W. L., 175
Gareis, E., 180
Gariépy, J. L., 210
Gartner, J. D., 545
Garton, A. F., 489, 499
Garvey, D., 488, 490
Garza, C., 45
Gaskins, S., 248, 515
Gatty, C. M., 72
Gauthier, B., 93
Gauvain, M., 11, 211, 241
Gaviria, M. B., 537
Gay, J. A., 394
Gazzaniga, M., 107
Ge, L., 103
Geary, D. C., 211, 262
Geber, M., 64, 65, 262
Geertz, C., 128, 129
Geldart, S., 102, 103, 104
Gelernter, J., 183

Gelman, R., 131
Gelman, S. A., 153
Gentner, D., 153
Georgas, J., 25, 31
Gerassimova, S., 412
Gerber, T. P., 410
Gergely, G., 197
Gerken, L. A., 99, 114, 151
Gershoff, E. T., 283, 288, 306, 512, 523
Gertner, S., 517
Gesell, A., 63, 64, 66, 262
Getz, J. G., 540
Gevers, J. M., 346
Ghalab, M. A., 360, 369
Ghanam, M. H., 372, 373
Ghazanfar, A. A., 95
Ghoniemah, H. A. M., 371
Giacoman, S. L., 74
Gibbons, J. L., 373
Gibson, E., 231
Gibson, J. J., 89
Gibson, R., 513
Gielen, U. P., 359, 363, 364, 368, 373
Gilbert, A., 114
Gilbert, J. H. V., 93
Gilbert, N., 543
Gill-Alvarez, F., 75
Gillberg, C., 334
Gillette, A., 168
Gillin, J., 329
Ginsburg, H. P., 213, 313
Gintis, H., 313
Girimaji, S. R., 518
Girnius-Brown, O., 306
Gitschier, J., 101
Gittleman, M., 507, 514, 517
Gittler, G., 26
Glasser, S., 410, 411
Gledhill, C., 6
Gleitman, H., 156
Gleitman, L., 112, 156
Glewwe, P., 44
Gliga, T., 94
Gluckman, P. D., 52
Gobet, F., 147
Godeau, E., 422
Godoy, R. A., 182
Goebert, D., 438
Golby, A., 106
Goldbart, J., 520
Goldberg, S., 83, 516
Golding, J., 72
Goldman, A. S., 51
Goldring, L., 543
Goldschmidt, W., 395
Goldsmith, D., 11, 303, 332
Goldsmith, H. H., 224
Goldstein, A., 105, 108

Goldstein, W. M., 10
Golimkoff, R. M., 95
Golinkoff, R. M., 95
Gómez, R. L., 151
Goncalves, V., 64
Göncü, A., 248
Gonzaga, G. C., 179
Gonzales, N. A., 312
Gonzalez, M., 522
Gonzalez, M. L., 327
Gonzalez, Y., 229
Gonzalez, Z., 261, 300
Gonzalez-Romos, G., 313
Goodenough, W., 127
Goodman, G. S., 291
Goodman, K. S., 165, 166
Goodnow, J. J., 4, 5, 7, 8, 10, 11, 12, 13, 14, 15, 26,
    48, 135, 139, 241, 260, 272, 280, 300, 306, 489,
    492
Goody, J., 162, 394
Goonetilleke, M. D. J., 214
Gootman, J. A., 311
Gopnik, A., 153
Gordon, D., 48
Gore, P., 53
Gorsuch, R. L., 279, 291
Gortmaker, S. L., 176
Gosling, S. D., 328
Goswami, U., 166
Gotowiec, A., 536
Gottlieb, A., 287–288
Gottlieb, G., 90f, 210
Gottman, J., 229
Gove, W. R., 520
Govinda, R., 473
Grabe, E., 97
Grajeda, R., 52
Gramsci, A., 5
Granger, D. A., 182
Grantham-McGregor, S. M., 44, 47, 48, 49, 508,
    516, 517
Grässmann, R., 31
Gratier, M., 536
Graves, T. D., 532
Gray, W. S., 163, 164
Graziano, A. M., 270
Green, C. S., 81
Green, M. C., 285
Greenberg, D., 166
Greene, M. E., 466
Greenfield, P. M., 23, 26–27, 82, 132, 135, 136, 215,
    218, 241, 249, 251, 253, 254, 264, 265, 303, 324,
    334, 335, 434
Greenough, W. T., 242, 263
Gregg, G. S., 362, 370
Grégoire, A., 144
Grese, M. A., 108
Gridley, H., 488

Griepentrog, G. J., 101
Grieve, K. W., 516
Grieve, R. W., 517
Griffin, P., 166
Griffiths, P., 470
Grigorenko, E. L., 415
Grimm, S. D., 25
Grinnell, E., 103
Grob, A., 350, 351, 420
Grön, G., 134
Grotpeter, J. K., 227, 232
Grusec, J. E., 243, 263, 306
Guberman, S. R., 334
Guerra, N., 228
Guerrero, A., 544
Guichard, J., 350
Guillot, M., 44
Guiton, G., 313
Gulati, J. K., 507, 512, 518
Güngor, D., 539
Gunnell, D., 51
Gunning, M., 507
Gunnoe, M. L., 269, 288, 290
Gutfreund, M., 147
Gvozdev, A. N., 144
Gwartney, J. D., 302
Gwatkin, D. R., 44

H

Habib, M. A., 370
Habicht, J. P., 41
Hacking, I., 53
Hadeed, J., 511, 515, 517
Hafez, N., 363, 372
Hagekull, B., 435
Haggerty, N., 309
Hahn, C. S., 204, 306
Haig, N., 103
Haight, W., 9, 248, 310
Hainline, L., 102
Haith, M. M., 102, 330
Hake, J. M., 388, 392
Hales, C. N., 52
Halgunseth, L. C., 511
Hallett, D., 8
Hallowell, A. I., 186
Halpern, D., 533
Halvorson, C. F., 7
Hamadani, J. D., 517
Hamblen, J. L., 270
Hambleton, R. K., 330
Hamilton, V. L., 218
Hamilton-Collins, J., 533
Hamilton-Giachritsis, C., 346
Hamm, J., 230
Hammen, C., 496
Hamza, J. M., 371

Han, J., 107, 204
Han, Y. O., 449
Hana, A. M., 364
Hanakawa, T., 139
Handy, T., 107
Hanish, L., 228
Hannermann, R. E., 67, 68f
Hannon, E. E., 99, 100
Hanover, B., 215
Hansche, L., 26
Hansen, K. K., 271
Hanson, K. M. P., 40
Hanson, M A., 52
Hansson, S. R., 183
Haraby, M. Kh., 368
Harb, P. B., 28
Harding, J. E., 52
Haredy, A. M., 371
Harel, R., 420
Harel, Y., 421
Harkness, S., 10, 48, 50, 65, 66, 195, 196, 224, 242,
    243, 244, 246, 252, 260, 264, 285, 299, 302, 323,
    389, 390, 395, 512, 518, 519, 523, 532
Harmon, M., 432
Harney-Boffman, J., 522
Harrid, R., 311
Harris, J., 489
Harris, P. L., 248, 334
Harris, S., 489
Hart, B., 148, 149
Hart, C. H., 227, 228, 232, 415, 416, 418, 438,
    439
Hartl, D., 187
Hartmann, S. U., 52
Hartup, W. W., 227, 230, 232, 311, 390, 391
Harvey, O. I., 180
Harwood, R. L., 81, 261, 300, 302, 304, 305, 333,
    507, 513, 538
Hasan, A. S., 368
Haselager, G. J. T., 232
Haspelmath, M., 145
Hassan, F., 454
Hastings, P. D., 202, 225, 243
Hatano, G., 11, 14, 15, 131, 138, 139, 241
Hatzichristou, C., 232
Hauck, F. R., 72
Hay, D. C., 102
Hayashi, K., 71
Hayatbakhsh, M., 496
Hayden, A., 103
Hayes, J., 510, 512, 515
Hayne, H., 495
Haynes, O. M., 204, 306
Hayward, W. G., 107, 108
Hazan, C., 520
He, H., 431, 432
He, Y., 229, 231, 433, 437, 439
Heath, D. T., 522

Heath, J., 146, 149
Heath, S. B., 9, 310
Heck, D., 230
Hedia, F. M. A., 365
Heglund, N. C., 76, 76f
Heinrichs, N., 176
Helen, M., 455
Hellawell, D., 102
Hemphil, L., 306
Hemphill, S. A., 225, 496
Henderson, H. A., 202, 225
Hendrix, L., 216
Henry, H., 366
Henthorn, T., 101
Hentschel, E., 31
Herbert, B., 301, 312
Herman-Stahl, M. A., 249, 312
Hernandez, D. J., 244, 300, 301, 531, 537, 540
Herrera, M. G., 331
Herskovits, M. J., 27, 111, 531
Hertz-Pannier, L., 92
Hespos, S. J., 112
Hess, R. D., 269
Hetherington, E. M., 288
Heuveline, P., 41, 44
Hewaidy, M., 365
Hewes, G. W., 78, 79f
Hewlett, B. S., 249, 261, 389
Hibbert, J. R., 353
Hibell, B., 341, 353, 354
Hidayat, S., 455
Hiebert , J., 432
Higgins, E. T., 292
Higgins, P. J., 211
Hill, K., 94
Hill, N. E., 249, 312, 511
Hillman, D. E., 177
Hinde, A., 470
Hinde, R. A., 223, 383
Hinton, D. E., 186
Hirsch, B., 230
Hirschman, C., 450
Hjelsel, D., 522
Ho, C. P., 81
Ho, D. Y. F., 436, 437, 438
Ho, L., 513
Hodes, R., 104
Hodsoll, J., 105
Hoehn-Saric, R., 176
Hofer, J., 24, 25, 29, 31, 284, 324
Hofferth, S. L., 248
Hoffman, B. J., 183
Hoffman, C., 212
Hoffman, J. M., 254
Hoffman, M. L., 306
Hoffmen, L. W., 280
Hofstede, G. H., 300, 302, 309
Hogan, M. J., 417

Höhle, B., 93
Hohn, G. E., 533
Holden, G. W., 272, 281, 283
Holding, P., 508, 511, 516
Holdstock, T. L., 386
Hole, G. T., 102, 107
Holland, D., 261, 270
Holland, P. W., 25
Holmes, A., 175
Honda, M., 139
Hondagneu-Sotelo, P., 539
Hong, Y. Y., 135
Honig, A. S., 448
Honing, H., 99
Hood, K. E., 210
Hood, R. W. J., 291
Hoogsteder, M., 535
Hopf, D., 232
Hopkins, B., 61, 64, 65, 66, 67, 68, 69f, 70, 72, 73, 264
Horwood, J., 496
Hosaka, T., 451, 453
Hostettler, K., 228
Hottes, J. H., 78
Hou, F., 545
House, R. J., 29
Houser, R., 51
Houser, R. F. Jr., 399
Houston, D., 98
Houthuys, S., 102
Howes, C., 228, 230
Howett, M. K., 52
Howitt, D., 384
Hox, J. J., 30
Hoyenga, K. B., 209, 210, 212
Hoyenga, K. T., 209, 210, 212
Hrdlicka, A., 77
Hrynevich, C., 492
Hsia, T. L., 180
Hseuh, Y., 451
Hu, D. Y. F., 434
Hu, W., 309, 313
Hubbard, M. L., 311, 312
Huber, J. K., 370
Huda, S. N., 517
Hudley, E. V. P., 9
Hudson, C., 74
Hugenberg, K., 106
Hughes, D., 7
Hughes, M., 520
Hui, C. H., 522
Humphrey, K., 93
Humphrey, N., 77, 77f, 78
Humphreys, G., 105
Humphries, T., 132
Hunsberger, B., 291, 305
Huron, D., 99
Hurst, N., 212

Husain, A., 288
Hussein, N., 371
Huston, A. C., 209, 213
Huteau, M., 22
Hutnik, N., 535
Hutt, C., 214
Hutt, S. I., 214
Huttenlocher, J., 148, 149
Hwang, C.-P., 212, 225, 389
Hwang, C. S., 451
Hwang, J. Y., 40
Hyde, D. M. G., 368
Hyman, I., 536, 545
Hymel, S., 232, 436
Hyun, J. H., 438, 448, 449

I

Iasnaia, L. V., 419
Ibrahim, A. S., 365
Ibrahim, B. L., 361
Ibrahim, F. F., 372
Ibrahim, I. M., 365
Ibrahim, M. A., 367
Iedema, J., 288
Iloeje, S. O., 64
Inagaki, K., 11
Inglehart, R., 29, 287
Inhelder, R., 395
Inoue, M., 43f, 44
Intons-Peterson, M. J., 215
Irizzary, Y., 188
Ishak, S., 71
Ismail, E. M. S., 371
Ispa, J. M., 414, 415, 417, 418, 511, 513
Ito, T., 106
Ivanova, T., 416
Iverson, J. R., 99
Ivey, P. K., 244, 519
Ivry, R., 114
Iyengar, S. S., 307, 312, 314
Izard, C., 411

J

Jacklin, C. N., 216
Jackson, D. N., 25
Jackson, L. M., 305
Jacobson, J. L., 514, 517
Jacoup, I. M., 365
Jacquart, D., 181
Jaffee, S. R., 512, 523
Jahoda, G., 330
Jain, A., 541
James, W., 197
Jameson, K., 113
Jancar, B. W., 420
Janelli, R. L., 448

Jang, S., 97
Jang, S. J., 290
Jang, Y., 517
Jansen, E. A., 227, 230, 453
Janssen, M. M. M., 533
Jantz, J., 72
Jaswal, S., 509
Javier, J. R., 534
Jeffery, L., 108
Jejeebhoy, S. J., 474
Jencks, C., 312
Jenkins, C. L., 50
Jenkins, L., 164
Jenni, O. G., 54
Jensen, H., 330
Jernegan, M. W., 300
Ji, G., 438
Ji, L., 134
Jiao, S., 438
Jimenez, E., 518
Jimerson, S., 508
Jin, S., 227, 415, 438
Jing, Q., 438
Johansson, E., 161
Johnson, A. N., 289
Johnson, B. R., 290
Johnson, F., 176
Johnson, F. A., 269
Johnson, G. D., 216
Johnson, J. A., 95
Johnson, J. G., 182
Johnson, K., 106
Johnson, K. E., 114
Johnson, M. H., 96, 102
Johnson, R., 346
Johnson, T. M., 282
Johnston, C., 542
Johnston, F. E., 45
Johnston, J., 153
Johnston, P. A., 101
Joiner, T. E., 176
Jones, C. H., 495
Jones, D. S., 182
Jones, E., 508
Jones, E. W., 187
Jones, G., 51
Jones, K., 167
Jones, P., 533
Jones, W. T., 181
Jose, P. E., 420
Joshi, H., 517
Joung, I. M. A., 533
Joyner, K., 230
Juang, L. P., 355
Judit, K., 514, 517
Jun, S. A., 97
Jungeblut, A., 164
Jusczyk, P. W., 93, 98, 99, 151

K

Kaani, B., 396
Kabat-Zinn, J., 288
Kabat-Zinn, M., 288
Kaffafi, A. M., 365
Kagan, J., 176, 177, 182, 183, 184, 186, 330, 334, 433–434, 506, 523
Kagan, S., 23, 227
Kagia, J., 64
Kagitcibasi, C., 27–28, 31, 196, 226, 245, 267, 314, 544
Kahne, J., 311
Kaine, W. N., 64
Kajantie, E., 52
Kajikawa, S., 96
Kakar, S., 468, 470, 472
Kalat, J. W., 211
Kaliaperumal, V. G., 518
Kalin, R., 535
Kallivayalil, D., 315
Kalmar, M., 517
Kamel, A. M., 371, 372
Kamil, M. L., 165
Kanbargi, R., 473
Kandiel, A., 177
Kaneko, R., 448
Kang, J. Y., 165, 166, 170
Kao, G., 230, 537
Kaping, D., 108
Kaplan, H., 71–72, 520
Kaplan, M. S., 542
Kapur, M., 518
Karasawa, M., 451
Karlekar, M., 475
Karlsen, S., 533
Karm- el-Din, L. A. E., 367, 368
Karmiloff-Smith, A., 96
Kärtner, J., 31, 198
Kasem, N. F., 363, 372
Kashima, Y., 536
Kashy, D. A., 254
Kaslow, F. W., 323
Kaspar, V., 231, 436
Kathuria, R., 396
Katigbak, M. S., 517, 521
Kattwinkel, J., 72
Katz, M. M., 218
Katz, P. A., 215
Kaur, B., 467, 468
Kaur, R. P., 518
Kavanaugh, K., 506
Kawamura, T., 111
Kay, J. B., 103
Kay, P., 113, 114
Kaye, B., 389
Kazi, S., 32
Kearins, J., 488, 489

Kearsley, R. B., 183, 433–434
Keats, D. M., 280, 491
Keats, J., 491
Keefe, R. C., 211
Keefe-Ormsby, V., 491
Keefer, C., 259
Keefer, C. H., 64, 323
Keenan, J. P., 100
Keenan, M. E., 72
Keener, M. A., 302
Keller, H., 23, 27, 28, 31, 73, 132, 196, 197, 198, 199, 303, 314, 324, 330, 332, 333, 335, 470, 477, 508
Keller, M., 226
Kelley, J., 284, 285, 289
Kellner, H., 7
Kelly, D., 104, 105, 109
Kelsey, R. M., 185
Keltner, D., 179
Kemmelmeier, M., 229, 302, 434
Kempe, V., 156
Kennard, B., 513
Kennedy, A., 534, 536
Kennedy, J., 262
Kenny, D. A., 254
Kenny, M. C., 513, 521
Kenrick, D. T., 211
Kent, S., 519
Kerestes, G., 227, 232
Kerig, P. K., 409
Kertes, J., 534
Keshaf, E. F., 373
Kessel, F., 5, 15, 48, 241, 272
Kessen, W., 112, 242, 254
Keynes, R., 77, 77f
Khalil, E. A., 371
Khan, L. K., 45
Kharchenko, V. I., 422
Khatri, P., 228
Khawaja, M., 487
Khetapal, N., 113
Khleefa, O. H., 370
Kidd, D., 394
Kidd, J. R., 183
Kidd, K. K., 183
Kiefer, M., 107
Kienbaum, J., 226
Kiessling, F., 24
Kilbride, C. P., 396
Kilbride, J. E., 64, 68, 73, 79, 395, 506, 509
Kilbride, K. M., 542
Kilbride, P. H., 64, 65, 66, 68, 73, 79, 506, 509
Kilbride, P. L., 395
Killen, M., 307
Kim, E. C., 448, 456
Kim, G. W., 448
Kim, H., 185, 266

Kim, H. S., 314, 453, 454
Kim, M. J., 452
Kim, M. U., 448
Kim, U., 226, 535, 542
Kim-Jo, T., 315
Kimmerling, B., 539
Kindermann, T. A., 231
King, A., 420, 421
King, A. Y. C., 225
King, M., 487, 491
King, P. E., 279, 285, 288, 290
King, V., 493
Kinzler, K. D., 111
Kirkland-Harris, A. M., 280
Kirsch, I., 164, 166
Kirschenbaum, L. A., 418
Kishani, B. T., 384, 396
Kisilevsky, B. S., 93
Kitayama, S., 111, 133, 196, 263, 300, 302, 505, 523
Kivlighan, K. I., 182
Klein, R. E., 93, 330
Klein-Allermann, E., 31
Kleis, A., 198
Klinnert, M. D., 110
Klugman, J., 412
Knight, G. P., 23, 227
Knight, N., 289
Knight, R., 260
Knightly, L. M., 97
Knutson, K., 53
Kochanska, G., 205, 306
Koentjaraningrat, 450, 454
Koestner, R., 270
Kogos, J., 411
Kohlberg, L., 213
Kohli, A., 518
Kohn, K., 537
Kohn, M. L., 300, 302
Kohrt, B., 54
Kojima, H., 269
Kojima., S., 97
Kolb, S., 70
Kolesnikov, J. S., 423
Kolev, A., 412
Koller, S. H., 331
Kolstad, A., 164
Kolsteren, P., 45
Konner, M. J., 68, 69, 70, 218
Kopp, C. B., 199
Korosec-Serafty, P., 506
Koslowski, B., 64
Kotchabhakdi, N. J., 260
Kotovskaia, M., 420
Kouptsov, O., 418
Koutsouvanou, E., 304
Kouyate, M., 290
Kouznetsove, N., 110
Kozma, R., 162, 169

Kracke, B., 31
Kraemer, H., 64
Krahn, H. J., 305
Krampe, R. T., 131
Kranzier, H., 183
Krappmann, L., 229
Kreher, S., 355
Krentz, U. C., 92
Kreutzberg, J., 70
Krieger, N., 50, 54
Kristel, O. V., 9
Kristeva, J., 6
Krohn, M. D., 259
Kruger, A. C., 239
Krugman, P., 312
Krupp, D., 110
Kuczynski, L., 306
Kuhl, P. K., 94, 95
Kuhn, A., 105
Kumar, K., 472
Kunz-Ebrecht, S. R., 182
Kuo, W. H., 542
Kupersmidt, J., 228
Kurdy, S. A. M., 365
Kurian, G. T., 282
Kurtines, W. M., 532, 542
Kurtz, B. E., 510, 518
Kurtz-Costes, B., 536
Kushnerenko, E., 95
Kuzara, D. L., 52
Kvalsvig, J., 516
Kwak, K., 533
Kwok, D. C., 432
Kyle, D. G., 52

L

Labbok, M. H., 51
LaBlanc, M., 13
Lacasa, P., 11
Lacerda, F., 94
Lacey, K., 185
Ladd, G. W., 249, 418
Ladd, R., 101
LaFleur, R., 94
Lagattuta, K. H., 307
Lagerspetz, K., 70, 227
Lagree, J. C., 348
Lahti, J., 188
Lai, D., 50
Laible, D. J., 202
Lally, C., 232
Lalonde, C. E., 8, 93, 94
Lam, M., 313
Lam, W., 269
Lamb, M. E., 212, 225, 261, 283, 288, 308, 333, 389, 391, 516
Lambert, W. W., 214, 217, 218

Lamborn, S. D., 21, 265
Lamm, B., 477
Lamy, D., 104
Lancaster, J. B., 50
Lancy, D. F., 248, 251
Landers, C., 470, 471
Landolt, P., 543
Lange, B., 518
Langinrichsen, J., 232
Lansford, J. E., 269, 286, 313, 523, 532, 534
Lanting, C. I., 524
Lanyasunya, A. R., 400
Laosa, L., 542
Larooy, D., 495
Larsen, J. T., 111, 179
Larson, D. B., 290
Larson, R., 249
LaScala, E. A., 416
Lasky, R. E., 93
Latz, S., 303
Lau, S., 269
Laude, M., 515
Laudon, M., 176
Laupa, M., 311
Laursen, B., 230
Lavallee, M., 395
Lave, J., 10, 139, 241
Lavi, I., 364
Laviola, G., 176
Law, C., 48
Lawn, J. E., 41, 44
Lawrence, J. A., 7, 13, 241
Lawson, R., 302
Lawton, A., 453
Layne, O., 334
Le, H. V., 449, 450, 452
Le, T. T. N., 449
Le Grand, R., 102, 103, 104
le Roux, J., 331
Ledebt, A., 75
Leder, H., 104
Lee, G. U., 448
Lee, H. C., 448
Lee, J., 510, 512, 517
Lee, J. C., 449
Lee, K., 103, 104, 434
Lee, K. H., 448
Lee, K. S., 456
Lee, S., 226, 229, 432
Lee, S. E., 449
Lee, S. H., 448, 454
Lee, S. M., 361
Lee-Shin, Y., 226, 228
Leichtman, M., 202, 204
Leiderman, G., 64
Leiderman, P., 64, 262
Leighton, A. H., 543
Leighton, M., 421

Leis, A., 103
Lendon, M., 489
Lens, W., 23
Leo, I., 102
Leodolter, U., 185
Leon, D. A., 52, 53
Leong, C., 539, 542, 543
Leopold, D. A., 108
Leopold, W. F., 144
Lepage, M., 93
Lepore, S. J., 520
Lepper, M. R., 307, 312, 314
Leprou, R, 53
Lerner, R. M., 211, 524
Lerner, Y., 534, 539, 542, 543
Lerude, M. P., 45
Lesolayia, M. S., 400
Leung, C., 104
Leung, K., 22, 23, 25, 26, 29, 269, 329, 342
Levak, M. D., 330
Leventhal, T., 249, 312, 313
Levesque, R. J. R., 271
Levin, D. T., 106, 134
Levin, H., 212
Levine, B., 181
LeVine, B. B., 71, 395
Levine, K., 163, 164, 168
LeVine, P. A., 451
LeVine, R. A., 15, 52, 71, 239, 241, 242, 243, 252, 259, 270, 383, 384, 388, 389, 394, 395, 396, 470
Levine, S., 148
LeVine, S. E., 52
Levinson, S., 111, 112
Levitin, D. J., 100, 101
Levitt, P., 541
Lew-Williams, C., 93
Lewko, J. H., 312
Lewkowicz, D. J., 95
Lewkowicz, K., 212
Leyendecker, B., 261, 333
Li, B., 264, 435, 437, 438
Li, B. S., 431
Li, D., 228, 229, 264, 433, 435, 438, 439
Li, H., 517
Li, J., 180, 432
Li, P., 112, 542
Li, S., 290
Li, S. C., 130
Li, Z., 228, 264, 435
Liamputtong, P., 542
Liang, C. H., 203, 265
Liang, S., 430, 436
Liberska, H., 419–420
Liddell, C., 516
Lieven, E., 148, 149, 156
Liew, J., 453
Liiceanu, A., 419

Lillard, A., 23–24
Lima, M., 515, 516, 517
Lin, C. C., 271
Lin, C. Y., 287
Lindahl, K. M., 269
Lindblom, B., 94
Lindgren, G., 45
Lindner, G., 144
Lindsay, R. C. L., 105, 108
Ling, X., 81
Link, B. G., 182
Linton, R., 531
Linver, M. R., 411
Lipton, E. L., 74
Lira, M. L., 508
Lira, P. I. C., 517
Litman, C., 311
Little, T. D., 350, 420, 422
Liu, H., 94, 437
Liu, J., 182
Liu, M., 200, 435, 437, 438, 439
Liu, P., 182
Liu, S., 97, 104
Lively, S. E., 96
Lizard, C. E., 109
Lloyd James, A., 97
Lo Coco, A., 232
Lo-oh, J. L., 398
Locke, J., 89
Lockwood, C. M., 254
Loeber, R., 13
Logan, J. S., 96
Logothetis, N. K., 95
Lohaus, A., 330
Long, J., 227
Lonner, W. J., 26, 28, 262, 324
Lopes, R., 509
Lopez, A. D., 40f, 41f, 42, 42f, 43f, 44
Lopez, N., 313
Lopez, S. R., 324
Losen, D., 312
Louie, J. M. C. P., 541
Louw, J., 385
Love, J. A., 540
Love, M., 493
Low, E. L., 97, 99
Lowin, A., 78
Lozoff, B., 303, 508, 510, 515, 516, 518
Lucca, N., 300
Luce, C. L., 211
Luce, P. A., 99
Luedtke, O., 30
Luhtanen, R. K., 305
Lukowski, W., 344
Lumey, L. H., 52
Lummis, M., 218
Lunn, P. G., 41
Lunney, G. S., 215

Luo, G., 430, 434, 436, 437
Luo, J., 103
Luster, T., 517
Lutz, C., 181
Luu, H. S., 450, 454
Lynam, D., 227
Lytton, H., 216, 218, 432

M

Macartney, S. E., 531
Macchi Cassia, V., 102
Maccoby, E. E., 212, 213, 216, 217, 253, 266, 506
MacDonald, J., 95
MacDonald, S., 492
MacDonald-Clark, N., 522
MacGaffey, W., 383
Macgregor, F. C., 64, 68, 72, 262
Macintyre, S., 486
MacKay, I. R. A., 97
Mackey, W. C., 218
Mackie, G., 79, 80, 81
MacKinnon, D. P., 254
MacLachlan, M., 403
Maclin, O. H., 106, 108
Macri, D., 366, 373
MacWhinney, B., 156
Maddieson, I., 145
Maddock, J. W., 417
Madduz, W., 110
Magnuson, K., 543
Magun, V. S., 419
Maha, A., 539
Mahindadasa, K. J., 214
Mahoney, A., 282, 286, 289, 291
Maital, S., 112
Majnemer, A., 72
Makableh, N. Y., 365
Makarenko, A. S., 414
Makrides, M., 513
Malcolm, G., 104
Malik, N. M., 269
Mallinckrodt, B., 307
Mallorie, L. A. M., 135
Malloy, M., 72
Maloiy, G. M. O., 76, 76f
Malpass, R., 105, 106
Malz, T. A., 270
Mana, V., 539
Mandler, J. M., 131, 151
Manganyi, N. C., 385
Manjrekar, N., 472
Manuck, S. B., 182
Maquet, J., 386
Marais, H. C., 385
Marcon, R. A., 308
Marcus, G. F., 151

Marin, B., 534
Marin, B. V., 25, 313
Marin, G., 25, 313, 534
Mariner, C. L., 269
Markham, S. S., 179
Markovits, H., 226
Markow, D. B., 114
Markowitz, F., 419, 420, 421, 422
Marks, G., 542
Marks, L. D., 281, 286
Markus, H. R., 5, 15, 196, 262, 300, 302
Marquis, A., 93
Marsella, A. J., 324
Marshall, F. B., 64
Martin, C. L., 209, 213
Martin, J. A., 266, 506
Martin, M. O., 29
Martin, R. M., 51
Martin-Jones, M., 167
Martini, M., 264
Martorell, R., 45, 52
Marturano, E., 517, 518
Marui, T., 183
Marvin, E., 101
Masaaki, A., 300
Masataka, N., 74
Mash, C., 112
Maslow, A. H., 303
Mason, C. A., 312
Massaro, D. W., 95
Massey, D. S., 313
Masten, A., 515
Masud, S., 517
Masuda, M., 532
Masuda, T., 110, 132, 134, 135
Mathers, C. D., 40f, 41f, 42f
Mathews, Z., 470
Matskovsky, M. S., 417
Matsumoto, D., 110, 224
Matsumoto, G. H., 532
Mattis, J. S., 280, 281, 285, 288
Mattock, K., 95, 100
Mattys, S. L., 99
Mauer, K. F., 385
Maurer, D., 102, 103, 104
Maye, J., 114
Mayer, M., 154
Mayer, S., 312
Maynard, A. E., 82, 132, 334, 398
Mazrui, A. A., 393
Mazur, L. J., 271
Mbiti, J. S., 397
McAdoo, H. P., 507
McBride, L., 108
McBride-Chang, C., 431, 438
McCabe, A., 166
McCandliss, B. D., 96
McCartney, K., 383

McClave, E., 266
McClelland, D. C., 23
McClelland, J. L., 96
McClintic, S., 201
McCollom, T. L., 231
McCrae, R. R., 29, 30
McCulloch, A., 517
McDade, T. W., 41, 43, 51f, 54
McDevitt, T. M., 269
McDonald, K., 453
McDougall, P., 228
McDougall, W., 176
McDowell, D. J., 249
McEachern, A. G., 513, 521
McEvoy, M., 279, 287
McGaugh, J. L., 189
McGillicuddy-De Lisi, A. V., 259, 272
McGraw, A. P., 9, 179
McGraw, M. B., 67, 70, 75
McGuffin, P., 539
McGurk, H., 95
McHale, J. P., 266, 478
McKay, H. D., 6, 15
McKelvey, R. S., 536
McKinnon, J., 228
McLellan, J. A., 311
McLeod, D. R., 176
McLoyd, V. C., 512
McMahon, W. W., 456
McMichael, A., 517
McMurray, B., 114
McNally, R. J., 186
McNaughton, S., 492
McNeilly-Choque, M. K., 415
McQueen, A., 540
McRoberts, G. W., 94, 96
Mead, G. H., 201
Mead, M., 64, 68, 72, 239, 243, 261–262
Meade, T. A., 209
Measelle, J., 201
Megreya, A. M., 366
Mehler, J., 91, 93, 97, 98, 151
Meissner, C., 105, 108
Mejía Arauz, R., 135, 138, 489
Melikian, L. H., 363
Meltzoff, A. N., 95
Melzer, W., 344, 349
Menard, S., 249
Mendelson, M., 230
Mendelson, S. E., 410
Mendoza, F. S., 534
Menon, E., 102
Menon, U., 477
Mensah, P., 52
Mensch, B. S., 361, 362, 373
Mensy, M. A., 373
Meredith, G. M., 532
Merrit, D. H., 416

Metzger, A., 310
Mezey, F., 183
Miao, X. C., 431
Michaels, S., 9
Michel, C., 107, 108, 109
Middleton, N., 51
Miedema, S., 288
Milanovic, A., 227, 232
Mildred, J., 72
Mileff, M., 266
Miller, J., 106
Miller, J. G., 26, 315
Miller, P. C., 283
Miller, P. J., 9, 10, 15, 48, 135, 203, 241, 265, 272, 305, 310
Miller, P. M., 259
Milman, A., 40, 54
Minagawa-Kawai, Y., 97
Minami, T., 264
Mincy, R. B., 312
Mineka, S., 187
Minow, M. L., 5
Minturn, L., 214, 217, 218
Mintz, J., 203, 265
Mischel, W., 212
Mishiev, V. G., 422
Mishra, R. C., 32, 328, 477
Misra, G., 517
Mistry, J., 266
Mitchell, P., 24
Mitchum, N. T., 266
Miura, K., 218
Miyake, K., 195, 265
Mizokami, Y., 108
Moffitt, T. E., 512
Moghaddam, F. M., 262
Mohammed, A. M., 366, 367, 370, 372
Mohanty, A. K., 467
Mohanty, M., 518
Moïse, L. A., 534
Moll, H., 152
Monasch, R., 387
Moncada, D., 177
Mondloch, C. J., 102, 103, 104
Mondragon, J. A., 335
Monteiro, C. A., 53
Montepare, J., 106
Moon, C., 93
Moon, R. Y., 72
Moon, Y. S., 449
Moore, C. C., 180
Moore, M. J., 102
Moore, S. G., 390
Moos, B. S., 248
Moos, R. H., 248
Mora, J. O., 331
Mordkowitz, E. R., 313
Morelato, G. S., 335

Morelli, G. A., 195, 244, 260, 264, 265, 268, 300, 303, 310, 332, 519
Moreno, C., 507, 512, 522
Moreno, D., 229
Morgan, J., 92
Morgan, J. L., 99
Mori, K., 97
Morley-Fletcher, S., 176
Morris, J. T., 308
Morris, M. W. Y., 135
Morris, P. A., 242, 245, 260, 267, 268, 285
Morris, R., 46, 46f
Morris, S. S., 41, 51, 517
Morrison, F. J., 330
Morsy, A. M. M., 366, 372
Morton, J., 102
Mosenthal, P. B., 165
Moser, E., 185
Moses, L. J., 24, 434
Mosier, C. E., 512, 522, 523
Mosley, W. H., 50
Motivans, A., 412
Motola, M., 350
Moumouni, A., 399
Mounts, N. S., 265
Moura, E. C., 53
Moussa, R. A., 361, 369
Mpofu, E., 396
Mugitani, R., 96
MuhammedAlly, S., 457
Mui-Ching, C., 209
Mukherjee, P., 539
Mukherjee, S., 520
Mukhopadhyay, C. C., 211
Mulder, P. G., 513, 524
Muldoon, M. F., 182
Mull, D. S., 332
Mullan, E., 343
Mullen, K., 290
Mullet, E., 365, 366, 373
Mullin, J. T., 102
Mullis, I. V. S., 29
Mulyadi, S., 452
Mundy-Castle, A. C., 395
Munieb, T. O., 373
Munroe, R. H., 211, 213, 218, 244, 395, 507, 510, 516
Munroe, R. L., 211, 213, 218, 244, 254, 395, 507, 510, 516
Murad, S. D., 533
Murcott, A., 420
Murdock, G. P., 217
Murphy, J. M., 543
Murray, C. J. L., 40f, 41f, 42, 42f
Muthén, B., 30, 254
Muthén, L., 254
Mwamwenda, T. S., 386
Myerberg, D., 72

N

Näätänen, C., 96
Nacuer, F., 372
Nagata, D. K., 536
Nagaty, M. D., 363
Naigles, L., 156
Nair, D. G., 185
Najarian, P., 71
Nakayama, K., 108
Nakazawa, J., 438, 447, 448, 451, 456
Nam, J. R., 449
Nambissan, G. B., 473, 474
Nancy, S., 48
Naoi, N., 97
Narayan, C., 94
Naser, A. G. K., 365, 381
Naser, R. N., 365
Nath, L. E., 182
Nauck, B., 542
Navarra, J., 97
Navarro, A., 331
Nazroo, J. Y., 533
Nazzi, T., 98
Neel, J., 53
Negayama, K., 264
Neider, J., 537
Nelson, C. A., 105, 110
Nelson, D. A., 227, 415, 416, 438
Nelson, K., 129, 201, 202, 203
Nelson, L. J., 415
Nespor, M., 91, 97
Neugarten, B., 12
New, R., 249
Newcomb, A. F., 229–230, 391
Newell, L. D., 418
Newport, E. L., 131
Ng, W. J., 105, 108
Ngaujah, D. E., 396
Ngo, P. Y. I., 270
Nguyen, D. H., 179
Nguyen, G. K., 449
Nguyen, L. H., 454
Nguyen, T. X., 449
Nhom Chan Troi Moi, 450
Ni, S., 431
Nichols, J., 146
Nichols, K. E., 306
Nicholson, J., 496
Nihira, K., 512, 518
Nilsson, K. W., 188
Nippon Hoso Kyokai, 451
Nisbett, R. E., 111, 132, 133, 134, 135, 263
Nishimura, M., 103
Nkaya, H. N., 22
Nkounkou-Hombessa, E., 73
Nkwi, P. N., 386
Noack, P., 31, 345

Nolan, F., 97
Norenzayan, A., 133, 135
Norris, K., 183
Norton, S., 302
Noyce, P., 489
Nsamenang, A. B., 283, 288, 384, 385, 386, 387, 388, 389, 390, 391, 392, 393, 395, 396, 397, 398, 399, 400, 401, 402, 516
Nucci, L. P., 310
Nunes, T., 334
Nurmi, J. E., 349, 419, 422
Nwokah, E., 150
Nygard, M., 70

O

Oakes, J., 313
Oakes, L. M., 114
Oberklaid, F., 496
Obiechina, E. N., 399
Obiekwe, V. U., 64
O'Brien, D. P., 334
Ochiltree, G., 494
Ochs, E., 149, 259, 310, 314
O'Connor, B. B., 54
O'Donnell, A., 512
Oettingen, G., 422
Ogbimi, G. E., 389, 390
Ogbu, J. U., 165, 269, 312, 398
Ogino, M., 198, 269, 303
Ogunaike, O. A., 399
Oh, J. S., 97
Ohgushi, K., 99
Öhman, A., 184, 211
Ohuche, R. O., 389, 395
Ojha, H., 288, 289
Ojiaku, M. O., 384
Okada, T., 139
Okagaki, L., 515
Okojie, C. E., 392
Olaniyan, R., 385
Olivier, D. C., 113
Ollen, J., 99
Olmedo, E. L., 532
Oloko, S. B. A., 392
Olsen, J. A., 415, 438
Olsen, S. F., 415, 418
Olweus, D., 228
Omar, A. M., 372
O'Neil, R., 249
Oney, B., 166
Ong, A., 539
Ongel, U., 28
Ontai, L. L., 202
Opeyo, A., 106
Oppenheim, D., 303, 332
Opper, S., 213
Orfield, G., 312

Orlick, T., 435
Ormsby, C., 491
Orr, E., 539
Osendarp, S. J., 517
Osgood, C. E., 179
Oshio, C., 512
Osmond, C., 43, 52
Osorio, S., 315
Ostergren, M., 346
Otaala, B., 389, 395, 398
Otero, G. A., 331
Otero-Sabogal, R., 313, 534
O'Toole, A. J., 108
Otrakkul, A., 517
Ottolini, M. C., 72
Oudenhoven, N. V., 450
Oura, Y., 11
Ouwaida, M. A., 371
Owen, C. G., 51
Owens, L. D., 227
Owusu-Bempah, J., 384
Oyserman, D., 229, 302, 434
Özgen, E., 114

P

Pachter, L. M., 268, 270, 515
Padden, C., 132
Padilla, A. M., 536
Padilla-Walker, L. M., 7
Page, J., 545
Pai, S., 469, 471, 472
Pakstis, A. J., 183
Palacios, J., 522
Palanza, P., 175
Palintinga, J., 101
Palkovitz, R., 288
Pallier, C., 97, 109
Palm, G., 288
Palmer, F. B., 64
Palsane, M. N., 520
Palti, H., 517
Paltiel, A. M., 534
Pancer, S. M., 305
Pandey, J., 466, 477
Paneth, N., 52
Pant, P., 472
Pantazis, C., 48
Panter-Brick, C., 52
Papousek, H., 266
Paquette, V., 184
Paradice, R., 489
Paradise, R., 135, 138
Paranjpe, A. C., 469
Parashar, S., 52
Pargament, K. I., 282
Park, A., 508
Park, I. S., 449

Park, K., 448
Park, N., 448
Park, S., 286
Park, Y. S., 448, 456
Parke, R. D., 248, 249, 253, 254, 262
Parker, J., 229
Parker, J. G., 201, 223, 436
Parker, R. D., 262
Parkhurst, J. T., 436
Parkin, M., 64
Parmigiani, S., 175
Parolaro, D., 176
Parrenas, R. S., 541
Parrinder, G., 285
Partington, J., 435
Pascalis, O., 102, 105, 110
Paschall, M. J., 311, 312
Patel, A. D., 99
Paterson, J., 497
Pathman, T., 102
Patrick, C. J., 189
Patterson, M. L., 95
Paulhus, D. L., 535
Paulter, K. J., 312
Paz, O., 315
Pearce, L. D., 288
Pearce, N., 491
Pearson, E., 266, 478
Pearson, P. D., 165
Pedersen, M., 412
Pedulla, J. J., 30
Pegg, J. E., 94
Pellegrini, A. D., 227, 240, 241, 242
Pelletier, D. L., 39, 41, 46, 46f, 47
Pellicano, E., 102
Pelosse, J. L., 78
Peltonen, T., 227
Peltzer, K., 384
Pemberton, S., 48
Pena, L. F., 515
Pena, M., 92
Peng, K., 133, 134
Penta, M., 76
Peper, M., 185
Pepler, D., 227, 228
Perese, L., 497
Perez, P., 507, 512
Perez-Cueto, A., 45
Perez-Stable, E., 534
Perin, D., 166
Perkins, C. C. D., 52
Perlis, R. H., 182
Perreault, S., 534
Peters, A., 155
Peters, A. M., 91
Peterson, M. F., 29
Petit, G. S., 259, 307
Petitto, L. A., 95

Petrie, S., 231
Petrova, P. K., 314
Pettit, G., 249
Petty, F., 189
Pezdek, K., 109
Pfaff, J. J., 176
Phalet, K., 23
Phatak, P., 471, 474
Phelan, P., 7
Phelps, E. A., 187
Philips, O., 392
Phillips, D. A., 13
Phillips, D. I. W., 52
Phillips, G., 492
Phillips, W. S. K., 475
Phinney, J. S., 315, 492, 535, 539, 540
Piaget, J., 89, 398
Piccinini, C., 509
Pich, V., 186
Pichard, C., 52
Pickens, J. N., 98
Pidada, S., 227, 349, 453
Pidada, S. U., 453
Pierce, S. H., 518
Pike, K., 97
Pikler, E., 73
Pilgrim, C., 335
Pilkington, H., 419
Pilling, M., 113
Pin, T., 72
Pinas-Hamel, O., 53
Pine, J., 150
Pine, J. M., 147
Ping, W., 80
Pinho, L., 509
Pinquart, M., 355
Pipe, M. E., 495
Pisoni, D. B., 90f, 94, 96, 114
Pivarnik, J. M., 52
Pjrek, E., 176
Platsidou, M., 32
Poasa, K. A., 307
Polanza, P., 176
Polka, L., 94
Pollack, M. H., 186
Pollo, C., 176
Pomare, E., 491
Pong, S-L, 450
Pons, F., 94
Poortinga, Y. H., 21, 23, 25, 27, 29, 31, 33, 179, 214, 239, 532
Popkin, B., 446
Popkin, B. M., 53
Porter, J. R., 215
Porter, L. S., 70
Portes, A., 301, 543
Porteus, S., 489
Posada, G., 323, 330

Pott, M., 195, 265
Potter, M. C., 134
Powell, C. A., 508, 516
Prabhakaran, D., 53
Prabhu, G. G., 518
Prager, L. M., 76, 76f
Prakash, D., 467
Prakash, K., 225, 227, 232
Pramanick, M., 288, 289
Pratt, M. W., 305
Preece, M. A., 45
Premack, D., 23
Preyer, W., 61, 144
Priestly, G., 495
Prince, A., 151
Prinsloo, R. J., 385
Prinstein, M., 227
Prior, M., 496, 498
Pripfl, J., 185
Prosser, G. V., 214
Protopapas, A., 96
Pryor, J., 494
Pumariega, A. J., 369
Pungello, E. P., 536
Purvis, C. C., 176
Pye, C., 147, 149

Q

Qin, D. B., 539, 542
Qin, J., 291
Qotyana, P., 516
Quartz, S. R., 129, 131
Qui, J., 438
Quin, N., 261, 270
Quinn, P., 104, 105, 109
Quixtan, Poz, P., 147

R

Rabain-Jamin, J., 67, 70, 73
Radan, A., 508
Radke-Yarrow, M., 306
Radwan, S. G., 372
Raffaelli, M., 331
Ragnarsdóttir, H., 155
Ramos-Jimenez, P., 53
Ramu, G. N., 470
Ramus, F., 97, 98
Rankin, B., 249
Rao, N., 266, 435, 478, 517
Raskin, L., 112
Rasmussen, F., 53
Ratha, D., 545
Ratner, H. H., 239
Ratner, N. B., 149
Rau, L., 212
Raudenbush, S. W., 30

Rebelsky, F. G., 262
Recchia, S., 201
Redanz, N., 98–99
Redd, A. J., 183
Reddy, N. N., 518
Redfield, R., 531
Reed, A., 103
Regenerus, M., 282
Regier, T., 114
Regnerus, M. D., 290
Reichel-Dolumatoff, A., 511
Reichel-Dolumatoff, G., 511
Reiger, T., 113
Reiser, M., 434
Reiss, D., 248, 288
Reissland, N., 67, 68
Reitz, J., 542
Reitzle, M., 350
Repetti, R. L., 250, 311–312
Res, H. T., 214
Resnick, D. P., 162
Resnick, L. B., 162
Restemeier, R., 31
Retschitzki, J., 395
Rhodes, G., 102, 107, 108
Riansari, M., 230, 453
Ribar, R. J., 114
Ribas, A. F. P., 332
Ribas, R. C., 332
Ricciuti, H. N., 520
Rich, G. J., 176
Richards, M. H., 249
Richardson, S., 498
Richerson, P. J., 129
Richman, A. L., 259, 509
Richmond, J. B., 74
Richter, L. M., 44, 393, 401, 516, 517
Riepe, M. W., 134
Rigby, K., 228
Rigg, A., 494
Riksen-Walraven, J. M., 346, 522
Riksen-Walraven, M. A., 232
Ripple, C. H., 309, 312
Risley, T. R., 148, 149
Risser, A. L., 271
Rivera-Gaxiola, M., 94, 96
Roazzi, A., 334
Robbins, M., 64
Roberfroid, D., 45
Roberson D., 113
Roberts, K., 345
Robey, J., 64
Robins, L., 13, 353
Robins, R. W., 328
Robinson, C., 308
Robinson, C. C., 415
Robinson, D. J., 326
Robinson, J., 492

Robinson, S., 185
Robinson, S. R. R., 75
Robson, P., 66
Roccas, S., 290
Rockel, C., 101
Rodgers, R. J., 175
Rodriguez, C. M., 412
Roehlkepartain, E. C., 279, 289
Roer-Strier, D., 537
Roeser, R. W., 253
Rogers, A., 262
Rogers, B., 494
Rogers, B. L., 51
Rogers, E. A., 51
Rogers, S. E., 100
Rogoff, B., 4, 11, 12, 27, 135, 138, 140, 196, 198,
    211, 216, 240, 242, 250, 251, 253, 254, 267,
    272, 300, 303, 310, 332, 399, 478, 489, 512,
    522, 523
Rohner, E. C., 218
Rohner, R. P., 26, 218, 267, 509
Romney, D. M., 216, 218
Romney, K., 180
Romney, K. A., 5
Roopnarine, J. L., 249, 470
Roosa, M., 511
Rosas, S., 13
Rosch Heider, E., 113
Rose-Krasnor, L., 230
Rosen, W., 110
Rosenberg, B. G., 438
Rosenblum, L. D., 95
Rosenfeld, A., 262
Rosenthal, D. A., 342, 492
Ross, A., 64
Ross, G., 251
Ross, J., 422
Ross, L., 212
Ross, S., 267
Rossion, B., 102, 107
Rothbart, M. K., 177, 225, 433
Rothbaum, F., 195, 260, 264, 265, 268
Rothstein-Fisch, C., 264, 434
Rouchkin, B. A., 412, 423
Roy, R., 226
Rozin, P., 211
Rubin, K. H., 15, 201, 202, 223, 225, 226, 228, 229,
    230, 232, 264, 433, 434, 436, 438, 439
Ruble, D. N., 209, 213
Rudy, D., 511
Rueda Riedle, A., 335
Ruel, M. T., 51
Rumbaut, R. G., 301, 327, 537, 543
Rusch, C. D., 180
Russell, A., 248
Russell, G., 248
Russell, J. A., 180
Russell, R., 262

Rutledge, K. E., 26
Rutstein, S. O., 44
Rutter, M., 13, 353
Ryan, J., 168
Ryan, R. M., 270, 307
Rydell, A. M., 435
Ryder, A. G., 535

S

Sabatello, E. M., 534
Sabatier, C., 67, 68, 69
Sabbagh, M. A., 24, 434
Sabogal, F., 313, 534
Sabry, E. M., 370
Sabry, Y. E., 366
Sachs, H., 100
Sachs, H. C., 72
Sadakata, M., 99
Saegert, S., 311
Saffran, J. R., 101, 131
Safonova, T. Y., 416
Safren, S. A., 186
Sagi, A., 212
Sai, F., 102
Saigh, P. A., 372
Sakamoto, A., 455
Salapatek, P., 102
Salazar, J. M., 328
Saleh, A. M. H., 363, 372
Saleh, S. Kh., 372
Saliev, R. Z., 419
Salls, J. S., 72
Salmon, K., 495
Salzman, P. C., 5
Sam, D. L., 531, 535, 536, 539
Sameroff, A. J., 13, 245, 249
Sampson, E. E., 302
Sampson, R. J., 9, 12
Sanchez, J. I., 535
Sandberg, J. F., 248
Sandel, T., 305
Sanders, M. G., 544
Sandler, B. E., 78
Sandy, J. M., 290
Sangrigoli, S., 104, 109
Sanson, A. V., 306, 486, 488, 490, 493, 496, 497
Santos, D., 64
Saraswathi, T. S., 243, 383, 445, 466, 467, 469, 470, 471, 472, 473, 474, 475
Saroglu, V., 287
Sarrafzadegan, N., 53
Sasso, S. E., 289
Satterly, D., 147
Saucier, G., 179
Saxe, G. B., 334
Saylor, M. M., 151–152
Scarlett, W. G., 279

Scarr, S., 383
Schafer, A., 177
Schank, R., 270
Scharrer, E., 251
Schaughency, E., 232
Scheffer, D., 31
Scheper-Hughes, N., 50, 52
Scherer, K. R., 175
Schiefele, U., 253
Schieffelin, B. B., 149, 150, 310, 314
Schienle, A., 177
Schiltz, C., 107
Schlegal, A., 241
Schliemann, A. L., 32, 334
Schmalzbauer, L., 541
Schmid, C., 226
Schmid, H., 423
Schmidt, K. L., 334
Schmidt, L., 225, 344
Schmuckler, M. A., 95
Schneider, B. H., 223, 226, 227, 229, 230, 232, 418
Schnell, B., 52
Schoeder, D. G., 45
Schoelmerich, A., 81, 261, 300, 304, 333
Schoff, K., 411
Schroeder, D. G., 41
Schul, D., 134
Schultheiss, O. C., 31
Schulze, P. A., 81, 261, 300, 304
Schütz, A., 15
Schwaninger, A., 107
Schwartz, D., 227, 228, 438
Schwartz, S. H., 29, 31
Sciarra, D. T., 533
Scoot, L. S., 110
Scott, J., 344
Scott, R., 540
Scott, W. A., 540
Scribner, S., 32, 136, 140, 161, 167, 168
Seagrim, G., 489
Sears, R. R., 212
Seavey, C. A., 215
Sebastián-Galles, N., 94, 97, 98
Sedwal, M., 473, 474
Seeck, M., 176
Seeman, T. E., 311–312
Segall, M. H., 26, 27, 111, 214, 239, 262, 324, 532
Seginer, R., 359, 365, 366, 371
Sejnowski, T. J., 129, 131
Sekyama, K., 95
Seligman, M. E. P., 211
Sellen, D. W., 51
Sellers, R. M., 250
Semba, R. D., 40
Sendioni, F., 368
Senecal, S., 534

Seo, D. I., 451
Sergeant, J., 334
Serpell, R., 25, 218, 241, 262, 386, 390, 391, 392, 395, 396, 400
Service, S. K., 101
Sesma, A., 515
Setiadi, B., 179
Setiloane, K., 509
Setiono, K., 230, 453
Settertobulte, W., 421
Sewell-Coker, B., 533
Seymour, S., 244, 470
Shabalala, A., 516
Shah, M., 469
Shalygina, N., 420
Shannon, D., 261
Shapiro, B. K., 64
Sharabany, R., 229
Sharan, P., 383
Sharma, A., 96, 474
Sharma, D., 353, 470
Sharma, N., 473
Sharma, V., 474
Sharp, D. W., 394
Sharp, E., 393
Shaver, P. K., 291
Shaw, C. R., 6, 15
Shaw, J., 53
Shebani, M. F. A., 21
Sheets, V., 254
Sheinberg, D. L., 106
Shejwal, B. R., 520
Shelov, S. P., 67, 68f
Shen, C., 30
Sherman, D. K., 314
Sherr, L., 393, 401
Shi, R., 92, 93
Shibasaki, H., 139
Shibuya, K., 41
Shih, N., 496
Shikanai, K., 30
Shimada, E., 536
Shimizu, H., 451
Shimmin, H. S., 213
Shin, U. J., 456
Shin, Y., 226
Shipler, D. K., 414
Shirley, M. M., 67
Shoham, R., 212
Shoji, J., 448
Shonkoff, J. P., 13
Shore, B., 48
Short, K., 542
Shoyer, S., 359, 365, 366, 371
Shrout, P. E., 75
Shu, H., 431
Shuval, J. T., 535, 540, 542
Shwalb, B. J., 447, 455

Shwalb, D. W., 438, 447, 448, 449, 455
Shweder, R. A., 5, 10, 15, 135, 196, 242, 383, 477
Sidorowicz, L. S., 215
Siegel, L. S., 166
Sigel, I. E., 272
Silbereisen, R. K., 350, 353, 355
Silberman, I., 292
Silburn, S., 490
Sills, S. J., 314
Silva, P. A., 176, 495
Silver-Isenstadt, J., 94
Silverman, I. N., 72
Simion, F., 102
Simm, R. W., 182
Simons, D. J., 134
Sinha, D., 467, 468
Sinha-Kerkhoff, K., 472
Sinisalo, P., 350
Siqueland, E. R., 93
Sithole, N. M., 96
Sivan, Y., 176
Skeels, H. M., 71, 513
Skinner, D. G., 289
Skinner, M., 289
Skodak, M., 71
Skoyles, J. R., 77, 77f
Slap, G. B., 41
Slater, A., 105
Slee, P., 228
Slijper, F., 513
Sliva-Pereyra, J., 94
Slobin, D. I., 152, 153, 154, 155
Slone, A., 105
Slone, M., 364
Small, M. F., 54
Smart, D. W., 496, 542
Smart, J. F., 542
Smeele, P. M. T., 95
Smetana, J. G., 307, 309, 310, 315
Smitasiri, S., 260
Smith, A. B., 494
Smith, C., 259, 282
Smith, C. B., 284
Smith, C. S., 331
Smith, D. J., 387, 388, 401
Smith, G. D., 51
Smith, J., 12
Smith, P. B., 28, 29, 328
Smith, P. K., 228
Smith, R., 178, 412
Smith L. T., 491
Smolensky, P., 151
Smoller, J., 310
Smyth, B., 493
Snider, J. B., 353
Sniderman, A. D., 53
Snidman, N., 177, 183, 184, 186
Snow, C., 306

Snow, C. E., 149, 165, 166, 170, 310
Sobolewski, J., 493
Soekanto, S., 457
Sokol, B. W., 8
Solari, F., 510
Solchany, J. E., 262
Soliman, A. S., 372
Sommerland, E., 489
Sommers, S. R., 305
Sondaite, J., 359, 361, 371
Sorce, J., 110
Soriano, G., 490
Sosa, J. J. S., 327, 328
Soteras-de Toro, M., 226
Soto-Faraco, S., 97, 98
Souas, P., 289
Soueif, M. I., 370, 371, 373
Spalding, T. L., 114
Spelke, E. S., 89, 111, 112, 131
Spence, M. J., 93
Spencer, M. B., 313
Sperli, F., 176
Spiegel, K., 53
Spilka, B., 291
Spinelli, L., 176
Spitz, R. A., 71
Sporte, A., 491
Sriram, R., 470
Sroufe, L. A., 267
Stabell, K. E., 182
Stallings, J. F., 50, 52
Stanat, P., 30
Stanislawski, D., 327
Stanley, F., 498
Stanley Hall, G. S., 279
Stansfield, B., 103
Stanton, W. R., 495
Stark, R., 185
Steel, Z., 492
Steggerda, M., 64
Stein, A. D., 52–53
Steinberg, J., 212
Steinberg, L., 6, 21, 265, 266, 269, 437
Steiner, G., 312
Steiner, I., 344
Steinscheider, A., 74
Steketee, R. W., 51
Steptoe, A., 182
Stern, G., 144
Stern, W., 144
Sternberg, K. J., 389
Sternberg, R. J., 396, 415
Sterne, J. A. C., 53
Stetsenko, A., 411, 414, 418, 419, 420, 421, 422, 423
Stevens, K. N., 94
Stevenson, H. W., 218, 226, 243, 305, 432, 439, 440
Stevenson-Hinde, J., 383
Stewart, J., 210

Stewart, S., 513, 523
Stewart, S. L., 202
Stewart, S. M., 287, 290, 435
Stewart-Gambino, H. W., 326
Stigler, J. W., 243, 305, 432
Stipek, D., 201
Stoll, S., 149
Stolnitz, G. J., 44
Stolz, H. E., 415
Stone, K., 81
Stoneman, Z., 250, 282
Stork, H., 477
Strandvik, C., 70
Straus, M. A., 270, 271
Strauss, C., 6
Streefland, P., 53
Street, B. V., 161, 164, 167, 168
Streeter, L. A., 93
Strömqvist, S., 154, 155
Strupp, B., 44
Strydom, N., 516
Stumpf, J., 540
Suarez-Orozco, C., 301, 314, 541, 542
Suarez-Orozco, M. M., 301, 314, 542
Subbotskii, E. V., 415
Subramanian, S., 259
Suci, G. J., 179
Sugawara, A. I., 214
Sugawara, M., 447
Sugie, S., 455
Sullivan, H. S., 436
Sulmont-Rosse, C., 179
Sumida,. M., 451
Sun, L., 228
Sun, S. L., 433, 436
Sun, Y., 228, 436
Sundaresam, J., 472
Super, C. M., 10, 24, 48, 50, 65, 66, 68, 70, 75, 195, 196, 224, 242, 244, 246, 252, 260, 262, 264, 285, 299, 302, 331, 389, 390, 395, 512, 518, 519, 523, 532
Suppal, P., 470
Sutherland, R., 495
Suwanlert, S., 228
Suzuki, L. A., 307
Suzuki, L. K., 264, 434
Swafford, M., 412
Swank, A. B., 282
Swanson, C. B., 312
Swartz, L., 262
Sweeting, H. N., 290
Swift, D., 227
Swingley, D., 96
Sylva, K., 511, 515, 517
Symons, L. A., 104
Syrdal-Lasky, A., 93
Szapocznik, J., 532, 542
Szechter, T., 103

T

Tagoilelagi-Leota, F., 492
Taher, C., 371
Tajfel, H., 6
Tak, S. Y., 456
Takahashi, K., 11, 447
Takata, T., 30
Takayama, T., 518
Takeuchi, S., 110
Takriti, R. A., 285, 290
Tal, D., 534
Talmy, L., 154
Tamahori, L., 491
Tamair, D., 517
Tamang, B. L., 289
Tamer, R., 266
Tamis-LeMonda, C. S., 71, 198, 204, 269, 270, 303, 304, 305, 306, 308, 316, 437
Tan, U., 77, 78
Tanaka, J. W., 102, 103, 104, 105, 107, 109
Tani, F., 230
Tannenbaum, P. H., 179
Tanner, J., 40
Tanon, F., 251
Tanzer, N. K., 22, 25, 26
Tao, G., 438
Tao, K., 438
Tape, G., 396
Tarakeshwar, N., 282
Tardif, T., 153, 431
Tasali, E., 53
Tash, J., 96, 114
Tatur, Y., 418
Tauman, R., 176
Taylor, A., 512
Taylor, C. R., 76, 76f
Taylor, I., 170
Taylor, J., 290
Taylor, S. E., 304, 311–312
Tchernof, A., 53
Te Puni Kokiri, 491
Team, A. S., 72
Tees, R. C., 93, 94
Teinonen, T., 95
Tellegen, A., 189
Tepper, D., 517
Tesch-Romer, C., 131
Tetlock, P. E., 9
Tham, B., 349
Thang, N. M., 446
Thapar, R., 465
Thelen, E., 63, 245
Theuring, C. F., 66
Thind, S. K., 509
Thomas, L., 176
Thomas, R., 74
Thomasset, C., 181

Thompson, R. A., 7, 195, 197, 201, 202, 203
Thorne, B., 7, 14
Tienda, M., 544
Tietze, W., 346
Tikoo, M., 474
Tilak, J. B. G., 473, 475
Tippie, J., 508, 512, 515
Titma, M., 355
Tiwari, B. K., 517
Toan, A., 449
Tobin, J., 451
Toda, S., 198, 303
Todorova, I. L. G., 541
Tokoro, M., 11
Tomada, G., 227, 230, 232
Tomaka, J., 185
Tomasello, M., 131, 147, 149, 152, 156, 239
Tomilson, M., 262
Tomiyasu, Y., 512
Tomkins, A., 52
Tonkura, Y., 95
Torralva, T., 510, 512, 517
Torres-Farton, C., 176
Torsheim, T., 352
Tousignant, M., 545
Townsend, P., 48
Trainor, L. J., 99, 101
Tran, V. Q., 449
Trawick, M., 465
Trefil, E., 517
Trehub, S. E., 93, 99, 100, 101
Trettien, A. W., 61, 63, 66
Trevarthen, C., 266
Triandis, H. C., 6, 22, 26, 196, 226, 229, 230, 232, 300, 302, 314, 522, 536
Tripathi, R. C., 477
Trivers, R. L., 211
Trommsdorff, G., 226
Tronick, E., 64, 74, 259
Tronick, E. D., 266
Tronick, E. Z., 244, 519
Tru, L. N., 183
Truong, T. X., 457
Trzesniewski, K. H., 305
Tsai, Y. M., 542
Tsao, F., 94
Tseng, C., 94
Tseng, V., 202, 313, 314
Tsimbal, E. I., 416
Tsushima, T., 94
Tudge, J. R. H., 331, 415
Tudor-Smith, C., 420
Tuijnman, A., 166
Tukuitonga, C., 497
Tulkin, S. R., 262
Tulviste, P., 32
Tuma, N. B., 355
Tupuola, A. M., 492

Turati, C., 102
Turiel, E., 311
Turk, D., 107
Turkmen, S., 77, 78
Turner, B., 53
Turner, J. C., 6
Turner, R. A., 179
Tymchuk, A. J., 332
Tynelius, P., 53

U

Uba, L., 314, 543
Udvari, S., 226
Uka, N., 389
Ulijaszek, S., 45
Ungerer, J., 493
Unwin, J., 72
Urland, G., 106
Uzgiris, I., 198

V

Vaitl, D., 177
Valderrama, P., 327
Valderrama Iturbe, P., 327
Valdez Medina, J. L., 335
Valentin, D., 179
Valentine, T., 105, 106
Valenza, E., 102
Valenzuela, M., 323, 331
Valera, R. E., 521
Valian, V., 146
Valsiner, J., 7, 48, 241, 507
Valyasevi, A., 260
van Baar, A., 517
Van Cauter, E., 53
van de Vijver, F. J. R., 21, 22, 23, 25, 26, 27, 28, 29, 31, 32, 33, 284, 324, 328, 329, 330, 335, 342, 477, 537, 541
Van den Broeck, C. T., 373
van der Ende, J., 533
van der Pal-de Bruin, K., 52
Van der Vyer, R., 494
Van Hemert, D. A., 25
van Hemert, D. A., 328
van IJzendoorn, H. W., 227
Van Langen, A., 30
Van Leeuwen, M. S., 212
van Leijenhorst, L., 181
van Lenthe, F. J., 533
van Lieshout, C. F., 227, 232, 522
van Sleuwen, B. E., 74
Van Walsum, S., 543
Van Zonneveld, R., 22
Vance, B., 369
Vandenberg, B., 225
Vandenbroack, M., 401

Vang, T. F., 537
Vannatta, K., 232
Vasilyeva, M., 148
Vaughan, E., 332
Vazsonyi, A. T., 345, 351, 353
Vedder, P., 535
Veii, K., 396
Venables, L., 176
Venezky, R. L., 166, 169
Venture-Cook, E., 304
Ventureyra, V., 97, 109
Venzky, R. L., 161
Verdun, K., 180
Vereijken, B., 66, 75
Verhoef, H., 310
Verhoeven, L., 154
Verhulst, F. C., 533
Verma, S., 472, 473, 474, 475
Vermigli, P., 227
Vetter, T., 108
Victor, A., 229
Vigaro, D., 176
Vigorito, J., 93
Vihman, M., 151
Vijayan, S., 151
Vilhjalmsdottir, P., 315
Villareal, M., 229, 300, 536
Viola, H., 177
Visaria, P., 475
Vishton, P. M., 151
Voelker, S., 73
Volein, A., 95
Vollebergh, W. A. M., 531, 537, 539
Vorotnikova, O., 423, 424
Vouloumanos, A., 92, 102
Vreugdenhil, H., 513, 524
Vu, K., 449
Vu, L. M., 450
Vu, N., 536
Vuong, T. X., 449
Vuorela, U., 541
Vygotsky, L. S., 10, 246, 267, 398, 429

W

Wachs, T. D., 519, 524
Wachtel, R. C., 64
Waggoner, L., 279
Wagner, D. A., 161, 162, 165, 166, 167, 169, 171
Wagner, R. K., 431
Wahdan, A., 371
Wainer, H., 25
Wake, M., 498
Wald, J., 312
Waldinger, R., 545
Waldman, R. J., 47
Walker, B. R., 53
Walker, P., 103, 105, 106

Walker, S. P., 44, 508, 512, 515, 516
Wall, S., 304
Wallace, C. S., 242, 263
Walt, G., 53
Walter, B., 228
Wampler, K. S., 7
Wang, B., 430
Wang, L., 180, 225, 433, 435, 436, 440, 445
Wang, Q., 202, 203, 204
Wang, S., 304, 305
Wang, W., 182
Wang, Y., 182, 434
Wang, Z., 440
Wanner, B., 350, 420
Ward, C., 534, 535, 536
Ward, W. D., 100
Wardle, J., 351
Warren, N., 64
Wartofsky, M., 128
Wassenaar, D. R., 517
Wasserman, G., 517
Wat, C. P., 431
Waters, E., 304
Waters, M. C., 315
Watson, J., 197
Watson, J. A., 308
Watson, T. L., 108
Watson-Gegeo, K. A., 6
Watt, I., 162
Waxman, S. R., 114
Way, N., 230, 539
Wearing, A. J., 350, 420
Weatherford, J., 520, 521
Webb, P., 51
Weber, E. K., 310
Weber, M., 302
Webster, M. A., 108, 109
Webster, N., 495
Weikum, W., 98
Weinraub, M., 214
Weinstein, H., 268
Weisglas-Kuperus, N., 513, 524
Weiskopf, S., 112
Weisner, T. S., 10, 15, 217, 244, 260, 262, 389, 390, 396
Weiss, M. J., 70
Weissenborn, J., 93
Weisz, J., 195, 228, 265
Weller, S. C., 5
Wellman, H. M., 431
Wells, G., 147
Wendelken, C., 181
Wenger, E., 139
Wenk, B. J., 99
Werker, J. F., 92, 93, 94, 95, 96, 102, 104, 114
Werner, E. E., 64, 243, 244, 471
Wertsch, J. V., 6, 9
West, J., 301

West, P. B., 290
West, S. G., 254
West, U., 10
Westermeyer, J., 537
Weston, R., 493
Westra, T., 64, 65, 66, 67, 68, 69f, 70, 72, 73, 264
Wexler, K., 147
Whincup, P. H., 51
White, D. R., 217
White, R. W., 303
Whiteside-Mansell, L., 521
Whiting, B. B., 29, 132, 195, 214, 216, 217, 243, 244, 252, 268, 310, 394, 395, 472, 506, 516, 521
Whiting, J. W. M., 132, 195, 224, 243, 244, 268, 395
Whitmore, J. K., 313
Whorf, B., 112
Whybrow, P. C., 545
Wiens, S., 179, 184
Wierzbicka, A., 180
Wiesner, M., 350
Wiesner-Hanks, M. E., 209
Wigfield, A., 253
Wikström, P. O. H., 9, 12
Wilcox, W. B., 286, 288
Wilczynska-Ketende, K., 41
Wilde, P. E., 51
Wiley, A. R., 203
Wiley, P. J., 265
Wilkes, J. K., 533
Wilkins, R., 180
Wilkinson, R. G., 48
Willems, P. A., 76
Williams, J., 309
Williams, J. E., 210, 212, 214, 215
Williams, L. M., 176, 186
Williams, M., 497
Williams, P., 517
Williams, P. K., 94
Williams, R. G. A., 290
Williams, W. L., 210
Williamson, I., 515
Willis, E., 108
Willis, P., 312
Willis, T. A., 290
Wilson, E. O., 211, 259
Wilson, R., 486
Wilson, S. P., 304
Wilson, W. J., 249
Wimbarti, S., 450
Winichagoon, P., 260
Winkler, C., 107
Winn, D. G., 332
Winter, D. G., 23
Winter, J., 24
Wise, S., 493
Witte, J., 285
Wittek, A., 156
Wober, M., 389, 394

Wodarski, J. S., 416
Wojslawowicz Bowker, J. C., 230
Wold, B., 420
Wolf, A., 166, 508
Wolf, A. W., 303
Woo, N. H., 456
Wood, D. J., 251, 267
Wood, W., 212
Woods, B., 102
Woodburn, S., 226
Woodruff, G., 23
Woodson, R., 520
Wornham, W. L., 67, 70, 73
Worthman, C. M., 43, 45, 50, 51f, 52, 54
Wright, C., 182
Wright, S., 214
Wu, D. H., 437
Wu, F., 230
Wu, S. P., 81
Wunderlich, A. P., 134

X

Xie, H., 227, 231
Xu, A., 431
Xu, F., 24, 153, 434
Xu, H. S., 101
Xu, Y., 100, 227, 231, 232

Y

Yablokova, O., 417
Yager, A. M., 290
Yahr, J., 105
Yamamoto, T., 438, 448
Yang, C., 227, 415, 418, 438, 455
Yang, J. H., 449
Yang, K. S., 434, 435
Yates, M., 311
Yau, J., 315
Ye, W., 431
Yen-Komshian, G. H., 97
Yeung, W. J., 248
Yew, W., 315
Yim, D. H., 448
Yin, R. K., 104
Ying, Y. W., 543
Yoo, H., 97
Yoon, G., 226
Yoshida, K. A., 94
You, E. C., 448
Youatt, J., 517
Young, A. W., 102
Young, J. W., 75
Young, P. T., 178
Young, S., 106
Younger, B. A., 114
Youngstrom, E., 411
Youniss, J., 310, 311
Youssef, G. S., 365
Yovsi, R., 27, 198, 330
Yovsi, R. D., 73
Yu, A., 23
Yu, F. Y. K., 79, 80, 81
Yu, H. C., 7
Yu, L., 232
Yu, R., 439
Yuki, M., 110
Yust, K. M., 289, 291

Z

Zack, M., 73
Zajac, R., 495
Zakharov, S., 411
Zakirova, V., 416
Zalk, S. R., 215
Zaman, R., 513
Zan, B., 307
Zappulla, C., 232, 436
Zarebina, M., 144
Zarger, R. K., 251
Zatorre, R. J., 101
Zayas, L. H., 313, 510
Zeanah, C. H., 302
Zeitler, P., 53
Zeitlin, M. F., 509, 516, 517
Zelazo, N. A., 70
Zelazo, P. D., 70
Zelazo, P. R., 70, 75, 183, 433–434
Zempleni-Rabain, J., 391
Zeng, W., 438
Zevalkink, J., 511, 522
Zhang, J., 22
Zhang, Y., 436
Zheng, S., 436
Zheng, S. J., 228
Zhmurov, V., 416
Zhou, A., 431
Zhou, M., 313
Zhou, Q. Y., 434, 435
Zhou, S., 513
Ziegler, J., 166
Zigler, E., 304, 309, 312
Zilber, N., 534, 542
Zimba, R. F., 389, 398, 399
Zimmerman, D., 10
Zimmet, P., 53
Zinbarg, R., 187
Zisapel, N., 176
Ziv, T., 104
Zoqan, G. F. T., 369
Zubkov, V., 411, 414, 422
Zubrick, S. R., 498
Zupan, J., 41
Zybert, P. A., 52

Subject Index

Page numbers followed by f indicate figure; those followed by t indicate table.

A

Aboriginal people
    child development research on, 488–490
    historical considerations, 485–486
Absolute pitch, perception of, 100–101
Academic achievement
    in Chinese children, 432–433
    in Japanese children, 455
    in Korean children, 456
Acceptance, in peer groups, 231–232
Acculturation, 531–546. *See also* Immigration
    of adolescents, 539–540
    culture and, 532
    defined, 531
    developmental research on, 537–540
        future directions, 544–545
        measurement issues, 540–541
    domain specificity and, 536–537
    family separation and, 533, 541–542
    gender differences in, 539–540
    historical and theoretical perspectives, 533–534
    integration and, 536
    orientations, 535–536
    outcomes, 536–537
    parenting and, 270–271, 537–539
    policy implications of, 543–544
    setting conditions, 534–535
    social-cognition approaches to, 534
    social learning theory and, 533–534
    stress related to, 542–543
Achievement
    academic
        in Chinese children, 432–433
        in Japanese children, 455
        in Korean children, 456
    in United States of America, 302–305
        optimism and, 304–305
        self-esteem and, 304–305
Acquired immunodeficiency syndrome (AIDS), in Afrique Noire, 386–388
Activities, in child development research, 10–12
Administration bias, 24
Adolescents
    acculturation of, 539–540
    European youth employment, 348–349
    home environment of, 507–508
    in India, 474–475
    in North Africa and Middle East, 361
    problem behavior in
        Japan, 453
        Korea, 453–454
        Vietnam, 454
    in Russia, 419–423
        gender differences, 420
        peer relationships, 420–422
        physical health, 422–423
        religion, 422
        schooling, 420–422
    in United States of America, equality and, 310–311
Africa
    North. *See* North Africa and Middle East
    sub-Saharan. *See* Afrique Noire
African developmental niche, 393
African theory of the universe
    child development research and, 397–399
    demographic considerations, 387–388
    overview, 386–387
Afrique Noire, 383–402
    acquired immunodeficiency syndrome (AIDS) in, 386–388
    African developmental niche, 393
    African theory of the universe, 386–387
        child development research and, 397–399
    child care in, 389–390
    child development research in, 393–396
        African theory of the universe and, 397–399
        challenges and opportunities in, 399–401
        cognitive development, 394–395
        developmental learning, 397–398
        developmental processes, 398–399
        indigenization movement in, 396
        physical development, 394
        social development, 395–396
    cultural variation in, 385–386
    education in, 389–390, 392–393
    family in, 388–389
    geography of, 385
    peer relationships in, 390–391
    poverty in, 388, 401
    psychology in, 384–385
    youth employment in, 391–393
Aggression
    in Chinese children, 335–436
    peer groups and, 227–228

Alcohol use
    in European Union, 353
    in Russian youth, 422–423
Anxiety, emotion and, 178
Artifacts
    in culture, 128
    scripts as, 128–129
    secondary, 128
Asia. See East and Southeast Asia
Attachment theory, self and personality and, 195
Attention control, in Central and South America, 334
Attitudes, in European Union, 349–350
Auditory–visual speech perception, 95
Australasia. See Australia; New Zealand
Australia
    child development research in
        central issues, 488–495
        future of, 498–499
        indigenous, 488–490
        longitudinal, 496–498
        migrant children, 491–492
    demographic considerations, 485–487
    family in, 493–494
    historical considerations, 485–487
Australian Temperament Project (ATP), 496
Autobiographical self-awareness, 197, 203–204
Autonomous model for literacy, 167

B

Bias
    in child development research, 22–26
    construct, 22–24, 26
    defined, 23
    item, 25–26
    method, 24–26
    strategies to remedy, 25–26
Biological–cultural influences, in child development research, 14
Biological determinism, in gender development, 210
Black Africa. See Afrique Noire
Books, exposure to, in home environment, 514–516
Boundary lines, perceptions about, in child development research, 7–8
Brain state, emotion as a, 184–186
Bullying, peer groups and, 227–228

C

Central and South America, 323–336
    child development research in
        challenges, 329–330
        cognitive development, 333–334
        mother–child interaction, 332–333
        overview, 327–329
        parenting, 331–332
        poverty, 331
        social behavior, 335
        street children, 331
    continued cultural changes in, 330–331
    demographic considerations, 325t, 327
    historical considerations, 324, 326–327
    religion in, 325t, 327
Change
    effects on child development research, 3
    innovation and, in child development research, 11
    opportunities and, in child development research, 13
Child abuse
    in New Zealand, 494–495
    in Russia, 416
Child care
    in Afrique Noire, 389–390
    in Australia, 493
    in European Union, 346–347
    in New Zealand, 494
    in Russia, 417–418
Child development research. See also specific country or region
    biological–cultural influences in, 14
    change in, 3
    culture and, 3–15, 26–27
    methodology, 21–33
        bias and equivalence, 22–26
        context in, 27–28
        culture and data analysis, 29–30
        culture in, 26–27
        integrative approaches, 31
        multilevel designs, 30
        natural experiments, 31–32
        sampling, 28–29
    nationality in, 4
    specifying cultural context in, 4–13. See also Cultural contexts
    universality in, 3–4
Child feeding, child health and, 50–52, 51f
Child health, 39–55
    child feeding and, 50–52, 51f
    child nutrition, 44–47, 46f, 47f
    culture and, 48–53
    developmental niche and, 48–50, 49f
    global effort for improvement, 46–47, 46f, 47f, 53–54
    goals for, 47–48
    health burden, 42–43, 42f
    indices of, 39–47
        growth standards, 45–46
        health burden, 42–43, 42f
        mortality rates, 40–41, 40f, 41f
    intergenerational effects, 52–53
    physical
        of European children, 352
        of Russian adolescents, 422–423

physical development, 44–45
as population welfare indicator, 39–40
psychosocial development and, 47–48
Childhood, middle
   in India, 471–474
   in Russia, 418–419
Childrearing. *See also* Parenting
   religion and, 286–289
      cognitions, 287–288
      practices, 288–289
China, 429–440
   academic achievement in children, 432–433
   child development research in
      future of, 440
      social and cultural changes and, 439–440
   demographic considerations, 429–430
   economic considerations, 430–431
   family in, 431
   historical considerations, 429–430
   only children prevalence in, 438
   parenting in, 437–438
   peer relationships, 436–437
   religion in, 430
   socialization goals, 437
   socioemotional development, 433–437
Choice, in United States of America, 302, 305–307
   cultural variation, 314–315
   economic considerations, 312
Christchurch Health and Development Study (CHDS), 495–496
Cigarette use
   in North Africa and Middle East, 370–371
   in Russian youth, 422
Climate conditions, home environment and, 520
Cognition, defined, 129
Cognitive development, 128–140
   in Afrique Noire children, 394–395
   biological contexts, 130–132
   in Central and South America, 333–334
   cultural practices and, 135–139
   language development and, 51–154
   large population comparisons, 132–135
   in North Africa and Middle East, 367–368
   schooling and, 32
   universal processes in, 129–130
Cognitive stage theory, on gender development, 213
Cognitive styles
   cultural differences in, 133–135
   cultural practices and, 135–139
   describing, 132–133
Collectivism
   in China, 434
   in Indonesia, 454–455
   in Korea, 451
   vs. individualism, in North Africa and Middle East, 370
Color perception, 112–114

Communal relationships, 9
Competition, peer groups and, 226–227
Composite face effect, in face processing, 102–103
Conceptual self, 197
   defined, 197
   development of, 200–203
Confucianism
   in China, 430
   in East and Southeast Asia, 459
   in Vietnam, 456–457
Construct bias, 22–24, 26
Construct equivalence, 23–24
Contest, in child development research, 5–8
Convenience sampling, 28
Cooperation, peer groups and, 226–227
Core grammar, 146
Counterfactual thinking, 9
Crowding
   effects of, in North Africa and Middle East, 372
   home, 520–521
Cultural adaptation, in acculturation, 535
Cultural contexts
   biological–cultural influences in, 14
   description of, in child development research, 27–28
   interconnections of, 14–15
   specifying, 4–13
      challenges in, 4–5
      ideologies, values and norms, 8–10
      multiplicity and contest, 5–8
      paths, routes, and opportunities, 12–13
      practices, activities, and routines, 10–12
Cultural maintenance, in acculturation, 535
Cultural practices
   cognitive styles and, 135–139
   defined, 135
Cultural variation
   in Afrique Noire, 385–386
   in child development research, 21, 29–30
   in East and Southeast Asia, 445–446, 455–459
   in India, 465–466
   in United States of America, 299, 313–315
Culture, 3–15
   artifacts in, 128
   child development and, 383
   child development research and
      data analysis, 29–30
      effects on, 3–15
      sampling, 28–29
      specifying cultural context in, 4–13. *See also* Cultural contexts
   child health and, 48–53
   defining, 127–129
   home environment and, 505, 521–524
   ideal–material dichotomy in, 128
   molar view of, 26–27, 29

molecular view of, 27, 29
parenting and, 259–260
temperament and, 182–184

D

Data analysis, culture and, 29–30
Day care. *See also* Child care
    in India, 470
Development, defined, 129
Developmental learning, in Afrique Noire, 397–398
Developmental niche
    African, 393
    child health and, 48–50, 49f
    cultural determinants of, 48
    defined, 48–50
    home environment and, 519
    religion and, 285
    socialization and, 246–247, 252
Developmental tasks, universal, 27–28
Developmental trajectories, in motor development, 74–78
    endpoints, 76–78, 76f, 77f
    periods of intermittent expression, 75
    shape of, 75–76
Dimensionality, in acculturation, 535
Discipline
    in European Union, 344
    in home environment, 510–513
    physical, 269–271
    in Russia, 415
    in United States of America, 306–307
Domain specificity, acculturation and, 536–537
Dunedin Multidisciplinary Health and Development Study (DMHDS), 495
Dynamic systems theory, socialization and, 245, 247–249

E

East and Southeast Asia, 445–459
    child development research in, 446–447
    demographic considerations, 445, 446t
    family in, 447–450, 458
    peer relationships in, 451–453, 458
    problem behavior in, 453–455, 458–459
    variation in, 445–446, 455–459
Ecological theory
    parenting and, 267–268
    religion and, 285
    socialization and, 245–246, 249–250
Economic variation, in United States of America, 299, 301, 311–313
Education
    in Afrique Noire, 389–390, 392–393
    in Central and South America, 334
    in China, 432–433
    in European Union, 347–348
    gender development and, 218
    in India, 476
        in adolescence, 474–475
        in middle childhood, 472–473
    in Japan, 455
    in Korea, 456
    in North Africa and Middle East, 362
Emergentist theory, in language development, 147
Emotion, 175–1911. *See also* Temperament
    anxiety and, 178
    as a brain state, 184–186
    central issues in, 184–187
    concept of, 175–176
    defined, 175
    developmental constraints, 181–182
    future directions in research, 190–191
    historical and demographic influences on, 177–178
    language and, 179–181
    socioemotional development
        in China, 433–437
        in North Africa and Middle East, 365–367
    theoretical considerations, 187–190
Emotional development, religion and, 289–290
Employment
    in India, 476–477
        in adolescence, 475
        in middle childhood, 473–474
    youth
        in Afrique Noire, 391–393
        in European Union, 348–349
Epigenesis, in gender development, 210
Equality, in United States of America, 302, 308–311
    economic considerations, 312
    gender differences, 308–309
    racial differences, 309
    social structure, 309–311
Equivalence
    in child development research, 22–26
    construct, 23–24
    full score, 25
    measurement unit, 24–25
European Union, 341–355
    child care in, 346–347
    child development research in
        attitudes and values, 349–350
        physical health, 352
        problem behavior, 352–354
        psychosocial development, 350
        psychosocial health, 350–352
    education in, 347–348
    family in, 343–345
    friendship and peers in, 345–346
    historical considerations, 342–343
    members of, 342
    youth employment in, 348–349

Evolutionary theories, on gender development, 211–212
Exchange relationships, 9

F

Face processing, 101–110
    composite face effect, 102–103
    experience in, 103–104
    facial expressions, 109–110
    other-race effects, 104–109
        in adults, 105–107
        in children, 109
        contact hypothesis, 108
        experience and, 107–109
        in infants, 104–105
    whole/part advantage, 102
Facial expressions, perception of, 109–110
Family. *See also* Parenting
    in Afrique Noire, 388–389
    in Australia, 493–494
    in China, 431
    in European Union, 343–345
    in India, 471–472
    in Indonesia, 450, 458
    interconnections of, in child development research, 14–15
    in Japan, 447–448, 458
    in Korea, 448–449, 458
    in New Zealand, 494–495
    religion and, 286
    in Russia
        adolescents in, 419–420
        characteristics of, 413–417
        child abuse, 416
        economic well-being and, 410–411
        marriage trends, 411–412
        parenting, 414–416
        single parents, 412
        violence, 416
    separation of, immigration and, 533, 541–542
    in United States of America
        choice and, 305–306
        equality and, 310
    in Vietnam, 449–450, 456–458
Family violence
    in European Union, 344
    in Russia, 416
Feelings. *See also* Emotion
    defined, 175
Filial piety
    in East and Southeast Asia, 459
    in Vietnam, 456–457
Fine motor development, 81
Footprints in Time, 490
Friendship. *See also* Peer relationships
    in European Union, 345–346
    functions of, 229–230
    prevalence and stability of, 230
Full score equivalence, 25

G

Gender, 209–219
    biological aspects of, 210
    development of
        central issues in, 210–211
        historical and demographic considerations, 209–210
    developmental research about, 214–218
        caregiving and, 217–218
        cultural influences, 215
        education, 218
        parental influences, 215–216
        peer influences, 216–217
        play, 214
        socialization, 214
        task assignment, 217
        trait stereotypes, 214–215
    developmental theories about, 211–214
        cognitive stage theory, 213
        evolutionary theories, 211–212
        gender schema theories, 213
        pancultural model, 214
        social learning theory, 212–213
        social role theory, 212
    psycho-socio-cultural aspects of, 210–211
    sex *vs.*, 209
Gender differences
    in acculturation, 539–540
    in India, 469–470
    in North Africa and Middle East, 361–362
    in Russia, 420
    in United States of America, equality and, 308–309, 315
Gender schema theories, 213
Genetic aspects
    of gender, 210
    of temperament, 176, 187–188, 190
Glasnost, 410
Gross motor development, 81–82
Growing Up in Australia, 497
Growth standards, child health and, 45–46
Guan, 513

H

Happiness, in North Africa and Middle East, 367
Health, child. *See* Child health
Health burden, child, 42–43, 42f
Helplessness, in European Union, 351
Heretical thinking, 9
Heterogeneity, in child development research, 5
Hierarchical relationships, 9

Home environment, 505–524
　culture and, 505, 521–524
　defining, 506
　discipline/punishment in, 510–513
　Home Observation for Measurement of the Environment (HOME) Inventory instrument for, 505–506
　household arrangements, 519–521
　stimulation/teaching in, 513–519
　warmth and responsiveness in, 506–510
Homogeneity, in child development research, 6–7
Household arrangements, 519–521

I

Ideological model for literacy, 167
Ideologies, in child development research, 8–10
Immigration, 531–546. *See also* Acculturation
　culture and, 532
　defined, 531
　family separation and, 533, 541–542
　historical and theoretical perspectives, 533–534
　literacy and, 169–170
　parenting and, 270–271, 537–539
Impulse control
　in Central and South American children, 334
　in Chinese children, 334–436
India, 465–479
　adolescence in, 474–475
　child development research in
　　applied, 475–477
　　central issues in, 467–468
　　future of, 477–478
　　Integrated Child Development Scheme (ICDS), 476
　　theory, 468–469
　cultural variation in, 465–466
　demographic considerations, 466–467
　education, 476
　　in adolescence, 474–475
　　in middle childhood, 472–473
　employment
　　in adolescence, 475
　　in middle childhood, 473–474
　employment in, 476–477
　family in, 471–472
　infancy in, 469–471
　middle childhood in, 471–474
　psychology in, 467–468
Indigenization movement, in Afrique Noire, 396
Individualism, collectivism *vs.*, in North Africa and Middle East, 370
Indonesia
　child development research in, 447
　demographic considerations, 446, 446t
　family in, 450
　peer relationships in, 452–453
　poverty in, 457
　problem behavior in, 454–455
Infant feeding, child health and, 50–52, 51f
Infants
　development of self in, 197–199
　emotions in, 181–182
　face processing, 102–110. *See also* Face processing
　in India, 469–471
　language development in, 150–152
　motor development
　　augmented practice and, 67–70, 68f, 69f
　　developmental norms, 63–64, 63f
　　restricted practice and, 71–73
　responsiveness to, 507
　in Russia, 417–418
　speech perception, 92–99. *See also* Speech perception
　temperamental bias of, 176–177
　in United States of America, 303–304, 306
Innovation, change and, in child development research, 11
Instrument bias, 24–25
Integrated Child Development Scheme (ICDS), 476
Integrative approaches, in child development research, 31
Intelligence, in North Africa and Middle East, 367–368
Internet use, in North Africa and Middle East, 372
Intersubjective self, 197
Intratypological approach, to language development, 154–155
Islam, in North Africa and Middle East, 360–362
Item bias, 25–26
Izzat, 287

J

Japan
　child development research in, 447
　demographic considerations, 445–446, 446t
　education in, 455
　family in, 447–448
　peer relationships in, 451
　problem behavior in, 453
Judgmental approach, to remedy bias, 25–26

K

Kami, 454
Kita, 454
Korea
　child development research in, 447
　demographic considerations, 445–446, 446t
　education in, 456

family in, 448–449
peer relationships in, 451–452
problem behavior in, 453–454

L

Language
　development of self and, 202–203
　differences in, 91–92
　emotions and, 179–181
　fundamental properties of, 91
　official, literacy and, 171
　second, perception of, 96–97
　stress-timed, 91–92
　syllable-timed, 91–92
Language development
　argument structure, 155–156
　child-directed speech in, 147–150
　cross-cultural research in, 143–157
　　central issues in, 145–146
　　historical and demographic issues in, 144–145
　　practical issues in, 156
　　research constraints, 144–145
　developmental prerequisites for, 150–151
　early production, 151
　emergentist and usage-based theories, 147
　intratypological approach to, 154–155
　linguistic influences on conceptual structure, 153–154
　literacy acquisition and, 165–166
　nativist-linguistic theory, 146–147
　nouns vs. verbs, 153
　Slobin's cross-linguistic project, 152–155
　sociocognitive development and, 51–152
　structure of language environment, 147–150
　"thinking for speaking" hypothesis, 154
Language processing, perception and, 91–101
　auditory–visual, 95
　caveats, 96
　perceptual biases at birth, 92–93
　phonetic, 93–97
　rhythmical, 97–99
　second language, 96–97
　sign language, 95
　tones, 94–95
Learning. *See also* Education
　developmental, in Afrique Noire, 397–398
　in home environment, 513–519
Literacy, 161–171
　adult rates for, 162, 163t
　autonomous model for, 167
　defining, 163–165
　developmental theory in, 169–170
　formal schooling and, 162
　future research directions, 170–171
　historical perspectives on, 161–162
　ideological model for, 167

immigration and, 169–170
informal schooling and, 161–162
literacies *vs.*, 167–168
necessity of, 168–169
official languages and, 171
Literacy acquisition, 165–166
　language skills and, 165–166
　reading skills, 165–166
　　adult *vs.* children, 166
　　phonics in, 166, 170
　sociocultural contexts, 166–168
Longitudinal Study of Australian Children (LSAC), 497

M

Manga (Japanese comics), 455–456
Maori
　child development research on, 491
　historical considerations, 485–487
Marijuana use, in European Union, 354
Marketing-pricing relationships, 9
Marriage
　in India, 474
　in Russia, 411–412
Mater-University of Queensland Study of Pregnancy (MUSP), 496
Math skills, in Central and South America, 334
Measurement unit equivalence, 24–25
Mestizos, defined, 327
Method bias, 24–26
Methodology, in child development research, 21–33
Middle childhood
　in India, 471–474
　in Russia, 418–419
Migrants. *See also* Immigration
　child development research on
　　in Australia, 491–492
　　in New Zealand, 492–493
Molar view, of culture, 26–27, 29
Molecular view, of culture, 27, 29
Moral development, in North Africa and Middle East, 368
Mortality rates
　adult, 40–41, 40f, 41f
　causes, 41, 41f
　child, 39, 40–41, 40f, 41f
Mother–child interaction
　in Central and South America, 332–333
　in Japan, 447–448
　in United States of America, 303–304
Motor development, 61–83
　central issues in, 65–67
　　dependent measures in, 67
　　natural experiments, 65–66
　　universals in, 66–67

cross-cultural studies on, 61, 62f, 64–65, 82–83
describing, 61, 63
developmental norms, 63–64, 63f
developmental trajectories, 74–78
    endpoints, 76–78, 76f, 77f
    periods of intermittent expression, 75
    shape of, 75–76
fine, 81
gross, 81–82
movement forms, 78–81
    explicit shaping of, 78–81
    implicit effects on, 78
onset ages, 67–74
    augmented practice and, 67–70, 68f, 69f
    expectations about, 73–74
    restricted practice and, 71–73
Mulattoes, defined, 327
Multilevel designs, in child development research, 30
Multiplicity, in child development research, 5–8
Music perception, 99–101
    absolute pitch, 100–101
    pitch, 100
    tone, 99–100
Muslim
    in Indonesia, 455
    in North Africa and Middle East, 360–362

N

National principles, shared, United States of America, 299–300, 302–311
    achievement, 302–305
    choice, 302, 305–307
    equality, 302, 308–311
Nationality, in child development research, 4
Nativist-linguistic theory, in language development, 146–147
Natural experiments
    in child development research, 31–32
    in motor development, 65–66
Neighborhood, interconnections of, in child development research, 14–15
New Zealand
    child development research in
        future of, 498–499
        indigenous, 491
        longitudinal, 495–497
        migrant children, 492–493
    demographic considerations, 485–487
    family in, 494–495
    historical considerations, 485–487
Nonparticipation, in child development research, 11–12
Norms, in child development research, 8–10
North Africa and Middle East, 359–374
    child development research in
        central issues in, 362–363
        cigarette use, 370–371
        cognitive development, 367–368
        collectivism *vs.* individualism, 370
        effects of crowding, 372
        moral development, 368
        parenting, 363–364
        political attitudes, 369–370
        practical information about, 372–373
        psychological disorders, 371–372
        religiosity, 369
        socialization, 363–364
        socioemotional development, 365–367
        street children, 371
        substance abuse, 370–371
        values and needs, 364–365
        violence, 371
    demographic considerations, 359–360
    religion in, 360–362, 369
Nutrition, child health and, 44–47, 46f, 47f

O

Only child prevalence, in China, 438
Onset ages, motor development, 67–74
    augmented practice and, 67–70, 68f, 69f
    expectations about, 73–74
    restricted practice and, 71–73
Opportunities, in child development research, 12–13
Optimism, in United States of America, achievement and, 304–305
Other-race effects, in face processing, 104–109
    in adults, 105–107
    in children, 109
    contact hypothesis, 108
    experience and, 107–109
    in infants, 104–105

P

Pacific Islands Families (PIF) Study, 497
Pancultural model, of gender development, 214
Parenting, 259–272. *See also* Childrearing; Family; Home environment
    across cultures, 263
    in Central and South America, 331–332
    central issues in, 263–365
    in China, 437–438
        academic achievement and, 432–433
        authoritative, 21
    cognitions, 260–261, 263–264
    cross-cultural research on, 268–271
    culture and, 259–260
    expectations and, 260–261
    gender development and, 215–216
    historical and demographic considerations, 261–263
    immigration and, 270–271, 537–539

in India, 471–472
mechanisms of, 267
mother–child interaction. *See* Mother–child interaction
mother *vs.* father roles, 262–263
in North Africa and Middle East, 363–364
practical considerations in, 271
practices, 264–265
in Russia, 414–416
theory in, 265–268
  ecological, 267–268
  form *vs.* function, 265–267
Participation, in child development research, 11–12
Paths, in child development research, 12–13
Peer groups
  acceptance in, 231–232
  functions of, 231
  rejection in, 231–232
  as social context, 231
Peer relationships, 223–233
  in Afrique Noire, 390–391
  aggression and, 227–228
  bullying and, 227–228
  in China, 436–437
  competition and, 226–227
  cooperation and, 226–227
  culture and, 224
  in European Union, 345–346
  friendship and, 229–230
  gender development and, 216–217
  in Indonesia, 452–453, 458
  in Japan, 451, 458
  in Korea, 451–452, 458
  prosocial behavior and, 226
  in Russia, 418, 420–422
  social participation and, 225–226
  social withdrawal and, 228–229
  temperament and, 224–225
  theories about, 223–224
  in Vietnam, 452, 458
Perception, 89–114
  attunement model for, 90–91, 90f
  color, 112–114
  defined, 89
  face processing, 101–110
    composite face effect, 102–103
    experience in, 103–104
    facial expressions, 109–110
    other-race effects, 104–109
    whole/part advantage, 102
  induction model for, 90, 90f
  language processing, 91–101
    auditory–visual, 95
    caveats, 96
    perceptual biases at birth, 92–93
    phonetic, 93–97
    rhythmical, 97–99
    second language, 96–97
    sign language, 95
    tones, 94–95
  music, 99–101
    absolute pitch, 100–101
    pitch, 100
    tone, 99–100
  perceptual attunement, 110–111
  visual–spatial processing, 111–112
Perceptions, about boundary lines, in child development research, 7–8
Perceptual attunement, 110–111
Perestroika, 410
Personal achievement. *See* Achievement
Personal choice. *See* Choice
Phonetic perception, 93–97
Phonics (decoding), in literacy acquisition, 166, 170
Physical development
  child, in Afrique Noire, 394
  child health and, 44–45
  growth standards and, 45–46
Physical discipline, 269–271, 511–513
Physical health
  of European children, 352
  of Russian adolescents, 422–423
Piagetian studies, in North Africa and Middle East, 367–368
Pitch perception, 100
Play, gender development and, 214
Political attitudes, in North Africa and Middle East, 369–370
Poverty
  in Afrique Noire, 388, 401
  in Central and South America, 331
  in European Union, 343
  in India, 470
  in Indonesia, 457
Practices, in child development research, 10–12
Problem behavior
  in European Union, 352–354
  in Indonesia, 454–455, 458–459
  in Japan, 453, 458–459
  in Korea, 453–454, 458–459
  in Vietnam, 454, 458–459
Prosocial behavior
  in Chinese children, 435
  peer groups and, 226
Psychological disorders, in North Africa and Middle East, 371–372
Psychological needs, in North Africa and Middle East, 364–365
Psychology
  in Afrique Noire, 384–385
  in India, 467–468
Psychosocial development
  in European Union, 350
  in North Africa and Middle East, 366

Psychosocial health, child, in European Union, 350–352
Punishment, in home environment, 510–513

R

Racial equality, in United States of America, 309
Random sampling, 28–29
Reading. *See also* Literacy
    exposure in home environment, 514–516
Rejection, in peer groups, 231–232
Relative pitch, perception of, 100–101
Religion, 279–292
    across cultures, 283–284, 283f
    in Central and South America, 325t, 327
    childrearing and, 286–289
        cognitions, 287–288
        practices, 288–289
    in China, 430
    cultural research on, 285–290
        future directions in, 290–291
        methodological issues, 282–284, 283f, 284f
        theories about, 285
    by culture, 284, 284f
    culture and, 279–281, 280f
    families and, 286
    historical and demographic considerations, 281–282
    identity development and, 289–290
    in Indonesia, 455
    influences on cultural level, 285–286
    in North Africa and Middle East, 360–362, 369
    role in child development, 279–281, 280f, 289–290
    in Russia, 422
    social and behavioral adjustment and, 290
Religions within culture, 283, 283f
Religiosity, in North Africa and Middle East, 369
Responsiveness, in home environment, 506–510
Rhythmical perception, in language development, 97–99
Routes, in child development research, 12–13
Routines, in child development research, 10–12
Russia, 409–424
    adolescence in, 419–423
        gender differences, 420
        peer relationships, 420–422
        physical health, 422–423
        religion, 422
        schooling, 420–422
    child care in, 417–418
    demographic considerations, 410–413
    family
        adolescents in, 419–420
        characteristics of, 413–417
        child abuse, 416
        economic well-being and, 410–411
        marriage trends, 411–412
        parenting, 414–416
        single parents, 412
        violence, 416
    infancy in, 417–418
    middle childhood in, 418–419
    modern societal upheaval in, 409–410
    peer relationships in, 418, 420–422
    population decline in, 412–413

S

Sample bias, 24
Sampling
    in child development research, 28–29
    convenience, 28
    random, 28–29
    systematic, 28
Schema, defined, 128
Schooling. *See also* Education
    cognitive development and, 32
    in European Union, 347–348
    in Russia, 420–422
Scripts
    as artifacts, 128–129
    defined, 128
Secondary artifacts, 128
Self
    autobiographical, 197, 203–204
    conceptual, 197, 200–203
    development of
        autobiographical self-awareness, 197, 203–204
        conceptual, 200–203
        intersubjectivity, 197–198
        self-recognition, 197–199
        self-regulation, 197, 199–200
        subjective self-awareness, 197–198
    intersubjective, 197
Self and personality, 195–205
    attachment theory and, 195
    culture and, 196–197
Self-awareness, subjective
    defined, 197
    development of, 197–198
Self-control
    in Central and South American children, 334
    in Chinese children, 433–436
Self-esteem, in United States of America, achievement and, 304–305
Self-recognition, featural
    defined, 197
    development of, 198–199
Self-regulation
    defined, 197
    development of, 199–200
Sex, gender *vs.*, 209
Sex typing, 209
Sexuality, in India, in adolescence, 474

Shared national principles, United States of America, 299–300, 302–311
  achievement, 302–305
  choice, 302, 305–307
  equality, 302, 308–311
Shy–sensitivity, in Chinese children, 436
Sign language, perception of, 95
Single parents
  in Australia, 493
  in Russia, 412
Slobin's cross-linguistic project, 152–155
Smoking
  in North Africa and Middle East, 370–371
  in Russian youth, 422
Sociability, in Chinese children, 435
Social behavior, in Central and South America, 335
Social-cognition theory, acculturation and, 534
Social development, in Afrique Noire children, 395–396
Social initiative, in Chinese children, 433–435
Social isolation, in North Africa and Middle East, 367
Social learning theory
  acculturation and, 533–534
  in gender development, 212–213
Social participation, peer groups and, 225–226
Social role theory, on gender development, 212
Social skills, in North Africa and Middle East, 367
Social withdrawal, peer groups and, 228–229
Socialization, 239–254
  cultural research on
    central issues in, 247–252
    historical considerations, 243–245
    methodological issues, 254
    theoretical issues, 252–254
  cultural theories on, 245–247
    developmental niche, 246–247, 252
    dynamic systems theory, 245, 247–249
    ecological systems theory, 245–246, 249–250
    sociocultural approaches, 246, 250–252
  dynamic nature of, 241–242
  gender development and, 214
  human development and, 239–240
  in Indonesia, 457
  in North Africa and Middle East, 363–364
  outcomes of, 242
  process of, 240–243
Socialization goals, in China, 437
Sociocultural approaches, socialization and, 246, 250–252
Sociocultural orientation, in child development research, 27–28
Socioemotional development
  in China, 433–437
  in North Africa and Middle East, 365–367
South Africa. See Afrique Noire

South America. See Central and South America
Southeast Asia. See East and Southeast Asia
Speech perception, 91–101
  auditory–visual, 95
  caveats, 96
  perceptual biases at birth, 92–93
  phonetic, 93–97
  rhythmical, 97–99
  second language, 96–97
  sign language, 95
  tones, 94–95
Spiritual development, 289–290
Spirituality. See also Religion
  African theory of the universe and, 386–387
Statistical approach, to remedy bias, 26
Stereotypes, in gender development, 214–215
Stimulation, in home environment, 513–519
Street children
  in Central and South America, 331
  in North Africa and Middle East, 371
Stress, related to acculturation, 542–543
Stress-timed language, 91–92
Subjective self-awareness, 197–198
Substance abuse
  in European Union, 353–354
  in North Africa and Middle East, 370–371
  in Russian youth, 423
Suicide rates, in European Union, 351–352
Survival, child
  child feeding and, 51
  global effort for improvement, 43–44, 43f
  mortality rates and, 39
Syllable-timed language, 91–92
Systematic sampling, 28

T

Taboo thinking, 9
Taoism, in China, 430
Teaching. See also Education; Learning
  in home environment, 513–519
Temperament, 175–191. See also Emotion
  central issues in, 184–187
  culture and, 182–184
  defined, 224
  developmental constraints, 181–182
  future directions in research, 190–191
  genetic aspects of, 176, 187–188, 190
  neurochemical aspects of, 176–177, 187–190
  peer groups and, 224–225
Temperamental bias
  cultural and maturational influences, 186–187
  defined, 176–177
  infant, 176–177
Theocentric theory, African theory of the universe, 386–387
Theory-guided sampling, 28
"Thinking for speaking" hypothesis, 154

Tone perception
  in language development, 94–95
  musical, 99–100
Trait stereotypes, in gender development, 214–215
Tusovka, 421

U

United States of America, 299–316
  child development in, 302
  cultural variation in, 299, 313–315
  economic variation in, 299, 301, 311–313
  historical considerations, 300–302
  shared national principles, 299–300, 302–311
    achievement, 302–305
    choice, 302, 305–307
    equality, 302, 308–311
Universal developmental tasks, 27–28
Universal grammar, 146
Universality, in child development research, 3–4
Universals, in motor development, 66–67
Urbanization, in Indonesia, 457–458
Usage-based theory, in language development, 147

V

Values
  in child development research, 8–10
  in European Union, 349–350
  in North Africa and Middle East, 364–365

Variation
  cultural
    in Afrique Noire, 385–386
    in child development research, 21, 29–30
    in East and Southeast Asia, 445–446, 455–459
    in India, 465–466
    in United States of America, 299, 313–315
  in North Africa and Middle East, 360
  in United States of America
    cultural, 299, 313–315
    economic, 299, 301, 311–313
Video games, in Japan, 455–456
Vietnam
  child development research in, 447
  demographic considerations, 446, 446t
  family in, 449–450, 456–457
  peer relationships in, 452
  problem behavior in, 454
Violence
  family
    in European Union, 344
    in Russia, 416
  in North Africa and Middle East, 371
Visual–spatial processing, perception and, 111–112

W

Warmth, in home environment, 506–510
Weight, child health and, 45–46

Printed in the USA/Agawam, MA
January 25, 2013